Introduction to Banking

Second Edition

Introduction to Banking

Barbara Casu
Cass Business School, City University London

Claudia Girardone
Essex Business School, University of Essex

Philip Molyneux
Bangor Business School, Bangor University

PEARSON

Harlow, England • London • New York • Boston • San Francisco • Toronto • Sydney
Auckland • Singapore • Hong Kong • Tokyo • Seoul • Taipei • New Delhi
Cape Town • São Paulo • Mexico City • Madrid • Amsterdam • Munich • Paris • Milan

Pearson Education Limited
Edinburgh Gate
Harlow CM20 2JE
United Kingdom
Tel: +44 (0)1279 623623
Web: **www.pearson.com/uk**

First published 2006 (print and electronic)
Second edition published 2015 (print and electronic)

© Pearson Education Limited 2006, 2015 (print and electronic)

The *Financial Times*. With a worldwide network of highly respected journalists, *The Financial Times* provides global business news, insightful opinion and expert analysis of business, finance and politics. With over 500 journalists reporting from 50 countries worldwide, our in-depth coverage of international news is objectively reported and analysed from an independent, global perspective. To find out more, visit **www.ft.com/pearsonoffer**.

ISBN: 978–0–273–71813–0 (print)
      978–0–273–78064–9 (eText)
      978-0-273-77656-7 (PDF)

British Library Cataloguing-in-Publication Data
A catalogue record for the print edition is available from the British Library

Library of Congress Cataloging-in-Publication Data
Casu, Barbara.
  Introduction to banking / Barbara Casu, Claudia Girardone, Philip Molyneux. —Second edition.
   pages cm
  ISBN 978-0-273-71813-0
 1. Banks and banking—Europe. 2. Bank management—Europe. I. Girardone, Claudia. II. Molyneux, Philip. III. Title.
HG2974.C375 2015
332.1—dc23
                              2014045195

10 9 8 7 6 5 4 3 2 1
19 18 17 16 15
Cover image: Rain from Golden Coins © Rashevskyi Viacheslav/Shutterstock

Print edition typeset in Charter ITC Std 9.5/12.5 by 71

Print edition printed by Ashford Colour Press Ltd, Gosport

NOTE THAT ANY PAGE CROSS REFERENCES REFER TO THE PRINT EDITION

To Martin, Lila, Milan, Kika and Beth. And to my parents and sister (BC)

To Marc, Matteo and Leonardo. To my parents Nieves and Sandro (CG)

To Delyth, Alun, Catrin, Gareth, Gethin, Lois and Rhiannon (PM)

Contents

Part 1 Introduction to banking

Part 3 Issues in bank management

Contents

Part 5 Advanced topics in banking

List of figures

List of tables

List of boxes

Preface

It is well enough that people of the nation do not understand our banking and monetary system, for if they did, I believe there would be a revolution before tomorrow morning.

Henry Ford

The aim of this textbook is to provide a comprehensive introduction to theoretical and applied issues relating to the global banking industry. Despite the fears of Henry Ford, we do not think reading this book will cause a revolution, but we do hope it will at least provide you with an enjoyable and interesting insight into the business of banking.

A major motivation for writing this text has been to fill a gap in the market. For a number of years we have all taught banking courses and we have become aware of students' frustration about the lack of a comprehensive yet accessible textbook that deals with a broad spectrum of introductory banking issues. Most introductory texts that cover banking issues tend to be broad-based, focusing on economics and finance, and these (in our view) do not provide sufficient detail or coverage of the theoretical and institutional detail that is essential for an accurate understanding of critical banking issues. While there are textbooks that provide such coverage targeted at advanced undergraduates and the postgraduate market, there is no text that has comprehensive coverage of such issues for those new to the study of banking. In addition, many textbooks that cover banking as part of a broadly based money and banking course tend to give only limited attention to international experiences. As such, we have written this text to provide (we hope) an essential teaching and learning resource for anyone who has to lecture introductory undergraduates as well as for professional banking courses.

The first edition of this book (2006) described a world where the banking industry experienced marked changes and deregulation allowed banking firms to diversify into broader financial services areas. Commercial banks became full-service financial firms, offering a range of non-traditional financial services including insurance, securities business, pensions and the like. Many banks dropped the word 'Bank' from their titles to emphasise their much broader role in the provision of financial services to households and corporations. In addition, various trends such as industry consolidation, securitisation and disintermediation were having a significant effect, resulting in a smaller number of major players operating in credit, capital and money markets business that increasingly overlapped. As banking systems opened up, many institutions were pursuing international strategies, thereby changing the traditional focus on banking as a mainly domestic business. This rapidly evolving environment posed both threats and opportunities to bank managers and owners. The former had to be increasingly aware of both domestic and international developments in the management process, and in particular of the various risk–return trade-offs in all areas of a bank's activities. Capital needed to be managed effectively to adhere to minimum regulatory requirements and also to generate returns in excess of the cost of capital to boost shareholders' returns. The market pressure on banks to generate good returns for shareholders was a key element of bank strategy – bankers were forced to cut costs, boost revenues (mainly through fee and commission income sources) and manage their capital resources much more efficiently.

This golden era of banking came to an abrupt end in the summer of 2007, when the demise of the US sub-prime mortgage lending market led to financial losses, government bailouts of banks (and other financial institutions), a credit crunch and a prolonged economic recession, mainly in developed countries, ensued. Since the onset of the crisis in 2007, there has been a large body of research investigating its causes and consequences. What had started as trouble in a small segment of the US financial markets became a fully fledged global financial crisis, following the demise of the US investment bank Lehman Brothers in September 2008. The unfolding of the sub-prime crisis and how it became a financial crisis, and its impact on European countries in the form of a sovereign debt crisis, can be described in various phases or waves that include (i) the US sub-prime crisis (August 2007 to September 2008); (ii) the systemic or global crisis (September 2008 to March 2009); (iii) the economic crisis (March 2009 to January 2010); and (iv) the sovereign debt crisis (January 2010 to June 2012). In this textbook, we will refer to the sub-prime crisis period as the 2007 crisis, to the global financial crisis period as the 2008–2009 crisis and to the sovereign debt crisis or eurozone crisis as the period 2010–2012. Because of the timing of different events, the period of financial market turbulence is also indicated as the 2007–2009 financial turmoil.

These crisis years have had a tremendous impact on the world of banking and have brought about dramatic changes in the global financial architecture. Against this background of global changes, the need to revise the book became apparent. As the dust has begun to settle on the crisis periods and the new shape of the world's banking markets has started to take form, we have thoroughly revised this textbook to account for all these recent changes.

The text is organised into five main parts:

- Part 1 Introduction to banking
  - Chapter 1 What is special about banks?
  - Chapter 2 Bank activities and services
  - Chapter 3 Types of banking
  - Chapter 4 International banking

This part of the text provides an introduction to the nature of financial intermediation and covers the main reasons why banks exist, focusing on key issues such as adverse selection, moral hazard and delegated monitoring. It also covers the information production, liquidity transformation and consumption smoothing role of banks as well as various other issues relating to the bank intermediation process. We then go on to give a detailed account of the main activities and services provided by banks, changes in the payment systems and the growing importance of ethical investments and sustainable banking strategies. As the financial sector in many countries comprise a wide range of different types of banking firms, these are then explained, covering commercial banks, mutual banks, investment banks, private banks and different forms of banking activity such as universal versus specialist banking and 'interest-free' Islamic banking. Given the increasing role of banks on the global scene, the final chapter of this part (Chapter 4) looks at the main features of international banking, highlighting the reasons why banks locate overseas or conduct international activity. We also outline the main services provided by international banks, covering payments, credit, money and capital markets activity and highlighting the role of the Euromarkets – Eurobonds and Eurocurrency activity – and also syndicated lending.

The main aim of Part 1 is to familiarise students with the reasons why banks exist, the main services they offer, recent trends impacting on business areas, types of banking firms and the differences between domestic and international banking business. This part provides the reader with the relevant knowledge of global banking business and should heighten awareness of contemporary banking issues that put the following parts into context.

- Part 2 Central banking and bank regulation
  - Chapter 5 Theory of central banking
  - Chapter 6 Central banks in practice
  - Chapter 7 Bank regulation and supervision
  - Chapter 8 Bank failures and banking crises

As the banking system is the main conduit of monetary policy, it is important that students of banking are aware of the main roles of a central bank, its monetary policy role and its other functions. The first chapter of Part 2 deals with the theory of central banking, outlining the roles and functions of central banks, as well as the rationale for their existence. We also discuss the conduct of monetary policy, distinguishing between instruments, targets and goals, as well as the benefits of central bank independence. Chapter 6 moves on to discuss how the Bank of England, the European Central Bank and the US Federal Reserve conduct monetary policy and the role of banks in this process. Chapter 7 focuses on bank regulation and supervision. We discuss the pivotal role played by banks in the economy to understand the rationale for regulation, and outline the aims and objectives of regulation and different types of regulation. We next discuss the elements of the financial safety net as well as the limitations of regulation and the possible reasons behind regulatory failure. In this chapter we also review the causes for regulatory reform and discuss key international policy initiatives, such as the Basel Capital Adequacy Accords. The final chapter of Part 2 focuses on bank failures and banking crises. This chapter is new to the second edition. The impact of the global financial and eurozone crises on the world's banking markets made it all the more relevant to include a detailed discussion of the determinants of bank failure. We then discuss the main strategies used to identify problem banks, with a focus on early warning systems (EWS) for bank soundness and the recently introduced stress tests. We outline the key issues of bank restructuring and the regulatory toolkits to intervene in the banking sector. Finally, we discuss the causes and consequences of banking and financial crises.

By the end of Part 2 students should be aware of the pivotal role played by monetary policy and supervisory regulation and their impact on the banking sector (and economy as a whole). The reader should be familiar with the rationale for central banking, the main tools and instruments of monetary policy and how various major central banks undertake their operations. Students should be able to identify the reasons why banks are so heavily regulated and why adequate solvency and liquidity are critical to maintain a safe and sound banking system. In particular, readers should understand the important role played by capital in the banking sector as well as the relevance of the Basel Capital Accords. Readers should become aware of the determinants of bank failure as well as the toolkits at regulators' disposal to supervise bank risk taking. Readers should also become familiar with the causes of banking and financial crises as well as effective crisis-management mechanisms.

- Part 3 Issues in bank management
  - Chapter 9 Banks' balance sheet and income structure
  - Chapter 10 Bank financial management
  - Chapter 11 Banking risks
  - Chapter 12 Bank risk management

Part 3 of the text is organised to provide a detailed insight into the financial features of banking firms. The first chapter focuses on the balance sheet and income features of both commercial and investment banks, highlighting the main differences between the two types of institutions. Substantial attention to detail is paid to the components of the financial statements of these types of banks. In addition, we outline the role of traditional ratio analysis for evaluating bank performance and asset quality as well as performance indicators relating to shareholder value creation. Chapter 10 provides a detailed introduction to bank financial management issues, covering asset and liability management, capital management, liquidity management and off-balance sheet management. The important role played by derivative business is introduced, together with a discussion of loan sales and securitisation. We then go on to discuss the various forms of risks faced by banks (including credit, interest rate, foreign exchange, market, operational and other risk types). The final chapter in the part introduces a number of key approaches to bank risk management. It also includes a discussion of the growing importance of banks' corporate governance frameworks in setting the standards of good practice and risk culture within banking organisations.

By the end of Part 3 students should be familiar with the main components of banks' balance sheet and income statements, be aware of off-balance sheet activity and be able to analyse bank performance and other issues using traditional ratio analysis. In addition, they should have an insight into how banks manage their on- and off-balance sheet positions and be familiar with the main risks faced in banking operations. After reading this part, students should be familiar with the main risk-management approaches undertaken in banking.

- Part 4 Comparative banking markets
  - Chapter 13 Banking in the UK
  - Chapter 14 Banking in Europe
  - Chapter 15 Banking in the US
  - Chapter 16 Banking in Japan
  - Chapter 17 Banking in emerging markets

Part 4 focuses on the features of various banking systems, highlighting the main institutional features of these systems (types of banks, non-bank deposit firms, role of other financial firms) as well as various structural trends (number of banks, branches, mergers and acquisitions (M&As) activity, market concentration and such like). We have tried to cover systems that (we hope) will be of interest to as wide an audience as possible, covering the UK, Europe, the US, Japan and various emerging banking markets. We have paid particular attention to regulatory developments in the wake of the global financial and eurozone crises. The emerging regulatory financial architecture is discussed in detail for the UK, the European Union and the United States. It is interesting to note that similar trends are apparent in most of these systems, namely, a decline in the number of banks, consolidation and concentration, the increased role of foreign banks, the broadening of banks' business into other financial services areas, greater disintermediation and the ongoing and omnipresent role of regulatory change. The final chapter provides a discussion of the relationship between finance and growth, illustrating how a sound and efficient financial system can aid economic development. We also offer a detailed insight into various emerging banking systems which we hope will be of interest and also of practical use for anyone curious to learn about banking sector features and developments across the globe. These include a discussion of the main forces of change and how these have influenced the structure of the banking industries in emerging and transition economies in terms of deregulation and the liberalisation process, the role of the state, M&As and the entry of foreign banks.

By the end of Part 4 students should be familiar with the institutional features of the banking/financial systems of the UK, the US, Europe, Japan and various emerging markets and transition economies. They should be aware of how the institutional features of the different banking systems are changing and the trends that are common to all systems. A full understanding of these characteristics will give students the relevant framework to analyse and discuss the structural and performance features of these (and other) banking systems.

● Part 5 Advanced topics in banking
  – Chapter 18 Banks and markets
  – Chapter 19 Mergers and acquisitions
  – Chapter 20 Bank competition and financial stability

This part is new to the second edition of this textbook. Part 5 focuses on some key issues in banking markets. Specifically, in the first chapter of this part we focus on the bank intermediation process, on the increasing integration of banks and markets, and we discuss the growth of the 'shadow banking' system. The aim of this chapter is to outline the key linkages between banks and markets, with a particular focus on the recent rise and fall of securitisation. We then move on to explain the main processes involved in issuing mortgage-backed securities (MBS) (and other asset-backed securities (ABS)). We note the broad impact of securitisation on bank activities and highlight how it has come under increased regulatory scrutiny. The next chapter in this part focuses on mergers and acquisitions in banking markets, providing a classification of the different types of bank mergers as well as a summary of the main reasons why banks merge. We outline the trends in bank M&A activity as well as the impact of M&As on bank performance. The final chapter focuses on the possible trade-off between banking sector competition and stability. We provide a comparative analysis of the different measures of competition in banking markets. Next we discuss different indicators of bank risk, including accounting indicators and market-based measures of risk. We then explore the link between competition and risk in banking systems and outline the competition-fragility view, which posits that competition induces increased risk taking and therefore is detrimental for stability, and the competition-stability view, which argues that competition promotes financial stability.

By the end of Part 5 students should be familiar with some of the current issues in banking and with the academic literature that has sought to investigate these issues empirically.

We have written this text to provide an introductory grounding to the theory and practice of banking and we hope it will serve as a useful guide for anyone studying banking subjects at an introductory level and for those who are perhaps considering a career in the banking/financial services industry.

We hope you enjoy reading the text and we encourage correspondence regarding any omissions or any recommendations regarding improvement of the content.

Barbara Casu (Cass Business School, City University London)
Claudia Girardone (Essex Business School, University of Essex)
Phil Molyneux (Bangor Business School, Bangor University)

Acknowledgements

This text could never have been completed without the direct and indirect help and support of a wide range of individuals. First and foremost we must acknowledge the role of our students in helping to develop our course and lecture material, which has been a critical element in encouraging us to write this text. In addition, numerous discussions with fellow banking researchers and professionals have helped us greatly. We want to acknowledge the support of our home institutions: Cass Business School, City University London; Essex Business School, University of Essex; and Bangor Business School, Bangor University.

Particular thanks must go to members of the European Association of Banking and Finance Professors (known as the Wolpertinger Club), who have emphasised the need for a comprehensive introductory book on banking issues – we hope this text goes some way to meeting this objective.

We would also like to offer a tribute to the late Shelagh Heffernan, an outstanding banking scholar, a great teacher and a good friend.

In compiling this textbook we would like to acknowledge the comments and discussions provided by various individuals with whom we have undertaken collaborative banking research in the past. In addition, thanks to the many colleagues who have discussed teaching and other matters relating to the study of banking and also to those who have given us valuable feedback on the text, including outside referees. We would like to thank a number of individuals who have given us help and suggestions and provided feedback on draft chapters: Yener Altunbas, Francesca Arnaboldi, Elena Beccalli, Thorsten Beck, Allen N. Berger, Dimitris Chronopoulos, Marta Degl'Innocenti, Bob DeYoung, Daniela Fabbri, Alessandra Ferrari, Franco Fiordelisi, Ted Gardener, John Goddard, Jens Hagendorff, Iftekhar Hasan, Hong (Frank) Liu, David Maude, David Marquez-Ibanez, Donal McKillop, Anna Sarkisyan, Steven Ongena, Fotios Pasiouras, Nemanja Radic, Amine Tarazi, Alexia Ventouri, Dmitri Vinogradov, Jonathan Williams, John O.S. Wilson. Thank you to Adam Fehd and John-Paul Conway of SNL Financial Ltd for their help with data collection.

Finally, thanks also to our families for the encouragement and support in accommodating our academic foibles and helping us to complete a large project of this kind.

Barbara Casu thanks her husband, Martin, for endless patience and support (and lots of hours on childminding duties!). And her children, despite their best attempts to make sure this second edition was never completed – they are all very proud of it.

Claudia Girardone thanks her husband, Marc, for his encouragement and patience at the weekends and nights she worked on this textbook. She also thanks her wonderful sons, Matteo and Leonardo, for their endless curiosity ('Is a bank like a big money box?') and enthusiasm, which drive her forward and motivate her. She is grateful to her parents, Nieves and Sandro, for being a constant source of strength and inspiration. She also thanks Annie and Jean for their continued support. To the 'LV' girls: Enrica, Maura, Patrizia and Sonia, a special thank you for being there over the years despite the distance.

Philip Molyneux thanks his children (who are now no longer children) and his wife, Del, for their kind and generous support during the completion of this text. They still cannot understand how he finds the subject of banking of any interest – he is sure they will 'see the light' soon?

Publisher's acknowledgements

We are grateful to the following for permission to reproduce copyright material:

Figures

Figure 2.2 from Payments Council; Figure 2.3 from Press 1 for modernity, *The Economist*, 28/04/2012, © The Economist Newspaper Limited, London 28/04/2012; Figure 2.7 from *World Retail Banking Report*, Capgemini and Efma (2011) p.25, Capgemini; Figure 2.8 from *World Retail Banking Report*, Capgemini and Efma (2012) p.12, Capgemini; Figure 3.3 from SNL Financial and Bankscope; Figure 3.4 from *World Wealth Report 2012* Capgemini and RBC Wealth Management, Capgemini and RBC Wealth Management; Figure 3.5 from http://www.chapsco.co.uk/about_chaps/chaps_statistics/ CHAPS, © CHAPS Co; Figure 3.6 from *World Islamic Banking Competitiveness Report*, Ernst and Young (2014) p.14, Ernst and Young; Figure 4.1 from *BIS Quarterly Review*, BIS (McCauley, R. 2010) p.26, BIS, contains public sector information licensed under the Open Government License v1.0 http://www.nationalarchives.gov.uk/doc/open-government-licence/version/1/open-government-licence.htm; Figure 4.3 from *Subsidiaries or Branches: Does One Size Fit All?*, IMF (Fiechter, J., Ötker-Robe, I., Ilyina, A., Hsu, M., Santos, A., and Surti, J.) p.14, IMF; Figure 4.4 from *Subsidiaries or Branches: Does One Size Fit All?*, IMF (Fiechter, J., Ötker-Robe I., Ilyina A., Hsu, M., Santos A., and Surti J.) IMF; Figure 4.7 from *BIS Quarterly Review*, September 2010, Graph 5, p.44, Bank for International Settlements (BIS); Figure 4.8 from *BIS Quarterly Review*, September 2010, Graph 6, p.44, Bank for International Settlements (BIS); Figure 4.9 from *BIS Quarterly Review*, September 2010, Graph 2, p.41, Bank for International Settlements (BIS); Figure 4.10 from *BIS Quarterly Review*, September 2010, Graph 3, p.42, Bank for International Settlements (BIS); Figure 5.1 from 'Issues in the Governance of Central Banks', A report from the Central Bank Governance Group, May 2009, Figure 2, p.21, Bank for International Settlements (BIS); Figure 5.5 from The Red Book: The Bank's current operations in the sterling money markets. p.1, http://www.bankofengland.co.uk/markets/Documents/money/publications/redbookosf.pdf Bank of England, contains public sector information licensed under the Open Government Licence v1.0.http://www.nationalarchives.gov.uk/doc/open-government-licence/version/1/open-government-licence.htm; Figure 5.10 from *Central Banks in Times of Crisis: The Fed vs. the ECB,* CEPS Policy Briefs, Centre for European Policy Studies (Gros, D., Alcid C. and Giovanni A.) pp.3&5, CEPS; Figure 6.1 from *Bank of England Quarterly Bulletin, Q1*, Bank of England (2013) p.21, © Bank of England 2013, http://www.bankofengland.co.uk/publications/Documents/quarterlybulletin/2013/qb1301.pdfcontains public sector information licensed under the Open Government Licence v1.0.http://www.nationalarchives.gov.uk/doc/open-government-licence/version/1/open-government-licence.htm; Figure 6.2 from *Bank of England Quarterly Bulletin Q1* Bank of England (2013) p.21, © Bank of England 2013, http://www.bankofengland.co.uk/publications/Documents/quarterlybulletin/2013/qb1301.pdf contains public sector information licensed under the Open Government Licence v1.0.http://www.nationalarchives.gov.uk/doc/open-government-licence/version/1/open-government-licence.htm;

Acknowledgements

Figure 6.4 from *Handbook-No.29 State of the art of inflation targeting – 2012*, Bank of England (Hammond, G. 2012) pp.7–8, © Bank of England 2012, http://www.bankofengland.co.uk/education/Documents/ccbs/handbooks/pdf/ccbshb29.pdf contains public sector information licensed under the Open Government Licence v1.0.http://www.nationalarchives.gov.uk/doc/open-government-licence/version/1/open-government-licence.htm; Figure 6.5 from Twenty years of inflation targeting, Speech, The Stamp Memorial Lecture, London School of Economics, http://www.bankofengland.co.uk/publications/Pages/speeches/2012/606.aspx, Bank of England, contains public sector information licensed under the Open Government Licence v1.0.http://www.nationalarchives.gov.uk/doc/open-government-licence/version/1/open-government-licence.htm; Figure 8.4 from Moody's Analytic 2011 Banking Industry Survey on Stress Testing, p. 9, http://www.efma.com/ressources/studies/2011/1-IQFY4_E_study.pdf, Moody's Analytics, © Moody's Investor Service Inc., and /or its affiliates. Reprinted with permission. All Rights Reserved; Figure 8.5 from *Systemic Banking Crises Database: An Update,* International Monetary Fund Working Paper, Fig. 3. IMF (Laeven, L. and Valencia, F. 2012) p.10, IMF; Figure 10.4 from *Unified Financial Analysis: The Missing Links of Finance*, Wiley & Sons (Brammertz, W., Akkizidis, I., Breymann, W., Entin, R. and Rustmann, M. 2011) © Wiley and Sons; Figure 10.10 from 'Triennial Central Bank Survey of foreign exchange and derivatives market activity', BIS (2013) p.6, Bank for International Settlements (BIS); Figure 11.5 from Accenture (2013), Regulatory Implications of Rogue Trading, Fig. 1 http://www.accenture.com/us--en/blogs/regulatory_insights_blog/archive/2013/03/22/rogue-trading.aspx, Accenture; Figure 12.2 from UK Department of Community and Local Government Statistics, https://www.gov.uk/government/organisations/department-for-communities-and-local-government/about/statistics, Gov.UK, contains public sector information licensed under the Open Government Licence v1.0, http://www.nationalarchives.gov.uk/doc/open-government-licence/version/3/; Figure 13.1 from *Financial Stability Report, figures from Northern Rock Interim and Annual Reports,* Chart 1, Bank of England (2007) p.10, © Bank of England 2007, http://www.bankofengland.co.uk/publications/Documents/fsr/2007/fsrfull0710.pdf contains public sector information licensed under the Open Government Licence v1.0.http://www.nationalarchives.gov.uk/doc/open-government-licence/version/1/open-government-licence.htm; Figure 13.2 from *The Creation and Sale of Northern Rock plc* National Audit Office (2012) p.5, National Audit Office; Figure 13.4 from *The Comptroller and Auditor General's Report to the House of Commons (HM Treasury Resource Accounts 2012–13,)* p.8, Fig. 2, National Audit Office (2013) National Audit Office; Figure 14.1 from *Review of the Lamfalussy Process. Strengthening supervisory convergence. Communication from the Commission to the European Parliament and the Council* (COM (2007) 727). Annex 1, p.14, European Commission (2007) p.14, European Commission; Figures 15.1, 18.6 and 18.7 from The Securities Industry and Financial Markets Association (www.sifma.org); Figure 15.4 from Share of industry assets according to bank size, Federal Deposit Insurance Corporation, https://www.fdic.gov/regulations/resources/cbi/report/cbi-full.pdf, FDIC; Figures 15.5 and 15.6 from Federal Deposit Insurance Corporation. Historical Statistics on Banking, Commercial Banks, http://www2.fdic.gov/hsob/index.asp, FDIC; Figure 16.1 from The structure of the Japanese banking sector, http://www.zenginkyo.or.jp/en/banks/principal/index.html, Japanese Bankers Association; Figure 16.2 from Total assets of Japanese domestic banking groups, http://www.zenginkyo.or.jp/en/banks/principal/index.html, Japanese Bankers Association; Figure 16.6 from Bank of Japan (2012) Payment, clearing and settlement systems in Japan, p. 270, https://www.boj.or.jp/en/paym/outline/pay_boj/pss1212a.pdf, Bank of Japan; Figure 16.8 from *The performance of Japanese bank .SNL Financial data for Q2*, SNL Financial (2013) SNL Financial; Figure 16.9 from *Capitalisation of Japanese bank,s* Bank of Japan (2013) Bank of Japan; Figure 17.1 from *Benchmarking Financial Systems around the World*, World Bank Policy Research Working Paper 6175, August, Washington DC, Fig. 6, World Bank (Cihák, M., Demirgüç-Kunt, A., Feyen, E. and Levine, R. 2012) p.31, http://documents.worldbank.org/curated/en/2012/08/16669897/benchmarking-financial-systems-around-world © World Bank. License: Creative Commons Attribution license (CC BY 3.0 IGO); Figure 17.2 from *The Future of Banking in Emerging Markets*, Exhibit 4, Oliver Wyman (2011) p.4, London: Oliver Wyman; Figure 17.3 from Bank for International Settlements 83rd Annual Report, Graph lll, (2013), p.28, Bank for International Settlements (BIS); Figure 17.4 from https://openknowledge.worldbank.org/bitstream/handle/10986/11848/Global%20Financial%20Development%20Report%202013.pdf?sequence=1, © World Bank 2012, Global Financial Development Report 2013: Rethinking the Role of the State in Finance. Washington, DC: World Bank. doi:10.1596/978-0-8213-9503-5. License: Creative Commons Attribution CC BY 3.0; Figure 17.5 from https://openknowledge.worldbank.org/bitstream/handle/10986/11848/Global%20Financial%20Development%20Report%202013.pdf?sequence, © World Bank 2012. Global Financial Development Report 2013: Rethinking the Role of the State in Finance. Washington, DC: World Bank. doi:10.1596/978-0-8213-9503-5. License: Creative Commons Attribution CC BY 3.0; Figure 17.6 from Foreign bank presence *Journal of Money, Credit and Banking*, 46(1), Fig. 3 (Claessens, S. and van Horen, N 2014), © Wiley & Sons; Figure 18.2 from *The Great Credit Squeeze: How It Happened, How to Prevent Another,* Brookings Institution (Baily, M. N., Elmendorf, D. W. and Latin, R. E. 2008) Fig 5, Brookings Institution; Figure 19.1 from *Bank M&As in Europe and the US (value of transactions $ billion)*, Fig. 1 (DeYoung, R., Evanoff, D. and Molyneux, P. 2009) Robert DeYoung; Figure 19.3 from *Bank M&As in the US (2007–2013)* SNL Financials (2013) SNL Financials; Figure 20.2 from *Herfindahl Index: equity derivatives, bank-to-non-bank,* Fig. 2.11, OECD (2011) © OECD.

Tables

Table 2.4 from Committee on Payment and Settlement Systems Statistics on payment, clearing and settlement systems in the CPSS countries, Figures for 2012, December 2013, Table 7, p.445 (2013) Bank for International Settlements (BIS); Table 3.5 from 18/07/2012, http://www.managersofwealth.com/uploads/whitepapers/120718_ScorpioPartnership_Private_Banking_Benchmark_FINAL.pdf, The Scorpio Partnership; Table 4.1 from http://www.lma.eu.com/uploads/files/Syndicated_Loan_glossary[1].pdf Loan Market Association (LMA) © Loan Market Association (LMA). All Rights Reserved; Table 7.5 from Calibration of the Capital Framework, Bank for International Settlements, Basel Committee on Banking Supervision. Annex 1 p.64, http://www.bis.org/press/p100912a.pdf, Bank for International Settlements (BIS); Table 7.6 from Bank for International Settlements, Basel Committee on Banking Supervision, http://www.bis.org/bcbs/basel3/basel3_phase_in_arrangements.pdf, Bank for International Settlements (BIS); Table 7.7 from Basel III phase-in arrangements – Liquidity http://www.bis.org/bcbs/basel3/basel3_phase_in_arrangements.pdf, Bank for International Settlements (BIS); Table 8.5 adapted from *Financial Crises: Causes, Consequences and Policy Responses,* Table 13.4, IMF (Claessens, S., Kose, M.A., Laeven, L. and Valencia, F. 2014) p.417, IMF; Table 9.4 from Barclays Bank assets, 2008–2012 (£m) http://www.investorrelations.barclays.co.uk, Barclays Bank; Table 9.5 from Barclays Bank liabilities, 2008–12 (£m) http://www.investorrelations.barclays.co.uk, Barclays Bank; Table 9.6 adapted from *Bank Management*, 7th edn, Cengage Learning (Koch, T.W. and MacDonald, S.S. 2009) p.504. Reproduced with permission of South-Western CENGAGE Learning in the format Republish in a book via Copyright Clearance Center; Table 9.8 from Barclays Bank PLC profit and loss account 2008–12 (£m) http://www.investorrelations.barclays.co.uk, Barclays Bank; Table 9.12 from *Competition Commission Report (2002) Supply of Banking Services by Clearing Banks to Small and Medium-Sized Enterprises,* Competition Commission, contains public sector information licensed under the Open Government Licence v1.0, https://www.nationalarchives.gov.uk/doc/open-government-licence/version/3/; Table 12.2 from Department of Community and Local Government (DCLG), Live table 1300, https://www.gov.uk/government/statistical-datasets/live-tables-on-repossession-activity, Gov.UK, contains public sector information licensed under the Open Government Licence v1.0, http://www.nationalarchives.gov.uk/doc/open-government-licence/version/3/; Table 13.5 from *Competition and Choice in Retail Banking: Ninth Report of Session 2010–11*, House of Commons, Treasury Committee (2011) p.11, © Parliamentary Copyright, contains Parliamentary information licensed under the Open Parliament Licence v1.0, http://www.parliament.uk/site-information/copyright/open-parliament-licence/; Table 14.6 from Dexia: un sinistre coûteux, des risques persistants (Dexia: a high cost with persistent risks), http://www.ccomptes.fr/Publications/Publications/Dexia-un-sinistre-couteux-des-risques-persistants, Cour des comptes; Table 15.1 from Data from Freddie Mac, reported by the IMF p.1, http://www.imf.org/external/pubs/ft/fmu/eng/2007/charts.pdf IMF, Provided by Freddie Mac®; Tables 15.7 and 15.8 from FDIC, Historical Statistics on Banking, Commercial Banks, http://www2.fdic.gov/hsob/index.asp, FDIC; Table 15.9 from http://www.fdic.gov/, FDIC; Table 16.7 from http://www.zenginkyo.or.jp/en/stats/, Japanese Bankers Association; Table 16.8 from Income Statement (March 2012, values in million yen), http://www.zenginkyo.or.jp/en/stats/, Japanese Bankers Association; Table 17.1 from *Benchmarking Financial Systems around the World World Bank Policy Research Working Paper 6175,* Washington DC, Table 1, http://documents.worldbank.org/curated/en/2012/08/16669897/benchmarking-financial-systems-around-world © World Bank. License: Creative Commons Attribution license (CC BY 3.0 IGO); Tables 17.4 and 17.5 from http://data.worldbank.org/about/country-classifications/country-and-lending-groups, © World Bank, License: Creative Commons Attribution license (CC BY 3.0 IGO); Table 17.8 adapted from *Oxford Handbook of Banking,* 2nd edn, N. Berger, P. Molyneux and J.O.S. Wilson (eds), Chapter 39, Table 2, Oxford: OUP (Bonin, J., Hasan, I. and Wachtel, P. 2014) © OUP; Table 17.10 Reprinted from Foreign Bank Entry in South East Asia, *International Review of Financial Analysis*, Table 2 (Molyneux, P., Nguyen, L.H. and R. Xie 2013) © 2013, with permission from Elsevier; Table 20.3 from *Recent Developments in European Bank Competition.* IMF Working Paper WP/11/146, Table 3, IMF (2011) p.20, IMF; Table 20.5 Reprinted from Bank Competition and Financial Stability in Asia Pacific, *Journal of Banking & Finance*, 38, 64–77 (Fu, X., Lin, Y. and Molyneux, P. 2014) © 2014 , with permission from Elsevier; Tables 20.6 and 20.7 adapted from Competition in Banking: Measurement and Interpretation, Ch 8 in Bell, A.R., Brooks, C. and Prokopczuk, M. (eds) *Handbook of Research Methods and Applications in Empirical Finance.* (Liu, Molyneux and Wilson 2013) Edward Elgar.

Text

Box 2.3 from Press 1 for modernity *The Economist* 28/04/2012, © The Economist Newspaper Limited, London 28/04/2012; Extract on page 57 from http://www.bsa.org.uk., The Building Societies Association; Box 3.4 from http://www.goldmansachs.com/media-relations/press-releases/archived/2008/bank-holding-co.html, Goldman Sachs; Box 8.5 from Mexican banks: From tequila crisis to sunrise *The Economist*, 22/09/2012, © The

Economist Newspaper Limited, London 22/09/2012; Box 11.4 from What caused China's cash crunch? *The Economist*, 04/07/2013, © The Economist Newspaper Limited, London 04/07/2013; Box 16.1 from Japan scales back Japan Post privatisation *Reuters*, 24/03/2010 (Sano, H. and Hirata, N.), Reuters; Box 17.2 from https://openknowledge.worldbank.org/bitstream/handle/10986/11848/Global%20Financial%20Development%20Report%20 2013.pdf?sequence=1, © World Bank 2012, Global Financial Development Report 2013: Rethinking the Role of the State in Finance. Washington, DC: World Bank. doi:10.1596/978-0-8213-9503-5. License: Creative Commons Attribution CC BY 3.0; Extract on page 598 from High-quality securitisation for Europe - The market at a crossroads, June 2014 p.5, http://www.afme.eu/WorkArea/DownloadAsset.aspx?id=10823, AFME.

Financial Times

Figure A1.2 from UK Government Yield Curve, *Financial Times*, 13/05/2014 © The Financial Times Limited. All Rights Reserved; Figure 18.1 from A history of Freddie Mac and Fannie Mae, FT.com 8 September 2008 http://www.ft.com/cms/s/0/e3e1d654-5288-11dd-9ba7-000077b07658.html#axzz3GJUemWbO, © The Financial Times Limited. All Rights Reserved; Figure 19.2 from JPMorgan's US acquisitions pack punch, *Financial Times*, 21/09/2010 (Guerrera, F.) © The Financial Times Limited. All Rights Reserved; Table A1.1 from Financial Times, 18 March 2014 www.ft.com/gilts © The Financial Times Limited. All Rights Reserved; Table A1.2 from UK benchmark government bond yields, *Financial Times*, 13/05/2014 © The Financial Times Limited. All Rights Reserved; Table 3.3 from 15 commercial banks (December 2012) http://www.thebankerdatabase.com/, The Financial Times, © The Financial Times Limited. All Rights Reserved; Tables 3.7 and 3.8 from http://markets.ft.com/investmentBanking/tablesAndTrends.asp?ftauth=1413279770282 © The Financial Times Limited. All Rights Reserved; Box 2.2 from Decision to abolish cheques reversed, *Financial Times*, 12/07/2011 (Moore, E.) © The Financial Times Limited. All Rights Reserved; Box 2.5 from Peer-to-peer lending – done deal, *Financial Times*, 03/01/2013 © The Financial Times Limited. All Rights Reserved; Box 2.6 from Nothing was separated and explained, *Financial Times* 13/05/2011 (Moore, E) © The Financial Times Limited. All Rights Reserved; Box 3.2 from Germany's small banks fight to keep privileges, *Financial Times*, 02/12/2012 (Wilson, J.) © The Financial Times Limited. All Rights Reserved; Box 3.3 from UK Credit Easing, *Financial Times*, 03/10/2011 © The Financial Times Limited. All Rights Reserved; Box 3.4 from After 73 Years: the last gasp of the broker-dealer, *Financial Times*, 15/09/2008 (Gapper, J.) © The Financial Times Limited. All Rights Reserved; Box 3.5 from Wall Street: Leaner and Meaner, *Financial Times*, 30/09/2012 (Braithwaite, T.) © The Financial Times Limited. All Rights Reserved; Box 7.7 from NSFR implementation uncertain after Basel III compromise on LCR phase-in, *Financial Times*, 22/01/2013 (Teitelbaum, H.) © The Financial Times Limited. All Rights Reserved; Box 12.7 from Risk management progress has been small, says banking study, *Financial Times*, 28/07/2013 (Masters, B.) © The Financial Times Limited. All Rights Reserved; Box 13.4 from Just the facts: the Vickers report, *Financial Times*, 12/09/2011 (Goff, S.) © The Financial Times Limited. All Rights Reserved.; Box 14.6 from EU reaches deal on final piece of Banking Union, *Financial Times*, 20/03/2014 (Barker, A.) © The Financial Times Limited. All Rights Reserved; Box 14.7 from EU agrees Deposit Guarantee Scheme deal, *Financial Times*, 18/12/2013 (Barker, A.) © The Financial Times Limited. All Rights Reserved; Box 15.3 from Volcker rule comes of age in spite of protests, *Financial Times*, 10/12/2013 (Braithwaite, T. and Chon, G.) © The Financial Times Limited. All Rights Reserved; Box 16.2 from Japan's biggest banks profit under Abenomics, *Financial Times*, 31/07/2013 (Soble, J.), © The Financial Times Limited. All Rights Reserved; Box 17.3 from Scope for consolidation in overcrowded Gulf banking markets, *Financial Times*, 09/10/2013 (Hunter, G. S.) © The Financial Times Limited. All Rights Reserved; Box 18.3 from CDS: modern day weapons of mass destruction, *Financial Times*, 11/09/11 (John Chapman) © The Financial Times Limited. All Rights Reserved; Box 18.4 from AIG saga shows dangers of credit default swaps, *Financial Times*, 06/03/2009 (Sender, H.) © The Financial Times Limited. All Rights Reserved; Box 19.2 from Santander in talks to sell stake in asset arm, Financial Times, 05/05/13 (Daniel Schäfer). © The Financial Times Limited. All Rights Reserved; Box 19.3 from Consolidation: Fragmented business offers huge potential for mergers, *Financial Times*, 07/05/2013 (Schäfer, D) © The Financial Times Limited. All Rights Reserved; Box 19.5 from A winner's curse that haunts the banking behemoths, *Financial Times*, 12/07/2009 (Plender, J.) © The Financial Times Limited. All Rights Reserved; Box 19.6 from Bank diversification, Financial Times, 19/02/09 (Lex column). © The Financial Times Limited. All Rights Reserved; Box 19.7 adapted from Out to break the banks, *Financial Times*, 30/04/2013 (Nasiripour, S. and Braithwaite, T.) © The Financial Times Limited. All Rights Reserved.

In some instances we have been unable to trace the owners of copyright material, and we would appreciate any information that would enable us to do so.

List of abbreviations and acronyms

$bn	billions of United States dollars
£bn	billions of Great Britain pounds
€bn	billions of euros
$mil	millions of United States dollars
£mil	millions of Great Britain pounds
€mil	millions of euros
2-BCD	EU Second Banking Co-ordination Directive
ABCP	asset-backed commercial paper
ABS	asset-backed securities
ACH	automated clearing house
ACP	Autorité de contrôle prudentiel
AES	advanced execution services
AGP	asset guarantee programme
AIG	American International Group
AIM	Alternative Investment Market
ALCO	asset and liability committee
ALM	asset–liability management
AMA	advanced measurement approach
ANZ	Australia and New Zealand Banking Group Ltd
APACS	Association for Payment Clearing Services
APF	asset purchase facility
APRA	Australian Prudential Regulation Authority
ARM	adjustable-rate mortgage
ASEAN	Association of Southeast Asian Nations
ASF	American Securitisation Forum
ATM	automated teller machine
B2B	business-to-business
BACS	Banks Automated Clearing System
BBA	British Bankers' Association
BBAA	British Business Angels Association
BBVA	Banco Bilbao Vizcaya Argentaria
BCB	Banco Central do Brasil
BCBS	Basel Committee on Banking Supervision
BCCSs	bill and cheque clearing systems
BCRA	Banco Central de la Republica Argentina
BFP	Business Finance Partnership
BHC	bank holding company
BHCA	Bank Holding Company Act
BIP	Bank Insolvency Procedure
BIS	Bank for International Settlements

BoE	Bank of England
BOJ-NET	Bank of Japan Financial Network System
bps	basis points
BRRD	Bank Recovery and Resolution Directive
BSC	Banking Supervision Committee
BTS	Binding Technical Standards
BU	Banking Union
BU	bottom-up approach
BVCA	British Private Equity & Venture Capital Association
C&CC	cheque and clearing company
C/I	cost-to-income ratio
CAD	EU Capital Adequacy Directive
CAGR	compound annual growth rate
CAMELS	Capital, Asset, Management, Earnings, Liquidity, Sensitivity to Market Risk
CAP	Capital Assistance Programme
CAPM	capital asset pricing model
CBA	Commonwealth Bank of Australia
CBFA	Commission Bancaire, Financière et des Assurances
CBO	collateralised bond obligations
CBPP	covered bond purchase programme
CBR	Central Bank of the Russian Federation
CBRC	China Banking Regulatory Commission
CC	Competition Commission
CCAR	comprehensive capital analysis and review
CCB	China Construction Bank
CCBM	Correspondent Central Banking Model
CCBS	Centre for Central Banking Studies
CCCL	Cheque and Credit Clearing Company Limited
CD	certificate of deposit
CDCI	Community Development Capital Initiative
CDFIs	Community Development Financial Institutions
CDIC	Canada Deposit Insurance Corporation
CDO	collateralised debt obligations
CDS	credit default swaps
CEBS	Committee of European Banking Supervisors
CEE	Central and Eastern Europe
CEIOPS	Committee of European Insurance and Occupational Pensions Supervisors
CEO	chief executive officer
CESR	Committee of European Securities Regulators
CFO	chief financial officer
CFPB	Consumer Financial Protection Bureau
CGFS	Committee on the Global Financial System
CGS	credit guarantee scheme
CHAPS	Clearing House Automated Payments System
CHIPS	Clearing House Interbank Payments System
CI	credit institutions
CIBC	Canadian Imperial Bank of Commerce

CLO	collateralised loan obligations
CLS	Continuous Linked Settlement
CME	Chicago Mercantile Exchange
CMGs	crisis management groups
CML	Council of Mortgage Lenders
COAGs	cross-border co-operation agreements
CORF	corporate operational risk function
CP	commercial paper
CPP	Capital Purchase Programme
CPSS	Committee on Payment and Settlement Systems
CRA	credit-rating agencies
CRAM	country risk assessment model
CRD	Capital Requirements Directive
CRDs	cash ratio deposits
CRIS	control risks information services
CR-n	n-firms concentration ratio
CRR	Capital Requirements Regulation
CV	conjectural variations
DD	distance to default
DEFRA	Department for Environment, Food & Rural Affairs
DFAST	Dodd–Frank Act stress tests
DG	duration gap
DGS	deposit guarantee scheme
DIS	deposit insurance scheme
DMO	debt management office
DNB	De Nederlandsche Bank
DTI	debt-to-income ratio
DTIs	deposit-taking institutions
DWF	discount window facility
EBA	European Banking Authority
EBC	European Banking Committee
ECB	European Central Bank
ECOFIN	Economic and Financial Affairs Council
ECSC	European Coal and Steel Community
ECTR	extended collateral term repo facilities
EDF	expected default frequency
EDI	electronic data interchange
EDP	excessive deficit procedure
EEA	European Economic Area
EEC	European Economic Community
EFDI	European Forum of Deposit Insurers
EFN	European Forecasting Network
EFSF	European Financial Stability Facility
EFTPOS	electronic fund transfer at point of sale
EIOPA	European Insurance and Occupational Pensions Authority
EIOPC	European Insurance and Occupational Pensions Committee
EIRIS	Ethical Investing Research Service

EIU	Economist Intelligence Unit
EL	expected loss
ELs	eligible liabilities
ELA	emergency liquidity assistance
EM	equity multiplier
EMI	European Monetary Institute
EMS	European Monetary System
EMU	economic and monetary union
EPS	earnings per share
ERM	Exchange Rate Mechanism
ERM II	Exchange Rate Mechanism II
ESAs	European Supervisory Authorities
ESC	European Securities Committee
ESCB	European System of Central Banks
ESRC	European Systemic Risk Council
ESF	European Securitisation Forum
ESFS	European Financial Stability Facility
ESFS	European System of Financial Supervision
ESFS	European System of Financial Supervisors
ESM	European Stability Mechanism
ESMA	European Securities and Markets Authority
ESRB	European Systemic Risk Board
ESS	efficient scale hypothesis
ESX	efficient structure hypothesis (x-efficiency)
EU	European Union
Euro area	EU member states that have adopted the euro
Eurozone	EU member states that have adopted the euro
EVA	economic value added
EVCA	European Private Equity & Venture Capital Association
EVE	economic value of equity
EWS	early warning systems
F gap	financing gap
FAC	Federal Advisory Council
FCA	Financial Conduct Authority
FCC	Financial Conglomerates Committee
FDI	foreign direct investment
FDIC	Federal Deposit Insurance Corporation
Fed	Federal Reserve Bank
FEDNET	Federal Reserve's national communications network
FFIEC	Federal Financial Institutions Examination Council
FHFA	Federal Housing Finance Agency
FHLMC	Federal Home Loan Mortgage Corporation (Freddie Mac)
FICC	Fixed Income, Currencies and Commodities Department
FINMA	Swiss Financial Market Supervisory Authority
FLS	Funding for Lending Scheme
FMSA	Federal Agency for Financial Market Stabilisation
FNMA	Federal National Mortgage Association (Fannie Mae)

FOMC	Federal Open Market Committee
FPC	Financial Policy Committee
FPS	Faster Payments Service
FR	Federal Reserve
FRA	forward rate agreement
FRB	Federal Reserve Board
FRNs	floating rate notes
FROB	Fondo de Reestructuración Ordenada Bancaria
FRS	Federal Reserve System
FSA	Financial Services Agency (Japan)
FSA	Financial Services Authority (UK)
FSAP	Financial Services Action Plan
FSB	Financial Stability Board
FSCS	Financial Services Compensation Scheme
FSF	Financial Stability Forum
FSMA	Financial Services and Markets Act 2000
FSOC	Financial Stability Oversight Council
FSU	Former Soviet Union
FTP	fund transfer pricing
FXYCS	Foreign Exchange Yen Clearing System
G10	Group of Ten
GAO	Government Accountability Office
GCC	Gulf Co-operation Council
GDP	gross domestic product
GNI	gross national income
GNMA	Government National Mortgage Association (Ginnie Mae)
GSE	government-sponsored enterprise
G-SIBs	global systemically important banks
G-SIFIs	global systemically important financial institutions
HHI	Herfindahl–Hirschman index
HICP	Harmonised Index of Consumer Prices
HKMA	Hong Kong Monetary Authority
HNWI	high net worth individual
HQLA	high-quality liquid assets
IADI	International Association of Deposit Insurers
IAIS	International Association of Insurance Supervisors
IASB	International Accounting Standards Board
IBFs	international banking facilities
ICAEW	Institute of Chartered Accountants in England and Wales
ICB	Independent Commission on Banking
ICBC	Industrial and Commercial Bank of China
ICICI	Industrial Credit and Investment Corporation of India
ICRG	International Country Risk Guide
IDIC	Indonesia Deposit Insurance Corporation
IFC	International Finance Corporation
IFRS	International Financial Reporting Standards
ILTROs	indexed long-term repo open market operations

IM	information memo
IMA	Investment Management Association
IMF	International Monetary Fund
IMM	International Money Market
IOSCO	International Accounting Standards Board
IPAB	Instituto para la Protección al Ahorro Bancario
IPO	initial public offering
IRB	internal ratings based
IRS	interest rate swap
ISAs	individual savings accounts
ISD	Investment Services Directive
ISP	internet service provider
KA	key attributes
KDIC	Korea Deposit Insurance Corporation
KPIs	key performance indicators
KYC	Know Your Customer
L gap	liquidity gap
LBO	leveraged buyouts
LBS RMS	London Business School Risk Measurement Service
LCBGs	large and complex banking groups
LCDS	loan credit default swaps
LCFIs	large and complex financial institutions
LCR	least-cost resolution
LCR	liquidity coverage ratio
LDA	loss distribution approach
LGD	loss given default
LGE	loss given event
LIBOR	London Interbank Offered Rate
LOC	letter of credit
LOLR	lender of last resort
LPFCs	limited-purpose finance companies
LRAC	long-run average cost
LRMC	long-run marginal cost
LSAPs	large-scale asset purchases
LTRO	longer-term refinancing operation
LTV	loan-to-value ratio
M gap	maturity gap
M&As	mergers and acquisitions
M1	narrow money
M2	intermediate money
M3	broad money
MAC	material adverse change
MAS	Monetary Authority of Singapore
MBBGs	Major British Banking Groups
MBS	mortgage-backed securities
MC	marginal cost
MCOB	mortgage conduct of business

MEW	mortgage equity withdrawal
MFIs	monetary financial institutions
MHFG	Mizuho Financial Group
MiFID	Markets in Financial Instruments Directive
MIP	macroeconomic imbalance procedure
MLA	mandated lead arranger
MMF	money market fund
MMOLR	market maker of last resort
MNC	multinational company
MPC	Monetary Policy Committee
MPs	Members of Parliament
MROs	main refinancing operations
MTFG	Mitsubishi Tokyo Financial Group
MUFJ	Mitsubishi UFJ Financial Group
MVE	market value of equity
NAB	National Australia Bank
NBB	National Bank of Belgium
NCAs	national competent authorities
NCB	national central bank
NCUA	National Credit Union Administration
NDTI	non-deposit taking institution
NEIO	New Empirical Industrial Organisation
NIF	note issuance facilities
NII	net interest income
NIM	net interest margin
NIM-8	five Central and Eastern European countries and three Baltic States
NMSs	new member states
NOPAT	net operating profit after tax
NPLs	non-performing loans
NRAM	Northern Rock Asset Management
NSFR	net stable funding ratio
NYSE	New York Stock Exchange
OBA	open bank assistance
OBS	off-balance-sheet
OCC	Office of the Comptroller of the Currency
OECD	Organisation for Economic Co-operation and Development
OFHEO	Office of Federal Housing Enterprise Oversight
OFT	Office of Fair Trading
OIS	overnight index swap
OLA	Orderly Liquidation Authority
OMOs	open market operations
OSFs	operational standing facilities
OTC	over the counter
OTS	Office of Thrift Supervision
P&A	purchase and assumption
P&L	profit and loss
P2P	peer-to-peer

P/B	price to book value
PBC	People's Bank of China
PC	personal computer
PD	probability of default
PIN	personal identification number
PLL	provision for loan losses
POP	persistence of profits
PPI	payment protection insurance
PPIP	public–private investment programme
PPT	partial property transfers
PRA	Prudential Regulation Authority
PSPs	private sector purchasers
PwC	PricewaterhouseCoopers
QE	quantitative easing
R&D	research and development
RAMSI	Risk Assessment Model of Systemic Institutions
RAPM	risk-adjusted performance measurement
RAR	risk–asset ratio
RAROC	risk-adjusted return on capital
RBI	Reserve Bank of India
RBS	Royal Bank of Scotland
RBSG	Royal Bank of Scotland Group
REPO	repurchase agreement
RMBS	residential mortgage-backed securities
RMP	relative market power
ROA	return on assets
ROCHs	recognised overseas clearing houses
ROE	return on equity
ROIEs	recognised overseas investment exchanges
RPD	relative profit differences
RSA	rate-sensitive assets
RSL	rate-sensitive liabilities
RTGS	real-time gross settlement
S&LA	Savings and Loan Association
S&Ls	savings and loans
S&P	Standard & Poor's
SAMA	Saudi Arabian Monetary Agency
SBA	scenario-based approach
SCAP	Supervisory Capital Assessment Programme
SCP	structure-conduct-performance
SDGS	Single Deposit Guarantee Scheme
SDM	Single Deposit Guarantee Mechanism
SEE	South-Eastern Europe
SEPA	Single Euro Payments Area
SFT	securities financing transaction
SGP	Stability and Growth Pact
SHIBOR	Shanghai Interbank Offered Rate

SIFIs	systemically important financial institutions
SIFMA	Securities Industry and Financial Markets Association
SIVs	structured investment vehicles
SLS	special liquidity scheme
SMEs	small and medium enterprises
SMFG	Sumitomo Mitsui Financial Group
SMP	Securities Markets Programme
SMTB	Sumitomo Mitsui Trust Bank Ltd
SPV	special-purpose vehicle
SRB	Single Resolution Board
SRF	Single Bank Resolution Fund
SRM	Single Resolution Mechanism
SRR	special resolution regime
SRU	Special Resolution Unit
SSM	Single Supervisory Mechanism
SWIFT	Society for Worldwide Interbank Financial Telecommunication
TAF	term auction facility
TARGET	Trans-European Automated Real-time Gross settlement Express Transfer system
TARP	Troubled Asset Relief Program
T-bills	Treasury bills
T-bonds	Treasury bonds
TBTDA	too-big-to-discipline-adequately
TBTF	too-big-to-fail
TD	top-down approach
TIP	targeted investment programme
TITF	too important to fail
TITF	too interconnected to fail
TPO	temporary public ownership
TRS	total-return swaps
TSTF	too systemic to fail
UCITS	Directive Undertaking for Collective Investment in Transferable Securities
UKFI	UK Financial Investments Limited
UKPA	UK Payments Administration Ltd
VaR	value at risk
WBC	Westpac Banking Corporation
WOCCU	World Council of Credit Unions
WSE	Warsaw Stock Exchange
WTO	World Trade Organization
YTD	year to date
YTM	yield to maturity
AT	Austria
BE	Belgium
BG	Bulgaria
CY	Cyprus
CZ	Czech Republic

DE	Germany
DK	Denmark
EE	Estonia
ES	Spain
FI	Finland
FR	France
GB	Great Britain (which consists of England, Wales and Scotland)
GR	Greece
HR	Croatia
HU	Hungary
IE	Ireland
IT	Italy
LT	Lithuania
LV	Latvia
MT	Malta
NL	the Netherlands
PL	Poland
PT	Portugal
RO	Romania
SE	Sweden
SI	Slovenia
SK	Slovakia
UK	United Kingdom (which consists of Great Britain together with Northern Ireland)
US	United States (of America)

PART 1

Introduction to banking

Chapter 1

What is special about banks?

Learning objectives

- To understand the role of financial intermediaries in the economy
- To understand lenders' and borrowers' different requirements and how banks can help to bridge such differences
- To understand how financial intermediaries reduce transaction, information and search costs
- To analyse the theories of financial intermediation

1.1 Introduction

The first question one may ask when reading this book is: 'What is special about banks?' This chapter aims to offer some insights into the nature of the banking business and what makes banks 'special'. A bank is a financial intermediary that offers loans and deposits, and payment services. Nowadays banks offer a wide range of additional services, but it is these functions that constitute banks' distinguishing features. Because banks play such an important role in channelling funds from savers to borrowers, in this chapter we use the concepts of 'bank' and 'financial intermediary' almost as synonyms as we review the role of banks and their main functions: size transformation, maturity transformation and risk transformation. The difference between banks and other financial intermediaries is introduced in Chapter 2. The second part of this chapter gives an overview of some important concepts in information economics as they apply to banking. The final sections present five theories to explain why banking exists and the benefits of financial intermediation.

1.2 The nature of financial intermediation

To understand how banks work, it is necessary to understand the role of financial intermediaries in an economy. This will help us to answer the question about why we need banks. Financial intermediaries' and financial markets' main role is to provide a mechanism by which funds are transferred and allocated to their most productive opportunities.

Figure 1.1 The intermediation function

A bank is a financial intermediary whose *core* activity is to provide loans to borrowers and to collect deposits from savers. In other words, banks act as *intermediaries* between borrowers and savers, as illustrated in Figure 1.1.

By carrying out the intermediation function, banks collect surplus funds from savers and allocate them to those (both people and companies) with a deficit of funds (borrowers). In doing so, they channel funds from savers to borrowers, thereby increasing economic efficiency by promoting a better allocation of resources.

Arguably, savers and borrowers do not need banks to intermediate their funds: in **direct finance**, as shown in Figure 1.2, borrowers obtain funds directly from lenders in financial markets.

A **financial claim** is a claim to the payment of a future sum of money and/or a periodic payment of money. More generally, a financial claim carries an obligation on the issuer to pay interest periodically and to redeem the claim at a stated value in one of three ways:

1 on demand;

2 after giving a stated period of notice;

3 on a definite date or within a range of dates.

Financial claims are generated whenever an act of borrowing takes place. Borrowing occurs whenever an economic unit's (individuals, households, companies, government bodies, etc.) total expenditure exceeds its total receipts. Therefore borrowers are generally referred to as **deficit units** and lenders are known as **surplus units**. Financial claims can take the form of any **financial asset**, such as money, bank deposit accounts, bonds, shares, loans, life insurance policies, etc. The lender of funds holds the borrower's financial claim and is said to hold a financial asset. The issuer of the claim (borrower) is said to have a **financial liability**.

The borrowing–lending process illustrated in Figure 1.2 does not require the existence of financial intermediaries. However, two types of barriers can be identified to the direct financing process:

1 The difficulty and expense of matching the complex needs of individual borrowers and lenders.

2 The incompatibility of the financial needs of borrowers and lenders.

Lenders are looking for safety and liquidity. Borrowers may find it difficult to promise either.

Figure 1.2 Direct finance

Lenders' requirements:

- The *minimisation of risk*. This includes the minimisation of the risk of default (the borrower not meeting repayment obligations) and the risk of assets dropping in value.
- The *minimisation of cost*. Lenders aim to minimise their costs.
- *Liquidity*. Lenders value the ease of converting a financial claim into cash without loss of capital value; therefore they prefer holding assets that are more easily converted into cash. One reason for this is the lack of knowledge of future events, which results in lenders preferring short-term to long-term lending.

Borrowers' requirements:

- Funds *at* a particular specified date.
- Funds *for* a specific period of time; preferably *long-term*. (Think of the case of a company borrowing to purchase capital equipment which will achieve positive returns only in the longer term or of an individual borrowing to purchase a house.)
- Funds at the *lowest possible cost*.

In summary, the majority of lenders want to lend their assets for short periods of time and for the highest possible return. In contrast, the majority of borrowers demand liabilities that are cheap and for long periods.

Financial intermediaries can bridge the gap between borrowers and lenders and reconcile their often incompatible needs and objectives. They do so by offering suppliers of funds safety and liquidity by using funds deposited for loans and investments. Financial intermediaries help minimise the costs associated with direct lending – particularly **transaction costs** and those derived from **information asymmetries** (these concepts will be analysed in more detail in Section 1.4).

Transaction costs relate to the costs of searching for a counterparty to a financial transaction;[1] the costs of obtaining information about them; the costs of negotiating the contract; the costs of monitoring the borrowers; and the eventual enforcements costs should the borrower not fulfil its commitments. In addition to transaction costs, lenders are faced with the problems caused by asymmetric information. These problems arise because one party has better information than the counterparty. In this context, the borrower has better information about the investment (in terms of risk and returns of the project) than the lender. Information asymmetries create problems in all stages of the lending process.

Transaction costs and information asymmetries are examples of market failures; that is, they act as obstacles to the efficient functioning of financial markets. One solution is the creation of organised financial markets. However, transaction costs and information asymmetries, though reduced, remain. Another solution is the emergence of financial intermediaries. Organised financial markets and financial intermediaries co-exist in most economies; the flow of funds from units in surplus to units in deficit, in the context of direct and **indirect finance**, is illustrated in Figure 1.3.

Having discussed the advantages of financial intermediation over direct finance, it is necessary to point out that financial intermediaries create additional costs for borrowers and

---

[1] Transaction costs can be defined as the costs of running the economic system (Coase, 1937). In particular, it is common to distinguish between co-ordination costs (e.g. costs of search and negotiation) and motivation costs (e.g. costs due to asymmetric information and imperfect commitment). Transaction costs can be measured in time and money spent in carrying out a financial transaction.

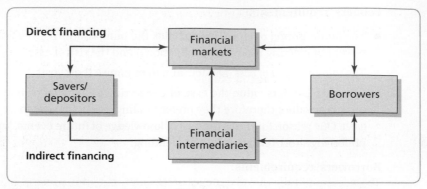

Figure 1.3 Direct and indirect finance

lenders who use their services. Therefore, in order to be able to state that intermediated finance is more advantageous than direct finance, it is necessary that the benefits of such activity outweigh the costs associated with intermediation.

The role of financial intermediation has now become more complex as financial intermediaries perform additional roles, such as brokerage services (i.e. buying and selling stocks and bonds for clients), leasing and factoring. Prior to the 2007–2009 financial turmoil, banks also engaged in a wide process of securitisation (i.e. the pooling and repackaging of illiquid financial assets into marketable securities), thus creating an extra layer of intermediation, as illustrated in Figure 1.4. When financial intermediaries hold claims issued by other financial intermediaries, then an extra layer of financial intermediation is created. Nowadays, given the increased complexity of credit flows, it is not uncommon to have more than two layers of intermediation.

In the decade leading up to the 2007–2009 financial crisis, financial markets also witnessed the rapid growth of a different form of financial intermediation, which became known as **shadow banking**. The term 'shadow banking' was first used at the 2007 Jackson Hole Symposium, an annual meeting sponsored by the Federal Reserve Bank of Kansas City. The Financial Stability Board (2011) defines shadow banking broadly as 'credit intermediation involving entities and activities outside the regular banking system'. This is, however, a very broad definition and both the scope and the economic relevance of shadow banking are still little understood. This has spurred an academic and policy debate on the role of banks in the financial system, and renewed the need to understand banks' operations, their economic

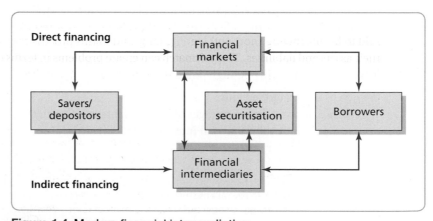

Figure 1.4 Modern financial intermediation

role, their risk-management systems as well as the activities that are carried out outside the scope of the current regulatory framework. It is widely recognised that the two shadow banking activities that are most important economically and in terms of financial stability are securitisation and collateral intermediation (Claessens *et al.*, 2012). These issues will be discussed in more detail in Chapter 18.

1.3 The role of banks

To understand fully the advantages of the intermediation process, it is necessary to analyse what banks do and how they do it. We have seen that the main function of banks is to collect funds (deposits) from units in surplus and lend funds (loans) to units in deficit. Deposits typically have the characteristics of being small-size, low-risk and high-liquidity. Loans are of larger size, higher risk and illiquid. Banks bridge the gap between the needs of lenders and borrowers by performing a transformation function:

(a) size transformation;

(b) maturity transformation;

(c) risk transformation.

(a) Size transformation

Generally, savers/depositors are willing to lend smaller amounts of money than the amounts required by borrowers. For example, think about the difference between your savings account and the money you would need to buy a house. Banks collect funds from savers in the form of small-size deposits and repackage them into larger-size loans. Banks perform this size-transformation function exploiting **economies of scale** associated with the lending/borrowing function because they have access to a larger number of depositors than any individual borrower (see Section 1.4.2).

(b) Maturity transformation

Banks transform funds lent for a short period of time into medium- and long-term loans. For example, they convert demand deposits (i.e. funds deposited that can be withdrawn on demand) into 25-year residential mortgages. Banks' liabilities (i.e. the funds collected from savers) are mainly repayable on demand or at relatively short notice. Banks' assets (funds lent to borrowers), meanwhile, are normally repayable in the medium to long term. Banks are said to be 'borrowing short and lending long' and in this process they are said to 'mismatch' their assets and liabilities. This mismatch can create problems in terms of **liquidity risk**, which is the risk of not having enough liquid funds to meet one's liabilities.

(c) Risk transformation

Individual borrowers carry a risk of default (known as credit risk), that is the risk that they might not be able to repay the amount of money they borrowed. Savers wish to minimise risk and prefer their money to be safe. Banks are able to minimise the risk of individual loans by diversifying their investments, pooling risks, screening and monitoring borrowers and holding capital and reserves as a buffer for unexpected losses.

The tools and techniques used by banks to perform these transformations and to minimise the risks inherent with such transformations will be illustrated in Chapter 12.

1.4 Information economies

As discussed earlier, banks provide an important source of external funds used to finance business and other activities. One of the main features of banks is that they reduce transaction costs by exploiting scale and scope economies and often they owe their extra profits to superior information. Sections 1.4.1 and 1.4.2 look into information economies as they apply to the banking industry.

1.4.1 Transaction costs

Banks traditionally differ from other financial intermediaries for two main reasons: (1) bank liabilities (i.e. deposits) are accepted as a means of exchange; and (2) banks are the only intermediaries that can vary the level of deposits and can create and destroy credit. Modern views on financial intermediation indicate as a crucial function of financial intermediaries the transformation of primary securities issued by firms (deficit units) into secondary securities that are more attractive to surplus units.

In this context, financial intermediation can be explained in terms of reduction of transaction costs: secondary securities will be less risky, more convenient and more liquid than primary securities because banks benefit from economies of scale in transaction technologies and are able to carry out a rational diversification of risks. This allows them to offer lower loan rates relative to direct financing. However, most bank assets are illiquid (non-negotiable) and this can be explained by issues relating to asymmetric information (see Section 1.4.3).

1.4.2 Economies of scale and economies of scope

Financial intermediaries reduce transaction, information and search costs mainly by exploiting economies of scale. By increasing the volume of transactions, the cost per unit of transactions decreases. Moreover, by focusing on growing in size, financial intermediaries are able to draw standardised contracts and monitor customers so that they enforce these contracts. They also train high-quality staff to assist in the process of finding and monitoring suitable deficit units (borrowers). It would be difficult, time-consuming and costly for an individual to do so.

Financial intermediaries can reduce risks by 'pooling', or aggregating, individual risks so that in normal circumstances, surplus units will be depositing money as deficit units make withdrawals. This enables banks, for instance, to collect relatively liquid deposits and invest most of them in long-term assets. Another way to look at this situation is that large groups of depositors are able to obtain liquidity from the banks while investing savings in illiquid but more profitable investments (Diamond and Dybvig, 1983).

Economies of scope refer to a situation where the joint costs of producing two complementary outputs are less than the combined costs of producing the two outputs separately. Let us consider two outputs, Q_1 and Q_2, and their separate costs, $C(Q_1)$ and $C(Q_2)$. If the joint cost of producing the two outputs is expressed by $C(Q_1,Q_2)$, then economies of scope are said to exist if:

$$C(Q_1, Q_2) < C(Q_1) + C(Q_2) \qquad (1.1)$$

This may arise when the production processes of both outputs share some common inputs, including both capital (for example, the actual building the bank occupies) and labour (such as bank management). Consider, for example, the economies derived from the joint supply of banking and insurance services. A bank might sell both mortgages and life insurance policies that go with them, therefore creating cross-selling opportunities for the bank (for more details on bancassurance, see Section 3.2.1). However, the literature indicates that economies of scope are difficult to identify and measure.

1.4.3 Asymmetric information

Information is at the heart of all financial transactions and contracts. Three problems are relevant:

- Not everyone has the same information.
- Everyone has less than perfect information.
- Some parties to a transaction have 'inside' information that is not made available to both sides of the transaction.

Such 'asymmetric' information can make it difficult for two parties to do business together, and this is why regulations are introduced to help reduce mismatches in information.

Transactions involving asymmetric (or private) information are everywhere. A government selling a bond does not know what buyers are prepared to pay; a bank does not know how likely a borrower is to repay; a firm that sells a life insurance policy does not know the precise health of the purchaser (even though they have a good idea); an investor that buys an equity in Apple does not know the full details of the company's operations and prospects. These types of informational asymmetries can distort both firms' and users' incentives that result in significant inefficiencies.

Information is at the centre of all financial transactions and contracts. Decisions are made beforehand (*ex ante*) on the basis of less than complete information and sometimes with counterparties who have superior information with the potential for exploitation. In any financial system, information is not symmetrically distributed across all agents, which implies that different agents have different information sets. Put another way, full and complete information is not uniformly available to all interested parties. In addition, not all parties have the same ability to utilise the information that is available to them. In particular, parties have more information about themselves (including their intentions and abilities) than do others. The problem arises because information is not a free good and the acquisition of information is not a costless activity. If either were the case, there would never be a problem of asymmetric information.

Asymmetric information, and the problems this gives rise to, are central to financial arrangements and the way financial institutions behave to limit and manage risk. Information asymmetries, or the imperfect distribution of information among parties, can generate **adverse selection** and **moral hazard** problems, as explained in Section 1.4.3.1. Another type of information asymmetry relates to the **agency costs** between the principal (e.g. bank) and the agent (e.g. borrower). These issues are analysed in Section 1.4.3.2.

1.4.3.1 Adverse selection and moral hazard

One problem that often arises from asymmetric information is adverse selection. The better informed economic agent has a natural incentive to exploit his informational advantage. Those who are uninformed should anticipate their informational handicap and behave accordingly.

It is the interaction between the inclination of the informed to strategically manipulate and the anticipation of such manipulation by the uninformed that results in distortion away from the 'first best' (the economic outcome in a setting where all are equally well informed). Adverse selection is a problem at the search/verification stage of the transaction (*ex ante*); it is sometimes referred to as the 'lemon' problem (Akerlof, 1970). In his famous study entitled 'The market for "lemons"', George Akerlof explains the consequences of asymmetric information in a situation where the buyer, and not the seller, does not know the quality of the commodity being exchanged. In this context, the vendor is aware that they are the only one knowing the true characteristics of the commodities and can exaggerate the quality. Conversely, the buyer can form an opinion on the quality of the commodities only after buying the commodity (i.e. *ex post*). Akerlof demonstrates that if there are a relatively high number of bad commodities in the market, the market will function poorly, if at all. A common example of this phenomenon is in the second-hand car market – here the sellers know whether or not their car is a lemon (a bad car) but the buyers cannot make that judgement without running the car. Given that buyers cannot tell the quality of any car, all cars of the same type will sell at the same price, regardless of whether they are lemons or not. The risk of purchasing a lemon will lower the price buyers are prepared to pay for a car, and because second-hand prices are low, people with non-lemon cars will have little incentive to put them on the market.

One possible solution to the adverse selection problem is to offer a warranty, as it would be viewed as a signal of quality. Hence '**signalling**' refers to actions of the 'informed party' in an adverse selection problem. The action undertaken by the less informed party to determine the information possessed by the informed party is called '**screening**' (for example, the action taken by an insurance company to gather information about the health history of potential customers).[2]

Economic transactions often involve people with different information. In the context of financial markets, for example, those who buy insurance or take out bank loans are likely to have a better idea of the risks they face than the insurance company or bank. As such, it is often those who face the bigger risks who are more likely to want to buy insurance and those with the riskiest business proposals who are more likely to seek bank loans and therefore are more likely to be selected. Adverse selection in financial markets results in firms attracting the wrong type of clients; this in turn pushes up insurance premiums and loan rates to the detriment of lower-risk customers. Financial firms such as banks and insurers therefore seek to screen out/monitor such customers by assessing their risk profile and adjusting insurance premiums and loan rates to reflect the risks of individual clients.

In banking, adverse selection can occur typically as a result of loan pricing. As shown in Figure 1.5, the relationship between the return the bank can expect from a certain loan and the loan price is increasing and positive up to a certain point (for example, an interest rate of 12 per cent). Any prices above that level (the shaded area in the figure) will decrease the expected return for the bank because of adverse selection: only the most risky borrowers (i.e. those with a low probability of repayment, such as speculators) will be ready to accept a loan at a very high price.

Another issue relating to information asymmetries is moral hazard (or hidden action). Superior information may enable one party to work against the interests of another. In general, moral hazard arises when a contract or financial arrangement creates incentives for parties to behave

---

[2] In 2001 the Nobel Prize in Economic Sciences was awarded to three economists 'for their analyses of markets with asymmetric information': G.A. Akerlof, A.M. Spence and J.E. Stiglitz.

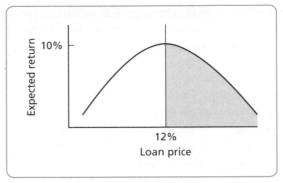

Figure 1.5 Adverse selection in loan pricing

against the interest of others. For example, moral hazard is the risk that the borrower might engage in activities that are undesirable from the lender's point of view because they make it less likely that the loan will be repaid and thus harm the interest of the lender. A classic example is the use of funds originally borrowed for a 'safe' investment project (a car purchase, a home improvement) which are then gambled in a high-risk project (for example, invested in a 'get rich quick' scheme). Thus, for a bank, moral hazard occurs after the loan has been granted (*ex post*) and is associated with the monitoring and enforcement stages. Those that obtain some form of insurance may take greater risks than they would do without it because they know they are protected, so the insurer may get larger claims than expected. Examples of moral hazard in banking relate to deposit insurance and the lender-of-last-resort function of the central bank (see Chapter 7).

Monitoring is required whenever there are the problems of moral hazard and adverse selection. A standard example often given is the case of bank loans where lenders screen out excessively high risks, and regularly monitor the performance of the borrowers by obtaining various types of financial information – for example, companies are often required to submit periodic reports detailing the performance of their business. In addition, for loans to large companies, there are credit rating agencies (such as Standard & Poor's and Moody's) that provide information on firm performance and credit ratings, that is an estimate of the amount of credit that can be extended to a company or person without undue risk (see Table 4.3 Credit risk ratings – Moody's and Standard & Poor's). Banks also send inspectors to firms to monitor their progress. However, it is particularly difficult for consumers/investors to monitor financial firms to see how they are performing and what they are doing with their deposits or investments. This is one reason why we have regulators to monitor financial firm behaviour.

1.4.3.2 Principal–agent problems

Financial transactions often create **principal–agent problems** of one sort or another. This is also related to the problem of incentive structures in that the central issue is how a principal is able to rely on the agent acting in the interests of the principal employing him rather than in his own selfish interests and against those of the principal. The problem arises because the agent often has superior information and expertise (which may be the reason the principal employs them). The agent can choose his or her behaviour after the contract has been established, and because of this the agent is often able to conceal the outcome of a contract. Agency problems also arise because the agent cannot be efficiently or costlessly monitored. Unless these problems can be solved, the agency costs involved can act as a serious deterrent to financial contracting, with resultant losses. The challenge is to create financial contracts or arrangements that align the interests of the principal and the agent.

A typical example of principal–agent problem refers to a situation of separation of ownership and control in a firm. Managers in control (the *agents*) may act in their own interest rather than in the interest of shareholders (the *principals*) because the managers have less incentive to maximise profits than shareholders do.[3] A firm acting in the interest of the shareholders has an incentive to undertake investments that benefit the shareholders at the expense of creditors. However, as observed by Jensen and Meckling (1976), the assumption that managers act in the best interest of the shareholders is questionable. As an agent of the shareholders, the manager can do many things that may not be in the best interests of the shareholders. For example, managers may select low-risk investment projects with a view towards protecting their positions and reputations. To summarise, the principal (the shareholder) is unable to completely control the agent's behaviour. If it were possible to costlessly observe the agent's action, there would be no moral hazard. It is obvious that the principal anticipates the agent's behaviour. Therefore, the principal attempts to design a contract that aligns the agent's incentives with his own.

The example above shows that principal–agency issues are inextricably linked to information asymmetry and moral hazard. The behaviour of contracting parties (counterparties) needs to be monitored after a contract has been agreed to ensure that information asymmetries are not exploited by one party against the interest of the other, and also because frequently a fiduciary relationship (a relationship of trust and confidence) is created by a financial contract. In both cases, parties need to be monitored to ensure that their behaviour is consistent with both their interests. A special characteristic of many financial contracts is that the value (for example, the future returns on an investment; the amount of loan repayments to a bank – some of which may suffer from default; returns on long-term savings products) cannot be observed or verified at the point of purchase, and that the post-contract behaviour of a counterparty determines the ultimate value of the contract. This also creates a need for monitoring. In addition, monitoring is needed because many financial contracts are long-term in nature and information acquired before a contract is agreed may become irrelevant during the course of the contract as circumstances and conditions change. Above all, the value of a contract or financial product cannot be ascertained with certainty at the point the contract is made or the product is purchased. This often distinguishes financial contracts from other economic contracts such as purchases of goods. While the need for monitoring is accepted, it is an expensive activity and parties involved need to balance the costs and benefits of such monitoring.

As the cost of monitoring principal–agent relationships can be expensive and difficult for the market to resolve, public regulatory agencies help perform this task – for instance, they monitor financial service firms to minimise conflicts between principals (financial firms) and agents (customers).

1.4.3.3 The free-rider problem

One general solution to information problems is for those involved in financial transactions to invest in information. However, this is not a costless activity and free-rider problems may emerge as, in some cases, no one party can appropriate the full value of the costly information acquired.

Free-rider problems occur when people who do not pay for information take advantage of the information that other people have paid for. For example, you purchase information that

---

[3] Note that shareholders in the US are referred to as stockholders. Also it is useful to remember that equities or ordinary shares in the UK are referred to as common stock in the United States.

tells you which firms are good and which are bad. You believe the purchase is worthwhile because you can buy securities of good firms that are undervalued so you will gain extra profits. But free-rider investors see that you are buying certain securities and will want to buy the same.

Governments could produce information to help investors distinguish good from bad firms and provide it to the public free of charge. The main drawback is that this action may be politically difficult. Moreover, it never completely eliminates the problem. By encouraging bank lending, a bank can profit from the information it produces by making private loans (i.e. avoiding free-rider problems).

1.4.3.4 Relationship and transaction banking

In credit markets one way to overcome agency and adverse selection problems is for the parties to enter a *relational contract*. Relational contracts are informal agreements between the bank and the borrowers sustained by the value of future relationships. Modern financial intermediation theory has emphasised the role of banks as relationship lenders: this is when banks invest in developing close and long-term relationships with their customers. Such relations improve the information flow between the bank and the borrower and thus are beneficial to both parties. If the customer has a 'history' (e.g. they have borrowed previously from the bank over a long period of time), then the bank's screening and monitoring costs will be much lower compared with the cost associated with new customers. Meanwhile, borrowers will find it easier to get future loans at (relatively) low rates of interest.[4]

The benefits of **relationship banking** over **transactional banking** arise from a reduction of agency problems by long-term loan contracts and the use of information reusability over time. Relationship banking improves upon information flow, thus mitigating information asymmetries, and allows for flexibility.

The literature (see Boot, 2000; Boot and Thakor, 2014) has indicated that relationship banking can be sustained in the face of significant competitive pressures. In other words, the informational savings derived from relationship lending can be considered as a primary source of competitive advantage for existing banks over new market participants – this is because by drawing relational contracts, banks can 'isolate' themselves from competition from other banks and/or non-bank financial intermediaries.

Our discussion above seems to suggest that the creation of strong links between banks and companies might be beneficial to both businesses. Indeed, in bank-based systems such as Japan and Germany, banks hold equity stakes in companies they lend to and banks in turn have members on the board of directors of these companies. In Anglo-Saxon countries (such as the United States and the United Kingdom), such arrangements are highly restricted.

The intense disintermediation process that has characterised the financial and banking markets, coupled with the increasingly common *transaction banking*, has started to challenge the importance of banks as relationship lenders. Transaction banking involves a pure funding transaction where the bank essentially acts as a 'broker' – an example is that of a mortgage loan made by a bank and then sold on to an investor in the form of a security. This process is known as securitisation and it is explained in more detail in Chapter 18. It is obvious that in transaction banking there is no relationship between the parties and no flexibility in the contract terms.

---

[4] It has been observed (e.g. Heffernan, 2005, p. 7), however, that in the presence of relationship banking there could be more scope for borrower opportunism.

1.5　Why do banks exist? Theories of financial intermediation

There are five theories that explain why financial intermediation (banking) exists. These theories relate to delegated monitoring, information production, liquidity transformation, consumption smoothing and the role of banks as a commitment mechanism.

1.5.1　Financial intermediation and delegated monitoring

One of the main theories put forward as an explanation for the existence of banking relates to the role of banks as 'monitors' of borrowers. Since monitoring credit risk (likelihood that borrowers default) is costly, it is efficient for surplus units (depositors) to delegate the task of monitoring to specialised agents such as banks. Banks have expertise and economies of scale in processing information on the risks of borrowers and as depositors would find it costly to undertake this activity, they delegate responsibility to the banks.

One of the most relevant studies explaining why banks exist on the basis of contract theory is by Diamond (1984), according to whom **delegated monitoring** on behalf of small lenders provides the *raison d'être* of banking:

> An intermediary (such as a bank) is delegated the task of costly monitoring of loan contracts written with firms who borrow from it. It has a gross cost advantage in collecting this information because the alternative is either duplication of effort if each lender monitors directly or a free-rider problem in which case no lender monitors. Financial intermediation theories are generally based on some cost advantage for the intermediary. Schumpeter assigned such a *delegated monitoring* role to banks.
>
> Diamond (1984, p. 393)

Diamond's study investigates the determinants of delegation costs and develops a theoretical model in which a financial intermediary (typically a bank or an insurance company) has net cost savings relative to direct lending and borrowing. Diamond's approach is essentially developed around two interconnected factors:

1 Diversification among different investment projects – this is crucial in explaining why there is a benefit from delegating monitoring to an intermediary that is not monitored by its depositors.
2 The size of the delegated intermediary that can finance a large number of borrowers.

Since usually diversification will increase with the number of bank loans, larger delegated intermediaries will generate higher economies of scale in monitoring and this will allow for greater portfolio diversification than any individual lender could achieve.

One issue that arises, however, relates to who is 'monitoring the monitor'. Surplus units (depositors) can reduce monitoring expense if the costs of monitoring the intermediary are lower than the costs of surplus units lending direct to borrowers and therefore directly incurring the monitoring costs. As a financial intermediary increases in size, it can commit to offer deposit facilities to surplus units only if the intermediary is undertaking the appropriate monitoring activity.

1.5.2 Information production

If information about possible investment opportunities is not free, then economic agents may find it worthwhile to produce such information. For instance, surplus units could incur substantial search costs if they were to seek out borrowers directly. If there were no banks, there would be duplication of information production costs as surplus units would individually incur considerable expense in seeking out the relevant information before they committed funds to a borrower. An alternative is to have a smaller number of specialist agents (banks) that choose to produce the same information.

Banks have economies of scale and other expertise in processing information relating to deficit units – this information may be obtained upon first contact with borrowers but in reality is more likely to be learned over time through repeated dealings with the borrower. As banks build up this information (e.g. the knowledge of credit risk associated with different types of borrowers – 'customer relationships') they become experts in processing this information. As such they have an information advantage and depositors are willing to place funds with a bank knowing that these will be directed to the appropriate borrowers without the former having to incur information costs.

1.5.3 Liquidity transformation

Banks provide financial or secondary claims to surplus units (depositors) that often have superior liquidity features compared with direct claims (such as equity or bonds). Banks' deposits can be viewed as contracts offering high liquidity and low risk that are held on the liabilities side of a bank's balance sheet. These are financed by relatively illiquid and higher-risk assets (e.g. loans) on the assets side of the bank's balance sheet. It should be clear that banks can hold liabilities and assets of different liquidity features on both sides of their balance sheet through diversification of their portfolios. In contrast, surplus units (depositors) hold relatively undiversified portfolios (e.g. deposits typically have the same liquidity and risk features). The better banks are at diversifying their balance sheets, the less likely it is that they will default on meeting deposit obligations.

1.5.4 Consumption smoothing

The three aforementioned theories are usually cited as the main reasons why financial intermediaries (typically banks) exist. However, studies have suggested that banks perform a major function as consumption smoothers – namely, banks are institutions that enable economic agents to smooth consumption by offering insurance against shocks to a consumer's consumption path. The argument goes that economic agents have uncertain preferences about their expenditure and this creates a demand for liquid assets. Financial intermediaries in general, and banks in particular, provide these assets via lending and this helps smooth consumption patterns for individuals.

1.5.5 Commitment mechanisms

Another theory that has developed aims to provide a reason why illiquid bank assets (loans) are financed by demand deposits that allow consumers to arrive and demand liquidation of those illiquid assets. It is argued that bank deposits (demand deposits) have evolved as a necessary device to discipline bankers. To control the risk-taking propensity of banks, demand deposits have developed because changes in the supply and demand of these instruments will be reflected in financing costs and this disciplines or commits banks to behave prudently (ensuring banks hold sufficient liquidity and capital resources).

1.6 The benefits of financial intermediation

Financial intermediation, as noted previously, is the process of channelling funds between those who wish to lend or invest and those who wish to borrow or require investment funds. Financial intermediaries act as principals, creating financial assets and liabilities.

A wide range of financial institutions are engaged in financial intermediation, including banks, insurance and pension firms, securities houses and others. Many of the services offered by financial institutions include both intermediation and non-intermediation activities (e.g. payment services, fund management services and so on).

An important distinguishing characteristic of financial intermediation is that financial assets and liabilities are created. In the case of a bank deposit, the nature of the claims and liabilities created is usually straightforward. The depositor has a claim for a given amount of money, perhaps to be repaid on demand, while the bank has a matching liability to repay a given amount of money. If the bank on-lends deposits, it has a claim against the borrower for a given amount of money, to be repaid (with interest) at a given point in time in the future. The borrower, naturally, has a liability to repay that sum of money with interest on the specified date.

The significance of financial intermediation within the financial system is best appreciated in terms of the benefits that it generates. These benefits accrue to ultimate lenders (surplus units), to ultimate borrowers (deficit units) and to society as a whole.

1.6.1 The benefits to ultimate lenders (surplus units)

These benefits may be summarised as follows:

- Greater liquidity is generally achieved by lending to a financial intermediary rather than directly to an ultimate borrower.

- Less risk is involved, due to the pooling of risk inherent in financial intermediation, the improved risk assessment that intermediaries are able to undertake and the portfolio diversification that can frequently be achieved. This reduction in risk may be reflected in guaranteed interest rates on deposits with a financial intermediary.

- Marketable securities may be issued as the counterpart to deposits with a financial intermediary. For example, a certificate of deposit (CD) is a type of time deposit where the bank issues a certificate that a deposit has been made (this is particularly common in the US). The certificate of deposit can then be sold in the market whenever an individual/firm needs cash. Hence depositors, instead of waiting until maturity of the securities, may sell them in the market to regain the cash. This clearly enhances the liquidity of the depositors' funds (in the broadest sense).

- Transaction costs associated with the lending process are likely to be reduced significantly, especially where straightforward deposit facilities are utilised.

- The lending decision is simplified, since there are fewer lending opportunities to financial intermediaries than there are ultimate borrowers. In addition, the assessment of the opportunities for lending to intermediaries is generally a simpler procedure than the assessment of the opportunities for lending to ultimate borrowers.

1.6.2 The benefits to ultimate borrowers (deficit units)

These benefits may be summarised as follows:

- Loans will generally be available for a longer time period from financial intermediaries than from the ultimate lenders.
- Financial intermediaries will generally be prepared to grant loans of larger amounts than will ultimate lenders.
- Using financial intermediaries will generally involve lower transaction costs than would be incurred if borrowers had to approach ultimate lenders directly.
- The interest rate will generally be lower when borrowing from financial intermediaries, compared with borrowing directly from ultimate lenders. As we have seen, financial intermediaries, through the minimisation of information costs and the diversification of risk, can actually reduce the cost of intermediation.
- When borrowing from financial intermediaries, there is a greater likelihood that loans will be available when required.

1.6.3 The benefits to society as a whole

Financial intermediation is beneficial not only to borrowers and lenders but it is considered likely to:

- cause a more efficient utilisation of funds within an economy, since the evaluation of lending opportunities will be improved;
- cause a higher level of borrowing and lending to be undertaken, due to the lower risks and costs associated with lending to financial intermediaries;
- cause an improvement in the availability of funds to higher-risk ventures, due to the capability of financial intermediaries to absorb such risk. High-risk ventures are widely considered to be important for creating the basis of future prosperity for an economy.

1.7 Conclusion

This chapter has analysed the key features of financial intermediation. Banks, as other financial intermediaries, play a pivotal role in the economy, channelling funds from units in surplus to units in deficit. They reconcile the different needs of borrowers and lenders by transforming small-size, low-risk and highly liquid deposits into loans which are of larger size, of higher risk and illiquid (transformation function). We have discussed the main reasons banks have advantages in the intermediation process relating to matching the needs of ultimate lenders (depositors) and borrowers. In particular, we have explored the concepts of transaction costs, economies of scale and economies of scope.

The relevance of information costs and the notion of information asymmetries were also introduced. These are costs due to imperfect distribution of information among parties and can be defined as situations in which one or more of the parties to a transaction do not have all or part of the relevant information needed to tell whether the terms of the contract are mutually acceptable and/or are being met. Situations of this kind give rise to adverse selection and moral hazard problems. Another type of information asymmetry relates to the agency costs between the principal (bank) and the agent (borrower).

The reasons for the existence of banks are then related to five theories that concern delegated monitoring, information production, liquidity transformation, consumption smoothing and the role of banks as a commitment mechanism. The chapter concludes with an overview of the main benefits of financial intermediation.

Key terms

Adverse selection	Financial asset	Moral hazard	Surplus unit
Agency costs	Financial claim	Principal–agent	Transactional
Deficit unit	Financial liability	problems	banking
Delegated monitoring	Indirect finance	Relationship banking	Transaction costs
Direct finance	Information	Screening	
Economies of scale	asymmetries	Shadow banking	
Economies of scope	Liquidity risk	Signalling	

Key reading

Akerlof, G.A. (1970) 'The market for "lemons": Quality uncertainty and the market mechanism', *Quarterly Journal of Economics*, 84(8), 488–500.

Allen, F. and Carletti, E. (2014) 'The roles of banks in financial systems', in Berger, A.N., Molyneux, P. and Wilson, J.O.S. (eds), *The Oxford Handbook of Banking*, 2nd Edition, Oxford: Oxford University Press, Chapter 2.

Boot, A.W.A. (2000) 'Relationship banking: What do we know?', *Journal of Financial Intermediation*, 9(1), 7–25.

Boot, A.W.A. and Thakor, A. (2014) 'Commercial banking and shadow banking: The accelerating integration of banks and markets and its implications for regulation', in Berger, A.N., Molyneux, P. and Wilson, J.O.S. (eds), *The Oxford Handbook of Banking*, 2nd Edition, Oxford: Oxford University Press, Chapter 3.

Claessens, S., Pozsar, Z., Ratnovski, L. and Singh, M. (2012) 'Shadow banking: Economics and policy', *IMF Staff Discussion Note*, 4 December.

Coase, R. (1937) 'The nature of the firm', *Economica*, 4(16), 386–405.

Diamond, D.W. (1984) 'Financial intermediation and delegated monitoring', *Review of Economics Studies*, 51(3), 393–414.

Financial Stability Board (FSB) (2011) 'Shadow banking: Strengthening oversight and regulation', Recommendations of the Financial Stability Board, Basel: Bank for International Settlements.

Jensen, M. and Meckling, W. (1976) 'Theory of the firm: Managerial behavior, agency costs and ownership structure', *Journal of Financial Economics*, 3(4), 305–360.

REVISION QUESTIONS AND PROBLEMS

1.1 What is the role of financial intermediaries in an economy?

1.2 What is special about banks?

1.3 How do lenders' and borrowers' requirements differ? How can financial intermediaries bridge the gap between them?

1.4 Explain how banks can lower transaction costs.

1.5 Explain the relevance of information asymmetries in the intermediation process.

1.6 How do adverse selection and moral hazard affect the bank lending function? How can banks minimise such problems?

1.7 How are banks affected by agency problems?

1.8 Describe the main theories put forward to explain the existence of financial intermediaries.

1.9 Explain the concept of delegated monitoring.

1.10 What are the costs and benefits of financial intermediation?

Chapter 2

Bank activities and services

Learning objectives

- To understand what modern banks do
- To describe the main services offered by banks
- To understand the importance of the payment system
- To understand the growing relevance of ethical banking
- To identify the different aspects of bank sustainability in relation to good business performance

2.1 Introduction

This chapter offers some insights into the nature of the banking business. It reviews the main services offered by banks (loans and deposits, and payment services) as well as a wide range of additional services, such as insurance and investment services. In this context, special attention is given to the significant changes in payment systems with an extensive discussion on the major instruments and services that modern banks provide to their customers, from plastic money to **e-banking**. The last section provides a synopsis of ethical and sustainable banking and explains why banks represent a key channel in directing financial capital to sustainable activities.

2.2 What do banks do?

We have seen in Chapter 1 that financial intermediaries channel funds from units in surplus to units in deficit. In order to better understand how banks work, we need to examine their assets and liabilities. Table 2.1 summarises a typical retail bank balance sheet (details of banks' balance sheet and income structure are presented in Chapter 9).

For traditional retail banks, the main source of funding is customer deposits (reported on the liabilities side of the balance sheet); this funding is then invested in loans, other investments and fixed assets (such as buildings for the branch network) and it is reported on the

Table 2.1 A simplified bank balance sheet

Assets	Liabilities
Cash	Customer deposits
Liquid assets	Equity
Loans	
Other investments	
Fixed assets	
Total	Total

assets side of the balance sheet. The difference between total assets and total liabilities is the bank capital (equity). Put very simply, banks make profits by charging an interest rate on their loans that is higher than the one they pay to depositors.

As with other companies, banks can raise funds by issuing bonds and equity (shares) and saving from past profits (retained earnings). However, the bulk of their money comes from deposits. It is this ability to collect deposits from the public that distinguishes banks from other financial institutions, as explained in Section 2.3.

2.3   Banks and other financial institutions

Banks are **deposit-taking institutions** (DTIs) and are also known as *monetary financial institutions* (MFIs). Monetary financial institutions play a major role in a country's economy as their deposit liabilities form a major part of a country's money supply and are therefore very relevant to governments and central banks for the transmission of monetary policy (see Chapter 5). Banks' deposits function as money; as a consequence, an expansion of bank deposits results in an increase in the stock of money circulating in an economy (see Box 2.1). All other things being equal, the money supply – that is the total amount of money in the economy – will increase.

The monetary function of bank deposits is often seen as one of the main reasons why DTIs are subjected to heavier regulation and supervision than their **non-deposit-taking institution** (NDTI) counterparts (such as insurance companies, pension funds, investment companies, finance houses and so on).

One further feature that distinguishes monetary financial institutions from other financial corporations lies in the nature of financial contracts: deposit holdings are said to be *discretionary*, in the sense that savers can make discretionary decisions concerning how much money to hold and for how long. Depositors are free to decide the frequency and amount of their transactions. Meanwhile, holding assets from other financial institutions requires a contract which specifies the amount and frequency of the flow of funds. For example, the monthly contributions to a pension fund or to an insurance provider are normally fixed and pre-determined. Therefore the flow of funds in and out of other financial intermediaries is described as *contractual*.

Figure 2.1 illustrates the classification of financial institutions in the UK. However, it is important to keep in mind that there is no unique, universally accepted classification of financial intermediaries. Furthermore, distinctions are becoming blurred as deregulation, financial conglomeration, advances in information technology and financial innovation, increased competition, globalisation and the fallout from the global financial crisis of 2007–2009 have all contributed to change the industry.

BOX 2.1 HOW BANKS CREATE MONEY: THE CREDIT MULTIPLIER

In order to understand how banks create money we illustrate a simple model of the **credit multiplier** based on the assumption that modern banks keep only a fraction of the money that is deposited by the public. This fraction is kept as reserves and will allow the bank to face possible requests of withdrawals. Suppose that there is only one bank in the financial system and suppose that there is a mandatory reserve of 10 per cent. This means that the bank will have to put aside as reserves 10 per cent of its total deposits. The balance sheet of this bank over three time periods is illustrated in Table 2.2.

Table 2.2 The case of a single bank under a 10 per cent reserve ratio (£mil)

		Initial period (a)	Intermediate period (b): increase deposits by £50,000	Final period (c): adjust reserve ratio
Liabilities	Deposits	50	50.05	50.05
Assets	Reserves	5	5.05	5.005
	Loans	45	45	45.045
Reserve ratio		10%	10.1%	10%

In the initial position (a) we assume that the bank has £50 million of deposits and is adhering to a 10 per cent reserve ratio. That is, for every £10 it receives in deposits, it keeps £1 in cash and can invest the other £9 as loans. In this case the bank's £50 million of deposits are broken down into £5 million cash and £45 million loans. Position (b) shows the effect of an increase in deposits by £50,000. Initially, this extra £50,000 of deposits is kept as reserves. However, as the bank earns no money by simply holding excess reserves, it will wish to reduce it back to 10 per cent. In position (c) the bank returns to the initial 10 per cent reserve holding as required by the reserve ratio. At the same time, the bank will increase its loans by £45,000. In this example, the credit multiplier is defined as the ratio of change in deposits to the change in level of reserves:

$$\text{Credit multiplier} = \frac{\Delta DEPOSITS}{\Delta RESERVES} = \frac{50.05 - 50}{5.005 - 5} = \frac{0.05}{0.005} = 10$$

where:

Δ Deposits = the change in the level of deposits

Δ Reserves = the change in the level of reserves.

The credit multiplier is the same as the reciprocal of the reserve ratio (i.e. $1/0.10 = 10$).

Considering that most banking systems operate with more than one bank, we can assume that if bank A gets a £50,000 increase in its deposit, 10 per cent will be kept as reserves and the remaining £45,000 will be lent out and will find its way to another bank. Let us suppose that such an amount is lent to an individual who deposits it in bank B. In turn, bank B will hold 10 per cent in cash (£4,500) and invest the rest, which finds its way to bank C. As illustrated in Table 2.3 at each stage the growth in deposits is exactly 90 per cent of what it was at the previous stage. The sum of the additional deposit created in a system with n banks can also be represented as:

$$50 + (50 \times 0.9) + (50 \times 0.9^2) + (50 \times 0.9^3) + (50 \times 0.9^4) + \ldots + (50 \times 0.9^n)$$

This geometric series will sum to: $\dfrac{50}{(1 - 0.9)} = 500$

Since the deposit multiplier equals the reciprocal of the required reserve ratio (1/0.1), then following an injection of £50,000 of cash in the system (i.e. new deposits), the process will end

2.1 How banks create money (*continued*)

Table 2.3 The banking system under a 10 per cent reserve ratio (£,000)

	Δ Deposits	Δ Loans	Δ Reserves
Bank A	50.00	45.00	5.00
Bank B	45.00	40.50	4.50
Bank C	40.50	36.45	4.05
Bank D	36.45	32.81	3.64
Bank E	32.81	29.53	3.28
—	—	—	—
Total all banks	500.00	450.00	50.00

(achieve equilibrium) when an additional £500,000 of deposits has been created. It should be noted that this multiple deposit-creation process acts also in reverse, i.e. multiple deposit contraction.

The credit multiplier explained above has several drawbacks. As with most theories, the assumptions behind this simple model are not very realistic. The creation of deposits is much less 'mechanical' in reality than the model indicates and decisions by depositors to increase their holdings in currency or by banks to hold excess reserves will result in a smaller expansion of deposits than the simple model predicts. Further, there are leakages from the system: for example, money flows abroad; people hold money as cash or buy government bonds rather than bank deposits. These considerations, however, should not deter from the logic of the process, which is: bank deposits 'create' money.

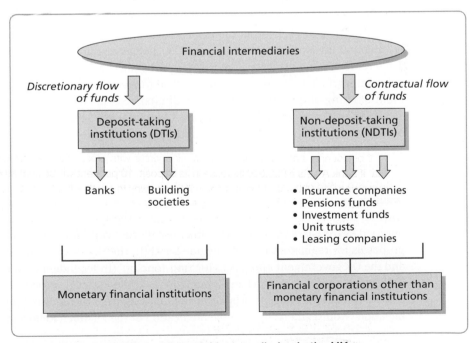

Figure 2.1 Classification of financial intermediaries in the UK

All countries have regulations that define what banking business is. For example, in all EU countries banks have been permitted to perform a broad array of financial services activity since the early 1990s and since 1999 both US and Japanese banks are also allowed to operate as full-service financial firms. A good example of the breadth of financial activities that banks can undertake is given by the UK's Financial Services and Markets Act 2000, which defines the range of activities that banks can engage in, including:

- accepting deposits;
- issuing **e-money** (or digital money), i.e. electronic money used on the internet;
- implementing or carrying out contracts of insurance as principal;
- dealing in investments (as principal or agent);
- managing investments;
- advising on investments;
- safeguarding and administering investments;
- arranging deals in investments and arranging regulated mortgage activities;
- advising on regulated mortgage contracts;
- entering into and administering a regulated mortgage contract;
- establishing and managing collective investment schemes (for example, investment funds and mutual funds);
- establishing and managing pension schemes.

Conglomeration has become a major trend in financial markets, emerging as a leading strategy for banks. This process has been driven by technological progress, international consolidation of markets and deregulation of geographical or product restrictions. In the EU, financial conglomeration was encouraged by the Second Banking Directive (1989), which allowed banks to operate as **universal banks**, enabling them to engage, directly or through subsidiaries, in other financial activities, such as financial instruments, factoring, leasing and investment banking. In the US, the passing of the Gramm-Leach-Bliley Act in 1999 removed the many restrictions imposed by the Glass-Steagall Act of 1933. Since 1999 US commercial banks can undertake a broad range of financial services, including investment banking and insurance activities. Similar reforms have taken place in Japan since 1999. As banks nowadays are diversified financial services firms, when we think about banks we should now think more about the particular type of financial activity carried out by a specialist division of a large corporation rather than the activity of an individual firm.

Since the immediate aftermath of the 2007–2009 financial crisis, a growing number of academics and policy makers are debating on whether the size and permissible activities of financial institutions should be re-constricted due to increased systemic risk. Narrowing the scope of large financial institutions would require the re-introduction of firewalls like those imposed by the Glass-Steagall Act to limit the risks that depositors are exposed to. The current proposals for regulatory reforms include Basel III, the Dodd-Frank Act in the United States and the UK government's proposals for '**ring-fencing**' (Independent Commission on Banking (ICB), also known as the Vickers Commission). At the EU level, structural reforms were discussed by an Expert Group led by Governor Liikanen from the Bank of Finland (the so-called Liikanen Group) and resulted in the publication of the Liikanen Report in October 2012.

2.4 Banking services

Modern banks offer a wide range of financial services, including:

- payment services;
- deposit and lending services;
- investment, pensions and insurance services;
- e-banking.

The following sections offer an overview of such services.

2.4.1 Payment services

An important service among banks' offerings is the facilities that enable customers to make payments. A **payment system** can be defined as any organised arrangement for transferring value between its participants. Heffernan (2005) defines the payment system as a by-product of the intermediation process, as it facilitates the transfer of ownership of claims in the financial sector. These payment flows reflect a variety of transactions, for goods and services as well as for financial assets. Some of these transactions involve high-value transfers, typically between financial institutions. However, the highest number of transactions relates to transfers between individuals and/or companies. If any of these circulation systems failed, the functioning of large and important parts of the economy would be affected. Banks play a major role in the provision of payment services (see also Section 3.5.1.1).

For personal customers the main types of payments are made by writing **cheques** from their current accounts (known as 'checking accounts' in the United States) or via debit or credit card payments. In addition, various other payment services are provided, including giro (or **credit transfers**) and automated payments such as **direct debits** and **standing orders**. Payments services can be either paper-based or electronic and an efficient payments system forms the basis of a well-functioning financial system. In most countries the retail payments systems are owned and run by the main banks. Note that the importance of different types of cashless payments varies from country to country, as illustrated in Tables 2.4 and 2.5.

Cheques are widely used as a means of payment for goods and services. If individual A buys goods and gives a cheque to individual B, it is up to B to pay the cheque into their own bank account. Individual B's bank then initiates the request to debit individual A's account. Individual A's bank authorises (clears) the cheque and a transfer of assets (settlement) then takes place. Cheque payments are known as debit transfers because they are written requests to debit the payee's account. Although not all accounts come with a cheque book, the vast majority do and in some countries (such as the UK) they are provided for free. Nowadays cheques are primarily used to pay small businesses and bills, although in this latter case discounts are frequently available if alternative methods are chosen, such as the direct debit. Cheques are often refused in shops because of the risk that they may bounce back if not covered with enough liquidity in the payee's current account, although shops may ask for a cheque guarantee card, which guarantees the cheque up to a certain amount. However, the

Table 2.4 Use of payment instruments by non-banks: number of transactions per payment instrument (millions, total for the year)

	Credit transfers				Direct debits			
	2000	2005	2011	2012	2000	2005	2011	2012
Belgium	511	816	1,025	939	166	219	264	286
Canada	565	857	1,043	986	444	626	673	699
France	2,094	2,408	2,977	3,097	1,969	2,513	3,533	3,543
Germany	5,585	6,713	6,090	6,154	4,766	6,662	8,661	8,812
Italy	320	1048	1261	1,261	326	463	600	602
Japan	1,217	1,354	1,438	1,500	n.a.	n.a.	n.a.	n.a.
Netherlands	1,170	1,263	1,686	1,694	836	1,059	1,340	1,369
Singapore	15	22	38	40	17	51	55	56.4
Sweden	793	654	830	859	91	160	289	297
Switzerland	545	595	753	776	46	52	46	48
United Kingdom	1,845	2,984	3,601	3,693	2,010	2,722	3,322	3,417
United States	3,775	5,475	7,914	8,638	2,368	7,193	11,796	13,088.9
	Cheques				E-money payment transactions			
Belgium	71	16	7	5.5	51	102	51	46
Canada	1,658	1,353	871	748	n.a.	n.a.	n.a.	36
France	4,494	3,916	2,971	2,806	3	17	47	52
Germany	393	107	40	34	27	38	36	34
Italy	565	466	291	256	n.a.	20	152	191
Japan	226	146	88	77	n.a.	n.a.	2,342	n.a.
Netherlands	14	n.a.	n.a.	n.a.	25	147	177	148
Singapore	92	86	77	75	100	1,622	2,888	3,015
Sweden	2	1	0.4	0.2	3	n.a.	n.a.	n.a.
Switzerland	11	2	0.3	0.3	18	19	10	2.8
UK	2,701	1,931	970	848	n.a.	n.a.	n.a.	n.a.
US	41,900	32,704	21,277	18,334.5	n.a.	n.a.	n.a.	n.a.

Source: Bank for International Settlements (2013, 2012, 2007, 2006) 'Statistics on payment and settlement systems in selected countries', Table 7.

relative importance of these cards is fading and, for example, in the UK in June 2011 they were phased out. This move was part of a broader plan from the UK Payments Council (the organisation that sets strategy for UK payments) to close the central cheque clearing by the target date of 2018. This plan provoked reactions from various groups that would have been affected by the move, such as consumers' groups, organisations representing the elderly, charities (which receive a large proportion of their donations by cheque) and other bodies. After a Treasury inquiry in July 2011 the Payments Council abandoned the plan to phase out cheques and announced that cheques would continue for 'as long as customers need them' (see Box 2.2). Figure 2.2 illustrates the decline in cheque volumes for personal and business transactions in the UK between 2003 and 2012.

Table 2.5 Number of plastic cards (000s)

	Cards with a cash function				Cards with a debit function				Cards with a credit function				Cards with an e-money function			
	2000	2005	2010	2012	2000	2005	2010	2012	2000	2005	2010	2012	2000	2005	2010	2012
AT	7,200	8,859	10,788	12,215	6,050	6,700	8,105	8,559	n.a.	n.a.	1,255	1,167	6,496	7,154	8,891	9,818
BE	13,930	15,931	19,448	20,647	10,960	12,672	15,132	16,197	n.a.	n.a.	n.a.	n.a.	7,931	9,617	11,660	12,115
BG	990	4,682	7,616	8,260	980	4,428	6,623	7,282	11	254	992	977	n.a.	n.a.	n.a.	n.a.
CY	435	747	1,254	1,266	163	380	805	783	279	363	492	433	n.a.	n.a.	n.a.	93
CZ	3,977	5,706	9,374	10,069	3,960	6,556	7,889	8,280	39	872	1,588	1,882	n.a.	334	1,984	361
DE	109,450	109,071	130,223	135,344	92,810	88,478	102,197	105,594	n.a.	n.a.	3,728	3,685	60,700	63,960	95,280	97,990
DK	3,677	4,839	7,461	8,275	3,018	3,882	5,978	6,467	458	957	1,482	1,809	593	n.a.	n.a.	n.a.
EE	858	1,420	1,793	1,792	811	1,143	1,401	1,432	43	266	394	356	n.a.	n.a.	n.a.	n.a.
ES	46,682	66,236	72,405	69,139	29,744	31,835	28,617	27,468	n.a.	n.a.	n.a.	n.a.	10,496	6,815	2,781	717
FI	6,109	6,212	7,448	7,874	3,000	4,700	3,000	6,805	n.a.	n.a.	n.a.	n.a.	623	1,482	n.a.	n.a.
FR	40,945	81,912	96,066	92,609	n.a.	38,911	71,054	80,110	n.a.	31,159	31,613	26,843	319	22,340	37,258	26,722
GB	120,682	164,440	165,065	168,993	49,730	66,990	84,642	88,553	47,080	69,858	55,601	56,443	n.a.	n.a.	n.a.	n.a.
GR	6,488	11,910	14,078	12,615	3,524	5,917	9,013	9,982	3,030	6,045	5,127	3,342	n.a.	n.a.	n.a.	n.a.
HU	4,446	7,381	8,550	8,341	4,192	6,336	7,553	7,677	270	1,028	1,368	1,256	n.a.	n.a.	n.a.	n.a.
IE	3,089	4,396	5,014	6,538	798	1,273	3,385	3,989	1,352	2,028	2,228	2,055	n.a.	n.a.	n.a.	n.a.
IT	21,172	35,059	49,715	60,042	20,204	30,728	36,174	39,707	n.a.	n.a.	n.a.	n.a.	n.a.	3,275	12,362	18,804
LT	505	3,082	4,270	3,633	402	2,803	3,705	3,233	9	147	566	400	94	133	n.a.	n.a.
LU	590	768	1,339	1,954	303	403	535	610	287	366	804	1,344	303	458	595	n.a.
LV	635	1,732	2,426	2,378	533	1,576	1,946	1,874	n.a.	n.a.	395	331	n.a.	n.a.	n.a.	n.a.
MT	328	467	688	798	240	345	508	601	86	121	173	185	n.a.	n.a.	n.a.	n.a.

(continued)

Table 2.5 continued

	Cards with a cash function				Cards with a debit function				Cards with a credit function				Cards with an e-money function			
	2000	2005	2010	2012	2000	2005	2010	2012	2000	2005	2010	2012	2000	2005	2010	2012
NL	26,000	31,453	30,220	30,510	21,000	25,405	24,413	24,663	n.a.	n.a.	n.a.	n.a.	20,900	17,533	23,823	24,306
PL	11,265	19,325	31,171	33,291	9,906	15,369	22,752	26,550	376	4,384	8,901	6,448	n.a.	n.a.	n.a.	n.a.
PT	10,895	16,316	18,889	18,708	n.a.	n.a.	n.a.	n.a.	n.a.	n.a.	n.a.	n.a.	3,500	615	300	519
RO	1,076	7,254	12,582	13,684	1,027	6,614	10,477	11,421	48	722	2,123	2,273	n.a.	n.a.	n.a.	n.a.
SE	4,892	8,725	11,100	12,034	4,570	6,659	8,333	8,857	2,802	3,610	6,157	5,361	593	n.a.	n.a.	n.a.
SI	1,837	2,859	3,375	3,171	1,392	2,330	2,742	2,529	33	89	123	112	n.a.	n.a.	n.a.	6
SK	1,720	3,866	5,072	5,426	1,713	3,111	4,249	4,683	3	732	848	812	n.a.	n.a.	n.a.	14
Euro area	286,062	388,125	466,022	480,648	184,869	247,022	309,930	333,711	1,639	39,599	46,391	40,334	110,950	133,249	192,949	191,114
EU	418,124	612,712	727,430	749,605	245,711	364,500	471,229	503,904	55,009	122,025	125,959	117,515	112,136	133,717	194,933	191,475

Notes:
AT = Austria; BE = Belgium; BG = Bulgaria; CY = Cyprus; CZ = Czech Republic; DE = Germany; DK = Denmark; EE = Estonia; ES = Spain; FI = Finland; FR = France; GB = Great Britain;
GR = Greece; HU = Hungary; IE = Ireland; IT = Italy; LT = Lithuania; LU = Luxembourg; LV = Latvia; MT = Malta; NL = the Netherlands; PL = Poland; PT = Portugal; RO = Romania;
SE = Sweden; SI = Slovenia; SK = Slovakia.

Source: ECB Statistical Data Warehouse, http://sdw.ecb.europa.eu

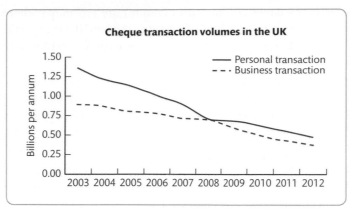

Figure 2.2 Cheque volumes in the UK (trend 2003–2012)
Source: Payments Council (2013).

BOX 2.2 DECISION TO ABOLISH CHEQUES REVERSED

A controversial plan to abolish cheques has been scrapped, after banks were warned in parliament that they had "scared the pants off middle England". Worried members of the public sent more than one thousand letters and emails to MPs after it was announced that the 350-year-old payment system was to be phased out by late 2018.

The U-turn came after the government indicated it would intervene unless a suitable alternative was found. The UK Payments Council, an industry-dominated financial body, said on Tuesday that cheques would now continue to be available "for as long as customers need them". But MPs expressed dissatisfaction with the industry-dominated body, pointing out that of the organisation's 15 members, 11 are industry directors.

"This is only stage one," said Andrew Tyrie MP, chairman of the Treasury select committee which investigated the future of cheques. "We have now got to establish that the Payments Council cannot spring a surprise like this again. They need to be brought in as part of the regulatory framework."

Cheque use has fallen since the 1990s, when 4bn were written. Banks claim the system is slow and prone to fraud and estimate they would save £200m if payments became paperless. The Payments Council had planned to shut the central system used to clear cheques, which it said was designed to process a far higher volume than the 1bn cheques written last year, in 2018. But the announcement caused instant uproar from consumer groups, charities and small businesses.

In a contrite appearance before the committee, Richard North, chairman of the Payments Council, said the decision to set an end date for cheques had been taken to stimulate innovation to find a better alternative payment system. Mark Hoban MP, financial secretary to the Treasury, wrote that the decision had caused much alarm across the country, particularly among the elderly or housebound people, schools, clubs and charities, rural communities, and small businesses. "Our members were very concerned," said Federation of Small Businesses spokesperson Andrew Cave. "There was no alternative to cheques that is trusted as much." The Institute of Fundraising, which had run a "save our cheque" campaign, said the decision to maintain cheques was a major success for charities, which currently receive up to 80 per cent of their funding by cheques.

- **Credit transfers** (or bank giro credits) are payments where the customer instructs their bank to transfer funds directly to the beneficiary's bank account. Consumers use bank giro transfer payments to pay invoices or to send payment in advance for products ordered.

- **Standing orders** are instructions from the customer (account holder) to the bank to pay a fixed amount at regular intervals into the account of another individual or company. The bank has the responsibility for remembering to make these payments. Only the account holder can change the standing order instructions. Some banks will accept instructions by telephone or internet banking.

- **Direct debits** are originated by the supplier of the goods/service and the customer has to sign the direct debit. The direct debit instructions are usually of a variable amount and the times at which debiting takes place can also be either fixed or variable (although usually fixed). If a payment is missed, the supplier can request the missed payment on a number of occasions. If the payments are continually missed over a period of time, the customer's bank will cancel the direct debit. Many retail customers pay utility bills (electricity, gas, water) in this way.

- **Plastic cards** include credit cards, debit cards, cheque guarantee cards, travel and entertainment cards, shop cards and 'smart' or 'chip' cards. Technically, **plastic cards** do not act themselves as a payment mechanism – they help to identify the customers and assist in creating either a paper or electronic payment.

- **Credit cards** provide holders with a pre-arranged credit limit to use for purchases at retail stores and other outlets. The retailer pays the credit card company a commission on every sale made via credit cards and the consumer obtains free credit if the bill is paid off before a certain date. If the bill is not fully paid off, it attracts interest. Visa and MasterCard are the two most important bank-owned credit card organisations. Credit cards have become an increasingly important source of consumer lending, particularly in the UK and the US. For example, in 1971 there was only one type of credit card (Barclaycard) available in the UK and by the early 2000s there were around 1,300. The use of cashless instruments continued to grow in the first decade of the new millennium, as shown in Table 2.5.

- **Pre-paid credit cards** are a form of *pay-as-you-go* credit card on to which you need to first deposit your money, then use it to pay for goods or services. Unlike normal credit or debit cards, you spend only the amount that you put on the card. Pay-as-you-go credit cards are becoming increasingly popular for several reasons. The requirements for approval are very basic (in some cases it is as simple as being a UK resident) and the cards are therefore available to people with poor credit history or to those who cannot legally obtain credit cards (for example, teenagers). They are also used by people who wish to be more in control of their finances, for example using a specified, pre-charged amount, such as holiday money.

- **Debit cards** are issued directly by banks and allow customers to withdraw money from their accounts. They can also be used to obtain cash and other information when used through automated teller machines (ATMs).

- **Delayed debit cards** (sometimes called deferred debit cards) are issued by banks and enable the holder to make purchases and withdraw money up to an authorised limit. The delayed debit cards allow the cardholder to postpone payment, but the full amount of the debt incurred has to be settled at the end of a pre-defined period.

- **Cheque guarantee cards** were introduced because of retailers' reluctance to accept personal cheques. Typically, the payer provides further identification by presenting the cheque guarantee card and the retailer writes details from the card on to the cheque in order to guarantee payment. Most of these types of cards also act as debit cards. In the UK these cards were phased out in June 2011.

- **Travel and entertainment cards (or charge cards)** provide payment facilities and allow repayment to be deferred until the end of the month, but they do not provide interest-free credit. Unlike credit cards, all bills have to be repaid at the end of the month and no rollover is allowed. Typically, unpaid balances are charged at a higher interest rate than for credit cards, to discourage late payment. The most widely used charge cards include American Express and Diners Club.

- **Smart, memory or chip cards** are cards that incorporate a microprocessor or a memory chip. The microprocessor cards can add, delete and otherwise manipulate information on the card and can undertake a variety of functions and store a range of information. Memory-chip cards (for example, pre-paid phone cards) can undertake only a pre-defined operation. There are more than 20 million smart cards issued by banks in Europe that perform various functions, although the main characteristic of the microprocessor technology is that it provides extra security features for card payment. Various schemes offer store value cards for small transactions.

Note that the importance of different types of cashless payments varies from country to country, as illustrated in Table 2.4 – for example, in the European Union cheques are more widely used in Britain and France compared with elsewhere. (Also remember that businesses as well as consumers use these payment services.) A report (Bank for International Settlements, 2012) of the Working Group on Innovations in Retail Payments provides an extensive overview of the key developments.

Table 2.5 illustrates the usage of plastic cards in various EU countries. It highlights the widespread use of credit cards and illustrates major increases between 2000 and 2012 (by 74 per cent for credit cards with cash functions and 129 per cent for cards with a credit function). Table 2.5 also shows that smart cards (listed as cards with e-money functions) are relatively commonplace in Germany, France and the Netherlands.

In contrast, poorer countries in the world are compensating for the lack of infrastructure by using a new mobile money-transfer technology or m-payments (see Box 2.3). Mobile phones are widespread in the developing world and the potential for growth of these novel payment services is high and attractive. The success of M-Pesa (M for mobile, pesa is Swahili for money), a mobile phone-based money-transfer and microfinancing service for Safaricom (a mobile network operators in Kenya), and its counterparty in Tanzania, Vodacom, has spurred established banking institutions to follow. M-Pesa allows users with a national ID card or passport to deposit, withdraw and transfer money easily with a mobile device, thereby offering banking services to previously unbanked customers in the form of e-wallets and person-to-person money transfers. The banking industry is under pressure to establish a presence in mobile banking as it is at risk of losing market share to non-bank entities, such as mobile phone operators, seeking to take advantage of the mobile phone's ubiquity and convenience to offer banking services (Capgemini, 2012).

Recent years have also witnessed an unprecedented growth in the use of a new form of digital currency and payment method, known as **Bitcoin**. Box 2.4 outlines its key characteristics, recent trends and main advantages and disadvantages.

BOX 2.3 PRESS 1 FOR MODERNITY

Many people know that 'mobile money' – financial transactions on mobile phones – has taken off in Africa. How far it has gone, though, still comes as a bit of a shock. Three-quarters of the countries that use mobile money most frequently are in Africa, and mobile banking in some of them has reached extraordinary levels.

A survey of global financial habits by the Gates Foundation, the World Bank and Gallup World Poll found 20 countries in which more than 10% of adults say they used mobile money at some point in 2011. Of those, 15 are African (see Figure 2.3). In Kenya, Sudan and Gabon half or more of adults used mobile money. In contrast, in countries with more developed financial systems, the share of adults who use mobile money is tiny – 1% in Brazil and Argentina. If you think of banking by phone as just a way of using financial services, then these African countries – where people sometimes live

several days' walk from the nearest branch – are much more financially literate than you might think just by looking at how many banks they have.

Most mobile-phone transactions are tiny. Market traders, for example, use mobile phones to pay peasant farmers for a single bag of cassava or maize-meal. One of the most successful mobile-phone products in Kenya is a SIM card costing just a few cents – but that is all people need for the occasional transaction. Mobile phones are also used to accept bank remittances from family members abroad. This may explain why mobile money has done so well in Somalia, a country which barely has a government, but where a third of adults said they used mobile money last year. Somalia is one of the countries that most depends on remittances: one study found that 80% of the capital for start-up firms came from the

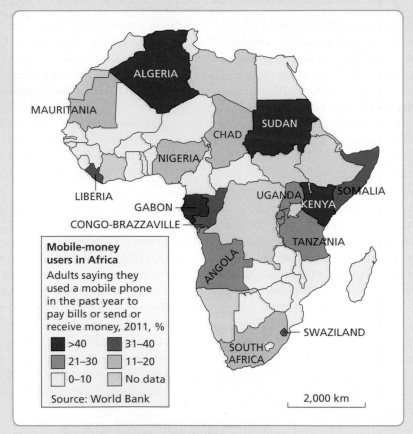

Figure 2.3 Mobile-money users in Africa
Source: The Economist (2012).

Box 2.3 Press 1 for modernity (*continued*)

diaspora. Without mobile banking, this lifeline would be weaker than it is.

For the most part, mobile-phone money is a substitute both for paper-based banks and for, say, sending cash via a bus driver. It enables people who cannot get to a branch or ATM to use financial services. This helps offset the bias of the banking system towards the well educated. In Africa only about 10% of people with primary or no education have bank accounts, compared with 55% of those with tertiary education. But rates of phone banking in some countries are high enough to prove that the practice is spreading beyond university graduates to the rest of the population.

Sometimes, though, mobile banking goes hand in hand with the familiar kind. In Kenya, where a staggering 68% of adults use mobile money (by far the highest rate in the world, partly because regulation is extremely light), more than 40% also have ordinary bank accounts. The leapfrogging technology can also help the old-fashioned kind it has just vaulted over.

Source: Adapted from *The Economist* (2012).

BOX 2.4 BITCOIN: A NEW FORM OF ELECTRONIC MONEY

Bitcoin was created in 2009 as a virtual currency based on a decentralised network of participating computers.[1] Bitcoin uses innovative peer-to-peer (P2P) payment technology and is not issued by any central authority or bank. The process of creation of bitcoins is called 'mining' and employs computing power to process transactions, secure the network, and keep everyone in the system synchronized together. Users create a Bitcoin digital 'wallet' on their computer desktop or smart phone that allows them to buy, use and accept bitcoin tokens through a secure online address or a third party service such as Multibit or Bitpay. Behind the scenes, the Bitcoin network is sharing a public ledger called the 'block chain' that keeps a record of all transactions and avoids that the digital money is used more than once.

Bitcoin is still in its experimental phase but has been enjoying an exceptional growth in popularity worldwide as more and more businesses and individuals accept 'crypto-currency'. At the end of March 2014, the total bitcoins in circulation exceeded 12.5 million for a total value of over $5.5 billion. Bitcoin is very volatile. In 2013 alone it fluctuated from $13 in January to $1,151 in December.

The trend in market price of Bitcoin over the two years from 2012 to 2014 is illustrated in Figure 2.4.

There are a number of pros and cons to using Bitcoin as a payment system. Table 2.6 summarises the key ones.

The table shows that the many benefits of Bitcoin are offset by some serious concerns, particularly in relation to money laundering and other criminal purposes (e.g. online drug dealing) that are likely to result in greater regulation and compliance costs in the near future. The European Banking Authority (2013) has also warned consumers of the many risks unregulated virtual currencies like Bitcoin pose for unprotected users.

In relation to the potential threats to banks posed by a more widespread use of Bitcoin, the detailed report of a large Swiss bank, UBS (2014), identifies two key factors: the disintermediation process and the competition over transaction fees. On one hand, depositors could be attracted by Bitcoin as they are put off by taxes and levies on deposits and by greater uncertainty about their banks' stability. On the other, individuals and businesses could prefer to use Bitcoin for the efficient, secure and low-cost transfers it provides. According to the report, banks should not be concerned about these threats 'given Bitcoin's limited viability as a currency' and could perhaps learn from the technology used by Bitcoin to reduce the costs and improve the security of transfers, particularly at the international level. This, however, could not occur in the short term as banks' fee income would suffer considerably as a result.

Sources: Nakamoto (2009); European Banking Authority (2013); UBS (2014).

[1]Bitcoin is an open-source project created by Satoshi Nakamoto (a pseudonym) and is currently in beta development stage (see **https://bitcoin.org/bitcoin.pdf**). Bitcoin, capitalised, refers to the system, the software and the network, and bitcoin, lower case, refers to the currency units.

Box 2.4 Bitcoin: A new form of electronic money (*continued*)

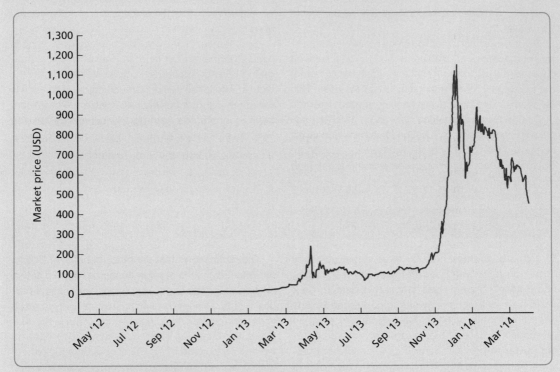

Figure 2.4 Market price of Bitcoin

Source: **https://blockchain.info/charts/market-price**

Table 2.6 Key advantages and disadvantages of Bitcoin

Advantages	Disadvantages
● Ease and speed of transactions	● Not widely accepted
● No banks or other financial inter-mediaries involved in the process (disintermediation)	● Use of bitcoins for money laundering, financing of terrorism and other criminal activities
● Low transaction costs	● Payments are irreversible
● Little or no processing fees	● Volatile volumes
● No geographical and/or time limitations	● Digital wallets may be lost or exposed to viruses
● Encrypted transactions that guarantee some anonymity	● No consumer protection
● Transparency via the block chain (https://blockchain.info/)	● No guarantee of minimum valuation
● Reduced risk of fraud	● To shop in most physical stores they would have to be converted into other currencies (e.g. $)
	● Still in Beta development stage
	● Technical and regulatory challenges
	● Capped at 21m bitcoin units

2.4.2 Deposit and lending services

In addition to payment services, personal banking includes the offer of a broad range of **deposit and lending services**. These are summarised as follows:

- **Current or checking accounts** that typically pay no (or low) rates of interest and are used mainly for payments. Banks offer a broad range of current accounts tailored to various market segments and with other services attached. As an example, Figure 2.5 illustrates how a typical current account can be used in the UK.

- **Time or savings deposits** that involve depositing funds for a set period of time for a pre-determined or variable rate of interest. Banks offer an extensive range of such savings products, from standard fixed term and fixed deposit rate to variable term with variable rates. All banks offer deposit facilities with features that are a combination of time and current accounts whereby customers can withdraw their funds instantly or at short notice. Typically, deposits that can be withdrawn on demand pay lower rates than those deposited in the bank for a set period.

- **Consumer loans and mortgages** are commonly offered by banks to their retail customers. Consumer loans can be *unsecured* (that is, no collateral is requested – such loans are usually up to a certain amount of money and for a short to medium time period: for example, in the UK unsecured loans are up to £25,000 and repaid over five years) or *secured on property* (typically from £20,000 to £100,000 and repaid over ten years) and interest rates are mainly variable (but can be fixed). In addition, banks of course offer an extensive array of mortgage products for the purchase of property. The main types of UK mortgages (that typically extend for 20–25 years) include *variable rate* (interest payments vary relative to a benchmark rate such as the bank's standard lending rate or those determined by outside bodies such as the Bank of England's base rate or LIBOR); *fixed rate* (rates are fixed for a set period, usually 2–5 years, and then revert to variable rate); *capped* (rates vary but a cap is placed on the maximum rate paid over a specified period); *discount mortgages* (where rates vary but are discounted at a few percentages below a benchmark rate over a period – e.g. 1 per cent discount to the base rate over the first two years); and *cashback mortgages* (where those taking out the mortgage receive a single lump sum or cashback generally based on the value of the loan). Mortgages can also be obtained in foreign currency, for the purchase of overseas properties, and also for 'buy-to-let' property.

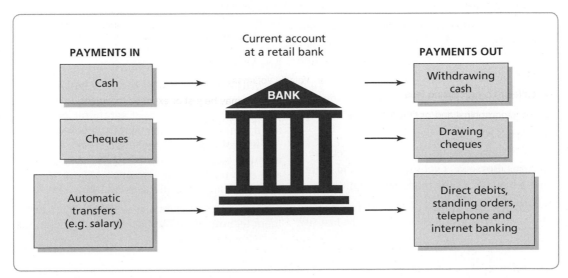

Figure 2.5 Typical current account usage

BOX 2.5 PEER-TO-PEER (P2P) LENDING ORGANISATIONS

In 2008, the overall winner of an *FT Money* readers' competition for the 'Next Big Investment Idea' was peer-to-peer (P2P) lending, via the internet. It was proposed by Jeff Norton, a creative producer from north-west London. P2P lenders provide a marketplace for social lending and thus represent an alternative to traditional banking. Essentially with this system, regular people exchange cash with the help of an online facilitator.

The nitty gritty of the lending process is well summarised here (see **www.zopa.com**).

- We look at the credit scores of people looking to borrow and work out whether they fit into the A*, A, B, C or Young market. If they're none of these, then Zopa's not for them.

- Lenders make lending offers – 'I'd like to lend this much to A-rated borrowers for this long and at this rate.'

- Borrowers size up the rates offered to them, and snap up the ones they like the look of. If they don't like the rates today, they can come back tomorrow to see if things have changed.

- To reduce any risk, Zopa lenders only lend small chunks to individual borrowers. A lender lending £500 or more would have their money spread across at least 50 borrowers.

- Borrowers enter into legally binding contracts with their lenders.

- Borrowers repay monthly by direct debit. If any repayments are missed, a collections agency uses the same recovery process that the high street banks use.

- Zopa earns money by charging borrowers a £130 transaction fee and lenders a 1% annual servicing fee.

- And everyone's happy – lenders get great returns, borrowers get great rates, and there's not a bank or a bank manager in sight.

The relative importance of P2P lending organisations has grown significantly over the last five years or so and P2P lending seems to be set to stay (see below). The financial turmoil and the failure of large institutions with the credit crunch that followed has no doubt helped this process. The best known electronic P2P lending sites are: Prosper and Lending Club in the US; Zopa in the UK, US, Japan, and Italy; and Qifang in China. Other successful social lending sites are RateSetter and Funding Circle in the UK, while Smava in Germany and Boober in the Netherlands have not enjoyed similar success.

Peer-to-peer lending – done deal

Tired of banks? Join the queue. Depositors want better interest rates. Consumers want alternative sources of finance. Governments want more lending, but banks must deleverage to meet global capital rules. Cue peer-to-peer (P2P) lending, online platforms that match investors with borrowers. With no bank overheads, P2P lenders offer higher rates than mainstream banks. Never mind the attempts by UK policy makers to egg on challengers to the status quo, P2P is already on the case.

In seven years, Zopa, the UK's largest such lender, has lent almost £260m gross. Another P2P lender, RateSetter, has lent nearly £50m gross. True, the market – at £380m – is still tiny, but its growth spurt has attracted the government's attention. Last month it agreed to provide £10m to Zopa to match investor funding to the UK's 3.5m sole traders, to help kick-start small business lending. Peer-to-business lender Funding Circle is already on that case: it lends only to small businesses. In its two-year life, it has lent £70m. The government just allocated it £20m for on-lending.

Returns for P2P investors can be relatively high. Zopa quotes an average of 5.5 per cent a year after adjusting for its 1 per cent set-up fee and average default rate of 0.5 per cent (well below that of mainstream banks). RateSetter quotes a similar amount, adjusted for its own 0.3 per cent default and set-up charge. It also operates a provision fund that has shielded investors from default.

Although P2P lenders use similar credit assessment techniques to those of the banks, default is

Alternative mortgage products, that is mortgages that are different from the traditional principal and interest repayment schedule, have been identified as some of the culprits of the 2007 sub-prime crisis (mainly the adjustable-rate mortgages – ARM – which earned the nickname of 'toxic mortgages'). However, recent research by Cocco (2013) argues that because of their lower initial mortgage payments relative to loan amount, they may be a valuable tool for households that expect higher and more certain future labour income, and that wish to smooth consumption over the life cycle.

In addition to deposit and lending services, many banks have diversified into a broader range of areas, offering a 'one-stop' facility to meet all retail customer financial needs. This includes the offer of an extensive array of investment products, pensions, insurance and other services.

2.4.3 Investment, pensions and insurance services

- **Investment products** offered to retail customers include various securities-related products: mutual funds (known as unit trusts in the UK), investment in company stocks and various other securities-related products (such as savings bonds). In reality there is a strong overlap between savings and investments products and many banks advertise these services together.

- **Pensions and insurance services** are widely offered by many banks. Pension services provide retirement income (in the form of annuities) to those contributing to pension plans. Contributions paid into the pension fund are invested in long-term investments, with the individual making contributions receiving a pension on retirement. The pension services offered via banks are known as private pensions to distinguish them from public pensions offered by the state. Usually there are tax advantages associated with pensions contributions as most governments wish to encourage individuals to save for their retirement. Insurance products protect individuals (policyholders) from various adverse events. Policyholders pay regular premiums and the insurer promises compensation if the specific insured event occurs. There are two main types of insurance – life insurance and general (or property and casualty) insurance. The latter is insurance that does not involve death as the main risk. It includes home, travel, medical, auto and various other types of insurance. Banks offer both life and non-life insurance products, the latter being mainly travel, property, mortgage repayment and other types of protection. In the UK, there has also been substantial growth in income protection insurance (insurance that replaces earnings if individuals are unable to work) and critical illness insurance (that covers medical costs and/or income loss due to illness).

BOX 2.6 CASE STUDY: PPI MISSELLING – 'NOTHING WAS SEPARATED AND EXPLAINED'

Paul Fielder, 33, is one of hundreds of thousands of customers who unwittingly took out a payment protection insurance (PPI) policy along with a personal loan. In 2006, Fielder, who runs a property company in Hull, borrowed £25,000 to refurbish one of his properties. The loan was to be repaid over 10 years at a rate of 12.9 per cent.

"I didn't realise at the time that the PPI was included. Nothing was separated and explained – it was a matter of 'Here's the total sum for the loan, these will be your monthly repayments, sign here.'" Not only had PPI been included in the loan, the company also failed to ask him if he had any medical condition that would have excluded him from claiming on the policy.

Fielder only found out that he had a PPI policy when a friend mentioned media coverage of the issue a year ago. "I called the loan company and found that the monthly repayments I'd been making of £488.98 included nearly £130 for PPI," he said. Fielder contacted Brunel Franklin, the claims company, which arranged for him to receive full compensation for the cost of PPI, plus 8 per cent interest for the payment period. In total, he received just under £7,600. "I don't feel animosity necessarily towards the banks, but it was a bonus to have that cheque arrive in the post," he says. "I used the money to buy my girlfriend an engagement ring, so it is happy endings all round."

Source: Case study: PPI misselling – 'nothing was separated and explained', *Financial Times*, 13/5/11 (Elaine Moore).
© The Financial Times Limited. All Rights Reserved.

- **Payment protection insurance** (also known as PPI) is an insurance product that is often designed to cover a debt that is currently outstanding (this debt is typically in the form of a loan or an overdraft). PPI is sold by banks and other credit providers as an add-onto product. It typically covers the borrower against an event (for example, accident, sickness, unemployment or death) that may prevent them from earning and therefore servicing the debt. However, PPI covers repayments for a finite period only (typically 12 months). PPI has become highly controversial because of banks' mis-selling practices, typically encouraged by large commissions. The number of complaints received by the Financial Ombudsman increased steadily, hitting a record number of 378,699 in the financial year 2012/2013.[2] The Office of Fair Trading (OFT) referred the market for PPI to the Competition Commission (CC) in 2007. After years of legal battles, a high court ruling in April 2011 opened the way for an estimated consumer payout of £4.5 billion. In May 2011, the British Bankers' Association said it would not appeal and therefore several million people became eligible for a compensation payment.

---

[2] http://financial-ombudsman.org.uk/publications/ar13/about.html

2.4.4 E-banking

A number of innovative financial products have been developed taking advantage of rapid technological progress and financial market development. Transactions made using these innovative products are accounting for an increasing proportion of the volume and value of domestic and cross-border retail payments. Mainly, we can refer to two categories of payment products:

● **E-money** includes reloadable electronic money instruments in the form of stored value cards and electronic tokens stored in computer memory.

● **Remote payments** are payment instruments that allow (remote) access to a customer's account.

Figure 2.6 exemplifies the role of **e-banking** in the world of business conducted through electronic networks.

E-banking is now regarded as part of an overall distribution strategy, particularly in retail banking, and it is offered by all major banks. Overall, banks' involvement in remote banking can be summarised as follows:

● Major institutions offer 'traditional' remote banking services (ATMs and telephone banking) and have started to offer a growing number of online PC banking and internet banking services.

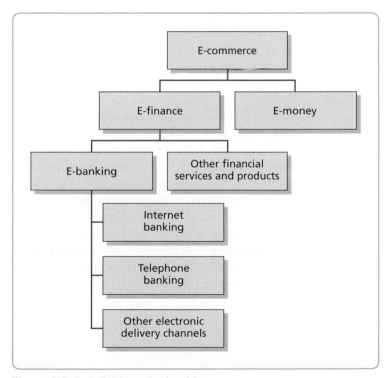

Figure 2.6 A definition of e-banking

- Some small-sized specialised banks operate without branches exclusively via remote banking channels. In most cases these banks are subsidiaries of existing banking groups (for example, in the UK the virtual bank First Direct is part of the HSBC group).

- Some banks, particularly in developing countries, have started to offer mobile banking, taking advantage of advanced mobile features and the increased popularity of smart phones (see Box 2.3). While mobile banking is still at an early stage, it is poised to grow in a similar way to that in which internet banking grew in the last decade (Capgemini and Efma, 2012).

The intensity with which banks have promoted various remote banking 'models' differs significantly from one country to another. Even though electronic banking, in the form of ATMs, telephone and mobile banking, is not a new phenomenon, it is only with the increased usage of the internet that the number of banks offering services and customers using online banking services has increased substantially. Firms have had varying levels of success and failure in their efforts to embrace remote banking. The internet is still preferred for carrying out standardised tasks (such as information gathering, looking up account status, etc.), while the branch is still the preferred channel when it comes to more complex tasks (Capgemini and Efma, 2011). As a consequence, most internet strategies have been developed especially for the retail segment, although some banks have developed services to target the corporate segment as well.

The branch survived a phase during the late 1990s when the industry briefly contemplated a future without branches. Some banks experimented with branches that steered customers away from live tellers and towards automated systems, in an attempt to wean customers away from human interaction. Many banks opened internet-only banks that had no branches at all, but offered low fees and high interest rates. However, a Capgemini and Efma (2011) study indicates that a shift is under way in customers' perceptions as branches are now seen as fulfilling an advisory role. Branches are pulling customers back for more personalised products and services. Banks are repositioning their retail strategy, changing branch layout and design, increasing the use of technology and changing practices for sales and services (see Figure 2.7).

One of the consequences of the greater use of technology in retail banking has been the increased competition in the sector. While in the past, banks relied upon their brand to defend against new entrants, today strong non-bank brands (e.g. Tesco, a leading retailer in the UK) continue their expansion into payments and other banking services. In addition, the financial crisis has damaged the 'brand' of many retail banks.

Banks seeking to increase their customer base (or at least retain existing customers) need to understand the importance of different channels to increase customer satisfaction. While customers seem to see phone and mobile channels as less important, they also report greater customer satisfaction through these channels (see Figure 2.8).

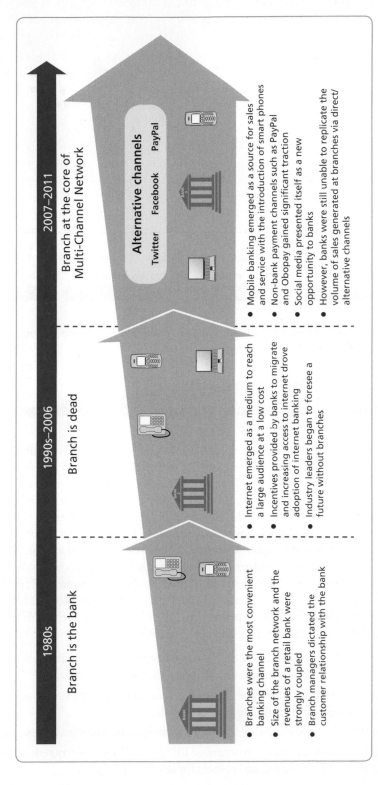

Figure 2.7 Evolving role of the branch in a multi-channel environment, 1980–2011

Source: Capgemini and Efma (2011) p. 25.

1980s

Branch is the bank

- Branches were the most convenient banking channel
- Size of the branch network and the revenues of a retail bank were strongly coupled
- Branch managers dictated the customer relationship with the bank

1990s–2006

Branch is dead

- Internet emerged as a medium to reach a large audience at a low cost
- Incentives provided by banks to migrate and increasing access to internet drove adoption of internet banking
- Industry leaders began to foresee a future without branches

2007–2011

Branch at the core of Multi-Channel Network

Alternative channels

Twitter   Facebook   PayPal

- Mobile banking emerged as a source for sales and service with the introduction of smart phones
- Non-bank payment channels such as PayPal and Obopay gained significant traction
- Social media presented itself as a new opportunity to banks
- However, banks were still unable to replicate the volume of sales generated at branches via direct/ alternative channels

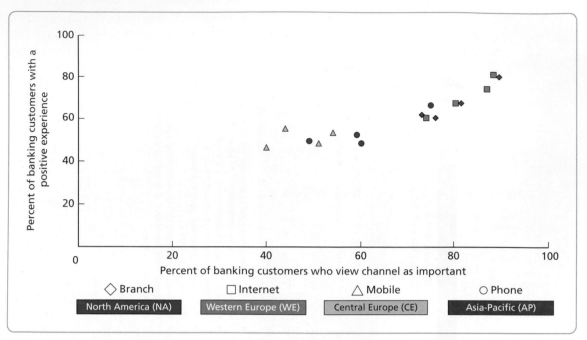

Figure 2.8 Positive customer experience of channels vs. channel importance by region, 2012

Source: Capgemini and Efma (2012) p. 19.

2.5 Sustainable and ethical banking: a brief overview

For years the mainstream banking sector has largely overlooked sustainability issues. Today the increased pressure from shareholders and environmental organisations has resulted in more banks taking up the challenge and offering investment products that are ethical or sustainable. These are investments in companies that have demonstrated socially responsible practices, are respectful of the environment and human rights, do not lend to oppressive regimes or companies making weapons and are not dealing with 'immoral' products such as alcohol, gambling and tobacco. More formally, **sustainable banking** can be defined as 'a decision by banks to provide products and services only to customers who take into consideration the environmental and social impacts of their activities' (Bouma *et al.*, 2001). According to the International Finance Corporation (IFC), a member of the World Bank group, the definition of sustainability as applied to financial institutions should include four aspects in relation to 'good' business performance (International Finance Corporation, 2007, p. 9):

● the *financial* sustainability of the financial institution and its client-companies, so that they can continue to make a long-term contribution to development;

● the *economic* sustainability of the projects and companies the financial institution finances, through their contribution to host economies;

● *environmental* sustainability through the preservation of natural resources;

● *social* sustainability through improved living standards, poverty reduction, concern for the welfare of communities, and respect for key human rights.

The UK-based Investment Management Association (IMA) provides an effective guide to ethical investing and clarifies that ethical funds have different objectives and thus follow both positive and negative criteria in order to meet the different values of investors. This is because some people want to invest in companies that make a positive contribution to green and ethical issues, while others prefer to avoid companies that may carry out activities that diverge from their ethical principles. Box 2.7 reports the list of positive and negative investment criteria published by the IMA.

BOX 2.7 POSITIVE AND NEGATIVE INVESTMENT CRITERIA

Negative criteria (activities that the funds may seek to avoid):

Animal testing	The testing of cosmetic finished products and ingredients on animals is no longer allowed in the UK, but continues abroad. Some consumers believe animal testing to be equally unacceptable in the production of other chemical products.
Genetic engineering	Genetic engineering and modern biotechnology are perceived by some to be an unacceptable way of manipulating nature.
Health and safety breaches	Investors can show their disapproval of companies that break the rules by avoiding investment in those that have been successfully prosecuted by the Health and Safety Executive.
High environmental impact	Public concern about the degradation of the environment is becoming increasingly widespread.
Human rights	Investors have traditionally boycotted certain countries, but increasingly it is being argued that countries need investment to improve basic social and economic rights. Against this background some people have concerns about the activities of certain companies.
Intensive farming	Many people are concerned about food quality, particularly food contamination (in the wake of BSE), antibiotic residues and the use of growth hormones and pesticides.
Military	Some people believe that the use of military force is unacceptable, either for defensive or offensive purposes.
Nuclear power	The threat of radioactive contamination from an incident at a nuclear power station typifies the concerns many people have about nuclear power.
Pesticides	Excessive pesticide use can lead to the build-up of chemical residues through the food chain, damage to birds and insects, injuries and deaths among farm workers and damage to animal and human immune systems. Some chemicals are also ozone depleting.
Pollution convictions	There has been increasing concern in the last few years about the effects of environmental pollution on health. A small number of prosecutions are carried out against companies each year as a result of non-compliance with a legally issued notice or following a serious pollution incident.
Pornography and adult films	People often object to pornography on the grounds that it may deprave, corrupt and degrade, contributing to sexual violence and sex discrimination. There has been rising public concern about internet pornography and worries about children using the internet and accessing offensive material.
Sustainable timber	Deforestation, including the clearance of land for agriculture, plantations and development, commercial logging and the collection of fuel wood, can have damaging effects on the environment and threaten the survival of certain wildlife.

BOX 2.7 Positive and negative investment criteria (*continued*)

Third world concerns	Many investors are concerned that too many companies put profits before principles in their dealings with the third world, and that by doing so they are actually contributing to third world poverty and its dependence on developed economies.
Traditional ethical concerns	The production and sale of alcohol and tobacco as well as profiting from gambling have concerned some ethical investors for many years.
Water pollution	Often caused by industrial discharges, water pollution has both environmental and social impacts.

Positive criteria (activities that a fund may actively choose to invest in):

Communal involvement	There are arguments in favour of identifying and encouraging companies that make a positive effort to contribute to the communities they work in and to society at large, whether via donations or by other means. However, not all investors will necessarily share the same priorities as companies in choosing which causes to support.
Corporate governance	Corporate governance provides a framework of accountability to a company's owners, investors and shareholders. Fundamentally, good corporate governance should facilitate good company performance, ensuring that it is managed in the best interests of its owners.
Disclosure	Investors, the public and government increasingly recognise the need for quality information on corporate policy and practice. For investors to be able to pick and choose between companies it is essential that they have sufficient information to make an informed decision.
Environmental	Public concerns about the degradation of the environment are becoming increasingly widespread. Companies have responded to this in a variety of ways, with a number of initiatives and approaches being adopted.
Equal opportunities	Some companies may have improved their equal opportunity records, i.e. by developing a system to monitor effectiveness of equal opportunity policies.
Positive products and services	EIRIS (Ethical Investing Research Service) has identified five groups of activity which can be seen as providing basic necessities, environmental products and other services that help in solving problems and making the world a safer place. The five groups are: ● environmental technology, including products such as machinery for recycling, wind power generators and pollution abatement technology; ● waste disposal companies; ● public transport and bicycles, including provision of bus services and maintenance of railway tracks; ● safety and protection, for example, alarm systems for elderly people living alone, fire alarms, life jackets and protective clothing; ● healthcare, including medicines, hearing aids and spectacles, housing, food and clothing.
Supply chain issues	The quality of working conditions in global supply chains is a high-profile issue of concern to many investors. Because many companies are yet to actively address some of these concerns, a helpful indicator of progress is the extent to which a company has developed policies to encourage, maintain and improve working conditions in its supply chain.

Source: Investment Management Association (2011).

Banks have begun to pursue sustainable strategies. Yet the special role that they have in financing businesses implies that they are key drivers in the context of social and environmental sustainability across all industrial sectors in the economy. A study on the role of financial services in sustainable development commissioned by the UK's Department for Environment, Food & Rural Affairs (DEFRA) states: 'The financial sector is a critical channel through which price signals, regulation, and civil society pressure can direct financial capital to more or less sustainable economic activity' (Corporation of London, 2002).

One notable example of this policy framework that has been adopted by many international banks operating in developing countries is the **Equator Principles**, in relation to project financing.[3] Project finance lending techniques are often employed in developing/emerging countries to provide funding to various industrial sectors. Typically, these tend to be asset-rich projects in sectors such as oil and gas, mining, utility and energy. The Equator Principles are a voluntary set of rules aimed at the development of socially responsible projects that reflect sound environmental management practices. These principles, first set out in 2003, follow the environmental and social guidelines of the IFC and have been restated and reviewed in a document published in July 2006. In extreme cases, signatory banks will avoid lending to borrowers that fail to comply with the Equator Principles. However, the purpose of the Equator Principles is to encourage those seeking funds to approach projects, from inception, in a way that is consistent with the principles. Further, when such an approach is found to be deficient, the aim is to work towards appropriate changes to ensure compliance (Girardone and Snaith, 2011).

There is no doubt that some progress has been made over the last decade in relation to sustainable and **ethical banking**. The public interest in investments that are useful to society has increased, as have the worries about climate change and other long-term issues about our planet. Some banks have responded by committing to sustainability programmes; nevertheless, a lot still needs to be done.

2.6 Conclusion

The nature of the banking business has changed dramatically. From traditional lending institutions, thanks to deregulation banks can now offer a wide variety of financial services and products. This means that they now compete with non-bank financial institutions and operate as universal banks offering non-banking products such as insurance and asset management. Similarly, there has been a considerable evolution in the payment systems, mainly as a result of technological advancements and innovations and a change in consumer demand.

In the rich world, the youngest generations appear increasingly more comfortable with using electronic means of payment such as plastic cards and automatic transfers. Not surprisingly, cheques usage has dropped sharply in most countries while the relative importance of electronic banking services has increased. In the poorer world, the challenge that operators should try to seize appears to lie on a relatively simple device: the mobile phone. The experience of M-Pesa in Kenya has been extremely positive. Essentially, with this system people are allowed to transfer money and pay for goods and services with their mobile phones and without the need to have a bank account. Given the potential for economic growth derived from this novel mobile money payments service, it is anticipated that it will soon become popular in the vast majority of developing and emerging countries.

---

[3] See **www.equator-principles.com/**

Last but not least, a chapter on the nature of the modern banking business cannot ignore issues related to ethics and sustainable development. The special role of banks in any economy, and the fact that they are often exclusive providers of financing for businesses, means that banks represent a key channel in directing financial capital to more or less ethical and sustainable activities. Although some banks have committed to sustainability programmes, there is no doubt that more will need to be done as the public interest in investments that are useful in society increases along with the worries over long-term global issues such as climate change.

Key terms

Bitcoin	Deposit-taking	Insurance services	Plastic cards
Cheques	institution	Investment products	Ring-fencing
Credit multiplier	Direct debit	Non-deposit-taking	Standing order
Credit transfers	E-money/e-banking	institution	Sustainable banking
Deposit and lending	Equator Principles	Payment system	Universal bank
services	Ethical banking	Pension services	

Key reading

Bank for International Settlements (2012) 'Innovations in retail payments', Report of the Working Group on Innovations in Retail Payments, May.

Cocco, J.F. (2013) 'Evidence of the benefits of alternative mortgage products', *Journal of Finance*, 68(4), 1663–1690.

Girardone, C. and Snaith, S. (2011) 'Project finance loan spreads and disaggregated political risk', *Applied Financial Economics*, 21(23), 1725–1734.

REVISION QUESTIONS AND PROBLEMS

2.1 What is a deposit-taking institution?

2.2 Why is the ability to collect retail deposits such an important feature?

2.3 How do banks create money? Explain the theory of the credit multiplier.

2.4 Define universal banking. Discuss the advantages and disadvantages of a universal banking system. Has the 2007–2009 financial crisis exposed the weaknesses of the universal bank business model?

2.5 Discuss the main services offered by banks.

2.6 Define a payment system. Discuss the main contemporary changes in payment systems.

2.7 Describe the main characteristics of different types of plastic cards.

2.8 P2P lending organisations clearly cut out the 'middle man' by effectively disintermediating the transactions. Discuss the following questions:

(a) What are the benefits and risks of the P2P lending process?

(b) In what way(s) is it different from traditional banking?

(c) Could this system potentially produce a better outcome for all parties involved?

2.9 What is e-banking? How has the use of technology changed the retail banking industry?

2.10 What is meant by ethical and sustainable banking?

Chapter 3

Types of banking

3.1 Introduction

This chapter outlines the main types of firms that undertake **modern banking** business and identifies the key features of commercial and **investment banking**. The first part of the chapter describes the trend towards the development of financial service conglomerates and the widespread acceptance of the **universal banking** model (as opposed to **specialist banking**) during the 1990s and early to mid-2000s. We then go on to outline the main types of banks and focus on the products and services offered to personal (including private banking) and corporate banking customers. Discussion on corporate banking services is split between services offered to small companies and corporate and investment banking products offered to mid-sized and large companies. We also briefly highlight the main aspects of the investment banking business and describe why the 2007–2009 crisis resulted in the 'end of an era' for US investment banks. Finally, the chapter looks into some aspects of non-interest-based Islamic banking.

A major theme throughout the chapter is the blurring of distinctions between particular areas of banking and financial services provision, the focus on customer relationships and meeting the increasingly complex and diverse needs of clients. Post crisis, however, financial reforms (for example, the Dodd-Frank Act in the US and the recommendations of the UK Independent Commission on Banking, chaired by Sir John Vickers) are calling once again for the separation of investment and retail banking activities (the so-called ring-fencing of retail banking).

3.2   Traditional versus modern banking

The banking business has experienced substantial change over the last 30 years or so as banks have transformed their operations from relatively narrow activities to full-service financial firms. **Traditional banking** business consisted of taking deposits and making loans and the majority of their income was derived from lending business. Net interest margins (the difference between interest revenues from lending minus the interest cost on deposits) was the main driver of bank profitability. In such an environment banks sought to maximise interest margins and control operating costs (staff and other costs) in order to boost profits. Banks strategically focused on lending and deposit gathering as their main objectives.

Up until the 1990s many banking markets were highly regulated and competition was restricted. In the UK, banks were restricted from carrying out certain securities and investment banking business until 1986, when various reforms allowed commercial banks to acquire stockbroking firms. In continental Europe, branching restrictions were in place in Spain and Italy until 1992 and banks were also limited in terms of the types of business they could conduct. The implementation of the EU's Second Banking Directive in 1992 established a formal definition of what constituted banking business throughout Europe and this introduced the so-called universal banking model. Under this model, the banking business is broadly defined to include all aspects of financial service activity, including securities operations, insurance, pensions, leasing and so on. This meant that from 1992 onwards banks throughout the European Union could undertake a broad range of financial services activity.

A similar trend has also occurred in the United States. For example, there were nationwide branching restrictions in place until the passing of the Riegle-Neal Interstate Banking and Branching Efficiency Act in 1994, which allowed national banks to operate branches across state lines after 1 June 1997. Also the Gramm-Leach-Bliley Act in November 1999 allowed commercial banks to undertake securities and insurance business, thus establishing the possibility of universal banking activity for US banks. Similar legislation was enacted in Japan in 1999.

The type of business banks can undertake has therefore expanded dramatically. As detailed in Chapter 2, in addition to deregulation various other factors have had an impact on banking business globally. Capital restrictions that limited the free flow of funds across national boundaries gradually disappeared throughout the 1980s, facilitating the growth of international operations. The role of state-owned banks in Europe and elsewhere declined as a result of privatisation and various balance sheet restrictions (known as portfolio restrictions) were lowered or abolished, allowing banks greater freedom in the financial management of their activities. These global trends have been complemented by advances in technology that have revolutionised back-office processing and front-office delivery of financial services to customers. The general improvements in communication technology and the subsequent decline in costs allowed dissemination of information throughout a widespread organisation, making it practical to operate in geographically diversified markets. Lower communication costs also increased the role of competitive forces, as physically distant financial service providers became increasingly relevant as local competitors.

Technology has continued to blur the lines of specialisation among financial intermediaries. Advances in computing power allowed investment banks and other financial service firms to offer accounts with characteristics similar to bank accounts. Technological developments, therefore, have generally facilitated growth in the range of financial services available and heightened the competitive environment.

Table 3.1 Traditional versus modern banking

Traditional banking	Modern banking
Products and services: LIMITED ● Loans ● Deposits	Products and services: UNIVERSAL ● Loans ● Deposits ● Insurance ● Securities/investment banking ● Pensions ● Other financial services
Income sources: ● Net interest income	Income sources: ● Net interest income ● Fee and commission income
Competitive environment: ● Restricted	Competitive environment: ● High competition
Strategic focus: ● Asset size and growth	Strategic focus: ● Returns to shareholders ● Creating shareholder value (generating Return-on-equity, ROE, greater than the cost of capital)
Customer focus: ● Supply led	Customer focus: ● Demand led ● Creating value for customers

Table 3.1 shows that the nature of the banking business has changed from being relatively restricted and uncompetitive to a much more dynamic activity. Banks are now regarded as full-service financial firms – and many banks have even dropped the word 'bank' from their name in their promotional material, such as Barclays in Britain and JPMorgan Chase in the United States. The transformation of banks into full-service financial institutions has been motivated by the strategic objective of banks to be able to meet as broad a range of customer financial service demands as possible. The increase in products and services that can be sold to customers helps strengthen client relationships and (as long as customers value the services being provided) should boost returns to the bank over the longer term.

In an increasingly competitive environment banks have sought to diversify their earnings – complementing interest revenues from lending activity with fee and commission income from selling non-traditional banking products such as insurance. The greater emphasis on building client relationships means that banks have had to become much more demand-oriented, focusing on meeting the needs of a more diverse and financially sophisticated client base.

Until the 2007–2009 crisis, banks had to pay much greater attention to the performance of their operations and in particular to rewarding their owners (shareholders). Traditionally, when banking markets were relatively restricted and uncompetitive there was less pressure on banks to generate high profits in order to boost their stock prices and keep shareholders happy. Typically, banks focused on strategies based on asset growth – in other words, they sought to become larger as this was viewed as the main indicator of commercial success. Banks have strategically focused on creating value for shareholders (the bank's owners) and strategies based solely on asset growth were no longer deemed appropriate. The main reason for this shift in emphasis was because demands from shareholders increased, as did banks' demand for capital. In banking, capital is a resource available to the bank to protect itself against potential losses and to finance acquisition or expansion. Regulators set minimum capital requirements (e.g. Basel ratios) so banks should have sufficient resources to bear losses incurred from bad loans or from other activities. As such, banks need to generate sufficient performance for their equity to increase in value in order to attract new shareholders as well as keeping established shareholders. Senior managers therefore prioritise strategies that seek to increase the overall value of the bank (reflected in the share value of the bank and its overall market capitalisation). Prior to the 2007–2009 crisis, strategies expected to boost banks' stock prices were therefore prioritised. Today, modern banks' approach has had to be realigned with the changes triggered by the US sub-prime crisis in 2007. The demand for tighter regulation in financial services and a greater focus on the risks associated with banks' business have increased sharply.

Following the 2007–2009 financial crisis, there have been calls to narrow the scope of large financial institutions, which would require the reintroduction of firewalls such as those imposed by the Glass-Steagall Act, to limit the risks that deposits are exposed to. In a similar vein, the notion of increased systemic risk – arising from the broadened scope of banking activities – has been gaining ground in both theoretical debates and empirical contributions. However, constraining the degree of product diversification of financial institutions does not eliminate the risk of future systemic crises. An important issue for policy makers is to understand the distinction between types of bank diversification that add value for shareholders without adding to systemic risk, and those that might pose a threat to financial stability irrespective of the possible benefit to the individual firms' shareholders. One of the most successful channels of diversification has been the emergence and expansion of bancassurance, as detailed in Section 3.2.1.

3.2.1 Universal banking and the bancassurance trend

A key feature of the deregulation trend is that it has allowed banks to compete in areas of the financial services industry that were previously prohibited. While the universal banking model has been an integral feature of European banking since the early 1990s, it has been a more recent development in the United States and Japan. One area that deserves particular attention regarding the adoption of the universal banking model has been the increased role of commercial banks in the insurance area (see Genetay and Molyneux, 1998). The experiences of European banks provide a neat example of how the combination of banking and insurance business has developed. The combination of banking and insurance is known as **bancassurance**.

Bancassurance is a French term used to define the distribution of insurance products through a bank's distribution channels. Bancassurance – also known as allfinanz – describes a package of financial services that can fulfil both banking and insurance needs at the same time. A high street bank, for example, might sell both mortgages and life insurance policies to go with them (so that if the person taking out the mortgage dies then the life insurance will pay up to cover the outstanding mortgage).

Since the 1980s, the trend towards bancassurance has been increasing steadily. Some of the reasons put forward to explain such a trend are:

- cross-selling opportunities for banks (scope economies);
- non-interest income boosted at a time of decreasing interest margins;
- risk diversification;
- banks converting into full-service financial firms (deregulation).

Until the 1980s, banks in many countries sold insurance guarantees that were a direct extension of their banking business. For example, credit insurance on consumer loans was common in France. Banks were also selling buildings insurance and home/contents insurance for property purchase funded by mortgages.

During the 1980s major developments occurred, particularly in France, where banks started offering capitalisation products (for example, endowment products). However, despite the existence of an insurance component, it was a support factor to the savings objectives of these products. The 1990s brought greater customer orientation in the financial sector and banks in several EU countries attempted to exploit better the synergies between banking and insurance. By the end of the 2000s, bancassurers in Europe had an approximate 36 per cent share of the life insurance market (5 per cent of the non-life), with a market share reaching a record high of 92 per cent in Malta, followed by other southern European countries, with shares over 50 per cent, as shown in Figure 3.1. Bancassurance is not generally common in Eastern Europe, while in the UK, which is the largest European life insurance market, bancassurance is estimated to account for only 15–20 per cent of new business.

Nowadays, the term 'bancassurance' encompasses a variety of structure and business models. The development of each model has largely occurred on a country-by-country basis as the models are tailored to the individual market structures and traditions. In broad terms, bancassurance models can be divided between 'distribution alliances' and 'conglomerates'.

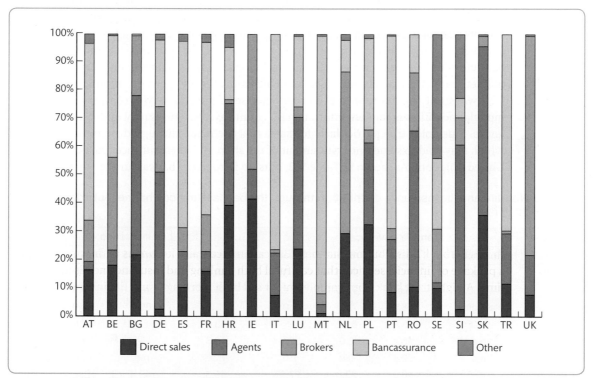

Figure 3.1 Life insurance distribution channels 2010 (gross written premiums)

Source: Insurance Europe (2013).

Note: AT = Austria; BE = Belgium; BG = Bulgaria; DE = Germany; ES = Spain; FR = France; HR = Croatia; IE = Ireland; IT = Italy; LU = Luxembourg; MT = Malta; NL = the Netherlands; PL = Poland; PT = Portugal; RO = Romania; SE = Sweden; SI = Slovenia; SK = Slovakia; TR = Turkey; UK = United Kingdom.

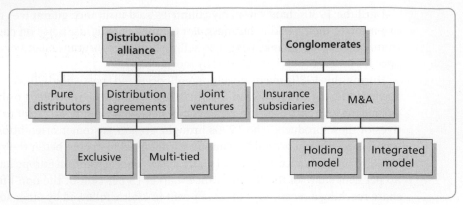

Figure 3.2 Bancassurance models

As shown in Figure 3.2 the 'conglomerate' model goes beyond the traditional bancassurance model of 'distribution alliances', which is the simple cross-selling of insurance products to banking customers, as it involves retaining the customers within the banking system and capturing the economic value added, that is a measure of the bank's financial performance, rather than simply acting as a sales desk on behalf of the insurance company. The conglomerate model is where a bank has its own wholly owned subsidiary to sell insurance through its branches whereas the distribution channel is where the bank sells an insurance firm's products for a fee.

In practice, the use of conglomerate and distribution alliance models is influenced by the role of the banking sector in the particular country. In countries such as Italy, France, Spain and Britain, where people visit banks on a regular basis, the conglomerate model is likely to be preferred. In general, most of the major European markets have seen a rapid rise in the market share of bancassurance for sales of life assurance and pensions products.

However, it is important to note that because of the complexity of the bancassurance models and different implementation in EU countries, the figures may understate real sales levels. This holds true particularly for sales that are made through distribution alliances, which may lead to some understatement of the share of bancassurance, particularly in the United Kingdom. As shown in Table 3.2, outside Europe the bancassurance model appears

Table 3.2 Non-life and life insurance distribution through the bancassurance channel outside Europe in 2010 (%)

Country	Non-life insurance				Life insurance			
	Bancassurance	Agents	Brokers	Others	Bancassurance	Agents	Brokers	Others
Australia	n.a.	21.0	74.0	5.0	43.0	-	57.0	-
Brazil	13.3	n.a.	71.6	n.a.	55.0	n.a.	30.0	n.a.
Canada	negligible	18.0	74.0	8.0	1.0	60.0	34.0	5.0
Chile	18.8	-	81.2	-	13.0	-	87.0	-
China	n.a.	45.4	2.0	52.6	16.3	-	83.7	-
Japan	n.a.	92.8	0.2	7.0	n.a.	n.a.	n.a.	n.a.
Malaysia	10.0	40.0	23.0	27.0	45.3	49.4	2.4	2.9
Mexico	10.0	25.0	50.0	15.0	10.0	-	90.0	-
Taiwan	n.a.	62.0	30.0	8.0	33.0	11.7	6.6	48.7
US	n.a.	n.a.	n.a.	n.a.	2.0	n.a.	n.a.	n.a.

Source: CEA (2010).

successful in both life and non-life business in two large Latin American countries: Brazil and Chile. In general, however, the bancassurance channel is typically more successful for the distribution of life products. While many European life insurance markets were dominated by bancassurance, this was not the case in other large markets. In 2010 bancassurance represented only 2 per cent of the market in the US and only 1 per cent in Canada. As in non-life, this low penetration was related to a change in legislation and to the attachment of consumers to traditional intermediaries.

3.3   Retail or personal banking

Retail or personal banking relates to financial services provided to consumers and is usually small-scale in nature. Typically, all large banks offer a broad range of personal banking services, including payments services (current account with cheque facilities, credit transfers, standing orders, direct debits and plastic cards), savings, loans, mortgages, insurance, pensions and other services (these services have been reviewed in Section 2.4).

A variety of different types of banks offers personal banking services. These include:

- commercial banks;
- savings banks;
- co-operative banks;
- building societies;
- credit unions;
- finance houses.

3.3.1   Commercial banks

Commercial banks are the major financial intermediary in any economy. They are the main providers of credit to the household and corporate sector and operate the payments mechanism. Commercial banks are typically joint stock companies and may be either publicly listed on the stock exchange or privately owned.

Commercial banks deal with both retail and corporate customers, have well-diversified deposit and lending books and generally offer a full range of financial services. The largest banks in most countries are commercial banks and they include household names such as Citibank, HSBC, Deutsche Bank and Barclays. Table 3.3 illustrates the ranking of the top 15 commercial banks in the world, as at December 2012, ranked by Tier 1 capital and total assets.

While commercial banking refers to institutions whose main business is deposit taking and lending, it should always be remembered that the largest commercial banks also engage in investment banking, insurance and other financial services areas. They are also the key operators in most countries' retail banking markets. Box 3.1 illustrates the business model of one of the world's largest banks, Bank of America.

Table 3.3 Top 15 commercial banks (December 2012)

Rank	Company	Country	Tier 1 capital ($mil)	Total assets ($mil)
1	Bank of America	US	159,232	2,136,577
2	JPMorgan Chase	US	150,384	2,265,792
3	ICBC	China	140,027	2,456,294
4	HSBC Holdings	UK	139,590	2,555,579
5	Citigroup	US	131,874	1,873,878
6	China Construction Bank Corporation	China	119,135	1,949,219
7	Mitsubishi UFJ Financial Group	Japan	117,017	2,664,170
8	Wells Fargo & Co	US	113,952	1,313,867
9	Bank of China	China	111,172	1,877,520
10	Agricultural Bank of China	China	96,413	1,853,318
11	BNP Paribas	France	91,857	2,542,879
12	Royal Bank of Scotland (RBS)	UK	88,112	2,329,767
13	Crédit Agricole	France	80,221	2,431,931
14	Banco Santander	Spain	79,897	1,619,349
15	Barclays	UK	78,036	2,417,369

Source: The Banker Database. Available at **www.thebankerdatabase.com**, *Financial Times*. © The Financial Times Limited. All Rights Reserved.

BOX 3.1 BANK OF AMERICA

Bank of America is one of the world's largest financial institutions, serving individual consumers, small- and middle-market businesses and large corporations with a full range of banking, investing, asset management and other financial and risk management products and services. The company serves approximately 53 million consumer and small business relationships with approximately 5,500 retail banking offices and approximately 16,300 ATMs, and award-winning online banking with 30 million active users.

Bank of America is among the world's leading wealth management companies and is a global leader in corporate and investment banking and trading across a broad range of asset classes, serving corporations, governments, institutions and individuals around the world. Bank of America offers industry-leading support to approximately 3 million small business owners through a suite of innovative, easy-to-use online products and services. The company serves clients through operations in more than 40 countries. Bank of America Corporation stock (NYSE: BAC) is a component of the Dow Jones Industrial Average and is listed on the New York Stock Exchange.

Figure 3.3 illustrates the structure of Bank of America's balance sheet and profit and loss (P&L) account at end of year 2012. The bank finances are mainly deposits and short-term funding (67 per cent), while the asset side of the balance sheet is more diversified, with an almost equal distribution of lending and non-lending activities.

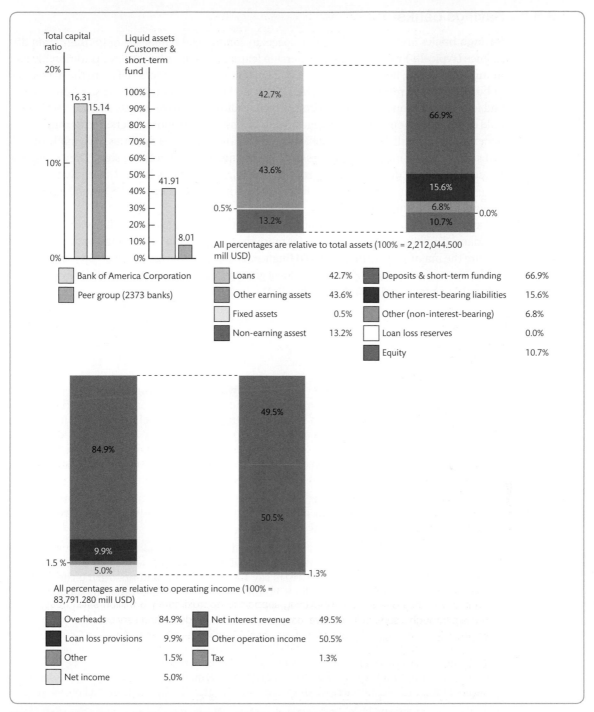

Figure 3.3 Structure of balance sheet and P&L of Bank of America (2012)

Source: SNL Financial and Bankscope.

3.3.2 Savings banks

Savings banks are similar in many respects to commercial banks although their main difference (typically) relates to their ownership features – savings banks have traditionally had mutual ownership, being owned by their 'members' or 'shareholders', who are the depositors or borrowers. The main types of savings banks in the United States are the so-called savings and loan associations (S&Ls or thrifts), which traditionally were mainly financed by household deposits and lent retail mortgages. Their business is now more diversified as they offer a wider range of small firm corporate loans, credit cards and other facilities. Originally the US S&Ls were mainly mutual in ownership, but now many have become listed. They represent the second largest deposit-taking group of financial institutions in the United States: there were 987 saving institutions in December 2012 with assets of more than $1tn and employing around 150,000 employees.[1]

Savings banks are also important in various other countries, particularly in Europe. In Germany, for instance, they account for more than 50 per cent of the retail banking market and are the major players in household finance. The German savings banks (Sparkassen) are public institutions owned by federal or local governments and represent politically powerful networks of small public banks (see Box 3.2).

BOX 3.2 GERMANY'S SMALL BANKS FIGHT TO KEEP PRIVILEGES

Ask those outside the Sparkassen group about why they complain of its privileges and one thing that crops up is its member banks' right to consider loans to each other – or the closely linked Landesbanken where many regional savings bank associations are co-owners – as, in effect, risk-free. It means no capital needs to be held against such exposures. That anomaly "leads to a de facto underestimation of capital requirements" and could encourage more leverage and interconnectedness to the detriment of stability, the International Monetary Fund argued last year.

At the same time, the 423 savings banks do not need to file combined accounts as a single financial group. Their accounts are first overseen by auditors from within the savings bank group, not external auditors.

The savings banks have also argued they should be able to remain outside of European deposit insurance plans, saying their traditional unlimited guarantees for each other's survival is more than adequate. Critics say Landesbanken bailouts during the crisis show that the robustness of the joint liability scheme is exaggerated. In some cases savings banks did not contribute a share of aid that reflected their ownership stakes.

Savings banks also enjoy a lower cost of capital than rivals: they are under no obligation to make payouts to their local municipalities.

Their donations to local sports clubs or cultural events partly make up for the lack of dividends – but Ralph Brinkhaus, a CDU MP, says savings banks' low level of dividends "is not going to be sustainable when so many local authorities are in financial problems".

 Source: Germany's small banks fight union plans, *Financial Times*, 02/12/12 (James Wilson).
© The Financial Times Limited. All Rights Reserved.

---

[1] www.fdic.gov/bank/statistical/stats

It should be noted that savings banks (in Europe and elsewhere) adhere to the principle of mutuality and pursue objectives relating to the social and economic development of the region or locality in which they operate. Unlike commercial banks, they may pursue strategic objectives other than maximising shareholder wealth or profits. Typically their business focuses on retail customers and small businesses, but as some have become very large (especially in Germany and Spain) they closely resemble commercial banks in their service and product offerings.

3.3.3 Co-operative banks

Another type of institution similar in many respects to savings banks are the **co-operative banks**. These originally had mutual ownership and typically offered retail and small business banking services. Co-operative banks are an important part of the financial sector in Germany, Austria, Italy, France, the Netherlands, Spain and Finland. A trend has been for large numbers of small co-operative banks to group (or consolidate) to form a much larger institution, examples of which include Rabobank in the Netherlands and Crédit Agricole in France – both of these are now listed and have publicly traded stock. In Britain, the Co-operative Bank also is publicly listed. However, after the 2007–2009 crisis, the virtues of banking consolidation and demutualisation have been undergoing a drastic reassessment. Various commentators are now calling for more diversity in types of banks, with different banking models suiting different types of customers, and therefore supporting the real economy, contributing to systemic stability and promoting inclusion (Ayadi *et al.*, 2009; Ayadi *et al.*, 2010).

3.3.4 Building societies

Another type of financial institution offering personal banking services prevalent in the United Kingdom and various other countries (such as Australia and South Africa) are **building societies**. These are similar to savings and co-operative banks as they have mutual ownership and focus primarily on retail deposit taking and mortgage lending.

As noted by the UK Building Societies Association:

> A building society is a mutual institution. This means that most people who have a savings account, or mortgage, are members and have certain rights to vote and receive information, as well as to attend and speak at meetings. Each member has one vote, regardless of how much money they have invested or borrowed or how many accounts they may have. Each building society has a board of directors who run the society and who are responsible for setting its strategy.
>
> Building societies are different from banks, which are companies (normally listed on the stock market) and are therefore owned by, and run for, their shareholders. Societies, which are not companies, are not driven by external shareholder pressure to maximise profits to pay away as dividends. This normally enables them to run on lower costs and offer cheaper mortgages and better rates of interest on savings than their competitors.
>
> The other major difference between building societies and banks is that there is a limit on the proportion of their funds that building societies can raise from the wholesale money markets. It is illegal for a building society to raise more than 50% of its funds from the wholesale markets. The average proportion of funds raised by building societies from the wholesale markets is around 20%.

Building Societies Association (2013) **www.bsa.org.uk**

There are around 46 building societies in the UK at the time of writing (2014), with total assets of £325bn. In addition, there are around 50 mutual lenders and deposit takers. Statistics show that the number of building societies fell substantially during the 1990s as the largest converted from mutual to publicly listed companies and therefore became banks. More detail on the UK building society sector can be found in Chapter 13.

3.3.5 Credit unions

Credit unions are another type of mutual deposit institution that is growing in importance in a number of countries. These are non-profit co-operative institutions that are owned by their members who pool their savings and lend to each other. They are usually regulated differently from banks. Many of their staff are part-time. As illustrated in Table 3.4, the growth in the number of credit unions worldwide over the five-year period 2005–2010 was remarkable (24 per cent overall). In many cases (as in Europe and Oceania), although the number of institutions has fallen considerably, the number of members and the volumes of savings and loans have kept growing significantly everywhere.

Table 3.4 Credit unions in the world, 2005–2010 (% changes)

Countries	Number of credit unions	Number of members	Savings (US$)	Loans (US$)
Africa	135.1	77.9	125.0	125.1
Asia	18.8	21.0	126.1	146.1
Caribbean	42.8	67.4	75.3	90.0
Europe	−16.4	23.1	25.5	26.4
Latin America	−12.0	26.6	154.3	163.3
North America	−11.2	12.4	54.1	47.5
Oceania	−18.8	0.3	96.2	108.1
Credit unions worldwide	**24.0**	**19.7**	**61.0**	**56.8**

Source: WOCCU (World Council of Credit Unions), and authors' calculations. Data available at **www.woccu.org/publications/statreport**

The total number of credit unions worldwide in 2012 was 56,000, serving 200 million members. In the United States there were 6,960 as of December 2012, with more than 95 million members with deposits exceeding $1 trillion and loans of over $850 billion. In the UK, 397 credit unions (down by 153 units since 2005) served an estimated 1,025,000 members in 2012 (up by more than 500,000 members since 2005; the increasing trend is remarkable, as members were up by 10.4 per cent between 2010 and 2011, equivalent to an increase of 15.19 per cent in total assets).[2]

3.3.6 Finance houses

Finance companies provide finance to individuals (and also companies) by making consumer, commercial and other types of loans. They differ from banks because they typically do not take deposits and raise funds by issuing money market (such as commercial paper) and capital market (stocks and bonds) instruments. In the UK these are sometimes referred to as hire

---

[2] World Council of Credit Unions, Statistical Reports, available at **www.woccu.org/publications/statreport**

purchase firms, although their main types of business are retail lending and (in the UK and continental Europe) **leasing** activity. All major retail firms and motor companies have their own finance house subsidiaries – for example, General Motors' finance house used to fund car purchase is known as GMAC Financial Services. A distinction is usually made between sales finance institutions (loans made by a retailer or car firm to fund purchases), personal credit institutions (that make loans to 'non-prime' or high-risk customers who usually cannot obtain bank credit) and business credit **finance houses** that use **factoring** (purchasing accounts receivables) and leasing to finance business activity.

The largest finance houses in the UK are subsidiaries of the major banks and they are significant operators in the unsecured consumer loan business. For instance, in 2012 finance houses provided more than £76.4 billion to consumers, representing almost 30 per cent of all unsecured lending in the UK. Within that total, finance houses provided £23.3 billion of motor finance to consumers and financed more than 70 per cent of all new private car registrations.[3]

3.4   Private banking

So far we have discussed personal banking business, outlining the various services on offer and the main types of financial institutions undertaking such activity. Another area of banking closely related to personal banking that has grown substantially over the last decade or so is known as **private banking**.

Private banking concerns the high-quality provision of a range of financial and related services to wealthy clients, principally individuals and their families. Typically, the services on offer combine retail banking products such as payment and account facilities plus a wide range of up-market investment-related services. Market segmentation and the offering of high-quality service provision forms the essence of private banking. Key components include:

- tailoring services to individual client requirements;
- anticipation of client needs;
- long-term relationship orientation;
- personal contact;
- discretion.

High net worth individuals (HNWIs) are defined as those with $1 million or more in investable assets (that is, assets at their disposal for investing). An important feature of the private banking market relates to client segmentation. The bottom end of the market is referred to as the 'mass affluent' segment – typically individuals with $100,000 to $1 million in investable assets. The top end of the market are often referred to as 'ultra HNWIs', with more than $30 million in investable assets, and in between lie HNWIs (investable assets of $1 million or more) and mid-tier millionaires, who are HNWIs having $5 million to $30 million. The level of service and the range of products on offer increase with the wealth of the respective client.

---

[3] See the consumer finance section of the UK's Finance & Leasing Association website at **www.fla.org.uk** for more details.

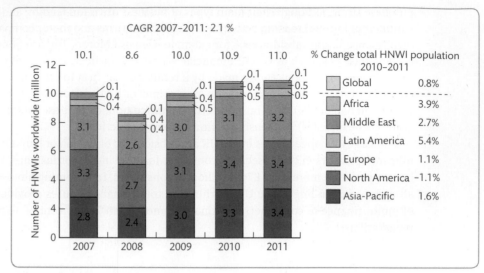

Figure 3.4 HNWI population (2007–2011)

Source: World Wealth Report 2012. Capgemini and RBC Wealth Management.

Figure 3.4 illustrates the HNWI population by region, as well as the change in the period 2007–2011.[4]

The Capgemini and RBC Wealth Management (2012) World Wealth Report highlights various features of the market for HNWIs:

● At the end of 2011, 11 million people globally each held at least US$1million in financial assets.

● HNWIs' wealth totalled US$42 trillion, surpassing the 2007 pre-crisis peak (although the aggregate investable wealth declined by 1.7 per cent in 2011, reflecting the impact of losses among higher wealth brackets – the 'ultra HNWIs', that is those with US$30 million or more in investable assets).

● Regionally:

  – the population of HNWIs in Asia-Pacific hit 3.37 million individuals, surpassing North America for the first time (3.35 million individuals) to become the largest in the world;

  – North American HNWIs, however, still account for the largest regional share of invest-able assets (US$11.4 trillion), although that declined by 2.3 per cent from 2010;

  – the combined wealth of Asia-Pacific HNWIs (US$10.7 trillion in 2011) had already topped Europe's in 2009, and that gap widened (US$10.1 trillion in 2011). This despite the fact that the number of HNWIs increased by 1.1 per cent in Europe to 3.17 million, due to growing numbers in Russia, the Netherlands and Switzerland.

● Over time, the HNWI population is gradually becoming more fragmented across the globe, but its geographic distribution in 2011 was much the same overall as it had been, and 53.3 per cent of the world's HNWIs were still concentrated in the US, Japan and Germany.

Table 3.5 lists the major private banks taken from a Scorpio (2012) ranking. The market for private banking services has been targeted by many large banks because of the growing

---

[4] www.capgemini.com/sites/default/files/resource/pdf/The_16th_Annual_World_Wealth_Report_2012.pdf

Table 3.5 Top 20 global private banks by assets under management

Rank	Institution	Assets under management ($ billion)	Growth 2011
1	Bank of America	1,671.00	−2.17%
2	UBS	1,554.53	−0.34%
3	Wells Fargo	1,300.00	−7.07%
4	Morgan Stanley	1,219.00	−0.81%
5	Credit Suisse	843.32	−2.51%
6	Royal Bank of Canada	573.32	0.68%
7	HSBC	377.00	−3.33%
8	Deutsche Bank	348.60	−5.41%
9	BNP Paribas	316.20	−7.11%
10	JPMorgan	291.00	2.46%
11	Pictet	262.11	−5.48%
12	Goldman Sachs	227.00	−0.87%
13	Citigroup	208.00	47.83%
14	ABN AMRO	189.98	−13.67%
15	Barclays	182.71	−1.72%
16	Julius Baer	178.79	0.12%
17	Northern Trust	173.70	12.5%
18	Bank of New York Mellon	168.00	1.20%
19	Crédit Agricole	163.67	−4.74%
20	Lombard Odier Darier Hentsch	151.30	−1.18%

Source: Scorpio (2012).

wealth of individuals and the relative profitability of private banking business. The wealth management industry is performing relatively well in spite of growing regulatory pressure and economic instability. However, the costs associated with assets under management are increasing, reflecting the changing global regulatory framework. Indeed, market trends for cost-to-income ratios were in the region of 78–85 per cent, much higher than the pre-2008 era. The top five firms in the private banking industry still come from America and Switzerland, led by Bank of America Merrill Lynch. Wealth management is increasingly seen as a reliable revenue stream as investment banking comes under pressure, with Goldman Sachs saying in 2012 that it planned to expand in private banking.

3.5 Corporate banking

Corporate banking relates to banking services provided to companies, although typically the term refers to services provided to relatively large firms. HSBC's activities with firms are divided into three size categories: firms with turnover up to £2 million (Business Banking), £2 million to £30 million (Commercial Banking) and greater than £30 million (Corporate Banking). Services offered to the latter, namely the largest firms, are referred to as corporate and structured banking services. Note that this distinction is not clear-cut and some banks do not explicitly distinguish between 'business banking' and 'corporate banking', although one should be aware that the term 'corporate banking' is used mainly to refer to services provided to relatively large firms whereas business banking may relate to a wide range of activities, from financial services offered to small start-up firms to services offered to larger companies.

Banking services provided to small and medium-sized firms are in many respects similar to personal banking services and the range of financial products and services on offer increases and grows in complexity the larger the company. Below we highlight the main banking services used by different sizes of firms.

3.5.1 Banking services used by small firms

There are four main types of banking service on offer to small firms:

1 Payment services.
2 Debt finance.
3 Equity finance.
4 Special financing.

3.5.1.1 Payment services

As noted earlier, banks play a pivotal role in the payments system. They provide clearing services to businesses and individuals, making sure that current account transactions are processed smoothly, issue credit and debit cards that enable customers to make payments, and offer instant access to cash through their ATMs and branch networks. In many respects the payments services on offer to small firms are similar to those offered to retail customers. The former are given business current accounts that allow firms access to current accounts providing a broad range of payment services. In the UK these include:

● cash and cheque deposit facilities;
● cheque writing facilities;
● access to the CCCL (Cheque and Credit Clearing Company), which deals with paper-based payments and processes the majority of cheques and paper-based credits;
● access to BACS (Banks Automated Clearing System), an automated clearing house responsible for clearing of electronic payments between bank accounts, and for processing direct debits, direct credits and standing orders. In 2012 BACS schemes accounted for 5.66 billion payments, equating to £4.15 trillion.[5]

In May 2008, the **Faster Payments Service (FPS)** went live. This is a payment system, developed by the UK banking industry, which enables electronic payments, typically initiated via the internet or phone, to be processed in hours. The service runs alongside the existing BACS service. Twelve banks and one building society, accounting for about 95 per cent of payments traffic, initially committed to use the service.[6] This system has improved money

---

[5] www.bacs.co.uk

[6] The original founding members of the new service were: Abbey (now Santander UK), Alliance and Leicester (now Santander UK), Barclays, Citi, Clydesdale and Yorkshire Banks (National Australia Group), Co-operative Bank, HBOS, HSBC, Lloyds TSB, Nationwide Building Society, Northern Bank (Danske Bank), Northern Rock, and Royal Bank of Scotland Group (including NatWest and Ulster Bank). Santander does offer this service in the UK now.

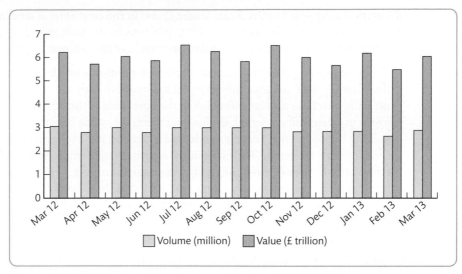

Figure 3.5 CHAPS monthly volumes and values (2012–2013)
Source: www.chapsco.co.uk/about_chaps/chaps_statistics/

transfer speeds between different banks in the UK, enabling account holders with one bank to make virtually instant payments to those with another bank.

● Access to CHAPS Clearing Company (Clearing House Automated Payments System) that provides electronic same-day transfer of high-value payments. (Small firms, however, rarely use CHAPS as transaction costs are prohibitively expensive.) While CHAPS is mainly used for high-value business-to-business payments, consumers can use the system to buy or sell high-value items, such as a house or car. CHAPS represents 0.5 per cent of total clearing volumes but 93 per cent of total clearing sterling values. In 2012, CHAPS volumes were at 34 million annually; on average 134,700 payments per day (see Figure 3.5).

These are core payment services for which there are no substitutes. The supply of payment services to small firms is dominated by the main UK banks and these also control the wholesale networks for many transaction services.

One of the critical features of the payments system relates to small firm access to cash and the ability to make payments in cash and cheque form. Like retail customers, small firms use their business current accounts via the branch network to make cash and cheque payments into their current accounts. They also use the ATM network to obtain cash. In terms of the types of payments made by small firms in the UK, cheques and automated transactions such as direct debits and standing orders predominate. Nevertheless, cash and plastic card payments are growing among small firms and estimates put them at 15–20 per cent (**www.paymentscouncil.org.uk**).

3.5.1.2 Debt finance for small firms

The access to external finance is a critical success ingredient in the development of any business and to this extent small firms are no different from their larger counterparts. Traditional bank loan and overdraft finance are the main sources of external finance for small firms, although one should bear in mind that many small firms rely on internal funding to finance their operations. With regards to lending to small firms, features can obviously vary from country to country – in the UK, for instance, the majority of bank lending is at variable rates of interest (as opposed to fixed-rate lending) and in the case of term lending, typically has a maturity of more than five years.

The other main sources of external finance include the following:

- **Asset-based finance** – this includes both **hire purchase** and leasing. These two types of financial services are generally grouped together but they are two distinct types of product. Hire purchase agreements result in the purchaser of the goods building up ownership over a pre-determined period. On final payment, the goods belong to the individual or firm making the payments. Leasing products are similar, but the legal ownership of the good remains with the lessor. For example, a lease is an agreement where the owner (lessor) conveys to the user (lessee) the right to use equipment (e.g. vehicles) in return for a number of specified payments over an agreed period of time. Unlike a bank loan, a lease is an asset-based financing product, with the equipment leased usually the only collateral for the transaction. Typically, a firm will be offered a leasing agreement that covers not only the equipment costs but also the delivery, installation, servicing and insurance.

- **Factoring and invoice discounting** – factoring is the purchase by the factor and sale by the company of its book debts on a continuing basis, usually for immediate cash. The factor then manages the sales ledger and the collection of accounts under terms agreed by the seller. The factor may assume the credit risk for accounts (the likelihood that sales invoices will not be paid) within agreed limits (this is known as *non-recourse factoring*), or this risk may remain with the seller (*factoring with recourse*). (It is best to think of a factoring firm as a company's debt collector – the factor takes on responsibility for recovering payments on sales made.) **Invoice discounting services** are similar to factoring but here the sales accounting functions are retained by the seller.

- **Shareholders and partners** – these are individuals who provide their personal finance to the firm and this confers ownership rights.

- **Trade credit** – this is credit given to firms by trading partners, allowing the former to delay payment.

- **Venture capital** – this is long-term external equity provided by **venture capital** firms. The venture capitalist is an equity partner who places greater emphasis on the final capital gain (dependent on the market value of the company). According to the British Private Equity & Venture Capital Association (BVCA) investments typically last for three to seven years.[7] In addition to finance, the venture capital firm (or individual) will provide expertise, experience and contacts to help develop the business.

- **Other sources** – this category includes a broad variety of alternative finance sources ranging from credit card borrowing, loans from private individuals conferring no ownership (e.g. a loan from a member of a family), various government grants for small business and so on.

3.5.1.3 Equity finance for small firms

Most small firms rely on bank- and asset-based financing for their external financing and few access either public or private equity finance. **Private equity finance** can be distinguished according to two main types: formal and informal. Formal equity finance is available from various sources, including banks, special investment schemes, and private equity and venture capital firms. The informal market refers to private financing by so-called '*business angels*' – wealthy

[7] See **www.bvca.co.uk/**

individuals who invest in small, unquoted companies. As pointed out by the British Private Equity & Venture Capital Association (2010), the terms 'private equity' and 'venture capital' can be used to refer to different stages in the investments. For example, in Europe the term 'venture capital' is often used to cover the private equity industry as a whole, i.e. encompassing both venture capital and management buy-outs and buy-ins. In the US, venture capital refers only to investments in early-stage and expanding companies.

All the main UK banks offer a range of equity products to small firms, although there are differences in their willingness to undertake direct equity investments. For instance, in the late 1990s HSBC operated a network of HSBC Enterprise Funds mainly aimed at making investments in the £5,000 to £250,000 range. The Fund, which supported 39 businesses across a wide range of sectors and stages, including start-ups and management buy-outs, is now closed to new investments. All the other main banks offer some form of private equity investment services, although these tend to be geared towards larger firms or those in certain sectors, such as high-tech start-ups.

It is interesting to note that the British Bankers' Association (BBA) has a section on its website dedicated to offering information on small firm financing.[8] It also provides links to those wishing to know about equity investments to the BVCA and the UK Business Angels Association.[9] The UK Business Angels Association is supported by key players in the financial community, such as the BBA, the £2.5 billion Business Growth Fund, Capital for Enterprise Ltd, Nesta and Lloyds TSB Commercial.

In addition to bank equity finance and that provided by business angels, Britain has the largest formal venture capital market in the world outside the United States. According to the European Private Equity & Venture Capital Association (EVCA), investments into European companies reached €46 billion in 2011, although investment decreased by 19 per cent in 2012, due to the economic uncertainty in Europe. The number of private equity-backed European companies remained stable at almost 5,000 at the end of 2012.[10] However, one should not forget that there are a number of public equity markets that provide funding for small firms with strong growth potential. In the United Kingdom, the main public equity market is the Official List of the London Stock Exchange. Smaller firms are categorised in the FTSE Small Cap (consisting of companies outside of the FTSE 350 Index and representing approximately 2 per cent of the UK market capitalisation) or FTSE Fledgling (UK companies listed on the main market of the London Stock Exchange that are too small to be included in the FTSE All-Share) indices. There is also a small market index that combines the FTSE Fledgling, Small Cap and other indices.[11]

While access to the Official List is (in most cases) limited to medium-sized firms, fast-growth firms seeking a UK stock market listing are most likely to access the Alternative Investment Market (AIM). This is the second tier of the stock market and it has less onerous admission and trading requirements than the Official List.

---

[8] See **www.bba.org.uk**

[9] The UK Business Angels Association is the national trade association representing angel and early-stage investment in the UK (England, Wales and Northern Ireland). It has superseded the BBAA (British Business Angels Association) and was relaunched in its new strengthened role in July 2012 (see **www.ukbusinessangelsassociation .org.uk**).

[10] See **www.evca.eu**

[11] techMARK was launched in November 1999 as the London Stock Exchange's index for innovative technology companies. Two years later, techMARK Mediscience was launched to focus on companies whose business is dependent on innovation in the development or manufacture of pharmaceuticals, or products or services that are wholly or substantially dedicated to the healthcare industry. See **www.londonstockexchange.com/**

Other sources of public equity finance in the UK include OFEX, an off-market trading facility provided by JP Jenkins Limited, that has lower requirements than the AIM and provides seed capital to firms that may be contemplating an AIM or Official Listing in the future.

3.5.1.4 Special financing

In addition to all the above-mentioned means of finance available to small firms, many countries have a range of government initiatives that seek to promote entrepreneurship and the development of the small firm sector. Britain is no exception – there is a plethora of initiatives aimed at promoting the development of the small firm sector.

Such schemes in the UK include initiatives geared to:

- financing small businesses in economically deprived areas;
- financing technology-based small firms;
- financing ethnic minority firms.

The government also offers a wide range of fiscal advantages aimed at stimulating small firm growth, and especially start-ups.

As a consequence of the 2007–2009 financial crisis, the UK government introduced measures to help small and medium-sized enterprises facing credit constraints by launching a Small Business Finance Scheme to support up to £1 billion of bank lending to small exporters, a £50 million fund to convert businesses' debt into equity, and a £25 million regional loan transition fund (see also Chapter 13). As part of the Autumn Statement in November 2011, a proposal unveiled by the UK Chancellor, George Osborne, was *credit easing* (see Box 3.3).

BOX 3.3 UK CREDIT EASING

If not the banks, then who? That has been the question for businesses seeking loans ever since the credit crisis started in 2007. One source of new lending might be the UK government. Chancellor George Osborne has unveiled a plan for 'credit easing' – making it easier for small and medium companies to borrow. Within Mr Osborne's sketchy announcement were several ideas about how to achieve this. The general idea should be applauded. The question will be whether the mandarins can get the details right.

One of the proposals is to revive that demon of the credit crisis: securitisation. By this scheme, the government would become a buyer of securitised loans that banks make to SMEs. Another is for the government to offer loan guarantees to SMEs. A third is some version of the US scheme whereby the government lends money to investors to buy certain types of bonds. These last two proposals involve officials deciding which borrowers are worthy of financing. And they do not address the long-term need to develop new lending channels as alternatives to bank credit. The best way to achieve Mr Osborne's goal would be to rehabilitate securitisation – a market that suffers rather unjustly from its 'toxic' label. If deals involving US subprime mortgages are excluded, securitised bonds are performing well. To be successful, however, credit easing will need the involvement of big investors, including pension funds and insurers. If bank lending is to be constrained by their own high borrowing costs and regulation – as it will for some time – then other long-term direct lenders must be found.

Companies can recover the confidence to invest in long-term growth if they believe there are committed investors. Mr Osborne's proposal will only work if those lenders show up.

Source: UK credit easing, *Financial Times* 03/10/11.

In March 2012, the Chancellor launched the National Loan Guarantee Scheme, to help smaller businesses to access finance. This includes:

- Funding for Lending Scheme (FLS) to provide incentives to banks to boost their lending to households and businesses; and
- Business Finance Partnership (BFP) to stimulate non-bank lending to mid-size and small businesses.

3.5.2 Banking services for mid-market and large (multinational) corporate clients

The mid-market and multinational corporate sector is served by a variety of financial service firms, including mainly commercial banks, investment banks and asset finance firms. These firms offer a broad range of services at varying levels of sophistication. The core banking products and services typically focus on the following range of needs:

1 Cash management and transaction services.

2 Credit and other debt financing facilities – loans, overdrafts, syndicated loans, commercial paper, bonds and other facilities.

3 Commitments and guarantees.

4 Foreign exchange and interest rate-related transactions.

5 Securities underwriting and fund management services.

At the bottom end of the middle-market sector, companies generally require the services provided to the small firm sector, but as they become larger they increasingly need a broader array of more sophisticated products.

3.5.2.1 Cash management and transaction services

An important area in which larger company banking services differ from those for small firms is in the provision of cash management and transaction services. Cash management services have grown mainly as a result of (a) corporate recognition that excess cash balances result in a significant opportunity cost due to lost or foregone interest, and (b) firms needing to know their cash or working capital position on a real-time basis. These services include the following:

- **Controlled disbursement accounts.** These current accounts are debited early each day so that firms get an up-to-date insight into their net cash positions.
- **Account reconciliation services.** A current account feature that provides a record of the firm's cheques that have been paid by the bank.
- **Wholesale lockbox facilities** whereby a centralised collection service for corporate payments is used to reduce the delay in cheque payment and receipt (i.e. clearing).
- **Funds concentration.** Redirects funds from accounts in a large number of different banks or branches to a few centralised accounts at one bank.
- **Electronic funds transfer.** Includes overnight wholesale payments via a variety of different mechanisms depending on the country in which the bank is based. In the UK, overnight wholesale payments are made through CHAPS and automated payment of payrolls or dividends by automated clearing houses (such as BACS). In the US, overnight wholesale payments are made through the Clearing House Interbank Payments System (CHIPS) and

Fedwire, and automated payroll payments are made through various automated clearing houses. International banks also conduct automated transmission of payments messages by the Society for Worldwide Interbank Financial Telecommunication (SWIFT), an international electronic message service owned and operated by US and European banks that instructs banks to make various wholesale payments.

- **Cheque deposit services.** Encoding, endorsing, microfilming and handling cheques for customers.

- **Electronic sending of letters of credit.** Allows corporate clients to access bank computers to initiate letters of credit.

- **Treasury management software.** Allows efficient management of multiple currency portfolios for trading and investment services.

- **Computerised pension fund services.**

- **Online corporate advisory and risk management services.**

- **Electronic data interchange (EDI).** An advanced application of electronic messaging that allows businesses to transfer and transact invoices, purchase orders, shipping notices and so on, automatically, using banks as clearinghouses.

3.5.2.2 Credit and other debt financing

Large companies often have to decide whether they are going to raise funds in the domestic or foreign currency. For instance, they may raise finance in a foreign currency in order to offset a net receivable position in that foreign currency. For example, consider a UK company that has net receivables in euros. If it requires short-term finance it can borrow euro and convert them into pounds for which it needs funds. The net receivables in euro will then be used to pay off the loan. In this particular example, foreign currency financing reduces the company's exposure to exchange rate fluctuations. This strategy, of course, is attractive if the interest rate of the foreign currency loan is low. The main point to emphasise is that both short- and longer-term borrowings, whether they relate to standard loan facilities or to the issue of short- or longer-term debt instruments, can be denominated in either local or foreign currency.

Short-term financing

All companies have to raise short-term finance (for less than one year) periodically and in most cases this is usually provided by banks. Typically, small firms will arrange extended overdraft facilities or negotiate term loans to meet short-term financing needs. In contrast, larger firms can negotiate credit lines with a number of banks so they are not dependent on one sole supplier of funds. Bank credit, of one form or another, may be denominated in the domestic currency of the firm or in a foreign currency. Large firms can also raise short-term funds in the capital markets by issuing various types of short-term paper. The arrangement of bank credit lines, overdraft facilities and the issue of short-term funding instruments are the responsibilities of the Treasury function.

Commercial paper

Large firms have access to various markets for short-term finance through the issuance of tradable instruments. One method that has been increasingly used by large firms to raise short-term finance has been through the issue of **commercial paper** (CP). Dealers issue this paper without the backing of an underwriting syndicate, so a selling price is not guaranteed to the issuers. Maturities can be tailored to the investor's preferences. Dealers make a secondary market in commercial paper by offering to buy the paper before maturity. The US commercial paper market is the largest in the world and is the main way (outside bank credit) that large US firms raise short-term finance.

Commercial paper issues denominated in currency outside the country of issue (such as a yen or Eurocommercial paper issues made in London) are known as Eurocommercial paper. (Note that this is not to be confused with the European currency – a Euro CP issue can be denominated in any currency as long as the issue of the paper is made outside of the country or area of issue of the currency.) Commercial paper issues are often preferred to bank credit, especially when large firms have better credit ratings than banks, and this means that the former can borrow on cheaper terms. As only a handful of international banks have the highest credit rating (for example, AAA given by Standard & Poor's credit rating agency), this means that many large firms – such as General Motors and Coca-Cola – are perceived as being more creditworthy than the banks with which they do business. As such, these firms can issue short-term financial instruments at finer terms than their relationship banks.

Euronotes

Euronotes are another type of instrument that large firms can issue to raise short-term funds. They are unsecured debt securities with interest rates based on interbank rates (mainly LIBOR – the London Interbank Offered Rate – which is the rate banks charge for lending wholesale funds to one another). These instruments typically have one-, three- or six-month maturities, although they are often rolled over as a form of medium-term financing. In the case of Euronotes, commercial banks usually underwrite the issue of these instruments guaranteeing an issue price. Banks and other companies purchase these as part of their investment portfolios.

Repurchase agreements (repos)

In addition to the aforementioned types of short-term financing there are numerous other types of techniques that companies can use to raise short-term finance. Many large firms have developed their repo (repurchase agreement) activities. A **repo** deal involves pledging collateral (usually government bonds or some low-risk instrument) in return for short-term wholesale funds. At a set date, the funds will be repaid and the collateral 'released'. There are various types of repurchase agreements that involve varying agreements concerning the sale and buy-back of wholesale funds backed by various types of collateral agreements. A main attraction of this type of business is that it allows companies to raise short-term funds at wholesale rates by pledging longer-term financial assets. (It is a technique widely used by banks to facilitate liquidity in the money market.)

Long-term financing

Companies also have to raise long-term finance (for more than one year) in order to finance long-term investments. Large companies have access to a broad array of credit facilities, including overdraft and both secured and unsecured lending facilities. For large lending requirements companies can borrow via the syndicated lending market. In addition, the largest companies can issue bonds – either domestic or **Eurobonds**.[12]

---

[12] For a brief introduction to the bond market, see Appendix A1.

Syndicated lending

Syndicated loans are a special category of loans in which an arranger, or group of arrangers, forms a group of creditors on the basis of a mandate to finance the company (or government) borrower. The main corporate borrowers in the syndicated loan market tend to be the largest multinational firms. Large firms typically choose this type of loan primarily because the required loan size is too great to be obtained from one bank (see also Section 4.6.1.3).

Eurobonds

Eurobonds are defined as securities that are issued, and largely sold, outside the domestic market of the currency in which they are denominated. Eurobonds are similar in many respects to domestic corporate bonds, consisting of largely fixed-rate, floating-rate and equity-related debt (convertibles) with maturities usually around 10–15 years. Unlike domestic corporate bonds (that are denominated in the home currency and issued in the home market), the Eurobond market is subject to lower regulation and is instead effectively self-regulated by the Association of International Bond Dealers. The 'Euro' prefix in the term Eurobond simply indicates that the bonds are sold outside the countries in whose currencies they are denominated.

Eurobonds are issued by multinational firms, large domestic companies, sovereign governments, state firms and other international institutions. These are not to be confused with the proposals to create euro bonds (also called e-bonds or European sovereign bonds), that is for all eurozone governments to jointly guarantee each other's debts, in the form of common bonds.

3.5.2.3 Commitments and guarantees

Commitments relate to services where a bank commits to provide funds to a company at a later date for which it receives a fee. Such services include unused overdraft facilities and the provision of credit lines. Banks also provide facilities that enable companies to raise funds by issuing marketable short-term instruments such as commercial paper, Euronotes and (for longer maturities) medium-term notes. In the United States, many large companies issue commercial paper to raise short-term funds and these facilities are almost always backed up by a line of credit from a bank. In other words, the bank has a commitment to provide credit in case the issuance of commercial paper is not successful.

Guarantees relate to a bank underwriting the obligations of a third party and thereby assuming the risk of the transaction. Default by a counterparty on whose behalf a guarantee has been written may cause an immediate loss to the bank. Examples include such things as a standby letter of credit. This is an obligation on behalf of the bank to provide credit if needed under certain legally pre-arranged circumstances. Commercial letters of credit are widely used in financing international trade. This is a letter of credit guaranteeing payment by a bank in favour of an exporter against presentation of shipping and other trade documents (see also Section 4.6.1.7.1). In other words, it is a guarantee from the importer's bank ensuring that payment for the goods can be made.

3.5.2.4 Foreign exchange and interest rate services offered to large firms

Banks can offer their corporate clients a variety of tools to manage their foreign exchange and interest rate risk. These instruments, broadly referred to as derivatives (also see Chapter 10), involve transactions such as the following:

- **Forward foreign exchange transactions** – these are contracts to pay and receive specified amounts of one currency for another at a future date at a pre-determined exchange rate. Default by one party before maturity exposes the other to an exchange rate risk.

- **Currency futures** – these are contracts traded on exchanges for the delivery of a standardised amount of foreign currency at some future date. The price for the contract is agreed on the purchase or selling date. As with forward contracts, gains or losses are incurred as a result of subsequent currency fluctuations.

- **Currency options** – these allow the holder of the contract to exchange (or equally to choose not to exchange) a specific amount of one currency for another at a pre-determined rate during some period in the future. For a company buying an option, the risk lies in the ability of the counterparty not to default on the agreement (credit risk). For the bank writing the option, the risk lies in its exposure to movements in the exchange rate between the two currencies (a market risk).

- **Interest rate options** – these are similar to currency options. The buyer has the right (but not the obligation) to lock into a pre-determined interest rate during some period in the future. The writer of the option (typically a bank) is exposed to interest rate movements, the buyer to counterparty default.

- **Interest rate caps and collars** – a bank (or other lender) guarantees the maximum rate (cap) or maximum and minimum rate (collar) on variable rate loans.

- **Interest rate and currency swaps** – in a currency swap two parties contract to exchange cash flows (of equal net present value) of specific assets or liabilities that are expressed in different currencies. In the so-called 'plain vanilla' interest rate swap, two parties contract to exchange interest service payments (and sometimes principal service payments) on the same amount of indebtedness of the same maturity and with the same payment dates. One party provides fixed interest rate payments in return for variable rate payments from the other, and vice versa.

Note that many companies engage in **risk management** with the use of such financial instruments provided via their banks. Companies can also go direct to the market to hedge various interest rate and exchange rate positions. Companies engaged in substantial international trade have greater need to hedge their foreign currency positions and therefore make wider use of currency-related options, futures and forward transactions.

3.5.2.5 Securities underwriting and fund management services

As companies become larger they increasingly seek funding direct from the capital market and as such they require banks to arrange and underwrite equity and bond issues. **Securities underwriting** was traditionally the preserve of investment banks (or so-called merchant banks in the United Kingdom), but during the 1990s universal banking became the 'norm' and now nearly all large commercial banks have an investment banking operation that underwrites issues.

In the case of securities underwriting, the underwriter undertakes to take up the whole or a pre-agreed part of a capital market issue (equity or bonds) at a pre-determined price. The main risk is that the underwriter will be unable to place the paper at the issue price.

Banks also can provide their corporate clients with **asset management** services, not only to manage a company's own investments but also to manage the pension funds of the firm's employees. The main investment banks are leaders in institutional fund management – this refers to the management of pension, insurance, corporate and other large-scale investments.

A major attraction for banks to provide services such as commitments, guarantees, foreign exchange and interest rate-related transactions, securities underwriting and fund management is that they are all fee-based and off-balance sheet (see Chapter 9). All the services listed above earn banks commissions and fees. In addition, they do not relate to any asset (e.g. a loan or investment) that has to be booked on the bank's balance sheet – hence the term 'off-balance sheet'.

As the above suggests, the range of products and services offered has grown rapidly over the last 20 years or so. This increase in products can be explained partially by the growing overlap of commercial and investment banking services on offer to medium-sized and larger companies.

3.6 Investment banking

The previous sections provide an overview of the main banking services offered to companies, some of which are similar to those provided to retail customers but on a larger scale. However, we have also briefly discussed a range of services – such as securities underwriting (including the issue of commercial paper, Eurobonds and other securities) – that may be less familiar. These activities have traditionally been undertaken by investment banks (or the investment bank subsidiaries of commercial banks) and relate generally to large-scale or wholesale financing activities. Investment banks deal mainly with companies and other large institutions and traditionally they do not deal with retail customers – apart from the provision of upmarket private banking services, as noted earlier.

While we have already outlined various investment banking products and services available to the corporate sector, it is best at this stage to explain the main features of investment banking activity to show how it differs from commercial banking and to highlight the changes resulting from the 2007–2009 financial crisis.

The main role of investment banks is to help companies and governments raise funds in the capital market, either through the issue of stock (otherwise referred to as equity or shares) or debt (bonds). Their primary business relates to issuing new debt and equity that they arrange on behalf of clients as well as providing corporate advisory services on mergers and acquisitions (M&As) and other types of corporate restructuring. Typically, their activities cover the following areas:

- Provision of financial advisory services (advice on M&A and other financial transactions).
- Asset management – managing wholesale investments (such as pension funds for corporate clients) as well as providing investment advisory services to wealthy individuals (private banking) and institutions.
- Other securities services – brokerage, financing services and securities lending.

Investment bankers represent important trading intermediaries for clients as they help raise funds on the capital markets, manage investment portfolios and carry out strategic planning. They are involved in virtually all large financial transactions and produce research and develop opinions on markets and securities. The investment banking business includes trading and investing in securities (i.e. issue, buy, sell) with their own capital (this is known as proprietary trading) or for their clients. This activity consists of trading and investments in a wide range of financial instruments, including bonds, equities and derivatives products. Note that sometimes financial advisory and underwriting is referred to as investment banking to distinguish this from trading and other securities-related business. It is also important to remember that investment banks did not use to hold retail deposits and their liabilities were mainly securities and short-term wholesale financing. The situation has changed,

Table 3.6 The end of an era for US investment banks

Investment banks	Outcome	Date
Bear Stearns	Sold to JPMorgan	March 2008
Lehman Brothers	Filed for bankruptcy	September 2008
Merrill Lynch	Sold to Bank of America	September 2008
Goldman Sachs	Converted to BHC	September 2008
Morgan Stanley	Converted to BHC	September 2008

particularly after the US financial giants (and so-called 'pure play' investment banks) Bear Stearns, Lehman Brothers and Merrill Lynch filed for bankruptcy protection or were rescued through large government bailouts. In September 2008 the US Federal Reserve accepted the request of the two largest free-standing investment banks, Goldman Sachs and Morgan Stanley, to change their status into bank holding companies (BHCs) to qualify for government assistance, as described in Box 3.4. This has been defined as the 'end of an era' for Wall Street investment banks (see Table 3.6).

BOX 3.4 THE END OF AN ERA: US INVESTMENT BANKS AND THE CONVERSION INTO BHCS

In the past, investment banking used to be in sharp contrast with commercial banking that was licensed only for the traditional banking business, i.e. accepting retail deposits and granting loans. The deregulation carried out over the 1990s reduced the differences across these two types of banks by allowing commercial banks to offer investment banking services. Large banking conglomerates took advantage of this opportunity as they were aiming to transform into 'one-stop shops'. Similarly, investment banks developed as large full-service institutions and enjoyed at least three decades of prosperity, until the financial crisis began in the summer of 2007, and intensified in September 2008, as described by John Gapper in the *Financial Times* (2008):

Investment banks went on to enjoy 30 years of prosperity. They grew rapidly, taking on thousands of employees and expanding around the world. The big Wall Street firms swept through the City of London in the 1990s, picking up smaller merchant banks, such as Warburg and Schroders, on their way. Under the surface, however, they were ratcheting up their risk-taking. It was increasingly hard to sustain themselves by selling securities – the traditional core of their business – because commissions had shrunk to fractions of a percentage point

per trade. So they were forced to look elsewhere for their profits.

They started to gamble more with their own (and later others') capital. Salomon Brothers pioneered the idea of having a proprietary trading desk that bet its own money on movements in markets at the same time as the bank bought and sold securities on behalf of its customers.

Banks insisted that their safeguards to stop inside information from their customers leaking to their proprietary traders were strong. But there was no doubt that being "in the flow" gave investment banks' trading desks an edge. Goldman Sachs' trading profits came to be envied by rivals.

Investment banks also expanded into the underwriting and selling of complex financial securities, such as Collateralised Debt Obligations (CDOs). They were aided by the Federal Reserve's decision to cut US interest rates sharply after September 11, 2001. That set off a boom in housing and in mortgage-related securities. The catch was that investment banks were taking what turned out to be life-threatening gambles. They did not have sufficient capital to cope with a severe setback in the housing market or markets generally. When it occurred, three (so far) of the

Box 3.4 The end of an era: US investment banks and the conversion into BHCs (*continued*)

five biggest banks ended up short of capital and confidence.

The US financial turmoil has resulted in what many have described as 'the end of Wall Street investment banks' as regulatory consent was given in autumn 2008 to investment houses (as well as credit card companies) to convert their status into bank holding companies.[13] Goldman Sachs and Morgan Stanley were the first two large investment banks to announce that they would become BHCs. This is how the chairman and CEO of Goldman Sachs, Lloyd C. Blankfein, commented on the move in September 2008:

When Goldman Sachs was a private partnership, we made the decision to become a public company, recognizing the need for permanent capital to meet the demands of scale. While accelerated by market sentiment, our decision to be regulated by the Federal Reserve is based on the recognition that such regulation provides its members with full prudential supervision and access to permanent liquidity and funding. We believe that Goldman Sachs, under Federal Reserve supervision, will be regarded as an even more secure institution with

an exceptionally clean balance sheet and a greater diversity of funding sources.

There is no doubt that by converting to BHCs the investment banks wanted to give a strong signal to investors and to the financial community in general about their commitment to a safer and sounder banking business. These banks have had to accept increased regulation, supervision and monitoring, including strict limits in the level of risk that they can take, as well as capital and management requirements. In exchange they obtained several advantages, including the access to protection and funding from the Fed (i.e. the federal deposit insurance scheme, discount window and TARP – the Troubled Asset Relief Program). Besides, by converting into BHCs the investment banks can better diversify their sources of financing by strengthening the retail business and thus making money from borrowing from depositors.

Sources: After 73 Years: the last gasp of the broker-dealer, *Financial Times*, 15/09/08 (John Gapper). © The Financial Times Limited. All Rights Reserved; Goldman Sachs (2008) 'To become the fourth largest bank holding company', 21 September, press release.

Since September 2008, the similarities with commercial banks have increased as US investment firms are now allowed to expand their funding through deposits, and are subject to higher capital reserves, more disclosure and less risk taking.

Table 3.7 lists the top global investment banks based on revenue for 2012. US investment banks predominate, although one should be aware that traditionally the main US investment banks (which tended to dominate global investment banking) were the so-called 'bulge bracket' firms, including Goldman Sachs, Merrill Lynch and Morgan Stanley. Because legislation (Glass-Steagall Act of 1933) prohibited commercial banks from doing investment banking business, the market was dominated by the specialist investment banks. However, since 1999 and the abandonment of Glass-Steagall, US commercial banks have acquired investment banks. This means that banks such as Citi, JPMorgan Chase and Bank of America Merrill Lynch offer both commercial and investment banking services, as do Goldman Sachs and Morgan Stanley now that they have converted into BHCs. As explained earlier, intermediaries that undertake a wide range of financial services business

---

[13] Under the Bank Holding Company Act of 1956 (BHCA) these are defined as companies owning 25 per cent or more of the voting stock in a bank or controlling a majority of its directors.

Table 3.7 Largest investment banks by revenue (2012)

	Revenue	M&A	Equity	Bonds	Loans
	$m	%	%	%	%
JPMorgan	5,505.42	23	18	34	25
Bank of America Merrill Lynch	4,695.86	19	19	34	28
Goldman Sachs	4,171.14	41	21	27	11
Morgan Stanley	3,738.53	32	24	32	11
Citi	3,622.18	19	19	40	22
Credit Suisse	3,476.67	32	17	30	20
Deutsche Bank	3,342.76	22	20	38	20
Barclays	3,256.05	27	15	36	22
UBS	2,193.81	28	26	34	13
Wells Fargo	1,997.40	10	14	40	36
Total	**77,650.76**	**33**	**17**	**28**	**22**

Source: FT.com/leaguetables © The Financial Times Limited. All Rights Reserved.

(such as commercial and investment banking, insurance, pensions and so on) are referred to as universal banks. Universal banking is common practice in Europe and we can also see from Table 3.7 that a variety of European commercial banks do substantial investment banking business. Structural differences among investment banks are apparent, with Goldman Sachs and Morgan Stanley barely competing in the loans market and earning the majority of their fees from traditional investment banking activities such as M&As and advisory services.

The main difference between commercial banking and investment banking is that the former refers to deposit and lending business while the latter relates to securities underwriting and other security-related business. Banks such as Barclays or Deutsche Bank are referred to as commercial banks because their main business is deposit- and lending-related – although they both have substantial investment banking operations. In terms of services offered to large companies, commercial banks typically provide cash management, payments and credit facilities whereas investment banks arrange other types of financing through the issue of equity and debt to finance company expansion. They also offer an extensive array of other securities-related services, including risk management products (such as interest rate and foreign exchange derivatives) and advice on company M&A activity as well as other company restructuring. These distinctions have become blurred as large commercial banks have either acquired or expanded their investment banking services to meet the increasing demands of corporate clients. Also the growth in global stock market activity has encouraged many commercial banks to develop asset management and private banking operations to deal with the growing demand for securities-related services from both institutional investors and wealthy private clients.

In the years after the 2007–2009 financial crisis, the investment banking industry has changed substantially, with most institutions' market value shrinking considerably (see Table 3.8).

Table 3.8 The changing face of investment banking (September 2008 to September 2012)

Investment banks	Market cap. change	Revenue change	Employee change
Bank of America	−37.5%	+40.3%	+16.0%
Barclays	−12.9%	+0.4%	−9.7%
Citi	−1.5%	−0.2%	−18.6%
Credit Suisse	−44.8%	−9.5%	+4.0%
Deutsche Bank	−9.3%	+7.4%	+25.5%
Goldman Sachs	−10.4%	−37.3%	−0.1%
JPMorgan	+8.9%	+36.2%	+15.6%
Morgan Stanley	−20.6%	+15.8%	+31.8%
Royal Bank of Scotland	−60.4%	−20.4%	−26.4%
UBS	−18.7%	+8.0%	−16.7%

BOX 3.5 WALL STREET: LEANER AND MEANER

Banks confront a post-crisis world of tougher regulations and lower profits

When Jamie Forese started out at Salomon Brothers in 1985, being an investment banker was not a guaranteed ticket to riches. "A career on Wall Street was considered a stable income, same as a lawyer, a doctor, an accountant," he recalls. What changed, he says, was banks' addiction to leverage – the cheap debt that fattened profits and bonuses, financed mega-mergers and ultimately fuelled the global financial crisis. In the boom years, leverage convinced people that "banking was the gravy train", he says.

Today, amid a regulatory clampdown and a turbulent global economy, the industry is contemplating a future that looks more like the lower-key profession Mr Forese remembers. Securities firms are cutting jobs. Bonuses are down sharply. The prestige of being a Wall Street banker has plummeted. And the profits that underpinned the heady years of the past are harder to come by. For Wall Street's critics, these are not all bad developments. Now aged 49 and the head of Citigroup's investment bank, Mr Forese is one of the executives trying to determine the future of Wall Street. But many of the events shaping the industry are well outside his reach.

Four thousand miles from Mr Forese's Manhattan office, regulators in Basel, Switzerland, have banned all banks from carrying as much debt as they did in the past. That changes the economics of the business, particularly in the fixed-income trading divisions that have been prized profit centres for the past two decades.

The big five US banks on Wall Street made more than $50bn a year in combined revenues between 2005 and 2010 from fixed income trading, with the exception of 2008. This was far more than in equities trading, underwriting or advisory work. Last year, according to Credit Suisse, their combined revenue fell 22 per cent. As the Basel III rules are phased in, the business is set to come under further pressure.

Basel III enforces greater levels of loss-absorbent equity capital for the banks but also lasers in on the structured credit businesses at the heart of the last crisis, ascribing particularly punitive capital levels to those areas. With less leverage it is difficult, perhaps impossible, to make the returns on equity that banks used to enjoy – with the happier trade-off that it is also harder for them to fail.

When Goldman Sachs went public in 1999, it was able to boast an ROE of more than 40 per cent, although it was never again to reach such levels. Last year it racked up its worst ever ratio: 3.6 per cent. Understandably, this affects shareholders' appetite for the stock. In 2006 both Goldman and

BOX 3.5 Wall Street: leaner and meaner (*continued*)

Morgan Stanley traded at more than twice their book value. Now Goldman trades at 0.9 times book; Morgan Stanley at about half. This means investors no longer believe the companies are worth more than the stated value of their assets.

On top of Basel III, US banks must contend with the Volcker rule, also aimed at limiting risk-taking in fixed income divisions. Banks contend that this will damage their traditional ability to act as market makers, bringing together investors wanting to buy with those who want to sell.

The banks are struggling to identify a cash cow that grazes between the new rules. The equivalent of the junk bonds of the 1980s or the credit derivatives of the 1990s has not been discovered. "We're waiting really for the unveiling for what the new bank models are going to be. I'm surprised that there hasn't been more forced innovation," says John Studzinski, who spent most of his career at Morgan Stanley and now runs the advisory group at Blackstone, the private equity firm.

Given some of the results of the last round of experimentation, there may be good reasons for the financial scientists to be held at bay. "Innovation? God, look where that got us," says one hedge fund executive. With no wizardry to rely on, banks are behaving like other mature companies in a straitened economy – they are cutting costs. But they also face a structural dilemma: is it possible to fine-tune the fixed-income divisions in the new environment or will it require a more radical overhaul?

Making savings will require cutting the headcount and reducing pay – which accounts for more than 40 per cent of revenues at investment banks.

Where there is innovation, it is in technology. While stocks, and much foreign exchange, are now electronically traded, most bonds and other fixed-income instruments remain opaque and reliant on human beings. Shifting from telephone to electronic trading offers a significant cost-cutting opportunity and a plausible route to increased revenue growth – but also, as greater transparency and efficiency leads to lower fees, to thinner margins. And then there is the risk someone will ask: why do we need the banks as a go-between?

At BlackRock, the asset manager, that conflict is already in evidence. The company is pioneering its electronic Aladdin Trading Network to match buyers and sellers of bonds without an investment bank standing in the middle. BlackRock stresses over and over again that the "dealer" banks are its "partners", and it does not wish to sideline them. The banks are not sure it will be successful but are convinced BlackRock – despite its denials – is taking them on.

Banks and asset managers, though, have a mutual interest in electronic trading expanding to take over more business. According to the Federal Reserve, the volume of bonds held by the traditional dealer banks has fallen sharply, from $200bn in 2007 to $90bn in 2011 and $45bn today. Institutional investors complain that this is reducing liquidity in the market, and is part of the reason for them to expand their own trading platforms, allowing them to trade among themselves.

Gary Cohn, chief operating officer at Goldman, calls this decline "the most fascinating chart". He and his peers are trying to decide how to satisfy their counterparties' demand for liquidity while complying with new regulations, and what products can be traded electronically.

Not all businesses demand as much soul-searching as fixed income trading. Goldman has the biggest mergers and acquisitions operation by revenues on Wall Street. In M&A, the problem is cyclical, not structural – corporate clients are too troubled by the world economy to do many deals.

But overall, particularly at Morgan Stanley, which is number two in M&A and also has a strong underwriting business, there is more radical surgery under way. The bank last month agreed to buy the rest of Smith Barney, the brokerage whose 15,000 advisers sell stocks and bonds to retail investors. It is also reducing its fixed income trading operation.

This shift from trading, combined with a push into advising retail clients, should help produce more stable revenues. It will also ease the bank's funding costs: investors and credit rating agencies such as Moody's prefer less volatile businesses.

The trading that remains, according to chief executive James Gorman, will be all about institutions servicing clients rather than making

BOX 3.5 Wall Street: leaner and meaner (*continued*)

money on their own account. This produces lower margins than some of the trading Morgan Stanley undertook in the past, but it is also safer.

Goldman, on the other hand, appears to be fine-tuning, looking to profit from the surrender of its rivals in fixed income trading. Risk, its executives say, will return.

"You go through periods of the cycle where clients want the most levered instrument they can possibly create," says Mr Cohn. "We're in the opposite part of the cycle now. You would think people want to get leverage back into the system, with interest rates so low, but clients have gotten more conservative."

He is betting this will change, and that the decision to do nothing drastic will benefit Goldman. "As the cycle changes, cash will diminish in importance and leverage will gain in importance. A lot of firms have laid off expensive derivatives talent so they're not tooled for that part of the cycle."

Both Mr Cohn, whose background is in commodities and fixed income, and Mr Gorman, who cut his teeth in retail brokerage, seem comfortable with their very different strategies.

There is one area where senior bankers do agree, and it is surprising in the current environment: despite the onslaught of regulation, they say, officials will loosen the fetters if the rules restrict business too much.

Mr Cohn and Mr Forese note that securitisation, which allowed banks to shift mortgages from their balance sheets and write new loans, has dried up. Run amok, mortgage-backed securities

turned into instruments such as the infamous collateralised debt obligations, whose risks were ill-understood by banks and their counterparties. But the first wave of securitisation brought down the cost of loans for ordinary Americans as well as generating profits for issuers.

"The securitisation business is closed," says Mr Cohn. "It's going to stay closed until central banks want to create more consumer-related credit." Bank executives say that eventually those central banks will revise Basel III to make the job easier.

Meanwhile, Mr Forese is confident that either the Volcker rule will be less stringent than feared or that Congress will step in to change it. "It may prove to be workable as it's written today or, if not, legislators will fix it if it needs to be fixed," he says. "If there's one thing that resonates in Washington it's the competitiveness of our capital markets."

So Wall Street today is divided on how drastic the job of reinvention will prove, and how much risk it is wise to take. But the banks are united in the hope that regulators, despite their tough post-crisis stance, will go the way of their predecessors and eventually heed pleas for leniency.

If the institutions adjust to the new financial landscape, the employees who remain are going to have to adjust, too. Their bosses insist that bonuses will have to fall if banks are to deliver a decent return for investors. Some bankers are finding it hard to adapt to the new Wall Street.

"I'm bemused when I hear about people getting upset with their $600,000 pay cheque because it's down from $800,000," says Mr Forese. "For banks, the greatest lever is compensation."

3.7   Islamic banking

So far this chapter has focused entirely on Western-based or conventional interest-based banking business. However, it would be remiss of us not to mention the development of **Islamic banking** business that is occurring in various parts of the world and is based on non-interest principles. Islamic *Shariah* law prohibits the payment of *riba* or interest but does encourage entrepreneurial activity. As such, banks that wish to offer Islamic banking services have to develop products and services that do not charge or pay interest. Their solution is to offer various profit sharing-related products whereby depositors share in the risk of the bank's lending. Depositors earn a return (instead of interest) and borrowers repay loans based on the profits generated from the project on which the loan is lent.

An example of a commonly used profit-sharing arrangement in Islamic banking is known as *Musharakah*, which is an arrangement where a bank and a borrower establish a joint commercial enterprise and both contribute capital as well as labour and management as a general rule. The profit of the enterprise is shared among the partners in agreed proportions while the loss will have to be shared in strict proportion of capital contributions. The basic rules governing the *Musharakah* contract include:

- The profit of the enterprise can be distributed in any proportion by mutual consent. However, it is not permissible to fix a lump sum profit for anyone.
- In case of loss, it has to be shared strictly in proportion to the capital contributions.
- As a general rule all partners contribute both capital and management. However, it is possible for any partner to be exempted from contributing labour/management. In that case, the share of profit of the sleeping partner has to be a strict proportion of their capital contribution.
- The liability of all the partners is unlimited.

There is a wide variety of Islamic banking products and services based on profit sharing and other forms of arrangements that enable financial intermediation without the use of interest. Globally, there are around 100 Islamic banks and financial institutions working in the private sector, excluding those in the three countries that have declared their intention to convert their entire banking sector to Islamic banking, namely, Pakistan, Iran and Sudan. An idea of recent trends in global Islamic banking assets is given in Figure 3.6.

In addition to the development of Islamic banking practices in parts of the world where the Islamic faith is an integral feature of the socio-economic make-up of the population, there has been growing interest among Western banks in developing such services for their customers. HSBC, for instance, was the first to offer an Islamic mortgage to its UK customers and Lloyds TSB followed suit by introducing a similar product in March 2005, details of which are summarised in Box 3.6.

BOX 3.6 LLOYDS TSB'S ISLAMIC MORTGAGE PRODUCT

On 21 March 2005 Lloyds TSB launched its debut *Shariah*-compliant Islamic home finance scheme at five branches in London, Luton and Birmingham, all cities with large Muslim populations.

Lloyds TSB, one of the top three banking groups in the UK, instead of developing its own standalone Islamic mortgage product, is utilising and co-branding a product off the shelf, the Alburaq Home Financing Scheme, which is based on the diminishing *Musharakah* contract (a declining equity participation scheme between buyer and lender), which was pioneered last year by ABC International Bank and Bristol & West, a subsidiary of the Bank of Ireland Group in London.

The Lloyds TSB scheme will be test-marketed by selected branches of the high street bank. The added value which Lloyds TSB brings, stresses a spokesman, is bespoke service elements. 'We only offer Islamic home finance from a single provider.' According to Sheikh

> ### Box 3.6 Lloyds TSB's Islamic mortgage product (*continued*)
>
> Nizam Yaquby, 'the diminishing *Musharakah* offers the most viable solution for housing finance. This particular contract has been successfully implemented by mortgage providers in the US, the UK and Pakistan.'
>
> Under this mode, the financial institution and client jointly purchase the house. The ownership of the house is split between the bank and the customer, and it is agreed that the customer will purchase the bank's share in the house gradually, thus increasing his own share until all the bank's share is purchased by him, thus making him the sole owner of the asset after a specified period. But during the financing period, the bank's share is leased to the customer, who pays rent for using the bank's share in the asset.
>
> The Alburaq Home Financing Scheme, which typically has a tenor of up to 25 years, offers two payment options to the customer. In the first option, the rent is fixed for an initial period of six months and is then reviewed every six months. In the second option, the rent is fixed for two years and is then reviewed every six months.
>
> *Source*: Adapted from **www.arabnews.com**

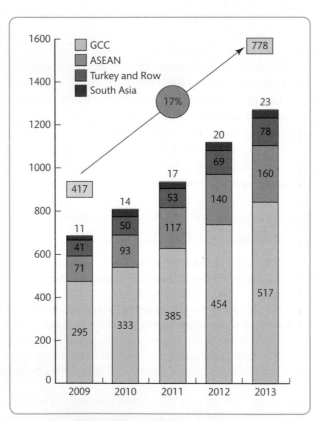

Figure 3.6 Global Islamic banking assets, 2009–2013

Source: Ernst and Young (2014).

3.8 Conclusion

This chapter outlines the main types of banking business undertaken globally. The focus has been on commercial and investment banking activities, although the last part of the chapter briefly highlights some features of non-interest Islamic banking practices. Prior to the 2007–2009 crisis, the trend towards the development of financial service conglomerates and the universal banking model was encouraged by favourable regulation (and mostly by deregulation). A major feature was the blurring distinction between different types of banking business and the emergence of full financial service conglomerates that offer an extensive array of retail, corporate and investment banking products. Many banks also offer insurance, pensions and other non-banking financial services. Even traditional Western banks nowadays offer various Islamic banking products and services to meet the needs of their customers.

Over the 1990s and early 2000s this change in the features of the banking business simply reflected the desire of banks to meet the ever increasing and divergent needs of their customers – both personal and corporate. It also reflected the trend to diversify earnings, supplementing traditional commercial banking interest income with fee- and commission-based revenues from other sources. The ultimate aim was to offer clients a spectrum of products and services that strengthen customer relationships and provide services that clients value. Nowadays the trend towards universal banking is under question as large banks are 'deleveraging' and selling 'non-core' activities. The 2007–2009 crisis highlighted the importance of having business models that lead to long-term sustainable activities and profitability.

Key terms

Asset-based finance
Asset management
Bancassurance
Bank holding companies (BHCs)
Building societies
Commercial banks
Commercial paper
Commitments
Co-operative banks
Corporate banking
Credit unions
Eurobond
Euronote
Factoring
Faster Payments Service (FPS)
Finance houses
Guarantees
High net worth individuals (HNWIs)
Hire purchase
Investment banking
Invoice discounting services
Islamic banking
Leasing
Modern banking
Private banking
Private equity finance
Proprietary trading
Repos
Retail or personal banking
Risk management
Savings banks
Securities underwriting
Specialist banking
Syndicated loans
Traditional banking
Universal banking
Venture capital

Key reading

Ayadi, R., Arbak, E., De Groen, W.P. and Llewellyn, D.T. (2010) *Investigating Diversity in the Banking Sector in Europe: Key developments, performance and role of cooperative banks*. Brussels: Centre for European Policy Studies.

Ayadi, R., Schmidt, R.H. and Carbó Valverde, S. (2009) *Investigating Diversity in the Banking Sector in Europe: The performance and role of saving banks*. Brussels: Centre for European Policy Studies.

Capgemini and RBC Wealth Management (2012) *World Wealth Report*.

European Central Bank (2010) 'Beyond ROE – how to measure bank performance'. Appendix to the report on EU banking structures, September.

Iqbal, M. and Molyneux, P. (2005) *Thirty Years of Islamic Banking*. London: Macmillan.

REVISION QUESTIONS AND PROBLEMS

3.1 In what ways does traditional banking differ from modern banking?

3.2 What is bancassurance?

3.3 Explain the main characteristics of the different types of banks that offer personal (retail) banking services.

3.4 What are the primary features of private banking?

3.5 What are the main features of corporate banking?

3.6 What are venture capitalists? To what extent are they similar to private equity finance?

3.7 What are the typical services offered by banks to the large (multinational) corporate sector? Distinguish between short- and long-term financing.

3.8 What services do investment banks typically offer to customers?

3.9 What is proprietary trading?

3.10 What are the pros and cons of the conversion of the US investment firms into BHCs?

3.11 What are the benefits of universal banking compared with specialist banking?

3.12 What distinguishes Islamic banking from Western banking?

Chapter 4

International banking

Learning objectives

- To outline the main features of international banking
- To describe the history of international banking
- To understand the reasons for the growth of international banking
- To understand the main theories on the rationale for international banking
- To describe the most common international banking products and services
- To introduce the loan syndication market
- To understand the impact of the credit crisis on international banking activity

4.1 Introduction

The growth in foreign bank activity and international banking in general has been a major factor in financial system development. This chapter gives an insight into the main characteristics of international banking and highlights its diverse and dynamic features. The first part of the chapter defines international banking, provides a brief history and then discusses the range of products and services offered by international banks. Here the focus is on banking services provided to large corporations – namely treasury management services, credit, debt and equity financing as well as trade finance and various risk management products. More detailed attention will be given to the loan syndication market. The chapter concludes by discussing the growing presence of foreign bank activity and the impact of the credit crisis on international bank activity.

4.2 What is international banking?

International banking refers to business undertaken by banks across national borders and/ or activities that involve the use of different currencies. A more precise definition of international banking is provided by Lewis and Davis (1987), who classify international banking into two main types of activity – traditional foreign banking and Eurocurrency banking.

Traditional foreign banking involves transactions with non-residents in domestic currency that facilitates trade finance and other international transactions. **Eurocurrency banking** involves banks undertaking wholesale (large-scale) foreign exchange transactions (loans and deposits) with both residents and non-residents. The definition above suggests that international banks are involved with financing trade, transacting foreign exchange business and making wholesale (large) short-term Eurocurrency loans and deposits.

While banks engaged in international banking are typically involved in these types of activities, the definition is rather broad and does not really take account of the fact that many banks have operations in various countries. Traditional foreign banking and Eurocurrency banking, for instance, do not require banks to have a physical presence in a foreign country – such activity can be conducted within a single country. For example, UK banks can undertake domestic currency transactions with customers in Hong Kong without any physical presence in the latter. Similarly, wholesale Eurodollar loans (wholesale loans denominated in US dollars) can be made between banks based in London without any of those banks needing a physical presence in the US.

In order to account for the fact that many banks have physical operations in various countries, a distinction is made between **multinational banking** and international banking. Multinational banking refers to banks having some element of ownership and control of banking operations outside their home market. The main feature of multinational banking is that it requires some form of **foreign direct investment (FDI)** by banks in overseas markets reflecting a physical presence. (As one can guess, the definition comes from the literature on multinational enterprises and FDI.)

If a bank were to follow a multinational banking model, it would operate sizeable foreign branches and subsidiaries in multiple jurisdictions and, in its extreme form, fund those positions locally in the host countries. In contrast, the international bank model refers to banks that operate out of the home country or in a (major) financial centre and conduct mostly cross-border business. The 2008 crisis put these two models to the test. A summary review of the key developments is presented in Box 4.1.

We should note that the terms 'international banking' and 'multinational banking' are used interchangeably to refer to banks that have global activities. For the purpose of this chapter we will use international banking as it is a more commonly used term, although one needs to be aware that the following sections discuss international activities of banks in the broadest sense. Box 4.2 gives some definitions.

BOX 4.1 FROM INTERNATIONAL TO MULTINATIONAL BANKING?

After the 1980s' Latin American debt crisis inflicted losses on cross-border loans, banks shifted towards the multinational model. Establishing or acquiring a local bank in order to borrow and lend locally avoided transfer risk, if not country risk. As a result, the share of local currency claims in foreign claims on emerging market economies rose from 7% in 1983 to 25–30% in the 1990s. After the Asian financial crisis of 1997–1998, the local currency share of claims globally was even higher. The shift to local banking slowed in the 2000s. In emerging markets, bank flows across borders resumed in the mid-2000s in response to higher yields and US dollar depreciation. Elsewhere, the introduction of the euro, spurring an area-wide interbank market, and European banks' heavy investment in US asset-backed securities had a similar effect. However, if factors promoting cross-border lending are transitory, then local claims as a share of foreign claims may rise (see Figure 4.1). This may occur even in the absence of any regulatory changes that might favour multinational over international banking.

The global financial crisis of 2007–2009 reinforced the previous trend towards local and multinational

BOX 4.1 From international to multinational banking? (*continued*)

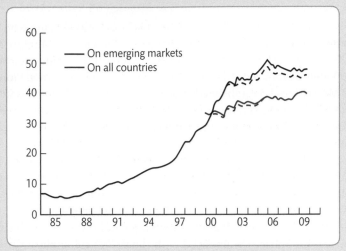

Figure 4.1 Local currency claims as a share of foreign claims
Source: McCauley *et al*. (2010) p. 26.

banking, especially in emerging markets. With the drying-up of the international interbank market, claims on unaffiliated banks shrank. Cross-border claims and locally booked foreign currency claims (often funded cross-border) dropped more abruptly than local currency claims. The same pattern on the liabilities side suggests that local funding proved more resilient during the crisis. Developments by currency differed slightly, reflecting the greater dislocation in dollar funding markets and the high cost of dollars in foreign exchange swap markets.

According to the BIS banking statistics, cross-border interbank lending fell from $22.7 trillion at end-March 2008 to $17.0 trillion at end-September 2013. While this contraction affected most countries worldwide, it was largest for borrowers in Europe, especially those in the euro area. Lending to banks in the United Kingdom dropped by $1.7 trillion, or 35%. Claims on banks in the United States and Switzerland fell sharply as well, by $415 billion (16%) and $346 billion (42%), respectively.

Source: Adapted from McCauley *et al*. (2010); Bank for International Settlements (2014).

BOX 4.2 SOME DEFINITIONS

Global banks are institutions with the widest reach – either through subsidiaries or branches they provide services in several world countries and have a presence in all continents.

International banks are institutions that provide cross-border services, but operate in too few countries, or are relatively too small, to be defined as global.

Local banks (also called domestic banks) are institutions providing services only in the country in which they are headquartered.

A bank is international if:

● it has branches and/or subsidiaries overseas;

● it conducts business in a foreign currency irrespective of its location;

● it has international customers.

4.3   Brief history of international banking

The origins of international banking date back over 4,000 years when various civilisations used **letters of credit** and bills of exchange issued across sovereign boundaries to finance trade. The history of banks having a physical presence outside their home country is more recent, widely acknowledged as starting in the 15th century when Florentine bankers (notably the Medici family) established subsidiaries or foreign branches in other jurisdictions to help finance trade, scientific, military, artistic and other endeavours. From the 14th to the 16th century, Florence was regarded as the scientific and cultural capital of the Western world and the city gave birth to the Renaissance and modern European art. It has been argued that commercial and artistic developments were inextricably linked by a change in social attitudes that emphasised the creation of wealth and conspicuous consumption. This not only prompted the development of regional banking business but also encouraged international activity because financing requirements could not be met locally.[1]

The modern era of international banking can be viewed as occurring in two distinct phases. The first phase commenced with the rise of colonialism during the 19th century, which continued into the 20th century. The second phase of international bank expansion was linked to the growth of US multinational firms and the changing financial regulatory landscape from the late 1950s and early 1960s onwards:

● **Colonial banking** – British banks opened branches in their Australian, Caribbean and North American colonies in the 1830s. Further expansion took place starting from the 1850s and by the end of the century British banks had operations in South Africa, Latin America, India and parts of Asia as well as in the Middle East and some European countries. Other colonial powers also expanded their banking activities in the latter part of the 19th century, particularly Belgian, French and German banks that set up operations in Latin America, Africa and China as well as in London. One noticeable difference between the British banks and their European counterparts was that the former established **colonial banks**, otherwise known as 'British overseas banks' or 'Anglo foreign banks' that provided services outside the UK only. In contrast, the European banks undertook both domestic and foreign activity, often via the acquisition of banks or through the establishment of subsidiaries. In other words, European bank expansion overseas was more similar to the type of activity conducted nowadays – domestic banks acquiring foreign operations or setting up subsidiaries through which business could be undertaken whereas British banks were specifically set up to do banking only in the colonies. Various Japanese and Canadian banks also developed international activities in the latter part of the 19th and the early 20th centuries.

● **Modern international banking** – the expansion of banks overseas during the first half of the 20th century was somewhat limited due to the decline of the British and other colonial empires, economic uncertainty brought about by the World Wars, and the changing political landscape in many countries that sought to establish their own banking systems by restricting (even nationalising) foreign banks. It was not until the emergence of the US as a major economic power and the growth of its multinational companies that the

---

[1] Banca Monte dei Paschi di Siena, the oldest bank in the world, was founded in 1472. Also see Parks (2005) for an excellent insight into the role of the Medici family in banking, art and other matters in 15th-century Florence.

second wave of international banking activity took place. This occurred from the late 1950s and early 1960s onwards, when US banks began to expand overseas to meet the financial requirements of multinational firms but also to take advantage of cheaper financing outside the home market. US banks were subject to limits on how much interest they could pay on deposits (known as Regulation Q) and also had to maintain onerous reserve requirements. They found that by establishing subsidiaries outside the US (typically in London), these operations were not subject to home regulations – so US banks could pay more interest on dollar deposits and could do more dollar lending at finer terms via their overseas subsidiaries as these were not subject to the home regulations. US banks were attracted to London because substantial dollar deposits were located there – some say this was because the anti-communist sentiment in the US (characterised by the so-called 'McCarthy witch hunts' from 1947 to 1954) encouraged the Russian, Chinese and other governments to move large-scale dollar funds out of New York to London as they thought these might be frozen. In any event, US banks flocked to London and, to a lesser extent, other major financial centres (e.g. Paris) during the 1960s. This was the birth of the **Eurocurrency** markets – markets where wholesale foreign currency deposits and lending take place. US banks continued to dominate international banking during the 1970s, although from the late 1970s and throughout the 1980s Japanese banks replaced them as the major international lenders (reflecting the growth of Japanese multinational companies over the period). The 1990s witnessed a decline in the relative importance of Japanese banks on the international scene due to problems in their home market, and their position was taken by European banks that expanded their international operations as a result of various factors (including the creation of the European Union's single market).

Next we look at some fundamental issues for understanding the international banking business. First, we focus on the main theories and strategic motives that make banks expand abroad. We then present the different types of entry in foreign markets and finally we explain the banking products and services offered by international banks.

4.4 Why do banks go overseas?

An extensive body of literature has examined the rationale for the expansion of companies overseas. This literature spans the economic literature on the determinants of foreign direct investment, studies on the strategic behaviour of firms as well as empirical evidence on the performance and efficiency advantages of international companies. Many of the theories applicable to the overseas expansion of non-financial firms can be applied to banks.

The main theories describing the motives for overseas expansion relate to:

- factor price differentials and trade barriers;
- arbitrage and the cost of capital;
- ownership advantages;
- diversification of earnings;
- excess managerial capacity;
- location and the product cycle.

These theories are briefly discussed below.

4.4.1   Factor prices and trade barrier theories

The theoretical and empirical literature on the determinants of foreign direct investment focuses on two main motives for overseas expansion – factor price differentials
and trade barriers that inhibit exports. The former, known as **vertical FDI**, suggests that
overseas activity occurs so that firms can take advantage of international factor price
differences. Headquarter services require substantial physical and human capital inputs
whereas production is mainly manual labour intensive. Companies become multinational
when they establish production in lower manual labour cost countries and headquarters where skilled labour costs are low. The alternative motivation for the existence of
multinationals relates to trade barriers that make exporting costly. Where trade costs
are high, the firm establishes itself in countries to access markets and this is referred to
as **horizontal FDI**.

One can see that these two main motives for FDI derive from study of the real sector. In the
case of banking, evidence would seem to suggest that horizontal FDI is likely to be a much
more important motive for cross-border activity than vertical FDI. For instance, the strategic
reasons for banks to establish multinational operations are most likely to be based on advantages associated with 'internalising' informational advantages as opposed to trading at arm's
length. Because it is difficult to find efficient markets for long-distance transactions in some
areas of banking (such as retail banking, lending to small firms, specific credits to companies
operating in different regulatory and economic environments), investment overseas is likely
to be an important feature of the industry.

Regulations governing many areas of business are also country-specific and act as substantial trade barriers. This means that in many areas of business (and particularly in banking) it
may be difficult to undertake cross-border activity without a physical presence within a country. For example, differences in tax treatments, consumer protection legislation, marketing
rules, definition of products and so on mean that the cross-border selling of many financial
services products is problematic unless the bank has a physical presence in the market in
which it wishes to sell its products. Box 4.3 highlights how trade barriers impact on banks'
decisions to locate overseas.

BOX 4.3 TRADE BARRIERS AND BANKING

Many jurisdictions prohibit the sale of financial services without establishment – a bank
must have a physical presence before it can enter the market. These barriers may be
less onerous when banks operate in areas that have a more international dimension such
as investment and international banking, although it is noticeable that even the world's
largest investment banks typically have extensive physical market presence in many
countries.

In general, domestic regulations dictate that banks must have a physical presence in the
country before they can access various markets – this therefore acts as a substantial trade
barrier. At the same time, it also incentivises cross-border establishment as well as M&A activity, as banks attempt to circumvent restrictive regulations. Cross-border activity in banking
can mainly be characterised by horizontal FDI, as it allows bank to exploit the informational
advantages associated with having a market presence and to avoid the barriers brought about
by domestic financial services regulation.

4.4.2 Arbitrage and the cost of capital

One of the main theories explaining the overseas investment decision of firms relates to the **arbitrage** activities of firms in that companies that raise their finance in strong currency markets can borrow relatively cheaply and they can invest their proceeds in markets where currencies are weak and firms can be acquired relatively cheaply. For a simple example, the substantial 20–30 per cent depreciation of the US dollar against the euro and British sterling during 2003 meant that European investors could acquire US banks for 20–30 per cent cheaper than they could do previously. All other things being equal, this means that overseas banks can be purchased cheaper due to currency depreciation and the overall returns from the acquired firm will be boosted – as return on capital will obviously be higher. (The theoretical argument is the same as the reason why European holidaymakers flock to destinations with relatively weak currencies and may be deterred from visiting destinations with strong currencies.)

More formally, the **cost of capital** argument focuses on the cost of raising finance (see Chapter 9 for more details). At any one time, some currencies are relatively strong whereas others are weak. Investors require a lower return or interest rate for securities issued in the stronger currency. As such, firms that issue securities in strong currencies require a lower cost of capital (it is cheaper for them to borrow via the issue of equity or debt instruments). Subsequently, these firms can acquire overseas assets at higher prices than local firms that issue securities in local currencies, and still appear to be buying foreign firms relatively cheaply. So if the euro is strong compared with the dollar, European firms can raise funds for acquisition more cheaply than their US counterparts and therefore can acquire stakes or outbid them to make purchases, say in the US market.

While the cost of capital arguments have been put forward as the main reason for the acquisition of US banks by their UK and European counterparts from the late 1990s to the mid-2000s, this theory cannot really explain the following:

- why some firms invest overseas in markets that have the same currency (for example, within the eurozone);
- why there is cross-investment at the same time, for instance, why UK firms invest in the US and why US firms invest in the UK;
- why firms incur substantial costs in setting up operations overseas instead of just making an acquisition.

As a consequence, various other theories have been proposed to explain overseas expansion of banks (and other firms).

4.4.3 Ownership advantages

Given the limitations of the cost of capital argument, attention has been placed on identifying why foreign banks seek to operate overseas when they seem to have various disadvantages compared with domestic/indigenous banks. Typically, the main disadvantages for foreign banks entering overseas markets can be identified as follows:

- Indigenous banks are likely to be better informed regarding the demand features of the local markets as well as the legal and institutional framework under which business is conducted. Foreign banks, therefore, can only acquire this expertise at a cost.
- Foreign banks have to incur costs associated with operating at a distance and these include such things as management, regulatory and other costs.

Given that these disadvantages are likely to be evident, the argument goes that banks that locate overseas must have some type of compensating advantages that enable them to compete with indigenous firms on equal terms – these are referred to in general as ownership advantages.

These so-called ownership advantages, which may be related to technological expertise, marketing know-how, production efficiency, managerial expertise, innovative product capability and so on, must be easily transferable within the bank and the skills and other ownership advantages diffused effectively throughout the organisation.

The concept of 'ownership advantages' is a rather broad concept. It is by no means clear how long it takes banks to build such advantages, whether such advantages relate mainly to innovative products and services, or whether they emanate mainly through the operation of more efficient organisational or production processes. There is also little evidence on the costs associated with developing such advantages. However, the fact that banks do expand into markets where they at first appear to have an inherent disadvantage compared with incumbent firms means that they must have some form of advantage compared with domestic operators.

4.4.4 Diversification of earnings

An obvious motive for foreign expansion relates to the aim of management to diversify business activity. This theory states that the investment decisions of banks stem from a conscious effort by managers to diversify earnings and therefore reduce risk. By expanding into different markets, banks expose their operations to the risk and return profile of specific business areas. If a German bank believes the prospects for retail banking in the US are more attractive than retail banking in its home market then it makes sense to consider expansion in the US. This will diversify earnings and make the German bank less exposed to its home market.

Diversification of bank earnings and risk reduction can be brought about by expansion into foreign markets and risk will be reduced the less correlated earnings in the foreign country are to those in the home market. You should be aware that finance theory tells us that investors wish to construct diversified portfolios of shares so that all their investments are not exposed to the same adverse shocks – hence they construct portfolios by choosing an array of investments, looking for low correlations between the price movements of the stock so as to maximise diversification benefits to yield a given expected return and risk (see Appendix A2). This principle is the same for banks (and other firms) when they consider expanding overseas. Also remember that banks can diversify by doing similar business activity in different countries (**geographical diversification**) and also by expanding into new areas (such as insurance, mutual funds, investment management, investment banking and so on) both at home and abroad (**product diversification**).

4.4.5 Theory of excess managerial capacity

Another theory of foreign investment relates to the desire of companies to use up **excess managerial capacity**. A bank may require the use of certain managerial and other resources that can be only fully utilised when they achieve a certain size. For instance, if a firm has a highly specialised management team it may not get the best use of this team if it focuses only on business in one particular geographical market. Companies can extend their scale of operations by expanding overseas and into new markets and these managerial resources will be more efficiently utilised.

4.4.6 Location and the product life cycle

In addition to the theories mentioned above, another school of thought focuses on location theories that are linked to the **product life cycle**. Here the focus is on the nature of the product (or services) produced and the changing demand and production cost features of the product in different markets.

The product life cycle has three main stages (see Figure 4.2):

1 Innovative or new product.

2 Maturing product.

3 Standardised product.

The **innovative (or new product) stage** is when a good or service is produced to meet a new consumer demand or when a new technology enables the creation of innovative goods. Typically, these new demands are first met by banks located in mature and well-established markets – also generally those with higher gross domestic product (GDP) per capita income. In the first instance, the product may not be standardised and communication between the production process and selling arm of the company needs to be close and frequent as the product establishes a market presence. As the communication costs increase with distance, the new product is likely to be produced and sold in the home market before any international expansion is considered.

As the bank gains from 'learning by doing' and the most efficient forms of production, distribution and selling are identified, the product becomes more standardised. This is known as the **mature product stage**. Customers are more aware of the product's features and also are likely to become more price-sensitive (demand for the product in the home market becomes more elastic). As the market expands, the producer is likely to benefit from scale economies so production costs fall. When the product or service reaches maturity and foreign customers become aware of the new good, then demand is likely to grow (especially from those in relatively more prosperous overseas markets). Usually, investment is first likely to take place in high-income countries that have demand features similar to the home market although where the costs of producing and operating locally exceed those

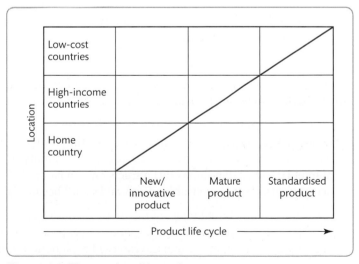

Figure 4.2 The product life cycle

of exporting. This pattern of **production diffusion**, whereby innovative products are first produced and sold in prosperous economies then trickle down to (relatively) less wealthy markets, characterises overseas expansion in the mature product stage. This feature is common to many retail financial services, such as credit cards, that originated in the US in the 1960s, spread to Europe in the 1970s and 1980s, and in the 1990s became commonplace in many developing countries.

The final stage of the product life cycle is that of the **standardised product** where the product is uniform and undifferentiated and competition between producers is based solely on price. In this case knowledge about foreign markets is not important and the main issue for the producer is to find the lowest cost of production. In this stage of the product life cycle production is transferred to the lowest-cost country so the firm can maintain competitive advantage.

4.4.7 Other theories on the rationale for international banking

While there is a host of theories explaining why international banking exists, no one theory seems to adequately explain all types of foreign expansion. Banks may wish to simultaneously diversify their income streams and find the lowest-cost production base. Many banks and other financial firms have developed services with strong brand images through effective differentiation strategies, but they still may wish to charge relatively high prices and also produce at the lowest cost.

In fact, if one reviews the literature on the motives for foreign expansion, it can be seen that all the theories come up with some form of explanation that tries to determine why banks seek to produce and sell their own products and services through foreign operations rather than exporting from the home market. Other theories concerning the rationale for international banking relate to the following:

- **Firm-specific advantages** – some banks have advantages (whether financial, based on distribution and production expertise, selling experience, etc.) that make foreign expansion easier. Size often confers such advantages as large banks typically have a wide array of financing sources, may benefit from scale and scope economies, and have more expert management and systems that make foreign expansion easier. They also are more likely to have the relevant financial and personal resources to undertake large-scale overseas activity.

- **Location advantages** – there may be a variety of attractions associated with overseas location that the aforementioned theories do not cover. We mentioned a couple of location advantages when we talked about the product life cycle above, but other location benefits relate to a variety of production, distribution and selling attributes of the product or service in question. For instance, banks like to group together in financial centres (as in London, New York and Tokyo) to benefit from the close proximity of the foreign exchange market and other Eurocurrency activities. The liquidity of London's foreign exchange market (the largest in the world) attracts foreign banks and other service firms (such as accountants, lawyers, consulting firms and so on) because of the business available.

Overall, there is a broad range of theories to choose from in explaining the rationale for foreign bank expansion. In reality, we can probably pick a variety of theories to explain the motives for foreign expansion and the choice of explanations are likely to vary on a case-by-case basis.

4.4.8 Practice of bank expansion in foreign markets

Complementing the theories noted above, we can identify a host of strategic reasons why banks may wish to establish foreign operations. These are outlined as follows:

- **Customer-seeking strategies** – banks seek to undertake overseas expansion in order to obtain new customers or to follow established clients. The reason why banks are more likely to seek new customers through foreign establishment (either through M&A activity or establishing new operations themselves) relates to the barriers associated with the cross-border selling of products and services without a physical presence. Typically, this view suggests that the decision to invest overseas is linked to the higher costs associated with meeting clients' needs from a distance as opposed to investment in the foreign market. The rush of banks into the Chinese market (with a customer base equivalent to 22 per cent of the world's population) is a good example of how the world's largest firms have been motivated by the commercial opportunities afforded by a relatively underdeveloped retail and commercial banking market.

- **Obtaining a foothold strategy** – foreign expansion can be motivated by the desire to establish a presence in order to test the market. Information can be obtained by making experimental foreign investment and over time banks can decide on whether to expand or contract their activities. For instance, various US and European investment banks have made relatively modest acquisitions of securities firms in the Japanese market to see whether they can develop their private banking business.

- **Follow-the-leader strategy** – when a large bank undertakes investment in a foreign market it may well encourage others to follow. There is anecdotal evidence that various multinational firms (including large banks) emulate their competitors' cross-border strategies regarding investment decisions in major markets. Some form of herd instinct seems apparent vis-à-vis the rush of many banks and other large firms into the Chinese and other Asian economies. The move of commercial and investment banks acquiring asset management firms across Europe and the US, as well as Spanish bank expansion in Latin America, are two examples of the herd instinct in international banking activity.

- **Customer-following strategies** – it has been argued that banks in their home markets have information advantages associated with their on-going client relationships. The nature of these relationships puts these firms in a privileged position to follow their customers abroad. If a bank's major corporate customer enters a new market, it may wish to obtain its banking services locally and this is likely to encourage foreign expansion. Customer-follower strategies are common in banking – big firms need big banks so they can meet their growing financing needs. The capital markets, of course, can meet certain financing requirements of large firms – especially when markets are buoyant. When capital markets become less accommodating, then companies turn to their banks. In other words, when companies become larger and industries more concentrated, the banking industry will follow suit.

- **Performance and efficiency advantages** – the most obvious reason justifying foreign expansion is that it adds to overall firm performance and shareholder value. That is, returns generated from cross-border operations will add to group returns, boosting profits and ultimately increasing the bank stock price for its shareholders. Given that a major strategic objective of banks is to generate sufficient risk-adjusted returns to their owners, one would expect that there is evidence to suggest that foreign operations add value in some way. Cross-border expansion can therefore be expected to add value to the bank by improving operating costs and/or increasing market power in setting prices.

- **Managerial motives** – international banking activity may, of course, be motivated by managerial motives rather than the objective of maximising profits and shareholder value. Entrenched managers may make international investment decisions based on their own preferences for pay, power, job security, risk aversion and so on. In general, international expansion may either strengthen or weaken the hands of entrenched managers directly by affecting the market for corporate control or governance, or indirectly by changing the market power of the firm. Put simply, managers may seek to expand internationally so they control larger firms – salaries and benefits being higher in bigger firms/banks. Managers may wish to expand in order to make their companies less prone to hostile takeovers, or they may believe that geographical diversification helps improve their managerial prospects, but this may not necessarily be the same as increasing the share price or profits of the bank.

- **Government motives** – it could be argued that a major factor that has motivated the growth of international banking activity has been deregulation aimed at fostering a more competitive, innovative and open market. The deregulation of many over-protected banking markets has had the effect of encouraging foreign bank entry and this, in theory at least, should boost competition and encourage domestic banks to become more efficient. For example, one of the main objectives of the EU's Single Market Programme has been to reduce barriers to trade in banking and financial services across all member countries in order to encourage foreign bank expansion.

4.5 Types of bank entry into foreign markets

When undertaking business in foreign markets banks have a number of choices with regards to the structure of their activities. The choice of structure depends on a broad range of considerations, including the amount of investment the bank wishes to undertake, the level of market experience, the volume of international business, tax and other factors, and the bank's overall strategic plans. There are five main types of structure that banks can choose when they undertake business in foreign markets:

- correspondent banking;
- representative office;
- agency;
- branch;
- subsidiary.

4.5.1 Correspondent banking

The lowest level of exposure to the foreign market can be achieved through a **correspondent banking** relationship. This simply involves using a bank located in the overseas market to provide services to a foreign bank. Typically, banks will use correspondent banks to do business in markets where they have no physical presence and as such these types of

BOX 4.4 CANADIAN IMPERIAL BANK OF COMMERCE (CIBC) CORRESPONDENT BANKING SERVICES

Canadian Imperial Bank of Commerce is a leader in payment processing and is a major provider of funds-transfer services for correspondent banks globally. CIBC's main correspondent banking services include:

(a) Current account services, including multi-currency accounts, a full range of statements and pooling services.

(b) Payment services in all major currencies to any bank or other beneficiary, anywhere in Canada or through its subsidiaries in the Caribbean. These include treasury settlement, cash settlement of securities, customer transfers to beneficiaries in Canada, disbursements, international bulk payments and pension payments.

(c) Cash letter clearing services, including clean collections.

(d) Documentary business such as letters of credit, documentary collections and guarantees.

Customer service teams are specialists in the investigation of client account activities, including payments, cash letters, collections, compensation claims, mail and pension payments, drafts and money orders.

CIBC delivers account and wire payment services reliably and efficiently and has made the bank a valued partner to banks throughout the world. In addition, CIBC has strengths in related areas such as trade finance and institutional trust and custody services.

CIBC has established strong clearing relationships with a multitude of banks around the globe. It has been providing correspondent banking services to foreign banks for nearly a century.

Source: Adapted from **www.cibc.com/ca/correspondent-banking**

services are widely used by smaller banks. Box 4.4 illustrates the correspondent banking services provided by one of Canada's largest banks, the Canadian Imperial Bank of Commerce.

It can be seen that the sorts of services offered via a correspondent banking relationship relate mainly to the offer of payment and other transaction services as well as various trade credit facilities. Correspondent banks like CIBC earn a fee from the foreign banks for providing these services. It should be clear that foreign banks have only minimal exposure to foreign markets via correspondent banking relationships.

4.5.2 Representative office

Banks can obtain slightly greater exposure to a foreign market via a **representative office**. Representative offices are usually small and they cannot provide banking business – that is, they cannot take deposits or make loans. Representative offices are used to prospect for new business and they usually act simply as marketing offices for parent banks. Typically, a bank will set up a representative office in risky markets as the cost of running such small offices is negligible and they can easily be closed if commercial prospects are not good.

4.5.3 Agency

The term **agency** mainly refers to a separately incorporated branch of a foreign bank in the United States. Agencies are similar to branches in that they form an integral part of the parent bank. They lie somewhere between branches and representative offices as they can do less than the former and more than the latter. In the US, for example, agency banks cannot make loans or take deposits in their own name; rather, they do so on behalf of the parent bank in the foreign country.

Just as a clarification, an 'agent bank' is a bank that acts in some capacity on behalf of another bank. It can refer to:

- the bank in a loan syndicate that advises other participating banks of advances taken and changes in interest rates for a foreign or domestic borrower;

- a bank that participates in the credit card programme of another bank by issuing credit cards;

- as explained above, a foreign bank doing business in the US on behalf of its parent bank.

4.5.4 Branch office

Establishing a **branch** usually indicates a higher level of commitment to the foreign market compared with the representative office. A branch is a key part of the parent bank and acts as a legal and functional part of the parent's head office. In many respects a foreign branch is similar to a domestic branch, although the former is likely to have more autonomy in making commercial decisions tailored to the specific features of the foreign market. Branches can perform all the functions that are allowed by the banking authorities of the host country, namely taking loans and making deposits, as well as selling other types of products and services.

Branches are the most common form of foreign bank expansion as the costs are less than establishing a wholly-owned subsidiary and they enable banks to conduct a full range of business activity.

4.5.5 Subsidiary

A **subsidiary** is a separate legal entity from the parent bank, has its own capital and is organised and regulated according to the laws of the host country. Where branches and agencies expose the whole capital of the parent bank to risk from overseas activity, the risk exposure of a subsidiary is limited by its own capital exposure. (Of course, if a foreign bank subsidiary faced difficulties, the regulators would expect the parent bank to provide support – although legally they do not have to do this given that subsidiaries have separate corporate identities.)

Subsidiaries may be the result of acquisition or organic start-ups (*greenfield*) – they also tend to be costly as the business has to be capitalised separately from the parent. One main advantage of having a subsidiary is that it generally signals a stronger commitment to do business in a country compared with other forms of entry and reflects the foreign company's more positive assessment of prospects for the market. In addition, subsidiaries are usually allowed to undertake a broad range of banking business subject to the rules and regulations of the host country. For example, prior to 1999 US commercial banks were

Table 4.1 Type of entry in foreign markets

Type of entry	Advantages	Disadvantages
Correspondent banking	• Low-cost market entry • Minimal staff expense • Local banking opportunities • Network of local contacts	• Customers might be given low priority • Some forms of credit not allowed
Representative office	• Low cost • Attracts additional business and maintains existing business	• Difficult to recruit and train qualified staff • Limited ability to expand foreign markets operations
Branch	• Greater control over foreign operations • Better customer relationship • Greater ability to offer products and services	• Expensive • Difficult to recruit and train qualified staff
Subsidiary	• Separate legal entity • No legal obligation to support if in distress	• Expensive • Decentralised management functions with possible duplication of roles

prohibited from undertaking full-scale investment banking business in their home market, so many of the largest banks established subsidiaries overseas where they could undertake this type of business.

Table 4.1 summarises the main advantages and disadvantages of the different types of entry in foreign markets.

Despite a clear legal distinction between branches and subsidiaries, however, they may in practice sometimes be operated and managed in a similar fashion. In some countries, branches work effectively as independent entities. In others, subsidiaries may function similarly to branches, subject to centralised risk management and funding decisions. Practices such as group-wide guarantees and supervisory ring-fencing often blur the distinctions between branches and subsidiaries.

4.5.6 Branches vs. subsidiaries

Both branch and subsidiary structures have certain features that make them attractive for cross-border banks, regardless of their business model (see Fiechter *et al.* (2011), p. 14):

● For the banking group as a whole, costs of doing business may be lower under the branch structure than under the subsidiary structure.

● The subsidiary structure may, in principle, be better for containing losses in the event of distress (or failure) of an affiliate.

● All else being equal, one could expect global retail banks to have a preference for subsidiarisation, while global universal banks for branching.

● In practice, when choosing a legal form of incorporation in foreign jurisdictions, banking groups also take into account a range of home/host country characteristics that may outweigh the business model considerations.

Actual practice is often complex, with cross-border banking groups choosing to branch into some jurisdictions and incorporate as subsidiaries in others. For example, a banking group might prefer branching when local financial markets are less developed and less able

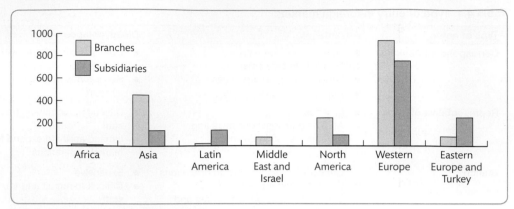

Figure 4.3 Branches and subsidiaries: geographical distribution, 2008

Source: Fiechter *et al.* (2011) p. 14.

to support a subsidiary; the entry to local markets targets credit extension and provision of risk management services to existing clients; political risks are high; and tax and regulatory treatments of branches are more favourable. In the case of advanced host countries, banking groups may prefer branching into countries that host major money centres (e.g. US or UK markets) or into markets for wholesale deposit sourcing (e.g. Germany).

Figure 4.3 illustrates the geographical distribution of subsidiaries and branches of foreign banks at the end of 2008, while Figure 4.4 shows the number of foreign branches and subsidiaries in selected financial centres.

Integrated cross-border banking groups may achieve efficiency gains arising from the scale and diversification of their operations, but their failure can also generate spillovers that threaten financial stability in countries in which they operate (see also Chapter 8). Cross-border expansion by banking groups through integrated branch networks appears to be less costly and, in some cases, more efficient than establishing a series of legally independent subsidiaries. In the event of failure of a banking group, however, it appears that a subsidiary structure would generally be less costly to resolve. A key consideration for policy makers, then, is whether the trade-off between efficiency and financial stability argues for policies that reflect a preference for certain cross-border banking structures.

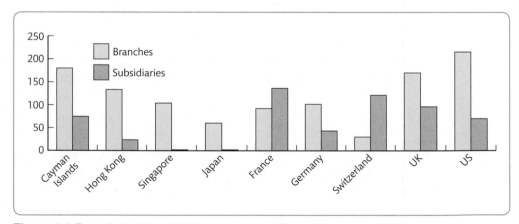

Figure 4.4 Branches and subsidiaries: selected financial centres, 2008

Source: Fiechter *et al.* (2011) p. 14.

4.6 International banking services

Banks can offer a wide range of different types of banking and financial services via their international operations. One of the difficulties in describing types of international banking activity relates to its diversity. Traditionally, the role of banks in providing services to multinational companies has been emphasised as the main feature of international banking, but as many banks have expanded overseas their customers now span the full spectrum of services, ranging from niche retail banking products to wholesale investment and commercial banking activity. Bearing this in mind, the following sections focus on banking products and services provided to international business.

4.6.1 Products and services to international business

All international businesses are served by a variety of financial service firms, including mainly commercial banks, investment banks and asset finance firms. The core banking products and services are similar (but not exclusively) to those offered to large corporate clients, which were reviewed in Section 3.5.2. These typically focus on the following range of needs:

- money transmission and cash management;
- credit facilities – loans, overdrafts, standby lines of credit and other facilities;
- syndicated loans (only available to large companies and multinational firms);
- debt finance via bond issuance (only available to large companies and multinational firms);
- other debt finance, including asset-backed financing;
- domestic and international equity (the latter typically only available to large companies and multinational firms);
- securities underwriting and fund management services;
- risk management and information management services;
- foreign exchange transactions and trade finance.

4.6.1.1 Money transmission and cash management

An important area where firms conducting international activities differ from smaller domestic-orientated firms is in the provision of **cash management and transaction services**, as they have to deal with remittances and payments in both the domestic and foreign currency. Although many companies may not be large enough to have well-developed treasury activities, they are likely to have more advanced cash management systems than their domestic counterparts. The cash management function in firms has developed mainly as a result of (a) corporate recognition that excess cash balances result in a significant opportunity cost due to lost or foregone interest, (b) the firm needing to know its cash or working capital position on a real-time basis and (c) foreign currency flows of cash needing to be managed effectively so as to minimise possible exchange rate risk.

The extent to which such services are used obviously depends on the scale of the firm's activities and the extent of its international operations. The largest companies will have treasury functions that resemble small banks conducting this type of business, whereas mid-sized companies are likely to have a limited array of cash management activities.

4.6.1.2 Credit facilities – loans, overdrafts, standby lines of credit and other facilities

Firms of all sizes have a broad array of bank **credit facilities** available to use to finance their operations. These range from standard loan facilities that may be fixed or floating rate, secured or unsecured, and can have short- to long-term maturities. In many respects these types of loan facilities are not really any different to consumer loans apart from their size. Companies also, of course, have access to on-going overdraft facilities to meet short-term financing needs.

In addition to these standard products, larger companies will have access to Eurocurrency markets. The Eurocurrency markets are essentially a high-volume, low-risk borrowing and depositing market. The main segment of the market is the interbank market where a relatively small number of large commercial banks undertake deposit and lending activity. Other important participants include companies and governments which use the market to fund short-term deficits and invest short-term surpluses. Various other financial institutions, such as investment banks, also use the market to fund large-scale holdings of securities through pledging these in repurchase (repo) agreements. Unlike banks, which issue certificates of deposits, large non-financial companies can fund their short-term deficits by issuing commercial paper or by discounting trade receivables in the form of banker's acceptances. These are techniques used for raising short-term wholesale funds denominated in a currency other than the home currency. For instance, a UK multinational company may issue $5 million of commercial paper to raise short-term finance or can simply borrow in the interbank market – the latter is a dollar Eurocurrency loan. (Similarly, the UK firm may have access to dollar funds and place, say, a $5 million deposit with a bank – this is known as a Eurocurrency deposit.) Access to the Eurocurrency markets is mainly the preserve of banks and large international companies.

In addition to standard loan products, banks will provide their corporate clients with various commitments and guarantees (see Section 3.5.2.3).

4.6.1.3 Debt finance via bond issuance

In addition to the credit facilities mentioned above, large companies can raise funds in the capital markets by issuing debt instruments known as **bonds**.[2] Bonds are simply contracts between a lender and a borrower by which the borrower promises to repay a loan with interest (see also Section 3.5.2.2). Typically, bonds are traded in the market after issue so their price and yields vary. Bonds can take on various features and a classification of bond types depends on the issuer, priority, coupon rate and redemption features, as shown in Figure 4.5.

Large companies as well as governments and international organisations all issue bonds to raise medium- to long-term finance. The most important feature relating to a bond is the credit quality of the issuer – typically governments (especially in the developed world) are believed to be lower risk than firms and so their bonds pay lower interest than those of commercial concerns. Of course, some of the world's largest companies have better credit ratings than some fragile economies so this means that the former can raise bond finance cheaper than the latter. Nearly all bond issuers have to be credit rated to assess their ability to make interest (and ultimately principal) payments for their bond financing. The credit rating process is the same as that outlined for syndicated credits and shown in Table 4.3. There are many types of corporate bonds that a firm can issue; bond finance can be used to raise funds

---

[2] For an introduction to bonds and bond markets, see Appendix A1.

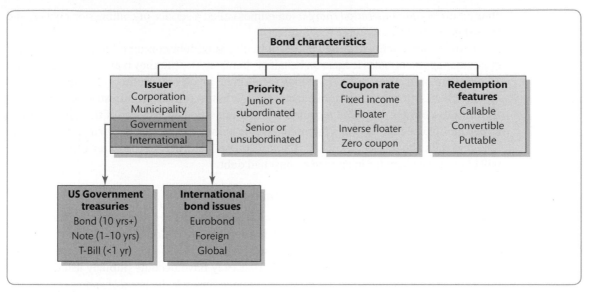

Figure 4.5 Bond features

in the home market (and currency) by issuing domestic bonds, or a company may wish to issue an international bond.

4.6.1.4   Other debt finance

The access to external finance is a critical success ingredient in the development of any business. Traditional bank loan and overdraft finance are the main sources of external finance for relatively small firms that conduct international business, whereas bond and syndicated loans form a major feature of multinational financing. In addition to these sources of debt finance, all firms (irrespective of size) have access to other forms of debt finance that can involve both domestic or/and international relationships and they include:

● asset-based finance;

● factoring and invoice discounting.

As introduced in Section 3.5.1.2, asset-based finance encompasses both **leasing** and hire purchase. The main difference between them is that in the former the asset remains the property of the leasing company at the end of the contract, whereas in the case of hire purchase the firm making payments obtains ownership.

Other sources of finance for companies are through the use of **factoring** and **invoice discounting services**. As illustrated in Section 3.5.1.2, factoring is a lending product that enables a company to collect money on credit sales. The factor purchases the company's invoice debts for cash, but at a discount, and subsequently seeks repayment from the original purchaser of the company's goods or services. Factoring involves the factor managing the sales ledger of a company, whereas invoice discounting is a narrower service where the discounting firm collects sales receipts but the firm still manages its ledger. Factors and invoice discounters charge for providing an advance to the company and this is usually around 80 per cent of the total value of the invoices. When the factor/invoice discounter receives the invoice payments they release the 20 per cent residual to the client, less charges. The main charges are an *administration charge*, sometimes called a service or commission charge, and a *discounting or finance charge* (i.e. interest).

Factors make administration charges for collecting debt contained in invoices and for credit management/sales ledgers on behalf of clients. In the UK, they typically charge around 1–3 per cent of invoice values. As already mentioned, invoice discounters also advance funds against clients' invoices, but unlike factors, they do not provide administration services. A factor or discounter may have recourse to the client when a customer of that client refuses to pay an invoice that has been factored – this is known as recourse factoring. If there is no recourse then the service is known as non-recourse factoring. In the latter case, the factor will charge the client for insurance against bad debt.

4.6.1.5   Domestic and international equity

Once they get to a certain size, companies have the choice of diversifying their sources of external finance by accessing the capital market. We have already noted that the largest firms can issue bonds and raise funds in the syndicated loans market, but before they can access these markets it is more than likely that they have become publicly listed on their domestic stock exchanges and raised equity finance through the issue of shares (or stock as it is known in the US). The next step may be to consider a listing in a foreign market – known as a **Euroequity** issue. However, most firms are not known well enough overseas to attract foreign investors so they may first try a Eurobond issue where the market is for professional investors and if this is a success they may progress to a cross-listing of their shares on another stock exchange.

There was substantial growth in the cross-listing of shares during the 1990s and the US market has been a popular destination for such listings. In particular, European and Asian companies are keen to seek out US investors by listing not only in their home market but also in the US. The main rationale is that a foreign listing gives the company access to a more liquid capital market and a cheaper source of funding. There is also substantial prestige associated with obtaining a foreign listing on a major international stock market such as the London and New York exchanges. Firms also seek to cross-list to diversify their source of funding and to tap new investor segments – such as various institutional investors that may not be prevalent in home markets. A cross-listing of equity in another market may also establish a secondary market for shares used to acquire other firms in the host market and such shares can be used to compensate local management and employees in foreign subsidiaries.

4.6.1.6   Securities underwriting, fund management services, risk management and information management services

In addition to the financial services already mentioned, international banks provide a variety of sophisticated services that complements traditional credit and debt finance facilities. These services are numerous but they can be broadly grouped into three main categories: guarantees, foreign exchange and interest rate-related transactions, and securities underwriting and fund management services (the main features of such services have been illustrated in Section 3.5.2.5).

4.6.1.7   Foreign exchange transactions and trade finance

Firms involved in international trading activity can rely on the banking system to provide various forms of trade finance that help facilitate the import and export of goods. The three main types of trade finance relate to the provision of letters of credit, forfaiting and **countertrade**.

4.6.1.7.1 Letters of credit

A letter of credit (LOC) is a legal banking agreement that allows importers to offer secure terms to exporters (see also Section 4.6.1.3). Letters of credit have been used for centuries in international trading transactions. A letter of credit from a bank guarantees the seller that, if various documents are presented, the bank will pay the seller the amount due. It is simply an undertaking given by the issuing bank on behalf of the buyer to pay the seller a specific amount of money on presentation of specified documents representing the supply of goods within certain time limits. These documents must conform to terms and conditions set out in the letter of credit and documents must be presented at a specified place.

Such an agreement offers security to the seller, as it is an assurance of payment from an international bank, on the condition that the terms of the letter of credit are complied with. In addition, the seller can raise extra finance using the letter of credit as collateral if need be. The attraction from the buyer's perspective is that they do not have to pay cash up front to a foreign country before receiving the documents of title to the goods purchased. This, of course, is helpful when the buyer is unfamiliar with suppliers overseas. In addition, a letter of credit protects the buyer's interest as the bank will pay the supplier only if specific documents are presented. Payment will be given if these documents comply with the terms and conditions set out in the letter of credit. The buyer can also include safeguards into the letter of credit, such as inspection of the goods, quality control and set production and delivery times. Table 4.2 sets out the main features of a standard letter of credit agreement.

An *irrevocable letter of credit* provides a guarantee by the issuing bank in the event that all terms and conditions are met by the buyer. A *revocable letter of credit*, in contrast, can be cancelled or altered by the buyer after it has been issued by the buyer's bank.

4.6.1.7.2 Forfaiting

In a **forfaiting** transaction, the exporter agrees to surrender the rights to claim for payment of goods or services delivered to an importer under a contract of sale, in return for a cash payment from a *forfaiting bank*. The forfaiting bank takes over the exporter's debt and assumes the full risk of payment by the importer. The exporter is thereby freed from any financial risk in the transaction and is liable only for the quality and reliability of the goods and services provided. The buyer's obligation is usually supported by a local bank guarantee and can in certain cases be guaranteed by the government. As in the case of letters of credit, the documentation requirements are relatively straightforward. These cover evidence of the underlying transaction, copies of shipping documents and confirmations from the bank guaranteeing the transaction. Forfaiting transactions can be on a fixed or floating interest rate basis. The exporter will receive the funds upon presentation of all the relevant documents, shortly after shipment of goods, and payment will usually be made in the form of a letter of credit.

4.6.1.7.3 Countertrade

Countertrade is a general term used to cover a variety of commercial mechanisms for reciprocal trade. Simple barter is probably the oldest and best-known example; however, other techniques such as switch-trading, buy-back, counter-purchase and offset have developed

Table 4.2 Letters of credit

Step 1	Buyer and seller agree terms, including means of transport, period of credit offered, latest date of shipment and other relevant terms to be used.
Step 2	Then the buyer applies to the bank for a letter of credit to be issued.
Step 3	The bank evaluates the buyer's credit rating and may require a cash cover and/or a reduction of other lending limits.
Step 4	The issuing bank will issue a letter of credit. This will be sent to the advising bank by airmail, telex or SWIFT.
Step 5	The advising bank will establish authenticity of the letter of credit using signature books or test codes, then informs seller (beneficiary).
Step 6	The advising bank may confirm the letter of credit, i.e. add its own payment undertaking.
Step 7	The seller should check that the letter of credit matches the commercial agreement and that the terms and conditions can be satisfied in good time.
Step 8	If there is anything that may cause a problem, an amendment should be requested.
Step 9	The seller ships the goods and gathers together all the documents asked for in the letter of credit, such as the invoice and the transport document.
Step 10	Before presenting the documents to the bank, the seller should check them for discrepancies against the letter of credit, and correct the documents where necessary.
Step 11	The documents are presented to a bank, often the advising bank.
Step 12	The advising bank checks the documents against the letter of credit. If the documents are compliant, the bank pays the seller and forwards the documents to the issuing bank.
Step 13	The issuing bank will also check the documents. If they are in order, the issuing bank will reimburse the seller's bank immediately.
Step 14	The issuing bank debits the buyer and releases the documents (including transport document), so that the buyer can claim the goods from the carrier.

Notes: 1) The letter of credit refers to documents representing the goods – not the goods themselves. 2) Banks are not in the business of examining goods on behalf of their customers. 3) Typically, the documents requested will include a commercial invoice, a transport document such as a bill of lading or airway bill, an insurance document and many others.

to meet the requirements of a more integrated global world economy. The main types of countertrade include:

- *simple barter* – direct exchange of physical goods between two parties;
- *switch-trading* – involves transferring use of bilateral balances from one country to another. For instance, an export from the US to Libya will be paid for with a dollar amount paid into an account at a bank in Libya. This in turn can be used only to buy goods from Libya. The original US exporter may buy unrelated goods from Libya or may sell the dollars at a discount to a 'switch trader' who buys Libyan goods for sale elsewhere;
- *buy-back* – this is an agreement where the exporter of plant or equipment agrees to take payment in the form of future production from the plant;
- *counter-purchase* – involves an initial export whereby the exporter receives 'payment' in goods unrelated to what the exporter manufactures;
- *offset* – refers to the requirement of importing countries that their purchase price be offset in some way by the seller; this can include requirements to source production locally, to transfer technology or to increase imports from the importing country.

There is a wide range of countertrade mechanisms that aims to facilitate trade in goods. This type of activity is usually more prevalent in countries that limit FDI and are subject to greater political risk.

4.6.2 Syndicated loans

Syndicated lending is when a lead bank persuades a number of other banks to contribute to a loan. Normally a syndicate of banks will provide very large loans to finance projects such as infrastructure, or sovereign loans to developing/emerging countries. While syndicates have many variations, the basic structure involves a lead manager (the agent bank) that will represent, and operate on behalf of, the lending group (the participating banks), as illustrated in Figure 4.6. Although there is only a single loan agreement contract, every syndicate member has a separate claim on the borrower. Typically, access to the syndicated loans market is restricted to only the largest firms as the smallest loans on average exceed $50 million.

At the most basic level, arrangers serve the role of raising finance for a borrower in need of capital. The borrower pays the arranger a fee for this service and this fee increases with the complexity and riskiness of the loan. Usually each participant funds the loan at identical conditions and is responsible for its particular share of the loan. Overall, syndicated loans lie somewhere between relationship loans and public debt, where the lead bank may have some form of relationship with the borrower – although this is less likely to be the case for banks participating in the syndicate at a more junior level.

Developments in the syndicated loan market have made a clearer distinction between syndicated loans and bilateral bank loans. One significant change was the growth in the regulated and standardised secondary market during the 1990s, which supplied significant amounts of liquidity to the syndicated loan market. Another major factor has been the rising number of syndicated loans rated by independent rating agencies. As a result of stronger secondary market activity, combined with independently rated syndicated loans, there has been greater recognition of these assets by institutional investors as an alternative investment to bonds (Altunbas *et al.*, 2010). Changes in the syndicated loan market – including its volume, its capacity to provide sizeable medium- and long-term funding and increased transparency – have shifted it closer to the corporate bond market and further away from bilateral bank lending.

These developments in turn have led the market to grow exponentially. Currently, syndicated loans are the only alternative to bond financing for large firms on account of the size and maturity of the funds that can be provided. The syndicated loan market is, therefore, a hybrid of the commercial banking and investment banking worlds. It is globally one of the largest and most flexible sources of capital. The syndicated lending market has become one of the dominant ways for large corporate and sovereign borrowers to raise funds.

The syndicated loan market has developed its own lexicon: Appendix 4.1 presents a selected glossary to explain the participants and functions and their sometimes odd names.

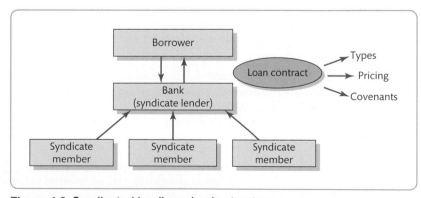

Figure 4.6 Syndicated lending – basic structure

The Standard & Poor's (2011) *Guide to the Loan Market* identifies three main types of syndication:

- **Underwritten deal**: this is one for which the arrangers guarantee the entire commitment and then syndicate the loan to other banks and institutional investors. If they cannot fully subscribe the loan, they absorb the difference and may later try again to sell to investors.

- **'Best efforts' syndication**: this is one for which the arranger group commits to underwrite less than the entire amount of the loan, leaving the credit to the market. Traditionally, best-effort syndications have been used for risky borrowers or for complex transactions.

- **Club deal**: this is a loan syndicated by a small number of participating banks, which are not entitled to transfer their portion of the loan to a third party. Smaller syndicates result in lower restructuring and monitoring costs, and are thus preferred by lead arrangers when default is more likely.

The relative reliance on these underwriting techniques can vary, depending on current market developments. For example, the underwriting approach is used more often in an active deal-making environment, where there are frequent mergers and acquisitions. Corporations are willing to pay the higher fees for the assurance of knowing that the entire financing for such a transaction is committed. In a less active or nervous market environment, the best-efforts approach tends to be the primary distribution technique of choice: borrowers may feel no need to pay the higher fees or lead banks may be more reluctant to assume the higher risks of the firm-commitment underwriting. There are also regional differences. For example, the European leveraged syndicated loan market almost exclusively consists of underwritten deals, whereas the US market is mostly best-efforts. Club deals gained importance, indicating both growing bank risk aversion and higher credit risk at a time of economic uncertainty. During the post-crisis period, club deals of more than €150 million became common.

Figure 4.7 illustrates club deals and loan issuance by the top five arrangers (ranked by the total value of arranged deals) between 2003 and 2010 (Chui *et al.*, 2010). The syndicated loan market is struggling to recover post 2008, as large companies are increasingly turning to bond finance.

4.6.2.1 The syndication process[3]

The syndication process can be broken down into: (i) before, (ii) during and (iii) after the syndication.

(i) Before awarding a mandate, a borrower (also known as the issuer) might solicit bids from arrangers. The banks will outline their syndication strategy and qualifications, as well as their view on the way the loan will price in market. This is also known as the *underwriting phase*.

(ii) Once the mandate is awarded, the syndication process starts. The arranger will prepare an **information memo** (IM) describing the terms of the transactions. This is also known as the sub-underwriting phase.

---

[3] A more in-depth description of the syndication process, as summarised in this section, can be found in Standard & Poor's *A Guide to the Loan Market* (2011). Also, see Standard and Poor's *A Guide to the European Loan Market* (2010).

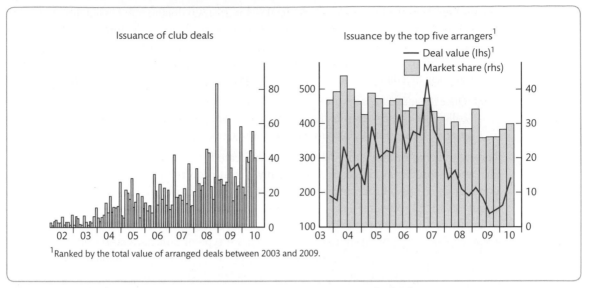

Figure 4.7 Club deals and loan issuance by the top five arrangers (in $bn)
Source: Chui *et al.* (2010).

The IM or *bank-book* typically will include:

- an executive summary;
- investment considerations;
- a list of terms and conditions;
- an industry overview;
- a financial model.

The executive summary will include a description of the issuer, an overview of the transaction and rationale, sources and uses, and key statistics on the financials. Investment considerations will be the management's sales 'pitch' for the deal. The list of terms and conditions will be a preliminary term sheet describing the pricing, structure, collateral, covenants and other terms of the credit (covenants are usually negotiated in detail after the arranger receives investor feedback). The industry overview will be a description of the company's industry and competitive position relative to its industry peers. The financial model will be a detailed model of the issuer's historical, pro-forma and projected financials, including management's high, low and base case for the issuer.

Because loans are not securities, this will be a confidential offering made only to qualified banks and accredited investors. As the IM is being prepared, the syndicate desk will solicit informal feedback from potential investors on what their appetite for the deal will be and at what price they are willing to invest. Once this intelligence has been gathered, the agent will formally market the deal to potential investors.

Most new loans are kicked off at a bank meeting at which potential lenders hear bank management and the sponsor group (if there is one) describe what the terms of the loan are and what transaction it backs. Bank management will provide its vision for the transaction and, most importantly, tell why and how the lenders will be repaid on or ahead of schedule. In addition, investors will be briefed regarding the multiple exit strategies, including second ways out via asset sales. Once the loan is closed, the final terms are then documented in detailed credit and security agreements. It is important to note that loans, by their very nature, are flexible documents that can be revised and amended from time to time (subject to different levels of approval). One or several lenders will typically act as an **arranger** or *lead manager*, instructed by the borrower to bring together the consortium of banks prepared to lend money at a given set of terms.

(iii) Once the mandate is awarded, the arranger is ready to start the syndication process. This is called the primary-distribution phase of the loan. The syndication unfolds as a multi-step process that is similar, in many ways, to the underwriting of a corporate bond or stock issue.

There are three primary investors in the syndicated loan market: banks, finance companies and institutional investors. Additionally, private equity funds, hedge funds, high-yield bond funds, pension funds, insurance companies and other proprietary investors participate opportunistically in loans.

Institutional investors in the loan market are principally structured vehicles known as **collateralised loan obligations** (CLOs) that are a type of **collateralised debt obligations** (CDOs). CLOs are special-purpose vehicles (SPVs) set up to hold and manage pools of leveraged loans. The SPV is financed with several tranches of debt (typically a 'AAA' rated tranche, a 'AA' tranche, a 'BBB' tranche and a mezzanine tranche) that have rights to the collateral and payment stream in descending order. CLOs are usually rated by two of the three ratings agencies (see Section 18.4.2 for more details on tranching).

In the wake of the 2007–2009 financial crisis, the funding of structures used to securitise syndicated loans, particularly CLOs, evaporated but by 2014 CLO issuance had demonstrated a full recovery with issuance of $90 billion by August, an amount equalling the previous record set in 2007.

4.6.2.2 Syndicated loans facilities

There are various types of syndicated loan facilities:

- A term loan – where the loan amount is specified for a set time. A term loan is simply an instalment loan, similar to a personal loan one would use to buy a car or a mortgage. The borrower may draw on the loan during a short commitment period and repays it based on either a scheduled series of repayments or a one-time lump-sum payment at maturity (bullet payment).

- A revolving credit facility – where part of the loan can be drawn down, repaid and then redrawn depending on the borrower's discretion.

- Letters of credit – guarantees provided by the syndicate group to pay off debt or obligations if the borrower cannot. There are several different types of LOC. The most common – a fee for standby or financial LOCs – guarantees that lenders will support various corporate activities (see Section 4.6.1.8 for more details on LOCs).

- Acquisitions or equipment lines – (a delayed-draw term loan) credits that may be drawn down for a given period to purchase specified assets or equipment or to make acquisitions.

- Bridge loans – loans provided to offer short-term financing to 'bridge' financial needs (for example, before bond/equity issuances).

4.6.2.3 Pricing of a syndicate loan

Pricing a loan requires arrangers to evaluate the risk inherent in the loan and to gauge investor appetite for that risk. There are various factors driving the pricing of a syndicated loan, including market liquidity, relative yield of other loans and other asset classes, creditor quality, sector, size of the deal, etc.

Table 4.3 Credit risk ratings – Moody's and Standard & Poor's

Moody's	S&P	Quality of issue
Investment grade		
Aaa	AAA	Highest quality. Very small risk of default.
Aa	AA	High quality. Small risk of default.
A	A	High–medium quality. Strong attributes, but potentially vulnerable.
Baa	BBB	Medium quality. Currently adequate, but potentially unreliable.
Leveraged		
Ba	BB	Some speculative element. Long-run prospects questionable.
B	B	Able to pay currently, but at risk of default in the future.
Caa	CCC	Poor quality. Clear danger of default.
Ca	CC	High speculative quality. May be in default.
C	C	Lowest rated. Poor prospects of repayment.
D	–	In default.

The market is divided, roughly, into two segments: investment grade (loans rated 'BBB' or higher) and leveraged (borrowers rated 'BB+' or lower), as shown in Table 4.3. Pricing of the loan is set at a margin above the interbank rate (usually LIBOR or Euribor, depending on the currency) according to the perceived credit risk of the borrower and fees are also paid by the borrower to the syndicate for arranging the loan. The fees increase in line with the complexity and riskiness of a loan. While large investment grade borrowers would typically pay little or no fees, a leveraged borrower would normally pay somewhere in the region of 1–5 per cent of the total loan commitment depending on the complexity of the transaction, market conditions and whether the loan is underwritten.

Higher credit risk borrowers (that is, customers with high probability of default) pay larger margins above LIBOR (or Euribor) for their syndicated loans. Pricing also varies according to the type of borrower, purpose of the loan, whether the loan is secured or not and other factors. Pricing on many loans is tied to *performance grids*, which adjust pricing by one or more financial criteria.

The pricing mechanism of a syndicated loan differs between the US and Europe. In the US, the pricing of a syndicated loan is a complex capital market negotiation that balances the needs and interests of the different players in the market at the given time. Pricing loans in Europe is a simpler (but less efficient) process because pricing is not as flexible and market-driven as it is in the US. However, Europe has moved closer to the US practice of using **market flex language** to adapt pricing during general syndication to market conditions.

For many years, the European market had a well-established pricing 'standard' where most deals started out. The pro-rata tranches usually began general syndication at Euribor + 225 basis points (bps). During the credit crunch of 2008–2009, opening spreads increased to Euribor + 400–500 bps across the different terms, in response to the higher return requirements of investors. Figure 4.8 illustrates trends in syndicated loans and bond issuance by credit rating between 2002 and 2010.

In addition to the spread over LIBOR, the borrower has to pay a variety of fees. The arranger and other members of the lead management team generally earn some upfront fee for putting the deal together – this is known as a *praecipium* or *arrangement fee*. The underwriters similarly earn an *underwriting fee* for guaranteeing the availability of funds. Other participants (those on at least the manager or co-manager level) may also expect to receive

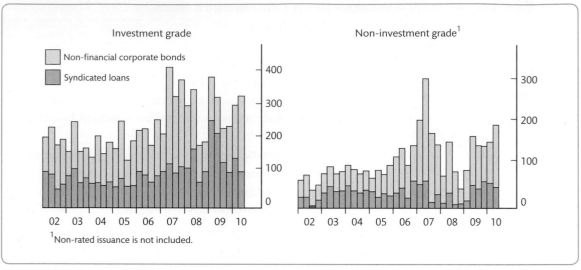

Figure 4.8 Syndicated loans and bond issuance by credit rating (in $bn)
Source: Chui *et al.* (2010).

a *participation fee* for agreeing to join the facility. The actual size of the fee generally varies with the size of the commitment. The most junior syndicate members typically earn only the spread over LIBOR or over a comparable market reference rate.

Once the credit is established, and as long as it is not drawn, the syndicate members often receive a *commitment or facility fee* (to compensate for the cost of regulatory capital that needs to be set aside against the commitment), again proportional to the size of the commitments. As soon as the facility is drawn, the borrower may have to pay a *utilisation fee*. This is paid, for instance, if the company draws more than a pre-agreed proportion of the facility – for example, it may be agreed that if the borrower draws more than 50 per cent of a facility it will have to pay its lenders an additional 5 bps utilisation fee on top of the margin. The agent bank typically earns an *agency fee*, usually payable annually to cover the costs of administering the loan. Loans sometimes also include penalty clauses whereby the borrower agrees to pay a prepayment fee or otherwise compensate lenders in the event that it reimburses its debt prior to the specified term.

Finally, market flex language is included in legal documents as additional protection for the bank. Market flex language may include *price flex* (which allows for a change in pricing of a loan) or a *structural flex* (which allows for a shift of amounts between various tranches of a loan). In addition, loan documentation normally incorporates a number of clauses that are in place to protect lenders against a deterioration in a borrower's financial/operational performance, changing market conditions and various other occurrences and takes the form of covenants, mandatory prepayments and collateral.

Syndicated loans have become an important source of corporate funds. Like many other credit markets, syndicated loan markets grew rapidly in the run-up to the 2007–2009 financial crisis. The main advantages of this form of borrowing are:

- arranging a syndicated loan is less costly, in terms of set-up fees, compared with a bond issuance;

- borrowers can achieve lower spreads than they might have to pay to individual banks if they intended to borrow through a series of bilateral bank borrowing;

- syndication can provide a more flexible funding structure which guarantees the availability of funds in the currency of their choice;
- it widens a company's circle of lenders through syndicates that include foreign banks;
- a syndication provides the borrower with a stable source of funds, which is of particular value in the event that other capital markets (such as the bond market) are subject to disruption;
- it allows borrowers to raise larger sums than they would be able to obtain through either the bond or equity markets under a time constraint;
- the facilities can be arranged quickly and discreetly, which may be of value for certain transactions such as takeovers;
- commitments to lend can be cancelled relatively easily compared with borrowing via securities markets where such actions could have an adverse impact on investor confidence.

Nonetheless, following the Lehman bankruptcy, syndicated loan markets collapsed. During the second half of 2008, gross syndicated lending declined by 67 per cent, both in developed economies and in emerging markets, with Africa and the Middle East particularly affected (see Figure 4.9).

The crisis of 2007–2009 was also associated with a substantial widening of syndicated loan spreads. Following a period of low spreads in the mid-2000s, average primary market spreads of both investment grade and leveraged syndicated loans rose sharply in late 2008, although by less than those on similarly rated corporate bonds. Towards the end of 2008, BBB-rated syndicated loan spreads reached 400 bps, compared with about 750 bps on corporate bonds with the same rating. However, while corporate bond spreads have fallen

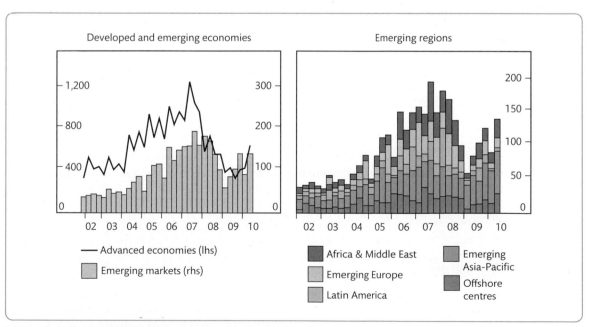

Figure 4.9 Gross syndicated loan issuance (in $bn)
Source: Chui *et al*. (2010).

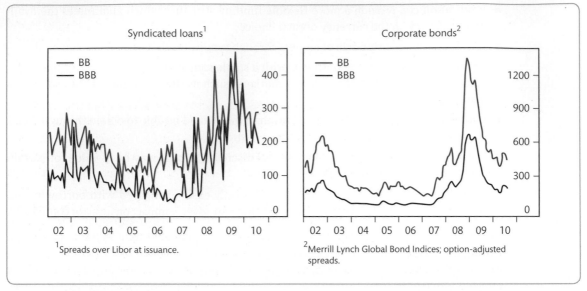

Figure 4.10 Syndicated loans and corporate bonds spreads
Source: Chui *et al*. (2010).

significantly since early 2009, syndicated loan spreads seem to have remained wide until recently (see Figure 4.10).

4.6.3 New credit products and securitisation

The growing corporate emphasis on capital market financing is also driving the development of a wider range of 'new' credit products (see also Chapter 18). For instance, corporate debt is widely traded in the US, as bonds, syndicated loans or securitised assets – loans that are bundled together and sold as a security in the market. In the US, a broad array of loans is being securitised, including corporate loans, mortgages, credit card receivables, computer leases and so on. The growth in credit derivatives business has also helped boost the market for tradable corporate credit products. Credit derivatives are tradable instruments that can be used to manage credit risk – the likelihood of default. The growth of such business means that nowadays around 50–60 per cent of all credits to US firms are tradable. This contrasts with the situation in Europe, where around 20 per cent of credits are tradable.

European corporate bond markets have long been underdeveloped compared with the US and up until the credit crisis many analysts predicted that there would be rapid growth of this business, although the market has stalled since mid-2007.

4.7 Conclusion

This chapter provides an insight to the reasons as to why banks undertake international business and highlights the evolution of foreign bank activity. It can be seen that a major feature of international banking is to provide commercial and investment banking and other services to global companies as well as to undertake a range of commercial banking and other activities in overseas markets. In terms of the products and services offered to large international companies, banks provide payments and treasury management services and also facilitate access to international financing, either short term via the Eurocurrency markets or longer term via bond, equity and syndicated lending markets.

International banks and corporations have benefited substantially from the growth in securitisation activity and structured credit products that have enabled them to raise funds and restructure their credit books. Access to credit ballooned up until the onset of the credit crisis in mid-2007. The securitisation of credits, international lending, syndicated lending and bond financing fell dramatically over 2008 and 2009 but has increased since then to recover to a market size of $3.7 trillion by the end of 2014. We have also noted that foreign bank presence has grown markedly and can take various forms. The range of services on offer can vary substantially from bank to bank. It is important to remember that international banking activity nowadays spans the full spectrum of the financial services industry and incorporates a wide range of players. Foreign banks are present in nearly every country and their importance had generally increased up to the start of the credit crisis.

Since 2008, many major banks have sought to boost their capital positions and therefore have been looking at ways to raise large amounts of cash quickly. As a consequence they have considered divesting some of their 'non-essential' international activities. This is a common feature of banking crises in general – when the Japanese banking industry suffered losses in the 1990s it divested foreign assets to concentrate on domestic business (as did US banks in the mid-1980s savings and loans crisis). It is highly likely that many international banks will seek to raise capital via this route and it is likely to stem the foreign expansion of US and European institutions in the near future.

Key terms

Agency	Correspondent	Geographical	Modern international
Arbitrage	banking	diversification	banking
Arranger	Cost of capital	Hire services (hire	Multinational banking
Best efforts	Countertrade	purchase)	Ownership
syndication	Credit facilities	Horizontal FDI	advantage
Bond	Eurocurrency	Information memo	Product
Branch	Eurocurrency	Innovative (or new	diversification
Cash management	banking	product) stage	Product life cycle
and transaction	Euroequity	Invoice discounting	Production diffusion
services	Excess managerial	services	Representative office
Club deal	capacity	Leasing	Standardised
Collateralised debt	Factoring	Letters of credit	product
obligations (CDOs)	Firm-specific	Location advantages	Subsidiary
Collateralised	advantages	Market flex	Traditional foreign
loan obligations	Foreign direct	language	banking
(CLOs)	investment (FDI)	Mature product	Underwritten deal
Colonial banks	Forfaiting	stage	Vertical FDI

Key reading

Chui, M., Domanski, D., Kugler, P. and Shek, J. (2010) 'The collapse of international finance during the crisis: Evidence from syndicated loan markets', *BIS Quarterly Review*, September, 39–49.

Claessen, S. and van Horen, N. (2012) 'Foreign banks: Trends, impact and financial stability', IMF Working Paper, WP/12/10.

Claessen, S. and van Horen, N. (2014) 'Location decisions of foreign banks and competitor remoteness', *Journal of Money, Credit and Banking*, 46(1), 145–170.

Fiechter, J., Ötker-Robe, I., Ĺyina, A., Hsu, M., Santos, A. and Surti, J. (2011) 'Subsidiaries or branches: Does one size fit all?', IMF Staff Discussion Note, March (SDN/11/04).

McCauley, R., McGuire, P. and von Peter, G. (2010) 'The architecture of global banking: From international to multinational?', *BIS Quarterly Review*, Bank for International Settlements, March, 25–37.

REVISION QUESTIONS AND PROBLEMS

4.1 In what ways does traditional foreign banking differ from Eurocurrency banking?

4.2 Why do banks go overseas? What are the main theories on the rationale for international banking?

4.3 Explain the main strategic reasons why banks may wish to establish foreign operations.

4.4 What do correspondent banking relationships involve?

4.5 Explain why banks engage in syndicated lending. Use information from the most recent BIS 'Annual Report' to illustrate your answer.

4.6 Discuss the different stages of a syndicated lending process.

4.7 Outline the main type of bonds that an international banking institution can issue.

4.8 What is a Euroequity issue?

4.9 In what way(s) can the banking sector provide trade finance that helps facilitate the import and export of goods for firms involved in international trading?

4.10 Explain the impact of the 2007–2009 financial crisis on international bank lending.

Appendix

Term	
Agen...	...nk per annum, payable by the borrower to ...rational work performed by that bank under the
Arrange...	...riginating and syndicating a transaction. The ... is also the agent and, if required, usually ...pating, although not always at the most
Availability...	...nt and the expiry of the lender's commitment ...w down advances or, if applicable, issue ...ent have been satisfied and the repeated
AXE sheet	...of borrower, type of facility, term of facility
Basis point (b...	...ent used to describe fees or spreads in
Bookrunner	...ution phase of syndication, with ...ssminating information to interested banks and informing ...he management group of underwriters of daily progress. It is a high-profile ...and it is generally considered the most desirable syndication task.
Bracket	A level of commitment and related title offered to banks and other investors invited into a syndicated loan agreement.
Bullet	A facility where the repayment is in one amount on the final maturity date of the syndicated agreement.
Clear market	An agreement by a borrower at the mandate stage of a syndicated loan not to engage in other public financings that could compete with the syndicated loan being arranged.
Club loan	A loan where a group of lenders agrees to take and hold an asset at the outset of the transaction with no intention of reducing its commitments through subsequent syndication.
Collateral	The particular assets of a borrower that are pledged to secure a loan(s) provided to it.
Commitment fee	An annual percentage fee payable to a bank on the undrawn portion of a committed loan facility. Typically paid quarterly in arrears.
Extension fee	The fee charged when an existing committed facility is extended beyond the original maturity date.
Facility fee	An annual percentage fee, payable by the borrower, pro rata to banks providing a credit facility to that borrower. It is calculated on the full amount of the facility, whether or not the facility is utilised.
Front-end fee	A fee, calculated as a percentage of the principal amount, that is payable once, generally at signing of the loan agreement or shortly thereafter.
General syndication	The syndication stage following the underwriting of a facility leading to the final distribution of amounts among the lenders participating in the primary stage of a syndicated loan.
Grace period	The period between signing the loan agreement and the first repayment of principal. Also, the period during which a borrower may be allowed to remedy an event of default.
Haircut	A situation where a borrower has fallen into financial difficulties and lenders have agreed to accept a reduction in interest and/or fees, or, on occasions, principal itself, to help prevent the borrower falling into bankruptcy. Also a situation where a borrower has fallen into financial difficulty and a lender has decided to sell its exposure in the secondary market at a significant discount to its par value.

Appendix 4.1 continued

Term	Explanation
IM	Information memo. A document describing the terms of the transactions. The IM typically will include an executive summary, investment considerations, a list of terms and conditions, an industry overview and a financial model. Also known as the bank book.
Intercreditor agreement	A document that sets out the agreement between various financiers providing loans or credits to a borrower and reconciles their different interests. It deals with the commercial behaviour of the parties and also the ranking of their debt and security, particularly on insolvency, by subordinating junior lenders and regulating the rights of lenders.
Investment grade	A borrower, or the specific debt instrument or class of debt of a borrower, given a rating from one of the major rating agencies of Baa3/BBB − or higher.
Jumbo	A very large syndicated loan, usually defined as a loan in excess of €5 billion or US$5 billion or equivalent.
Know Your Customer (KYC)	Various checks and investigations required of your customers as part of the procedures to prevent money laundering.
Lead manager	A bank committing to a senior level of participation.
Leveraged loan	A loan that has higher levels of debt leverage when compared with an investment grade credit. Various institutions may define a leveraged loan in different ways, although it is reasonably common to be determined against a bank loan rating (i.e. Ba1/BB+ or lower from one or more of the major rating agencies), or, for non-rated borrowers, a margin of around 125 to 150 bps p.a. or more.
Loan credit default swaps (LCDS)	A product that is similar to credit default swaps (CDS) but referenced against loans. This is a relatively new product and steps to standardise processes are being considered by market players. Note: there are differing contracts for European and US LCDS.
Mandated lead arranger (MLA)	A mandated bank at the highest level. The MLA, or at least one MLA in cases when there is more than one MLA, will act as the bookrunner.
Margin	The extra percentage rate of interest charged by lenders over the relevant basis rate reflecting the credit quality of the borrower.
Market flex	Underwriters' right to revise the structure and conditions of a mandate if the syndication of a loan fails to raise the required level of commitment from participants.
Material adverse change (MAC)	A reference to a clause sometimes included in loan agreements seeking to provide lenders with a degree of protection against adverse change in a borrower's circumstances.
On the break	The point in time when a syndicated loan becomes free to trade.
Out of the box	The pricing on a facility as notified to the market at the start of primary syndication.
Participation	A single lender's share of the overall loan facility.
Participation fee	A credit-related fee; normally paid on or within 30 days of signing, calculated on each bank's final allocated commitment. Also commonly known as a front-end fee.
Praecipium	A portion of the front-end fee, calculated on the nominal amount of the loan and paid to the MLA in recognition of the human resources and technical skills commitment required to conclude a successful transaction. In any multi-bank bidding group, the fee is usually shared equally among the MLAs without regard to the unequal commitment of resources to the transaction.
Pricing grid	When a borrower agrees to pay a margin and, where applicable, a commitment fee, the levels of which vary by reference to a specific financial ratio (e.g. leverage) or external credit rating, the transaction is said to include a pricing grid.
Private placement	A group of lenders which agrees to take and hold an asset at the outset of the transaction. There is no intention of reducing the amount of the commitment to lend through subsequent syndication. In a loan market context this is often referred to as a 'take and hold' strategy or a 'club loan'.
Ratchet	The movement from one pricing level to another on the pricing grid.

Appendix 4.1 continued

Term	Explanation
Snooze you lose	A clause in the loan agreement that disenfranchises a lender's voting right in relation to a specific amendment or waiver request if that lender has not responded to the agent within a certain pre-defined period of time.
Transfer fee	The fee charged by an agent bank for transferring a portion of a loan from one lender of record to another lender of record.
Underwriter	A lender that commits in advance of drawdown to take on a portion of the overall facility.
Underwriting fee	The fee charged by an underwriter. It is calculated on the basis of the amount committed.
Utilisation fee	A fee paid to the lender to increase its return on drawn assets. The payment is generally linked to the average utilisation of the facility exceeding a specified percentage or amount during a defined period of time.
Yank the bank	A clause in a loan agreement permitting the borrower(s) to buy out a lender who does not accept a waiver or amendment request to the loan agreement.
YTD	Year to date.

Source: Adapted from Loan Market Association, **www.lma.eu.com/uploads/files/Syndicated_Loan_glossary[1].pdf** © Loan Market Association (LMA). All Rights Reserved.

PART 2

Central banking and bank regulation

Chapter 5

Theory of central banking

Learning objectives

- To understand the crucial role of central banks in the financial sector
- To describe the main functions of the central bank
- To understand the monetary policy functions of central banks
- To understand the arguments put forward by the free banking theorists
- To discuss the arguments for and against an independent central bank
- To understand the relevance of central banks during financial crises

5.1 Introduction

The core functions of central banks in any countries are to manage monetary policy with the aim of achieving **price stability**, to prevent liquidity crises, situations of money market disorders and financial crises, and to ensure the smooth functioning of the payments system. This chapter explores these issues and focuses in particular on the conduct of monetary policy, distinguishing between instruments, targets and goals. Furthermore, it examines some basic concepts as they relate to central banking theory. Specifically, the chapter investigates the following fundamental areas:

- What are the monetary policy functions of a central bank?
- Why do banks need a central bank?
- Should central banks be independent from government?

The chapter presents an introduction to these topics. The specific functions, organisation and roles of the Bank of England (BoE), the European Central Bank (ECB) and the US Federal Reserve System (Fed) are described in Chapter 6.

5.2   What are the main functions of a central bank?

A central bank can generally be defined as a financial institution responsible for overseeing the monetary system for a nation, or a group of nations, with the goal of fostering economic growth without inflation. The main functions of a central bank can be listed as follows:

1 The central bank controls the issue of notes and coins (legal tender). Usually, the central bank will have a monopoly on the issue, although this is not essential as long as the central bank has power to restrict the amount of private issues of notes and coins.

2 It has the power to control the amount of credit-money created by banks. In other words, it has the power to control, by either direct or indirect means, the money supply.

3 A central bank should also have some control over non-bank financial intermediaries that provide credit.

4 Encompassing both points 2 and 3, the central bank should effectively use the relevant tools and instruments of monetary policy in order to control:
   (a) credit expansion;
   (b) liquidity; and
   (c) the money supply of an economy.

5 The central bank should oversee the financial sector in order to prevent crises and act as a **lender of last resort (LOLR)** in order to protect depositors, prevent widespread panic withdrawals and otherwise prevent the damage to the economy caused by the collapse of financial institutions.

6 A central bank acts as the government's banker. It holds the government's bank account and performs certain traditional banking operations for the government, such as deposits and lending. In its capacity as banker to the government it can manage and administer the country's national debt.

7 The central bank also acts as the official agent to the government in dealing with all its gold and foreign exchange matters. The government's reserves of gold and foreign exchange are held at the central bank. A central bank, at times, intervenes in the foreign exchange markets at the behest of the government in order to influence the exchange value of the domestic currency.

Central banks differ from country to country in their organisation and structure as well as in the specific tasks carried out; their main task nowadays is to carry out a country's monetary policy function. Central banks usually also have important financial stability functions, which become more prominent during times of financial turmoil. Figure 5.1 summarises the weight of central bank objectives in central bank laws for nearly 50 central banks – it is apparent that objectives related to monetary policy are far more frequent than objectives related to other functions. Section 5.3 briefly introduces monetary policy objectives.

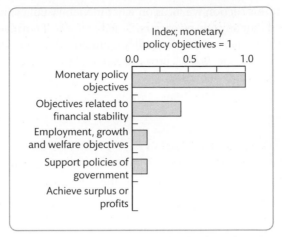

Figure 5.1 Weight of central bank objectives in central bank laws

Source: Bank for International Settlements (2009b) p. 21.

5.3   How does monetary policy work?

There are five major forms of economic policy (or, more strictly, macroeconomic policy) conducted by governments that are of relevance. These are monetary policy, fiscal policy, exchange rate policy, prices and incomes policy, and national debt management policy.

- **Monetary policy** is concerned with the actions taken by central banks to influence the availability and cost of money and credit by controlling some measure (or measures) of the money supply and/or the level and structure of interest rates.[1]

- **Fiscal policy** relates to changes in the level and structure of government spending and taxation designed to influence the economy. As all government expenditure must be financed, these decisions also, by definition, determine the extent of public sector borrowing or debt repayment. An expansionary fiscal policy means higher government spending relative to taxation. The effect of these policies would be to encourage more spending and boost the economy. Conversely, a contractionary fiscal policy means raising taxes and cutting spending.

- **Exchange rate policy** involves the targeting of a particular value of a country's currency exchange rate, thereby influencing the flows within the balance of payments. In some countries it may be used in conjunction with other measures such as exchange controls, import tariffs and quotas.[2]

- A **prices and incomes policy** is intended to influence the inflation rate by means of either statutory or voluntary restrictions upon increases in wages, dividends and/or prices.

- **National debt management policy** is concerned with the manipulation of the outstanding stock of government debt instruments held by the domestic private sector with the objective of influencing the level and structure of interest rates and/or the availability of reserve assets to the banking system.

---

[1] See also Appendix A1.

[2] Note that exchange controls, tariffs and quotas are restricted or forbidden under a number of trade agreements (such as those implemented by the EU and the World Trade Organization).

In this section we focus on what monetary policy involves. However, it must be remembered that any one policy mentioned above will normally form part of a policy package, and that the way in which that policy is employed will be dependent upon the other components of that package. Box 5.1 provides essential background reading for this section on the concept and functions of **money**.

BOX 5.1 THE CONCEPT AND FUNCTIONS OF MONEY AND MONETARY AGGREGATES

In general, money is represented by the coins and notes that we use in our daily lives; it is the commodity readily acceptable by all people wishing to undertake transactions. It is also a means of expressing a value for any kind of goods or service. For economists, money is referred to as 'money supply' and includes anything that is accepted in payment for goods and services or in the repayment of debts.

In an economic system money serves four main functions: 1) medium of exchange; 2) unit of account; 3) store of value; and 4) standard of deferred payment.

1 **Medium of exchange** is probably the main function of money. If barter were the only type of trade possible, there would be many situations in which people would not be able to obtain the goods and services that they wanted most. The advantage of the use of money is that it provides the owner with generalised purchasing power. The use of money gives the owner flexibility over the type and quantities of goods they buy, the time and place of their purchases, and the parties with whom they choose to deal. A critical characteristic of a medium of exchange is that it be acceptable as such. It must be readily exchangeable for other things. It is usual for the government to designate certain coins or paper currency as the medium of exchange.

2 If money is acceptable as a medium of exchange it almost certainly comes to act as a **unit of account** by which the prices of all commodities can be defined and then compared. This, of course, simplifies the task of deciding how we wish to divide our income between widely disparate items. For this reason it is sometimes said that money acts as a measure of value, and this is true if value is taken to mean both price and worth, the latter being a much more subjective concept.

3 Money is also a liquid **store of value** in that it provides individuals with a means of holding and accumulating their wealth in a form that can, at any time, be converted immediately into goods and services. When a person holds money as a store of value they are effectively treating it as a substitute for holding alternative forms of financial assets such as bonds or deposit accounts. The holder of money therefore foregoes the payment of an explicit yield in return for the acceptance of an implicit yield in the form of convenience and certainty.

4 Money can also act as a **standard of deferred payment**. Due to this function it is possible to undertake a number of transactions in the present and actually settle the account (or bill) at some time in the future, e.g. buy now and pay later. The production and sale of goods is made easier by money performing this function since goods and services can be acquired prior to payment being made. Because money acts as a standard of deferred payment, labour, raw materials and other goods and services can be acquired and the various parties will know the sums involved and payments to be made at a future date. Although this particular function of money is not essential for lending, borrowing and production to take place, it certainly makes such activities easier. Money's function as a standard for deferred payment may be questioned in times of high inflation where the real value of money declines rapidly. In such situations the debtor would benefit from a deferred payment. However, the meaning of the function of money as a standard for deferred payment is that it permits commercial lending to take place. A borrower can agree that if a lender supplies him with ten units of money today, he will pay back eleven units in (say) three months' time. The charging of interest has become possible.

BOX 5.1 The concept and functions of money and monetary aggregates (*continued*)

The formal definition of what constitutes money is summarised by central banks' definitions of what they call **monetary aggregates**. In the UK, for example, official estimates of the money supply have been published since 1966. The earliest definition of the money supply was a broad one covering notes and coin held by UK non-banks and deposits (in both sterling and foreign currency) held by UK residents with banks in the United Kingdom. Since 1970, this definition has been amended and supplemented on a number of occasions, reflecting developments in the financial system and policy. Common practice among central banks is to construct monetary aggregates from a list of monetary assets by adding together those that are considered to be likely sources of monetary services. The monetary aggregates play a role in the formulation of the monetary policy. In the UK, M0 is the narrowest measure of money stock and M4 the broadest.

M0 = Sterling notes and coin in circulation
+ Banks' operational deposits with the Bank of England

M4 = Notes and coin held by the private sector in sterling
+ Private sector £ non-interest-bearing sight bank deposits
+ Private sector £ interest-bearing sight and time bank deposits
+ Private sector holdings of £ certificates of deposit
+ Private sector holdings of building society shares and deposits and £ certificates of deposit
+ Building society holdings of bank deposits and bank certificates of deposit and notes and coins.

Note that sight deposits include funds that can be converted immediately and without restrictions into cash (see also Chapter 2); time deposits are funds that are deposited at a bank for a fixed period of time and that the depositor cannot access until the end of an agreed period (e.g. 30- and 60-day savings accounts). Certificates of deposit are negotiable certificates confirming that a (usually large) deposit has been made for a specified period of time with a bank.

M4 can be analysed either in terms of its components—cash and deposits—or of its asset counterparts, which represent the other side of the banks' and building societies' balance sheets (and must, as an accounting identity, sum to the same). These counterparts include banks' and building societies' lending to the private sector and their transactions with the public sector and with overseas residents.

The European Central Bank's definition of monetary aggregates is slightly different from the Bank of England's detailed above. In line with international practice, the euro-system has defined a narrow aggregate (M1), an 'intermediate' aggregate (M2) and a broad aggregate (M3). These aggregates differ with regard to the degree of 'moneyness' of the assets included. These are defined as follows:

- **Narrow money (M1)** includes currency (i.e. bank notes and coins), as well as balances that can immediately be converted into currency or used for cashless payments (i.e. overnight deposits).

- **Intermediate money (M2)** comprises narrow money (M1) and deposits with a maturity of up to two years and deposits redeemable at a period of notice of up to three months. The definition of M2 reflects the particular interest in analysing and monitoring a monetary aggregate that, in addition to currency, consists of deposits that are liquid.

- **Broad money (M3)** comprises M2 and marketable instruments issued by the MFI sector. Certain money market instruments, in particular money market fund (MMF) shares/units and repurchase agreements, are included in this aggregate. A high degree of liquidity and price certainty makes these instruments close substitutes for deposits. As a result of their inclusion, M3 is less affected by substitution between various liquid asset categories than narrower definitions of money and is therefore more stable.

See Table 5.1.

BOX 5.1 The concept and functions of money and monetary aggregates (*continued*)

Table 5.1 Definitions of euro area monetary aggregates

Liabilities	M1	M2	M3
Currency in circulation	x	x	x
Overnight deposits	x	x	x
Deposits with an agreed maturity of up to 2 years		x	x
Deposits redeemable at a period of notice up to 3 months		x	x
Repurchase agreements			x
Money market fund shares/units			x
Debt securities up to 2 years			x

Sources: Adapted from Bank of England (2007b) and from 'The ECB's definition of euro area monetary aggregates', **www.ecb.int/stats/money/aggregates/aggr/html/hist.en.html**

Monetary policy relates to the control of some measure (or measures) of the money supply and/or the level and structure of interest rates. Nowadays much greater emphasis is placed on monetary policy within a government's policy package. This is because a broad consensus has emerged that suggests that price stability is an essential pre-condition for achieving the central economic objective of high and stable levels of growth and employment. Monetary policy is viewed as the preferred policy choice for influencing prices.

Although traditionally the choice of monetary policy over fiscal policy as the main policy tool was viewed as a matter of ideology, today it is seen more as a pragmatic solution. As it is widely recognised that high and variable inflation harms long-term growth and employment, policy makers have tended to focus on those policies that appear to be most successful in dampening inflationary pressures. Price stability, therefore, has become a key element of economic strategy, and monetary policy is widely accepted as the most appropriate type of policy to influence prices and price expectations.

The preference for using monetary policy over other types of policy relates to two main factors – the role of the monetary authorities (central banks) as sole issuers of banknotes and bank reserves (known as the monetary base) and the long-run neutrality of money (see below).

The central bank is the monopoly supplier of the monetary base and as a consequence can determine the conditions at which banks borrow from the central bank. The central bank can influence liquidity in the short-term money markets and so can determine the conditions at which banks buy and sell short-term wholesale funds. By influencing short-term money market rates, the central bank influences the price of liquidity in the financial system and this ultimately can impact on various economic variables such as output or prices.

In the long run a change in the quantity of money in the economy will be reflected in a change in the general level of prices but it will have no permanent influence on real variables such as the level of (real) output or unemployment. This is known as the *long-run neutrality of money*. The argument goes that real income or the level of employment are, in the long term, determined solely by real factors, such as technology, population growth or the preferences of economic agents. Inflation is therefore solely a monetary phenomenon.

As a consequence, in the long run:

● a central bank can contribute to raising the growth potential of the economy only by maintaining an environment of stable prices;

- economic growth cannot be increased through monetary expansion (increased money supply) or by keeping short-term interest rates at levels inconsistent with price stability.

In the past it has been noted that long periods of high inflation are usually related to high monetary growth. While various other factors (such as variations in aggregate demand, technological changes or commodity price shocks) can influence price developments over the short period, over time these influences can be offset by a change in monetary policy.

5.4 Monetary policy functions of a central bank

The most important function of any central bank is to undertake monetary control operations. Typically, these operations aim to administer the amount of money (money supply) in the economy and differ according to the monetary policy objectives they intend to achieve. These latter are determined by the government's overall macroeconomic policies (see Box 5.2).

Typically, the most important long-term monetary target of a central bank is price stability that implies low and stable inflation levels. As shown in Figure 5.2, such a long-term goal can be attained only by setting short-term *operational targets*. Operational targets are usually necessary to achieve a particular level of interest rates, commercial banks' reserves or exchange rates.

BOX 5.2 MONETARY POLICY OBJECTIVES

Monetary policy is one of the main policy tools used to influence interest rates, inflation and credit availability through changes in the supply of money (or liquidity) available in the economy. It is important to recognise that monetary policy constitutes only one element of an economic policy package and can be combined with a variety of other types of policy (e.g. fiscal policy) to achieve stated economic objectives. Historically, monetary policy has, to a certain extent, been subservient to fiscal and other policies involved in managing the macro economy, but nowadays it can be regarded as the main policy tool used to achieve various stated economic policy objectives (or goals).

The main objectives of economic (and monetary) policy include the following:

- **High employment** – often cited as a major goal of economic policy. A high level of unemployment results in the economy having idle resources that leads to lower levels of production and income, lower growth and possible social unrest. However, this does not necessarily mean that zero unemployment is a preferred policy goal. A certain level of unemployment is often felt to be necessary for the efficient operation of a dynamic economy. It will take people a period of time to switch between jobs, or to retrain for new jobs, and so on – so even near full employment there may be people switching jobs who are temporarily out of work. This is known as *frictional unemployment*. In addition, unemployment may be a consequence of mismatch in skills between workers and what employers want – known as *structural unemployment*. (Typically, although structural unemployment is undesirable, monetary policy cannot alleviate this type of unemployment.) The goal of high employment, therefore, does not aim to achieve zero unemployment but seeks to obtain a level above zero that is consistent with matching the demand and supply of labour. This level is known as the *natural rate of unemployment*. Milton Friedman (1968) defined the natural rate of unemployment as the level of unemployment that resulted from real economic forces, the long-run level of which could not be altered by monetary policy. There is a large economic literature on measuring the natural rate of unemployment, although with little consensus on a measure, as shifts in local labour market conditions, and changes in both labour supply and labour demand, can influence the natural rate of unemployment.

BOX 5.2 Monetary policy objectives (*continued*)

- **Price stability** – considered an essential objective of economic policy, given the general wish to avoid the costs associated with inflation. Price stability is viewed as desirable because rising price levels create uncertainty in the economy and this can adversely affect economic growth. Many economists (but by no means all) argue that low inflation is a necessary prerequisite for achieving sustainable economic growth.

- **Stable economic growth** – provides for the increases over time in the living standards of the population. The goal of steady economic growth is closely related to that of high employment because firms are more likely to invest when unemployment is low – when unemployment is high and firms have idle production they are unlikely to want to invest in building more plants and factories. The rate of economic growth should be at least comparable to the rates experienced by similar nations.

- **Interest rate stability** – another desirable economic objective because volatility in interest rates creates uncertainty about the future and this can adversely impact on business and consumer investment decisions (such as the purchase of a house). Expected higher interest rate levels deter investment because they reduce the present value of future cash flows to investors and increase the cost of finance for borrowers.

- **Financial market stability** – also an important objective of public policy and one major concern of central banks. A collapse of financial markets can have major adverse effects on an economy. The crisis that hit the global financial system in 2007–2009 caused a sharp contraction in output, weakened the effectiveness of the transmission mechanism (Box 5.5) and contributed to inefficient capital allocation. A similar crisis occurred in 1929, when the Wall Street Crash in the US resulted in a fall of manufacturing output by 50 per cent and an increase in unemployment to 25–30 per cent of the US workforce by 1932. (More than 11,000 banks closed over this period.) Such major crises may be rare, but they do highlight the serious consequences of financial crises. A less dramatic example of how policy makers view the adverse effects of

a crisis in financial markets relates to the case of the US-based hedge fund Long-Term Capital Management. In September 1998 the US Federal Reserve organised a rescue of Long-Term Capital Management, a large and prominent hedge fund on the brink of failure. The monetary authorities intervened because they were concerned about the serious consequences for world financial markets if they allowed the hedge fund to fail. Note that financial market stability is influenced by stability of interest rates because increases in interest rates can lead to a decrease in the value of bonds and other investments, resulting in losses in the holders of such securities.

- **Stability in foreign exchange markets** – has become a policy goal of increasing importance, especially in the light of greater international trade in goods, services and capital. A rise in the value of a currency makes exports more expensive (an increase in the value of sterling relative to the dollar means that consumers in the United States have to pay more for UK goods), whereas a decline in the value of a currency leads to domestic inflation (if sterling declines relative to the dollar, US goods sold in the United Kingdom become more expensive). Extreme adverse movements in a currency can therefore have a severe impact on exporting industries and can also have serious inflationary consequences if the economy is open and relatively dependent on imported goods. Ensuring the stability of foreign exchange markets is therefore seen as an appropriate goal of economic policy.

At first glance it may appear that all these policy objectives are consistent with each other; however, conflicts do arise. The objective of price stability can conflict with the objectives of interest rate stability and full employment (at least in the short run) because as an economy grows and unemployment declines, this may result in inflationary pressures forcing up interest rates. If the monetary authorities do not let interest rates increase, this could fuel inflationary pressures, yet if they do increase rates then unemployment may occur. These sorts of conflicts create difficulties for the authorities in conducting monetary and other macroeconomic policy.

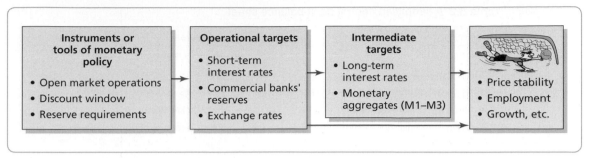

Figure 5.2 Monetary policy instruments, targets and goals

Often they are complemented by *intermediate targets* such as a certain level of long-term interest rates or broad money growth (monetary aggregates). In choosing the intermediate targets, policy makers should take into account the stability of money demand and the controllability of the monetary aggregate. The chosen target should also be a good indicator of the effect of the monetary policy decision on the price stability target. Broad aggregates normally show higher stability and display better indicator properties than narrow aggregates. In contrast, in the short term narrow aggregates are easier to control via official interest rates than broad aggregates. Although central banks cannot use monetary policy instruments directly to affect intermediate targets, they can use them to affect operating targets, such as reserve money and short-term interest rates, which influence movements in intermediate variables.

Let us now focus on the tools or instruments of monetary policy. In the past, it was common for central banks to exercise direct controls on bank operations by setting limits either on the quantity of deposits and credits (e.g. ceilings on the growth of bank deposits and loans) or on their prices (by setting maximum bank lending or deposit rates). As a result of the significant financial liberalisation process aimed at achieving an efficient allocation of financial resources in the economy, there has been a movement away from direct monetary controls towards indirect ones (Gray and Talbot, 2006).

Indirect instruments influence the behaviour of financial institutions by affecting initially the central bank's own balance sheet. In particular the central bank will control the price or volume of the supply of its own liabilities (reserve money) that in turn may affect interest rates more widely and the quantity of money and credit in the whole banking system.

To understand how a central bank can direct and control the money supply through indirect instruments it is essential to first evaluate the role and importance that the different classes of assets and liabilities detailed in its balance sheet have for monetary policy.

As with any other bank, the central bank has to produce a financial statement each year (for more details on banks' accounts see Chapter 9) and the items contained in its balance sheet do not differ substantially from those of commercial banks. Table 5.2 illustrates a simplified central bank balance sheet.

The asset side of the balance sheet of any central bank includes two asset types: net foreign reserves and domestic claims. These are typically represented by loans and advances (to banks and other institutions) and debt securities. On the liability side, it is possible to identify the so-called 'high-powered' money or monetary base (currency and reserves), other deposits of banks and other institutions (e.g. the government), the central bank's own securities and equity capital. This latter includes accumulated profits/losses and transfers of resources from the government.

Table 5.2 A simplified central bank balance sheet

Assets	Liabilities
Foreign assets	Reserve money
Domestic assets	Currency in circulation
Claims on government and public enterprises	Reserves of commercial banks
Claims on the private sector	Foreign liabilities
Claims on domestic money banks	Other deposits of commercial banks, etc.
Claims on other financial sector entities	Central bank securities, etc.
	Government deposits
	Others
	Equity capital

Source: Adapted from Filardo and Yetman (2011) Table 1.

Central banks' balance sheets have expanded markedly. Financial crises and economic downturns have resulted in unusual and/or extraordinary measures that are reflected in substantial changes in both the structure and size of central banks' balance sheets. In the UK, the money market reforms of 18 May 2006 and the measures implemented after the 2007–2009 crisis have had a substantial effect on the Bank of England's balance sheet. 'Unprecedented' expansion trends in central banks' balance sheet are found both in the developed (US and Eurozone) and the developing world, e.g. in Asia Pacific, with China leading the trend. In most cases changes have been driven by the growth in net foreign assets, particularly US dollar-denominated bonds. Box 5.3 reports selected balance sheet data for the Bank of England as published on 29 February 2012.

If we focus on the asset side, it is possible to see that the item 'other loans and advances' represents the most significant asset of the Bank of England (90.8 per cent), while on the liability side, deposits from banks and other financial institutions are the largest proportion (69.7 per cent). These latter are the reserve balances, i.e. current account balances held by commercial banks at the Bank of England. As discussed in Box 5.4, commercial banks earn an interest on their reserves that is equal to the Bank official rate and this represents a key part in the implementation of the UK's monetary policy. Since March 2009 there has been a sharp increase in reserves balances and this reflects the fact that asset purchases under the Monetary Policy Committee (MPC)'s policy of **quantitative easing (QE)** have been financed by increasing reserves balances (see Section 5.4.5 for a specific discussion of unconventional monetary policy tools). To steer the quantity towards the required target, the Bank of England uses its **open market operations (OMOs)**.

The indirect instruments used by central banks in monetary operations are generally classified into the following:

- open market operations;
- discount windows (also known as **standing facilities**);
- reserve requirements.

5.4.1 Debt securities and open market operations

Debt securities are mainly represented by Treasury securities (i.e. government debt) that central banks use in open market operations. These operations are the most important tools by which central banks can influence the amount of money in the economy.

BOX 5.3 BALANCE SHEET, BANK OF ENGLAND (2012)

	(£mil)
Assets	
Cash and balances with other central banks	372
Loans and advances to banks and other financial institutions	15,157
Other loans and advances	286,582
Securities held at fair value through profit and loss	4,782
Available for sale securities	5,340
Derivative financial instruments	461
Property, plant and equipment	218
Intangible assets	10
Retirement benefit assets	564
Other assets	1,986
Total assets (100%)	315,472
Liabilities	
Deposits from central banks	14,806
Deposits from banks and other financial institutions	217,623
Other deposits	70,163
Foreign currency bonds in issue	5,104
Derivative financial instruments	232
Current tax liabilities	44
Deferred tax liabilities	201
Retirement benefit liabilities	252
Other liabilities	3,660
Total liabilities (100%)	312,085
Equity	
Capital	15
Retained earnings	2,477
Other reserves	895
Total equity attributable to shareholder	3,387
Total liabilities and equity	315,472

Source: Bank of England (2012a).

Although the practical features of open market operations may vary from country to country, the principles are the same: the central bank operates in the market and purchases or sells government debt to the non-bank private sector. In general, if the central bank sells government debt, the money supply falls (all other things being equal) because money is taken out of bank accounts and other sources to purchase government securities. This leads to an increase in short-term interest rates. If the government purchases (buys back) government debt, this results in an injection of money into the system and short-term interest rates fall. As a result, the central bank can influence the portfolio of assets held by the private sector.

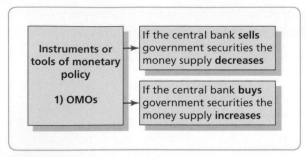

Figure 5.3 Open market operations

This will influence the level of liquidity within the financial system and will also affect the level and structure of interest rates.

The main attractions of using open market operations to influence short-term interest rates are that:

- they are initiated by the monetary authorities who have complete control over the volume of transactions;
- open market operations are flexible and precise – they can be used for major or minor changes to the amount of liquidity in the system;
- they can easily be reversed;
- open market operations can be undertaken quickly.

Open market operations are the most commonly used indirect instruments of monetary policy in developed economies. One of the main reasons for their widespread use relates to their flexibility in terms of both the frequency of use and scale (i.e. quantity) of activity. These factors are viewed as essential if the central bank wishes to fine-tune its monetary policy. In addition, OMOs have the advantage of not imposing a tax on the banking system.

In the United Kingdom, the Bank of England uses OMOs (buying and selling of securities) to supply, in aggregate, the reserves that banks need to meet their collected targets. However, the amount of reserves that the Bank of England aims to supply is affected by the banks' reserves targets as well as the expected impact of other factors that may influence the supply, such as an increase in the demand for banknotes (Bank of England, 2012a). The Bank of England may also supply banks with funds by using 'repo' agreements, i.e. sale and repurchase agreements relating to financial assets. For example, in gilt repo transactions, the Bank purchases gilt-edged securities from private sector counterparties with a legally binding commitment that the securities will be repurchased by the counterparties at a pre-determined price and date. Gilt repos are, in effect, cash loans with the gilt-edged securities used as collateral. While the stance of monetary policy is expressed as the level of the bank rate (see Box 5.4), under the current operational framework two types of open market operations can be used to supply reserves: short-term and long-term. The former are aimed to ensure that the Bank of England rate does not diverge from the interbank rate and to steer the quantity of reserves to the amount necessary for the banking system as a whole to meet its targets. The latter have been introduced to provide a sort of liquidity insurance as the Bank of England offers to lend reserves for longer periods against a broad range of collateral (Clews *et al.*, 2010).

5.4.2 Loans to banks and the discount window

The second most important monetary policy tool of a central bank is the so-called **discount window** (in the United Kingdom this tool is often referred to as 'standing facilities'). It is an instrument that allows eligible banking institutions to borrow money from the central bank, usually to meet short-term liquidity needs.

By changing the discount rate, that is, the interest rate that monetary authorities are prepared to lend to the banking system, the central bank can control the supply of money in the system. If, for example, the central bank is increasing the discount rate, it will be more expensive for banks to borrow from the central bank so they will borrow less, thereby causing the money supply to decline. Vice versa, if the central bank is decreasing the discount rate, it will be cheaper for banks to borrow from it so they will borrow more money (see Figure 5.4).

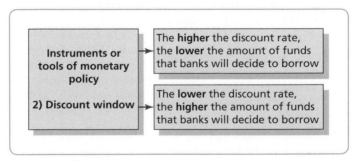

Figure 5.4 Discount window

BOX 5.4 BANK OF ENGLAND AND THE OFFICIAL INTEREST RATE

The Bank of England's Monetary Policy Committee (MPC) announces the interest rate decision the first Thursday of every month, reviewing the short-term 'official bank rate' (also referred to as 'policy rate' or 'base rate') in response to economic conditions. In the United Kingdom, the Bank Rate (0.5 per cent since March 2009) is the overnight interest rate at which the Bank of England lends to financial institutions. In setting this key rate, the Bank considers the amount at which banks borrow from each other overnight.

The official bank rate replaces the *repo rate* that was used prior to the May 2006 reforms to the Bank's framework for its operations in the sterling money market. These changes allow banks and building societies that hold cash ratio deposits (CRDs) at the Bank of England to place additional deposits overnight in an account at

the central bank.[3] These assets are called reserve balances and they represent claims on the central bank. Their role includes the following: 1) they are the most liquid risk-free assets in the economic system, together with banknotes; 2) they are the ultimate assets for settling payments between customers of different banks; and 3) they facilitate banks' liquidity management that derives from typical lending and borrowing bank activities. In recent years, as a result of the quantitative easing, the holding of reserves has increased significantly.

Since 2009 the Bank of England pays reserves balances an interest that is typically the bank rate. By doing so the Bank keeps market interest rates in line with the bank rate and establishes an important benchmark short-term risk-free rate. Banks can decide to change their holdings of reserves daily to meet day-to-day

---

[3] Cash ratio deposits (CRD) are non-interest-bearing deposits lodged with the Bank of England by eligible institutions (i.e. banks and building societies), which have reported average eligible liabilities (ELs) of more than £600 million over a calculation period. The level of each institution's CRD is calculated twice-yearly (currently in May and November) at 0.18 per cent of average ELs, over the previous six end-calendar months, in excess of £600 million. The value bands and ratios were specified by HM Treasury in the Cash Ratio Deposits (Value Bands and Ratios) Order 2013 (No. 1189).

BOX 5.4 Bank of England and the official interest rate (*continued*)

liquidity needs. The bank rate will affect the rates banks are willing to charge or pay on short-term loans or borrowing in the money market. In the longer term, money markets rates will be influenced by expectations about future bank rates. Consumer and business demand (i.e. the aggregate spending) will be affected by changes in the bank rate through several channels in the transmission mechanism of monetary policy, namely by changes in: 1) the deposit and lending rates charged by commercial banks and building societies; 2) financial assets prices (e.g. bonds and equities); and 3) exchange rates (for more details, see Box 5.5).

In this context, operational standing facilities (OSFs) have two roles:

1 To provide an arbitrage mechanism in normal market conditions to prevent money market rates moving far away from the bank rate (and therefore they are a vital part of implementing monetary policy).

2 To provide means for participating banks to manage unexpected payment shocks that may arise due to technical problems in banks' own systems or in the market-wide payments and settlements infrastructure.

The OSFs allow participating institutions to deposit reserves with or borrow reserves directly from the Bank on a bilateral basis throughout each business day. The operational standing lending facility takes the form of an overnight repo transaction against high-quality, highly liquid collateral. The operational standing deposit facility takes the form of an unsecured deposit with the Bank. On those terms, the OSFs are available in unlimited size. Commercial banks borrowing from the lending facility are required to pay a premium over bank rate, while those placing reserves in the deposit facility are remunerated at a rate below bank rate. Commercial banks will typically be unwilling to deal in the market on worse terms than those available at the Bank – for example, if market rates are above the lending facility rate, banks will tend to borrow from the Bank in preference to the market. So the OSF rates establish a corridor around bank rate and help limit volatility in overnight market interest rates while incentivising banks to manage their liquidity prudently. Figure 5.5 illustrates this mechanism.

Additional reading

Bank of England (2012b) 'The framework for the Bank of England's operations in the sterling money markets', June.

Clews, R., Salmon, C. and Weeken, O. (2010) 'The Bank's money market framework', *Quarterly Bulletin*, Bank of England, Q4.

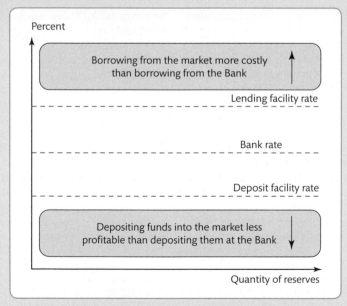

Figure 5.5 Bank of England operational standing facilities

Source: Bank of England (2012b) Extract from the 'Red Book: The Bank's current operations in the sterling money markets'. Available at **www.bankofengland .co.uk/markets/Documents/money/publications/redbookosf.pdf**

Table 5.3 Eurosystem monetary policy operation

Monetary policy operations	Types of transactions		Maturity	Frequency	Procedure
Open market operations					
Main refinancing operations	● Reverse transactions		1 week	Weekly	Standard tenders
Longer-term refinancing operations	● Reverse transactions		3 months	Monthly	Standard tenders
Fine-tuning operations	● Reverse transactions ● Foreign exchange swaps	● Reverse transaction ● Collection of fixed-term deposits ● Foreign exchange swaps	Non-standardised	Non-regular	Quick tenders Bilateral procedures
Structural operations	● Reverse transactions	● Issuance of ECB debt certificates	Standardised and non-standardised	Regular and non-regular	Standard tenders
Monetary policy operations	● Outright purchases	● Outright sales		Non-regular	Bilateral procedure
Standing facilities					
Marginal lending facility	● Reverse transactions		Overnight	Access at the discretion of counterparties	
Deposit facility		● Deposits	Overnight	Access at the discretion of counterparties	
Minimum reserves					

The Eurosystem requires credit institutions to hold minimum reserves on accounts with the national central banks. The reserve ratio is 2 per cent for the majority of the items for which the reserve base applies (deposits, debt securities and money market paper). Reserve holdings are remunerated at the Eurosystem's rate on its main refinancing operations.

Source: 'Guideline of the European Central Bank on Monetary Policy Instruments and Procedures in the Eurosystem' (2011) *Official Journal of the European Union* (L 331/17).

Manipulation of the discount rate can therefore influence short-term rates in the market. For instance, the eurozone's discount rate is known as a 'marginal lending facility', which offers overnight credit to banks from the Eurosystem. Table 5.3 summarises the Eurosystem monetary policy operations.

In the United States, when the Federal Reserve System was established (see Chapter 6), lending reserve funds through the discount window was intended to be the most important instrument of central banking operations, but it was soon replaced by open market operations. Indeed, today banks are discouraged from using this type of borrowing.[4] Direct lending to banks can also occur through the central bank's lender-of-last-resort function. By acting as an LOLR the central bank provides liquidity support directly to individual financial institutions if they cannot obtain finance from other sources. Therefore it can help to prevent financial panics. Some drawbacks of this function are discussed in Section 5.5.1.

---

[4] For more details, see **www.frbdiscountwindow.org/**

5.4.3   Reserve requirements

Banks need to hold a quantity of reserve assets for prudential purposes. If a bank falls to its minimum desired level of reserve assets it will have to turn away requests for loans or else seek to acquire additional reserve assets from which to expand its lending. The result in either case will generally be a rise in interest rates that will serve to reduce the demand for loans.

The purpose of any officially imposed **reserve requirements** is effectively to duplicate this process. If the authorities impose a reserve requirement in excess of the institutions' own desired level of reserves (or else reduce the availability of reserve assets), the consequence will be that the institutions involved will have to curtail their lending and/or acquire additional reserve assets. This will result in higher interest rates and a reduced demand for loans that, in turn, will curb the rate of growth of the money supply.

By changing the fraction of deposits that banks are obliged to keep as reserves, the central bank can control the money supply. This fraction is generally expressed in percentage terms and thus is called the *required reserve ratio*: the higher the required reserve ratio, the lower the amount of funds available to the banks. Vice versa, the lower the reserve ratio required by the monetary authorities, the higher the amount of funds available to the banks for alternative investments (see Figure 5.6).

The advantage of reserve requirements as a monetary policy tool is that they affect all banks equally and can have a strong influence on the money supply. However, the latter can also be a disadvantage, as it is difficult for the authorities to make small changes in money supply using this tool. Another drawback is that a call for greater reserves can cause liquidity problems for banks that do not have excess reserves.[5] If the authorities regularly make decisions about changing reserve requirements it can cause problems for the liquidity management of banks. In general, an increase in reserve requirements affects banks' ability to make loans and reduces potential bank profits because the central bank pays no interest on reserves.

In some countries, such as the United States, Japan and the eurozone, central banks use reserve requirements now and again as a monetary policy tool. However, in reality they are rarely used compared with OMOs and the discount window. In fact, various central banks (such as those in Switzerland, New Zealand and Australia) have eliminated them. The main reason for this is that the application of reserve ratios discriminates against banks (as other financial firms do not have to hold reserves at the central bank). Also many banks may have internal resources well in excess of minimum reserve requirements and so any call to increase reserves from the authorities can easily be achieved without affecting bank behaviour in a significant fashion.

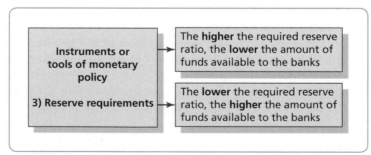

Figure 5.6 Reserve requirements

---

[5] 'Excess reserves' can be defined as additional reserves that banks decide to hold over the present mandatory requirements.

In the United Kingdom, compulsory reserve requirements were used during most of the post-war period but were abandoned as a monetary policy tool in the late 1970s especially as a result of the processes of deregulation and innovation. There are, however, compulsory *cash ratio deposits* – not used for monetary policy purposes – determined by the Bank of England that are non-interest-bearing deposits of eligible institutions (i.e. banks and building societies) that have reported average liabilities greater than £600 million over a calculation period. The level of CRD is calculated twice-yearly (currently in May and November) at 0.18 per cent of average eligible liabilities (see Box 5.4).

Reserve requirements are often referred to as **instruments of portfolio constraint**. It means that they may be imposed by the authorities on the portfolio structure of financial institutions, with the purpose of influencing credit creation and, possibly, the type of lending taking place. Other instruments of portfolio constraint that are potentially available for use include special deposits, moral suasion and direct controls.

5.4.4 Other instruments of portfolio constraint

5.4.4.1 Special deposits

In the United Kingdom, special deposits are deposits that the Bank of England may require from certain banking institutions. These deposits, equal to a specified proportion of certain elements of a bank's deposit liabilities, are then 'frozen' at the Bank of England and may not be used as part of the reserve asset base for lending purposes. While they are particularly discriminatory as regards the institutions to which they apply, they do have a rapid impact upon the ability of these institutions to create credit and are useful for drawing off any excess reserve assets within the system. At present, they are not used for monetary policy purposes. During the 1970s the Bank of England used a scheme known as 'supplementary special deposits'. These were deposits that banking institutions had to make at the Bank of England if the growth rate of some interest-bearing deposit liabilities exceeded an upper limit set by the Bank. The Bank of England operated this mechanism, referred to as the 'corset', on a periodic basis between 1973 and 1980. Institutions exceeding the specified growth rate for liabilities were required to make supplementary special deposits with the Bank on a scale dependent upon the extent of the overshoot. Supplementary special deposits could not be used as part of the reserve asset base by banks and they attracted no interest payment. The main objective of special deposits is to remove excess liquidity from the system if bank deposit growth (and therefore loan growth) is increasing too rapidly.

5.4.4.2 Moral suasion

Moral suasion refers to the range of informal requests and pressure that the authorities may exert over banking institutions. The extent to which this is a real power of the authorities relative to direct controls is open to question, since much of the pressure that the authorities would exert involves the institutions having to take actions that might not be in the bank's commercial interests. However, the position and potential power of the authorities probably provides them with some scope to use moral suasion, which may perhaps be utilised most effectively in the context of establishing lending priorities rather than absolute limits to credit creation.

5.4.4.3 Direct controls

Direct controls involve the authorities issuing directives in order to attain particular intermediate targets. For example, the monetary authorities might impose controls on interest rates payable on deposits, may limit the volume of credit creation or direct banks to prioritise lending according to various types of customer. Although these direct controls have the benefits of speed of implementation and precision, they are discriminating towards the institutions involved and are likely to lead to disintermediation as both potential borrowers and potential lenders seek to pursue their own commercial interests. Their use, therefore, is perhaps best reserved for short-term requirements, not least since their effectiveness will tend to decline the longer they are applied. Such controls, however, are widely used in many developing countries where the authorities may force banks to (say) lend a certain percentage of loan book to 'priority sectors'.

5.4.4.4 The decline in use of portfolio constraints

In contrast to market intervention instruments (OMOs and standing facilities), instruments of portfolio constraint tend to have a narrow and therefore distorting impact. Although in principle they could be applied to a wide range of financial institutions, in the past in the UK and in the US they have been applied only to banking institutions. The result of this is that banks have, in effect, been discriminated against. It should also be noted that disintermediation has often occurred as potential borrowers have sought alternative sources of funds, from outside of the monetary control regime.

As we noted in the case of reserve requirements, there has generally been a decline in the use of portfolio constraints as a tool of monetary policy in the world's largest economies (although they are still prevalent in many developing countries).

Portfolio constraints are less widely used in the developed world for the following reasons:

- Deregulation and increasing competition in the provision of financial services and products traditionally offered by banks have broadened considerably the number and type of institutions that would need to be brought within the control regime. Defining and implementing effective portfolio constraints would be difficult and open to controversy.

- Disintermediation, primarily involving large companies, has undermined portfolio constraints. By contrast, the use of market intervention allows the authorities to influence all relevant parts of the financial system, with monetary control coming via the price of credit.

- Throughout the 1950s, 1960s and 1970s, when portfolio constraints were used extensively, most countries maintained a system of foreign currency exchange control. This restriction on the movement of funds to and from abroad prevented borrowers from seeking finance from overseas when domestic monetary policy was restrictive. These exchange controls had the effect of supporting the portfolio constraints, but (for many countries) they now no longer exist, with the result that domestic borrowers have much greater scope to seek funds from overseas.

- Portfolio constraints are regarded as inimical to competition because they place restrictions, of one kind or another, on the business freedom and growth of banks and other intermediaries falling within the constraints. Also, markets are distorted and economic efficiency tends to be undermined.

BOX 5.5 MONETARY POLICY: TRANSMISSION MECHANISM, FIXED RULES AND DISCRETION

How does the monetary transmission mechanism work?

The **monetary transmission mechanism** consists of the several channels through which policy-induced changes in money supply and interest rates influence real economic activity and in particular the price level.

Understanding the channels through which monetary policy actions and strategies impact output and inflation and the time needed for a policy action to be effective is crucial for the design and implementation of sound monetary policy strategies (see Figure 5.7). The transmission mechanism of monetary policy includes several different channels.

Figure 5.8 shows that changes in the official interest rates first alter money market rates and the public's expectations. These in turn affect bank rates, asset prices, the availability of bank loans and the foreign exchange rate. Specifically:

1 The first indirect effect of a change in official bank rate is on the cost of borrowing. Changes in retail banks' rates for conventional financial products such as mortgages, loans and deposits have an impact on consumption and investment.

2 Another channel is through prices of financial and other assets. This is also known as wealth channel because higher interest rates depress bond, stock and real estate prices, thereby decreasing households' wealth.

3 A third channel is money and credit availability as higher interest rates increase borrowers' default risk so households and businesses may be subject to credit rationing, thus reducing their consumption and investments.

4 Finally, in an open market, changes in the official policy rate affect foreign exchange markets. For example, in the UK, an increase in interest rates relative to rates in other countries makes the pound stronger and more attractive to investors while British products become more expensive so their demand drops.

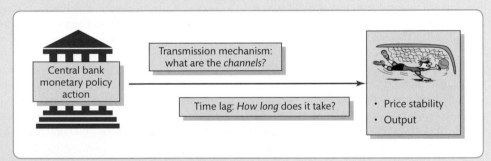

Figure 5.7 The key issues in monetary policy transmission

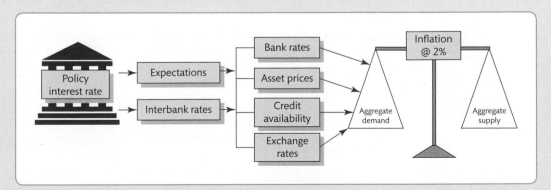

Figure 5.8 Channels of monetary policy transmission

BOX 5.5 Monetary policy: transmission mechanism, fixed rules and discretion (*continued*)

Figure 5.8 also shows that eventually changes in policy rate influence the overall spending in the economy, i.e. the aggregate demand (AD). This is the sum of consumers' spending (C), firms' investments (I), government spending (G) and net exports (NX) so that AD = C + I + G + NX. The general price levels are affected by the relationship between AD and the ability of the economy to supply them (aggregate supply, or AS). If AD > AS then prices will increase, so the monetary authorities may intervene to raise the policy rate to reduce growth and avoid inflation going above the government target (2 per cent in the UK at the time of writing). Vice versa, if AD < AS then monetary authorities may be inclined to ease monetary policy to stimulate spending and keep inflation from falling below the target.

To sum up, changes in monetary policy ultimately alter the propensity and the ability to consume and invest of households, businesses, the government and foreign economic agents and shift aggregate demand and supply. *How long* it takes for monetary policy actions to impact output and price levels depends on a number of factors, including 1) public expectations on long-term interest rates and inflation; and 2) the extent to which markets have been able to anticipate monetary policy actions and factor in future price increases.

While changes in policy rates affect bank rates, asset prices and exchange rates relatively quickly, the impact of monetary policy actions on output can take anything from three months to two years, and on inflation from one to three years or more (see Figure 5.9). This is why the central banks' decisions

typically have to be made with a view to the future, taking into account associated uncertainty.

How is monetary policy implemented?

Monetary authorities operate with almost complete discretion in the conduct of monetary policy. This means that although they are expected to achieve various goals in terms of sustainable economic growth, employment and price stability, current institutional settings enable them to freely weight and pursue these goals using their own judgement.

For example, the committee in charge of setting the US monetary policy (the Federal Open Market Committee or FOMC) meets eight times a year to evaluate the current state of the economy and assess the forecast of future economic and financial conditions. Based on these considerations, the FOMC sets the Federal fund rate and then the Fed adjusts the money supply to reach that interest rate target.

Some economists advocate that monetary policy made by a precise, legislated *rule* would be more successful in ensuring a stable macroeconomic environment than using discretionary powers. A classic example of a tight, fixed rule is Friedman's constant money (*k*%) growth rule.[6] As pointed out by Bernanke (2003), although they have never been implemented, 'rule-like monetary policy arrangements have existed in the real world', such as the international gold standard.

Although it is not in the remit of this textbook to go into the details of the rules vs. discretion debate over monetary policy, it is useful to summarise some of the most important pros and cons (see Table 5.4).

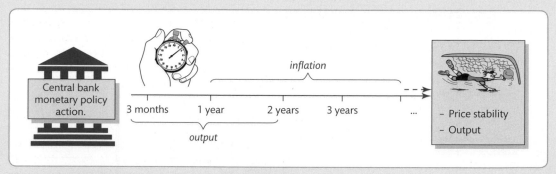

Figure 5.9 Transmission lags of monetary policy

---

[6] Friedman (1969). There are other well-known rules such as the Taylor rule and the McCallum rule. For more details see Bernanke (2003) and Mishkin (2011).

BOX 5.5 Monetary policy: transmission mechanism, fixed rules and discretion (*continued*)

Table 5.4 Pros and cons of discretion vs. fixed rules in monetary policy

	Discretion (subjective judgement)	Fixed rule-based policy
Pros	• Flexible and adaptable to changing economic conditions • Active approach that works without rules • Policy makers can respond quickly to events	• Transparent and predictable • Removes the active role of the policy maker • Leaves less room for policy makers' mistakes
Cons	• Time inconsistency 'trap' and trend to forbearance, especially during downturn • Long lags between problem observation and policy implementation • Unclear what monetary authority should do in case of unexpected shock • Works only if the public trust the policy maker • Requires accurate knowledge and measure of current and future economic conditions (forecast)	• Too mechanical and unpractical • Passive approach that lacks flexibility in case of unexpected shock • If too strict it cannot accommodate special circumstances. This may result in the rules being inapplicable • Requires a high degree of confidence that the variables will perform as expected • Needs 'escape clause' in case of exceptional event (such as a war) and thus could be liable to abuse

The time inconsistency problem viz. 'eat your soup or no TV'

One of the most important problems of discretion is the time inconsistency that was analysed first by economics Nobel Prize winners Finn Kydland and Edward Prescott in the article 'Rules rather than discretion: The inconsistency of optimal plans', published in the *Journal of Political Economy* in 1977.

Time inconsistency of policy occurs when monetary authorities decide to announce *ex ante* the policy they want to pursue to influence the expectations of private economic agents. However, *ex post*, i.e. when these latter have acted based on their expectations, monetary authorities may be tempted to revoke their decision. The outcome of this situation is that when private economic agents realise that monetary authorities' may be inconsistent over time, they lose their trust in policy makers' announcements. In order to gain credibility for their announcements, policy makers may find it optimal to commit to a fixed policy rule.

Examples of time inconsistencies can be found in different scenarios, even in relation to parenting, where the parent (policy maker) announces a punishment for bad behaviour for a child (the economic agent), e.g. 'eat your soup or no TV'. The purpose of the threat is to affect the expectations of the child and therefore their behaviour. Although there is a clear threat, the parent may have incentives to give concessions to the child. However, the parent will be better off sticking to the behavioural rule of 'no TV' as the best outcome for the parent is to never relent to avoid undermining their credibility and prevent time inconsistency. The corollary is that policy makers can better achieve their goals by having the discretion taken away from them.

In the monetary policy practice, one way of approximating this outcome might be to give the policy maker (central bank) a simple rule which is a reasonable approximation to the optimal rule. In this way if the central bank wants to deviate from this rule by more than some pre-specified amount, it is allowed to, but at the cost that it must explain its rationale for so doing (e.g. Athey *et al.*, 2005).

Going back to Table 5.4, it is clear that there are a number of pros and cons of the two extreme cases of pure discretion and fixed rules. This is why many countries have adopted hybrid regimes of 'constrained discretion' in monetary policy that combine elements of both fixed rules and discretion.

A classic example is inflation targeting that involves 'a strong, credible commitment by the central bank to stabilize inflation in the long run, often at an explicit numerical level, but also allows for the central bank to pursue policies to stabilize output around its natural rate level in the short run' (Mishkin, 2011). The key requirements for sound inflation-targeting policies are that central banks 1) have some degree

---

BOX 5.5 Monetary policy: transmission mechanism, fixed rules and discretion (*continued*)

of independence; and 2) are committed (and allowed) not to target other indicators (e.g. employment or exchange rates). In the case of inflation targeting, the 'constrained discretion' framework combines two distinct elements: a precise numerical target for inflation in the medium term and a response to economic shocks in the short term. For more information on inflation targeting see Jahan (2012) and Box 5.2 in Chapter 6.

Note: Most countries' central banks provide illustrations of the transmission mechanism of monetary policy. These documents are often available from the central banks' websites. For example, see Bank of England ('The transmission mechanism of monetary policy', **www.bankofengland.co.uk/publications/Documents/ other/monetary/montrans.pdf**); European Central Bank ('Transmission mechanism of monetary policy', **www.ecb.europa.eu/ mopo/intro/transmission/html/index.en.html**) and Bank of Canada ('How monetary policy works: The transmission of monetary policy', **www.bankofcanada.ca/wp-content/uploads/2010/11/ how_monetary_policy_works.pdf**).

5.4.5 Unconventional tools of monetary policy and the 'zero-bound'

In 'normal' times, monetary policy aims at setting a target for the overnight interest rate in the money market and adjusting the supply of central bank money to that target through open market operations. In doing so, the central bank controls the liquidity levels in the market without having to lend to the private sector or the government. But what if interest rate and money supply, i.e. the 'conventional' monetary policy tools, are not effective in providing monetary stimulus to the economy and in limiting inflationary forces? What if interest rates reach zero or near-zero levels and although the economy is struggling the monetary authorities cannot cut interest rates any further?

If a central bank reaches the 'zero-bound', i.e. cannot cut policy rates any further, then 'unconventional' or 'non-standard' policies may be used to try to spur lending and spending in the economy. In general terms this can be achieved by 1) providing assurance to financial investors that short rates will be lower in the future than they currently expect; 2) changing the relative supplies of securities (such as Treasury notes and bonds) in the marketplace by shifting the composition of the central bank's balance sheet; and 3) increasing the size of the central bank's balance sheet beyond the level needed to set the short-term policy rate at zero ('quantitative easing').[7]

Quantitative easing can be defined as an unconventional monetary stimulus designed to inject money directly into the economy to counterbalance a sharp fall in aggregate demand as spending has declined. In practical terms, the central bank purchases assets (mainly government bonds) from private business using new money created electronically. The institutions selling those bonds (such as commercial banks, other financial intermediaries and non-financial firms) will have new money in their account that is expected to stimulate the money supply.

In the UK the MPC introduced quantitative easing for the first time in history in March 2009, when the bank rate was reduced to its all-time low of 0.5 per cent. The series of asset purchases undertaken between March 2009 and February 2012 injected money directly into the system with the aim of boosting nominal demand and giving a monetary stimulus to the economy. Table 5.5 summarises the purchases of government debt ('gilts') as well as corporate bonds authorised by the MPC since 2009 as part of the quantitative easing programme to date (December 2012). The Bank of England purchases gilts from private investors (typically non-bank financial intermediaries) that have an interest in selling low-yielding assets, i.e. gilts, so that they can purchase other assets such as corporate bonds and shares. This process should lower longer-term borrowing costs and encourage the issuance of new equities and bonds, thus improving the functioning of the corporate credit market (Joyce *et al.*, 2011).

---

[7] See Bernanke and Reinhart (2004).

BOX 5.6 QUANTITATIVE EASING IN JAPAN

The first experiment of quantitative easing was pioneered in Japan in the first half of the 2000s following what has been defined as a 'lost decade' of economic stagnation. Japan's problems started in the 1980s when the economy experienced an unsustainable boom – a 'bubble economy' – accompanied by several 'mistakes' in monetary policy decisions. (For a thorough discussion of the Bank of Japan's monetary policy options during the asset price bubble see Ito and Mishkin (2004).) During the boom period banks expanded considerably their lending activity to riskier customers in different industrial sectors, including real estate and construction, and small and medium businesses. Banks' lending decisions were typically based on collateral requirements and, unsurprisingly, a high proportion of these collaterals were real estate (Kanaya and Woo, 2000).

When the bubble burst in the early 1990s, non-performing loans had reached alarming levels and Japan entered a period of virtually zero growth and high deflationary pressures. The highly overvalued stock and real estate markets fell dramatically, and bad loans, capital erosion and a slow policy response resulted first in the failure of small to medium-size financial institutions in the first half of the 1990s, then a major banking crisis in 1997–1998 that saw the collapse of several large Japanese banks. Monetary authorities resorted to unconventional monetary policies when the Bank of Japan's official rate (the 'uncollateralised call rate') was lowered to virtually zero in 2001 and even this failed to reverse the process.

The Bank of Japan changed its main operating target for money market operations from the uncollateralised call rate to the current account (reserves) balances held by commercial banks, in excess of the required reserves. Initially the target amount of current account balances was set at 5 trillion yen, while the required reserves were about 4 trillion yen. By January 2004 the target amount had been raised in several steps to a range of 30–35 trillion yen and remained unchanged until the quantitative easing policy was terminated in March 2006. The Bank also expanded the amount of monthly outright purchase of long-term Japanese government bonds, from 400 billion yen to 600 billion yen, in August 2001, and in several steps to 1,200 billion yen in October 2002. In addition, purchases of some private debts, including asset-backed securities (ABS), as well as stocks held by financial institutions, were introduced (Ito and Mishkin, 2004; Shiratsuka, 2010).

Although back in 2001 the Bank of Japan committed to maintain these policies until the core inflation stopped declining, many economists reckon that quantitative easing did not provide a sufficient stimulus to aggregate demand to overcome the risk of persistent consumer price deflation. In contrast, some analysts (Bowman et al., 2011) argue that quantitative easing policies have had some (albeit small) positive effects on Japan's economy, but this was weakened by various factors, not least severe problems in the banking sector.

While both the Japanese and the UK's quantitative easing experience has implied the use of both sides of the central bank balance sheet, the US Federal Reserve bank policy appears to focus more on the asset side, a fact that explains why it is sometimes referred to as credit (rather than quantitative) easing. The US Federal Fund rate was lowered to near-zero levels in December 2008, amid the financial crisis and economic slowdown. At that time, the Federal Reserve started the first programme of large-scale asset purchases that ended in March 2009 and reached $1.725 trillion (see Table 5.5).

In theory, a narrow definition of quantitative easing implies an increase in the size of the central bank balance sheet without changing its composition. Conversely, **credit easing** (narrowly defined) corresponds to changes in the composition of the balance sheet without

Table 5.5 UK and US asset purchase programmes (in figures)

Month/Year	US	UK
December 2008	$1.725 trillion	
March 2009		£200 billion
November 2010	$600 billion	
October 2011		£75 billion
February 2012		£50 billion
September 2012	$40 billion (per month)[a]	

[a] Purchases of government mortgage-backed securities until price stability is achieved.

Source: Bank of England, 'Quantitative easing explained'. Available at **www.bankofengland.co.uk/monetarypolicy/ Pages/qe/default.aspx**; **www.federalreserve.gov/faqs/what-are-the-federal-reserves-large-scale-asset-purchases. htm**

changing its size, i.e. by replacing conventional assets with unconventional ones. Shiratsuka (2010) argues that in practice, to be an effective non-standard policy, both sides (assets and liabilities) of the balance sheet should interact and the two elements of the balance sheet (size and composition) should be combined.

Generally speaking, the ECB's actions in the aftermath of the 2007–2009 global financial crisis were similar to those implemented by the BoE and the Fed as they were primarily aimed at extending the range of available facilities and designing novel mechanisms to ensure that banks could easily access the liquidity they needed. Since August 2007 the ECB has engaged in exceptional monetary policy measures known as *enhanced credit support* to stimulate the economy of the eurozone states (ECB, 2010b). The ECB's main objectives have been to increase liquidity and to improve the functioning of money markets in the euro area. Importantly, the ECB has broadened the scope of its standard refinancing operation by using 'fixed-rate full allotment' provisions (rather than variable-rate tender procedures) with a longer maturity of maximum one year. With these operations, the interest rate is set in advance and the ECB provides as much liquidity as the banks require provided they offer suitable collateral.

However, with the sovereign debt crisis that developed in late 2009 (see Chapter 14 for more details of the eurozone crisis), the ECB took a different approach to the Fed's and BoE's easing programmes and implemented first a **Securities Markets Programme** (SMP) in spring 2010 and then a set of **longer-term refinancing operations (LTROs)** in December 2011. In addition, the ECB introduced two programmes in 2009 and 2011 to purchase **covered bonds** (covered bond purchase programme, or CBPP) for a total of €100 billion. Covered bonds are debt obligations secured by a cover pool of high-quality collateral (mortgage loans or public sector debt) that the issuer is required to maintain on balance sheet, as opposed to asset-backed securities where the credit risk can be transferred and the assets are taken off-balance sheet (ECB, 2008a). The aims of the covered bond purchase programme are 1) to ease funding conditions for banks and firms; and 2) to stimulate bank lending (see also Chapter 6). For a detailed account of the ECB's non-standard monetary policy measure, we refer the readers to Cour-Thimann and Winkler (2013).

Figure 5.10 reports the exceptional growth in central banks' balance sheets over the period 2008–2012. The BoE's balance sheet, for example, expanded by 300 per cent since 2006, against 230 per cent for the Fed and 170 per cent for the ECB (panel a).

Gros *et al.* (2012) observe that a crude comparison between the sizes of the balance sheets would not be accurate as, after 2010, the ECB had to respond to a crisis specifically occurring in the euro area. Panel (b) of Figure 5.10 illustrates that the extent of the Securities Markets

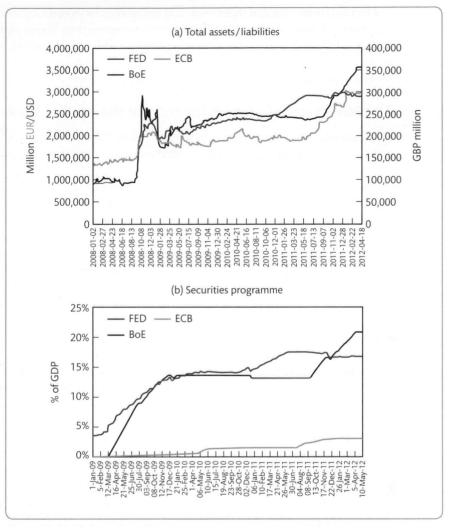

Figure 5.10 Total assets/liabilities expansion and securities programme of the BoE, Fed and ECB

Source: Gros *et al.* (2012) pp. 3–5.

Programme (as a percentage of GDP) for the three central banks was very different, being particularly limited for the ECB.

5.5 Why do banks need a central bank?

The banking sectors of most countries have a pyramid structure where a central bank is at the apex and the ordinary banking institutions are at the base of the pyramid. Central banks can also be thought of as 'super-banks', at the centre of the financial system, responsible for both 'macro' functions, such as monetary policy decisions, and 'micro' functions, including the LOLR assistance of the banking sector. Over time the roles and functions of central banks have developed and evolved, as has the environment in which banks operate.

Liberalisation, financial innovation and technology have contributed to major changes in the operating environment. Many banks have converted their status to private institutions – that by definition are demand- or customer-driven – while the global riskiness and uncertainty of the sector have increased significantly. The next section focuses on the LOLR function of central banks and how this has changed following the 2007–2009 financial crisis.

5.5.1 The lender-of-last-resort function of the central bank

The lender-of-last-resort function of a central bank is often subject to controversial debates and criticisms because it implies direct intervention of the monetary authorities in the banking markets.

In its role as a LOLR, the central bank will provide reserves to a bank (or banks) experiencing serious financial problems due to either a sudden withdrawal of funds by depositors or a situation where the bank has embarked on highly risky operations and thus cannot find liquidity anywhere else (i.e. no other institutions will lend to a bank considered near collapse). Technically, this important function of central banks derives from the discount window tool that, as illustrated in Section 5.4.2, is one of the instruments used to influence reserves and money supply in the banking sector. However, central banks operate under different frameworks in conducting the LOLR activities. These differences can reflect various country-specific factors such as public policy objectives, historical experience or other elements.

It is clear that a central bank will extend credit to an illiquid bank to prevent its failure only in exceptional circumstances and in doing so it also carries out a 'macro' function by preventing potential financial panics. However, the central bank cannot guarantee the solvency of every banking institution in a country. (On the relationship between liquidity and solvency, see Box 5.7.) This is because it would encourage bankers to undertake undue risk and operate imprudently, especially if banks knew that they would always be bailed out (by taxpayers' money) were they to become insolvent. In other words, the security of the LOLR function could induce or increase moral hazard in banks' behaviour.

One of the most famous examples of the direct support given by the Bank of England to the banking sector was offered in 1973–1974 where the Bank organised help for 26 fringe (or secondary) banks facing severe liquidity problems. In the United States, famous examples of the Fed acting as an LOLR include the rescue effort of two troubled banks: Franklin National Bank in 1974 and Continental Illinois National Bank in 1984.

Since 2007, the Bank of England, the Fed and the European Central Bank have injected substantial amounts of liquidity into their respective banking systems; these market interventions have placed their actions increasingly under the spotlight. In an unprecedented move, on 1 December 2010, the Federal Reserve released previously confidential information about its function as LOLR during the 2007–2009 period, including the names of the financial institutions and foreign central banks that received financial assistance, the amounts borrowed, the dates credits were extended, the interest rates charged, information about collateral, and a description and rationale of the credit terms under each Federal Reserve emergency facility.[8]

---

[8] The release of data was as a consequence of a Bloomberg request for the data under the Freedom of Information Act. After a series of appeals, the Fed conceded the issue and in December 2010 it released detailed information about individual credit and other transactions conducted during the financial crisis. In accordance with the Dodd–Frank Wall Street Reform and Consumer Protection Act of 2010, transaction-level details for discount window loans and open market transactions will be made available on a quarterly basis and with an approximately two-year lag. Information is available through the Federal Reserve Board's website and the Federal Reserve Bank of New York's website.

BOX 5.7 RELATIONSHIP BETWEEN LIQUIDITY AND SOLVENCY

As we noted earlier, the liquidity of a bank relates to its ability to meet short-term obligations (expected and unexpected) when they fall due. For example, banks can predict with a certain degree of accuracy how much cash they need to hold to meet such things as payment of utility bills (electricity, water), rent on buildings and (under normal market conditions) deposit withdrawals. In addition to these expected calls on liquidity, banks have to hold a cushion above this amount to meet unexpected liquidity requirements and this is why liquidity risk management is a key feature of banking business (see Sections 11.4 and 12.6).

Solvency is the ability of a bank ultimately to meet all its obligations. This means that the value of assets has to be greater than liabilities – the difference between the two being the bank's capital. If some assets go bad (e.g. loans are not repaid) then the bank must make charges against the loan portfolio (loan loss provisions) that are paid for from retained profits. As long as profits are sufficient to cover these provisions, the level of bank capital and its capital adequacy ratio (the Basel risk-weighted capital–asset ratio) remain unchanged. However, when profits do not cover provisions, then losses will have to be written out of capital (the amount of capital the bank has declines) or alternatively, shareholders will be asked to provide additional capital to restore the capital ratio to the required level.

The liquidity and solvency position of a bank are related because a severe liquidity shortfall can ultimately result in a solvency problem. For example, a continuous liquidity shortage could lead a bank to tighten its lending policy, for instance by not renewing short-term revolving lines of credit. This would force borrowers to repay their loans earlier than expected and those unable to do so would default on their loan payments. In turn, the quality of the loan portfolio would deteriorate, requiring additional loan loss provisions. If the bank does not have sufficient provisions then the losses will be written out of capital resources, thus reducing the solvency of the bank. In general, if a bank is unable to meet its liquidity requirements it will first attempt to obtain support through the LOLR facility by borrowing from the central bank. However, if this option is not available, the bank will have to consider bearing the losses from its capital resources, thus reducing the bank's capital position.

A liquidity crisis can quickly change into a solvency crisis. For example, if a bank has actual (or even perceived) liquidity difficulties, and this becomes known to other banks, the latter will withdraw their wholesale interbank deposits from the illiquid bank, leading to a wholesale deposit run, which may then spread to retail deposit withdrawals. In this case the bank would not be able to meet its short-term obligations and would have to resort to using capital resources to bear any losses. Ultimately the bank might not have sufficient capital resources to meet these losses, resulting in insolvency.

In the case of an individual bank failure, the decision as to whether a bank is illiquid or insolvent is a critical judgement that the regulators have to make in order to decide whether to support a troubled bank or to let it fail. For example, if a small bank is facing financial difficulties, the regulator has to decide whether this is a result of a short-term liquidity problem or a longer-term solvency issue. If the authorities decide the problems are caused by liquidity problems, they are more likely to offer support through the LOLR facility (providing new liquidity to the bank to help it get through its liquidity problem). If the bank is deemed to have a solvency problem, the authorities are more likely to consider letting the bank go bankrupt or organising some form of rescue. In theory, regulators should consider supporting banks with a liquidity problem but not with a solvency problem – although we know in reality that this is not always the case. Another point to note is that regulators have a very difficult task in deciding whether a bank that is in trouble is either illiquid or insolvent as often a decision has to be made very quickly on whether liquidity support should be provided or not. Often regulators have to decide in a matter of days the liquidity and solvency position of a troubled bank and they will also have to take into consideration whether a decision not to provide liquidity will result in failure and serious systemic repercussions. In general, the relationship between liquidity and solvency is at the heart of bank regulation and is a critical feature of the bank supervisory process.

The depth and length of the global financial crisis transformed the role of LOLR to what is now discussed as a **market maker of last resort (MMOLR)** function. The traditional Bagehot rule of central banking (LOLR activities should be limited to solvent but illiquid banks with good collateral, to avoid moral hazard problems) has been stretched to the limit in order to meet the liquidity needs of increasingly dysfunctional financial markets. Some commentators have welcomed this transition, as it reflects the evolution of the LOLR function to meet the reality of modern financial systems. Others are more critical of the explosion of central banks' balance sheets, as well as of the collateral policies central banks followed during and after the 2007–2009 crisis. Other concerns include the inflationary consequences of this expansion of central bank credit and the lack of transparency of the decision-making process. Some have criticised central banks for bailing out insolvent institutions, and many have noted that quasi-fiscal support has been provided through generously priced bank support packages (Moe, 2012).

5.5.2 The free-banking hypothesis

The presence of a central bank acting as a 'super-bank' has been investigated by the so-called 'free-banking school'. **Free banking** theorists argue that regulation should be left to the market. Therefore, they object to a single central bank being given the 'privilege' – or monopoly – in issuing banknotes.

Similarly, a number of researchers in the field argue that the possibility for modern banks of 'refinancing' at the central bank is not in line with the current developments of a banking market that is increasingly driven by the objective of shareholders' wealth maximisation. In particular, they claim that in market-based economies the availability of the LOLR function of the central bank is detrimental to the good functioning and efficiency of the banking system as a whole because it may give rise to distortions and misallocation of resources.

In the words of Dowd (1996, pp. 35–36):

> Once the government intervenes in the economy, the banking system becomes weaker and inefficient; the currency becomes debauched, and so on. The banking system becomes weak because the government preys on it, or because it sets up a system of deposit insurance or lender of last resort that undermines the banks' own incentives to maintain their financial health.

This argument begs the question: could the market function efficiently without a central bank? Yes, according to the laissez-faire economists whose main ambitions are to prohibit government 'predation' on the financial system, to abolish all rules distorting the free functioning of the financial sector, including capital adequacy regulation, and to eliminate deposit insurance and the LOLR function. The free-banking school theorists argue that depositors would adapt to the competitive nature of the banking sector and accept that they would lose funds if their bank failed. However, bank managers would want to keep depositors' confidence for the usual reason that if investors had any doubts about the safety of their bank, they would react by withdrawing their money. As a result, bank managers would be willing to maintain adequate capital as well as other measures necessary to reassure depositors. This process would ensure an acceptable level of safety and soundness of the banking sector.

An interesting theoretical explanation for the existence of central banks is given by Charles Goodhart (1987). He highlights three possible reasons that might lead banks to prefer to form interbank organisations (a banking club) to which to delegate certain functions. First, the transaction and monitoring costs for interbank loans would be reduced if the central bank arranged them centrally. Second, banks would be obliged to hold a sort of 'socially optimum' amount of reserves that they most probably would not keep otherwise. Finally, they would mitigate potential negative externalities derived by bank contagion effects.

In Goodhart's view, central banks are needed for two main reasons. First, because banks provide two essential functions: they operate the payment systems and undertake portfolio management services. These are considered to be 'public goods' and hence need to be preserved. The second reason is that bankers themselves have an economic interest in protecting the reputation of the banking sector as a whole and in keeping the confidence of investors. A central bank also aims to prevent the collapse of the banking sector that could arise from information problems, abuses by bankers and excessive risk taking.

However, Goodhart's argument challenges the conventional view that the joint provision of payments services together with portfolio management functions of banks exposes the monetary system to contagious failure, which a central bank should prevent. Instead, the author maintains that it is the special nature of banks' assets, largely non-marketable, fixed nominal-value loans of uncertain true worth, that makes them more vulnerable than other non-banking firms.

While there is debate about the merits and demerits of central banks, it is a fact that there is a central bank in virtually every country in the world. One of the key issues is whether central banks should be given independence from governments, and if so, to what extent.

5.6   Should central banks be independent?

There has been a significant trend towards **central bank independence** in many countries and the issue has generated substantial debate all over the world. Theoretical studies seem to suggest that central bank independence is important because it can help produce a better monetary policy. For example, an extensive body of literature predicts that the more independent a central bank, the lower the inflation rate in an economy.

Central bank independence can be defined as independence from political influence and pressures in the conduct of its functions, in particular monetary policy. It is possible to distinguish two types of independence: *goal independence*, that is, the ability of the central bank to set its own goals for monetary policy (e.g. low inflation, high production levels), and *instrument independence*, that is, the ability of the central bank to independently set the instruments of monetary policy to achieve these goals (Mishkin, 2000).

It is common for a central bank to have instrument independence without goal independence; however, it is rare to find a central bank that has goal independence without having instrument independence. In the United Kingdom, for example, the Bank of England is currently granted instrument independence and practises what is known as *inflation targeting*. This means that it is the government that decides to target the inflation rate (at the time of writing – 2014 – set at 2 per cent) and the Bank of England is allowed to independently choose the policies that will help to achieve that goal. Such a situation is only acceptable in a democracy because the Bank of England is not elected and thus goals should only be set by an elected government.

While central bank independence indicates autonomy from political influence and pressures in the conduct of its functions (in particular monetary policy), dependence implies subordination to the government. In this latter case, there is a risk that the government may 'manipulate' monetary policy for economic and political reasons. It should be noted, however, that all independent central banks have their governors chosen by the government; this suggests that to some extent central banks can never be entirely independent.

BOX 5.8 WHO OWNS THE CENTRAL BANK?

There is no general answer to this question, it depends on the specific case. For example, the Bank of England is a 'public sector institution wholly owned by the government'. This means that the entire capital of the Bank is held by the Treasury solicitor on behalf of HM Treasury. Current regulations provide that the Bank is required to pay to HM 'on the fifth day of April and October, a sum equal to 25% of the Bank's post-tax profit for the previous financial year or such other sum as the Bank and HM Treasury may agree. The overall effect is that the Bank and HM Treasury will normally share post-tax profits equally' (see the Bank of England Act 1946 and 1998 amendments).

While the Bank of England is owned by the British government, the ECB is owned by the central banks of member states, as clearly reported in its Statute. This means that member central banks have voting powers as shareholders (article 10.3 on Governing Council) and share the profits and losses of the ECB (article 33.1). But who owns the national member state central banks then? The answer can be found in their own statutes: they are owned by the major financial institutions in a country.

Another interesting example is that of the US Federal Reserve System. Using the FAQ on its website and typing 'Who owns the Fed?' in the internal search engine brings the following answer: 'The Federal Reserve System fulfils its public mission as an independent entity within government. It is not "owned" by anyone and is not a private, profit-making institution.' It then adds that: 'As the nation's central bank, the Federal Reserve derives its authority from the Congress of the United States. It is considered an independent central bank because its monetary policy decisions do not have to be approved by the President or anyone else in the executive or legislative branches of government, it does not receive funding appropriated by the Congress, and the terms of the members of the Board of Governors span multiple presidential and congressional terms. However, the Federal Reserve is subject to oversight by the Congress, which often reviews the Federal Reserve's activities and can alter its responsibilities by statute. Therefore, the Federal Reserve can be more accurately described as "independent within the government" rather than "independent of government." The 12 regional Federal Reserve Banks, which were established by the Congress as the operating arms of the nation's central banking system, are organised similarly to private corporations – possibly leading to some confusion about "ownership." For example, the Reserve Banks issue shares of stock to member banks. However, owning Reserve Bank stock is quite different from owning stock in a private company. The Reserve Banks are not operated for profit, and ownership of a certain amount of stock is, by law, a condition of membership in the System. The stock may not be sold, traded, or pledged as security for a loan; dividends are, by law, 6 percent per year.' This means that the concept of ownership in the case of member banks takes some unique connotations.

Since the financial crisis, the growing consensus on the positives of central bank independence has come under increasing pressure. For example, after the collapse of Lehman Brothers in 2008, the independence of the Fed has been under scrutiny. The Fed's performance during and after the 2007–2009 crisis has been severely criticised. As a consequence of growing political pressure, the Dodd–Frank Act amended Section 13(3) to require the Treasury's approval for its exercise of LOLR activities. The ECB independence has also been compromised by the adoption of the Outright Monetary Transmission Programme (OMT), which entails a promise to purchase sovereign debt of individual euro member states. While the programme has helped recover market confidence, some see it as a 'fiscalisation of

Table 5.6 Central bank independence (CBI)

In favour	Against
• As monetary policy works with lags, it is necessary to take a long-term view when making decisions. CBI offers a safeguard against short-term political interests.	• Lack of democratic governance.
• CBI can prevent governments from using central banks to finance government spending. Given the large public debt in many countries, CBI should act as a safeguard against deficit increases.	• Constraints of central banking (i.e. central banks may be too cautious for fear of political interference and for fear of losing independence and credibility).
• Political pressures can damage the credibility of a central bank and distort inflation expectations, which goes against central banks' ultimate goal to maintain price stability.	• Poor social outcomes (deflation).
• Many empirical studies have shown that higher levels of CBI result in economic growth and price stability.	
• CBI also allows the central bank to move more swiftly and effectively in response to macroeconomic shocks.	

Source: Adapted from Toyoda (2013).

central banking', as it allows government intervention and may lead to the loss of the ECB's independence.[9]

It is possible to distinguish between the case 'for' and the case 'against' independence. In general terms, there are mainly political and economic reasons in support of central bank independence. Moreover, there is a principal–agent problem between the public (the principal) and the central bank and the government (the agents). The agents may have incentives to act against the interests of the public. According to the supporters of central bank independence it is the government in particular that has a strong incentive to act in its own interest. Only an independent central bank operating outside the day-to-day business of politics can be considered a guarantor of long-term economic stability. Table 5.6 summarises the arguments in favour of and against central bank independence.

5.7 Conclusion

A central bank's main function is to undertake monetary control operations and thus to administer the amount of money in the economy, given the specific monetary policy objectives set by the government. Modern central banks tend to use *indirect instruments*, or tools, in the conduct of their monetary policy and can generally choose between 1) open market operations; 2) the discount window; and 3) reserve requirements. OMOs are at present the most popular instruments used by central banks as they are tax-free (in that they do not place specific constraints on banks' operations) and flexible (in terms of their frequency of use and scale of activity). In particular, the main attractions for using OMOs to influence short-term

---

[9]See Bullard (2013) and Toyoda (2013).

interest rates are as follows: they are initiated by the monetary authorities who have complete control over the volume of transactions; they are flexible and precise – they can be used for major or minor changes in the amount of liquidity in the system; they can easily be reversed; and finally, they can be undertaken quickly.

The financial crisis of 2007–2009 brought to the fore the key role of central banks in responding to crises. In particular, unconventional policies such as quantitative and credit easing have been key monetary policy tools in the aftermath of the global financial crisis. While the role and core functions of central banks around the world keep evolving to adapt to the transformations in the operating environment, one school of thought, the free-banking school, has questioned whether central banks are needed. In essence, free bankers doubt the effectiveness of central banks in a demand-oriented banking market that is increasingly driven by the profit-maximisation culture. In particular, they criticise the use of the LOLR function and central banks' monopoly in issuing banknotes. Against this viewpoint, Goodhart (1987) confirms the need for a central bank using his theory of banking 'clubs'. He emphasises that banks are especially vulnerable to crises due to the special nature of their assets, which are largely non-marketable.

There has been a trend in both developed and developing countries towards increased independence of central banks from political pressure, although central bank independence has come under renewed scrutiny post financial crisis.

Key terms

Central bank independence	Instruments of port-folio constraint	Monetary aggregates	Price stability
Covered bonds	Lender-of-last-resort (LOLR)	Monetary policy	Prices and incomes policy
Credit easing	Longer-term refinanc-ing operations (LTRO)	Monetary transmis-sion mechanism	Quantitative easing (QE)
Discount window		Money	
Exchange rate policy	Market maker of last resort (MMOLR)	National debt man-agement policy	Reserve requirement
Fiscal policy		Open market opera-tions (OMOs)	Securities Markets Programme
Free banking			Standing facilities

Key reading

Bank for International Settlements (2009) 'Issues in the governance of central banks', a report from the Central Bank Governance Group. Available at **www.bis.org/publ/othp04.htm**

Cour-Thimann, P. and Winkler, B. (2013) 'The ECB's non-standard monetary policy measures. The role of institutional factors and financial structure', ECB Working Papers Series, No. 1528, April.

Dowd, K. (1996) *Competition and Finance: A new interpretation of financial and monetary economics.* London: Macmillan.

Friedman, M. (1968) 'The role of monetary policy', *American Economic Review*, 58(1), 1–17.

Gros, D., Alcidi, C. and Giovanni, A. (2012) 'Central banks in times of crisis: The FED vs. the ECB', CEPS Policy Briefs, No. 276, July.

Mishkin, F. (2000) 'What should central banks do?', Federal Reserve Bank of St Louis Review, November–December.

REVISION QUESTIONS AND PROBLEMS

5.1 What are the five major forms of economic policy?

5.2 What is money and what are the monetary aggregates?

5.3 Outline the differences between monetary policy tools, instruments and goals.

5.4 Why are OMOs the most popular monetary policy tool?

5.5 What is the Bank of England official rate?

5.6 Explain the meaning and limitations of the 'instruments of portfolio constraint'.

5.7 Discuss the key issues in the transmission of monetary policy. Briefly explain the channels through which monetary policy actions impact the economy.

5.8 Outline the advantages and disadvantages of discretion vs. fixed rules in monetary policy. Focus on the time inconsistency problem.

5.9 What are the unconventional monetary policy tools?

5.10 What is the lender-of-last-resort function? Why is it controversial?

5.11 What are the main arguments put forward by the free-banking theorists?

5.12 What are the arguments for and against an independent central bank?

Chapter 6

Central banks in practice

Learning objectives

- To describe the functions and roles of the Bank of England, the European Central Bank and the Federal Reserve System
- To describe the organisational structure and corporate governance of the Bank of England, the European Central Bank and the Federal Reserve System
- To understand the relationship between the European Central Bank and the national central banks of EU member states
- To understand the actions taken by the Bank of England, the European Central Bank and the Federal Reserve System during and after the 2007–2009 financial crisis
- To understand the actions taken by the European Central Bank during the eurozone crisis of 2010 and thereafter

6.1   Introduction

This chapter investigates the functions, structure and role of central bank operations. In particular, Section 6.2 focuses on the Bank of England, Section 6.3 looks at the European Central Bank and Section 6.4 investigates the US Federal Reserve System. We start by focusing on the structure and functions of these central banks, which are among the most important central banks in the world. We then look at the decision-making process within these organisations, to end with a discussion of some of the most relevant operational changes implemented.

6.2   The Bank of England

The Bank of England is the central bank of the United Kingdom. As we discussed in Chapter 5, a central bank is ultimately responsible for the organisation of its country's official financial policies, including the monetary policy, and acts as banker to the government and general overseer of the whole financial system.

The origins of the Bank of England can be traced back to 1694 when it received its charter as a joint stock company. The Bank of England, in fact, was established in order to improve the fund-raising capability of the British government. It was not until the Bank Charter Act of 1844, however, that it obtained full central bank status. The 1844 Act ultimately led to a monopoly for the Bank of England in the production of notes and coins in the United Kingdom.

During the nineteenth century the Bank of England consolidated its position as overseer of the British banking system by standing ready to purchase bills of exchange issued by other commercial banks, if the need arose. This lender-of-last-resort function helped maintain public confidence and credibility in the banking system. In fact, during the nineteenth century the Bank of England found itself performing many of the functions that are today thought commonplace for a central bank: the main issuer of bank notes and coins; lender of last resort; banker to the government and to other domestic banks; and guardian of the nation's official reserves. As well as providing banking services to its customers, the Bank of England managed the UK's foreign exchange and gold reserves and the government's stock register. The latter is a register of government securities (gilts). It must be remembered, however, that although the Bank of England performed these functions (as well as undertaking a larger role in the financial management of the economy), it remained a private joint stock company, operating for a profit. The Bank of England Act of 1 March 1946 nationalised the Bank and the state acquired all of the Bank's capital. In 1997, the government gave the Bank operational independence to set monetary policy and statutory responsibilities for the stability of the financial system as a whole. In 2012, the Bank was also given macro-prudential responsibility for oversight of the financial system and day-to-day prudential supervision of financial services firms (see Box 6.1).

6.2.1 Constitution of the Bank

The Bank of England is a public corporation with a fundamental role with regard to the objective of maintaining a stable and efficient monetary and financial framework. Like other nationalised organisations, the actual degree of operational freedom has always been rather limited. In May 1997, the Treasury proposed a number of institutional and operational

---

BOX 6.1 THE BANK OF ENGLAND – MORE THAN 300 YEARS OF HISTORY

- Established 1694 (The Royal Charter)
- 1734 the Bank moved to Threadneedle Street, London, its current premises
- 1781 renewal of the Bank's Charter – the banker's bank
- 1844 Bank Charter Act – the Bank took on the role of lender-of-last-resort
- 1946 Bank of England Act – the Bank was nationalised and formally recognised as a central bank
- Until 1997 the Bank was statutorily subordinate to the Treasury
- 1998 Bank of England Act – the Bank was granted operational independence
- 2012 Financial Services Act – a Financial Policy Committee was created at the Bank as part of a new system of financial regulation

changes to the Bank of England that were set out in the **Bank of England Act 1998** (1 June). Following the implementation of the 1998 Act, the Bank of England was given operational independence in setting interest rates that became the responsibility of the newly created **Monetary Policy Committee (MPC)** working within the Bank. However, the legislation provides that, in extreme circumstances and if the national interest demands it, the government will have the power to give instructions to the Bank on interest rates for a limited period.

Furthermore, in the 1998 Act, the regulation of the banking sector was taken away from the Bank and given to a newly established 'super' regulator called the **Financial Services Authority (FSA)**. As a result of these changes, the Bank's functions for the national debt management passed to the newly created UK **Debt Management Office (DMO)** that is legally and constitutionally part of HM Treasury.

In October 1997, the Bank, Her Majesty's Treasury and the FSA signed a 'Memorandum of Understanding' which made provisions for the establishment of a high-level standing committee that met regularly and provided a forum where the three organisations could develop a common position on financial stability issues. This structure became known as the 'tripartite', whereby the three authorities – the Bank of England, the Financial Services Authority and HM Treasury – were co-operating on the supervision and oversight of the banking sector. However, weaknesses of such a system were exposed during the 2007–2009 financial crisis and major reforms were implemented thereafter. The **Financial Services Act 2012**, which came into force on 1 April 2013, amends the Bank of England Act 1998, the Financial Services and Markets Act 2000 and the Banking Act 2009 and profoundly changes the UK regulatory structure. Most changes involve the Bank of England, which is experiencing its most important institutional and functional changes since 1997. This regulatory reform has resulted in the Bank of England gaining significant new responsibilities, as detailed in Section 6.2.2.

6.2.2 The 2012 Financial Services Act and the UK regulatory framework

The 2012 Financial Services Act brings the roles performed by the UK three regulatory bodies under one roof – the Bank of England's. The 2012 Act gives the Bank of England macroprudential responsibility for oversight of the financial system and day-to-day prudential supervision of financial services firms.[1] The FSA, which was established with the Financial Services and Markets Act of 2000, is abolished and three new regulatory bodies are created: the **Financial Policy Committee (FPC)**, the **Prudential Regulation Authority (PRA)** and the **Financial Conduct Authority (FCA)**. Two of the three new bodies, the FPC and the PRA, are subsidiaries of the Bank of England. These new responsibilities are in addition to the Monetary Policy Committee and its existing responsibilities for monetary policy, and the Bank's responsibilities for liquidity provision and resolution. Figure 6.1 illustrates the new UK regulatory framework.

The major changes introduced by the Financial Services Act of 2012 aim to protect and improve the UK economy. Figure 6.2 illustrates the main statutory decision-making bodies of the Bank of England.

6.2.2.1 The Prudential Regulation Authority (PRA)

The Prudential Regulation Authority is a subsidiary of the Bank of England in charge of the prudential regulation and supervision of about 1,700 financial institutions, including banks, building societies, credit unions, insurers and major investment firms. Its main role is to promote the safety and soundness of these financial firms and therefore it works closely with the

---

[1] www.legislation.gov.uk/ukpga/2012/21/pdfs/ukpga_20120021_en.pdf

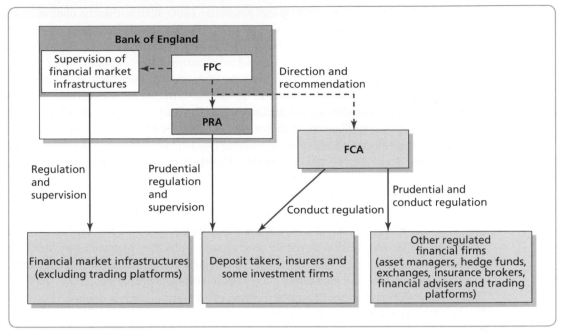

Figure 6.1 The new UK regulatory framework

Source: Adapted from Bank of England (2013b).

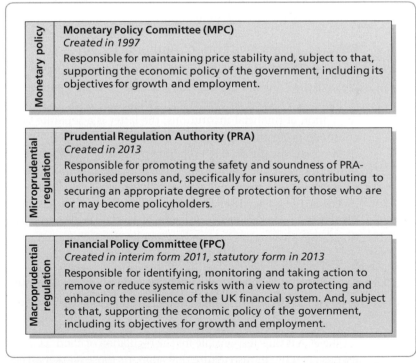

Figure 6.2 Statutory decision-making bodies of the Bank of England

Source: Adapted from Bank of England (2013b).

Financial Policy Committee and the Special Resolution Unit (SRU) within the Bank of England. The PRA is responsible for the supervision of both UK-headquartered and international financial firms, including firms with an 'EU passport' from within the European Economic Area, branches from other countries and UK-owned subsidiaries of international firms.

In terms of governance and accountability, the PRA, as part of the Bank of England, will be accountable to the Bank's Court of Directors for administrative matters. It will also have its own independent board, which comprises the Governor of the Bank of England, the CEO of the PRA, the Deputy Governor for Financial Stability, the CEO of the FCA and at least three independent non-executive members. The first Board meeting was held on 7 March 2013. Like the Bank's other statutory decision-making bodies, the PRA Board will be accountable to the UK Parliament.

6.2.2.2   The Financial Policy Committee (FPC)

The Financial Policy Committee is an official committee of the Bank primarily in charge of macro-prudential regulation. More specifically, the FPC is responsible for identifying, monitoring and taking action to remove or reduce systemic risks with a view to protecting and enhancing the resilience of the UK financial system (without impairing economic growth opportunities for the UK in the medium and long term). Subject to achieving its primary objective, the FPC also supports the economic policy of the government, particularly growth and employment.[2]

The FPC has four main functions:

- monitoring the stability of the UK financial system, with a view to identifying and assessing systemic risks;
- giving directions to the FCA or the PRA;
- making recommendations within the Bank of England, the FCA and the PRA;
- preparing financial stability reports.

6.2.2.3   Financial Conduct Authority (FCA)

From April 2013, the FSA ceased to exist and two separate regulatory authorities have been created: the Prudential Regulation Authority and the Financial Conduct Authority. While the former is an independent entity at the Bank of England that focuses on the micro-prudential regulation of financial institutions, the latter is a separate body responsible for business, consumer protection and market conduct.

More specifically, FCA is a separate regulatory entity whose main objectives are to maintain and ensure the integrity and the effective functioning of the markets, to ensure that financial services firms give their customers a fair deal and to promote competition.

The 2012 Financial Services Act provides the FCA with a single strategic objective: ensuring that the relevant markets function well. The Act also defines the FCA's three main operational objectives as market conduct regulator as follows:

- to secure protection for consumers;
- to protect and enhance the integrity of the UK financial system; and
- to promote effective competition in the interests of consumers.

These objectives are supported by a competition duty.

The FCA is thus responsible for the regulation of conduct in retail and wholesale financial markets and the infrastructure that supports those markets. The FCA also has responsibility

---

[2] www.bankofengland.co.uk/financialstability/pages/fpc/default.aspx

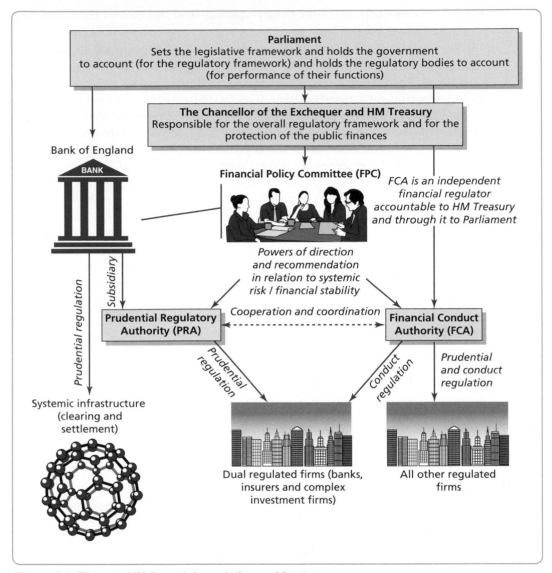

Figure 6.3 The new UK financial regulation architecture

for the prudential regulation of firms that do not fall under the PRA's remit, such as asset managers, hedge funds, exchanges, insurance brokers and financial advisers (see Figure 6.3). The FCA is thus the new prudential supervisor for approximately 23,000 other firms that were previously regulated by the FSA. Figure 6.3 summarises the new financial regulation architecture for the UK financial system.

6.2.3 Objectives and functions of the Bank of England

The Bank of England has two core purposes:

- monetary stability;
- financial stability.

6.2.3.1 Core purpose of monetary stability and the role of the Monetary Policy Committee

The first core purpose of the Bank is to ensure monetary stability by maintaining stable prices and confidence in the currency. *Price stability* is met by influencing the price of money, i.e. by setting an interest rate. Decisions are taken by the Monetary Policy Committee that aim to meet the government's annual inflation target (at the time of writing 2 per cent, as measured by the 12-month increase in the Consumer Price Index). With regard to *confidence in the currency*, the Bank is also responsible for safeguarding the value of the currency.

The Bank's MPC is made up of the governor, the two deputy governors, the Bank's chief economist, the executive director for market operations and four external members appointed directly by the Chancellor. The MPC meets every month and decides the level of interest rate at which it lends to financial institutions (0.5 per cent in 2014). As discussed in Chapter 5, this interest rate impacts the whole range of interest rates set by banks and building societies for their customers. It also tends to affect asset prices in financial markets and the exchange rate.

It is important to highlight that monetary authorities in all countries are concerned about the level of interest rates and the supply of bank reserves and they try to influence them by using the various tools at their disposal. Undoubtedly, all the main goals of macroeconomic policy (high employment, growth, financial stability and so on) can be better pursued in a low and stable interest rate environment. The point to emphasise is that while some monetary authorities (for example in the United States) explicitly target short-term interest rates as a major policy tool, the Bank of England focuses primarily on an inflation target.

A clear and stable inflation target is a relevant way of making the objectives of monetary policy credible, thus ensuring inflation expectations are consistent with price stability. In the UK, intermediate targets, such as monetary aggregates, have had an uncertain relationship with the main goal of maintaining price stability. This is why the Bank of England now uses inflation targets as the main feature of its monetary policy. Box 6.2 summarises the evolution of inflation targeting as the mainstay of UK monetary policy.

BOX 6.2 INFLATION TARGETING IN THE UNITED KINGDOM

What is inflation targeting? It is a framework of monetary policy based on the following five essential elements (Hammond, 2012):

1 Price stability is explicitly recognised as the main goal of monetary policy.

2 There is a public announcement of a quantitative target for inflation.

3 Monetary policy is based on a wide set of information, including an inflation forecast.

4 Transparency.

5 Accountability mechanism.

The adoption of formal inflation targets in 1992 marked an important break with the past. The other key date is 1997, when the Bank of England was granted operational independence; the institutional framework then put in place entrenched and enhanced the credibility of inflation targeting and has been widely admired. Hammond (2012) observes that most inflation-targeting central banks have statutory independence. Figure 6.4 (panel (a)) shows that in 2009 a total of 27 countries were operating a fully fledged inflation-targeting regime, of which 9 were industrialised countries. New Zealand was the first to adopt this framework and the most recent convert was Serbia in 2009. From Figure 6.4, (panel (b)) it is clear that in the majority of cases (15 out of 27) the inflation target is set jointly by the government and central bank. The only country

Box 6.2 Inflation targeting in the United Kingdom (*continued*)

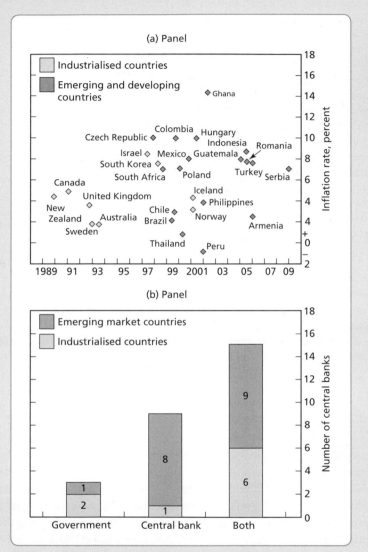

Figure 6.4 Inflation targeting

Source: Hammond (2012) pp. 7–8.

where the government is not involved in setting the target is Sweden.

In the UK, as in other inflation-targeting countries, a track record of success, built up over more than two decades, has progressively reinforced the credibility of these targets. As a result, people and firms have increasingly come to expect inflation to stay close to the official target – a belief that itself helps to keep it there. The institutional framework is set out in the 1998 Bank of England Act. The BoE is required to set interest rates so as 'to maintain price stability and subject to that to support the economic policy of HM government, including its objectives for growth and employment'. The government is required to specify what its economic objectives are, including what is meant by price stability. The remit of the MPC must be set out in writing at least annually and it must be published.

Box 6.2 Inflation targeting in the United Kingdom (*continued*)

The remit has always had important elements of flexibility. For example, while the MPC is directed to aim for the target 'at all times' and to treat deviations from target symmetrically, it is not expected to react mechanically. Instead, if inflation deviates from target by more than 1 per cent, the governor is required to write to the Chancellor explaining the circumstances and setting out what action the MPC considers necessary to return to target.

More than 20 years of inflation targeting (since 1992) and inflation rates look remarkably stable by post-war standards, as shown in Figure 6.5.

Despite the success of inflation targeting in the first 20 years after its adoption, the recent financial turmoil has posed serious doubts about its adequacy in guaranteeing economic and financial stability. The former governor of the Bank of England, Mervyn King, discussed these issues in a speech at the London School of Economics in 2012 (King, 2012). In the next two decades, he acknowledged, it will be necessary to focus on macro-prudential policies while guaranteeing low and stable inflation as a crucial *prerequisite* to achieve economic success. Nonetheless, Mr King argued, while changes will be necessary to

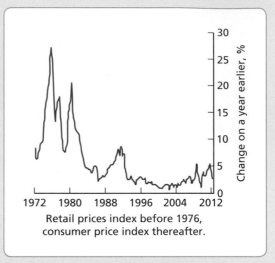

Retail prices index before 1976, consumer price index thereafter.

Figure 6.5 UK CPI inflation, 1972–2012
Source: King (2012).

minimise the impact of possible future crises, the case for price stability is still 'as strong today as it was twenty years ago – both in theory and practice'.

Sources: Hammond (2012); King (2012).

6.2.3.2 Core purpose of financial stability and the function of lender-of-last-resort

In broad terms, financial stability entails maintaining an efficient flow of funds within the economy and confidence in financial intermediaries. The Bank of England is responsible for maintaining the stability of the UK financial system. Since April 2013 the achievement of the financial stability objective within the Bank is the task of the FPC, which is charged with taking action to remove or reduce systemic risks with a view to protecting and enhancing the resilience of the UK financial system. The objective of financial stability is pursued through the Bank's financial operations, including as lender-of-last-resort, the decisions of the FPC, the PRA's prudential regulation of financial institutions, the Bank's role as resolution authority, and Bank oversight and regulation of key payment, clearing and settlement infrastructure.

6.2.3.2.1 *The Bank of England as lender-of-last-resort*

The Bank of England has acted as lender-of-last-resort for the banking system for more than a century. This means that the Bank stands ready to supply funds to the banking sector if liquidity or solvency problems arise (on the distinction between liquidity and solvency see Box 5.6 in Chapter 5).

However, this does not mean that the Bank guarantees the solvency of every banking institution in the UK. Rather, the situation is that the Bank stands ready to accommodate shortages of cash in the banking sector, perhaps resulting from the non-bank private sector or from an unusually large net flow of funds from private bank accounts to the government's accounts at the Bank of England. This view adopts a short-term view of the LOLR. It is argued that the Bank, in its role as LOLR, is not prepared to guarantee the solvency of every banking institution because this would encourage bankers to take undue risks and operate imprudently (i.e. increase moral hazard – see Chapter 7), especially if banks knew that they would be bailed out (by taxpayers' money) if they became insolvent. In other words, the Bank may lend money to a troubled institution to avoid a possible systemic crisis that may arise as a result of the bank failing. However, this 'safety net' is not meant to protect individual institutions or their managers and shareholders. Rather, it exists only to protect the stability of the financial sector as a whole.

The LOLR function of the world's largest central banks (Federal Reserve, European Central Bank and the Bank of England) has changed in consequence of the 2007–2009 financial crisis. The crisis forced central banks to implement the LOLR more comprehensively, including providing liquidity and collateral, loosening of collateral standards, supporting troubled financial institutions, opening special liquidity facilities, lowering interest rates, expansionary monetary policy and becoming market maker of last resort (see Chapter 5).

The Bank of England's actions during the 2007–2009 financial crisis were described as conservative by some commentators. The Bank's first intervention came in September 2007, in relation to the run on Northern Rock. The Bank's (delayed, according to some critics) response was to provide emergency liquidity assistance (ELA) of £27 billion and a guarantee of £40 billion of liabilities. These loans were later transferred to HM Treasury, therefore effectively financing the nationalisation of the troubled financial institution.[3] In October 2008, the Bank provided ELA to the Royal Bank of Scotland and HBOS (see Box 6.3). The Bank also used some unconventional lending facilities, thereby making the transition to MMLR. These facilities include (i) a Special Liquidity Scheme; (ii) a Discount Window Facility; (iii) indexed long-term repo open market operations; and (iv) extended collateral term repo facilities.

(i) Special liquidity scheme (SLS)

The Special Liquidity Scheme was introduced in April 2008 to improve the liquidity position of the banking system by allowing banks and building societies to swap their high-quality mortgage-backed and other securities for UK Treasury bills for up to three years. The SLS was initially designed to finance part of the overhang of illiquid assets on banks' balance sheets by exchanging them temporarily for more easily tradable assets. Although the drawdown period for the SLS closed on 30 January 2009, the scheme remained in place for a further three years. Treasury Bills with a face value of approximately £185 billion have been lent under the scheme, with 32 banks and building societies (accounting for more than 80 per cent of the sterling balance sheet of the financial institutions eligible to use the scheme) accessing it. Most of the collateral received has been residential mortgage-backed securities or residential mortgage-covered bonds. To borrow Treasury Bills under the scheme, banks and building societies were charged a fee based on the spread between three-month LIBOR and the three-month general collateral gilt repo rate. The average spread over the drawdown period was about 115 basis points. The SLS officially closed on 30 January 2012. All drawings under the scheme were repaid before the scheme closed.[4]

---

[3] In January 2012, Northern Rock was re-privatised and sold to Virgin Money.

[4] More information on the Special Liquidity Scheme can be found at **www.bankofengland.co.uk/markets/Documents/marketnotice090203c.pdf**

BOX 6.3 EMERGENCY LIQUIDITY ASSISTANCE TO HBOS AND RBS

In October 2008, as the financial crisis intensified rapidly following the failure of Lehman Brothers, HBOS and the Royal Bank of Scotland (RBS) received emergency liquidity assistance (ELA) from the Bank of England on a large scale, amounting at its intraday peak to £61.5 billion: HBOS first received ELA on 1 October 2008 and at peak on 13 November that year had drawn £25.4 billion. HBOS made final repayment of the facility on 16 January 2009. RBS first received ELA on 7 October 2008, initially in dollars, but subsequently from 10 October also in sterling. Its use of the dollar facility peaked at $25 billion on 10 October 2008, and of the sterling facility at £29.4 billion on 27 October 2008. RBS made final repayment of ELA on 16 December 2008.

The sterling ELA took the form of collateral swaps, under which the Bank of England lent the two banks UK Treasury bills (T-bills) against unsecuritised mortgage and loan assets. The structure was similar in form to the Special Liquidity Scheme (SLS), under which the Bank of England had been providing liquidity against an extended range of collateral on a market-wide basis since April 2008. The Bank charged a fee of 200 basis points on amounts drawn. The Bank also received an indemnity from HM Treasury for any additional amounts drawn after 13 October 2008. Before that indemnity was put in place, the full £51.1 billion of the Bank's exposure at that date was not indemnified. Even after the indemnity was in place, the Bank remained unindemnified for £50.9 billion of its peak intraday exposure of £61.5 billion on 17 October 2008. The ELA operation was conducted covertly; it was publicly disclosed on 24 November 2009, just over a year after it was initiated.

By the time ELA was needed to support HBOS and RBS in October 2008, the strains that were destabilising the financial system had been evident for more than a year; and the Bank had already had experience of extending ELA to Northern Rock the previous year.

Shortly after the commencement of the ELA, the UK government announced, on 8 October 2008, a package of support measures for the financial system, including a recapitalisation scheme for banks. As a result of government recapitalisation received under that scheme, RBS and Lloyds Banking Group (the result of HBOS's merger with Lloyds TSB, which was completed on 19 January 2009) were brought into partial public ownership, where they remain today. The government's ownership of Lloyds Banking Group stood at 40 per cent at end-March 2012. Recapitalisation of RBS occurred in a series of transactions, which eventually led to government ownership of 83 per cent of RBS. The government's ownership of RBS stood at 80 per cent in September 2014 (and Lloyds at 20 per cent), amid talks of a fresh push for a return of the bank to private ownership.

The actions of the Bank of England at the height of the financial crisis were the subject of one of three reviews commissioned by the Court of Governors of the Bank on 21 May 2012.

Source: Plenderleith (2012). Available at **www.bankofengland.co.uk/publications/Documents/news/2012/cr1plenderleith.pdf**

(ii) Discount window facility (DWF)

The Discount Window Facility offers liquidity insurance for idiosyncratic as well as system-wide shocks. It is a bilateral facility designed to address short-term liquidity shocks without distorting banks' incentives for prudent liquidity management. At the Bank's discretion, eligible banks and building societies may borrow gilts, for 30 or 364 days, against a wide range of collateral in return for a fee, which will vary with the collateral used and the total size and maturity of borrowings.[5]

(iii) Indexed long-term repo open market operations (ILTROs)

The Bank of England offers funds via an indexed long-term repo operation once each calendar month, usually on a Tuesday mid-month. Each operation offers a pre-announced fixed quantity at a single maturity. Normally, the Bank will conduct two operations with a three-month maturity and one operation with a six-month maturity in each calendar quarter. The ILTROs replace extended long-term repo operations and target the banking system as a whole.

Participants are able to borrow against two different sets of collateral: a 'narrow collateral' and a 'wider collateral'. The first set corresponds to securities eligible in the Bank's short-term repo operations and the second set contains a broader class of high-quality debt securities that, in the Bank's judgement, trade in viable liquid markets. Participants bid by submitting a nominal amount and a spread to bank rate expressed in basis points.[6]

(iv) Extended collateral term repo facilities (ECTR)

The extended collateral term repo facility is a contingency liquidity facility that the Bank can activate in response to actual or prospective market-wide stress of an exceptional nature. The ECTR facility enables the Bank to undertake operations against a much wider range of collateral than is eligible in the indexed long-term repo operations.[7]

6.2.3.2.2 The Bank of England as market maker of last resort

By using these facilities, the Bank of England not only used special lending facilities but also broadened the range of collateral and began to target liquidity stress in the markets in general. However, it is through the Asset Purchase Facility (APF) that the Bank of England became market maker of last resort. In January 2009, the Chancellor of the Exchequer authorised the Bank to set up an APF to buy high-quality assets financed by the issue of Treasury bills and the DMO's cash management operations. The aim of the facility was to improve liquidity in credit markets. The Chancellor also announced that the APF provided an additional tool that the MPC could use for monetary policy purposes. When the APF is used for monetary policy purposes, purchases of assets are financed by the creation of central bank reserves.[8] The APF continues to operate facilities for the purchase of private sector assets through the Corporate Bond Secondary Market Scheme and Secured Commercial Paper Facility, with purchases financed by the issue of Treasury Bills and the DMO's cash management operations. The Commercial Paper Facility closed on 15 November 2011, reflecting improvements in the market since commercial paper was first purchased on 13 February 2009. Figure 6.6 illustrates the cumulative net assets purchased by type since the APF was set up.

Box 6.4 reviews the tenure of Sir Mervyn King, former Governor of the Bank of England, who directed the Bank through a number of key changes.

---

[5] More information on the Discount Window Facility can be found at **www.bankofengland.co.uk/markets/Documents/money/publications/redbookdwf.pdf**

[6] More information on indexed long-term repo open market operations can be found at **www.bankofengland.co.uk/markets/Documents/money/publications/redbookiltr.pdf**

[7] More information on Extended collateral term repo facilities can be found at **www.bankofengland.co.uk/markets/Pages/sterlingoperations/redbook.aspx**

[8] More information on Asset Purchase Facility can be found at **www.bankofengland.co.uk/markets/Pages/apf/default.aspx**

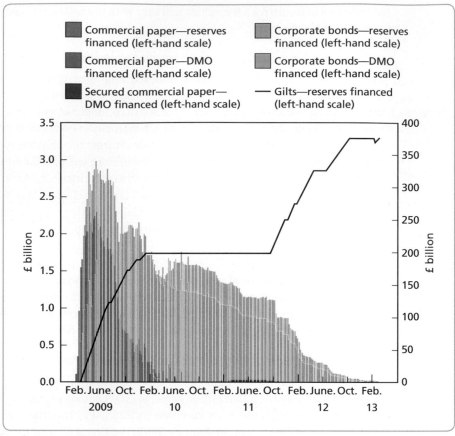

Figure 6.6 Cumulative net asset purchases by type (amounts outstanding), 2009–2013

Source: Bank of England (2013a) p. 2.

BOX 6.4 LEAVING THE OLD LADY

Among the 119 men who have run the Bank of England since 1694, Sir Mervyn King stands out in two ways. He has overseen exultant highs and terrible lows – from the 'great moderation' of inflation and steady growth to Britain's worst banking collapse. And he has profoundly changed not just the bank, but central banking around the world. In some ways Sir Mervyn, who steps down on June 30th 2013, has failed. In others he has succeeded so completely that it is hard to remember how bad things were before he arrived.

Before the early 1990s British monetary policy was chaotic. The bank and the Treasury set targets for things like money supply and credit growth, missed them, then dropped them. In desperation, they tried to import some credibility, first shadowing Germany's

Bundesbank, then, in 1990, joining the **Exchange Rate Mechanism**. If previous efforts had been faltering, this proved a disaster: the high interest rates needed to keep in line with Germany's currency drove Britain into recession. When Sir Mervyn arrived at the bank as chief economist in 1991, a new policy was being explored: inflation targeting.

He was the right man to push it through. He had studied at Cambridge, which then had an arrogant and insular economics department, driven by theoretical disputes. He rejected it, frequently decamping to America and becoming fascinated by practical microeconomics, particularly how firms respond to tax incentives. Martin Feldstein, a colleague at Harvard, recalls him being absorbed by the harmful effects of inflation. At the Bank of England he became (in the

Box 6.4 Leaving the old lady (*continued*)

words of Kenneth Clarke, Britain's chancellor from 1993 to 1997) the 'intellectual rock' on which the new policy was built.

Assessed narrowly, the regime worked brilliantly. Between 1992 and 2012 retail-price inflation averaged around 3%. Over the previous two decades it had averaged 10%. Cheap imported goods helped. But the system faced severe tests during Sir Mervyn's time, and held. Two oil-price surges, in 2008 and 2011, were comparable to those of the 1970s. They did not lead to anything approaching 1970s-style inflation (see Figure 6.5).

Sir Mervyn did not pioneer inflation targeting – New Zealand adopted it earlier than Britain – but he popularised it. The network of academic contacts he had built in America was tapped to fill top jobs in central banking and at the IMF. Those contacts, and Britain's success in controlling inflation, gave Sir Mervyn global clout. In 1992 there were just three inflation targeters. Today there are more than 30.

But the new system contained hairline cracks which would open later. Running through the inflation-targeting regime was the conviction, powerful in academic economics, that there must be at least one tool for each policy objective. Central banks' interest rates would simply target consumer prices. Asset prices – the cost of houses, bonds and equities – would not be part of the objective. The logic was that financial and economic cycles do not always line up. It would be pointless to drive a calm economy into recession just to tamp down a frothy housing market.

That narrow focus was new. It was enabled by the creation of an apparently neat regime for bank regulation. A new body, the Financial Services Authority, would ensure the stability of individual banks. The heads of both the Bank of England and the FSA would stake their reputations on hitting their targets, and had the weapons to do so. It made sense in theory.

Yet if Britain's inflation targeting was best of breed, its banking system became one of the worst. Between 2002 and 2007 British banks' balance-sheets almost tripled in size, fuelling a house-price boom. Equity buffers were low, and included 'efficient' new types of capital that turned out not to absorb losses at all. The banks' new funds were not deposits but short-term and flighty market borrowing. This cocktail of high leverage and short-term funding induced a colossal hangover.

Sir Mervyn failed to spot the crisis coming. And his initial reaction was ill-judged. When Northern Rock, a lender, experienced a run on its market borrowing, the central bank rightly bailed it out. But the governor chose to speak about the deeper causes of the crisis rather than the emergency, talking about the problems that occur when markets know that banks can lean on the state. He was right: the economics of 'moral hazard' do explain why they took on so much debt. But it was not the time for such lessons. Talking about abstract economic concepts in the teeth of the crisis made him look out of touch.

The failure of Northern Rock was just the start of Sir Mervyn's woes. By 2008 the Royal Bank of Scotland was not just Britain's biggest bank but the biggest in the world. Its assets, at £2.2 trillion ($3.5 trillion), were more than 150% of Britain's GDP. Yet its owners' equity was wafer-thin: the government was forced to add £45.5 billion more, giving it an 81% stake. Britain's banking sector moved from free-market to publicly owned overnight. Each Briton invested £740 in RBS, today that stake is worth just £470, a fact that cost Steven Hester his job [of CEO of RBS] this week.

Sir Mervyn has done better since the days of acute crisis. In particular, he has responded adeptly to a nasty combination of economic weakness and price pressures. Oil and regulated prices (things like VAT and university fees) have pushed inflation as high as 5%. Bringing inflation back to the 2% target by raising interest rates would kill Britain's feeble recovery. Some brands of monetary policy, notably the European Central Bank's, have been too hawkish. Sir Mervyn's is more subtle. He has allowed inflation to remain above target for the past four years while frequently confirming his commitment to that target. Somehow this has worked. The bank's credibility as an inflation targeter is intact: firms and workers still expect inflation to be close to 2%. The Bank of England's 120th governor, Mark Carney, who takes over on July 1st, will find it a difficult line to tread.

On banking, Mr Carney's arrival has echoes of 1992. The old system has been binned, the FSA split up. Bank regulation is now Mr Carney's remit, and he inherits a new, untested tool. A committee will vary banks' capital requirements in an attempt to

Box 6.4 Leaving the old lady (*continued*)

calm credit cycles. Here he is on even trickier ground, inheriting a banking system in need of more capital and an economy short of credit. Banks are bolstering themselves by cutting lending, threatening to suppress Britain's meagre growth. Although Sir Mervyn's solution, providing banks with cheap funds on condition that they lend to firms, may have eased the crunch, it has not ended it.

One way to ease the tension between capital and lending would be to encourage some new entrants.

During Sir Mervyn's stint at the top, Britain has seen huge bank mergers, including RBS–NatWest in 2000 and Lloyds–HBOS in 2009. In allowing the takeovers, he followed a centuries-old tradition: successive governors, stretching back to a crisis in 1825, have favoured consolidation. If Mr Carney can find a way to simplify setting up a new bank, he would end that custom. It would make his job, and his successor's, much easier.

Source: The Economist (2013) 15 June.

6.3 The European Central Bank (ECB)

Established on 1 June 1998 and based in Frankfurt, Germany, the **European Central Bank** is one of the world's youngest central banks and the central bank for Europe's single currency, the euro. The legal basis for the ECB is the Treaty establishing the European Community and the statute of the **European System of Central Banks (ESCB)** and of the ECB. According to its statute, the ECB's primary objective is price stability in the euro area, thus it is responsible for monitoring inflation levels and maintaining the purchasing power of the common currency.

The euro area (or eurozone) consists of those European Union countries that have adopted the euro as their currency. It comprises 18 EU member states: Austria, Belgium, Cyprus, Estonia, Finland, France, Germany, Greece, Ireland, Italy, Latvia, Luxembourg, Malta, the Netherlands, Portugal, Slovakia, Slovenia and Spain. Latvia became the eighteenth eurozone member state when it adopted the euro in January 2014.

The origin of the ECB can be traced back to the history of the Economic and Monetary Union (see Chapter 14, Box 14.2, on the creation of a single market for financial services in the European Union). In 1994 the EMI (European Monetary Institute) was created; the EMI was the precursor to the ECB. On 25 May 1998 the governments of the then 11 participating member states appointed the president, the vice-president and the four other members of the Executive Board of the ECB. Their appointment took effect from 1 June 1998 and marked the establishment of the ECB.[9]

The ECB and the **national central banks (NCBs)** of all EU member states, regardless of whether they have adopted the euro or not, constitute the European System of Central Banks.

The European Central Bank, together with the national central banks of the member states whose currency is the euro, constitute the **Eurosystem** (Article 282 of the Treaty on the Functioning of the European Union). The term Eurosystem was chosen by the Governing Council of the ECB to describe the arrangements by which the ESCB carries out its tasks within the euro area. As long as there are EU member states that have not yet adopted the euro, this distinction between the Eurosystem and the ESCB will need to be made.

[9] See **www.ecb.europa.eu/ecb/history/emu/html/index.en.html**

6.3.1 Organisational structure of the European Central Bank

There are three main decision-making bodies of the ECB: the Governing Council, the Executive Board and the General Council (see Figure 6.7).

The **Governing Council** is the main decision-making body of the ECB. It consists of the six members of the Executive Board plus the governors of all the NCBs from the euro area countries. The council's main responsibilities are: 1) to adopt the guidelines and take the decisions necessary to ensure the performance of the tasks entrusted to the Eurosystem; and 2) to formulate monetary policy for the euro area, including key interest rates and reserves in the Eurosystem. The statute (article 7) establishes independence from political interference of the ECB and the ESCB in the carrying out of their tasks and duties.[10]

The Executive Board consists of the president of the ECB, the vice-president and four other members, appointed by the European Council, acting by a qualified majority. It is responsible for implementing monetary policy, as defined by the Governing Council, and for giving instructions to the NCBs of the eurozone countries. It also prepares the Governing Council meetings and is responsible for the day-to-day management of the ECB.

The General Council is the ECB's third decision-making body. It comprises the ECB's president and vice-president and the governors of the NCBs of all EU member states. The General Council contributes to the ECB's advisory and co-ordination work and helps prepare for the future enlargement of the euro area. The General Council can be regarded as a transitional body and it will be dissolved once all EU member states have introduced the single currency.

In addition to the decision-making bodies, the corporate governance of the ECB encompasses a number of external and internal control layers. The ECB's functional units are grouped into business areas – Directorates General (DG) and Directorates (D) – that consist of Divisions and Sections. The overall responsibility for day-to-day business lies with the Executive Board.

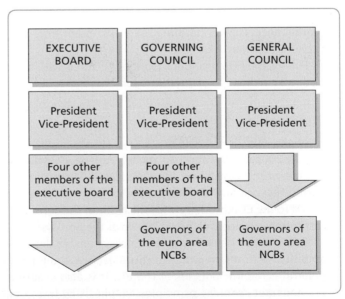

Figure 6.7 The decision-making bodies of the ECB

Source: Adapted from European Central Bank (2011) p. 18.

---

[10] See the 1/6/2004 Protocol on the Statute of the European System of Central Banks and of the European Central Bank at **www.ecb.int/ecb/legal/pdf/en_statute_2.pdf**

The organisational structure of the ECB reflects the tasks performed and can be divided between core processes, which are closely related to the tasks as defined in the Treaty, and enable processes, which support the work.

6.3.2 Core functions of the ECB

The functions of the ECB (and of the ESCB) are specified in the statute that is a protocol attached to the 1992 Treaty on the European Union: 'The primary objective of the ESCB shall be to maintain price stability.' Moreover, 'without prejudice to the objective of price stability, the ESCB shall support the general economic policies in the Community with a view to contributing to the achievement of the objectives of the Community as laid down in Article 2' (Treaty Article 105.1). Article 2 on the Treaty on European Union states the objectives of the Union as being a high level of employment and sustainable and non-inflationary growth.

More specifically, according to the Treaty establishing the European Union (article 105.2), the basic tasks of the ECB are to:

1 define and implement monetary policy for the euro area;
2 conduct foreign exchange operations;
3 hold and manage the official foreign reserves of the euro area countries (portfolio management); and
4 promote the smooth operation of payment systems.

In addition to the core tasks defined above, the ECB has the exclusive right to authorise the issuance of banknotes within the euro area. That means it is the monopoly supplier of the monetary base. Further, in co-operation with the NCBs, the ECB collects statistical information necessary for fulfilling the tasks, either from national authorities or directly from economic agents.

Finally, the ECB maintains working relations with relevant institutions, bodies and fora, both within the EU and internationally, in respect of tasks entrusted to the Eurosystem.

6.3.2.1 Monetary policy

By July 2002, 12 EU countries, namely Austria, Belgium, Finland, France, Germany, Greece, Ireland, Italy, Luxembourg, the Netherlands, Portugal and Spain, had replaced their national currencies with the euro. Responsibility for monetary policy within the eurozone was transferred to the ECB, working with the NCBs of the eurozone member states. This grouping of institutions, as noted above, is known as the Eurosystem.

The primary objective of the Eurosystem, as defined by statute, is to maintain price stability. Without prejudice to this objective, the Eurosystem is expected to support the general economic policies of the EU. It is also required to operate in accordance with open market economy principles, emphasising free competition and an efficient allocation of resources. According to the Treaty, a successful monetary policy by the ECB will ensure stable prices over time as the main pre-condition to the achievement of the objectives of high economic growth and full employment in Europe.

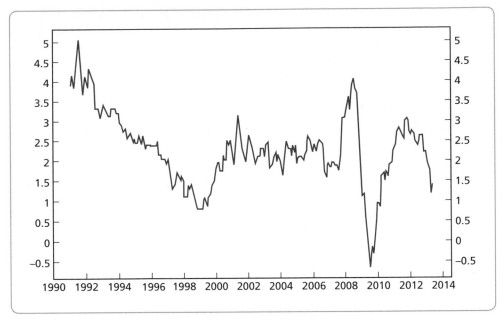

Figure 6.8 Inflation in the euro area (%), 1990–2014

Source: Eurostat data, available from the European Central Bank.

The ECB's Governing Council has defined price stability as 'a year-on-year increase in the Harmonised Index of Consumer Prices (HICP) for the euro area of below 2%.[11] Price stability is to be maintained over the medium term'. Figure 6.8 illustrates the inflation rate (in terms of HICP) since the early 1990s.

The ECB uses a set of monetary policy tools, including the following:

- Open market operations – normally in the form of repo transactions or secured loans. The most significant instrument is the so-called reverse transaction (applicable on the basis of repurchase agreements or collateralised loans) used via its main refinancing operations (MROs). For example, the interest rate on the MRO stood at 0.05 per cent in September 2014.

- Standing facilities – used to provide or to absorb overnight liquidity in the markets; they are controlled by the NCBs and include the marginal lending facility and the deposit facility.

- A minimum reserve requirement – applied to credit institutions established in the euro area and branches operating in the euro area of banks headquartered outside the euro area.

Figure 6.9 shows the trends in the key ECB's interest rates. It is possible to identify six phases in the conduct of monetary policy: 1) mid-1998 to mid-1999, the transition to the monetary union; 2) mid-1999 to end-2000 raised rates to contain inflationary pressures;

---

[11] From the time of its inception until May 2003, the ECB defined its statutory requirement to maintain price stability as keeping the rate of inflation at less than 2 per cent p.a. This chosen objective was not only regarded as having been excessively harsh when global inflationary pressures were low, but also it may be thought to have lacked the flexibility that would have been offered by the use of an inflation target band. In May 2003, the ECB effectively announced a loosening of its policy regime by indicating that henceforth it would seek to maintain the rate of inflation within the eurozone *close to* 2 per cent p.a. over the medium term.

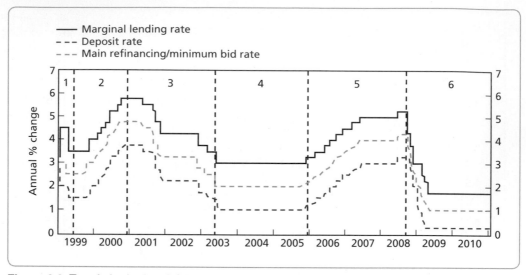

Figure 6.9 Trends in the key ECB interest rates, 1999–2010

Source: European Central Bank (2011a) p. 100. Annual percentage change, daily data.

3) early 2001 to mid-2003 downward adjustments to key interest rates in response to price pressures; 4) mid-2003 to end-2005 no changes to interest rates as price pressures are contained; 5) end-2005 to mid-2008 gradual reduction of monetary accommodation (i.e. low interest rates); 6) since autumn 2008: ECB response to the financial crisis.

The decision of what type of monetary policy has to be undertaken is made by the ECB's Governing Council. In addition, it includes an analytical framework for the assessment of the risks to price stability that is based on two key pillars of economic and monetary analysis.[12] The Governing Council's approach to organising, evaluating and cross checking all information relevant for assessing the risks to price stability is based on two analytical perspectives, referred to as the 'two pillars': economic analysis and monetary analysis:

● The first pillar focuses on the analysis of economic dynamics and shocks, and aims to identify the determinants of price developments over the short to medium term in relation to the real activity and financial conditions of the economy. A key element of this analysis is the interplay of supply and demand in the goods, services and factor market. Accordingly it encompasses an assessment of inflationary pressures based on a range of indicators such as economic growth, the euro exchange rate, demand and labour market conditions, business and consumer surveys and eurozone fiscal policies.

● The second pillar relates to monetary analysis and focuses on a longer-term perspective. The ECB uses a wide range of tools and instruments to examine the monetary and credit developments with the aim of determining the implication for future inflation and growth. In particular, it focuses on the close monitoring of the growth rate of a broad monetary aggregate (M3) relative to an announced medium-term target growth rate.

---

[12] European Central Bank (2011a).

It has been argued that the ECB may not have given enough weight to the monetary implications of the transition of eurozone economies to the use of a single currency and the effect of a single set of interest rates throughout the eurozone. In the first years of the single currency, a particular problem was the weakness of the German economy relative to the economies of some other members of the eurozone that experienced higher growth, employment rates and inflation. This caused problems for setting monetary policy in the eurozone as the ECB had to accommodate the diverse features of macroeconomic performance of all member countries when setting policy. For example, Ireland's booming economy over 1995–2008 (the *Celtic Tiger*) would probably have benefited more from a tighter monetary policy stance (hence dampening inflationary pressures) than the expansionary policy conducted by the ECB that was geared to boosting sluggish economic performance in Germany, France and Italy. Prior to the 2007–2009 crisis it was clear that structural adjustments in eurozone markets were needed, particularly in respect of freer market competition and the flexibility of labour markets and that the ECB was facing major challenges in implementing a 'one-size-fits-all' monetary policy in the eurozone.

A controversial issue about the Eurosystem relates to the extent and nature of democratic control over the ECB and its openness and accountability for its actions. Quite simply, it may be argued that the ECB has been given the power to determine its own inflation objective without recourse to the democratically elected governments of the eurozone countries, and on the basis of only limited disclosure of the underlying monetary policy decision-making processes. This is not to question the importance of independence from political pressure in respect of the implementation of policy once the objectives have been set. To be fair, the criticisms that may be made of the ECB should not be allowed to disguise its widely acknowledged achievements. The establishment of the eurozone and the practical aspects of launching a new currency have occurred with far fewer problems than might have been feared. The objective of price stability within the eurozone has been broadly achieved, although the 2 per cent target has been periodically overshot (see Figure 6.8).

Figure 6.10 illustrates the stability-oriented monetary policy strategy of the ECB. The conditions for maintaining price stability in the euro area have been tough due to the several adverse conditions (a period of strong global oil and commodity price movement), uncertainty (especially in the aftermath of the 11 September 2001 terrorist attacks in the US) and, more recently, the most severe financial crisis since the US Great Depression in the 1930s.

In its initial monetary policy strategy, the ECB placed considerable emphasis on intermediate targeting of monetary aggregates, particularly M3, its broad measure of money, for the eurozone. In setting a so-called *reference value* (intermediate target) for broad monetary growth, the Governing Council of the ECB has taken account mainly of price stability, i.e. inflation below 2 per cent, and of a growth rate of 2–2.5 per cent per annum for real GDP. Furthermore, the medium-term decline in the velocity of money (the ratio between the nominal GDP and nominal M3) is considered to lie in the approximate range of 0.5–1 per cent each year. Based on these considerations, the Governing Council decided to set the first reference value for monetary growth at 4.5 per cent.

Although the ECB was close to achieving the 2 per cent inflation target during the decade 1999–2008, the growth rate of M3 persistently exceeded the 4.5 per cent quantitative reference rate. As a result, the use of what is effectively an intermediate target for a broad

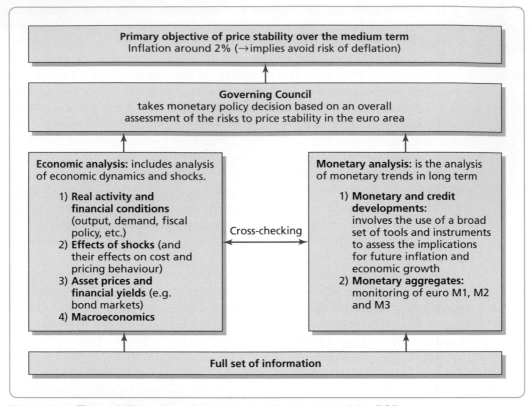

Figure 6.10 The stability-oriented monetary policy strategy of the ECB

Source: Adapted from **www.ecb.int**

monetary aggregate has been increasingly questioned. The reported overshooting of this target variable undoubtedly contributed to pressure for restrictive monetary policy and was expected to ultimately undermine the credibility of monetary policy and confidence in the monetary authorities. This may have been a factor in the ECB's decision to announce that it would put less emphasis on the M3 money supply measure and move towards indicators of the real eurozone economy in setting its policy. This is reflected in the current two-pillar structure and particularly the role of monetary factors described above.

A crucial phase in the eurozone's monetary policy is represented by the ECB's response to the financial and sovereign debt crises. Like other major central banks, the ECB dramatically cut interest rates to historically low levels and then undertook a series of so-called *unconventional* policy actions (see also Section 5.4.5 in Chapter 5). According to the IMF (2013c), these non-standard policies ultimately aim to ensure macroeconomic stability and specifically aim to: 1) restore the functioning of financial markets and intermediation; and 2) provide further monetary policy accommodation at the zero lower bound.

Box 6.5 gives some details on the non-standard measures the Eurosystem took in response to the crises.

Central banks' monetary policy conduct can be indirectly influenced by fiscal policy because this latter can ultimately affect fundamental macro variables such as GDP, inflation and the level of employment. It follows that monetary and fiscal policies should be coordinated to ensure economic and financial stability. In Europe, although 18 countries are 'married' by a common monetary policy, fiscal policy is the responsibility of the individual

BOX 6.5 THE ECB'S NON-STANDARD MEASURES OF MONETARY POLICY

1. Enhanced credit support

The ECB's Enhanced Credit Support is a set of non-standard measures to support financing conditions and the flow of credit beyond what could be achieved through reductions in key ECB interest rates alone. These measures were adopted in October 2008 and complemented in May 2009. Reflecting the financial structure of the euro area, these measures are primarily bank-based and help to ensure a more normal functioning of money markets. These include five elements: (a) extension of the maturity of liquidity provision; (b) fixed rate full allotment; (c) currency swap agreements; (d) collateral requirements; (e) covered bond purchase programme.

(a) Extension of the maturity of liquidity provision

The Eurosystem had already increased the amount of liquidity provided in longer-term refinancing operations (LTROs) after the ECB's decision to introduce supplementary refinancing operations with maturities of three and six months during the period of financial turmoil. After the collapse of Lehman Brothers (on 15 September 2008) the maximum maturity of the LTROs was temporarily extended to twelve months. This element, together with the fixed rate allotment (point 2 below), contributed to keeping money market interest rates at low levels and increased the Eurosystem's intermediation role aimed at easing refinancing concerns of the euro area banking system, especially for term maturities. Reduced uncertainty and lower liquidity costs, coupled with a longer liquidity planning horizon, were expected to encourage banks to continue providing credit to the economy.

(b) Fixed rate full allotment

A fixed rate full allotment tender procedure was also adopted for all refinancing operations during the financial crisis. Thus, contrary to normal practice, ten eligible euro area financial institutions had unlimited access to central bank liquidity at the main refinancing rate, subject to adequate collateral.

(c) Currency swap agreements

The Eurosystem also temporarily provided liquidity in foreign currencies during the financial crisis, most notably in US dollars, at various maturities against euro-denominated collateral. It used reciprocal currency arrangements with the Federal Reserve System to provide funding in US dollars against Eurosystem eligible collateral at various maturities at fixed interest rates with full allotment. This measure supported banks which otherwise faced a massive shortfall in US dollar funding during the period of financial crisis. Eurozone banks and associated off-balance sheet vehicles had significant liabilities in US dollars, having provided considerable financing to several US market segments, including subprime and real estate.

(d) Collateral requirements

The list of eligible collateral accepted in Eurosystem refinancing operations was extended during the financial crisis, and this allowed banks to use a larger range and proportion of their balance sheet to obtain central bank liquidity. The ability to refinance illiquid assets through the central bank provides an effective remedy to liquidity shortages caused by a sudden halt in interbank lending. This includes, for instance, asset-backed securities, which became illiquid when the market collapsed after the default of Lehman Brothers.

(e) Covered bond purchase programme

Within the scope of this programme, the Eurosystem purchased euro-denominated covered bonds issued in the euro area at a value of €60 billion over the period between May 2009 and June 2010. The covered bonds market had virtually dried up in terms of liquidity, issuance and spreads. The aim of the covered bond purchase programme was to revive the covered bond market, which is a very important financial market in Europe and a primary source of financing for banks. It is the largest and the most active segment of the fixed income market alongside the public sector bond market. Covered bonds are long-term debt securities that are issued by banks to refinance loans to the public and private sectors, often in connection with real estate transactions. Covered bonds – unlike mortgage-backed securities – have the specific legal characteristic of 'double protection': recourse to the issuer as well as additional security

> ### BOX 6.5 The ECB'S non-standard measures of monetary policy (*continued*)
>
> provided by the legal pledge of the assets financed. The size of the programme represented around 2.5% of the total outstanding amount of covered bonds, which in the given context was effective as a catalyst to restart activity in this market.
>
> #### 2. Securities Markets Programme (SMP)
>
> The Securities Markets Programme (SMP) was introduced in response to tensions in some segments of the financial market, in particular in the euro area sovereign bond markets (the Greek crisis) that started in May 2010. The aim was to ensure depth
>
> and liquidity in those market segments that were dysfunctional and restore the proper functioning of the monetary policy transmission mechanism. Under the SMP, Eurosystem interventions could be carried out in the euro area public and private debt securities markets. In line with the Treaty provisions on the functioning of the EU, purchases of government bonds are strictly limited to secondary markets. In addition, they were fully neutralised through liquidity absorbing operations, so as to not affect central bank liquidity conditions.
>
> *Source*: Cour-Thimann and Winkler (2013).

member states. The EU Treaty and various other provisions address the issue of monetary and fiscal interactions; however, the economic and financial crises have revealed the urgent need for an improved fiscal framework in Europe. In 2012 the ECB emphasised that such a framework must i) maintain a price stability-oriented monetary policy; ii) provide stronger safeguards for sustainable public finances and economic policies; and iii) include explicit provisions for ensuring financial stability and crisis management.[13]

These measures comprise changes to the EU's Stability and Growth Pact (SGP), an agreement signed by the EU governments in 1997 – and subsequently reformed in 2005 – with the primary aim to limit individual member states' fiscal policies and public financing regimes. The SGP was adopted mainly on the grounds that fiscal policies may conflict with the inflation objective, or may cause the economic performance of member states to diverge. According to the pact, member states must keep their public deficits below a 3 per cent deficit/GDP ratio and their debts below a 60 per cent debt/GDP ratio.[14]

The ineffectiveness of the SGP in securing fiscal health in the euro area resulted in a set of reforms that are summarised below:

● The Euro Plus Pact (March 2011), signed by the euro area heads of state or government and joined by Bulgaria, Denmark, Latvia, Lithuania, Poland and Romania to strengthen the economic pillar of economic and monetary union (EMU) and to achieve a new quality of economic policy coordination, with the objective of improving competitiveness, thereby leading to a higher degree of convergence. This pact includes the 'Six Pack' on the European Economic Governance Framework that was implemented in December 2011 and the reform of both the preventive and corrective arms of the SGP, new minimum requirements for national budgetary frameworks, the new Macroeconomic Imbalance Procedure (MIP), and a stronger enforcement mechanism through new financial sanctions, under both the SGP and the MIP.

---

[13] European Central Bank (2012b), July.

[14] However, in 2005 the pact's rules were made more 'flexible' across a range of areas. For example, member states will avoid an excessive deficit procedure (EDP) if they experience any negative growth at all (previously –2 per cent), can draw on more 'relevant factors' to avoid an EDP and will have longer deadlines if they do move into a deficit position greater than the stipulated minimum. See ECB (2008).

- The Two-Pack (November 2011), i.e. two regulations that aim at 1) improving budgeting surveillance in euro area countries through reviews of draft budget plans by the European Commission to ensure compliance with the SGP requirements; and 2) enhancing surveillance for troubled euro area countries at risk of financial instability. The decision to enforce greater surveillance will be taken by the European Commission and stress tests will be carried out in co-operation with the European Banking Authority (see Chapter 7).

- Finally, the Treaty on Stability Coordination and Governance, known as the 'Fiscal Compact' or 'Fiscal Stability Treaty', that was signed by most EU member states in March 2012.[15] There are four key elements of the compact (ECB, 2012a): 1) a balanced budget rule, including an automatic correction mechanism to be implemented in national law; 2) the strengthening of the excessive deficit procedure; 3) the inclusion of the numerical benchmark for debt reduction for member states with government debt exceeding 60 per cent of GDP; and 4) *ex ante* reporting on public debt issuance plans.

6.3.2.2 Foreign exchange operations

The second most important basic task of the ECB is the conduct of foreign exchange operations and this includes: 1) foreign exchange interventions; and 2) operations such as the sale of foreign currency interest income and so-called commercial transactions. At present (2014) the Eurosystem may decide, if and when needed, to conduct foreign exchange interventions either on its own (unilateral interventions) or within the framework of co-ordinated intervention involving other central banks (concerted interventions). In addition, interventions may be carried out either directly by the ECB (i.e. in a centralised manner) or by NCBs acting on behalf of the ECB in a decentralised manner.

6.3.2.3 Portfolio management

The ECB owns, manages and is responsible for the risk management of two portfolios: 1) the *foreign reserves portfolio*, that ensures that the ECB has sufficient liquidity to conduct its foreign exchange operations; 2) the *own funds portfolio*, that provides the ECB with revenue to help cover its operating costs. While trying to achieve the best possible portfolio returns, the ECB strictly separates portfolio management activities from other ECB activities. The ECB is responsible for the monitoring and management of the financial risks incurred either directly or by the NCBs of the Eurosystem acting on behalf of the ECB.

6.3.2.4 Payment system

The ECB, together with the Eurosystem, aims to achieve smooth and prudent operation of payment and settlement systems. This is considered essential for a sound currency and the conduct of monetary policy, for guaranteeing the effective functioning of financial markets and to ensure stability of the banking and financial sectors.

More specifically, the Eurosystem fulfils its task by:

- providing payment and securities settlement facilities: the Eurosystem runs a settlement system for large-value payments in euro (called *TARGET2*, i.e. the second generation of TARGET, Trans-European Automated Real-time Gross settlement Express Transfer system).

---

[15] The UK and the Czech Republic abstained. For more information see ECB (2012a).

It also provides a mechanism for the cross-border use of collateral (CCBM, Correspondent Central Banking Model);[16]

- overseeing the euro payment and settlement systems: the Eurosystem sets standards to ensure the soundness and efficiency of systems handling euro transactions. It also assesses the continuous compliance of euro payment and settlement systems with these standards;

- setting standards for securities clearing and settlement systems;

- ensuring an integrated regulatory and oversight framework for securities settlement systems (e.g. in the framework of the co-operation between the European System of Central Banks and the Committee of European Securities Regulators (ESCB–CESR). On 1 January 2011, the CESR officially became the European Securities and Markets Authority (ESMA).

- acting as a catalyst for change: the Eurosystem promotes efficiency in payment systems and the adaptation of the infrastructure to the needs of the **Single Euro Payments Area** (SEPA). It also promotes an efficient securities market by encouraging the removal of barriers towards integration.

As a consequence of the global financial crisis of 2007–2009 and the eurozone crisis that started in 2010, the European Commission put forward a long-term plan for a banking union (Chapter 14). The plan included the creation of the Single Supervisory Mechanism (SSM), the Single Resolution Mechanism (SRM) and the Single Bank Resolution Fund (SRF). Under the SSM, the ECB will be responsible for specific supervisory tasks related to the financial stability of all euro area banks. These key changes in the remit of the ECB and the European financial architecture are discussed in Section 14.4.2.

6.4   The Federal Reserve System

The **Federal Reserve System** (or the Fed), the central bank of the United States of America, was founded by Congress in 1913 with the signing of the Federal Reserve Act. It was created to provide the nation with 'a safer, more flexible, and more stable monetary and financial system'.[17]

As the United States' central bank, the Federal Reserve derives its authority from the US Congress. It is considered an independent central bank because its decisions do not have to be ratified by the president or anyone else in government, it does not receive funding from Congress, and the terms of the members of the **Board of Governors** span multiple presidential and congressional terms. However, the Federal Reserve is subject to oversight by Congress, which periodically reviews its activities and can alter its responsibilities by statute. Also, the

---

[16] TARGET2 is the real-time gross settlement (RTGS) system for the euro and one of the largest payment systems in the world. It is used for the settlement of central bank operations, large-value euro interbank transfers and other euro payments. It provides real-time processing and settlement in central bank money. All Eurosystem central banks and their banking communities are connected to TARGET2. Other EU national central banks may join TARGET2 on a voluntary basis, making TARGET2 accessible to a large number of participants from 23 EU countries. The CCBM ensures that all assets eligible for use either in monetary policy operations or to obtain intraday liquidity in TARGET are available to all its counterparties – regardless of where in the euro area the assets or the counterparty are situated.

[17] Board of Governors of the Federal Reserve System (2013).

Federal Reserve must work within the framework of the overall objectives of economic and financial policy established by the government. Therefore, the Federal Reserve can be more accurately described as 'independent within the government'.

6.4.1 Organisational structure of the Fed

The Fed is a federal system, composed of a central governmental agency, the Board of Governors, in Washington, DC, and 12 regional Federal Reserve Banks, located in major cities throughout the United States.[18] These components share responsibility for supervising and regulating certain financial institutions and activities, for providing banking services to depository institutions and to the federal government, and for ensuring that consumers receive adequate information and fair treatment in their business with the banking system.

A major element of the system is the **Federal Open Market Committee**, which is made up of the members of the Board of Governors, the president of the Federal Reserve Bank of New York, and presidents of five other Federal Reserve Banks, who serve on a rotating basis. The FOMC oversees open market operations, which is the main tool used by the Federal Reserve to influence money market conditions and the growth of money and credit.

In addition, the Federal Advisory Council (FAC) is a group of 12 representatives of the banking industry selected annually by the Board of Directors for each of the 12 Reserve Banks. The FAC's main duties are to consult with and advise the Board on its operations.

To sum up, the structure of the Federal Reserve System includes the following entities:

- Board of Governors;
- Federal Reserve Banks;
- Federal Open Market Committee;
- Federal Advisory Council;
- member banks.

6.4.2 The Board of Governors

The Board of Governors of the Federal Reserve System was established as a federal government agency. The Board comprises seven members, appointed by the president and confirmed by the Senate to serve 14-year terms of office. The appointments are staggered so that one term expires on 31 January of each even-numbered year. To avoid political interference, governors may serve only one full term. The president designates, and the Senate confirms, two members of the Board to be chairman and vice-chairman, for four-year terms. Each of the 12 Federal Reserve Districts can select only one member of the Board of Governors. It is a duty of the president of the United States to ensure that there is a fair representation of regional interests and the interests of various sectors of the public.

The primary responsibility of the Board members is to guide the monetary policy action. The seven Board members constitute a majority of the 12-member FOMC, the group that makes the key decisions affecting the cost and availability of money and credit

---

[18] The 12 regional Federal Reserve Banks are those of Atlanta, Boston, Chicago, Cleveland, Dallas, Kansas City, Minneapolis, New York, Philadelphia, Richmond, St Louis and San Francisco. See Section 6.4.3 for more details.

179

in the economy. The board sets reserve requirements and shares the responsibility with the Reserve Banks for discount rate policy. These two functions plus open market operations constitute the main monetary policy tools of the Federal Reserve System.

In addition to monetary policy responsibilities, the Federal Reserve Board has regulatory and supervisory responsibilities over banks that are members of the system, bank holding companies and international banking facilities in the United States.[19] (See Chapter 15 for more detail on regulation of the US banking system.) The Board also sets margin requirements, to prevent excess use of credit for purchasing or carrying securities. In addition, the Board plays a key role in assuring the smooth functioning and continued development of the nation's payments system.

The chairman of the Board advises the president of the United States on economic policy and may represent the United States in negotiation with other countries on economic matters. In January 2014, Janet Yellen was voted in by the US Senate to become the first woman to lead the Federal Reserve; she succeeded Ben Bernanke, who led the Fed during the global financial crisis.

6.4.3 The Federal Reserve Banks

Each of the 12 Federal Reserve Districts has a Federal Reserve Bank: Atlanta, Boston, Chicago, Cleveland, Dallas, Kansas City, Minneapolis, New York, Philadelphia, Richmond, St Louis, and San Francisco. Federal Reserve Banks operate under the general supervision of the Board of Governors in Washington. Each bank has a nine-member board of directors that oversees its operations. All reserve banks, except those in Boston, Philadelphia and – since 2008 – New York, have branches that help them carry out their work. There are 24 branches in all.

Five of the twelve presidents of the Federal Reserve Banks serve as members of the FOMC. The president of the Federal Reserve Bank of New York serves on a continuous basis; the other presidents serve one-year terms on a rotating basis. Each Federal Reserve Bank has a research staff to gather and analyse a wide range of economic data and to interpret conditions and developments in the economy to assist the FOMC in the formulation and implementation of monetary policy.

In terms of monetary policy, the boards of directors of the Federal Reserve Banks vote on discount rate recommendations. Requests to alter the discount rate must be approved by the Board of Governors.

6.4.4 The Federal Open Market Committee (FOMC)

The FOMC is composed of the seven members of the Board of Governors and five Reserve Bank presidents. Each year one member is elected to the committee by the boards of directors of Reserve Banks in each of the following groups: 1) Boston, Philadelphia and Richmond; 2) Cleveland and Chicago; 3) Atlanta, St Louis and Dallas; and 4) Minneapolis, Kansas City and San Francisco. The president of the New York Fed is a permanent voting member of the FOMC, and the presidents of the other Reserve Banks serve one-year terms as voting

---

[19] International banking facilities (IBFs) enable depository institutions in the United States to offer deposit and loan services to foreign residents and institutions free of Federal Reserve System reserve requirements, as well as some state and local taxes on income. IBFs permit US banks to use their domestic US offices to offer foreign customers deposit and loan services which formerly could be provided competitively only from foreign offices.

members on a rotation that is set by law. The permanent chairman of the FOMC is the chairman of the Board of Governors and the permanent vice-chairman is the president of the New York Federal Reserve Bank.

The FOMC regularly meets eight times each year in Washington, DC. At each scheduled meeting, the committee reviews economic and financial conditions and decides on the monetary policy to be carried out to meet its long-term goals of price stability and sustainable economic growth.

Before each meeting of the FOMC, written reports on past and prospective economic and financial developments are prepared and sent to committee members and to non-member Reserve Bank presidents. At the meeting itself, staff officers present oral reports on the current and prospective business situation, on conditions in financial markets, and on international financial developments. After these reports, the committee members and other Reserve Bank presidents turn to policy. Typically, each participant expresses his or her own views on the state of the economy and prospects for the future and on the appropriate direction for monetary policy. However, the monetary policy decisions are based on national rather than local economic conditions. At the meeting, economic developments, as well as the economic forecasts and conditions in the banking system, foreign exchange markets and financial markets, are discussed. The committee must reach a consensus regarding the appropriate course for policy, which is incorporated in a directive to the Federal Reserve Bank of New York – the bank that executes transactions for the System Open Market Account. The directive sets forth the committee's objectives for long-run growth of certain key monetary and credit aggregates.

Open market operations as directed by the FOMC are the major tool used to influence the total amount of money and credit available in the economy. The Federal Reserve attempts to provide enough reserves to encourage expansion of money and credit in keeping with the goals of price stability and sustainable growth in economic activity.[20]

6.4.5 The Board of Directors and the Federal Advisory Council

Reserve Bank boards of directors are composed of nine members and they are divided into three classes of three persons each. Class A directors represent the member commercial banks in the district, and most are bankers. Class B and class C directors are selected to represent the public. Class A and class B directors are elected by member banks in the district, while class C directors are appointed by the system's Board of Governors in Washington. All directors serve three-year terms.

The responsibilities of directors are broad, ranging from the supervision and management of the Reserve Banks (assigned by the Federal Reserve Act) to making recommendations on monetary policy. Directors review their Reserve Bank's budget and expenditures. They are also responsible for the internal audit programme of the bank.

The Federal Reserve Act requires directors to set the bank's discount rate every two weeks, subject to approval by the Board of Governors in Washington. Directors bring to the Federal Reserve a regional perspective, an independent assessment of the business outlook, and judgement and advice on the credit conditions of the districts they represent.

The board of directors appoints the members of the Federal Advisory Council. The FAC regularly meets four times a year with the Board of Governors to discuss economic and banking matters. The 12 members of the FAC serve three one-year terms.

---

[20] More information can be found at: **www.federalreserve.gov/pubs/frseries/frseri2.htm**

6.4.6 The member banks

All national banks (i.e. banks chartered by the Office of the Comptroller) are required to be members of the Federal Reserve System. Banks chartered by states are not required to be members, but they can be if they so choose.[21] While many large state banks have become Fed members, most state banks have chosen not to join. Member banks must subscribe to stock in their regional Federal Reserve Bank in an amount equal to 6 per cent of their capital and surplus. They receive a 6 per cent annual dividend on their stock and may vote for class A and class B directors of the Reserve Bank. However, the stock does not carry with it the control and financial interest that is normal for the common stock of a for-profit organisation. It offers no opportunity for capital gain and may not be sold or pledged as collateral for loans. The stock is merely a legal obligation that goes along with membership.

6.4.7 Functions of the Fed

Today the Federal Reserve's duties fall into four general areas: 1) conducting the nation's monetary policy; 2) supervising and regulating banking institutions and protecting the credit rights of consumers; 3) maintaining the stability of the financial system and containing systemic risk that may arise in financial markets; and 4) providing certain financial services to the US government, the public, financial institutions and foreign official institutions. This includes playing a major role in operating the country's payment system.[22]

The Fed's mission is 'to promote sustainable growth, high levels of employment, stability of prices'. Typically, macroeconomic policy in the US (as in the UK and the eurozone) emphasises economic policy packages where monetary policy is predominant. This is because price stability is viewed as an essential pre-condition for achieving the main economic objective of high and stable levels of growth and employment.

6.4.7.1 Monetary policy

Monetary policy in the United States (as in the United Kingdom) was dominated by targeting monetary aggregates in the second half of the 1970s and the early 1980s. This was based on the view that if the authorities could target the growth of (some measure of) money supply in the economy it could contain inflationary pressures. In the United States, for instance, targeted growth rates of various money measures were used (e.g. M1 − cash and notes + bank checking accounts and M2 − M1 + savings accounts and money market funds), with growth ranges being in the order of 3–6 per cent for the former and 4–7 per cent for the latter. In the United States, M3 (mainly reserves + bank deposits) is nowadays the most widely used broad measure of money. However, these are no longer used as major intermediate targets of monetary policy because since the mid-1980s the empirical relationship between monetary supply (aggregate) growth and inflation has been found to be weak at best.

---

[21] The US banking system is a 'dual banking system'. This refers to the fact that both state and federal governments issue bank charters (licences). The Office of the Comptroller of the Currency (OCC) charters national banks; the state banking departments charter state banks. As a consequence, in US banking 'National' or 'State' in a bank's name has nothing to do with where it operates, it refers to the kind of charter the bank has. The charter is an institution's primary regulator; the Comptroller of the Currency supervises approximately 3,191 national banks. State bank supervisors oversee about 7,524 commercial banks. See Chapter 15 for more details on bank licensing and regulation in the United States.

[22] More information can be found at **www.federalreserve.gov/aboutthefed/mission.htm**

To carry out monetary policy, the Federal Reserve employs three tools:

- open market operations;
- the discount rate;
- reserve requirements.

Open market operations refer to the purchases and/or sales of US Treasury and Federal Agency securities. These largely determine the federal funds rate – the interest rate at which depository institutions lend balances at the Federal Reserve to other depository institutions overnight. The federal funds rate, in turn, affects monetary and financial conditions, which ultimately influence employment, output and the overall level of prices. Decisions regarding open market operations are taken by the FOMC. The discount rate is the interest rate charged to commercial banks and other depository institutions on loans they receive from their regional Federal Reserve Bank's lending facility: the discount window. Reserve requirements are the amount of funds that a depository institution must hold in reserve against specified deposit liabilities. Depository institutions must hold reserves in the form of vault cash or deposits with Federal Reserve Banks. The Board of Governors of the Federal Reserve System is responsible for the discount rate and reserve requirements. Since the early 1990s, the United States has targeted its federal funds rate as its primary tool of monetary policy. Box 6.6 briefly notes this main feature of US monetary policy.

6.4.7.2 Supervision and regulation

The Federal Reserve Board is responsible for implementing the Federal Reserve Act, which established the Federal Reserve System, and a number of other laws relating to a range of banking and financial activities. As a consequence, the Federal Reserve Board has regulation and supervision responsibilities over banks. This includes monitoring banks that are members of the system, international banking facilities in the United States, foreign activities of member banks, and the US activities of foreign-owned banks. The Fed also needs to ensure that banks act in the public's interest.

However, the Fed is only one of several government agencies that share responsibility for ensuring the safety and soundness of the US banking system. (Chapter 15 discusses the role of the Fed and other agencies that regulate the US banking system.)

6.4.7.3 Financial stability

The Fed's goals with respect to supervision and regulation include promoting the safety and soundness of the banking system, fostering stability in financial markets, ensuring compliance with applicable laws and regulations, and encouraging banking institutions to responsibly meet the financial needs of their communities. The financial turmoil has highlighted the need to reform and strengthen the regulatory and supervisory system in the financial sector. The 2010 Dodd–Frank Act has indeed expanded the regulators' responsibilities to foster financial stability. The commitment to financial stability is now as important as price stability, as stated in a speech by Ben Bernanke in 2011:[23]

> My guess is that the current framework for monetary policy – with innovations, no doubt, to further improve the ability of central banks to communicate with the public – will remain the standard approach, as its benefits in terms of macroeconomic stabilization have been demonstrated.

---

[23] www.federalreserve.gov/newsevents/speech/bernanke20111018a.htm

However, central banks are also heeding the broader lesson, that the maintenance of financial stability is an equally critical responsibility. Central banks certainly did not ignore issues of financial stability in the decades before the recent crisis, but financial stability policy was often viewed as the junior partner to monetary policy. One of the most important legacies of the crisis will be the restoration of financial stability policy to co-equal status with monetary policy.

Chairman Ben S. Bernanke
Speech at the Federal Reserve Bank of Boston 56th Economic Conference,
18 October 2011

BOX 6.6 EFFICACY AND COSTS OF LARGE-SCALE ASSET PURCHASES

The 2007–2009 economic and financial turbulence has posed serious risks to the stability of financial institutions and markets globally. In an effort to restore stability and confidence in financial markets, the Fed responded by: 1) providing liquidity in the form of short-term secured loans (lender-of-last-resort policies); 2) coordinating with foreign central banks and creating foreign currency swaps. By swapping foreign currency with dollars foreign central banks could meet the dollar funding needs for their own financial institutions; 3) collaborating directly with the Treasury and federal regulatory agencies to improve the regulatory system; 4) carrying out *stress tests* on the biggest banks to improve their safety and soundness and reassure investors (see Chapter 7).

In an attempt to try to stabilise the economy, the Fed took a radical approach to the global financial crisis and when traditional monetary policy responses were ineffective and insufficient, the Fed turned to unconventional monetary policy tools in exercising and extending its function of LOLR. The use of non-conventional monetary policies became a necessity from September 2008 (after the default of Lehman Brothers). In December 2008 the Fed made the latest change to the target federal funds rate by reducing it to nearly zero (six years on, it still stands at near zero).

To affect long-term rates, the Fed announced a programme of large-scale asset purchases (a form of quantitative easing, see for more details Chapter 5) in March 2009 and then again in November 2010. Essentially, large-scale asset purchases (LSAPs) involve the purchase, in the private market, of long-term securities issued by the US government and by government-sponsored enterprises (GSEs) like Freddie Mac and Fannie Mae. With the funds rate near its effective lower bound, leaving little scope for further

reductions, in late 2008 the Federal Reserve began a series of LSAPs.

Between late 2008 and early 2010, the Federal Reserve purchased approximately $1.7 trillion in longer-term Treasury securities, agency debt, and agency mortgage-backed securities (MBS). From late 2010 to mid-2011, a second round of LSAPs was implemented, consisting of purchases of $600 billion in longer-term Treasury securities. Between September 2011 and the end of 2012, the Federal Reserve implemented the maturity extension program and its continuation, under which it purchased approximately $700 billion in longer-term Treasury securities and sold or allowed to run off an equal amount of shorter-term Treasury securities. And in September and December 2012, the Federal Reserve announced flow-based purchases of agency MBS and longer-term Treasury securities at initial paces of $40 billion and $45 billion per month, respectively.

These purchases were undertaken in order to put downward pressure on longer-term interest rates, support mortgage markets, and help to make broader financial conditions more accommodative, thereby supporting the economic recovery. One mechanism through which asset purchases can affect financial conditions is the 'portfolio balance channel', which is based on the premise that different financial assets may be reasonably close but imperfect substitutes in investors' portfolios. This assumption implies that changes in the supplies of various assets available to private investors may affect the prices or yields of those assets and the prices of assets that may be reasonably close substitutes. As a result, the Federal Reserve's asset purchases can push up the prices and lower the yields on the securities purchased and influence other asset prices as well. As investors

Box 6.6 Efficacy and costs of large-scale asset purchases (*continued*)

further rebalance their portfolios, overall financial conditions should ease more generally, stimulating economic activity through channels similar to those for conventional monetary policy. In addition, asset purchases could signal that the central bank intends to pursue a more accommodative policy stance than previously thought, thereby lowering investor expectations about the future path of the federal funds rate and putting additional downward pressure on longer-term yields.

A substantial body of empirical research finds that the Federal Reserve's asset purchase programs have significantly lowered longer-term Treasury yields. More important, the effects of LSAPs do not seem to be restricted to Treasury yields. In particular, LSAPs have been found to be associated with significant declines in MBS yields and corporate bond yields as well as with increases in equity prices.

While there seems to be substantial evidence that LSAPs have lowered longer-term yields and eased broader financial conditions, obtaining accurate estimates of the effects of LSAPs on the macro-economy is inherently difficult, as the counterfactual case – how the economy would have performed without LSAPs – cannot be directly observed. However, econometric models can be used to estimate the effects of LSAPs on the economy under the assumption that the economic effects of the easier financial conditions that are induced by LSAPs are similar to those that are induced by conventional monetary policy easing. Model simulations conducted at the Federal Reserve have generally found that asset purchases provide a significant boost to the economy. For example, a study based on the Federal Reserve Board's FRB/US model estimated that, as of 2012, the first two rounds of LSAPs had raised real gross domestic product almost 3 percent and increased private payroll employment by about 3 million jobs, while lowering the unemployment rate about 1.5 percentage points, relative to what would have been expected otherwise. These simulations also suggest that the program materially reduced the risk of deflation. Of course, all model-based estimates of the macroeconomic effects of LSAPs are subject to considerable statistical and modelling uncertainty and thus should be treated with caution. Indeed, while some other studies also report significant macroeconomic effects from asset purchases,

other research finds smaller effects. Nonetheless, a balanced reading of the evidence supports the conclusion that LSAPs have provided meaningful support to the economic recovery while mitigating deflationary risks.

The potential benefits of LSAPs must be considered alongside their possible costs. One potential cost of conducting additional LSAPs is that the operations could lead to a deterioration in market functioning or liquidity in markets where the Federal Reserve is engaged in purchasing. More specifically, if the Federal Reserve becomes too dominant a buyer in a certain market, trading among private participants could decrease enough that market liquidity and price discovery become impaired. As the global financial system relies on deep and liquid markets for US Treasury securities, significant impairment of this market would be especially costly; impairment of this market could also impede the transmission of monetary policy. Although the large volume of the Federal Reserve's purchases relative to the size of the markets for Treasury or agency securities could ultimately become an issue, few if any problems have been observed in those markets thus far.

A second potential cost of LSAPs is that they may undermine public confidence in the Federal Reserve's ability to exit smoothly from its accommodative policies at the appropriate time. Such a reduction in confidence might increase the risk that long-term inflation expectations become unanchored.

The Federal Reserve is certainly aware of these concerns and accordingly has placed great emphasis on developing the necessary tools to ensure that policy accommodation can be removed when appropriate. For example, the Federal Reserve will be able to put upward pressure on short-term interest rates at the appropriate time by raising the interest rate it pays on reserves, using draining tools like reverse repurchase agreements or term deposits with depository institutions, or selling securities from the Federal Reserve's portfolio. To date, the expansion of the balance sheet does not appear to have materially affected long-term inflation expectations.

A third cost to be weighed is that of risks to financial stability. For example, some observers have raised concerns that, by driving longer-term yields lower, non-traditional policies could induce imprudent risk taking by some investors. Of course, some

---

Box 6.6 Efficacy and costs of large-scale asset purchases (*continued*)

risk taking is a necessary element of a healthy economic recovery, and accommodative monetary policies could even serve to reduce the risk in the system by strengthening the overall economy. Nonetheless, the Federal Reserve has substantially expanded its monitoring of the financial system and modified its supervisory approach to take a more systemic perspective.

There has been limited evidence so far of excessive build ups of duration, credit risk, or leverage, but the Federal Reserve will continue both its careful oversight and its implementation of financial regulatory reforms designed to reduce systemic risk. The Federal Reserve has remitted substantial income to the Treasury from its earnings on securities, totalling some $290 billion since 2009. However, if the economy continues to strengthen and policy accommodation is withdrawn, remittances will likely decline

in coming years. Indeed, in some scenarios, particularly if interest rates were to rise quickly, remittances to the Treasury could be quite low for a time. Even in such scenarios, however, average annual remittances over the period affected by the Federal Reserve's purchases are highly likely to be greater than the pre-crisis norm, perhaps substantially so. Moreover, if monetary policy promotes a stronger recovery, the associated reduction in the federal deficit would far exceed any variation in the Federal Reserve's remittances to the Treasury. That said, the Federal Reserve conducts monetary policy to meet its congressionally mandated objectives of maximum employment and price stability and not primarily for the purpose of turning a profit for the US Department of the Treasury.

Source: Board of Governors of the Federal Reserve System (2012) Box 2, p. 23.

6.4.7.4 Services to the US government

The Fed serves as a bank not only for other banks but also for the federal government. The government maintains accounts at the Fed and makes its payments by writing cheques against these accounts or by transferring funds from the account electronically. The Fed helps the government borrow funds that it needs. It processes the vast majority of bids that individuals and institutions make to buy securities at the Treasury's weekly, monthly and quarterly auctions. The Fed also issues and redeems US savings bonds for the federal government.

Other services provided by the Reserve Banks include clearing cheques drawn on the Treasury's account and acting as fiscal agents for the government (i.e. the Reserve Banks sell, service and redeem Treasury securities). Furthermore, the Fed is responsible for issuing (and withdrawing) currency and coins from circulation.

6.5 Conclusion

The Bank of England is the central bank for the United Kingdom. It was established in 1694 and it is one of the world's oldest central banks. The Bank of England Act (1998) set forth a series of changes, including the definition of responsibilities of the Bank. With the 1998 Act, the Bank of England was also given operational independence in setting interest rates. The monetary policy function of the Bank is carried out by the MPC, which is responsible for setting short-term interest rates. The UK regulatory architecture has been reformed by the 2012 Financial Services Act and as a result the Financial Services Authority (FSA) was replaced by the Prudential Regulation Authority (PRA) and a Financial Conduct Authority (FCA). In addition, an expert macro-prudential authority was created within the Bank: the Financial Policy Committee (FPC). The main objectives of the Bank of England are to maintain the integrity and value of the currency, to maintain the stability of the financial system and to ensure the effectiveness of the UK financial services industry.

The European Central Bank was established in 1998 and it is one of the world's youngest central banks. It is the central bank for all the countries that have adopted the single currency, the euro. The ECB and the NCBs of all EU member states, regardless of whether they have adopted the euro or not, constitute the European System of Central Banks. The ECB and the NCBs of those countries that have adopted the euro form the Eurosystem. As long as there are EU member states that have not yet adopted the euro, this distinction between the Eurosystem and the ESCB will need to be made. The functions of the ECB (and of the ESCB) are specified in the Statute that is a protocol attached to the Treaty on the European Union. The primary objective of the ESCB is to maintain price stability.

The Fed is the central bank of the United States of America and was founded by Congress in 1913, with the signing of the Federal Reserve Act. The Fed is a federal system, composed of a central, governmental agency, the Board of Governors, in Washington, DC, and 12 regional Federal Reserve Banks, located in major cities throughout the United States. A major component of the system is the FOMC, which is responsible for conducting open market operations. The Fed explicitly targets short-term interest rates as its major tool of monetary policy, whereas the Bank of England and the ECB place greater emphasis on inflation targeting.

The 2007–2009 financial crisis and the economic downturn that followed resulted in significant changes in the way central banks help stimulate the economy. As traditional tools of monetary policy have proved ineffective, quantitative easing has become central in the monetary authorities' agenda. Remarkably, events have demonstrated that stable prices cannot grant financial stability and that preventing excesses in the financial markets should not be a secondary objective of central banks. There have been major reforms in the regulatory and supervisory frameworks to minimise the likelihood that a similar crisis may occur again in the future and these are discussed in Chapters 7 and 8.

Key terms

Bank of England Act 1998	Eurosystem	Financial Policy Committee (FPC)	National central banks (NCBs)
Board of Governors	Exchange Rate Mechanism	Financial Services Act 2012	Prudential Regulation Authority (PRA)
Debt Management Office (DMO)	Federal Open Market Committee (FOMC)	Financial Services Authority (FSA)	Single Euro Payments Area
European Central Bank (ECB)	Federal Reserve System (Fed)	Governing Council	
European System of Central Banks (ESCB)	Financial Conduct Authority (FCA)	Monetary Policy Committee (MPC)	

Key reading

Bank of England (2013) 'Asset purchase facility', *Quarterly Report*.

Board of Governors of the Federal Reserve System (2013) *The Federal Reserve System: Purposes and Functions*, 9th Edition.

Cour-Thimann, P. and Winkler, B. (2013) 'The ECB's non-standard monetary policy measures: The role of institutional factors and financial structure', ECB Working Papers Series, No. 1525, April.

European Central Bank (2011) *The Monetary Policy of the ECB*.

Hammond, G. (2012) 'State of the art inflation targeting, Bank of England', *CCBS Handbook*, No. 29, February.

International Monetary Fund (2013) 'Unconventional monetary policies: Recent experience and prospects', April.

REVISION QUESTIONS AND PROBLEMS

6.1 What are the main functions and objectives of the Bank of England?

6.2 How does the Bank of England meet its objective of price stability?

6.3 Describe the relationship between the ECB and the NCBs of EU member states.

6.4 What does the term Eurosystem refer to?

6.5 What are the core functions of the European Central Bank?

6.6 Describe the operational structure of the Federal Reserve Bank.

6.7 What is the role of the FOMC?

6.8 What are the core functions of the Federal Reserve Bank? How do they differ from those of the Bank of England and the European Central Bank?

6.9 Discuss the key actions taken by the Bank of England, the ECB and the Fed during and after the 2007–2009 global financial crisis.

6.10 Discuss the efficacy and costs of large-scale asset purchases (LSAPs).

Chapter 7

Bank regulation and supervision

Learning objectives

- To understand the rationale for financial regulation
- To appreciate different types of regulation
- To understand the elements of the financial safety net
- To understand the limitation and costs of regulation
- To understand the causes for regulatory reform
- To understand bank capital regulation
- To understand the increased importance of the international dimension

7.1 Introduction

The regulation of financial markets in general, and of banking institutions in particular, is considered a controversial issue. The financial sector is one of the most heavily regulated sectors in the economy and banking is by far the most heavily regulated industry. In Chapter 1, we presented some of the reasons why banks are considered 'special', outlined the existence of market imperfections (such as information asymmetries, moral hazard and adverse selection) and noted how the existence of banks can help minimise such problems. In this chapter we note the pivotal role played by banks in the economy to understand the rationale for regulation (Section 7.2). We investigate the aims and objectives of regulation, and the different types of regulation in Section 7.3. Section 7.4 describes the elements of the financial safety net. The limitations of regulation and the possible reasons behind regulatory failure are discussed in Section 7.5. Section 7.6 reviews the causes of regulatory reform. International policy initiatives, such as the Basel Capital Adequacy Accords, are reviewed in Section 7.7.

Before we discuss the rationale for regulation it is useful to introduce various terms that are often used to describe the regulatory environment. **Regulation** relates to the setting of specific rules of behaviour that firms have to abide by – these may be set through legislation (laws) or be stipulated by the relevant regulatory agency. **Monitoring** of these regulations refers to the process whereby the relevant authority assesses financial firms to evaluate whether these rules are being obeyed. **Supervision** is a broader term used to refer to the general oversight of the behaviour of financial firms. In practice, one should note that these terms are often used interchangeably in general discussion of the regulatory environment.

7.2	The rationale for regulation

Financial systems are prone to periods of instability. A number of financial crises around the world (South East Asia, Latin America and Russia) have brought about a large number of bank failures. Further, the 2007–2009 crisis and the widespread financial turmoil that it caused have brought these issues to the fore. These occurrences, some argue, suggest a case for more effective regulation and supervision. Others attribute many of these crises, including the global financial crisis of 2007–2009, to the failure of regulation. Advocates of so-called 'free banking' argue that the financial sector would work better without regulation, supervision and central banking.[1] In the absence of government regulation, they argue, banks would have greater incentives to prevent failures.

However, the financial services industry is a politically sensitive one and relies largely on public confidence. Because of the nature of their activities (illiquid assets and short-term liabilities), banks are more prone to troubles than other firms. Further, because of the interconnectedness of banks, the failure of one institution can immediately affect others.

This is known as bank **contagion** and may lead to **bank runs**. Banking systems are vulnerable to **systemic risk**, which is the risk that problems in one bank will spread through the whole sector (bank failures and financial crises will be analysed in detail in Chapter 8).

Bank runs occur when a large number of depositors, fearing that their bank is unsound and about to fail, try to withdraw their savings within a short period of time. A bank run starts when the public begins to suspect that a bank may become insolvent. This creates a problem because banks keep only a small fraction of deposits in cash – they lend out the majority of deposits to borrowers or use the funds to purchase other interest-bearing assets. When a bank is faced with a sudden increase in withdrawals, it needs to increase its liquidity to meet depositors' demands. Banks' reserves may not be sufficient to cover the withdrawals and banks may be forced to sell their assets. Banks assets (loans) are highly illiquid in the absence of a secondary market and if banks have financial difficulties they may be forced to sell loans at a loss (known as 'fire-sale' prices in the United States) in order to obtain liquidity. However, excessive losses made on such loan sales can make the bank insolvent and bring about bank failure.

Bank loans are highly illiquid because of information asymmetries: it is very difficult for a potential buyer to evaluate customer-specific information on the basis of which the loan was agreed. The very nature of banks' contracts can turn an illiquidity problem (lack of short-term cash) into insolvency (where a bank is unable to meet its obligations – or to put this differently, when the value of its assets is less than its liabilities).

In summary, regulation is needed to ensure consumers' confidence in the financial sector. According to Llewellyn (1999), the main reasons for financial sector regulation are:

- to ensure systemic stability;
- to provide smaller, retail clients with protection;
- to protect consumers against monopolistic exploitation.

---

[1] See section 5.5.2 for more discussion on free banking.

Systemic stability is one of the main reasons for regulation, as the social costs of bank failure are greater than the private costs. The second concern is with consumer protection. In financial markets *caveat emptor* (a Latin phrase meaning 'Let the buyer beware') is not considered adequate, as financial contracts are often complex and opaque. The costs of acquiring information are high, particularly for small, retail customers. Consumer protection is a particularly sensitive issue if customers face the loss of their lifetime savings. Finally, regulation serves the purpose of protecting consumers against the abuse of monopoly power in product pricing.

7.3   Types of regulation

It is possible to identify three different types of regulation:

1 systemic (or macro-prudential) regulation;
2 prudential (or micro-prudential) regulation;
3 conduct of business regulation.

7.3.1   Systemic (macro-prudential) regulation

Goodhart *et al.* (1998) define systemic regulation as regulation concerned mainly with the safety and soundness of the financial system. Under this heading we refer to all public policy regulation designed to minimise the risk of bank runs that goes under the name of the financial safety net. In particular, the safety net encompasses two main features – **deposit insurance** arrangements and the **lender of last resort** function (see also Section 7.4):

● Deposit insurance is a guarantee that all or part of the amount deposited by savers in a bank will be paid in the event that a bank fails.

● The lender of last resort (LOLR) function is one of the main functions of a central bank. The central bank, or other central institution, will provide funds to banks that are in financial difficulty and are not able to access any other credit channel. A more detailed discussion of the functions of central banks was presented in Chapter 5. Through the LOLR mechanism, the authorities can provide liquidity to the banking sector at times of crises.

Macro-prudential supervision is concerned with the aggregate effect of individual banks' actions. Because it aims to generate an overall picture of the functioning of the financial sector, macro-prudential supervision is also referred to as 'top-down supervision'.

7.3.2   Prudential and conduct of business regulation

Prudential regulation is mainly concerned with consumer protection. It relates to the monitoring and supervision of financial institutions, with particular attention paid to asset quality and **capital adequacy**. The case for prudential regulation is that consumers are not in a position to judge the safety and soundness of financial institutions due to imperfect consumer information and agency problems associated with the nature of the intermediation business.

Micro-prudential supervision checks that individual financial firms are complying with financial regulation. It involves the collection and analysis of information about the risks that the firms take, their systems and their personnel. Because micro-prudential supervision uses firm-specific information to generate a picture of risk and its management, it is also referred to as 'bottom-up supervision'.

Conduct of business regulation focuses on how banks and other financial institutions conduct their business. This kind of regulation relates to information disclosure, fair business practices, competence, honesty and integrity of financial institutions and their employees. Overall, it focuses on establishing rules and guidelines to reduce the likelihood that:

- consumers receive bad advice (possible agency problem);
- supplying institutions become insolvent before contracts mature;
- contracts turn out to be different from what the customer was anticipating;
- fraud and misrepresentation take place;
- employees of financial intermediaries and financial advisors act incompetently;
- insider trading takes place;
- money will be laundered.

7.4 The financial safety net

One of the consequences of the 2007–2009 global financial crisis was that more attention is now being paid to financial regulation, and that holds true both regarding the protection of the stability of individual banks (micro-prudential regulation) and the system overall (macro-prudential regulation).

A financial safety net is a comprehensive system for enhancing and ensuring a country's financial stability. It often consists of five elements (see Figure 7.1), which complement and strengthen each other (Bernet and Walter, 2009):

- regulation and supervision;
- deposit insurance schemes;

Figure 7.1 Elements of the financial safety net
Source: Adapted from Bernet and Walter (2009).

- lender of last resort;
- bank insolvency/resolution laws;
- cooperation and resolution processes.

The distribution of powers and responsibilities between the financial safety-net participants is a matter of public policy choice and individual country circumstances.

7.4.1 Deposit insurance

As mentioned, deposit insurance is a guarantee that all or part of the amount deposited by savers in a bank will be paid in the event that a bank fails. The guarantee may be explicitly given in law or regulation, offered privately without government backing or inferred implicitly from the verbal promises and/or past actions of the authorities. The level and coverage of deposit insurance is country specific. In some countries there are no statutory rules regarding the eligibility of bank liabilities, the level of protection provided or the form that reimbursement will take.

The United States was the second country (after Czechoslovakia) to introduce deposit insurance in the 1930s; a substantial number of countries adopted deposit insurance schemes (DIS) between 1970 and 2011.[2] According to the International Association of Deposit Insurers (IADI), 113 jurisdictions had deposit insurance schemes in place by January 2014.[3] In Europe, the first EU Directive on deposit guarantee schemes was issued in 1994 (Directive 94/19/EC), setting minimum levels of deposit insurance that had to be in place. However, a number of countries do not have an explicit DIS – for example, in the run-up to the 2007–2009 global financial crisis, Australia, China, Saudi Arabia and South Africa, among others, had no explicit deposit protection systems.

The 2007–2009 financial crisis also exposed some fundamental weaknesses in the deposit insurance schemes operating at the time. In addition, for a number of years the IMF and the World Bank have been posing questions concerning the adjustment of deposit insurance schemes to the rapidly changing national and international conditions of financial markets. In nearly all countries hit by the crisis, there began a fundamental revision of the existing deposit insurance schemes. The financial crisis also caused a range of other supranational institutions to concern themselves with questions relating to the structure and implementation of national deposit insurance schemes. A report by the Financial Stability Forum (FSF) in early 2008 stressed the necessity of internationally recognised basic principles and conditions for the structure of DIS (Financial Stability Forum, 2008). In response, in the summer of 2008, the Basel Committee on Banking Supervision (BCBS), together with the IADI, issued the revised version of the so-called *Core Principles for Effective Deposit Insurance Systems*. The results of this work – a set of 18 principles in total, which together define the target function of a modern DIS – were presented in the summer of 2009. Since then, IADI has been collaborating with the BCBS, the European Forum of Deposit Insurers (EFDI), the IMF, the World Bank and the European Commission (EC) to develop a robust methodology to assess compliance with the Core Principles. A final version of the *Core Principles* was submitted to the Financial Stability Board (FSB) in December 2010 (Basel Committee on Banking Supervision and International Association of Deposit Insurers, 2010).

---

[2] The Federal Deposit Insurance Corporation was created in 1933 in response to the thousands of bank failures that occurred in the 1920s and early 1930s.

[3] **www.iadi.org/di.aspx**

These *Core Principles* are intended as a voluntary framework for effective deposit insurance practices. National authorities are free to put in place supplementary measures that they deem necessary to achieve effective deposit insurance in their jurisdictions. The *Core Principles* (summarised in Box 7.1) are not designed to cover all the needs and circumstances of every deposit insurance system or prescribe a single specific form of deposit insurance but are designed to be adaptable to a broad range of country circumstances, settings and structures.

Following the development of the *Core Principles* and their assessment methodology, the FSB agreed to undertake a peer review of deposit insurance systems in 2011. The results of the review as well as the recommendation of the FSB can be found in the Report 'Thematic review on deposit insurance systems' (Financial Stability Board, 2012d).

An explicit DIS is considered preferable to implicit protection if it clarifies the authorities' obligations to depositors and limits the scope for discretionary decisions that may result in arbitrary actions. A DIS scheme should cover all those deposits that can lead to a liquidity problem for a bank; these include all kinds of saving accounts and short-term deposits held by private individuals and business customers (excluding financial institutions). In the European Union, deposits are defined in Article 1(1) of Directive 94/19/EC. In 2008, the need to restore confidence in the financial sector was vital and the European Commission put forward a revision of EU rules to promote convergence of deposit guarantee schemes within member states in order to improve depositor protection, including increased level of coverage for deposits (from €20,000 to €100,000), the removal of co-insurance (i.e. where

BOX 7.1 CORE PRINCIPLES FOR EFFECTIVE DEPOSIT INSURANCE SYSTEMS

1 Public policy objectives: formally specified and integrated in the DIS design
2 Mitigating moral hazard
3 Mandate: clear and formally specified
4 Powers: clear and formally specified
5 Governance: operationally independent, transparent and accountable
6 Relationship with other safety net participants: clear and formally specified
7 Cross-border issues: clear recognition of responsibilities
8 Compulsory membership: for all financial intermediaries accepting deposits
9 Coverage: clear and formally specified
10 Transition from a blanket guarantee to a limited coverage DIS
11 Funding: to ensure prompt reimbursement of depositors
12 Public awareness
13 Legal protection
14 Dealing with parties at fault in a bank failure
15 Early detection and timely intervention and resolution
16 Effective resolution processes
17 Reimbursing depositors
18 Recoveries

Source: BCBS and IADI (2010).

the depositor bears part of the losses) and the reduction of the payout period from three months to three days. These proposals were adopted by the European Council in February 2009. However, the evolution of the eurozone crisis highlighted the need for more drastic improvements, leading to the creation of a Single Deposit Guarantee Scheme (SDGS). The EU SDGS deal is discussed in Section 14.5.

In general terms, the deposits that are repayable by the DIS are called *eligible deposits*. Not all eligible deposits are repayable, as some countries apply a coverage limit. For example, in the UK if a bank, building society or credit union were to default, the Financial Services Compensation Scheme (FSCS) would automatically refund savings up to £85,000 within seven days. According to the FSCS, around 98 per cent of the UK population have less than £85,000 in savings and are therefore covered by the protection limit.

Figure 7.2 illustrates the level of coverage for the FSB's member countries.[4] A lesson from the 2007–2009 financial crisis was that a low level of coverage can increase financial

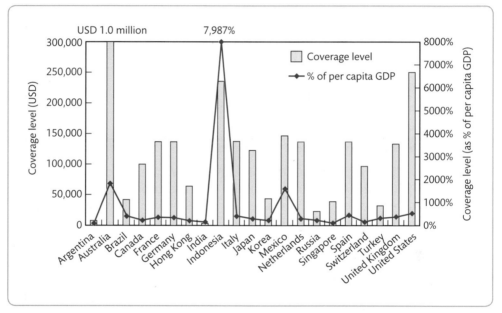

Figure 7.2 Cross-country comparison of coverage levels at end-2010 (absolute level and per capita GDP)

Source: Financial Stability Board (2012d) p. 19.

---

[4] The Financial Stability Board was established in April 2009 as the successor to the Financial Stability Forum (FSF). The FSF was founded in 1999 by the G7 finance ministers and central bank governors. In November 2008, the leaders of the G20 countries called for a larger membership of the FSF. In April 2009, an expanded FSF was re-established as the Financial Stability Board, with a broadened mandate to promote financial stability. The FSB member institutions are the central banks and/or Treasuries (or equivalent government departments) from the following countries: Argentina, Australia, Brazil, Canada, China, France, Germany, Hong Kong SAR, India, Indonesia, Italy, Japan, Mexico, the Netherlands, Republic of Korea, Russia, Saudi Arabia, Singapore, South Africa, Spain, Switzerland, Turkey, United Kingdom and United States. It also includes the following international organisations: Bank for International Settlements, European Central Bank, International Monetary Fund, Organisation for Economic Co-operation and Development and the World Bank. In addition, the following international standard-setting bodies are members: Basel Committee on Banking Supervision, Committee on the Global Financial System, Committee and Payment and Settlement Systems, International Association of Insurance Supervisors, International Accounting Standards Board and the International Organisation of Securities Commissions.

instability. While a high level of coverage might reduce depositors' incentive to run, it also reduces market discipline. The *Core Principles* do not prescribe a preferred coverage level. However, they suggest that limits should be set so that the vast majority of small-scale retail depositors are covered in full (so they have no incentive to run) but that a significant portion of the value of total deposit liabilities remains uncovered and exposed to market discipline.

To contribute effectively to the stability of a country's financial system a DIS needs to be: (i) credible; (ii) properly designed; (iii) well implemented and understood by the public; (iv) supported by strong prudential regulation and supervision; (v) supported by sound accounting and disclosure regimes; and (vi) supported by the enforcement of effective laws (Bernet and Walter, 2009).

It is necessary to point out that a deposit insurance system can deal with a limited number of simultaneous bank failures, but cannot be expected to deal with a systemic banking crisis. The practical organisation of a DIS is country-specific; it can be either private or public, depending on a country's legal circumstances.

7.4.1.1 Types of deposit insurance schemes

There are different types of deposit insurance schemes, of which the most common are the following:[5]

- the paybox model;
- the cost reducer model (or loss minimiser);
- the resolution facilitator model;
- the supervisor model (or risk minimiser).

In the *paybox model* the role of the deposit insurance institution is narrowly based and limited to a *settlement function* (that is, limited to paying out the depositors and ensuring an orderly settlement of all claims). A number of countries adopt this narrow mandate, including Australia, Germany, Hong Kong, India, the Netherlands, Singapore and Switzerland. The UK (together with Argentina and Brazil) adopts a so-called 'paybox plus' model, where the deposit insurer has some additional responsibilities, such as a resolution function.

In the *cost reducer model*, the deposit insurance institution retains the settlement function of the paybox model and, in addition to it, takes on the role of handling any occurrence of insolvency in an insured institution with the lowest possible costs and externalities for the financial system. Nine countries adopt this loss-minimiser approach, where the deposit insurer is tasked with pursuing the least-cost resolution strategy: Canada, France, Indonesia, Italy, Japan, Mexico, Russia, Spain and Turkey.

In the *resolution facilitator model*, the deposit insurance institution has additional powers: it can intervene to support a bank in difficulties (but not an illiquid or insolvent bank); it can facilitate a corporate restructuring or even a merger in order to protect depositors.

Finally, in the *supervisor model*, the deposit insurance institution has a broad mandate, as it is part of the supervisory system (for example, the Federal Deposit Insurance Corporation (FDIC) in the US and the Korean Deposit Insurance Corporation (KDIC)).

Following the 2007–2009 financial crisis, the mandates of many deposit insurers have been revised and expanded and many countries have adopted versions of the 'cost minimiser' approach.

---

[5] For a detailed discussion of different types of deposit insurance, see Bernet and Walter (2009) and FSB (2012d).

The financial crisis also illustrated that depositors' confidence depended, in part, on knowing that adequate funds would always be available to ensure the prompt reimbursement of their claims (*Core Principle 11*). While the primary responsibility for paying the cost of deposit insurance should be borne by banks, adequate emergency funding arrangements were also considered important (Financial Stability Board, 2012d). The main issues policy makers have to address in relation to the funding of a DIS is whether it should be funded *ex ante* (where a fund it set up so that it can be drawn upon to secure payments) or *ex post* (where there is no fund and the participants in the DIS will be required to contribute in the event of a claim). Both *ex-ante* and *ex-post* funding have a number of advantages and disadvantages. *Ex-post* funding fosters market discipline, as banks have an incentive to monitor each other's activities. However, there may be delays when the funds are needed. In addition, requests for contributions to the DIS may come at a time of economic instability, triggering a domino effect of bank failures.

Ex-ante financing, meanwhile, might boost public confidence, smooth premium payments and reduce moral hazard if it incorporates risk-adjusted premiums (see Box 7.2 for a discussion of how safety net arrangements can increase moral hazard). Drawbacks of setting up an insurance fund *ex ante* include the difficulty in establishing and managing a fund of adequate size to guarantee deposits of large financial institutions. In addition, while depositors seem to have a clear preference for a DIS based on *ex-ante* financing, this type of funding requires the definition of a deposit insurance premium. The key unanswered questions in this context are how to price the deposit insurance premiums; how to arrive at a 'fair' premium; what the premium should cover; and how to incorporate systemic risk in the deposit insurance premiums.

The investigation of risk-based models for computing contributions of DIS members has become a crucial goal for regulators in the aftermath of the global financial crisis. For example, the European Commission Joint Research Centre, in co-operation with the EFDI, has investigated potential models and assessed their potential impact across EU member states (European Commission, Joint Research Centre, 2009). In addition, the Financial Stability Board (2012d) has undertaken a comprehensive review of the reforms carried out to ensure depositors' protection as well as the structure of possible arrangements going forward. Table 7.1 presents a cross-country comparison of DIS features.

7.4.2 Lender of last resort (LOLR)

The lender of last resort function is typically one of the main functions of a central bank (see Section 5.5.1). The central bank, or other central institution, will provide funds to banks that are in financial difficulty and are not able to access any other credit channel. Through the LOLR mechanism, the authorities can provide liquidity to the banking sector at times of crises. The lender of last resort normally operates at the domestic level. The growing internationalisation of banking institutions and the banking and financial crises have raised the issue of an *international lender of last resort*. However, there is little agreement on the desirability of such a cross-country institution. In the case of a global scheme it is not clear whether it would be appropriate for the IMF to play such a role. However, a number of elements of a global financial safety net are at various stages of approval (the IMF, for example, has introduced a new precautionary line of credit and improved its existing flexible line of credit for countries that meet a rigorous set of criteria). The IMF publishes a *Global Financial Stability Report* that examines current risks facing the global financial system and highlights policy actions that may mitigate these (see also Chapter 8).

Table 7.1 DIS cross-country comparison

Country	Coverage level (US $)[1]	Public policy objectives formalised	Admin	Multiple agencies/ systems	Type/Mandate	Type/ Funding
Argentina	7,545	In law	Private	No	Paybox plus	*Ex ante*
Australia	1,016,300	In annex to law	Public	No	Paybox	*Ex ante*
Brazil	42,000	In statutes	Private	Yes	Paybox plus	*Ex ante*
Canada	100,000	In law	Public	Yes	Loss minimiser	*Ex ante*
France	136,920	In law and regulation	Mixed	No	Loss minimiser	*Ex ante*
Germany	136,920	In law	Mixed	Yes	Paybox	*Ex ante*
Hong Kong	64,000	In law	Public	No	Paybox	*Ex ante*
India	2,240	Preamble of law, annual report	Public	No	Paybox	*Ex ante*
Indonesia	235,294	In law	Public	No	Loss minimiser	*Ex ante*
Italy	136,920	In law	Private	Yes	Loss minimiser	*Ex ante*
Japan	122,775	In law	Mixed	Yes	Loss minimiser	*Ex ante*
Korea	43,902	In law	Public	No	Risk minimiser	*Ex ante*
Mexico	146,606	In law	Public	No	Loss minimiser	*Ex ante*
The Netherlands	136,920	In law	Public	No	Paybox	*Ex post*
Russia	23,064	In law	Public	No	Loss minimiser	*Ex ante*
Singapore	38,835	Ministerial statement, preamble of law	Public	No	Paybox	*Ex ante*
Spain	136,920	In law	Private	No	Loss minimiser	*Ex ante*
Switzerland	96,830	In law and statutes	Private	No	Paybox	*Ex post*
Turkey	32,341	In law	Public	No	Loss minimiser	*Ex ante*
UK	133,068	In law and statutes	Public	No	Paybox plus	*Ex post*
US	250,000	In law	Public	Yes	Risk minimiser	*Ex ante*

Note: [1]Using the exchange rate as of end-2010.
China has announced that it will introduce a deposit insurance scheme in 2015–2016.

Source: The information shown in this table is collated from different tables in Annex C of the 'Thematic Review on Deposit Insurance Systems', Financial Stability Board (2012d).

7.4.3 Bank insolvency and resolution laws

As part of the regulation specific to the financial industry, bank insolvency and resolution laws refer to the legal provisions that regulate the conditions for the handling of bank failures and insolvencies. Bankruptcy laws applicable for general types of companies are generally not suited for balancing or preventing the negative externalities to the real economy triggered by bank insolvency. For this reason, most countries have enforced a bankruptcy law or insolvency regime aimed specifically at banks and financial institutions (Bernet and Walter, 2009). These are also known as *special resolution regimes* (SRR). The design and implementation of bank insolvency regulations are subject to strong political influence and there is a wide range of approaches adopted in EU countries and elsewhere. Since the onset of the global financial crisis in 2007, many countries have enacted major regulatory reforms to develop new, or revise existing, resolution regimes. In the UK, the Banking Act of 2009 created an SRR that gives the UK authorities (HM Treasury, Bank of

England and Prudential Regulation Authority) a permanent framework, providing them with tools for dealing with failing UK banks and building societies. The Act also gave the Bank of England a key role in implementing resolution using statutory tools. The PRA, in consultation with the Bank of England and the Treasury, makes the decision to put a bank into the SRR. A number of regulatory authorities then play a role in the SRR. HM Treasury decides whether to put a bank into temporary public ownership. If a bank is not temporarily nationalised, the Bank of England, in consultation with the other authorities, decides which of the tools to use and implements the resolution. This work is done by the Special Resolution Unit (SRU) within the Bank of England. The SRU was established in February 2009 to specifically deal with distressed banks and building societies. The Financial Services Compensation Scheme (FSCS) also has a role in the SRR, paying out depositors covered by its depositor compensation scheme, and its funds may be used also to support a non-payout resolution provided that is no more costly to the FSCS, net of recoveries, than a payout.

The 2009 UK Banking Act sets out five key objectives that must be considered in choosing which resolution tools to use (Bank of England, 2008):

- to protect and enhance the stability of the financial systems of the UK;
- to protect and enhance public confidence in the stability of the banking systems of the UK;
- to protect depositors;
- to protect public funds;
- to avoid interfering with property rights in contravention of the Human Rights Act 1998.

In the United States and Canada, the Federal Deposit Insurance Corporation and the Canada Deposit Insurance Corporation (CDIC) are subject to least-cost resolution (LCR) requirements, whereby they must adopt the resolution method that costs the least to the deposit insurance fund regardless of other objectives (although these requirements can be overridden in circumstances that trigger 'financial stability exceptions'). Some countries, including New Zealand and Hong Kong, specify public interest objectives in their SRRs. Other countries, for example EU countries, do not specify financial stability of public interest objectives in legislation relating to the resolution of failing banks.

In the EU, a Single Resolution Mechanism (SRM) was established in 2013 in the context of the creation of the Banking Union (see Chapter 14). The SRM regulation builds on the 'Rulebook on bank resolution' set out in the 2013 **Bank Recovery and Resolution Directive (BRRD)**; it comprises establishing a Single Resolution Board (SRB) and a Single Bank Resolution Fund (SRF); these are discussed in Section 14.4.4. The harmonisation of the EU legislation in this area should ensure that future bank failures could be managed with minimal disruption for financial stability and public finances. Given the present diversity in European resolution legislation and practice (see Table 7.2), this seems a necessary step forward for the EU banking systems. Even outside the EU, the growing internationalisation of banking requires closer co-operation between national deposit insurance institutions, regulators and resolution authorities.

Table 7.2 illustrates the administrative authority responsible for restructuring banks in a number of countries. There are substantial cross-country differences, in terms of scope, mandates and powers of authorities, which reflect differences in the regulatory environment. While there is no preferred resolution regime, there are significant divergences and

economic functions. They set out essential features in 12 areas that should be part of the resolution regimes of all jurisdictions, which relate to:

1 scope of the resolution regime;

2 resolution authority (existence, mandate and governance);

3 resolution powers;

4 legal framework governing set-off rights, contractual netting, collateralisation arrangements and segregation of client assets;

5 the existence of safeguards;

6 funding arrangements to support the resolution of firms;

7 legal framework conditions for cross-border co-operation;

8 crisis management groups (CMGs);

9 institution-specific cross-border co-operation agreements (COAGs) – these mainly apply to global systemically important financial institutions (G-SIFIs);

10 resolvability assessments;

11 recovery and resolution planning;

12 access to information and information sharing.

7.4.4 Co-operation and resolution processes

Finally, the viability of a safety net in case of crisis also depends on efficient communication and co-operation between all network elements (see Figure 7.1). This requires appropriately standardised and clearly regulated processes that at best are also internationally harmonised. The 2007–2009 global financial crisis highlighted the need for further work in this area, as information exchange and a co-ordinated decision-making process have proven difficult at the national level, let alone internationally.

7.5　Limitations of regulation

So far, we have highlighted the case for financial regulation, which depends mainly on various market imperfections and failures (information asymmetries, agency problems, etc.), which, in the absence of regulation, would produce sub-optimal results and reduce consumer welfare. As a consequence, the purpose of regulation should be limited to correcting for identified market imperfections and failures. There are, however, a number of arguments against regulation.

Regulatory arrangements, in particular the 'safety net' arrangements, create moral hazard. The concept of moral hazard was introduced in Chapter 1. Deposit insurance and the LOLR can cause people to be less careful than they would be otherwise. For example, with 100 per cent deposit insurance, depositors will not be concerned about the behaviour of their bank. Similarly, the belief that the LOLR will eventually bail out troubled banks may encourage institutions to take greater risks in lending. Box 7.2 illustrates these concepts. Other examples of the moral hazard caused by the **government safety net** are known as the **too big to fail (TBTF)** and the too important to fail (TITF) cases. Because the failure of a large (or strategically important) bank poses significant risks to other financial institutions and

BOX 7.2 MORAL HAZARD AND GOVERNMENT SAFETY-NET ARRANGEMENTS

Financial regulation and supervision are needed because moral hazard can be associated with government safety net arrangements that are designed to protect the banking and financial system. For example, banks that face liquidity problems and cannot borrow from other banks in the market may approach the regulators to act as a 'lender of last resort' in order to provide emergency liquidity assistance (ELA). This, in principle, seems a good thing as the authorities have a mechanism for providing liquidity to the banking system at times of crises. However, moral hazard arises in that if banks all believe they have access to the LOLR, they may be inclined to take on excessive risks, knowing that in the event of trouble they will be bailed out by the authorities (in other words, the taxpayer, as these are public funds being used). To mitigate this moral hazard problem the authorities need to establish a regulatory framework that assures access to the LOLR facility is by no means guaranteed for banks.

Linked to this is the *too big to fail* argument whereby the largest banks are viewed as being too big to be allowed to fail and therefore they must have guaranteed access to the LOLR – which could cause moral hazard problems. No financial regulatory authority will ever provide guaranteed access to the LOLR financing, although history does tell us that (for systemic and other reasons) large banks are likely to be bailed out more than small banks. In addition, the *too important to fail* view argues that size by itself is not the relevant criterion for bailing out troubled banks – rather, the significance or importance of banks in specific markets and the expected scale/impact of potential failure should be the main criteria in providing support.

Similar moral hazard issues relate to the design of appropriate deposit insurance and other investment (and insurance) compensation schemes. As noted earlier, if deposit insurance is too generous it creates incentives for banks to take on more risk as they know their customers' deposits will be protected in the event of a bank failure. Similar arguments can be put forward for other compensation schemes. Financial regulations need to be designed to reduce the possibility of such possible moral hazards occurring; it is important to note that regulation can never eliminate all information asymmetries, but it can (and should) be formulated in order to minimise the potential adverse effects of such market failures.

to the financial system as a whole, policy makers may respond by protecting bank creditors from all or some of the losses they otherwise would face. If managers of large (or important) banks believe that they will be bailed out by the authorities (with taxpayers' money) if they get into financial difficulty, this increases the moral hazard incentives for big banks, resulting in banks taking on even greater risks to increase profits and executive remuneration. Executives maybe less concerned about taking big risks if they know depositors and the bank will ultimately be protected by government bailouts if thing go wrong.

Banks may also benefit from **regulatory forbearance**. Regulatory forbearance (or renegotiation) is an example of time inconsistency. Time inconsistency refers to the problem that it may not be optimal *ex post* (after an event occurs) to implement regulations that were optimal *ex ante* (before the event occurred). When financial intermediaries are in trouble, there may be pressures not to apply existing regulations, for example to impose higher capital or liquidity requirements. This is because it could worsen the institution's problems. If the bank was allowed to fail, this could drain the deposit insurance fund. Furthermore, publicity surrounding a bank facing difficulties may worry the public, who may be induced to withdraw their savings, thereby aggravating the bank's problems (with a possible domino effect on other institutions leading to further bank failures). Also, there might be political costs associated with enforcing regulations and therefore an incentive to delay action. There are some benefits of forbearance. First, not publicising the bank's problems may help avoid systemic risk caused by bank runs. In addition, the bank may be worth more as a 'going concern', that is, remaining in operation rather than going out of business and liquidating its assets. To stay operational, a bank must be able to generate enough resources. As we have seen, banks' assets are highly illiquid and therefore their sale might not generate enough cash to satisfy creditors.

There are, however, costs associated with forbearance. First, it may cause moral hazard: forbearance in one case may lead to expectations of similar behaviour in future cases, causing other financial institutions to observe regulations less carefully. Furthermore, regulators and regulated firms may become locked into an ever-worsening spiral, resulting in a loss of public confidence in how banks and the financial system in general are being regulated.

Regulation can create problems of **agency capture** – that is, the regulatory process can be 'captured' by producers (in this case by banks and other financial institutions) and used in their own interest rather than in the interests of consumers. For example, some have argued that the Basel II Capital Accord had too much input from banking sector participants and large banks in particular. The Basel II capital rules allowed the largest banks to use their own internal models for assessing risk and capital adequacy positions – which led to the biggest banks holding less capital for regulatory purposes (see also Section 7.7.3). The fact that major banks have had a significant say in devising regulations that govern their own operations is a possible indicator of agency capture.

Regulation is a costly business and the costs of compliance with the regulatory process will be passed on to consumers, resulting in higher costs of financial services and possibly less intermediation business. In addition, regulatory costs may act as a barrier to entry in the market and this may consolidate monopoly positions.

The notion of incremental **compliance costs** is set out in Alfon and Andrews (1999, p. 16) as follows:

> Compliance costs are the costs to firms and individuals of those activities required by regulators that would not have been undertaken in the absence of regulation. Thus the term 'compliance costs' as used here refers to the incremental costs of compliance caused by regulation, not to the total cost of activities that happen to contribute to regulatory compliance. Examples of compliance costs include the costs of any additional systems, training, management time and capital required by the regulator.

Table 7.3 Bank regulation: key concepts

Objectives	Reasons	Rationale	Costs
Sustain systemic stability	Key position of banks in the financial system	Market imperfections and failures	Moral hazard
Maintain the safety and soundness of financial institutions	Consumer demand	Potential systemic problems	Agency capture
Protect consumers		Monitoring of financial firms	Compliance costs Costs of entry/exit
		Ensuring consumers' confidence	Control over products/ activities/prices

However, none of these criticisms is enough to reject financial regulation. Regulation is always about making judgements and considering trade-offs between costs and benefits. While it is important to recognise the limitations of regulation, a well-designed regulatory framework is necessary to ensure consumers' confidence in the financial sector.

Although there are costs involved, there is also evidence that consumers and other users demand appropriate regulation: public pressure to introduce regulations may derive from the view that market solutions to regulations do not provide users with the appropriate reassurance that they are being protected appropriately.

7.6 Causes of regulatory reform

The scope and complexity of financial regulation have tended to grow almost continually. This has been partially in response to public reaction to financial scandals and the consequent political pressures generated (i.e. increased consumer demand for regulation).

Another factor that can change regulations is financial innovation. As new financial products and services emerge and gain in market significance, there are often calls for new regulation – for instance, the US Federal Reserve in early 2005 called for greater regulation of hedge funds (which are private investment funds that trade and invest in various assets such as securities, commodities, currency and derivatives on behalf of their clients) due to their rapid growth and potentially destabilising activity. Similar examples can be given regarding the regulation of derivatives activity and other financial instruments. The global financial crisis of 2007–2009 attracted regulatory attention to innovations such as derivatives, off-balance-sheet vehicles, hedge funds, private equity firms, etc.

One of the reasons financial innovations tend to attract regulatory attention is that often the innovations are due to regulatory avoidance. In other words, financial firms and markets create new products not only to meet new demands but also to circumvent regulations. For example, the growth of off-balance-sheet activities (derivatives trading, securities underwriting, foreign exchange trading and so on) during the first half of the 1980s can be explained by the fact that this business was not subject to capital regulations, in contrast to on-balance-sheet business. Similarly, the flow of US dollars to the United Kingdom during the 1960s and the start of the dollar Eurobond market has been explained mainly because restrictive regulations in the United States (reserve requirements, limits on deposit rates – Regulation Q, and other limits on US domestic bond issues) encouraged dollars to flow to London and borrowers to raise dollar debt finance by issuing Eurobonds. Firms innovate to get around regulations and the regulators are always one step behind the market – this is known as the *regulatory dialectic*.

As mentioned earlier, other factors impacting on regulatory reform are internationalisation and globalisation trends. The increased international activity of financial firms means that foreign institutions play an increasing role in many domestic financial sectors. Throughout the world financial liberalisation has provided a passport for banks to offer services cross-border.

The increased presence of foreign financial firms raises issues relating to how they should be regulated. The main concern relates to who is ultimately responsible if a foreign bank faces difficulties in an overseas market – should it be the host or the home country regulator? Generally, for large complex banks, the host regulator will supervise foreign subsidiary activity but it is the home country that is ultimately responsible if the bank faces difficulties (see also Chapter 4 for more details).

In addition to the issue of regulatory responsibility, the internationalisation trend has encouraged much greater debate about convergence of rules – so as to ensure that banks operate under similar regulations in different jurisdictions. It has been argued that minimal harmonisation (regulation based on minimum standards) allows for greater flexibility in implementing legislation and is likely to result (or sustain) more competitive playing fields than if one chooses maximum harmonisation. Harmonisation should always result in some form of convergence in national rules and at the same time should increase actual and potential competition (as well as the safety of the system) if it is to be effective. Many commentators recognise the need for greater co-operation between supervisory authorities and improved relations between supervisory authorities, market participants and consumers.

Another factor impacting on regulatory reform – and closely linked to the internationalisation trend – is the globalisation phenomenon. The growth in international activities and trade of multinational corporations has increased the demand for services from financial institutions that operate cross-border and therefore financial firms continue to expand their international presence. This means that various financial firms operate globally (e.g. HSBC, Santander, Citibank, Goldman Sachs, etc.). As a result, banks are increasingly exposed to risks originating from abroad, and risks to financial stability are less and less confined to national borders. This calls, at the minimum, for greater regulatory oversight and co-ordination between national regulators. Further, consolidation in the global banking industry has resulted in the emergence of financial conglomerates that conduct an extensive range of businesses with a group structure. The formation of financial conglomerates is forcing regulators to re-think the way in which the financial sector should be supervised.

In addition to the aforementioned factors, various other forces can have a marked impact on the regulatory environment. Major financial crises can have a big impact on regulatory changes, mainly because the occurrence of a crisis is an indication that regulation in place prior to the difficulties was not sufficient. However, not all countries tightened regulatory restrictions following the global financial crisis. A survey carried out by Barth *et al.* (2013) showed that 80 per cent of countries tightened such restrictions following the crisis, while others, including Brazil, Portugal and Switzerland, actually eased overall restrictions.

One of the mainstays of banking sector policy around the world is capital regulation. Many rules and policies determine the precise amount and nature of capital that banks must hold. These are analysed in detail in Section 7.7.

7.7 Bank capital regulation

The role of capital in the financial sector, and for banks in particular, is a central element of regulation. A bank's capital may be defined as the value of its net assets (i.e. total assets minus total liabilities). In practice, this capital is the sum of the bank's paid-up share capital and its accumulated capital reserves. A bank's capital is vital for the protection of its depositors, and hence for the maintenance of general confidence in its operations, and the underpinning of its longer-term stability and growth.

The role of capital in banking can be illustrated by a simple balance sheet diagram as shown below where Bank Greedy has assets of £55 billion and £5 billion of capital. The bank has £54 billion in loans and £50 billion held in deposits.

A) Bank Greedy balance sheet

Liabilities (£)		Assets (£)	
Capital	5 billion	Cash and liquid assets	1 billion
Deposits	50 billion	Loans	54 billion
Total	55 billion	Total	55 billion

Now let us assume that the bank has made some risky loans and £4 billion worth of loans go bad. The bank believes they will never be repaid (the bank cannot recover these loans). Bank Greedy has to take a 'hit' and the losses can be borne by the capital cushion. As shown below in B), assets shrink by £4 billion and capital falls to £1 billion.

B) Bank Greedy balance sheet after £4 billion in loans go bad

Liabilities (£)		Assets (£)	
Capital	1 billion	Cash and liquid assets	1 billion
Deposits	50 billion	Loans	50 billion
Total	51 billion	Total	51 billion

In this case Bank Greedy can bear the loss of £4 billion as it has sufficient capital to cover these losses. Note that we assume that cash and liquid assets remain at £1 billion.

If, however, the losses exceed £5 billion then Bank Greedy does not have enough capital to cover these losses and it cannot meet depositor obligations. See what happens if instead of a £4 billion loss Bank Greedy has £7 billion in loans go bad. This is shown in C.

C) Bank Greedy balance sheet after £7 billion in loans go bad

Liabilities (£)		Assets (£)	
Capital	0 billion	Cash and liquid assets	1 billion
Deposits	48 billion	Loans	47 billion
Total	48 billion	Total	48 billion

It can be seen that Bank Greedy has used all its £5 billion capital to cover these losses and deposits of £2 billion have also had to be used to make up the shortfall. This means that the bank cannot repay all its depositors as the value of deposits has fallen from the original £50 billion to £48 billion – in theory the bank would have to tell its depositors that it had some bad news and unfortunately some will not be able to withdraw their deposits (or that all depositors will bear a loss). Of course, in reality this does not happen as the bank is insolvent.

The main point to stress is that any losses incurred by a bank – whether these are caused by bad loans, securities trading, the failure of a subsidiary, fraudulent activity or whatever – have to be met out of its capital as deposits have to be protected at all costs in order to maintain confidence in the bank, as well as the banking system overall. This is why bank regulators spend so much time and energy focusing on the capital adequacy of banks.

The adequacy of any given amount of capital not only depends upon the absolute volume of assets to be covered but is also affected by the quality of those assets. The more risky the assets, the greater must be the cushion of capital funds, all other things being equal, in order to maintain a given level of capital adequacy.

For a number of years, the Bank of England specified for each UK bank individually a minimum required ratio of capital to risk-weighted assets. If the actual ratio were to fall below this 'trigger' ratio, the Bank of England would be likely to intervene in the bank's activities. This regulatory capital ratio was set to take account of the Bank of England's assessment of the bank's managerial capacity with regard to its risk position, its profitability and its over-all prospects. In addition, it was expected that, in normal circumstances, each bank would maintain a 'target' capital ratio that included a margin over the value of its trigger ratio. The UK banking sector regulator has modified this approach in the light of evolving international standards. Moves at an international level to harmonise the capital adequacy ratios of banks in different countries have led to a more rigorously defined framework for capital adequacy. The Committee on Banking Regulations and Supervisory Practices of the Bank for International Settlements put forward a framework in July 1988 for the harmonisation of standards of capital adequacy. This framework has become known as the Basel I Accord. The objective of this framework was to strengthen the world's banking system and place it in a better position to withstand any future problems in world financial markets. In addition, the requirements were intended to provide a more equal basis for competition between banks in different countries and to remove the incentive for banks to relocate activities to other countries in order to take advantage of relatively lax regulatory requirements.

Capital adequacy ratios are a measure of the amount of a bank's capital expressed as a percentage of its risk-weighted credit exposures. The Basel I Accord recommends minimum capital adequacy ratios to ensure banks can absorb a reasonable level of losses before becoming insolvent. Applying minimum capital adequacy ratios serves the purpose of protecting depositors and promoting the stability and efficiency of the financial system. As such, minimum capital standards can be seen as a vital tool in reducing systemic risk.

Although the Basel Committee does not have any powers to impose the Accord, more than 100 countries have implemented its guidelines in one form or another.

7.7.1 The 1988 Basel Capital Accord (Basel I)

The Basel Committee on Banking Supervision was created at the end of 1974 and was charged by the Group of Ten (or G-10, the ten largest industrialised countries in the world: Belgium, Canada, France, Germany, Italy, Japan, the Netherlands, Sweden, the United Kingdom and the United States), plus Luxembourg and Switzerland, central bank governors to seek a common approach among its members towards measuring capital adequacy and the prescription of minimum capital standards.[6] In July 1988, the Basel Committee on Banking Supervision introduced its 1988 Capital Accord (the Basel I Accord). The majority of the world's leading central banks undertook to implement the Basel Accord by the end of 1992. (The EU implemented almost all of the features of the Basel Accord into EU, and therefore member states', law by the end of 1992.)

---

[6] The Basel Committee is the committee of central banks and bank supervisors from the major industrialised countries that meets every three months at the BIS in Basel, Switzerland. Note the French spelling of the name of the Swiss city is Basle, whereas the German spelling is Basel. The latter is more commonly used.

The Accord reflected the culmination of the committee work on international convergence of capital adequacy and is based on a risk–asset ratio (RAR) approach (see Box 7.3). The committee stated that 'a weighted risk ratio in which capital is related to different categories of asset and off-balance sheet exposure, weighted according to broad categories of relative riskiness, is the preferred method for assessing the capital adequacy of banks' (Basel Committee on Banking Supervision, 1988, paragraph 9).

The 1988 Capital Accord established an international standard around a capital ratio of 8 per cent and focused on risks associated with lending (credit risks), thereby ignoring other types of risk. The Basel I definition of capital is made up of two elements: Tier 1 ('core capital') and Tier 2 ('supplemental capital'). Bank total capital is the sum between Tiers 1 and 2 ('capital base').

Specifically, the elements of capital are:

Tier 1

(a) Ordinary paid-up share capital/common stock

(b) Disclosed reserves

Tier 2

(a) Undisclosed reserves

(b) Asset revaluation reserves

(c) General provisions/general loan loss reserves

(d) Hybrid (debt/equity) capital instruments

(e) Subordinated term debt

More details on the definitions of capital elements can be found in Box 7.3. The sum of Tier 1 and Tier 2 elements is eligible for inclusion in the capital base, subject to various

BOX 7.3 DETAILS OF CAPITAL ELEMENTS (ESTABLISHED 1988 AND APPLIED IN 1992)

Tier 1 (core capital) = common stockholders' equity + non-cumulative perpetual preferred stock + any surplus + minority interest in the equity accounts of consolidated subsidiaries − goodwill and other intangibles (deduction is carried out only if some conditions are met).
REQUIRED TIER 1 CORE CAPITAL IS EQUAL TO RISK WEIGHT × 4% OF WEIGHTED RISK ASSETS.

Tier 2 (supplementary capital) = allowance for losses on loans and leases (reserves) + cumulative perpetual, long-term and convertible preferred stock + perpetual debt and other hybrid debt/equity instruments + intermediate-term preferred stock and term subordinated debt. The total of Tier 2 is limited to 100% of Tier 1. Other limitations are specified in the 1992 revised guidelines.
Deductions from total capital (Tier 1 + Tier 2) consist of investments in unconsolidated banking and financial subsidiaries, reciprocal holdings of capital securities, and other deductions (such as other subsidiaries or joint ventures) as determined by supervisory authorities with handling on a case-by-case basis or as a matter of policy after formal rule making.
REQUIRED TOTAL CAPITAL (TIER 1 + TIER 2 − DEDUCTIONS) IS EQUAL TO RISK WEIGHT × 8% OF WEIGHTED RISK ASSETS

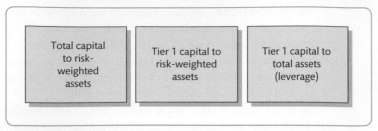

Figure 7.3 Measures of bank capital

limits described in the 1988 Basel report. Figure 7.3 illustrates the different measures of bank capital.

The general framework for capital adequacy risk-weighted assets can be summarised as follows. There are four risk classes in the weighted-risk system that reflects credit risk exposure:

1 No risk: 0% (e.g. cash or equivalents; bonds issued by OECD governments).

2 Low risk: 20% (e.g. short-term claims maturing in a year or less; bonds issued by agencies of OECD governments).

3 Moderate risk: 50% (e.g. mortgages).

4 Standard risk: 100% (e.g. commercial loans; claims by non-OECD banks and government debts).

BOX 7.4 RAR (RISK–ASSET RATIO) APPROACH

The RAR is a relatively simple approach that sets out to appraise capital adequacy on the basis of banks' relative riskiness. Banks' assets are divided by the supervisory authorities into a number of equivalent risk classes. Different 'risk weights' are assigned to each of the equivalent risk classes of assets. Total weighted risk assets are calculated as follows:

1 $W = \sum a_i r_i$ where $A = \sum a_i$ and

2 $RAR = C/W$ where W = total weighted assets

RAR = risk–asset ratio

A = bank total assets

a_i = risk classes of assets

r_i = risk weights

C = capital as defined by the supervisory authorities

Moreover, conversion factors were set for calculating credit-equivalent amounts for off-balance-sheet (OBS) items.

(a) 0% (e.g. unused portion of loan commitments).

(b) 20% (e.g. commercial letters of credit).

(c) 50% (e.g. revolving underwriting facilities).

(d) 100% (e.g. standby letters of credit).

> ## Box 7.4 RAR (risk–asset ratio) approach (*continued*)
>
> Essentially, the capital adequacy scheme is based on a four-step approach:
>
> 1 **Classify** assets into one of four risk categories described above.
> 2 **Convert** OBS commitments and guarantees on their on-balance-sheet 'credit equivalent' values and classify them in the appropriate risk category.
> 3 **Multiply** the £ amount of assets in each risk category by the appropriate risk weight; this equals 'risk-weighted assets'.
> 4 **Multiply** 'risk-weighted assets' by the minimum capital percentages, either 4% for Tier 1 capital or 8% for total capital for a bank to be adequately capitalised.
>
> *For example*: take a bank with the following assets:
>
> - cash: $100m (0% risk weighting);
> - loans to other banks: $500 m (20% risk weighting);
> - mortgage loans to owner-occupiers: $800m (50% risk weighting);
> - commercial loans: $1,500m (100% risk weighting).
>
> Its minimum capital ratio under Basel I can be calculated as follows:
>
> Total risk-weighted assets (RWA)
> $$= (\$100m \times 0) + (\$500m \times 0.2) + (\$800m \times 0.5) + (\$1,500m \times 1)$$
> $$= \$0 + \$100m + \$400m + \$1,500m$$
> $$= \$2,000m$$
>
> Minimum capital requirement is 8% of $2,000m = $160m, of which at least 50% needs to be held in the form of Equity (Tier 1) capital.

If the RAR calculated by the bank falls below the minimum ratio stipulated by the regulatory authorities then this obviously indicates the institution has inadequate capital. A summary of the minimum capital adequacy requirements is given below. Box 7.5 shows how to distinguish well-capitalised banks from those that are undercapitalised.

The Basel Accord was generally regarded as a step forward in the regulation of bank capital adequacy. It involved international agreement and it became the basis for most nations' capital regulations for all banks. Nevertheless, almost immediately debate began as to its efficiency and effectiveness. Questions were raised on capital ratios appearing to lack economic foundation, risk weights not accurately reflecting the risk associated with assets (e.g. the riskiness of loans) and the lack of recognition of asset portfolio diversification. It should also be noted that many nations chose to set capital adequacy ratios somewhat higher than the Accord's minimum, reflecting their own assessment of the risk associated with individual banks' activities.

7.7.2 The 1996 amendments to the 1988 Accord

The original capital Accord focused on risks arising from the lending activity of banks, thereby ignoring other types of risks (for an overview of the main bank risks see Chapter 11). A proposal for changing the original Accord to include capital charges for market risk incurred by banks was issued by the Basel Committee in April 1995. The objective was to provide 'an explicit capital cushion for the price risks to which banks are exposed, particularly those

BOX 7.5 FIVE CAPITAL-ADEQUACY CATEGORIES OF BANKS

1 **Well capitalised:**

Total capital to risk-weighted assets 10%

Tier 1 capital to risk-weighted assets 6%

Tier 1 capital to total assets 5%

2 **Adequately capitalised (fulfilling minimum requirements):**

Total capital to risk-weighted assets 8%

Tier 1 capital to risk-weighted assets 4%

Tier 1 capital to total assets 4%

3 **Undercapitalised:**

Fails to meet one or more of the capital minimums for an adequately capitalised bank

4 **Significantly undercapitalised:**

Total capital to risk-weighted assets <6%

Tier 1 capital to risk-weighted assets <3%

Tier 1 capital to total assets <3%

5 **Critically undercapitalised:**

[(Common equity capital + perpetual preferred stock − Intangible assets)/total assets] = <2%

arising from trading activities'. The Basel Committee defined market risk as the risk of losses in on- and off-balance-sheet positions arising from movements in market prices.

In particular, the risks covered by the proposed framework were: (a) the bank's trading book position in debt, equity instruments and related off-balance-sheet contracts; and (b) commodity and foreign exchange positions held by the bank. The amendments to the Accord to incorporate market (trading) risk resulted in the inclusion of an 'ancillary' or Tier 3 capital to support trading book activities. Moreover, a significant innovation in the market risk requirements consisted in the opportunity given to banks to use their internal risk assessment models (see Chapter 12 for more details) for measuring the riskiness of their trading portfolios.

Overall, these regulatory changes in the minimum capital required for market risk came into force in 1996 and represented a significant step forward for the Committee in strengthening the soundness and stability of the international banking and financial systems.

7.7.3 The second Capital Accord (Basel II)

In response to the criticisms of the original Accord, a number of changes were made. On 3 June 1999, the Basel Committee on Banking Supervision formally launched proposals for a new capital adequacy framework (which was to become known as Basel II). The first version of the proposed Accord received strong criticism from bankers and academics, which prompted the committee to make substantial changes to the new framework. In May 2004, central bank governors and the heads of bank supervisory authorities in the Group of Ten (G10) endorsed the publication of the 'International Convergence of Capital Measurement and Capital Standards: A Revised Framework' (Basel Committee on Banking Supervision, 2004).

Table 7.4 Rationale for Basel II: more flexibility and risk sensitivity

Basel I	Basel II
Focus on a single risk measure	More emphasis on banks' internal methodologies, supervisory review and market discipline
One size fits all	Flexibility, menu of approaches, incentives for better risk management
Broad-brush structure	More risk sensitivity

In June 2006, the Committee released a comprehensive version of the Accord, incorporating the June 2004 Basel II Framework, the elements of the 1988 Accord that were not revised during the Basel II process, the 1996 amendment to the Capital Accord to incorporate Market Risks, and the 2005 amendments (Basel Committee on Banking Supervision, 2006). This was the outcome of the Basel Committee's work over the years to secure international convergence on revisions to supervisory regulations governing the capital adequacy of internationally active banks. The Accord's main aim was to introduce a more comprehensive and risk-sensitive treatment of banking risks. In particular, the setting of minimum capital requirements was based on an update of the risk-weighting approach, including the use of banks' internal risk ratings and external credit risk assessments. Table 7.4 summarises the key differences between Basel I and Basel II, highlighting the main reasons put forward to revise the first capital accord.

Basel II is built on three main pillars. Pillar 1 deals with the quantification of new capital charges and relies heavily on banks' internal risk-weighting models and on external rating agencies. Pillar 2 defines the supervisory review process and Pillar 3 focuses on market discipline, imposing greater disclosure standards on banks in order to increase transparency. Figure 7.4 summarises the three pillars approach.

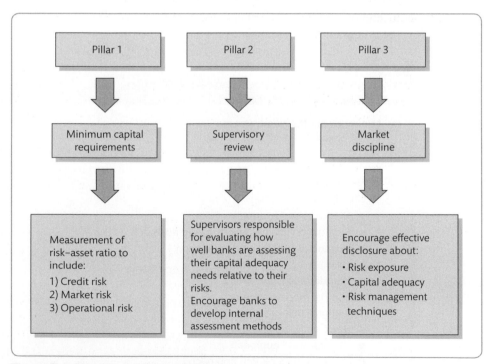

Figure 7.4 Basel II: the three pillars

Pillar 1

The first pillar seeks to amend the old rules by introducing risk weightings that are more closely linked to the borrower's credit standing. The Basel II refines the methodology to reflect with greater precision the varying underlying risks against which banks are required to hold capital. The second Accord does not change the definition of capital or the minimum requirement of 8 per cent capital to risk-weighted assets. It mainly affects how banking risks (credit risk, which is risk of a borrower's default; operational risk, which is the risk associated with the potential for systems failure; and market risk, which is the risk that the value of investments will decrease due to movements in market factors) are measured. The biggest changes relate to the calculation of capital backing for credit risk. Under Basel II, banks would be able to choose from what is known as the 'menu of approaches', including the 'standardised approach' and the internal ratings based (IRB) approach (see Box 7.6). In the standardised approach the Basel II defines risk weights within broad categories of sovereigns, banks and companies, by reference to an external credit assessment firm (credit rating agency) subject to strict standards. Under IRB banks are allowed to use their internal credit risk assessments subject to strict methodological and disclosure requirements.

Pillar 2

Pillar 2 identifies the roles of the national supervisors to ensure banks use appropriate methodology to determine capital adequacy ratios and have a strategy to maintain such ratios. These are defined as follows:

- to review banks' internal assessment procedures and strategies, taking appropriate action if these fall below standard;
- to encourage banks to hold capital above the minimum requirements;
- to intervene as early as possible to ask banks to restore their capital levels if they fall below the minimum.

BOX 7.6 PILLAR 1

(a) **Minimum capital requirements**

$$\frac{Total\ capital\ (unchanged)}{Credit\ risk\ +\ Market\ risk\ +\ Operational\ risk} = the\ bank's\ capital\ ratio\ (min\ 8\%)$$

(b) **Menu of approaches**

1 Credit risk
  - Standardised approach
  - Foundation internal ratings based approach
  - Advanced internal rating approach

2 Market risk
  - Standardised approach
  - Internal models approach

3 Operational risk
  - Basic indicator approach
  - Standardised approach
  - Internal measurement approach

The supervisory review process aims to ensure that a bank's capital adequacy position is consistent with its overall risk profile. To this end, bank regulators must be able to make qualitative judgements on the ability of each bank to measure and manage its own risks. Supervisors should also have the ability to require banks to hold capital in excess of minimum regulatory requirements.

Pillar 3

The third pillar seeks to enhance effective market discipline by introducing high disclosure standards with regard to bank capital. This requires banks to provide more reliable and timely information, enabling market participants to make better risk assessments. Banks are expected to disclose:

- risk exposure;
- capital adequacy;
- methods for computing capital requirements;
- all material information.

Taken together, Pillar 1 provides the rules for quantifying risk sensitivity and the minimum capital charges associated with these risks. This is balanced by the supervisory judgements available under Pillar 2 and market disclosure rules of Pillar 3. Ultimately, the Basel II Accord aimed to create a more comprehensive and flexible regulatory framework, without sacrificing the safety and soundness achieved by the Basel I Accord.

7.7.3.1 Criticisms of Basel II

Basel II was subject to a number of early criticisms. They can be summarised as follows:

1 It is pro-cyclical, i.e. it moves with the economic cycle. The literature on the pro-cyclical effects of Basel II suggests that the rules may exacerbate downturns in the business cycle. For instance, as credit risk increases in a recession, capital requirements are likely to rise, inducing credit rationing.

2 Basel II could increase the amount of systemic risk for banks using the standardised approach. These banks have little incentive to diversify, as they are not rewarded for it.

3 Some suggested that there was a danger of banks that are part of a financial conglomerate to move their credit risk to another non-bank financial subsidiary to reduce the amount of capital they have to set aside.

4 Another concern is that Basel II requirements could encourage banks to transfer credit risk off their balance sheets (see Chapter 18 on the use of asset-backed securitisation and the use of financial derivatives).

5 Small and medium-size enterprises and firms located in developing countries may find it difficult to raise finance, as they are not listed and therefore do not have official credit ratings.

6 There is a potential conflict of interest as rating agencies also act as advisors to big banks on their risk management systems.

Some of these early criticisms were brought to the fore by the 2007–2009 global financial crisis. Since then, a number of amendments have been proposed. Responses to the global financial crises have called for tighter and 'more global' regulation of financial institutions. However, some doubts remain as to whether the attempts to regulate globally (i.e. Basel II) have if not caused then worsened the 2007–2009 crisis.

7.7.4 The third Capital Accord (Basel III)

Basel II, to all intents and purposes, never came fully into effect. The global financial crisis laid bare the shortcomings of the existing prudential framework and made a thorough overhaul an overriding necessity. In July 2009, less than two years after Basel II came into force in the EU, the Basel Committee complemented its Basel II rules on trading books (also known as Basel 2.5).[7]

The G20 approved the new Basel III solvency and liquidity rules at its Seoul summit in November 2010. In December 2010 and June 2011, the BCBS published its latest recommendations on bank solvency and liquidity (Basel Committee on Banking Supervision, 2011a).

According to the BCBS, Basel III is a comprehensive set of reform measures, developed by the Basel Committee on Banking Supervision, to strengthen the regulation, supervision and risk management of the banking sector. These measures aim to:

- improve the banking sector's ability to absorb shocks arising from financial and economic stress, whatever the source;
- improve risk management and governance;
- strengthen banks' transparency and disclosures.

The reforms target:

- bank-level, or micro-prudential, regulation, which will help raise the resilience of individual banking institutions to periods of stress;
- macro-prudential, system-wide risks that can build up across the banking sector as well as the pro-cyclical amplification of these risks over time.

The new proposal was first published in December 2010, with a revised version issued in June 2011. In addition, the Basel Committee issued the full text of the revised liquidity coverage ratio (LCR) in January 2013 (Basel Committee on Banking Supervision, 2013a).

Being a new and complex set of rules, in the remainder of this section we will introduce the main changes under the new regulatory standards, as well as the timetable that has been set forth for their implementation.

The Basel III Accord addresses several issues. It proposes many new capital, leverage and liquidity standards to strengthen the regulation, supervision and risk management of the banking sector. The capital standards and new capital buffers will require banks to hold more capital and higher quality capital than under Basel II. The new leverage and liquidity ratios introduce a non-risk-based measure to supplement the risk-based minimum capital requirements and measures to ensure that adequate funding is maintained in case of crisis.

The enhanced capital ratios prescribed by the BCBS relate to the ratio of a firm's eligible regulatory capital divided by a regulatory prescribed calculation of risk-weighted assets. As illustrated in Figure 7.5, all three parts of this have changed, putting more pressure on a firm's compliance with the ratio. The capital ratio requirement has increased; the eligibility of capital has been tightened so reducing the types of capital firms can use to meet the required ratio; and the calculation of risk weighted assets has changed leading to an increase for many organisations.

---

[7] The European Union implemented the Basel II Accord via the following EU Capital Requirements Directives: Directive 2006/48/EC of 14 June 2006 relating to the taking up and pursuit of the business of credit institutions and Directive 2006/49/EC of 14 June 2006 on the capital adequacy of investment firms and credit institutions.

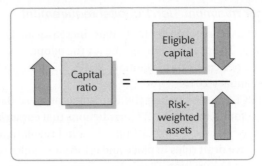

Figure 7.5 Elements of the capital ratio affected by Basel III

Basel III builds upon the Basel II three pillars approach and strengthens the three pillars, especially Pillar 1, with enhanced minimum capital and liquidity requirements. Figure 7.6 illustrates the key changes compared with Basel II.

7.7.4.1 The key elements of Basel III

The Basel III regulations aim to raise the quality, consistency and transparency of banks' capital base. Alongside the higher capital requirements and increased capital ratios, Basel III introduces liquidity and leverage ratios.

The main elements of the Basel III capital framework are:

(i) higher minimum Tier 1 capital requirement;

(ii) a capital conservation buffer;

(iii) a countercyclical capital buffer;

(iv) higher minimum Tier 1 common equity requirement;

(v) minimum total capital ratio.

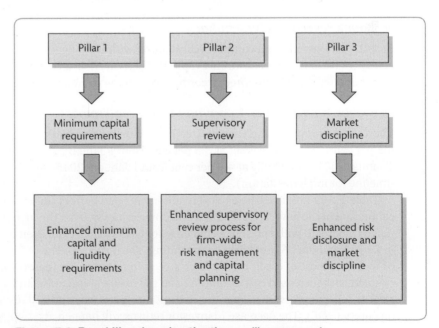

Figure 7.6 Basel III: enhancing the three-pillar approach

i. Higher minimum Tier 1 capital requirement

The proposed requirements include increases in Tier 1 capital ratio from 4 per cent to 6 per cent. The proposed timetable for the adoption of the higher minimum Tier 1 ratio was set at 4.5 per cent from 1 January 2013, 5.5 per cent from 1 January 2014 and 6 per cent from 1 January 2015.

The BCBS is monitoring the implementation of Basel III regulatory reforms. In a 2013 report, it found that of the 27 jurisdictions that comprise the Basel Committee, 25 have now issued the final set of Basel III-based capital regulations. The remaining two, Indonesia and Turkey, have draft rules in place and efforts are under way to finalise them (Basel Committee on Banking Supervision, 2013c).

The crisis revealed that certain Tier 1 capital instruments – classed as core capital – were unable to absorb losses. To address this issue, Basel III has therefore tightened its definitions of regulatory capital. Tier 1 capital will now be comprised predominantly of common equity and retained earnings. Common equity will now reach 82.3 per cent of Tier 1 capital, inclusive of the capital conservation buffer. Basel III abandons the 'core Tier 1' concept in favour of the stricter 'common equity Tier 1'.

ii. New capital conservation buffer

A new capital conservation buffer of 2.5 per cent will be used to absorb losses during periods of financial and economic stress. This requirement, which is designed to help banks withstand future periods of stress, will bring the total common equity requirement to 7 per cent. This is the sum of 4.5 per cent common equity requirement and the 2.5 per cent capital conservation buffer.

It should be noted that the capital conservation buffer must be met exclusively with common equity and banks that do not maintain the capital conservation buffer will face restrictions on payouts of dividends, share buy-backs and bonuses. Most large banks will probably maintain such a buffer, as falling below it will lead to additional regulatory scrutiny.

iii. Countercyclical capital buffer

Basel III also introduces a countercyclical buffer within a range of 0–2.5 per cent of common equity (or other fully loss-absorbing capital). This is in effect an extension of the conservation buffer and will be implemented according to national circumstances.

iv. Higher minimum Tier 1 common equity requirement

There was a proposed increase of Tier 1 common equity requirements from 2 per cent to 4.5 per cent. This ratio was set at 3.5 per cent from 1 January 2013, then at 4 per cent from 1 January 2014 and finally at 4.5 per cent from 1 January 2015 (see Table 7.6 for a proposed timeline for implementation).

Table 7.5 summarises the capital requirements and buffers (in per cent) required for the calibration of the new capital framework. Some critics say that the higher capital ratios mandated by Basel III will represent a challenge for banks to meet and even well-capitalised banks in Europe and the US could find it demanding. The result could be reduced credit availability or increased cost of credit on the high street. In addition, increased capital requirements, coupled with increased cost of funding and the need to reorganise and deal with regulatory reform, will put pressure on margins and operating capacity and will result in reduced return on equity (ROE). The decrease in investor returns will happen at a time when firms need to encourage enhanced investment to rebuild and restore capital buffers.

Table 7.5 Calibration of the capital framework

	Common equity Tier 1	Tier 1 capital	Total capital
Minimum	4.5	6.0	8.0
Conservation buffer	2.5		
Minimum plus	7.0	8.5	10.5
Conservation buffer			
Countercyclical buffer range	0–2.5		

Source: Bank for International Settlements, Basel Committee on Banking Supervision, **www.bis.org/publ/bcbs189.pdf**

v. Minimum total capital ratio

The minimum total capital ratio will remain at 8 per cent. As illustrated in Table 7.6, the addition of the capital conservation buffer increases the total amount of capital a bank must hold to 10.5 per cent of risk-weighted assets, of which 8.5 per cent must be Tier 1 capital.

In addition, Tier 2 capital instruments will be harmonised, whereas Tier 3 capital will be phased out, according to the timetable illustrated in Table 7.6.[8]

7.7.4.2 Basel III liquidity standards

The introduction of liquidity ratios is one of the main innovations of Basel III. Specifically, the new regulations propose a liquidity coverage ratio and a net stable funding ratio (NSFR).

i. Liquidity coverage ratio (LCR)

The **LCR** is designed to ensure that sufficient high-quality liquid assets (HQLA) are available for one-month survival in case of a stress scenario. HQLA are defined as cash or assets that can be converted into cash at little or no loss of value in private markets to meet a bank's liquidity needs for a 30-calendar-day liquidity stress scenario.

Table 7.6 Basel III phase-in arrangements – capital

Phases	2013	2014	2015	2016	2017	2018	2019
Leverage ratio	Parallel run 2013–2015 Disclosure starts 1 January 2015					Migration to Pillar 1	
Minimum common equity ratio	3.5%	4.0%	4.5%				4.5%
Capital conservation buffer				0.625%	1.25%	1.875%	2.5%
Minimum common equity plus conservation buffer	3.5%	4.0%	4.5%	5.125%	5.75%	6.375%	7.0%
Minimum Tier 1 capital	4.5%	5.5%	6.0%				6.0%
Minimum total capital	8.0%						8.0%
Minimum total capital plus conservation buffer	8.0%			8.625%	9.25%	9.875%	10.5%
Capital instruments that no longer qualify	Phased out over 10-year horizon beginning 2018						

Source: Adapted from Bank for International Settlements, Basel Committee on Banking Supervision, **www.bis.org/publ/bcbs189.pdf**

---

[8] See Sections 7.7.1 and 7.7.2 for definitions of Tier 1, Tier 2 and Tier 3 capital.

The LCR has two components: a) the value of the stock of HQLA and b) the total net outflows, and it is expressed as:

$$LCR = \frac{Stock\ of\ HQLA}{Total\ net\ outflows\ over\ the\ next\ 30\ calendar\ days} \geq 100\%$$

According to the BIS definition, HQLA comprise Level 1 and Level 2 assets.[9] Level 1 assets are typically of the highest quality and the most liquid and generally include cash, central bank reserves, and certain marketable securities backed by sovereigns and central banks, among others. Level 2 assets are comprised of certain government securities, covered bonds and corporate debt securities. Level 2 assets may also include lower-rated corporate bonds, residential mortgage-backed securities and equities that meet certain conditions (these latter are known as Level 2B assets). Level 2 assets may not in aggregate account for more than 40 per cent of a bank's stock of HQLA. Level 2B assets may not account for more than 15 per cent of a bank's total stock of HQLA.

The total net outflows (over the next 30 days) are defined as:

$$Total\ net\ cash\ outflows\ =\ Total\ expected\ cash\ out\ flows\ -$$
$$Min\ (total\ expected\ cash\ inflows;\ 75\%\ of\ total\ expected\ cash\ outflows)$$

The Basel III standard requires that, in normal conditions, the value of the LCR be no lower than 100 per cent (that is, the stock of HQLA should at least equal total net cash outflows). During periods of financial stress, however, banks may use their stock of HQLA, thereby temporarily falling below 100 per cent. The timetable for the implementation of the liquidity ratio is illustrated in Table 7.7.

ii. The net stable funding ratio (NSFR)

The NSFR is designed to promote resiliency over longer-term time horizons by creating additional incentives for banks to fund their activities with more stable sources of funding on an ongoing structural basis. In addition, the NSFR aims to limit over-reliance on short-term wholesale funding during times of buoyant market liquidity and encourage better assessment of liquidity risk across all on- and off-balance-sheet items.

The new proposal includes additional liquidity monitoring metrics focused on maturity mismatch, concentration of funding and available unencumbered assets. Reviews to the implementation of the NSFR were being discussed at the time of writing (2014), as illustrated in Box 7.7. In January 2014, the BCBS issued a consultative document (Basel Committee on Banking Supervision, 2014) with proposed revisions to the Basel framework's NSFR.

Table 7.7 Basel III phase-in arrangements – liquidity

Phases	2013	2014	2015	2016	2017	2018	2019
Liquidity coverage ratio – minimum requirements			60%	70%	80%	90%	100%
Net stable funding ratio						Introduce minimum standards	

Source: Adapted from Bank for International Settlements, Basel Committee on Banking Supervision, **www.bis.org/publ/bcbs238.htm**

---

[9] See **www.bis.org/press/p130106a.pdf**

BOX 7.7 NSFR IMPLEMENTATION UNCERTAIN AFTER BASEL III COMPROMISE ON LCR PHASE-IN

The implementation of the Net Stable Funding Ratio (NSFR), a significant part of the Basel III bank liquidity regime, is likely to be delayed and could even be dropped, credit analysts and banking industry sources told dealReporter.

The NSFR aims to ensure banks are able to survive an extended closure of wholesale funding markets. It establishes a minimum acceptable amount of stable funding based on the liquidity characteristics of an institution's assets and activities over a one year horizon. The observation period for considering possible changes to the formulation, announced in 2010, began last year and implementation is scheduled for 2018.

But two credit analysts and two banking industry sources said that a compromise agreement with The Basel Committee on Banking Supervision on the Liquidity Coverage Ratio (LCR) announced on 6 January has altered the landscape into which the NSFR rules were to be implemented.

Most significant among the announced changes to the LCR was to allow banks a wider range of assets, including equities and high quality residential mortgage backed securities, to count as easy-to-sell assets in the calculation of their funding requirements for surviving a 30-day liquidity crisis. Prior to the compromise, banks were to be restricted to holding cash and easy-to-sell assets such as government securities to meet the minimum standard.

The compromise also gives banks more flexible implementation terms and a longer phase-in period for the LCR. Banks are now only required to meet a minimum funding requirement of 60% in 2015, with this rising in equal annual steps of 10 percentage points to reach 100% on 1 January 2019.

The analyst and industry sources agreed that the changes to the LCR not only increase the likelihood of a delay in the NSFR, they set the stage for a larger re-think of the controversial measure.

"There is a correlation" between the two measures and their implementation, said one of the credit analysts, because the NSFR is supposed to pick up where the LCR leaves off. He noted that at the very least, the extended phase-in period for the LCR gives banks more time to monetize their long-term capital.

But it also gives them reason to expect that lobbying for more flexible terms on the NSFR would be similarly effective, especially as memories of the 2007 financial crisis recede.

For its part, the Basel Committee says it remains committed to the current implementation schedule for the NSFR and to the principle that requiring banks to hold high quality liquid assets for up to a year is necessary to prevent a future systemic collapse.

A person familiar with the Basel Committee's plans also insisted that the implementation of the LCR and NSFR is not linked, but that the committee has prioritised its work on the LCR because it was due to be implemented earlier.

NSFR is in many ways more intrusive than LCR because it examines banks' business models and practices. This requires banks to better match their assets and liabilities to prevent them from running out of funding if an extended crisis restricts their access to funding markets for up to a year. Such prolonged crisis conditions were responsible for the collapse of Northern Rock in 2007 and to a large extent Lehman Brothers the following year.

But two banking industry sources said they consider the current draft of the NSFR fundamentally flawed for several reasons. One of these sources said the NSFR as it is drafted really doesn't work, in part because its "one-size-fits-all" approach makes otherwise stable funding facilities such as repurchase agreements (repos) unviable. At the same time, he said, the new standard creates "perverse incentives" that would cause banks to load up on potentially riskier assets simply because they match liabilities and allow the bank to meet the minimum standard.

One example of this is that a bank holding blue chip equities would be required to hold more stable funding (50%) than it would for a nine-month loan to a hedge fund, which can be held at a 0% weighting. Similarly, he said marketable securities held for less than a year are risk weighted at 5% under NSFR, while a retail mortgage loan

---

BOX 7.6 NSFR implementation uncertain after Basel III compromise on LCR phase-in *(continued)*

somehow falls into the "all other assets" category, thereby requiring a 100% risk weighting.

Both industry sources said that while they welcome the compromise on the LCR and the longer implementation time frame, they feel the kind of issues that the NSFR tries to manage are more effectively addressed through the Basel III framework's existing Pillar 2 requirements. These requirements include regular reporting of liquidity risks by the banks along with closer monitoring of cash flow forecasts and stress testing by the supervisor.

The second industry source said that regulators globally are already monitoring bank liquidity "much more closely than previously" by looking at their models and monitoring the maturity of assets they hold, as well as by stress testing cash flows.

He expects Pillar 2 reporting and national supervision to become the cornerstone of bank liquidity monitoring under Basel III.

This source cited a recent example of intensifying regulatory commitment to maintaining adequate liquidity in a recent note sent by the UK's FSA to bank fund managers. He said that in the letter, the FSA asked fund managers to avoid putting retail clients into term deposits so as to "make sure deposits are on call" as well as to protect depositors from losses in the event of a crisis.

The second industry source said he now expects that NSFR "will fade into the background over the next few years" as further lobbying by banks convinces regulators that implementation is both unnecessary and counter-productive. FSA declined to comment.

7.7.4.3 Basel III leverage ratio

In addition to the solvency ratio, a leverage ratio between capital and a denominator made up of balance-sheet and off-balance-sheet items could be integrated into Pillar on 1 January 2018. This is a supplemental 3 per cent non-risk-based leverage ratio which serves as a backstop to the measures outlined above.

The main theoretical justification for the leverage ratio lies in the fact that risk-based ratios cannot completely prevent the undervaluation of certain risks in the denominator. It must be noted that the leverage ratio remains controversial and there remains ambiguity about certain aspects of the exact mechanics. In June 2013 the BIS issued a consultative document for a revision of the proposed leverage ratio (Basel Committee on Banking Supervision, 2013b). At the time of writing (2014), the new rules were still under discussion.

According to the BIS, a leverage ratio is intended to:

- restrict the build-up of leverage in the banking sector to avoid destabilising deleveraging processes that can damage the broader financial system and the economy;

- reinforce the risk-based requirements with a simple, non-risk-based 'backstop' measure.

The Basel Committee is of the view that a simple leverage ratio framework is critical and complementary to the risk-based capital framework and that a credible leverage ratio is one that ensures broad and adequate capture of both the on- and off-balance-sheet leverage of banks.

The proposed leverage ratio, expressed as a percentage, is defined as

$$Leverage\ ratio = \frac{Capital\ measure}{Exposure\ measure}$$

The capital measure is the Tier 1 capital as defined by Basel III. The exposure measure, in addition to on-balance-sheet exposures, will consider derivative exposures, securities financing transaction (SFT) exposures and other off-balance sheet exposures.

Implementation of the leverage ratio requirement began with bank-level reporting to supervisors of the leverage ratio and its components from 1 January 2013 and will proceed with public disclosure starting on 1 January 2015. Any final adjustments to the definition and calibration of the leverage ratio will be made by 2017, with a view to migrating to a Pillar 1 treatment on 1 January 2018 based on appropriate review and calibration.

7.7.4.4 Basel III and G-SIFIs

The Basel III regulations will affect all banks; however, the impact may differ across bank type and size. Most banks will be impacted by the increase in quantity and quality of capital, liquidity and leverage ratios, amended Pillar 2 and capital preservation. The more sophisticated banks will be affected by the amended treatment of counterparty credit risk, more robust market risk framework and, to some extent, the amended treatment of securitisations.

Systemically important financial institutions and global systemically important financial institutions will have to cope with higher capital requirements or be subject to additional supervision. The terms **SIFIs**, **G-SIFIs** and **G-SIBs** (global systemically important banks) are used to define banks or financial institutions that are deemed too big to fail. The Financial Stability Board has provided a tentative definition as well as a list of the 29 financial institutions considered to be SIFIs.

G-SIFIs are defined as:

> Financial institutions whose distress or disorderly failure, because of their size, complexity and systemic interconnectedness, would cause significant disruption to the wider financial system and economic activity. To avoid this outcome, authorities have all too frequently had no choice but to forestall the failure of such institutions through public solvency support. As underscored by this crisis, this has deleterious consequences for private incentives and for public finances.
>
> (Financial Stability Board, 2011b)

The FSB and BCBS identified an initial group of 29 G-SIBs in 2011 (Financial Stability Board, 2011b). The group of G-SIFIs will be updated annually and published by the FSB each November – Table 7.8 illustrates the 2012 and 2013 lists. There are a few changes from the original list – compared with the group of G-SIBs published in 2011, two banks were added: Banco Bilbao Vizcaya Argentaria (BBVA) and Standard Chartered. The Industrial and Commercial Bank of China (ICBC) was added in 2013. Three banks were removed in 2012: Dexia (as it was undergoing an orderly resolution process), Commerzbank and Lloyds, as a result of a decline in their global systemic importance. No bank was removed in 2013.

The G-SIBs will be subject to more intensive supervision, including stronger supervisory mandates, resources and powers, and higher supervisory expectations for risk management functions, data aggregation capabilities, risk governance and internal controls. Capital requirements for G-SIFIs and G-SIBs will need to have additional loss-absorption capacity tailored to the impact of their default, rising from 1 per cent to 2.5 per cent of risk-weighted assets (with an empty bucket of 3.5 per cent to discourage, in the words of the FSB, further 'systemicness', that is, how much the failure of one bank can impact on the rest of the financial system), to be met with common equity.

The additional loss absorbency requirements will initially apply to those banks identified in November 2014 as globally systemically important by the FSB using the BCBS methodology.

Table 7.8 G-SIBs and additional capital requirements

Bucket		G-SIBs in alphabetical order within each bucket	
		2012	2013
5	3.5%	(Empty)	(Empty)
4	2.5%	Citigroup Deutsche Bank HSBC JPMorgan Chase	HSBC JPMorgan Chase
3	2.0%	Barclays BNP Paribas	Barclays BNP Paribas Citigroup Deutsche Bank
2	1.5%	Bank of America Bank of New York Mellon Credit Suisse Goldman Sachs Mitsubishi UFJ FG Morgan Stanley Royal Bank of Scotland UBS	Bank of America Credit Suisse Goldman Sachs Group Crédit Agricole Mitsubishi UFJ FG Morgan Stanley Royal Bank of Scotland UBS
1	1.0%	Bank of China BBVA Groupe BPCE Group Crédit Agricole ING Bank Mizuho FG Nordea Santander Société Générale Standard Chartered State Street Sumitomo Mitsui FG Unicredit Group Wells Fargo	Bank of China Bank of New York Mellon BBVA Groupe BPCE Industrial and Commercial Bank of China Limited ING Bank Mizuho FG Nordea Santander Société Générale Standard Chartered State Street Sumitomo Mitsui FG Unicredit Group Wells Fargo

Source: Adapted from FSB (2013b).

They will be phased in starting in January 2016, with full implementation by January 2019. Table 7.8 lists the G-SIBs and the allocation to buckets corresponding to the required level of additional loss absorbency, as detailed above. The methodology used to define the buckets is based on an 'indicator-based' measurement approach. The selected indicators (which include the size of banks, their interconnectedness, lack of readily available substitutes or financial institution infrastructure for the services they provide, their global (cross-border) activity and their complexity) are chosen to reflect the different aspects of what generates negative externalities and makes a bank critical for the stability of the financial system.[10]

---

[10] Details on the indicator-based measurement approach can be found in Basel Committee on Banking Supervision (2011c).

7.8   Conclusion

In this chapter we have reviewed the issue of financial regulation. The chapter began with a review of the rationale for regulation, introducing the reader to different types of regulation. The limitations of regulation were also analysed, in particular the moral hazard issue connected with the government safety net arrangements such as deposit insurance and the lender of last resort function. The chapter also focused on the Basel Capital Accord and the efforts of the Basel Committee to provide common regulatory standards for internationally active banks.

Bank regulation cannot prevent financial crises, but the regulatory framework that is currently being shaped will influence the development of the banking system for many years to come. Measures by governments to purchase impaired assets, recapitalise troubled banks and inject liquidity into the system have commanded support among many banking academics and practitioners.

Key terms

Agency capture	Compliance	Government	Regulatory
Bank Recovery	costs	safety net	forbearance
and Resolution	Contagion	Lender of last resort	SIFIs
Directive (BRRD)	Deposit insurance	(LOLR)	Supervision
Bank runs	G-SIBs	Monitoring	Systemic risk
Capital adequacy	G-SIFIs	Regulation	Too big to fail

Key reading

Barth, J.R., Caprio, G. and Levine, R.E. (2013) *Measure It, Improve It: Bank regulation and supervision in 180 countries 1999–2011*. Milken Institute, April.

Basel Committee on Banking Supervision (2011b) 'Basel III: A global regulatory framework for more resilient banks and banking systems', **www.bis.org/publ/bcbs189.pdf**

Bernet, B. and Walter, S. (2009) 'Design, structure and implementation of a modern deposit insurance scheme', *SUERF Studies*, 5.

Brunnermeier, M.K., Crocket, A., Goodhart, C., Persaud, A. and Shin, H. (2009) *The Fundamental Principles of Financial Regulation,* Geneva Reports on the World Economy. London: Centre for Economic Policy Research.

Goodhart, C.A.E., Hartmann, P., Llewellyn, D., Rojas-Suarez, L. and Weisbrod, S. (1998) *Financial Regulation: Why, How and Where Now?* London: Routledge.

Llewellyn, D. (1999) 'The economic rationale for financial regulation', FSA, Occasional Papers Series, No. 1, **www.fsa.gov.uk/pubs/occpapers/op01.pdf**

REVISION QUESTIONS AND PROBLEMS

7.1 Is there a rationale for the regulation of financial intermediaries and financial markets?

7.2 What is a bank run?

7.3 What are the main types of financial regulation?

7.4 Why are the 'safety net' arrangements said to increase moral hazard in financial markets?

7.5 What are the main limitations of financial regulation?

7.6 What is regulatory forbearance? Describe the main costs and benefits of engaging in forbearance.

7.7 What is the financial safety net? Why is deposit insurance the central element of a well-functioning financial safety net?

7.8 What are the main drivers of regulatory reforms?

7.9 Discuss the 'too big to fail' hypothesis. Can you give some recent examples?

7.10 Illustrate the main features of the Basel Capital Accords, with a focus on the reforms introduced by Basel III.

Chapter 8

Bank failures and banking crises

Learning objectives

- To define bank and financial failures
- To evaluate strategies to identify problem banks
- To identify successful bank restructuring procedures
- To identify the main causes of banking crises
- To evaluate the costs of banking and financial crises
- To understand the different approaches taken to resolve a banking crisis
- To identify the key regulatory initiatives to reduce systemic risk

8.1 Introduction

Banks are profit-maximising firms and bank management is all about seeking profits and managing risks. Bank managers routinely deal with risk management issues and strategic planning. On occasions, bank managers take on excessive risks or implement value-destroying strategies, thereby causing the bank to run into trouble. Like any other firm, banks do fail. The reasons why banks fail are numerous and often interlinked. Managerial deficiencies are often an important reason behind the failure of financial institutions. For this reason, bank risk management is also the focus of regulatory concerns. In addition, because of the potential for systemic risk arising from bank failures, regulators tend to intervene in the banking sector.

Before we discuss the determinants of bank failure and the strategies adopted by regulators to identify problem banks, it is useful to introduce a definition of bank failure. A bank, as a profit-maximising firm, is considered insolvent when its liabilities exceed its assets and its net worth becomes negative. A bank is deemed to have failed if it is liquidated, merged with a healthy bank under government supervision/pressure, or rescued with state financial support. Whereas some think that failing banks should be treated as any other failing firms, the potential for systemic effects arising from bank failures has entailed a varying degree of intervention in the banking system (ranging from deposit insurance to lender of last resort functions of the central bank, to direct state intervention and financing).

How to deal with bank failures is a controversial issue. Banks play such a critical role in the economy that they are subject to more intense regulation than other sectors. As we discussed in Chapter 7, regulation of the banking system is justified by market failures, which can be caused by asymmetric information and negative externalities. Bank regulation can take a number of forms, from deposit insurance to capital requirements (namely, the Basel Capital Adequacy Accords), bank licensing and regular examinations of banks. The main concern of regulators is that the failure of one bank can have a contagious domino effect, leading to the failure of other banks, and this, therefore, can adversely affect the whole financial system. In reality, the transition from the failure of an individual bank to the collapse of a country's banking system is rare (although possible – a recent example is the collapse of Icelandic banks in 2008). Nonetheless, there have been frequent systemic crises in developed and emerging economies in recent years. These will be analysed in more detail later on in this chapter. We first discuss the determinants of bank failure in Section 8.2. The main strategies used to identify problem banks are explained in Section 8.3, with a focus on early warning systems for bank soundness and the recently introduced stress tests. Section 8.4 presents the key issues of bank restructuring and will discuss the regulatory toolkit. Section 8.5 discusses the causes and consequences of banking and financial crises and Section 8.6 concludes the chapter.

8.2   The determinants of bank failure

It is rare to find a single reason for a bank's failure; rather, there are often a number of contributing factors. Nevertheless, a clear understanding of the main reasons as to why a financial institution has run into trouble is necessary to enable regulators to use appropriate tools and ensure success of the proposed solutions. To give a very simple example, if a bank is facing a temporary liquidity problem, the extension of a liquidity line by the central bank (or access to the discount window) might help in solving the bank's problem. However, if the bank faces solvency rather than liquidity problems, then allowing the bank to access the discount window is unlikely to solve the bank's problems and it can have costly consequences for taxpayers.

The academic and policy literature identifies the key determinants of bank failure as follows:

(i)   poor management;

(ii) fraud;

(iii) regulatory forbearance;

(iv) too big to fail;

(v)   clustering;

(vi) macroeconomic and systemic factors.

i. Poor management

Deficiencies in the management of banks are a contributing factor in virtually all cases of bank troubles. In most bank failure cases, the senior management will appear as the culprits. For example, in the case of Barings in 1995, even though the bank was eventually brought down by a 'rogue trader', the underlying problem was bad senior management. Indeed, head office allowed Nick Leeson to run both the front and the back office of the Singapore branch simultaneously, despite an internal audit report recommending that the trader should stop managing the back office. This allowed Leeson to hide huge losses. More recently, the trading incident at Société Générale in January 2008, which involved the trader Jérôme Kerviel and resulted in a loss of €4.9 billion – the largest in banking history – calls Société Générale's management into question (see Box 8.1).

BOX 8.1 ROGUE TRADERS AND BANK LOSSES

In 1995 Mr Nick Leeson was the rogue trader who brought down Barings Brothers, a British merchant bank, by uncovered exposures in the derivatives market. He went into the red by $1.2bn by trading on Asian markets, after what he claimed was a well-intentioned attempt to cover up losses in a client's account. He was jailed for fraud.

Also in 1995, Mr Toshihide Iguchi at Daiwa Bank in Japan lost around $1.1bn (after more than 10 years of illicit trading) while dealing in US Treasury bonds. Daiwa Bank did not fail because it sold its assets and had considerable reserves, however it was a massive hit for its reputation. Mr Iguchi was fined $2.6m and sentenced to four years in prison.

In 2002 Mr John Rusnak caused losses of some $750m to Allied Irish Bank, Ireland's largest bank, in unauthorised foreign exchange dealing at its American subsidiary, Allfirst. Mr Rusnak expected the Yen to strengthen against the dollar but this did not occur. The bank thought that options contracts were purchased as the internal system showed. Instead they weren't actually bought. Therefore, there was no insurance against the loss. The bank's solvency was not threatened but the bank absorbed the losses at a price of a significant reduction in earnings and capital.

Another rogue trader, Mr Peter Young, a fund manager of investment bank Morgan Grenfell Asset Management, a Deutsche Bank company, lost some $380m from the funds he ran, after hiding a series of unauthorised investments. Deutsche Bank had to inject $300m in cash to replace the fund; however, they incurred huge losses after a third of the investors left the fund within a few weeks.

In 2002 Central Europe had its own rogue trader in Mr Eduard Nodilo, a dealer at Rijecka Banka, Croatia's third-biggest bank, which accumulated $98m in foreign exchange losses, wiping out the bank's capital.

In January 2004, Australia's biggest bank, the National Australian Bank, revealed that some of its foreign currency options traders in Melbourne and London had engaged in unauthorised trading. Losses have been estimated at $445m.

More recently, in January 2008, the trading incident at Société Générale, involving the trader Jérôme Kerviel, resulted in a loss of €4.9 billion. This event sparked the question as to whether it was a case of an isolated rogue trader or a more complex case of a 'rogue business model'.

> Société Générale uncovered a fraud, exceptional in its size and nature: one trader had taken massive fraudulent directional positions in 2007 and 2008, beyond its limited authority. Aided by its knowledge of control procedures, he managed to conceal these positions though a scheme of elaborate fictitious transactions … which eventually resulted in the largest trading loss in banking history.
>
> *Financial Times*, 24 January 2008

A similar question was raised in 2011 in the case of Kweku Adoboli's actions at UBS.

> UBS has discovered a loss due to unauthorized trading by a trader in its Investment Bank. The matter is still being investigated, but UBS's current estimate of the loss on the trades is in the range of USD 2 billion. It is possible that this could lead UBS to report a loss for the third quarter of 2011. No client positions were affected.
>
> *Financial Times*, 15 September 2011

In November 2012, Adoboli was jailed for the UK's biggest bank fraud, while UBS was fined £29.7 million over its conduct in the case.

A 2011 report by the UK Financial Services Authority, which aimed to identify the multiple factors resulting in the failure of the Royal Bank of Scotland in October 2008, identifies

> errors of judgement and execution made by RBS executive and management, which in combination, resulted in RBS being one of the banks that failed amid the general crisis. These were decisions for whose commercial consequences RBS executive and Board were ultimately responsible.
>
> (Financial Services Authority, 2011a)

The FSA report concludes that, even taking into account deficiencies in regulation and the macroeconomic conditions at the time, RBS's failure ultimately resulted from poor decisions made by the management and Board of Directors (see also Box 13.2 on the failure of RBS).

Beside these extreme examples, poor management can cause asset-side problems (e.g. bad loans, investment losses), liability-side problems (e.g. liquidity problems, deposit withdrawals, bank runs) and off-balance-sheet problems (e.g. derivative losses). Poor asset management, or a weak loan portfolio because of excessive exposure in one or more sectors, can eventually lead to failure.

The IMF identifies five types of loan performance categories for external reporting purposes:

1 **Standard.** Credit is sound and payments current.

2 **Watch.** Subject to conditions that, if uncorrected, could raise concerns about full repayment.

3 **Substandard.** Full repayment is in doubt due to inadequate protection. Interest or principal overdue (90 days +).

4 **Doubtful.** Assets for which collection is considered improbable. Interest or principal overdue (180 days +).

5 **Loss.** Virtually uncollectible. Interest or principal overdue (1 year +).

Substandard, doubtful and loss are considered as **non-performing loans (NPLs)** and remain so until either the loan is written off or principal and interest payments are received. More specifically, the IMF (2004) defines non-performing loans as loans on which debtors have failed to make contractual payments for a pre-determined time.[1]

It should be noted that a loan classified as non-performing does not necessarily lead to losses. If there is adequate collateral, losses might not occur. Conversely, loans may be lost even though they were never classified as non-performing.

Not all countries adopt the same definition of NPLs and there may even be different definitions in use within a single country depending on the sector involved (financial institutions, quoted corporations, small enterprises, government entities and so forth). In addition, international accounting and banking standards refer to loans being *impaired* rather than non-performing.[2] Proper recognition and provisioning for NPLs are essential for crisis management and prevention. However, while there is broad consensus on the need for more rigorous loan classification rules, there is some controversy over the timing and tightening of rules. The fear is that markets might overreact to the full disclosure of NPLs, particularly in emerging markets

---

[1] The International Monetary Fund posted on its website a 'Guide' ('Compilation guide on financial soundness indicators') in 2004 (and then published it in 2006 and revised it in 2007) with the purpose of providing information and advice on concepts and definitions, as well as sources and techniques, for the compilation and dissemination of financial soundness indicators. See IMF (2007).

[2] Impairment is a specific term used in the International Accounting Standard 39 (IAS 39) and by the Basel Committee on Banking Supervision.

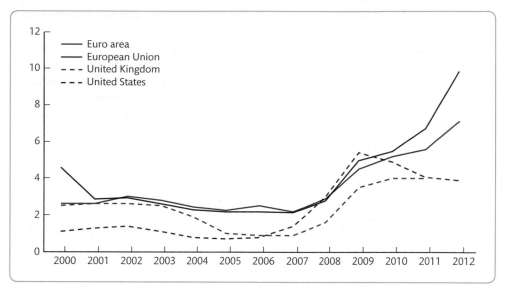

Figure 8.1 Bank NPLs to total loans ratio (%)

Source: World Bank data and authors' calculations.

or in markets where the existing economic conditions are difficult. Yet suspicions that the true scale of the problem is being hidden can hurt market confidence. Figure 8.1 illustrates the trend in NPLs (defined as the value of non-performing loans divided by the total value of the loan portfolio) for the eurozone, the EU, the UK and the US between 2000 and 2012.

From Figure 8.1, we can see that the credit quality of loan portfolios remained relatively stable at around 4 per cent of total loans, until the global financial crises. From 2007, average bank asset quality deteriorated sharply, with eurozone banks faring worse than their US and UK competitors from 2009 onwards.

An essential step in any bank restructuring programme is to measure correctly the amount of non-performing loans. This is a major task, due to the varying practices of loan classification and different regulatory environments. Some regulatory authorities use quantitative criteria, such as the number of days loan repayments are overdue, others rely on qualitative norms, such as the clients' financial status, or on management judgement about future loan repayments.

An area of concern during bank restructuring is the valuation of **collateral**. In theory, most bank loans are collateralised (typically on real estate) and this should provide available resources to any restructuring agency. In practice, collateral is often worth considerably less than book value and can be recovered only if bankruptcy procedures operate efficiently. As aggregate demand weakens during banking crises, collateral values (such as property prices) drop steeply. Moreover, a large number of simultaneous 'fire sales' may force the value of collateral to drop even further. This raises the question of how long a restructuring agency should hold the assets of distressed banks. Finally, the value of the collateral depends also on the credibility of the legal process to enforce repayments.

ii. Fraud

Fraud has long being recognised as a key cause of bank failure. A 1986 study commissioned by the American Bankers Association to identify the main reasons for US bank failure noted (Benston *et al.*, 1996): 'Because fraud has been the single most important cause of bank failures, both in the past and in the present, it is distinguished from excessive risk-taking.'

Along similar lines, Barker and Holdsworth (1993) reported a study by the US House Committee on Government Operations which found about 50 per cent of bank failures and 25 per cent of thrift failures in the 1980s were principally due to fraud. However, it is often difficult to secure a conviction because of the fine line between fraud and bad management. Box 8.1 highlights some of the largest episodes on fraud in financial institutions.

iii. Regulatory forbearance

When financial intermediaries run into trouble, regulators may be under pressure to not apply existing regulations too strictly. As discussed in Section 7.5, this is known as regulatory forbearance and it arises when applying regulations (for example, imposing compliance with capital adequacy ratios) could worsen the institution's problems and could result in failure, possibly triggering a run on other financial institutions. Regulatory forbearance itself may even cause a banking crisis as bank regulators may become locked into an ever-worsening spiral, resulting in a loss of public confidence in how banks and the financial system in general are being regulated. Regulatory forbearance for poorly managed banks may result in damage to the regulator's credibility and authority. In addition, the moral hazard risk associated with regulatory forbearance could provide incentives for excessive risk taking.

In the context of bank failures, when bank auditors and regulators 'miss' important signals from the distressed bank, or they put the interests of the regulated bank ahead of taxpayers, they are 'guilty' of forbearance. In many cases of failures, subsequent investigations show that exposure limits were exceeded with the knowledge of the regulators – suggestive of widespread forbearance in dealing with troubled banks.

iv. Too big to fail (TBTF)

'Too big to fail' refers to the viewpoint whereby the largest banks in a banking system are viewed as being too big to be allowed to fail and therefore they have guaranteed access to the lender of last resort. The idea of TBTF is not new – the term became used in the 1980s following the bailout of the US bank Continental Illinois. Since the 1980s though, financial institutions have grown much larger and more interconnected. Indeed, it is often argued that size by itself is not the relevant criterion for bailing out troubled banks – rather, it is the significance or importance of banks in specific markets and the expected scale/impact of potential failure. This is what prompted the rescue of US investment bank Bear Stearns (in March 2008) and the government bailout of American International Group (AIG) (in September 2008), once the world's largest insurer. This has prompted the use of other acronyms, such as too systemic to fail (TSTF) or too interconnected to fail (TITF).

While no financial regulatory authority will ever provide guaranteed access to lender of last resort financing, history does tell us that (for systemic and other reasons) large banks are likely to be bailed out more than small banks. The policy of the TBTF applies, to a certain degree, in all countries. Critics argue that the implicit government guarantees for the biggest banks encourage them to take excessive risks and therefore makes them more likely to fail.

Following the 2007–2009 global financial crisis, the concept of TBTF has emerged from the regulatory and academic debate and has moved into the public arena and there have been calls to break up big banks. For example, the 2010 Dodd–Frank Wall Street Reform and Consumer Protection Act (Dodd–Frank) is the US government's attempt to resolve the TBTF problem for US banks. At the global level, in 2011 the Financial Stability Board identified an initial group of 29 banks as systemically important financial institutions, to be subjected to more stringent prudential standards (see also Section 7.7.4.4). Similarly, the BCBS set forth an additional capital requirement for global systemically important banks. Most of these regulatory reforms are still works in progress at the time of writing (2014) and the future of large banks is therefore uncertain (see also Section 8.4.2).

v. Clustering

Clustering refers to the fact that bank failures in a country tend to be clustered around a few years rather than being spread evenly over time. The presence of a so-called 'herd instinct' or 'contagion effect' among depositors and investors may help explain a run on several banks over a short period of time. However, macroeconomic factors are also important in explaining clustering effects.

Another reason for clustering may relate to the failure of timely intervention by the government or regulatory authorities. The Japanese banking crisis of the 1990s offers an example of the interaction of macroeconomic factors and badly timed regulatory intervention.

vi. Macroeconomic and systemic factors

There are a number of factors that do not slot easily in any of the previous categories. There is a vast literature on the causes of bank failures and banking crises; this literature is fairly divided between advocates of microeconomic factors and supporters of macroeconomic reasons and systemic factors. These are discussed in more detail in Section 8.5.3.

Qualitative reviews of bank failure, as the ones described in this section, give some insight into what causes a bank to fail. Quantitative approaches provide econometric models of bank failure, borrowing from the literature on corporate bankruptcy. These models aim to measure bank soundness and provide early warning indicators of trouble. These early warning systems (EWS) are discussed in Section 8.3.

8.3 Early warning systems for bank soundness

Recent episodes of turmoil in the international financial markets have called attention to the need for better tools to monitor bank risk taking as well as the vulnerabilities in the financial system. From a regulator's perspective, the key is to anticipate the next bank failure by identifying those institutions that display underlying vulnerabilities, taking into account potential triggers in the wider economic environment (for example, contagion from other banks/countries, trade shocks, political instability, etc.).

Put simply, **early warning systems (ESW)** are models designed to draw regulators' attention to certain key variables associated with past crisis. These variables can reflect the risk of a single financial institution (micro-prudential approach) or the risk of the financial system as a whole (macro-prudential approach).

Bank supervisors have traditionally concentrated on assessing the risk profile and soundness of individual financial institutions. This micro-prudential approach has focused mainly on the following:

1 Standard balance sheet and income statement financial ratios. This includes the so-called CAMELS variables (see Section 8.3.2).

2 Market prices of financial instruments, such as bank stocks and subordinated debt.

3 Measures of bank risk and financial strength, such as deposit rates.

In addition, regulators collect key macroeconomic indicators. However, critics say that the emphasis on micro surveillance prior to 2007 failed to spot the risk arising from the growing interconnectedness of financial institutions, both domestically and across borders.

Although the use of EWS is not new in policy making, the 2007–2009 financial crisis prompted national regulatory authorities and international organisations, such as the IMF and the FSB, to work together to revise the existing tools to anticipate systemic problems. Among these initiatives are the ongoing efforts to develop and use macro-prudential indicators, defined broadly as indicators of the health and stability of financial systems.

EWS can be generally divided into models based on financial ratio analysis or peer group analysis and statistical models (for example, models predicting failure or survival rates, models estimating ratings and the probability of rating downgrades, and models estimating expected losses).

8.3.1 Financial ratio analysis based models

Financial ratio analysis is an important tool for bank management and it is used both internally and externally to evaluate bank performance – it investigates areas such as profitability, asset quality, liquidity, solvency and capital adequacy (see Section 9.4 for details on bank financial ratio analysis).

In terms of EWS, a bank's financial condition is related to a set of key financial ratios, which should be within a certain range for the bank to be operating in a safe and sound manner. If one or more of these key financial ratios exceeds a pre-determined critical level or lies within a set interval, then the EWS generates a warning signal, a 'red flag' that indicates that more attention should be paid to that particular bank.

In this context, a bank's performance is benchmarked both against its past performance (that is, checking whether a particular ratio – or set of ratios – is an outlier with respect to past performance) and/or against the performance of a *peer group* of banks. A peer group is normally defined based on some common characteristics, such as bank size (large banks vs. small banks), bank specialisation (co-operative banks, saving banks, commercial banks, investment banks) or other characteristics that might be relevant in some countries (domestic vs. foreign banks, listed banks vs. non-listed banks, state-owned vs. privately owned banks).

Peer group analysis is undertaken on the basis of financial ratios for a group of banks together. This is then used to establish whether an individual bank is performing in a significantly different manner from its peers, with a view to identifying the reasons for such significant difference, which may or may not imply supervisory concerns. Within each peer group, a first step in peer analysis is a simple identification of the best/worst performers compared with the peer average. In addition, financial ratios are ranked from best to worst, and percentile rankings are calculated with the aim of providing regulators an overall view of a bank's performance compared with similar institutions. Individual banks whose financial ratios have deteriorated relative to the averages of their respective peer group can then be identified and action taken if necessary. Some regulators follow a formalised procedure for the use of financial ratio analysis for regulatory purposes. The best known of these models is the CAMELS rating, adopted by the US Federal Reserve.

Table 8.1 CAMELS rating

CAMELS	Variables
Capital adequacy	Total risk-based capital ratio; Tier 1 ratio; charge-offs to loan loss reserves
Asset quality	NPLs/total assets; non-current loan ratio; loans secured by commercial real estate/total assets; other loans/total assets
Management quality	Non-interest expenses to revenue (net interest income plus non-interest income)
Earnings	Return on assets (ROA), net interest margin (NIM)
Liquidity	Core deposits/total assets; volatile liabilities ratio (long-term assets/short-term liabilities)
Sensitivity to market risk	Non-interest income/total assets (proxy returns on risky assets)

8.3.2 CAMELS rating

In the US, bank supervisors rate an individual bank's overall safety and soundness to produce what are commonly referred to as **CAMELS** ratings. CAMELS is the abbreviation for the components of a bank's condition that are assessed: **C**apital adequacy; **A**sset quality; **M**anagement quality; **E**arnings; **L**iquidity; **S**ensitivity to market risk.

Table 8.1 summarises the key financial ratios used to evaluate a bank's financial condition. The Fed uses a mix of publicly available information (from bank financial statements) and private information supplied by bank management to assign a composite rating. CAMELS ratings range from 1 (best rating) to 5 (worst rating). These ratings are disclosed only to bank senior management and are not made public, except in the event of a bank's failure.

Figure 8.2 illustrates the average and distribution of CAMELS ratings of US banks between 1990 and 2011. Strong banks have a CAMELS rating of 1 or 2, while weak banks have ratings of 3, 4 and 5.[3] The data show that bank average ratings were low during the credit crunch of the early 1990s, then recovered during the late 1990s and early 2000s, only to deteriorate quickly from 2007 onwards.

Figure 8.3 shows how the pattern in the average rating reflects the changes in the number of banks in each of the five CAMELS rating categories. More specifically, the data show a larger decrease in 'strong banks' (particularly banks achieving the highest rating of 1) mirrored by an increase in banks rated worst with a rating of 5. Also worrying for regulators is the steady increase in the percentage of weak banks with a rating of 3, which may indicate a worsening of financial condition for banks across the system.

Since the global financial crisis, US regulators have also introduced **stress testing** as a supervisory tool. The first stress testing exercise, known as the Supervisory Capital Assessment Programme (SCAP), was conducted in 2009. After the SCAP, US regulators introduced

---

[3] More specifically, a composite CAMELS rating of 1 means that the bank is basically sound in every respect. A CAMELS rating of 2 means that the bank is fundamentally sound but may have modest weaknesses correctable in the normal course of business. A CAMELS rating of 3 means that a bank has a combination of financial, operational or compliance weaknesses ranging from moderately severe to unsatisfactory. A CAMELS rating of 4 means that a bank has an immoderate volume of serious financial weaknesses or a combination of other conditions that are unsatisfactory to supervisors. Finally, a CAMELS rating of 5 means that the bank has an extremely high immediate or near-term probability of failure (Bassett *et al.*, 2012).

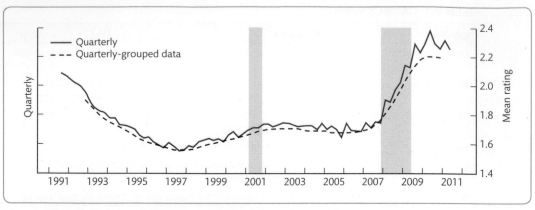

Figure 8.2 Average and distribution of CAMELS ratings, 1990–2011

Note: Bars relate to periods of recession.

Source: Bassett *et al.* (2012) p. 8.

two distinct but related supervisory programmes that rely on stress testing: (i) DFAST – the so-called Dodd–Frank Act stress tests, which aim to quantitatively assess how bank capital levels would fare in stressful economic and financial scenarios; (ii) CCAR (Comprehensive Capital Analysis and Review), which combines the quantitative results from the stress tests with more qualitative assessments of the capital planning processes used by banks.

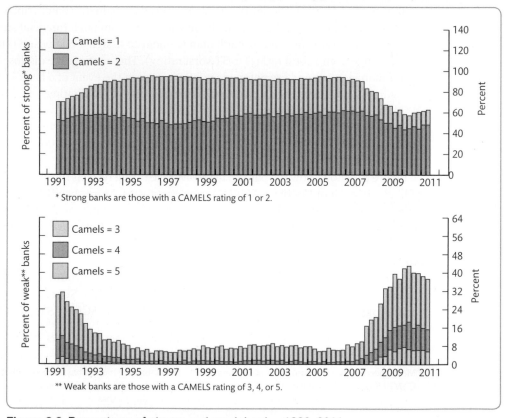

Figure 8.3 Percentage of strong and weak banks, 1990–2011

Source: Bassett *et al.* (2012) p. 8.

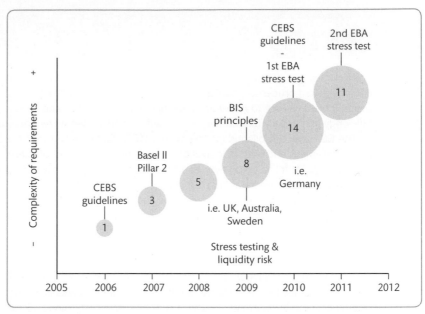

Figure 8.4 The growth of domestic and international stress testing regulations

Source: Moody's Analytics (2011) p. 9.

Stress testing has become a popular regulatory tool in many countries, as the global financial crises shifted the focus of regulation from the risks faced by individual financial institutions to systemic risk.

8.3.3 Stress testing

In recent years, stress testing has grown in importance, due to increased regulatory requirements and an uncertain economic environment in many countries. Figure 8.4 illustrates the growth of domestic and international stress testing regulations. The Moody's Analytic (2011) 'Banking industry survey on stress testing' indicates that the number of country-specific regulations or guidelines increased fourfold between 2007 and 2011. Regulatory requirements have increased not only in number but also in complexity and banks now have to manage multiple requests from different regulatory agencies.

In general terms, stress testing is designed to complement standard Basel capital ratios by adding a more forward-looking perspective and by helping to ensure that banks will have enough capital to keep lending even under highly adverse circumstances. In addition, the disclosures of stress test results can help promote market discipline by providing consistent and comparable information about banks' financial conditions. The Basel Committee on Banking Supervision introduced stronger testing guidelines in 2009 with the objective of ensuring that financial institutions are able to meet capital and liquidity requirements under stressed conditions. These guidelines were followed by those from the CEBS (Committee of European Banking Supervisors, now European Banking Authority (EBA)) in 2010, as discussed in Box 8.2.

Despite their growing popularity, stress tests raise a number of issues, including problems with data collection, the use of different methodologies and the need to reconcile internal

BOX 8.2 THE EUROPEAN BANKING AUTHORITY AND EU-WIDE STRESS TESTS

The European Banking Authority is an independent EU authority that works to ensure effective and consistent prudential regulation and supervision across the European banking sector. Its overall objectives are to maintain financial stability in the EU and to safeguard the integrity, efficiency and orderly functioning of the banking sector (see **www.eba.europa.eu/**).

The EBA was established in November 2010 (Regulation Number 1093/2010 of the European Parliament and of the Council of 24 November 2010) and officially came into being on 1 January 2011. It has taken over all existing and ongoing tasks and responsibilities from the Committee of European Banking Supervisors.

The EBA has some broad competences, including strengthening international supervisory co-ordination, promoting supervisory convergence and providing advice to the EU institutions in the areas of banking, payments and e-money regulation. Its main task is to contribute to the creation of the *European Single Rulebook* in banking, which is to provide a single set of harmonised prudential rules for financial institutions throughout the EU.

The EBA is part of the European System of Financial Supervision (ESFS), which comprises three supervisory authorities: the European Securities and Markets Authority (ESMA), the European Banking Authority and the European Insurance and Occupational Pensions Authority (EIOPA). The ESFS also comprises the European Systemic Risk Board (ESRB) and the Joint Committee of the European Supervisory Authorities as well as the national supervisory authorities of EU member states.

The main decision-making body of the EBA is the Board of Supervisors. At the time of writing it was chaired by Andrea Enria; EU member states are represented by officials of the national central bank. The Board of Supervisors also includes observers from the European Commission, the ESRB, the ECB and other regulatory authorities that are part of the ESFS. The EBA is headquartered in the City of London.

The EBA's main competencies are in three broad areas: (i) regulation; (ii) oversight; (iii) consumer protection.

Within its main competencies, one of the responsibilities of the EBA is to ensure the stability of the financial system in the EU. To this end, the EBA is mandated to monitor and assess market developments as well as to identify trends, potential risks and vulnerabilities stemming from the micro-prudential level. One of the EBA's primary supervisory tools is the EU-wide stress test exercise.

In co-operation with the ESRB, the EBA conducts EU-wide stress tests in a bottom-up fashion, using methodologies, scenarios and key assumptions developed by the EBA with the ESRB, the ECB and the EU Commission. The aim of such tests is to assess the resilience of financial institutions to adverse market developments, as well as to contribute to the overall assessment of systemic risk in the EU financial system. In 2011 they tested 90 banks in 21 countries, covering 65 per cent of banking assets and at least 50 per cent of banking assets in each country. The results of the exercise were made public and provide an unprecedented level of transparency on banks' exposures and capital composition (see **www.eba.europa.eu/risk-analysis-and-data/eu-wide-stress-testing/2011/results**).

expert judgement and external benchmarks as well as national and international regulatory requirements. From a bank's point of view, stress testing can be an expensive and time-consuming exercise; banks criticise both the methodologies and data used. The long-term aim of regulators is to embed stress testing in bank risk management practices rather than it simply being a regulatory tool.

8.3.3.1 Different approaches to stress testing

There are different approaches to stress testing, the main ones being:

1 the bottom-up approach (BU);
2 the top-down approach (TD);
3 the reverse approach.

In a bottom-up approach, banks conduct regular evaluations of their positions relative to a set of common scenarios (provided by the authorities). This is the approach followed by the EBA. One of the advantages of the BU tests is their use of extremely granular information on individual banks' trading portfolios and overall exposures. This permits a more detailed insight into how an individual bank might be affected by worsening macroeconomic and market conditions. On the flip side of the coin, BU tests are institution-specific and therefore it is difficult to compare results across banks.

In the top-down approach, the regulatory authorities set the macroeconomic scenarios and conditions under which the test should be run, and calculate the results without the involvement of the banks themselves. The focus with TD tests is as much on the banking system as a whole as it is on individual institutions. A TD stress test first draws on macroeconomic scenarios and on statistical estimates of the impact of adverse economic conditions on credit and market exposures. Second, it builds formal 'maps' of transmission of economic shocks onto the financial system. By applying the same scenario, on the same model, with the same assumptions and at the same time, TD tests allow for comparisons across banks, as well as offering a framework for understanding and identifying particular areas of vulnerability in the banking system as a whole. TD models lack the balance sheet granularity of the BU models. The TD approach is favoured by many central banks, including the Bank of England, whose RAMSI model (Risk Assessment Model of Systemic Institutions) is an example of a top-down stress testing model and is one part of the Bank's risk assessment toolkit.[4]

Reverse stress tests require a bank to assess scenarios and circumstances that would render its business model unviable, thereby identifying potential business vulnerabilities. Reverse stress testing starts from an outcome of business failure and identifies circumstances where this might occur. This is different to general stress and scenario testing which tests for outcomes arising from changes in circumstances. Reverse stress tests were introduced by the UK Financial Services Authority in December 2012 and are now the remit of the PRA within the Bank of England. Reverse stress tests are to be used by banks as a risk management tool to help managers to overcome 'disaster myopia' and improve contingency planning.

8.4　Bank restructuring

Despite regulators' efforts to identify vulnerabilities in the financial systems, bank failures do happen. A crucial question on regulators' mind is: 'What is the best policy option for rescuing a troubled bank?' In this section we are going to discuss the tools in the regulatory toolkit to deal with bank failure.

Bank restructuring has many (sometimes conflicting) aims and as a consequence, there is no universally accepted way to carry out a successful restructuring exercise. The ultimate

---

[4] For more details on the Bank of England RAMSI model see Burrows *et al.* (2012).

goal of bank restructuring is assumed to be a lower probability of the bank's default with a minimal taxpayer burden (Landier and Ueda, 2009).

Before we start discussing the bank resolution mechanisms available to policy makers, we need to introduce some basic bank resolution terminology. Some terms related to bank resolution have a range of meanings and different terms are used in different countries. The terminology presented in Table 8.2 is used in most of the IMF literature on banking crises and resolution.

The toolkits designed to assist authorities in resolving troubled banks are generally country-specific, as are the various steps in the resolution of a troubled bank. Within each

Table 8.2 Bank resolution terminology

Intervened bank	An insolvent or non-viable bank where the authorities have taken over the powers of management and shareholders. Such a bank may be closed or may stay open under the control of the authorities while its financial condition is better defined and decisions are made on an appropriate resolution strategy.
Resolved bank	A bank undergoing a resolution strategy, including liquidation, merger or sale, transfer to a bridge bank, recapitalisation by the government, and sales or transfers of blocks of assets or liabilities.
Bank closure	When a bank ceases to carry on its business as a legal entity. Withdrawal of the banking licence typically accompanies a closure. A closure may be part of a legal process of achieving the orderly exit of a weak bank through a range of resolution options, including liquidation or a complete or partial transfer of its assets and liabilities to other institutions.
Bank liquidation	The legal process whereby the assets of an institution are sold and its liabilities are settled to the extent possible. It can be voluntary or forced, within or outside general bankruptcy procedures, and with or without court involvement. In liquidation, assets are sold to pay off the creditors in the order prescribed by the law. Liquidation can take place under a country's bankruptcy or company laws or pursuant to a **special resolution regime (SRR)** for banks.
Merger (or **sale**)	When all the assets and liabilities of the firm are transferred to and absorbed into another institution. Mergers can be voluntary or government assisted.
Purchase and assumption (P&A)	When a solvent bank purchases all or a portion of the assets of a failing bank, including its customer base and goodwill, together with all or part of its liabilities. In a P&A operation, the government typically will pay with securities to the purchasing bank the difference between the value of the assets and liabilities. The process usually involves the withdrawal or cancellation of the licence of the troubled bank, the termination of the owners' rights in the bank, the assumption of the troubled bank's deposits and good assets, and the takeover of the bank's problem assets by the resolution authority. In the UK, a similar procedure is known as private sector purchaser.
Bridge bank	A form of P&A, it involves the use of a temporary financial institution to receive and manage the good assets of one or several failed institutions. A bridge bank may be allowed to undertake some banking business, such as providing new credit and restructuring existing credits. A bridge bank does not require the authorities or state to acquire the shares of a failed bank, merely part or all of its property.
Deposit payoff	When the deposit insurer makes sure that customers of a failed bank receive the full amount of their insured deposits.
Open bank assistance	OBA occurs when a distressed financial institution remains open with government financial assistance. This operation is similar to temporary public ownership (TPO) in the UK (although the TPO tool involves the UK government acquiring all the shares of the failing bank).

Table 8.2 continued

Good bank/Bad bank	When a troubled bank is split into a 'good bank', which continues to operate and it is typically acquired by a healthy bank, and a 'bad bank', which goes into administration. Insured deposits usually go with the 'good bank'. All other creditors typically travel with the 'bad bank' and become claimants in the insolvency procedure. This is also known as partial property transfers (PPT).
Nationalisation	Occurs when the government assumes ownership of an institution.
Bailout	When a troubled bank receives financial help or liquidity from outside investors or from public funds in order to avoid bankruptcy.
Bail-in	A resolution mechanism that gives regulators the ability to impose losses on bondholders while ensuring the critical parts of the bank can keep running.

Sources: Brierley (2009); Hoelscher and Quintyn (2003); McGuire (2012).

country, the legal framework defines the organisations that must be involved in the restructuring operations, their roles and their powers.

It is a generally accepted principle that the resolution should be carried out in a manner that minimises the cost for the resolution authority or the government (**least-cost resolution**). To determine the least-cost resolution, authorities will have to compare the different resolution mechanisms, taking into account the macroeconomic and market conditions at the time, which may render some of the options unfeasible. The Financial Stability Board (2011a) has issued the 'Key attributes of effective resolution regimes for financial institutions' to promote effective and consistent implementation across countries and to support regulatory authorities to resolve financial institutions 'in an orderly manner without taxpayer exposure to loss from solvency support, while maintaining continuity of their vital economic functions'. The implementation of the 'Key attributes' is particularly relevant for cross-border bank resolution and the resolution of SIFIs (see Section 8.4.2). Box 8.3 outlines the aims of an effective bank resolution regime.

8.4.1 Bank resolution techniques

A resolution procedure is initiated when a bank is no longer viable (or likely to be no longer viable). A number of techniques can be used for dealing with problem banks; these tools may in some cases be alternatives and in other cases complementary. These are:

(i) liquidation (bank insolvency procedure);

(ii) mergers and acquisitions;

(iii) purchase and assumption;

(iv) bridge bank;

(v) open bank assistance.

i. Liquidation (bank insolvency procedure)

When a bank is no longer viable, if a rescue is not possible or there is no prospect of restoring its longer-term viability, the bank may have to be liquidated under the country's general insolvency framework or a bank SRR. Depositors are likely to be paid off and creditors will be paid according to the hierarchy of claims. The resolution authority will dispose of all of the

BOX 8.3 AIMS OF AN EFFECTIVE BANK RESOLUTION REGIME

An effective resolution regime (interacting with applicable schemes and arrangements for the protection of depositors, insurance policy holders and retail investors) should:

(i) ensure continuity of systemically important financial services, and payment, clearing and settlement functions;

(ii) protect, where applicable and in coordination with the relevant insurance schemes and arrangements, such depositors, insurance policy holders and investors as are covered by such schemes and arrangements, and ensure the rapid return of segregated client assets;

(iii) allocate losses to firm owners (shareholders) and unsecured and uninsured creditors in a manner that respects the hierarchy of claims;

(iv) not rely on public solvency support and not create an expectation that such support will be available;

(v) avoid unnecessary destruction of value, and therefore seek to minimise the overall costs of resolution in home and host jurisdictions and, where consistent with the other objectives, losses for creditors;

(vi) provide for speed and transparency and as much predictability as possible through legal and procedural clarity and advanced planning for orderly resolution;

(vii) provide a mandate in law for cooperation, information exchange and coordination domestically and with relevant foreign resolution authorities before and during a resolution;

(viii) ensure that non-viable firms can exit the market in an orderly way; and

(ix) be credible, and thereby enhance market discipline and provide incentives for market-based solutions.

Source: Financial Stability Board (2011a).

failed bank's assets, which can be a costly and time-consuming process. In addition, assets sold in a fire sale will yield less than their fair market value. A liquidation or bankruptcy procedure is most likely to be used for a bank whose failure is unlikely to have adverse systemic consequences and for which there is unlikely to be a buyer.

ii. Mergers and acquisitions

In the context of bank resolution, a merger of a troubled bank occurs when all the assets and liabilities of the firm are transferred and absorbed into another (healthy) institution. Mergers can be unassisted (voluntary) or government assisted. In an *unassisted merger,* regulators encourage the deal without providing any financial assistance. The plus side of this strategy is that there is no cost for regulators. A drawback is that the acquisition of a weak bank results in the weakening of an initially strong acquirer bank and therefore may leave regulators with a much larger weak bank to resolve. In *government-assisted mergers*, the government will offer some form of direct financial assistance in order to find a buyer for the troubled bank. The provision of direct financial assistance needs to be carefully structured so as not to benefit stockholders of the acquired institution at the expenses of taxpayers.

iii. Purchase and assumption

Purchase and assumptions are one of the most efficient methods for resolving troubled banks. A P&A involves a healthy financial institution 'purchasing' some or all of a failed institution's assets and 'assuming' some or all of the institution's liabilities, usually insured deposits (where there is explicit deposit insurance) and potentially all deposits and even other liabilities (McGuire, 2012). There are many types of P&A transactions. In a basic P&A transaction, the assuming institution generally takes on only limited assets, usually cash and cash equivalents. The liabilities are then matched to the assets taken and consist of either all or some of the deposits. In a 'whole bank P&A' the acquirer purchases the entire portfolio of the failed bank on an 'as-is' basis with no guarantees. P&A operations can also include some form of put option, entitling the acquiring bank to return certain assets within a specified time period, or a contractual profit- or loss-sharing agreement related to some or all of the assets.

iv. Bridge bank

A **bridge bank** is a variation of P&A. In this scenario, the resolution authority acts as the acquirer by creating a new, temporary, full-service bank that is designed to bridge the gap between the failure of a bank and the time when the resolution authority can implement a satisfactory acquisition by a third party (McGuire, 2012). This resolution is used when the failure of a bank is unexpected (for example, in the case of the discovery of a fraud or the onset of a liquidity crisis). The bridge bank is designed to provide an immediate change in ownership and it is usually operational for a limited period of time (normally one or two years). Transfer to a bridge bank may be the best option if a private sector solution requires more time to arrange, for example because potential **private sector purchasers** (PSPs) need to carry out further due diligence on the bank's books.

v. Open bank assistance

Under certain circumstances, the government or the resolution authority may provide direct financial assistance to a bank in danger of failing. This 'assistance' may take the form of a loan, an asset purchase, a capital injection or the purchase of other debt instruments. In some circumstances the regulatory authorities might opt to exercise regulatory forbearance, particularly with respect to capital adequacy. In some specific circumstances, it may be necessary to take a bank into **temporary public ownership (TPO)** if there is no reasonable prospect of selling it to a PSP (either directly or through a bridge bank) and in the short run the bank's failure could represent a serious threat to financial stability.

Table 8.3 summarises the pros and cons of the different resolution tools. Regulators will have to make decisions based on the bank's financial condition, the reasons behind the financial troubles, market conditions at the time and the risk to systemic stability posed by the event of bank failure.

8.4.2 Resolution of large and complex financial institutions

The resolution methods discussed in Section 8.4.1 are not designed to cope with the failure of large and complex financial institutions (LCFIs). LCFIs (also called systemically important financial institutions) are large financial institutions that operate across borders and in many business areas; they have complex capital structures and can be funded by multiple types of liabilities (the definition of SIFIs was discussed in Section 7.8.4.4).

Table 8.3 Bank resolution methods

Resolution methods	Benefits	Costs
Liquidation (bank insolvency procedure – BIP)	• Customers with insured deposits receive money quickly from the deposit insurance fund	• Customers with uninsured deposits and creditors have to wait for the (often lengthy) proceeds of the liquidation • Customers with uninsured deposits may not be paid the full uninsured amount • Customers must find a new bank • It is usually considered a 'last resort' because of high costs involved
Mergers and acquisitions (M&As)	• Unassisted mergers come at no cost to the authorities • There is no interruption to banking services	• Healthy banks can become overburdened with the problems of the troubled bank
Purchase and assumption (P&A)	• Customers with insured deposits suffer no losses • Acquiring bank has the opportunity for new customers	• The majority of the assets might need to be liquidated • Uninsured depositors may suffer losses
Bridge bank	• Gives regulators time to arrange a permanent transaction • Gives purchaser time to assess the bank's condition	• Duplicates part of the resolution process • Regulator becomes responsible for the operation of the bridge bank, which can be labour intensive and time consuming • May require ongoing liquidity support from the government • Difficult to retain best employees and customers • If a subsequent sale is not made, operating a bridge bank may exceed the costs of liquidation
Open bank assistance (OBA)	• Can be implemented relatively quickly • Could prevent systemic issues • Assets are kept in the private sector	• Promotes a belief in the TBTF • Government funds could benefit private shareholders

The first issue concerning the resolution of an LCFI is that it is likely to stretch government skills and resources. The second crucial issue is how to handle the resolution of large and internationally active banks. LCFIs are usually cross-border banking groups, whose resolution can be hampered by the fact that countries have their own SRRs and SRR tools cannot automatically be applied extra-territorially.

A third problem is that existing SRRs are not designed to cope with the failure of investment banks (for example, a standard SRR could not effectively and orderly run down massive, complex derivatives or trading portfolios). As demonstrated by the Lehman Brothers and AIG episodes, unwinding a derivatives book is particularly complicated, as it requires dynamic hedging to preserve value, and that is very difficult to achieve in liquidation proceedings when counterparties take flight and funding dries up.

Major reforms are being considered domestically and internationally to address these problems, in order to safeguard the stability of the financial system in the case of an LCFI failure. Key regulatory reforms are designed to reduce the systemic risk contribution of LCFIs and include proposals to impose additional capital charges on SIFIs (see Section 7.8.4.4), as well as proposals to facilitate the resolution of cross-border institutions. Regulatory measures that affect the structure, organisation or scope of the activities of LCFIs are also being discussed. Table 8.4 summarises these key regulatory initiatives at the national and international levels and the proposed timeline to implementation.

Table 8.4 Regulatory initiatives

Key reforms	Aim	Timeline
Global reforms		
Basel III capital standards	● Changes the definition of capital	2019
Basel III capital charges	● Better valuation of risk	2019
	● Incremental risk charge for trading book activity	
	● Higher capital charges for counterparty exposures in derivatives and repo trading	
	● Additional capital surcharge for G-SIFIs	
	● Capital charge assessed on (clearing member) banks' central counterparty default fund exposures	
G-SIBs surcharge	● Additional amount of common equity for systemically important banks	2019
Basel III liquidity requirements	● Liquidity coverage ratio: requires high-quality liquid assets sufficient to meet 10 days' outflows	2015
	● Net stable funding ratio: requires better maturity matching of assets and liabilities	2018
Basel III leverage ratio	● Sets a ceiling on the measure of exposures (regardless of risk weighting) against capital (3% of Tier 1 capital over total exposure)	2019
FSB compensation guidelines	● Responsibility of boards for compensation policies	Implemented
	● Compensation should be aligned with risks and time horizons	
	● Supervisors should monitor compensation policies	
Corporate governance	● Emphasis on robust corporate governance, including the role of banks' boards	
Resolution of G-SIFIs	● Reduce the likelihood that G-SIFIs will need to use public funds when they fail	
National reforms		
Volcker Rule (Dodd–Frank Act) (US)	● Deposit-taking institutions restricted from trading activities, ownership of private equity and hedge funds	Law passed, Implementation pending
Vickers Report (UK)	● Ring-fencing of UK retail banks from investment banking activities	2019
	● Additional capital for ring-fenced entity	
Bank Recovery and Resolution Directive (EU Directive 27.06.2013)	● Establishing a common framework for the recovery and resolution of credit institutions and investment firms	Directive approved Implementation pending
	● Institutions required to draw up recovery plans	
	● Resolution authorities to prepare resolution plans for each institution	
	● Enables resolution authorities to use the bail-in tool	
	● Member states to set up *ex-ante* resolution funds	

Source: Adapted from IMF (2012c) and authors' updates.

The measures illustrated in Table 8.4 aim to reduce the systemic risk contribution of SIFIs and to introduce measures to improve regulators' capacity to resolve SIFIs.

8.5 Banking crises

When the default or failure of a bank brings about a loss of confidence in the banking system that leads to a run on banks as individuals and companies withdraw their deposits, authorities are faced with a banking crisis. In the past 20 years, several countries have suffered systemic banking crises of different severities. IMF economists Luc Laeven and Fabian Valencia (2012) identify 147 banking crises over the period 1970–2011. They also count 218 currency crises and 66 sovereign crises over the same time period.

During the period 1980–1993, liberalisation and deregulation led to the failure of 1,300 US 'thrifts' and 1,500 commercial banks (the so-called savings and loan crisis). During the mid-1990s, the Swedish, Norwegian and Finnish banking systems went from deregulated boom to bust, rescued by the state by means of varying forms of government indemnity, and final recovery. There were no bank defaults but the cost to taxpayers was high. Altogether the banking crises and the consequent support measures had a profound impact on the three countries' economies, more particularly for Finland and Norway than for Sweden.

The French crisis of the early 1990s was centred mainly on real estate, causing the failure of seven rated banks. From the mid-1990s onwards the Japanese banking system also experienced a period of crisis, with no bank defaults. The enormous inflation and subsequent crash (in the early 1990s) in Japanese real estate prices severely damaged the major banks. At no period in their post-Second World War history have the Japanese banks needed government support more than from the mid-1990s to the present day (see also Chapter 16 for more details on the Japanese banking crisis).

Bulgaria, the Czech Republic, Hungary, Poland, Romania and Slovakia experienced banking crises during the 1990s, particularly during the period of transition from communism to capitalism and prior to EU accession.

In 1997, a number of emerging economies in South East Asia were affected by a severe financial crisis, which started in Thailand and then spread to Indonesia, Malaysia, South Korea and Vietnam.

In more recent times, the US and the UK experienced a banking crisis in 2007, which then spread to a number of other countries between 2008 and 2010.

The literature indicates that banking crises happen in waves, often preceded by a credit boom. Figure 8.5 illustrates the cycles of banking crises between 1970 and 2010.

Governments, central banks and external agencies have dealt with banking crises in a number of ways, often according to the circumstances, as described in Section 8.4. Although there is no unique recipe, there are some common ingredients to successful crisis management:

● Governments must be willing to recognise the scale of the problem as soon as possible.

● Governments should support supervisory authorities that want to close insolvent banks.

● Governments should be willing to commit substantial fiscal resources to the banking system.

● Transparent actions with regards to NPLs should be adopted at an early stage.

● Improved regulatory and supervisory frameworks are often necessary.

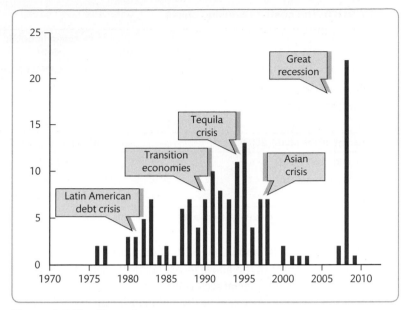

Figure 8.5 Banking crises

Source: Laeven and Valencia (2012) p. 10.

8.5.1 Systemic banking crises

The success of crisis management and bank restructuring depends, ultimately, on a favourable macroeconomic environment and the wherewithal of the authorities to make hard (often politically unpopular) decisions regarding banking system restructuring. Sometimes though, things do not go according to the regulators' plans and the failure of one or more banks triggers a number of defaults, with profound consequences on the economy. The failure of a key bank can prompt runs on other banks as bank customers withdraw their savings, unable to distinguish between sound and troubled institutions. Further, because of the interconnectedness of banks, the failure of one institution can immediately affect others. This is known as *bank contagion* and may lead to *bank runs*.

Banking systems are vulnerable to *system risk*, which is the risk that problems in one bank will spread through the whole sector, and crises can become 'systemic'. This vulnerability to systemic risk is one of the main reasons for bank regulation (see Chapter 7).

Systemic banking crises are rare events, according to Boissay *et al.* (2013), who estimate that they occur on average every 40 years. However, they cause recessions that are deeper and last longer than other recessions.

According to Laeven and Valencia (2012), banking crises can be defined as 'systemic' if there are: 1) significant signs of financial distress in the banking system (as indicated by significant bank runs, losses in the banking system and/or bank liquidations); or 2) significant banking policy intervention measures in response to major losses in the banking system. More specifically, the authors consider a crisis episode to be systemic if at least three out of the following six measures have been used by regulators: (i) extensive liquidity support (5 per cent of deposits and liabilities to non-residents); (ii) bank restructuring costs (at least 3 per cent of GDP); (iii) significant bank nationalisations; (iv) significant guarantees put in place; (v) significant asset purchases (at least 5 per cent of GDP); (vi) deposit freezes and/or bank holidays. Using these metrics, they identify 17 countries that experienced a systemic banking

Table 8.5 The costs of banking crises

	Direct fiscal costs	Increase in public debt	Output losses
Previous crises (1970–2006)		**Medians (% of GDP)**	
Advanced economies	3.7	36.2	32.9
Emerging markets	11.5	12.7	29.4
All	10.0	16.3	19.5
Recent crises (2007–2009)		**Medians (% of GDP)**	
Advanced economies	5.9	25.1	24.9
Emerging markets	4.8	23.9	4.7
All	4.9	23.9	24.5

Source: Adapted from Laeven and Valencia (2014), Chapter 13.

crisis between 2007 and 2011, with eight more countries experiencing a borderline case (i.e. less than three of the above measures were used). In the past, however, some countries intervened in their financial sectors using a combination of less than three of these measures, but on a large scale (for example, by nationalising all major banks in the country). Therefore, a banking crisis can be considered systemic if: (i) a country's banking system exhibits significant losses resulting in a share of NPLs above 20 per cent; (ii) there are bank closures of at least 20 per cent of banking system assets; or (iii) fiscal restructuring costs of the banking sector are sufficiently high, exceeding 5 per cent of GDP.

Over the past 20 years, a number of economies have suffered systemic banking crises, with far-reaching negative economic implications. These crises resulted in substantial losses in terms of wealth, output and jobs. For example, the average cumulative output losses in Argentina (2001–2002), Indonesia (1998) and Turkey (1999–2001) have been estimated in the range of 12–15 per cent of GDP. The economic cost of the new crises is on average much larger than that of past crises, both in terms of output losses and increases in public debt, as illustrated in Table 8.5. These differences in part reflect an increase in the size of financial systems and the fact that the 2007–2009 crisis was concentrated in high-income countries, whereas previously banking crises seemed to affect mainly developing and transition economies (with some notable exceptions, such as the Japanese banking crisis).

Table 8.6 compares the costs, in terms of output losses and fiscal costs, of the two largest and most recent crises, the 1997 Asian crisis and the 2007–2009 crisis. In 1997, a number of South East Asian economies suffered a severe financial crisis, causing substantial output losses. At the time of writing (2014), the global economy is still trying to recover in the aftermath of the 2007–2009 financial crisis, or global financial crisis, which triggered the deepest recession since the Second World War and has become known as the 'Great Recession'. The majority of the countries affected by the global crisis have been in recession since 2007 or early 2008, with the economic outlook worsening from 2010 for a number of eurozone countries.

8.5.2 Financial crises

These recent crisis episodes have not been confined to the banking sector but have involved other financial markets. As a consequence, some economists broaden the definition of financial crisis to include features of financial fragility, bank panics and contagion, when financial markets experience volatility and financial firms suffer illiquidity and insolvency.

Table 8.6 Comparing the costs of the Asian and global crises

	Country	Year start	Year end	Output loss	Fiscal costs (% of GDP)	Fiscal costs (% of financial sector assets)	Peak NPLs
Asian crisis	Indonesia	1997	2001	69.0	56.8	105.4	32.5
	Malaysia	1997	1999	31.4	16.4	12.7	30.0
	Thailand	1997	2000	109.3	43.8	30.6	33.0
	Overall			69.9	39.0	49.6	31.8
Global financial crisis	United Kingdom	2007	ongoing	25.0	8.8	2.5	4.0
	United States	2007	ongoing	31.0	4.5	2.1	5.0
	Benelux	2008	ongoing	26.0	8.8	1.7	2.5
	Germany	2008	ongoing	11.0	1.8	0.6	3.7
	Greece	2008	ongoing	43.0	27.3	15.8	14.7
	Iceland	2008	ongoing	43.0	44.2	5.0	61.2
	Ireland	2008	ongoing	106.0	40.7	4.6	12.9
	Spain	2008	ongoing	39.0	3.8	1.3	5.8
	Overall			40.5	17.5	4.2	13.7

Notes: Output loss in % of GDP. Output losses are computed as the cumulative sum of the differences between actual and trend real GDP over the period [T, T+3], expressed as a percentage of trend real GDP, with T the starting year of the crisis. Fiscal costs are defined as the component of gross fiscal outlays related to the restructuring of the financial sector. They include fiscal costs associated with bank recapitalisations but exclude asset purchases and direct liquidity assistance from the Treasury. NPL as expressed in % of total loans. NPLs data come from IMF staff reports and financial soundness indicators.

Source: Authors' calculations. Database made available by Laeven and Valencia (2012).

In addition to banking crises, financial crises can come in many forms. Reinhart and Rogoff (2009) distinguish two types of crises: (i) currency and sudden stop crises; and (ii) debt and banking crises.

A **currency crisis** involves a speculative attack on the currency resulting in a devaluation or sharp depreciation. This will force the authorities to defend the currency by selling foreign exchange reserves, raising domestic interest rates or imposing capital controls.

Currency crises have been relatively common in the past. The most remarkable episodes include the crisis of the British pound in 1976 and the European Exchange Rate Mechanism (ERM) crisis in 1992–1993. A sharp depreciation from a fixed exchange rate was also central to the Mexican peso crisis (which became known as the Latin American Tequila Crisis) in 1994–1995 and the Thai crisis of 1997, which marked the beginning of the Asian financial crisis of 1997–1998.

A **sudden stop** (also known as a capital account or balance of payments crisis) can be defined as a sudden (and often large) decrease in international capital inflows or a sharp reversal in aggregate capital flows to a country, likely taking place in conjunction with a sharp rise in its credit spreads. Sudden stops are usually followed by a sharp decrease in output, private spending and credit to the private sector, and real exchange rate appreciation. Sudden stops hit many emerging economies, particularly in the aftermath of financial crisis.

Claessens and Kose (2013) define a *foreign debt crisis* as an episode of financial turbulence that takes place when a country cannot (or does not want to) service its foreign debt.

It can take the form of a *sovereign debt crisis* or *private debt crisis* (or both in some cases). The most recent episode was the European sovereign debt crisis, which started in 2008 with the collapse of Icelandic banks (see Box 8.4) and spread to Greece, Ireland and Portugal and subsequently to Italy and Spain, leading to a crisis for the eurozone (the eurozone troubles will be discussed in more detail in Chapter 14).

Crises episodes often occur together, currency crises followed by banking crises (for example in the case of the Asian crises), or banking crises followed by sovereign debt crises, as in the case of the eurozone crisis. These occurrences are defined as **twin crises**. Rarer are episodes of 'triplet crises' (i.e. the simultaneous occurrence of three or more crises). Since the early 1970s, Laeven and Valencia (2012) have identified 99 episodes of banking crises, 18 debts crises and 153 episodes of currency crises. They also identified 68 episodes of twin crises, of which 28 were the result of the simultaneous occurrence of currency and banking crises, 29 currency and debt crises, and only 11 banking and debt crises. Finally, they identified only 8 episodes of triplet crises since 1970.

BOX 8.4 THE ICELANDIC MELTDOWN

Relative to the size of its economy – Iceland's population is just over 300,000 – the collapse of Iceland's banking system in autumn 2008 has been adjudged the largest of all time by the IMF. Following financial deregulation in 2001, Iceland's three major banks, Landsbanki, Kaupthing and Glitnir, developed a business model that circumvented the constraints on growth implied by the small size of the Icelandic economy, by attracting funding from international capital markets. Between 2006 and 2008 Landsbanki and Kaupthing set up online banking operations offering high-interest internet accounts to depositors in the UK and the Netherlands in the case of Landsbanki's Icesave brand, and through subsidiaries trading under the Kaupthing Edge brand in nine European countries.

Prior to the banking crisis, Iceland's current account deficit was clearly unsustainable, having reached 25% of GDP in 2006, and 15% in 2007. Between January and September 2008, consumer price inflation was running at around 14%, and domestic interest rates reached 15.5%. Despite a 35% decline in value against the euro during the first nine months of 2008, the krona was still significantly overvalued, bolstered by short-term capital inflows attracted by the high domestic interest rate. When liquidity in the interbank markets dried up in mid-September 2008 following the liquidation of Lehman Brothers in the US, the Central Bank of Iceland had inadequate reserves to be able to guarantee the banks' debts as lender of last resort. The European Central Bank, US Federal Reserve, Bank of England and the three Nordic central banks collectively declined to provide sufficient assistance to avert the imminent crisis.

On 29 September 2008 it was announced that the Icelandic government was to acquire a 75% stake in Glitnir. This part-nationalization was not completed, however, and a few days later Glitnir was placed into receivership. Reports in the British press over the weekend of 4–5 October 2008 appear to have triggered a run on savings in Icesave by UK and Dutch online depositors, and Landsbanki was placed into receivership on 7 October. Since Icesave was a branch of Landsbanki, its UK depositors were not protected under UK deposit insurance; however, on 8 October the UK government froze Landsbanki's UK assets, and announced it would compensate UK retail depositors in full. A number of UK local authorities and other governmental organisations, which had deposited spare funds with Icelandic banks, would not be guaranteed reimbursement, and the full extent of their losses remains unknown at the time of writing. Meanwhile, on 8 October the UK's Financial Services Authority placed Kaupthing's UK subsidiary into administration and sold its internet bank Kaupthing Edge to the Dutch group ING Direct. In Iceland Kaupthing followed into receivership on 9 October, and over

8.5 Banking crises

BOX 8.4 The Icelandic meltdown (*continued*)

the next few days Kaupthing's other subsidiaries were either wound up or taken into public ownership by the respective national authorities.

With the krona continuing to fall precipitously against the euro, the Icelandic government applied for IMF assistance in late-October 2008. In November the IMF agreed to provide a $2.1bn standby programme over two years, supplemented by assistance in the form of loans and currency swaps from the governments of the Nordic countries, Russia, Poland, the UK, the Netherlands and Germany, which brought the headline value of the full package to over $10bn. The terms of the IMF package impose obligations on the Icelandic government in the areas of currency stabilization and inflationary control, bank restructuring and fiscal retrenchment. A sharp fall in GDP was anticipated in 2009, projected at around 10% at the time of writing. Several years of austerity appeared inevitable.

A new Icelandic government elected in April 2009 was committed to applying for full EU membership and adoption of the euro as soon as possible. Membership of a global reserve currency was viewed as offering future protection against the exposure that destroyed the Icelandic banking system in 2008, and may alleviate the banks' difficulties in raising short-term foreign funds to cover their foreign debts. Iceland applied to join the EU on 16 July 2009. However, contentious issues, particularly relating to fisheries, remained unresolved. On 13 September 2013 the Icelandic government dissolved its accession team and suspended its application to join the EU.

Source: Adapted from Goddard *et al.* (2009b) and authors' updates.

8.5.3 Identifying the causes of banking and financial crises

The identification of the causes of banking and financial crises is important in terms of crisis management and effectiveness of the proposed solutions. The nature of the underlying causes may have important bearings in the optimal official response. There is a vast literature on the causes of banking crises; this literature is fairly divided between advocates of microeconomic factors and supporters of macroeconomic reasons.

The often-cited microeconomic reasons include:

- poor banking practices (inadequate capital, inadequate credit risk assessment resulting in non-performing loans, insufficient diversification of the lending portfolio, excessive mismatching of maturity and currency);
- principal–agent incentive problems (particularly when loan officers are rewarded on the volumes of loans granted);
- over-staffing (particularly in state-owned banks);
- restrictive labour practices (sometimes delaying the adoption of IT).

Macroeconomic reasons, although not relieving bank management of their responsibilities, are often seen as a catalyst of crises. Macroeconomic shocks, such as the oil crisis in the 1970s, can strain even properly managed banks.

A third set of causes is the so-called system-related, in the sense that the environment is not conducive to the development of an efficient banking sector. For example:

- large state ownership in the banking sector can distort the industry. If state-owned banks enjoy special privileges, this may distort competition and limit banks' diversification possibilities;
- government direction of credit may prevent banks from developing credit risk management skills;

- restrictions on foreign banks' entry;
- poor market discipline (due to moral hazard and excessive deposit insurance);
- weak corporate governance;
- poor supervision;
- an inadequate legal framework may limit the effectiveness of the banking system;
- an underdeveloped securities market may concentrate too much risk on the banking system;
- high market power of incumbent banks, leading to lack of competition.

Banking crises may result from rapid changes in the environment in which banks operate. For example, in the early 1990s Mexico experienced a rapid privatisation process of its commercial banks, coupled with financial liberalisation measures and sudden reduction of the borrowing requirement of the public sector. The rapid expansion of credit that followed these changes, coupled with weak supervision, led to a financial sector crisis in 1994.

Much has been written on the causes of the 2007–2009 global financial crisis. While academics' and policy makers' views may differ on the importance of different factors, most list the following as the key reasons (Claessens and Kose, 2013):

1 asset price increases that turned out to be unsustainable;

2 credit booms that led to excessive debt burdens;

3 build-up of marginal loans and systemic risk; and

4 the failure of regulation and supervision to keep up with financial innovation.

These triggers have been present even in previous crises. However, the 2007–2009 global financial crisis was also brought about by new factors, including: (1) the widespread use of complex and opaque financial instruments; (2) the increased interconnectedness of financial markets, nationally and internationally; (3) the high degree of leverage of financial institutions; (4) the central role of the household sector; and (5) the emergence of an unregulated 'shadow banking' sector. These factors, in combination with the ones common to previous crises, led to the worst financial crisis since the Great Recession, the consequences of which are still being felt in many countries.

8.5.4 Crisis management

Crisis management can be summarised in three distinct phases:

1 the containment phase;

2 the resolution phase;

3 the structural reform phase.

Crisis management starts with the containment phase, when the crisis is unfolding and a speedy regulatory response is critical. The first step is the control of liquidity pressures on the banking sector, via emergency liquidity lines to troubled financial institutions. In this phase, the main aim is to stabilise the markets, which sometimes entails government blanket guarantees to financial institutions.

In the *resolution phase* a broad range of measures (such as those described in Section 8.4.1) is implemented to restructure banks. The final phase is the reform phase, when fundamental changes to the regulation and supervision of the financial sectors are enacted.

The specific actions taken by domestic and international regulatory bodies in response to the global financial crises have been discussed elsewhere in this textbook. In general terms, the policy responses during the 2007–2009 crisis were similar to those used in the past. The first action of many national central banks and governments was to ease liquidity pressures, through liquidity support and guarantees on bank liabilities. During the bank resolution phase, a broad array of resolution techniques was used, including asset purchases, asset guarantees and equity injections. All these methods, to some extent, have been used in the past. Some of the measures put in place have been more innovative (see, for example, the discussion of the ECB's non-standard measures of monetary policy in Box 6.5). The current phase is the structural reforms phase and the key reforms are summarised in Table 8.4.

One key feature of the 2007–2009 global financial crisis was that it predominantly affected advanced economies with large, internationally integrated financial institutions that were deemed too big and/or interconnected to fail. The large international networks and cross-border exposures of these financial institutions helped propagate the crisis to other countries. Failure of any of these large financial institutions could have resulted in the failure of other systemically important institutions, either directly by imposing large losses through counterparty exposures or indirectly by causing a panic that could have generated bank runs. This prompted unprecedented large-scale government interventions in the financial sector in many countries.

How successful have these interventions been? This is a complex question to answer, as it is difficult to compare the success of crisis resolution policies given differences across countries and time in the size of the initial shock to the financial system, the size of the financial system, the quality of institutions, and the intensity and scope of policy interventions. There is, however, some hope going forward. A positive example was set by Mexican banks, which were hit by a severe banking crisis in 1994–1995. Box 8.5 discusses the recovery and growth of Mexican banks and the lessons learned.

BOX 8.5 MEXICAN BANKS: FROM TEQUILA CRISIS TO SUNRISE

Mexican banks have historically not been safe places in which to leave money lying around. When they collapsed in 1995, following the devaluation of the peso and the 'tequila crisis', bankers in Europe and America shook their heads in disbelief at the irresponsible lending that had gone on. A $50 billion bail-out was rustled up by tutting friends and neighbours.

How things have changed. As banks in Europe and America scrabble to meet stricter capital requirements, made necessary by the failures of their own exotic lending practices, Mexico is offering some a lifeline. On September 26th Santander, a Spanish bank, plans to list a quarter of its Mexican subsidiary on stock exchanges in Mexico City and New York. It has already listed subsidiaries in Brazil, Chile and Peru, as well as selling its Colombian unit. These sell-offs have helped to increase its core-capital ratio to 10.1%; the Mexican listing, which is set to raise around $4 billion, will add another half a percentage point.

The offering, priced at two times book value, is a better deal than most European or American banks could get for issuing new shares at home. That's because Mexico's banks are very profitable.

BOX 8.5 Mexican banks: from tequila crisis to sunrise (*continued*)

Santander Mexico gives a return on equity of almost 20%, about double the rates commonly found in Europe. Bancomer, the Mexican arm of Spain's BBVA, contributes a third of BBVA's worldwide profits. The Mexican subsidiaries of BBVA, Citibank and Santander are all graded as less risky than their parents by Moody's, a ratings agency. BBVA and Canada's Scotiabank might float their own Mexican operations before too long, suspects Bill Rudman of Blackfriars Asset Management.

Mexican banks' smooth negotiation of the financial crisis owes much to a favourable economic environment and to conservatism in their own lending. First, the economy. After spending much of the past decade in Brazil's shadow, Mexico is moving into the limelight. Last year it outpaced its great Latin American rival; this year it is expected to grow nearly twice as fast, at about 4%.

The countries' changing fortunes are partly due to slowing growth in China, a big buyer of Brazilian commodities and bitter rival of Mexican manufacturers. Thanks to higher Chinese wages and the rising cost of shipping across the Pacific, Mexico is increasingly attractive to foreign investors. Although the American market is sluggish, Mexico is taking a bigger bite of it. HSBC reckons that by 2018 Mexico will overtake Canada and China to become America's main source of imports.

Despite bouncy growth in a middle-income country of 115m people, Mexican banks have also been helped by their own caution. Private debt is equal to only about 20% of GDP, one of the lowest ratios in Latin America (Brazil's is above 50%). Only a third of all Mexican firms have access to commercial-bank loans; among small firms, the proportion is lower still. Many businesspeople complain that Mexico's banks have been playing things too safe.

Part of the stinginess is due to a strict credit-scoring regime, operated by two private agencies that are owned mainly by the banks themselves. Rather than be graded, customers are classed simply as creditworthy or not. There is no lower limit on the default necessary to trigger a blacklisting, so a missed phone-bill could render someone ineligible for loans. Fines for missed tax payments can also land people on the blacklist. 'So because you were fined 500 pesos ($40) by the tax authorities, you cannot get credit to buy a car, which would contribute 10,000 pesos in VAT,' complains Giulliano Lopresti of Crea México, an organisation that helps small businesses to get off the ground.

The lucky few who do qualify for credit face steep rates. Although the base rate of interest is 4.5%, most credit cards charge upwards of 40%, plus an annual fee. Most deposit accounts offer below-inflation rates of interest. Customer service is patchy. Queues at branches are scores-deep ahead of holiday weekends; Banamex, a big bank, has called your correspondent every day for two years because its call centre is unable to correct wrong numbers.

With five banks controlling about three-quarters of the market, there is more competition than in many other sectors. But with so many potential new customers, the banks do not need to work that hard to turn a profit. Santander is adding more than 100 branches a year to its network. New laws have allowed supermarkets to turn themselves into banks, though uptake was slowed by an outbreak of credit-card defaults in 2009. Lending is rising by 15% per year, about the fastest a country can manage without giving ratings agencies the jitters. By 2020 it will equal 35% of GDP, thinks Nomura, a Japanese bank.

There are obstacles ahead. Banks will have to overcome a culture in which businesses get most of their credit from suppliers, which offer poor value but are seen as easier to deal with. And family firms will have to meet banks' requirements for accounting and corporate governance. At the moment small firms' accounts are often designed to look bad, for tax purposes, rather than good, to secure credit.

If these problems can be solved, the economy will benefit. Five to six consecutive years of loan growth, in tandem with macroeconomic stability, could add half a percentage point to Mexico's annual growth rate, says Agustín Carstens, the central-bank governor. More foreign-bank listings will be good news for Mexico's modest stock exchange, too. At the moment only one of the country's big banks, Banorte, is traded. Santander's flotation 'means more options for investors,' says Jorge Lagunas of Interacciones, a trading house. Plenty for Mexico to celebrate, then – just go easy on the tequila.

Source: The Economist (2012a).

8.6   Conclusion

Bank regulation cannot prevent financial crises, but the regulatory framework that is currently being shaped will influence the development of the banking system for many years to come. Bank resolution measures recently implemented by governments (including the purchase of impaired assets, the recapitalisation of troubled banks and liquidity injections into the financial system) have possibly avoided even more serious consequences, despite concerns that publicly funded bank bailouts sent the wrong signals to bank investors and executives who caused the problems.

At the time of writing, the roadmap to recovery in Europe and the US remains uncertain, and there are fears that many EU banks still have long distances to travel before the consequences of the 2007–2009 global financial and eurozone crises are completely overcome. Many predict that banks will become leaner, more capitalised, less leveraged and more heavily regulated than they have been in the past. If the banking system that emerges from the recent period of severe instability is more reliable and efficient, then the lessons of the 2007–2010 crises may have been learned.

Key terms

Bridge bank	Early warning system	Peer group analysis	Stress testing
CAMELS	(EWS)	Private sector	Sudden stop
Collateral	Least-cost resolution	purchaser	Temporary public
Currency	Non-performing	Special resolution	ownership (TPO)
crisis	loans (NPLs)	regime (SRR)	Twin crises

Key reading

Bassett, J.L., Lee, S.J. and Spiller, T.W. (2012) 'Estimating changes in supervisory standards and their economic effect', Finance and Economics Discussion Series, Federal Reserve Board, 2012–2055.

Claessens, S. and Kose, M.A. (2013) 'Financial crises: Explanations, types, and implications', IFM WP/13/28.

Koopman, G.-J. (2011) 'Stability and competition in EU banking during the financial crisis: The role of state aid control', *Competition Policy International*, 7, 8–21.

Laeven, L. and Valencia, F. (2012) 'Systemic banking crises database: An update', IMF WP/12/163.

Stolz, S.M. and Wedow, M. (2010) 'Extraordinary measures in extraordinary times. Public measures in support of the financial sector in the EU and the United States', ECB Occasional Paper Series, No. 117, July.

REVISION QUESTIONS AND PROBLEMS

8.1 The reasons why banks fail are numerous and often interlinked. Managerial deficiencies are often important and there is a very fine line between bad management and fraud. Discuss.

8.2 Discuss the different approaches to the resolution of a failed bank. Discuss the principle of 'least-cost resolution' and how it applies to the choice of regulatory tool.

8.3 Discuss the use of EWS in the context of the anticipation and prevention of banking problems. How useful are stress tests?

8.4 What are non-performing loans? Discuss the relevance of NPLs in the context of bank failure and bank restructuring.

8.5 Discuss the pros and cons of bank resolution tools, giving examples of successful and not so successful outcomes.

8.6 Discuss the different problems posed by the failure of a purely domestic bank and of an internationally active bank. What are the main issues associated with cross-border bank supervision?

8.7 Define the process of crisis management. What elements influence the success of crisis management and bank restructuring?

8.8 Briefly discuss major regulatory developments that have impacted LCFIs since 2007.

PART 3

Issues in bank management

Chapter 9

Banks' balance sheet and income structure

Learning objectives

- To understand the importance of banks' financial statements
- To identify the main assets and liabilities of commercial and investment banks
- To understand the sources of revenue for commercial and investment banks
- To understand the importance of economic capital
- To describe the concept of shareholder value creation and the cost of equity capital
- To become familiar with the most commonly used bank financial ratios

9.1 Introduction

Traditionally, the business of banks is to intermediate funds between surplus units and deficit units, thereby linking depositors with borrowers. Banks also provide pooling of risk, liquidity services and undertake delegated monitoring. Financial intermediaries can be classified according to their different **balance sheet** structures. For deposit-taking institutions, the main source of funding (customer deposits) is reported on the liabilities side of the balance sheet, while the allocation of these funds (cash, loans, investments and fixed assets) is detailed on the assets side. Banks' profits are derived from the **income statement (profit and loss account)**, a document that reports data on **costs** and revenues and measures bank performance over two balance sheet periods. This chapter focuses on understanding commercial and investment banks' financial statements and describes the main characteristics of their balance sheet and income statements. The last part of the chapter investigates the most common bank financial ratios such as **return on assets (ROA)**, **return on equity (ROE)**, **net interest margin (NIM)** and the **cost–income ratio**.

9.2   Retail banks' balance sheet structure

The **balance sheet** is a financial statement of the wealth of a business or other organisation on a given date. This is usually at the end of the financial year. For commercial banks the balance sheet (also known as *Report of Condition* in the US) lists all the stock values of sources and uses of banks' funds. Banks' funds come from:

(a) the general public (retail deposits);

(b) companies (small, medium and large corporate deposits);

(c) other banks (interbank deposits);

(d) equity issues (share issues, conferring ownership rights on holders);

(e) debt issues (bond issues and loans); and

(f) saving past profits (retained earnings).

The above is generally classified as banks' **liabilities** (debt) and **capital** (equity). These funds are then transformed into financial and, to a lesser extent, real **assets**:

(a) cash;

(b) liquid assets (securities);

(c) short-term money market instruments such as Treasury bills, which banks can sell (liquidate) quickly if they have a cash shortage;

(d) loans;

(e) other investments; and

(f) fixed assets (branch network, computers, premises).

Table 9.1 summarises the assets and liabilities in a simplified commercial bank balance sheet.

Bank liabilities (e.g. retail deposits) tend to have shorter maturities than assets (e.g. mortgage loans). This mismatch derives from the different requirements of depositors and borrowers: typically, the majority of depositors want to lend their assets for short periods of time and for the highest possible return. In contrast, the majority of borrowers require loans that are cheap and for long periods. The asset transformation function of banks is derived from these characteristics. To recap, banks have the primary function of being asset transformers because they intermediate between depositors and borrowers by changing the characteristics of their liabilities as they move from one side of the balance sheet to the other.

Table 9.1 Simplified commercial bank balance sheet

Assets	Liabilities
Cash	Deposits: retail
Liquid assets	Deposits: wholesale
Loans	
Other investments	
Fixed assets	
	Equity
	Other capital terms
Total assets	Total liabilities and equity

Capital (see also Section 9.2.1.3) is sometimes referred to as equity capital or net worth and is equal to the difference between assets and liabilities.

9.2.1 Assets and liabilities of commercial banks: main components

The balance sheet provides information about the bank's financial position at the end of the accounting period. It comprises three principal components: a) the assets the bank controls; b) the liabilities the bank is obliged to meet; and c) the equity interests of the bank's owners.

Tables 9.2 and 9.3 show the combined balance sheet for UK banks as reported by the Bank of England. The tables show aggregate assets and liabilities of all financial institutions recognised by the Bank of England as UK banks for statistical purposes.

9.2.1.1 The assets side

On the assets side, banks store a relatively small amount (about 0.3 per cent of total assets in 2012) of cash in the form of *notes and coins* to meet daily commitments. In the United Kingdom, according to current regulation, both banks and building societies with average eligible liabilities of £600 million or more are required to hold non-operational, non-interest-bearing deposits with the Bank of 0.18 per cent. The purpose of these deposits (known as *cash ratio deposits*) is to ensure banks' liquidity. Banks can also keep other balances with the Bank of England (i.e. other than cash ratio deposit); these deposits give the central bank a source of income.

In case of cash shortage, banks can ask for a loan in the interbank market. The interbank market constitutes an important portion of the money markets and it is the place where banks meet each day to exchange liquidity. Therefore, the item *market loans* in the asset side of a bank balance sheet includes wholesale loans that are typically very short-term (i.e. overnight or 'call' loans), very liquid (they allow banks to lend money and call it back at short notice) and characterised by large volumes (typically >£1 million).

Bankers' acceptances are negotiable time drafts, or bills of exchange, that have been accepted by a bank that, by accepting, assumes the obligation to pay the holder of the draft the face amount of the instrument on the maturity date specified. They are used primarily to finance the export, import, shipment or storage of goods. *Acceptances granted* comprise a claim on the party whose bill the banks have accepted, except for bills both accepted and discounted by the same bank that are included as lending (unless subsequently rediscounted).

Another important source of liquidity is provided by *bills*. As shown in Table 9.2, the main bills held by UK banks are Treasury bills (or T-bills), that are essentially a form of short-term government borrowing, bank bills (usually eligible for rediscounting at the Bank of England) and other short-term bills including local government bills and public corporation bills.

Further liquidity is provided by the item claims under *sale and repurchase agreements*. This item comprises cash claims arising from the purchase of securities for a finite period with a commitment to re-sell.

By far the most important item on the asset side, *advances*, includes all balances with, and lending to, customers not included elsewhere. Despite the dramatic changes that have characterised the banking sector in recent years, loans are still the primary earning assets of banks and account for a relatively large proportion of total assets. As reported in Table 9.2, in 2012 loans were the largest items on the balance sheet: sterling advances held on the asset side of banks in the United Kingdom totalled more than £2 trillion, which was more than 54 per cent of total sterling assets. Typically, UK banks lend to individuals, financial and non-financial firms. The major categories of loans are: commercial loans (such as short-term

Table 9.2 Bank of England aggregate assets of UK banks (end-year 2012, £bn amounts)

Assets	£bn end-year 2012	% over total sterling assets
Notes and coins	11.2	0.30%
With UK central bank	271.8	7.36%
– Cash ratio deposit	2.5	0.07%
– Other	269.3	7.29%
Market loans	583.2	15.79%
– UK banks	461.3	12.49%
– UK banks' CDs and commercial paper	6.0	0.16%
– Non-residents	115.9	3.14%
Acceptances granted	0.3	0.01%
– UK banks	0.0	0.00%
– UK public sector	-	-
– Other UK residents	0.3	0.01%
– Non-residents	0.1	0.00%
Bills	13.2	0.36%
– Treasury bills	8.4	0.23%
– UK bank bills	0.0	0.00%
– Other UK residents	0.3	0.01%
– Non-residents	4.5	0.12%
Sale and repurchase agreements	253.8	6.87%
– UK banks	84.1	2.28%
– UK public sector	0.0	0.00%
– Other UK residents	121.2	3.28%
– Non-residents	48.5	1.31%
Advances	2,005.0	54.27%
– UK public sector	7.9	0.21%
– Other UK residents	1919.2	51.95%
– Non-residents	77.9	2.11%
Investments	487.0	13.18%
– UK government bonds	91.2	2.47%
– Other UK public sector	0.3	0.01%
– UK banks	84.0	2.27%
– Other UK residents	267.9	7.25%
– Non-residents	43.7	1.18%
Items in suspense and collection	24.6	0.66%
Accrued amounts receivable	18.6	0.50%
Other assets	25.9	0.70%
Total Sterling Assets	3,694.5	100.00%
Total foreign currency assets	4,104.3	
– Of which total euro assets	1,754.5	
Total Assets	7,798.8	

Note: Figures may not add due to rounding.

Source: Bank of England, Monetary and Financial Statistical Interactive Database and authors' calculations.

loans to businesses), consumer loans (for example, overdrafts and credit card loans), mortgage lending and real estate loans (such as long-term loans to finance commercial real estate such as office buildings).

The next item on the asset side of the balance sheet is *investments*. These include all longer-term securities beneficially owned by the reporting institution and include securities that the reporting institution has sold for a finite period but with a commitment to repurchase (i.e. repos), but exclude securities that have been bought for a finite period but with a commitment to re-sell (i.e. reverse repos). Securities are defined as marketable or potentially marketable income-yielding instruments including bonds, floating rate notes (FRNs), preference shares and other debt instruments, but excluding certificates of deposit and commercial paper that are shown as market loans.

The remaining assets include the following:

- *Items in suspense and collection* that include, for example, debit balances awaiting transfer to customers' accounts and balances awaiting settlement of securities transactions. Collections comprise cheques drawn, and in course of collection, on other UK banks and building societies.

- *Accrued amounts receivable* are gross amounts receivable but have not yet been received, and include interest and other revenues.

- *Other assets* include holdings of gold bullion and gold coin, other commodities, together with land, premises, plant and equipment and other physical assets owned, or recorded as such, including assets leased out under operating leases. Assets leased out under finance leases are included as loans.

- *Eligible banks' total sterling acceptances* comprise all bills accepted by a reporting institution whose bills are eligible for rediscount at the Bank of England, including those that the reporting institution has itself discounted.

Finally, in 2012, UK banks had about £4,104 billion in foreign currency assets (e.g. foreign currency loans), of which approximately 43 per cent were euro-denominated. As shown in Table 9.2, foreign currency assets and liabilities account for a significant proportion of total bank assets.

9.2.1.2 The liability side

On the liabilities side, as illustrated in Table 9.3, the first item reported is *notes outstanding and cash-loaded cards*. This includes all notes and cash held by banks, including the sterling notes issued by Scottish and Northern Irish banks and cash-loaded cards issued by banks (these are electronic cards, smart cards, etc.).

The largest proportion of bank liabilities is in the form of deposits that are typically made by individuals and firms, including deposits by other UK banks. The majority of deposits are represented by sight and time deposits, as shown in Figure 9.1. Sight deposits comprise those deposits where the entire balance is accessible without penalty, either on demand or by close of business on the day following the one on which the deposit was made. Time deposits comprise all other deposits and they include, for example, 30- and 60-day savings bank deposits and ISA deposits.[1] As shown in Figure 9.1, deposits encompass all credit balances on customers' accounts, including acceptances granted, liabilities under sale and repurchase agreements, and certificates of deposit.

---

[1] ISAs (Individual Savings Accounts) were introduced in the United Kingdom in 1999. They are tax-free savings and investment accounts that can be used to save cash, or invest in stocks and shares.

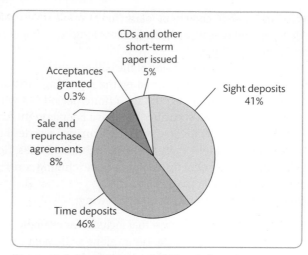

Figure 9.1 Breakdown of UK banks' sterling deposits, end-year 2012

Note: Figures may not total 100% due to rounding.

Source: Bank of England, Monetary and Financial Statistical Interactive Database and authors' calculations.

Acceptances granted represent the banks' liabilities to the owners of bills. Liabilities under *sale and repurchase agreements* comprise cash receipts arising from the sale of securities or other assets that the bank has sold temporarily with a commitment to repurchase. A bank's liabilities under sale and repurchase agreements with UK banks account for more than 34 per cent of the total.

CDs and other short-term paper issued: certificates of deposits are certificates given to depositors in return for a (wholesale) deposit. The holder of the CD receives interest at a fixed or floating rate. CDs are short-term securities and are re-saleable in the market. This item also contains promissory notes issued by the reporting institutions, unsubordinated capital market instruments (except debentures and secured loan stocks) of any maturity and subordinated loan stocks with maturity of five years or less. Other subordinated loan stocks and debentures are included in capital and other funds (see below for the details on the capital item).

The remaining non-deposit liabilities, as reported in Table 9.3, include the following:

- *Items in suspense and transmission*, such as balances awaiting settlement of securities transactions, standing orders and credit transfers debited to customers' accounts, and other items for which the corresponding payment has not yet been made by the reporting institution.

- *Net derivatives*, which comprise the overall net derivatives position of contracts that are included within the trading and banking books of the reporting institutions.

- *Accrued amounts payable*, which are gross amounts payable that have not yet been paid or credited to accounts.

- *Capital and other internal funds*, which consist primarily of shareholders' funds, reserves and long-term debt.

Finally, Table 9.3 shows that in 2012 UK banks had more than £4 trillion in foreign currency liabilities (e.g. foreign currency sight and time deposits), of which approximately 42 per cent were euro-denominated.

Table 9.3 Bank of England aggregate liabilities of UK banks (end-year 2012, £bn amounts)

Liabilities	£bn end-year 2012	% over total sterling assets
Notes outstanding and cash-loaded cards	6.7	0.18%
Sight deposits	1,282.0	35.24%
– UK banks	181.3	4.98%
– UK public sector	13.6	0.38%
– Other UK residents	951.8	26.17%
– Non-residents	135.3	3.72%
Time deposits	1,461.1	40.17%
– UK banks	281.8	7.75%
– UK public sector	18.5	0.51%
– Other UK residents	912.7	25.09%
– Non-residents	248.0	6.82%
Sale and repurchase agreements	267.6	7.36%
– UK banks	91.7	2.52%
– UK public sector	3.6	0.10%
– Other UK residents	109.6	3.01%
– Non-residents	62.8	1.73%
Acceptances granted	0.3	0.01%
CDs and other short-term paper issued	149.1	4.10%
Total Sterling Deposits	3,160.2	86.88%
Items in suspense and transmission	26.3	0.72%
Net derivatives	−25.0	−0.69%
Accrued amounts payable	25.9	0.71%
Capital and other internal funds	443.5	12.19%
Total Sterling Liabilities	3,637.6	100.00%
Total foreign currency liabilities	4,161.2	
– Of which total euro liabilities	1,757.7	
Total Liabilities	7,798.8	

Note: Figures may not add due to rounding.

Source: Bank of England, Monetary and Financial Statistical Interactive Database and authors' calculations.

The assets and liabilities side of a major UK bank

Tables 9.4 and 9.5 illustrate the consolidated financial data over 2008–2012 for a major UK credit institution, Barclays Bank. Figures 9.2 and 9.3 illustrate the breakdown of the major components of Barclays Bank's assets and liabilities in 2012.

A few remarks about Barclays' recent past are necessary before commenting on these financial results. In recent years Barclays Bank switched to the new financial reporting standards that were approved by the EU Commission with effect from 1 January 2005 and are compulsory for all listed companies. Accordingly, the valuation of some assets and liabilities and the format of the income statements were subject to significant modifications. For instance, trading and financial assets and liabilities are now designated at **fair value**. Box 9.1 explains the meaning of adopting fair value compared with book value.

Table 9.4 Barclays Bank assets, 2008–2012 (£mil)

Assets	2008	2009	2010	2011	2012
Cash and balances at central banks	30,019	81,483	97,630	103,087	81,996
Items in course of collection from other banks	1,695	1,593	1,384	1,634	1,076
Trading portfolio assets	185,637	151,344	168,867	85,048	74,719
Financial assets designated at fair value	121,199	42,568	41,485	44,552	82,237
Derivative financial instruments	984,802	416,815	420,319	546,921	476,129
Available for sale investments	64,976	56,483	65,110	47,979	61,753
Loans and advances to banks	47,707	41,135	37,799	52,287	51,175
Loans and advances to customers	461,815	420,224	427,942	517,780	474,723
Reverse repurchase agreements and other similar secured lending	130,354	143,431	205,772	161,436	174,284
Prepayments, accrued income and other assets	6,302	6,358	5,269	10,384	12,019
Investments in associates and joint ventures	341	422	518	174	174
Investments in subsidiaries	-	-	-	22,073	14,718
Property, plant and equipment	4,674	5,626	6,140	1,937	1,906
Goodwill and intangible assets	10,402	8,795	8,697	4,333	4,564
Current and deferred tax assets	3,057	2,652	2,713	1,270	1,414
Retirement benefit assets	-	-	-	1,708	2,276
Total assets	2,052,980	1,378,929	1,489,645	1,602,603	1,515,163

Source: www.investorrelations.barclays.co.uk

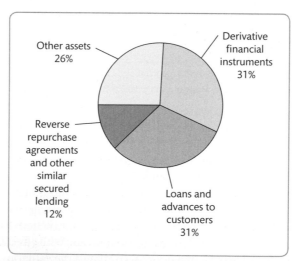

Figure 9.2 Barclays Bank assets, end-year 2012 (£mil)

Source: Data available at www.investorrelations.barclays.co.uk and authors' calculations.

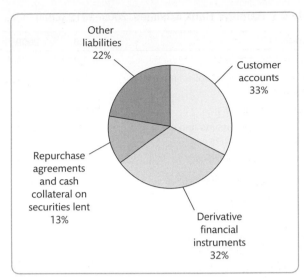

Figure 9.3 Barclays Bank liabilities, end-year 2012 (£mil)

Source: Data available at **www.investorrelations.barclays.co.uk** and authors' calculations.

In addition, during 2008 Barclays bought Lehman Brothers' North American investment banking and trading operations. The acquisition of hundreds of billions of dollars of derivatives positions as a result of the deal was one of the main factors that contributed to an impressive balance sheet growth at end-year 2008 compared with previous years. Other factors that played a role were loans and advances, increased volatility, movements in yield curves during the year and a substantial depreciation in sterling against other major currencies (Barclays Plc, 2008). In December 2009, Barclays Global Investors, the asset management business of Barclays, was acquired by BlackRock, which became the world's largest and most prominent fund manager with more than 10,000 employees and $3.79 trillion in asset under management. Barclays retained nearly 20 per cent stake in BlackRock until 2012, when the firm completed a secondary offering of 26.1 million shares of Barclays' common stock and repurchased 6.4 million of the shares to eliminate Barclays' ownership in the firm.

Figure 9.2 shows the breakdown of Barclays' asset side of the balance sheet in 2012. About 31 per cent of the bank's assets derive from loans to retail and corporate customers (compared with 64 per cent at end-year 2004, according to Barclays' 2004 *Annual Report*). Specifically, these items include home loans, credit cards, unsecured and other retail lending (about 40 per cent of the item total 'loans and advances to customers') and corporate loans (60 per cent). Derivative financial instruments represent the second largest item in Barclays' assets side of the balance sheet (31 per cent of total assets).

Tables 9.4 and 9.5 show that the total size of the bank's balance sheet at end-year 2012 was more than £1.5 trillion; if we exclude 2008, which was a special year due to the acquisition of Lehman's investment business, over 2009–2012 the size of the balance sheet grew by 10 per cent.

On the liability side, customer deposits account for nearly 33 per cent of the total. Only 6 per cent of total liabilities are represented by short- and long-term debt securities (e.g. commercial paper, CDs and bonds). As for the asset side, the relative importance of derivative financial instruments is again large (around 32 per cent). Table 9.5 also shows details on shareholders' equity (see Chapter 7 on bank capital regulation).

Table 9.5 Barclays Bank liabilities, 2008–2012 (£mil)

Liabilities	2008	2009	2010	2011	2012
Deposits from banks	114,910	76,446	77,975	108,816	83,740
Items in the course of collection due to other banks	1,635	1,466	1,321	966	1,231
Customer accounts	335,505	322,429	345,788	454,522	481,126
Repurchase agreements and cash collateral on securities lent	182,285	198,781	225,534	193,453	187,148
Trading portfolio liabilities	59,474	51,252	72,693	28,632	30,105
Financial liabilities designated at fair value	146,075	87,881	97,729	101,069	91,376
Derivative financial instruments	968,072	403,416	405,516	535,837	466,321
Debt securities in issue	149,567	135,902	156,623	83,939	85,173
Subordinated liabilities	29,842	25,816	28,499	26,764	22,941
Accruals, deferred income and other liabilities	14,792	14,241	13,233	15,471	14,996
Provisions	535	590	947	939	2,405
Current tax liabilities	1,520	1,462	1,160	1,327	750
Retirement benefit liabilities	1,357	769	365	109	146
Total liabilities	2,005,569	1,320,451	1,427,383	1,551,844	1,467,458
Shareholders' equity					
Shareholders' equity excluding non-controlling interests	36,618	47,277	50,858	50,759	47,705
Non-controlling interests	10,793	11,201	11,404	-	-
Total shareholders' equity	47,411	58,478	62,262	50,759	47,705
Total liabilities and shareholders' equity	2,052,980	1,378,929	1,489,645	1,602,603	1,515,163

Source: www.investorrelations.barclays.co.uk

BOX 9.1 ASSETS AND LIABILITIES VALUATION IN BANKING

Fair value is an accounting term that indicates how a bank values certain assets and liabilities. Under fair value these are stated in the bank's accounts at the current market values and if an active market is unavailable, the bank will use estimates. Historical cost accounting is the main alternative to fair value and it refers to the original purchase price paid by the bank to acquire an asset (or received for a liability). However, historical cost also implies that the amount recorded in the financial statements should not exceed the amount expected to be recovered from either its use or its sale.

To understand these principles, it is useful to provide a simple example. Take a Bank ABC that in 2012 buys 1,000 shares in a listed bank for €12 per share. Assume that at the end of the year the price per share has increased to €20 and that at the end of 2013, due to a sharp recession, the price drops to €5. Under the two accounting principles Bank ABC would report the following figures in its balance sheet:

Balance sheet	Shares' fair value	Shares' historical cost
End-year 2012	€20,000	€12,000
End-year 2013	€5,000	€5,000

Source: Adapted from ICAEW.

BOX 9.1 Assets and liabilities valuation in banking (*continued*)

The recent shift towards the use of fair value accounting in banking has been driven by several factors, including a greater involvement in capital markets activity, rapid financial innovation and the embrace of market-based risk management. Regulatory developments have been led by the US Financial Accounting Standards Board (FASB) and the International Accounting Standards Board (IASB), responsible for two distinct sets of accounting standards: the US GAAP and the IAS/IFRS, respectively. Under both the International Financial Reporting Standards (IAS39) and the US Generally Accepted Accounting Principles (FAS159), banks held a range of financial instruments valued using either fair values or historical value. Assets that banks intend to hold to maturity are valued at historic cost. In contrast, assets for sale or trading assets are valued at market prices (fair value). Any gains or losses relative to sale or trading assets are reported in accumulated other comprehensive income. Fair values are established using level 1 inputs (observable prices in active markets), level 2 inputs (using prices for similar assets in active or inactive markets) and level 3 inputs (using modelling assumptions based on assumed prices, otherwise referred to as 'mark-to-model').

As shown in the table above, in contrast to historic cost, fair value reporting allows increases in value above cost. Vice versa, losses can be overstated when values fall. This implies that one of the major drawbacks often attributed to fair value accounting principles is that financial statements become pro-cyclical as they follow market swings. This is particularly relevant for banks compared with other industries because they hold proportionally higher amounts of financial assets and liabilities on their balance sheets.

(For more information see The Institute of Chartered Accountants in England and Wales (ICAEW), **www.icaew.com/en**)

9.2.1.3 Bank equity capital

Defined as the value of assets minus the value of liabilities, the capital (or 'net worth' or 'equity capital') represents the ownership interest in a firm.

$$\text{Capital} = \text{Assets} - \text{Liabilities}$$

Bank capital and liabilities represent the specific sources of funds (see Figure 9.3). However, compared with manufacturing firms, typically banks are highly **leveraged** and thus hold a lower proportion of equity to assets (see Box 9.2). If a relatively small amount of loans are not repaid, this can seriously affect the level of equity and leave the bank technically insolvent. This is because if loans are not repaid then losses have to be borne by the capital cushion that banks hold to protect against such losses. The greater the level of capital relative to the losses incurred, the greater protection the bank will have. If losses exceed the level of capital then a bank will become technically insolvent because even if it could liquidate all its assets there would not be sufficient funds to cover deposits. In such circumstances, the need to ensure depositors' confidence (a major issue for the banking sector) may result in one of the following:

1 other banks can engage in a rescue package to pump new capital into the troubled bank; or

2 the authorities can decide to rescue the troubled bank using taxpayers' money. The potential repercussions on the whole banking sector are such that regulatory authorities monitor bank behaviour and try to ensure that banks have adequate capital and that they are run in a safe and sound manner (see also Section 7.7).[2]

---

[2] Adequate capital corresponds to the 'C' in the CAMELS structure that includes also Asset quality, Management quality, Earnings, Liquidity, Sensitivity to market risk. For more details see Section 8.3.2.

In general, the primary function of capital is to reduce the risk of failure by providing protection against operating and any other losses. It does this in five ways by:

1 providing a cushion for firms to absorb unanticipated losses with enough margin to inspire confidence and enable the bank to remain solvent;

2 protecting uninsured depositors (depositors not protected by a deposit insurance scheme that covers small depositors) in the event of insolvency and liquidation;

3 protecting bank insurance funds and taxpayers;

4 providing ready access to financial markets and thus guarding against liquidity problems caused by deposit outflows; and

5 limiting risk taking.

Capital is also needed to acquire plant and other real investments that are necessary to provide financial services. For example, a bank will need capital for its technological investments, branching network and the management of the payment systems. A bank can also use its capital resources to finance acquisitions.

Capital and risk are strictly connected. Generally speaking, more risk requires more capital, so capital adequacy should be a function of risk exposure, all other things being equal. Today banks are exposed to many different financial risks – this is because their activities are increasingly taking place in markets that can be affected by changes in interest and exchange rates as well as variations in credit conditions that can affect both on- and off-balance-sheet positions. In such a context banks' need for capital is much higher than it was in the past. The recent turmoil in the global marketplace has prompted regulatory authorities and policy makers to revise the capital rules so that banks' financial statements reflect more adequately the level of risks undertaken (see Section 7.6).

BOX 9.2 TYPICAL CAPITAL STRUCTURE OF A MANUFACTURING FIRM VERSUS A RETAIL BANK

Table 9.6 illustrates the typical balance sheet composition of a bank versus a manufacturing firm (see also Figure 9.4). Banks have a higher proportion of short-term assets over total assets and a smaller proportion of fixed assets. On the liability side, banks, on average, have a higher proportion of short-term liabilities (deposits). One major difference relates to the amount of leverage. Manufacturing firms hold a much higher proportion of capital to assets compared with banks.

Table 9.6 Banks vs. manufacturing firms – balance sheet composition

Manufacturing firm	%	Bank	%
Assets		Assets	
Short-term assets	55	Short-term assets	70
Fixed assets	45	Long-term and fixed assets	30
Total assets	100	Total assets	100
Liabilities		Liabilities	
Short-term liabilities	25	Short-term liabilities	80
Long-term debt	35	Long-term debt	12
Shareholders' equity	40	Shareholders' equity	8
Total liabilities	100	Total liabilities	100

BOX 9.2 Typical capital structure of a manufacturing firm versus a retail bank (*continued*)

The value of the manufacturing firm would have to decline by more than 40 per cent before the firm would become insolvent while a decline of only 8 per cent would make the bank insolvent.

The debt/equity ratio (or financial leverage) of the manufacturing firm is 60/40 = 1.5 and the debt/equity ratio of the bank is 92/8 = 11.5.

The structure of the balance sheet is extremely important for all firms. It is obvious that the way it is leveraged affects the value of the firm; it is an objective for financial managers to achieve a level of debt/equity that maximises the value of the company.

Source: Adapted from Koch and MacDonald (2009) p. 504.

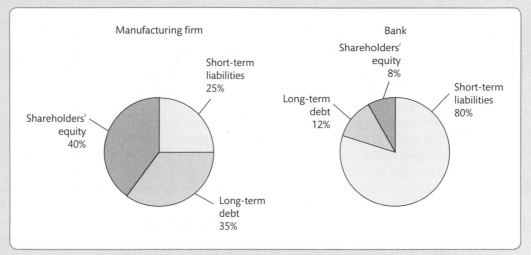

Figure 9.4 Balance sheet of a manufacturing firm vs. a bank

9.2.1.4   Banks' income structure

The profitability of a bank can be derived from its income statement. Also known as its **profit and loss account** (or *Report of Income* in the US), this measures bank performance between two year-end balance sheets. The relationship between the balance sheet and income statement relates to the fact that the balance sheet reports stock values (e.g. the amount of outstanding loans) whereas the income statement represents cash flow values for a particular year (e.g. the interest received on outstanding loans). Therefore, the income statement reflects the revenue sources in banking as well as the costs.

The **costs**, derived from the liabilities side of the balance sheet, relate to the payments that banks have to undertake, such as payment of interest on deposits, dividends to shareholders, interest on debt, provision for loan losses and taxes. The **revenues**, generated by the assets, include interest earned on loans and investments, and fees and commissions (interest and non-interest revenue). Then, as any other firm, banks also incur staffing and other operating costs.

$$\text{Bank profits} = \text{Income} - \text{Costs}$$

In the relationship above, income is equal to interest and non-interest income; costs are the sum of interest costs, staff costs and other operating costs. Table 9.7 shows a simplified income statement and how **profits** are calculated for a retail bank.

The *interest income* is the income generated on all banks' assets, such as loans, securities and deposits lent out to other institutions, households and other borrowers. *Interest expense* is the sum of interest paid on all interest-bearing liabilities, such as all deposit accounts, CDs, short-term borrowing and long-term debt. The difference between interest income (revenues) and interest expenses (costs) is the *net interest income* (NII).

Provision for loan losses (PLL) is the amount charged against earnings to establish a reserve sufficient to absorb expected loan losses. It can be subtracted from net interest income in recognition that some of the reported interest income overstates what will actually be received after loan defaults. Thus, net interest income after provisions for loan losses (PLL) is calculated as the difference between NII and PLL.

Non-interest income is the income generated by fee income, commissions and trading income and has become important due to increased emphasis on this source of revenue in recent years. It includes, for example, fees and deposit service charges, such as fees paid on safe deposit boxes, commissions (e.g. from insurance sales) and gains/losses from trading in securities, and other non-interest income sources such as gains/losses on foreign transactions and from undertaking other OBS activities (such as securities underwriting).

Non-interest expenses include salaries and fringe benefits paid to employees, property and equipment expenses, and other non-interest expenses (such as deposit insurance premiums and depreciation). *Net non-interest income* will be the difference between non-interest income and non-interest expenses.

As we move down Table 9.7 we find the item *pre-tax net operating profit,* which is the sum of interest income minus PLL plus net non-interest income. *Profit before taxes* will be equal to *pre-tax net operating profit* $\pm$ the *securities gains (losses)* that may occur when the bank sells securities from its portfolio at prices above the initial cost to the bank. By deducting taxes and other net extraordinary items (which are unusual or infrequent events that can include, for

Table 9.7 A simplified bank income statement

a	Interest income
b	Interest expense
$c \ (= a - b)$	Net interest income (or 'spread')
d	Provision for loan losses (PLL)
$e \ (= c - d)$	Net interest income after PLL
f	Non-interest income
g	Non-interest expenses
$h \ (= f - g)$	Net non-interest income
$i \ (= e + h)$	Pre-tax net operating profit
l	Securities gains (losses)
$m \ (= l \pm l)$	Profit before taxes
n	Taxes
o	Extraordinary items (net)
$P \ (= m - n - o)$	Net profit
q	Cash dividends
$r \ (= p - q)$	Retained profits

example, the net revenue from the sale of real assets), it is possible to obtain the *net profit*, which is the profit after tax.

Finally, *retained profits* will be equal to net profit minus dividends.

Table 9.8 shows a profit and loss account for Barclays over 2008–2012 using the IFRS standards.

Table 9.8 Barclays Bank Plc profit and loss account 2008–2012 (£mil)

	2008	2009	2010	2011	2012
Interest income	28,010	21,236	20,035	20,589	19,199
Interest expense	16,595	9,567	7,517	8,393	7,564
Net interest income	11,415	11,669	12,518	12,196	11,635
Fee and commission receivable	9,489	9,946	10,368	10,208	10,216
Fee and commission payable	1,082	1,528	1,497	1,586	1,634
Net fee and commission income	8,407	8,418	8,871	8,622	8,582
Net trading income	1,260	6,994	8,080	7,738	3,028
Net investment income	680	283	1,490	2,322	663
Net premiums from insurance contracts	1,090	1,172	1,137	1,076	896
Other income	454	1,389	118	39	335
Total income	23,306	29,925	32,214	33,123	25,139
Net claims and benefits incurred on insurance contracts	237	831	764	741	600
Total income net of insurance claims	23,069	29,094	31,450	32,382	24,539
Credit impairment charges and other credit provisions	5,419	8,071	5,672	5,602	3,596
Net income	17,650	21,023	25,778	26,780	20,943
Employment costs	7,779	9,948	11,916	11,407	10,447
Administration and general expenses	5,662	5,558	6,581	6,351	6,638
Depreciation, amortisation and other costs	921	1,206	1,470	3,014	3,899
Operating expenses	14,362	16,712	19,967	20,772	20,984
Share of post-tax results of associates and joint ventures	14	34	58	60	110
Loss/Profit on disposal of subsidiaries, associates and joint ventures	327	188	81	(94)	28
Gains on acquisitions	2,406	26	129	-	2
Profit before tax	6,035	4,559	6,079	5,974	99
Tax	786	1,047	1,516	1,928	(483)
Loss/Profit after tax from continued operations	5,249	3,512	4,563	4,046	(384)
Profit for the year from discontinued operations	-	6,777	-	-	-
Loss/Profit after tax	5,249	10,289	4,563	4,046	(384)
Other comprehensive income (net)	-	547	(63)	794	(121)
Total comprehensive profit for the year	5,249	10,836	4,500	4,840	(505)

Source: www.investorrelations.barclays.co.uk

At year-end 2012 Barclays Bank had total income of more than £25 billion, an increase of about 9 per cent from 2008. The increase had been brought about by a rise in net trading income (+140 per cent). Barclays' net profits peaked in 2009 and were inflated by the sale of Barclays Global Investors to BlackRock. Note that Barclays after tax profit exceeded £4 billion in 2011 but fell to a loss of £384 million in 2012.

While the income statement gives a good indication of the profitability of a commercial bank, **bank performance** over time is usually measured in relation to ratio analysis, which uses the information contained in both the balance sheet and the income statements. Section 9.4 focuses on the importance of ratio analysis and how to interpret the most common financial ratios.

Before moving on to ratio analysis, Section 9.3 illustrates the main characteristics of investment banks' financial statements and how they compare with those of commercial banks.

9.3   Investment banks' financial statements

We saw in Chapter 3 that large-scale wholesale financing activities are typically carried out by investment banks. Moreover, investment banks offer a range of services such as securities underwriting (including the issue of commercial paper, Eurobonds and other securities) and provide corporate advisory services on mergers and acquisition and other types of corporate restructuring. In a nutshell, investment banks mainly deal with corporations and other large institutions and they typically do not deal with retail customers, apart from the provision of upmarket private banking services.

As a result of the global financial crisis of 2007–2009, US investment banks have converted to bank holding companies (BHCs) to qualify for government assistance (as did Goldman Sachs and Morgan Stanley), or they have been acquired by commercial banks (as in the Merrill Lynch acquisition by Bank of America). In the remainder of this section, we use the term 'investment bank' to describe a financial institution that engages mainly in the investment banking business, either as a standalone institution or as part of a group. As of 2013, the world's largest investment bank (by share of revenues) was JPMorgan Chase, followed by Goldman Sachs. In the UK, one of the most successful investment banks is Barclays, as the bank has a large investment bank division (Barclays Investment Bank, formerly known as Barclays Capital).

To understand in some detail the nature of investment banks' business, it is useful to examine the composition of their statements. This is relatively straightforward when looking at the annual reports of investment banks that have recently converted to BHCs (such as Goldman Sachs – see Box 9.3). It becomes slightly more complicated for banks that have been acquired by BHCs, since their business has been deconstructed across various business segments, as in the case of Merrill Lynch, whose original bank name is used only for the private banking/wealth management of Bank of America, but the investment banking business has been allocated to two business lines: Global Banking and Global Markets.[3]

---

[3] In addition to Global Banking and Global Markets, Bank of America has another three business segments: Consumer and Business Banking, Consumer Real Estate Services, and Global Wealth and Investment Management. The most profitable in terms of net revenues in 2012 was Consumer and Business Banking, which is comprised of deposits to consumers and small businesses, credit and debit card services, and business banking, and offers a diversified range of credit, banking and investment products and services to consumers and businesses.

9.3.1 Investment banks' balance sheet

Table 9.9 shows a simplified investment bank balance sheet.

9.3.1.1 Assets side

On the assets side, investment banks keep *cash and other non-earning assets*. These assets include, for example, short-term highly liquid securities along with assets set aside for regulatory purposes.

Another key item is *trading assets*. These are the banks' trading activities that consist primarily of securities brokerage, trading and underwriting, and derivatives dealing and brokerage. Generally, trading assets include cash instruments (e.g. securities) and derivatives instruments used for trading purposes to manage risk exposures. Other cash instruments can include, for instance, loans held for trading purposes (i.e. loans that can be traded in the secondary market).

Investment banks enter into secured lending in order to meet customer needs and obtain securities for settlement. Under these transactions, they can receive collateral from resale agreements and securities borrowed transactions, customer margin loans and other loans. *Securities financing transactions* are collateralised securities that the bank can sell or re-pledge.

Securities owned for non-trading purposes are classified as *investment securities*. They are marketable investment securities and other financial instruments the bank owns and can include highly liquid debt securities such as those held for liquidity management purposes, equity securities and other investments such as long-term ones held for strategic purposes. Investment banks' lending and related activities such as loan originations, syndications and securitisations (see Chapter 18) are reported under *loans, notes and mortgages*.

Other investments include other receivables such as amounts due from customers on cash and margin transactions. *Fixed assets* consist of equipment and facilities. Typical examples are technology hardware and software and owned facilities (e.g. premises). *Other assets* consist of intangible assets and goodwill as well as assets generated from any unrealised gains on derivatives used to hedge the bank's borrowing and investing activities. They can also include prepaid expenses and real estate purchased for investment purposes.

Table 9.9 A simplified investment bank balance sheet

Assets	Liabilities
Cash and other non-earning assets	Commercial paper and other short-term borrowing
Trading assets	Trading liabilities
Securities financing transactions (receivable)	Collateralised securities
Investment securities	Long-term borrowing
Loans, notes and mortgages	Deposits
Other investments	Other payables
Fixed assets	
Other assets	
	Equity
	Other capital terms
Total assets	Total liabilities and equity

9.3.1.2 Liabilities and equity

As shown in Table 9.9, investment banks' funding derives from various sources. The main items are as follows:

● *Collateralised securities* – derived from the bank entering secured borrowing transactions and securities sold under agreement to repurchase; these include payables under repurchase agreements and payables under securities loaned transactions. (This item corresponds to securities financing transactions on the assets side.)

● *Trading liabilities* – include activities that the investment bank undertakes based on future expectations, such as trading securities and derivatives dealing and brokerage.

● *Commercial paper* – consists of short-term negotiable debt instruments that the bank issues to raise unsecured funding and that are traded in the money market.

The investment bank can issue *other short-term debt instruments* – that may be linked to the performance of equity or other indices – and *medium- and long-term debt instruments*.

Another liability is *deposits* (savings and time deposits), which are typically high-volume corporate deposits, followed by *other liabilities* to customers, brokers and dealers, etc., and finally, *stockholders' equity*.

9.3.2 Investment banks' income statements

Investment banks, like commercial banks, are required to publish their profit and loss accounts (or 'statement of earnings') that report all costs, revenues and net profits for the financial year. Investment banks' revenues derive from the following four sources:

● trading and principal investments;

● investment banking;

● asset management, portfolio service fees and commissions; and

● interest income.

The first components of *trading and principal investments* relate to income generated from trading in equities and equity derivatives, corporate debt, debt derivatives, mortgage and municipals, government and agency obligations, and foreign exchange. *Principal investments* are those securities held over time for general investment purposes. *Investment banking* (in the US) generally includes underwriting and financial advisory services (e.g. M&A advice). *Asset management and portfolio services* can originate revenues in the form of commissions (e.g. agency transactions for clients on main stock and futures exchanges). More specifically, asset management is a source of fees for investment banks generated by providing investment management (e.g. managing company pension funds and other investments) and advisory services to both individuals and institutions.

Securities services can also generate fees from various activities such as brokerage, financing services and securities lending, and matched book businesses. Finally, *interest income* derives primarily from the bank's wholesale lending activity.

On the cost side, interest expenses can be relatively high due to investment banks' obligations on borrowings as well as bond and short-term paper instruments (compared with commercial banks), while the bulk of operating expenses relates to staff costs. Other costs include, among others:

● communication and technology;

● occupancy and related depreciation;

- brokerage, clearing and exchange fees;
- professional fees;
- marketing;
- other expenses.

Box 9.3 illustrates the financial statement composition of Goldman Sachs.

BOX 9.3 GOLDMAN SACHS' FINANCIAL STATEMENTS (2012)

Founded in 1869 by a German immigrant, Marcus Goldman, Goldman Sachs today 'is a leading global investment banking, securities and investment management firm that provides a wide range of financial services to a substantial and diversified client base that includes corporations, financial institutions, governments and high-net-worth individuals' (**www .goldmansachs.com**). As of December 31, 2012 the company had 32,400 staff members throughout the world and net revenues of US$34.6 billion.

Goldman Sachs provides a variety of services, from capital markets services, investment banking and advisory services, wealth management, asset management, banking and related products and services. In 2008 Goldman Sachs converted into a Bank Holding Company and thus is subject to consolidated regulatory capital requirements administered by the Fed.

Figure 9.5 illustrates the assets and liabilities composition for Goldman Sachs in 2012.

On the asset side, relevant items are trading assets at fair value that comprise, for example, securities and financial derivatives held by the bank for trading purposes. These constitute the bulk of total assets (43 per cent). Other relevant items are collateralised agreements, i.e. securities borrowed and securities purchased under agreement to resell, amounting to 15 per cent overall. It is also worth noting that Goldman Sachs holds a relatively high proportion of liquid assets (around 8 per cent).

The traditional banking activity of selling loans and collecting deposits does not seem as important as other activities for the bank: wholesale deposits are relatively small, amounting to 8 per cent of total liabilities. This is because unlike commercial banks, whose main activity has traditionally been to transform the

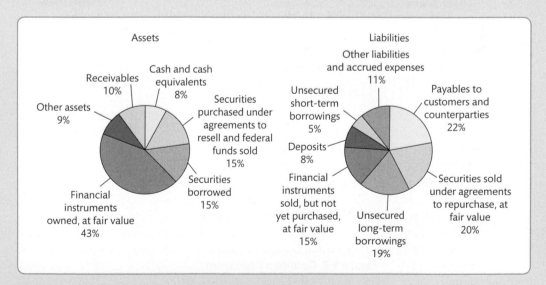

Figure 9.5 Asset and liability composition of Goldman Sachs, 2012

Source: Goldman Sachs, *Annual Report, 2012* and authors' calculations.

BOX 9.3 Goldman Sachs' financial statements (2012) (*continued*)

maturity and size of deposits into loans, investment banks operate by reshuffling a broad range of securities transactions. Therefore the assets and liabilities structure of investment banks usually indicates shorter maturity characteristics on the assets side of the balance sheet compared with a traditional commercial bank. Goldman Sachs's funding derives mainly from long-term borrowing (19 per cent), payables to customers and counterparties (22 per cent) and trading liabilities (15 per cent).

The revenue sources of Goldman Sachs for 2012 are shown in Figure 9.6.

The figures show that most revenues derive from market making and other principal transactions (50 per cent), asset management and commissions (24 per cent) and investment banking activities (15 per cent). It is notable that Goldman Sachs earns nearly 60 per cent of its net revenues in the US (see Figure 9.7). Operations in Europe, the Middle East and Africa account for 25 per cent.

On the operating costs side, staff expenses (in the form of employee compensation and benefits) are prevalent (56 per cent) (see Figure 9.8). It is worth noting that on the cost side the proportion of non-interest to interest expenses is about 75:25 of total costs (see Figure 9.9).

Source: Goldman Sachs, *Annual Report*, 2012.

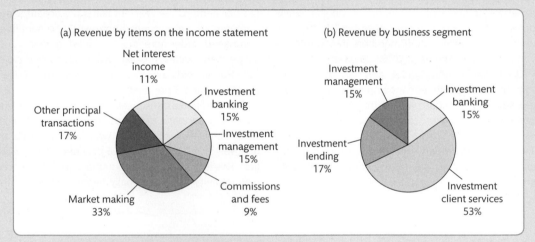

Figure 9.6 Goldman Sachs: sources of revenue, 2012

Source: Goldman Sachs, *Annual Report, 2012* and authors' calculations.

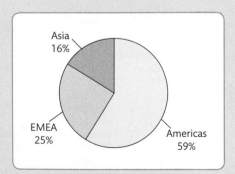

Figure 9.7 Goldman Sachs: net revenues by geographic regions, 2012

Source: Goldman Sachs, *Annual Report, 2012* and authors' calculations.

BOX 9.3 Goldman Sachs' financial statements (2012) (*continued*)

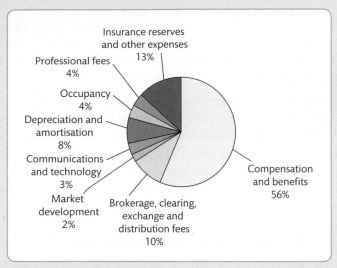

Figure 9.8 Goldman Sachs: non-interest expenses, 2012

Source: Goldman Sachs, *Annual Report, 2012* and authors' calculations.

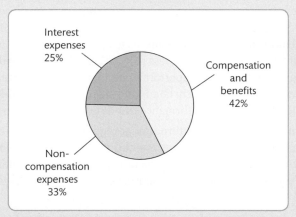

Figure 9.9 Goldman Sachs: breakdown of costs, 2012

Source: Goldman Sachs, *Annual Report, 2012* and authors' calculations.

9.4 Bank performance and financial ratio analysis

The significant changes that have occurred in the financial sector in all advanced economies have increased the importance of performance analysis for banking institutions. The current operating environment is characterised by more intense competition, greater pressures for banks to control costs and manage risks while at the same time maximise revenues. For publicly listed banks, the objective of shareholders' wealth maximisation (maximising the returns to investors holding equity shares in the bank) is still a priority, restrained merely by increased regulatory constraints (forcing banks to hold more capital reduces returns on capital). It is not surprising that the 2007–2009 financial turmoil and the recession that followed have increased the demand for prudential regulation (see Chapter 7).

Performance analysis is an important tool used by various agents either operating internally to the bank (e.g. managers) or who form part of the bank's external operating environment (e.g. regulators), as shown in Figure 9.10.

- **Shareholders, bondholders:** investors in shares and in bonds issued by the bank, and bank managers and other employees have an obvious economic and strategic interest in the current and future prospects of the banking firm.

- **Direct competitors:** peer group analyses compare the profitability of similar banking institutions operating in similar operating environments; in some cases the homogeneity of the groups being analysed allows for the use of sophisticated statistical techniques.

- **Other market participants:** competitors (or other firms) that represent potential takeover or merger possibilities will rely on **financial ratio analysis** to assess the viability of potential M&A activity and to evaluate potential economic synergies.

- **Financial markets:** capital and money market participants use ratio analysis to monitor the performance of banks. Money market participants, especially those involved with lending in the interbank market, will need to assess the creditworthiness of the banks they are lending to. Deterioration in bank performance may increase credit risk and therefore interbank lenders will require higher returns on their loans. Banks with higher capital ratios will more likely be able to achieve cheaper finance in the interbank markets (as such banks will be perceived as being less risky). Capital market participants and analysts also use ratio analysis to assess the performance of banks as a change in bank performance can alter the valuation of long-term bonds and shares issued by banks. For example, potential bondholders will rely on performance trends as a guide to their investments.

- **Regulators:** domestic and international regulatory authorities will also be concerned about the performance of banking institutions. For example, financial regulators need to evaluate the solvency, liquidity and overall performance of banking firms to gauge the likelihood of potential problems. Competition authorities also investigate bank performance

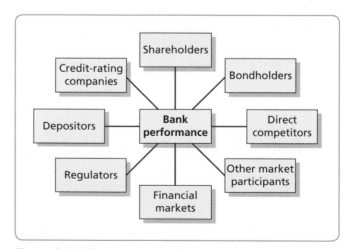

Figure 9.10 Who is interested in bank performance?

indicators to analyse whether banks are making excess profits and behaving in an uncompetitive manner.

- **Depositors:** The smooth performance of banks is valuable for depositors who trust their bank will remain profitable and not expose itself to too much risk.

- Finally, **credit-rating companies** – such as Moody's, Standard & Poor's and Fitch IBCA – analyse performance information to compile analyses and ratings of banks operating in a certain country or group of countries.

Bank performance is calculated using ratio analysis and assessed with the aim of 1) looking at past and current trends; and 2) determining future estimates of bank performance. Financial ratio analysis investigates different areas of bank performance, such as profitability, asset quality and solvency.

In addition, over recent years greater emphasis has been placed on **key performance indicators (KPIs)**.[4] These can be defined as 'factors by reference to which the development, performance or position of the business of the company can be measured effectively' (UK Companies Act 2006, Section 417: 6). This definition implies that KPIs can be financial and non-financial (e.g. customer satisfaction), as described in Box 9.4, and should be monitored and reviewed by management in light of the company's strategic objectives.

BOX 9.4 WHAT ARE KEY PERFORMANCE INDICATORS (KPIS)?

A report by PwC (2007) stresses the importance of financial and non-financial KPIs for *narrative reporting* to ensure corporate transparency and clarifies their main features and scope as follows:

With reference to the specific banking industry, the key strategic drivers rotate around the following six critical aspects: customer retention, customer penetration, capital adequacy, assets under management, asset quality and loan losses.

Source: Adapted from PwC (2007).

Key performance indicators

(1) How many KPIs should be reported?	Typically, there are likely to be between four and ten measures. However, in order to aid corporate transparency, KPIs should reflect the company-specific business and its strategy so there is no 'one size fits all'.
(2) Segmental or group KPIs?	In some cases, it may be more useful to report separate KPIs by business segments (e.g. retail banking, commercial banking, asset management, insurance, etc.). For example, in diversified organisations reporting the KPIs only at the group level may be meaningless.
(3) How rigid is the choice of KPIs?	Since strategies and objectives evolve over time, it may be appropriate to allow the KPIs to adapt to these changes, so there is no requirement to continue reporting the KPIs identified in previous periods.
(4) Does reliability matter in choosing KPIs?	Particularly for non-traditional and less well-known indicators, it is important that management ensure the reliability and clarity of the information, so any limitations should be stated and, if possible, explained to the reader.

---

[4] In the UK, the Business Review legislation requires companies to enhance good practice in narrative reporting, using financial and other KPIs. More details can be found in the Accounting Standards Board 'Reporting statement on operating and financial reviews', released in January 2006.

The traditional financial ratios for measuring bank performance are discussed below. The tools that can be used to calculate performance are derived from the information revealed by periodic financial reports produced by the accounting system: the balance sheet and the income statement.

9.4.1 Profitability ratios

Profitability ratios traditionally used in banking are return on equity (ROE), return on assets (ROA), net interest margin (NIM) and C/I (cost-to-income) ratio.

ROA is calculated as net income/total assets (or alternatively average assets over two financial years); this ratio indicates how much net income is generated per £ of assets.

$$ROA = \text{net income/total assets} \tag{9.1}$$

ROE is probably the most important indicator of a bank's profitability and growth potential. It is the rate of return to shareholders or the percentage return on each £ of equity invested in the bank.

$$ROE = \text{net income/total equity} \tag{9.2}$$

Box 9.5 shows the decomposition of ROE into return on assets and equity multiplier. It also summarises briefly the key points of a report by the European Central Bank (2010a) on the shortcomings of this widely used ratio.

BOX 9.5 THE ROE DECOMPOSITION

ROE can be decomposed using a traditional method in corporate finance known as the 'Du Pont Model', from the name of the US corporation that first applied it in the 1920s. This decomposition is important because it allows financial analysts to understand the interrelationship between various ratios and helps banks to invest in areas where the risk-adjusted returns are greater.

We specified in equation (9.2) that accounting ROE is equal to net income divided by total (or, alternative, average) equity. By multiplying ROE by total assets, it is possible to decompose it into two parts: the ROA (= net income/total assets), which measures average profit generated relative to the bank's assets, and the so-called equity multiplier (EM), i.e. a measure of a bank's leverage. Specifically:

$$ROE = \left(\frac{\text{net income}}{\text{total assets}}\right) \times \left(\frac{\text{total assets}}{\text{total equity}}\right) \tag{9.3}$$

where

$$EM = \text{total assets/total equity} \tag{9.4}$$

so that

$$ROE = ROA \times EM \tag{9.5}$$

BOX 9.5 The ROE decomposition (*continued*)

ROA can also be split into two parts: profit margin (= net income/total revenue) and total revenue over total assets, which can be defined as the asset yield or asset 'utilisation' ratio. By multiplying ROA by the bank's total revenue, we obtain:

$$ROA = \left(\frac{\text{net income}}{\text{total revenue}} \right) \times \left(\frac{\text{total revenue}}{\text{total assets}} \right) \tag{9.6}$$

Substituting:

$$ROE = \left(\frac{\text{net income}}{\text{total revenue}} \right) \times \left(\frac{\text{total revenue}}{\text{total assets}} \right) \times \left(\frac{\text{total assets}}{\text{total equity}} \right) \tag{9.7}$$

It is possible to depict the ROE decomposition graphically, as shown in Figure 9.11.

Over the crisis period, banks that had previously generated high ROE performed rather poorly. An ECB report (2010a) acknowledges the need to better understand the potential trade-off between risk and return in bank performance analysis and discusses the reliability of using ROE as a benchmark, particularly in periods of high volatility and weak economic conditions. The major shortcomings of ROE identified by the report can be summarised as follows:

1 There are unbalances in the drivers of ROE (namely ROA and leverage); in particular, ROE is not risk-sensitive.

2 Crucial risk elements are missing in ROE, such as the proportion of risky assets and the level of solvency.

3 ROE fails to distinguish the best-performing banks from others because it is essentially a short-term indicator and thus cannot measure the potential for sustainable (long-term) results of the bank.

4 Last but not least, like other accounting metrics ROE may be prone to manipulations from the markets since data are not always reliable and there are significant seasonal factors that can affect them.

Source: ECB (2010a).

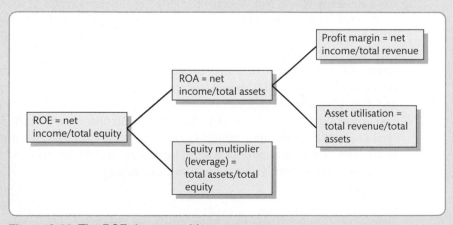

Figure 9.11 The ROE decomposition

Another key performance measure for institutions engaged in traditional banking activities is the NIM, which measures the net interest income relative to the bank's total, average or earning assets.

$$\text{NIM} = [(\text{interest income} - \text{interest expense})/\text{total assets}] \qquad (9.8)$$

It reflects the difference between interest earned on assets minus interest costs per £ of assets. The NIM measures the bank's spread per £ of assets. High NIM suggests that the difference between deposit rates and loans (+ other interest-earning assets) rates are high, and vice versa. As we have noted in earlier chapters, NIM has been falling in many banking markets, reflecting increased competition in the deposits and loans markets – the difference between how much banks pay on deposits and how much they earn on loans is declining.

Finally, the cost-to-income ratio is a quick test of efficiency that reflects bank non-interest costs as a proportion of income.

$$\text{C/I} = \text{non-interest expenses}/(\text{net interest income} + \text{non-interest income}) \quad (9.9)$$

where non-interest expenses are considered as the main inputs to the production process of a bank and total operating income is the output.

If the bank is listed in the capital markets, some additional useful measures of performance are earnings per share (EPS), price to book value (P/B) and credit default swaps (CDS) spreads.

$$\text{EPS} = \text{net income}/\text{average shares outstanding} \qquad (9.10)$$

It measures the portion of a bank's profit net of tax allocated to each share in issue of common stock. Higher EPS means better profitability for shareholders.

$$\text{P/B} = \text{stock price}/\text{book value of equity per share} \qquad (9.11)$$

Price to book value (also known as market-to-book) is the ratio between the market prices of a bank's shares and the accounting value of shareholders' equity per share. The lower the number, the better for investors because if, for example, the bank's current share price is £4 and shareholders' equity per share is £2, investors are ready to pay for one share twice the book value.

Table 9.10 gives the financial highlights for Australia's four major banks: Australia and New Zealand Banking Group Ltd (ANZ), Commonwealth Bank of Australia (CBA), National Australia Bank (NAB) and Westpac Banking Corporation (WBC). It is possible to note that ROA ranges between 0.72 per cent and 1.03 per cent while ROE is around 16 per cent and NIM 2.16 per cent.[5] Usually the benchmark for ROA level is around 1 per cent while ROE is considered good when over 10 per cent. High-performing banks typically adopt a target ROE figure of 15 per cent plus. Generally speaking, the higher these ratios, the better from a bank's perspective, as higher NIM should feed through into greater net income, thus boosting ROA and ROE. However, as highlighted in Box 9.5, very high ROE can also indicate high risk taking and unsustainable business models. Table 9.10 also illustrates that the top four Australian banks have been performing relatively well in terms of C/I ratios that are below 50 per cent in all cases. The benchmark for the C/I ratio is around 50–70 per cent, i.e. a low C/I ratio indicates that the bank is operating in an efficient way.

---

[5] It is not unusual to find ratios expressed in basis points. One basis point is 1/100th or 0.01 per cent. For example, a ratio of 0.055 per cent is 5.5 basis points.

Table 9.10 Top Australian banks' performance at a glance (2012)

	ANZ	CBA	NAB	WBC
Ranking				
Ranking by total assets	4	2	1	3
Ranking by market capitalisation	3	1	4	2
Profitability and efficiency				
Return on assets	0.96	1.03	0.72	0.98
Return on equity	15.6	18.6	14.2	15.5
Net interest margin (basis points)	231	209	210	216
Cost-to-income ratio	48.1	46	49.8	44
Asset quality				
Impaired loans to total loans	1.01	0.85	1.36	0.84
Capital adequacy ratios				
Tier 1	10.8	10.01	10.27	10.3
Total capital	12.2	10.98	11.67	11.7

Source: KPMG (2013).

Table 9.11 reports the 2012 key profitability ratios for three large former investment banks. It is noticeable that Morgan Stanley's performance is not as strong as that of the other two banks. ROE exceeds 10 per cent for both JPMorgan and Goldman Sachs and is just 1 per cent for Morgan Stanley; in addition, JPMorgan's ROA (0.9 per cent) is ten times higher than the figure reported for Morgan Stanley. Typically, net interest margin has a secondary role for investment banks compared with commercial and retail banks. A more suitable measure of profitability for investment banks is **profit margin**, which is equal to earnings before income taxes to total operating income and takes into account both interest and non-interest income.

Table 9.11 also reports the two market-based measures of performance mentioned above (EPS and P/B). It seems clear that JPMorgan is the best bank at generating high EPS while

Table 9.11 Selected ratios for three former large US investment banks (%)

End-year 2012	JPMorgan	Goldman Sachs	Morgan Stanley
Return on assets	0.92	0.80	0.09
Return on equity	10.98	10.23	1.02
Net interest margin	2.22	0.52	−0.03
Cost-to-income ratio	66.71	67.20	98.03
Other operating income/average assets	2.25	3.25	3.44
Profit margin[a]	25.97	22.23	4.11
Liquid assets/deposits	55.87	180.57	150.56
Tier 1 ratio	12.59	16.70	17.70
Total capital ratio	15.27	20.10	18.50
Equity/Total assets	8.65	8.07	8.93
EPS (June 2013)[a]	5.98	1.19	0.52
P/B (June 2013)[a]	1.06	1.09	0.85

Note: [a]Data from Yahoo Finance (**https://uk.finance.yahoo.com**) at June 2013.
Source: Bankscope.

keeping the level of equity in line with the other two banks. In contrast, the ratio of liquid assets over total deposits and short-term funding appears significantly lower (56 per cent) than that of its peers (>150 per cent).

Finally, spreads on CDS provide useful information, as they represent the cost of insuring an unsecured bond issued by the institution over a specific period of time. CDS spreads are considered a direct indicator of a firm's credit risk (European Central Bank, 2009a).

9.4.2 Asset quality

Lending is still one of the most important activities of banks. While it is expected that all banks will have to bear some positive levels of bad loans and loan losses, one of the key objectives of bank management is to minimise such losses. In the context of the income–expense statement, financial analysts can control the provisions for loan losses to manipulate their accounting earnings. For example, more conservative bankers may understate their accounting earnings by building a large and above-average loan-loss reserve, while more aggressive bankers may overstate their accounting earnings by keeping the loan-loss reserve low.

The drop in profitability that banks have experienced in recent years has often been due to a poor assets quality that has continued to worsen in a number of European countries as a consequence of the eurozone troubles (see Chapter 14 for a discussion). Box 9.6 reviews and discusses the main sources of underperformance for EU countries for the 40 largest banking institutions over 2007–2011.

BOX 9.6 SOURCES OF UNDERPERFORMANCE IN EUROPEAN BANKING

Using a sample of the 40 largest European banks over 2007–2011, McKinsey (2012) identifies a number of sources of underperformance of the sector that resulted in a drop in: (1) banks' market value (by 50 per cent since 2007); and (2) total return to shareholders by over 15%. These include:

- a general decline in operating profitability;
- major write-downs/write-offs of assets;
- rising loan-loss provisions (LLPs);
- increasing cost-to-income ratios;
- increased regulatory burden, including higher capital ratios, liquidity ratios and other restrictions.

As a result, ROE levels have also suffered, thus destroying value from an economic-value-added perspective. As shown in Figure 9.12, panel (a), ROE remained well below the cost of equity from 2008 to 2011. Panel (b) reports that in the face of €179 billion in value created over 2001–2006, with the crisis some €278 billion were destroyed after 2007.

In order to remain profitable, banks should respond on one hand by conserving capital and therefore complying with the new rules and regulations, and on the other hand by focusing on improving their efficiency. Specifically, McKinsey identifies the tactical responses and actions needed in order to create value and improve profitability and some are summarised below:

1 Optimising portfolios, including improved hedging and sale of capital-intensive portfolios and controlling the risk profile of the credit portfolios.

2 Improving risk and capital models and elevating data quality, including amendments to the VaR model to calculate stressed VaR, and new internal risk model processes.

3 Improving financial efficiency, including balance-sheet optimisation and enhancements to current capital (so as to generate an acceptable leverage), liquidity, and funding stocks.

4 Boosting operational efficiency, including both traditional cost-efficiency measures (reducing head count, shrinking IT costs) and driving greater use of electronic trading.

5 Rethink strategies with regard to noncore activities.

Sources: McKinsey (2011, 2012).

BOX 9.6 Sources of underperformance in European banking (*continued*)

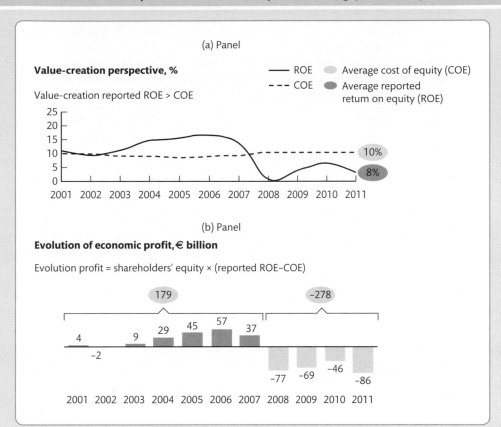

Figure 9.12 Value destruction in European banking
Source: McKinsey (2012).

9.4.3 Cost of capital and shareholder value creation in banking

While the above discussion of bank performance focuses on traditional and market-based measures, one important indicator that is now widely used by banks (and other companies) relates to what is known as 'shareholder value creation'. The main strategic objective of a profit-oriented bank is to generate value for its owners (shareholders) – see Box 9.7.

A bank can create **shareholder value** by pursuing a strategy that maximises the return on capital invested relative to the (opportunity) **cost of capital** (the cost of keeping equity shareholders and bondholders happy). In other words, if a bank invests in a project that generates greater returns than the cost to shareholders of financing the project then this should boost returns to holders of the bank's shares (in terms of capital appreciation of stock and higher dividends). The concept can be applied to an individual project, such as a bank considering making a strategic investment in another country, or for the whole bank's performance overall.

287

BOX 9.7 VALUE MAXIMISATION FOR THE BANKING FIRM

As with any other commercial firms listed on the stock market, one of the main objectives of a banking firm is to maximise its value. This is because if the bank meets investors' expectations then it will be able to raise the capital it needs to sustain its future growth. It is well known that the value of the stock (V_0) for any firm will be equal to the present value of expected future stream of dividends $E(D)$ (see Appendix A1 on the concept of present value):

$$V_0 = \frac{E(D_t)}{(1 + r)^t} + \frac{E(D_1)}{(1 + r)^1} + \ldots + \frac{E(D_2)}{(1 + r)^2} = \sum_{t=1}^{\infty} \frac{E(D_\infty)}{(1 + r)^\infty} = \sum_{t=1}^{\infty} \frac{E(D_t)}{(1 + r)^t} \qquad (9.12)$$

where r is the minimum acceptable – or required – rate of return on the stock, given the bank's riskiness and the returns available on other investments. The rate of return r is the bank's cost of capital.

The valuation model above is the well-known dividend discount model, which assumes that the amount of dividends paid in each period varies over time. It also implies that we need dividend forecasts for every year into the indefinite future. By assuming that dividends are trending upwards at a stable growth rate that we call 'g', the model can be simplified as follows:

$$V_0 = \frac{D_0(1 + g)}{r - g} = \frac{D_1}{r - g} \qquad (9.13)$$

This is known as the 'Gordon' model and essentially implies that a bank's stock is expected to grow at the same rate as dividends. For example, suppose the most recently paid dividend for Bank Delta was $D_0 = \$5$, $g = 0.04$ and the appropriate discount rate is 12 per cent. By applying the formula Bank Delta's current share value will be:

$$V_0 = \$5/(0.12 - 0.04) = \$0.625 \text{ per share}$$

So shareholder value is created when:

Return on capital invested in the project $>$ Cost of capital to the firm

or

Return on capital (ROC) $>$ Cost of capital

In order to add shareholder value, firms must invest in projects that generate returns exceeding their cost of capital. A common measure of shareholder value is economic value added, as described in Box 9.8.

To calculate the cost of capital we can use the CAPM where:

$$R_i = R_f + \beta(R_m - R_f) \qquad (9.14)$$

where

R_i is the required rate of return on an investment;

R_f is the risk-free rate;

R_m refers to the market return; and

β is a measure of the volatility of the company's equity relative to the overall market.

BOX 9.8 WHAT IS EVA?

Bank shareholders rely on performance measures to evaluate how well they are doing in relation to their wealth-maximising objectives. However, profit-based measures ignore the cost of equity capital and are calculated based on accounting standards that do not reflect truly the amount of wealth created. Economic Value Added (EVA) is a performance measurement system that overcomes these two limitations.

EVA was developed by the US consulting firm Stern Stewart & Co and is now commonly used both by practitioners and academics to investigate shareholder value. To increase shareholder value the financial firm has to produce at least a positive equity spread which can be converted into EVA. Specifically, EVA expresses the surplus created by a banking firm (or division within a bank) in a given period, i.e. the firm's profit net of the cost of all capital. It is always a useful measure to calculate the value creation in a specific division or business segment within the bank.

Following Fiordelisi (2007), EVA can be calculated for each bank over the period t and $t - 1$ using a procedure accounting for bank peculiarities, specifically:

$$EVA_{(t-1, t)} = NOPAT_{t-1, t} - (CI_{t-1} * K^e_{t-1, t}) \tag{9.15}$$

where NOPAT is net operating profits after tax, CI = bank's capital invested and K^e = cost of capital (shareholders' expected rate of return).

The calculation of EVA requires that NOPAT and capital invested (CI) are expressed on an economic (rather than accounting) basis. Normally, adjustments are carried out on accounting data, particularly relating to Loan Loss Provision and Loss Reserves, R&D and training costs, taxes and so on.

Concerning CI and its cost, various studies suggest the use of equity capital, while for the cost of capital (K) it is possible to employ the book value of shareholder equity. Finally, the cost of equity is estimated using capital asset pricing model (CAPM) models and looking at investors' expected returns.

A bank pursuing a focused EVA strategy will have the following priorities:

1 raise the rate of return on assets via revenue-enhancing and cost-containment (e.g. branch closures) strategies;

2 the development of capital-free business to raise the measured ROE (e.g. increasing non-interest fee incomes that can be generated with low capital expenditure);

3 the removal of assets from the balance sheet if they do not meet the target ROE established as the bank's objective (e.g. via securitisation);

4 being prepared, if necessary, to radically change organisational structure (e.g. by outsourcing part of the business);

5 exiting business areas that do not generate a rate of return equal to the target set;

6 repaying capital to shareholders (e.g. by repurchasing stocks from its shareholders).

Sources: CIMA (2004); Fiordelisi (2007).

The CAPM (see Appendix A2) states that investors require a return from holding a company's shares that exceeds the risk-free rate (Rf), to compensate them for holding equity over bonds (this is Rm – Rf, otherwise known as the equity risk premium) and for the riskiness of the company relative to the whole market (β).[6]

For example, if a company has beta (β) of 1.5, and assuming a risk-free rate of 6 per cent (given by the US long-bond rate) and an equity premium of 5 per cent (Rm – Rf), then the cost of capital to the firm will be 13.5 per cent. In other words, to maintain shareholder value, this firm will have to invest in projects that generate returns greater than 13.5 per cent if they are to add to shareholder wealth. Investments that generate returns of less than 13.5 per cent will destroy shareholder value. The equity market premium (the difference between equity and bond returns) is usually calculated over a 20- or 25-year period and there is much debate as to how large this premium is, although the US equity market premiums are almost always found to be greater than those in the UK, and they are even lower in continental Europe. Betas (β) should also be calculated over long periods as short-term estimates may yield unreliable cost of capital estimates.

Box 9.9 explains the calculation of the cost of capital. Cost of capital calculations can be done for the whole bank or divisions/business areas within a bank in order to determine the allocation of capital within the organisation. For example, if a bank's mortgage business is generating returns greater than the cost of capital but credit card activities are making returns less than the cost of capital, the bank should consider dedicating more capital resources to the former and also should think of ways of boosting returns in (or divesting) its credit card business.

BOX 9.9 CALCULATING THE COST OF EQUITY CAPITAL

In 2002, the Competition Commission Report on the 'Supply of banking services by clearing banks to small and medium-sized enterprises' presented an evaluation of the cost of capital for British banks NatWest and the Royal Bank of Scotland Group (RBS). The study followed the methodology explained below.

CAPM 'standard' cost of equity capital

The standard model for the cost of equity capital is the CAPM. Despite some drawbacks, this model continues to be the most widely used tool for business decision making. In 2002, RBS was asked by the Competition Commission to provide the cost of capital used by the bank. However, the appropriate benchmark is not the cost of equity capital currently used but the cost of equity capital rates that should be used for making assessments about performance in each year. This should be the cost of equity capital prevailing at the start of each year. The Competition Commission study therefore starts by setting out the cost of equity capital as it would have been for

NatWest and RBS (according to the CAPM) at the beginning of each of the years 1998, 1999 and 2000.

Risk-free rate

The study considered 31 December 1997, 1998 and 1999 six-month LIBOR as the risk-free rates applying at the start of 1998, 1999 and 2000. Six-month LIBOR is used because it avoids some of the liquidity problems that are evident with government bill rates.

Equity risk premium

A wide range of equity premiums can be quoted from the literature, ranging from 3 per cent to 9 per cent. For this analysis a rate of 4 per cent was used to reflect lower expected returns in the future.

CAPM beta figures

For a beta figure, the Competition Commission consulted the London Business School Risk Management Service to get the start-of-year betas for NatWest and

➡

---

[6] A beta of less than one indicates lower risk than the market; a beta of more than one indicates higher risk than the market.

BOX 9.9 Calculating the cost of equity capital (*continued*)

Table 9.12 'Standard' cost of equity capital for NatWest and RBS

NatWest	1998	1999	2000
Risk-free rate (six-month LIBOR)	7.7%	5.9%	6.2%
Equity risk premium (%)	4.0%	4.0%	4.0%
Beta (start of year from LBS RMS)*	1.14	1.20	1.12
CAPM 'standard' cost of equity capital (%)	**12.3%**	**10.7%**	**10.7%**
RBS			
Risk-free rate (six-month LIBOR)	7.7%	5.9%	6.2%
Equity risk premium (%)	4.0%	4.0%	4.0%
Beta (start of year from LBS RMS)*	1.02	1.27	1.24
CAPM 'standard' cost of equity capital (%)	**11.8%**	**11.0%**	**11.2%**

Notes: The term 'standard' is used as the report goes on to make various adjustments to these estimates.

*LBS RMS stands for London Business School Risk Measurement Service, see **www.london.edu/facultyandresearch/subjectareas/finance/research.html**

Source: Competition Commission (2002) Appendix 13.3. Charles River Associates' note on 'normal' profits and rates of return (referred to in paragraph 13.240 of the main report), pp. 148–154.

RBS. The cost of equity capital for NatWest and RBS for the years 1998–2000 are shown in Table 9.12.

Following the same methodology, we re-ran the exercise and evaluated the cost of capital for some of the largest US and European banks in 2013. The results of this exercise are reported in Table 9.13.

The overall cost of capital for banks, ten years later, is surprisingly similar on average. However, there seem to be substantial differences particularly among European banks.

Table 9.13 'Standard' cost of equity capital for selected US and EU banks

US banks	Goldman Sachs	Morgan Stanley	JPMorgan Chase	Citigroup	Bank of America Merrill Lynch
Risk-free rate (T-bill rate)	0.05%	0.05%	0.05%	0.05	0.00%
Equity risk premium (%)	5.78%	5.78%	5.78%	5.78%	5.78%
Beta	1.87	2.45	1.8	2.09	2.39
CAPM 'standard' cost of equity capital (%)	10.86%	14.21%	10.45%	17.08%	13.81%
European banks	Deutsche Bank	UBA AG	Banco Santander	HSBC	RBS
Risk-free rate	0.50%	0.50%	0.50%	0.34	0.34
Equity risk premium (%)	5.9	3.4	3.1	4.3	4.3
Beta	2.01	1.58	1.75	1.32	2.25
CAPM 'standard' cost of equity capital (%)	11.86%	5.38%	5.43%	6.02%	10.02%

Note: See Appendix A2 for more details about the beta.

Source: Data on risk-free rates and equity premia from Damodaran (2013). Available at SSRN: **http://dx.doi.org/10.2139/ssrn.2238064**. Beta (Yahoo Finance, Key Statistics accessed on 19 July 2013).

Note that this is just the equity cost of capital and we can extend the analysis to include the cost of debt to present what is known as a weighted cost of capital. Also, one should note that there is a variety of other approaches that can be used to calculate the cost of capital (including a wide range of various accounting and other adjustments) and it should be stressed that cost of capital calculations are never definitive – they vary according to the calculation method used.

9.4.4   Solvency ratios

The Basel III Accord (detailed in Chapter 7) requires banks to hold a minimum overall risk-weighted capital ratio of 8 per cent, of which Tier 1 capital should be at least 6 per cent. Total capital adequacy ratio measures Tier 1 capital + Tier 2 capital; this ratio should be at least 8 per cent. The addition of the capital conservation buffer increases the total amount of capital a bank must hold to 10.5 per cent of risk-weighted assets, of which 8.5 per cent must be Tier 1 capital.

The total capital adequacy ratio cannot be calculated simply by looking at the balance sheet of a bank, as the bank has to classify its assets and off-balance-sheet business according to certain risk categories and varying amounts of capital have to be held according to these risks. Recall from Section 7.8, for example, cash has a 0 per cent risk weighting requiring no capital backing, whereas unsecured loans require 8 per cent capital backing. Both Tier 1 and Tier 2 ratios can only be calculated internally by the bank. Banks have the option of publishing these ratios in their annual reports. Financial ratios shown in Tables 9.10 and 9.11 illustrate that in 2012 banks in Australia and the US were able to set aside a level of Tier 1 and total capital significantly above the 6 and 8 per cent minimum requirements.

Finally, we can say that as equity is a cushion against asset malfunction, the simple equity/ assets measure (which we can calculate from bank balance sheets) indicates the amount of protection afforded to the bank by the equity it invested in it. It follows that the higher this figure, the more protection there is. However, remember that this is a crude measure of a bank's financial strength because, unlike the Basel Tier 1 and Tier 2 measures, this ratio does not take into account the riskiness of banking business.

9.4.4.1   The trade-off between safety and the return to shareholders

The amount of capital affects the returns to equity holders and ROE is a good measure for shareholders to know how much profit the bank is generating on their equity investments. Indeed, as we discussed in Box 9.5, the ROE is related directly with ROA, as follows:

$$\text{ROA} \times \text{EM} = \text{ROE} \qquad (9.16)$$

rearranging:

$$\text{EM} = \text{ROE} \times \frac{1}{\text{ROA}} \qquad (9.17)$$

substituting:

$$\text{EM} = \frac{\text{Total assets}}{\text{Total equity capital}} \qquad (9.18)$$

Table 9.14 An illustration of the trade-off between solvency and profitability

Bank	Total assets (a)	Total capital (b)	EM = (a)/(b)	ROA	ROE = EM × ROA
Bank Alpha	£50,000,000	£5,000,000	10	1.5%	15%
Bank Beta	£50,000,000	£2,500,000	20	1.5%	30%

where EM measures the extent to which a bank's assets are funded with equity relative to debt. To understand the importance of EM, consider two banks, both having total assets (with the same risk features) equal to £50 million and earning a ROA of 1.5 per cent, as shown in Table 9.14.

The table illustrates the trade-off between total capital and ROE. In particular, Bank Alpha displays the highest level of total capital and the lowest level of EM and ROE relative to Bank Beta. However, while the shareholders of Bank Beta will be earning twice as much as those of Bank Alpha, it is not necessarily true that Bank Beta is the most desirable for shareholders as Bank Beta is more risky as it has half the amount of capital backing the same amount of risky assets. There is clearly a trade-off between safety and returns to shareholders.

9.4.5 Limitations of financial ratios

Financial ratios have their own limitations. First, generally one year's figures are insufficient to evaluate the performance of banks, and financial analysts typically look at trends to evaluate the ratios and their fluctuations over a timespan of at least five years. Second, precise comparisons between similar banks may be difficult as they often compete in different markets, have varying product features and customer bases, and so on. As such, ratio analysis may be misleading as it is often difficult to compare 'like with like'. Despite these problems, financial analysts often undertake *peer analysis of* similar banks and this involves the creation of peer groups (see also Section 8.3.1 on peer analysis). Third, ratios do not stand in isolation: they are interrelated. For example, poor profitability may affect liquidity and capital ratios. A bank that performs poorly may have to use its liquid assets (if it has an excess of such assets) to fund future lending, thus reducing its liquidity ratios. Large losses may be written out of capital, thus reducing capital ratios.

Another important factor is that ratios relate to a particular point in time and there are seasonal factors that can distort them. Moreover, figures in the financial statements may be 'window-dressed' – that is, made to look better than they really are (as was the case mentioned earlier, referring to banks over- or under-provisioning for bad loans). Similarly, financial statements may be manipulated and may not reflect accepted accounting procedures. That is why both domestic and international regulatory authorities have pointed out the need for more transparency, disclosure and uniformity of bank accounts as the markets become increasingly global. For example, at the EU level all listed companies that are required to publish consolidated accounts are also required to prepare their accounts in accordance with adopted IFRS for accounting periods beginning on or after 1 January 2005. Last but not least, particularly in cross-country analyses, the usefulness of some financial ratios (e.g. those having income net of tax as numerator like ROE and ROA) can be influenced by tax laws that may differ substantially from country to country.

9.5 Conclusion

This chapter examined the main items contained in banks' financial statements and introduced the key financial ratios used by banks to compare performance. It also highlighted the role of bank capital, simply defined as the difference between assets and liabilities. Typically, banks are highly leveraged compared with non-financial firms; therefore capital management techniques are vital to ensure the solvency of banking institutions. In the chapter we also briefly discussed the concept of shareholder value creation and the cost of equity capital.

Furthermore, the analysis of the income statement (or profit and loss) account has shown the various sources of income (interest and non-interest) and cost structure for banks and how to determine the profitability. The chapter also focused on the different activities that investment banks perform and how these are reflected in the structure of their financial statements. We noted that investment banks' balance sheet structure and income statements differ substantially from those of commercial banks.

Many different agents operating either internally or externally to the banks (from managers to regulators and credit-rating companies) will be interested in their performance, thus the last part of this chapter introduced a selection of key ratios used to gauge bank performance, focusing particularly on profitability, asset quality and solvency.

Key terms

Assets	Fair value	Leverage	Return on assets
Balance sheet	Financial ratio	Liabilities	(ROA)
Bank performance	analysis	Net interest margin	Return on equity
Capital	Income statement	(NIM)	(ROE)
Cost of capital	(profit and loss	Profit margin	Revenues
Cost–income ratio	account)	Profit and loss	Shareholder
Costs	Key performance	account	value
Credit-rating	indicators	Profits	
companies	(KPIs)		

Key reading

ECB (2010) 'Beyond ROE – how to measure bank performance', Appendix to the Report on EU Banking Structures, September.

Fiordelisi, F. (2007) 'Shareholder value efficiency in European banking', *Journal of Banking and Finance*, 31(7), 2151–2171, July.

Koch, T.W. and MacDonald, S.S. (2009) *Bank Management*, Mason, OH: South-Western Cengage Learning.

REVISION QUESTIONS AND PROBLEMS

9.1 What is a bank balance sheet? What are the main items in a commercial bank's balance sheet?

9.2 What is equity capital? What are the functions of capital?

9.3 What is a bank income statement?

9.4 What are the main differences between a bank balance sheet and income statement?

9.5 What are the main differences between commercial and investment banks' financial statements?

9.6 Using the information contained in Tables 9.4 and 9.5, calculate Barclays' ROA, ROE, NIM and C/I ratios.

9.7 Download the annual reports of two large banking groups and critically analyse the pages that describe the KPIs. During your seminar class, discuss in groups the KPIs reported by the two banking institutions and try to identify and explain the PwC's six critical aspects described in Box 9.4 in light of the major strategies stated in the annual reports of the respective banks.

9.8 Explain how to calculate the cost of equity capital for a bank. Outline the main advantages of this approach to bank performance measurement compared with using standard profitability ratios.

9.9 Explain the trade-off between solvency and profitability.

9.10 What are the main limitations of bank financial ratios?

Chapter 10

Bank financial management

Learning objectives

- To understand the basics of asset–liability management
- To identify the main management concerns on the balance sheet
- To identify the main off-balance-sheet management concerns
- To describe the features of the most common derivative contracts

10.1 Introduction

The main objective of any private firm is the maximisation of profits and shareholders' wealth. In achieving this aim, the role of financial management is threefold: 1) to make investment decisions (how to allocate finance); 2) to undertake financing decisions (how to acquire finance); and 3) to control resources (how to conserve finance). Investment and financing decisions are vital elements used in the planning process to achieve the objectives of an organisation. For a manufacturing firm, for example, these objectives are measured in sales and profit goals over a specific period, supported by financial targets. For banks, the goal is to manage assets and liabilities in a way that maximises profits while being generally 'safe and sound'. Prudence in banking is needed due to the special role that banks play in the economy and the potential 'domino' effects that a bank's failure may cause to the financial sector as a whole (see Chapter 8). More specifically, bank managers will have the following concerns:

- **Asset management**: the bank must make sure that its portfolio of assets (mainly loans) includes low-risk assets and that it is well diversified.
- **Liability management**: the bank must acquire funds (raise deposits) at the lowest possible cost.
- **Liquidity management**: the bank must predict with the lowest possible margin of error the daily withdrawals and other payments by customers in order to keep enough cash and other liquid assets readily available.
- **Capital management**: the bank must keep an adequate level of capital to comply with regulatory requirements in order to maintain the appropriate level of solvency. Bank capital refers to funds that can be used as a cushion against losses – if loans are not repaid it is

the capital that takes the loss. The more capital a bank has, in theory at least, the safer it is as it has a bigger cushion to absorb losses.

- **OBS management**: the bank must control and limit the exposures derived from off-balance-sheet transactions.

The function of financial management is to monitor actual performance against planned goals and targets. In doing so, managers rely on the information revealed by periodic financial reports produced by various accounting systems. As discussed in Chapter 9, these are the balance sheet and profit and loss account. As we will see throughout this chapter, bank financial management includes all five main points described above. In recent years, the development of the financial systems in most advanced economies, together with the widespread use of technology, have meant that banks can now use a relatively large variety of negotiable financial instruments (for example, certificates of deposits) and processes (for example, securitisation) to manage their asset and liability positions. Most institutions nowadays employ a combined management on both sides of the balance sheet, involving a wide range of sophisticated risk management instruments and procedures (see Section 10.7).

Other important aspects introduced in this chapter relate to banks' off-balance-sheet commitments and derivative instruments. OBS activities are transactions that are not recorded on a bank's balance sheet, such as letters of credit, unused overdraft facilities and guarantees. Bank managers' objectives of achieving relatively high levels of profitability and safety have induced them to engage increasingly in OBS business that provides fee income; this includes derivatives business, securities underwriting and foreign exchange trading. These latter activities may expose the bank to new risks and, as discussed in Chapter 9, recent changes in the international accounting standards demand that they should appear *on* balance sheet at fair value.

10.2 Asset–liability management (ALM)

Over the past few decades, two sets of transformations have affected the composition of banks' balance sheets: on the one hand, the growing importance of the liability side, and on the other hand, the significant expansion of the interbank markets, where banks can easily buy and sell excess liquidity, even overnight. As a result of these major changes, modern banks have become more likely to undertake a co-ordinated management of both sides of the balance sheet rather than focusing on just the asset side. The main concerns and objectives of a bank manager on the asset and liability sides are summarised in Figure 10.1.

A bank manages its assets well when it maximises the returns on loans and securities, for example by increasing loan screening and monitoring activities and by choosing low-credit-risk/high-return customers. Moreover, a bank will aim to diversify its portfolio of assets to avoid over-investing in a single sector. Another important objective of asset management involves decisions concerning the amount of liquid assets and reserves to keep on hand, taking into account the trade-off between profitability and liquidity. (Recall that liquid assets tend to yield low returns, so a bank that holds a high proportion of liquid assets on its balance sheet is likely to have lower income and profits.) On the liability side, a bank manager will aim to acquire funds at low cost when operating in the money markets (by borrowing from

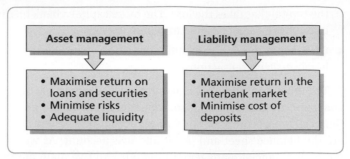

Figure 10.1 Forms of asset management versus liability management

other banks or by offering negotiable CDs) and at the same time minimising the interest paid on deposits.

The co-ordinated and simultaneous decision on financing and investing is the essence of **asset–liability management**. ALM is typically associated with the management of interest rate risk and bank liquidity and its goals include controlling a bank's value and profits, subject to taking a certain level of risk and maintaining an appropriate level of safety, as shown in Figure 10.2. Box 10.1 illustrates the ALM process in practice.

Post the 2007–2009 crisis, it has become apparent that banking institutions should take a more 'holistic' view of their balance sheet. A survey of 43 leading financial institutions carried out by PwC (2009a) emphasised several key challenges to the way in which banks manage their balance sheet. Among the main concerns are that in recent years banks have evolved to become more silo-driven organisations, with an increased focus on lines of business as 'profit centres' (see Box 10.2). Equally, bank risk departments have become progressively more concerned about the measurement, management and monitoring of individual risk classes. One of the lessons from the global financial crisis has been the need for banking institutions to expand the scope of balance sheet management and to take a more corporate-wide strategic focus. A key finding of PwC's (2009a) survey is that leading banks are indeed moving in this direction.

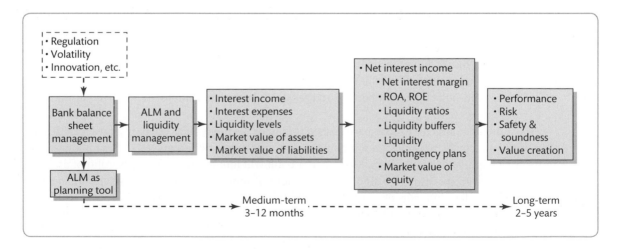

Figure 10.2 Goals of ALM and liquidity management

BOX 10.1 ASSET–LIABILITY MANAGEMENT IN PRACTICE

Sinkey (2002) defines ALM as an intermediate-term planning function (3–12 months) designed to move the bank in the direction of its long-run plan (2–5 years) while maintaining the flexibility to adapt to short-run (monthly) changes. In addition to the planning aspect of ALM, direction and control of the levels, changes (flows) and mix of assets, liabilities and capital are integral parts of overall balance sheet management. From an accounting point of view, the key variables of ALM are NII (net interest income), ROA (return on assets) and ROE (return on equity). From an economic point of view the key variable is the MVE (market value of equity). Sinkey (2002) identifies a three-stage approach to balance sheet co-ordinated management.

Stage I is a general approach that focuses on co-ordinated management of a bank's assets, liabilities and capital. Stage I requires co-ordination of the various specific functions that can be identified in Stage II.

Stage I: Global (or general) approach	
Asset management	Liability management
	Capital management

Stage II distinguishes between the various components of a bank's balance sheet used in co-ordinating its overall portfolio management. Stage II is based on planning, directing and controlling the levels, changes and mix of the various balance sheet accounts, which generate the bank's income–expense statement (Stage III).

Stage II: Identification of specific components	
Reserve-position management	Liability management
Liquidity management	Reserve-position liability management
Investment/securities management	Loan-position liability management
Loan management	Long-term debt management
Fixed-asset management	Capital management

Stage III illustrates a bank's profit and loss account as generated by its on- and off-balance-sheet items, given prices and interest rates.

Stage III: Balance sheet generates profit and loss account
Profit = Interest revenue − interest expenses − provision for loan losses + non-interest revenue − non-interest expense − taxes.

Policies to achieve objectives:

1 Spread management.
2 Loan quality.
3 Generating fee income and service charges.
4 Control of non-interest operating expenses.
5 Tax management.
6 Capital adequacy.

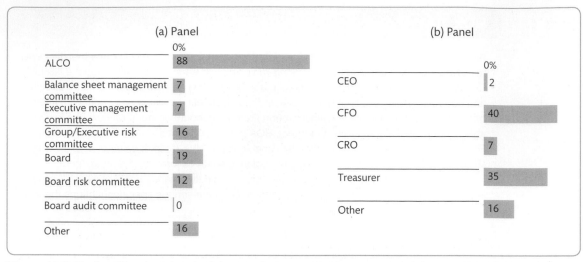

Figure 10.3 Body with primary oversight over balance sheet management (panel a) and ALM unit reporting line (panel b)

Source: PwC (2009a).

Typically, the ALM role is carried out by a bank's asset and liability committee (ALCO). This committee can be considered the single most important management group and function in a bank. The committee should also consider the importance of the management of capital (see Section 10.4). The aforementioned PwC survey highlighted the fact that most banks had recently done so by either creating dedicated 'capital management committees' or ensuring a broader mandate for the existing ALCO to focus on capital. The responsibility for the ALM unit is typically split between the **Treasury** and the chief financial officer (CFO) functions (see Figure 10.3). The next section highlights the importance of ALM in the context of liquidity management.

BOX 10.2 THE 'BANK WITHIN THE BANK' AND THE FUND TRANSFER PRICING (FTP) PROCESS

The Treasury division has a crucial role in the management of a bank as it has to ensure that it 1) has a sufficient amount of cash (liquidity management); 2) holds an adequate level of capital (capital management); and 3) can raise funds as and if needed (funding management).

The functions of the Treasury department are evolving rapidly, mainly due to the post-crisis regulatory reforms that increased the liquidity constraints (i.e. Basel III) and the ongoing economic instability.

Among the key challenges of modern banks are to raise margins and create shareholder value in a constrained environment – recent reports emphasise how the Treasury function is expected to play an increasingly critical role in shaping banks' strategies towards these goals.[1] A useful way to interpret the role of the Treasury is as a 'bank within a bank', as depicted in Figure 10.4. It shows that the FTP technique considers assets and liabilities simultaneously as they both are needed to produce the bank's income.

---

[1] In addition to improving risk–return ratios the Treasury has other challenges such as the process of maximising capital efficiency and deleveraging banks' balance sheets.

BOX 10.2 The 'bank within the bank' and the fund transfer pricing (FTP) process (*continued*)

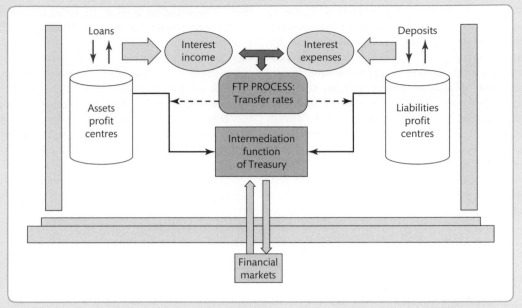

Figure 10.4 Profit centres and the FTP process

Source: Adapted from Brammertz *et al.* (2011).

The focus on FTP has intensified because it is considered as a framework through which the Treasury function can become more of a strategic balance sheet management function that can significantly contribute to optimise the banks' risk/return profiles. This means that internal funds pricing governance and internal funding policy will increasingly have implications for liquidity risk management and the overall bank ALM. The Treasury has a central function in the FTP process because it acts as an intermediary between the asset profit centres and the liability profit centres within the bank; outside the bank the Treasury intermediates with the markets. Brammertz *et al.* (2011) give a useful example

that helps understand how the Treasury makes margins and helps mitigate market risk thanks to the FTP framework.

Table 10.1 shows the case of a bank that at time *t* enters two transactions simultaneously at different rates with the respective margins.

The Treasury essentially acts as an intermediary between the asset profit centre and the liability profit centre because it finances the three-year loan at the current risk-free rate of 5.6 per cent and buys the one-year deposit at the risk-free rate of 5 per cent. FTP has the advantage of allocating profitability between profit centres, including the Treasury which at the end of the process gains a net margin

Table 10.1 Profit centres and the FTP process: a simple example

	Transactions	Interest rate (received and paid)	Interest-free market rate paid to Treasury	Margins
Asset profit centre	3-year loan	6%	5.6%	0.4%
Liability profit centre	1-year deposit	4.5%	5%	0.5%
Treasury			0.6%	

Source: Adapted from Brammertz *et al.* (2011).

> **BOX 10.2 The 'bank within the bank' and the fund transfer pricing (FTP) process** (*continued*)

of 0.6 per cent. This margin can be considered as its reward for acting as an intermediary and for mitigating market risk. This is because after one year the deposit has matured, so if we assume that the liability profit centre will have to pay higher rates to new customers, to leave the margin relatively stable the Treasury will make fewer profits, while the asset and liability profit centres will not be affected by market changes. Of course, if after one year rates move in the opposite direction, the Treasury will make a profit (Brammertz *et al.,* 2011).

More generally, FTP can be defined as a complex 'internal measurement and allocation system that assigns a profit contribution to funds gathered,

lent, or invested by a bank'. Transfer pricing is a critical component of risk transfer, profitability measurement, capital allocation and specifying business unit incentives, as it allocates net interest income to the various products or business units of a bank. Most banking institutions utilise **funds transfer pricing (FTP)** in different forms and to varying degrees of complexity. Accordingly, a wide range of practical application and sophistication exists across the banking industry. As a critical component of a bank's profitability measurement process, FTP allocates net interest income to various products or business units (Moody's Analytics, 2011b).

10.3   Liquidity management and the importance of reserves

Liquidity in banking is a key factor because a bank needs to ensure that it keeps enough cash or other liquid assets to meet its obligations to depositors and to satisfy customer loan demand. Essentially, a bank must always be able to meet both normal and abnormal shortfalls in anticipated cash flows. Two issues are particularly important in the context of bank liquidity. First, there is a trade-off between liquidity and profitability. This means that the bank should calculate the opportunity cost of the amount kept as liquid assets because these assets are typically either non-earning or low-yielding. Second, banks' reserves are an insurance against the costs associated with deposit outflows. Normally there are two types of reserves: required and excess. It is obvious that if the bank has only modest excess reserves, in the case of a large deposit outflow it will need changes in other parts of the balance sheet and will require a co-ordinated ALM approach. In particular, in the event of a bank having to obtain liquidity it has four options:

- borrowing from other banks;
- selling some of its securities;
- selling some of its loans; or
- borrowing from the central bank.

A bank experiencing a liquidity problem normally has to act quickly and discreetly to meet any shortfalls. If other institutions or depositors were to become aware that the bank had a liquidity shortage, it could create a run on the bank and possibly lead to insolvency. That is why selling off or calling in loans may be problematic for the troubled bank and the option of borrowing funds from the central bank may be a last resort (see Chapter 5 on the LOLR function of the central bank). It follows that liquidity and solvency are inextricably linked.

10.4 Capital adequacy management

In Chapter 9 we illustrated a simple way to define bank capital as the value of assets minus the value of liabilities. Capital in banking is one of the major balance sheet concerns because it signals to what extent the bank is safe and sound, in other words 'solvent'. In contrast to bank liquidity, that is the ability of a bank to pay its obligations when they fall due, solvency is the ability of a bank to repay its obligations ultimately. As for bank liquidity, there is a trade-off between safety and returns because the higher the capital, the lower the ROE.

However, from the bank's point of view, capital is costly because higher capital means lower returns for equity holders. From the point of view of regulators, capital is a necessary buffer to absorb possible losses.

The distinction between regulatory and economic capital is often made. *Regulatory capital* is the amount of capital required by regulators. (Recently the issue of how much capital is adequate has become an area of substantial discussion, due to the interest that domestic and international regulators have in ensuring a safe and sound financial sector. For details on recent developments on this issue see Chapter 7.) *Economic capital* is the capital that a bank believes it should hold to cover the risks it is undertaking.

Banks manage their economic capital, directing capital resources to different areas of business that aim to generate the highest risk-adjusted returns. So if a bank feels there are two business areas that carry the same risk, say unsecured lending to consumers and unsecured lending to SMEs, but the former generates higher returns, more capital should be held against the former to develop this business to boost returns as the risks are the same as in SMEs lending but returns are higher. Assuming that regulatory capital requirements are the same, the bank should reduce capital dedicated to SMEs lending and redirect it to unsecured consumer lending. The efficient allocation of capital throughout the bank is critical if the bank wishes to maximise performance. Banks will scrutinise all areas of their business, looking at where economic capital can best be employed to generate the best risk-adjusted returns.

10.5 Off-balance-sheet (OBS) business in banking

Nowadays banks do a considerable amount of OBS business. Typically, these activities have no asset backing and are sometimes referred to as contingent liabilities business. They generally refer to promises or commitments to undertake certain types of business in the future (by definition, *contingent* means 'dependent on something that may or may not occur'). For instance, an unused overdraft facility will be recorded as an OBS activity. In addition, banks can transfer risk off balance sheet by underwriting business and various other commitments and guarantees.

For the bank, the earnings generated from OBS operations are fee-related and so long as the activity is contingent, it would not (until recently at least – see Box 10.5) be reported on the bank's balance sheet as there is no asset or liability. However, when a contingent event occurs, the item or activity will be written in the asset (or liability) side of the balance sheet or a non-interest income item (or expense) will be generated in the income statement. Prior to the 1988 Basel Accord, no capital reserves or advancing were required for these types of operations. Moreover, OBS banking does not involve deposit funding (cash asset reserves are not needed).

In recent years, bank managers' increasing concerns about earnings and safety induced them to engage in OBS activities, securitisation and loan sales. Recall from Chapter 9 that a bank ROE is calculated as net income/total equity and can be decomposed into two parts: the ROA (net income/total assets) – which measures average profit generated relative to the bank's assets – and the equity multiplier (EM = assets/equity), so that $ROE = ROA \times EM$. If banks wish to increase their profitability, they can engage in OBS business so that they restrain asset growth and increase fee income. These effects tend to increase ROA and reduce EM, all other things being equal, and meet the regulators' requirements of improved profitability and stronger capital positions.[2]

10.5.1 Loan commitments, guarantees and letters of credit

There are a number of other OBS activities that banks undertake to generate fee income (some of which were introduced in Chapter 4), including:

- loan commitments (including overdrafts);
- financial guarantees (including letters of credit);
- securities underwriting;
- other financial services.

Loan commitments are promises to lend up to a pre-specified amount to a pre-specified customer at pre-specified terms. Many business loans are made under loan commitments. For example, a bank may avail £20 million to GlaxoSmithKline Ltd over a period of two years for building a brand new chemical plant. Over the set period the borrower may decide to use only part (or even none) of the loan commitment. The terms of the contract will also specify how the interest rate will be computed and whether the rate is fixed or variable. Typically, loan commitments involve large amounts and generate relatively low bank margins. Banks are compensated by the fees charged for making such commitments. The bank generally receives compensation for a loan commitment in a variety of ways (Greenbaum and Thakor, 2007), including:

- a commitment fee: expressed as a percentage of the total commitment and paid up front by the borrower;
- a usage fee: levied on the unused portion of the credit line;
- servicing fees: on the borrowed amount to cover the bank's transactions costs; and
- compensating balances requirements: deposit balances the borrower must keep at the bank during the commitment, computed as a fraction of the total commitment and on which the bank pays below market interest rates.

It is also common to distinguish between the following types of loan commitments:

- Revolving lines of credit: where a bank gives a line of credit and commits for several years ahead.

---

[2] The Basel Capital Accord, however, requires banks to convert the OBS activities into credit or asset equivalents in the calculation of risk-weighted assets. For more information, see Chapter 7.

- Unused overdraft facility: an agreed amount by which a bank account can be overdrawn; the bank, however, can withdraw the agreed facility under certain circumstances. Typically, the customer will be charged a set fee for the provision of an overdraft facility. This fee is often calculated as a fairly high percentage of the total value of the overdraft.

- Note issuance facilities (NIF): essentially the bank (or a syndicate of banks if it is a large loan) arranges and guarantees the availability of funds from the issue of a succession of short-term notes (commonly three or six months). In the case of these notes not being taken up by the market, the bank will provide the funds.

Financial guarantees are instruments used to enhance the credit standing of a borrower to help ensure a lender against default and lower the cost of borrowing. They are designed to ensure the timely repayment of the principal and interest from a loan even if the borrower goes bankrupt or cannot perform a contractual obligation. With a financial guarantee a bank underwrites the obligations for a third party, thus relieving the counterparty from having to assess the ability of the customer to meet the terms of the contract. Common examples of financial guarantees are commercial letters of credit and banker's acceptances (see also Chapter 4).

A **commercial letter of credit** is a document issued by a bank stating its commitment to pay someone a specific amount of money on behalf of a buyer as long as the seller meets certain terms and conditions. LOCs are used to facilitate trade where there is uncertainty, for instance in international dealings when an exporter based (say) in Canada has limited knowledge of the European importer's ability to pay and limited ability to enforce contracts across borders. The importer arranges an LOC to be issued by its bank guaranteeing payment in exchange for a fee for bearing the risk that the importer may default, as shown in Figure 10.5. By reducing the default risk confronting the exporter, the issue of an LOC reduces the asymmetric information problems between the two parties. It should be noted that with a commercial LOC the importer's bank usually advances the payment and is repaid by its customer.

Upon presentation of the necessary documents, the importer's bank will issue either an immediate payment (a 'sight draft') or a 'time draft' promising payment at some future date. In the latter case, the instrument becomes a **banker's acceptance**, which is marketable and usually quite liquid. If the exporter decides to hold the acceptance, it essentially extends the loan to the importer. Alternatively, if the acceptance is sold in the secondary market, the holder of the acceptance will provide funding, but the bank guarantees payment.

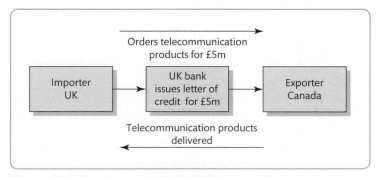

Figure 10.5 Simple example of a letter of credit

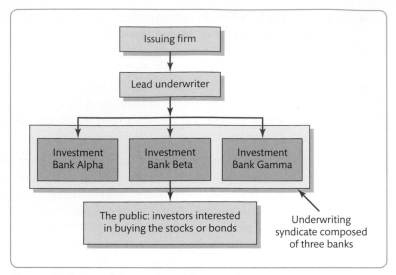

Figure 10.6 Securities underwriting syndicate

A **standby letter of credit** is similar to the commercial LOC in that it is a financial instrument that guarantees the performance of a party, say the importer as in the previous example, in a commercial or financial transaction. However, while a LOC always involves a funding transaction, in a standby LOC the importer's bank makes a payment only if its customer fails to fulfil their obligations (i.e. in case of default). Therefore, the standby LOC issued by the importer's bank creates an obligation for the bank to compensate the exporter only in the event of a performance failure. The importer will obviously pay a fee for this service and will be liable to its bank for any payments made by the bank under the standby LOC.

Securities underwriting is a type of business typically undertaken by investment banks whereby a bank agrees to buy a set amount of the securities that are not taken up in an issue. For instance, investment banks charge a compensation fee for taking IPOs (initial public offerings) to market (sometimes there is an underwriting syndicate, as shown in Figure 10.6); they also issue stocks and bonds for established listed companies in the secondary market. This guarantees the issuer that the whole of the issue is taken up and a fee is paid to the banks providing the underwriting service (see Chapter 4 for details on syndicated lending).

Other financial services that generate fee income and do not lead to a balance sheet entry can include, for example, the advisory services that banks give to organisations that are planning to merge with other institutions or to acquire other firms. In Europe, all commercial banks have been allowed by the Second Banking Co-Ordination Directive to provide these services that in the past were undertaken only by investment banks (as have US commercial banks by the Gramm–Leach–Bliley Act of 1999 and Japanese commercial banks by Japan's 'Big Bang' reforms of 1999).

Another example of a financial service that generates non-interest income is the case where the bank originates a loan in exchange for a fee and then transfers it to another bank, which will provide funding and servicing for the loan (see Box 10.3 on the **process of deconstruction**). Similarly, a loan sale involves a contract whereby the bank that originated the loan removes it from its balance sheet by selling all or part of the cash streams to an outside buyer. An introduction to these activities is given in Section 10.8.

BOX 10.3 THE PROCESS OF DECONSTRUCTION OF LENDING ACTIVITY

Banks' lending activity has traditionally been composed of the following four main parts:

- Loan origination:
  - administration and processing of paperwork and documentation related to the loan application;
  - undertaking risk analysis (screening) and assessing the creditworthiness of the potential borrower;
  - design of loan contracts and loan pricing.
- Provision of funding to the borrower:
  - raising finance;
  - holding the asset on the balance sheet;
  - allocating capital to the risk.
- Servicing:
  - collecting loan payments;
  - bookkeeping.
- Undertaking monitoring activity:
  - post-lending monitoring to control for credit risk;
  - diversification to control default risk.

As a result of changes in regulation and financial innovation, modern banking institutions can specialise in providing only some of the component parts of the lending function described above. This process of 'deconstruction' of the lending function has two main effects. On the one hand, it allows individual parts of the process of providing loans to be transferred to highly specialised separate financial firms (not necessarily banks) that would have not been able to enter the banking market otherwise due to high barriers to entry. On the other hand, it encourages banks to sell individual loans or pool together a bundle of homogenous loans and securitise them for risk management and other purposes.

Over the past two decades, financial innovation has transformed intermediation from a process involving a single financial institution to a process now broken down into several steps, each step carried out by a different specialised institution. As pointed out by Adrian *et al.* (2013), with specialisation have come significant reductions in the cost of intermediation, together with improvements in the terms of liquidity offered to borrowers. However, the aim to reduce costs has also pushed this type of financial activity 'into the shadows', in order to reduce or eliminate the cost associated with prudential supervision and regulation, investor disclosure and taxes. This relatively recent development, the so-called shadow banking system, quickly grew to become equal in size to that of the traditional system. However, the process was not without problems, as became apparent during the 2007–2009 global financial crisis.

10.6   Loan sales and the process of securitisation

Loan sales have existed for many years. A loan sale occurs when a bank originates a loan and then decides to sell it to another legal entity, usually a financial intermediary. Where the bank is selling only part of the loan the operation is called loan participation or loan

Table 10.2 Simplified bank balance sheet before and after loan sales (in £mil)

Balance sheet before loan sale (with or without recourse)			
Assets		**Liabilities**	
Cash assets	£5	Deposit	£45
Loans	£45	Equity	£5
Total	£50	Total	£50
Balance sheet after loan sale (with or without recourse)			
Assets		**Liabilities**	
Cash assets	£5	Deposit	£45
Loans	£35		
New investments	£10	Equity	£5
Total	£50	Total	£50
Off-balance sheet (loan sale with recourse only)			
		Contingent credit risk liability	
		Loan sale	£10

Source: Adapted from Saunders and Cornett (2012).

syndication (see also Chapter 4). As the loan is sold or transferred, it is removed from the bank's balance sheet. However, the risk may stay with the originating bank if the loan is sold *with recourse.* In this case, the buyer can put the loan back to the selling bank if it goes bad; thus the bank retains the contingent liability. If the loan is sold without recourse then the loan buyer bears all the risk. Table 10.2 shows a simplified bank balance sheet before and after the loan sale. If the loan is sold without recourse it is removed from the bank balance sheet, and the bank has no explicit liability if it eventually goes bad. This means that the buyer – and not the bank originating the loan – bears the credit risk in full. In the (less frequent) case of a loan sold with recourse, the bank retains a contingent liability, which is written off balance sheet. Correspondingly, the buyer can put the loan back on the bank balance sheet.

It is possible to distinguish between three main types of loan sales contracts:

- **Participations in loans:** the loan purchaser is not a partner to the loan contract between the bank selling the loans and the borrower so that the initial contract between loan seller and borrower remains in place after the sale. The buyer of a participation in an existing loan can exercise only partial control over changes in the loan contract's terms and bears significant risks in case of failure of either the bank or the borrower.

- **Assignments:** refers to buying a share in a loan syndication with some contractual control and rights over the borrower. The ownership of the loan is transferred to the buyer, who thereby acquires a direct claim against the borrower. The borrower in some cases has to agree to the sale of the loan before an assignment can be made.

- **Loan strips:** a third and less common type of loan sale is a loan strip. These are short-dated pieces of a longer-term loan. The buyer of a strip is entitled to a fraction of the expected income from a loan while the bank retains the risk of borrower default.

From the point of view of a bank manager, selling loans to outside investors is an important method of funding bank operations, for various reasons (Saunders and Cornett, 2012):

- they allow the replacement of lower-yielding assets with higher-yielding assets when market interest rates increase;

- they can increase the bank's liquidity if loans are replaced with more marketable assets such as government securities;

- they help in the management of credit and interest rate risk;

- they slow the growth of banks' assets, which helps maintain the balance between capital and credit risk;

- they help diversify the bank's assets and lower its cost of capital (on this last issue, see Section 9.4.3).

In particular, banks trying to comply with the Basel capital regulation will find it cheaper to boost their capital-to-asset ratio by reducing assets instead of increasing capital since equity capital is more costly than debt for tax reasons.

PwC (2013) has noted how loan sales are being strategically used by European banks that are deleveraging (see Box 10.4).

In contrast to loan sales the process of **securitisation** is more recent. The first issue took place in the United States in the 1970s, compared with 1985 in the United Kingdom (see

BOX 10.4 LOAN SALES AND MODERN BANKS' STRATEGIES

The growing market for loan transactions will play an increasingly important role in banks' strategic decision-making over the next few years. Banks in Western Europe, and to a lesser extent the US, are likely to remain the major source of loan sales. European banks' non-core loans at the end of 2011 were estimated at more than €2.5tn, equivalent to 6% of total banking assets. Non-performing loans were valued at more than €1tn, and the current slowdown in many eurozone economies suggests this figure may grow.

The past two years have seen European banks dispose of loans with total face values in the tens of billions of euro. We expect the pace of loan sales to accelerate over the next few years, as banks seek to deleverage and maximise their returns on assets.

Transactions will not only come from markets like the US, the UK, Ireland and Spain where loan sales are already running at significant levels, but also from markets such as Germany and Italy where non-core loans are substantial but deal activity has so far been comparatively low. Loan portfolio transactions will be stimulated by growing investor appetite, and by the increasing willingness of banks facing refinancing hurdles to ring-fence assets for disposal. A fresh wave of provisioning by European banks could also help to stimulate transactions by reducing bid-ask spreads.

Of course, sales are not the only means of deleveraging open to banks. Many non-core loans will refinance in the normal way or be subjected to accelerated workout, and asset swaps or structured arrangements will also play a role. Even so we expect loan transactions, already more significant than in previous credit downturns, to become an increasingly important tool of banking strategy.

Source: PwC (2013).

Table 10.3 Simplified bank balance sheet before and after securitisation (in £mil)

Balance sheet before securitisation			
Assets		Liabilities	
Cash reserves	£ 5.33	Deposits	£53.33
Long-term mortgages	£50.00	Capital	£ 2.00
Total	£55.33	Total	£55.33
Balance sheet after securitisation			
Assets		Liabilities	
Cash reserves	£ 5.33	Deposits	£53.33
Cash proceeds from mortgage securitisation	£50.00	Capital	£ 2.00
Total	£55.33	Total	£55.33

Source: Adapted from Saunders and Cornett (2012).

Chapter 18 for more details on securitisation). Until the 2007–2009 crisis, securitisation markets were growing rapidly; however, the US market was significantly more developed than the UK and the EU. Securitisation is a structured finance technique whereby a bank transforms its illiquid assets (traditionally held until maturity) into securities, which are then sold to investors. The bank achieves this by pooling the assets and selling them to a special-purpose vehicle (SPV), which in turn finances the purchase of the assets via the issuance of securities (commonly known as asset-backed securities). As shown in Table 10.3, securitisation removes financial assets (in this example a pool of mortgage loans) from the balance sheet.

In Table 10.3, the commercial bank's long-term mortgages have been replaced on the balance sheet by the cash received, which can then be used to pay down liabilities. In the example below, the bank has increased its liquidity by £50 million. Therefore after securitisation the balance sheet shows fewer assets and liabilities (or at the margin does not add assets to it) than it would if the bank originating the mortgages had used a straight debt offering as a means of raising money. This improves ROE and the capital-to-assets ratio and prevents these from declining, all other things being equal.

10.7 Derivative business in banking

Financial derivatives markets have been growing rapidly in recent years. Derivatives are contracts involving rights or obligations relating to purchases or sales of underlying real or financial assets (e.g. gold and shares respectively), or relating to payments to be made in respect of movements in indices (e.g. the London FTSE 100). These rights and obligations are related to – or derived from – the underlying transactions, so they have been given the general name of *derivatives*. The major types of derivatives are futures, forwards, options and swaps and these are discussed in more detail in Sections 10.7.1 to 10.7.4. With these contracts a bank has the potential to generate a profit or suffer a loss on an asset that it currently does not own (and therefore these transactions were traditionally recorded as off-balance-sheet business). Recent developments in international accounting standards have brought radical changes to the way in which companies listed on the stock market present their financial

BOX 10.5 FINANCIAL DERIVATIVES FROM OFF TO ON THE BALANCE SHEET

Until recently financial derivatives did not appear on listed banks' balance sheets. They were accounted for using historical cost accounting and presented in the *Notes* to their financial statements. In the mid-2000s the way in which listed banks account for their derivatives and other contracts was radically transformed.

The reasons for these changes in accounting requirements are linked to two main factors: (1) the urgency of international harmonisation of accounting standards in an increasingly global financial marketplace; and (2) the general need for more transparency in disclosing banks' real exposures, particularly on derivative contracts that often do not attract an initial cost. As a result banks must report all derivatives, other held-for-trading financial assets/financial liabilities and available-for-sale financial assets *on* the balance sheet measured at fair value. As explained in Chapter 9, derivatives can represent a relatively large proportion of banks' total assets. Figure 9.2 shows that in 2012 the asset side of Barclays Bank's balance sheet is evenly divided between loans and financial derivatives, and they represent around 31 per cent of the total, both in terms of assets and liabilities.

In terms of accounting standards, the key requirements are set out in the 1998 US Financial Accounting Standards (FAS 133): *Accounting for Derivative Instruments and Hedging Activities* and in the International Accounting Standards (IAS 39): *Financial Instruments: Recognition and Measurement.* These standards are quite complex and have been subject to a number of modifications and amendments over the last decade (PwC, 2009b). In 2008, the work began to replace IAS 39. The first two instalments of the new standards deal with the classification and measurement of financial assets and liabilities and were issued as IFRS 9 *Financial Instruments* in November 2009 and October 2010, respectively. The IFRS 9 standards aim to provide an improved and simplified set of requirements for financial instruments and will require application for annual periods beginning on or after 1 January 2015 (**www.ifrs.org**).

Source: PwC (2009b).

instruments. As a result banks are required to report financial derivatives *on* balance sheet (see Box 10.5).

The rights and obligations associated with derivatives contracts are relatively complex but these instruments often have the ability of being able to smooth out price changes in the underlying assets – on the *cash market* as it is often termed. Typically, for there to be a derivatives market, the associated cash market needs to be liquid – easy to trade in without moving the price of an asset (although prices can change for other reasons) – and volatile. 'Volatile' in this instance means 'changeable in price'. If the price cannot be moved then there is no opportunity to make a short-term profit by trading in that asset. The link between the cash market and the derivatives market is a process of buying and selling between the two, known as **arbitrage** – buying in one market and selling in another in order to exploit price differentials. If purchases are made in the lower price market and simultaneous sales are achieved in the higher price market, then as purchases will tend to raise prices and the sales will tend to lower them, the outcome will be that price differences will diminish.

Derivative products that are traded in organised exchanges are described as 'standard' contracts. However, banks may want to strengthen customer relationships by offering products that are tailored to customers. For example, forwards contracts can only be traded over the counter (OTC) (see Box 10.7 on the differences between trading derivatives in official exchanges and OTC).

Derivative products can be used by banks to manage positions or 'hedge' for risk management purposes. **Hedging** involves reducing the risk of exposure to changes in market prices or rates that may affect bank income and value, through taking an offsetting position. For instance, a bank will be hedging risk if it engages in a financial transaction that offsets a long position (i.e. a market position in which a bank has bought an asset and thus owns it) by taking an additional short position at some future date (that is, the sale of an asset that will be delivered at a future date). Alternatively, the bank can offset a short position (the bank has sold an asset that will be delivered at a future date) by taking an additional long position (that is to buy an asset) at some future date.

Box 10.6 gives a brief overview of how credit derivative instruments can be used in bank financial management.

BOX 10.6 HOW CAN CREDIT DERIVATIVES BE USED IN BANK FINANCIAL MANAGEMENT?

Credit derivatives

Credit derivatives are swap, forward and option contracts that transfer risk and return from one counterparty to another without actually transferring the ownership of the underlying assets. Similar products have been around for centuries and include letters of credit, government export credit and mortgage guarantees.

Credit derivatives differ from their predecessors because they are traded separately from the underlying assets; in contrast, the earlier products were contracts between an issuer and a guarantor.

Credit derivatives are an ideal tool for lenders who want to reduce their exposure to a particular borrower but find themselves unwilling (say, for tax- or cost-related reasons) to sell outright their claims on that borrower.

Types of credit derivatives

The three major types of credit derivatives are credit default swaps, total-rate-of-return swaps and credit-spread put options.

Credit default swaps transfer the potential loss on a 'reference asset' that can result from specific credit 'events' such as default, bankruptcy, insolvency and credit-rating downgrades. Marketable bonds are the most popular form of reference asset because of their price transparency. While bank loans have the potential to become the dominant form of reference asset (because of their sheer quantity), this is impeded by the fact that loans are more heterogeneous and illiquid than bonds.

CDS involve a 'protection buyer', who pays a periodic or upfront fee to a 'protection seller' in exchange for a contingent payment if there is a credit event (see Figure 10.7). Some CDS swaps are based on a basket of assets and pay out on a first-to-default basis, whereby the contract terminates and pays out if any of the assets in the basket are in default. CDS are the largest component of the global credit derivatives market.

Total-return swaps (TRS) transfer the returns and risks on an underlying reference asset from one party to another. TRS involve a 'total return buyer', who pays a periodic fee to a 'total return seller' and receives the

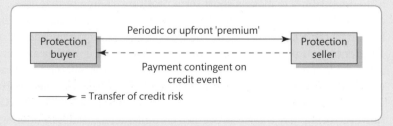

Figure 10.7 A default swap

BOX 10.6 How can credit derivatives be used in bank financial management? (*continued*)

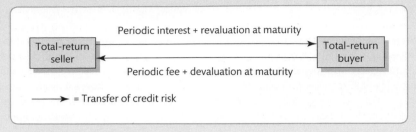

Figure 10.8 A total-rate-of-return swap

total economic performance of the underlying reference asset in return. 'Total return' includes all interest payments on the reference asset plus an amount based on the change in the asset's market value. If the price goes up, the total-return buyer gets an amount equal to the appreciation of the value, and if the price declines, the buyer pays an amount equal to the depreciation in value (see Figure 10.8). If a credit event occurs prior to maturity, the TRS usually terminates and a price settlement is made immediately.

Credit-spread put option contracts isolate and capture devaluations in a reference asset that are independent of shifts in the general yield curve. Essentially, they are default swaps that stipulate spread widening as an 'event' (see Figure 10.9). The spread is usually calculated as the yield differential between the reference bond and an interest rate swap of the same maturity. Unlike default or total-rate-of-return swaps, counterparties do not have to define

the specific credit events – the payout occurs regardless of the reasons for the credit spread movement. Spread puts usually involve the 'put buyer' paying an upfront fee to a 'put seller' in exchange for a contingent payment if the spread widens beyond a pre-agreed threshold level.

The advantage of the spread put's detachment from defined credit events became particularly apparent during the periods of turmoil in Asian, Latin American and Eastern European financial markets during the late 1990s, where spreads widened dramatically in the absence of any 'event' as defined in typical default-swap documentation. However, credit-spread derivatives can be difficult to hedge and very complicated to model and price, and most investors and hedgers can accomplish their objectives with cheaper CDS.

For a more detailed treatment of how banks use a variety of derivatives to manage risk, see Bessis (2009).

Source: Adapted from Kiff and Morrow (2000).

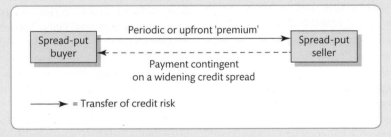

Figure 10.9 A credit-spread put option

It is also common to distinguish between **micro-hedging**, which is when a bank hedges a transaction associated with an individual asset, liability or commitment, and **macro-hedging**, which is when a bank uses futures (or other derivatives) to hedge the entire balance sheet (e.g. the aggregate portfolio interest rate risk). It is obvious that the bank could also use derivatives to speculate (i.e. to take a position with the objective of making a profit) on anticipated price moves.

BOX 10.7 DERIVATIVE PRODUCTS: OFFICIAL EXCHANGES AND OTC MARKETS

Derivatives can be traded either on an official exchange or OTC. In Europe the major derivative exchanges are currently the Eurex Exchange (owned by Deutsche Börse) and IntercontinentalExchange (ICE) who acquired NYSE Euronext in 2013 and through this owns LIFFE, the London International Financial Futures and Options Exchange). In the United States, the major exchanges include the US Chicago Board Options Exchange and Chicago Mercantile Exchange. London remains the main centre for OTC derivatives transactions.

The first derivatives markets to be developed were the exchange-based markets and clearing houses. These are highly organised markets regulated by their owners who are usually traders. It is the exchange that decides on the:

- standard units – currency, size, maturity – to be traded, and the times when trading begins and ceases each day;

- rules of the clearing house, through which all deals are routed, with the result that a deal between (say) X who sells to Y becomes a deal between X selling to the clearing house which in turn sells to Y. Conversely, Y pays the clearing house, which pays X (irrespective of whether Y pays the clearing house or X delivers to the clearing house). The clearing house interposes itself between all counterparties, thereby shouldering the burden of default and lessening the risk. In effect, it standardises the counterparty, just as deals are for standard products. It also facilitates delivery;

- margin requirements, which all members have to deposit with the clearing house, to ensure that default is unlikely. In addition, all investors must maintain margins with their brokers who are, of course, members of the exchange. The initial margin required is usually 2–10 per cent of the value of the contract. However, if the contract involves a party making a loss that is greater than the initial margin, further deposits are required on a daily basis from the losing party. These are called 'variation margins'. So, as the price moves they (the current loser) must pay the counterparty each day a variation margin based on the day-end settlement price;

- marking to market – a process by which all outstanding deals are revalued daily because prices may change frequently. In other words, historic pricing/costing is not used because prices may be volatile. Marking to market is done by the clearing house for all the exchange's members and, again, by members who act as brokers. The latter 'mark to market' all their transactions with their clients. As margin payments are adjusted according to the price changes in the underlying asset on a daily basis, the exposure to risk experienced by the exchange is limited.

Derivative products can also be traded OTC. These markets have no official membership, and banks, non-bank financial firms and (typically) large corporations deal with each other via telephone, fax and computer links. Regulation is undertaken by each country's regulator and coordinated by the Bank for International Settlements. Within these markets private contracts are established between sets of parties without any clearing house involvement.

OTC markets are characterised by the existence of *quote vendors,* providing real-time price information on computer screens. Firms providing this service include Reuters, Bloomberg News Service and the McClatchy Company. Quote vendors also link into the exchange markets, thus providing a comprehensive price information service. They get their OTC prices from dealers in the markets.

To summarise, the main advantages of trading in an organised exchange versus OTC markets are:

Organised exchange	OTC market
• Guarantees every contract, meaning that counterparty risk of default is reduced	• Investors obtain a contract which is tailored exactly to their required quantity and maturity, unlike an exchange's standard contract
• Usually requires capital base and margins (initial and variation) to be taken	• The impact of deals on prices tends to be more gentle than on an exchange where liquidity is said to be more 'concentrated'
• Constantly monitors players and holds a clearing fund	• When the counterparty is a well-established commercial bank regulated by a competent regulatory body, the counterparty risk is believed to be minimal

Box 10.7 Derivative products: official exchanges and OTC markets (*continued*)

However, trading OTC has a number of disadvantages that can be summarised as follows:

- There is no clearing house to eliminate counterparty risk, although banks are increasingly seeking security from counterparties.

- There is no daily margining, which increases the risk arising from counterparty default.

- There is a limited secondary market.

- Documentation can be more complex than on an exchange.

- Prices can be less transparent than on an exchange, although quote vendors provide as much information as possible – at a price.

Figure 10.10 shows recent trends in the OTC derivative markets. A distinction is made between six types of derivative contracts: foreign exchange, interest rate, commodities, equity, credit derivatives and other. The notional amounts (left-hand chart)

measure the overall size of the derivatives market and show that at end-June 2013 it reached $693 trillion. Among all types of derivative contracts in the global OTC market, the interest rate contracts have the highest notional amounts, totalling $577 trillion as at end-June 2013. Gross market value is the cost of replacing all outstanding contracts at current market prices. It provides an estimation of 'market risk' in terms of potential for gains (or losses) from derivative operations. Gross market value has historically proved to be a quite volatile measure – in six months alone from end-year 2012 to June 2013 it declined by $5 trillion to $20 trillion.

Finally, gross credit exposure can be defined as the gross market values after legally enforceable bilateral netting but before collateral. Recently it increased, as shown in the chart on the right-hand side. Relative to gross market values, exposures increased by four points to 19 per cent, which was the highest percentage reached since 2007.

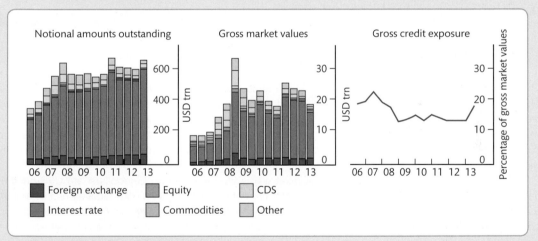

Figure 10.10 Global OTC derivatives market
Source: Bank for International Settlements (2013d) p. 6.

10.7.1 Financial futures

Financial futures are standardised contracts to deliver and pay for a real or financial asset on a pre-arranged date in the future for a specified price. Futures relate to a broad variety of financial instruments, including bonds, CDs, currencies and indexes. One of the most widely traded futures contracts is that on government Treasury bonds (T-bonds). For example, say that on 1 December 2014 a bank sells one £100,000 March T-bond futures contract at a price of £115,000. The buyer of the contract agrees to pay £115,000 for £100,000 face value of long-term bonds. At the end of March 2015, if interest rates go up, the price of the bond will fall to, say, £110,000 (on the inverse relationship between bond prices and interest rates, see Appendix A1). So the buyer of the contract will have lost £5,000 because the bank can now sell the bonds to the buyer for £115,000 and have to pay only £110,000 in the market. Box 10.8 illustrates an example of three-month Eurodollar time deposit futures.

There are various points relating to futures:

- They are traded on organised markets (futures markets) so they carry standardised terms, amounts and maturities.

- They are also highly liquid because they can be sold and bought in the secondary market.

- They are not usually intended to result in the delivery of a commodity or currency.

- They are usually offset, e.g. a purchase offset by a sale, or vice versa, before delivery.

- The clearing house requires both parties to deposit cash against the transaction and this is known as the 'initial margin'.

- If the contract involves a party making a loss that is greater than the initial margin, further deposits are required on a daily basis from the losing party. These are called 'variation margins' – so, as the price moves, the current loser must pay the counterparty each day a variation margin based on the day-end settlement price.[3]

- If a counterparty defaults on a futures contract, the exchange assumes the defaulting party's position and the payment obligations.

BOX 10.8 EXAMPLE OF THREE-MONTH EURODOLLAR TIME DEPOSIT FUTURES

The Eurodollar time deposit future is a short-term interest rate contract traded on the International Money Market which has been part of the Chicago Mercantile Exchange (CME) since 1981. In Europe this product was launched in March 2004 by the former Euronext.liffe and soon established growing liquidity while providing trading opportunities to a wide variety of market participants. Total open interest (i.e. the amount of outstanding contracts) exceeded 8 million in 2012, making this one of the most successful products in the derivatives industry.

The underlying asset is a Eurodollar time deposit with a 90-day maturity. 'Eurodollars' are US$-denominated bank deposits that are deposited in banks that are not subject to US banking regulations.[4] Therefore, Eurodollar time deposits generally pay a higher interest rate than US bank CDs and T-bills. The bet in such contracts concerns the changes in short-term interest rates relative to those rates at the time the contract is negotiated.

Table 10.4 reports the quotes for the three-month Eurodollar futures contracts from the *Financial Times* (16 September 2013). In particular, it shows the following information: the delivery date, the opening and closing settlement price, and the change in settlement price from the previous day. The next two columns report the highest and lowest price reached for the contract on the day, followed by the estimated number of contracts entered into during the day. The last column reports the open interest, which is the number of outstanding contracts at the end of the day.

---

[3] The process of restating the value of an asset or contract to reflect the market value of the asset or the value of the underlying asset is called 'marking to market'.

[4] Originally, these deposits were held, almost exclusively, in Europe, hence the collective name: Eurodollars. However, Eurodollars are now used as a collective name for US dollars held anywhere other than in the United States.

BOX 10.8 Example of three-month Eurodollar time deposit futures (*continued*)

Table 10.4 Eurodollar interest rate futures

Sep 20	Delivery	Open	Sett.	Change	High	Low	Est. vol.	Open int.
Eurodollar 3m	Oct	99.735	99.75	+0.010	99.745	99.735	16,569	21,128
Eurodollar 3m	Jan	99.705	99.70	+0.010	99.705	99.705	977	607
Eurodollar 3m	Mar	99.645	99.66	+0.015	99.675	99.645	169,621	805,657
Eurodollar 3m	Jun	99.560	99.58	+0.025	99.615	99.555	245,400	902,967

Source: Financial Times (2013) 16 September.

The contract's main characteristics are:

- each Eurodollar futures contract represents $1 million of initial face value of Eurodollar deposits maturing 90 days after contract expiration;

- contracts expire in October, January, March and June;

- they are referenced to the LIBOR for three-month sterling deposits at 11 a.m. on the last trading day (that is, the third Wednesday of the delivery month);

- they trade according to an index that equals 100 minus the rate of interest (an index of 95, for example, indicates a futures interest rate of 5 per cent);

- each basis point change in the futures rate equals a $25 change in the value of the contract (0.01% × $1 million × 90/360). Note that the change in value of the contract of $25 is known as the 'tick value'. For example, a profit of 5 ticks will be equal to $25 × 5 = $125;[5]

- gains/losses are calculated by multiplying the profit/loss on the futures trade, times the number of contracts traded, times $1 million, times 90/360. For example, a buyer of 40 contracts at 94.50, offset at 96, will:
  - gain on each futures transaction = 1.5 (150 basis points);
  - gross profits = 40 × 150 × 25 = $150,000;
  - alternatively the profit can be calculated as follows: 40 × (0.96 − 0.945) × $1,000,000 × 90/360 = $150,000;

- Eurodollar contracts are cash settled, which means that the contracts are settled with the payment of the cash difference between the future and the market price.

As a general rule,

and vice versa. Specifically as a result of a Eurodollar time deposit future contract the buyer owns a commitment from the seller to pay cash if the price of the underlying asset rises; therefore the buyer expects futures rates to fall. In contrast, the seller owns a commitment from the buyer to pay cash if the asset price falls (thus the seller expect futures rates to increase). To recap:

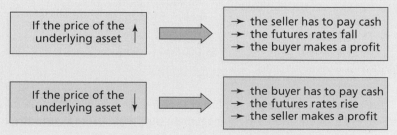

---

[5] However, trading can also occur for example in .0025 increments ($6.25/contract) or '1/4 tick' in the expiring front-month contract, and in .005 increments ($12.50/contract).

BOX 10.8 Example of three-month Eurodollar time deposit futures (*continued*)

Table 10.5 Example of long hedge using Eurodollar futures

Date	Cash market	Futures market	Basis
30/06/2014 (initial futures position)	Bank anticipates investing $1 million in Eurodollars in 5 months; current cash rate = 4.15%	Bank buys one December 2014 Eurodollar futures contract at 4.24%; price = 95.76	4.24% − 4.15% = 0.09%
09/11/2014 (close futures position)	Bank invests $1 million in 3-month Eurodollars at 3.90%	Bank sells one December 2014 Eurodollar futures contract at 4.05%; price = 95.95	4.05% − 3.90% = 0.15%
Net effect	Opportunity loss: 4.15% − 3.90% = 0.25%; 25 basis points worth $25 each = $625	Futures gain: 4.24% − 4.05% = 0.19%; 19 basis points worth $25 each = $475	Basis change: 0.15% − 0.09% = 0.06%

Interest rate futures can be used to hedge against current or future interest rate risk. This is done by taking a position that will generate profits to cover (or offset) losses related to an adverse movement in interest rates. Moreover, participants can use futures to speculate. The trader will either buy or sell the future depending on whether the contract is perceived to be undervalued or overvalued. Typically, a borrower would sell futures to protect against a future increase in interest rates, whereas a lender would purchase futures to hedge against a fall in interest rates.

Take the following example of a long hedge:

Suppose that on 30 June 2014 HSBC expects to receive a $1 million payment on 9 November 2014 and anticipates investing the funds in three-month Eurodollar time deposits. If the bank had the cash available in June it would immediately buy Eurodollar deposits; however, it will not have access to the funds for five months and over this period interest rates may fall.

In order to hedge, HSBC should buy futures contracts such that if interest rates decline, futures rates will also typically fall and the long futures position will increase in value. Table 10.5 summarises the hedge results assuming that on 30 June HSBC buys one December Eurodollar futures contract (the first to expire after November 2014) at 4.24 per cent while current interest rates are 4.15 per cent (note the 0.09 per cent 'basis' difference in rates). On 9 November HSBC sells the December 2014 Eurodollar futures because it receives the $1 million payment and invests in three-month Eurodollars in the cash market. Over the period there is effectively a decrease in interest rate by 0.25 per cent and the bank is obliged to invest at a rate of 3.90 per cent. However, the opportunity loss in the cash market ($625) is offset by a net gain in the futures market ($475) because the bank can sell the futures contract at a higher price. Overall, the bank has a cumulative income from the investment of $10,225 and its effective return is equal to 4.09 per cent.

Cumulative investment income:

Interest at 3.90% = $1,000,000 (.0390) (90/360) = $9,750

$$\text{Profit from futures trade} = \$475$$

$$\text{Total} = \$10,225$$

$$\text{Effective return} = \frac{\$10,225}{\$1,000,000} \times \frac{360}{90} = 4.09\%$$

Source: Adapted from Koch and MacDonald (2010).

The following is an example of futures contracts employed by banks to manage positions or 'hedge' for interest rate risk management purposes. (Note that future contracts can also be used to hedge foreign exchange risk.)

Assume that a bank expects interest rates to rise in the next six months. In order to protect itself, the bank can decide today to sell interest rate future contracts that are due for delivery in six months' time, that is, to promise to sell a set amount of Treasury bills at a specific price in the future. After six months the bank buys back the contracts from the exchange and thus agrees to take delivery of the same securities in the future at a specific price. As a result, the two contracts are closed out (i.e. cancelled out or 'reversed') by the futures exchange clearing house and if interest rates do not change the bank is clear of all commitments to buy or sell. If, as expected, interest rates rise in the first six months, this will imply that bond prices will decrease. The bank will make a profit, or at least will be able to offset all or part of the loss in value of the securities, because after six months these will be obtainable at a lower price. (More details on interest rate risk management can be found in Chapter 12.)

10.7.2 Forward contracts

In the case of **forward** contracts two parties directly agree to sell a real or financial asset on a pre-arranged date in the future for a specified price. They differ from financial futures contracts because they are tailor-made, privately traded over the counter and less regulated. An example of a forward contract from the foreign exchange market would be for a party to agree on 30 March to sell to another party £100,000 worth of US dollars on 31 December at a rate of (say) £1 to $1.67. The forwards:

- are non-standard contracts traded OTC entered bilaterally by two negotiating partners such as two banks;

- imply private agreements between two parties so they are customised to the specific needs of the parties;

- are highly illiquid: non-negotiable, there is no secondary market;

- are contracts where all cash flows are required to be paid at one time (on contract maturity);

- are such that if one party cannot deliver from stock, then it must buy the commodity or currency on the spot market in order to fulfil the forward contract.

The clearing house does not guarantee the operation so there is a risk of default by the counterparty.

One common type of forward contract is the **forward rate agreement (FRA)**, which gives the agents involved the opportunity to hedge against interest rate risk, thereby 'locking in' the future price of the assets. Therefore, FRAs can be used to manage interest rate risk in a way similar to that used for financial futures. Suppose that a bank has a long position in long-term bonds currently selling at par value. In order to remove the interest rate risk from the future price of the bonds the bank can decide to enter a forward contract and sell those bonds at a future date at the current price. (The buyer must have different expectations and worry that the rate on the bonds might decline in the same period.)

Other important types of forward contracts are **currency forwards**, which allow both the buyer and the seller to hedge against the risk of future fluctuations in currencies. For example, the holder of a four months' long position in dollars can offset it by entering a forward contract that requires him to sell in four months the equivalent amount, in say Euros, at the current exchange rate. This currency forward will ensure that the transaction is protected from exchange rate fluctuations that may occur over the four months. An example of a forward rate agreement is discussed in Box 10.9.

BOX 10.9 EXAMPLE OF FORWARD RATE AGREEMENT

Assume that:

- Company X expects to have to borrow £1 million in three months' time for a six-month period;

- short-term rates, say sixth-month LIBOR,[6] are at 6 per cent but Company X expects this to rise over the following three months;

- to protect against this expected rise in rates, Company X buys an FRA to cover the six-month period starting three months from now – known as a '3 against – 9 month' or 3 × 9 FRA;

- a bank quotes a rate of 6.25 per cent for such an FRA and this would enable Company X to lock into the borrowing rate of 6.25 per cent in three months' time for six months, so Company X buys the FRA;

- six-month LIBOR increases to 7 per cent in three months' time. Despite having the FRA, Company X is still forced to borrow in the market and pay the going 7 per cent rate. Over a six-month period the borrower would have to pay approximately £35,000 interest in the underlying borrowing. This is the difference between 7 per cent LIBOR borrowing minus 6.25 per cent for the FRA divided by 2 (because the borrowing is for six months);

- under the FRA Company X would receive approximately £3,750 to compensate for the extra 0.75 per cent interest payable on the £1 million loan over the six-month period – this is known as the settlement sum that effectively offsets the higher borrowing costs. This is paid on the settlement date, which is the date at which the contract starts.

Note that while the FRA has not guaranteed Company X the interest rate on the specific financing, it has managed to secure its finance at the 6.25 per cent fixed rate from the FRA.

The standard formula for calculating the payment or settlement sum can be shown as:

$$\text{Payment} = \text{notional principal} \left(\frac{(\text{reference rate} - \text{forward rate})(\text{days}/360)}{\text{reference rate }(\text{days}/360) + 1} \right)$$

where:

notional principal = notional amount of loan

reference rate for the period of the forward rate = LIBOR, EURIBOR or another floating rate underlying the agreement

forward rate = fixed rate agreed on the FRA

days = length of the contract period.

For further illustration if we take the aforementioned example, the formula is as follows:

Payment or settlement amount =

Numerator (interest saving) = $(0.07 - 0.0625) \times (180/360)$

$= 0.0075 \times 0.5 = 0.00375$

Denominator (discount factor) = $(0.07 \times (180/360)) + 1 = 1.035$

Settlement amount = $1,000,000 \times (0.00375/1.035) = £3,623.10$

---

[6] Note there are many different LIBOR rates: overnight, one week, two weeks, one month, two months and so on.

10.7.3 Options contracts

Options give holders the right but not the obligation to buy or sell an underlying security (a financial instrument or a commodity) at a specified price known as the exercise or strike price. The purchase price of an option is called its *premium*. A contract that gives the right to buy is known as a *call option,* a contract that gives the right to sell is a *put option*. It is common to distinguish between American options, which can be exercised at any time during their life, and European options, which can be exercised only at the end of their life, i.e. on the expiry date.

- Options can be OTC or exchange traded.

- Exchange-traded or listed options are standardised contracts with pre- determined exercise prices and expiry dates.

- If the options are traded on exchanges, such as bond options, a clearing house is responsible for the settlement of debits and credits for the members (so they are virtually default risk free).

- Options may be purchased that effectively give the right to borrow or to lend (deposit funds) at a specified rate of interest (the striking rate) for an agreed period at a future date, or to purchase/sell currencies at agreed exchange rates at agreed future dates.

An illustration of option contracts payoffs and profits profiles is provided Box 10.10.

BOX 10.10 OPTION CONTRACTS: PAYOFF AND PROFIT PROFILES

The most common option contracts are options on individual stocks (stock options). For example, consider an April 2014 maturity call option on a share of Barclays with an exercise price of £50 per share selling on 3 January 2014 for £2. Until the expiration day (the third Friday of the expiration month, that is 21 April), the purchaser of the calls is entitled to buy shares of Barclays for £50 and thus stands to gain from a *rise* in the price of the underlying share. If at expiration Barclays stock sells for a price above the exercise price, say for example £55, then the option holder could acquire the Barclays share at £50 under the terms of the option and sell it in the spot market at £55. In this case the profit to the call holder will be equal to £3 – that is, the payoff (£5) minus the premium paid to purchase the option (£2).

The relationship between market and exercise price is as follows:

- In the money – exercise of the option would be profitable

    Call: market price > exercise price ($S_T > x$)
    Put: exercise price > market price ($x > S_T$)

- Out of the money – exercise of the option would not be profitable

    Call: market price < exercise price ($S_T < x$)
    Put: exercise price < market price ($x < S_T$)

- At the money – exercise price and asset price are equal ($x = S_T$)

Figure 10.11 shows the payoff and profits from the point of view of the holder of the call option. For example, if the exercise price is £50 and Barclays is now selling the shares at the market price of £60, the holder of the option will clear £10 per share. The profit will be equal to the payoff (£10) – the premium (£2) = £8. Yet if the shares sell any amount equal to or below £50 the holder can sit on the option and do nothing, realising no further gain or loss. To summarise:

Payoff to call holder
$(S_T - X)$ if $S_T > x$

0 if $S_T = x$

Profit to call holder
Payoff − Purchase price (premium)

Figure 10.12 illustrates the payoffs and profits from the point of view of the holder of the put option. If the

---

BOX 10.10 Option contracts:payoff and profit profiles (*continued*)

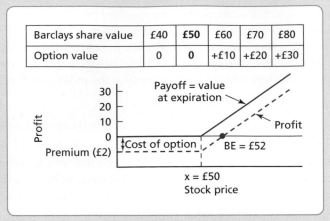

Barclays share value	£40	**£50**	£60	£70	£80
Option value	0	0	+£10	+£20	+£30

Figure 10.11 Payoffs and profits on call options at expiration (from the perspective of the buyer of the option)

exercise price is £50 per share and Barclays is now selling at, say, £30, the holder of the put option will earn £20 per share (the profit will be £20 − £2 = £18). If the shares sell any amount equal to or above £50 the holder can sit on the option and do nothing, realising no further gain or loss. To recap:

Payoff to put holder
0 if $S_T = x$
$(x - S_T)$ if $S_T < x$
Profit to put holder
Payoff − Premium

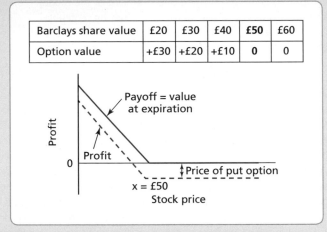

Barclays share value	£20	£30	£40	**£50**	£60
Option value	+£30	+£20	+£10	0	0

Figure 10.12 Payoffs and profits on put options at expiration (from the perspective of the buyer of the option)

Options on assets other than stocks include:

- 'index options', which are calls or puts based on a stock market index such as the London FTSE 100;
- 'futures options', which give their holders the right to buy or sell a specified futures contract, using as futures price the exercise price of the option;

- 'foreign currency options', which offer the right to buy or sell a quantity of foreign currency for a specified amount of domestic currency;
- 'interest rate options' – options that are also traded on T-bills, bonds and CDs.

One common application of options contracts relates to the protection of banks' bond portfolios against rising interest rates. The main advantage of using options, as opposed to futures and forwards, to manage interest rate risk is that there is no delivery obligation, so the bank can decide to keep its bonds if interest rates fall and bond prices rise. For example, in order to protect itself against rising interest rates (and falling market values of bank assets, rising borrowing rates and so on) a bank can decide to buy a put option on securities. The put option grants the bank the right to deliver the securities at a set price 'P'. If interest rates do rise, the market price of the securities will fall, so the bank will be able to buy them at the current price and deliver them to the option writer at the (higher) price 'P'. The profit for the bank will be equal to P less the current price and the premium paid to exercise the option. Note that, typically, banks are buyers rather than sellers of puts and calls because of the considerable risks involved if interest rates move against the sellers.

10.7.3.1 Caps, floors and collars

Caps and **floors** are effectively types of options. They may be thought of as giving the holder a right to purchase a forward rate agreement (forward contract in interest rates) 'with hindsight'. **Collars** are hybrid products, being part forward contract and part option.

An interest rate cap may be purchased from a bank in order to protect the holder of an existing floating-rate loan from the interest rate moving upwards beyond the level specified by the cap contract. The holder (borrower) is still able to benefit if interest rates fall, but may claim any excess interest charge over the cap level from the seller of the cap.

An interest rate floor has the same characteristics as a cap, except that it protects an investor or depositor against a floating rate of interest falling below the specified floor level. The seller of the floor will pay the purchaser any interest losses below the floor rate. The purchaser is still able to benefit from increases in interest rates.

An interest rate collar is effectively a combination of a cap and a floor. A collar may be purchased by a company wishing to protect itself against the interest rate on outstanding debt going beyond a capped level but prepared to forego the gain from the interest rate falling below a lower specified level in exchange for a lower premium on the cap.

10.7.4 Swaps

Swaps are agreements between two parties to exchange two differing forms of payment obligations. They can be thought of as exchanges of cash flows used to manage their asset–liability structure or to reduce their cost of borrowing. The most common types of swaps are interest rate swaps and currency swaps.

10.7.4.1 Interest rate swaps

Interest rate swaps occur between borrowers and swap dealers (normally banks). The swap dealer is the counterparty to the swap transaction with the borrower. It is important to understand that only debt servicing commitments are swapped, not the underlying borrowed funds. Hence, swaps are used as a risk management instrument whereby a company can change the profile of its interest rate liabilities without disturbing the underlying borrowing. In addition, swaps can be used as a basis for speculation when they are taken out without any matching exposure in the cash market.

The main features of interest rate swaps are:

- only interest payments are swapped so there is no exchange of principal;
- interest payments are swapped at rates and for a term agreed at the outset based on a specified notional principal;
- transactions are usually governed by a standardised swap contract (but the amount and terms are not standardised);
- the rights and obligations under a swap contract are entirely separate from the rights or obligations associated with any underlying borrowing;
- interest swaps normally cover initial periods of anything from one to ten years or more.

Among other applications, swaps give counterparties the ability to:

- convert floating-rate debt to fixed or fixed-rate to floating-rate;
- lock in an attractive interest rate in advance of a future debt issue;
- position fixed-rate liabilities in anticipation of a decline in interest rates; and
- arbitrage or speculate on debt price differentials in the capital markets.

As stated above, swaps are normally arranged through a swap dealer, with the dealer acting as a principal rather than an agent. The dealer makes a return on this activity through the bid–ask spread.[7] Interest rate swap prices are quoted on a range of currencies for periods of up to 30 years and are published in the *Financial Times*. The quotes will, in general, move in the same direction as changes in the yields on gilt-edged securities with a similar maturity to the swap.

10.7.4.2 Currency swaps

Currency swaps transfer the obligation for payment in one currency to another party who, in turn, undertakes an obligation for payment in another currency.

Typically, a currency swap involves:

- an initial exchange of principal amounts of two currencies at the spot exchange rate;
- the exchange of a stream of fixed or floating interest rate payments in their swapped currencies for the agreed period of the swap; and
- re-exchange of the principal amount at maturity at the initial spot exchange rate. Sometimes, the initial exchange of principal is omitted and instead a net amount or 'difference' is paid.

In a currency swap, counterparties agree to exchange an equivalent amount of two different currencies for a specified time. These can be negotiated for a wide range of maturities up to at least ten years. As in the case of other foreign exchange contracts, if the cost of borrowing in one currency is higher than it would be in another then a fee may be required to compensate for the interest differential.

---

[7] Most financial instruments traded in the market have a bid–ask spread. The bid price is the price at which you can sell the instrument. The ask price is the price you would have to pay to buy the instrument. Alternatively one can view the bid price as the highest price that somebody will pay for (say) a share at a particular point in time, whereas the ask price is the lowest price at which someone is willing to sell the share. The difference between the bid and the ask price is known as the bid–ask spread. Market makers that offer to buy and sell shares create the spread so they can earn income from trading.

The usual reason for a financial intermediary wishing to engage in a currency swap is so that it can replace cash flows in an undesired currency with flows in a desired currency. Global banks and other large financial intermediaries often raise finance in the international markets and may have to service debt in a variety of currencies. Box 10.11 gives an example of interest rate swap while Box 10.12 illustrates a fixed–floating currency swap.

BOX 10.11 EXAMPLE OF INTEREST RATE SWAP

Suppose a UK-based bank has recently agreed a total of £100 million of mortgage loans at a rate that will remain fixed at 7 per cent per annum for the next five years. Also, suppose that the funding is in the form of wholesale deposits with three-month maturity paying interest at LIBOR that is currently 6.6 per cent. As long as its mortgage loans are at 7 per cent fixed, the bank will gain if LIBOR falls and it will lose out if LIBOR rises.

A swap dealer may offer the bank the following deal:

- Swap dealer to pay the bank each year, for the next five years, a sum of money calculated on the interest that would have been paid on £100 million at LIBOR.

- Bank to pay swap dealer each year, for the next five years, a sum of money calculated on the interest that would have been paid on £100 million at 6.6 per cent fixed.

- The bank may then use the swap to fix its interest rate margin between the mortgage loans and the three-month deposits for a five-year period.

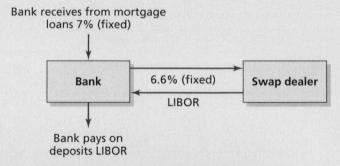

As long as the notional principal and the maturity date of the swap match the amount and maturity of the fixed-rate mortgage loans, the interest margin is fixed at 0.4 per cent. Consequently, the bank's profit margin is insulated from the risk that LIBOR could rise. However, if LIBOR falls, the margin will remain at 0.4 per cent and the bank will not be able to benefit from this fall in market rates. The interest margin is fixed, irrespective of the level of LIBOR.

A possible problem could arise for the bank if interest rates were to fall and this created pressure for early repayment of the fixed interest mortgage loans. If the mortgage loans were to be repaid early, the bank would cease to need the wholesale deposits. However, with the swap obligations still in force, a LIBOR rate of, say, 4 per cent would lead to a loss for the bank of £2.6 million on the transaction. That is, the bank would still have to pay the swap dealer £6.6 million, but would receive only £4 million from the swap dealer. To prevent this problem, the bank could incorporate early repayment penalties in mortgage loan agreements, although it would need to ensure that it did not contravene any related consumer protection legislation.

This example illustrates clearly the basic rule that derivatives can reduce risk if they match a position in the underlying cash markets, but they increase risk if there is no underlying obligation in the cash market or if the underlying obligation does not come to fruition for whatever reason.

BOX 10.12 EXAMPLE OF FIXED–FLOATING CURRENCY SWAP

Suppose that a US-based bank has partly financed its asset portfolio with a total of £60 million three-year note issue with fixed 10 per cent annual coupons denominated in sterling. Also, suppose that this US bank holds mostly floating-rate short-term US dollar-denominated assets.

- A UK-based bank has partly financed its asset portfolio with a total of $100 million short-term dollar-denominated Euro CDs whose rates reflect changes in one-year LIBOR + 1 per cent premium. Also, suppose that this UK bank holds mostly fixed-rate long-term sterling-denominated assets.

Both banks are faced with interest rate and foreign exchange exposure if the following situations occur:

- for the US bank, if dollar short-term rates fall, and the dollar depreciates against the pound;

- for the UK bank, if US interest rates rise, and the dollar appreciates against the pound.

- Therefore the two banks may wish to engage in a fixed–floating currency swap whereby:

- the US bank transforms its fixed-rate sterling-denominated liabilities into variable-rate dollar liabilities;

- the UK bank transforms its variable-rate short-term dollar-denominated liabilities into fixed-rate sterling liabilities.

Each year the two banks swap payments at some pre-arranged dollar/sterling exchange rate, assumed to be $2/£1. The UK bank sends fixed payments in pounds to cover the cost of the US bank's pound note issue, while the US bank sends floating payments in dollars to cover the UK bank's floating-rate dollar CD costs. Table 10.6 shows that the realised cash flows from the swap result in a net nominal payment of $3 million by the US bank to the UK bank over the life of the swap.

Table 10.6 Fixed–floating rate currency swap (millions)

Year	LIBOR %	LIBOR + 3	Floating-rate payment by US bank ($mil)	Fixed-rate payment by UK bank		Net payment by US bank ($mil)
				($mil)	$mil (at $2/£1)	
1	8	11	11	6	12	−1
2	9	12	12	6	12	0
3	10	13	130	66	132	−2
Total net payment						−3

Source: Adapted from Saunders and Cornett (2012).

A Japanese bank, for instance, may have to service most of its debt in fixed-rate yen, whereas a UK bank has to (say) service mainly fixed-rate British pound debt. If the Japanese bank has some fixed-rate British pound debt and the UK bank has fixed-rate yen debt, this could provide an opportunity for both banks to swap principal and interest payments – so the UK bank obtains an income stream paying fixed-rate yen and the Japanese firm fixed-rate British pounds. Put simply, both banks are swapping cash flows in different currencies. Currency swaps come in various forms:

- fixed-for-fixed currency swaps – where the interest rate payments on the two currencies that are swapped are fixed at the start of the swap agreement;

- fixed-for-floating swaps (cross-currency swaps) – where the interest rate on one currency is floating and usually linked to the London Interbank Offered Rate (the average of interest rates that major international banks charge each other to borrow US dollars in the London money market) and the other is fixed;

- floating-for-floating currency swaps – where both interest rates are floating.

The main reasons for the development of currency swaps business is that some financial and other firms have an advantage in generating cash flows in specific currencies and it is in the interest of these firms to trade these cash flows if they desire other currency streams. As business has become more international, and financing and investment requirements more diversified, the need to have access to a wider array of cash flows in different currencies has heightened.

10.8 Conclusion

Bank managers' role is to implement decisions that maximise the profitability of their institutions' and shareholders' wealth. In order to achieve these aims, bank managers should pursue strategies in several areas, such as asset and liability management, liquidity management and capital management. This chapter describes these on-balance-sheet concerns of banks and then provides an account of the different types of off-balance-sheet business that modern banks undertake, such as loan sales and other contingent commitments. In the past, financial derivative products have been referred to as off-balance-sheet activities. In recent years, the need for more disclosure and transparency has implied changes in the way these items are recorded in banks' financial statements. The current trend in international accounting standards is to require banks to record derivatives at fair value on the balance sheet and to report any gain (loss) on hedged instruments in the income statement whenever derivatives are used as a hedge against underlying assets or liabilities.

A related area of strategic decision that carries a high potential for affecting bank profits, value and safety is risk management. The following two chapters outline the main risks that banks have to face (Chapter 11) and discuss the techniques used by banks to measure and manage these risks (Chapter 12).

Key terms

Arbitrage	Currency forward	Hedging	Options
Asset management	Financial	Liability	Process of
Asset–liability	derivatives	management	deconstruction
management	Financial futures	Liquidity	Securities
Banker's acceptance	Financial guarantees	management	underwriting
Capital management	Forward rate	Loan commitments	Securitisation
Caps, floors and	agreement	Loan sales	Standby letter of
collars	Forwards	Macro-hedging	credit
Commercial letter of	Funds transfer	Micro-hedging	Swaps
credit	pricing (FTP)	OBS management	Treasury

Key reading

Deloitte (2013) 'Future of bank treasury management: A profession in focus', March. Available at **www.deloitte.com/assets/Dcom-UnitedKingdom/Local%20Assets/Documents/ Industries/Financial%20Services/uk-fs-future-bank-treasury-management.pdf**

Koch, T.W. and MacDonald, S.S. (2010) *Bank Management,* 7th Edition, Mason, OH: Southwestern Cengage Learning.

Saunders, A. and Cornett, M. (2012) *Financial Institutions Management: A Risk Management Approach,* New York: McGraw-Hill/Irwin.

REVISION QUESTIONS AND PROBLEMS

10.1 What is asset–liability management?

10.2 Why is there a trade-off between liquidity and profitability?

10.3 What are the main functions of the Treasury division within the bank and what is the FTP process?

10.4 What are the main concerns in capital management?

10.5 Explain loan sales with and without recourse.

10.6 Explain the changes in a bank's balance sheet before and after securitisation.

10.7 Broadly describe what is meant by derivative products and explain the different implications of trading in organised exchanges versus OTC.

10.8 How can banks use futures and forwards for hedging an interest rate exposure?

10.9 What are the primary features of options contracts and how can they be used for risk management purposes?

10.10 What are the main differences between interest rate and currency swaps?

Chapter 11

Banking risks

Learning objectives

- To define the most common risks in banking
- To distinguish between the various risks in banking
- To understand the importance of the interrelation among banking risks

11.1 Introduction

For any privately owned bank, management's goal is to maximise shareholders' value. If the institution is publicly listed and markets are efficient, returns are proportional to the risks taken; if the bank is small and unlisted, managers will try to maximise the value of the owner's investments by seeking the highest returns for what they deem to be acceptable levels of risk. With increased pressure on banks to improve shareholders' returns, banks have had to assume higher risks and, at the same time, manage these risks to avoid losses.

The processes of deregulation, globalisation and conglomeration have offered productive opportunities for banks in terms of profitability and value creation activities (see Chapter 9) but have also posed serious risk challenges. The financial crisis in the second half of the 2000s demonstrated on one hand the fragilities of the banking sector globally and, on the other, the potential systemic risks associated with the interconnectedness of banking activities. In this chapter we describe the main types of risks modern banks have to face. An introduction to the prevailing risk management techniques will be provided in more detail in Chapter 12.

11.2 Credit risk

According to the Basel Committee on Banking Supervision (2000) **credit risk** is defined as 'the potential that a bank borrower or counterparty will fail to meet its obligations in accordance with agreed terms'. Generally, credit risk is associated with the traditional lending activity of banks and it is simply described as the risk of a loan not being repaid in part or in full. However, credit risk can also derive from holding bonds and other securities.

Credit risk is the risk of a decline in the credit standing of a counterparty. Such deterioration does not imply default, but means that the probability of default increases. Capital markets value the credit standing of firms through the rate of interest charged on bonds or other debt issues, changes in the value of shares, and ratings provided by the **credit-rating agencies** (such as Standard & Poor's, Moody's and Fitch IBCA). However, banks also face credit risk in a number of other financial instruments such as derivative products and guarantees. This particular type of credit risk is sometimes referred to as **counterparty risk**. Resti and Sironi (2010) define the risk associated with deterioration in the counterparty's creditworthiness as a 'migration' risk that becomes effectively a 'downgrading' risk if the rating agency that issued the public credit rating downgraded it. According to the authors, in the context of credit risk, it is also useful to distinguish between spread risk, recovery risk, pre-settlement (or substitution) risk and country risk (see Section 11.7). Spread risk is the risk connected with an increase in the spreads required of borrowers, such as bond issuers, by the market. When risk aversion increases due, for example, to instability, crisis or shocks, the spread differential between good-quality and bad-quality bonds may rise (so-called 'flight to quality'). In case of insolvent assets of the counterparty, there is also the recovery risk that can occur when the recovery rate is lower than initially predicted because of lower liquidation value or unexpected delays in cashing in bad assets. A bank also runs a pre-settlement or substitution risk, which is the risk that may occur when the bank counterparty in an over-the-counter derivative transaction becomes insolvent prior to maturity, forcing the bank to substitute it at less favourable conditions.

In general terms, bank managers should minimise credit losses by building a portfolio of assets (loans and securities) that diversifies the degree of risk. This is because very low default risk assets are associated with low credit risk and low expected return, while higher expected return assets have a higher probability of default (i.e. a higher credit risk). Focusing on loans that constitute the largest proportion of a bank's assets, in Chapter 10 we mentioned that the traditional lending function involves four different components (Sinkey, 2002; Greenbaum and Thakor, 2007):

1 Originating (the application process).
2 Funding (approving the loan and availing funds).
3 Servicing (collecting interest and principal payments).
4 Monitoring (checking on borrowers' behaviour through the life of the loan).

Banks must investigate borrowers' ability to repay their loans before and after the loan has been made (these activities are known as screening and monitoring functions of banks) because of their aim to maximise value and the responsibility they have towards their depositors and deposit insurers to be safe and sound.

To recall, banks are said to act as *delegated monitors* on behalf of lenders and to this end they use technology and innovation in the design and enforcement of contracts. These contracts are costly for the banks but they are essential for the protection of both banks' owners and lenders. However, *agency problems* may arise as a result of functions (1) and (4). As shown in Chapter 1, agency problems imply potential contractual frictions between principals (lenders) and agents (borrowers) because of asymmetric information, moral hazard and adverse selection. Banks need to account for these problems while aiming to minimise losses in lending.

While it is accepted that all banks experience some loan losses, the degree of risk aversion varies significantly across institutions. All banks have their own **credit philosophy** established in a formal written **loan policy** that must be supported and communicated with an appropriate credit culture. The lending philosophy could reflect an emphasis on aggressive loan growth based on flexible underwriting standards. Alternatively, it could reflect the goals of a more conservative management aiming at achieving a consistent performance of a high-quality loan portfolio. Loan policies reflect the degree of risk bank management is ready to take and may change over time. A credit culture is successful when all employees in the bank are aligned with the management's lending priorities (Hempel and Simonson, 2008) – see Box 11.1.

BOX 11.1 CREDIT CULTURE AND EQUITY CULTURE IN BANKING

Credit culture refers to the fundamental principles that drive a bank's lending activity and the way management analyses risk. Credit culture relates specifically to the way management sets the values of a bank in relation to the credit risk management process and seeks to communicate with and influence the organisation. In this context, senior executives and particularly the CEO (chief executive officer) play a key role in determining a bank's credit culture and in setting the tone and direction of their organisations.

This special role of the CEO was also emphasised in an unpublished speech at Bangor Business School (September 2010) by Lord Mervyn Davies, former Government Minister and Chairman of Standard Chartered Bank Plc. Lord Davies stressed the importance of the functions and responsibilities of a bank CEO in giving clear signals appropriate for the credit culture that they have decided to pursue. In line with the existing relevant literature, Lord Davies confirmed the role of the CEO as protector of a bank's value system, and in preserving prudent discipline, guidelines and accountability.

In Mueller's (1994) words, credit culture can be defined as the true 'spirit behind the rules [. . .] with many moving parts embracing everything that has to do with credit extension. It is rooted in ideas, traditions, skills, attitude, philosophies and standards'. So credit culture relates not only to the tangible written policies and procedures but also to the intangible. In addition, 'a credit culture is developed over time and communicated and passed on'. That is, a strong credit culture will permeate the organisation throughout and people will know intuitively what is acceptable and what is not.

The 2007–2009 financial turmoil has demonstrated that an equity culture in banking took over from the credit culture in the run-up to the collapse. Equity culture implies a bank's behaviour that encourages excessive risk taking and leverage and is characterised by short-term (and short-sighted) strategies. In a study published in the *OECD Financial Market Trends* paper series, Blundell-Wignall *et al.* (2009) attempt to identify the main factors that brought about a greater focus on equity culture at the expense of the credit culture. These include factors such as excess liquidity, poor regulation, competition and governance frameworks, structured products and derivative growth drivers, often motivated by tax considerations. What Blundell-Wignall *et al.* (2009) define as 'the levels of damage' brought about by the equity culture in the banking industry translated over recent years into massive capital and liquidity injections, asset purchases and debt guarantee facilities for banking sectors in virtually all developed countries.

Blundell-Wignall *et al.*'s study denounces not only the damage of pursuing an equity culture in banking but also the risks of 'leaving it unconstrained' for the future. The research emphasises the need for essential reforms to avoid too-big-to-fail risk and ensure stability. These reforms include, among others, a more transparent and comparable set of accounting rules and improvements in corporate governance.

Sources: Blundell-Wignall *et al.* (2009); Davies (2010); Mueller (1994).

If internal data are available, credit risk can be monitored by looking at the changes in the ratio of medium-quality loans to total assets. The bank can choose to lower its credit risk by lowering this ratio. If the data on medium-quality loans are not available, traditional proxies for credit risk include, for instance:

- total loans/total assets;
- non-performing loans/total loans;
- loan losses/total loans;
- loan loss reserves/total assets.

These types of ratios can be calculated for different types of loans the bank holds on its balance sheet – for example, a bank may look at its mortgage loan book and see what proportion of such loans it holds relative to total assets, the amount on non-performing mortgage loans, losses on mortgage loans and so on.

However, Hempel and Simonson (2008) argue that these indicators can be subject to criticism because they lag in time behind the returns gained by taking higher risk. Therefore one should look at lead indicators such as:

- loan concentration in geographic areas or sectors;
- rapid loan growth;
- high lending rates;
- loan loss reserves/non-performing loans.

Another key credit-risk measure is the ratio of total loans to total deposits. The higher the ratio, the greater the concerns of regulatory authorities, as loans are among the riskiest of bank assets. A greater level of non-performing loans to deposits could also generate greater risk for depositors.

Since in the presence of credit risk the mean return on the bank's asset portfolio is lower than if the loan portfolio was entirely risk-free, the bank will find it necessary to minimise the probability of bad outcomes in the portfolio by using a diversification strategy. Diversification will decrease **unsystematic** or firm-specific credit risk. This is derived from 'micro' factors and thus is the credit risk specific to the holding of loans or bonds of a particular firm. While diversification decreases firm-specific credit risk, banks remain exposed to **systematic credit risk**. This is the risk associated with the possibility that default of all firms may increase over a given period because of economic changes or other events that have an impact on large sections of the economy/market (e.g. in an economic recession firms are less likely to be able to repay their debts).

11.3 Interest rate risk

An interest rate is a *price* that relates to *present* claims on resources relative to *future* claims on resources. An interest rate is the price that a borrower pays in order to be able to consume resources now rather than at a point in the future. Correspondingly, it is the price that a lender receives to forego current consumption. Like all prices in free markets, interest rates are established by the interaction of supply and demand; in this context, it is the supply of future claims on resources interacting with the demand for future claims on resources. An interest rate may, therefore, be defined as a price established by the interaction of the supply of, and the demand for, future claims on resources. That price will usually be expressed as a proportion of the sum borrowed or lent over a given period.

Interest rates have a crucial role in the financial system. For example, they influence financial flows within the economy, the distribution of wealth, capital investment and the profitability of financial institutions (also see Chapter 5 for more details on the implementation of monetary policy). For banks, the exposure to interest rate risk, that is the risk associated with unexpected changes in interest rates, has grown sharply in recent years as a result of the increased volatility in market interest rates, especially at the international level.[1]

However, not all banks' assets and liabilities are subject to **interest rate risk** in the same way. Important distinctions should be made between **fixed-rate assets and liabilities** and **rate-sensitive assets and liabilities:**

- Fixed rate assets and liabilities carry rates that are constant throughout a certain period (e.g. one year) and their cash flows do not change unless there is a default, early withdrawal or an unanticipated pre-payment.

- Rate-sensitive assets and liabilities can be re-priced within a certain period (e.g. 90 days); therefore the cash flows associated with rate-sensitive contracts vary with changes in interest rates.

Other banks' assets and liabilities can be categorised into non-earning assets (i.e. assets that generate no explicit income, such as cash) and non-paying liabilities (i.e. liabilities that pay no interest, such as current accounts or, as they are known in the United States, 'checking accounts').

A rise in market interest rates has the effect of increasing banks' funding costs because the cost of variable rate deposits and other variable rate financing increases. If loans have been made at fixed interest rates this obviously reduces the net returns on such loans. Meanwhile, banks will be vulnerable to falling rates if they hold an excess of fixed-rate liabilities. In the case of bonds, as interest rates increase this reduces the market value of a bond investment. Typically, long-term, fixed-income securities subject their holders to the greatest amount of interest rate risk (see Appendix A1 for more details on the relation between bond prices and interest rates). In contrast, short-term securities, such as Treasury bills, are much less influenced by interest rate movements.

Recently, regulators and bankers have been assessing how damaging a US rate increase might be specifically for banks that have now adapted their strategies to a low interest rate environment, as shown in the article in Box 11.2.

Traditional interest rate risk analysis compares the sensitivity of interest income to changes in asset yields with the sensitivity of interest expenses to changes in interest costs of liabilities. In particular, it is common to refer to the ratio of rate-sensitive assets to rate-sensitive liabilities: when rate-sensitive assets exceed rate-sensitive liabilities (in a particular maturity range), a bank is vulnerable to losses from falling interest rates. Conversely, when rate-sensitive liabilities exceed rate-sensitive assets, losses are likely to be incurred if market interest rates rise. Typically, if a bank has a ratio above 1.0, the bank's returns will be lower if interest rates decline and higher if they increase. However, given the difficulty in forecasting interest rates, some banks conclude that they can minimise interest rate risk with an interest

---

[1] Note that interest rate risk is faced by both borrowers, who do not want to pay higher rates on loans, and lenders, who may suffer losses if rates fall.

BOX 11.2 WATCH OUT FOR THE RATE HIKE HIT TO BANKS

Earlier this year, officials at America's mighty Federal Deposit Insurance Corporation (FDIC) engaged in a bout of brainstorming with bank leaders about interest rate risk. The message was sobering.

Back then, in April, the FDIC did not seriously expect US rates to jump soon. Little wonder: at that stage, the 10-year yield was still below 2 per cent – and sinking – while Ben Bernanke, the US Federal Reserve chairman, seemed committed to quantitative easing (QE).

But if rates were to rise, the fallout could be painful, the regulator warned. Or as Dan Frye, an FDIC official, told the bankers: "If rates started going up today it could have serious consequences for some of our banks . . . a lot of banks would get hurt." Indeed, the FDIC felt so uneasy about the issue that it begged banks to start scrutinising their balance sheets, in readiness for that day.

Investors – not to mention bankers – should take note. After all, a rate increase is no longer an entirely hypothetical idea. On the contrary, in the past couple of months 10-year Treasury yields have jumped 60 basis points, amid speculation that the Fed could embark on a "tapered" end to QE next year.

That increase has already inflicted painful losses on bond investors and some hedge funds. And though banks have remained out of the spotlight, as bond market volatility rises, the issue raised by the FDIC is now looking doubly pertinent; notably, what regulators and some bankers are trying to assess is just how damaging a rate increase might be – not just for big banks, but small ones too.

Opinions are mixed. In theory, a return to more normal levels of US interest rates in future years should be beneficial for many banks. After all, low rates typically cause banks' net interest margins to shrivel. And in the past two years the margin squeeze has been so painful that some Fed officials say banks actually want QE to stop, as soon as possible. "In my district, the banks are saying that low interest rates are killing them – they want higher rates," says one regional Fed president.

But there is a crucial catch. Precisely because of that margin collapse, many banks have quietly been adopting novel – if not desperate – strategies to boost earnings. Some have been extending more long-term loans, often at fixed rates, or investing in risky bonds or complex structured products. And that could potentially create big losses if rates rise, particularly if this swing occurs dramatically, as in 1994.

For the moment, at least, most regulators appear to think, or hope, that the largest US banks are fairly well protected against that risk. That is partly because large banks have rebuilt their capital reserves since 2008, but also because many have engaged in sophisticated hedging strategies.

However, one problem for investors is that banks' balance sheets are so opaque that it is difficult for outsiders to judge the resilience of such hedging. And for the smaller banks there are other risks. Right now, according to FDIC research, just 3 per cent of community banks use sophisticated financial products to hedge interest rate risk; instead, they typically try to respond by managing their assets and liabilities sensibly. However, this task is becoming much harder. One reason is that banks have extended more long-term mortgage and commercial loans, often at low(ish) fixed rates. But another issue is a growing use of short-term debt and non-maturity deposits; in the past couple of years some $1,500bn has moved from money market funds to bank deposits, due to those low rates.

The net result of this, as the FDIC says, is that "the current structure of bank balance sheets suggests greater sensitivity to higher rates" than in 2004, or the last time that interest rates started rising sharply. Back in 2004, long-term assets were just 17 per cent of banks' portfolios; now they are 28 per cent. Similarly, in 2004 non-maturity deposits were 48 per cent; now they stand at 59 per cent. However, if rates rise, money could flood out of those non-maturity assets, just as banks get hit by the costs of long-term, fixed loans. "Some banks are doing crazy things, to chase yield," mutters the chairman of one small bank. Or as Mr Frye says: "There is still this tendency to seek short-term gains with long-term costs."

Of course, for the moment, these risks and costs are merely hypothetical; the Fed insists that it

---

Box 11.2 Watch out for the rate hike hit to banks (*continued*)

wants to keep rates low for some time. And if it does that, then banks should have enough time to adjust. But, there again, the longer that the Fed staves off that day of monetary policy reckoning, the more that some banks may be tempted to keep

chasing yield – and ignore those FDIC appeals. It is just one more reminder, if any were needed, of how fiendishly difficult it will be to "exit" from QE without triggering shocks; even with that infamous "taper".

 Source: Gillian Tett (2013) *Financial Times*, 13 June.

---

sensitivity ratio close to 1.0. As pointed out by Hempel and Simonson (2008), such a ratio may be difficult for some banks to achieve and often can be reached only at the cost of lower returns on assets.

These traditional measures of interest rate risk have a number of limitations. Bank managers nowadays use sophisticated measures of interest rate management such as the gap buckets analysis, maturity models and duration analysis. Details of these models are provided in Chapter 12. It is important to note that interest rate risk measurement and management will always imply an ALM approach (see Chapter 10).

Section 11.3.1 follows Saunders and Cornett's (2012) examples of the two types of interest rate risk that banks may have to face – **refinancing risk** and **reinvestment risk** – and also focuses on the impact on a bank's profitability.

11.3.1 Refinancing risk and reinvestment risk

Interest rate risk is the risk arising from the mismatching of the maturity and the volume of banks' assets and liabilities as part of their asset-transformation function. As we saw in Chapter 1, one of the main functions of financial intermediaries is to act as asset transformers, e.g. they transform short-term deposits into long-term loans.

Typically, the maturity of banks' assets (e.g. loans) is longer than the maturity of banks' liabilities (e.g. deposits). This means that banks can be viewed as 'short-funded' and have to run the risk of refinancing their assets at a rate that may be less advantageous than previous rates. Saunders and Cornett (2012) define refinancing risk as 'the risk that (the) cost of rolling over or re-borrowing funds will rise above the returns being earned on asset investments'.

For example, assume the cost of funds (liabilities) for a bank is 7 per cent per annum and the interest return on an asset is 9 per cent. In year 1 by borrowing short (1 year) and lending long (2 years) the profit spread is equal to the difference between the lending and borrowing rates, i.e. 2 per cent, as in situation (a) in Figure 11.1. In year 2 profits are uncertain because if the interest rate does not change then the bank can refinance its liabilities at 7 per cent per annum and as in year 1 have a profit of 2 per cent. However, if interest rates increase as in situation (b), the bank can borrow at 8 per cent and profits will be only 1 per cent.

Another type of mismatch could occur when the maturity of banks' liabilities is longer than the maturity of the assets. This means that banks can be viewed as 'long-funded' and have to run the risk of reinvesting their funds in the second period at a rate that may be less advantageous than the previous rate and that they were unable to forecast in advance. Such a situation can often occur in banking within specific maturity buckets (i.e. intervals of consecutive maturities, such as a 3–6 months' maturity bucket). Accordingly, Saunders and

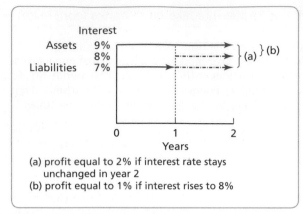

Figure 11.1 Refinancing risk

Source: Adapted from Saunders and Cornett (2012).

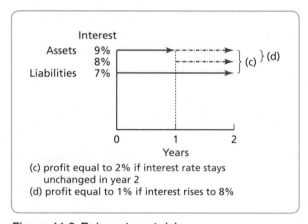

Figure 11.2 Reinvestment risk

Source: Adapted from Saunders and Cornett (2012).

Cornett (2012) define reinvestment risk as 'the risk that the returns on funds to be reinvested will fall below the cost of funds'.

For example, assume the interest return on an asset for a bank is 9 per cent per annum and the cost of funds (liabilities) is 7 per cent. In year 1 by borrowing long (2 years) and lending short (1 year) the profit spread is equal to the difference between lending rate and borrowing rate, that is 2 per cent, as in situation (c) in Figure 11.2. In year 2 profits are uncertain because if the interest rate does not change then the bank can reinvest its assets at 9 per cent per annum and as in year 1 have a profit of 2 per cent. However, if interest rates go down as in situation (d), then the bank can lend at 8 per cent and profits will be only 1 per cent.

11.4 Liquidity (or funding) risk

A liquid asset may be defined as an asset that can be turned into cash quickly and without capital loss or interest penalty. Most bank deposits are therefore very liquid, but investment in, for example, property is highly illiquid. The liquidity that is required by a lender will depend on a number of factors, including in particular the range of liquidity inherent in other securities held. Moreover, a bank needs liquidity to cover a possible surge in operating expenses and to satisfy loan demand. All other things being equal, lenders will wish to have a high level of liquidity in their loans.

Liquidity risk is generated in the balance sheet by a mismatch between the size and maturity of assets and liabilities. It is the risk that the bank is holding insufficient liquid assets on its balance sheet and thus is unable to meet requirements without impairment to its financial or reputational capital. Banks have to manage their liquidity to ensure that both predictable and unpredictable liquidity demands are met and taking into account that the immediate sale of assets at low or 'fire sale' prices could threaten the bank's returns.[2]

If a bank cannot meet depositor demands there will be a bank run, as depositors lose confidence and rush to withdraw funds. This may then make it difficult for the bank to obtain funds in the interbank market and before long a **liquidity crisis** will turn into a solvency crisis and possible failure (on the distinction between liquidity and solvency see Chapter 5, Box 5.6). Hence it is common to distinguish two types of liquidity risk:

- Day-to-day liquidity risk relates to daily withdrawals. This is usually predictable (or 'normal') because only a small percentage of a bank's deposits will be withdrawn on a given day. Very few institutions ever actually run out of cash because it is relatively easy for the bank to cover any shortage of cash by borrowing funds from other banks in the interbank markets.

BOX 11.3 LIQUIDITY RISK AND INFORMATION ASYMMETRIES

Consider a bank that has made loans of €1 million with three-year maturity financed with uninsured demand deposits. The bank has an informational advantage compared with outsiders on the credit risk and overall quality of its loan portfolio. Suppose that one year later €500,000 of deposits are withdrawn and the bank's stock of cash assets is only €100,000. The bank will need €400,000 to fund the deposit withdrawal. Two cases can occur: 1) potential new depositors have a good perception about the bank's loan portfolio and the bank will easily acquire the €400,000 in new deposits; 2) outsiders have received unfavourable information about the bank's loans despite the bank's belief that the quality is good. Here the bank will either not be able to acquire new deposits (in extreme cases it will lose all existing deposits!) or have to pay too high a price for the risk associated with the loan portfolio. Informational asymmetries about asset quality create liquidity risk. If outsiders knew as much as the bank does about the quality of the loan portfolio, then the bank would be able to acquire deposits at the appropriate price given the risk of the loan portfolio.

Information asymmetries can also affect interbank lending and indeed evidence has shown that the actions taken during the 2007–2009 financial turmoil did little to restart the frozen interbank markets. These measures included central bank monetary policy decisions to lower rates, quantitative easing and bank recapitalisations. Each day banks exchange liquidity in the interbank markets and this process is crucial to guarantee a smooth functioning of monetary policy and for the healthy management of bank liquidity.

Source: Adapted from Greenbaum and Thakor (2007).

---

[2] Greenbaum and Thakor (2007) point out that the most extreme manifestation of liquidity risk is that the seller of the asset is unable to sell the asset at any price. This is known as *credit rationing* and occurs when a bank refuses credit to a borrower irrespective of the price that they are willing to pay.

- A liquidity crisis occurs when depositors demand larger withdrawals than normal. In this situation banks are forced to borrow funds at an elevated interest rate, higher than the market rate that other banks are paying for similar borrowings. This is usually unpredictable (or 'abnormal') and can be due to either a lack of confidence in the specific bank or some unexpected need for cash. Liquidity crises can ultimately hinder the ability of a bank to repay its obligations and in the absence of central bank intervention or deposit insurance it could result in a 'run' and even the insolvency of the bank.

Typically, banks can reduce their exposure to liquidity risk by increasing the proportion of funds committed to cash and readily marketable assets, such as T-bills and other government securities, or use longer-term liabilities to fund the bank's operations. The difficulty for banks, however, is that liquid assets tend to yield low returns, so if a bank holds sub-optimal levels of such assets its profits will decline. This is the trade-off between liquidity and profitability: the opportunity cost of stored liquidity is high and holding low-yielding assets (and/or zero-yielding assets such as cash) on the balance sheet reduces bank profitability (this issue will be considered further in Chapter 12).

One measure banks can use to monitor liquidity risk relates short-term securities, a proxy for a bank's liquidity sources, to total deposits – this provides an approximate measure of a bank's liquidity needs. Another traditional ratio of liquidity risk is the loan/deposits ratio. This ratio tends to focus on the liquidity of assets on the balance sheet. A high ratio of short-term securities/deposits and a low loan/deposits ratio indicate that the bank is less risky but also less profitable.

There are, however, other indicators that are more suited to proxy for a bank's liquidity needs, based on actual or potential cash flows. For example, a good indication of the bank's need for liquidity may be given by the amount a bank has in purchased or volatile funds and the amount the bank has used of its potential borrowing reserve.

Liquidity shortage can potentially cause a credit crunch (or credit squeeze), but usually actions are taken by central banks to avoid or limit the reduced availability of credit in the system. Recently, though, the markets were surprised by the delayed action of the Central Bank of China when a group of domestic banks found it increasingly difficult to satisfy their liquidity needs in the interbank market (see Box 11.4).

BOX 11.4 WHAT CAUSED CHINA'S CASH CRUNCH?

Last month some Chinese banks found it excruciatingly difficult to borrow the money they required from their fellow banks. The interest rate for an overnight loan from one bank to another briefly hit 30% on June 20th, compared with a typical rate of about 2.5% earlier in the year. This cash crunch or 'SHIBOR shock' (SHIBOR stands for Shanghai Interbank Offered Rate, a benchmark interest rate) raised immediate fears of bank defaults. It also highlighted broader concerns about financial excesses in China, where the supply of credit has been growing faster than the economy.

What caused the sudden cash crunch? Banks keep cash in reserve both to satisfy regulatory requirements and to meet their obligations to customers, creditors and each other. If a bank runs short of money, it typically borrows cash from other banks that have more than they need. Although banks can run out of money, China cannot. Its central bank, the People's Bank of China (PBC), can 'print' all the yuan it needs. It transfers this freshly created money to the banks by buying something from them, such as foreign currency, bonds or other safe financial assets. It can also lend it to them. But when China's banks ran short of cash last month, the central bank surprised everyone by refusing to help. Instead of adding more money to the banking system it sat on its hands, causing the crunch.

BOX 11.4 What caused China's cash crunch? (*continued*)

Exactly why it did so is still in dispute. A central bank may be reluctant to print money if it fears inflation. But inflation in China is quite low. The PBC was instead worried about something else. In its public statements, it argued that the banks as a group had plenty of money between them. If one or two of them were running short that was because they were behaving badly. Perhaps they had lent too much, in one form or another. Or perhaps they were taking out a lot of short-term loans from their fellow banks in order to make a lot of longer-term ones.

Banks can get away with this kind of overstretch and mismatch if they know they can always borrow easily and cheaply. Perhaps the PBC wanted to shake their complacency by creating a cash squeeze. But instead it caused an unexpectedly severe crunch. As interest rates spiked, the central bank was slow to react or to clarify its intentions. That allowed fear and uncertainty to spread. Eventually the central bank did intervene, ordering big banks to lend to smaller ones and promising to stabilise the market. But the banks remain shaken by its hesitation.

What will be the lasting consequences for China's economy? The direct damage will be limited. The shock was sharp but short. Interest rates have fallen a lot (although they remain higher than they were pre-crunch). The stock market, which plunged on June 24th and 25th, has risen by more than 7% from its lowest point. But the indirect consequences could be profound. The central bank's foot-dragging shows that China's leadership is worried about rapid credit growth. This excess lending is contributing little to the economy. Instead of financing consumer spending or business expansion it appears to be financing the purchase of existing assets instead. That adds nothing to growth. The government's efforts to curb lending could, however, subtract quite a lot from growth. The director of GK Dragonomics, a consultancy in Beijing, has predicted that China will grow by little more than 6% in 2014 at best. Barclays Capital argues that quarterly growth could briefly fall to 3% at some point in the next few years. Neither outfit is known for its bearishness. China has not run out of money, but its double-digit growth model has run out of steam.

Source: The Economist (2013) 4 July.

11.5   Foreign exchange risk

As banking markets become more global, the importance of international activities in the form of foreign direct investment and foreign portfolio investments has increased sharply. However, the actual return banks earn on foreign investment may be altered by changes in exchange rates. Changes in the value of a country's currency relative to other currencies affect the foreign exchange rates. Like other prices, exchange rates (which essentially reflect the price of currencies) tend to vary under supply and demand pressure.

Foreign exchange relates to money denominated in the currency of another nation or group of nations. Any firm or individual that exchanges money denominated in the 'home' nation's currency for money denominated in another nation's currency can be said to be acquiring foreign exchange. This is the case whether the transaction is very small, involving, say, a few pounds, or whether it is a company changing $1 billion for the purchase of a foreign company. In addition, the transaction is viewed as acquiring foreign exchange if the type of money being acquired is in the form of foreign currency notes, foreign currency bank deposits, or any other claims that are denominated in foreign currency. Put simply, a foreign exchange transaction represents a movement of funds, or other short-term financial claims, from one country and currency to another.

Foreign exchange can take many forms. It can be in the form of cash, funds available on credit cards (credit card payments when on holiday overseas are usually made in the foreign currency but the card is debited in the home currency), bank deposits or various other short-term claims. In general, a financial claim can be regarded as foreign exchange if it is negotiable and denominated in a currency other than that in which it resides, for instance, a US dollar bank deposit in Paris. Box 11.5 gives a more formal definition and explanation of exchange rates and foreign exchange markets.

BOX 11.5 EXCHANGE RATES AND FOREIGN EXCHANGE MARKETS: WHAT IS AN EXCHANGE RATE?

The exchange rate is a *price* – the number of units of one nation's currency that needs to be surrendered in order to acquire one unit of another nation's currency. There is a wide range of 'exchange rates', for example the US dollar, Japanese Yen, British pound and the Euro. In the spot market, there is an exchange rate for every other national currency traded in that market, as well as for a variety of composite currencies such as the International Monetary Fund's Special Drawing Rights (SDRs). There is also a variety of 'trade-weighted' or 'effective' rates designed to show a currency's movements against an average of various other currencies.

In addition to the spot rates, there is a wide range of exchange rates for transactions that take place on other delivery dates, in the forward markets. While one can talk about, say, the Euro exchange rate in the market, it is important to note that there is no single or unique Euro exchange rate in the market, as the rate depends on when the transaction is to take place, the spot rate being the current rate and forward rates being influenced by various factors, most noticeably the Euro interest rate compared to the official interest rate in other currencies.

The market price is determined by supply and demand factors, namely, the interaction of buyers and sellers, and the market rate between two currencies is determined by the interaction of the official (mainly central banks) and private (banks, companies, investment firms, and so on) participants in the foreign exchange market. For a currency with an exchange rate that is set by the monetary authorities, the central bank or another official body is the key participant, standing ready to buy or sell the currency as necessary to maintain the authorised rate.

What are the features of the foreign exchange markets?

While most people are familiar with the aforementioned features of foreign exchange they are less familiar with what is known as the foreign exchange market. The foreign exchange market represents an international network of major foreign exchange dealers (central banks, commercial banks, brokers and other operators) that undertakes high-volume (wholesale) trading around the world. These transactions nearly always take the form of an exchange of bank deposits of different national currency denominations. If one bank agrees to sell Euro for US dollars to another bank, there will be an exchange between the two parties of a Euro bank deposit for a US dollar bank deposit.

There is no physical location for the foreign exchange market, and transactions are carried out via computer screens based in banks, large companies and various other organisations throughout the world. The majority of foreign exchange turnover takes place in the main financial centres of London, New York and Tokyo. The main market participants include banks, non-financial firms, individuals, official bodies and other private institutions that are buying and selling foreign exchange at any particular time. Some of the buyers and sellers of foreign exchange may be involved in physical goods transactions and need foreign exchange to make purchases (such as a UK importer of car parts from Japan that needs to make a purchase in Yen). However, the proportion of foreign exchange transactions related to goods trade is generally believed to be very small – less than 5% of all foreign exchange transactions. Other participants in the market may wish to undertake foreign exchange transactions to undertake direct investment in plant and equipment, or in portfolio investment (dealing across borders in stocks and bonds and other financial assets), while others may operate in the money market (trading short-term debt instruments internationally).

Overall, the motives of participants in the foreign exchange market are wide and varied. Some participants are international investors or speculators while others may be financing foreign investments or

BOX 11.5 Exchange rates and foreign exchange markets: what is an exchange rate? (*continued*)

trade. Many participants also use foreign exchange transactions for risk management purposes in order to hedge against the risks associated with adverse foreign exchange movements. Transactions may be very short-term or long-term, and can be conducted by official bodies (such as central banks) or by private institutions, the motives for conducting business can vary and the scale of activity can alter substantially over time. All these combined features make up the supply and demand characteristics of the global foreign exchange market.

Given the diverse make-up of the supply and demand features of the market, predicting the future course of exchange rates is a particularly complex and uncertain business. In addition, since exchange rates influence such an extensive array of participants and business decisions, it is a critically important price in an economy, influencing consumer prices, investment decisions, interest rates, economic growth, the location of industry, and much more. It should be clear that for a firm wishing to undertake international activity knowledge of the foreign exchange market, predictions about future exchange rates and the risks associated with foreign exchange are essential elements that senior managers must understand if they are to be successful in overseas expansion.

The foreign exchange market consists of a wholesale (or interbank) market and a retail market. Transactions in the wholesale market are dominated by bank-to-bank transactions that involve very large transactions, typically greater than $1 million. In contrast, the retail market, where clients obtain foreign exchange via their banks, involves much smaller sums.

According to the 2013 Triennial Survey by the Bank for International Settlements (BIS), global foreign exchange market turnover was 61% higher in April 2013 than in April 2007, with average daily turnover of $5.3 trillion compared to $4.0 trillion in 2010 and $3.3 trillion in 2007. FX swaps were the most actively traded instruments in April 2013, at $2.2 trillion per day, followed by spot trading at $2.0 trillion. The growth of foreign exchange trading was driven by financial institutions other than reporting dealers. Smaller banks (not participating in the survey as reporting dealers) accounted for 24% of turnover, institutional investors such as pension funds and insurance companies 11%, and hedge funds and proprietary trading firms another 11%. Trading with non-financial customers, mainly corporations, contracted between the 2010 and 2013 surveys, reducing their share of global turnover to only 9%. The US dollar remained the dominant vehicle currency; it was on one side of 87% of all trades in April 2013. The euro was the second most traded currency, but its share fell to 33% in April 2013 from 39% in April 2010. The turnover of the Japanese yen increased significantly between the 2010 and 2013 surveys. So too did that of several emerging market currencies, and the Mexican peso and Chinese renminbi entered the list of the top 10 most traded currencies. Trading is increasingly concentrated in the largest financial centres. In April 2013, sales desks in the United Kingdom, the United States, Singapore and Japan intermediated 71% of foreign exchange trading, whereas in April 2010 their combined share was 66%.

Source: Bank for International Settlements (2013b).

Foreign exchange risk is the risk that exchange rate fluctuations affect the value of a bank's assets, liabilities and off-balance-sheet activities denominated in foreign currency. We have seen in Chapter 9 that UK banks have significant amounts of foreign currency assets and liabilities in their balance sheet – this is mainly from the assets and liabilities of foreign banks based in London that do predominantly wholesale foreign currency-related business (see Tables 9.2 and 9.3). A bank may be willing to take advantage of differing interest rates or margins in another country, or simply to invest abroad in a currency different from the domestic one. A bank that lends in a currency that depreciates more quickly than its home currency will be subject to foreign exchange risk.

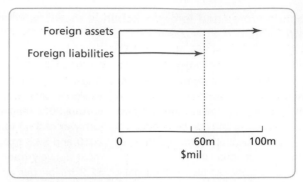

Figure 11.3 The foreign asset and liability position
of a Spanish bank: a net long asset position in US$

Suppose a Spanish bank has a net 'long' assets position in dollars (e.g. a loan in dollars) of $100 million, as illustrated in Figure 11.3. (If the bank is *net long* in foreign assets it means it holds more foreign assets than liabilities. Conversely, the bank would be holding a *net short* position in foreign assets if it had more foreign liabilities than assets.) On the liability side, the Spanish bank has $60 million in Spanish CDs. These CDs are denominated in euros. The Spanish bank will suffer losses if the exchange rate for dollars falls or depreciates against the euro over this period because the value of the US dollar loan assets would decrease in value by more than the Euro CDs.

To measure foreign exchange risk, banks calculate measures of net exposure by each currency. It will be equal to the difference between the assets and liabilities denominated in the same currency. In the case above the bank is exposed to the risk that its net foreign assets may have to be liquidated at an exchange rate lower than the one that existed when the bank entered into the foreign asset/liability position.

11.6 Market (or trading) risk

Market risk is the risk of losses in on- and off-balance-sheet positions arising from movements in market prices. It pertains in particular to short-term trading in assets, liabilities and derivative products, and relates to changes in interest rates, exchange rates and other asset prices.

Modern conditions have led to an increase in market risk due to a decline in traditional sources of income and a greater reliance by banks on income from trading securities. This process has increased the variability in banks' earnings due to the relatively frequent changes in market conditions. International regulators have acknowledged the importance of market risk since 1996 when the Basel Capital Accord was changed to incorporate capital requirements for market risk in its capital adequacy rules (see Chapter 7).

Heffernan (2005) distinguishes between:

- general or systematic market risk, caused by a movement in the prices of all market instruments due to macro factors (e.g. a change in economic policy); and

- unsystematic or specific market risk, which arises in situations where the price of one instrument moves out of line with other similar instruments because of events related to the issuer of the instrument (e.g. an environmental law suit against a firm will reduce its share price but is unlikely to cause a decline in the market index).

Market risk is the risk common to an entire class of assets or liabilities. It is the risk that the value of investments may decline over a given period simply because of economic changes or other events that affect large portions of the market. Typically, market risk relates to changes in interest rates, exchange rates and securities' prices driven by the market overall. In the case of bank lending, credit risk is the most important, but for banks lending to companies that are investing in securities (such as bank loans to hedge funds), bank assessment of credit risk will be influenced by the hedge funds' exposure to market risk. (The banks' own investments and securities trading activity will also be subject to market risk.)

Bonds and equity are especially sensitive to the movements in market interest rates and currency prices and this affects the investors' perception of a bank's risk exposure and earnings potential. Important indicators of market (or price) risk in banking are (Rose and Hudgins, 2010):

- book value assets/estimated market value of those same assets;
- book value of equity capital/market value of equity capital;
- market value of bonds and other fixed-income assets/their value as recorded on a financial institution's book;
- market value of common and preferred stock per share, reflecting investor perceptions of a financial institution's risk exposure and earnings potential.

Box 11.6 discusses the revised market risk framework proposed by the Basel Committee on Banking Supervision in 2013.

Large banks perform VaR (value-at-risk) analysis to assess the risk of loss on their portfolios of trading assets while small banks measure market risk by conducting sensitivity analysis. VaR is a technique that uses statistical analysis of historical market trends and volatilities to estimate the likely or expected maximum loss on a bank's portfolio or line of business over a set period, with a given probability. The aim is to get one figure that summarises the maximum loss faced by the bank within a statistical confidence interval. For instance, it can be estimated that 'there is a 0.5 per cent chance that a portfolio will lose £1 million in value

BOX 11.6 REFORMING THE BOUNDARIES BETWEEN BANKING BOOK AND TRADING BOOK: A NEW BASEL IV?

Market risk emphasises the risks for banks that trade their assets, liabilities and derivative contracts actively and frequently in the markets. For regulatory purposes these highly liquid positions in different financial instruments (such as bonds, equities and derivatives) typically belong to the **trading book** of the bank. In contrast, the **banking book** includes deposits, cash, loans and other illiquid assets, as shown in Figure 11.4.

Although the nature of the activities reported in the trading and banking book is not fundamentally different, they are subject to separate regulatory treatment. In general, market-based activities are less onerous in terms of capital requirements and this has generated distortions in the system by incentivizing banks to move items from the banking book to the trading book,

thereby adding risks. In other words, the lack of precise boundaries between banks' banking books and trading books has resulted in regulatory arbitrage and inadequate capital levels with regards to the trading books.

Post-Basel III the Basel Committee has circulated a second consultative paper (October 2013) – that could become a new Basel IV or at least a Basel 3.5 – that aims to review the methods used to calculate regulatory capital with regard to market risk. The proposal is issued for comments by 31 January 2014. It concentrates on the design of the trading book regime and addresses the shortcomings of both standardized and internal model approaches. Finally it offers ideas about capital requirements to cover banking book Interest Rate Risk (ALM).

BOX 11.6 Reforming the boundaries between banking book and trading book: a new Basel IV? (*continued*)

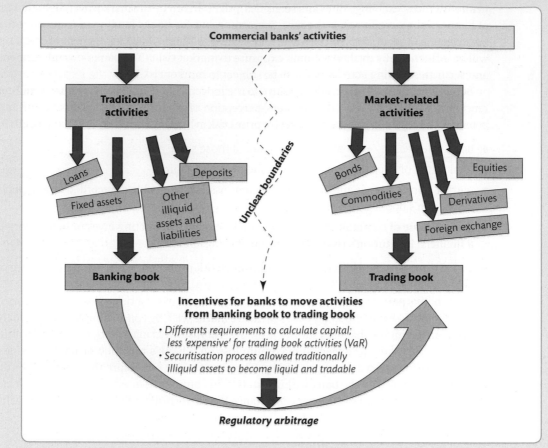

Figure 11.4 Banking vs. trading books

Source: Basel Committee on Banking Supervision (2013c).

over the next quarter'. In contrast, sensitivity analysis refers to the more traditional methods of assessing the price sensitivity of assets and liabilities to changes in interest or other rates and the corresponding impact on stockholders' equity.

11.7 Country and sovereign risk

Country risk is the risk that economic, social and political conditions of a foreign country will adversely affect a bank's commercial and financial interests. It relates to the adverse effect that deteriorating macroeconomic conditions and political and social instability may have on the returns generated from overseas investments. International lending always carries 'unusual' risks; however, it is generally accepted that a loan to a foreign government is safer than a loan to a private sector borrower (Hempel and Simonson, 2008).

Nonetheless, it is possible that even governments will default on debt owed to a bank or government agency. This is the **sovereign risk** and refers to the possibility that governments, as sovereign powers, may enforce their authority to declare debt to external lenders void or modify the movements of profits, interest and capital. Such situations typically arise when foreign governments experience some sort of economic or political pressures and decide to divert resources to the correction of their domestic problems. Clearly the fact that governments generally benefit from a particular 'immunity' from legal process makes international lending extremely risky for banking institutions that in case of default find it very difficult, if not impossible, to recover some of the debt by taking over some of the country's assets.

Sovereign risk can result in the re-scheduling and re-negotiation of the debt, with considerable losses for the lending banks. These types of new agreements are usually obtained with the intervention of international organisations (e.g. the International Monetary Fund and the World Bank). The extreme case for sovereign risk is *debt repudiation,* when the government simply repudiates its debts and no longer recognises its obligations to external creditors.

To help investors measure country and sovereign risks, rating-company agencies provide tables of sovereign (credit risk) ratings. Table 11.1 shows sovereign credit ratings as of December 2012 according to Standard & Poor's for a selection of countries. It can be seen that

Table 11.1 Selected sovereign foreign currency ratings

Country	Rating	Country	Rating	Country	Rating
Argentina	B−(−)	Hong Kong	AAA	Pakistan	B−
Australia	AAA	Hungary	BB	Philippines	BB+(+)
Austria	AA+(−)	Iceland	BBB-	Poland	A−
Belgium	AA(−)	India	BBB−(−)	Portugal	BB(−)
Brazil	BBB	Indonesia	BB+(+)	Russia	BBB
Bulgaria	BBB	Ireland	BBB+(−)	Singapore	AAA
Canada	AAA	Israel	A+	Slovenia	A(−)
Chile	AA−	Italy	BBB+(−)	South Africa	BBB+(−)
China	AA−	Japan	AA−(−)	Spain	BBB−(−)
Colombia	BBB−(+)	Jordan	BB(−)	Sweden	AAA
Croatia	BB+	Korea	A+	Switzerland	AAA
Cyprus	CCC+(−)	Lithuania	BBB	Taiwan, China	AA−
Czech Rep.	AA−	Malaysia	A−	Thailand	BB+
Denmark	AAA	Mexico	BBB	Turkey	BB
Finland	AAA(−)	Netherlands	AAA(−)	United Kingdom	AAA(−)
France	AA+(−)	New Zealand	AA	United States	AA+(−)
Germany	AAA	Norway	AAA	Venezuela	B+
Greece	A−	Peru	BB−	Zambia	B+

Note: The best-quality credits are rated AAA, followed by AA, A, BBB, BB, B and although not shown in the table, CCC, CC, and finally D for in default. The + and − signs simply reflect a little fine-tuning, so BB+ has a higher credit rating than BB, but not as good as BBB, etc.

(+) and (−) indicate positive (negative) outlook according to S&P.

Source: Standard & Poor's (2012).

over the period studied China (AA−) had a higher sovereign risk rating than India (BBB−, with a negative outlook), suggesting that in the credit-rating agency's view the Indian government is a higher credit risk than China's. The governments of Pakistan and Cyprus, with credit ratings of B− and CCC+, should be viewed as the worst credit risks (i.e. of the countries listed in Table 11.1, these are the governments most likely to default on interest and principal repayments on their bond issues).

11.8 Operational risk

Another important risk in banking is **operational risk**. The Risk Management Group of the Basel Committee on Banking Supervision (2001) defines operational risk as 'the risk of loss resulting from inadequate or failed internal processes, people and systems or from external events'. In general terms, this is the risk associated with the possible failure of a bank's systems, controls or other management failure (including human error).

The definition of operational risk given above includes **technology risk**; however, there are some differences between the two that are outlined below (Saunders and Cornett, 2012, p. 192):

- Technology risk occurs when technological investments do not produce the anticipated cost savings in the form of either economies of scale or scope. This risk also refers to the risk of current delivery systems becoming inefficient because of the developments of new delivery systems.

- Operational risk occurs whenever existing technology malfunctions or back-office support systems break down.

Operational risk was one of the main innovations in Basel II, requiring banks to hold capital for such risks along with credit and market risk. Table 11.2 shows a list of operational risk event types that the Basel Committee, in consultation with the industry, has identified as having the potential to result in substantial losses. As shown in the table, operational risk includes a number of risk event types, from employee fraud to natural disaster, that may damage a bank's physical assets and reduce its ability to communicate with its customers.

11.9 Off-balance-sheet risk

So far, we have analysed banking risks that arise through on-balance-sheet activities. For example, bad loans on the asset side, and deposit withdrawals and bank runs on the liability side. But they can also derive from off-balance-sheet exposures that can potentially translate into significant losses.

Off-balance-sheet (OBS) risk relates to the risks incurred when banks deal in activities that imply the increase in contracts that obligate them to perform in various ways but do not appear in the bank balance sheet. Examples of such activities are financial guarantees and letters of credit (as described in Chapter 10) that involve the creation of contingent assets and liabilities. It is also reasonable to think that the volatility in market values and complexity of many derivative instruments imply that they carry a considerable degree of OBS risk.

Table 11.2 Operational risk event types

Risk event types	Examples include
Internal fraud	Intentional misreporting of positions, employee theft, and insider trading on an employee's own account.
External fraud	Robbery, forgery, cheque kiting* and damage from computer hacking.
Employment practices and workplace safety	Workers' compensation claims, violation of employee health and safety rules, organised labour activities, discrimination claims and general liability.
Clients, products and business practices	Fiduciary breaches, misuse of confidential customer information, improper trading activities on the bank's account, money laundering and sale of unauthorised products.
Damage to physical assets	Terrorism, vandalism, earthquakes, fires and floods.
Business disruption and system failures	Hardware and software failures, telecommunication problems and utility outages.
Execution, delivery and process management	Data-entry errors, collateral management failures, incomplete legal documentation, unapproved access given to client accounts, non-client counterparty mis-performance and vendor disputes.

Note: *'Cheque kiting' is a fraudulent method to draw against uncollected bank funds.

This may still occur despite new accounting standards requiring banks to disclose the fair value of their financial derivatives in their balance sheet.

Given the nature of OBS activities and the fact that they have become increasingly widespread, it can be difficult for investors and regulators to identify the actual level of risk a bank is taking in any given period. Paradoxically, derivative products were introduced to reduce the amount of risk taken by a business, but recent history has shown that while they can provide some protection against important risks such as interest rate or currency risk, excessive OBS commitments can result in spectacular losses, due to mismanagement or speculative use of financial instruments. The Barings Bank failure in 1995 is an often-quoted example of insolvency of a British investment bank due to the misuse of derivatives activities. The Barings case and some other well-known examples of losses caused by 'rogue traders' in derivatives and other OBS items (foreign exchange trading and investment fund business) are discussed in Chapter 8 (Box 8.1).

Given the potential huge losses that can be derived from excessive OBS trading, the regulators' approach has been to incorporate OBS commitments (using an on-balance-sheet or credit equivalent) in calculating bank capital adequacy requirements (see Chapter 7). In addition, as mentioned above, the most recent approach to accounting standards has been to require banks to disclose the amount of derivative commitments in the balance sheet at fair value.

11.10 Other risks

There are a number of other risks that banks face. It is common to distinguish between macro and micro risks. Macro risks are also known as environmental risks and some of them are common to all businesses. They can include the risk of an economic recession, a sudden change in taxation or an unexpected change in financial market conditions, due for example to war, revolution, stock market crashes or other factors. Additional examples include the following:

- **Inflation risk** – the probability that an increase in the price level for goods and services will unexpectedly erode the purchasing power of a bank's earnings and returns to shareholders.

- **Settlement or payment risk** – a risk typically faced in the interbank market; it refers to the situation where one party to a contract fails to pay money or deliver assets with another party at the time of settlement. It can include credit/default risk if one party fails to settle. It can also be associated with any timing differences in settlement between the two parties.

- **Regulatory risk** – the risk associated with a change in regulatory policy. For example, banks may be subject to certain new risks if deregulation takes place and barriers to lending or to entry of new firms are lifted. Changing rules relating to products and dealing with customers are other examples of potential regulatory risk.

- **Competitive risk** – the risk that arises as a consequence of changes in the competitive environment, as bank products and services become available from an increasing number of new entrants, including non-bank financial firms and retailers.

Microeconomic risks are generally due to factors inside the bank, rather than external factors, such as:

- **Operating risk** – the possibility that operating expenses might vary significantly from what is expected, producing a decrease in income and the bank's value.

- **Legal risk** – the risk that contracts that are not legally enforceable or documented correctly could disrupt or negatively affect the operations, profitability or solvency of the bank.

- **Reputation risk** – the risk that strategic management's mistakes may have consequences for the reputation of a bank. It is also the risk that negative publicity, either true or untrue, adversely affects a bank's customer base or brings forth costly litigation, thereby affecting profitability.

- **Portfolio risk** – the risk that the initial choice of lending opportunities will prove to be poor, in that some of the alternative opportunities that were rejected will turn out to yield higher returns than those selected.

- **Call risk** – the risk that arises when a borrower has the right to pay off a loan early, thus reducing the lender's expected rate of return.

Sometimes risks may be due to both internal and exogenous factors. Earnings risk, for example, is the risk that earnings may decline unexpectedly and this may be due to bad management or a change in laws and regulation.

Finally, it is worth mentioning **management risk**. This is the risk that management lacks the ability to make commercially profitable and other decisions consistently. It can also include the risk of dishonesty by employees and the risk that the bank will not have an effective organisation.

11.11 Capital risk and solvency

Capital risk should not be treated as a separate risk because all risks described in this chapter can potentially affect a bank's capital. In other words, excessive credit risk, interest rate risk, operational risk, liquidity risk, OBS risk, etc. could all result in a bank having insufficient capital to cover such losses. As noted in Chapter 8 (Box 8.1) in the case of Barings Bank, in such an instance the bank's solvency is impaired and failure can occur.

A bank will be insolvent when it has negative net worth of stockholders' equity. We learned in Chapter 9 that this is the difference between the market value of its assets and liabilities. Therefore, capital risk refers to the decrease in market value of assets below the market value of its liabilities. In case of liquidation the bank would not be able to pay all its creditors and would be bankrupt.

Capital risk is closely tied to financial leverage (debt/equity) and banks are typically highly leveraged firms. It also depends on the asset quality and the overall risk profile of the institution. One should realise by now that the amount of capital a bank holds is positively related to the level of risk, that is, the more risk taken, the greater the amount of capital required. Banks with high capital risk (that is, banks that have low capital to assets ratios) also normally experience greater periodic fluctuations in earnings.

Capital risk, therefore, is the same as the risk of insolvency or the risk of failure. The following are some early indicators of failure risk (Rose and Hudgins, 2010, p. 187):

- The interest rate spread between market yields on bank debt issues and market yields on government securities of the same maturity: if the spread increases then investors believe that the bank in question is becoming more risky relative to government debt – investors in the market expect a higher risk of loss from purchasing and holding the bank's debt.

- The ratio of stock price per share to annual earnings per share: the ratio will often fall if investors come to believe that a bank is undercapitalised relative to the risks it has taken on.

- The ratio of equity capital to total assets: a low level of equity relative to assets may indicate higher risk exposure for debt holders and shareholders.

- The ratio of purchased funds to total liabilities: purchased funds usually include uninsured deposits and short-term borrowings in the money market.

- The equity capital to risk-weighted assets ratio: indicates how well a bank's capital covers potential losses from the assets that are most likely to decline in value.

11.12 Interrelation of risks

In this chapter we have presented the characteristics of the main risks that modern banks face. While we have described each risk independently, risks are often correlated. For example, an increase in interest rates may increase default risk because companies may find it more difficult to maintain the promised payments on their debt. It may also increase liquidity risk for the bank if the defaulted payments were important for liquidity management purposes. Ultimately, this will affect banks' earnings and capital. Similarly, market risk and **rogue trader risk** (operational risk) can be highly interrelated, as outlined in Box 11.7.

Note that banks face a plethora of risks and these risks are not mutually exclusive. They face credit risk when lending, market risk when trading in securities, interest rate risk in their funding operations, operational risks in undertaking all activities, and so on.

BOX 11.7 INTERACTIONS BETWEEN MARKET RISK AND ROGUE TRADER RISK

Rogue trading can be defined as the situation where traders engage 'in fraudulent practices, while trading on behalf of their institutions with a view of deliberately violating an institution's trading related rules/mandates, with the intention of deriving superior monetary benefits for themselves' (see also Chapter 8).

According to the Basel Committee on Banking Supervision, rogue trader risk is a type of operational risk that falls specifically under 'people risk', accounts for errors and misdeeds of employees and is classified as 'internal fraud' [see also Table 11.2].

In an interesting article on the regulatory implications of rogue trading it is noted that large losses due to rogue trading are often triggered by adverse movements in market risk factors (for example: interest rates, foreign exchange rates, commodity, and equity prices). In this typical interaction between operational and market risk factors, severity of losses due to rogue trading is determined by market risk factors (Figure 11.5). Therefore, unless accompanied by adverse movements in relevant market risk factors, rogue trading positions would result in relatively low losses as purely operational risk events. For instance, the penalty levelled by a regulator would most likely be less than an adverse market movement. Appreciating the risk interactions and their impacts is crucial to devise necessary controls and monitoring of positions to effectively manage rogue trader risks.

Source: Adapted from Accenture (2013).

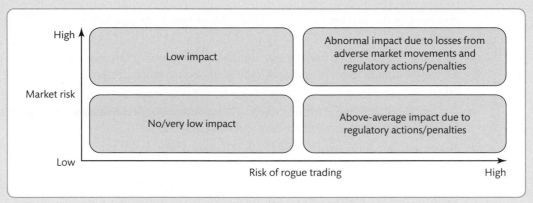

Figure 11.5 Interaction between rogue trading and market risks: impact on losses
Source: Accenture (2013).

11.13 Conclusion

Risks are part of any economic activity. In financial services they assume a particular relevance because the business of banking is linked to uncertain future events and the risk of a bank failure is always a possibility in a system essentially run on confidence.

We have shown in this chapter that banks have to face a number of often interrelated risks, such as interest rate risk, credit risk and liquidity risk, and that banks' attempts to cope with risks have often brought about other risks. One such case is derivative products that were designed to control risk through various hedging techniques, and have demonstrated themselves, in certain cases, to be highly risky instruments.

There are various ways for a well-managed bank to protect against risk. One way is through diversification, in all its forms (e.g. portfolio diversification and geographic diversification).

In addition, a bank will have to carry out appropriate asset/liability management practices and hedging strategies. Finally, there is capital that can act as a financial buffer, thus minimising the likelihood of bank failure. The next chapter discusses these and other issues and focuses on the various approaches to managing the main risks in modern banking.

Key terms

Banking book	Fixed-rate assets	Management risk	Reinvestment risk
Call risk	and liabilities	Market risk	Reputation risk
Capital risk	Foreign exchange	Off-balance-sheet	Rogue trader risk
Competitive risk	risk	(OBS) risk	Settlement or
Counterparty risk	Inflation risk	Operating risk	payment risk
Country risk	Interest rate	Operational risk	Sovereign risk
Credit culture	risk	Portfolio risk	Systematic/
Credit philosophy	Legal risk	Rate-sensitive assets	unsystematic
Credit-rating	Liquidity crisis	and liabilities	credit risk
agencies	Liquidity risk	Refinancing risk	Technology risk
Credit risk	Loan policy	Regulatory risk	Trading book

Key reading

Hempel, G.H. and Simonson, D.G. (2008) *Bank Management,* New York: John Wiley & Sons.

Resti, A. and Sironi, A. (2010) *Risk Management and Shareholders' Value in Banking,* Chichester: John Wiley & Sons.

Rose, P.S. and Hudgins, S.C. (2010) *Bank Management & Financial Services,* 8th Edition, Singapore: McGraw-Hill.

Saunders, A. and Cornett, M.M. (2012) *Financial Institutions Management: A risk management approach,* New York: McGraw-Hill/Irwin.

Sinkey, J.F. Jr (2002) *Commercial Bank Financial Management,* London: Prentice Hall International.

REVISION QUESTIONS AND PROBLEMS

11.1 What is credit risk and what is meant by credit culture?

11.2 Define interest rate risk and distinguish between reinvestment and refinancing risk.

11.3 What are rate-sensitive assets and liabilities?

11.4 Why is liquidity risk one of the most important concerns for bank management?

11.5 Is it correct to state that the root of liquidity risk lies on information asymmetries?

11.6 What is exchange rate risk? What are the main features of foreign exchange markets?

11.7 What is a commercial bank's banking book? Why should the boundaries between banking books and trading books be reviewed?

11.8 What are the differences between country and sovereign risk?

11.9 What distinguishes operational risk from technology risk? Explain the interactions between market risk and rogue trader risk.

11.10 Explain the importance of capital risk.

Chapter 12

Bank risk management

Learning objectives

- To define risk measurement and risk management
- To understand the role of corporate governance in determining banks' risk culture
- To understand the importance of risk management
- To identify the main risk management techniques

12.1   Introduction

This chapter focuses on risk management as a central management tool to ensure banks' soundness and profitability. Risk management is a complex and comprehensive process, which includes creating an appropriate environment, maintaining an efficient **risk measurement** structure, monitoring and mitigating risk-taking activities and establishing an adequate framework of internal controls. As we have noted in previous chapters, the management of banking risks is becoming increasingly important in the light of the recent market turbulence, which many consider to be the result of a failure of **risk management** systems. The need for a broad new risk management approach in banking is being discussed by policy makers globally. In particular, one issue that has come to the spotlight relates to the need to tackle the problem of excessive bank risks at its roots, by setting standards of good practice in relation to **corporate governance** and regulating bank managers' remuneration packages. In addition, the Basel Committee has proposed a series of capital and liquidity reforms to make banks safer (see also Chapter 7). Among the key objectives are raising the quality, consistency and transparency of the capital base, enhancing banking risk coverage, introducing a leverage ratio, promoting forward-looking provisioning and holding buffers above the minimum required. Accordingly, banks will be required not only to adopt more formal and quantitative risk measurement and risk management procedures and processes but also to make sure that they adopt appropriate risk practices and are more transparent in relation to their risk exposure. Another related crucial aspect concerns the financial instruments used for risk management purposes, whose notional value may not be directly related to the extent of bank risk exposure. We discussed derivative products extensively in Chapter 10 and, although not covered in this chapter, the reader should be aware of their key role in the banks' risk management process.

It is not only regulators that have placed increased emphasis on risk management in an attempt to foster financial stability and economic development, it is also all the more important for bankers to manage their capital more efficiently in order to maximise risk-adjusted returns from their business activities.

There are several aspects of risk management in banking and this chapter does not aim to analyse them all in detail, but rather to highlight the main issues. While Section 12.2 introduces the general issues of risk management, Sections 12.3 to 12.6 outline the main techniques used by banks to manage risks, including credit risk, interest rate risk and liquidity risk. Sections 12.7 and 12.8 illustrate the techniques that are used to manage market and operational risk. Finally, the management of country risk is discussed in Section 12.9.

12.2 General risk management

This section focuses on how the risk management function is handled within the banking organisation and highlights the importance given to this function by managers and the institutional environment influencing its effectiveness and efficiency. Here we aim to provide an overview of systems and practices that cut across the major types of risks faced by banks. These systems and processes include such items as the allocation of resources to risk management activities, governance issues, record keeping, communications within the organisation and internal audit. As pointed out by Cumming and Hirtle (2001), the difference between risk measurement and risk management is that while risk measurement deals with the quantification of risk exposures, risk management deals with the overall process that a financial institution follows to define a business strategy, to identify the risks to which it is exposed, to quantify those risks and to understand and control the nature of risks. In Chapter 11 we reviewed the main risks faced by financial institutions; for each class of risk, banks need to estimate the expected losses and the probability of unexpected losses, so that an appropriate amount of capital may be held.

It is important to recall that the main objective of bank risk managers is that of shareholders' wealth maximisation and in pursuit of such an objective they have to manage carefully the trade-off between risk and returns. In order to increase shareholders' wealth a company has to generate returns greater than its opportunity cost of capital. The opportunity cost of capital is the perceived cost to the bank of raising equity and keeping shareholders happy (see also Section 9.4.3). For example, if a bank makes an acquisition that generates a ROE of 8 per cent, but the cost of obtaining the capital funds needed to undertake the acquisition is 10 per cent, then this destroys shareholders' wealth. Alternatively, if returns exceed 10 per cent, then the acquisition creates value for shareholders. Typically, higher returns (ROE) are reflected in higher market valuations of a company's shares – or to put it another way, investors rank profitable firms more highly and this is reflected in greater equity prices. The aim of bank managers therefore is to maximise ROE relative to its cost of capital and this will maximise shareholders' wealth. Note that banks can do these sorts of calculations for all parts of their business in order to identify how capital is being used within the bank and what parts are generating the best or worst returns.

Investors, meanwhile, can expect a higher rate of return only by increasing the risk they are prepared to bear. Risk measures are therefore related to profitability measures, as banks must take risks to earn adequate returns. As Sinkey (2002) points out, the essence of modern banking is the measuring, managing and accepting of risk and the heart of bank financial management is risk management. The task then becomes: how to set appropriate targets for a bank's returns and the corresponding risks undertaken. Hempel and Simonson (2008), while cautioning that there is no exact answer, suggest three steps:

- Assess how other similar individual banks and groups of banks have made their risk/return decisions.
- Compare the bank's performance measure to those of similar banks.
- Set reasonable objectives against the backdrop of a bank's historic performance, the performance of its peers and its external environment.

These steps, in turn, are essentially based on the following analysis:

- stock market expectations (if the bank is quoted);
- trend analysis of past performance;
- trend and comparative analysis of peers' performance allowing for factors such as business mix, available production technology and external environment (macroeconomic and regulatory).

One of the underlying issues in most banking systems is the fact that deregulation, globalisation and internationalisation have increased the (real or perceived) degree of competition in banking markets, requiring banks to take on more risk to achieve satisfactory returns.

Given their special role in any economy, banks should be run in a safe and sound manner. As discussed in Section 8.3.2, US regulatory authorities monitor banks' behaviour and try to ensure that they achieve a good CAMELS rating (adequate Capital, good Asset quality, competent Management, good Earnings, sufficient Liquidity and Sensitivity to market risk). Banks are rated 1 (essentially sound) to 5 (basically insolvent). Banks with ratings of 1 or 2 are considered to present few, if any, supervisory concerns, while banks with ratings of 3, 4 or 5 present moderate to extreme degrees of supervisory concern. A bank's CAMELS rating is highly confidential; it is evaluated by the bank's senior management and disclosed only to the appropriate supervisory staff. However, the public may infer such information based on subsequent bank actions or specific disclosures.

The main elements of modern risk management processes and strategies include identifying, measuring and monitoring risk exposures. The overall risk management process should be a comprehensive one, which creates a risk management culture in all departments of the financial institution. The specific asset–liability management function (its coverage and functions) varies from bank to bank. However, as detailed in Chapter 10, the ALM function takes an overall risk management view of the bank. Specifically, ALM is concerned with explicit managerial and risk functions such as liquidity, capital management, funding and cost of funds, and managing the bank's security portfolio.

Interest rate risk management and lending and credit risk management are key components of a bank's overall risk management function and are also part of the ALM function, but they are usually managed specifically by separate units or divisions within a bank. For this reason, and because of the relative importance of such risks for financial institutions, we will analyse in detail their management processes. Before we move on to specific risk management techniques, let us outline the basic concepts of the risk management process.

Following the publication of the comprehensive set of 'core principles' for effective banking supervision in 1997 (BCBS, 1997a) and as part of an ongoing effort to enhance sound practices in banking organisations, the BCBS has issued a number of publications – in the form of core principles, standards and guidelines – to highlight the practices and criteria that should underpin the risk management process. In recent years, the BCBS's response to the 2007–2009 crisis has resulted in the compilation of a set of documents that forms the basics of a new Accord, including:

- 'Basel III: A global regulatory framework for more resilient banks and banking systems' (June 2011);
- 'Basel III: Towards a safer financial system' (September 2010).

A full list of reports can be found at the Bank for International Settlements online publications archive at **www.bis.org/bcbs**. It is noticeable that one of the most recent objectives of the Basel Committee is to ensure better corporate governance and control of remuneration practices. Publications in these areas include:

- 'Principles for enhancing corporate governance' (October 2010);
- 'Range of methodologies for risk and performance alignment of remuneration' (May 2011).

Corporate governance and remuneration policies are particularly sensitive topics in banking for two main reasons: first because the **risk culture** shared in any corporation is ultimately determined and monitored by corporate governance frameworks and second, because performance-related managers' remuneration can potentially increase the risk-taking incentives and this can produce undesirable outcomes, particularly in a sector like banking that relies heavily on confidence. Box 12.1 looks into these issues in some detail; however, first it is useful for the reader to reflect on the concept of risk culture as defined in Table 12.1.

According to Power *et al.* (2013), the common thread that runs through almost all definitions of risk culture is that it concerns people's behaviour within an organisation in relation to risk management. Corporate governance and leadership should design, express and

Table 12.1 Selected definitions of risk culture

Definitions from the 'practice literature'	Source
The values, beliefs, knowledge and understanding about risk shared by a group of people with a common purpose, in particular the employees of an organisation or of teams or groups within an organisation.	IRM (2012)
The combined set of individual and corporate values, attitudes, competencies and behaviour that determines a firm's commitment to and style of operational risk management.	BCBS (2011d)
The system of values and behaviour present throughout an organisation that shapes risk decisions. Risk culture influences the decisions of management and employees, even if they are not consciously weighing risks and benefits.	KPMG (2010)
The norms and traditions of behaviour of individuals and of groups within an organisation that determine the way in which they identify, understand, discuss, and act on the risks the organisation confronts and the risks it takes.	IIF (2009)
Organisational behaviour and processes that enable the identification, assessment and management of risks relative to objectives ranging from compliance to operational, financial and strategic.	PwC (2012)

Source: Adapted from Power *et al.* (2013).

impart the company's propensity to risk. However, the governance implications in banks are different from those of other financial organisations for a number of reasons, as discussed in Box 12.1.

BOX 12.1 THE CORPORATE GOVERNANCE OF BANKS

Since the financial crisis of 2007–2009, much has been said about the way in which banks are governed and how senior executives are remunerated. There is a general belief that some CEOs and other senior executives had perverse incentives that encouraged them to formulate strategies to pursue excessive risks (so as to boost their pay and other benefits) at the expense of the ultimate bank owners – the shareholders. There has also been criticism that some banks had too powerful CEOs that had undue influence on chairmen and boards resulting in little checks to their (sometimes) excessive risk-taking behaviour. Recent EU policy has been directed to limiting bank executive pay – by restricting bonus payments – and over the last decade or so there has been a general trend to improve the way in which publicly listed companies are governed. This section briefly highlights these topical issues relating to bank corporate governance.

How to define corporate governance?

There is no generally accepted definition of what corporate governance is, but typically it relates to the way outside investors and other stakeholders, such as employees and government, exercise control over senior management and other corporate insiders in order to protect their interests. The main focus of the academic literature, prompted by the seminal work of Jensen and Meckling (1976), has tended to focus on the tensions that arise between corporate insiders and shareholders and also between equity holders and other creditors (such as banks and bondholders) over the appropriate amount of risk that firms (including banks) should take. As shareholders own the residual claims in the firms they invest in (this is a formal way of saying that creditors, like banks and bondholders, are paid before shareholders when firms make any payout – in both the good and bad times), so this structure creates a strong incentive for shareholders to emphasise risk-taking – shareholders want firms to take on risks to earn higher returns so that other creditors are first paid off and then they can earn higher dividends. More risk and greater returns

will also likely boost share prices, thus feeding capital gains for shareholders.

Of course, excessive risk-taking can lead ultimately to bankruptcy and failure – an outcome that shareholders and other stakeholders are unlikely to be keen on. The key issue is how to balance insider and outsider interests so firms do not take on too much risk and the benefits of all parties are optimised.

Is the governance of banks different from other firms?

The situation of governance in banking is more complicated than for other types of firms for three main reasons:

1 Banks are highly leveraged – they have much less capital than other industries.

2 Banks have opaque business models – some activities are particularly difficult to evaluate, such as the amount of non-performing loans, the value of derivatives and trading activities, and so on.

3 Safety-net subsidies, such as deposit insurance, too-big-to-fail and lender-of-last-resort backstops, mean that senior executives of banks may be incentivised to take on excessive risk as the downside is not too bad/limited. To put another way, if senior executives take on too much risk and the bank fails, they may be not too concerned as they believe that most depositors will be protected by deposit insurance and/ or the government will bail out the bank if it's too big to fail. So the upside of taking more risk (big bonuses and higher pay for executives), and the limited downside resulting from safety-net subsidies, creates skewed incentives – encouraging bankers to take on too much risk.

Despite these differences, and as pointed out by Hagendorff (2014), traditionally, the corporate governance codes for banks were not much different from those applied to non-banking firms.

BOX 12.1 The corporate governance of banks (*continued*)

What are the functions of the board of directors?

The board of directors of publicly listed firms is regarded as the main internal control mechanism that promotes and protects shareholder interests. Typically, the main role of the board should be to act as a check on managerial excess, to monitor senior manager behaviour and to support management if the board sees fit. Boards also evaluate the performance of senior executives, decide on remuneration packages and can fire poor performers. It is generally accepted that a board that has more outsiders (non-executive directors) with diverse backgrounds has the best chance of being independent in its actions. Typically, the more the board is insider controlled (for instance, if there is a high proportion of company senior managers on the board), the more likely it is to be captured by incumbents and the more likely it is to act on behalf of insiders (senior company managers). In contrast, the more independent the board, the more likely it is that the company will be run in the interests of shareholders. (There is a big consulting industry that advises chairmen and CEOs on the make-up of their boards.)

What are the key changes with respect of corporate governance since the banking crisis?

In February 2009, Sir David Walker was asked by the UK government to review the corporate governance of the UK Banking Industry (Walker, 2009). The report (which became known as the *Walker Review* and was published in November 2009) outlined the following key issues: role and constitution of the board; board size, composition and qualifications of board members; functioning of the board and evaluation of its performance; role of institutional shareholders; and the governance of risk and remuneration. Many of the recommendations emanating from the report have since been implemented – particularly those on pay and the qualifications of board members. Reviews of bank corporate governance have been carried out also in other countries. For example, in the Netherlands in 2010, new governance codes were

introduced to cover banks to complement those that apply to firms.

Specifically on executive compensation, in 2010 the former FSA (now Prudential Regulation Authority) circulated the first version of a remuneration code that controls both level and structure of executive pay in all UK financial services firms (around 2,700 banks, building societies and some investment firms) (Financial Services Authority, 2010). The revised version of this code was issued in 2011 (Financial Services Authority, 2011b); however, although the UK is not part of the eurozone, as an EU member state it is subject to the CRD IV, the Fourth Capital Requirement Directive, agreed in February 2013 by the European Parliament. This controversial legislative act was implemented in January 2014 and introduced a pay cap on bankers' bonuses throughout the EU. This is impacting a big chunk of the industry and has implications for centres that seek to attract highly paid financial sector employees, like the City of London. It should be noted that the decision to limit top bankers' pay has not been imitated in the US, thus is likely to lead to either movement of activity to the detriment of the City (see *FT* article reproduced below) or to regulatory avoidance via an increase in fixed pay 'allowances' for top bankers, as HSBC has done in February 2014.[1]

Structural change is the answer to the problem of bankers' bonuses
(Article from the FT)

It is bonus time in the City of London. This annual ritual used to be about bankers, brokers and traders positioning themselves for a life-changing payout. But since the crash, the payouts are smaller and the actors have another role, which involves dodging the bullets from regulators and politicians. It is an intriguing drama with three distinct subplots: how EU bonus rules affect the City's competitiveness; the unique case of Royal Bank of Scotland, taken into state control during the crisis; and, most importantly, identifying and addressing the underlying cause of the bonus rumpus.

---

[1] Arnold (2014) 'HSBC fixed pay soars as bonus paradox bites', *Financial Times*, 24 February.

BOX 12.1 The corporate governance of banks (*continued*)

The issue has been flushed out by a new EU law that allows bankers' bonuses up to a maximum of two times salary with shareholders' permission. This law is aimed at investment banks, where very high bonuses are most common, and by implication at the City, Europe's only global investment banking capital. New York shows no sign of following this route, thus opening up pay arbitrage opportunities between Europe and the US. As this law bites, highly paid bankers will prefer to work in New York rather than London and US banks will tend to repatriate significant parts of their investment banking operations from the City to Wall Street. City vested interests exaggerate the importance of the financial services industry to the UK economy but there is no doubt that such a development would threaten the London boom and ripple out to the rest of the economy of the country's southeast, with unknown effects. The mitigating factor, of course, would be to load less of the British economy on to such a volatile and destabilising activity.

RBS has been caught in the political headlights as a result of this law. It is a unique case because it is the only leading British bank controlled by the state. George Osborne, Chancellor of the Exchequer, has an awkward decision to make if, as principal shareholder, he is asked to approve a request from the bank to pay a double-salary bonus to certain employees. On the one hand, he will need to weigh up public outrage at high pay in the City and the need for state-controlled institutions to set an example. On the other, he has a responsibility to maximise value for the taxpayer. To achieve that, RBS needs a small number of specialist debt and advisory experts in both its Treasury and its residual investment banking businesses. Such skills do not come cheap, and the chancellor will need to do a cost-benefit analysis involving political as well as economic factors if RBS pops the bonus question. He must be hoping against hope that the bank spares his blushes by capping bonuses below the ceiling.

Setting aside the cut-and-thrust of domestic and European politics, the more interesting question is the surprising resilience of bankers' pay globally to normal market forces. In any other sector that had just been bailed out, customers and shareholders would have demanded that employee remuneration drop to levels comparable with other professions. Banking pay has indeed fallen from the peaks and shareholders are still grumbling, yet there remains a substantial pay premium in banking over other industries. The fundamental reason for this is that the banking model is still very favourable for participants, allowing the possibility for super-returns in the industry as a whole and within specific pockets at any given time. Until this structural issue is addressed, the bonus question will persist.

We are not there yet because – although increased capital ratios, restrictions on over-the-counter trading and partial bans on proprietary trading have done little to dull the banks' edge – the integration of sales, trading and advisory services in single institutions gives them a powerful informational advantage. It also conceals the true profitability of product lines, and means that customers do not know what they are paying for individual products and services. They can exert pricing pressure on the part of the trade they can see but it is the hidden turn, facilitated by the edge that integrated banks enjoy, that creates the potential for super-returns and thus super-pay.

Regulators and governments have done a little to make the world's financial institutions safer but they need to require the separation of trading and advisory businesses to restore transparency to the industry and thus open up pay rates to conventional market forces. Failure to do this will mean public attention will continue to focus on bonuses, which are a symptom but not the cause of an industry that is still flawed.

In sum, the corporate governance of banks remains a topical issue and over the last decade or so there has been an explosion of research looking at aspects relating to board features, the role of CEOs, executive pay and a whole host of related issues. Figure 12.1 summarises some of the key areas investigated for banks.

Key references

Hagendorff (2014); Jensen and Meckling (1976); Walker (2009).

Source: Philip Augar (2014) *Financial Times*, 16 January.

BOX 12.1 The corporate governance of banks (*continued*)

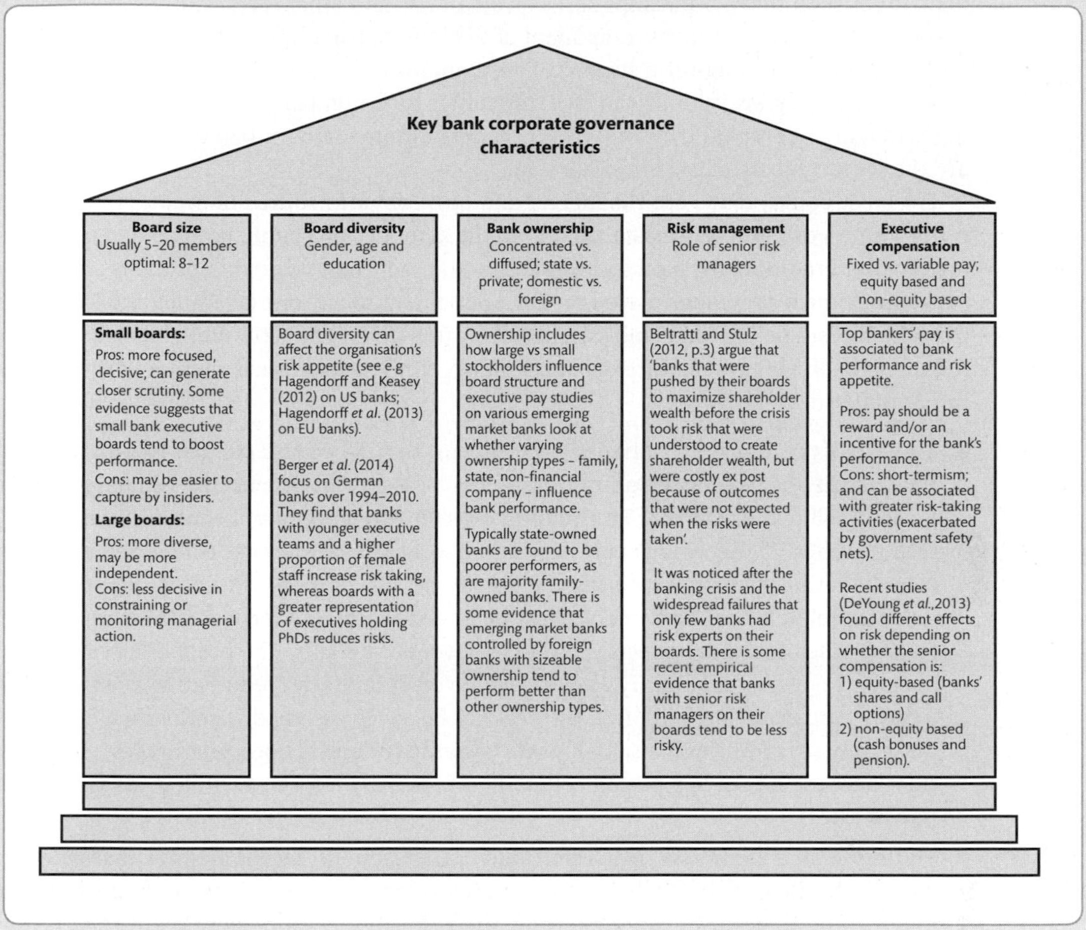

Figure 12.1 Corporate governance in banking

As mentioned in Chapter 11, the total risk a financial institution faces can be assigned to different sources. In the next sections we detail the management process of specific risks.

12.3 Credit risk management

Credit risk, defined as the potential that a bank borrower or counterparty will fail to meet its obligations in accordance with agreed terms, is the most familiar of banking risks (and it remains the most difficult to quantify).

According to the BCBS (2000), the goal of credit risk management is 'to maximise a bank's risk-adjusted rate of return by maintaining credit risk exposure within acceptable parameters'. Banks need to manage the credit risk arising both from individual creditors and individual transactions and the risk inherent in their entire portfolio. Furthermore, banks need to consider the relationships between credit risk and other risks. The effective management of credit risk is a critical component of a comprehensive approach to risk management and essential to the long-term success of any banking organisation.

While financial institutions can face difficulties for a number of reasons, in normal times loans that are not repaid (referred to as non-performing loans, or bad debts, or loan losses) are the most frequent cause of bank losses.

For most banks, loans are the largest and most obvious source of credit risk; however, other sources of credit risk exist throughout the activities of a bank, both on and off the balance sheet. Traditionally, banks have monitored credit risk through a number of standard procedures, such as ceilings placed on the amount lent to any one customer and/or customers within a single industry and/or customers in a given country. While such procedures have long been a central feature of bank lending, credit risk measurement does raise several important issues:

- The size of the loan is not sufficient to measure the risk because risk has two dimensions – the quantity of risk, or the amount that can be lost, plus the quality of the risk, which is the likelihood of default. The quality of risk is often appraised through some form of credit ratings. These ratings may be internal to a bank or external when they come from a credit-rating agency. Measuring the quality of risk ultimately leads to quantifying the default probability of customers, plus the likelihood of any recovery (how much of the loan or other debt can be recovered) in the event of default. The probability of default is obviously not easy to quantify. Historical data on defaults by credit-rating class and/or by industry are available, but often they cannot be easily assigned to individual customers. The extent of recoveries is also unknown. Losses may depend upon guarantees, either from third parties or from any posted collateral, of recovery after bankruptcy and the liquidation of assets.

- The cumulated credit risk over a portfolio of transactions, either loans or market instruments, is difficult to quantify because of diversification effects. If the defaults of all customers tend to occur at the same time, the risk is much more significant than if those default events are not related (or independent). All banks, of course, protect themselves against risk through diversification, which makes simultaneous defaults very unlikely. However, the quantitative measurement of the impact of diversification remains a modelling challenge.

Banks are increasingly facing credit risk (or counterparty risk) in various financial instruments other than loans, including acceptances, interbank transactions, trade financing, foreign exchange transactions, financial futures, swaps, bonds, equities, options, in the extension of commitments and guarantees, and the settlement of transactions.

Market transactions also generate credit risk. For instance, the inability of a company to service a swap, futures or options agreement, or make dividend repayments on bonds, is also regarded as a credit risk. The loss in the event of default depends on the value of these instruments and their liquidity. If the default is totally unexpected, the loss is the market value of the instruments at the time of default. If the credit standing of the counterparty falls, e.g. Standard & Poor's reduces the credit rating of a counterparty from AAA to AA, it will still be possible to sell their instruments in the market at a discount. For financial instruments with more limited marketability, such as OTC transactions, for example swaps and options, sale is not usually feasible. The credit risk of these types of instruments changes constantly with market movements during their lifespan. Therefore, the potential values of the transactions during the period of the contracts are at risk. Clearly, there is a relationship between credit risk and market risk during this period because values depend on market movements.

Over the last decade banks have been seeking ways to measure credit risk more accurately, a need that has been strongly driven by a variety of factors:

- the growth of securitised loans and the secondary loan trading market (see Section 4.6.2 and also Chapter 17);
- the evolution of credit derivatives business;
- the increased emphasis on risk-adjusted performance measurement systems (where performance for different parts of the firm/bank is assessed relative to the risk taken and capital backing) and the desire to transfer credit risk;
- the desire of companies to manage more effectively the risk/return characteristics of their debt funding.

These factors have all contributed to the development of an increasingly liquid and transparent market in tradable bank loans and other credit instruments. Such a market enables banks and large firms to trade their credit risk more effectively and therefore improve returns. It also provides banks with greater flexibility in meeting client needs as loan portfolios can be restructured in a more efficient manner, thereby releasing resources to be directed to higher-demand (and more profitable) areas. The growth in credit market instruments and the demand from banks to better assess the risks associated with their credit business has led to the development of various modelling techniques, similar in many respects to those previously developed to calculate market risk (such as JPMorgan's CreditMetrics™ or Credit Suisse First Boston's CreditRisk+™).[2]

Undoubtedly the 2007–2009 financial crisis has proved that these developments, particularly the growth in securitised lending, off-balance-sheet business and the increased reliance on external assessments by rating agencies in managing credit risk, resulted in banks' exposures being seriously understated. Typically, banks used complex quantitative modelling techniques to assess the risks associated with their credit business and indeed for their trading strategies too. One of the main problems, in this context, is that these models largely relied on 'normal' distributions, that although realistic in periods of prolonged stability and moderate growth (as in the *Great Moderation* era, between the late 1980s and 2007) can have devastating consequences in case of an unexpected (negative) shock to the system. It is possible that banks' over-reliance on sophisticated risk management processes increased moral hazard and encouraged banks to take on higher exposures as a result.

In a provocative speech, a member of the executive board of the ECB, Mr González-Páramo (2010), emphasised that one of the causes of the severity of the global financial crisis was banks' deviation (or even abandonment in some cases) from some well-established rules in the management of risk, and particularly credit risk.[3] These are common-sense risk management

---

[2] See Bessis (2011) for an overview of the main features of credit risk models.

[3] 'The challenges of credit risk management – lessons learned from the crisis', Speech available at **www.bis .org/review/r100528d.pdf**

practices such as 'know your counterparties', 'invest only in products you understand', 'do not outsource credit risk management by relying exclusively on external credit assessments', 'do not rely exclusively on quantitative models, however sophisticated'. Again, as we discussed in Box 11.1, the development of an appropriate credit culture within banks is crucial in ensuring a more stable and reliable banking sector.

The BCBS (2000) document identifies sound practices in the management of credit risk and specifically addresses the following areas:

1 establishing an appropriate credit risk environment;

2 operating under a sound credit-granting process;

3 maintaining an appropriate credit administration, measurement and monitoring process; and

4 ensuring adequate controls over credit risk.

Although specific credit risk management practices may differ among banks depending upon the nature and complexity of their credit activities, a comprehensive credit risk management programme will address these four areas. These practices should also be applied in conjunction with sound practices related to the assessment of asset quality, the adequacy of provisions and reserves, and the disclosure of credit risk.

12.4 Managing the lending function

Managing credit risk in retail banking, although based on the same broad principles, differs from wholesale banking in several ways. One first, obvious difference concerns the size of the loan commitments. Bad corporate loans can be very serious for banks because of the vast sums of money involved. Big corporate failures in the early 2000s caused more than a serious headache to banks. High-profile failures such as Enron, WorldCom and a group of other big, mainly US telecoms and energy companies have left banks with a large amount of bad loans. Past crises in Latin America and Asia have also led to substantial write-offs. The global crisis of 2007–2009 had major consequences on the balance sheets and performance of non-financial corporate businesses, and this affected significantly the cash flow and capital of the banking sector. Retail lending, meanwhile, while unlikely to create serious consequences for a bank in case of individual loan defaults (although it can still create problems if a large number of retail loans default, say, as a result of a bank being overexposed to a particular sector of the economy, particularly real estate), is more difficult to assess because of the lack of information on the creditworthiness of individual potential borrowers.

12.4.1 Retail lending

An accurate credit decision, given a bank's credit standards, is the one that maximises the value of the loan for the bank and minimises the risk of default. Consequently, gathering, processing and analysing information on potential borrowers are key steps in credit risk management.

Prior to making a lending decision, banks need to assess the risk–return trade-off of a loan. This process involves both an assessment of the risk of the applicant and the applicant's business, an analysis of the external environment, the purpose of the loan and the particular loan structure requested by the applicant. One key step in this process is pricing the loan, where the 'price' (**loan rate**), assuming there are no other costs, should be:

$$R^L = \frac{1 + r}{1 - d} - 1 \qquad (12.1)$$

where:

R^L = profitable loan rate

r = risk-free interest rate (i.e. the rate of return on a 'risk-free' investment, such as government bonds)

d = expected probability of default.

Equation (12.1) shows that the profitable loan rate increases with the borrower's expected probability of default. From a lender's perspective, the gross return on the loan should take into account several key factors:

1 interest rate on the loan;
2 fees relating to the loan;
3 credit risk premium on the loan;
4 collateral backing of the loan; and
5 other non-price terms (e.g. clauses and conditions on the use of the loan).

Following a general model along the lines developed by Saunders and Cornett (2012), the gross return on a loan is:

$$1 + k = 1 + \frac{f + (L + M)}{1 - [b(1 - R)]} \qquad (12.2)$$

where:

k = contractually promised gross return on the loan per £ lent

f = administration fee

L = base lending rate

M = credit risk premium on the loan

b = compensating balance requirement (as a percentage of the loan)

R = reserve requirement.

L in formula (12.2) reflects the bank's marginal cost of funds (or the so-called prime lending rate in the United States – the interest rate a bank charges its best or 'prime' customers). Compensating balances (b) is the portion of a loan that a borrower may be required to hold as deposit at the bank. They are commonly used in corporate lending business. Reserve ratios (R) are effectively a tax on deposits and can cause the loan price to rise, as banks are not earning income for every £ of reserves. Finally, the loan price should include a credit risk premium (M) and an administration fee (f). The former should reflect the risk profile of the borrower: the riskier the borrower, the higher the premium. The latter should cover all the costs incurred in the origination and administration of the loan.

Another factor that influences the price of the loan is the presence of any collateral (assets backing the loan that can include such things as residential property, other real estate, securities, etc.): the rate charged should be lower than in the case of no collateral. However, in times of economic trouble the price of collateral can become very volatile and banks may have to raise either the loan price or the amount of collateral required. If collateral values fall dramatically there can be a banking sector collapse – as was the case in the Japanese banking system crisis that occurred in 1997–1998 (discussed in Chapter 16). Obviously, if the value of the collateral is linked to the ability of the borrower to repay, a decrease in the value of the collateral will increase the probability of default. Box 12.2 illustrates how the fall in UK property prices in the early 1990s and in the aftermath of the 2007–2009 crisis resulted in loan losses and negative equity.

BOX 12.2 MORTGAGE MARKET, EQUITY WITHDRAWAL AND NEGATIVE EQUITY

Over the past forty years or so the UK housing market has experienced persistent volatility (rapid fluctuations in house prices) that resulted in major economic and social costs. During the late 1980s, UK house prices soared, boosting people's confidence in the housing market and prompting them to borrow against the value of their homes. Between 1980 and 1990, average mortgage debt in the UK more than doubled relative to income.

A **mortgage equity withdrawal** relates to homeowners borrowing against the increased value of their property (capital gains), by taking out additional housing equity loans. The Bank of England's estimate of mortgage equity withdrawal (MEW) measures the part of consumer borrowing from mortgage lenders that is not invested in the housing market. Levels of mortgage equity withdrawal reached very high levels in the late 1980s; mortgage equity loans were a major factor behind the consumer boom of 1987–88. However, the collapse in the housing market in the early 1990s led to over 1.5 million homeowners being in **negative equity** – a situation where the market value of their property was less than the outstanding mortgage loan. The slump in the UK

housing market coincided with record increases in mortgage arrears and repossessions. Between 1989 and 1993, as both interest rates and unemployment rose, the number of households in mortgage arrears increased. Arrears peaked in 1992 when over 350,000 households owed six or more months' payments. Repossessions were highest in 1991 at 75,450, falling to 58,540 by 1993.

As shown in Figure 12.2, by the mid-2000s, following a period of sharp increases in housing prices, repossessions were relatively low by historical standards. However, the financial turmoil that started in 2007, and the global credit crunch and recession that followed, profoundly affected the UK housing market and repossessions peaked in 2009 at nearly 49,000 homes.

The volatility of the early 1990s and late 2000s caused distorted housing choices and increased risks. From the lenders' point of view these housing market problems resulted in costly losses to banks and building societies (see Table 12.2). Falling nominal house prices reduced the amount of equity in housing and provided incentives for borrowers to accumulate arrears and for lenders to repossess property that had been used to secure loans.

Box 12.2 Mortgage market, equity withdrawal and negative equity (*continued*)

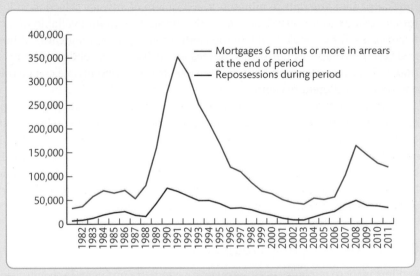

Figure 12.2 Home repossessions in the UK, 1982–2011

Source: UK Department of Community and local government statistics.

Table 12.2 Mortgages outstanding, arrears and repossessions 1994–2012

	Total number of mortgages at end of period	Mortgages 6–12 months in arrears at end of period		Mortgages 12 months or more in arrears at end of period	
		Number	%	Number	%
1994	10,410,000	133,700	1.28	117,100	1.12
1995	10,521,000	126,700	1.20	85,200	0.81
1996	10,637,000	101,000	0.95	67,000	0.63
1997	10,738,000	73,800	0.69	45,200	0.42
1998	10,821,000	74,000	0.68	34,900	0.32
1999	10,987,000	57,100	0.52	29,500	0.27
2000	11,177,000	47,900	0.43	20,800	0.19
2001	11,251,000	43,200	0.38	19,700	0.18
2002	11,368,000	34,100	0.30	16,500	0.15
2003	11,452,000	31,000	0.27	12,600	0.11
2004	11,515,000	29,900	0.26	11,000	0.10
2005	11,608,000	38,600	0.33	15,000	0.13
2006	11,746,000	34,900	0.30	15,700	0.13
2007	11,852,000	40,500	0.34	15,300	0.13
2008	11,667,000	72,000	0.62	29,500	0.25
2009	11,504,000	93,900	0.82	69,500	0.60
2010	11,478,000	80,500	0.70	63,700	0.55
2011	11,384,000	72,200	0.63	54,400	0.48
2012	11,284,000	69,900	0.62	48,500	0.43

Source: Department of Community and Local Government (DCLG), Live table 1300.

Loans availability in retail markets may not be linked simply to the loan price but restricted to a selected category of borrowers. This is a method for managing credit risk (**credit rationing**) that attempts to minimise the problem of adverse selection in loan markets. To reduce risk exposure, banks can limit the amount of credit available to a certain class of borrowers – for example, think of the credit limit on your credit card. Although it is illegal to discriminate against borrowers for reasons such as race, gender, religion, sexual orientation and address, there is no automatic 'right' to credit and people can be refused credit for a number of different reasons.

As we have seen, a loan evaluation process focuses on evaluating the prospective risk and return on a loan. There are several techniques or models for assessing credit risk, but they can be broadly divided into qualitative models and quantitative models. Qualitative models are normally used when there is limited available information on a borrower. Bank managers have to gather information from private sources and the amount of information needed will be proportional to the size of the loan. Quantitative models are to assess borrowers' creditworthiness based on the estimated probability of default.

12.4.2 Credit checking and credit scoring

Lenders want to minimise the information asymmetry problems in the retail loan market and therefore aim to ensure that potential borrowers are a good risk and do not have a history of bad debts and unpaid loans. To do this they will do two things: **credit checking** and **credit scoring**.

12.4.2.1 Credit checking

Lenders will check the applicant's entry on credit registers. **Credit reference agencies** in the United Kingdom such as Experian, Equifax and Callcredit hold factual information on retail customers and this allows a lender to check individuals' names and addresses and credit history, including any county court judgments or defaults recorded against the individual.[4] This process will provide a person's so-called *credit reference*.

12.4.2.2 Credit scoring

To obtain information on a potential borrower, banks will initially adopt a qualitative approach, which involves asking the applicant a number of questions. They will then allocate points (weights) to the answers. Questions may concern the applicant's employment history, the length of time as a customer of the bank, the number and type of accounts held, the length of time at their present address and so on. Personal judgement on behalf of loan officers based on the 'five Cs' (character, capacity, capital, collateral and conditions) is now commonly replaced by a quantitative approach based on the use of the information provided by the applicant to calculate the probability of default.[5] Using statistical programs, creditors

---

[4] Experian and Equifax are also among the major national credit bureaus in the US, together with TransUnion.

[5] The so-called five Cs of a credit decision can be described as follows: 1) *character*, which refers to the willingness of the borrower to repay the loan; 2) *capacity*, which refers to the borrower's cash flow and the ability of that cash flow to service that debt; 3) *capital*, which refers to the strength of the borrower's balance sheet; 4) *collateral*, which refers to the security backing up the loan; and 5) *conditions*, which refer to the borrower's sensitivity to external forces such as interest rate and business cycles and competitive pressures (Saunders and Cornett, 2012; Sinkey, 2002).

compare the information to the credit performance of consumers with similar profiles. A credit-scoring system awards points for each factor that helps predict who is most likely to repay a debt. A total number of points – a credit score – helps predict how creditworthy the applicant is, that is, how likely it is that they will repay a loan and make the payments when due. Lenders will never divulge how their credit scoring works for fear of fraud and each lender will have their own system. The fact that your loan application has been turned down by one lender does not necessarily imply that it will also be declined by other lenders.

Although such a system may seem arbitrary or impersonal, when it is properly designed it can help make decisions faster, more accurately and more impartially than individuals. In marginal cases, applicants are referred to a credit manager who decides whether the company or lender will extend credit. This may allow for discussion and negotiation between the credit manager and the consumer. Box 12.3 illustrates how a credit scoring system works in practice.

Credit scoring can be applied both to individuals and to corporations; obviously the variables used to define the scoring system will differ. Sinkey (2002) and Saunders and Cornett (2012) provide detailed overviews of the main credit scoring models.

BOX 12.3 CREDIT SCORING: HOW TO SCORE HIGH

● Have you paid your bills on time?

Payment history typically is a significant factor. It is likely that your score will be affected negatively if you have paid bills late, had an account referred to collections, or declared bankrupt, if that history is reflected on your credit report.

● What is your outstanding debt?

Many scoring models evaluate the amount of debt you have compared with your credit limit. If the amount you owe is close to your credit limit, it is likely that it will have a negative effect on your score.

● How long is your credit history?

Generally, models consider the length of your credit track record. An insufficient credit history may have an effect on your score, but that can be offset by other factors, such as timely payments and low balances.

● Have you applied for new credit recently?

Many scoring models consider whether you have applied for credit recently by looking at 'inquiries' on your credit report when you apply for credit. If you have applied for too many new accounts recently, it is likely that it may negatively affect your score. However, not all inquiries are counted. Inquiries by creditors who are monitoring your account or looking at credit reports to make 'pre-screened' credit offers are not counted.

● How many and what types of credit accounts do you have?

Although it is generally good to have established credit accounts, too many credit card accounts may have a negative effect on your score. In addition, many models consider the type of credit accounts you have. For example, under some scoring models, loans from finance companies may negatively affect your credit score.

Source: Adapted from the Federal Trade Commission (**www.ftc.gov**).

12.4.2.3 Linear probability models

Loans are divided in two groups, those that defaulted ($Z_i = 1$) and those that did not ($Z_i = 0$). These observations are then regressed on a set of n variables reflecting quantitative information about the ith borrower.

$$Z_i = \sum_{j=1}^{n} \beta_j X_{ij} + \epsilon \tag{12.3}$$

Logit (and Probit) models

These constrain the cumulative probability of default on a loan between zero and one and assume the probability of default to be logistically distributed (or have a normal distribution in the Probit case).

Linear discriminant models

These models (which include the Altman Z-score model) divide borrowers according to their derived Z-scores into high or low default risk classes, contingent on their observed characteristics (X_j).

$$Z_i = \sum_{j=1}^{n} \alpha_i X_{ij} \tag{12.4}$$

12.4.3 Managing the loan portfolio

Moving from individual loans to a bank's loan portfolio, the first step in credit risk management is diversification. The principle behind portfolio diversification is the same as the one behind the old saying 'don't put all your eggs in one basket'. Bank managers should diversify their lending to different sectors of the economy, different geographical locations, different types of industry, different maturities and so on. By diversifying their loan portfolios, i.e. by owing assets whose returns are not statistically correlated, banks can reduce the impact of any failure by diversifying away the unsystematic risk. A heavy concentration of loans in one sector of the economy can cause serious trouble for banks. For example, in the United Kingdom, building societies have historically concentrated the majority of their lending to finance residential property purchase and have therefore suffered a high number of non-performing loans when the housing market collapsed (see Chapter 8 and Box 12.2). If loans are not correlated, banks can expect to increase the expected returns on their loan portfolio by diversifying across asset classes. In other words, it is possible to apply standard portfolio theory to obtain a measure of aggregate credit risk exposure.[6]

When assessing the credit risk of the aggregate loan portfolio, bank managers need to calculate the following:

- the expected loss, for each loan and for the whole portfolio, over a specific time horizon;
- the unexpected loss for each loan and for the whole portfolio (i.e. the volatility of loss);
- the probability distribution of credit loss for the portfolio and the capital requirement for a given confidence level and time horizon (see Figure 12.3).

---

[6] For an introduction to portfolio theory, see Appendix A2.

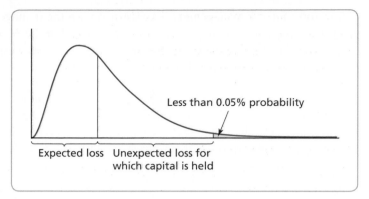

Less than 0.05% probability

Expected loss   Unexpected loss for
which capital is held

Figure 12.3 Probability distribution of portfolio losses

There are three factors that drive expected and unexpected losses on a credit portfolio:

● customer default risk – determined by the risk-grade profile of the portfolio;

● exposure – the amount that is likely to be outstanding at the time of default;

● loss given default – determined by the level of security cover, the effectiveness of the recovery process and the credit cycle.

The calculation of the expected loss is based on the current risk profile of the portfolio, possibly ignoring historical loss rates. Banks that rely on their average loss experience to derive expected loss are assuming that the risk profile, business mix and risk management processes remain constant over time. However, the existing profile might be considerably better than the one that created the losses in the past.

The main problem with applying portfolio theory to banks' loan portfolios is that, in the vast majority of cases, bank loans are non-tradable assets. As we noted earlier, there are several products in the market that attempt to deal with these issues. The best known are Credit Suisse First Boston CreditRisk+™, CreditPortfolioView™ by McKinsey and JPMorgan's CreditMetrics™. In addition, firms such as KMV[7] and KPMG are actively participating in the debate and are openly sharing many of their analytical engines. KMV was taken over by Moody's in 2002 and since then this portfolio model is called M-KMV. Moody's has several products on the market, including Credit Monitor™ and Porfolio Manager™. KPMG's contribution is the Loan Analysis System™.[8]

12.5   Managing interest rate risk

Interest rate risk can be defined as the exposure of a bank's financial condition to adverse movements in interest rates (BCBS, 2004). For banks, interest rate risk derives from mismatching the maturities of assets and liabilities, as part of their asset-transformation function. Banks use funds raised in the form of short-term deposits to issue or buy longer-term assets (loans and bonds) but typically their prices and income react differently to interest rate fluctuations compared with short-term prices and interest expenses.

---

[7] KMV is the acronym for Kealhofer, McQuown and Vasicek, the originators of the KMV methodology.
[8] For more information on these products, see Credit Suisse First Boston (1997); Bessis (2011).

Interest rate risk management is concerned with the management of the interest rate exposure of a bank. Traditionally, it is managed within the ALM function but, given the increased volatility of interest rates, together with the increased interest rate risk arising from off-balance-sheet activities, it is now often managed by a dedicated department. As seen in Section 11.3, interest rate risk arises from potential variations in banks' returns that derive from unanticipated changes in interest rates. Changes in interest rates also affect a bank's underlying economic value. The value of a bank's assets, liabilities and off-balance-sheet business is affected by a change in rates because the present value of future cash flows, and in some cases the cash flows themselves, are altered.[9] A bank interest rate risk exposure refers to market value changes in its equity position as a result of unexpected changes in market interest rates. When attempting to measure and manage interest rate risk, it is important to note that the exposure to such risk concerns *future* losses (or gains) and therefore some uncertainty will always be present. Some interest rate management techniques involve a forecast of possible interest rate scenarios and, as in every attempt to forecast the future, there is no such thing as 100 per cent accuracy. In other words, managing interest rate risk is about identifying, measuring and controlling such risk, taking uncertainty into account.

There are two broad management approaches that are used to measure interest rate risk and these are known as 'gap' and 'duration' analysis.

12.5.1 Gap analysis

Gap analysis is possibly the best-known interest rate risk management technique. The 'gap' (Figure 12.4) refers to the difference between interest rate-sensitive assets and interest rate-sensitive liabilities over a specific time horizon. If the interest rate-sensitive liabilities are greater than the interest rate-sensitive assets, then an increase in interest rates will reduce

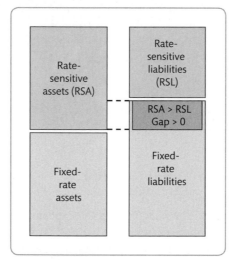

Figure 12.4 Rate-sensitivity and positive gap

---

[9] This occurs, for example, when the bank funds a one-year loan, then re-prices monthly based on the one-month T-bill rate, with a one-year deposit that re-prices monthly based on one-month LIBOR. Interest rate changes can result in unexpected changes in the cash flows and earnings spreads between assets and liabilities. This type of interest rate risk is referred to as 'basis risk'.

a bank's profit and vice versa. In the basic gap analysis, the focus is on the maturity of the rate-sensitive assets and liabilities.

$$\text{GAP} = \text{RSA} - \text{RSL} \qquad (12.5)$$

where:

RSA = rate-sensitive assets

RSL = rate-sensitive liabilities.

An asset or a liability is defined as rate sensitive if the cash flow from the asset or liability changes in the same direction as changes in interest rates. The gap ratio derived from equation (12.5) is also called the *interest-sensitivity ratio*. If this ratio is equal to one, then the rate sensitivity of assets and liabilities is perfectly matched. However, most banks have a positive gap (RSA > RSL) since they borrow short and lend long, and therefore have assets that will mature later than liabilities. The main aim of gap analysis is to evaluate the impact of a change in interest rates on the bank net interest income and net interest margin. Ideally, the gap should be managed in such a way as to expand when interest rates are rising and contract when interest rates are declining. However, it is difficult for bank managers to know what phase of the interest rate cycle they are facing. Furthermore, bank customers may be seeking opposite interest rate positions compared with the bank.

Up to now, we have defined the gap as being related to (or a function of) a specified time horizon (for example, 90 days). However, this is rather arbitrary, as it does not clearly indicate what time period is appropriate for determining the interest rate sensitivity of assets and liabilities. For instance, focusing on a short-term gap may ignore reinvestment risk (the risk that loans are repaid early). One extension of the basic gap model is the *maturity bucket* approach. Each of the bank assets and liabilities is classified according to its maturity and placed into 'maturity buckets', for example overnight, 3 months, 3–6 months and so on. Analysts compute both incremental and cumulative gap results. An incremental gap is defined as RSA − RSL in each time bucket; the cumulative gap is the cumulative subtotal of the incremental gaps.

As illustrated in Table 12.3, as total assets equal total liabilities by definition, the incremental gaps must total to zero and therefore the last cumulative gap must be zero. The maturity bucket approach allows bank managers to concentrate on the cumulative gaps for the different time buckets.

One extension is the maturity gap (M Gap).

$$\text{M Gap} = W_A\text{RSA} - W_A\text{RSL} \qquad (12.6)$$

Table 12.3 Maturity bucket gap (£mil)

	Assets	Liabilities	Gap	Cumulative gap
1 day	40	30	+10	−10
More than 1 day less than 3 months	50	60	−10	0
More than 3 months less than 6 months	90	110	−20	−20
More than 6 months less than 12 months	110	120	−10	−30
More than 1 year less than 5 years	80	70	+10	−20
Over 5 years	30	10	+20	0
	400	400		

where:

$W_A RSA$ = weighted average rate-sensitive assets

$W_A RSL$ = weighted average rate-sensitive liabilities.

This model better reflects the economic reality or the true value of assets and liabilities if the bank portfolio was liquidated at today's prices. If the maturity of a bank's assets is greater than the maturity of its liabilities, an increase in interest rates will cause the value of the assets to fall more than the value of the liabilities because the assets mature later. The bigger the maturity gap, the more a bank's net worth will suffer by an increase in interest rates. Figure 12.5 reports a simple summary for gap and maturity models in the form of a strategic matrix to maximise banks' earnings (in terms of NII and NIM) when interest rates fluctuate.

Another extension is the so-called 'dynamic gap analysis' approach, which involves forecasting interest rate changes and expected changes in the bank's balance sheet for several periods in the future. Software models provide bank managers with simulation tools to inform them of the way in which gaps are expected to be structured at certain times in the future.

Gap analysis was one of the first methods developed to measure a bank's interest rate risk exposure and continues to be widely used by banks. Despite the extensions, the gap model has been defined as 'naïve' and has been subject to a number of criticisms as the approach:

- fails to take into account the market value effect (i.e. the new value of the asset given changes in interest rates);
- suffers from over-aggregation, that is, it fails to consider for intra-bucket effects;
- fails to deal with run-offs, which is the periodic cash flow of interest and principal amortisation payments on long-term assets;
- ignores banks' exposure to pre-payment risk (the risk that loans will be repaid early);
- ignores differences in spreads between interest rates that could arise as the level of market interest rates changes (basis risk);
- does not take into account any changes in the timing of payments that might occur as a result of changes in the interest rate environment;
- generally oversimplifies the complexity of a bank's ALM.

For these reasons, gap analysis provides only a rough approximation of the actual impact of changes in interest rates.

	Gap	Maturity
If interest rates ↑	RSA>RSL	Assets < Liabilities
If interest rates ↓	RSA<RSL	Assets > Liabilities

Figure 12.5 Strategic matrix for profit maximisation

12.5.2 Duration analysis

Duration is a measure of the average life of an asset's (or liability's) cash flow. **Duration analysis** takes into account the average life of an asset (or liability) rather than its maturity. It is a technique borrowed from bond portfolio management, where duration is defined as a weighted average of the maturities of the individual coupon payments. In this context, duration may be different from maturity if, for example, an asset repayment schedule includes interest and principal. A three-year car loan that is repaid with monthly instalments will have duration different from its maturity. Maturity and duration are only ever equal in the case of single payment assets and zero coupon bonds. Higher duration implies that a given change in the level of interest rates will have a larger impact on economic value. The duration of a coupon bond is expressed by the formula (known as Macaulay duration – see Box 12.4):

$$D = 1*\frac{C_1/(1 + Y)^1}{V} + 2*\frac{C_2/(1 + Y)^2}{V} + \cdots + n*\frac{(C_n + P_n)/(1 + Y)^n}{V} \qquad (12.7)$$

where:

Y = the bond's internal yield or yield to maturity (YTM)

C_1 = annual coupon payment in year 1

P_n = principal payment

n = number of years to maturity

V = current market value of the bond.

Estimates derived from a standard duration approach may provide an acceptable approximation of a bank's exposure to changes in economic value for relatively non-complex banks. However, there are a number of problems arising from the use of the duration measure:

- Convexity – the duration formula implies a linear relationship between changes in interest rate and changes in bond price; in reality the relationship is convex. Duration is a good approximation for small changes but it becomes less accurate for larger changes.

- Data requirements – the calculation of the duration gap can be data demanding.

- Duration generally focuses on just one form of interest rate risk exposure – re-pricing risk – and ignores interest rate risk arising from changes in the relationship among interest rates within a time band (basis risk).

- The simplifying assumptions that underlie the calculation of standard duration mean that the risk from off-balance-sheet activities may be underestimated.

12.5.3 Simulation approaches

Many large banks employ more sophisticated interest rate risk measurement systems than those based on simple maturity/re-pricing schedules. These simulation techniques typically involve detailed assessments of the potential effects of changes in interest rates on earnings and economic value by simulating the future path of interest rates and their impact on cash flows. Simulation approaches typically involve a more detailed breakdown of various categories of on- and off-balance-sheet positions, so that specific assumptions about the interest and principal payments and non-interest income and expense arising from each type of position can be incorporated. In addition, simulation techniques can incorporate more varied

BOX 12.4 EXAMPLE OF MACAULAY DURATION

Consider a bond with the following characteristics:

- £ 100 annual coupon;
- 2 years to maturity;
- YTM = 10%;
- market value £ 1,000.

The Macaulay duration for this bond is 1.909 years.

$$1.909 = 1 * \frac{£100/(1.1)}{£1000} + 2 * \frac{£1100/(1.1)^2}{£1000}$$

The formula provides the weighted average payment stream, where the maturity of each payment is weighted by the fraction of the total value of the bond accounted for by the payment. As the example illustrates, the emphasis in duration analysis is on the market value rather than on the book value, as was the case in gap analysis.

Using formula (12.7) it is possible to compute the duration of the entire asset and liability portfolios of a bank (see Box 12.5 for an example). By matching the duration of assets and liabilities, movements in interest rates should have roughly the same effect on both sides of the balance sheet. Duration gap (DG) measures the mismatch between the duration of a bank's assets and its liabilities.

$$DG = \left(D_A - \frac{L}{A} D_L \right) \tag{12.8}$$

where:

A = market value of assets

L = market value of liabilities

D_A = duration of assets

D_L = duration of liabilities

L/A = leverage or gearing ratio.

The impact of a change in interest rates on the value of a bank's equity can be calculated from equation (12.9) as follows:

$$\Delta E = -DG \left(\frac{\Delta r}{(1 + r)} \right) A \tag{12.9}$$

where:

ΔE = change in the value of bank equity

DG = duration gap

Δr = change in interest rate

A = market value of assets.

BOX 12.5 EXAMPLE OF DURATION GAP

Consider a bank with the following characteristics:

- £500 million of assets;
- £400 million of liabilities;
- £100 million of own equity;
- the duration of assets is five years;
- the duration of liabilities is three years.

Let's suppose that bank management expect an interest rate increase of 0.25 per cent to 4.5 per cent following the next meeting of the Bank of England's Monetary Policy Committee (MPC).

$$DG = [5 - (400/500)3] = 2.6$$

$$\Delta E = -2.6 \, [0.0025/(1 + 0.0425)] \, 500 = -3.12 \text{ million}$$

In this case, an increase in interest rates from 4.25 per cent to 4.5 per cent will decrease the equity value by £3.12 million.

and refined changes in the interest rate environment, ranging from changes in the slope and shape of the yield curve to interest rate scenarios derived from (relatively complex) statistical approaches such as Monte Carlo simulations.[10]

We can distinguish between:

- static simulations, where only the cash flows arising from the bank's current on- and off-balance-sheet positions are assessed; and
- dynamic simulations, where the model builds in more detailed assumptions about the future course of interest rates and the expected changes in a bank's business activity over that time.

The usefulness of simulation-based interest rate risk measurement techniques depends on the validity of the underlying assumptions and the accuracy of the basic methodology. In its document 'Principles for the management of interest rate risk' (1997), the BCBS warns that the output of sophisticated simulations must be assessed in the light of the validity of the simulation's assumptions about future interest rates and the behaviour of the bank and its customers (BCBS, 1997b). One of the primary concerns of BCBS is that such simulations could become 'black boxes' that lead to false confidence in the precision of the estimates.

Recent recommendations of the Federal Reserve Board (2010) include the need to run dynamic earning simulations together with static ones in order to have a complete profile of the bank's interest rate risk, as well as the use of economic value-based methodologies to broaden the assessment in quantifying interest rate risk exposures and overcome the limitations of static and dynamic models. Specifically, the economic-value approaches focus on

---

[10] A Monte Carlo simulation is a computerised technique which is the basis for probabilistic risk analysis, and which replicates real-life occurrences by mathematically modelling a projected event.

a longer time horizon and capture all future cash flows expected from current assets and liabilities. They are also regarded as more effective in considering embedded options in a typical institution's portfolio.

To summarise:

● Economic value of equity (EVE) models measure the degree to which the economic values of a bank's positions change under different interest rate scenarios and can include dynamic technique to provide forward-looking estimates of economic value.

Overall, the most recent guidelines encourage banks to use a range of measurement approaches. The aim is to ensure that the interest rate risk measurement system captures all on- and off-balance-sheet positions and incorporates stress-testing processes to identify and quantify the institution's exposure and potential problem areas.

12.6   Managing liquidity risk

As defined in Section 11.4, a bank faces liquidity risk when, because of lack of confidence or unexpected need for cash, withdrawals are higher than normal and the bank is unable to meet its liabilities. Sound liquidity management can reduce the probability of serious problems. The importance of liquidity goes beyond the individual bank, since a liquidity shortfall at a single institution can have system-wide repercussions. Systemic risk and the problems of contagion and bank runs have been discussed in Chapter 7 and elsewhere in this text.

If a bank experiences a temporary liquidity problem, and it is either unable or unwilling to borrow on the interbank market, the central bank can provide funds, in the form of loans and advances. However, central bank borrowing is costly not only in terms of the interest rates charged but also in terms of the bank's reputation.

Liquidity pressures can arise from both sides of the balance sheet. On the liability side, unexpectedly high cash withdrawals can cause solvent banks to have liquidity problems. On the asset side, liquidity problems can be caused by unexpectedly high loan defaults and by customers unexpectedly drawing down lines of credit. Liquidity pressures can arise from off-balance-sheet activities as well as from problems in the payment system. Contingent liabilities, such as letters of credit and financial guarantees, represent a potentially significant drain of funds for a bank, but are usually not dependent on a bank's liquidity position. Other potential sources of cash outflows include payments relating to transactions involving swaps, OTC options, other interest rate and forward foreign exchange rate contracts, margin calls and early-termination agreements.

Liquidity management is an integral part of the ALM function. Liquidity risk management aims at protecting a bank against liquidity risk, that is, to avoid a situation of negative net liquid assets.

To avoid liquidity problems, a bank can hold liquid assets. However, increased liquidity comes at a cost. There is a trade-off between liquidity and profitability, as the more liquid the asset, the lower the rate of return. Instead of holding liquid funds, a bank could make more profitable loans. Despite the costs, however, the holding of liquid assets is necessary as it:

● reassures creditors that the bank is safe and able to meet its liabilities;

● signals to the market that the bank is prudent and well managed;

● ensures that all lending commitments can be met;

- avoids forced sale of the bank's assets;
- avoids having to pay excessive borrowing costs in the interbank markets;
- avoids central bank borrowing.

Banks can minimise withdrawal risk by diversifying funding sources (liability management). Prudent banks will also seek to minimise their volatility ratio:

$$VR = (VL - LA)/(TA - LA) \tag{12.10}$$

where:

VL = volatile liabilities

LA = liquid assets

TA = total assets.

Prudent banks will have a volatility ratio lower than zero.

In measuring and managing a bank's liquidity exposure, the following techniques may be used:

- cash flow projections of daily liquidity positions;
- cash flow projections of daily liquidity sources;
- scenario analysis and simulation models;
- liquidity gap analysis.

12.6.1 Liquidity gap analysis and financing gap

Liquidity gap analysis is the most widely used technique for managing a bank's liquidity position. As we have already discussed, liquidity risk is generated in the balance sheet by a mismatch between the size and maturity of assets and liabilities. It is the risk that the bank is holding insufficient liquid assets on its balance sheet to meet requirements. The liquidity gap is defined as the difference between net liquid assets and unpredictable (or volatile) liabilities. If a bank's net liquid assets are less than liabilities then the bank needs to purchase funds in the market to fill the shortfall in liquid assets. Banks typically will examine the maturity profile of their assets and liabilities to identify mismatches in liquidity that require funding.

$$L\,Gap = NLA - VL \tag{12.11}$$

where:

NLA = net liquid assets

VL = volatile liabilities.

The liquidity gap analysis is similar to the maturity bucket approach we have discussed for interest rate risk management. In this case, balance sheet items are placed in a bucket according to the expected timing of cash flows. Net mismatched positions are accumulated over time to produce a cumulative net mismatch position. In this way, the bank can monitor the amount of cash that becomes available over time.

Another useful measure of bank liquidity is the financing gap (F Gap):

$$F\,Gap = Average\ loans - Average\ deposits \tag{12.12}$$

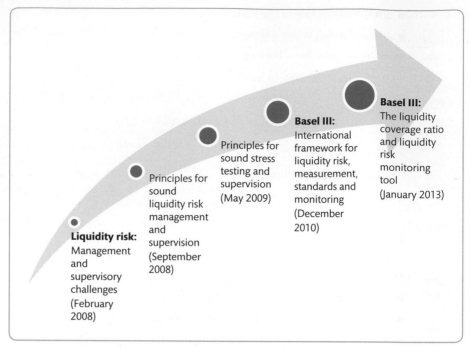

Figure 12.6 Basel and liquidity risk timeline

If the F Gap is positive, the bank needs cash and will have either to sell some assets or borrow on the interbank market. The bigger the F Gap, the more a bank needs to borrow and the greater its exposure to liquidity risk. However, technological and financial innovations have provided banks with new ways of funding their activities and managing their liquidity. A declining ability to rely on core deposits, together with increased reliance on wholesale funds, has changed the way banks view liquidity.

During the early stages of the sub-prime crisis in 2007 many banks, despite being adequately capitalised, suffered significant difficulties, mainly due to the lack of prudent liquidity management. The crisis has shown that markets can become illiquid very quickly and that the illiquidity can last for long periods. The Basel Committee responded by setting out key principles, detailed guidelines and a framework for effective liquidity risk management and supervision in banking and the key documents in a timeline are shown in Figure 12.6. The two fundamental minimum standards of the most recent Basel liquidity framework are the liquidity coverage ratio and the net stable funding ratio, explained in detail in Chapter 7 (Section 7.7.4.2).

12.7 Managing market risk

Market risk is the risk resulting from adverse movements in the level or volatility of market prices of interest rate instruments, equities, commodities and currencies (see Section 11.6). Market risk is usually measured as the potential gain/loss in a position/portfolio that is associated with a price movement of a given probability over a specified time horizon.

Financial institutions have always faced market risk; however, the sharp increase in asset trading since the 1980s has increased the need to ensure that these institutions have the

Table 12.4 The trading book review

Proposed revisions to Basel 2.5	Description
Trading book and banking book	Create a more objective boundary that remains aligned with banks' risk management practices and reduces the incentives for regulatory arbitrage.
Risk measurement approach and calibration	Shift in the measure of risk from value at risk to expected shortfall so as to better capture 'tail risk', and calibration based on a period of significant financial stress.
Risk of market illiquidity	Introduce 'liquidity horizons' in the market risk metric, and an additional risk assessment tool for trading desks with exposure to illiquid, complex products.
Standardised approach	Ensure a standardised approach that is sufficiently risk-sensitive to act as a credible fallback to internal models, yet appropriate for banks that do not require sophisticated measurement of market risk.
Internal models-based approach	A more rigorous model approval process and more consistent identification and capitalisation of material risk factors. Hedging and diversification recognition will also be based on empirical evidence that such practices are effective during periods of stress.
Relationship between the standardised and the models-based approaches	Align standardised and models-based approaches by establishing a closer calibration, requiring: • calculation of the standardised approach by all banks; • public disclosure of standardised capital charges by all banks.

Source: Basel Committee on Banking Supervision (2013c).

appropriate management systems to control (and the capital to absorb) the risks posed by market-related exposures. As a risk, market risk gained a high profile when the Basel Committee on Banking Supervision published 'The supervisory treatment of market risks' (1993), in which for the first time it was proposed that market risk, in addition to credit risk, needed to be taken into account for the calculation of bank capital requirements (this updated the 1988 Basel Capital Adequacy Accord).

The 1993 BCBS consultative document put forward a standardised measurement framework to calculate market risk for interest rates, equities and currencies which differentiates capital requirements for specific risk from those for general market risk. The BCBS (1996) document 'Amendment to the capital Accord to incorporate market risks' provides the framework for capital charges relative to market risk. It sets forth two approaches for calculating the capital charge to cover market risks: *the standardised approach* and *the internal models approach*. The methodology for banks using the standardised approach is based on a 'building blocks' approach, in which the specific risk and the general market risk arising from securities positions are measured separately. Meanwhile, the focus of many internal models is on the bank's general market risk exposure, leaving specific risk (i.e. exposures to specific issuers) to be measured largely through separate credit risk measurement systems. Post the 2007–2009 crisis the market risk framework has been revised by the BCBS (2010b) to include the following changes in the calculation of market risk capital:

- **stressed value at risk** that takes into account a one-year observation period relating to significant losses (in addition to the value at risk based on the most recent observation period);
- **incremental risk charge** that includes default risk and migration risk (for unsecuritised credit products with issuer risk such as bonds, CDs, equities, etc.).

In addition the BCBS has published two consultative documents (BCBS, 2013b) to improve trading book capital requirements.

The central component of market risk management is **value at risk (VaR)** and it is discussed in Section 12.7.1. Although VaR was originally developed to manage market risk, it has now been extended to incorporate other risks, including credit risk. Following the global financial crisis, the importance of scenario analysis and stress testing for managing market risk has become very relevant. In particular, the Committee is proposing key changes, including the replacement of VaR, and these are summarised in Table 12.4.

12.7.1 Value at risk (VaR)

VaR is the principal portfolio measure of market risk – it provides an estimate of the potential loss on the current portfolio from adverse market movements. Originally developed by JPMorgan in the context of its RiskMetrics product, it builds on modern portfolio theory. VaR is a statistical measure of potential trading revenue volatility, and a change in the general level of VaR would normally be expected to lead to a corresponding change in the volatility of daily trading revenues. The distinguishing feature of VaR is that it uses the volatility of assets.

The basic formula of VaR is as follows:[11]

$$\text{VaR}_x = V_x \, (dV/dP) \, \Delta P_t \tag{12.13}$$

where:

V_x = the market value of portfolio x

dV/dP = the sensitivity to market prices movements per £ of market value

ΔP_t = the adverse price movement over a specific time horizon t (under the Basel Agreement t = 10 days).

It expresses the 'maximum' amount a bank might lose, to a certain level of confidence (q), as a result of changes in risk factors (i.e. changes in interest rates, exchange rates, equity and commodity prices). The basic time period t and the confidence level q are the two major parameters that should be chosen in an appropriate way. The time horizon can differ from a few hours for an active trading desk to a year for a pension fund. In simple terms, the VaR approach aims to answer the following question: 'How much can I lose with x per cent probability over a pre-set horizon?'

Suppose that a bank portfolio manager has a daily VaR equal to £1 million at a 99 per cent confidence interval. This means that there is only one chance in 100 that a daily loss bigger than £1 million occurs under normal market conditions.

The calculation of VaR specified in equation (12.13) involves several assumptions:

● prices of financial instruments are assumed to be normally distributed;

● price changes are assumed to be statistically uncorrelated;

● the volatility (standard deviation) of the price or rate changes is stable over time;

● the interrelationship between two different price movements follows a joint normal distribution.

---

[11] A general introduction to VaR can be found in Jorion (2007).

Box 12.6 gives an example of VaR.

Most VaR calculations, however, are not concerned with annual value at risk. The main regulatory and management concern is with the loss of portfolio value over a much shorter period (typically several days).

After the introduction of market risk measurement in the 1996 Amendment to the Basel I Capital Adequacy Accord, regulators have encouraged the use of VaR. The required VaR measure is for every ten days with a confidence interval of 99 per cent. However, the ten-day VaR measure takes no account of the mitigating action that can be taken in the event of adverse market moves, nor does it express the worst outcome that could occur as a result of extreme, unusual or unprecedented market conditions. The absolute level of VaR should not, therefore, be interpreted as the likely range of daily trading revenues.

As there is no general consensus on the 'best way' to carry out a VaR analysis, the approach allows various options for the choice of the underlying frequency distributions:

- parametric methods (e.g. RiskMetrics™);
- non-parametric methods (historic approach);
- simulation approaches (such as using Monte Carlo techniques);
- hybrid models (e.g. historic simulation with parametric model).

BOX 12.6 EXAMPLE OF VAR

Suppose a portfolio manager manages a portfolio that consists of a single asset. The return of the asset is normally distributed with annual mean return of 15 per cent and annual standard deviation of 25 per cent. The value of the portfolio today is £100 million. We want to answer various simple questions about the end-of-year distribution of the portfolio's value:

1 What is the probability of a loss of more than £20 million by year-end – i.e. what is the probability that the end-of-year value is less than £95 million (£115 million minus £20 million)?

2 With 1 per cent probability, what is the maximum loss at the end of the year? This is the VaR at 1 per cent.

To answer these questions keeping in mind the assumptions made above, we need to employ a statistical package (for example, Microsoft Excel):

1 In Excel, you need to employ the formula giving standard normal cumulative distribution. In this example:

$$\text{NORMDIST (95, 115, 25, TRUE)} = 0.211855$$

The probability of a loss of more than £20 million is 21 per cent.

2 In Excel, you need to employ the formula giving the inverse of the normal cumulative distribution. In this example:

$$\text{NORMINV (0.01, 115, 25)} = 56.841325$$

There is 1 per cent probability that the end-of-year value will be less than £56.84 million, which means that the maximum loss is equal to:

$$£115 \text{ million} - £56.84 \text{ million} = £58.16 \text{ million}$$

Because of the different approaches that might be followed, i.e. financial institutions may use different confidence levels or holding periods, may have different sources of historical data or use longer or shorter time-series and may use approximate changes in individual risk factors following different distribution, direct comparisons between VaR numbers produced by different institutions can be misleading. A recent formal survey of US and international commercial banks suggests that the most popular VaR estimation methodology is by far historical simulation, followed by the Monte Carlo based method (Perignon and Smith, 2010).

In order to determine the overall or net position, a portfolio can be divided according to its sensitivity to certain risk (the so-called Greeks):

(a) Delta risk (absolute price risk): is the risk that the price of the underlying asset will change.

(b) Gamma risk (convexity risk): allows for the existence of a non-linear relationship between the change in the price of the underlying asset and the change in the value of the portfolio.

(c) Vega risk (volatility risk): is the risk arising from a change in the expected volatility in the price of the underlying instrument.

(d) Theta risk (time-decay risk): is the risk of a change in the value of the portfolio simply connected with the passing of time.

(e) Rho risk (discount risk): is the risk associated with a change in the risk-free rate.

To arrive at a VaR, the portfolio components are disaggregated according to the above risk factors, netted out and then re-aggregated.

To illustrate how VaR is reported by banks, Table 12.5 gives the figures from UBS (2012). It shows that UBS group's management VaR halved between end-year 2011 and end-year 2012. This was driven primarily by the efforts taken by the investment bank to reduce trading risk as part of the group's overall strategy. In terms of volumes, the average management VaR was CHF33 million (US$37.7 million) for 2012 (compared with CHF60 million – or US$68.5 million – in the previous year).[12]

Table 12.5 Value at risk at UBS

(CHF million)*	Year ended 31 December 2012				Year ended 31 December 2011			
	Min	Max	Avg.	31 December	Min	Max	Avg.	31 December
Wealth Management Americas	1	2	2	2	1	2	1	2
Investment Bank	15	164	30	15	30	219	75	34
Global Asset Management	0	0	0	0	0	0	0	0
Corporate centre	3	17	11	10	4	14	7	4
Diversification effect			(10)	(9)			(7)	(4)
Total management VaR, group	18	167	33	18	31	222	76	36

Note: *CHF = Swiss Franc.

Source: UBS (2012).

---

[12] These figures exclude the effect of the September 2011 trading incident within UBS' Investment Bank that resulted in a total loss of US$2.3 billion. This unauthorised trading was conducted by a trader on the exchange traded funds (ETF) desk, part of the equities business in the investment bank in London. The trader involved was charged by the UK authorities and sentenced to seven years in prison.

Some authors (Taleb, 1997; Danielsson, 2000; Danielsson, 2002) have expressed the following concerns over the use of VaR:

- VaR does not give the precise amount that will be lost.
- The assumption that financial returns are normally distributed and uncorrelated may not hold.
- VaR measures are seemingly easy to manipulate.
- It does not provide an indication of the probability of a bank failure.
- If all traders are using the same approach to minimise market risk, this can result in increased liquidity risk.

The reputation of VaR was also seriously damaged in the 2007–2009 financial crisis as banks and policy makers realised that markets under stress can generate losses well above the maximum predicted by VaR.

For these reasons, **back testing** (that is, an *ex-post* comparison of the risk measure generated by the model against actual daily changes in portfolio value) is advocated by the BCBS. Given the limitations of VaR highlighted above, most banks also employ scenario analysis and stress testing.

In simple terms, back testing compares actual revenues arising from closing positions (i.e. excluding intra-day revenues, fees and commissions) with the VaR calculated on these positions, and is used to monitor the quality of the VaR model.

Figure 12.7 shows these daily revenues and the corresponding 1-day 99 per cent confidence level regulatory VaR for UBS over the 12 months of 2012.

As illustrated in Figure 12.7, the revenue volatility over 2012 was within the range predicted by the VaR model. If we focus on the exceptions, these occur when back testing revenues are negative and the absolute value of those revenues is greater than the previous day's VaR. UBS experienced one such back testing exception in 2012 due to an incident relating to the Facebook IPO in May 2012 where the Swiss bank allegedly lost more than $350 million due to technical glitches at the Nasdaq Stock Exchange (see also Section 12.8 as this can be considered a *classical* case of operational risk).

Scenario analysis and stress testing are based on simulated forecasts of plausible unfavourable scenarios to compute how much a bank would lose in the event of a 'worst-case scenario' and tests the bank's ability to withstand possible shocks.

12.7.2 Risk-adjusted return on capital (RAROC)

The concept of **risk-adjusted return on capital (RAROC)** was introduced by Bankers Trust in the late 1970s as a planning and performance management tool, in the context of risk-adjusted performance measurement (RAPM). Several approaches, defined as 'asset-volatility-based approaches' as opposed to the traditional risk-based and ROE-based approaches, were developed in response to the need to target shareholders' value and to allocate banks' internal resources more efficiently. The RAROC measures the risk inherent in each banking activity, and the risk factor is computed taking into account the asset price volatility, calculated on historical data. An interesting feature of RAROC is that it can be employed to estimate the relative capital allocation of all types of banking risks.

$$\text{RAROC} = \frac{\text{Revenues} - \text{Cost} - \text{Expected losses}}{\text{Total Equity Capital}} \qquad (12.14)$$

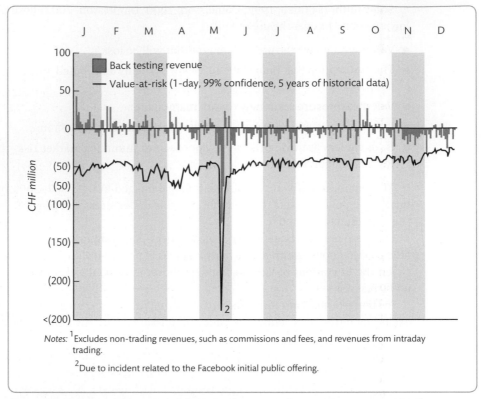

Figure 12.7 Back testing VaR (UBS), 2 January 2012 to 31 December 2012[1]
Source: UBS (2012).

In the context of the Basel II Capital Accord (explained in Section 7.8), which encouraged the use of internal risk models to set banks' capital requirements, the RAROC measure helped bank managers to assess in what areas they should allocate more capital. As the Basel III phase-in has begun, and considering the major credit losses and recent banking crises, it is clear that the current approaches to RAROC need to be revised to take account of **tail risk** and stress testing (see Box 12.7). Tail risk can be defined as a higher than anticipated risk of an investment moving more than three standard deviations away from the mean.

12.8 Managing operational risk

The Basel Committee on Banking Supervision (2011a) broadly defines operational risk as 'the risk of loss resulting from inadequate or failed internal processes, people and systems or from external events'. In general terms, this is the risk associated with the possible failure of a bank's systems, controls or other management failure (including human error). This definition focuses on the causes of operational risk, and it is aimed at facilitating operational risk measurement and management.

Various factors have contributed to increase the operational risk in the environment where banks operate over recent years. External forces include the progress in trading technology (e.g.

BOX 12.7 RISK MANAGEMENT PROGRESS HAS BEEN SMALL, SAYS BANKING STUDY

Banks, insurers and asset managers have made only incremental progress towards tying pay to risk and improving their data so that they can spot looming dangers, despite substantial increases in their risk management spending, a global Deloitte survey has found. Only 55 per cent of the 86 financial institutions surveyed include risk management in the performance goals and compensation for their senior managers, little changed from a similar 2010 survey. Risk management mattered even less for business unit and personnel and middle managers, with only one-third of companies reporting that it officially factored into compensation decisions.

Financial groups are doing a better job of making sure they can take back bonuses when things go wrong, with 41 per cent of them reporting they now include so-called 'clawback' provisions in executive pay, up from 26 per cent in 2010. 'It's a work in progress in this area,' said Edward Hida, the Deloitte partner who led the survey work. Mr Hida said that banks also continue to struggle to improve the quality of their data, even though getting a better handle on counterparty exposures and other data has been a top priority since at least the September 2008 collapse of Lehman Brothers. Fully 40 per cent of survey respondents said they were 'extremely or very concerned' about the data management capabilities at their institution. 'Data are one of the biggest challenges for a lot of these institutions,' he said. The Deloitte survey also found that less than one-third of the banks surveyed were fully prepared to meet the requirements of the new Basel III bank capital and liquidity reforms, which started phasing in this year.

The slow progress comes despite the fact that nearly half the institutions have increased their risk management budgets in the past year, and 58 per cent expect to spend more over the next three years. Mr Hida said the continually increasing spending reflects a shift in focus among the regulatory community. Right after the 2008 financial crisis, banking supervisors concentrated on forcing the very largest banks to improve their risk management, so risk management budgets in that part of the sector grew quickly. Now new regulatory requirements are starting to catch medium-sized institutions, so they too are having to ramp up.

The Deloitte survey results dovetail with results of another survey of top financial services executives released late last week by Protiviti and the Economist Intelligence Unit, which found that only 20 per cent of financial institutions feel they have integrated risk awareness into their corporate culture. Just 15 per cent thought they were making substantial improvements to comprehensive, enterprise-wide risk-management.

high-frequency trading) and the increased complexities and interconnectedness in the financial marketplace globally. Losses can be quite substantial – Figure 12.7 exhibits the considerable losses (more than $350 million) suffered by the investment bank business line of UBS during the IPO of Facebook in July 2012. UBS said the cause of the loss was 'gross mishandling of Facebook's market debut by Nasdaq', which it accused of 'substantial failures to perform its duties'.[13]

The increased importance of operational risk in financial institutions was recognised in the past decade by the Basel Committee and a new capital charge was incorporated in Basel II.

---

[13] Shotter *et al.* (2012) 'UBS updates Facebook status', *Financial Times*, 31 July.

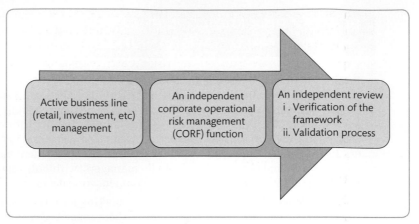

Figure 12.8 The three lines of defence for sound operational risk management

Source: Adapted from Basel Committee on Banking Supervision (2011c).

Although operational risk is not yet a well-defined concept, recent years have seen significant progress in setting a framework for an effective measurement and management of operational risk in banking. In June 2011 the Basel Committee published two key documents: 'Principles for the sound management of operational risk' (2011c) and 'Operational risk – supervisory guidelines for the advanced measurement approaches' (2011b). The former focuses on the importance of adopting sound operational risk governance practices and the latter on setting out supervisory guidelines relating to governance, data and modelling. Following these documents, the sound management of operational risk should rely on three lines of defence, as illustrated in Figure 12.8.

First line of defence is business line management, which is responsible for identifying and managing the risks inherent in the products, activities, processes and systems for which it is accountable. Second line of defence is the creation of a specialised and independent internal committee, the corporate operational risk management function (CORF), responsible for the design, maintenance and ongoing development of the operational risk framework within the bank. CORF's functions include operational risk measurement and reporting processes, risk committees and responsibility for board reporting. The third line of defence is an independent review of the bank's operational risk management controls, processes and systems. It includes two interrelated aspects: (i) periodic verification and (ii) validation. The former is usually carried out by the bank's internal and/or external audit and is in charge of testing the effectiveness and consistency of the operational risk management framework. The latter is an independent process performed by audit and/or external staff and should confirm the robustness and reliability of the quantification procedures and risk measurement methodology used by the bank.

In line with the management of other banking risks, a capital provision should be set aside to cover for unexpected losses due to operational risk. However, explicit pricing of the losses relating to operational risk is uncommon.

The Basel II framework proposes three methods for calculating operational risk capital charges, which present increasing sophistication and risk sensitivity:

1 The basic indicator approach.

2 The standardised approach.

3 The advanced measurement approach.

The basic approach allocates capital using a single indicator (gross income) as a proxy for a bank's overall operational risk exposure. Gross income is defined as net interest income plus net non-interest income and the bank is expected to set aside a capital provision to cover for unexpected losses due to operational risk equal to the average of the previous three years of a fixed percentage ('alpha') of positive gross annual income.

In the standardised approach, a bank's activities are divided into eight standard business units and business lines and all use gross income as a common indicator. These are:

1 Corporate finance (18 per cent).

2 Trading and sales (18 per cent).

3 Retail banking (12 per cent).

4 Commercial banking (15 per cent).

5 Payment and settlement (18 per cent).

6 Agency services (15 per cent).

7 Asset management (12 per cent).

8 Retail brokerage (12 per cent).

Within each business line, the capital charge is calculated by multiplying a bank's broad financial indicator by a percentage factor 'beta' (in brackets above). This is a rough proxy for the relationship between the industry's operational risk loss experience for a given business line and the broad financial indicator for the bank's activity in that business line. The total capital charge is the sum of the capital charges in each business line.

The advanced measurement approach (AMA) allows individual banks (subject to supervisory approval) to employ their own internal operational risk measurement systems using quantitative and qualitative criteria to calculate the required capital. Banks apply different AMA models depending on the way they combine the following four 'data elements':

1 Internal loss data.

2 External loss data.

3 Scenario analysis.

4 Business environment and internal control factors.

The Basel Committee on Banking Supervision (2011b) recognises that there are various ways that an AMA model can be constructed to use these four data elements and a bank should ensure that the resulting level of operational risk capital is adequate given the bank's level of exposure. It also suggests that the most popular methods in modelling operational risk are the loss distribution approach (LDA) followed by scenario-based approaches (SBA).

In terms of actual measurement methodologies, the Basel Committee has identified three sub- approaches that banks can choose from:

1 **Scorecard approach:** relies primarily on qualitative analysis across business lines and less on historical loss data in determining capital. The process is constantly updated and aims at creating risk indicators that are combined into a score that reflects the degree of the operational risk. Risk loss data are used to validate results of scorecards.

2 **Loss distribution approach:** is based on the historical database of operational loss for capital calculation. It requires the determination of the probability distribution of the frequency of operational loss events and the conditional probability distribution of the

severity of operational losses given an operational loss event. This is calculated for each business unit and type of event; the capital charge is based on the sum of all operational risk for each business line/event type.

3 **Internal measurement approach:** see Box 12.8.

BOX 12.8 STRUCTURE OF THE INTERNAL MEASUREMENT APPROACH

In the internal measurement approach, a bank's activities are categorised into a number of business lines, and a broad set of operational loss types is defined and applied across business lines. Within each business line/loss type combination, the supervisor specifies an exposure indicator (EI), which is a proxy for the size (or amount of risk) of each business line's operational risk exposure.

For each business line/loss type combination, banks measure, based on their internal loss data, a parameter representing the probability of loss event (PE) as well as a parameter representing the loss given that event (LGE). The product of EI*PE*LGE is used to calculate the expected loss (EL) for each business line/loss type combination.

The supervisor supplies a factor (the 'gamma term', γ) for each business line/loss type combination, which translates the expected loss (EL) into a capital charge. The overall capital charge for a particular bank is the simple sum of all the resulting products. This can be expressed in the following formula:

$$\text{Required capital} = \sum i \sum j \, [\gamma(i,j) * \text{EI}\,(i,j) * \text{PE}\,(i,j) * \text{LGE}\,(i,j) \qquad (12.15)$$

where:

  i = the business line

  j = the risk type.

To facilitate the process of supervisory validation, banks supply their supervisors with the individual components of the expected loss calculation (i.e. EI, PE, LGE) instead of just the product EL. Based on this information supervisors calculate EL and then adjust for unexpected loss through the gamma term to achieve the desired soundness standard.

Source: Adapted from Basel Committee on Banking Supervision (2001) p. 8.

12.9 International risk assessment

Banks engaged in international activities face a plethora of risks, in addition to the ones already discussed, including among others foreign currency risk, regulatory risk, strategic and reputation risk. These risks are not mutually exclusive and any product or service provided either domestically or internationally may expose the bank to multiple risks. For banks contemplating an international investment or for those already with substantial overseas operations the risks associated with operating in a foreign country need to be evaluated. Put simply, firms that operate internationally have to evaluate the country risk associated with their investments and/or overseas operations.

Country risk is the risk that economic, social and political conditions and events in a foreign country will adversely affect a firm's commercial/financial interests. In addition to the adverse effect that deteriorating macroeconomic conditions and political and social instability may have on the returns generated from an overseas investment, country risk includes the possibility of nationalisation or expropriation of assets, governments revoking licences, imposition of exchange controls, and the likelihood of currency depreciation or devaluation.

Country risk can have a critical effect on a firm's international activities and therefore needs to be explicitly taken into account in the risk assessment of all overseas investments/activities. Even the risk associated with what are perceived to be the most stable (or safe) investments will increase if, for instance, the political or macroeconomic conditions change and cause the exchange rate to depreciate, resulting in lower cash flows (and therefore profits) from overseas investments. Country risk is also not necessarily limited to a firm's exposure to overseas operations. A firm may have commercial relationships in its home country with a foreign firm that may be subject to such risks. For instance, country risk factors should also be taken into account when assessing the creditworthiness of domestic trade creditors. One should also be aware that country risk factors are critical for all types of international firms, non-financial and financial. Borrowers in higher-risk countries pay higher premiums for their debt compared with those located in lower-risk countries.

In banking, country risk is regarded as the exposure to a loss in cross-border lending, caused by events in a particular country that are (at least to some extent) under the control of the government but are not under the control of a private enterprise or individual. This contrasts with what is known as sovereign risk, which relates to the risk associated with a government default on bond or loan repayments. A broader definition of country risk relates to any loss associated with international activity due to adverse changes in the overseas operating environment beyond the control of the firm. Transfer risk is another form of risk that is believed to be one of the most important drivers of country risk. This is simply the risk associated with the restriction of foreign payments from overseas to the home company or bank. Transfer risk refers to restrictions on payments between private agents whereas sovereign risk is associated with a government default on payments. In reality, sovereign and transfer risks are closely related as a government default on payments may lead private parties to renege on their payment obligations – especially if the government default leads to a major depreciation or crisis scenario.

12.9.1 Managing country risk

In order to effectively control the level of risk associated with their international operations, firms must have in place a procedure that systematically evaluates the country risk features of their business. This includes having in place a country risk evaluation process that has:

- effective oversight by senior managers;
- appropriate risk management policies and procedures;
- an accurate system for reporting change in country risk and potential exposures;
- an effective process for analysing country risk;
- a country risk-rating system;
- regular monitoring of country conditions.

While the details and complexity of country risk assessment will vary from bank to bank, senior management must be suitably qualified to evaluate the bank's international activities.

If country risk is to be managed effectively then senior bank managers, up to board level, must oversee the process. It is likely that a team of senior project appraisers will review the bank's international operations in order to ensure that they are consistent with the company's major strategic objectives. Decisions to extend international operations and exposure to different countries' risk will ultimately be up to the company board, as they should have a view of the sorts of country exposure required, and it is the responsibility of the board to make sure that country risk (as well as other risks) is effectively managed.

Senior bank management are responsible for implementing policies and procedures for managing country risk. This involves:

- identifying investments and other activities exposed to country risk;
- identifying desirable and undesirable opportunities that can be used to complement or be substituted for current operations, resulting in a reduction of country risk;
- establishing country risk limits if necessary;
- identifying clear lines of responsibility and accountability for country risk management decisions.

Senior management are ultimately responsible for country risk management policies, standards and practices and also need to make sure that these are communicated effectively to relevant parts of the organisation.

In order to effectively manage country risk, banks need to have reliable systems for capturing and categorising the volume and nature of their foreign activities. Such a reporting system should cover all aspects of the company's international operations. Banks, for example, have to have country exposure reporting systems to support regulatory reporting of foreign exposure requirements.

The level of resources dedicated to the country risk analysis process will vary from bank to bank depending on the size and sophistication of the company's international activities. In order to construct an effective country risk evaluation process, senior managers need to ask the following questions:

- Is there a quantitative and qualitative assessment of the risk associated with each country in which the firm is conducting or planning to undertake activities?
- Is any formal country risk analysis undertaken on a regular basis and are changes in country risk monitored in any way?
- Is the country risk analysis adequately documented, with the findings communicated to the relevant parties?
- Are adequate resources devoted to country risk evaluation procedures?
- Do the company's country risk assessments concur with the risk ratings of third-party assessors, such as rating agencies?

If the answers to these questions are in the affirmative then the bank is well placed to use the results of its country risk analysis effectively in strategic and operational decision making. In order to arrive at a conclusion about the level of country risk faced by a bank, managers need to evaluate the current (and possible future) economic, political and social characteristics of a country. For this they are likely to use some form of country risk-rating system.

12.9.2 Country risk rating

Country risk ratings simply summarise the main findings of the country risk analysis process. While large firms and banks are likely to have teams evaluating country risk, smaller firms are more likely to rely heavily on the country risk assessments done by specialist third-party firms. Because there is a wide range of factors that can affect country risk, it is often difficult for smaller firms to dedicate the relevant resources to assess somewhat complex issues.

Macroeconomic and political environments can change rapidly and it is often difficult to keep abreast of these developments, especially if one is considering or monitoring projects in a number of countries. Box 12.9 provides a broad indication of the various factors that affect country risk.

BOX 12.9 FACTORS AFFECTING COUNTRY RISK

Macroeconomic factors

- Size and structure of the country's external debt in relation to its economy
- Level of international reserves
- Potential for extreme adverse exchange rate movements and the effect on the relative price of the country's imports and exports
- GDP growth and inflation levels, current and forecast
- Role of foreign sources of capital in meeting the country's financing needs
- Country's access to international financial markets and the potential effects of a loss of market liquidity
- Country's relationships with private sector creditors
- Country's current standing with multilateral and official creditors such as the IMF
- Trends in foreign investments and the country's ability to obtain foreign investment in the future
- Privatisation of government-owned entities
- Extent to which the economy of the country may be adversely affected through the contagion of problems in other countries
- Size and condition of the country's banking and financial system
- Extent to which state-directed lending or other government intervention may have adversely affected the soundness of the country's financial system and economy.

Socio-political factors

- Country's natural and human resource potential
- Willingness and ability of the government to recognise economic or budgetary problems and implement appropriate remedial action
- Extent to which political or regional factionalism or armed conflicts are adversely affecting government of the country
- Any trends towards government-imposed price, interest rate or exchange controls

BOX 12.9 Factors affecting country risk (*continued*)

- Extent to which the legal system of the country can be relied upon to fairly protect the interests of foreign creditors and investors
- Accounting standards and the reliability and transparency of financial information
- Level of adherence to international legal and business practice standards
- Level of corruption
- Level of corporate social responsibility.

Institution-specific factors

- Bank's business strategy and its plans for investment in the country
- Types of investments, FDI or portfolio investments, joint ventures, licensing agreements and so on
- Economic outlook for any specifically targeted business opened within the country
- Extent to which political or economic developments are likely to affect the bank's chosen lines of business
- Degree to which political or economic developments are likely to affect the credit risk of individual counterparties in the country. For instance, foreign firms with strong export markets in developed countries may have significantly less exposure to the local country's economic disruptions than do other firms operating in the country
- Institution's ability to effectively manage its country risk through in-country or regional representation, or by some other arrangement that ensures the timely reporting of, and response to, any problems.

One can see from Box 12.9 that there is a whole host of factors that affect a country's risk rating, including various economic, financial and socio-political risks, as well as those risks that may be relevant to the specific bank or firm in question. In quantifying the broad economic/financial and socio-political risks, companies can do their own risk evaluation but can also cross-check these with a variety of ratings calculated by third-party firms.

There are many firms that provide services that measure country risk. The main providers include:

- Control Risks Group;
- Economist Intelligence Unit (EIU);
- Euromoney;
- Institutional Investor;
- Moody's Investor Services;
- OECD;
- Political risk services: International Country Risk Guide (ICRG);
- Political risk services: Coplin-O'Leary Rating System;
- Standard & Poor's Rating Group.

Apart from the OECD, all act as 'rating agencies' and sell their country risk ratings via the web or through other media. Each of these firms produces risk ratings using a variety of qualitative and quantitative information so as to construct a single index or country risk-rating schedule. For example, Institutional Investor's credit ratings are based on a survey of leading international bankers who are asked to rate each country on a scale from zero to 100 (where 100 represents maximum creditworthiness). Institutional Investor averages these ratings, providing greater weights to respondents with greater worldwide exposure and more sophisticated country analysis systems. ICRG compiles monthly data on a variety of political, financial and economic risk factors to calculate risk indices in each of these categories as well as a composite risk index. Five financial, thirteen political and six economic factors are used. Each factor is assigned a numerical rating within a specified range. In the case of ICRG country risk weightings, political risk assessment scores are based on subjective staff analysis of available information. Economic risk assessment scores are based upon objective analysis of quantitative data, and financial risk assessment scores are based upon analysis of a mix of quantitative and qualitative information.

Of the non-commercial country risk ratings, those provided on a regular basis by the OECD are widely used and often these will be cross-checked against a firm's own internal risk assessment and those of a private third-party provider. How the OECD calculates its country risk ratings is outlined in Box 12.10 and Table 12.6 reports its country risk ratings at January 2014.

BOX 12.10 OECD COUNTRY RISK-WEIGHTING CALCULATIONS

The OECD produces a regular country credit risk assessment that classifies countries into eight risk categories (0 to 7), with 7 being the most risky. The Country Risk Classification Method measures the country credit risk, i.e. the likelihood that a country will service its external debt.

The classification of countries is achieved through the application of a methodology comprised of two basic components: (1) the Country Risk Assessment Model (CRAM), which produces a quantitative assessment of country credit risk, based on three groups of risk indicators (the payment experience of the participants, the financial situation and the economic situation), and (2) the qualitative assessment of the model results, considered country-by-country to integrate political risk and/or other risk factors not taken (fully) into account by the model. The details of the CRAM are confidential and not published.

The final classification, based only on valid country risk elements, is a consensus decision of the sub-group of country risk experts that involves the country risk experts of the participating export credit agencies.

The sub-group of country risk experts meets several times a year. These meetings are organised in such a way as to guarantee that every country is reviewed whenever a fundamental change is observed and at least once a year. While the meetings are confidential and no official reports of the deliberations are made, the list of country risk classifications is published after each meeting.

Source: **www.oecd.org**

Table 12.6 Example of OECD country risk classification of the participants to the arrangement on officially supported export credits (as of 31 January 2014)

Country code	Country name	Previous	Current prevailing
ALB	Albania	6	6
DZA	Algeria	3	3
AGO	Angola	5	5
ATG	Antigua and Barbuda	6	6
ARG	Argentina	7	7
ARM	Armenia	6	6
ABW	Aruba	4	4
AUS	Australia	0	0
AUT	Austria	0	0
AZE	Azerbaijan	5	5
BHS	Bahamas	3	3
BHR	Bahrain	4	4
BGD	Bangladesh	6	6
BLR	Belarus	7	7
BEL	Belgium	0	0
BLZ	Belize	6	6
BEN	Benin	6	6
BOL	Bolivia	6	6
BIH	Bosnia and Herzegovina	7	7
BWA	Botswana	2	2
BRA	Brazil	3	3
BRN	Brunei	2	2
BGR	Bulgaria	4	4
BFA	Burkina Faso	7	7
CMR	Cameroon	6	6
CAN	Canada	0	0
CPV	Cape Verde	6	6

Source: Adapted from www.oecd.org/tad/xcred/cre-crc-current-english.pdf

While banks have a wide range of resources at their disposal to evaluate country risk, they also have to ensure that this risk is monitored on an ongoing basis as country circumstances can change rapidly. International banks therefore should have a system in place to monitor current conditions in each of the countries where they have significant operations and also reconcile their risk assessments with those provided by other parties (such as the rating scores given by the firms listed in the previous section). The quantity of resources devoted to monitoring conditions within a country should, of course, be proportionate to the firm's level of overseas activity and the perceived level of risk. Information provided by senior managers in the foreign country is a valuable resource for monitoring country conditions, as are regular reports by regional or country managers. There also needs to be regular contact between parent senior management and those responsible for the operations in the foreign market. All banks conducting international business should not rely solely on informal and ad hoc lines of communication, and established procedures should be in place for dealing with operations that are faced with troubled overseas environments. Also, various contingency plans should be put in place for dealing with problems associated with increases in country risk; if necessary these should include various exit strategies.

It should be stressed that international banks must have adequate internal controls in place so that there is a reporting mechanism ensuring the integrity of the information used by senior management to monitor country risk positions and to comply with any pre-determined country risk exposure limits.

12.10 Conclusion

This chapter reviewed various aspects of bank risk management. The basic principles of bank management, including asset and liability management, were reviewed in Chapter 10, whereas Chapter 11 analysed the main banking risks. This present chapter introduced the general concepts of bank risk management in Section 12.2. This section included an extensive discussion of the growing importance of banks' corporate governance frameworks in setting the standards of good practice and the risk culture within banking organisations. The chapter then considered the management of specific banking risks, focusing particularly on the banking risk included in the calculation of regulatory capital in the most recent Basel documents (credit risk, market risk and operational risk) and the management of the 'traditional' ALM function (interest rate risk and liquidity risk). Finally, given the growing importance of international banking activities, Section 12.9 outlined the main features relating to the management of country risk.

Risk management is a complex and comprehensive process, which includes creating an appropriate environment, maintaining an efficient risk measurement structure, monitoring and mitigating risk-taking activities, and establishing an adequate framework of internal controls. Banks will increasingly need to adopt more formal and quantitative risk measurement and risk management procedures and processes.

Key terms

Back testing	Credit scoring	Negative equity	Tail risk
Corporate governance	Duration analysis	Risk culture	Value-at-risk (VaR)
Credit checking	Gap analysis	Risk management	
Credit rationing	Loan rate	Risk measurement	
Credit reference agencies	Mortgage equity withdrawal	Risk-adjusted return on capital (RAROC)	

Key reading

Basel Committee on Banking Supervision (2010a) 'Principles for enhancing corporate governance', October, **www.bis.org/publ/bcbs176.htm**

Basel Committee on Banking Supervision (2011a) 'Basel III: A global regulatory framework for more resilient banks and banking systems', December, **www.bis.org/publ/bcbs189.htm**

Basel Committee on Banking Supervision (2011d) 'Range of methodologies for risk and performance alignment of remuneration', May, **www.bis.org/publ/bcbs194.pdf**

Beltratti, A. and Stulz, R.M. (2012) 'The credit crisis around the globe: Why did some banks perform better during the credit crisis?', *Journal of Financial Economics*, 105(1), 1–17.

DeYoung, R., Peng, E. and Yan, M. (2013) 'Executive compensation and business policy choices at US commercial banks', *Journal of Financial and Quantitative Analysis*, 48(1), 165–196.

Hagendorff, J. (2014) 'Corporate governance in banking', in Berger, A.N., Molyneux, P. and Wilson, J.O.S. (eds), *The Oxford Handbook of Banking*, 2nd Edition, Oxford: Oxford University Press, Chapter 4.

Hagendorff, J., Keasey, K. and Vallascas, F. (2013) *Size, Risk and Governance in European Banking*, Oxford: Oxford University Press.

Jensen, M.C. and Meckling, W.H. (1976) 'Theory of the firm: Managerial behavior, agency costs and ownership structure', *Journal of Financial Economics*, 3, 305–360.

Walker, D. (2009) 'A review of corporate governance in UK banks and other financial industry entities, final recommendations', London: HMSO.

REVISION QUESTIONS AND PROBLEMS

12.1 What do you understand by 'risk culture'?

12.2 Why is corporate governance in banks more complicated than for other types of firms?

12.3 What is the bonus cap and why is it controversial?

12.4 What is described as 'sound practice' in the management of credit risk?

12.5 Explain the process of credit scoring and describe its main applications.

12.6 What are the main limitations of the GAP approach?

12.7 Why should prudent banks seek to minimise their volatility ratio?

12.8 What are the main techniques used to manage a bank's liquidity exposure?

12.9 What is VaR?

12.10 What are the difficulties inherent in the measurement and management of operational risk?

12.11 What are the main factors affecting country risk?

PART 4

Comparative banking markets

Chapter 13

Banking in the UK

Learning objectives

- To understand the main structural features of the UK banking market

- To identify the main trends in the recent performance of UK banks

- To discuss the implications of increased concentration on competition in the UK banking sector

- To understand how the financial crisis has impacted on UK banks

- To understand the characteristics of the UK payment system

- To describe the regulatory changes that have impacted the UK banking sector pre- and post-financial crisis

13.1   Introduction

UK banking was badly hit by the 2007 global financial crisis. What was once a profitable, innovative and dynamic industry virtually collapsed, exposing a series of weaknesses that increased the severity of the crisis and its impact on the real economy. The **Turner Review** (2009) identified five key issues that played a crucial role in the downfall of UK banking. A first reason is the rapid growth of the financial sector, particularly in terms of the relative size of wholesale financial services within the overall economy. The increasing size of the financial sector went hand in hand with an increase in leverage (asset to capital) and in the complexity of the financial system (for example, the growth in securitised credit and shadow banking; these are discussed in detail in Chapter 18). In addition, the growing scale of banking (particularly of investment banking activities) was accompanied by changing forms of maturity transformation, which led to an underestimation of risk, compounded by the reliance on sophisticated risk management techniques (such as VaR). It is a commonly held opinion that the very complexity of the mathematical models used to assess and manage risk made it difficult for bank management to fully understand the risks banks were taking. Finally, the use of such models to guide management decisions and trading strategies created strong interconnections, which amplified the impact of the downturn. As a leading financial centre, the UK was greatly exposed to these factors, which played a crucial role in reinforcing the severity of the financial crisis.

The events of 2007–2009 also revealed the weaknesses of the existing regulatory system and set the agenda for regulatory reform. Banking sector reforms are the second step in the UK government's programme for reform. The first step was the reform of financial services regulation, which culminated with the **2012 Financial Services Act**. The 2012 Act abolished the existing financial regulator, the Financial Services Authority, and created three new regulatory bodies: the Financial Policy Committee (FPC), the Prudential Regulation Authority (PRA) and the Financial Conduct Authority (FCA). Two of the three new bodies, the FPC and the PRA, are subsidiaries of the Bank of England, while the FCA is a separate body responsible for business, consumer protection and market conduct (see Section 6.2.2 for a detailed discussion of the 2012 Financial Services Act). At the time of writing (2014) the UK government was legislating to reform the structure of the UK banking system, through the **Financial Services (Banking Reform) Act (2013)**. It is expected that the Banking Reform Act will deliver the most significant reform of the UK banking sector in a generation, largely based on the recommendations of the **Independent Commission on Banking** (ICB), which reported in September 2011 (also known as the **Vickers Report**).

In this context of fast-paced changes, this chapter aims to offer an overview of the UK banking industry, including an analysis of the 2007–2009 financial crisis and how it unravelled in the UK (Section 13.2). We then move on to discuss the key regulatory changes and examine their potential impact on UK banking in Section 13.3. Section 13.4 illustrates the structure of the sector, highlighting recent trends. Section 13.5 reviews the financial structure of UK banks, with a particular focus on the **Major British Banking Groups (MBBGs)**. The performance of UK banks is analysed in Section 13.6, while Section 13.7 illustrates the main characteristics of the UK payment system. Section 13.8 discusses the competitive conditions in UK banking and Section 13.9 concludes the chapter.

13.2 The crisis in UK banking

The financial turmoil that hit several countries since mid-2007 impacted severely on the UK's banking sector. This section highlights the key crisis events that unfurled between mid-2007 and mid-2009.[1]

The US sub-prime crisis that started in the summer of 2007 raised international concerns about banks' exposure to real estate lending and about the value of asset-backed securities (see Chapter 15 on the crisis in US banking). All banks with significant real estate exposure came under scrutiny by analysts, depositors and investors. These concerns spread rapidly from the US to other banking markets. In the UK the first casualty of the crisis was Northern Rock in early September 2007 (see Box 13.1). The underlying causes of the failure of Northern Rock included over-aggressive growth in mortgage lending and over-dependence on short-term wholesale funding. In September 2007, Northern Rock faced the first run on

---

[1] A detailed account of the crisis in UK banking can be found in Goddard *et al.* (2009a). Parts of this section are based on their analysis.

BOX 13.1 THE FAILURE AND RESOLUTION OF NORTHERN ROCK

The failure of Northern Rock

Northern Rock was originally a building society based in Newcastle upon Tyne, in the North of England. It was formed in 1965 following the merger of the Northern Counties Permanent Building Society and the Rock Building Society and operated mainly in the north of the country. In 1997, Northern Rock (and a number of other large building societies) converted to bank status, following the process of **demutualisation** that led to a shift of assets from the mutual to commercial banking sector (see Appendix 13.1). In the ten years between 1997 and 2007, the bank's business plan was extremely ambitious and involved a dramatic change of focus from a traditional mortgage lender to a bank pursuing an aggressive expansion in the retail mortgage market, funded via short-term money market funding and securitisation (see Figure 13.1). Northern Rock grew rapidly in the early 2000s, roughly trebling its share of the UK mortgage market. In 1999 Northern Rock accounted for 3.6 per cent (gross) and 6 per cent (net) of UK mortgage lending; at the onset of the crisis in 2007, these shares had increased to 9.7 per cent (gross) and 18.9 per cent (net) (Bank of England, 2007a).

Northern Rock's rapid lending growth and funding concentration came at the cost of its lending spreads, both in absolute terms and compared with other lenders. It was nonetheless considered a well-capitalised bank with a good-quality mortgage book. Both Standard & Poor's (in August 2006) and Moody's (in April 2007) increased its debt rating by one notch. Market perceptions of its risk (measured by its CDS spreads) were also stable and in early 2007 Northern Rock was able to raise £10.7 billion through its principal securitisation programme, Granite, and it

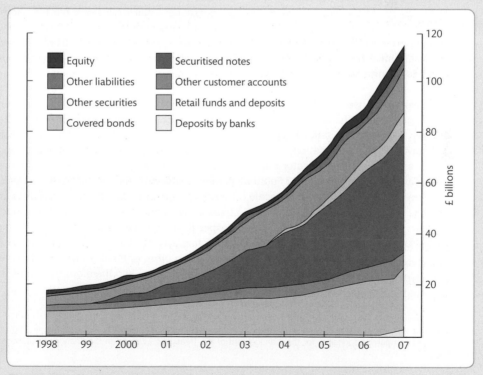

Figure 13.1 Northern Rock balance sheet growth and liability structure, June 1998–June 2007

Source: Bank of England (2007a), figures from Northern Rock *Interim* and *Annual Reports*.

Box 13.1 The failure and resolution of Northern Rock (*continued*)

completed three covered bond (where the mortgage loans remain on the balance sheet) issues totalling £2.2 billion. In 2007, Northern Rock's securitisations accounted for more than 17 per cent of all residential mortgage-backed securities (RMBS) issuance by UK-based issuers (Bank of England, 2007).

However, while Northern Rock's credit spread remained stable, its share price had been under pressure from early 2007. As the conditions in worldwide credit and money markets began to deteriorate, Northern Rock's CDS spread began to rise, while its share prices decreased further. Liquidity became a problem due to the need to constantly roll over its maturing short-term debt. By mid-September 2007, it had become apparent that Northern Rock's vulnerability was increasing and it could no longer access longer-term funding markets. At that time Northern Rock sought an assurance of liquidity support from the Bank of England. On 14 September 2007, Northern Rock issued a warning about its profits and on the same day the Tripartite (the Bank of England, the UK Treasury and the Financial Services Authority) issued a joint statement that they would provide liquidity support to Northern Rock. While the announcement should have been positive news, it confirmed the public's worst fears and triggered a run on the bank.

The UK government response included an extension of the deposit guarantee scheme to all deposits at Northern Rock. However, the unfolding of the crisis limited the government's options: on 17 February 2008 attempts to find a private sector buyer for Northern Rock came to an end and on 22 February 2008 the UK government announced a full-scale nationalisation.

From nationalisation to sale

At the time of the nationalisation, Northern Rock had assets of just over £100 billion, government guarantees covering customer deposits and an outstanding emergency loan from the government of more than £25 billion. In public ownership, the bank was expected to run down its mortgage assets to repay the emergency loan and the deposit guarantees would be removed by the end of 2011. It was also expected that Northern Rock would then enter a period of growth, followed by a return of the business to the private sector. However, following higher than expected losses, the government decided to review its options and split Northern Rock into two businesses: Northern Rock plc, a bank that could be returned to private sector ownership, and Northern Rock Asset Management (NRAM), to be retained in public ownership and eventually wound down. On 1 January 2010, the existing £21 billion of retail deposits, matched by £10 billion of the best-performing mortgages and £11 billion of cash, were transferred to Northern Rock plc. In 2010, oversight of the new companies transferred to **UK Financial Investments Ltd (UKFI)**.[2]

Performance while in public ownership was below expectations – Northern Rock plc fell short of its lending targets in both 2010 and 2011 and incurred higher than expected losses. In 2011, UKFI reviewed all the options and a sale at the earliest opportunity appeared to be the best available option to minimise losses. Finally, at the end of 2011, the Treasury sold Northern Rock plc to Virgin Money (for between £863 million and £977 million, depending on the size and timing of future payments agreed as part of the sale). The sale was announced in November 2011 and finalised in January 2012. Figure 13.2 summarises the process of creation and sale of Northern Rock plc.

A 2012 report by the National Audit Office and HM Treasury (National Audit Office, 2012) concludes that, despite the fact that the sale resulted in a further loss to the taxpayer of £232 million, delaying the sale or considering other options would have incurred significant uncertainty and therefore concludes that the sale was justified.

➡

---

[2] UKFI is a Treasury-owned company responsible for the management of the Treasury's interests in the financial institutions supported directly by the taxpayer.

Box 13.1 The failure and resolution of Northern Rock (*continued*)

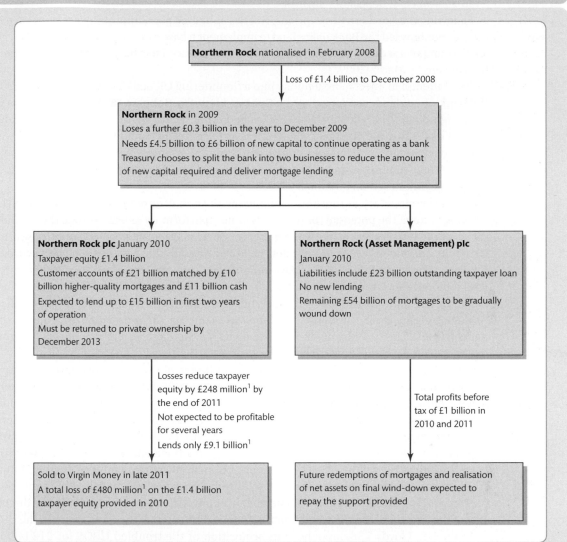

Figure 13.2 Northern Rock: from nationalisation to sale

Note: Latest available estimates of Northern Rock plc's lending, 2011 book values and the midpoint loss on the sale.

Source: National Audit Office (2012).

a UK bank for more than a century. To stem depositor panic, the UK government announced a full guarantee of depositors' savings.

Following the Northern Rock episode, worries about the possibility of a major slowdown in the UK economy led the Bank of England to implement a base rate cut in December 2007; this was the first of a series of cuts that saw the base rate reduced to a historically unprecedented 0.5 per cent by March 2009.

In an attempt to inject more liquidity into a floundering UK banking system, in April 2008 the Bank of England also introduced a **Special Liquidity Scheme (SLS)** to allow banks to swap high-quality, illiquid mortgage-backed and other securities for Treasury bills (see also Box 6.3 discussing the emergency liquidity assistance to HBOS and RBS). The scheme was intended as a temporary measure, to give banks time to strengthen their balance sheets and diversify their funding sources, although it remained in place for almost four years before being officially closed on 30 January 2012.

While the monetary authorities continued with their efforts to inject liquidity into the banking system, the potential for write-offs of non-performing assets to erode the capitalisation of the UK's largest banks was a growing concern. Over the next few months, several UK banks announced plans to raise new capital, although these were not always successful. For example, in July 2008 Barclays announced that only 18 per cent of the shares in a £4.5 billion rights issue had been taken up, with the rest acquired by an investment group including the Qatar Investment Authority. In July 2008 HBOS attempted to raise £4 billion through a rights issue, but only 8 per cent was taken up, the remainder reverting to the underwriters. The inability of UK banks to convince their shareholders to invest in rights issues provided a clear signal that further serious difficulties lay ahead.

Indeed, the worst was still to come and global financial markets experienced the most momentous events in more than a century in September 2008, which became known as 'meltdown month': two major US government-sponsored organisations, Fannie Mae and Freddie Mac, were placed in 'conservatorship' (effective government ownership); Lehman Brothers, the fourth largest US investment bank, filed for bankruptcy. The Lehman collapse triggered a spectacular sequence of events that brought the global financial system to the brink of collapse, including the failure of AIG (the largest US insurance firm) and Washington Mutual (the largest US savings and loan institution) as well as various bank bailouts in Europe (Fortis, Dexia, Hypo Real Estate and Commerzbank among others – see Chapter 14 for a discussion of the crisis in EU banking and Chapter 15 for a discussion of the crisis events in the US).

In the UK, Lloyds TSB announced its acquisition of the troubled HBOS for £12 billion (at the behest of the government). And at the end of September 2008, the UK government announced that it was acquiring the mortgage-lending arm of Bradford & Bingley and selling the still-viable depositor base and branch network to the Spanish Santander Banking Group. On 13 October 2008, capital injections were announced for RBS (£20 billion), and Lloyds TSB and HBOS (£17 billion combined), increasing the government stakes in their ownership to around 60 per cent and 40 per cent, respectively. In return for government capital injections, the UK banks were required to make commitments to lend at competitive rates to homeowners and small businesses, reschedule mortgage payments for homeowners facing difficulties and exercise restraint over executive compensation. Meanwhile, Barclays announced that it planned to raise £6.5 billion by private means, avoiding the need for partial nationalisation. On 3 November 2008, the UK government set up a new 'arm's-length' company, UK Financial Investments Ltd (UKFI), to manage the banks in public ownership, Northern Rock and Bradford & Bingley (see Box 13.1).

On 21 February 2009 the **Banking Act** established a permanent **Special Resolution Regime (SRR)**, providing the authorities with tools to deal with banks facing financial difficulties. Details of the **Special Liquidity Scheme (SLS)**, the **Credit Guarantee Scheme (CGS)** and the **Asset Protection Scheme (APS)** were unveiled shortly afterwards. The first failure of a UK bank in 2009 occurred on 30 March, when the Treasury announced its acquisition of around £1.5 billion of non-performing mortgages and commercial property loans from Dunfermline Building Society. The rest of the Dunfermline's loans portfolio, and its deposits and branch network, were taken over by Nationwide Building Society.

Table 13.1 summarises the main actions of the UK Treasury to support the banks. The list excludes loans and commitments to other countries and interventions to support the wider economy (for example, the Bank of England's quantitative easing). It is possible to distinguish the support given to banks as (i) provision of cash (for example, loans to the Financial Services Compensation Scheme; loans to insolvent banks and the recapitalisation of RBS and Lloyds Banking Group) and (ii) the provision of guarantees and other non-cash support (for example, the CGS, the SLS and the APS). The National Audit Office provides figures for estimates of the total peak support provided to banks at £1,162 billion.

Table 13.1 Government support to UK banks, 2007–2012

Intervention type	Intervention	Purpose
Cash outlay	Recapitalisation	Recapitalisation of Lloyds Banking Group (Lloyds) and Royal Bank of Scotland (RBS) to avoid bank failure. This was achieved through a series of transactions eventually acquiring 83 per cent of RBS and 41 per cent of Lloyds.
	Lending through the Financial Services Compensation Scheme	To guarantee customer deposits of up to £50,000.
	Direct lending to insolvent banks	Lending directly to insolvent banks so they could repay customer deposits of over £50,000. Banks that benefited included London Scottish Bank and Dunfermline Building Society and the Icelandic banks with UK depositors: Heritable, Kaupthing, Singer and Friedlander, and Landsbanki.
	Nationalisation	Nationalisation of Northern Rock and Bradford & Bingley to protect their depositors and facilitate the orderly unwinding of their obligations and the Treasury's guarantees.
Guarantee commitments	Special Liquidity Scheme	The scheme (April 2008 to January 2012) aimed to increase the liquidity of UK banks. It was a BoE scheme, supported by a Treasury guarantee, under which banks swapped assets for more liquid Treasury bills in return for a fee.
	Credit Guarantee Scheme	The scheme (October 2008 to October 2012) aimed to help restore investor confidence in bank wholesale funding by providing short-term liquidity by guaranteeing certain unsecured debts in return for a fee.
	Asset Protection Scheme	The scheme (January 2009 to October 2012) was designed to protect assets on banks' balance sheets. The scheme originally involved two banks, RBS and Lloyds, but in the end only RBS joined as Lloyds Banking Group paid £2.5 billion to exit the scheme in November 2009 and instead raised additional capital from shareholders. The scheme was only a partial success in terms of encouraging lending.

Source: Adapted from the National Audit Office, Taxpayers support for UK banks (**www.nao.org.uk**).

One can see that a lot has happened since the onset of the crisis in mid-2007, and while the implications of these dramatic changes are just becoming apparent, it is clear that we have a remarkably different UK banking system than we had just a few years ago. By the end of 2009 two of the country's largest banks, Royal Bank of Scotland (see Box 13.2) and Lloyds Group, were in state majority ownership while Northern Rock and Bradford & Bingley were nationalised. Even those banks not under state ownership have benefited directly or indirectly from the massive capital and liquidity provision granted by the government via the Bank of England.

BOX 13.2 WHY DID RBS FAIL?

In October 2008, the Royal Bank of Scotland (RBS) in effect failed and was part nationalised. From the 7 of October, it relied on the Bank of England Emergency Liquidity Assistance (ELA) to fund itself; and on the 13 of October, the government announced that it would provide up to £20bn of new equity to recapitalise RBS. Subsequent increases in government capital injections amounted to £25.5bn. RBS's failure thus imposed significant direct costs on British taxpayers. In addition, the failure played an important role within an overall financial crisis which produced a major recession.

In March 2009, the FSA's Enforcement Division initiated enquiries into a number of firms which had in effect failed during 2007 to 2008. While the results of these investigations were not disclosed to the public, the FSA also produced a comprehensive report into the causes of RBS's failure, with the additional aim to identify and report on any key deficiencies in the FSA's own regulation and supervision of RBS in the years running up to failure.

The results of the FSA report can be summarised as follows:

Why did RBS fail? Poor management decisions, deficient regulation and a flawed supervisory approach.

The FSA (2011) report concludes that failure of RBS can be explained by a combination of six key factors:

1 **Capitalisation.** Significant weaknesses in RBS's capital position, as a result of management decisions and permitted by an inadequate regulatory capital framework.

2 **Liquidity.** Over-reliance on risky short-term wholesale funding.

3 **Asset quality.** Concerns and uncertainties about RBS's underlying asset quality, which in turn was subject to little fundamental analysis by the FSA.

4 **Trading activities.** Substantial losses in credit trading activities, which eroded market confidence. Both RBS's strategy and the FSA's supervisory approach underestimated how bad losses associated with structured credit might be.

5 **The ABN AMRO acquisition.** RBS proceeded with the acquisition without appropriate heed to the risks involved and with inadequate due diligence.

6 **Systemic risk.** An overall systemic crisis in which the banks in worse relative positions were extremely vulnerable to failure. RBS was one such bank.

Capitalisation

The immediate cause of RBS's failure was a liquidity run. But concerns about the bank's capital adequacy (as well as about capital adequacy across the banking system) were crucial to its failure. It is now apparent that the global regulatory capital framework in place before the crisis was severely deficient, and the reforms introduced by Basel II added major complexity without addressing the fundamental problem of inadequate capital across entire banking systems. However, even in the context of that capital regime, RBS chose to be lightly capitalised relative to its peers and made considerable use of lower-quality forms of capital (see Figure 13.3). In addition, the acquisition of ABN AMRO further weakened its capital position.

BOX 13.2 Why did RBS fail? (*continued*)

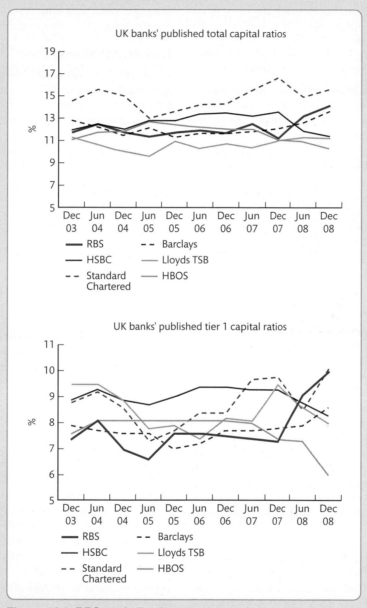

Figure 13.3 RBS capitalisation

Source: 2003 to 2008 published annual reports and interim results; FSA (2011a).

As an example, the FSA Review Team estimated that, if the Basel III definitions of capital had been in place before the crisis, RBS would have recorded a common equity tier 1 ratio at end-2007 of around 2% (instead of the new minimum standard of 4.5% and the higher standard of 9.5% that the Financial Stability Board and the Basel Committee have agreed for Systemically Important Banks (see Section 7.7.4 for

BOX 13.2 Why did RBS fail? (*continued*)

a discussion of Basel III). In this instance, it is evident that RBS's capital position before the crisis was grossly inadequate.

Liquidity

RBS entered the crisis with extensive reliance on wholesale funding. Its short-term wholesale funding gap was one of the largest in its peer group, and it was more reliant on overnight funding and unsecured funding than most of its peers. The acquisition of ABN AMRO increased its reliance on short-term wholesale funding.

Again, as an example, if the Basel III liquidity coverage ratio (LCR) had been in place, the FSA Review Team estimated that RBS's liquidity position at end-August 2008 would have translated to an LCR (as currently calibrated) of between 18% and 32%, versus a future standard requirement of 100%.

Asset quality

In addition, RBS's balance sheet and leverage increased rapidly in the years leading up to the financial crisis, in a period of fast growth in credit extension and leverage across the banking sector. While RBS's investment banking division, Global Banking and Markets, was the most rapidly growing area, RBS's loan portfolio in its other divisions also expanded. Significant loan losses were subsequently incurred in many areas of business, with a particular concentration in commercial property. Indeed, impairments incurred on loans and advances eventually amounted to £32.5bn over the period 2007–10, significantly exceeding the £17.7bn of losses on credit trading activities.

Trading activities

By early 2007, RBS had accumulated significant exposures containing credit risk in its trading portfolio, following its strategic decision in mid-2006 to expand its structured credit business aggressively. The acquisition of ABN AMRO increased RBS's exposure to such assets just as credit trading activities were becoming less attractive. This increased the firm's vulnerability to market concerns.

The ABN AMRO acquisition

The acquisition of ABN AMRO by a consortium led by RBS greatly increased RBS's vulnerability. The decision to fund the acquisition primarily with debt, the majority of which was short-term, rather than equity, eroded RBS's capital adequacy and increased its reliance on short-term wholesale funding. The acquisition significantly increased RBS's exposure to structured credit and other asset classes on which large losses were subsequently taken. In the circumstances of the crisis, its role as the leader of the consortium affected market confidence in RBS.

Systemic risk

The intensification of market uncertainties during the summer of 2008, culminating in the acute loss of confidence following the collapse of Lehman Brothers in September, affected all banks in some way. But those most affected were those that were, or were perceived as being, in a worse position, in terms of capital, liquidity or asset quality. They included RBS.

Overall

Some of the causes of RBS's failure were systemic – common to many banks or the consequence of unstable features of the entire financial system. But with hindsight it is clear that poor decisions by RBS's management and Board during 2006 and 2007 were crucial to RBS's failure.

FSA Review Team concludes that it was individual poor decisions that caused RBS to fail. These poor decisions, at the time or with hindsight, were also considered indicative of underlying deficiencies in the bank's management capabilities and style; governance arrangements; checks and balances; mechanisms for oversight and challenge; and in its culture, particularly its attitude to the balance between risk and growth.

Source: Adapted from FSA (2011) available at **www.fsa.gov.uk/pubs/other/rbs.pdf**

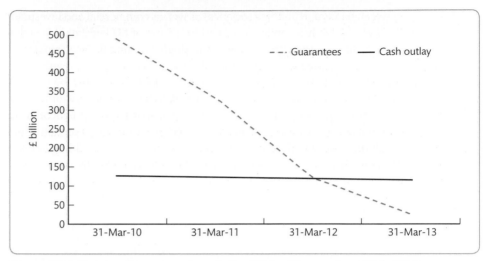

Figure 13.4 Outstanding guarantees to the UK banking sector, 2010–2013

Source: National Audit Office (2013).

The UK's National Audit Office (2013) report gives an update on the financial support granted by the Treasury to the UK banking sector since 2007: how much support had been provided, how much was still outstanding and how much it was costing the taxpayer. As of March 2013, the total outstanding support stood at £141 billion (down from the total a year before of £242 billion and a peak of £1.2 trillion). Of the £141 billion, £115 billion was provided as cash and £26 billion constitutes outstanding guarantee commitments. In return for providing the support, the Treasury has charged fees for the financial guarantee schemes and received interest on the loans. Once the opportunity cost and risks are factored in, the schemes have represented a transfer of at least £5 billion from taxpayers to the financial sector since 2008. The National Audit Office states that had the support not been provided, the potential costs would have been difficult to forecast and therefore this £5 billion can be regarded as part of the cost of preserving financial stability in the crisis. At its peak, support for the banks totalled more than £1 trillion. However, the scale of these interventions, particularly the guarantees outstanding, reduced substantially in 2012–2013, as illustrated in Figure 13.4. This resulted mainly from the closure of the APS and the CGS (see Table 13.1). In addition, Northern Rock Asset Management and Bradford & Bingley repaid £3.1 billion of loans and recoveries of loans from other financial institutions totalling £1.5 billion (National Audit Office, 2012).

13.3 Regulatory reforms and the changing face of UK banking

The regulatory environment in the UK banking and financial services industry has changed dramatically since the mid-1980s. To understand the ongoing changes brought on by the events discussed in Section 13.2, it is necessary to step a little further back in time and discuss the changes that shaped the UK financial sector from the 1980s to the mid-2000s.

In general, legislation has covered three main areas. First, a range of regulatory changes has sought to reduce demarcation lines between different types of financial services firms (especially between banks and building societies) as well as commercial and investment banking business. Second, the UK has implemented various pieces of EU legislation into domestic banking law, thus facilitating the introduction of the single banking licence (making it easier for banks to do business throughout Europe) and harmonising prudential regulation for both commercial banks and investment firms. Third, legislation laid down in the Financial Services and Markets Act (2001) put in place the transfer of regulatory responsibility for the whole financial system to a 'super regulator' – the Financial Services Authority – in the light of the Labour government's announcement to make the Bank of England independent for monetary policy purposes.

Changes governing the regulatory treatment of the building society sector have had a major impact on the competitive environment in the retail banking sector. Ironically, reforms that were put in place to improve the competitive stance of the mutual sector vis-à-vis commercial banks led to a systematic decline of the former. This is because most of the largest building societies embraced demutualisation, leading to a shift of assets from the mutual to commercial banking sector (see Appendix 13.1).

Another area where the changes in legislation have had a big impact is in the restructuring of the domestic merchant banking industry. Prior to the 1986 **'Big Bang'** reforms, investment banking and securities business was dominated by UK-owned banks – mainly partnerships operating in the City. Independent UK firms such as Morgan Grenfell, Kleinwort Benson and SG Warburg dominated domestic business. The 'Big Bang' reforms allowed commercial banks to be members of the London Stock Exchange and the legal separation between stockbroking and jobbing firms (those operating on the floor of the exchange) was abandoned. This led to a frenzy of domestic and foreign commercial banks (as well as the main US investment banks) acquiring UK securities firms. The merger and acquisition frenzy faltered, to a certain extent, after the 1987 stock market crash – although Deutsche Bank acquired Morgan Grenfell in 1989. It commenced again post UK recession, particularly from 1995 onwards, and by 2005 there were hardly any significant independent UK merchant banks. Since the mid-2000s, investment banking and securities business in the UK has been dominated by the US 'bulge bracket' firms (Goldman Sachs, Morgan Stanley, Merrill Lynch) as well as by various Swiss (Credit Suisse and UBS) and German banks (Deutsche Bank). UK banks such as Barclays and RBS invested heavily in the investment banking business to become credible competitors.

The gradual structural deregulation relating to commercial banking, investment banking, securities business and insurance meant that financial firms had the choice of being universal operators. The decision by the government to create a single financial services regulator in 1999 (the Financial Services Authority) was another reflection of the universalisation of the UK banking industry.

Many of the above-mentioned regulatory initiatives aimed to create a more competitive and innovative banking and financial system. Domestic banks became engaged in non-interest business on a bigger scale and competed with other domestic financial firms, as well as foreign banks and even new non-banking firms that had moved into financial service provision. An area for excess competition was the real estate lending market where a boom in mortgages fed a property price bubble. When the bubble burst in the US and spread across the Atlantic in mid-2007, UK banks were over-exposed to the property market.

The UK regulatory response to the crisis has been rapid and (as documented in Section 13.2) aimed to re-establish stability in a crisis situation. In addition, it had become apparent that the tripartite regulatory structure between the Bank of England, the Treasury and the FSA did not work well during the crisis. As such, the UK authorities set out proposed legislation in 2011 called 'A new approach to financial regulation – the blueprint for reform' that became law in 2012 as the Financial Services Act. The 2012 Act abolished the Financial Services Authority and created the Financial Policy Committee (FPC), the Prudential Regulatory Authority (PRA) and the Financial Conduct Authority (FCA) – the 2012 Act is discussed in detail in Section 6.2.2.

In 2012, the UK banking system was involved in a different type of crisis: the largest UK credit institutions were allegedly involved in the LIBOR fixing scandal as described in Box 13.3. As a result of this scandal, the UK government put in place new legislation to regulate the LIBOR and to ensure that any wrongdoing in relation to benchmark setting is now treated as a criminal offence in the UK.

13.3.1 A new approach to regulation in UK banking

As a response to the recognition that the structural and other features of the UK banking system needed reform, in June 2010 the Treasury set up an Independent Commission on Banking, chaired by Sir John Vickers. The ICB was requested to make recommendations on:

- reducing systemic risk in the banking sector, exploring the risk posed by banks of different size, scale and function;

- mitigating moral hazard in the banking system;

- reducing both the likelihood and impact of firm failure, as well as promoting competition in both retail and investment banking with a view to ensuring that the needs of banks' customers and clients are efficiently served, and in particular considering the extent to which large banks gain competitive advantage from being perceived as too big to fail.

BOX 13.3 LIBOR FIXING

Understanding LIBOR

LIBOR (London Interbank Offered Rate) is an interest rate set in London and used as a global benchmark to price financial products worth some $350 trillion. Its origins relate to the importance of London as a global financial centre: over 30% of global foreign exchange trading is done in London and more than 20% of international bank lending.

LIBOR had traditionally been set by the British Bankers' Association (up until February 2014) as follows:

1 Each day a panel of global banks submitted rates at which they could borrow various currencies over different time periods.

2 Individual bids were submitted daily at 11a.m.

3 Thomson Reuters processed the bids by rejecting some of the highest and lowest and used the middle two quartiles to calculate the average. This process was repeated 150 times to

create the day's LIBOR rates for 15 borrowing periods and 10 currencies.

4 Once calculated the LIBOR figures were published at midday.

5 Libor rates set the basis for a range of financial instruments including a broad array of wholesale instruments including derivative products as well as retail home mortgages, credit cards and company loans.

Problems arose when it was revealed that the global banks submitting rates to fix LIBOR were colluding to manipulate rates that would favour their own pricing of certain derivative instruments. The scandal is outlined below.

Gargantuan task of LIBOR probes becomes clearer

Last year, when Barclays became the first bank to admit to rigging LIBOR, politicians, regulators and bankers

BOX 13.3 LIBOR fixing (*continued*)

loudly jumped on the enforcement bandwagon, promising to clean up the interbank lending market and other survey-based indices vulnerable to manipulation.

Fifteen months later, the gargantuan nature of that task is becoming clearer. Four banks and an interdealer broker have paid more than $3.5 billion in fines on LIBOR alone, with more settlements expected. Rate-rigging has been documented on three continents, with traders in cities as far-flung as Singapore, New York and London captured on emails and in chat rooms openly discussing their efforts to influence the daily rate-setting process to make money on derivatives.

Nor has the misbehaviour been confined to the high-flying investment banks. Rabobank, which has its roots in a Dutch farmers' co-operative, this week paid $1 billion in penalties, the second-largest settlement to date, and lost its chief executive.

Meanwhile, efforts to replace LIBOR with a transaction-based rate that would be less susceptible to manipulation are faltering, dragged down by three problems. The first was known up front, the holders of a number of existing LIBOR contracts, including 30-year home mortgages, are reluctant to accept a new rate that could change their position. Second, the interbank lending market remains so barren that there are not many transactions to anchor a new rate. The third reason became depressingly clear this week – transaction-based rates may not solve the problem.

Several of the world's biggest banks – including several LIBOR players – confirmed that they are co-operating with a global probe into alleged manipulation of foreign exchange rates. Employees at Barclays, Royal Bank of Scotland, JPMorgan Chase and Citigroup have all been put on leave, and several other banks are conducting internal investigations. Regulators are said to be focusing on instant messages among traders at different banks. While the investigation is still in its infancy, the revelations to date are reminiscent of the early days of the still-unfolding LIBOR scandal.

But this time the scandal cannot be blamed on surveys or lack of trading. The forex markets are among the most liquid in the world and the rates in question are based on actual transactions during specified windows.

If rates cannot be engineered to prevent manipulation, what are regulators to do? The Swiss gave a clue to the answer this week when UBS revealed that it had been ordered to bump up the capital it holds against litigation, compliance and operational risks by 50 per cent. Global regulators are thinking along similar lines – the Basel Committee on Banking Supervision warned last year that it was considering bumping up worldwide capital requirements for this area.

The optimistic view of this development is that regulators are using the big stick of higher capital requirements to force banks to take their conduct and compliance duties more seriously. The glass half-empty version is that authorities have thrown up their hands and given up. Essentially, regulators seem to be saying that if they cannot stop bad behaviour, they will at least make sure banks have enough cash on hand to pay for the lawsuits and enforcement penalties that will inevitably follow.

New LIBOR arrangements

On February 1st 2014, the responsibility for administering LIBOR was transferred from the British Bankers' Association to ICE Benchmark Administration Limited (IBA), a company owned by Intercontinental Exchange (ICE), which owns the New York Stock Exchange (NYSE) Euronext. ICE was granted the business after an independent enquiry set up by the UK government. IBA is authorised by the UK's Financial Conduct Authority (FCA). ICE takes over from Thomson Reuters as the primary publisher of the LIBOR rates, using a new Secure File Transfer Protocol (SFTP) service. The new arrangements (see Figure 13.5) aim to:

● return credibility, trust and integrity to LIBOR by bringing together a strong regulatory and governance framework and market-leading validation techniques;

● implement a new post-publication surveillance system and tests designed to assess the credibility of LIBOR submissions and rates;

● introduce new surveillance approaches to vary to changing market conditions and employ sophisticated analytical tools to operate the benchmark price setting process with transparency.

Sources: Ben Freese and Johanna Kassel (2013) 'Understanding LIBOR', *Financial Times*; Brooke Masters (2013) *Financial Times*, 1 November; ICE Benchmark Administration, **www.theice.com/iba**

BOX 13.3 LIBOR fixing (*continued*)

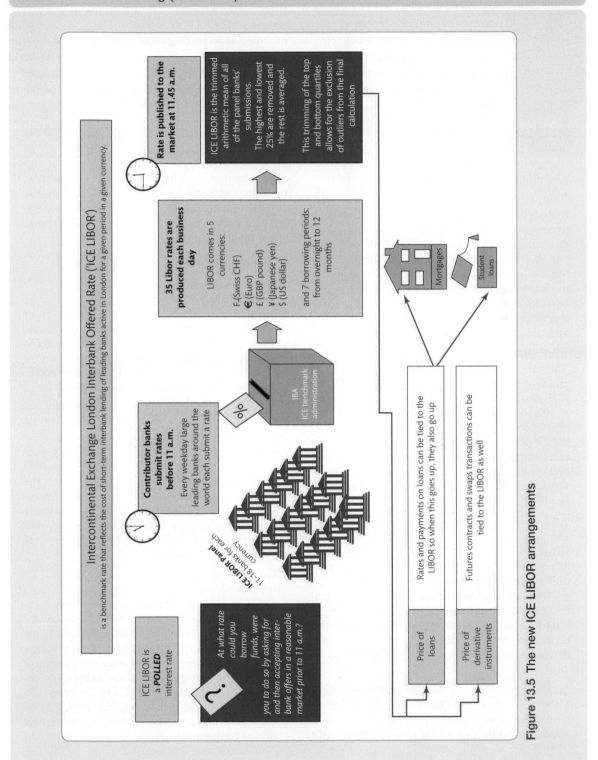

Intercontinental Exchange London Interbank Offered Rate ('ICE LIBOR')

is a benchmark rate that reflects the cost of short-term interbank lending of leading banks active in London for a given period in a given currency.

ICE LIBOR is a **POLLED** interest rate

At what rate could you borrow funds, were you to do so by asking for and then accepting inter-bank offers in a reasonable market prior to 11 a.m.?

ICE LIBOR panel
11–18 banks for each currency

Contributor banks submit rates before 11 a.m.

Every weekday large leading banks around the world each submit a rate

%

IBA
ICE benchmark administration

35 Libor rates are produced each business day

LIBOR comes in 5 currencies:

Fr (Swiss CHF)
€ (Euro)
£ (GBP pound)
¥ (Japanese yen)
$ (US dollar)

and 7 borrowing periods: from overnight to 12 months

Rate is published to the market at 11.45 a.m.

ICE LIBOR is the trimmed arithmetic mean of all of the panel banks' submissions.
The highest and lowest 25% are removed and the rest is averaged.

This trimming of the top and bottom quartiles allows for the exclusion of outliers from the final calculation

Price of loans

Rates and payments on loans can be tied to the LIBOR so when this goes up, they also go up

Price of derivative instruments

Futures contracts and swaps transactions can be tied to the LIBOR as well

Mortgages

Student loans

Figure 13.5 The new ICE LIBOR arrangements

The Vickers Commission produced its final Report in September 2011 (Independent Commission on Banking, 2011). Its main recommendations related to **ring-fencing** retail banking, boosting capital resources and various measures relating to competition. Most attention has been placed on the ring-fencing argument aimed at protecting retail depositors and separating higher-risk investment banking activities. In simple terms, ring-fencing will exclude banks that accept retail deposits from undertaking a range of activities not directly connected to providing payment services and making loans. The *Financial Times*' assessment of the report is illustrated in Box 13.4.

BOX 13.4 JUST THE FACTS: THE VICKERS REPORT

The ring-fence

What has been announced?
British banks must separate their high street and investment banking operations. The ring-fence must contain all retail and small business deposits and their overdrafts. Investment banking activities including derivatives, debt and equity underwriting and investing and trading in securities must fall outside. Banks are free to place other activities including lending to consumers and businesses and trade finance on either side of the fence.

Who will be most affected?
The reforms will trigger far-reaching structural changes for every one of the big UK banks. The ICB's estimate for the amount of assets that will be held behind the ring-fence is between £1,500bn and £2,300bn. Allowing individual institutions to decide where they draw the line will mean they can adapt the rules to suit their own models. Nevertheless, as the two banks with the largest and most diversified UK businesses, Barclays and RBS are likely to be hardest hit.

What do the critics say?
Ring-fencing UK retail operations may encourage banks to take greater risks with activities that are grouped inside the fence, such as mortgages and corporate and personal loans, because they are more confident of being bailed out. Bankers complain that the UK is "going it alone" on ring-fencing at the worst possible time, when economic growth is slowing and without enough detail about the impact of the changes.

FT verdict
Making the ring-fence flexible in allowing banks a degree of choice over where it is placed – and, in particular, over whether to include big corporate deposits and loans – was a sensible compromise by the commission in pursuit of its fundamental aim: curtailing the implicit government subsidy that stems from the prospect that universal banking groups will be bailed out by the taxpayer when they run into difficulty.

Capital requirements

What has been announced?
Banks will have to hold equity capital – the highest quality kind – of at least 10 per cent of risk-weighted assets in the ring-fenced business. On top, Vickers recommends that both parts of the bank have total loss-absorbing capital of at least 17–20 per cent. This could include 'bail-in bonds' – or long-term loss unsecured debt – and contingent capital or "cocos", as well as equity and other capital.

Who will be most affected?
All British banks will be hit, although they were generally already moving in this direction. The Vickers proposals are slightly higher than the existing Basel III rules for the ring-fenced business. Analysts estimate that banks typically already have between 15 and 25 per cent of loss-absorbing debt, in addition to their top layer of highest quality capital.

What do the critics say?
That these capital requirements are out of step with internationally agreed measures. Only Switzerland has gone this far in increasing banks' capital buffers. The banks themselves are likely to be the biggest critics, arguing that introducing tougher regulation in the UK could damage their ability to compete globally. Some others, including the CBI employers' group, say the proposals could increase the cost of lending for UK businesses, putting them at a disadvantage to their overseas competitors.

➡

BOX 13.4 Just the facts: the Vickers Report (*continued*)

FT verdict

The biggest cause of bank failures during the recent financial crisis was too little capital, so it is hard to argue that levels should not be increased. While the proposals for the ring-fenced business go further than the Basel III rules, the commission has aligned the minimum equity requirements for the non-ring-fenced with international standards. The further layer of loss-absorbing capital should not cause too many problems as banks already hold high buffers.

Costs

What has been announced?

The commission put the costs to the banking industry at £4bn–£7bn per year. However, it expects the social cost – the amount that will actually translate into lower growth – to be between £1bn and £3bn. Much of this comes from higher funding costs, largely in the non-ring-fenced business. Operational changes – through setting up an independent board for the retail arm, for example – will also increase costs, although to a lesser degree.

Who will be most affected?

Banks' shareholders, creditors, employees and customers will all be affected to some degree. The commission expects the effect to be greatest in the non-ring-fenced business, which is more vulnerable to rises in funding costs. The impact on UK borrowers should therefore be lower. Overall, the commission says borrowing costs could rise by an average of 0.1 of a percentage point – far less than other estimates.

What do the critics say?

Banks and some business groups argue that hitting the industry with billions of pounds of additional costs at a time when their business models are already under pressure could undermine lending and the recovery. They are concerned that in spite of the delayed target date for implementation of 2019, banks will be under pressure to start restructuring their businesses sooner, which could put pressure on their ability to lend.

FT verdict

The commission estimates the annual benchmark cost of financial crises at about £40bn, so paying up to about £7bn to avoid that looks worthwhile. The commission's estimates are far lower than some of the banks' own figures, which suggested annual costs could be as much as £10bn. The impact should be largely mitigated by the decision to delay implementation until 2019 at the latest. Still, the costs are clearly only worth paying if the proposals are successful in averting another crisis.

Competition

What has been announced?

A range of measures largely focused on improving access to bank accounts for retail and small business customers. The commission wants to ensure the branch portfolio being sold by Lloyds Banking Group creates a strong new challenger in the market. It has endorsed a new industry-wide switching service that should enable customers to move providers within seven days and has recommended that banks provide more detail on charging structures and that the regulator takes charge of competition.

Who will be most affected?

As the biggest high-street lender, Lloyds has always been at the centre of the commission's competition proposals. The final recommendations are less harsh than feared: Lloyds must ensure the business it is selling has at least a 6 per cent share of UK current accounts, but it does not have to sell more branches. For the market as a whole, new entrants and smaller lenders, who have long complained that it is hard to win market share from the big banks, should see most benefit from the new switching service.

What do the critics say?

Generally, measures to promote competition for consumers and small businesses are widely supported. However, consumer organisations are concerned that it will take a long time to implement the changes, and even longer for them to make a real difference in the market. Also, some say the recommendations on Lloyds were watered down. Initially, the commission had wanted to shrink Lloyds' own share of current accounts, which may not be achieved through its final recommendations.

BOX 13.4 Just the facts: the Vickers Report (*continued*)

FT verdict

Lloyds has dodged a bullet. It does not have to sell more branches and its share of the current account market – expected to be 25 per cent following the branch disposal – has been left intact. Also, its efforts to dispose of the branches specified by the EU should not be disrupted. Lloyds can still sell to a new entrant as long as it ensures the new entity has a 6 per cent share of current accounts. An easier and faster switching service is clearly sensible. A survey from Firstsource Solutions shows that half of those polled would consider moving provider if there were a seven-day deadline.

Source: Just the facts: the Vickers Report, *Financial Times*, 12/09/11 (Sharlene Goff).

Based on the recommendations of the ICB, the UK government published a White Paper (HM Treasury, 2012) titled 'Banking reform: Delivering stability and supporting a sustainable economy', which sets out the proposal for reform of the UK banking sector.

Following a period of consultation, in February 2013 the UK Chancellor presented the Banking Reform Bill to Parliament. The Bill incorporates many of the ICB's recommendations; it aims to separate the retail and investment arms of UK banks and erect a ring-fence around the retail bank so that essential operations continue even if the whole bank fails. There have also been promises that the legislation, if passed, would 'electrify the ring-fence', that is it would incorporate provisions to allow regulators to split up a bank if it were found to flout the rules.

The Banking Reform Act (which received Royal Assent in December 2013) will:[3]

- introduce a 'ring-fence' around the deposits of people and small businesses, to separate the high street from the dealing floor and protect taxpayers when things go wrong;

- make sure the new Prudential Regulation Authority can hold banks to account for the way they separate their retail and investment activities, giving it powers to enforce the full separation of individual banks;

- give depositors, protected under the Financial Services Compensation Scheme, preference if a bank enters insolvency and give the government power to ensure that banks are more able to absorb losses.

In summary, it is expected that the Bill will ring-fence the deposits of individuals and small businesses to separate important everyday banking activities from volatile investment bank activities, give insured depositors preference if a bank enters insolvency and give the government power to ensure banks are more able to absorb losses. However, it will not implement ICB key recommendations on higher capital requirements for large ring-fenced banks, as these are being pursued at the European level (**www.gov.uk**).

Overall, the Banking Reform Act of 2013 aims to establish a more resilient, stable and competitive banking sector.[4] The current structure of the UK banking sector is reviewed in Section 13.4.

---

[3] See **www.gov.uk** under the Policies heading 'Creating stronger and safer banks'.

[4] The full text of the Financial Services (Banking Reform) Act of 2013 can be found at **www.legislation.gov .uk/ukpga/2013/33/pdfs/ukpga_20130033_en.pdf**

13.4 The structure of the UK banking sector

This section aims to review the structural features of the UK banking industry, with particular focus on the major British banking groups (which are now also known as 'the main high street banking groups'), highlighting recent trends. The impact of the increased consolidation in the sector, and possible adverse market power effects, have become more pressing from a **competition policy** perspective given the banking sector restructuring that has taken place since mid-2007.

13.4.1 Number and types of banks

In contrast to other large European countries, the UK has a relatively small number of banks. As Figure 13.6 illustrates, the total number of authorised banking institutions fell from around 600 in 1985 to 298 by 2013. The figure also shows the decline in the number of mutual building societies over the same period.

The decline in the total number of banks is attributable to foreign banks acquiring UK banks as well as consolidation in the domestic retail banking market. Table 13.2 shows that during the second part of the 1990s the decline in the number of foreign banks was greater than that for UK incorporated banks, although mergers and acquisitions between UK incorporated banks resulted in a fall in their number from 202 in 1999 to 157 by the end of 2008. Post-crisis numbers continued to decrease, reaching 146 by 2012. During the second half of the 1990s, a decline in the number of non-European banks (particularly Japanese banks) was counteracted by the increased presence of European institutions, whose number increased

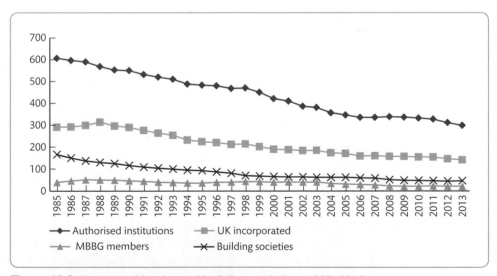

Figure 13.6 Number of banks and building societies, 1985–2013

Note: MBBG refers to major british banking groups.

Sources: Figures for end of February. Adapted from British Bankers' Association (2013) Table 1.04; (2012) Table 1.04; (2011) Table 1.04; (2004) Table 1.04; (1999) Table 1.04; (1996) Table 6.01. Building Societies Association (**www.bsa.org.uk**). Financial Services Authority Building Society Statistics, **www.fsa.gov.uk/pubs/ other/bs_stats/table1_08.pdf**; **www.fsa.gov.uk/pubs/annual/ar04_05/table1.pdf**

Table 13.2 Number of banks in the United Kingdom, 1995–2013

	1995	1996	1997	1998	1999	2000	2001	2002	2003	2004	2005	2006	2007	2008	2009	2010	2011	2012	2013
Number of authorised institutions of which:	481	478	466	468	449	420	409	385	380	356	346	335	335	338	336	332	327	311	298
UK incorporated	224	220	212	214	202	190	188	184	185	174	171	159	160	157	157	154	154	146	141
European authorised institutions	102	103	105	105	109	103	97	89	92	89	87	93	93	97	97	98	93	90	78
Incorporated outside the European Economic Area	155	155	149	149	138	127	124	112	103	93	88	83	82	84	82	80	80	75	79
MBBG members and their banking sector subsidiaries (included above) (a)	37	40	41	44	43	41	42	41	42	35	32	30	28	23	22	22	23	22	22
BBA member banks (included above)	307	306	311	337	327	302	295	265	244	236	218	206	199	203	196	186	180	182	n.a.

Notes: Lists of authorised institutions are published by the Bank of England

(a) MBBGs in 1999 included the following: Abbey National Group, Alliance & Leicester Group, Barclays Group, Bradford & Bingley plc (from 2000), the HBOS Group, HSBC Bank Group, Lloyds TSB Group, Northern Rock Group (from 1999) and the Royal Bank of Scotland Group. In February 2012 they comprised: Santander UK Group, Barclays Group, HBOS Banking Group, Lloyds Banking Group, the Royal Bank of Scotland Group.

(b) As at end-February.

Source: Adapted from British Bankers' Association (2012) Table 1.04; (2005) Table 1.04, p. 6; (1999) Table 1.04, p. 6; (1996) Table 6.01, p. 6.

from 79 to 105 between 1993 and 1999. However, the number of European banks subsequently fell to 90 by 2012. The total number of foreign banks operating in the UK fell from 257 to 165 between 1995 and 2012.

Foreign banks typically do little sterling-denominated business, focusing mainly on wholesale foreign currency activity relating to investment banking activity. The main UK retail banks – otherwise known as the MBBGs – dominate sterling-denominated banking business. Up until the end of 2007 the MBBGs included Abbey National, Alliance & Leicester, Barclays, Bradford & Bingley, HBOS, HSBC Bank, Lloyds TSB, Northern Rock and the Royal Bank of Scotland. Four of these were mutual building societies that converted to bank status – Abbey National (converted in 1989), Alliance & Leicester (1997), Northern Rock (1997) and Bradford & Bingley (2000). HBOS was formed by the merger of Halifax (that converted into plc and bank status in June 1997) and the Bank of Scotland in September 2001.

As discussed in Section 13.2, since mid-2007 the MBBGs have experienced turmoil and there have been significant developments adversely affecting their activities. Northern Rock was the first casualty of the crisis in September 2007 (see Box 13.1). Later the same month Lloyds TSB announced that it was to acquire HBOS for £12 billion, creating a merged entity with a market share of around one-third in the UK savings and mortgage markets. The aim of preventing the collapse of HBOS overrode antitrust concerns that would otherwise stem from the merger of two large high-street retail banks. On 29 September 2008 the UK government announced that it was acquiring the mortgage-lending arm of Bradford & Bingley and selling the still-viable depositor base and branch network to the Spanish Santander banking group.

The British Bankers' Association (2012) has changed the definition of major British banking groups to 'the main high street banking groups', which now comprise: Santander UK Group, Barclays Group, HBOS Banking Group, Lloyds Banking Group, the Royal Bank of Scotland Group (see note to Table 13.2 that reports members of the MBBGs in February 2013).

13.4.2 Trends in branch numbers, ATMs and employment

Over the last 25 years or so (notwithstanding the forced impact of the financial crisis), UK banks and building societies have engaged in significant reorganisation. This is characterised by the decline in branch numbers that has occurred since the late 1980s. The financial crisis further accelerated the decrease in the number of UK branches, with a fall from 10,051 in 2006 to 8,837 in 2012 (British Bankers' Association, 2013). Figure 13.7 shows the trends in branch and ATM numbers in the UK since 1985 and illustrates that during the 1990s, while branch numbers were declining, the introduction of ATMs (at the branch and in 'remote' locations) grew significantly.[5]

---

[5]The total number of ATMs stood at 66,619 in 2013. The number of pay-to-use machines represented 30 per cent of the total cash machine estate and 43 per cent of off-site machines. Meanwhile, free-to-use machines increased to 46,444. Around 70 per cent of all cash machines were 'off-site' by the end of 2013 (Q2). The majority of these (60 per cent or 28,274 ATMs) were in retail locations, with 17,296 in convenience stores and a further 7,273 in supermarkets. A further 21 per cent of 'off-site' ATMs (9,451 machines) were located in the services sectors, which include social and leisure; 11 per cent were located in the transport sectors, which comprise petrol stations and railway/bus termini; there were 2,907 (6 per cent) ATMs in post offices, £48.7 billion were withdrawn from cash machines during 2013 Q2 spread over 753 million withdrawals. The average withdrawal amounted to £65. The volume of withdrawals at pay-to-use machines was 2.4 per cent of the total. These figures are from **www.paymentscouncil.org.uk/**

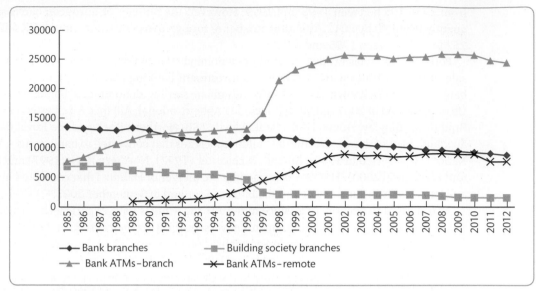

Figure 13.7 Number of branches and ATMs, 1985–2012

Note: Branch and ATM/cash dispenser numbers are for MBBG (parents only) and exclude data on smaller banks. The jump in ATM figures for 1998/1999 is due to the inclusion of various converted building societies into banks and other re-classifications.

Sources: Adapted from British Bankers' Association (2013) Tables 5.02 and 5.03; (2012) Tables 5.02 and 5.03; (2011) Tables 5.02 and 5.03; (1999) Tables 5.02 and 5.03; (1996) Table 5.02.

Although not shown in the figure, there was also a substantial growth in electronic funds transfer at point-of-sale (EFTPOS) terminals, further reflecting the trend to supplement traditional with new distribution channels. These are terminals placed in stores, petrol stations and so on that process credit and debit card payments.

The reason for the shift from branches to other means of financial service delivery mainly relates to UK retail financial services firms' desire to improve operating efficiency as well as customers' increasing demands to access banking services outside traditional (rather limited) banking hours.

The largest branching network in 2012 was that of Lloyds TSB (1,749 branches), followed by that of Barclays (1,593 branches). However, a ruling of the European Commission in 2009 on the conditions for state aid raised the issue of forced divestments through the sale of branches. The aim of the ruling was to increase competition and customer choice in the UK banking sector (see also Section 13.8). The Co-operative Bank had agreed earlier in 2012 to buy 632 Lloyds Bank branches, although the deal fell through in May 2013. In September 2013 Lloyds Banking Group announced the launch of TSB as a separate bank. The standalone TSB has a network of 631 branches in England, Wales and Scotland (see Box 13.5).

Together with the general decline in branch numbers, the restructuring of the system has led to a fall in bank and building society employment, as shown in Figure 13.8. The drop in staff employed is particularly noticeable for retail banks (it fell by around 75,000 between 1990 and 1996), increasing to a peak of around 350,000 in 1999 and then systematically

BOX 13.5 A BRIEF HISTORY OF TSB

- 1810: 'Trustee Savings Bank' was founded by the Reverend Henry Duncan to help working people in Dumfriesshire manage their annual wages.

- 1951: TSBs had combined deposits of more than £1bn.

- 1961: The 'three circles' TSB logo was commissioned as part of the bank's 150th anniversary celebrations.

- 1986: TSB Group floated on the London Stock Exchange for £1.2bn.

- 1995: Lloyds Bank and TSB merged to form Lloyds TSB.

- 2008: Lloyds TSB was bailed out by the government following its disastrous rescue of HBOS.

- 2009: Lloyds TSB was ordered by the European Commission to sell 600-plus branches.

- 2013: Lloyds TSB's plan to sell the branches to the Co-operative collapsed in April.

- 2013: Lloyds launched TSB as a separate, standalone business with 632 branches on September 9. Along with the branches, TSB will have 5m customers, 8,500 staff, about £20bn of loans and deposits and 4.3 per cent of the UK current account market. The bank is preparing for flotation in 2014.

 Source: Adapted from Sharlene Goff (2013) 'Born from the Reverend Henry Duncan, a brief history of TSB', *Financial Times,* 6 September.

falling to below 200,000 by the end of 2012. The increase in employment after 1996 is attributable to building society conversions to bank status. The figure also reveals that there was a substantial increase in employment by foreign banks from 1996 up to 2001 to 2002, reflecting the booming capital markets activity of foreign-owned investment banks in London. Figure 13.8 also clearly illustrates the big fall in employment from 2008 onwards as a result of the crisis, although there are some signs of recovery in the sector.

A clearer picture of employment trends at the top UK retail banks is given in Figure 13.9. This shows that all the main banks maintained relatively stable staff levels up until 2007. Note the large decline for NatWest is mirrored by the increase at the Royal Bank of Scotland, which acquired NatWest in 2000. It is also interesting to note that of the 292,600 staff employed by the MBBGs in 2012, nearly 60 per cent were female, of which 36 per cent were part-time workers (while only 3.3 per cent of male workers were employed part-time). Since the early 1990s there has been a gradual increase in the number of part-time staff employed in the banking sector – mainly in the retail sector. Again, the general decline in total employment in the banking sector and the increase in part-time employment are indicators of the banks' desire to improve their operating efficiency.

The global financial crisis, of course, has had a serious negative impact on UK banking sector employment. The main UK banks have shed around 25,000 staff since mid-2007 and

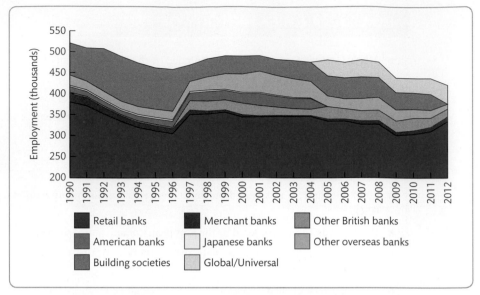

Figure 13.8 Employment in the UK banking sector, 1990–2012

Note:

a) Employment figures relate to banks that are members of the British Bankers Association. In 1997, the incorporation of all banking subsidiaries of members which were not previously members resulted in a marked increase in the total staff numbers for BBA members.

b) Figures for Other overseas bank, Japanese banks, American banks, Other British banks and Merchant banks are up to 2005.

c) Classification changes in 2005. All overseas banks are reported in the Other overseas banks category. A new group of banks, Global/Universal banks are included from 2005 onwards. Wholesale/investment bank figures reported in the 'merchant bank' category.

Source: Adapted from British Bankers' Association (2013) Table 5.01; (2012) Table 5.01; (2011) Table 5.01; (2005) Table 5.01; (1999) Table 5.01; (1996) Table 5.01.

this put total employment down from 318,300 to 292,600 by 2012. The average staff costs accounted for 0.6 per cent of total assets and remained at a stable proportion for the period 2009–2012 (British Bankers' Association, 2013). The largest employer in 2012 was Lloyds Banking Group (110,295 employees), followed by HSBC Bank (74,190 employees). The Royal Bank of Scotland was the largest employer in 2007 with 203,500 but had only 71,200 by the end of 2012 (see Box 13.2 for a discussion of RBS's troubles).

13.5 Financial structure of the UK banking sector

The balance sheet structure of the UK banking system differs from that of many other European systems mainly because of the significant presence of foreign banks. The latter primarily engage in foreign currency-denominated business (known as Eurocurrency

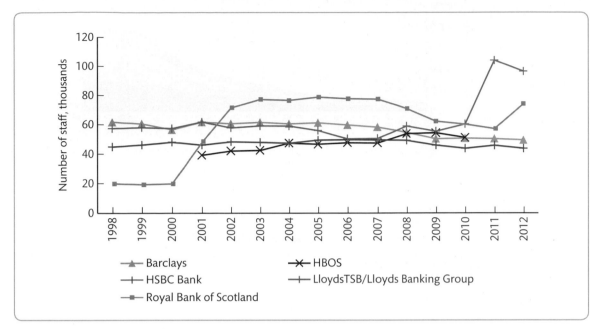

Figure 13.9 Number of staff: major UK banks, 1998–2012

Notes:

a) HBOS was formed after the merger of Halifax and Bank of Scotland in 2001.

b) Lloyds TSB figures and HBOS figures run to 2010. They are combined and reported as Lloyds Banking Group just for 2011.

c) Royal Bank of Scotland acquired National Westminster Bank plc in 2000.

Source: Adapted from British Bankers' Association (2013) Table 5.01; (2012) Table 5.01; (2011) Table 5.01; (2005) Table 5.01; (1999) Table 5.01.

business) and undertake only modest sterling banking operations.[6] In contrast, the UK banks primarily engage in sterling-denominated activity. Given the important presence of foreign banks, this means that a substantial proportion of total balance sheet activity is foreign currency orientated. This can be seen in Figure 13.10, which shows that foreign currency business is at least as important as sterling activity in the banking sector's balance sheet. Similarly, Figure 13.11 illustrates the importance of foreign currency deposits in the UK system.

Regarding foreign bank presence in the domestic banking sector, the share of other European banks has increased significantly since the 1990s, mainly as a result of the EU single market programme (see Chapter 14 for details), whereas the assets share of Japanese banks has fallen (mainly because of retrenchment related to problems in their domestic market) and US banks' share has remained relatively constant during the past two decades. In addition,

---

[6]Eurocurrency business includes foreign currency interbank deposits as well as other debt instruments denominated in foreign currencies, including commercial paper, Treasury bills, certificates of deposits and repurchase agreements.

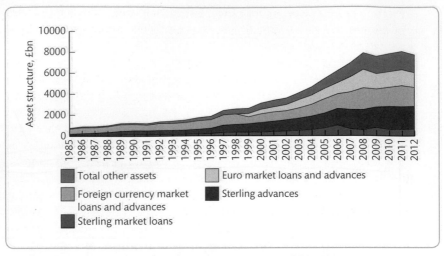

Figure 13.10 All banks in the UK: asset structure, 1985–2012

Note: Foreign currency market loans and advances include all types of foreign currency loans and advances up to 1998, from 1999 euro–denominated loans and advances are reported separately, so from 1999 onwards the foreign currency segment includes all non-euro loans and advances.

Source: Adapted from British Bankers' Association (2013) Table 5.01; (2012) Table 5.01; (2011) Table 5.01; (2005) Table 5.01; (1999) Table 5.01; (1996) Table 5.01.

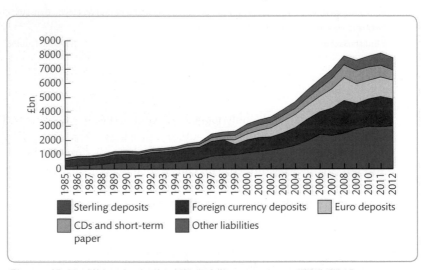

Figure 13.11 All banks in the UK: liability structure, 1985–2012

Notes: Foreign currency deposits include all types of foreign currency deposits up to 1998, from 1999 euro–denominated deposits are reported separately, so from 1999 onwards the foreign currency deposits segment includes all non-Euro deposits.

Source: Adapted from British Bankers' Association (2013) Table 5.01; (2012) Table 5.01; (2011) Table 5.01; (2005) Table 5.01; (1999) Table 5.01; (1996) Table 5.01.

many large European banks headquartered their capital markets operations, as well as built up substantial private banking and asset management businesses, in London during the latter half of the 1990s.

The MBBGs dominate sterling business in the UK and the make-up of their lending business is shown in Figure 13.12. The figure shows that since the mid-1990s there has been substantial growth in domestic mortgage lending relative to other types of lending. There also appears a spike in lending to financial intermediaries from 2006 onwards – a reflection of increased bank lending to hedge funds and private equity companies – and a decline post 2008, due to the financial crisis. The relatively low level of lending to the manufacturing sector is also noticeable and this has raised policy concerns about inadequate bank funding available to small and medium sized enterprises (SMEs). Although not shown, individual sterling deposits comprise around 52 per cent of MBBGs' non-bank sterling deposits, followed by company deposits (22 per cent). Over the last decade or so the proportion of individual sterling deposits, as a percentage of total sterling deposits, has increased. This trend reflects the growing focus of UK banks on retail

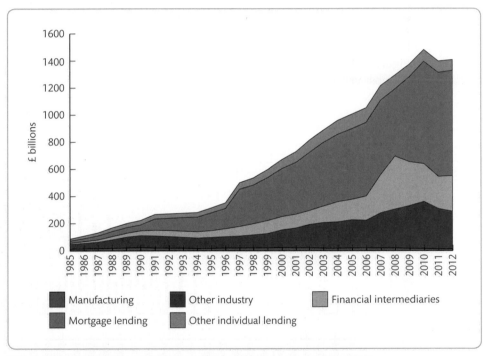

Figure 13.12 MBBGs' sterling lending to UK residents, 1985–2012

Note: Prior to 2011 the industry groups are based on the Office for National Statistics' 'Standard Industrial Classification, 1992' with the addition of the 'Individuals' category. From 2011 onwards the industry groups are based on the Office for National Statistics' 'Standard Industrial Classification, 2007' with the addition of the 'Individuals' category.

Source: Adapted from British Bankers' Association (2013) Table 5.01; (2012) Table 5.01; (2011) Table 5.01; (2005) Table 5.01; (1999) Table 5.01; (1996) Table 5.01.

banking activity at the expense of corporate and investment banking business. The substantial profits earned by UK banks from 1995 to the early 2000s were mainly driven by retail banking business and this has encouraged all the top banks to emphasise this business area, as well as to diversify into other retail financial services such as insurance and private pensions. The (relatively) low funding cost of retail deposits, coupled with the healthy margins generated through mortgage and other consumer lending, encouraged the main banks to prioritise retail banking/financial services and to de-emphasise other areas (for example, the former NatWest significantly reduced its investment banking operations because of poor performance at the end of 1997, and all the MBBGs are reducing their exposure to investment banking and higher risk securities activities since the 2007–2009 crisis).

The main UK banks have been particularly aggressive in competing with the building societies and other lenders in the consumer credit and mortgage areas. Figures 13.13 and 13.14 illustrate net lending trends in these two sectors since 1985. The cyclical nature of the two areas is clearly evident – rapid growth in consumer lending up to 2004 and a decline thereafter. In contrast, the mortgage lending cycle of the 2000s is much more exaggerated than that experienced during the late 1980s and early 1990s and this appears to have peaked in 2006–2007 – a clear precursor of the financial crisis (note the collapse of specialist mortgage lenders in 2008). The figures also reveal that banks dominate net lending for consumer credit from 1997 up until 2006, thereafter specialist lenders became more important. Banks have been the main net lenders in the mortgage area. Figures 13.13 and 13.14 clearly reveal the collapse in new consumer and mortgage lending post-crisis.

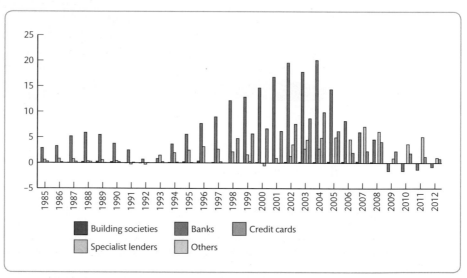

Figure 13.13 Net lending for consumer credit, 1985–2012

Note: From 2004 data on specialist lenders is included in the 'Others' consumer lenders category.

Source: Adapted from British Bankers' Association (2013) Table 5.01; (2012) Table 5.01; (2011) Table 5.01; (2005) Table 5.01; (1999) Table 5.01; (1996) Table 5.01.

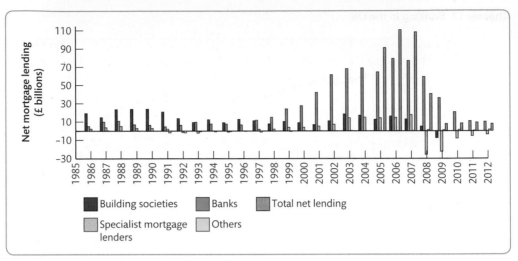

Figure 13.14 Net mortgage lending, 1985–2012

Note: From 2010 separate data is no longer available for banks and building societies separately.

Source: Adapted from British Bankers' Association (2013) Table 5.01; (2012) Table 5.01; (2011) Table 5.01; (2005) Table 5.01; (1999) Table 5.01; (1996) Table 5.01.

13.6 Balance sheet features and the performance of UK banks

Up until mid-2007, UK banks had been among Europe's best-performing financial firms. This was because they benefited from the buoyant domestic economy and also managed to maintain relatively high interest margins (the difference between interest revenue and interest cost). In addition, costs had been reduced and provisioning (the amount of funds set aside to cover loans that are not repaid) had fallen noticeably. The lack of foreign competition in the retail banking market contributed to boosting profitability. These factors together resulted in substantial banking sector profitability up until year-end 2007. As discussed in Section 13.2, UK banks were severely affected by the global financial crisis and profitability collapsed in 2008. While UK banks' profitability remained constrained, particularly because of the impairment charges for loans and receivables, the sector also showed resilience and performance improved from 2009 onwards (see Figure 13.15).

Table 13.3 shows the impairment charge for loans and receivables, available for sale investments and other credit provisions for the UK's largest banks between 2006 and 2012.

On the cost side, the main UK banks had been, on average, successful at reducing their cost-to-income ratios, from around 65 per cent in 1994 to 54 per cent in 1999. These costs increased to around 60 per cent by 2004 (presumably caused by the expenditures incurred associated with M&A activity and other restructuring) but then fell to just under 54 per cent by 2007. The impact of the financial crisis on UK banks' costs can be clearly seen in Figure 13.16, which shows that cost-to-income levels increased to 109 per cent in 2008, although these declined relatively quickly to around 57 per cent from 2009 onwards. Staff costs as a proportion of total income also declined to around 27 per cent of gross income by 2006 but increased thereafter. In addition, the net costs of provisioning fell from 1992, acting as a strong boost to overall profitability, although these increased gradually from 2000 onwards and then rocketed to record levels in 2008.

So far we have discussed income and cost trends in UK banking and as we all know, income minus costs equals profits. Before we go on to discuss the profitability of UK banks it is important to understand how bank profits are derived.

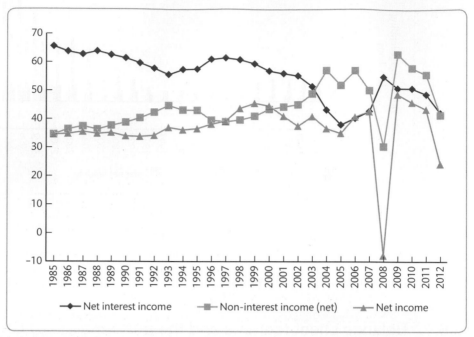

Figure 13.15 Income of major British banking groups, 1985–2012 (% of gross income)

Source: Adapted from British Bankers' Association (2013) Table 5.01; (2012) Table 5.01; (2011) Table 5.01; (2005) Table 5.01; (1999) Table 5.01; (1996) Table 5.01.

Table 13.3 Impairment charges, 2006–2012 (£mil)

	2006	2007	2008	2009	2010	2011	2012
Abbey National	407	344	365				
Alliance & Leicester	105	253	1,071				
Barclays	2,154	2,795	5,419	8,071	5,672	3,802	3,596
Bradford & Bingley	7	117	699	687			
HBOS	1,813	2,072	12,050				
HSBC Bank	983	1,043	1,835	3,364	1,951	1,623	1,245
Lloyds TSB	1,555	1,796	3,012				
Lloyds Banking Group				16,673	10,952	8,094	5,149
Northern Rock	81	472	1,162	1,093	2		
Santander UK				842	712	565	1,009
The Royal Bank of Scotland	1,878	1,968	8,072	13,899	9,256	8,709	5,279

Note: Statistics collected by the BBA for the main high street banking groups (formerly MBBGs). The restructuring of the UK banking sector since 2006 makes it difficult to compare figures. The key changes are highlighted as follows: Santander Group UK includes retail deposits of Bradford & Bingley from 2008; Alliance & Leicester from 2008. HBOS Banking Group included the Halifax plc, up to and including 2006; Bank of Scotland up to and including 2008. Lloyds Banking Group included the Halifax plc up to and including 2006; Bank of Scotland from 2009; Lloyds TSB bank from 2009; Cheltenham & Gloucester up to and including 2006; Scottish Widows Bank from 2009. HSBC Bank Group includes Marks & Spencer Financial Services from 2011. Lloyds TSB Group includes Lloyds TSB Bank Plc (up to and including 2008); Cheltenham & Gloucester plc (up to and including 2006); Scottish Widows Bank plc (up to and including 2008). Northern Rock Group includes only Northern Rock plc from 2009 and excludes the assets moved to Northern Rock Asset Management (NRAM). The Royal Bank of Scotland Group includes Direct Line Financial Services (up to and including 2006); Tesco Personal Finance Ltd (up to and including 2008); National Westminster Bank Plc and Ulster Bank Ltd.

Source: Adapted from British Bankers' Association (2013) Table 3.08; (2012) Table 3.08.

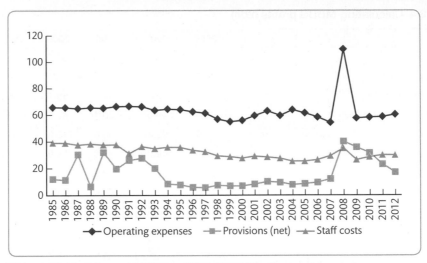

Figure 13.16 Costs of MBBGs, 1985–2012 (% of gross income)

Source: Adapted from British Bankers' Association (2013) Table 5.01; (2012) Table 5.01; (2011) Table 5.01; (2005) Table 5.01; (1999) Table 5.01; (1996) Table 5.01.

To calculate the profitability of UK banks we have to identify income sources and costs. This calculation is summarised in Box 13.6 (for more details on banks' financial accounts see Chapter 9).

BOX 13.6 COMPONENTS OF BANK PROFITS

Interest Income includes interest earned on loans; on investments held by the bank that pay interest (such as bonds); interest paid to the bank on interbank deposits it holds at other banks and other sources of interest income.

Interest Expense includes interest paid to depositors; interest paid to holders of bonds that the bank has issued itself to raise debt finance and other interest costs.

Net Interest Income = Interest Income **minus** Interest Expense.

Non-Interest Income includes fee and commission income (from selling insurance, share dealing, private pensions, processing various payments, sales of assets and all income unrelated to interest earnings).

Gross Income = Net Interest Income + Non Interest Income.

Operating Expenses includes Staff Costs and other expenses associated with running branch networks and headquarters.

Net Income = Gross Income **minus** Operating Expenses.

Provisions include funds set aside by the bank to cover losses on loans that are expected to not be repaid (as well as other types of losses). Provisions are made on a regular basis and are charged against current earnings. The total accumulated stock of provisions is known as loan-loss reserves. This is a cost to the bank and so they are deducted from Net Income to arrive at bank profits.

Profit before Tax = Net Income minus Provisions.

Profit after Tax = Profit before Tax **minus** Tax.

Retained Profit = Profit after Tax **minus** Distributed Profit (dividends to shareholders, the owners of the bank).

Table 13.4 Calculating MBBG profits (£bn)

	2006	2007	2008	2009	2010	2011	2012
Interest Income	116.8	147.0	172.3	107.2	90.7	87.7	79.6
Interest Expense	76.8	104.4	117.6	56.5	40.0	39.1	37.6
Net Interest Income	40.0	42.5	54.7	50.7	50.7	48.6	41.9
Non-Interest Income (net)	56.9	49.9	30.1	62.9	58.0	55.6	42.1
Gross Income	96.9	92.4	84.8	113.6	108.7	104.2	84.1
Operating Expenses	56.2	49.9	92.8	64.9	63.0	60.8	60.0
(of which Staff Costs)	25.5	27.1	29.7	30.0	31.0	31.2	29.8
Net Income	40.6	42.5	−7.9	48.7	45.9	43.4	24.1
Impairments & Provisions (net)	8.9	10.9	33.7	46.7	33.9	23.7	16.7
Profit before Tax	31.7	31.7	−41.7	8.3	12.0	10.2	0.0
Tax	9.2	7.2	−4.2	0.0	4.2	3.4	−0.6
Profit after Tax	22.5	24.5	−37.5	8.3	7.6	6.8	−0.6
Profitability Ratios (%)							
Return on Assets – ROA (Net Income/Assets)	1.1	0.8	−0.1	0.9	0.9	0.8	0.9
Profit before Tax/Assets	0.9	0.6	−0.6	0.2	0.2	0.2	0.0
Profit before Tax/Gross Income	32.7	34.3	−49.1	7.3	11.1	9.8	0.0
Profit after Tax/Net Income	55.4	57.6	471.9	17.1	16.6	15.6	−2.5
Impairments & Provisions/Net Income	22.0	25.5	−424.2	83.0	73.8	54.5	69.5
Profit after Tax/Assets	0.6	0.5	−0.6	0.2	0.2	0.1	0.0
Profit after Tax/Gross Income	23.2	26.5	−44.2	7.3	7.0	6.5	−0.7

Note: The average total assets of MBBGs amounted to around £735,899 million in 2007.
MBBGs in 2008 included the following: Abbey National Group, Alliance & Leicester Group, Barclays Group, Bradford & Bingley plc, the HBOS Group, HSBC Bank Group, Lloyds TSB Group, Northern Rock Group and the Royal Bank of Scotland Group.
Source: Adapted from British Bankers' Association (2013) Table 3.07; (2012) Table 3.06; (2008) Table 3.06.

Using the combined figures for the major British banking groups for 2006–2012, Table 13.4 shows the calculation of profit figures. The figures presented in Table 13.4 are averages for the sector. Pre-tax losses of £5.7 billion for RBS and Lloyds Banking Group exactly offset profits of other banking groups, thus resulting in an aggregate flat position for 2012.

As already noted, the relatively high margins, lower costs and buoyant economic conditions feeding through into increased loan demand led to a sustained increase in the profitability of UK banks (see Figure 13.7). After-tax returns hovered between 20 per cent and 25 per cent between 2000 and 2007. The relatively high level of profitability experienced in 2006 and 2007 was the end to the UK banking boom. For instance, Barclays posted ROE of 20.5 per cent in 2007 and this fell to 14.6 per cent in 2008; Lloyds Group reported ROE of 34 per cent in 2007 and this fell to 8 per cent in 2008; and most spectacularly, Royal Bank of Scotland's ROE declined from 18.6 per cent in 2007 to −43.7 per cent in 2008 (hence the government bailout). UK bank profitability has rebounded since then, although the heady days of the mid-2000s appear a long way off, with banks posting returns around the 10 per cent level (at best).

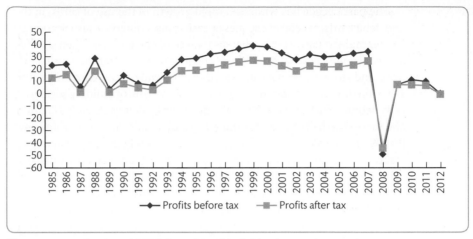

Figure 13.17 Profits of MBBGs, 1985–2012 (% of gross income)

Source: Adapted from British Bankers' Association (2013) Table 5.01; (2012) Table 5.01; (2011) Table 5.01; (2005) Table 5.01; (1999) Table 5.01; (1996) Table 5.01.

13.7 The UK payment system

As we have seen in Chapter 2, a payment system can be defined as any organised arrangement for transferring value between its participants. Some of these transactions involve high-value transfers, typically between financial institutions. However, the highest number of transactions relates to transfers between individuals and/or companies (they include the payment and receipt of wages, salaries and government benefits, direct debits, cheques, debit and credit card payments).

In 2012, more than 40 billion cash and non-cash payments took place in the UK, with a total value of £9.5 trillion.[7] The main UK payment systems are CHAPS, BACS, Faster Payments Service (FPS), CREST, LCH.Clearnet Ltd (Protected Payment System), ICE Clear Europe (Assured Payment System) and CLS.

The UK Payments Administration Ltd (UKPA) is a trade body responsible for promoting the UK payments industry and maximising the industry's effectiveness[8] There is also the Payments Council, which sets the strategy for the sector.[9]

Under the Banking Act of 2009, the payment systems oversight is carried out by the Bank of England (Part 5, Banking Act, 2009). The Bank of England currently oversees the seven recognised payment systems – the three main sterling payment schemes (BACS, CHAPS and FPS); the foreign exchange settlement scheme CLS; and the payment arrangements embedded in the CREST securities settlement system (SSS) operated by Euroclear UK and Ireland (EUI) and the central counterparties (CCPs) operated by LCH.Clearnet Ltd and ICE Clear Europe. In addition, following the Financial Services Act of 2012, the responsibility for supervision of CCPs and SSSs was moved from the FSA to the Bank of England, with effect from 1 April 2013. Following a period of consultation, in February 2013 the UK Chancellor announced plans to regulate payment systems.

---

[7] UK Payments Council, **www.paymentscouncil.org.uk/**

[8] Up until July 2009, it was known as APACS – Association for Payment Clearing Services. See **www.ukpayments.org.uk/**

[9] **www.paymentscouncil.org.uk/**

The past decade has witnessed rapid growth in the use of cards, in the form of both credit and debit cards, instead of cheques or cash transactions (see also Section 2.4.1). Cash payments have remained fairly stable whereas the use of cheques has fallen significantly. UK businesses and consumers have switched from cheques to cards: transactions using plastic cards (credit, debit and store cards) have increased dramatically. Debit cards were introduced in the UK in 1985, linking transactions directly to the holder bank or building society account and automatically debiting such account. By 1994, debit card volumes exceeded credit cards for the first time and more than half of all cash acquired by individuals came from withdrawals at cash machines. By 1998 there were more debit card payments than cheque payments made by personal customers. By 2001, more than 6 million adults in the UK accessed their banks accounts online (one in four internet users). The year 2002 witnessed the largest annual decline in cheque volumes and the largest ever increase in the number of credit cards issued. By the mid-2000s all UK credit and debit card transactions had been authorised by customers keying in their personal identification number (PIN) rather than signing for the receipt of goods and services.[10]

A relatively recent innovation is **Faster Payments:** it was introduced in 2008 and it was the first new payments service to be introduced in the UK for more than 20 years. By the end of 2011 more than 85 per cent of phone and internet payments were being processed through Faster Payments. Scheme membership is open to credit institutions with a settlement account at the Bank of England which can connect their payment system to the central infrastructure 24 hours a day, 7 days a week.[11] FPS is operated by Faster Payments Scheme Limited and is owned by the ten members of FPS. The current members of the scheme are: Barclays, Citi, Co-operative Bank, Clydesdale and Yorkshire Banks (National Australia Group), HSBC, Lloyds Bank, Nationwide Building Society, Danske Bank, Royal Bank of Scotland Group (including NatWest and Ulster Bank) and Santander UK. The number of Faster Payments rose from 198 million in 2012 Q2 to 239 million in 2013 Q2 while the combined value of Faster Payments continued to increase as they have done since 2008 but particularly so throughout 2012. Annual payment volumes grew by 35 per cent and values by 65 per cent, with the latter reaching a quarterly figure of £190 billion in 2013 Q2. The average value of a Faster Payment was £795.[12]

The increasing reliance on electronic payments does not come without glitches, as discussed in Box 13.7.

BOX 13.7 RBS TECHNOLOGY BREAKDOWN

On Monday, December 2nd, 2013, also known as 'Cyber Monday' by busy internet shoppers, the Royal Bank of Scotland experienced its fourth technology breakdown in two years, which left millions of customers unable to pay for goods using their credit or debit cards.[13]

Royal Bank of Scotland's boss Ross McEwan admitted the bank had failed to invest properly in systems as he was forced to apologise for yet another embarrassing IT failure on the busiest online shopping day of the year. The IT glitch – the bank's fourth in two years – left millions of

➡

---

[10] The source for all figures cited is APACS, Payment Developments and Innovations Milestones since 1985.

[11] **www.fasterpayments.org.uk/**

[12] **www.paymentscouncil.org.uk/**

[13] 'Cyber Monday' has become the online equivalent of 'Black Friday'. In the US, Black Friday is an established shopping tradition: it is the day after Thanksgiving Day when retailers discount thousands of items. It is the US equivalent of the UK sales on Boxing Day. Cyber Monday is the first Monday after Thanksgiving, when US consumers head online, rather than to the shops, to grab bargains. Although a US tradition, it is fast spreading to the UK and other parts of the world due to the global presence of retailers such as Amazon, Apple, Wal-Mart and others.

BOX 13.7 RBS technology breakdown (*continued*)

customers of RBS and its NatWest and Ulster Bank subsidiaries unable to use credit and debit cards for three hours on Monday.

The embarrassing breakdown was an unwelcome reminder of a large-scale computer systems failure at RBS in June 2012, which left millions of customers without access to their accounts. A faulty software update crashed RBS's system, causing a huge backlog of payments and locking about 17m customers of NatWest, RBS and Ulster Bank out of their accounts. Some customers in Ireland were unable to get back in for three weeks. The bank struggled to resolve a backlog of tens of millions of transactions after the failed software update disrupted processing systems for three weeks.

Despite promises to increase investment, similar, although smaller scale, episodes happened in March 2013. On March 7, 2013, a hardware fault left RBS customers unable to withdraw cash from ATMs or access their accounts overnight. A few weeks later, on March 28, 2013, NatWest, RBS and Ulster Bank's mobile banking applications also stopped working for about six hours during a working day.

In April 2013, the Financial Conduct Authority (FCA) took the unusual step of announcing a formal investigation into the IT failure, which could result in big fines. The FCA has not yet decided whether enforcement action should follow.

Critics say banks have failed to invest properly in technology over the years. Severe outages are rare, however, although a number have suffered less extreme IT failures, often as a result of bedding down acquisitions.

Santander, for example, encountered problems when it integrated Abbey, the UK building society. Bank of Scotland customers also suffered disruption when they joined the Lloyds TSB platform last year.

Unite, the trade union, said: 'Since the start of the financial crisis, RBS has announced over 30,000 job losses. IT problems will do nothing to reassure customers that RBS's commitment to quality customer service is backed up by proper investment in staff and systems.'

 Source: Adapted from Lina Saigol (2013) 'RBS apologises for Cyber Monday technology breakdown', *Financial Times,* 3 December.

13.8   Competition in UK banking

The UK banking market, like many other European systems, is relatively concentrated, with the top four banks accounting for more than 60 per cent of all banking sector assets by 2012. The level of concentration, as measured by the share of the top four banks (assets) to the whole banking system, is illustrated in Figure 13.18. Concentration remained relatively stable throughout the 1980s up to 1997; this trend was contrary to concentration developments in various other European markets (see Chapter 14). However, from 1997 onwards concentration increased. It can be seen that the market share of the top banks, as a proportion of UK bank and building society assets, grew rapidly from 1997 onwards due to various large-scale mergers and acquisitions – for example, Bank of Scotland merged with Halifax to form HBOS and the Royal Bank of Scotland acquired NatWest.

In addition to these broad trends, concentration in specific market segments is substantial. Moreover, one can see that the share of the top four banks increased more rapidly since 2005 than in previous years. The forced 2008 merger between Lloyds TSB and HBOS that gave the newly formed institution an estimated one-third of the UK retail savings market is testimony to this point. Further reorganisations and restructurings have highlighted the dominant role played by a handful of institutions.

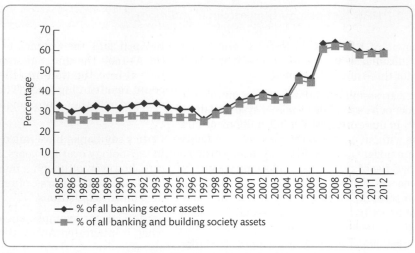

Figure 13.18 Share of top four banks' assets, 1985–2012

Source: Adapted from British Bankers' Association (2013) Table 5.01; (2012) Table 5.01; (2011) Table 5.01; (2005) Table 5.01; (1999) Table 5.01; (1996) Table 5.01.

While the above discussion suggests that the degree of concentration in the UK banking market may appear excessive, various international comparisons of broad concentration indicators suggest that this may not be so. However, the 2007–2009 financial crisis resulted in significant further consolidation of the UK retail market. Since the bailout of RBS and Lloyds TSB, and worries about 'too-big-to-fail' banks and the perverse risk-taking incentives that this can create, it is widely recognised that some UK banks are simply too big. Excessive concentration is an ongoing policy concern for regulators overseeing the stability of the UK and other banking systems. Table 13.5 summarises the M&As in UK banking that took place between 2008 and 2010, at the peak of the financial turmoil.

Table 13.5 Mergers and acquisitions in UK banking

Year	Acquirer	Target
2008	Santander	Alliance & Leicester
2008	Santander (Abbey)	Bradford & Bingley
2008	ING Direct Heritable	Kaupthing Singer & Friedlander
2008	Chelsea Building Society	Catholic Building Society
2008	Nationwide Building Society	Cheshire Building Society
2008	Nationwide Building Society	Derbyshire Building Society
2008	Lloyds TSB	HBOS
2008	Yorkshire Building Society	Barnsley Building Society
2009	Co-operative Financial Services	Britannia Building Society
2009	Yorkshire Building Society	Chelsea Building Society
2009	Nationwide Building Society	Dunfermline Building Society
2009	Skipton Building Society	Scarborough Building Society
2010	Barclays	Standard Life Bank
2010	Coventry Building Society	Stroud and Swindon Building Society

Source: Adapted from House of Commons, Treasury Committee (2011) 'Competition and Choice in Retail Banking' Ninth Report of Session 2010–11.

Concerns about competitive conditions in the UK banking sector are not a result of recent turmoil and reorganisation of the UK banking system post-crisis; concerns about the effectiveness of competition in the banking market go back many years. A Treasury report entitled 'Competition in UK banking', published in 2000, aimed to investigate these issues (Cruickshank, 2000). The report (known as the **Cruickshank Report** as it was headed by Don Cruickshank) examined a broad range of issues relating to competitive conditions in the UK banking market. However, the main focus was on three areas – money transmission services, services to retail customers and services to SMEs. Since then the Office of Fair Trading (OFT) and **Competition Commission** (CC) have conducted almost 20 inquiries into competition in different parts of the retail banking market. Many of these inquiries and investigations have focused on particular segments of the market, such as the personal current account market (Office of Fair Trading, 2008), cash ISAs (Office of Fair Trading, 2010a) and store card credit services (Office of Fair Trading, 2004; Competition Commission, 2006). There have been two studies on SME banking: Competition Commission (2002) and Office of Fair Trading (2007). The Office of Fair Trading conducted a market study on a 'Review of barriers to entry, expansion and exit in retail banking' (2010b) and a 'Review of the personal current account market' (2013). In addition, there have been a number of EU inquiries into the banking sector, including the European Commission's 2007 inquiry into retail banking (European Commission, 2007).

The following briefly summarises the findings of the key reports and highlights concerns about the effectiveness of competition in the UK banking market (see Chapter 20 for an analysis of the various methods used to evaluate competitive conditions in banking).

The Cruickshank Report

Published in March 2000, the Cruickshank Report found that there were important limitations to competition in various key markets and that the established regulatory environment was inappropriate to deal with this. Recommendations were therefore made for a major overhaul of bank regulation in order to improve competition and innovation in UK banking.

One area that came in for particular criticism was the market for money transmission services (cheque payments, credit transfers and other payments media) where 'profound competition problems and inefficiencies' were found to exist. The report argued that money transmission services were dominated by a handful of major banks and the current arrangements restricted entry and resulted in high costs to retailers for accepting credit and debit cards as well as excessive charges for cash withdrawals (up to six times their cost). Money transmission services were also found to be 'cumbersome and inflexible' and slow to adapt to the new demands of e-commerce.

In the supply of retail banking services, it was found that competition had increased in the mortgage, personal loan and credit card areas, although the prices charged by new entrants had had only a limited impact on established bank pricing. In addition, the dominant role played by the major banks in the current account market was believed to restrict competition in many other product areas. Significant barriers to switching current accounts remained. The report voiced concerns about the inadequate representation and redress for consumers in the event of disputes. It also referred to 'significant information problems', citing the fact that consumers were rarely aware of the terms and conditions of the products they bought.

The market for SME banking services was found to be much less competitive than the retail sector. Problems associated with switching current accounts, financial product information, representation and redress were found to be acute. The market for SME services was much more concentrated than the retail sector and entry barriers were found to be high (it is noticeable that the building societies that converted to banks did not enter the SME market in any significant fashion). Money transmission costs for UK SMEs were also found to be high on an international basis and access to risk capital for high-growth firms was perceived to be limited.

Taking together the report's findings on retail and SMEs' banking services, a broad range of recommendations were made, including:

- strengthening the current arrangements for customer redress and representation, including the establishment of a new Financial Services Consumer Council;
- improving customer information by publishing, via the FSA, a broad range of benchmark retail and SME services according to price (providing both regional and UK prices);
- various initiatives to improve the flow of equity finance to high-growth SMEs.

Other, more controversial, recommendations included:

- that until UK merger law is reformed, the government should refer all mergers between financial suppliers to the Competition Commission if the merging firms have 'material shares of the market';
- calling for a Competition Commission inquiry into banking for SMEs.

An important theme throughout the report was the highly concentrated nature of the UK current account and SME markets as well as the structure of the domestic payments system. All these areas, the report argued, were characterised by high entry barriers as well as limited price and non-price competition. The large market shares held by a handful of banks were put as a major reason for the high profitability of UK banks during the 1990s. Market structure and adverse competitive outcomes were most pressing in the SME market. The Cruickshank Report stated that the competition problems were so significant that a change in market structure might be the only way of achieving an effectively competitive marketplace. It went on to argue that the only mechanism for delivering such a change was action following a complex monopoly reference to the Competition Commission.

Overall, the report argued that there was substantial scope for increased competition as well as the opportunity for competing banks to make adequate returns even in the provision of basic banking services. The recommendations, although unpalatable to the main UK banks at the time, were thought to go a long way to promote more effective competition in the UK banking market; in reality, however, the report has had little actual effect.

Competition Commission Report

The UK Competition Commission report (2002) into the 'Supply of banking services by clearing banks to small and medium-sized enterprises' followed on from the Cruickshank Report. The Report recommended a number of measures to apply to all the eight main clearing groups to reduce barriers to entry and expansion in the SME banking area. Primary among these were measures to ensure fast error-free switching of accounts regarded as crucial to a more competitive market. In addition, it was recommended that measures should be taken to limit bundling of services, and to improve information and transparency and an examination of the scope for sharing of branches. The report concluded that the four largest clearing groups (Barclays, HSBC, Lloyds TSB and Royal Bank of Scotland Group) were charging excessive prices (including interest foregone on non-interest-bearing current accounts) and therefore making excessive profits, in England and Wales, of about £725 million a year, with adverse effects on SMEs or their customers. For the most part, the report found no such excessive prices in Scotland or Northern Ireland. The Commission recommended that the four largest clearing groups be required to pay interest on current accounts or alternatively to offer SMEs accounts that are free of money transmission charges, or to offer SMEs a choice between the two options.

The banking sector's response to the above recommendations has been to introduce **Banking and Business Banking Codes**, which are voluntary codes that set standards of good banking practice for banks and building societies to follow when they are dealing with personal or business customers in the United Kingdom. As voluntary codes, it was argued that they allow competition and market forces to work to encourage higher standards for the benefit of customers. Various measures have been implemented to make it easier for retail and small business customers to switch accounts and free banking services are now generally available to new customers, although the banks did not adopt the recommendation that market rates be paid on current accounts and access to payment systems still appears relatively limited. In short, there has been no noticeable improvement in competition as a result of the Competition Commission's report.

The Independent Commission on Banking

The Independent Commission on Banking (also known as the Vickers Commission as it was chaired by Sir John Vickers) was established by the government in June 2010 to 'consider the structure of the UK banking sector, and look at structural and non-structural measures to reform the banking system and promote competition'. While its main recommendations related to ring-fencing retail from investment/wholesale banking, boosting capital resources (see Section 13.3.1), it also included various measures relating to increasing the competitive conditions in UK banking. Although we have touched on this already in this chapter, here we focus in a little more detail on the competition issues. The ICB report aimed to distinguish between 'good competition' (which increases consumers' choice and serves them well) and 'bad competition' (which exploits customer unawareness or, for example, 'creates a race to the bottom on lending standards'). The report painted a depressing picture:

- Most of the bad issues highlighted in the Cruickshank Report remain.
- The competition authorities have had to intervene on several occasions in recent years.
- The industry is more concentrated post crisis than it was before.
- Consumer satisfaction levels are low and the perceived costs of exercising market choice by switching accounts are 'remarkably' low.

The Commission recommended:

- that the divestment of RBS and Lloyds Banking Group should be enhanced to create a major new 'challenger' in the market;
- the introduction of an account 'redirection' service for personal and small business accounts to 'boost confidence in the ease of [account] switching';
- improved transparency of the costs of an account, including interest foregone indicators;
- that competition should be central to financial regulation.

The UK government accepted all the Commission's recommendations concerning increased competition, apart from that the divestiture of Lloyds should exceed the EC requirements (see also Section 13.3 for a discussion of the new regulatory landscape and the impact of the Vickers Report).

13.9 Conclusion

Up until mid-2007 the changing features of the UK banking system were mainly a consequence of the evolving market environment and also the result of various domestic regulatory reforms. Since the global financial crisis hit in the summer of 2007, all has changed. UK banks have been transformed from highly profitable, well-managed and innovative institutions to pariahs – subject to public and private derision. There is extensive debate surrounding the longer-term implications of the crisis for the future architecture of the UK (and global) banking and financial system. Support has been expressed for a 'return to basics' involving greater emphasis on simple leverage and liquidity ratios, more realistic risk assessment as the basis for risk-based capital regulation, greater transparency and the curtailment of opaque business models (e.g. complex securitisation and derivatives activity), and the development of systems and other procedures to identify problem institutions for early intervention in cases of financial distress.

The proposals made by the Independent Commission on Banking in September 2011 have been incorporated in two major new pieces of legislation: the 2012 Financial Services Act and the 2013 Financial Services (Banking Reform) Act. The 2012 Act abolished the existing financial regulator, the Financial Services Authority, and created three new regulatory bodies: the Financial Policy Committee (FPC), the Prudential Regulation Authority (PRA) and the Financial Conduct Authority (FCA). The 2013 Act, among other measures, introduces the ring-fencing of retail banking activities.

Whatever changes take place, there is no doubt that these momentous events will resonate for many years to come and that UK banks are likely to experience limitations to their business activities and risk-taking capabilities in the future.

Key terms

Asset Protection Scheme (APS)	Credit Guarantee Scheme (CGS)	Financial Services (Banking Reform) Act (2013)	Special Liquidity Scheme (SLS)
Banking Act (2009)	Cruickshank Report	Independent	Special Resolution Regime (SRR)
Banking and Business Banking Codes	Demutualisation	Commission on Banking	Turner Review
'Big Bang'	Faster Payments	Major British	UK Financial
Competition Commission	Financial Services Act (2012)	Banking Groups (MBBGs)	Investments Ltd (UKFI)
Competition policy	Financial Services and Markets Act (2001)	Ring-fencing	Vickers Report

Key reading

Goddard, J., Molyneux, P. and Wilson, J.O.S. (2009) 'Crisis in UK banking: Lessons for public policy', *Public Money and Management,* 29, 276–284.

Financial Services Authority (2011) 'The failure of the Royal Bank of Scotland', Financial Services Authority Board Report.

The Independent Commission on Banking (2011) 'Final report recommendations'.

The Turner Review (2009) 'A regulatory response to the global banking crisis', March, London: Financial Services Authority.

REVISION QUESTIONS AND PROBLEMS

13.1 Why did the global financial crisis affect UK banking so severely? Discuss the main features of UK banks in the 1990s and early 2000s and explain why these features made the UK banking sector particularly vulnerable.

13.2 Describe how changes in the regulatory structure contributed to the banking crisis and outline the key issues of current and future reform.

13.3 Read Box 13.3 and answer the following questions:
  (a) What is the LIBOR and how was it traditionally fixed?
  (b) What do you understand by 'rate rigging'?
  (c) What are the two main motivations for banks to misreport LIBOR rates?
  (d) What reforms have been introduced in the UK as a result of this scandal?

13.4 Why did RBS fail? Discuss the main reasons of the failure of one of the largest UK banks.

13.5 What are the main drivers of UK banks' profitability and how has the global financial crisis affected performance?

13.6 What are the implications of increased concentration in the UK banking market? Is it reasonable to trade off competition for stability?

13.7 Are we likely to witness any more M&As among MBBGs in the near future? What implications does this have for competition and innovation in the UK banking sector?

13.8 What were the main recommendations of the Independent Commission on Banking and how do you think the banking industry responded?

13.9 What are the main features of the UK payment system?

13.10 Discuss the key threats to the city of London as a global financial centre.

Appendix 13.1
Demutualisation of the UK building society sector

Year	Building society name	Assets size	Nature of conversion or acquisition
1989	Abbey National	£38.9 billion (end 1989)	Converted to plc and bank status in July 1989
1995	Cheltenham & Gloucester	£19.4 billion (end 1994)	Acquired by Lloyds TSB in August 1995
1996	National & Provincial	£14.1 billion (end 1995)	Acquired by Abbey National in August 1996
1997	Alliance & Leicester	£22.3 billion (end 1996)	Converted to plc and bank status in April 1997
1997	Halifax	£102.1 billion (end 1996)	Halifax and Leeds Permanent Building Societies merged in 1995; the new Halifax then converted into plc and bank status in June 1997. Halifax merged with the Bank of Scotland in September 2001 to form HBOS
1997	Woolwich	£29.3 billion (end of 1996)	Converted to a bank in July 1997 and acquired by Barclays in October 2000
1997	Bristol & West	£9.4 billion (end of 1996)	Acquired by the Bank of Ireland in July 1997
1997	Northern Rock	£13.7 billion (end of 1996)	Converted to bank status in October 1997
1999	Birmingham Midshires Building Society	£8.22 billion (end of 1999)	Acquired by Halifax in April 1999 The Halifax merged with the Bank of Scotland in September 2001 to form HBOS
2000	Bradford & Bingley	£24.7 billion (end of 2000)	Converted to bank status in December 2000

Note: The year 1997 was the most significant for building society conversions into banks, when five of the eight largest societies demutualised. These five societies accounted for around 60 per cent of the total assets of the building society sector.

Chapter 14

Banking in Europe

Learning objectives

- To understand the main structural features of the European banking market
- To analyse the implications of the 2007–2009 financial crisis on European banks
- To analyse the implications of the eurozone crisis on European banks
- To describe the regulatory changes that have affected the European banking sector
- To understand the key building blocks of the Banking Union
- To understand the main trends in the recent performance of European banks

14.1 Introduction

Since the introduction of the First Banking Directive in 1977, the **deregulation** of financial services in the European Union (EU) – together with the establishment of the Economic and Monetary Union (EMU) and the introduction of the euro – aimed at fostering integration through the creation of a level playing field in the provision of banking services across the EU. Financial integration is considered to be one of the key factors for making Europe more efficient and competitive and, ultimately, for contributing to sustainable economic growth. During this time, European banking markets have experienced marked changes – the number of banks has fallen substantially as a result of mergers and acquisitions and industry concentration has increased. Banks have shifted their business focus on generating revenue through non-interest sources of income and there has been widespread diversification into areas such as insurance, pensions, mutual funds and various securities-related areas. Technological developments reshaped the way in which banks distribute products and services to their customers and also re-organised back-office functions for the processing of financial transactions and information.

The EU's financial integration has been an ongoing process during the last decade and has made substantial progress, particularly in the wholesale financial sector. This process has also fostered the growth of many large banking groups, which combine investment, commercial, retail and investment banking. These provide a range of services in several countries, both inside and outside the EU. The European model of integration is based on the

441

single EU passport (introduced by the Second Banking Directive in 1989), thanks to which financial institutions have the freedom to determine where they want to be established and under which legal form. Over time, many financial institutions have expanded their operations across national borders, through branches and subsidiaries.

Ten years into the introduction of the euro, the global financial crisis of 2007–2009 triggered a swing of the pendulum for the process of integration and the sustainability of the bank business model fostered by the EU agenda has come under question. In addition, the **eurozone crisis**, which has been affecting eurozone countries since late 2009, has combined banking sector fragilities with a sovereign debt crisis, deepening the impact of the global financial crisis on EU growth and competitiveness. The crises have also highlighted a number of issues with the existing EU regulatory architecture. Debates on the necessary reforms needed to strengthen the EU regulatory framework to limit future risks arising from banks' activities are ongoing. European authorities have initiated substantial reforms to strengthen simultaneously the three pillars of financial stability: surveillance, crisis prevention and crisis management. The reforms come under the umbrella of the EU's **Banking Union**, which include three main parts: (i) plans to place eurozone banks under the overarching supervision of the ECB, (ii) the creation of a common bank resolution scheme, and (iii) a common deposit scheme.

This chapter discusses the key developments in the European Union (Section 14.2) and the creation of the single market for financial services (Section 14.3). In Section 14.4 we look at the impact of the global financial and eurozone crises on EU banks and discuss the various developments in response to the 2007–2009 banking crisis and 2010–2013 sovereign debt problems. Structural trends in European banking are discussed in Section 14.5 and Section 14.6 gives an overview of the recent performance features of European banks. Section 14.7 concludes the chapter.

14.2 The European Union

The origins of the European Union date back to the 1950s: in 1951 Belgium, France, Germany, Italy, Luxembourg and the Netherlands formed the European Coal and Steel Community (ECSC) and in 1957 the Treaty of Rome established the European Economic Community (EEC). Since then, the European Union (formally established by the Maastricht Treaty in 1993) has grown to a union of 28 member states, through a number of enlargements, as summarised in Table 14.1. The last amendment to the constitutional basis of the EU came into force in 2009 and was the Lisbon Treaty.[1] To join the EU a country must meet the so-called Copenhagen criteria, which require a stable democracy, a respect of human rights and the rule of law, a functioning market economy and the acceptance of the obligations of membership, including EU law.

---

[1] The Treaty of Lisbon was signed on 13 December 2007, but could enter into force only when ratified by all member states. The last country to ratify the treaty was the Czech Republic, which completed the process on 3 November 2009. The treaty became law on 1 December of that year. The Lisbon Treaty amends both the Treaty establishing the European Community (Treaty of Rome, 1957) and the Treaty on European Union (Maastricht Treaty 1992). These two Treaties will continue to be the basis on which the EU functions. The Treaty of Lisbon simplifies the structure of the EU, which currently consists of three 'pillars': the Community, the common foreign and security policy, and justice and home affairs. In the new Treaty, these pillars cease to exist and the Community is replaced by the Union, which will have legal personality. The Treaty establishing the European Community is renamed the Treaty on the Functioning of the Union.

Table 14.1 The European Union: a timeline

Year	Member states	Enlargement
1957	Belgium, France, Germany, Italy, Luxembourg and the Netherlands	Founding six
1973	Denmark, Ireland, United Kingdom	First enlargement
1981	Greece	Second enlargement
1986	Portugal, Spain	Third enlargement
1995	Austria, Finland, Sweden	Fourth enlargement
2004	Cyprus, Czech Republic, Estonia, Hungary, Latvia, Lithuania, Malta, Poland, Slovakia, Slovenia	Fifth enlargement (part one)
2007	Bulgaria, Romania	Fifth enlargement (part two)
2013	Croatia	
2014	Iceland, the Former Yugoslav Republic of Macedonia, Montenegro, Serbia and Turkey	Official candidates
	Albania, Bosnia and Herzegovina and Kosovo	Applied for membership

On 1 May 2004, Cyprus, the Czech Republic, Estonia, Hungary, Latvia, Lithuania, Malta, Poland, Slovenia and the Slovak Republic joined the European Union. Bulgaria and Romania joined in 2007. This was the biggest ever enlargement of the EU and a historic step towards unifying Europe after several decades of division resulting from the Cold War. Finally, Croatia became the 28th EU country on 1 July 2013. Over the past two decades, these countries have faced a great degree of change and have made remarkable progress towards convergence to EU standards on a number of economic indicators. Between 1999 and 2003, for example, they recorded an average GDP growth of 3.2 per cent compared with 2.0 per cent for the EU-15 countries. Despite growth and continuing convergence, GDP levels per capita on average still lag behind those of the old EU member states. Indeed, EU membership is only the first of the many major milestones that these countries will be facing over the next several years.

At the time of writing (2014), Iceland, Montenegro, Serbia, the former Yugoslav Republic of Macedonia and Turkey are official candidate states. Albania, Bosnia and Herzegovina and Kosovo have also applied for membership and are considered potential candidates. Since the break-up of Yugoslavia and the civil war in the 1990s, countries in the Balkans have been prioritised for EU membership. While Turkey has been negotiating since the 1980s, Iceland has only recently applied for EU membership, following the 2008 financial crisis.

14.2.1 The economic outlook

The European Union covers a large part of the European continent, with 28 member states and a population of more than half a billion citizens, the world's third largest after China and India. Although standards of living have improved considerably over the past decade, significant differences among member states remain. GDP per capita is highest in Luxembourg and lowest in Bulgaria. The EU is striving to narrow the gap between its rich and poor members and GDP growth is currently higher in the countries that have joined the EU since 2004 than in the older member states.

Table 14.2 summarises the main macroeconomic indicators for the 28 EU member states and shows the considerable growth in both total and per capita GDP in the run-up to accession

Table 14.2 Macroeconomic outlook

Country	Population[1]		GDP at current prices[2]		Real GDP growth rate[3]		Employment rate[4]	
	2005	2012	2005	2012	2005	2012	2005	2012
BE	10,474	11,041	303,435	375,881	1.8	−0.1	66.5	67.2
BG	7,719	7,327	23,256	39,668	6.2	0.8	61.9	63.0
CZ	10,234	10,505	104,629	152,926	6.3	−1.0	70.1	75.4
DK	5,419	5,580	207,367	245,252	2.4	−0.4	78.0	75.4
DE	82,464	81,844	2,224,400	2,666,400	0.8	0.7	69.4	76.7
EE	1,348	1,340	11,182	17,415	9.4	3.9	72.	72.1
IE	4,160	4,583	162,897	163,938	6.2	0.2	72.6	63.7
GR	11,104	11,291	193,050	193,749	2.3	−6.4	64.6	55.3
ES	43,398	46,496	909,298	1,029,002	3.6	−1.6	67.2	59.3
FR	62,958	65,398	1,718,047	2,032,297	1.9	0.0	69.4	69.3
IT	58,607	60,821	1,436,380	1,567,010	0.7	−2.5	61.6	61.0
CY	758	862	13,598	17,887	3.9	−2.4	74.4	70.2
LV	2,300	2,042	12,928	22,257	10.6	5.2	70.3	68.1
LT	3,414	3,008	20,969	32,940	7.8	3.7	70.6	68.5
LU	465	525	30,270	42,918	5.4	−0.2	69.0	71.4
HR	4,669	4,383	36,030	43,904	4.3	2.0	60.0	55.4
HU	10,087	9,958	88,766	96,968	4.0	−1.7	62.2	62.1
MT	403	416	4,931	6,851	3.9	0.9	57.9	63.1
NL	16,317	16,730	513,407	599,338	2.0	−1.2	75.1	77.2
AT	8,225	8,443	245,243	307,004	2.5	0.9	71.7	75.6
PL	38,161	38,538	244,420	381,204	3.6	1.9	60.1	64.7
PT	10,549	10,541	154,269	165,108	0.9	−3.2	72.3	66.5
RO	21,624	21,355	79,802	131,579	4.2	0.7	63.6	63.8
SI	2,001	2,055	28,731	35,319	4.5	−2.5	71.1	68.3
SK	5,387	5,404	38,489	71,096	6.7	1.8	64.5	65.1
FI	5,245	5,401	157,429	192,350	2.9	−1.0	73.0	74.0
SE	9,030	9,483	298,353	407,820	3.3	0.9	78.1	79.4
GB	60,238	62,990	1,867,129	1,932,702	2.2	0.3	75.2	74.2

Notes: [1]In thousand inhabitants; [2]in millions of euros; [3]percentage change over previous year; [4]percentage. AT = Austria; BE = Belgium; BG = Bulgaria; CY = Cyprus; CZ = Czech Republic; DE = Germany; DK = Denmark; EE = Estonia; ES = Spain; FI = Finland; FR = France; GB = Great Britain; GR = Greece; HR = Croatia; HU = Hungary; IE = Ireland; IT = Italy; LT = Lithuania; LU = Luxembourg; MT = Malta; NL = the Netherlands; PL = Poland; PT = Portugal; RO = Romania; SE = Sweden; SI = Slovenia; SK = Slovakia.

Source: Eurostat and DG ECFIN.

for central, eastern and southern European countries. Indeed, growth in these countries has been higher than in the old member states over the same period. However, most economies show a contraction in recent years, with some of the new member states being badly hit by the global recession.

Income per capita rose from 40 per cent of the old member states' average in 1999 to 52 per cent in 2008. Research estimates indicated that the accession process boosted economic growth in the new member states by about $1\frac{3}{4}$ percentage points per year over 2000–2008, when growth increased from 3.5 per cent, on average, in 1999–2003 to 5.5 per cent in 2004–2008.[2]

Growth in the old member states also benefited from enlargement, in particular in those countries that increased trade and investment in the new member states. A key driver of growth was institution building. Institutional reforms were introduced by the adoption of the **acquis communautaire**, which is the body of principles, practices, obligations, objectives and legal and other acts agreed or developed over the years by the European Union. These include the EU Treaties in their entirety, as well as all existing EU legislation and Court of Justice judgments. These have improved the regulatory framework and increased the effectiveness of public administration in the new member states.

However, the sovereign debt crisis, which followed on from the global financial crisis in 2010, posed major new challenges for all member states through declining trade, reduced availability of financing, falling household wealth and deteriorating market confidence. Although EU membership, and even more so euro area membership, provides some degree of protection and stability, all member states have developed similar vulnerabilities. There are fears that in the wake of both crises, the convergence process could slow down. But the economic situation also offers opportunities for reform which could mitigate the adverse social and economic impacts and provide a strong underpinning for a quick and sound recovery.

The EU has enacted a series of initiatives to promote growth. *Europe 2020* is the EU's growth strategy for the coming decade (see Box 14.1). The strategy includes seven 'flagship

BOX 14.1 EUROPE 2020 IN A NUTSHELL

The European Union is working hard to move decisively beyond the crisis and create the conditions for a more competitive economy with higher employment. Europe 2020 is the European Union's ten-year growth strategy. It is about more than just overcoming the crisis which continues to afflict many European economies. It is about addressing the shortcomings of the EU growth model and creating the conditions for a different type of growth that is smarter, more sustainable and more inclusive.

To render this more tangible, five key targets have been set for the EU to achieve by the end of the decade. These cover: (1) employment, with a target of 75% of the 20–64 year olds to be employed; (2) education; the targets are reducing the rates of early school leaving to below 10% and increasing the rate of 30–34 years old with third level (university) education to 40%; (3) research and innovation, with a target of 3% of the EU's GDP to be invested in R&D; (4) social inclusion and poverty reduction, aiming to have fewer than 20 million people in or at risk of poverty and social exclusion; and (5) climate change and energy sustainability, aiming at reducing the rates of greenhouse gas emissions 20% (or even 30%, if the conditions are right) lower than in 1990; to obtain 20% of energy from renewables and to increase energy efficiency by at least 20%. These targets are then translated into national targets, so that each member state can check its own progress towards these goals.

To achieve these goals, EU policies and instruments include the deepening of the Single Market, to overcome bottlenecks to cross-border activity, increase interconnections and enforce Single Market Rules.

Source: Adapted from European Commission (2013).

---

[2] European Commission (2009) 'Five years of an enlarged EU: Economic achievements and challenges' DG Economic and Financial Affairs.

initiatives' providing a framework through which the EU and national authorities mutually reinforce their efforts in areas supporting the Europe 2020 priorities in areas such as innovation, the digital economy, employment, youth policy, industrial policy, poverty and resource efficiency.

14.3 The Single European Market for financial services

Since the passing of the First Banking Co-ordination Directive in 1977, EU legislation has been directed towards creating an integrated and competitive European banking system. To assist banks in confronting challenges posed by the ever-changing economic environment, financial authorities throughout Europe have become more aware of the importance of financial regulation. Possibly the most far-reaching legislation for EU banking, the 1989 **Second Banking Co-ordination Directive (2BCD)** sought to enhance competition by establishing EU-wide recognition of single banking licences. The 1992 Maastricht Treaty created the European Union and led to the establishment of the euro currency and the European Central Bank in 1999.

In this respect, EU legislation creating a **Single Market** and the introduction of **Economic and Monetary Union (EMU)** in 1999 (see Box 14.2 for more details) further liberalised financial market activity.

BOX 14.2 THE CREATION OF A SINGLE MARKET FOR FINANCIAL SERVICES IN THE EUROPEAN UNION

Until the 1980s the European financial and banking sectors were mainly domestically oriented. National governments invariably acted as protectors of their banks from foreign influences and sometimes were themselves owners of major banks. Interest rate restrictions and capital controls were common, and branching restrictions existed in some countries. The objective of harmonisation of laws and practices of the member states reflected wider changes in the domains of economic policy, internationalisation, technological advances and globalisation. The integration process embodied extensive financial liberalisation and was aimed at creating a single market for financial services.

In a report to the House of Lords, the Select Committee on the European Union (2003) clarifies the meaning of a single market in financial services for providers and consumers:

A single market in financial services means that a financial services provider authorised to provide financial services in one member state is able to offer the same services throughout the EU competing on an equal basis within a regulatory framework that is consistent across the Union. On the other side, the consumer would have access to a wider range of more competitively priced products and would be able to shop with confidence and safety in the market place.

A milestone in the harmonisation of EU banking laws was the 1989 Second Banking Co-ordination Directive, which established EU-wide recognition of single banking 'passports' issued in any member state as well as the principle of home-country supervision with minimum standards (including capital) at EU level. In addition, the directive allowed banks to operate as *universal banks:* that is, to engage directly in other financial activities, such as financial instruments, factoring, leasing and investment (merchant) banking. A number of other directives were enacted in an attempt to harmonise the details (e.g. setting minimum standards for deposit guarantee schemes). The single market for financial services implied also liberalisation of non-bank financial intermediaries. Insurance companies and investment firms were granted

Box 14.2 The creation of a single market for financial services in the European Union (*continued*)

a single EU 'passport' with mutual recognition as a result of directives enacted in the early 1990s. Mutual recognition is a system that allows licensed banks to set up branches across states while being subject to each state's rules and regulations.

A major barrier to the formation of a single European market for financial services was that countries still had their own national currencies and monetary policy. As part of the EU's single market programme, the introduction of a single currency was viewed as a central element in the harmonisation process. A further step towards a single market in financial services was finally taken on 1 January 1999, with the launch of the third stage of EMU. The three stages of EMU are detailed in the report of the committee chaired by the then President of the European Commission, Jacques Delors.

- Stage 1 of EMU began on 1 July 1990. Member states had to abolish all remaining capital controls. It required also a higher co-operation among national central banks and underlined the need for a new treaty to permit the realisation of an economic union ('Treaty on European Union', agreed December 1991 and signed in Maastricht on 7 February 1992).

- Stage 2 of EMU began on 1 January 1994, a few months after the coming into force of the Maastricht Treaty. Member states made significant progress towards economic policy convergence. As a precursor to the European Central Bank (ECB), the EMI (European Monetary Institute) was created. Its task was to strengthen co-operation between the national central banks and to carry out the necessary preparations for the introduction of the single currency.

- Stage 3 of EMU began on 1 January 1999. Exchange rates between national currencies were fixed and a European Central Bank created. The transition to the third stage of the monetary union was made on the basis of a series of 'convergence criteria' set out in the Maastricht Treaty on European Union, with the objective of establishing an economic environment of sustainable low inflation in all the member countries.

The Euro replaced national currencies by 1 July 2002: 11 countries made up the euro area when the euro was introduced in 1999; there are now 18 member states.

The 11 euro area (also known as the eurozone) countries originally participating in EMU were Austria, Belgium, Finland, France, Germany, Ireland, Italy, Luxembourg, the Netherlands, Spain and Portugal. In July 2000 the conversion rates between the euro and the Greek drachma were set as Greece fulfilled the conditions for joining the EMU. Denmark and the UK negotiated an 'opt-out' Protocol to the EU Treaty, granting them the option of joining the euro area or not. Sweden initially did not meet the necessary conditions for entry and in September 2003 rejected the euro in a national referendum.

Since then, six more countries have adopted the euro: Slovenia on 1 January 2007, Cyprus and Malta on 1 January 2008, Slovakia on 1 January 2009. Estonia joined the euro area on 1 January 2011, when the euro replaced the Estonian kroon. Latvia became the 18th member state of the eurozone on January 2014.

Euro banknotes and coins were introduced on 1 January 2002 in 12 member states of the EU. The irrevocably fixed conversion rates between the euro and the currencies of the 12 initial member states adopting the euro are shown in Table 14.3 (OJ L 359, Vol. 41, 31/12/1998 and OJ L 167, 07/07/2000). Table 14.3 also indicates the irrevocably fixed conversion rates for the newer eurozone members.

Box 14.2 The creation of a single market for financial services in the European Union (*continued*)

Table 14.3 Euro area member states

Country	Conversion rate of 1 EUR	Member of the eurozone since
Austria	13.7603 ATS	1999
Belgium	40.3399 BEF	1999
Cyprus	0.585274 CYP	2008
Estonia	15.6466 EEK	2011
Finland	5.94573 FIM	1999
France	6.55957 FRF	1999
Germany	1.95583 DEM	1999
Greece	340.750 GRD	2002
Ireland	0.787564 IEP	1999
Italy	1936.27 ITL	1999
Latvia	0.702804 LVL	2014
Luxembourg	40.3399 LUF	1999
Malta	0.429300 MTL	2008
Netherlands	2.20371 NLG	1999
Portugal	200.482 PTE	1999
Slovakia	30.1260 SKK	2009
Slovenia	239.640 SIT	2007
Spain	166.386 ESP	1999

A major aim of EU legislation has been to reduce the barriers to cross-border trade in the banking and financial services area, with the ultimate aim of creating a single market in financial services. The liberalisation of structural obstacles has been accompanied by financial deregulation through the reduction of direct government control. Table 14.4 shows the main regulatory measures that have aimed at establishing a harmonised framework for European financial services in the pre-crisis period. (The regulatory changes triggered by the global financial crisis and eurozone crisis are discussed in Section 14.4.)

Table 14.4 Regulatory measures affecting the EU banking and financial sectors

Year	Regulation
1977	**First Banking Directive (77/780/EEC)** – adoption of regulations, norms and procedures, which removed obstacles to the provision of services across the borders of member states and to the establishment of branches. It also harmonised the rules and conditions for issuing a licence to operate as a bank and defined the authorities that supervise banks and branches of foreign banks, as well as the procedures for co-operation among these authorities.
1985	**White Paper 'Completing the internal market' (COM 85/310)** – proposed to abolish all remaining non-tariff barriers to the free circulation of goods, services, people and capital.
1988	**Basel Capital Adequacy Regulation** – established minimum capital adequacy requirements for banks, the so-called 8 per cent ratio. Established definitions of capital including Tier 1 (equity) and Tier 2 (near-equity) capital. Devised risk weightings based on credit risk for bank business. These were incorporated into European law by the Council Directive 89/299/EEC on the own funds of credit institutions.

Table 14.4 Regulatory measures affecting the EU banking and financial sectors (*continued*)

Year	Regulation
1988	**Deregulation of capital movements in the European Monetary System (EMS)** – enabled the free flow of capital cross-border within the EU (Council Directive 88/361/EEC).
1989	**Second Banking Directive** (Second Council Directive 89/646/EEC) – established the rules for a single banking licence within the EU and introduced the principles of home-country control (home regulators have ultimate supervisory authority for the foreign activity of their banks) and mutual recognition (EU bank regulators recognise that their rules and regulations are equivalent). The Second Banking Directive was passed in conjunction with the Own Funds and Solvency Directives that effectively introduced capital adequacy requirements similar to those proposed by Basel into EU law.
1993	**Investment Services Directive** (Council Directive 93/22/EEC) – set the legislative framework for investment firms and securities markets in the European Union, providing for a single passport for investment services.
1994	**Deposit Guarantee Scheme** – Directive 94/19/EC introduced minimum harmonisation for deposit guarantee schemes.
1999	**Financial Services Action Plan (FSAP)** – aimed at developing a legislative framework for the single market in financial services. Between its endorsement by the European Council in Lisbon in March 2000 and the end of April 2004, 38 out of the 42 FSAP measures were adopted in the EU.
2000	**Directive on e-money** – Directive 2000/46/EC was conceived and adopted at the height of the e-commerce boom and was intended to facilitate access by non-credit institutions to the business of e-money issuance. Dealt with harmonising rules and standards relating to such things as payments by mobile telephone, payments using transport cards, as well as Basel payment facilities.
2001	**Directive on the Re-organisation and Winding-Up of Credit Institutions** – Directive 2001/24/EC created rules to ensure that reorganisation measures or winding-up proceedings adopted by the home state of an EU credit institution are recognised and implemented throughout the Community.
2001	**Regulation on the European Company Statute** (Council Regulation (EC) No 2157/2001) – established a legal framework for a new form of company, the European Company or 'Societas Europaea (SE)', and consisted of an EU regulation (setting out the core company law framework and which has direct effect throughout the Community) and an accompanying EU Directive dealing with employee involvement in SEs. Aimed to establish standard rules for company formation in the EU.
2004	**Directive on Takeover bids (Directive 2004/25/EC)** – established a common framework for cross-border takeover bids.
2004	**Markets in Financial Instruments Directive (Directive 2004/39/EC)** – known as **MiFID**, the Directive proposed harmonised regulation for investment services across the European Economic Area (EEA). It introduced a 'passport' for trading venues and investment firms to operate throughout the EEA on the basis of authorisation in their home member state. It also introduced various investor protection measures.
2006	**Basel II – solvency (capital adequacy) framework** – to update the original international bank capital accord (Basel I), which has been in effect since 1988. The new rules aim to improve the consistency of capital regulations internationally, make regulatory capital more risk sensitive, and promote enhanced risk management practices among large, internationally active banking organisations. These were incorporated into European law by Directive 2006/49/EC and Directive 2006/49/EC, also known as CRD (Capital Requirement Directives).
2007	**Payment Services Directive (Directive 2007/64/EC)** – the Directive known as PSD sets the basis for a harmonised legal framework for the creation of an integrated payments markets. It was seen as an additional step towards the single market and aimed at increasing consumer protection and market transparency and at enhancing competition in payment markets by removing market entry barriers. It is also a key step towards the completion of the Single Euro Payments Area (SEPA).

In this respect, the launch of the EU's **Financial Services Action Plan (FSAP)** in 1999 acted as a catalyst for the realisation of the single market – the ultimate aim of the FSAP was to promote a more competitive and dynamic financial services industry with better regulation and this would be expected to feed through into enhanced economic growth. Consumers of financial products should obtain lower prices, and producers of such services will benefit from lower costs. The original document put forward indicative priorities and a timetable for specific measures to achieve three strategic objectives:

- establishing a single market in wholesale financial services;
- making retail markets open and secure; and
- strengthening the rules on prudential supervision.

A range of other regulatory actions focused on establishing more uniform fiscal treatment of financial products and business in order to 'obtain wider conditions for an optimal single financial market'. Good progress was made on the proposed measures and by the start of 2005, 38 out of the original 42 measures outlined in the FSAP had been adopted and were being implemented into EU law.

In 2005, the Financial Services Action Plan was replaced by the *White Paper on Financial Services,* which set out the Commission's objectives from 2005 to 2010. In the White Paper, the EC states the main aims of its policy for the period 2005–2010, which include:

- consolidation of the progress achieved;
- completion of current measures;
- enhancement of supervisory co-operation and convergence;
- removal of remaining barriers to integration.

The White Paper set the following priorities: 1) strengthening the achievements made under the FSAP; 2) strengthening the regulatory framework; 3) enhancing convergence of supervisory practices and improving the supervisory architecture; 4) fostering competition in EU financial services; and 5) enhancing the EU's role in global capital markets.

One of the key objectives was to ensure the coherence of the regulatory framework and the development of consistent legislation. Co-ordination and harmonisation of financial supervision in the EU were pursued through the so-called **Lamfalussy process**, which aimed to simplify and speed up the complex and lengthy EU legislative process. In the words of the European Commission, the launch of the Lamfalussy process in 2001 aimed to put in place 'an efficient mechanism to begin converging European financial supervisory practice and enable financial services legislation to respond rapidly and flexibly to developments in financial markets'. Under this approach, financial regulation is passed at four levels, as discussed in Box 14.3. A broad review of the process was carried out in 2007 and found that although the process had broadly met its overall objectives, some essential changes were required in order to make it more efficient.

While the creation of a single financial market is an admirable aim, it has long been recognised that this may be difficult to achieve for certain financial products – especially those that are essentially national in nature. Since the earliest assessments of conditions in European financial services there has been the recognition that retail financial services markets are segmented by national boundaries. A study by the Single Market Observatory (European Economic and Social Committee, 2012) indicates that after 20 years of existence, the single market is still a work in progress; while a number of barriers have been abolished, new ones have appeared.

Table 14.5 shows an outline of the integration obstacles classified by demand- and supply-side factors. In general, most seem to be a result of natural or policy-induced elements. Such obstacles to further integration are apparent in a wide range of areas; some of these barriers are natural and they can be only partially influenced by policy makers, others require further regulation (e.g. new capital adequacy rules).

Various studies have identified that there remain substantial price differences in retail financial services across the EU. These price differences reflect a broad array of factors, not least the different institutional, legal and risk features in the various national markets. They also reflect varying degrees of competition and the lack of cross-border trade in retail products. Cross-border trade in retail financial services is marginal for unsecured loans, deposit and savings accounts, credit cards, pensions and insurance (although there is a modest amount of non-life business and retail mutual fund activity). All these factors point to a market that is far from integrated. A report from the EC to the European Parliament (2013b) finds that fragmentation of national rules relating to labour, taxation, health and safety, consumer protection and contract law remains an issue. In general, market fragmentation has increased since the 2007 sub-prime crisis. For example, fragmentation is evident when

BOX 14.3 THE LAMFALUSSY PROCESS

In July 2000, the French presidency of the EU initiated the appointment of a Committee of Wise Men chaired by Alexandre Lamfalussy, with the task of drafting proposals for improving the effectiveness of the EU's securities market regulatory process. In February 2001, the Wise Men's report proposed a four-level legislative process, where significant powers are delegated to implementing committees. The procedure, now known as the Lamfalussy process, aims to simplify and speed up the complex and lengthy regular EU legislative process by means of a four-level approach. It was extended to the entire EU financial sector in December 2002.

According to the Lamfalussy process, EU institutions adopt framework legislation under the auspices of the Commission (*level one*). The Commission then prepares the detailed technical implementing measures with the help of four specialist committees (*level two*). These are the European Banking Committee (EBC), the European Securities Committee (ESC), the European Insurance and Occupational Pensions Committee (EIOPC) and the Financial Conglomerates Committee (FCC) for supervisory issues relating to cross-sector groups. They decide on implementing measures put forward by the Commission.

In developing the implementing measures, the Commission is again advised by committees of experts at the **third level** of the Lamfalussy process. These are the Committee of European Banking Supervisors (CEBS), the Committee of European Securities Regulators (CESR) and the Committee of European Insurance and Occupational Pensions Supervisors (CEIOPS). The Banking Supervision Committee also includes representatives from the national central banks. Apart from advising and assisting the Commission in the development of technical implementing measures, the committees of experts also deal with the exchange of supervisory information, the consistent implementation of European legal acts and the harmonisation of supervisory practices in the European market for financial services. At the **fourth level,** the Commission – in close co-operation with the member states, the regulatory authorities involved in level three and the private sector – checks that Community law is applied consistently. The Lamfalussy process is illustrated in Figure 14.1.

A review of the Lamfalussy process was carried out in 2007, to identify some practical, necessary and achievable improvements to the process.

Following the outbreak of the global financial crisis in 2007, EU regulators identified supervisory convergence as a key objective not only from an integration point of view but also from a financial stability perspective.

Box 14.3 The Lamfalussy process (*continued*)

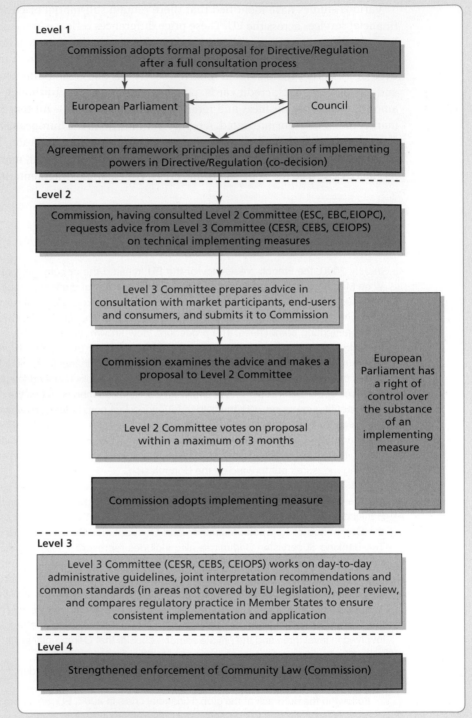

Figure 14.1 The Lamfalussy process
Source: European Commission (2007b).

Table 14.5 Obstacles to full integration of EU financial retail markets

	Natural	Policy-induced
Demand side	• Language, culture • Consumer trust in national suppliers • Distance and the desire for personal contacts	• Discriminatory tax treatment of foreign services/products • Existence of national currencies (e.g. UK) • Insufficient knowledge about cross-border redress procedures
Supply side	• Information costs caused by natural factors (e.g. cultural differences) • Bias for home products in established distribution channels • Smaller national EU market commercially not attractive	• Information and adjustment costs derived from national differences in regulation (e.g. consumer protection) • Obstacles to cross-border information flow (e.g. limited access to foreign credit registers) • Competitive privileges of domestic suppliers • Shortcomings of internal market rules (e.g. through slow EU legislative adjustments to new developments) • Particular costs of cross-border operations (e.g. money transfers)

Source: Adapted from Heinemann and Jopp (2002).

comparing interest rates on bank loans to households and SMEs across member states, as illustrated in Figure 14.2.

Regulations governing the retail financial services sector are also country-specific. It remains problematic to undertake cross-border activity without (physical) establishment. Differences in tax treatments, consumer protection legislation, marketing rules, definition of products, investor protection and so on substantially hinder the cross-border provision of many retail banking and other financial services. Banks that try to sell their retail services cross-border (without a physical presence), therefore, are likely to have a substantial competitive disadvantage. These barriers may be less onerous when banks operate in areas

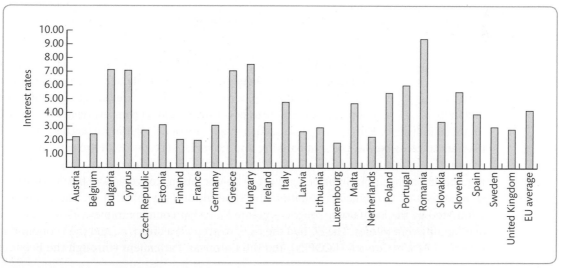

Figure 14.2 Interest rates, loans to non-financial corporates

Note: Up to 1 year to maturity, outstanding amount, average rates from January to August 2013.

Source: European Commission (2013b).

that have a more international dimension such as investment and international banking, although it is noticeable that even the world's largest investment banks typically have extensive physical market presence in many countries, suggesting that cross-border provision of services without establishment is also not the preferred strategy, even in wholesale business. In general, domestic regulations as well as institutional factors, culture, strength of banking relationships, the need for proximity in certain services and so on dictate that banks must have a physical presence in the country before they can access retail markets.

Overall, limited integration in the retail financial services in the European Union can be put down to:

● the nature of the retail banking/financial services relationship;

● limited cross-border consolidation (due to economic/business factors mainly);

● very limited cross-border provision without establishment, due to business reasons as well as obstacles such as double taxation or discriminatory taxation of financial products when sold across frontiers, consumer protection laws, data transfer issues, contract law differences, legal definitions of collateral for retail mortgages, definition of customers, difficulties in implementing 'know your customer rules', different ways of calculating prices (such as annual percentage rates or APRs) and so on.

The already existing fragmentation in retail financial services has also been in some cases exacerbated by the response of some national supervisors to potential stability concerns triggered by the eurozone crisis (starting in 2010), including prudential measures that have 'ring-fencing' effects, such as measures aimed at retaining liquidity, dividends and other bank assets within national borders. In reaction to concerns of decreased integration, EU regulators have promoted the development of a **Single Rulebook**, which should ensure uniform rules, supervision and resolution across the EU (this is discussed in Section 14.4.6). In addition, the creation of the Banking Union aims to restore confidence in the single market for financial services.

14.4   Building a new EU financial architecture

Based on the Nice Treaty and the Lisbon strategy, the EU has fostered liberalisation of financial services providers and financial markets.[3] The key principle behind this strategy has been stronger competition in EU markets, with the purpose of reducing financing costs and improving allocation of resources, thus boosting the global competitiveness of the EU's financial industry. As previously discussed, a major aim of EU legislation has been to reduce barriers to cross-border trade in banking and financial services, with the ultimate aim of creating a single market in financial services. Over the past two decades, a large body of EU regulation has been put in place to improve co-operation, convergence, harmonisation or standardisation of financial regulation and supervision (see Table 14.4). These initiatives – initiated by the Lamfalussy process – created a rather complex framework of sometimes overlapping committees. The EC had the right to propose a directive, and the Economic and Financial Affairs Council (ECOFIN) and the European Parliament (through the Economic

---

[3] The Treaty of Nice was signed in 2001 by European leaders and entered into force in February 2003. The treaty had a clear mandate to revise existing legislation in preparation for the European enlargement.

and Monetary Affairs Committee) had co-decision rights to adopt the directive. Once a directive was adopted, the EC and the member states played an important role in implementation. While the ECB had no legal mandate to regulate or supervise banks and other financial institutions, or financial markets, it was involved in many EU structures and institutions in an advisory function and was legally mandated to provide information in support of action on financial stability (see Box 14.3 on the Lamfalussy process).

During the financial turmoil and government interventions of the late 2000s, the weakness of the existing structure became clear. Many governments first took national measures before gradually co-ordinating EU-wide responses. This led to widespread criticism and major public debate about changes in EU institutional arrangements. To understand these regulatory changes, we need first to review the key events of the crisis in EU banking. Section 14.4.1 highlights the key crisis events and discusses their impact on the EU banking sector.

14.4.1 Crises in European banking

Some have argued that the crises that have hit EU countries since the late 2000s relate to three different crises – a banking crisis, a sovereign debts crisis and an economic growth crisis – and the three are highly interlinked (see Figure 14.3). The notion of multiple crises is not new (see Chapter 8 for crises definitions), although many argue that the case for the eurozone problems is different.

There has been much conjecture about the causes of eurozone troubles, with a number of critics pointing to the creation of the monetary union. The causes of the global financial crisis

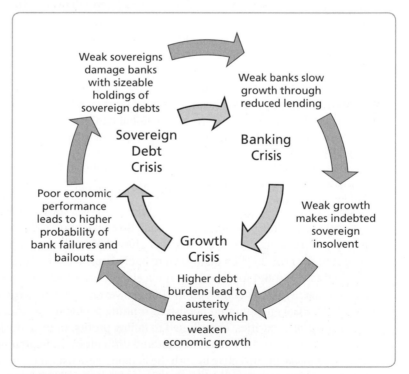

Figure 14.3 The three crises in the eurozone
Source: Adapted from Shambaugh (2012).

that started in mid-2007 in the United States are discussed in detail in Chapter 15 ('Banking in the US'). The unfolding of the financial crisis and how it became a European sovereign debt crisis and an economic crisis is often described in phases or waves, as follows:

(I)   Phase One: US sub-prime crisis (August 2007 to September 2008).

(II) Phase Two: systemic or global crisis (September 2008 to March 2009).

(III) Phase Three: economic crisis (March 2009 to 2010).

(IV) Phase Four: sovereign debt crisis (2010 to 2011).

(V)   Phase Five: 'crisis of confidence' in Europe (since 2011).

14.4.1.1   Phase One: US sub-prime crisis

The early phase of the global financial crisis impacted mainly US banking and became systemic or global from September 2008, with the failure of the investment bank Lehman Brothers. Eurozone banks, unlike UK banks, although exposed to sub-prime securitised products, were not immediately impacted (with some exception) by the bursting of the US real estate bubble and consequent loss of value of securitised products backed by US residential mortgages.

One notable exception was IKB Deutsche Industriebank, which became one of the first eurozone banks to be hit by the crisis. The German bank had built a large portfolio of asset-backed commercial paper (ABCP) funds whose investment strategy suffered from the losses announced by the US investment bank Bear Stearns in the summer of 2007. Bear Stearns then failed in March 2008 and was acquired by JPMorgan Chase. When the ABCP market collapsed in the summer of 2007, IKB was unable to roll over its funds' short-term debt and had to be rescued with a package arranged by the German central bank. Within days of IKB's rescue, the situation in the eurozone financial markets started to deteriorate and the ECB had to intervene with liquidity injections (the first in August 2007 and the second in December 2007).

In this first part of the financial crisis, the EU banking industry experienced losses due to significant write-downs when the price of mortgage-backed securities collapsed. During this phase, the total write-downs in the global banking system amounted to $720 billion, with euro area banks accounting for $131 billion, or 18 per cent, of the global amount (ECB statistics).

14.4.1.2   Phase Two: systemic or global crisis

A second phase or 'systemic' part of the financial crisis started in September 2008. In the 12 months following the collapse of Lehman Brothers, unprecedented state aid was directed towards the banking sector. During this phase UK banks (see Chapter 13 for a detailed account of the crisis in UK banking) were badly impacted and the banking sector in Iceland collapsed (see Box 8.4 for details on the Icelandic crisis). On average, credit losses of euro area banks generally remained low in 2008; however, eurozone **large and complex banking groups (LCBGs)** encountered persistent funding problems, which, coupled with sizeable write-downs on securities, contributed to falling profits. Indeed, during this period, a number of large cross-border banks encountered difficulties. In September 2008 Fortis, a large Benelux financial group active in both the banking and insurance markets and one of the top five financial institutions in the EU, experienced a sharp fall in its share price, amidst rumours of difficulties in raising liquid funds through the interbank markets. The rescue of Dexia Bank

BOX 14.4 THE FAILURE OF CROSS-BORDER BANKS: THE CASE OF FORTIS AND DEXIA

Fortis

Fortis Group was a Belgian–Dutch financial conglomerate with substantial subsidiaries in Belgium, the Netherlands and Luxembourg. Fortis was present in over 50 countries with more than 85,000 employees. In 2006, financial results amounted to a record €4 billion profit. The consolidating and coordinating supervisor was Belgium's Commission Bancaire, Financière et des Assurances (CBFA), as the banking activities within Fortis Group, headed by the Belgium-based Fortis Bank SA/NV, were the largest part of Fortis's operations. Fortis was deemed to be systemically relevant in the three countries, not only because of its large positions in domestic markets, but also because of its function as a clearing member at several major domestic and foreign stock exchanges.

In 2007, Fortis acquired portions of the operations of ABN AMRO through a consortium with Royal Bank of Scotland and Santander. In 2008 the international financial crisis intensified to such an extent that Fortis had difficulties realising its plans to strengthen its financial position and to finance the acquisition and integration of its acquisitions of portions of ABN AMRO. Starting in June 2008, there was increasing uncertainty in the market as to whether Fortis would be able to realise the intended steps. Over the summer, its share price deteriorated and liquidity became a serious concern.

In the last week of September 2008, its share price declined rapidly and institutional clients began to withdraw substantial deposits. Fortis lost access to the overnight interbank market, and had to turn to the marginal lending facility of the Eurosystem provided by the National Bank of Belgium (NBB). The combined effect made the finding of a solution imperative, triggering intervention by public authorities.

After the Dutch government purchased Fortis Bank Netherlands, Fortis Insurance Netherlands, Fortis Corporate Insurance and the Fortis share in ABN AMRO, the Belgian government raised its holding in Fortis Bank Belgium up to 99%. The Belgian government also agreed to sell a 75% interest to BNP Paribas (BNP) in return for new BNP shares, keeping a blocking minority of 25% of the capital of Fortis Bank Belgium. BNP also bought the Belgian insurance activities of Fortis and took a majority stake in Fortis Bank Luxembourg. A portfolio of structured products was transferred to a financial structure owned by the Belgian state, BNP and Fortis Group.

On 12 December 2008, the Court of Appeal of Brussels suspended the sale to BNP, which was not yet finalised, and decided that the finalised sales to the Dutch state and to the Belgian state as well as the subsequent sale to BNP had to be submitted for approval by the general assembly of shareholders of Fortis Holding in order for these three sales to be valid under Belgian law. After initial rejection by the shareholders, certain transactions were renegotiated and the financing of the portfolio of structured products was modified. The renegotiated transaction with the Belgian State and BNP was approved at the second general assembly of shareholders and the latter transaction was finalised on 12 May 2009.

The Fortis case illustrates the tension between the cross-border nature of a group and the domestic focus of national frameworks and responsibilities for crisis management. This led to a solution along national lines, which did not involve intervention through statutory resolution mechanisms. The Fortis case also illustrates the trade-off between the need to maintain financial stability, for which a bank under certain circumstances needs to be resolved in the public interest and with public support, and the position of the shareholders of such a bank. Despite a long-standing relationship in on-going supervision and information sharing, the Dutch and Belgian supervisory authorities assessed the situation differently. Differences in the assessment of available information and the sense of urgency complicated the resolution.

Dexia

Dexia was established in 1996 as a result of a merger between a Belgian and a French bank, respectively Crédit Communal de Belgique and Crédit Local de France, with a significant presence in Luxembourg. In 1999, the two listed holding companies – one French (Dexia France) and the other Belgian (Dexia Belgium) – merged to create Dexia SA, a financial company under Belgian law not operating with the status of a bank, which wholly owned the three main operating

Box 14.4 The failure of cross-border banks: the case of Fortis and Dexia (*continued*)

entities in France, Belgium and Luxembourg: Dexia Crédit Local, Dexia Banque Belgique and Dexia Banque Internationale à Luxembourg.

The growth years

Between 1999 and 2008, the size of the consolidated balance sheet increased by 2.7%. The group's net income improved continuously, reaching €2.75 billion in 2006. The group's growth was primarily driven by the increase in the portfolio of invested assets. In addition, the bank's funding structure was not based on long-term, stable funding or on deposits but more than 40% of the balance sheet was covered by short-term funding. The group was structurally dependent on wholesale liquidity.

The first bailout

During 2008, difficulties came in particular from: (i) the financing of long-term assets, and, in particular, of an important portfolio of bonds, by short-term funding; and (ii) its US subsidiary, Financial Security Assurance (FSA), a monoline insurer. Following a decision taken by Dexia's Board of Directors on 30 September 2008, Dexia increased its capital by €6.4 billion, of which Belgian and French public and private sector investors subscribed €3 billion each and the Luxembourg state subscribed €376 million under the form of convertible bonds. Following this recapitalisation, Dexia's chairman and the chief executive were replaced.

On 9 October 2008, Belgium, France and Luxembourg concluded an agreement on a joint guarantee mechanism – covered 60.5% by Belgium, 36.5% by France and 3% by Luxembourg – to facilitate Dexia's access to financing. On 14 November 2008, additional public Belgian and French guarantees were announced in the context of the sale of FSA, Dexia's US subsidiary, to US insurer Assured Guaranty, to insulate Assured Guaranty from any risk resulting from FSA's portfolio of riskier securities linked to sub-prime mortgages that were not included in the sale.

In the case of Dexia, authorities in Belgium, France and Luxembourg agreed to share the burden of guarantees in order to allow the institution to access financing and provide time for the sale of certain operations and the retrenching of others. In general terms, the division of the burden for guarantees among the three national authorities was premised on the proportions of share ownership held by the institutional investors and public authorities of the three countries. Before the crisis, public sector institutions and municipalities already had significant minority stakes in Dexia. These interests increased by virtue of capital injections during the crisis by these historical shareholders.

The eurozone crisis and the break-up of the Dexia Group

Despite the bailout, Dexia was to become the first victim of the eurozone crisis and the financial institution needed to be bailed out for the second time in 2011 and for a third time in 2012.

In October 2011 France, Belgium and Luxembourg agreed to a second bailout of the troubled bank, following fears it could go bankrupt. At the core of the crisis, Dexia had €3.4 billion of exposure to Greek government bonds (and analysts estimated it had a further €17.5 billion of exposure to sovereign debt issued by Italy, Spain, Portugal and other troubled eurozone economies). During the summer of 2011, Dexia wrote down the value of some of its long-term Greek holdings by 21%. However, this started speculations of a record loss and the inability of Dexia to absorb such loss, triggering a fall in the institution's share price to an all-time low. This prompted the decision of a second rescue. The Belgian government agreed to buy the bank's division in Belgium for €4 billion. A Qatari investment group was ready to buy the bank's Luxembourg unit.

Dexia also secured state guarantees of up to €90 billion to secure borrowing over the next 10 years. Belgium will provide 60.5% of these guarantees, France 36.5% and Luxembourg 3%.

Table 14.6 The development of Dexia's balance sheet and income (in €bn)

	1999	2000	2001	2002	2003	2004	2005	2006	2007	2008
Total assets	245	258	351	351	350	405	509	567	605	651
Net income	761	1,001	1,426	1,299	1,431	1,822	2,038	2,750	2,533	−3,326

Source: Court des Comptes (2013).

Box 14.4 The failure of cross-border banks: the case of Fortis and Dexia (*continued*)

In the aftermath of the second bailout, it became necessary to recapitalise Dexia, as the financial institution was incurring heavy losses following the discounted sale of several assets. The sale of its assets contributed to net losses of €11.6 billion in 2011 after units were sold at a discount. Dexia sold its Turkish bank DenizBank to Sberbank of Russia in June for about €3 billion.

In November 2012, France and Belgium agreed to a third bailout in four years and injected €5.5 billion of fresh capital into what was once the world's largest municipal lender. Up to 53%, or €2.9 billion, of the bailout was provided by Belgium and the balance by France. It is estimated that France lost €6.6 billion through the bailout of Dexia.

The failure of Dexia, three times bailed out by the French and Belgian authorities, showed the need for the eurozone to accelerate its plans to establish a single banking supervisor and resolution authority.

In July 2013, the French Court of Accounts (the competent authority) published a report into the Franco–Belgian banking groups' failure and highlighted the following:

● Dexia's management was pursuing a high-risk strategy (a financing model based on short-term funding; the search for ever-higher profitability

and the distribution of substantial dividends) that neither Dexia's internal governance nor the supervisory authorities were able to prevent.

● Failure of the restructuring plan put together in 2008. In exchange for accepting state aid, the European Commission wanted a restructuring plan whose main objective was to reduce Dexia's balance sheet size. While the objectives of the plan were met for the most part, Dexia's high exposure to sovereign debt meant that the group had to be dismantled once the sovereign debt crisis peaked in 2011.

● A high cost in terms of public spending, with added risks over the long term. To date, the direct cost of this banking debacle, for the French part alone, comes to €6.6 billion.

● A late and incomplete search for accountability. The 2008 bailout of Dexia was followed by a change in its management teams, then the substantial overhaul of the Board of Directors in 2009. However, members of Dexia top management nevertheless held onto substantial financial benefits.

Source: Adapted from Basel Committee on Banking Supervision (2010b); Court des Comptes (2013); authors' updates.

(a Franco–Belgian financial institution which was once the world's largest municipal lender) in September 2008 by the governments of Belgium, French and Luxembourg highlighted the need for state co-ordination for banks with substantial cross-border activities. The 2008 bailout was the first of a series of bailouts eventually needed by the Dexia group, which went on to become the first big casualty of the sovereign debt crisis (see Box 14.4).

During the same period, a major German commercial-property lender, Hypo Real Estate, had to be saved from the brink of collapse after its Irish subsidiary ran into short-term funding problems. Commerzbank, Germany's second-largest bank, also received public support between November 2008 and January 2009, required partly to cover losses emanating from the acquisition of Dresdner Bank in August 2008.

By the end of September, conditions in the euro area financial market had become extremely tense and banks were increasingly dependent on ECB liquidity operations and overnight borrowing, as interbank lending at longer maturities had ceased almost completely. Quick and co-ordinated policy actions by the ECB and eurozone national governments helped to stabilise the situation. A common eurozone framework and an action plan to support banks were agreed in October 2009. These measures included a strengthening of deposit guarantee schemes, government guarantees for bank debt issuance and capital provisions to relevant banks. In late 2009, around €2 trillion was pledged by governments in the euro area to guarantee banks' new debt issuance, support their recapitalisation or purchase their assets (European Central Bank, 2009b).

14.4.1.3 Phase Three: economic crisis

The extraordinary remedial actions taken by the European Central Bank and eurozone national central banks and governments since mid-2009 were successful in restoring confidence in financial markets. However, eurozone banks were still exposed to a number of potential vulnerabilities. In particular, the pressure on banks to deleverage was acute: they faced high funding costs in wholesale markets, difficulties in issuing debt, and were under increasing pressure to raise capital buffers. Eurozone banks responded to these pressures by tightening their lending standards and by cutting costs. This resulted in a sharp reduction in the growth of banks' risk-weighted assets, also due to slower growth in lending to both households and firms against the backdrop of weaker economic activity. Eurozone economies were heading towards a period of recession. In addition, concerns about the sustainability of public finances of some member states started to emerge.

14.4.1.4 Phase Four: sovereign debt crisis

Sovereign debt refers to debt incurred by governments – mainly through the issue of medium-to long-term bonds. Under certain circumstances, governments may suspend or fall behind on their debt payments. In other words, there are instances when governments default on their debt. A *sovereign debt crisis* can be defined as the inability or unwillingness of a government to repay its debt. Defaults and debt crises can be triggered by a number of different economic and political factors (for example, wars, economic recessions, changes in political leadership, currency depreciations, fluctuation in the price of imports, among other factors). A sovereign debt crisis may not result in an actual default if, for example, the country receives a bailout package or a loan (for example from the IMF) to allow it to stay current in its debt obligations.

Countries may be unwilling to repay their debt, based on a consideration of the relative costs and benefits of default. On the one hand, countries may be unable to repay their debt because they are either insolvent or illiquid. The perceived riskiness of a country (that is, its ability or willingness to repay its debt) can be measured by the 'spread' or additional interest that markets demand for holding the debt of a country compared with the bonds issued by a country that is deemed safe. Within the eurozone, the benchmark 'safe country' is Germany and the spread over ten-year German *bunds* is the standard measure of perceived risk and it can be used as a benchmark to compare the premium that markets/investors demand for holding, let's say, (risky) Greek bonds with the bonds issued by (safe) Germany.

During the second phase of the crisis, yields on eurozone sovereign bonds remained relatively unaffected. However, when the newly elected Greek government revealed the true size of the country's deficit and debt in November 2009, markets' attention moved to sovereign risk. After that, sovereign spreads rose sharply for most of the euro area countries, causing the biggest challenge for the European monetary union since its creation. As speculation on the ability of Greece to service its debt intensified, markets feared that most of Greece's debt was owned by large EU banks, thus establishing the link between sovereign and banking crises.

In May 2010, after lengthy negotiations, the Greek government eventually accepted a €110 billion EU/IMF-led rescue package. Simultaneously, a €750 billion emergency fund was created jointly by EU member states and the IMF to support other weaker EU economies. In November 2010, Ireland asked for financial assistance from that emergency fund. In April 2011, Portugal followed. The long political process to put together sufficient firewalls at

European level and to find a solution for Greece, Ireland and Portugal, combined with the attempts to restore market confidence, imposed significant costs on the European banking sector and European banks had to rely on covered bonds (bond issues backed by balance sheet capital) or secured short-term funding from the ECB (see Liikanen Report, 2012).

During the first half of 2011, it became apparent that the regulatory efforts put in place by EU authorities were not sufficient to restore confidence. Greece's sovereign debt was further downgraded by Standard & Poor's in June 2011, due to increasing concerns about the country's inability to meet targets set by the 'Troika' (the European Central Bank, the European Commission and the International Monetary Fund), and a second rescue package worth more than €100 billion became necessary in July 2011. During the summer of 2011, sovereign debt pressure also hit Italy and Spain, two of the largest economies in the euro area. Although the two countries' credit spread decreased by the autumn of 2011, the episode highlighted the need for a credible and permanent mechanism for providing financial assistance to EU members. The European Council adopted a comprehensive package of measures to respond to the crisis, as well as providing a backstop against future crises. To this end, the **European Stability Mechanism (ESM)** was designed to provide financial assistance to euro area member states experiencing or threatened by financing difficulties. The ESM replaces the **European Financial Stability Facility (EFSF)**, the temporary mechanism set up in 2010, which will cease to exist once all outstanding liabilities are repaid. Table 14.7 summarises the key financial assistance facilities put in place for eurozone countries during this phase of the crisis.

14.4.1.5 Phase Five: crisis of confidence

The events of 2011 put the European project in general and the euro in particular under severe strain. The process of integration was interrupted and there was an increased risk of fragmentation. Supervisors' focus on domestic financial stability exacerbated this process. For example, there had been a decline or reversal of some cross-border credit flows, banks increasingly focused on their home markets, and differences in wholesale financing costs and retail interest rates between member states increased (see Likaanen Report (2012) and European Commission (2012)).

In June 2012, the presidents of the European Council, the European Commission, Eurogroup and the ECB issued a joint report, 'Towards a genuine economic and monetary union', which sets out the four essential building blocks for the future of EMU: (i) an integrated financial framework; (ii) an integrated budgetary framework; (iii) an integrated economic policy framework; and (iv) strengthened democratic legitimacy and accountability (Van Rompuy, 2012). In June 2012 the European Council asked for a road map for the achievement of a genuine economic and monetary union; as a first step, legislative proposals were put forward for the establishment of a single supervisory mechanism in Europe, with a view of achieving a Banking Union going forward, the ultimate aim being to try to break the link between banking and sovereign debt crises.

14.4.2 The road to an EU Banking Union

The weaknesses of the EU regulatory framework became apparent during the early stages of the global financial crisis, particularly with respect to the resolution of cross-border groups. In the absence of a multinational resolution framework, national authorities will typically seek to protect national interests (that is, minimise the losses to domestic depositors, shareholders and other creditors, including losses to taxpayers and deposit insurers).

Table 14.7 Financial assistance facilities for euro area countries

	Euro area intergovernmental loans to Greece	European Financial Stabilisation Mechanism	European Financial Stability Facility	European Stability Mechanism
Legal/ institutional form	Intergovernmental agreement	EU mechanism	Private company owned by euro area countries	Intergovernmental organisation
Capital structure	None. Bilateral loans pooled by the European Commission	Guaranteed by EU budget (i.e. all member states)	Guarantees from euro area countries	€80 billion paid-in capital and €60 billion callable capital (payment of initial shares by euro area countries to be made in five annual instalments of 20 per cent of the total amount)
Lending capacity - *EU/euro area limit* - *Commitments*	- €80 billion - €80 billion	- €60 billion - €22.5 billion for Ireland and €26 billion for Portugal	- €440 billion - €17.7 billion for Ireland (plus €4.8 billion in bilateral loans) and €26 billion for Portugal	- €440 billion
Instruments	Loans	Loans, credit lines	Loans, bond purchases on the primary market	Loans, bond purchases on the primary market
Duration	Loans to be repaid after seven and half years after disbursement date in 22 equal quarterly payments	Until the end of June 2013	Until the end of June 2013, but will remain operational until all outstanding liabilities are repaid	Permanent mechanism from the beginning of July 2013 onwards
ECB involvement	Involved in programme design and monitoring and as paying agent	Involved in programme design and monitoring and as paying agent	Involved in programme design and monitoring and as paying agent	Involved in conducting sustainability analysis, programme design and monitoring and as paying agent
Main decision-making bodies	Eurogroup	ECOFIN Council, acting by qualified majority voting on proposal from EC	Eurogroup/EFSF Board of Directors	Eurogroup/ESM Board of Governors and ESM Board of Directors
Legal basis - *Financing* - *Conditionality*	- Intergovernmental decision and Treaty Article 136 - Treaty Articles 126 and 136	- Treaty Article 122 - EU Council decision on the basis of EFSM regulation	- Intergovernmental decision - EFSF framework agreement by cross-reference with Memorandum of Understanding and EU Council decision	- Intergovernmental treaty linked to amended Treaty Article 136 - EU Council decision under Treaty Article 136

Source: Adapted from European Central Bank (2011b).

In 2009, a high-level group on financial supervision in the EU, chaired by Jacques de Larosière, published a report outlining the proposals for reform of the EU regulatory framework. The report, known as the **de Larosière Report**, outlined 31 recommendations on regulation and supervision of EU financial markets (High-Level Expert Group on financial supervision in the EU, 2009). A key issue highlighted by the report related to the lack of a common rulebook across EU member states, which led to inconsistencies in crisis management and financial stability oversight. Therefore, the report proposed a two-level approach

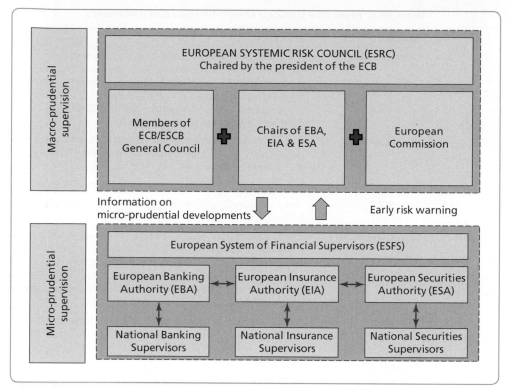

Figure 14.4 Proposals for EU financial supervision – de Larosière Report

Source: Adapted from de Larosière Report (2009).

to reforming the EU financial architecture centred around the creation of a new systemic risk board for the oversight of financial markets and high level co-ordination among national supervisors. The report recommended the creation of a European Systemic Risk Council (ESRC), chaired by the president of the European Central Bank. Figure 14.4 summarises the recommendations for regulatory changes made by the de Larosière Report.

The European Commission followed most of the report's recommendations and the new structure for European financial supervision started to grow. In November 2010 ECOFIN agreed upon the creation of a new **European Systemic Risk Board (ESRB)** and a **European System of Financial Supervisors (ESFS)**, comprising three functional authorities: the **European Banking Authority (EBA)**, the **European Insurance and Occupational Pensions Authority (EIOPA)** and the **European Securities and Markets Authority (ESMA)**. The ESRB was established on 16 December 2010 and the new regulatory system became operational as from 1 January 2011. Table 14.8 summarises the timeline of the key regulatory changes towards the establishment of a Banking Union.

The establishment of the European System of Financial Supervision, comprising the ESRB and the three European Supervisory Authorities, has contributed to improving co-operation between national supervisors in EU member states. It also contributed to the development of a Single Rulebook for financial services. However, the supervision of banks remains to a large extent within national boundaries and therefore fails to keep up with integrated banking markets. To further strengthen co-operation and improve supervision with the aim of restoring confidence in banking markets and in the euro, the European Commission put

Table 14.8 Towards a Banking Union: timeline and milestones

Timeline	Milestone
October 2008	The European Parliament called on the European Commission to fundamentally reform the supervisory structure of Level 3 Committees established in 2001 by the Lamfalussy process: the Committee of European Banking Supervisors (CEBS), the Committee of European Insurance and Occupational Pensions Supervisors (CEIOPS) and the Committee of European Securities Regulators (CESR).
November 2008	The European Commission mandated a high-level group chaired by Jacques de Larosière to make recommendations on how to strengthen European supervisory arrangements.
February 2009	Publication of the de Larosière Report on financial supervision in the EU.
June 2009	The European Council recommended establishing a 'Single Rulebook' for all financial institutions in the single market.
September 2009	The European Commission adopted proposals to strengthen financial supervision that would set up the European System of Financial Supervisors (ESFS) composed of the European Systemic Risk Board (ESRB) and the three European Supervisory Authorities (ESAs) for the banking (EBA), securities and markets (ESMA) and insurance and occupational pensions sectors (EIOPA).
December 2010	The three founding regulations (ESA Regulations) and the ESRB Regulation were published and entered into force in December 2010. The European Systemic Risk Board (ESRB) was established on 16 December 2010.
January 2011	The ESAs started their operations.
July 2011	The ESMA became the direct supervisor of credit rating agencies (CRAs).
September 2012	The European Commission presented a 'roadmap towards a Banking Union'. It proposed to set up a Single Supervisory Mechanism within the ECB and amend the EBA Regulation in order to strengthen the Economic and Monetary Union. The set of proposals is a first step towards an integrated Banking Union, which includes further components such as a Single Rulebook, common deposit protection and a single bank resolution mechanism.
December 2012	The Presidents of the European Council, the European Commission, the European Central Bank and the Eurogroup presented the report (known as the 'Four Presidents' Report') 'Towards a genuine Economic and Monetary Union'. The report sets out a road map for the creation of a genuine Economic and Monetary Union and builds on the vision presented by Herman Van Rompuy, President of the European Council, in June 2012.
March 2013	European Parliament and European Council agree on a Regulation amending the EBA regulation with regards to the interactions between the EBA and the ECB within the new Single Supervisory Mechanism (SSM).
July 2013	European Commission started a consultation of the ESFS review.
July 2013	The European Commission proposed a Single Resolution Mechanism for the Banking Union. The Single Resolution Mechanism complements the Single Supervisory Mechanism; it is set to centralise key competences and resources for managing the failure of any bank in the euro area and in other member states participating in the Banking Union.
November 2013	Regulation on the Single Supervisory Mechanism came into force.
January 2014	The EC adopted structural measures to improve the resilience of EU credit institutions.
March 2014	The European Parliament and the Council reached provisional agreement on the proposed Single Resolution Mechanism for the Banking Union.

BOX 14.5 EUROPEAN SYSTEM OF FINANCIAL SUPERVISION (ESFS)

Drawing on the lessons from the financial crisis and based on the recommendations of the de Larosière Report, the European System of Financial Supervision (ESFS) was created as a decentralised, multi-layered system of micro- and macro-prudential authorities. This supervisory system came into being in January 2011 and is currently (2014) undergoing major changes due to the introduction of a Banking Union.

The ESFS consists of two pillars: macro-prudential oversight and micro-prudential supervision (see Figure 14.5).

The micro-prudential pillar at the European level is formed by the European Supervisory Authorities (ESAs): the European Banking Authority (EBA), the European Securities and Markets Authority (ESMA), and the European Insurance and Occupational Pensions Authority (EIOPA), which work together in the Joint Committee of the European Supervisory Authorities (ESAs). These new authorities take over the assignments of the former Committee of European Banking Supervisors (CEBS), Committee of European Insurance and Occupational Pensions Supervisors (CEIOPS) and Committee of European Securities Regulators (CESR).

The three authorities have similar powers and competences in their respective fields. The EBA is headquartered in London; its scope includes *inter alia* credit institutions, financial conglomerates, investment firms and payment institutions (including e-money). The ESMA is located in Paris; its scope is directed at securities markets and their participating institutions. It is also responsible for supervising credit-rating agencies. The EIOPA's seat is in Frankfurt, Germany; its set-up is similar to that of the EBA, but its scope is directed at insurance undertakings, reinsurance undertakings, financial conglomerates, institutions for occupational retirement provision and insurance intermediaries. It is important to note that the responsibility for day-to-day supervision remains with the **National Competent Authorities (NCAs)**.

The Joint Committee ensures overall and cross-sectoral coordination in order to ensure cross-sectoral supervisory consistency. This includes: financial conglomerates, accounting and auditing, micro-prudential analyses of cross-sectoral developments, risks and vulnerabilities for financial stability, retail investment products, measures fighting money

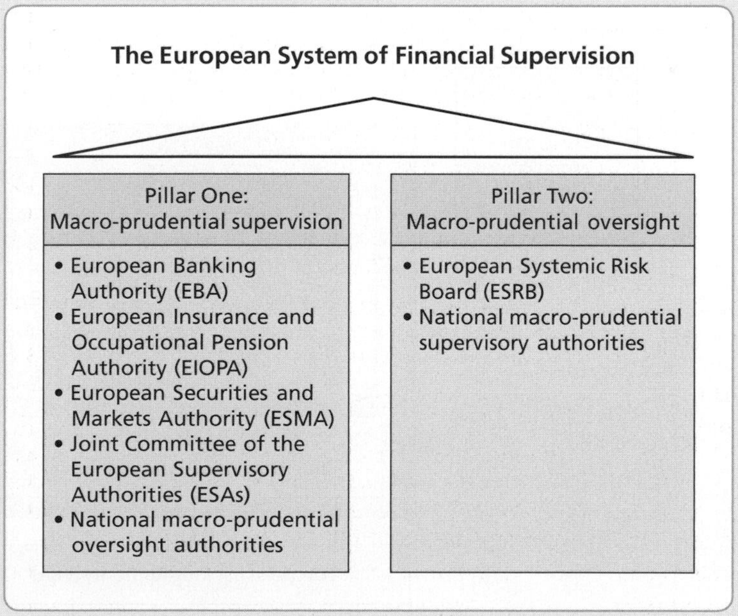

The European System of Financial Supervision

Pillar One: Macro-prudential supervision	Pillar Two: Macro-prudential oversight
• European Banking Authority (EBA) • European Insurance and Occupational Pension Authority (EIOPA) • European Securities and Markets Authority (ESMA) • Joint Committee of the European Supervisory Authorities (ESAs) • National macro-prudential oversight authorities	• European Systemic Risk Board (ESRB) • National macro-prudential supervisory authorities

Figure 14.5 The European System of Financial Supervision

Source: Adapted from European Systemic Risk Board (2011).

Box 14.5 European system of financial supervision (ESFS) (*continued*)

laundering, and information exchange between the ESRB and ESAs and developing relations between these institutions. The Joint Committee is responsible for the settlement of cross-sectoral disagreements between ESFS authorities.

The respective Member States' National Competent Authorities (NCAs) are also part of the EFSF. One objective of the ESFS is, *inter alia,* the development of a common supervisory culture and facilitating a single European financial market.

Macro-prudential oversight is conducted by the European Systemic Risk Board (ESRB), which is an independent EU body, seated in Frankfurt, Germany (within the ECB). The ESRB's task is to monitor the entire financial sector, to identify potential problems which could contribute to a crisis in the future, working in close cooperation with the European Supervisory Authorities (ESA).

Source: Adapted from European Parliament (2014).

forward a longer-term plan for a Banking Union. In June and December 2012, the European Commission presented its vision for the EU as part of a longer-term vision for economic and fiscal integration in the publication 'Towards a genuine Economic and Monetary Union', highlighting the following building blocks (this is also known as the Van Rompuy plan):[4]

1 An integrated financial framework.

2 An integrated budgetary framework.

3 An integrated economic policy framework to ensure growth, employment and competitiveness.

4 Ensuring democratic legitimacy and accountability in decision making in the EMU.

The Banking Union is the first of the four building blocks, which aim to deliver an integrated financial framework (see Figure 14.6). In September 2012 the European Commission

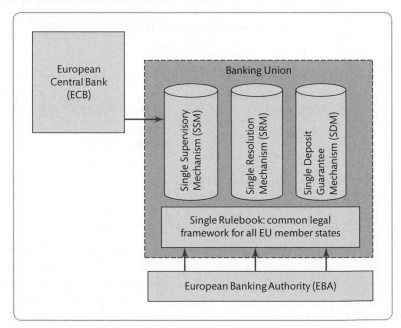

Figure 14.6 The Banking Union

[4] Van Rompuy (2012).

presented a detailed plan highlighting the central elements necessary to achieve its aim in the publication 'A roadmap towards a Banking Union' (European Commission, 2012). The central elements of the Banking Union are the following:

1 single European banking supervision (**Single Supervisory Mechanism – SSM**);
2 common deposit insurance (**Single Deposit Guarantee Mechanism – SDM**);
3 common resolution framework (**Single Resolution Mechanism – SRM**);
4 single rulebook (common legal framework, EBA single rulebook).

Before we discuss in detail the building blocks of the Banking Union, it is necessary to recall that the European Union includes countries that have adopted the single currency (the 18 countries forming the eurozone) and countries that are EU member states but have not adopted the euro (see Box 14.2). This distinction has caused EU reforms to follow a 'two-speed' path, one for the eurozone and one for all member states (some critics have gone as far as labelling it 'two Europes'). In this context 'two-speed Europe' does not mean creating a two-tier Europe, with first- and second-class citizens, it refers to the development of a closer integration among some member states while still pursuing objectives that are common to all EU member states.

In this respect, it is possible to classify the recent developments into two tiers:

1 Tier one – common to all EU member states: these include the creation of the European System for Financial Supervision, as discussed above. It also includes the 'Single Rulebook', comprising, for example, the Capital Requirements Directive (CRD IV) and the Capital Requirements Regulation (CRR), the Bank Recovery and Resolution Directive (BRRD) and the Deposit Guarantee Scheme (DSG).
2 Tier two – common to eurozone countries: these include more advanced integration measures towards the creation of the Banking Union, such as the Single Supervisory Mechanism, the Single Resolution Mechanism and the Single Bank Resolution Fund.

14.4.3 Single Supervisory Mechanism

In March 2013 the European Parliament and European Council agreed on regulation regarding the interaction of the EBA and the ECB's prudential supervision powers within the new SSM. The regulation came into force in November 2013 and was due to become fully operational in late 2014. The transfer of supervisory tasks to the ECB is based on Article 127 (6) of the Treaty on the Functioning of the European Union (also known as the Lisbon Treaty). More specifically, this regulation details:

- new competencies of the European Central Bank as supervisor;
- co-operation between the European Central Bank and the European Banking Authority.

The SSM is a component of the Banking Union; under the SSM, the ECB will be responsible for specific supervisory tasks related to the financial stability of all euro area banks as well as banks in other (non-euro area) member states voluntarily joining the SSM. The main aims of the SSM will be to ensure the safety and soundness of the European banking system and to increase financial integration and stability in Europe. The SSM confers to the ECB new supervision powers for the banks of the euro area. Under the SSM, the ECB will directly supervise 'significant' credit institutions and it will work closely with the national competent authorities to supervise all other credit institutions. Credit institutions will be classified as 'significant' based on:[5]

● total value of their assets;

● importance for the economy of the country in which they are located or the EU as a whole;

● significance of cross-border activities;

● whether they have requested or received financial assistance from the ESM or the EFSF.

On the basis discussed above, it is expected that the ECB will directly supervise all banks having assets of more than €30 billion or constituting at least 20 per cent of their home country's GDP, which includes around 130 credit institutions, representing almost 85 per cent of total banking assets in the euro area.[6] This number reflects a consolidated perspective; that is, banking groups that include a number of individual credit institutions are counted as one institution. All other credit institutions in the participating countries will continue to be supervised by the national competent authorities. However, the ECB can decide at any time to exercise direct supervision of any one of these credit institutions in order to ensure consistent application of high supervisory standards.

The main objective of an SSM is to centralise prudential supervision (in the hands of the ECB) to end national fragmentation and to ensure that the rules are applied in all cases and in the same way. The creation of an SSM should contribute to creating a more level playing field while decreasing the scope for regulatory arbitrage and the protection of 'national champions' in ways that breach the principles of the single market.

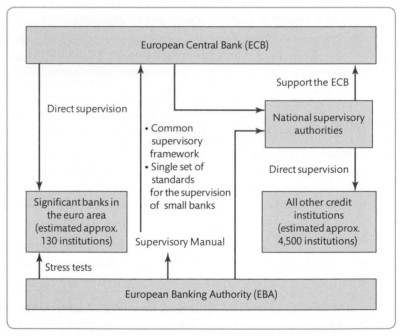

Figure 14.7 The Single Supervisory Mechanism

---

[5] See **www.ecb.europa.eu/ssm/html/index.en.html**

[6] Between December 2013 and autumn 2014 the ECB undertook stress tests on 128 eurozone banks under its Asset Quality Review.

In addition, it should improve the conditions for cross-border activity. Figure 14.7 summarises the main features of the SSM.

Non-euro area member states can also choose to participate in the SSM through their national competent authorities entering into 'close cooperation' with the ECB. For cross-border banks active both within and outside member states participating in the SSM, existing home/host supervisor co-ordination procedures will continue to exist.

The governance structure needs to ensure separation between the ECB's monetary and supervisory tasks, in order to eliminate potential conflicts of interests; to this end the SSM centres around a newly established separate Supervisory Board supported by a steering committee.

14.4.4 Single Resolution Mechanism

The second building block of the Banking Union is the Single Resolution Mechanism. As highlighted by the European Council in December 2012 and June 2013, it is not feasible to have a Single Supervisory Mechanism without a Single Resolution Mechanism. If bank resolution was left to national authorities, tensions between the supervisor (ECB) and national resolution authorities could emerge over how to deal with ailing banks. At the same time, as the 2013 financial crisis in Cyprus clearly highlighted, without an SRM market, expectations about member states' ability to deal with bank failure nationally could persist, reinforcing negative feedback loops between sovereigns and banks, and maintaining fragmentation and competitive distortions across the single market. Political agreement on the single resolution mechanism was reached in March 2014:

> Today's compromise allows us to complete the architecture of the Banking Union for the eurozone. It represents a major step towards the alignment of both banking supervision and banking resolution at a central level, whilst involving all relevant national players. Backed by an appropriate resolution funding arrangement, and an acceptable decision-making process, this second pillar of the Banking Union will allow bank crises to be managed more effectively. In case of cross-border failures, it will be much more efficient than a network of national resolution authorities and will help to avoid risks of contagion. The Single Resolution Mechanism might not be a perfect construction but it will allow for the timely and effective resolution of a cross border bank in the eurozone, thus meeting its principal objective.
>
> Together with reforms to the financial sector for all 28 countries, the completed banking union will put an end to the era of massive bailouts. It will further contribute to the return to financial stability, thus creating the right conditions for the financial sector to once again lend to the real economy which is essential to consolidate the economic recovery and to create jobs.

> Michel Barnier
> Internal Market and Services Commissioner
> Brussels, 20 March 2014

The proposed SRM applies only to banks that are covered by SSM; this means that the SRM would cover all banks established in all euro area member states and any other member state deciding to join the Banking Union.

The SRM Regulation builds on the Rulebook on bank resolution set out in the Bank Recovery and Resolution Directive (BRRD). It comprises establishing a **Single Resolution Board (SRB)** and a **Single Bank Resolution Fund (SBRF)**. In most cases, the ECB would notify that a bank is failing to the Board, the Commission and the relevant national resolution authorities. The Board would then assess whether there is a systemic threat and any private sector solution.

If not, it would adopt a resolution scheme including the relevant resolution tools and any use of the Fund. Once agreed, the national resolution authorities would then be tasked with the implementation of the resolution scheme. If resolution entails state aid, the Commission would have to approve the aid prior to the adoption by the Board of the resolution scheme.

One of the most controversial parts of the SRM is the creation of a Single Bank Resolution Fund to which all the banks in the participating member states would contribute (see Box 14.6). The Fund has a target level of €55 billion and would be owned and administrated by the SRB. There is a transitional period of eight to ten years, during which the Single Fund would reach a target level of at least 1 per cent of covered deposits. During this transitional period, the Single Fund would comprise national compartments corresponding to each participating member state. In the longer term, the resources accumulated in those compartments are to be progressively mutualised, starting with 40 per cent of these resources in the first year.

The proposed timeline for the SRM to come into force is 1 January 2015, whereas bail-in and resolution functions would apply from 1 January 2016, as specified under the BRRD.

BOX 14.6 EU REACHES DEAL ON FINAL PIECE OF BANKING UNION

Europe agreed the final piece of its banking union after marathon talks ended with a deal on a common system for handling bank crises that pushed Germany's red lines on cost sharing.

The breakthrough came after record-breaking 16-hour talks, ending a protracted political stand-off between the European Parliament and EU member states that threatened to delay the reforms.

Once formally approved by the parliament, the legislation will establish a single eurozone system to shut failing banks – the Single Resolution Mechanism – and a €55bn shared fund to cover costs, paid for by banks.

While the compromise falls well short of the parliament's opening position, the MEPs secured terms to ensure the fund is mutualised earlier and somewhat curbed the influence of finance ministers in decisions to close a lender.

MEPs hailed the compromise as showing they had the clout to make Wolfgang Schäuble, the German finance minister, make bigger concessions to them than his fellow finance ministers.

Although the compromise largely bends to Germany's vision for the system, some diplomats fear there is a small chance that the tentative deal could unravel, specifically over Berlin's discontent at being required to mutualise the fund more rapidly than it said was acceptable.

The reform is the final leg of an ambitious project launched almost two years ago to fuse financial oversight in the eurozone and improve the resilience of the currency bloc against the ravages of its debt crisis.

However, the resolution system has faced criticism, including from the European Central Bank, for being too complex and inadequately funded.

The final terms make hard-fought changes to the negotiating position of EU states, which was heavily influenced by Berlin resistance to German taxpayers being exposed to any bank bailout.

Michel Barnier, the EU commissioner responsible for the reforms, said the deal had been won through the "spirit of compromise".

"The Single Resolution Mechanism might not be a perfect construction but it will allow for the timely and effective resolution of a cross-border bank in the eurozone, thus meeting its principal objective," he said.

The main concession made to the parliament is accelerating the build-up of a common bank-paid fund from ten to eight years and front-loading its mutualisation, so that a bigger proportion of the fund is shared at an earlier stage. Under the provisional deal, 40 per cent of contributions are mutualised from the first year and 60 per cent from the second.

Box 14.6 EU reaches deal on final piece of Banking Union (*continued*)

This is the one area that significantly tests the position of Mr Schäuble, who said mutualisation should not be faster than the pace at which the fund is built up.

Some tweaks were also made to the decision-making structure. The Commission is given a formal role to approve resolution decisions recommended by an independent board. Finance ministers would be able to overturn the finding in limited cases.

The European Parliament and European Commission had pushed for a fully mutualised fund, with a strong external credit line, working under a system where Brussels rather than member states would have the final say on decisions.

Other revisions include giving the ECB, as top supervisor, the primary responsibility for triggering a resolution process when a bank is identified as facing difficulties. However, as demanded by member states, the resolution board would be able to push for the closure of a bank against the judgment of Frankfurt.

14.4.5 Single Deposit Guarantee Scheme

The third building block of the Banking Union is the creation of a Single Deposit Guarantee Scheme (SDGS). Recall that the aim of deposit insurance is to reimburse a limited amount of deposits to depositors whose bank has failed (see Section 7.4.1).

Deposit guarantee schemes in the EU were regulated according to a 1994 Directive (94/19/EC). In 2008, the need to restore confidence in the financial sector was paramount and the European Commission put forward a revision of EU rules and a proposal to promote convergence of deposit guarantee schemes within member states in order to improve depositor protection. The main changes proposed included the following:

- **Increased level of coverage for deposits.** The 1994 Deposit Guarantee Schemes Directive covered savings up to at least €20,000, although individual member states could choose to increase this level. The reforms proposed to increase the minimum level of coverage for deposits from €20,000 to €100,000.

- **Removal of co-insurance.** Co-insurance (i.e. where the depositor bears part of the losses) is to be abandoned. Member states must ensure that the deposit is reimbursed up to the coverage level. Under the 1994 Directive, member states had the option to decide that deposit guarantee covers only 90 per cent of savings.

- **Reduction of the payout period.** It was proposed that the time allowed for the deposit guarantee scheme to pay depositors in the event of bank failure should be reduced from three months to three days.

These proposals were adopted by the European Council in February 2009. The evolution of the eurozone crisis, however, highlighted the need for more drastic improvements, mainly aimed at increasing harmonisation of deposit insurance schemes within the EU, thus ensuring a uniform level of protection to depositors. In July 2010, the European Commission proposed changes to existing rules to further improve protection for bank account holders and retail investors. This involved amending the existing Deposit Guarantee Scheme Directive (94/19/EC). Specifically, the draft legislation proposes a harmonisation of the scope of coverage (type of deposits), the introduction of common standards on financing (where the lack of common standards has allowed for diverging models of *ex-ante* and *ex-post* funding schemes), a target fund size of 1.5 per cent of eligible deposits, the introduction of risk-based contributions, shorter payout periods (limited to seven working days), a clarification of responsibilities to improve insurance payments for cross-border banks, and limited cross-border borrowing arrangements between various national DGS. Moreover, in order to facilitate the payout process in cross-border situations, the EC has proposed that the host country DGS acts as a 'single point of contact' for depositors at branches in another member state (including paying out those depositors on behalf of the home country DGS, which would subsequently reimburse the host DGS).[7] The new draft legislation has been under discussion at the European Parliament and European Commission since 2010 and a deal was finally reached in December 2013 (see Box 14.7).

14.4.6 The Single Rulebook

An important piece of the puzzle in the integration process is the creation of a **Single Rulebook,** applicable to all financial institutions in the EU. The term 'Single Rulebook' was coined in 2009 by the European Council to refer to a unified regulatory framework for the EU financial sector that would complete the single market in financial services. The Single Rulebook aims to provide a single set of harmonised prudential rules which institutions throughout the EU must respect.

It is expected that the Single Rulebook will lead to a more resilient, transparent and efficient EU banking sector:[8]

- **Resilience:** a Single Rulebook will ensure that prudential safeguards are applied across the EU and not limited to individual member states.

- **Transparency:** a Single Rulebook will ensure that institutions' financial situation is more transparent and comparable across the EU for supervisors, deposit holders and investors. Lack of transparency is an obstacle to effective supervision but also to market and investor confidence.

- **Efficiency:** a Single Rulebook will ensure that institutions do not have to comply with 28 differing sets of rules.

While the creation of a Single Supervisory Mechanism represents a key step in strengthening Economic and Monetary Union by transferring the responsibility for the supervision of all the euro area banks to the European Central Bank, national supervisors will continue to play an important role in the day-to-day supervision of banks and in the implementation of ECB decisions. In addition, the fact that ten EU member states are not part of the eurozone has led EU authorities to propose that the European Banking Authority should develop a **Single Supervisory Handbook** to 'preserve the integrity of the single market and ensure coherence in banking supervision for all 28 EU countries'. The EBA is mandated to produce a number of Binding Technical Standards (BTS) for the implementation of the CRD IV package. BTS are legal acts which specify particular aspects of an EU legislative text (Directive or Regulation) and aim at ensuring consistent harmonisation in specific areas.

---

[7] See International Monetary Fund (2013a).

[8] **www.eba.europa.eu/regulation-and-policy/single-rulebook**

BOX 14.7 EU AGREES DEPOSIT GUARANTEE SCHEME DEAL

The EU is to finance better the guarantees offered to depositors under a long-delayed deal that will increase the levies that banks must pay to cover the costs of a lender failing.

After more than three years of stop-start negotiations, EU member states and the European parliament agreed on reforms to make available funds of up to 0.8 per cent of the banking sector's insured deposits for payouts.

The revision to the Deposit Guarantee Scheme Directive is one of a number of financial services reforms that Brussels is aiming to close in December. Last week preliminary approval was given to national rules on bank failure, which will require governments to impose fees on banks equivalent to 1 per cent of insured deposits, which will go towards the costs of resolving or rescuing banks.

While the EU deposit guarantee of €100,000 will remain the same, the rules will co-ordinate better the way governments arrange for that insurance to be paid. At present many countries have poorly funded or unfunded deposit guarantee schemes, which may ask for industry contributions after a payout is made.

"This is a good day for the taxpayer and for depositors. We have further severed the link between taxpayers and banks, and depositors will be able to receive their money more quickly," said Peter Simon, the parliament's lead negotiator.

Michel Barnier, the EU commissioner responsible for the reforms, said it was "another important step towards completing the single rule book on crisis management for credit institutions in the EU".

The weaknesses of the existing guarantees were brutally exposed after the 2008 financial crisis. The Cyprus bailout this year initially included plans to hit insured depositors, on the grounds that a tax would not trigger the €100,000 deposit guarantee. The revisions to the directive agreed on Tuesday night do not preclude the taxation of deposits.

The system of European deposit guarantees was also tested by the Icesave case, where Iceland refused to compensate UK and Dutch savers lured by high interest rates on the grounds that it faced a systemic crisis.

Under the deal, in principle, countries will need to build a bank-paid fund for deposit guarantees over the next decade, which could approach up to €53bn. The law requires this money raised from banks to be available in a crisis. Some countries would choose to set it aside in standalone funds, which often invest in sovereign debt.

With the approval of the European Commission, the fundraising target can fall from 0.8 per cent to 0.5 per cent of covered deposits in "concentrated banking sectors" – a concession that helps France.

Banks engaged in "risky" activities are required to pay a relatively higher fee, according to the deal. Up to 30 per cent of the fund can be in the form of "payment commitments".

The deadline for payouts is gradually reduced from 20 to seven working days by 2024. At least 70 per cent of this payment must be made in cash; the remainder can be deferred for a year.

 Source: EU agrees Deposit Guarantee Scheme deal, *Financial Times*, 18/12/13 (Alex Barker).

Key to the implementation of the Single Rulebook are stronger prudential requirements (the implementation of Basel III) and the implementation of a harmonised framework for bank recovery and resolution. More specifically:

- **CRD IV/CCR** (Capital Requirements Directive/Capital Requirements Regulation): the CRD IV package transposes – via a Regulation (CCR) and a Directive (CRD IV) – the new global standards on bank capital adequacy and liquidity issued by the Basel Committee on Banking Supervision in December 2010 (Basel III) into the EU legal framework. The regulatory package entered into force on 17 July 2013. While EU member states will have to transpose the Directive into national law, the CRR is directly applicable, without the need for any further action on the part of the national authorities. The CCR contains detailed and prescriptive provisions on capital, liquidity, leverage and counterparty credit risk. The Capital Requirements Directive (CRD IV), which must be implemented through national law, includes enhanced requirements for quality and quantity of capital, a basis for new liquidity and leverage requirements, new rules for counterparty risk, and new macro-prudential standards including a countercyclical capital buffer and capital buffers for systemically important institutions. CRD IV also makes changes to rules on corporate governance, including remuneration, and introduces standardised EU regulatory reporting which will specify the information firms must report to supervisors in areas such as own funds, large exposures and financial information. (For more details on Basel III see Section 7.7.4.)

- **BRRD (Bank Recovery and Resolution Directive):** this law, which applies to all 28 EU member states, is designed to ensure that failing banks can be wound down in a predictable and efficient way with minimum recourse to public money. It is fundamental to restoring confidence in Europe's financial sector. The Directive proposed a minimum harmonisation regime for the resolution of banks within the EU with the aim of ensuring a bank or an institution can be resolved speedily and with minimal risk to financial stability.

The global financial crisis and the eurozone crisis clearly have had a profound impact on the EU banking landscape. The regulatory framework has changed in the direction of a more integrated Banking Union. In the next section we will review the main structural features of EU banking markets as well as the proposed structural reform.

14.5 Structural features and the consolidation trend

The EU banking sector is large by international standards, both in absolute terms (€42.9 trillion as per January 2014) and relative to GDP. While total banking sector assets make up around 80 per cent of GDP in the US, and around 175 per cent in Japan, they are as much as 350 per cent in the EU (Liikanen Report, 2012). There is, however, significant cross-country heterogeneity; the largest banking sectors in absolute terms are those of the UK, Germany and France. However, relative to GDP, the largest banking sectors are those of Luxembourg, Ireland, Malta and Cyprus (all offshore financial centres). Figure 14.8 shows the total assets of euro area credit institutions in absolute terms (in million euros) and relative to country GDP. The credit institutions in the euro area had total assets of €34,516.5 million in 2013 and represented 361 per cent of the region's GDP.

Up until the late 1980s many European financial systems were characterised by relatively high levels of controls, where regulatory authorities maintained a protected banking environment

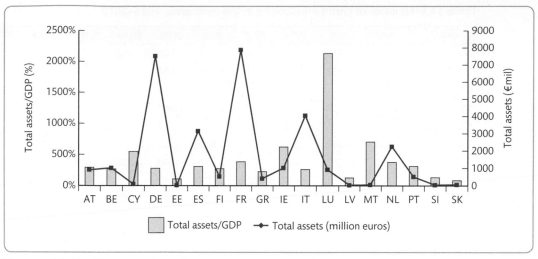

Figure 14.8 Total assets of credit institutions in the euro area, 2013

Notes: AT = Austria; BE = Belgium; CY = Cyprus; DE = Germany; EE = Estonia; ES = Spain; FI = Finland; FR = France; GR = Greece; IE = Ireland; IT = Italy; LU = Luxembourg; LV = Latvia; MT = Malta; NL = the Netherlands; PT = Portugal; SI = Slovenia; SK = Slovakia.

Source: Authors' estimates, ECB and Eurostat data.

that inhibited competition. However, market conditions have undergone extensive changes over recent years. On the demand side, customer preferences have changed substantially, becoming more sophisticated and price conscious. On the supply side (as noted in Chapter 2), the globalisation of financial markets has been accompanied by deregulation, financial innovation and automation. These factors imply an increasingly competitive environment. In addition, progress in technology has enabled financial firms to extend their activities beyond local or national boundaries and to increase their market share by providing competitive products to wider markets at a lower price. Technological advances have also enabled banks to reorganise their back-office activities, making the processing of financial information faster and more efficient. New suppliers of retail financial services, such as retailers, automobile manufacturers and so on, have entered the market. As such, banks are now faced with strong competition from both banks and non-bank institutions, and this also accentuates competition within the banking and financial services sector overall. This has been reflected in banks' efforts to rationalise their business, with pressures to cut costs. In addition, since 2008 EU banks have been undergoing a deleveraging process: for the euro area as a whole, banking sector assets in 2012 totalled €29.5 trillion, a decrease of around 12 per cent compared with 2008 (European Central Bank, 2013). This process of deleveraging was accompanied by a drop in the number of credit institutions following bank restructuring and resolution processes in many EU countries.

14.5.1 Structural indicators of banking capacity

Technological developments, deregulation at the EU level and the introduction of the single market for financial services, the global financial and eurozone crises have all played their part in restructuring European banking markets. This is reflected in the decline in the number of banks. ECB statistics indicate that the total number of credit institutions in the euro area at the end of 2013 stood at more than 5,846 (on a non-consolidated basis and including foreign branches), with a net decrease of 724 credit institutions over the period 2008–2013 (around

Table 14.9 Number of credit institutions in the euro area, 1995–2013

Country	1995	1999	2004	2007	2008	2009	2010	2011	2012	2013
AT	1,041	878	796	803	803	790	780	766	751	731
BE	145	117	104	110	105	104	106	108	103	103
CY			405	215	163	155	152	141	137	101
DE	3,785	2,996	2,148	2,026	1,989	1,948	1,929	1,898	1,869	1,842
EE			9	15	17	18	18	17	16	31
ES	506	386	346	357	362	352	337	335	314	290
FI	381	345	363	360	357	349	338	327	313	303
FR	1,469	11,163	897	808	728	712	686	660	639	623
GR	53	57	62	63	66	66	62	58	52	40
IE	56	80	80	81	81	492	489	480	472	458
IT	970	894	787	821	818	801	778	754	714	694
LU	220	209	165	155	153	174	146	141	141	147
LV			23	31	34	37	39	31	29	63
MT			16	22	23	23	26	26	28	27
NL	648	615	461	341	302	295	290	287	266	253
PT	233	223	197	175	175	166	160	155	152	151
SI			24	27	25	25	25	25	23	23
SK			21	26	26	26	29	31	28	28
Euro area	9,507	7,906	6,406	6,127	6,570	6,458	6,334	6,210	6,019	5,846

Notes: AT = Austria; BE = Belgium; CY = Cyprus; DE = Germany; EE = Estonia; ES = Spain; FI = Finland; FR = France; GR = Greece; IE = Ireland; IT = Italy; LU = Luxembourg; LV = Latvia; MT = Malta; NL = the Netherlands; PT = Portugal; SI = Slovenia; SK = Slovakia. The euro area total covers the EU member states that had adopted the euro at the time to which the statistics relate (see Table 14.3 for the date of adoption of the euro). The jump in the number of credit institutions in IE in 2009 is attributable to a reclassification of 419 credit unions as credit institutions.

Source: www.ecb.europa.eu/stats/money/mfi/general/html/mfis_list_102.en.html

11 per cent).While the reduction in the number of credit institutions has accelerated since 2008, the trend towards banking sector consolidation started long before the financial turmoil. This, in turn, has tended to increase the level of domestic market concentration where a handful of banks have a substantial share of banking sector assets. As Table 14.9 shows, a fall in the number of banks has been a shared tendency throughout Europe. Since the onset of the crisis, however, Greece, Spain and Portugal have recorded the largest decreases, followed by Italy, France and Cyprus.

Figure 14.9 illustrates the changing numbers of monetary financial institutions (MFIs) in the EU and euro area. The vast majority of euro area MFIs are credit institutions (i.e. commercial banks, savings banks, post office banks, credit unions, etc.), which represented 87 per cent of all MFIs (5,909 units) on 1 January 2014, while money market funds accounted for 12 per cent (816 units). Central banks (19 units including the ECB) and other institutions (46 units) together accounted for only 1 per cent of the total number of euro area MFIs (ECB statistics).

In the EU as a whole, credit institutions represented 88.3 per cent of MFIs on 1 January 2014, while money market funds accounted for 10.8 per cent (see Figure 14.10).

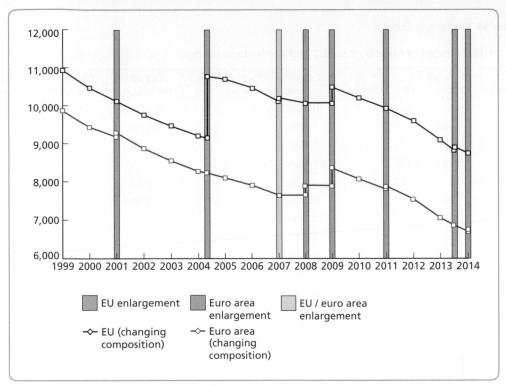

Figure 14.9 Number of MFIs in the EU and euro area, 1999–2014

Source: European Central Bank, Press Release, 21 January 2014, www.ecb.europa.eu/press/pr/date/2014/html/pr140121.en.html

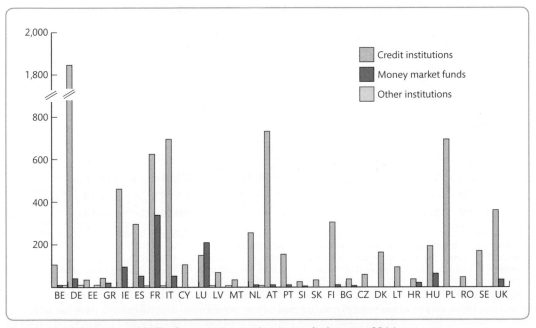

Figure 14.10 Number of MFIs (by country and category), January 2014

Notes: AT = Austria; BE = Belgium; BG = Bulgaria; CY = Cyprus; CZ = Czech Republic; DE = Germany; DK = Denmark; EE = Estonia; ES = Spain; FI = Finland; FR = France; GR = Greece; HR = Croatia; HU = Hungary; IE = Ireland; IT = Italy; LT = Lithuania; LU = Luxembourg; LV = Latvia; MT = Malta; NL = the Netherlands; PL = Poland; PT = Portugal; RO = Romania; SE = Sweden; SI = Slovenia; SK = Slovakia; UK = United Kingdom.

Source: European Central Bank, Press Release, 21 January 2014, www.ecb.europa.eu/press/pr/date/2014/html/pr140121.en.html

Table 14.10 Number of MFIs by country and percentage change

Country	2000	2004	2013	% of all MFIs euro area	% of all MFIs non-euro area	% of all MFIs EU	Change 2000–2013	Change 2004–2013
AT	910	827	741	10.68%	- -	8.47%	−18.6	−10.4
BE	153	126	116	1.67%	- -	1.33%	−24.2	−7.9
CY	- -	409	103	1.49%	- -	1.18%	- -	−74.8
DE	3,280	2,268	1,885	27.18%	- -	21.55%	−42.5	−16.9
EE	- -	25	35	0.50%	- -	0.40%	- -	40
ES	608	512	345	4.97%	- -	3.94%	−43.3	−32.6
FI	354	396	318	4.59%	- -	3.64%	−0.2	−19.7
FR	1,938	1,577	966	13.93%	- -	11.05%	−50.2	−38.7
GR	102	100	62	0.89%	- -	0.71%	−39.2	−38
IE	96	294	554	7.99%	- -	6.33%	477.1	88.4
IT	944	854	714	10.30%	- -	8.16%	−24.4	−16.4
LU	676	586	360	5.19%	- -	4.12%	−46.7	−38.6
LV	- -	52	73	1.05%	- -	0.83%	- -	40
MT	- -	17	31	0.45%	- -	0.35%	- -	82.4
NL	668	484	264	3.81%	- -	3.02%	−60.5	−45.5
PT	228	205	162	2.34%	- -	1.85%	−28.9	−21
SI	- -	27	29	0.42%	- -	0.33%	- -	7.4
SK	- -	28	30	0.43%	- -	0.34%	- -	7.1
Euro area	9,856	8,230	6,935	100.00%		79.29%	−10.2	−19.7
BG	- -		37	- -	1.89%	0.42%	- -	- -
CZ	- -	79	59	- -	3.02%	0.67%	- -	- -
DK	216	206	164	- -	8.38%	1.88%	−24.1	−20.4
LT	- -	74	92	- -	4.70%	1.05%	- -	24.3
HR	- -		56	- -	2.86%	0.64%	- -	- -
HU	- -	238	250	- -	12.78%	2.86%	- -	- -
PL	- -	659	692	- -	35.38%	7.91%	- -	5
RO	- -		42	- -	2.15%	0.48%	- -	- -
SE	179	255	174	- -	8.90%	1.99%	−2.8	- -
UK	556	475	390	- -	19.94%	4.46%	−29.9	−14.7
EU	10,909	10,856	8,746			100.00%	−19.8	−18.7

Notes: MFIs are central banks, credit institutions and other financial institutions whose business is to receive deposits, grant credit and/or make investments in securities. Money market funds are also classified as MFIs. AT = Austria; BE = Belgium; BG = Bulgaria; CY = Cyprus; CZ = Czech Republic; DE = Germany; DK = Denmark; EE = Estonia; ES = Spain; FI = Finland; FR = France; GR = Greece; HR = Croatia; HU = Hungary; IE = Ireland; IT = Italy; LT = Lithuania; LU = Luxembourg; LV = Latvia; MT = Malta; NL = the Netherlands; PL = Poland; PT = Portugal; RO = Romania; SE = Sweden; SI = Slovenia; SK = Slovakia; UK = United Kingdom

The euro area total covers the EU member states that had adopted the euro at the time to which the statistics relate (see Table 14.3 for the date of adoption of the euro). The EU total covers the countries that became members of the EU during the time to which the statistics relate (see Table 14.1). The jump in the number of credit institutions in IE is attributable to a reclassification of 419 credit unions as credit institutions in 2009.

Source: www.ecb.europa.eu/stats/money/mfi/general/html/mfis_list_102.en.html

In the euro area, Germany and France accounted for 42 per cent of all MFIs. Austria, Italy and Ireland accounted for a further 30 per cent. Over the period 1999–2013 there were relatively large declines in the number of MFIs in the Netherlands (−60.5 per cent), France (−50 per cent), Luxembourg (−46.7 per cent) and Spain (−43.3 per cent) and, to a lesser degree, in Portugal (−28.9 per cent), Italy (−24.4 per cent) and Belgium (−24.2 per cent). As illustrated in Table 14.10, among the non-euro area EU member states Poland had the largest number of MFIs (692 at the end of 2013), representing 8 per cent of MFIs in the EU, or 35 per cent of MFIs in the non-euro area. The other main contributors (in terms of the number of MFIs) among non-euro area EU member states were the United Kingdom (20 per cent), Hungary (13 per cent), Sweden (9 per cent) and Denmark (8 per cent). However, between 2000 and 2012, both the United Kingdom and Denmark witnessed considerable reductions (−30 per cent and −24 per cent, respectively).

Another indicator of the changing features of the banking sector relates to indicators of banking sector capacity, including the distribution of bank branches, the population per credit institution and per branch/ATM. The availability of banking services is also proxied by the population per bank employee and bank assets per bank employee. Table 14.11 illustrates these key indicators on banking capacity.

Table 14.11 Euro area indicators of banking sector capacity, 2012

Country	Number of branches	Population per credit institution	Population per branch	Population per ATM	Population per bank employee	Asset per bank employee	Population density
AT	4,460	11,220	1,889	1,028	109	12,592	100
BE	3,820	107,320	2,894	696	185	18,143	334
CY	866	6,375	1,009	1,219	68	9,969	94
DE	36,239	43,829	2,260	971	124	12,740	229
EE	176	83,731	7,612	1,523	241	3,536	30
ES	38,142	147,016	1,210	806	197	15,255	91
FI	1,404	17,293	3,855	2,404	240	26,524	16
FR	38,359	102,400	1,706	1,119	157	18,505	119
GR	3,629	217,117	3,111	1,321	198	7,743	86
IE	1,064	9,725	4,314	1,434	144	27,463	65
IT	32,528	85,247	1,871	1,171	197	13,604	202
LU	203	3,770	2,618	1,078	20	27,800	206
MT	107	14,945	3,911	2,128	105	13,320	1,308
NL	2,466	62,976	6,793	2,140	162	24,080	410
PT	6,258	69,752	1,694	616	185	9,692	115
SI	1,061	89,425	2,959	1,113	179	4,417	102
SK	695	193,080	5,095	2,245	290	3,201	110
Euro area	171,477	55,504	1,945	1,035	158	15,076	127

Notes: AT = Austria; BE = Belgium; CY = Cyprus; DE = Germany; EE = Estonia; ES = Spain; FI = Finland; FR = France; GR = Greece; HR = Croatia; IE = Ireland; IT = Italy; LU = Luxembourg; MT = Malta; NL = the Netherlands; PT = Portugal; SI = Slovenia; SK = Slovakia.

Assets per employees are in thousand euros. Population density is inhabitants per square kilometres.

Source: European Central Bank (2013). Available at http://sdw.ecb.europa.eu/home.do

The process of rationalisation and cost cutting during the crises period (2008–2012) brought about a decline in the number of bank branches by 8.7 per cent (in absolute terms, this represents a decline of 16,294 bank branches). The total number of branches at the end of 2012 stood at 171,477. In addition, the population per branch and the population per bank employee have increased steadily, in line with banks' efforts to reduce staff costs and branch networks.

14.5.2 Cross-border banking

The rapid growth of EU banking has been accompanied by an expansion in international activities, both within the EU and globally. The creation of the Single Market and the adoption of the euro fostered cross-border expansion, particularly prior to the financial crises.

On 1 January 2014 there were 645 branches of non-domestic credit institutions resident in the euro area, accounting for 11 per cent of all euro area credit institutions. Of these, 108 branches (17 per cent) were located in Germany. However, foreign branches in Germany account for only 6 per cent of the total number of German credit institutions and for 4 per cent of total assets, which is similar to the EU average. Belgium, Slovakia and Greece had the largest number of foreign branches as a proportion of the total number of credit institutions. Cross-border banking grew prior to the financial crises, but it differs substantially across member states. As Table 14.12 shows, in the largest EU economies the share of assets of non-domestic banks is limited, whereas in some smaller economies the foreign banking share is sometimes greater than 50 per cent of total banking sector assets. Post-crises, the share of domestic banking assets increased in Greece, Ireland, Portugal and Cyprus, due to the financial assistance programmes enacted by the respective governments under EU–IMF supervision.

Another factor that may be suggestive of the relative size of the banking sector is the amount of employment in the banking industry as a percentage of total employment. Traditionally, employment in the European banking sector has been substantially larger than in the United States or Japan. Having said this, however, it should be noted that the number of employees in the banking sector has fallen slightly in recent years – EU banking sector employment stood at 3.6 million in 2008 and had fallen to 3 million by 2012.

14.5.3 The consolidation trend

As already mentioned, a key feature of European banking systems in recent years has been the consolidation trend that has led to a small number of banks having dominant positions in various banking systems. During the 1990s the preference was for **national consolidation** as it appeared to offer clearer opportunities for reducing costs and fewer complications in terms of handling the merger due to a normally more homogeneous corporate culture. Besides, firms try first to establish a stronger national presence so that they are large enough to compete in cross-country consolidation. In the 2000s and up to the financial crises, emphasis was placed on **cross-border mergers** as domestic markets became increasingly concentrated. The EU's largest banks have grown even larger over time, leading to the emergence of large and complex banking groups (LCBGs). This term was introduced in 2006 by the European Central Bank (see Special Feature A, Financial Stability Report). The European Central Bank (2006) recognised the importance of identifying and monitoring the activities of large and cross-border banking groups, because their size and business model can have serious implications for financial stability in the case of failure.

Table 14.12 Number and total assets of foreign branches and subsidiaries in the euro area, 2012

Country	Branches			Subsidiaries		% foreign credit institutions	Total assets foreign owned	% foreign-owned assets
	Domestic	Other EU	Outside EU	Other EU	Outside EU			
AT	4,460	28	1	18	17	8.76%	216,389	22.20%
BE	3,820	35	24	21	6	83.50%	695,428	64.08%
CY	866	11	16	5	3	34.65%	44,307	34.58%
DE	36,239	88	20	22	15	7.87%	1,001,068	12.17%
EE	176	7	1	2	3	41.94%	6,749	34.31%
ES	38,142	77	8	33	10	44.14%	324,450	9.06%
FI	1,404	20	2	4	0	8.58%	399,730	66.59%
FR	38,359	65	22	56	61	32.74%	835,909	10.35%
GR	3,629	18	4	5	0	67.50%	72,329	16.36%
IE	1,064	35	1	15	11	13.54%	417,897	35.72%
IT	32,528	69	9	17	7	14.70%	567,687	13.45%
LU	689	8	0	66	34	73.47%	687,774	71.50%
LV	400	8	1	3	4	25.40%	20,546	72.49%
MT	107	1	2	11	2	59.26%	16,529	30.88%
NL	2,466	34	5	9	14	24.51%	273,274	10.99%
PT	6,258	22	2	7	4	23.18%	114,818	20.61%
SI	695	3	0	7	0	43.48%	14,902	29.34%
SK	1,061	14	0	12	0	92.86%	57,204	95.79%
Euro Area	171,477	557	123	310	187	16.97%	581,9643	17.78%
EU	217,716	743	228	439	289	19.43%	45,535,202	14.36%

Notes: AT = Austria; BE = Belgium; CY = Cyprus; DE = Germany; EE = Estonia; ES = Spain; FI = Finland; FR = France; GR = Greece; IE = Ireland; IT = Italy; LU = Luxembourg; LV = Latvia; MT = Malta; NL = the Netherlands; PT = Portugal; SI = Slovenia; SK = Slovakia.
Source: Authors' estimates. Data: ECB statistical data. Available at http://sdw.ecb.europa.eu/home.do

While some EU banking markets are dominated by large domestic banks (for example, France and the UK), others are dominated by foreign players, as discussed above. As per the end of 2013, the largest bank in the EU was HSBC (both in terms of total assets and market capitalisation), as the British bank overtook Germany's Deutsche Bank.

The large and complex group term has now been almost completely replaced by the systemically important financial institution definition, introduced in 2011 by the Financial Stability Board. Recall from Chapter 7 that SIFIs are determined based on four main criteria: (a) size, (b) cross-border activity, (c) complexity and (d) substitutability. The list of SIFIs (or G-SIFIs or G-SIBs) is published annually by the FSB. The November 2013 list identified 29 banks as G-SIBs, of which 14 were EU banks: Barclays (UK), BBVA (Spain), BNP Paribas (France), Deutsche Bank (Germany), Groupe BPCE (France), Group Crédit Agricole (France), HSBC (UK), ING Bank (the Netherlands), Nordea (Sweden), Royal Bank of Scotland (UK), Santander (Spain), Société Générale (France), Standard Chartered (UK) and Unicredit Group (Italy).

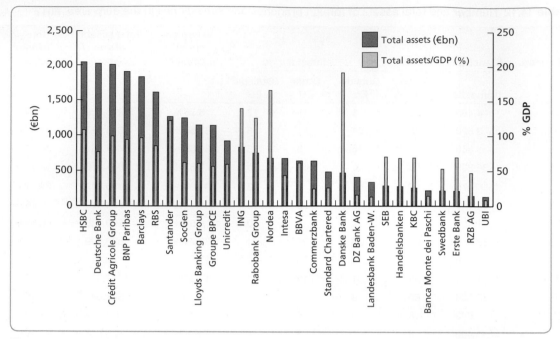

Figure 14.11 Size of selected EU banks, 2012 (assets in €bn and as % of national GDP)

Source: SNL Financial (total assets), Eurostat (GDP), Commission Staff Working Document Impact Assessment (http://eur-lex. europa.eu/legal-content/EN/TXT/?uri=CELEX:52014SC0030).

Figure 14.11 illustrates the size of selected EU banks (2012 assets in billion euros and as a percentage of national GDP). Particularly in smaller economies, large banks are bigger than the country's GDP, with important implications for financial stability.

Merger and acquisition activities have been declining since 2008 (both in the number and the value of transactions) and no substantial cross-border deal took place within the EU in 2012 and 2013. This trend is reflected in the concentration ratios across EU banking markets. When we compare the percentage of the banking and credit sector controlled by the five largest banks, measured in terms of total assets, we observe an increase in this figure for most countries. Banking sectors have become more concentrated in countries with relatively low levels of concentration as well as in countries undergoing banking sector restructuring processes (for example, Greece and Ireland). Yet concentration levels are decreasing in banking markets traditionally characterised by high concentration levels, for example in Belgium where the market share of the five largest banks decreased from 80.8 per cent in 2008 to 66.3 per cent in 2012 (see Table 14.13).

14.5.4 The Liikanen Report and structural reform of the EU banking sector

In November 2011 the European Commission mandated a High-Level Expert Group (HLEG), chaired by Erkki Liikanen, Governor of the Bank of Finland, with the remit to assess the need for structural reform of the EU banking sector. More specifically, the Group's mandate was to determine whether, in addition to ongoing regulatory reforms discussed in Section 14.4.2, structural reforms of EU banks would strengthen financial stability and improve efficiency and consumer protection. The Group delivered its report (known as the **Liikanen Report**)

Table 14.13 Five-firm concentration ratio as percentage of total banking sector assets and Herfindahl index

Country	Herfindahl index					CR-5 (total assets) %				
	2008	2009	2010	2011	2012	2008	2009	2010	2011	2012
AT	454	414	383	423	395	39.0	37.2	35.9	38.4	36.5
BE	1881	1622	1439	1294	1061	80.8	77.1	74.9	70.8	66.3
BG	834	846	789	766	738	57.3	58.3	55.2	52.6	50.4
CY	1019	1089	1124	1027	996	63.8	64.9	64.2	60.8	62.5
CZ	1014	1032	1045	1014	999	62.1	62.4	62.5	61.8	61.5
DE	191	206	298	317	307	22.7	25.0	32.6	33.5	33.0
DK	1229	1042	1077	1192	1130	66.0	64.0	64.4	66.3	65.6
EE	3120	3090	2929	2613	2494	98.8	93.4	92.3	90.6	89.6
ES	497	507	528	596	654	42.4	43.3	44.3	48.1	51.1
FI	3160	3120	3550	3700	3010	82.8	82.6	83.8	80.9	79.0
FR	681	605	610	600	545	51.2	47.2	47.4	48.3	44.6
GR	1172	1184	1214	1278	1487	69.5	69.2	70.6	72.0	79.5
HU	819	864	828	848	872	54.4	55.2	54.6	54.6	54.0
IE	800	90	900	800	1000	55.3	58.8	56.8	53.2	56.9
IT	307	298	410	407	410	31.2	31.0	39.8	39.5	39.7
LT	1714	1693	1545	1871	1749	81.3	80.5	78.8	84.7	83.6
LU	309	310	343	346	345	29.7	29.3	31.1	31.2	33.1
LV	1205	1181	1005	929	1027	70.2	69.3	60.4	59.6	64.1
MT	1236	1250	1181	1203	1314	72.8	72.8	71.3	72.0	74.5
NL	2168	2032	2052	2061	2026	86.7	85.1	84.2	83.6	82.1
PL	562	574	559	563	568	44.2	43.9	43.4	43.7	44.4
PT	1114	1150	1207	1206	1191	69.1	70.1	70.9	70.8	70.0
RO	922	857	871	878	852	54.0	52.4	52.7	54.6	54.7
SE	953	899	860	863	853	61.9	60.7	57.8	57.8	57.4
SI	1268	125	1160	1142	1115	59.1	59.7	59.3	59.3	58.4
SK	1197	1273	1239	1268	1221	71.6	72.1	72.0	72.2	70.7
UK	370	360	424	523	436	35.3	34.1	39.8	44.1	40.6

Notes: AT = Austria; BE = Belgium; BG = Bulgaria; CY = Cyprus; CZ = Czech Republic; DE = Germany; DK = Denmark; EE = Estonia; ES = Spain; FI = Finland; FR = France; GR = Greece; HU = Hungary; IE = Ireland; IT = Italy; LT = Lithuania; LU = Luxembourg; LV = Latvia; MT = Malta; NL = the Netherlands; PL = Poland; PT = Portugal; RO = Romania; SE = Sweden; SI = Slovenia; SK = Slovakia; UK = United Kingdom.

Source: Data: ECB statistical data. Available at http://sdw.ecb.europa.eu/home.do

in October 2012. The key recommendations included in the Liikanen Report can be summarised as follows:

- mandatory separation of proprietary trading and other high-risk trading activities;
- possible additional separation of activities conditional on the recovery and resolution plan;
- possible amendments to the use of bail-in instruments (where bonds convert to equity, in order to boost capital, in times of stress) as a resolution tool;

- a review of capital requirements on trading assets and real estate-related loans;
- a strengthening of the governance and control of banks.

Following a consultation period, the European Commission adopted a proposal for a regulation to stop the EU's largest banks from engaging in proprietary trading. The new rules also give supervisors the power to require banks to separate certain potentially risky trading activities from their deposit-taking business if the pursuit of such activities compromises financial stability. Note that these new rules apply only to the largest banks, those considered too big to fail, and in particular those with significant trading activities, whose failure could have a detrimental impact on the rest of the financial system and the whole economy. In this context, it applies to those EU banks that are deemed to be of global systemic importance (G-SIFIs) or to those institutions exceeding certain thresholds (€30 billion in total assets, and trading activities exceeding either €70 billion or 10 per cent of the bank's total assets).

After the consultation period, the EC agreed that imposing structural measures across the board would have disproportionate and unnecessary costs for smaller banks. It was expected that out of the 8,000 banks operating in the EU, only a handful (probably around 30) would be affected by the proposal, representing however more than 65 per cent of the total banking assets in the EU. With the aim of pursuing a level playing field, the proposal would apply to EU banks and their EU parents, including their subsidiaries and branches wherever they are located. It would also apply to foreign branches operating in the EU. It is expected that the proprietary trading ban will apply as of 1 January 2017 and the effective separation of other trading activities will not be compulsory before 1 July 2018. This reform is in line with those ongoing in the US (the so-called Volcker Rule) and the UK (the ring-fencing of core banking activities advocated by the Vickers Report). However, EU reforms do not question the universal banking model, nor do they call for a break-up of large EU banking groups.

14.6 Balance sheet structure and performance in European banking

The structure of EU banks' balance sheets was impacted substantially by the events of 2007–2010. On the asset side, the share of loans declined in the majority of countries, due to both the transfer of 'bad loans' to asset management companies and decreased lending. In addition, banks have been trying to build up capital and liquidity buffers, in preparation for Basel III. Cross-country differences are also stark; for example, the share of loans to total assets varies from 80 per cent in Ireland to only 49 per cent in France (European Central Bank, 2013). Differences are also attributable to bank size; for large banks, trading assets accounted for around 24 per cent of total assets whereas the percentage for small banks was around 2 per cent (and 4 per cent for medium-sized banks). The asset structure of small and medium-sized banks is, in turn, dominated by loans, particularly retail loans. These differences are illustrated in Table 14.14.

As regards the liability side, prior to the crises many banks increasingly relied on short-term wholesale funding. However, since 2008 banks have had to change their funding structures towards more stable sources, such as customer deposits and equity, while reducing their exposure to short-term wholesale and interbank funding. Banks adopted different strategies to reduce their reliance on interbank liabilities and to increase their liquidity and build up more stable funding.

Table 14.14 Selected balance sheet items (€bn and as a percentage of total assets), 2013

	All domestic banks		Large domestic banks		Medium-sized domestic banks		Small domestic banks		Foreign banks	
	€bn	% of total assets	€bn	% of total assets	€bn	% of total assets	€bn	% of total assets	€bn	% of total assets
Assets										
Cash and cash balances with central banks	1,343.3	3.90%	1,176.3	4.64%	155.3	1.95%	11.7	1.06%	307.5	4.10%
Financial assets held for trading	6,472.8	18.80%	6,328.9	24.95%	141.1	1.77%	2.8	0.25%	2,343.1	31.24%
Available-for-sale financial assets	1,764.5	5.12%	1,234.8	4.87%	509.7	6.41%	19.6	1.78%	338	4.51%
Intangible assets	235.5	0.68%	203.8	0.80%	30.77	0.39%	0.9	0.08%	18.4	0.25%
Total loans and advances	20,632.6	59.93%	14,515.5	57.22%	5,359.8	67.35%	757.4	68.75%	3,409.4	45.46%
Total debt instruments	5,840.1	16.96%	4,070.4	16.05%	1,555.9	19.55%	213.7	19.40%	1,547.3	20.63%
Total equity instruments	724.1	2.10%	512.07	2.02%	153.3	1.93%	58.7	5.33%	114.8	1.53%
Liabilities										
Total deposits from credit institutions	3,178.7	9.23%	2,039.9	8.04%	1,001.2	12.58%	137.5	0.124848	1,365.7	18.21%
Total deposits (other than from credit institutions)	15,163.2	44.05%	10,541.7	41.56%	3,831.9	48.15%	789.5	71.67%	2,229.2	29.73%
Total debt certificates (including bonds)	6,164.7	17.91%	4,744.9	18.71%	1,402.5	17.62%	17.4	1.58%	976.9	13.03%
Total equity	1,883.2	5.47%	1,326.2	5.23%	474.5	5.96%	82.5	7.49%	423.2	5.64%
TOTAL ASSETS	34,426.1		25,366.2		7,958.3		1,101.66		7,499.4	

Source: ECB statistical data. Available at http://sdw.ecb.europa.eu/home.do

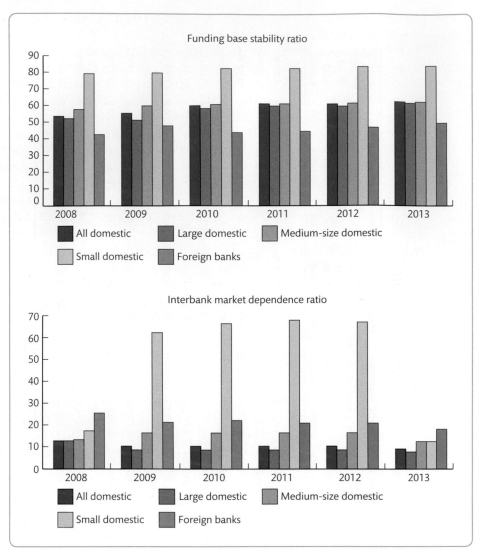

Figure 14.12 Funding base stability ratio and interbank market dependency ratio, 2008–2013

Note: The interbank market dependence ratio is defined as the ratio of deposits from credit institutions to total assets. The funding base stability ratio is defined as the ratio of total deposits (other than from credit institutions) to the sum of total deposits and total debt certificates.

Source: ECB and national central banks.

Figure 14.12 illustrates the trend of the interbank market dependence ratio (calculated as the ratio of deposits from credit institutions to total assets) and the funding base stability ratio (calculated as the ratio of deposits (other than from credit institutions) to the sum of total deposits and total debt certificates as indicators of bank liquidity.

The share of non-bank deposits to total liabilities has increased since 2008 for all bank types in most EU countries. However, there are still substantial cross-country differences:

the share of non-bank deposits to total assets ranges from 21.5 per cent in Ireland to 71.5 per cent in Slovakia (European Central Bank, 2013).

The performance of European banks has remained weak since 2008, although again this varies considerably from country to country, not least because of the different features of the specific markets as well as the general economic climate. However, there are some features common to all systems. Profitability levels have remained low since the onset of the crises (see Table 14.15), and ROA and ROE had returned to positive levels in most countries by 2013, however at values much lower than the pre-crisis peak of 2006 (only Greece, Cyprus, Portugal and Slovenia posted negative average ROE and ROA for their respective banking sectors).

Table 14.15 also illustrates recent trends in EU bank cost efficiency (as measured by the cost–income ratio). Cost–income ratios fell modestly between 2008 and 2013, from just over 70 per cent to around 60 per cent. Overall it appears that the trend is towards restructuring and cost cutting in order to drive improvements in bank efficiency. These figures, however, mask differences between countries and for various types and sizes of banks. For instance, typically cost–income ratios are higher for small banks compared with large banks, and are also generally greater for investment banks compared with commercial banks. Operating costs, as a share of total assets, also declined slightly between 2008 and 2013. Interestingly, these reductions were not driven by significant cost saving due to reductions in the number of employees – staff costs increased for large banks while they remained constant for small and medium sized-banks.

Cost reductions have been necessary as EU banks have been confronted by lower revenue (both interest and non-interest) since 2008.

Another factor negatively impacting EU bank profitability was the steady deterioration in asset quality during the crisis period, which forced banks to increase impairment charges and provisions (see Figure 14.13). However, higher provisioning did not keep pace with the increasing levels of non-performing loans. The latter were caused mainly by losses on loans and receivables, but also on other financial assets, including exposure to sovereign debts (particularly in the case of exposure to Greek debt).

Table 14.15 Selected income statement items (EU banks)

	2008	2009	2010	2011	2012	2013
Income structure (% of total assets)						
Interest income	4.4	3.2	2.84	2.96	2.75	2.46
Net interest income	1.1	1.3	1.34	1.27	1.1	1.09
Total operating income	0.1	2.2	2.2	2.15	1.9	2.03
Expenditure structure (% of total assets)						
(Total operating expenses)	−1.2	−1.3	−1.34	−1.34	−1.19	−1.23
Profitability (% of total assets)						
Operating profits	0.5	0.9	0.86	0.81	0.71	0.8
Efficiency indicators						
Cost-to-income ratio (%)	70.6	59.8	60.89	62.39	62.58	59.27
Return on equity (%)	3.2	0.3	3.9	−0.78	2.65	6.03
Return on assets (%)	−0.1	0	0.2	−0.04	0.13	0.33

Source: ECB statistical data. Available at http://sdw.ecb.europa.eu/home.do

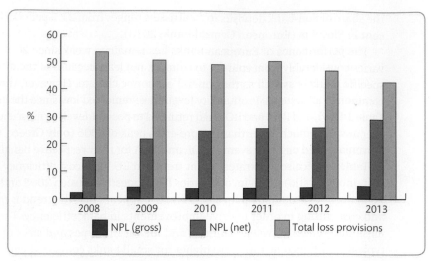

Figure 14.13 Non-performing loans and provisions

Note: NPL (gross) is: Total doubtful and non-performing loans (loans and debt securities) per Total loans and advances and Total debt instruments. NPL (net) is: Total doubtful and non-performing loans (loans and debt securities) per Total own funds for solvency purposes. Total loss provisions is Total loss provisions per Total (Gross) doubtful and non-performing loans.

Source: ECB statistical data. Available at http://sdw.ecb.europa.eu/home.do

EU banks have also been under pressure to increase their capital buffers, with some success: the median Tier 1 ratio increased from 8.7 per cent in 2008 to 12.7 per cent in 2012 (European Central Bank, 2013). These improvements were partly driven by the EBA capital exercise and by banks anticipating the Basel III requirements. Most EU banks decreased their leverage, through a combination of increased capital and reduced assets (by scaling back lending and selling assets) (see Figure 14.14).

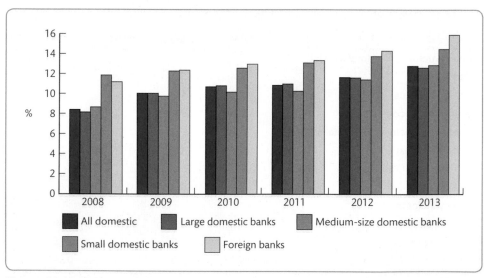

Figure 14.14 Tier 1 capital ratio

Source: ECB statistical data. Available at http://sdw.ecb.europa.eu/home.do

Overall, the EU banking sector was badly impacted by the 2007–2009 financial crisis and then by the eurozone crisis. EU banks are still struggling with low profitability and bad assets. Higher levels of uncertainty regarding changes in the regulatory structure as well as ongoing negative feedback loops between banks and sovereigns contribute to a more pessimistic outlook for EU banks compared with their US counterpars. On the positive side, EU banks have made significant progress in clearing up their balance sheets since the outbreak of the financial crisis in 2007 and a return to profitability seems likely in the near future.

14.7 Conclusion

Major changes are impacting on the global financial system and European banks are not immune from these developments. The EU banking sector is readjusting following a prolonged period of crises, which started in 2007 with the sub-prime crisis and evolved into a global financial crisis first and then a sovereign debt crisis. This badly affected all EU economies, and the eurozone in particular, leading to a number of bank failures and government bailouts.

In an evaluation of the causes of the crises, the Liikanen Report found that EU banks were taking excessive risks and relied excessively on short-term funding. Since then, a number of regulatory reforms have been initiated to ensure financial stability in the EU. The implementation of the new Capital Adequacy Directive (CRD IV/CCR) will encourage banks to improve their capital positions.

A significant step towards increased integration and enhanced financial stability was the creation of the European System of Financial Supervisors (ESFS), comprising three functional authorities: the European Banking Authority (EBA), the European Insurance and Occupational Pensions Authority (EIOPA) and the European Securities and Markets Authority (ESMA). To further strengthen co-operation and improve bank supervision, the European Commission put forward a longer-term plan for a Banking Union, comprising three pillars: a Single Supervisory Mechanism (SSM), a Single Deposit Guarantee Mechanism (SDM) and a Single Resolution Mechanism (SRM). All EU banks will also be supervised according to a common legal framework (a Single Rulebook). Ultimately, if the EU is to overcome the legacy of the sovereign debt crisis, the need to foster increased integration, particularly in the eurozone, appears paramount. It is also hoped that the new Banking Union will go a long way to break the link between banking and sovereign debt crises.

Key terms

acquis communautaire	Deregulation	European Financial Stability Facility (EFSF)	European Securities and Markets Authority (ESMA)
Banking Union	Economic and Monetary Union (EMU)	European Insurance and Occupational Pensions Authority (EIOPA)	European Stability Mechanism (ESM)
Cross-border mergers	European Banking Authority (EBA)		European Supervisory Authorities (ESAs)
de Larosière Report			

European System of Financial Supervisors (ESFS)	Large and complex banking groups (LCBGs)	Second Banking Co-ordination Directive (2BCD)	Single Resolution Board (SRB)
European Systemic Risk Board (ESRB)	Liikanen Report	Single Bank Resolution Fund (SBRF)	Single Resolution Mechanism (SRM)
Eurozone crisis	National Competent Authorities (NCAs)		Single Rulebook
Financial Services Action Plan (FSAP)	National consolidation	Single EU passport	Single Supervisory Handbook
Lamfalussy process		Single Market	Single Supervisory Mechanism (SSM)

Key reading

Allen, F., Beck, T., Carletti, E., Lane, P., Schoenmaker, D. and Wagner, W. (2011) 'Cross-border banking in Europe: Implications for financial stability and macroeconomic policies', London: Centre for Economic Policy Research (CEPR). Available at **www.voxeu.org/sites/default/files/file/cross-border_banking.pdf**

Beck, T. (2012) 'Banking union for Europe: Risks and challenges', London: CEPR.

Goddard, J., Molyneux, P. and Wilson, J.O.S. (2014) 'Banking in the European Union: Deregulation, crisis and renewal', in Berger, A.N., Molyneux, P. and Wilson, J.O.S. (eds), *Oxford Handbook of Banking,* 2nd Edition, Oxford: Oxford University Press, Chapter 35.

High-Level Expert Group on reforming the structure of the EU banking sector (2012) Final Report (Liikanen report), **http://ec.europa.eu/internal_market/bank/docs/high-level_expert_group/report_en.pdf**

REVISION QUESTIONS AND PROBLEMS

14.1 Describe the main trends that have influenced the structure of the European banking markets over the last ten years.

14.2 Starting from the 1977 First Banking Co-ordination Directive, what are the other important regulatory measures affecting the EU banking and financial sectors?

14.3 Discuss the impact of the global financial crisis and the eurozone crisis on the EU banking sector.

14.4 What are the lessons learned from the failure of large cross-border banks such as Fortis and Dexia?

14.5 Discuss the process of creation of a Banking Union for euro area countries.

14.6 Illustrate the European System of Financial Supervision and the interactions between macro-prudential and micro-prudential regulation.

14.7 Discuss the aims of a Single Rulebook in the context of the differences between euro area and non-euro area countries within the European Union.

14.8 Discuss the importance of cross-border banking in EU member states.

Chapter 15

Banking in the US

Learning objectives

- To distinguish between different types of bank depository institutions and investment companies operating in the US
- To understand the meaning of the disintermediation process
- To understand the characteristics of the US payment system
- To understand the main trends in the performance of US banks
- To understand the main tasks and organisation of the US regulatory authorities
- To understand the impact of the global financial crisis on US banking

15.1 Introduction

This chapter examines the main features of the US banking system, outlining recent structural and financial developments. Since mid-2007 the system has been involved in crises and has witnessed the biggest financial sector bailout in living memory. Since the onset of the sub-prime crisis, the US banking system has been transformed from one of the world's most profitable to teetering on bankruptcy. The first part of this chapter presents a brief analysis of the financial crisis and its impact on the US banking and financial sectors. We then look at the changing structure of the banking system, highlighting the consolidation trend, the increase in industry concentration and the radical post-crisis developments. We next outline the main types of banking and financial service firms operating in the US, discussing the major deposit-taking institutions and other financial firms. Since the passing of the **Gramm–Leach–Bliley Act** of 1999, US banks can establish financial holding companies and engage in the full range of financial services. The general adoption of the universal banking model and its implications for bank balance sheet structure, performance as well as regulation are discussed, and linked to the banking sector turmoil. The move to universal banking, however, has been reversed by the passing of the **Dodd–Frank Wall Street Reform and Consumer Protection Act** in July 2010 that limits commercial banks' activity in undertaking proprietary trading activities as well as owning hedge funds and private equity firms (under the so-called **Volcker Rule**). Under the new regulatory environment US banks are being forced to hold significantly more capital and liquidity, reduce their risk exposures and undertake increasingly conservative banking practices. Retail banking profits have become the main driver of commercial banks' performance since 2009, as returns from commercial and investment banking have dwindled.

The remainder of the chapter is organised as follows. Section 15.2 highlights the key events of the financial crisis in US banking. Section 15.3 reviews the structure of the US banking and financial systems while Section 15.4 focuses on the US payment system. The balance sheet features of US commercial banks are discussed in Section 15.5 while their performance characteristics are analysed in Section 15.6. The regulatory architecture of the US financial sector, including the changes brought forward by the passing of the Dodd–Frank Act of 2010, are discussed in Section 15.7, and Section 15.8 concludes.

15.2 The financial crisis in the US

The US banking system underwent a drastic transformation during the past two decades, driven by deregulation, financial innovation and a wave of mergers and acquisitions that led to increased consolidation and competition in the sector. These changes led to increased profitability and efficiency, increased provision of banking and financial services and to the international growth of US financial institutions. On the down side, these rapid changes also led to increased risk taking and instability which culminated with the financial crisis of 2007–2009. The crisis originated in the US banking system, with the demise of the **sub-prime mortgage lending** market, and led to financial losses, government bailouts and prolonged economic recession in many countries.

Since the onset of the crisis in 2007, much research has investigated the causes and consequences of it. In this section we aim to review the key events that led to the almost complete meltdown of US banking and the actions taken by regulators and policymakers to avoid it.

The origins of the 2007 crisis are linked to the housing market bubble and the development of the securitisation market (see Section 18.3). In the US, house prices had risen constantly from the mid-1990s until 2006, with the increased demand driven by low interest rates, rising household income and increased availability of mortgages. The increase in mortgage loan originations was coupled with a decrease in lending standards.

Sub-prime mortgage lending refers to loans made to relatively high-risk borrowers for property purchase. This market expanded rapidly from the early 2000s and was funded primarily by the securitisation of mortgages that were re-packaged and sold on to investors (see also Chapter 18). Box 15.1 illustrates the different type of mortgage loans available to would-be homeowners in the US.

BOX 15.1 US MORTGAGE BASICS

The mortgage industry in the US has some different characteristics from the UK or continental European industries. In the US, the Federal government created several government-sponsored entities (GSEs) to foster mortgage lending and encourage home ownership.

These include the Government National Mortgage Association (Ginnie Mae), the Federal National Mortgage Association (Fannie Mae) and the Federal Home Loan Mortgage Corporation (Freddie Mac). The GSEs do not originate mortgages themselves, but rather fulfil

BOX 15.1 US mortgage basics (*continued*)

their missions by purchasing mortgages originated by lenders, under the terms of separate, annually negotiated, contracts. The GSEs work by offering a guarantee on the mortgage payments of certain '*conforming loans*'. Whether or not a loan is conforming depends on the size and a set of guidelines implemented in an automated underwriting system.

The terminology used is typical of the US market and is illustrated below:

Conforming mortgages: a mortgage that is equal to or less than the amount established by the conforming loan limit set by Fannie Mae and Freddie Mac's Federal regulator, the Office of Federal Housing Enterprise Oversight (OFHEO), and meets the funding criteria of Freddie Mac and Fannie Mae. In 2013, for the eighth consecutive year, the one-unit (that is, a single-family residence) conforming mortgage loan limit is $417,000.

Non-conforming mortgages: mortgages that exceed the conforming loan limit are classified as non-conforming or Jumbo mortgages.

Jumbo mortgages: a Jumbo mortgage is a mortgage loan in an amount above conventional conforming loan limits. A **Super Jumbo** mortgage is classified as a mortgage in an amount greater than $650,000 (although this may differ between lenders).

Alt-A mortgages: Alt-A (Alternative A) mortgages are defined not according to the size of the loan, but according to the risk. In this case, the borrowers will typically have clean credit histories, but the mortgage itself will generally have some issues that increase its risk profile (for example, higher loan-to-value and debt-to-income ratios, investment properties, or inadequate documentation of the borrower's income). In this sense, Alt-A loans are 'alternatives' to the standard of conforming, GSE-backed mortgages.

Sub-prime mortgages: a type of mortgage that is normally given to borrowers with lower credit ratings. A borrower with a good credit rating will get what is called an A-paper loan (or conforming loan). Borrowers with less-than-perfect credit scores might be given A-minus, B-paper, C-paper or D-paper loans, with interest payments progressively increasing for borrowers' lower scores. Although there is no single, standard definition, in the US sub-prime loans are usually classified as those where the borrower has a FICO score below 640. FICO is a leading provider of credit scoring, decision management, fraud detection and credit risk score services.

The decrease in lending standards and the growth of the sub-prime market are well documented in the literature (Dell'Ariccia *et al.*, 2012). Table 15.1 illustrates the growth of adjustable-rate mortgages (ARM) (these are also known as variable-rate mortgages and are mortgages with interest rates periodically adjusted based on an index, which is designed to reflect the cost of borrowing for the lender), interest-only mortgages as well as low- or no-documentation mortgages.[1] Table 15.1 also documents the increase in the debt-to-income ratio (DTI – which represents the percentage of monthly of income that needs to be disbursed to cover mortgage payments and other debts) and in the loan-to-value ratio (LTV – the value of the house to the amount borrowed. For example, a mortgage of $150,000 on a house that is worth $200,000 results in an LTV of 75 per cent). Higher LTVs are often considered an indication of riskier lending practices.

These riskier mortgage loans were then used as collateral for the issuance of structured finance products, via securitisation (see Chapter 18 for a detailed discussion of securitisation). The issuance of sub-prime- and other mortgage loan-backed products grew from around

---

[1] In an interest-only mortgage, the monthly mortgage payment is made up only of interest on the outstanding debt, while the amount of capital borrowed is repaid on maturity. Low-documentation or no-documentation mortgages normally fall into the Alt-A classification.

Table 15.1 Sub-prime home purchase loans (%)

Year	Adjustable-rate mortgage (ARM)	Interest-only (ARM)	Low/No documentation (Alt-A)	Debt payment-to-income ratio	Average loan-to-value ratio
2001	73.8	0.0	28.5	39.7	84.04
2002	80.0	2.3	38.6	40.1	84.42
2003	80.1	8.6	42.8	40.5	86.09
2004	89.4	27.2	45.2	41.2	84.86
2005	93.3	37.8	50.7	41.8	83.24
2006	91.3	22.8	50.8	42.4	83.35

Source: Data from Freddie Mac, reported by the IMF at www.imf.org/external/pubs/ft/fmu/eng/2007/charts.pdf

$150 billion in 2000 to around $1.2 trillion by 2007. Up until mid-2007, the demand for these structured credit products increased exponentially: the market for mortgage-backed securities increased from around $2.4 trillion outstanding in 1995 to $7.1 trillion at year-end 2006.[2]

Figure 15.1 illustrates the increase in mortgage-related issuance. Recall that 'agency issuance' relates to issuance by government-sponsored entities (GSEs) such as Fannie Mae and Freddie Mac (more precisely, it includes issuance by the following: the Federal Home Loan Mortgage Corporation (FHLMC), known as Freddie Mac; the Federal National Mortgage Association (FNMA), commonly known as Fannie Mae; the Government National Mortgage Association (GNMA), known as Ginnie Mae; the National Credit Union Administration (NCUA), and the Federal Deposit Insurance Corporation – FDIC), whereas non-agency issuance, also known as private label issuance, includes issuance of non-conforming mortgages, i.e. mortgages which did not meet the limits set for conforming mortgages (see Box 15.1 for a discussion of US mortgage basics).

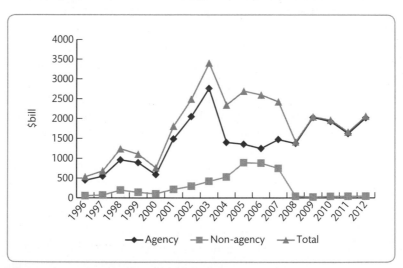

Figure 15.1 US mortgage-related issuance

Source: Securities Industry and Financial Markets Association (SIFMA).

---

[2] Data available from the Securities Industry and Financial Markets Association (**www.sifma.org**)

Figure 15.1 illustrates the rise of total issuance, mainly driven by agency issuance. Non-agency issuance started to become significant from 2002 onwards, reaching a peak in 2005 and 2006 and falling post-2007. Investors were attracted to these securities because they appeared to offer higher returns than similarly rated alternative investments.

At the top of the US credit cycle in 2006, around 20 per cent of US mortgage originations were sub-prime, and 75 per cent of these were securitised. When foreclosures and defaults on US sub-prime mortgages accelerated from late 2006 onwards, the value of the securities backed by such assets rapidly declined. Furthermore, property prices crashed, causing prime and sub-prime borrowers to increasingly default on their mortgages, further putting downward pressure on the value of securitised mortgage products and bank-loan books. This resulted in a liquidity gridlock in interbank markets and the subsequent 'credit crunch'. Key events relating to the US credit crisis are illustrated in Box 15.2.

BOX 15.2 KEY EVENTS IN THE US CREDIT CRISIS

December 2007 – the Federal Reserve introduced the Term Auction Facility (TAF). This was a temporary programme managed by the Federal Reserve aimed to 'address elevated pressures in short-term funding markets'. Under the TAF the authorities auctioned collateralised loans with terms of 28 and 84 days to depository institutions that are 'in generally sound financial condition' and 'are expected to remain so over the terms of TAF loans'. Eligible collateral included a variety of financial assets. The programme aimed to help banks raise short-term funds due to gridlock in interbank markets. (The initial programme envisaged $20 billion of loans under the TAF, but this ballooned – $1.6 trillion in loans to banks were made for various types of collateral under the TAF by November 2008.)

March 2008 – Bear Stearns became the largest casualty of the 'credit crunch' to that date when the failing investment bank was purchased by JPMorgan Chase for a nominal amount ($2 per share or $236 million) following the provisions of earlier liquidity support (a revised offer of $10 per share was made on 24 March enabling JPMorgan Chase to acquire 39.5 per cent of Bear Stearns). In addition, the Federal Reserve extended the safety net arrangement to ensure that JPMorgan Chase would not suffer significant losses on loans extended to Bear Stearns.

June 2008 – the FDIC took over IndyMac Bank, a large Alt-A mortgage lender (Alt-A mortgages are considered riskier than prime and less risky than sub-prime, and often do not require income verification of the borrower) that suffered large losses on these mortgages. The bank had $32 billion in assets,

making it the second-largest bank failure in US history. The estimated cost of the failure is $8.9 billion. The takeover followed a slow run or 'walk' on the bank of $1.3 billion in deposits withdrawn between 27 June and 10 July. This followed a public warning about the bank from Senator Charles Schumer. At the same time, Fannie Mae and Freddie Mac, which held or guaranteed more than $5 trillion in US mortgages (about half of the total), were having their own problems of a 'walk' on their outstanding stock and shares, both of which declined by more than 80 per cent in value from a year earlier.

July 2008 – Treasury Secretary Henry Paulson announced a plan to insure that Fannie Mae and Freddie Mac would continue to support the housing market. This consisted of a proposal that the Treasury would temporarily increase its credit lines to the organisations, that they may borrow from the Federal Reserve under certain circumstances, and that the Treasury would get temporary authority to buy their shares should that be necessary.

September 2008 – Freddie Mac and Fannie Mae were placed into conservatorship of the Federal Housing Finance Agency (FHFA).

September 2008 – Lehman Brothers collapsed and Merrill Lynch was sold to Bank of America. The two remaining large investment banks, Goldman Sachs and Morgan Stanley, converted into commercial banks. AIG, the world's largest insurance company, was rescued by the Federal Reserve courtesy of an $85 billion emergency loan, and in exchange the Federal government acquired a 79.9 per cent equity stake. Washington Mutual (WaMu) was acquired by

BOX 15.2 Key events in the US credit crisis (*continued*)

the US Office of Thrift Supervision (OTS) and the bulk of its untroubled assets sold to JPMorgan Chase.

October 2008 – the Federal Reserve announced that it was to expand the collateral it would lend against to include commercial paper, to help address ongoing liquidity concerns.

November 2008 – Citigroup failed and was rescued by the US government. In a complex deal, the US government announced it was purchasing $27 billion of preferred stock in Citigroup and warrants on 4.5 per cent of its common stock. The preferred stock carried an 8 per cent dividend. This acquisition followed an earlier purchase of $25 billion of the same preferred stock using Troubled Asset Relief Program (TARP) funds. The TARP was a plan under which the US Treasury would acquire up to $700 billion worth of mortgage-backed securities. After various revisions the plan was introduced on 20 September 2008 by Treasury secretary Paulson. Under the agreement, Citigroup and regulators would support up to $306 billion of mainly residential and commercial real-estate loans and certain other assets, which would remain on the bank's balance sheet. Citigroup would bear losses on the first $29 billion.

November 2008 – the Federal Reserve announced the $200 billion **Term Asset-Backed Securities Loan Facility**, a programme that supported the issuance of 'asset-backed securities' (ABS) collateralised by loans related to autos, credit cards, education and small businesses. In the same month, the Federal Reserve also announced a $600 billion programme to purchase MBS of government-sponsored entities (such as Freddie Mac and Fannie Mae) in a move aimed at reducing mortgage rates.

February 2009 – the US authorities presented plans for new comprehensive measures in support of the financial sector, including a **Public-Private Investment Program (PPIP)** of up to $1 trillion to purchase troubled assets.

March 2009 – the Federal Reserve announced plans for purchases of up to $300 billion of longer-term Treasury securities over a period of six months and increased the maximum amounts for planned purchases of US agency-related securities. The Treasury provided details on the PPIP proposed in February.

April 2009 – the US Federal Open Market Committee authorised new temporary reciprocal foreign currency liquidity swap lines with the Bank of England, ECB, Bank of Japan and Swiss National Bank.

The Federal Reserve released details on the stress tests conducted to assess the financial soundness of the 19 largest US financial institutions, declaring that most banks had capital levels well in excess of the amount required for them to remain well capitalised.

January 2010 – President Barack Obama announced plans to restrict commercial banks from carrying out securities business and to limit their size. The proposed reforms, encapsulated under the Dodd–Frank Act, prohibited commercial banks from doing proprietary trading (trading in securities on their own account) and from investing in hedge funds and private equity firms. No bank would be permitted to hold more than 10% of US bank deposits, with the definition of what constitutes deposits being narrowed to limit further concentration in the domestic US banking system.

December 2013 – US regulators approved the Volcker Rule, which aims to stop banks from making speculative bets from their own account (proprietary trading). This rule is one of the critical provisions of the 2010 Dodd–Frank Act. Despite its importance, it has taken almost four years for the rule to be finalised.

Source: Adapted from Valdez and Molyneux (2013) Table 10.3, pp. 294–295; BIS (2009a), Table 11.1, p. 19; and authors' updates.

The US response to the crisis is unprecedented in recent banking history. The US government attempted to tackle the crisis on several different fronts, with the overall aim of helping the economy. There have been a number of initiatives; the best known by far is the **Troubled Asset Relief Program** (TARP), through which the US government purchased assets and equity from financial institutions. The US Congress initially authorised $700 billion for TARP in October 2008; however, that authority was reduced to $475 billion by the Dodd–Frank Act. Of that amount, approximately $250 billion was committed to the stabilisation of the banking sector.

TARP measures aimed to remove bad or doubtful assets from bank balance sheets (or off-balance sheet) to strengthen banks' financial position – indirectly helping them to boost their soundness (capital strength) and provide greater confidence in the system so as to encourage lending. A report by the inspector-general for TARP carried out in January 2012 on the use of TARP funds by US banks confirmed that the programme was widely used and helped promote lending. The Treasury believed that TARP helped stabilise the financial system by providing capital to more than 700 banks. TARP funds were invested in both large and small banking institutions. At the time of writing (2014), US banks have paid back 99 per cent of the funds invested by the Treasury. And whereas banks participating in TARP at the height of the financial crisis held more than 98 per cent of all US banking assets, now that number is less than 1 per cent. Figure 15.2 illustrates the TARP funds outstanding. According to data from the Treasury, TARP's bank programmes earned significant positive returns for taxpayers. As of 31 December 2013, the Treasury had recovered $273.2 billion through repayments and other income – more than $28 billion more than the $245 billion originally invested.

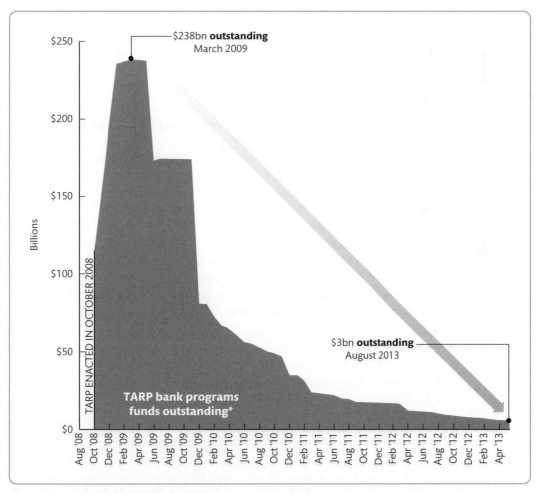

Figure 15.2 TARP funds outstanding

*TARP collections include $2 billion from loans refinanced under the Small Business Lending Fund.

Source: US Department of the Treasury (2013).

In addition to TARP, other programmes aimed at the banking sector included:

- Asset Guarantee Programme (AGP): under this programme, which began in January 2009 and is now closed, the US government supported institutions whose failure would have caused serious harm to the financial system and the broader economy. It was a joint programme between the Treasury, the Federal Reserve and the FDIC and it involved supporting the value of certain assets held by qualifying financial institutions by agreeing to absorb a portion of losses on those assets. Two institutions received assistance under the AGP – Bank of America and Citigroup.

- Supervisory Capital Assessment Programme (SCAP) and Capital Assistance Programme (CAP): these programmes were established to ensure that the US major banking institutions had adequate capital buffers to withstand losses and meet the credit needs of their customers in an adverse scenario (for example, a more severe recession than was anticipated). The SCAP was basically a stress test and it was conducted in early 2009. It assessed the 19 largest US bank holding companies (assets greater than $100 billion); 18 of them were found to have adequate capital buffers and therefore did not need further help under CAP, which closed in November 2009.[3] The SCAP proved to be a critical step to restore confidence in the financial system and get credit flowing again. Following the release of the stress test results, banks were able to raise hundreds of billions of dollars in private capital. A mid-cycle stress test was run in 2013.

- Capital Purchase Programme (CPP): this was launched with the aim of strengthening the capital position of solvent banks of all sizes, to help rebuild confidence in these institutions and in the US financial system as a whole. The Treasury initially committed $250 billion of TARP funding to the CPP; this was later reduced to $218 billion in March 2009. At the end of the investment period for the programme, the Treasury had invested approximately $205 billion under the CPP, providing capital to 707 financial institutions in 48 states. The final investment under the CPP was made in December 2009. According to the Treasury, taxpayers have already recovered more than the amount invested in banks through the CPP, and the Treasury is in the process of winding down its remaining bank investments.

- Community Development Capital Initiative (CDCI): this was launched in February 2010 to help viable certified Community Development Financial Institutions (CDFIs) and the communities they serve cope with effects of the financial crisis. CDFIs include community banks, thrifts and credit unions. Under CDCI eighty-four institutions received investments amounting to $570 million. The programme closed in September 2010.

- Targeted Investment Programme (TIP): this programme was established in December 2008 to help stabilise institutions considered systemically significant. Under the TIP, the Treasury purchased $20 billion in preferred stock from two institutions, Citigroup and Bank of America. The programme is now closed: Bank of America and Citigroup repaid their TIP investments in full in December 2009.

Economists seem to agree that the US response to the financial crisis, including the government fiscal stimulus, the bailouts of banks and other financial institutions, the introduction of

---

[3] The 19 largest US bank holding companies which were stress tested under SCAP in 2009 were Bank of America, JPMorgan Chase, Citigroup, Wells Fargo, Goldman Sachs, Morgan Stanley, Metropolitan Life Insurance Company, PNC Financial Services, US Bancorp, The Bank of New York Mellon, GMAC, SunTrust Bank, Capital One, BB&T, Regions Financial Corporation, State Street Corporation, American Express, Fifth Third Bank and KeyCorp.

bank stress tests and the Fed purchase of asset-backed securities, probably avoided a depression and saved millions of jobs (see, for example, Blinder and Zandi (2010), *How the Great Recession was brought to an end*).

However, while the financial crisis had for the most part ended by 2010, the post-crisis recovery has been very slow. In July 2010, President Obama passed the Dodd–Frank Act. The Act aimed to overhaul financial regulation and supervision in order to boost disclosure, transparency and the safety and soundness of the financial system. The Act's key changes include: the establishment of the **Financial Stability Oversight Council (FSOC)**; the introduction of new measures to deal with systemically important financial institutions (SIFIs); and the creation of a *Consumer Financial Protection Bureau*. In addition, the Act reformed the Federal Reserve; proposed ways to improve transparency in derivatives transactions by moving more over-the-counter transactions on to regulated exchanges; and introduced new rules on executive pay and credit rating agencies. Another important regulatory reform contained in the Dodd–Frank Act is the 'orderly liquidation authority' (OLA) granted to the FDIC. These key changes will be discussed in more detail in Section 15.7.

15.3 Structure of the US banking and financial systems

There is a wide range of financial intermediaries operating in the US system that provides a variety of banking and other financial services. A common way of distinguishing between such intermediaries is based on the main type of liabilities these institutions hold.

The main types of financial institutions include the following:

- **Depository institutions** – commercial banks, savings institutions and credit unions. The main types of liabilities these institutions hold are deposits.

- **Contractual savings institutions** – insurance companies and pension funds whose main liabilities are the long-term future benefits to be paid to policyholders and fund holders. These typically take the form of reserves that are listed on the company's balance sheet as part of liabilities.

- **Investment intermediaries** – mutual funds, investment banks and securities firms and finance houses whose liabilities are usually short-term money market or capital market securities.

The following provides an overview of the main features of these types of financial intermediaries.

15.3.1 Depository institutions

Commercial banks are the major financial intermediaries in the US economy. They are the main providers of credit to the household and corporate sectors and operate the payments mechanism. Commercial banks are typically joint stock companies and may be either publicly listed on the stock exchange or be privately owned.

As you should know already, their main liabilities are deposits (of different size, currency and maturity). Often a distinction is made between *demand deposits* (deposits payable on demand) and *time deposits* (deposits that have a term, e.g. three-month deposits). Deposits are either retail (small household deposits) or wholesale (large-value deposits from companies, banks and other institutions). Deposits can be denominated in the home or foreign currency.

Figure 15.3 shows that the number of commercial banks has fallen from just over 14,000 in 1935 to 5,876 in 2013. According to the FDIC's statistics on depositary institutions, commercial banks had $13.6 trillion in assets of which total loans amounted to over $7 trillion by the end of 2013.

The decline in the number of banks, a trend common in many other countries, has been mainly the result of M&A activity and recent years have witnessed deals between large banks that had the impact of increasing industry concentration. The share of banking sector industry assets controlled by the ten largest banks increased from 20 per cent in 1990 to 56.3 per cent by the end of 2012. Over the same period the market share of the top 100 banks has grown from around 50 per cent to 84.5 per cent. Figure 15.4 illustrates the number of small banks – those with less than $500 million – that witnessed a major decline in number over the last few decades. The passing of the Gramm–Leach–Bliley Act of 1999 also encouraged consolidation as it allowed the possibility of the creation of financial holding companies whereby banks can engage in securities underwriting, insurance sales and a broad range of investment banking and other financial services business. All major banks are part of financial holding companies, of which there were 489 by the start of 2014.

Table 15.2 illustrates the ten biggest US banks at different time periods. One can see that some banks have remained in the top slots since 1988 – Citicorp, Bank of America, JPMorgan (now merged with Chase Manhattan) and Wells Fargo. Others have disappeared – Chemical Bank (acquired by Chase Manhattan), Manufacturers Hanover (acquired by Chemical before the aforementioned Chase deal), Bankers Trust (acquired by Germany's Deutsche Bank) and First Interstate (acquired by Wells Fargo). Looking at the top US banks in December 2012 one can see Goldman Sachs (an investment bank that converted to a bank holding company status at the peak of the 2008 banking crisis), General Electric Capital (the banking subsidiary of

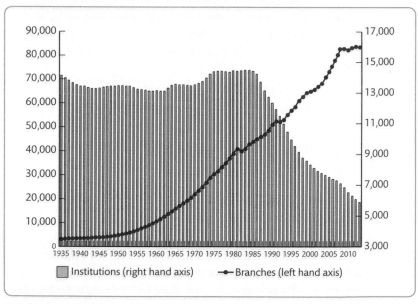

Figure 15.3 Number of commercial banks and branches in the U.S. (1935–2013)

Source: Federal Deposit Insurance Corporation. Historical Statistics on Banking, https://www2.fdic.gov/hsob/index.asp

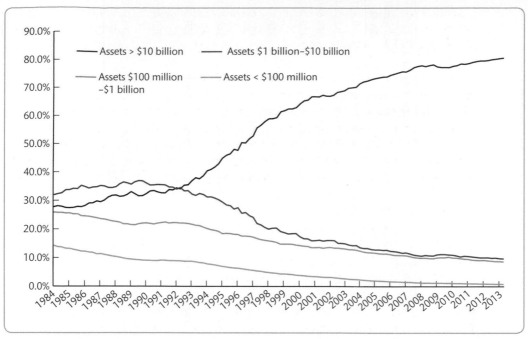

Figure 15.4 Share of industry assets according to bank size, 1984–2013

Source: Federal Deposit Insurance Corporation.

US conglomerate GE Capital) and Capital One Financial whose business has been built on credit cards and other consumer financial services.

Another interesting trend since the 1990s has been the increased international presence of US banks; and noticeably, non-bank subsidiaries have been the most rapidly growing source of foreign assets reported by US bank holding companies over the past decade or so. These subsidiaries undertake a range of activities, including securities underwriting, real estate brokerage and other commercial enterprises. The growth of these non-banking subsidiaries underscores the long-term trend towards diversification of earnings beyond traditional commercial banking products and services.

In general, the main strategic reasons for the foreign expansion of US banks relates to the desire to:

● grow profits by expanding distribution channels into new, potentially high-growth geographic markets and across demographic groups;

● provide commercial lending and capital markets products and services to complement the international expansion plans of corporate and commercial clients;

● increase revenue diversification; and

● cross-sell and leverage existing product expertise in foreign markets.

While major US banks have expanded overseas, it needs to be noted that liberalisation of the domestic banking market also fuelled increased foreign presence in the home market. In addition, the move to a universal banking model, whereby traditional commercial banking and markets become more closely entwined, is likely to have led to excessive risk taking – particularly in the securitisation of residential mortgage products and the granting of mortgage lending (see also Section 15.2).

Table 15.2 Ten largest US banking companies, ranked by assets ($mil)

	June 1988		December 1997		June 2007		December 2012	
	Bank	Total assets ($mil)	Bank	Total assets ($mil)	Bank	Total assets ($mil)	Bank	Total assets ($mil)
1	Citicorp	194,600	Chase Manhattan Corp.	365,531	Citigroup Inc.	2,220,866	JPMorgan Chase & Co.	2,359,141
2	Chase Manhattan Corp.	98,860	Citicorp	262,159	Bank of America Corp.	1,535,684	Bank of America Corp.	2,212,004
3	BankAmerica	96,923	NationsBank Corp.	260,159	JPMorgan Chase & Co.	1,458,042	Citigroup, Inc.	1,864,660
4	Chemical Banking Company	78,410	JPMorgan & Co.	157,274	Wachovia Corp.	719,922	Wells Fargo & Co.	1,422,968
5	JPMorgan & Co.	74,681	BankAmerica Corp.	140,102	Wells Fargo & Co.	539,865	Goldman Sachs	938,770
6	Manufacturers Hanover Corp	73,826	First Union Corp.	116,182	Washington Mutual Inc.	349,140	Morgan Stanley	780,960
7	Security Pacific Corp.	64,714	Bankers Trust New York Corp.	140,102	U.S. Bancorp	222,530	General Electric Capital Corp.	548,771
8	Bankers Trust New York Corp.	54,700	Banc One Corp.	116,182	SunTrust Banks Inc.	180,314	Bank of New York Mellon	359,301
9	First Interstate Bancorp	51,790	First Chicago NBD Corp.	114,096	Capital One Financial Corp.	145,938	U.S. Bancorp	353,855
10	Wells Fargo & Co.	44,721	Wells Fargo & Co.	97,456			Capital One Financial Corp.	313,040

Source: American Banker (www.americanbanker.com/data-tools).

The US financial system also hosts a variety of savings institutions that are similar in many respects to commercial banks, although the main difference (typically) relates to their ownership features – as savings institutions traditionally have mutual ownership. They are owned by their 'members' or 'shareholders', who are the depositors or borrowers. The main type of savings institutions in the US are the so-called **Savings and Loans Associations (S&Ls)** (or thrifts) which traditionally were mainly financed by household deposits and lent retail mortgages. Their business is more diversified nowadays, as they offer a wider range of corporate loans, credit cards and other facilities. Originally, the S&Ls were mainly mutual in ownership but now many have become listed. They compete directly with commercial banks, particularly in the retail and small to medium business sectors. There were 987 S&Ls by the end of 2012 with assets of $1.059 trillion – and they are the second-largest deposit-taking group of financial institutions in the US. Commercial banks and the S&Ls compete for personal and business banking services, although commercial banks focus more on larger-scale corporate banking activity.

Credit unions are another type of mutual deposit institution that are present in the US financial system and have grown in importance over the last decade or so. These are non-profit institutions that are owned by their members. Many staff are part-time. Member deposits are used to offer loans to the members. Credit unions focus almost entirely on the retail financial services segment and they usually are regulated differently to banks. In the US there were 7,165 at the end of 2012 with 93.7 million members with assets of more than $1,015 billion.

15.3.2 Contractual savings institutions

Although depository institutions constitute the main deposit-taking institutions in the US, it is also important to mention other financial services firms that also compete and/or complement banks in the provision of financial services. This is because these firms, especially pension funds and mutual funds, have become increasingly important relative to banks in the US financial system.

Insurance companies

Insurance products are an integral feature of the financial services sector and many US banks nowadays cross-sell insurance services to their banking clients. As discussed in Chapter 3, insurance companies protect individuals and firms (or policyholders) from various adverse events. They receive premiums from policyholders and promise compensation if an adverse event occurs. There are two main types of insurance company – life insurance and general or property and casualty insurance. The latter is insurance that does not involve death as the main risk. It includes home, auto and various commercial risks such as aviation insurance. A company that undertakes both life and non-life insurance is known as a *composite insurance company*.

According to the US Insurance Information Institute, the life insurance sector received net premiums of $568 billion and property and casualty insurance received $703 billion in 2012.[4] The US is the largest insurance market in the world, accounting for 27.5 per cent of global insurance premiums (followed by Japan, 14 per cent, UK, 7 per cent and China, 5.3 per cent). There were 2,660 property and casualty insurance companies and 913 life insurance companies in 2012. Tables 15.3 and 15.4 illustrate the main insurance companies operating in the US. Note that the fourth-largest property/casualty insurance firm in 2012 was AIG – this firm

---

[4]**www.iii.org**

Table 15.3 Leading US property and casualty insurance companies, 2012

Company	Direct written premiums[1] ($mil)
State Farm Mutual Automobile Insurance Company	53,654.20
Liberty Mutual Insurance Company	28,297.50
Allstate Insurance Group	26,531.00
American International Group, Inc.	23,596.40
Travelers Companies, Inc.	22,696.00
National Indemnity Company and its affiliated insurers[2]	20,236.50
Farmers Insurance Group of Companies[3]	18,311.40
Nationwide Mutual Insurance Company	17,042.90
Progressive Insurance Group	16,559.70
United Services Automobile Association	13,286.30

Notes: [1]Before reinsurance transactions, includes some state funds.

[2]Owned by Berkshire Hathaway.

[3]Data for Farmers Group and Zurich Financial Group (which owns Farmers' management company) are reported separately by SNL Financial.

Source: SNL Financial (**www.snl.com**).

Table 15.4 Leading US life insurance companies, 2012

Company	Direct written premiums[1] ($mil)
MetLife Inc.	102,321.50
Prudential Financial Inc.	85,852.80
Jackson National Life Group	24,206.90
New York Life Insurance Group	24,010.50
ING Groep N.V.	23,513.20
Lincoln National Corp.	21,004.30
Manulife Financial Corp.	20,965.70
Massachusetts Mutual Life Insurance Co.	20,751.70
AEGON NV	19,695.60
Principal Financial Group Inc.	18,337.00

Note: [1]Includes life insurance, annuity considerations, deposit-type contract funds, other considerations; excludes accident and health insurance from life/health insurers. Before reinsurance transactions.

Source: SNL Financial (**www.snl.com**).

failed on 16 September 2008. It suffered from a liquidity crisis as a result of its credit rating being downgraded due to its large exposure to losses in the credit default swaps market. AIG was a major underwriter of credit default swaps that were purchased to insure against bond defaults. When major defaults occurred AIG had to make substantial payouts – it had done little hedging to cover these risks. The Federal Reserve had to create an $85 billion credit facility to bail out the insurer (for 79.9 per cent of the equity) and later the US government revised the credit facility and it eventually amounted to $182.5 billion. Effectively these moves nationalised one of the world's largest insurance companies.

Pension funds

Pension funds provide retirement income (in the form of annuities) to employees covered by pension plans. They obtain their income from contributions made by employees and employers and invest these in a variety of long-term securities (bonds and equity) and other investments such as property. A distinction is made between private and public pension funds:

- **Private pension funds** are pension funds that are administered by a bank, life insurance firm or pension fund manager. Contributions paid into the fund by employers and employees are invested in long-term investments with the individual making contributions receiving a pension on retirement. Note, however, that many company pension plans are underfunded because they aim to meet pension obligations out of current earnings when benefits are due. If companies have sufficient earnings then this underfunding is not a problem but if not then they cannot meet pension obligations. Various pieces of legislation have been put in place, particularly in the US and UK, to try to minimise the likelihood of major underfunding but it continues to be an important issue for many large private pension funds.

- **Public pension funds** are the pension provisions of the government. In the US the most important public pension plan is the Social Security Old Age and Survivors Insurance Fund.

15.3.3 Investment intermediaries

Investment intermediaries are financial companies whose liabilities are usually short-term money market or capital market securities. These include mutual funds, investment banks and securities firms and finance houses.

Mutual funds

A mutual fund is a company that pools the money of many investors – its shareholders – so as to invest in a range of different securities. Investments may be in stocks, bonds, money market securities or some combination of these. Mutual funds are professionally managed on behalf of the shareholders, and each investor holds a share of the portfolio and is entitled to any profits (and losses) when the securities are sold.

There are two main segments of the mutual fund industry – long-term and short-term funds. Long-term funds include bond funds, equity funds and other hybrid funds that contain a mix of bonds and equity. Short-term funds are known as money market funds and they are comprised of a range of money market instruments – in the US (where the market for mutual funds in general is most developed) they also allow shareholders to write cheques against the value of money market funds (these are known as *money market fund checking accounts*).

The main attraction for investors is that mutual funds provide diversification benefits as their assets are invested in many different securities. Note that there are many different types of mutual funds with different risk-return objectives. In the US more than $13 trillion was invested in some 8,750 mutual funds by the end of 2012.[5]

Investment banks and securities firms

As we noted in Chapter 3, the world's largest investment banks come from the US, including such firms as Goldman Sachs and Morgan Stanley. Their main function is to help companies and governments raise funds in the capital markets and business relating to issuing new debt

---

[5] For more detail on the US mutual funds industry see **www.ici.org/research#statistics**

and equity, which they arrange on behalf of clients, as well as providing corporate advisory services on mergers and acquisitions and other types of corporate restructuring. Since the repeal of the Glass-Steagall Act in 1999 various US commercial banks have acquired investment banks. This means that banks such as Citigroup and JPMorgan Chase now offer both commercial and investment banking services.

Despite its long and successful pedigree, the US investment banking industry has been almost destroyed by the credit crisis. Bear Stearns and Lehman Brothers failed in 2008; Merrill Lynch merged with Bank of America; Goldman Sachs and Morgan Stanley converted into bank holding companies. By the end of 2009, none of the largest investment banks had the same corporate form they had at the start of 2007. The industry had been also blamed for the excesses that led to the crisis (see also Section 3.6).

Securities firms

Securities firms assist in the trading of existing securities. There are two main types of securities firms: *brokers* (agents of investors that match buyers with sellers of securities) and *dealers* (agents who link buyers and sellers by buying and selling securities). In the US there are specialist discount brokers, for instance, that undertake trading activities for clients without providing advice (like Charles Schwab) and specialist electronic trading securities firms (E*trade).

Table 15.5 provides a snapshot of the evolution and relative size of various types of financial firms in the US and highlights the relative long-term decline of depository firms compared to mutual funds between 1980 and 2012. The decline is a reflection of the **disintermediation** trend, where customers bypass intermediaries so as to obtain improved returns from direct financing. However, the increased market activity of banks in recent years (up to the crisis at least) reversed this trend, although mutual funds and pension funds have increased in relative importance post-crisis.

In formal terms, disintermediation occurs where ultimate borrowers and ultimate lenders by-pass the established financial intermediation channels and borrow/lend directly. Traditionally, for large corporate borrowers possessing high credit ratings, it may simply be cheaper to raise funds direct from savers/investors than via a financial intermediary. The costs associated with the intermediary are cut out of the transaction to the benefit of both borrowers and lenders. There are also other advantages for companies in terms of raising market profile and the diversification of sources of funds. However, these benefits must be weighed against the costs (i.e. financial intermediation foregone). A good example of disintermediation in this context is the use of commercial paper issues by large companies as a means of raising short-term funds.

While the cost factor is the main commercial driver of disintermediation, it may also occur on account of official restrictions being placed on normal intermediation activity, perhaps with the purpose of controlling the money supply. Borrowers may be turned away from financial intermediaries and hence may seek other sources of funds, directly from savers/investors. Whatever the cause, it is clear from Table 15.5 that the decline in depository institutions is a sign that the disintermediation process has been prevalent in the US.

One area where it seems that disintermediation has been prevalent is in the emergence of the so-called *shadow banking system* (see Chapter 18 for a detailed discussion). Many firms involved in the securitisation business – hedge funds, private equity firms, structured investment companies, money market funds – either traded with banks or undertook banking-type activities but were not subject to the same regulations. This meant that a large part of the

Table 15.5 US financial intermediaries (market share, total assets)

	1980	2012
Depository institutions (banks, thrifts, credit unions)	50.6	24.5
Pension funds (public and private)	18.0	18.5
Insurance companies	14.8	11.5
Mortgage finance companies and funds*	7.1	16.3
Finance companies	4.9	2.5
Mutual funds (stock, bond, money market)	3.3	19.9
Securities firms (brokers, dealers, funding corporations)**	1.4	6.9
Total	**100.0%**	**100.0%**

Notes: *Includes government-sponsored entities (GSEs) and pools they sponsor, private mortgage securitisers and pools they sponsor, mortgage banks, and real estate investment trusts (REITs).

** Includes assets held by investment banks.

Source: Federal Reserve System Flow of Funds Accounts.

financial system fell outside traditional banking sector regulations and therefore could operate in an unregulated environment. Shadow banking first emerged in the US on the back of the securitisation business.[6]

15.4   US payments systems

Having a well-functioning payments system is critical for the smooth running of an economy. The challenges posed by the ever-changing demands of individuals, firms and government, and technological advances, impact on the evolution of the payments system. As in most developed countries, the US has two main parts to its payments system – one that deals with wholesale large-value payments and another that deals with retail and relatively small-value payments.

15.4.1   Wholesale payments

In the US, payment and securities settlement systems involve a large number of financial intermediaries, financial services firms and non-bank businesses that create, distribute and process large-value payments. The bulk of the dollar value of these payments is processed electronically and is generally used to purchase, sell or finance securities transactions; to make or repay loans; settle real estate transactions; and make large-value, time-critical payments, such as those for the settlement of interbank purchases, settlement of foreign exchange transactions or other financial market transactions.

There are two main networks for interbank, or large-value, domestic, funds transfer payment orders. The first, **Fedwire**, is owned and operated by the Federal Reserve Banks, and is an important participant in providing interbank payment services as well as safekeeping and transfer services for US government and agency securities, and mortgage-backed securities.

---

[6] See Pozsar *et al.*, 2010 for an excellent account of shadow banking.

Fedwire is a real-time gross settlement (RTGS) system that enables participants to make final payments in central bank money.[7] Fedwire consists of a range of procedures and computer applications to route and settle payment orders: the system reviews payment orders and notifies participants of related credits and debits to their accounts. Fedwire is supported by the Federal Reserve's FEDNET national communications network.

An institution that holds an account with a Federal Reserve Bank generally can become a Fedwire participant. These participants use Fedwire to instruct a Federal Reserve Bank to debit funds from the participant's own Federal Reserve account and credit the Federal Reserve account of another participant. Fedwire processes and settles payment orders individually throughout the operating day. Payment to the receiving participant over Fedwire is final and irrevocable when the amount of the payment order is credited to the receiving participant's account or when the payment order is sent to the receiving participant, whichever is earlier. Fedwire participants send payment orders electronically or by phone to a Federal Reserve Bank. Payment orders must be in the proper syntax and meet the relevant security controls. An institution sending payment orders to a Federal Reserve Bank is required to have sufficient funds either in the form of account balances or overdraft capacity, or a payment order may be rejected.

The value of payments conducted via Fedwire amounted to more than $2.4 trillion per day (from an average of 524,452 daily transactions) during 2012.

The second major wholesale payments system is known as **CHIPS**, the Clearing House Interbank Payments System, and this is the main bank-owned payments system for clearing large-value payments. CHIPS is a real-time payments system for US dollars that uses bilateral and multilateral netting (where payments are netted out between bank participants). In 2013 CHIPS processed more than 420,000 payments a day with a gross value of $1.5 trillion. Much of CHIPS business relates to cross-border payments in US dollars. The number of participants using CHIPS has fallen from 104 in 1996 to 50 in 2013, reflecting consolidation between major banks. Also, the value of transactions conducted via CHIPS has declined since 1997 from around 40 times GDP to under 23 times by 2013 – as a result of the fall in the number of participating banks and also possibly due to the reduction in fees charged by Fedwire for wholesale payments.

The processing of large-value funds transfers involves two important elements: *clearing* and *settlement*. Clearing relates to the transfer and confirmation of information between the payer (sending financial institution) and payee (receiving financial institution). Settlement is the transfer of funds between the payer's financial institution and the payee's financial institution. Settlement discharges the obligation of the payer's financial institution to the payee's financial institution with respect to the payment order. Final settlement is irrevocable and unconditional. The finality of the payment is determined by the rules and the relevant laws that apply.

In general, payment messages may be credit transfers or debit transfers. Most large-value funds transfer systems are credit transfer systems in which both payment messages and funds move from the payer financial institution to the payee financial institution. An institution initiates a funds transfer by transmitting a payment order (a message that requests the transfer of funds to the payee). Payment order processing follows the rules and operating procedures of the large-value payment system used. Typically, large-value payment system operating procedures include identification, reconciliation and confirmation procedures necessary to

---

[7] A real-time gross settlement system is a payment system in which processing and settlement of transactions take place in real time (continuously).

process the payment orders. In some systems, financial institutions may contract directly with one or more third parties to help perform clearing and settlement activities on behalf of the institution.

15.4.2 Retail payments

In the United States, many payments traditionally made with paper instruments —cheques and cash – are now being made electronically with debit or credit cards or via the **Automated Clearing House (ACH)**. The ACH electronic funds transfer system provides for the clearing of electronic payments for participating banks and other depository institutions. ACH payments include such things as:

- direct deposits of payroll, social security and other government benefits, and tax refunds;
- direct payments of consumer bills such as mortgages, loans, utility bills and insurance premiums;
- business-to-business payments;
- e-cheques;
- e-commerce payments;
- federal, state and local tax payments.

Paper cheques once accounted for the majority of non-cash payments but since the mid-1990s they have been increasingly replaced by other means of non-cash payment. Table 15.6 shows that between 2000 and 2012 the number of cheque payments in the US fell substantially amid modest growth for credit card transactions, while debit card payments (particularly online transactions) increased rapidly. The Federal Reserve suggests that a variety of factors, such as growth in economic activity and population, has contributed to the increase in electronic payments. It also notes that some of the increase is probably also due to the replacement of some cash and cheque payments with electronic payments.

Moves to reduce paper-based processing of cheques are a major feature of the Check Clearing for the 21st Century Act ('**Check 21**') that became effective in October 2004. Check 21 is designed to foster innovation in the payments system and to enhance its efficiency by permitting banks greater flexibility in converting paper cheques into electronic form to speed up retail payments.

Table 15.6 Number of non-cash payments ($bn), 2000–2012

	2000	2003	2006	2009	2012
Non-cash payments	72.5	81.2	93.3	109.0	122.8
Cheque	41.9	37.3	30.6	24.5	18.3
Credit card	15.6	19	21.7	21.6	23.2
ACH	6.2	9.1	14.6	19.1	20.1
Debit cards	8.3	15.6	25.4	37.9	40.8
Prepaid Card	-	-	3.3	6.0	-

Notes: 1 The cheque estimates represent cheques paid, not cheques written. 2 ACH are Automated Clearing House transactions such as direct debits, standing orders and other payments. 3 Debit card payments include online debit (PIN-based), which includes purchases at the point of sale with ATM cards, and offline debit (signature based).

Source: Federal Reserve System (2011, 2013).

15.5 Balance sheet features of US commercial banks

The balance sheet structure of US commercial banks reflects the main assets and liability components of their business. An overview of the assets and liabilities of the commercial banking sector is shown in Tables 15.7 and 15.8 respectively. Table 15.7 shows the asset structure of banks and illustrates that loans constituted around 53 per cent of banking sector assets in 2012 compared with around 62 per cent in 1990 – in fact the proportion of loans over total assets was at its lowest level from 2008 onwards. Investment securities typically comprise 15 to 25 per cent of total assets, although they reached their lowest level of just over 14 per cent in 2007 and 2008. In addition, the amount of liquid assets (cash and due) fell systematically over the period from 9.4 per cent in 1990 to 4.3 per cent in 2007, then jumped markedly to 8.5 per cent in 2008 – the latter a clear reflection of banks' (and the regulatory authorities') desire to boost liquidity in the light of the credit crunch. It stood at around 10 per cent by end-2012. Other earning assets also increased from around 5 per cent in 1990 to 9 per cent by 2012.

Table 15.8 shows the changing liability features of US commercial banks, highlighting the greater reliance on borrowed funds (wholesale deposits acquired through the interbank market) up until 2004 (16 per cent of total liabilities), staying at this level until 2008, then falling to 8.5 per cent by 2012. Capital levels also increased over most of the period; the equity-to-assets ratio increased from 6.4 per cent to 8.5 per cent between 1990 and 2000, and reached 10.2 per cent by 2007. Figures for 2008 highlight the impact of the crisis, which reduced the equity-to-assets ratio to 9.4 per cent, but recapitalisations post-crisis increase the ratio to around 11 per cent by 2012.

It is important to remember that the above trends relate to the whole banking system and there are substantial differences in the balance sheet make-up of the largest banks compared to other banks. For instance, the ten largest banks, on average, do less lending, hold more securities and less capital compared with smaller banks. Also, as noted above, the lending structure of the banks also varies substantially with size – for example, small and medium-sized banks account for around 45 per cent of US commercial real estate lending, whereas the top 100 banks account for just under 20 per cent. As such, it is always important to remember that bank balance sheet features vary considerably according to different asset sizes of banks.

15.6 Performance of US commercial banks

US commercial banks have been among the most profitable banks in the developed world, with return on equity (ROE) varying between 11 per cent and 15 per cent for all but the smallest banks, between 1993 and 2006 (see Figure 15.5). From then on, as shown in Figure 15.6, the returns of the US banking sector have gradually fallen, to 8 per cent in 2007 and then collapsed to −1.1 per cent in 2008, −1.35 per cent in 2009. Mild improvements were recorded since, from 5.7 per cent in 2010 to just over 9 per cent by the end of 2013. Following a similar trend, return-on-assets fell to 0.1 per cent in 2008 and then to 0.08 per cent in 2009 – the lowest levels since 1991. Around 20 per cent of US banks suffered losses in 2008 and these institutions accounted for about 35 per cent of industry assets, the highest share since 1987.

Table 15.7 Assets of US commercial banks, 1990 to 2012 ($mil)

Year	No. of banks	Cash and due from banks	Investment securities	Total loans and leases	Allowance for losses	Net loans and leases	Other earning assets	Bank premises and equipment	Other real estate	Intangible assets	All other assets	Total assets
1990	12,343	318,016	604,622	2,110,170	55,532	2,054,638	194,601	51,437	21,607	10,646	133,923	3,389,490
1991	11,921	304,862	691,385	2,052,754	55,146	1,997,609	215,858	52,249	27,553	12,245	128,921	3,430,682
1992	11,463	298,083	772,941	2,032,494	54,519	1,977,975	238,970	53,104	26,377	15,559	123,163	3,506,171
1993	10,959	272,979	836,712	2,150,658	52,805	2,097,853	272,995	55,528	16,784	18,057	136,181	3,707,088
1994	10,452	303,577	823,028	2,359,813	52,217	2,307,596	343,051	58,922	10,177	24,009	141,747	4,012,107
1995	9,941	306,545	810,877	2,605,474	52,966	2,552,508	398,023	61,425	6,644	30,219	148,934	4,315,175
1996	9,528	336,052	800,656	2,815,090	53,647	2,761,444	404,770	64,613	5,451	44,721	164,457	4,582,165
1997	9,143	355,149	871,879	2,974,456	54,897	2,919,559	558,528	67,182	4,454	61,690	180,090	5,018,532
1998	8,774	356,703	979,867	3,236,642	57,255	3,179,386	563,908	71,311	3,656	80,222	207,552	5,442,604
1999	8,580	366,456	1,046,536	3,489,092	58,746	3,430,346	483,580	73,743	3,075	98,067	233,332	5,735,135
2000	8,315	369,931	1,078,985	3,815,498	64,120	3,751,377	584,102	75,794	3,210	103,803	278,358	6,245,560
2001	8,080	390,340	1,172,540	3,884,328	72,273	3,812,055	620,534	76,644	3,830	120,143	356,208	6,552,294
2002	7,888	383,846	1,334,727	4,156,250	76,983	4,079,267	709,197	79,235	4,431	124,850	361,358	7,076,912
2003	7,770	387,437	1,456,248	4,428,947	77,124	4,351,823	780,438	83,392	4,531	158,174	379,502	7,601,545
2004	7,631	387,555	1,551,101	4,906,362	73,496	4,832,866	889,529	86,799	3,853	275,726	388,186	8,415,615
2005	7,526	400,267	1,572,202	5,382,110	68,731	5,313,379	942,515	91,725	4,026	302,892	414,334	9,041,339
2006	7,401	432,960	1,666,204	5,981,812	69,060	5,912,753	1,149,123	96,829	5,467	358,512	470,109	10,091,958
2007	7,284	482,162	1,590,802	6,626,409	89,179	6,537,229	1,513,678	105,022	9,792	423,218	514,140	11,176,043
2008	7,087	1,041,803	1,746,327	6,838,447	156,659	6,681,788	1,627,921	109,681	22,916	392,528	685,933	12,308,897
2009	6,840	976,573	2,199,578	6,495,187	213,817	6,281,370	1,108,125	110,514	35,859	386,800	723,910	11,822,728
2010	6,530	922,704	2,351,738	6,594,996	217,973	6,377,023	1,177,980	110,664	46,653	373,186	705,541	12,065,489
2011	6,291	1,195,925	2,541,235	6,719,066	178,636	6,540,430	1,171,969	112,006	41,017	348,297	698,058	12,648,937
2012	6,096	1,333,764	2,750,150	7,047,941	152,158	6,895,783	1,227,730	112,657	34,887	351,250	684,896	13,391,116

Source: Federal Deposit Insurance Corporation, 'Historical statistics on banking, commercial banks', www2.fdic.gov/hsob/index.asp.

Table 15.8 Liabilities and equity capital of US commercial banks, 1990–2010 ($mil)

Year	No. of banks	Liabilities					Equity Capital					Total liabilities and equity capital
		Total deposits	Borrowed funds	Subord- inated notes	Other liabilities	Total liabilities	Perpetual preferred stock	Common stock	Surplus	Undivided profits	Total equity capital	
1990	12,343	2,650,150	385,292	23,920	111,511	3,170,873	1,673	30,858	92,382	93,703	218,616	3,389,490
1991	11,921	2,687,664	379,726	24,962	106,632	3,198,983	1,524	31,259	101,523	97,393	231,699	3,430,682
1992	11,463	2,698,682	407,095	33,731	103,196	3,242,704	1,610	32,130	117,409	112,319	263,467	3,506,171
1993	10,959	2,754,330	498,665	37,372	120,118	3,410,484	1,523	32,881	126,596	135,604	296,604	3,707,088
1994	10,452	2,874,439	563,674	40,756	221,012	3,699,881	1,505	34,630	136,168	139,923	312,226	4,012,107
1995	9,941	3,027,576	629,214	43,536	265,057	3,965,382	1,835	35,883	146,952	165,124	349,793	4,315,175
1996	9,528	3,197,139	681,616	51,167	276,657	4,206,578	2,001	35,105	167,751	170,729	375,586	4,582,165
1997	9,143	3,421,664	774,441	62,015	342,367	4,600,487	2,406	34,485	190,992	190,162	418,045	5,018,532
1998	8,774	3,681,391	853,188	72,785	373,010	4,980,373	2,698	34,713	217,730	207,090	462,231	5,442,604
1999	8,580	3,831,058	1,000,653	76,450	347,284	5,255,445	3,129	32,833	238,904	204,825	479,690	5,735,135
2000	8,315	4,179,567	1,047,273	87,043	401,320	5,715,204	3,377	31,245	260,557	235,177	530,356	6,245,560
2001	8,080	4,377,558	1,071,515	95,313	414,313	5,958,699	4,378	30,258	303,722	255,457	593,595	6,552,294
2002	7,888	4,689,847	1,171,190	94,744	473,736	6,429,516	6,000	30,005	320,342	291,221	647,395	7,076,912
2003	7,770	5,035,052	1,260,898	100,759	512,940	6,909,650	6,497	30,259	350,467	304,863	691,895	7,601,545
2004	7,631	5,593,175	1,315,668	110,138	546,450	7,565,430	6,237	29,811	493,502	320,818	850,185	8,415,615
2005	7,526	6,073,134	1,424,578	122,237	509,061	8,129,010	5,264	32,274	529,804	345,268	912,329	9,041,339
2006	7,401	6,731,411	1,589,614	149,790	591,214	9,062,029	5,122	33,835	625,625	365,732	1,029,930	10,091,958
2007	7,284	7,309,871	1,880,519	174,900	667,887	10,033,176	5,000	35,982	738,911	363,143	1,142,867	11,176,043
2008	7,087	8,082,230	2,079,101	182,982	810,406	11,154,719	6,391	45,410	851,030	251,631	1,154,177	12,308,897
2009	6,840	8,333,221	1,482,515	154,663	544,075	10,514,474	6,170	46,192	993,731	242,225	1,288,006	11,822,728
2010	6,530	8,514,285	1,448,435	144,824	593,769	10,701,314	6,480	45,952	1,026,855	258,468	1,337,530	12,065,489
2011	6,291	9,256,822	1,193,208	131,789	645,334	11,227,152	5,133	44,181	1,041,267	313,301	1,403,648	12,648,937
2012	6,096	10,014,144	1,141,104	117,533	615,621	11,888,402	4,814	43,446	1,064,166	375,002	1,487,188	13,391,116

Source: Federal Deposit Insurance Corporation, 'Historical statistics on banking, commercial banks', www2.fdic.gov/hsob/index.asp.

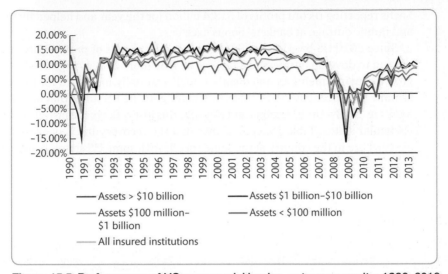

Figure 15.5 Performance of US commercial banks – return on equity, 1990–2013

Source: Federal Deposit Insurance Corporation, 'Historical statistics on banking, commercial banks', www2.fdic.gov/hsob/index.asp

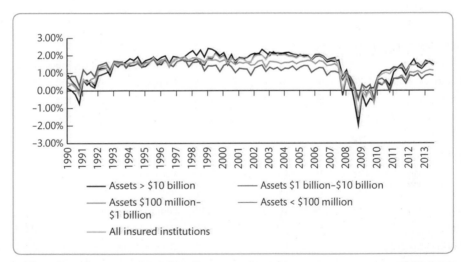

Figure 15.6 Performance of US commercial banks – return on assets, 1990–2013

Source: Federal Deposit Insurance Corporation, 'Historical statistics on banking, commercial banks', www2.fdic.gov/hsob/index.asp

The main reason for the collapse in profitability was the decline in non-interest income (particularly from securities trading losses) and the large increase in loan-loss provisions. The significant decline in profits is a clear indication of the adverse impact of the credit crisis.

During 2009 US commercial bank performance improved and by the start of 2010 some of the major recipients of TARP funds, as noted earlier, (Bank of America, Bank of New York Mellon, Citigroup, JPMorgan Chase and Wells Fargo) had repaid all their borrowed funds. The same was the case for the top investment banks including Goldman Sachs and Morgan Stanley. Throughout 2009 there was growing evidence that the business of major US (and European) investment banks' profits was improving. This eventually culminated in Goldman

Sachs reporting record profits of $13.4 billion for the year and helped further stoke political and public outrage at bankers' bonus excesses.

Since 2010 US banking has returned to modest levels of profitability and banks are continuing to develop business to adapt to the new more heavily regulated and slow economic growth environment. As noted earlier, ROE gradually increased for the whole industry to around 10 per cent by 2013. Table 15.9 highlights the US states that had the most profitable banks in 2013 – Utah, Arizona and Nevada; this just reflects the fast-growing nature of these particular states. Table 15.9 also shows that the recovery in US banking has not happened everywhere in the country at the same speed, with some US states' banking sectors still lagging behind.

Table 15.9 Bank profitability by state – return on assets (%)

	State	No. of banks	2013	2012	Change		State	No. of banks	2013	2012	Change
1	Utah	55	2.16	2.54	−38	28	Missouri	309	0.95	1.00	−5
2	Arizona	24	1.97	1.67	30	29	Louisiana	142	0.94	0.92	2
3	Nevada	20	1.69	3.04	135	30	Kansas	295	0.93	0.95	−2
4	Delaware	23	1.56	1.33	23	31	Ohio	232	0.93	0.93	0
5	Hawaii	9	1.43	1.24	19	32	New Mexico	48	0.92	1.02	−10
6	North Dakota	88	1.40	1.65	−25	33	Kentucky	185	0.89	1.06	−17
7	Oklahoma	229	1.34	1.42	8	34	Mississippi	86	0.88	0.90	−2
8	South Dakota	76	1.29	1.14	15	35	Florida	200	0.84	0.59	25
9	Montana	65	1.28	1.04	24	36	Massachusetts	154	0.82	0.90	−8
10	Arkansas	126	1.23	1.11	12	37	New York	165	0.77	0.78	−1
11	Texas	543	1.23	1.23	0	38	Georgia	224	0.76	0.58	18
12	Nebraska	210	1.17	1.24	−7	39	Maine	28	0.76	0.55	21
13	Michigan	126	1.16	1.61	−45	40	Vermont	14	0.75	0.79	−4
14	Iowa	333	1.14	1.20	−4	41	Idaho	16	0.71	0.45	26
15	Minnesota	364	1.14	0.8	34	42	Illinois	544	0.69	0.61	8
16	Oregon	28	1.13	1.22	−9	43	New Hampshire	20	0.69	0.66	4
17	North Carolina	79	1.11	0.89	22	44	Connecticut	46	0.67	0.77	−10
18	Wyoming	34	1.11	1.12	−1	45	District of Columbia	5	0.65	0.52	13
19	California	228	1.07	1.10	−3	46	Tennessee	180	0.65	0.53	12
20	Alaska	6	1.04	1.28	24	47	South Carolina	69	0.64	0.45	19
21	Colorado	100	1.03	0.95	8	48	New Jersey	108	0.61	0.27	34
22	Indiana	133	1.02	1.05	−3	49	Maryland	76	0.53	0.54	−1
23	Wisconsin	260	1.02	0.88	14	50	Pennsylvania	197	0.44	0.76	−32
24	West Virginia	61	1.01	0.92	9	51	Puerto Rico	6	0.01	0.55	−54
25	Alabama	136	1.00	0.92	8	52	Rhode Island	10	−3.74	0.65	−439
26	Virginia	106	0.99	0.43	56						
27	Washington	64	0.99	1.69	−70	Total		6,891	1.06	1.02	4

Source: Federal Deposit Insurance Corporation Statistics on Banking https://www2.fdic.gov/SDI/SOB/.

Regulation of the US banking system

The current system for regulating and supervising financial institutions in the US is diverse, relatively complex and increasingly under scrutiny given the turmoil the banking system has faced since the onset of the 2008 financial crisis. At the federal level, commercial banking organisations are regulated and supervised by three agencies which include the:

- **Office of the Comptroller of the Currency (OCC)**;
- **Federal Reserve System (Federal Reserve)**;
- **Federal Deposit Insurance Corporation (FDIC)**.

The 2008 global crisis highlighted a number of weaknesses in the US financial regulation framework. The roadmap for addressing these issues has been provided in the form of the Dodd–Frank Wall Street Reform and Consumer Protection Act.

The 2010 Dodd–Frank Act created the interagency Financial Stability Oversight Council and consolidated bank regulation from five agencies to four (it abolished the Office for Thrifts Supervision (OTS) and its responsibilities were transferred to other agencies). In addition, the Dodd–Frank Act granted the Federal Reserve oversight authority and the FDIC resolution authority over the largest financial firms. The 2010 Act also consolidated regulatory oversight of consumer protection, which had been dispersed among several federal agencies, by establishing the new **Consumer Financial Protection Bureau (CFPB)**.

Table 15.10 summarises the regulatory structure of the US financial system. In the US it is common to distinguish between 'prudential regulators' (which include the Federal Reserve, the OCC, the FDIC and the NCUA) and regulators which focus on 'disclosure' (that is monitoring the information the financial firms and exchanges provide to market participants). In addition, other financial regulators have the function to facilitate the exchange of information and co-ordination among agencies; these include the FSOC, the Federal Financial Institutions Examination Council (FFIEC) and the President's Working Group on Capital Markets.

15.7.1 Office of the Comptroller of the Currency (OCC)

The OCC charters, regulates and supervises all national banks. The OCC is an independent bureau of the Department of the Treasury, set up in 1863 to regulate all banks chartered by the Federal Reserve government. These banks, known as national banks, all have the word 'national' in their title or carry abbreviations 'NA' or 'NS&T'. The OCC also supervises the federal branches and agencies of foreign banks.

The OCC conducts on-site reviews of national banks and provides on-going supervision of bank operations. The agency issues rules, legal interpretations and regulatory decisions concerning banking, bank investments, bank community development activities and other aspects of bank operations. In regulating national banks, the OCC has the power to:

- examine the banks;
- approve or deny applications for new licences (or charters), branches, capital or other changes in corporate or banking structure;

Table 15.10 US financial regulators

Type of regulator	Regulatory agency	Institutions regulated	Powers
Prudential Bank Regulators	Federal Reserve	• Bank holding companies • Financial holding companies • State banks that are members of the Federal Reserve System • US branches of foreign banks • Foreign branches of US banks	Lender of last resort (through the discount window). In 'unusual circumstances' the Fed may extend credit to non-member banks and provide liquidity to the financial system. It may also initiate a resolution process to close firms that pose a great risk to financial stability.
	Office of the Comptroller of the Currency (OCC)	• National banks • US federal branches of foreign banks	Examine the national banks and federal thrifts. Approve or deny applications for changes in corporate or banking structure. Take supervisory actions against national banks and federal thrifts that do not comply with laws and regulations or that otherwise engage in unsound practices. Issue rules and regulations, legal interpretations, and corporate decisions governing investments lending and other practices.
	Federal Deposit Insurance Corporation (FDIC)	• Federally insured depository institutions, including banks that are not members of the Federal Reserve System	Operates a deposit insurance fund for federally and state-chartered banks and thrifts. In case of systemic risk, the FDIC may invoke a broad authority to use the deposit insurance funds to provide assistance to depository institutions.
	National Credit Union Administration (NCUA)	• Federally chartered or insured credit unions	Serves as liquidity lender to credit unions experiencing liquidity shortfalls through the Central Liquidity Facility. Operates a deposit insurance fund for credit unions, the National Credit Union Share Insurance Fund (NCUSIF).
Securities and Derivatives Regulators	Securities and Exchange Commission (SEC)	• Securities exchanges • Brokers and dealers • Mutual funds • Investment advisers	Authorised to set financial accounting standards. May unilaterally close markets or suspend trading strategies for limited periods. Registers corporate securities sold to the public.
	Commodity Futures Trading Commission (CFTC)	• Futures exchanges • Brokers • Pool operators • Advisers	May suspend trading, order liquidation of positions or raise margins.

Type of regulator	Regulatory agency	Institutions regulated	Powers
Other regulators of Financial Activities	Federal Housing Finance Agency (FHFA)	• Fannie Mae • Freddie Mac • Federal Home Loan Banks	Acting as conservator (since September 2008) for Fannie Mae and Freddie Mac.
	Consumer Financial Protection Bureau	• Non-bank mortgage-related firms • Private student lenders • Payday lenders • Other 'larger consumer financial entities'* • Consumer business of banks with more than $10 billion of assets	Writes rules, supervises companies and enforces federal consumer financial protection laws. Restricts unfair, deceptive or abusive acts or practices. Takes consumer complaints. Monitors financial markets for new risks to consumers. Enforces laws that outlaw discrimination and other unfair treatment in consumer finance.

Note: *Does not include insurers, SEC and CFTC registrants, auto dealers, sellers of non-financial goods, real estate brokers and agents, and agents and banks with assets of less than $10 billion.

Source: Adapted from Murphy (2013).

- take actions against banks that do not comply with laws and regulations or that otherwise engage in unsound banking practices. The agency can remove officers and directors, negotiate agreements to change banking practices, and issue cease and desist orders as well as civil money penalties;
- issue rules and regulations governing bank investments, lending and other practices.

By 2012 the OCC was responsible for regulating more than 1,900 national banks and 50 federal branches of foreign banks in the US. On 21 July 2011, under provisions of the Dodd–Frank Act, the OTS became part of the OCC. As a result, the OCC is now also responsible for the supervision of federal savings associations.

15.7.2 Federal Reserve System

In addition to its (central banking) monetary policy role (discussed in Chapter 6), the Federal Reserve is responsible for regulating and supervising various types of banks. These include:

- bank holding companies, including diversified financial holding companies formed under the Gramm–Leach–Bliley Act of 1999 and foreign banks with US operations;
- state-chartered banks that are members of the Federal Reserve System (state member banks);
- foreign branches of member banks;
- Edge Act and agreement corporations, through which US banking organisations may conduct international banking activities;
- US state-licensed branches, agencies and representative offices of foreign banks; and
- non-banking activities of foreign banks.

Typically, the Federal Reserve is responsible for regulating the largest and most complex US banks as it has responsibility for bank and diversified financial holding companies. It also regulates the operations of foreign banks, many of which are engaged in relatively complicated investment and corporate banking activity.

The 2010 Dodd–Frank Act reformed the Federal Reserve. The Act made the Fed the principal regulator for systemically important financial companies. The emergency lending powers of the Federal Reserve (established in 1932 under Section 13(3) of the Federal Reserve Act) give it authority to lend to non-depository institutions (investment banks, insurers) in 'unusual and exigent circumstances'. Dodd–Frank now makes this lending conditional on approval from the Secretary of the Treasury. The Federal Reserve will have to disclose all its Section 13(3) lending details and will be subject to a one-time Government Accountability Office (GAO) audit of emergency lending during the recent crisis. A new post of the Federal Reserve Vice Chairman for supervision will be created and the GAO will also examine governance issues and how directors are appointed.

15.7.3 Federal Deposit Insurance Corporation (FDIC)

The FDIC is the main federal regulator of banks that are chartered by the states that do not join the Federal Reserve System. It can also supervise the branches and agencies of foreign banks that take deposits. As an independent agency it is funded by premiums that banks and thrift institutions pay for deposit insurance coverage and from earnings on investments in US Treasury securities. By the end of 2012, the FDIC insured a record $7.4 trillion of deposits in more than half a billion accounts at more than 7,000 institutions. In general, deposit insurance protects the deposits of retail customers in the event of a bank failure. Savings, checking and other deposit accounts, when combined, were insured up to $100,000 per depositor in each bank or thrift up to the credit crisis. Also deposits held in different categories of ownership – such as single or joint accounts – may be separately insured. Given growing concerns about the state of US banking, the deposit insurance coverage was increased in May 2009 to $250,000.

The Dodd–Frank Act expanded the FDIC's role in liquidating troubled financial institutions which are considered to pose a 'systemic risk'.

15.7.4 Other regulatory agencies

In addition to the three major federal regulatory agencies mentioned above there are a number of other agencies that have responsibility for the other types of deposit-taking institution in the US. These included the OTS, which was established in 1989 as the main regulator of all S&Ls whether federally or state chartered. As already mentioned, the Dodd–Frank Act abolished the OTS and thrifts are now regulated by the OCC. The credit union sector is supervised by the NCUA which also insures credit union deposits.

Table 15.11 illustrates the regulatory responsibility of all the main bank regulatory bodies and highlights various overlaps. It can be seen that the regulatory structure is complex and apparently involves a duplication of resources. However, some have argued that this is a good thing as it allows for competition between regulators and acts against complacency. From banks' point of view, however, it has been argued that the system is burdensome and over-bureaucratic. The debate on the perceived costs and benefits of multiple regulators versus single regulators is far from resolved. As banks became larger, more complex and

Table 15.11 Supervisors and regulators of US banks

Component	Supervisor and regulator
Bank holding companies (including financial holding companies)	FR
Non-bank subsidiaries of bank holding companies	FR/ Functional regulator[1]
National banks	OCC
State banks	
Members	FR
Non-members	FDIC
Thrift holding companies[4]	OTS[4]
Savings banks	OTS[4]/FDIC/FR
Savings and loan associations	OTS[4]
Edge and agreement corporations	FR
Credit unions	NCUA
Government-sponsored entities	FHFA
Foreign banks[2]	
Branches and agencies[3]	
State licensed	FR/FDIC
Federally licensed	OCC/FR/FDIC
Representative offices	FR

Notes: FR = Federal Reserve; OCC = Office of the Comptroller of the Currency; FDIC = Federal Deposit Insurance Corporation; OTS = Office of Thrift Supervision; NCUA = National Credit Union Administration; FHFA = Federal Housing Finance Agency.

[1]Non-bank subsidiaries engaged in securities, commodities or insurance activities are supervised and regulated by their appropriate functional regulators. Such functionally regulated subsidiaries include a broker, dealer, investment adviser and investment company registered with and regulated by the Securities and Exchange Commission (or, in the case of an investment adviser, registered with any state); an insurance company or insurance agent subject to supervision by a state insurance regulator; and a subsidiary engaged in commodity activities regulated by the Commodity Futures Trading Commission.

[2]Applied to direct operations in the US. Foreign banks may also have indirect operations in the US through their ownership of US banking organisations.

[3]The FDIC has responsibility for branches that are insured.

[4]Note the Dodd–Frank Act abolished the OTS and moved regulatory responsibilities to the OCC.

Source: Federal Reserve System (2005) and authors' updates.

diversified into wider financial services areas (such as insurance, investment banking, pensions) through the financial holding company route, it had been argued that a more unified approach to bank regulation was needed. While this argument was hot on the agenda when US banks were performing well, the advent of the credit crisis raised questions as to whether a single regulator could do any better than a multitude of regulators. During the 2008 crisis, UK banks (which at the time were supervised by a single regulator, the Financial Services Authority) seem to have fared just as badly as their US counterparts (see Chapter 13 on the crisis in UK banking). The UK introduced a new regulatory structure moving bank supervision away from the FSA (which was abolished in 2013) back to the Bank of England. What is in no doubt, however, is that regulation between bank and non-bank regulators will become increasingly co-ordinated. As banks have become larger and more complex, the adverse effects of failure have become more pronounced and the governance issues associated with banks being 'too big to be allowed to fail' has become a reality (for example, Citigroup).

In general, it is important to note that the supervisor of a US domestic banking institution is generally determined by the type of institution and the governmental authority that granted it permission to undertake business. Given that there are a number of regulatory agencies performing similar tasks, the US authorities established the Federal Financial Institutions Examination Council (FFIEC). The FFIEC is composed of the chairpersons of the FDIC and the NCUA, the OCC, the director of the **Consumer Financial Protection Bureau**, and a governor of the Federal Reserve Board appointed by the Board chairman. The main purpose of the FFIEC is to ensure uniform federal principles and standards relating to the supervision of depository institutions and also to promote co-ordination of bank supervision among the federal agencies that regulate financial institutions. Also the FFIEC seeks to encourage better co-ordination of federal and state regulatory activities.

The Federal Housing Finance Agency (FHFA) was established in 2008 by the Housing and Economic Recovery Act to 'consolidate and strengthen' the regulation of housing finance-related GSEs. The FHFA was given similar powers to those of the federal bank regulators (including the ability to set capital standards; order the entity to cease any activity or divest any asset that poses a threat to financial stability; replace management and assume control if an entity becomes severely undercapitalised). One of the FHFA's first actions was to place Freddie Mac and Fannie Mae into conservatorship, in agreement with the Treasury.

The Consumer Financial Protection Bureau (CFPB) was established by the Dodd–Frank Act to 'bring consumer protection regulation of depository and non-depository institutions into closer alignment'. The CFPB is an independent entity within the Federal Reserve and acts as the primary federal consumer protection supervisor with authority over a range of financial products.

The Dodd–Frank Act also addressed the systemic risk oversight gap in the US regulatory framework by creating the *Financial Stability Oversight Council*. The council is accountable to Congress and is charged with: (i) identifying risks to the financial stability of the US; (ii) promoting market discipline; and (iii) responding to emerging risks to the stability of the US financial system. The council consists of ten financial regulators (voting members) and an independent insurance expert appointed by the US President and five non-voting members. The council is chaired by the Treasury secretary. Key responsibilities of the council are to recommend tougher capital, liquidity and risk management when banks get 'too big'. By two thirds' vote the council can require systemically important financial intermediaries to be regulated by the Federal Reserve.

Concerns about the appropriate regulatory structure needed to avoid a second credit crisis are far from resolved. As a first step, as in all banking crises, the system had to be re-capitalised and liquidity built up – but at the same time the new regulatory structure must not constrain banks excessively so they stop lending or innovating. Also, there needed to be much greater oversight of large banks so as to ensure that 'too-big-to-fail' subsidies would become the exception rather than the norm.

Since the crisis the US authorities have moved to close various gaps and weaknesses in the system for bank regulation and supervision. The passing of the Dodd–Frank Act in 2010, the biggest financial reform in the US since the Great Depression, was a key reflection of this trend.

One of the key changes introduced by the Dodd–Frank Act is the Volcker Rule. Named after former Federal Reserve chairman Paul Volcker, it prohibits banks from proprietary trading and limits investments in hedge funds/private equity fund sponsorship to 3 per cent of capital. Although the Volcker Rule was passed as part of the Dodd–Frank legislation, it faced difficulties in implementation, mostly due to opposition from the banking industry, and was formally approved only in December 2013 (see Box 15.3).

BOX 15.3 VOLCKER RULE COMES OF AGE IN SPITE OF PROTESTS

In the four years since Paul Volcker, former Federal Reserve chairman, first called for a ban on banks trading with their own money, the rule named after him has survived challenges from Wall Street, foreign governments and inter-agency warfare before being ratified by US regulators on Tuesday.

As drafts have gone back and forth between regulators in the past three months, the rule has broadly got tougher and its restrictions on trading will change banks' activities in far-reaching ways. But it is not the knockout blow to bank profits that some had feared.

Mr Volcker told the Financial Times in an interview that regulators had done 'pretty damn well' at drafting a rule that outlaws proprietary trading at banks. The idea is they should not be able to gamble government-insured deposits. Since proposing the rule in January 2010 Mr Volcker had dismissed the idea that it was complicated to identify proprietary trading, saying it was like the adage on pornography – you know it when you see it. 'They've gone beyond that and said there are detailed rules about how you approach [this] and what is legitimate market making once you do that it gets complicated, there's no question.'

The complexity of deciding what is market making – buying and selling stocks and bonds for clients – and what is proprietary trading has helped prolong the rulemaking. Too soft and banks will find ways to disguise proprietary trading; too harsh and activity essential to companies raising capital will be curtailed. Mr Volcker said some activity would doubtless move from banks such as JPMorgan Chase and Goldman Sachs to nimbler, less-regulated companies. But this was not necessarily a bad thing. 'They have no pretence of being supported by the Federal Reserve. They are bound hopefully by market pressure to be well capitalised. They have no responsibility for providing an essential public service.'

Though satisfied with the result, Mr Volcker was less happy about the protracted process. 'That is on my mind,' he said, adding that his new institute, the Volcker Alliance, would consider the issue. 'One of our first projects is to review the multiplicity of agencies,' he said. He said there was nonetheless value to having 'more than one group' as it added 'somebody else looking over your shoulder'.

The rule-writing involved the Fed, the Federal Deposit Insurance Corporation, the Commodity Futures Trading Commission, the Securities and Exchange Commission and the Office of the Comptroller of the Currency, with the US Treasury also playing a role. Regulators say they had an unprecedented barrage of comments – 18,000 in all – to a proposed rule last year. Each had to be considered. There were also delegations of bankers and officials. At one meeting last year, six JPMorgan executives warned that the proposed rule threatened the bank's ability to conduct the banal work of 'liquidity management', investing their funds in short-term assets.

Then, just a month later, the 'London whale' trading scandal hit JPMorgan and the industry's chances of escaping a new, stricter trading environment evaporated. JPMorgan eventually lost $6bn trading credit derivatives. The affair damaged the bank's reputation and led to the departure of some of the same executives who had been lobbying the Fed.

The mess also made Wall Street's pleas for leniency on the Volcker Rule harder to swallow. The credit derivatives strategy was a 'hedge' against other risks in the division supposed to be managing the bank's liquidity, demonstrating that risky trades were not confined to easily identified areas of the bank. Although the London whale undermined Wall Street's plea for broad leniency on hedging, the final rule does allow so-called 'portfolio hedging' – where banks take a broad offsetting position. But it forces them to meet numerous criteria to prove that the hedge is aimed at 'specific, identifiable risks' and to supply a correlation analysis to show the relationship between the risk and the hedge.

Banks also argued that the prohibition restricting banks from investing in hedge funds and private equity funds was too broad because it appeared to sweep in joint ventures and wholly owned subsidiaries which did not seem to be the aim of the original proposal. As a result, the final rule contains more specific definitions for covered funds and excludes joint ventures and other entities that do not engage in investing money for others. But the

Box 15.3 Volcker rule comes of age in spite of protests (*continued*)

measure also allows agencies to rescind an exemption 'if it is being used to evade the requirements of the statute'. Banks were not the only ones asking for changes to the rule. Governments from Mexico to Japan dispatched officials to press the Fed. Their targets: a provision that exempted US banks from the proprietary trading restrictions for US government debt, but not foreign sovereign debt, and the suggestion that roaming US regulators would seek to impose restrictions on foreign banks. The initial proposal exempted activities 'solely outside the US', but the definition was so narrow that it covered almost any trade elsewhere in the world.

The final version of the rule unveiled on Tuesday showed that the governments had been only partially successful in getting change. Deutsche Bank in New York will be allowed to take positions on German bonds but Goldman Sachs will not be able to do the same thing so easily. Overall, foreign banks' operations in New York are covered by the rule and, controversially, even the UK operations of a bank such as Barclays would be

covered when it engages in transactions with a US-based entity – though the final rule is softer than once proposed.

The rule now allows foreign banks to trade with overseas offices of US banks, in addition to activity on US exchanges via clearing houses. David Hirschmann of the US Chamber of Commerce complained that the rulemaking process was flawed, warning it would 'raise the costs of capital and place the United States at a competitive disadvantage in a global economy', and hinting at the prospect of legal action.

'We will now have to carefully examine the final rule to consider the impact on liquidity and market-making, and take all options into account as we decide how best to proceed,' he said.

Mark Van Der Weide, a senior Fed official, acknowledged that similar rules were unlikely to be adopted in Europe: 'Outside the US the major capital markets competitors of our big banks are unlikely to be subject to the Volcker Rule and that is something that we'll have to watch.'

In addition to the key changes discussed above, the Dodd–Frank Act includes a number of other provisions, particularly concerning systemically important institutions which will have to provide 'living wills' (their plans for rapid and orderly shutdown in case of bankruptcy). The Act also creates orderly liquidation mechanisms for the FDIC to unwind failing systemically significant companies.

Key provisions outside the banking sector include (i) improving transparency and accountability in derivatives, (ii) new rules for credit rating agencies and (iii) new rules on CEO compensation.

The Dodd–Frank Act is expected to dramatically alter the way in which the US banking system is regulated into the future with greater restrictions on the type of activities banks can undertake and continued pressure to bolster capital and liquidity strength with an end (in theory at least) to taxpayer bailouts. As illustrated in Box 15.4, however, the legislation is not without its critics who argue that the new rules are unlikely to significantly reduce systemic risk in the system.

BOX 15.4 FAILURES OF THE DODD–FRANK ACT

Last month, Friedrich Hayek's classic *The Road to Serfdom*, a warning against the dangers of excessive state control, was the number one bestseller on Amazon. At the same time, the foundation of much modern economics and capitalism – Adam Smith's *The Wealth of Nations* – languished around a rank of ten thousand. It is a telling reflection of the uncertain times we are in that precisely when confidence in free markets is at its all-time low that scepticism about the ability of governments and regulation to do any better is at its peak. It is thus no trivial task for Messrs Dodd and Frank to put up the Wall Street Reform and Consumer Protection Act and convince the suspecting audience that financial stability will be restored in the near future.

The backdrop for the Act is now well understood. When a large part of the financial sector is funded with fragile, short-term debt and is hit by a common shock to its long-term assets, there can be wholesale failures and disruption of intermediation to households and corporations.

Having witnessed such financial panics from 1850s till the Great Depression, Messrs Glass and Steagall enacted the Banking Act of 1934. They put in place the Federal Deposit Insurance Corporation to provide an orderly resolution of troubled depository institutions – 'banks' – before they failed. To guard against the risk that banks might speculate at the expense of the FDIC, they ring-fenced their activities to commercial lending, requiring riskier capital markets activity to be spun off into investment banks.

Over time, however, the banking industry nibbled at the perimeter of this separation and traditional banks morphed into large and complex financial institutions. A parallel banking system evolved, consisting of money-market funds collecting uninsured short-term deposits and funding financial firms, investment banks performing many functions of commercial banks, and a range of derivatives and securitisation markets providing tremendous liquidity for hitherto illiquid loans but operating in the shadow of regulated banks, remaining opaque and highly leveraged. The Banking Act began to be largely compromised, a development only accentuated by the increasing size and connectedness of traditional and shadow banks, many of which became too big to fail.

Fast forward to 2004 and a perfect storm developed with large global banks seeking capital flows in the form of short-term debt, financed at historically low interest rates, all taking a one-way bet on the housing market, joined in equal measure by the US government's own shadow banks – Fannie and Freddie and AIG, the world's largest insurer. While these institutions seemed individually safe by prudential standards, collectively they fuelled the largest credit boom of modern times and crashed together when the bet went bad. The first big banks to fail were put on oxygen, but when that ran out, a panic ensued, making it clear they all needed – and markets expected them to be given – a lifeline.

Distilled to its essence, the Dodd–Frank Act's task is to address the increasing propensity of the financial sector to put the system at risk and be eventually bailed out at taxpayer expense.

Does the Act do the job? It certainly has its heart in the right place. It sets up a Council that can deem non-bank financial firms as systemically important, regulate them, and as a last resort break them up; requires funeral plans and orderly liquidation procedures for unwinding of such institutions, ruling out taxpayer funding of wind-downs and instead requiring that costs be borne by shareholders, creditors and other large financial firms; restricts emergency Federal assistance to individual institutions; limits bank holding companies to *de minimis* investments in proprietary trading activities such as hedge funds and private equity; provides for central clearing of standardised derivatives, regulation of complex ones, transparency of both, and separation of non-vanilla positions into well-capitalised subsidiaries; puts in place an office under the Treasury to collect, analyse and disseminate relevant information for anticipating future crises; and, introduces a range of additional reforms for mortgage lending practices, hedge fund disclosure, conflict resolution at rating agencies, skin-in-the-game requirement for securitisation, and shareholder say on pay and governance.

However, when read in its full glory, the 2,000 plus page script falls flat on at least three important counts, even ignoring its somewhat misplaced – likely populist – diversion into consumer protection issues.

Box 15.4 Failures of the Dodd–Frank Act (*continued*)

First, the Act does not sufficiently discourage individual firms from putting the system at risk. Since the failure of systemically important firms imposes costs beyond their own losses, it is not sufficient to simply wipe out their stakeholders. They must pay in advance for contributing to the risk of the system. Not only does the Act rule this out, it makes the problem worse by requiring that other large financial firms pay for the costs, precisely at a time when they likely face the risk of contagion from failing firms. It makes little economic sense to charge neighbours for putting out a fire in the house of a habitual smoker.

Second, the Act falls into the familiar trap of regulating by form rather than function. For instance, it allows for provision of Federal assistance to bank holding companies under certain conditions, but restricts such assistance to other systemically important firms. This will create a push for the acquisition of small depositories when non-banks experience trouble, undermining the intent of restriction. And, if a large clearing house or swaps dealer were to face insolvency, the restriction on emergency liquidity assistance will prove disastrous, as any orderly liquidation must take several weeks, if not months.

Third, implicit government guarantees for large parts of the shadow banking sector remain unaddressed. Fannie and Freddie are the most glaring examples of systemically important financial firms whose risk choices went awry given access to guaranteed debt. There is no attempt at reforming them in the Act. Orderly resolution of runs in systemically important markets – such as the sale and repurchase agreements ('repo') – that now constitute several trillion dollars of intermediation flows, remains unplanned. And ditto for dealing with runs on money market funds whose redemption risk following the collapse of Lehman brought finance to a standstill. All of these remain too big to fail.

In a somewhat less known passage from *The Wealth of Nations*, Adam Smith explains beautifully that those 'exertions of the natural liberty of a few individuals, which might endanger the security of the whole society, are, and ought to be, restrained by the laws of all governments; of the most free, as well as of the most despotical. The obligation of building party walls, in order to prevent the communication of fire, is a violation of natural liberty, exactly of the same kind with the regulations of the banking trade which are here proposed.'

The Dodd–Frank Act is right in charging depository banks – and their prudential regulators – to build party walls. But alas the party can – and did – happen elsewhere in the shadow banking system.

For all its ambition and copious attempt to crack down on taxpayer-funded bailouts, it is somewhat unfortunate that the Dodd–Frank Act, the most ambitious overhaul of the financial sector regulation in our times, will be anachronistic in parts right from the day of its legislation.

 Source: Viral V. Acharya (2010) *Financial Times*, 15 July.

15.8   Conclusion

This chapter examines the structural features of the US financial system with a particular focus on the banking system. The industry has experienced marked changes over recent years characterised by a decline in the number of banks, growing concentration and an increasingly international focus (both in terms of foreign bank presence in the domestic market as well as growing US bank presence overseas). The largest banks have transformed themselves into full service financial firms offering an increasingly diversified range of products and services to retail and corporate clients. US banks posted record profits up until the mid-2000s and were among the best performing financial institutions in the world. Recent official estimates suggest that the cost of the credit crisis may be less than expected – around 1 per cent of GDP – although various commentators believe this estimate to be optimistic. Despite uncertainty about the true costs, however, the short-term policy responses appear to have been effective (so far) in minimising the likelihood of a deflationary spiral, although there is still extensive policy debate surrounding the longer-term implications of the crisis for the future architecture of the banking and financial system.

There has been much discussion about introducing new (simpler and tougher) capital and liquidity rules. There are new rules to restrict the securities activities of US banks. Regulators are also seeking to put structures in place to try to develop better early warning systems that look to identify and curtail excessive credit growth and bank expansion in general. Whatever changes take place there is no doubt that bank and financial sector regulation in the US has radically changed.

Key terms

Check 21	Federal Deposit	Gramm–Leach–Bliley	Sub-prime mortgage
CHIPS	Insurance	Act	lending
Consumer Financial	Corporation (FDIC)	Office of the	Term Asset-Backed
Protection Bureau	Federal Reserve	Comptroller of the	Securities Loan
(CFPB)	System (Federal	Currency (OCC)	Facility
Disintermediation	Reserve or 'Fed')	Public-Private	Troubled Asset
Dodd–Frank Wall	Fedwire	Investment	Relief Program
Street Reform	Financial Stability	Program (PPIP)	(TARP)
and Consumer	Oversight Council	Savings and Loans	Volcker Rule
Protection Act	(FSOC)	Associations (S&Ls)	

Key reading

Blinder, A.S. and Zandi, M. (2010) 'How the Great Recession was brought to an end'. Available at **www.economy.com/mark-zandi/documents/End-of-Great-Recession.pdf**

DeYoung, R. (2014) 'Banking in the United States', in Berger, A.N., Molyneux P. and Wilson, J.O.S. (eds), *The Oxford Handbook of Banking*, 2nd Edition, Oxford University Press, Chapter 34.

Federal Reserve Board (2014) *Consumers and Mobile Financial Services 2014*, Washington, DC: Federal Reserve.

Pozsar, Z., Tobias, A., Ashcraft, A. and Boesky, H. (2010) 'Shadow banking', Federal Reserve Bank of New York Staff Reports No. 458, February.

REVISION QUESTIONS AND PROBLEMS

15.1 What are the main features of the different types of depository institutions operating in the US?

15.2 What are the main savings institutions operating in the US?

15.3 Distinguish between different types of US investment institutions.

15.4 What is the disintermediation process that has characterised the US banking and financial sectors over the last decade?

15.5 How is the payment system organised for the wholesale and retail banking sectors?

15.6 How has the credit crisis impacted on the balance sheet structure and performance of US commercial banks?

15.7 What are the most important regulatory agencies in the US and how are they organised? Is there a case for a single banking sector regulator in the US?

15.8 What are the main challenges for the US banking sector post credit crisis?

15.9 Analyse how the US authorities injected liquidity into the banking system to help free-up interbank lending. Were these moves a success?

15.10 Outline the case for and against the state bail-out of major financial institutions like Citigroup and AIG.

Chapter 16

Banking in Japan

Learning objectives

- To distinguish between different types of financial institutions operating in Japan
- To understand the characteristics of the Japanese payment system
- To understand the main tasks and organisation of the Japanese regulatory authorities
- To understand the main trends in the performance of Japanese banks and the impact of the 1998–1999 banking crisis
- To understand the relevance of the 2007–2009 global financial crisis for the Japanese banking sector

16.1 Introduction

This chapter outlines the main features of the Japanese banking and financial systems. Japan has a bank-based financial system, where the banking system has traditionally played a more important role than the stock market. The banking system is also rather complex, with a wide array of different types of private, co-operative and public banks, all undertaking a range of banking business. The main private deposit-taking institutions are the city banks and the largest public bank is the **Japan Post Bank** (the former Post Office Savings Bank that was privatised in 2007). The system has undergone dramatic changes over recent years, mainly because of the major financial crisis that occurred in 1997–1998 and resulted in the failure of a number of banks and a substantial build-up of non-performing loans in the banking system. The parlous state of the banking system in the late 1990s resulted in a wide range of reforms aimed at improving banking and financial sector soundness, as well as restructuring the banking system. This chapter discusses these issues and also highlights how Japanese banks have been impacted and are dealing with the outcomes of the 2007–2009 global financial crisis.

The first part of the chapter outlines the structural features of the Japanese banking system and the various types of institutions that operate in the system. We then outline the main characteristics of payment systems and cover the impact of the 1998–1999 financial crisis, its regulatory impact, and then finish off by looking at how the 2007 credit crunch and ensuing financial crisis had only had a modest impact on Japanese banks.

16.2　Structure of the banking system

The Japanese banking system has experienced difficult times in recent years, mainly as a consequence of the downturn in the domestic economy that has resulted in banking sector failures and a mountain of bad debts for the banking system overall. The surge in bad debts in the 1990s resulted from a rapid increase in financial asset and property prices from the mid-1980s that led to excessive bank lending. The subsequent collapse in asset prices during the 1990s resulted in a high volume of non-performing loans, contributing to a major financial crisis between 1997 and 1998, when several large financial institutions went bankrupt. In 1998, laws were enforced to stabilise the financial system and measures that included temporary government control were developed to deal with bankrupt financial institutions (the Japanese banking crisis is discussed in detail in Section 16.4.1).

The late 1990s' crisis resulted in a large number of regulatory measures aimed at restructuring the banking sector, as well as protecting depositors; these issues will be covered in more detail later in this chapter. Given the weak operating climate, the Japanese banking system experienced a major transformation – especially noticeable by the decline in the number of banks and increasing number of mergers between the largest institutions. While the private financial institutions have suffered, various public financial institutions have expanded their lending and other activities.

The structure of the Japanese banking system is rather complex, with a wide range of deposit-taking institutions that perform particular functions. The current structure is illustrated in Figure 16.1. There are two main categories of financial institutions: private and public. The main distinction between the two relates to the fact that 'banks' are defined under the 1981 Banking Law whereas other types of financial institutions (including co-operative banks) are regulated by different specialised regulation (namely, the Shinkin Bank Law, the Co-operatives and Small and Medium Enterprises Law, the Norinchukin Bank Law).

The major institutions operating in the financial system can be classified according to three main groups:

- private deposit-taking institutions;
- private non-deposit-taking institutions;
- public financial institutions.

Private banks can be divided into several categories, based on their business function or historical background. The distinction between city, regional banks and second-tier regional banks (referred to as members of the second association of regional banks in Figure 16.1) is not a legal one but is a customary classification for the purposes of administration and statistics (Japanese Bankers Association).

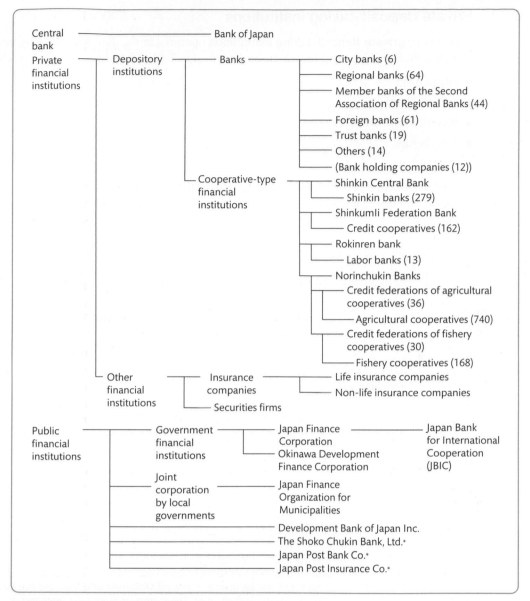

Figure 16.1 The structure of the Japanese banking sector

Note: *In the figure, Japan Post Bank Co. and Japan Post Insurance Co. are categorised as 'public financial institutions' because they are in a transition period toward final privatisation (the process started in 2007 and is scheduled to end in 2017). The Development Bank of Japan, Inc. and The Shoko Chukin Bank, Ltd. are treated in the same manner until the final privatisation (scheduled for the period 2017–2019).

Source: Japanese Bankers Association (**www.zenginkyo.or.jp/en/banks/principal/index.html**).

16.2.1   Private deposit-taking institutions

A variety of **private deposit-taking institutions** operates in the Japanese banking system and their main features and functions are described in Table 16.1. The main banks include:

- city banks;
- regional banks;
- second-tier regional banks;
- trust banks;
- foreign banks.

City, trust, regional (tier 1 and 2), foreign, **Shinkin banks** and credit co-operatives, as well as bridge and internet banks, are included in the definition of 'narrow banking system'. The broader system additionally includes the Japan Post Bank and Norinchukin bank.

Table 16.1 Licensed financial institutions in Japan (as of December 2012)

Features and functions	
A) Banks	
City banks	Major commercial banks comprising: Sumitomo-Mitsui Banking Corporation, Mitsubishi-Tokyo-UFJ, Mizuho Bank and Resona Bank. These are also known as the domestic 'mega-banks'. The city banks are Japan's largest banks and provide a full range of banking, investment and other financial services. They are the main corporate banking service providers in Japan. The Bank of Japan classification of city banks includes also Saitama Resona Bank.
Regional banks	Regional banks focus on retail and SME banking activity in different regions of Japan. The 64 regional banks have large branch networks, with 7,500 branches and 35,000 ATMs set up all over the country. While city banks' business has traditionally focused on urban areas, the regional banks operate in various regions or 'prefectures' throughout the country. They account for around 22 per cent of retail deposit taking. The three largest regional banks (by lending) are Bank of Yokohama Ltd, Fukuoka Financial Group Inc. and Chiba Bank Ltd.
Second-tier regional banks (Sogo banks)	Like traditional regional banks, these are smaller regional banks that also focus on retail and SME business within their immediate geographical regions. Most of these banks have converted from mutual savings banks to ordinary commercial banks.
Trust banks	Trust banks provide traditional commercial banking services but focus on trust business. A trust is an investment product in which an investor (trustor) entrusts funds to a trust bank, which invests the funds in various instruments (stocks, bonds, etc.) at its own discretion and returns the investment gains to the investor (trustor) as a dividend. All the city banks have trust banking subsidiaries, including Mitsubishi UFJ Trust and Banking, Mizuho Trust and Banking and Nomura Trust. The merger of Sumitomo Trust and Banking Corp., Chuo Mitsui Trust and Banking Co. and its affiliate Chuo Mitsui Asset Trust and Banking Co. in 2012 created Japan's largest trust bank, Sumitomo Mitsui Trust Bank Ltd (SMTB).
Former long-term credit banks	These are banks established in accordance with the Long-term Credit Bank Law of 1999, which restructured/nationalised these banks. Long-term credit banks provide long- and medium-term finance to the corporate sector. They had long been a feature of high-value lending at low rates to the corporate sector. Due to various factors, these banks became technically insolvent and were reorganised: Mizuho Corporate Bank was created from the Industrial Bank of Japan and others, Shinsei Bank (from the Long-Term Credit Bank of Japan) and Aozora Bank (from the former Nippon Credit Bank). Note that Mizuho Corporate Bank is part of the city bank group Mizuho.
Foreign banks	Foreign banks are mainly engaged in corporate and investment banking activity, although some undertake upscale retail (private banking) business.

Features and functions	
B) Co-operative financial institutions	
Shinkin banks	Shinkin banks are co-operative financial institutions. Their membership is composed of local residents and small and medium-sized companies. They are non-profit organisations that operate under the principle of mutual support. Shinkin banks limit their lending, in principle, to members. However, their functions are similar to commercial banks, and they also deal with many people who are not members, accepting deposits, providing exchange services, accepting various payments including those for public utilities, and engaging in over-the-counter sales of public bonds, investment trusts and insurance.
Credit co-operatives Labour banks Agricultural co-operatives Fishery co-operatives	A wide range of co-operative deposit-taking institutions operates in Japan. These provide services such as deposits, lending, bill discounting, domestic exchange and foreign exchange. As a rule credit associations only lend to members (deposits may be taken from non-members). Members have typically to be resident, working or owning a business in the co-operative's area. Generally membership is not open to large businesses. The co-operative banks serve various sectors, such as agriculture, fisheries and other groups.
C) Federations of co-operative financial institutions	
Shinkin Central Bank (Central institution for Shinkin banks) Shinkumi Federation Bank (National Federation of Credit Co-operatives) Rokinren Bank (National Association of Labour Banks) Norinchukin Bank (Central Bank for the Japanese Agricultural, Forestry and Fishery Co-operatives) Shoko Chukin Bank (the Central Co-operative Bank for Commerce and Industry)	These are the central organisations for the various co-operative banks listed above. They offer various products and services to their member banks, typically undertaking larger and more complex banking transactions. For instance, they provide investment and asset management services, as well as more sophisticated corporate banking services to their member banks.

Source: Compiled using information from various sources, including Community Bank Shinyo Kumiai, the Japanese Bankers Association, Japan Post, Japan Securities Dealers Association, Shinkin Central Bank Research Institute, the Norinchukin Bank, the Regional Banks Association of Japan and the Financial Services Agency.

16.2.1.1 City banks

The **city banks** are the largest banks in the Japanese banking system and account for more than 50 per cent of total banking sector assets. As Table 16.1 notes, they are commercial banks that offer the full range of banking services, including retail, corporate and investment banking services. Traditionally, they have focused on providing banking services to relatively large corporations and their retail banking activities are typically based in urban areas. All city banks offer nationwide branch banking services and have extensive foreign bank networks.

City banks have experienced substantial restructuring in recent years; these reorganisations have been aimed at bolstering the financial strength of the country's main banks and resulted in the creation of the three so-called '*mega-banks*' (Mitsubishi UFJ Financial Group, Sumitomo Mitsui Financial Group and Mizuho Financial Group) that now dominate the Japanese banking landscape. Figure 16.2 illustrates the trend in total assets (in trillions

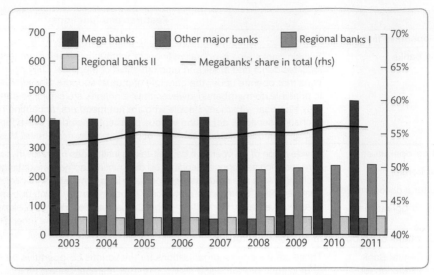

Figure 16.2 Total assets of Japanese domestic banking groups (in trillions of yen)

Source: Japanese Bankers Association (**www.zenginkyo.or.jp/en/banks/principal/index.html**).

of yen) for the major domestic banking groups (excluding Japan Post Bank and co-operative financial institutions).

16.2.1.2 Regional and second regional banks

Regional banks are medium-sized institutions whose banking activities are regionally focused. There are 64 of these banks and they have a much larger geographical presence than the city banks, with more than 7,000 branches nationwide. They tend to focus more on retail financial services and lending to SMEs in the various regions (or prefectures). The majority of regional banks are publicly quoted and the largest offer a full range of banking and financial services, although their business focuses on companies and households that operate within specific regions of Japan. Note that there are two types of regional banks, differentiated primarily by size (see Table 16.1), the second group being the second (tier) regional banks. Historically these were set up as mutual (Sogo) banks whose purpose was to finance small and medium-sized enterprises. Although they are no longer restricted to this area it remains their main focus. The 41 second-tier regional banks have more than 3,500 branches and in excess of 35,000 ATMs, and are important funders of small businesses (see Table 16.2).

16.2.1.3 Trust banks and long-term credit banks

In addition to the city and regional banks, there are a number of **trust banks**. These perform commercial banking activities, but their main function is asset management for retail and other customers. Japanese households place funds (or entrust funds) in these banks in the form of 'money trusts', which are a type of medium- to long-term time deposit. (Note that Bank of Japan statistics for the banking sector distinguish between banking account and trust account business when reporting features of the system.) These money trusts enable banks to undertake long-term commercial lending and investments in bonds, equities and other instruments. Trust banks have long-term liabilities that enable them to make long-term loans and as such they have played an important role in providing long-term credit to corporate borrowers.

Table 16.2 Total deposits and number of branches by bank type (as of March 2012)

Bank type	Total deposits outstanding (US$bn)	Number of branches
City banks	3,326	2,400
Regional banks	2,683	7,481
Shinkin banks	1,490	7,535
Agricultural co-operatives	1,072	755
Second-tier regional banks	725	3,136
Credit co-operatives	216	1,751
Labour credit associations	212	642

Source: Shinkin Central Bank (2012); The Norinchukin Bank (2012).

The merger between Sumitomo Trust and Chuo Mitsui Trust – announced in 2009 and which came into effect on 1 April 2012 – created Japan's largest trust bank, Sumitomo Mitsui Trust Bank Ltd (SMTB), with total assets of 32,839 billion yen. As a trust bank, the value of assets entrusted to SMTB by companies and individuals stood at 122 trillion yen (about $1.5 trillion) in 2012, more than 10 per cent larger than the amount held by Mitsubishi UFJ Trust. As a commercial bank, SMTB now ranks as the fifth largest in Japan, after the mega-banks. The integration of Sumitomo Trust and Chuo Mitsui represents the largest merger since Mitsubishi UFJ Financial Group, Japan's biggest banking group, was created in 2005.

The major **long-term credit banks** failed in 1999 and had to be reorganised as described in Table 16.1. The former three long-term credit banks have been restructured into the following entities: Mizuho Bank (created from the Industrial Bank of Japan and others), Mizuho Corporate Bank (created from the Industrial Bank of Japan and others), Shinsei Bank (formerly, the Long-Term Credit Bank of Japan), Aozora Bank (formerly, the Nippon Credit Bank). In 2009 it was announced that Shinsei Bank and the Aozora Bank would merge; however, the talks collapsed in May 2010.

16.2.1.4 Co-operative banks

The mutual co-operative banking sector also plays a major role in the Japanese banking system. These are co-operative organisations and non-profit-making financial institutions established for the benefit of SMEs in certain industries (such as agriculture and fisheries) and other groups including residents in various areas. They undertake mainly retail banking activity and SME services and are typically restricted to small areas (prefectures). Shinkin banks limit their lending, in principle, to members. However, their functions are almost the same as those of commercial banks. Total deposits outstanding at the 271 Shinkin banks (as of end of March 2012) reached approximately 122 trillion yen (equivalent to about $1,490 billion), making the Shinkin banks the third largest group of financial institutions in Japan, after city and regional banks (see Table 16.2). Shinkin banks also possess one of the largest branch networks among the financial business categories, forming a strong network throughout Japan.

The central organisations of the individual credit **co-operative banks** are relatively large banks in their own right and these provide services direct to their member banks. The main feature of co-operative banks is that they act as strong competitors to regional banks in local banking markets.

The Shinkin Central Bank serves as the central bank for Japan's 271 Shinkin banks as well as being an independent financial institution. The Shinkin Central Bank (with total assets of 30 trillion yen – around $365 billion – at the end of 2012) is one of Japan's leading financial institutions. In addition, it provides a wide range of financial services to support the Shinkin banking sector.

The Norinchukin Bank is a co-operative bank serving agricultural, fishing and forestry co-operatives. Its members include co-operative federations such as the Japan Agricultural and the Japan Fishery Co-operatives and the Japan Forestry (JForest) co-operatives. Its main function is to operate the co-operative banking business within the organisation. The bank is also one of Japan's largest institutional investors. By asset size, the Norinchukin Bank (the Nochu) is Japan's largest co-operative bank. In 2012 its total assets amounted to 72,262.8 billion yen (around $879.6 billion), more than double the size of the Shinkin Central Bank. Figure 16.3 illustrates the complex web of connections of the co-operative system.

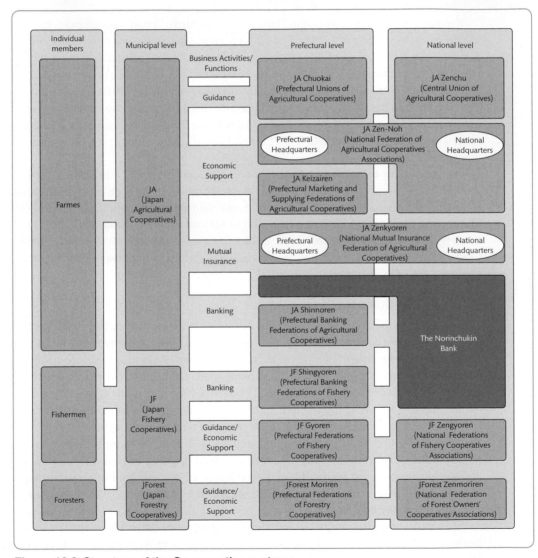

Figure 16.3 Structure of the Co-operative system

Source: The Norinchukin Bank (2012).

16.2.2 Private non-deposit-taking institutions

Private non-deposit-taking financial institutions in Japan comprise a wide variety of securities, insurance and other firms. Securities firms include major broking and investment banking type operations that offer securities services to both the corporate and the household sector. Their business is solely securities-related and they do not take deposits. In addition to these, there are insurance companies that transact life and non-life business as well as a range of other firms, including consumer finance, leasing, money market dealers (firms that trade short-term wholesale money market instruments) and mortgage securities firms (companies that deal in mortgage-backed securities). In many respects, the range and type of non-deposit-taking institutions are similar to those in other developed financial systems.

16.2.3 Public financial institutions

Japan also has a range of **public financial institutions**, which perform a significant role in the financial system. These are mainly **development banks** (close to government) that carry out direct lending (usually subsidised and medium- to long-term finance) to certain sectors of the economy. Such public institutions include:

- Development Bank of Japan (long-term financing for regional development);
- Japan Bank for International Cooperation (lending and other financial operations for the promotion of Japanese exports, imports or Japanese economic activities overseas):
- National Life Finance Corporation (lends to small businesses, students and others without access to traditional credit);
- Japan Finance for Small and Medium Sized Enterprises (subsidised lending to SMEs);
- Agriculture, Forestry, Fisheries Finance Corporation (lending to firms involved in the respective industries and 'to maintain and develop the productivity of agriculture, forestry and fisheries, and to secure stable food supply through supporting the food industry');
- Government Housing Loan Corporation (mortgage loans to individuals who have difficulty obtaining residential property finance through banks);
- Japan Financial Corporation for Municipal Enterprises (subsidised lending to local authorities);
- Okinawa Development Finance Corporation (subsidised loans for business development in Okinawa).

16.2.4 Japan Post Bank

Japan's postal savings system was the world's largest financial institution in terms of deposits. Postal savings had long been an important element in Japanese household savings and, given the crises in the banking sector over the last decade or so, the relative position of the Post Office in banking business increased. The Japanese government approved plans to privatise Japan Post in 2007, under the Postal Service Privatization Act. This resulted in the dissolution of Japan Post and the creation of the Japan Post Group and its five constituent companies: Japan Post Holdings, Japan Post Service, Japan Post Network, Japan Post Bank and Japan Post Insurance.

After it was established in 2007, the road towards the privatisation of the Japan Post Group did not go as smoothly as planned (see Box 16.1).

BOX 16.1 JAPAN SCALES BACK JAPAN POST PRIVATISATION

Japan scaled back plans to privatize the world's biggest financial conglomerate on Wednesday to keep control of the state-owned group, opening the way for it to buy more government bonds. That could provide a crutch for a government that issued a record amount of new bonds in the financial year to the end of March and which faces a public debt burden running close to 200 percent of GDP, the highest in the developed world.

Banking Minister Shizuka Kamei said the plan was not intended to create a megabank to regularly buy Japanese government bonds [JGB], but that view met with scepticism in some quarters. 'This is essentially a move to put money back to the public sector from the private sector. Japan Post money will be used to support public finance,' said Kazuo Ishikawa, senior research fellow at Tokyo Foundation. The JGB yield curve flattened on the prospects that Japan Post could become a bigger buyer of JGBs. The five-year to 20-year spread tightened 1.5 basis points to 163 basis points, shrinking from a decade high above 167 basis points earlier this month.

Japan Post is the world's biggest financial institution, based on the assets declared in earnings reports. It has financial assets of about 300 trillion yen ($3.3 trillion) – more than the GDP of France. The proposal of the six-month-old Democratic Party government of Prime Minister Yukio Hatoyama overturns a plan that the charismatic Junichiro Koizumi had begun rolling out when he led a Liberal Democratic Party government.

The previous plan envisioned spinning off the two financial subsidiaries, Japan Post Bank and Japan Post Insurance, and selling two-thirds of the holding company by 2017. Hatoyama froze that plan on the grounds it ignored the needs of consumers, saying it focused too much on profits and had already led to the closures of local post offices.

Under the new plan, the government will retain more than one-third of the shares of Japan Post's parent company, enough to allow the government to veto any major changes at the firm. 'Essentially, Japan Post will be a government-run company,' research fellow Ishikawa said.

Fund shift?

The plan allows Japan Post to roughly double the limit on the size of the company's deposits and insurance underwriting by June, although it may review

that around April 2012 depending on the impact the changes have on the banking sector. The plan has to be sealed by the cabinet and then parliament, but National Strategy Minister Yoshito Sengoku called for a rethink on doubling the deposit limits.

Bond dealers said the measures could draw funds from other banks into Japan Post accounts, especially as it is perceived as having an implicit government guarantee as a state controlled firm. Assuming Japan Post maintains a practice of investing roughly three-quarters of its financial assets in JGBs, the news is bullish for bonds, they said.

'The new plan is supportive to longer-dated Japanese government bonds as the duration of bond holdings in Japan Post Bank's portfolio is said to be longer than other banks. Japan Post Insurance is a life insurer so it is expected to invest more in longer-dated bonds,' said Chotaro Morita, head of Japan fixed-income strategy research at Barclays Capital. Although Japanese interest rates have been close to zero for much of the past decade, Japanese savers have been reluctant to take risks in shares and foreign assets, preferring to put most of their savings on deposit in Japan.

Only 1 percent of total household assets in Japan are held in foreign currency or foreign securities accounts. Otsuka Holdings, Japan's largest privately owned pharmaceutical company, said it would be up to the management of Japan Post to consider its investment stance but added it would be difficult for Japan Post to cut its government bond weighting near term.

Indeed, analysts said it was unrealistic for Japan Post to reduce its bond holdings because that could destabilize the market at a time when it is trying to cope with a sharp increase in government bond issuance.

Back-pedalling?

Otsuka said the government is likely to reduce its Japan Post stake in the future but had not decided on a timeframe. Japan Post's financial services are considered the golden goose because the traditional demand for mail services is under pressure from increased use of electronic mail and Japan's shrinking population.

BOX 16.1 JAPAN SCALES BACK JAPAN POST PRIVATISATION (*continued*)

As a state-backed bank, Japan Post Bank has long had a deposit limit of 10 million yen per person. But the government said it would double that to 20 million yen to support its profitability. The government also plans to merge deliveries and post office services into the parent company, hoping that profits from the two financial firms will subsidize deliveries and post office services.

Source: Sano and Hirata (2010).

In 2012, the Japanese government revived privatisation plans: on 27 April, around four and a half years after the original privatisation, it enacted the 'Act for Partial Revision of the Postal Service Privatisation Act and others'. The amended legislation was passed on 8 May 2012. This amended law will see Japan Post Service and Japan Post Network merge. The Japan Post Group will thus be restructured from five companies to four companies. Moreover, the 2012 law requires Japan Post Holdings Co. Ltd to aim to dispose of all shares of Japan Post Bank Co. Ltd and Japan Post Insurance Co. Ltd as soon as possible. Figure 16.4 illustrates the main changes to the Japan Post Group. All of the equity of the Japan Post Bank is owned by a government holding company (Japan Post Holdings) and the plan is for a sale and completion

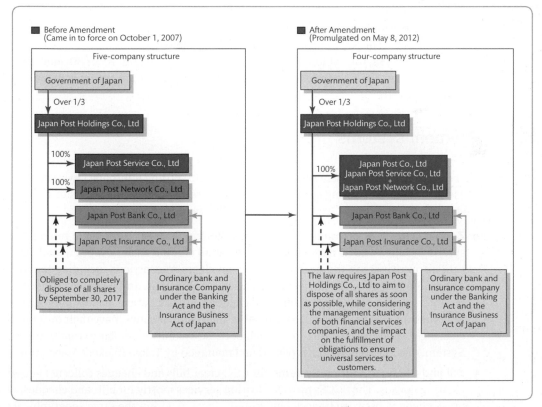

Figure 16.4 Changes to the structure of the Japan Post Group
Source: Japan Post Bank (2012) p. 25.

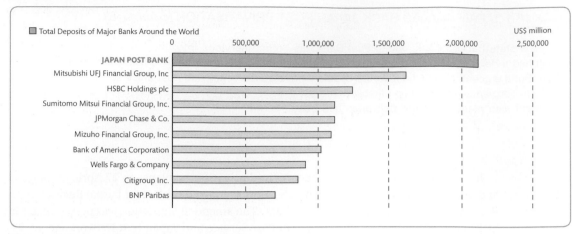

Figure 16.5 Japan Post Bank deposit base

Note: Japanese banks as of March 31, 2012, others as of December 31, 2011. Calculated based on foreign exchange rates as of the respective fiscal year-end.

Source: Japan Post Bank (2012) p. 11.

of the privatisation process by 2017. However, at the time of writing (2014), this is still a contentious political issue. A discussion of the key issues relative to the privatisation of Japan Post Bank can be found in Sawada (2013).

As a member of the Japan Post Group, Japan Post Bank offers financial services through a network comprising 234 branches and about 24,000 post offices across the country, as well as 26,557 ATMs. This vast branch network allowed the bank to build up a deposit base of 175 trillion yen ($2,136 billion) in 2012, the largest in the world. As of 30 June 2013, the bank's total assets were recorded at 203.129 trillion yen and total equity at 10.664 trillion yen (see Figure 16.5).

16.3   Payment systems

There are four major payment systems for clearing and settling interbank payments in Japan. These include three clearing systems in the private sector and a funds transfer system operated by the Bank of Japan. These clearing systems include the following:

- **Zengin Data Telecommunication System** (Zengin System) is the main retail payments system in Japan and its main task is to clear retail credit transfers. More than 2,000 institutions participate in the system. The system clears transactions including remittances, direct credits such as the payment of salaries and pensions, and payments resulting from the inter-regional collection of bills and cheques. Small financial institutions, such as the Shinkin banks and other small co-operative and regional banks, have their own interbank clearing systems. (The structure of each of these systems is similar to that of the Zengin System.) The Zengin System is owned and managed by Tokyo Bankers Association.

- **Bill and Cheque Clearing Systems** (BCCSs) clear bills and cheques collected at regional clearing houses. The BCCSs provide clearing services mostly for bills and cheques, which are exchanged between financial institutions located within the same geographical area.

Clearing houses are established and managed by their respective regional bankers' association. Large and medium-sized financial institutions, including banks and branches of foreign banks in Japan, participate directly. Small financial institutions participate indirectly through direct participants. BCCSs predominantly handle bills and cheques used for commercial transactions between firms.

- **Foreign Exchange Yen Clearing System (FXYCS)** clears mainly yen legs of wholesale foreign exchange transactions. The FXYCS was established in 1980 to facilitate clearing of yen payments for cross-border financial transactions. Clearing is undertaken through the BOJ-NET and the main participants are large banks and branches of foreign banks.

- **BOJ-NET (Bank of Japan Financial Network System) Funds Transfer System** is the central bank's funds transfer system used to settle wholesale interbank obligations, including those arising from the clearing systems. The BOJ-NET Funds Transfer System undertakes most of the payment services provided by the Bank of Japan, which are: 1) funds transfers among financial institutions stemming from interbank money market and securities transactions; 2) funds transfers between different accounts of the same financial institution; 3) settlement of net positions arising from privately owned clearing systems; and 4) funds transfers between financial institutions and the Bank of Japan, including those for monetary policy operations. Most funds transfers made through the BOJ-NET Funds Transfer System are credit transfers.

In November 2011, the Next-Generation RTGS (RTGS-XG) project was completed to bring new levels of safety and efficiency to large-value payments in Japan.

Figure 16.6 illustrates the Japanese payment systems while Table 16.3 presents some key statistics.[1]

With regards to retail payments, a key feature of the Japanese system relates to the high proportion of cash transactions compared with other developed countries. As Figure 16.7 shows, Japan has a much higher level of cash in circulation compared with the US, the UK and the euro area.

Retail payments in Japan differ from those in other major economies because of Japanese citizens' strong preference for cash payment. The use of cheques did not really develop in Japan and the large majority of non-cash payments are dominated by credit transfers (known as giro payments) and card payments.[2] This contrasts with the US, where cheques account for nearly 30 per cent of the total number of retail transactions. Credit transfers are widely used in Japan, for example, to pay wages, pensions, dividends and tax refunds. One area where Japan leads the world is in the use of smart card and mobile phone technology for retail payments. A wide range of smart cards is in use to make retail payments. Japanese households are the most avid users of smart cards and these have been introduced in a wide variety of applications, such as transport ticket payments, access control, electronic money and credit cards.

---

[1] For a detailed account of the operations of these systems see Bank of Japan (2012) 'Payment, clearing and settlement systems in Japan' available online at **www.boj.or.jp/en/paym/outline/pay_boj/pss1212a.pdf**

[2] Unfortunately the figures for Japan do not provide a breakdown for credit transfers and direct debits. See Bank for International Settlements (2013c), available at **www.bis.org/publ/cpss112.htm**

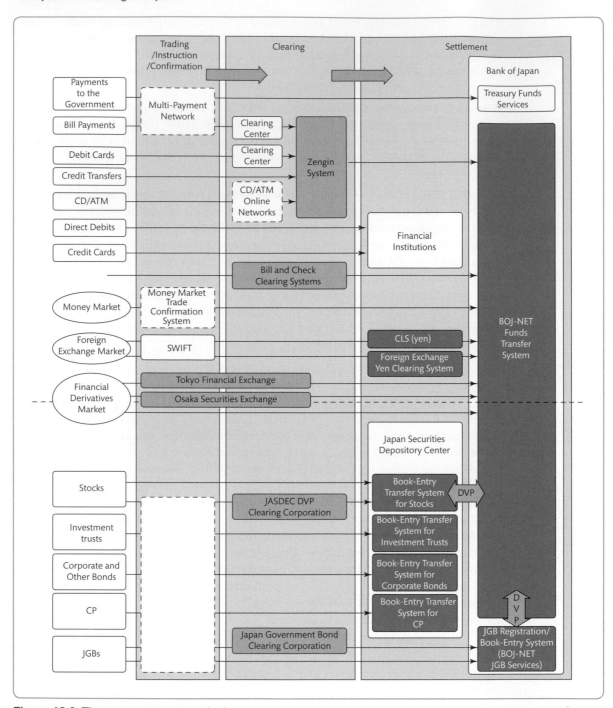

Figure 16.6 The payment systems in Japan

Source: Bank of Japan (2012).

Table 16.3 Payment system statistics: number and value of transactions

	2008	2009	2010	2011	2012
Number of transactions (millions)					
BOJ-NET	8.47	12.31	12.41	12.93	15.30
FXYCS	7.54	6.21	6.35	6.33	6.29
Zengin System	1,368	1,380	1,380	1,394	1,460
Tokyo Clearing House	36.65	31.17	28.51	26.64	24.97
Increase in the number of transactions (% change on previous year)					
BOJ-NET	25.3	45.4	0.8	4.2	18.3
FXYCS	−2.8	−17.7	2.3	−0.3	−0.7
Zengin System	1.1	0.9	0.0	1.0	4.7
Tokyo Clearing House	−10.0	−15.0	−8.5	−6.6	−6.3
Value of transactions ($ billions)					
BOJ-NET	285,589	291,305	291,496	311,549	341,479
FXYCS	50,080	33,957	32,859.0	35,399	30,848
Zengin System	25,974	25,703	28,266.8	32,204	33,252
Tokyo Clearing House	2,884	2,782	3,117.3	3,522	3,416
Average value per transaction ($ thousands)					
BOJ-NET	33,714	23,656	23,485	24,093	22,326
FXYCS	6,643	5,470.8	5,176	5,591	4,907
Zengin System	19	18.6	20.5	23	23
Tokyo Clearing House	79	89.3	109	132	137
Increase in the real value of transactions (% change on previous year, adjusted by CPI inflation)					
BOJ-NET	−1.2	−6.5	−5.5	−2.6	9.7
FXYCS	−9.3	−37.8	−8.6	−1.8	−12.8
Zengin System	0.9	−9.3	3.9	3.8	3.4
Tokyo Clearing House	−7.2	−11.6	5.8	3.0	−2.9
Value of transactions as a percentage of GDP (in %)					
BOJ-NET	5,894	5,784	5,300	5,277	5,727
FXYCS	1,034	674	597	600	517
Zengin System	536	510	514	545	558
Tokyo Clearing House	59	55	57	60	57

Source: Bank for International Settlements (2013c). Available at www.bis.org/publ/cpss112.htm

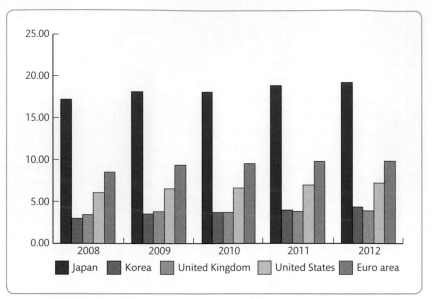

Figure 16.7 Banknotes and coins in circulation (to nominal GDP), 2008–2012

Source: Data from Bank for International Settlements (2013c).

16.4 Banking crises in Japan

Throughout this chapter we have mentioned how the banking crisis in the late 1990s severely impacted on the Japanese financial system. The regulatory features of the system have changed dramatically as a consequence of these events and as such it is best to highlight the main features of this crisis and its impact on the regulatory structure before we look in more detail at the impact of the 2007–2009 global financial crisis.

16.4.1 The Japanese banking crisis

The banking collapse that ensued during the 1990s was mainly a consequence of three main forces:

- **Excessive lending** – bank lending, much of which was secured against land and property, grew rapidly in the late 1980s. Bank lending activity was concentrated in the wholesale and retail trade, real estate, finance and insurance, and construction sectors. The fall in stock prices and reversal in the performance of the economy in the early 1990s made highly indebted firms in these sectors unable to repay their loans due to a decline in collateral values, thus creating a large pool of bad loans. However, despite these problems, bank exposure to certain sectors, such as real estate and construction, continued to grow due to the low interest rate environment until the second half of the 1990s. This resulted in a further increase in bank NPLs and the banking system fell into a systemic crisis in 1997–1998.

- **Negative impact of asset price deflation** – the rapid credit growth during the 1990s had been accompanied by a doubling of stock prices and a rapid rise in commercial estate prices, particularly in major cities. A sharp increase in interest rates and the introduction of various credit ceilings (limits on the amounts banks could lend) to real estate-related activity led to the bursting of the asset price bubble. This created substantial losses for firms that held equities and had borrowed from banks with real estate as collateral. As a consequence, this had the effect of converting a substantial portion of banks' loans into non-performing assets, and asset price **deflation** resulted (and has been a feature of the Japanese economy for nearly a decade).

- **Policy failure to contain problem** – various commentators have argued that the main government authorities (Bank of Japan and the Ministry of Finance) were too slow in dealing with the build-up of problem loans in the banking system. Throughout the 1990s banks were continuing to lend to the real estate sector despite signs of problems in their loan books as well as deflationary pressures in the economy overall. Interest rates had fallen to low levels and the government made various attempts to boost public spending in order to create demand in the economy, although little action was taken to deal with problems in the banking system until the crisis hit. The initial government approach was to stimulate demand by fiscal policy in the economy; it was assumed that it would restore economic growth and thus return the banks to a healthy position. However, the fiscal stimulus had only a marginal impact on the economy. There was also little international pressure on the authorities to resolve their banking problem, which was viewed mainly as a domestic issue.

The gradual culmination of these forces led to the collapse of the so-called '**convoy system**' where the Ministry of Finance 'encouraged' healthy banks to acquire those in trouble. In addition, while the Bank of Japan (the central bank) provided liquidity assistance to the banking system, this was not enough to stem the crisis that ensued. Major events relating to the crisis are illustrated in Table 16.4.

Since the banking crisis, a wide range of reforms has been put in place. These reforms have aimed to stabilise the banking system and to facilitate bank restructuring. The authorities introduced a blanket deposit insurance scheme (to protect all depositors in the event of bank failure), extended emergency liquidity assistance to troubled banks, provided financial assistance to promote mergers among troubled financial institutions, injected capital into weak but viable banks and allowed for the temporary nationalisation of non-viable banks.

Various features of reforms involved with bank restructuring include:

- public **recapitalisation** of various banks (in March 1998, March 1999 and May 2003) that amounted to around 9 trillion yen;
- more rapid recognition of NPLs (introduced in October 2002) – with tougher loan classification and loan loss provisioning rules which enabled the regulators to identify the size of bad loans but also encouraged faster disposals of non-performing loans (e.g. banks writing them off their balance sheets);
- disposal of bank NPLs, close to 90 trillion yen since 1998, although despite these disposals, bank NPLs have not declined as fast as expected due to the emergence of new NPLs;
- exit of a number of inefficient deposit-taking institutions;
- establishment of various public asset management companies that deal with the sale of bank NPLs.

In addition to these reforms, the authorities have been active in encouraging mergers between the leading banks, they withdrew the blanket deposit insurance guarantee in spring 2005 and continued to focus on measures aimed at reducing the level of non-performing loans in the system. We will focus on the impact of the global financial crisis in Section 16.4.2.

Table 16.4 Japan's 1998 banking crisis – major events

Year	Event
Mid-1995	Two large credit unions and a regional bank fail as a result of bad loans.
1995	A substantial number of housing loan companies, known as Jusen, failed and were bailed out by a group of banks and government funds. As a result of the Jusen collapse and concerns about growing levels of non-performing loans, bank stock prices declined relative to other stocks around the end of 1995, and credit-rating agencies began to downgrade the credit ratings of Japanese banks – increasing their cost of funds.
November 1997	On 3 November, Sanyo Securities defaulted in the interbank loan market, delivering another shock to the market.
November 1997	Hokkaido Takushoku Bank and Yamaichi Securities (one of the four large securities houses) failed, leading to a further downgrading of bank credit ratings.
March 1998	The Japanese government sought to deal with the undercapitalisation of banks by injecting capital into the banking sector in March 1998. A newly created Financial Crisis Management Committee handled this capital injection, which was successful in calming financial markets (until May).
Mid- to late 1998	The government attempted to pass several reform bills. One of these bills was the Financial Revitalisation Act, which was designed to deal with failed financial institutions. Under this law, a failed bank could either be placed under Financial Reorganisation Administration (FRA) or could be temporarily nationalised. This law formed the basis for the government's decision in late 1998 to nationalise two major banks, the Long Term Credit Bank of Japan and Nippon Credit Bank, both teetering on the verge of bankruptcy.
Late 1990s to early 2000s	The establishment of the Financial Supervision Agency (FSA) in June 1998 shifted the responsibility of financial supervision of private deposit institutions from the Ministry of Finance to an independent entity. The Agency changed its name to the Financial Services Agency in 2001.

16.4.2 Impact of the 2007–2009 financial crisis on Japanese banking

Japanese banks have been operating in a slow growing, near deflationary environment since the onset of the 1998 crisis. They have restructured their activities and reduced their levels of non-performing loans, although the system overall still posts low profitability by international standards (see Section 16.5.2). While still struggling to recover from the 1998 crisis, the Japanese banking system was hit by the fall-out from the US sub-prime crisis that emerged in mid-2007. Unlike the US, however, Japan did not have a high-risk segment of the mortgage market – securitisation of mortgages (or other loans) is not common and property prices had followed a different trend from those in the US and the UK for nearly two decades. The Japanese real-estate bubble burst in the early 1990s and after that prices in the major cities fell continuously. Although residential property prices in Japan did increase by around 25 per cent between 2004 and 2008, by the time the sub-prime bubble burst in 2008 prices were not at the level they had been in 2000. As a consequence, the country did not face a real estate bubble funded by securitisation and lending excesses. In addition, Japanese banks did not hold significant amounts of US sub-prime and other securitised securities. For instance, the largest three banking groups (Mizuho, Mitsui Sumitomo and Mitsubishi-Tokyo UFJ) are estimated to have had less than 1 per cent of their balance sheet invested in sub-prime mortgage-backed securities and sub-prime asset-backed securities or collateralised debt obligations by the end of March 2008. No Japanese bank failed as a consequence of the global financial crisis, although the downturn in the global economy and the adverse impact on the already weakened Japanese economy contributed to putting additional pressure on Japanese banks.

As noted above, although Japanese banks were not large buyers of sub-prime-related products, they still suffered in the financial fallout from the crisis. Bank margins decreased further, as did credit to the corporate sector, which forms the bulk of their business. When loan growth stalls, so does bank profitability. The stock market also fell 40 per cent between April 2008 and April 2009, creating losses that further reduced banks' capital. A major consequence was that all the main Japanese banks sought to raise more capital ($34 billion through the issue of new equity and preferred stock between January 2008 and April 2009).

Despite the aforementioned setbacks, Japanese banks came through the credit crisis relatively well compared with their US and UK counterparts. Their loss-absorbing capacity was higher, asset quality was more stable and reliance of wholesale funding was lower compared with US and eurozone banks.

Post global financial crisis, Japanese banks still face a number of challenges related to future profitability and business models (IMF, 2013d). In addition, Japanese banks have increased their foreign presence, thereby increasing their reliance on external funding. According to the IMF (2013d) figures, the Japanese banking system's external funding position – the difference between its foreign assets and liabilities – has increased to $1.6 trillion (US and UK banks have net surplus positions). This relatively large external funding position can expose Japanese banks to foreign currency shocks, in terms of availability, maturity and costs.

The major ongoing concern remains the state of the domestic economy and this poses the greatest threat to the performance of the banks.

16.5 Changing structure of the financial system

Given the turmoil in the Japanese economy in the late 1990s, it is perhaps of little surprise that financial activities shifted from private financial intermediaries to public financial intermediaries between 1989 and 1999, although there has been a slight reversal since then. Table 16.5 illustrates that financial institutions hold around 45–46 per cent of the country's financial assets, with the household sector having around 24 per cent (15 trillion yen) and non-financial firms holding around 15–16 per cent of financial assets. Of the 15 trillion yen of assets held by households, more than 45 per cent is in bank deposits. In the corporate sector, loans from private financial institutions comprise around 36 per cent of total debt and this is by far the most

Table 16.5 Financial assets of Japan by sectors, 2012 (trillion yen)

Sectors	March 2011	March 2012	Annual growth (%)
Domestic sectors	5707	5794	1.5
Financial institutions	2822	2869	1.7
Domestic non-financial sector	2886	2925	4.1
Non-financial corporations	845	488	2.8
General government	485	488	0.6
Households (incl. sole proprietorships)	1502	1513	0.7
Private non-profit institutions serving households	54	55	3.1
Overseas	347	380	9.6

Source: Statistics Bureau (2013).

important source of debt. For instance, corporate bonds and commercial paper borrowings account for less than 8 per cent of debt combined. (In the US the corporate bond and commercial paper amount to 22 per cent of corporate liabilities compared with only 9 per cent for bank loans.) Clearly Japan has a bank-based intermediation system where markets are much less important in funding the corporate sector. According to the Bank of Japan (2013), the fraction of financial assets held in banks has been on a downward trend throughout the past two decades, although the decline ended in the late 2000s as a consequence of the global financial crisis.

16.5.1 Regulation of Japanese banks

The regulatory environment under which Japanese banks operate has undergone substantial changes as a result of the 1998 crisis. Until the late 1990s, inspection and supervision of financial institutions, as well as the function of financial system planning, had been the responsibility of the Ministry of Finance. Traditionally, the Bank of Japan supervised the banking system and was instrumental in introducing various reforms known as the '**Big Bang**' which effectively introduced the universal banking model. The deregulation that occurred between 1998 and 1999:

● allowed the use of financial holding companies;

● eliminated many barriers between banking and other financial service sectors;

● liberalised stock brokerage fees;

● allowed banks to sell investment trust products.

As a result of these and other measures, financial institutions in Japan could offer a wide range of financial products and options to their customers. From April 1998, the Bank of Japan was given greater independence in relation to monetary policy and in June 1998 a new governmental agency called the Financial Supervisory Agency (which changed its name to the **Financial Services Agency** in 2001) was established and given supervisory and inspection functions with respect to private sector financial institutions. (Previously, both the Bank of Japan and the Ministry of Finance had supervisory responsibilities.)

The Financial Services Agency is responsible for the supervision and inspection of all private banks in Japan. It monitors the financial soundness of banks, including the status and performance of their control systems for business activities. The main functions of the agency are:

● planning and policy making concerning the financial system;

● inspection and supervision of private sector financial institutions, including banks, securities companies, insurance companies and market participants including securities exchanges;

● establishment of rules for trading in securities markets;

● establishment of business accounting standards and others concerning corporate finance;

● supervision of certified public accountants and audit firms;

● participation in activities on financial issues of international organisations and bilateral and multilateral forums to develop internationally co-ordinated financial administration;

● surveillance of compliance of rules governing securities markets.

The FSA is responsible for dealing with failed financial institutions and general oversight of the soundness of private banks in the Japanese system. There is also a Deposit Insurance Corporation that protects depositors' funds in the event of a bank failure.

Table 16.6 Regulation and supervision by bank type

Type of bank	Central bank	Legal foundation	Supervisory authority
Commercial banks	Bank of Japan (BoJ)	The 1981 Banking Law	Financial Services Agency
Shinkin banks	Shinkin Central Bank (SCB)	The 1951 Shinkin Bank Law (and 1981 revision)	Financial Services Agency
Credit co-operative banks (Shinkumi)	The Shinkumi Federation Bank (SFB)	The 1949 Small and Medium-Size Enterprise and Co-operative Act	Financial Services Agency
Labour banks	The Rokinren Bank (national federation of labour credit associations)	The 1953 Labour Bank Law	Financial Services Agency Ministry of Health, Labour and Welfare
Agricultural (JA), Fishery (JF) and Forestry (JForest) co-operatives	The Norinchukin Bank	The 1943 Norinchukin Bank Law	Ministry of Agriculture, Forestry and Fisheries of Japan

As discussed in Section 16.2, commercial banks in Japan are defined under the 1981 Banking Law. Although the FSA is the main supervisory authority for most financial institutions (with the exception of the Norinchukin Bank), other types of banks are defined under different legislation, as summarised in Table 16.6. More specifically, other types of financial institutions (including co-operative banks) are regulated by different specialised regulation (namely, the Shinkin Bank Law, the Co-operatives and Small and Medium Enterprises Law and the Norinchukin Bank Law).

16.5.2 Balance sheet features and performance

The Japanese economy has been stagnating since the late 1990s, when the country was hit by a deep economic and financial crisis (see Section 16.4.1). A mild recovery seemed to have started in the mid-2000s; however, the onset of the global financial crisis pushed Japan back into recession and deflation. Since then, the Japanese government has enacted various reforms to restore economic growth. The more recent of these reforms, a combination of monetary policy, fiscal stimulus and structural reforms, carried out by Prime Minister Shinzo Abe, have earned the nickname of '**Abenomics**' and are considered the most aggressive policy moves in Japan's history. These reforms aim to restore sustainable growth and seem to have been successful, but not without risks (see Box 16.2).

The balance sheet and performance features of the Japanese banking system were severely affected by the recession in the economy as well as the financial sector crises. Between 1996 and the mid-2000s, bank lending portfolios declined by around 30 per cent, reflecting the lack of demand and the increasing number of bad loans that had to be written off. On average, however, the Japanese banking system overall has been steadily improving since the mid-2000s (see Figure 16.8). Yet, given the high fragmentation of the sector, bank performance differs significantly by bank segment. Several regional banks are afflicted by low core profitability and a relatively thin capital position, making them particularly vulnerable to slow growth, as illustrated in Figure 16.9 (IMF, 2012a). Japan's mega-banks, meanwhile, seem to have enjoyed a period of high growth (see Box 16.2).

Tables 16.7 and 16.8 illustrate the financial statements of Japanese banks in 2012. Japanese banks hold large amounts of liquid assets as a share of both short-term liabilities (around 50 per cent) and total assets (about 20 per cent) (see Table 16.7). However, there

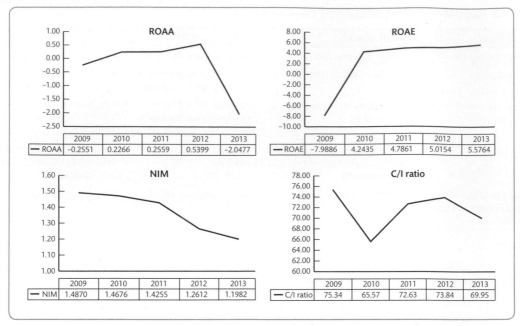

Figure 16.8 The performance of Japanese banks, 2009–2013

Source: SNL Financials, data for 2013 (Q2).

BOX 16.2 JAPAN'S BIGGEST BANKS PROFIT UNDER ABENOMICS

Japan's biggest banks are prospering in the drastically altered business environment created by "Abenomics", confounding – at least for now – fears that a loss of bond-trading income under the country's new monetary regime would lead to lower profits.

Mitsubishi UFJ and Mizuho, Japan's two largest banking groups by assets, reported stronger than forecast earnings for the quarter to June on Wednesday, as the benefits of a surging stock market and growing demand for corporate loans more than offset the decline in bonds.

Mitsubishi's net profit rose 40 per cent from a year earlier, to Y255bn ($2.6bn), while Mizuho's grew 35 per cent to Y248bn. Sumitomo Mitsui, Japan's third-biggest lender, said on Monday its net profit for the period more than doubled to Y288bn. In May 2013, the three banks forecast lower profits for the financial year that began on April 1. Their pessimism was a response to the aggressive monetary easing programme launched in April by the Bank of Japan and its newly installed governor, Haruhiko Kuroda.

As part of an effort to end Japan's prolonged consumer-price deflation, Mr Kuroda doubled the target for purchases of Japanese government bonds by the BoJ each month, turning the central bank into the dominant player in the JGB market by mopping up about 70 per cent of new issuance.

One result was that trading volumes collapsed and commercial banks were squeezed out of a market where they had previously made much of their profits. Japanese banks have for years counted on income from JGB trading to supplement the poorly paid business of lending to companies. Corporate Japan is flush with cash and, given chronically weak economic growth, has little need for new factories or equipment. When companies do turn to banks for funds, it is at rates so low as to make the loans barely profitable. Lending was still an ultra-low margin business last quarter: at Mitsubishi, the spread between domestic loans and deposits shrank 6 basis points to 1.05 per cent. Spreads at the other banks were similarly thin. Volumes increased, however, bringing in more income overall. Aggregate Japanese bank lending rose to its highest level in four years in June 2013 as a stronger economy and rock-bottom interest rates prompted some companies to seek funds for investment. Tax

Box 16.2 Japan's biggest banks profit under Abenomics (*continued*)

breaks promised by the government of Shinzo Abe, prime minister, could lift demand further.

"The environment is improving for Japanese companies to expand capital spending," Takeshi Kunibe, the president of Sumitomo Mitsui and chairman of the Japanese Bankers Association, said in July 2013.

Japanese banks are expanding overseas, with Mitsubishi in July offering to buy a majority stake in Thailand's Bank of Ayudhya. Banks are also benefiting from the Japanese stock market rally that began late last year, which has lifted the value of their share portfolios and attracted fee income from a growing roster of mutual-fund buyers. Mitsubishi reported stock-related gains of Y12.8bn in the quarter, compared with losses of Y54.5bn in the same quarter last year. The three banks' profits in the first quarter were equal to between a third and half of their full-year forecasts, which call for slightly weaker earnings than last year. Still, the lenders left those forecasts unchanged on Wednesday.

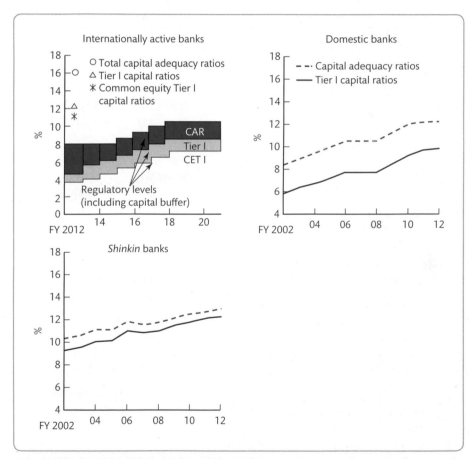

Figure 16.9 Capitalisation of Japanese banks

Notes:

1. CAR indicates total capital adequacy ratio. 'Domestic banks' excludes Shinkin banks. Data for banks are on a consolidated basis.

2. Figures of internationally active banks and domestic banks are based on the Basel III requirements (taking grandfathering measures into consideration) and the Basel II requirements, respectively.

Source: Bank of Japan (2013).

Table 16.7 Balance sheet, March 2012 (values in million yen)

	All banks	City banks	Regional banks
(a) LIABILITIES			
Deposits	616,711,968	291,289,365	220,991,780
Commercial papers	1,545,410	1,409,947	—
Trading liabilities	12,303,209	11,470,429	95,718
Borrowed money	36,687,441	27,576,925	3,776,241
Foreign exchanges	1,548,556	1,534,548	12,457
Short-term bonds payable	366,768	117,399	—
Bonds payable	15,869,202	13,400,981	788,164
Bonds with subscription rights to shares	58,502	—	51,402
Borrowed money from trust account	4,004,337	798,541	53,275
Other liabilities	19,256,332	15,046,382	1,812,739
Other reserves	296,047	136,126	78,041
Total liabilities	828,584,587	450,464,226	240,844,264
(b) EQUITY CAPITAL			
Capital stock	11,722,261	5,936,947	2,551,310
Retained earnings	15,573,253	5,216,822	7,599,969
Shareholders' equity	38,844,157	19,626,982	11,569,832
Total liabilities and equity capital	870,696,762	471,493,980	253,880,822
(c) ASSETS			
Cash and due from banks	39,974,851	23,103,467	9,424,581
Call loans	16,680,970	9,798,850	4,622,568
Receivables under resale agreements	1,896,980	1,776,253	32,090
Receivables under securities borrowing transactions	3,403,682	3,032,958	120,459
Trading assets	17,897,479	15,702,464	466,474
Trading account securities	117,674	40,793	63,524
Securities	278,652,128	166,266,403	71,084,654
Loans and bills discounted	458,254,205	209,926,763	161,973,978
Foreign exchanges	3,909,784	3,544,073	239,017
Other assets	21,695,168	17,044,054	1,716,099
Tangible fixed assets	6,509,877	2,699,097	2,552,118
Intangible fixed assets	1,341,973	816,800	282,536
Total assets	870,696,762	471,493,980	253,880,822

Source: Data from the Japanese Bankers Association, **www.zenginkyo.or.jp/en/stats/**

are concerns that the financial system's massive holdings of government bonds could leave it exposed to a spike in yields.

Japanese banks' capital ratios have improved steadily and the large regional banks have higher capital ratios compared with their city bank competitors. The top banks have capital levels similar to their Western counterparts, especially since the global financial crisis that forced banks to boost their capital strength. Concerns about the capital strength of some

Table 16.8 Income statement, March 2012 (values in million yen)

	All banks	City banks	Regional banks
Ordinary income	15,437,211	7,684,655	4,632,973
Interest income	9,934,733	4,566,816	3,488,779
Fees and commissions	2,638,849	1,479,003	677,024
Trading income	306,015	245,401	4,530
Other ordinary income	1,579,193	1,022,595	257,692
Other income	731,480	345,595	204,184
Ordinary expenses	11,619,848	5,463,470	3,607,725
Interest expenses	1,777,832	1,056,463	308,934
Fees and commissions payments	931,600	420,385	298,978
Other ordinary expenses	514,480	271,021	104,246
General and administrative expenses	6,855,170	2,974,512	2,456,403
Other expenses	1,535,907	740,403	438,571
Ordinary profit	3,817,305	2,221,182	1,025,215
Extraordinary income	46,856	18,883	18,146
Extraordinary loss	159,427	63,712	31,318
Income before income taxes	3,704,716	2,176,352	1,012,035
Total income taxes	1,223,453	609,034	432,551
Net income	2,481,210	1,567,316	579,452

Source: Data from the Japanese Bankers Association, **www.zenginkyo.or.jp/en/stats/**

Japanese regional banks, however, are ongoing and there may be more pressure on them to boost their solvency.

Probably the most important factor influencing Japanese bank performance in recent years has been the enormous levels of bad loans accumulated during the Japanese financial crisis. According to official figures from Japan's Financial Services Agency, the cumulative amount of losses by way of bad debts for all Japanese banks amounted to 100,263 billion yen by September 2008 (more than $1 trillion in 2008 dollar terms). Following significant restructuring among the large banks and insurance companies (described in Section 16.3), non-performing loans were reduced and capital positions improved. As shown in Figure 16.10, the proportion of non-performing loans had fallen from 9.6 per cent of total gross loans to 2.4 per cent by late September 2008 and remained stable thereafter – and provisioning also fell, reflecting this trend. The total losses from NPLs also decreased steadily, and despite a brief increase in 2008–2010, they have remained at low levels.

Turning to figures from the income statements of Japanese banks (see Table 16.8), net interest margins have been low, given the low interest rate domestic environment that has contributed to the overall level of bank performance, which remains below that of international peers. While NIMs have been decreasing steadily for several years in many advanced economies, the pressure on Japanese banks seems higher as they reported average NIMs of 1.2 in 2012, compared with 3.3 for US banks and 2.9 for UK banks.

To summarise, since the late 1990s, substantial progress has been made to strengthen and stabilise the Japanese banking system. The restructuring has resulted in a healthier banking sector, which withstood the output contraction deriving from the global financial crisis of 2007–2009. Capital positions improved and NPLs were reduced. The Japanese banking sector

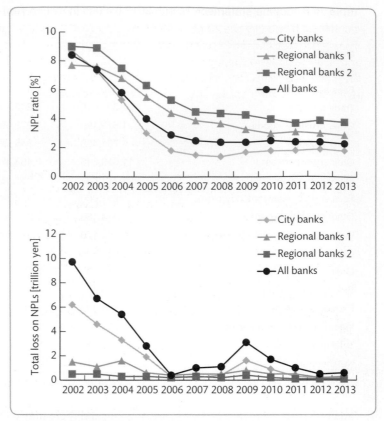

Figure 16.10 Japanese banks' non-performing loans and loan losses, 2002–2013

Source: Data from Japan's Financial Services Agency. Available at **www.fsa.go.jp/en/**

is now in better health than it has been for the past two decades, although some vulnerabilities are apparent, including the exposure of its banks to government debt, credit quality and regional weaker macroeconomic conditions.

16.6 Conclusion

The Japanese banking sector has endured dramatic changes over the last few decades, experiencing rapid growth during the 1980s and the mid-1990s, followed by a collapse between 1997 and 1998 and an ensuing long restructuring period thereafter, returning to respectable levels of profitability in 2005. The improvement in performance was short-lived and Japanese banks' profitability declined in the mid-2000s, and remained flat over 2009–2012 with ROE hovering around 4–5 per cent (mainly as a consequence of a slow growing economy and very low margins on corporate and other lending business). Since mid-2005 non-performing loan levels have fallen but weak revenue growth still hampers profitability.

There has been substantial consolidation between the largest banks, with five major city banks and the Japan Post Bank vying for market share in a congested market. Although capital levels have improved in recent years, there is ongoing market pressure for banks to strengthen their capital positions. Unlike its US and UK counterparts, Japanese banking was much less affected by the 2007–2009 global financial crisis. Japanese banks were not heavily engaged in securitisation activities and did not invest in sub-prime and other securitised assets; as a result no Japanese bank failed or needed any form of direct support because of the global financial crisis. The main threat to the banking system is the state of the domestic economy, which still battles strong deflationary pressures.

Key terms

Abenomics	City banks	Japan Post Bank	Public financial
'Big Bang'	'Convoy system'	Long-term credit	institutions
Bill and Cheque	Co-operative banks	banks	Recapitalisation
Clearing Systems	Deflation	Private deposit-	Regional banks
(BCCSs)	Development banks	taking financial	Shinkin banks
BOJ-NET (Bank of	Financial Services	institutions	Trust banks
Japan Financial	Agency	Private non-	Zengin Data
Network System)	Foreign Exchange	eposit-taking	Telecommunication
Funds Transfer	Yen Clearing	financial	System
System	System (FXYCS)	institutions	

Key reading

Bank of Japan (2013) 'Financial System Report', available at **www.boj.or.jp/en/research/brp/fsr/data/fsr131023a.pdf**

Bank of Japan (2012) 'Payment, clearing and settlement systems in Japan', available at **www.boj.or.jp/en/paym/outline/pay_boj/pss1212a.pdf**

Kanaya, A. and Woo, D. (2000) 'The Japanese banking crises of the 1990s: Sources and lessons', IMF Working Paper WP/00/7.

Uchida, H. and Udell, G. (2014) 'Banking in Japan', in Berger, A.N., Molyneux, P. and Wilson, J.O.S. (eds), *Oxford Handbook of Banking*, 2nd Edition, Oxford: Oxford University Press, Chapter 36.

REVISION QUESTIONS AND PROBLEMS

16.1 What are the main features of the different types of financial institutions operating in Japan?

16.2 To what extent has the disintermediation process impacted the Japanese banking and financial sectors?

16.3 How is the payment system organised for clearing and settling interbank payments in Japan?

16.4 What have been the most relevant changes to the Japanese banks' profitability since 2000?

16.5 Compare the impact of the 1998–2009 crisis with the 2007–2009 global financial crisis on Japanese banks.

16.6 Discuss why Japanese banks were less affected by the 2007–2009 global financial crisis than were US and UK banks. Can the latter learn any lessons from Japanese bankers?

16.7 Discuss recent trends in Japanese banking and highlight the performance implications of these developments.

16.8 Discuss Japan's economic prospects and how these are likely to impact the performance of Japanese banks.

Chapter 17

Banking in emerging markets

Learning objectives

- To understand how financial sector development aids economic growth
- To analyse the evolution of the finance and growth literature
- To provide an overview of the main structural features of banking systems in emerging markets
- To understand the main changes that have occurred in emerging banking markets in recent years
- To analyse the role of state ownership and foreign ownership in banking markets
- To understand how financial sector liberalisation and other forces have impacted banking sector consolidation and foreign entry in emerging markets

17.1 Introduction

Global banking markets have experienced major developments over the last few decades, in line with a transformation of the macroeconomic features of many countries. The fall of the Berlin Wall and decline of the communist states of Central and Eastern Europe from 1991 onwards gave major impetus for reform, as did the gradual acceptance of market forces and liberalisation in many Asian and Latin American countries. State banking has, in many cases, been replaced by privately owned banks, and foreign banks now play a key role in many systems. Heightened competition and consolidation trends have also been commonplace. Where emerging economies' banks once lagged their counterparts from developed countries, they increasingly rival them across a broad array of financial services, although typically the former first build expertise in consumer and SME financial services, developing more sophisticated commercial and investment banking services later.

Some developing and transition economies have had to actively attract foreign banks to inject capital in their banking systems because of scarce domestic resources – as in Central and Eastern Europe after the collapse of communism and in South East Asia after the banking crises of 1998–1999 (when the Malaysian, Indonesian and Thailand banking systems collapsed). Other economies have been more cautious. China insists on foreign banks having domestic partners – it limits single foreign ownership of its banks to 20 per cent and total foreign ownership to 25 per cent. India has a 10 per cent limit for individual investors, although total foreign ownership is not to exceed 74 per cent. Other countries also have limits on foreign ownership that can be increased after ministerial approval (Vietnam, for instance).

This chapter aims to address some of the important issues impacting the development of emerging banking markets. Deregulation and the general liberalisation of financial services at the national level and the opening up of many domestic sectors to foreign banks have all contributed to transforming economies as well as boosting competition and innovation (both financial and technological). Against the background of these developments, Section 17.2 examines the difference between bank-based and market-based financial systems and outlines different measures that can be used to compare financial sectors, with particular emphasis on emerging markets. Section 17.3 looks at the relationship between finance and growth, illustrating how a sound and efficient financial system can aid economic development – although it can also bring risks. In Section 17.4 we look at the macroeconomic outlook for emerging markets and highlight how following the 2007–2009 global financial crisis they have (typically) performed less well, although longer-term growth prospects remain above those of their developed country counterparts. Section 17.5 investigates the main forces of change and how these have influenced the structure of the banking industries in terms of deregulation and the liberalisation process, the role of the state, M&As and the entry of foreign banks. Section 17.6 gives the conclusions.

17.2   Benchmarking financial development

Before we examine how banks and financial markets contribute to economic development it is important to outline the broad characteristics of financial systems, including the relative importance of financial institutions and markets. Joseph Schumpeter, the famous Austrian–American economist, was the first to recognise that financial sector development contributed to economic growth (although he held the view that technological innovation was more important in the development process). From the early 1980s onwards there was much debate as to what type of financial system best served growth – was it a financial system where banks dominated or one where capital markets/stock markets were more important? This debate, first identified by Tad Rybczynski (1983), led to the discussion about **bank-based** and **market-based financial systems** (see also Section 18.2). From the 1960s through to the mid-1980s the German and Japanese economies (which had large banking sectors but small stock markets) had performed better than their US and UK counterparts (which typically had relatively much bigger stock markets). Also the former had universal-style banking, where banks owned substantial stakes in non-financial firms, both directly (Germany) or indirectly via a web of cross-holdings (Japan). It looked to some economists that the bank-based universal model was the type of financial system that best aided growth. This view, however, changed from the mid to late 1980s as the political economy of developed economies emphasised pro-market reforms and widespread liberalisation. Obstacles to trade in goods and services were also dismantled, aiding international capital flows. Both the International Monetary Fund (whose brief primarily focuses on alleviating balance of payments problems and general macroeconomic crises) and the World Bank (which aims to alleviate poverty and promote economic development) increasingly emphasised deregulation and liberalisation in policy actions aimed at broad-based market reforms.

The debate as to whether a bank-based or market-based system best serves economic development ran its course – ultimately a consensus emerged which concluded that it did not seem to matter whether an economy had a large banking sector or capital market, what was most important was that there was a sizeable, efficient and competitive financial system overall. Key policy organisations like the World Bank have made major efforts to measure and classify the importance of different attributes of banking and financial market activities in all the world's economies. Table 17.1 illustrates a classification from the World Bank identifying potential indicators to help benchmark the features of different financial systems. Note that the indicators for financial institutions relate mainly to banks and other deposit-taking institutions. The Čihák et al. (2012a) study provides a '4 × 2 framework for financial sector benchmarking', which aims to summarise the characteristics of financial systems along four dimensions:

1 **Depth** – financial depth relates to the size of the banking sector and/or financial markets. Looking at the indicators for financial institutions, these relate to variables such as (i) private sector credit to GDP (this is mainly bank lending to GDP); (ii) financial institutions' assets to GDP (this relates to the sum of assets of banks, insurance companies, pension companies and other non-bank financial firms over GDP); (iii) M2/GDP (where M2 is a measure of money supply equalling the sum of cash and current account deposits plus savings account deposits); (iv) gross value added of the financial sector to GDP (defined by how much financial institutions contribute to the economy overall – output minus intermediate consumption). The indicators for financial markets include measures of the size of the stock market (capitalisation – the amount of shares issued multiplied by the price) and debt markets, both private (bonds issued by companies) and public (bonds issued by governments). The stock traded/GDP indicator links the volume of shares traded to the size of the economy (GDP). Economists often talk about **financial deepening** when the financial sector overall gets bigger in relation to the overall size of the economy.

2 **Access** – this relates to how available financial services are to the population or the corporate sector. The proposed benchmark indicators for financial institutions relate to the proportion of the population with access to banking services. These indicators include, for example, commercial bank accounts per 100,000 adults and the percentage of individuals with bank accounts. Other indicators look at the proportion of firms with bank credit (for all firms and/or just small firms). Financial market indicators of access relate to the availability of market-based finance for companies other than for the largest firms. In addition, indicators of access include measures of stock market capitalisation outside the top ten firms, the value of stock/share trading outside the largest ten firms, new corporate bond issuance and the ratio of private to public debt (this latter indicator shows the relative importance of private company bond issuance to government bond issuance). Government bond yields are included as a market access indicator because the lower the rate, the easier it is for a government to borrow, and typically bank and company bond yields tend to follow government debt yields very closely (albeit higher) – so a low

Table 17.1 The World Bank's '4 × 2 matrix of financial system characteristics'

	Financial institutions	Financial markets
Depth	• Private sector credit to GDP • Financial institutions' assets to GDP • M2 to GDP • Deposits to GDP • Gross value-added of the financial sector to GDP	• Stock market capitalisation plus outstanding domestic private debt securities to GDP • Private debt securities to GDP • Public debt securities to GDP • International debt securities to GDP • Stock market capitalisation to GDP • Stock traded to GDP
Access	• Accounts per thousand adults (commercial banks) • Branches per 100,000 adults (commercial banks) • % of people with a bank account • % of firms with line of credit (all firms) • % of firms with line of credit (small firms)	• % of market capitalisation outside of top 10 largest companies • % of value traded outside of top 10 traded companies • Government bond yields (3 months and 10 years) • Domestic securities to total debt securities • Private securities to total debt securities • New corporate bond issuance to GDP
Efficiency	• Net interest margin • Non-interest income to total income • Overhead costs (% of total assets) • Profitability (ROA, ROE) • Concentration indicators (HHI) • Competition indicators (Boone indicator; H-Statistics)	• Turnover ratio (turnover/capitalisation) for stock market • Price synchronicity • Private information trading • Price impact • Liquidity/transaction costs • Quoted bid–ask spread for government bonds • Turnover of bonds (private, public) on securities exchange • Settlement efficiency
Stability	• Z-score (or distance to default) • Capital adequacy ratios • Asset quality ratios • Liquidity ratios • Other ratios (net foreign position to capital, etc.)	• Volatility (standard deviation/average) of stock price index, sovereign bond index • Skewness of the index • Vulnerability to earning manipulation • Price to earnings (P/E) ratio • Duration • Short-term bonds to total bonds (domestic, international) • Correlation with major bond returns (US, EU)

Source: Adapted from Čihák *et al.* (2012a).

government debt yield implies easier access for financial and other private sector firms to external bond finance.

3 **Efficiency** – these benchmark indicators relate to a range of factors, including (i) net interest margin (interest income minus interest costs divided by earning assets); (ii) lending–deposit spreads (the difference between lending rates and deposit rates); and (iii) the proportion of non-interest income to total income. In the case of net interest margins and loan–deposit rate spreads, the smaller these are, the more competitive (and therefore

efficient) the system is considered to be. The proportion of non-interest income to total income can also be considered an indicator of efficiency, as banks can generate non-interest income derived from the cross-selling of financial services. Other efficiency indicators relate to profitability measures (ROA and ROE) and various competition and concentration measures. In theory, greater competition should be linked to more efficiency (although there are limitations). (See Chapter 20 for an explanation of the various competition and concentration measures and for a discussion of the relationship between competition and efficiency in banking.) Nevertheless, one has to be careful with profits – high profits may reflect efficiency (revenues are much higher than costs), but so can low profits (low revenues and low costs). In this context, one would need to know about bank pricing behaviour to accurately interpret the profits measures as efficiency indicators. Overhead costs over total assets is a traditional efficiency indicator (overhead costs includes staff, rent and other non-interest costs); this latter is similar to the better known cost to income ratio – a measure widely used by the industry to gauge efficiency. The financial market indicators of efficiency relate to the volume of trading activity, namely turnover. The greater the volume of shares traded, the more efficient the trading process. Other suggested indicators relate to pricing, including bid–ask spreads, transaction costs and the speed with which transactions are processed (settlement efficiency). They are standard financial market efficiency indicators.

4 **Stability** – these indicators relate to bank capital and liquidity as well as asset quality. Lower capital and liquidity imply greater fragility. The Z-score, a distance to default measure, reflects the extent to which a bank's profit and capital levels can withstand volatile profitability (see Section 20.5.1.1). The higher the capital strength and profits, the more stable the bank – so higher Z-scores mean greater stability. These can be calculated for the whole banking system by simply calculating the Z-score for individual banks and then calculating the weighted average by bank size (usually assets). Indicators of stability for financial markets relate to various volatility measures (the more volatile, the less stable), as well as price to earnings (P/E) and price to dividend (duration) measures. These measures are interpreted as follows: more volatile P/E and price/dividend ratios suggest greater fragility.

Table 17.2 highlights a selection of the financial institution indicators reported in the Čihák et al. (2012) study, showing countries with the highest and lowest measures for selected indicators. It is interesting to note that the economies with the deepest financial systems (using the private credit to GDP indicator) include the offshore financial centre of San Marino (a microstate surrounded by Italy in the north east of the country) as well as Cyprus, Ireland, the UK and Spain (countries that have all experienced major banking sector problems since 2008). This seems to indicate that having too big a banking system can result in problems. Yet some of the world's poorest economies – Chad and Myanmar – also have the least deep financial sectors.

Although at first glance the different World Bank indicators may seem inconsistent, the study does show that the indicators for financial institution (and financial market) development tend to be highly correlated across all countries. However, advanced economies still dominate in terms of the size of financial sectors. This is illustrated in Figure 17.1, which shows a map of the world with countries drawn according to the size of their financial sectors – much of the developing world seems to shrink.

Table 17.2 Financial institution characteristics by country, 2008–2010 average

	Indicator	Lowest	Highest	Others
Depth	Private sector credit/GDP	Myanmar (3.3%) Chad (3.3%)	San Marino (361.7%) Cyprus (265.6%) Ireland (228.2%) UK (205.3%) Spain (203.7%)	Brazil (45.6%) China (111.1%) India (44.1%) Russia (41.3%) Germany (109.1%) Japan (103.7%) USA (60%)
Access	Accounts per thousand adults (at commercial banks)	Central African Republic (2.4) Republic of Congo (16.1)	Japan (7,185.2) South Korea (4,374) Greece (3,799.7)	India (747.3) Singapore (2070.3) Ukraine (3,176.4)
Efficiency	Lending–deposit spread	Iran (0.1%) The Netherlands (0.2%) Belarus (0.4%)	Democratic Republic of the Congo (41.5%) Madagascar (35.2%) Brazil (34.0%)	China (3.1%) Russia (6.0%) Japan (1.2%)
Stability	Z-score	Guinea (2.8) Latvia (3.0) Myanmar (3.2) Ireland (3.7) Lithuania (4.3) Kazakhstan (4.3)	Libya (77.3) Bahrain (48.6) Jordan (48.2) Namibia (41.1) Croatia (39.8)	Brazil (15.9) China (34.8) India (27.8) Russia (18.1) Germany (10.5) Japan (32.9) US (24)

Source: Constructed from Čihák *et al.* (2012).

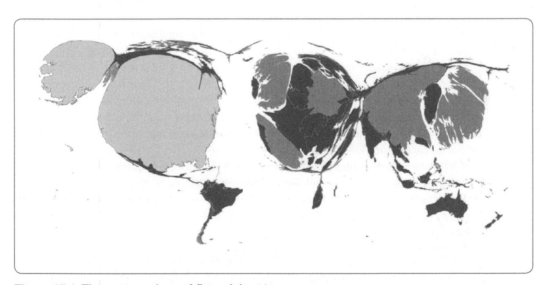

Figure 17.1 The uneven sizes of financial systems

Note: The map is for illustration purposes only. Country sizes are adjusted to reflect the volume of financial sector assets in the jurisdiction, measured in US $ at the end of 2010.

Source: Čihák *et al.* (2012) p. 31.

17.3 Finance and growth

Since the early work looking at the role of bank-based and market-based systems, economists have long been interested in how financial systems influence economic development. Seminal work by King and Levine (1993) investigated how features of financial sectors in 80 countries influenced development. Looking at the 30-year period between 1960 and 1989, they found that growing financial systems had a strong positive influence on real GDP per capita (and also on the rate of physical capital accumulation). This key finding then spawned an array of (mainly) empirical studies that sought to explain how financial systems drive growth and other features of the development process.

17.3.1 How does finance boost growth?

Following on from the finding that financial systems spur economic development, research emphasis focused on the route through which this took place. The literature finds that financial sector development helps boost firm productivity and improves the efficiency with which resources are allocated. Companies with wider access to finance – either through the banking sector or via financial markets – appear to become more efficient and productive, and it is through this process that economies grow. There is also evidence that firms become more innovative and entrepreneurial when the financial system develops – presumably they have to become more ingenious in formulating business plans in order to raise external finance, and this prompts the innovation/entrepreneurial process. Firms can use external finance to make acquisitions and improve the scale of operations, and this can also feed through into efficiency and productivity gains. In addition to promoting growth, there is evidence that financial sector development reduces its volatility. Having a broader-based financial system makes the economy less susceptible to financing shocks (if a country has a well-established banking system and stock market, then reduced financing by one part of the system may be counteracted with increased financing from the other part). There is also some evidence that a broader-based and well-developed financial system can aid policy formulation. According to the IMF (2012d), developed financial systems can promote the effectiveness of domestic monetary policy, create a wider base for fiscal policy and can allow for a greater choice of exchange rate regimes.

While it is widely found that financial sector development positively impacts economic growth, the influence has been found to be non-linear; namely, the most developed economies and biggest companies benefit least. Financial sector development appears to have its biggest impact in the least developed countries and for smaller firms. Five main arguments have been proposed to explain this phenomenon:

1 **Catch-up to best practice productivity and efficiency** – developing economies, characterised by many small firms, may be significantly less productive and efficient than developed economies. As developing economies have further to go in terms of improving firm and economic performance, developments in the financial sector (such as improved access to bank credit and services and to the stock market for equity and other external finance) have a greater impact on firm investment and growth.

2 **Traditional measures of financial sector development are limited** – measures of financial sector development, such as bank credit to GDP, bank assets to GDP and stock

market capitalisation to GDP (as well as the other measures shown in Table 17.1), are possibly too basic to pick up the subtleties of financial sector development. This may be increasingly an issue with the emergence of the shadow banking sector, namely, financial institutions (hedge funds, private equity firms, investment companies) that undertake banking-style activities – such as buying and selling securitised assets – but are not regulated like banks and whose activities are not typically recorded by regulatory organisations (see Chapter 18 for a discussion of shadow banking). Estimates of the size of the shadow banking industry vary: in the US in 2013 the estimated size of the shadow banking industry was about 50 per cent of the official banking sector assets, although prior to the crisis of 2008 it was 120 per cent of banking sector assets (Financial Stability Board, 2012a). Typically, measures of financial sector development do not pick up shadow banking activity and its subtle effects; this may result in the role of finance and its impact being understated in developed economies. However, it could also be argued that if one finds little influence of narrow definitions of financial sector development on growth, then the influence is going to be found to be weaker if broader measures are chosen.

3 **Finance to the corporate sector has a much bigger impact on growth compared with household finance** – there is strong evidence that the route through which finance impacts growth is via the corporate sector, and small to medium-sized firms in particular. Typically, lending to households – particularly residential mortgage lending – has been the major component of both the level and growth of commercial banks' credit portfolios in advanced economies. With a preference for retail/household financial services, this has a muted impact on economic growth compared with corporate lending.

4 **Developed financial systems extract talented employees who could be more productive working in other sectors** – as financial sectors become more developed, they tend to attract talented employees with high pay, for example in investment banking. The argument goes that this talented workforce would be better employed in other sectors, as it would yield greater productivity for the economy overall if they worked elsewhere. Here the focus is on the banking sector recruiting engineers, physicists, mathematicians and other scientists to develop increasingly complex products and systems that have little, or even negative, impact on economic performance. Recent research points to the 'absorption of talent into finance' and claims that as the banking and financial sectors grow, often following deregulation policies, the demand for skilled labour increases, thus diverting labour away from real sectors and therefore leading to overall productivity decline, particularly in those industries which are more reliant on a skilled workforce (Kneer, 2013).

5 **Exploitation of safety-net subsidies** – there is an incentive, as banks become larger, to seek to exploit safety-net subsidies (deposit insurance, lender-of-last-resort facilities, too big to fail) that provide protection to banks when they get into financial difficulties. Put simply, the senior managers of a very big (too-big-to-fail) bank may decide to take on excessive risks to boost profits (and their bonuses) if they believe the government will bail them out if things go bad. They may also be reassured that depositors will not be too worried about the excessive risk taking as most have deposit insurance. In general, the incentives to grow and take on too much risk are exacerbated by safety-net benefits. Rapid financial sector development and excessive risk taking are likely to lead to problems that ultimately reduce growth.

Finally, the mechanism through which financial sector development aids economic growth also makes economies more susceptible to shocks and financial fragilities. More open financial markets have greater capital flows that can exacerbate volatility in domestic capital markets. A fast growing banking sector can result in excessive risk taking that may feed through into solvency and liquidity problems. In sum, recent evidence seems to point to the fact that the more developed the financial system, the greater the chance of having banking or financial sector crises.

The evolution of the aforementioned finance and growth literature is summarised in Table 17.3 and a practical example of the finance and growth link is presented in estimates from Oliver Wyman (2011), reported in Figure 17.2. A detailed review of this literature can be found in Beck (2012b).

Table 17.3 Finance and growth: a review of the literature

A. Financial development boosts economic growth	
● King and Levine (1993)	Seminal empirical study that sought to investigate the view of Joseph Schumpeter that financial sector development aided economic growth. Examining 80 countries from 1960 to 1989, the authors found (using a variety of indicators) that the level of financial system development was strongly associated with real per capita GDP growth, the rate of physical capital accumulation and improvements in the efficiency with which economies employ physical capital. The study also found that current financial sector development boosts future economic growth.
B. How? Finance drives growth by positively impacting the productivity, resource allocation and innovative nature of firms	
● Claessens and Laeven (2003) ● Demirgüç-Kunt et al. (2006)	Financial sector development aids the efficiency of firms in choosing a better mix (more efficient and productive) of assets and better organisational forms (such as limited liability and publicly listed companies).
● Beck et al. (2006) ● Beck et al. (2008)	A more developed financial system characterised by a greater share of bank assets, or bank credit to GDP, or a larger stock market capitalisation to GDP, has a bigger impact on small and medium-sized than large companies.
● Rajan and Zingales (1998) ● Beck et al. (2006) ● Beck et al. (2008)	A more developed financial sector enables existing firms to take advantage of various growth and investment opportunities, and to achieve larger (more optimal) scale.
● Beck et al. (2000)	A more developed financial sector has a bigger impact on economic growth by boosting productivity growth and the allocation of resources (optimally allocating land, labour and capital) than through pure capital accumulation (developing physical infrastructure).
● Klapper et al. (2006) ● Aghion et al. (2007) ● Ayyagari et al. (2011)	Greater availability of external finance is positively linked to entrepreneurship, greater firm entry and more innovation.
C. Financial development also reduces the volatility of economic growth and increases the effectiveness of policy	
● Aghion et al. (2010)	A developed financial system can reduce liquidity constraints on firms and increase long-term investment, ultimately reducing volatility of investment and growth.

Table 17.3 continued

● Aghion *et al.* (2009)	Financial sector development reduces the negative impact that exchange rate volatility can have on firms' liquidity and therefore on their investment capacity.
● International Monetary Fund (2012d)	A more developed financial system can increase the effectiveness of domestic monetary policy, provide a broader base for fiscal policy and allow for a bigger choice of exchange rate regimes.

D. But – the impact of financial sector development on economic growth is non-linear – developed economies and the largest companies benefit least

● Rioja and Valev (2004a, 2004b) ● Aghion *et al.* (2005)	The impact of financial sector development on economic growth is strongest among middle-income countries.
● Arcand *et al.* (2012)	Finance has a weaker impact on growth as countries grow richer.

E. Five reasons why developed economies and large firms benefit least from financial sector development

1 Catch-up is faster the further economies are from best practice. Aghion *et al.* (2005)	Financial sector development may facilitate catch-up to more efficient levels of productivity, but provides little impetus for growth to those countries already producing at the most productive level.
2 Traditional measures of financial sector development are too simple. Bertay *et al.* (2013)	Traditional measures of intermediation are too limited to pick up the subtle impact of non-intermediated finance (shadow banking, other capital markets activity) that tends to be more important in more developed economies.
3 Finance to the corporate sector boosts growth more than household finance (the former is more prevalent in developed economies). Beck *et al.* (2012)	Financial development/deepening in emerging markets mainly relates to greater access to credit and finance for the corporate sector and (up until recently at least) less to the consumer/household sector. This may explain why developed economies benefit less from financial sector development.
4 Developed financial systems extract talent that has more productive uses elsewhere in the economy Philippon (2010); Kneer (2013)	Financial systems may grow too big in relation to the real economy, extracting too much young talent and other resources that become increasingly less productive. Or to put it simply, mathematicians, engineers and other scientists employed in the financial sector are less productive (in economic growth terms) than if employed in the real sector.
5 Exploitation of safety-net subsidies. Carbó-Valverde *et al.* (2013)	As economies develop, financial systems eventually start to grow excessively as banks seek to exploit various so-called safety-net subsidies (deposit insurance, lender-of-last-resort facilities, too-big-to-fail subsidies). As banks grow faster, they take on excessive risk, believing that regulators and the taxpayer will bail them out if they fail. This moral hazard problem creates incentives for senior managers to take on excessive risk to boost returns (from which they benefit in terms of bigger pay and bonuses) whereas the downside is somewhat limited (although it can end in executive job loss). Incentives to grow and take on too much risk are exacerbated by safety-net benefits. Rapid financial sector development and excessive risk taking are likely to lead to problems that ultimately reduce growth.

F. Mechanisms through which finance promotes economic growth also make the economy susceptible to shocks and fragility

● Laeven and Valencia (2008)	The impact of systemic banking crises can be significant, reaching more than 50 per cent of GDP in various cases in fiscal costs and more than 100 per cent in output loss. It has been shown that in these cases, industries that depend more on external finance are hurt disproportionately more, and this effect is stronger in countries with developed financial systems.
● Reinhart and Rogoff (2011)	Banking sector crisis usually precedes a broader sovereign debt crisis.

Figure 17.2 Banking and economic growth

Source: Oliver Wyman (2011).

17.4 The macroeconomic outlook

Before we describe the macroeconomic outlook of emerging economies, it is important, in this context, to provide some terminology. The term **emerging market** was originally coined by the International Finance Corporation (IFC) to describe a fairly narrow list of middle- to higher-income economies among the developing countries, with stock markets in which foreigners could buy securities.[1] The term's meaning has since been expanded to include more or less all developing countries. **Developing countries** are those with a gross national income (GNI) per capita of $12,615 or less. As per 2014, the World Bank classifies economies as low income (GNI $1,035 or less), lower-middle income (GNI $1,036–4,085), upper-middle income (GNI $4,086–$12,615) and high income (GNI $12,616 or more). Low-income and middle-income economies are sometimes referred to as developing countries.[2] The label **transition economies** is also sometimes used to describe former communist countries that have been transforming their planned economies to market economies. As a result, and for the purpose of this chapter, transition countries are considered emerging economies. In other words, the label 'emerging economies' encompasses all countries that are not included in the developed world.

---

[1] The IFC is a member of the World Bank Group and is headquartered in Washington, DC. The IFC's aim is to promote sustainable private sector investment in developing countries as a way to reduce poverty and improve people's lives.

[2] At the start of 2014, the World Bank had 188 member countries and also identified other economies with populations of more than 30,000 (another 26, making 214 countries/economies in the world in total).

Table 17.4 shows the geographical composition of countries that are included in the above definition of 'emerging and transition economies' and Table 17.5 classifies them according to income. From the number of countries in Tables 17.4 and 17.5, it is apparent that it would be impossible to describe in detail the banking sector and associated issues of each country. For this reason, we will analyse briefly the major emerging markets regions.

The performance of emerging economies has varied substantially since the mid-1990s, and although there is big variation in growth prospects from country to country, some clear pictures emerge. First, virtually all emerging economies grew faster than advanced

Table 17.4 Emerging economies – geographical region

East Asia and Pacific		
American Samoa	Malaysia	Samoa
Cambodia	Marshall Islands	Solomon Islands
China	Micronesia, Fed. Sts	Thailand
Fiji	Mongolia	Timor-Leste
Indonesia	Myanmar	Tuvalu
Kiribati	Palau	Tonga
Korea, Dem. Rep.	Papua New Guinea	Vanuatu
Lao PDR	Philippines	Vietnam
Europe and Central Asia		
Albania	Hungary	Romania
Armenia	Kazakhstan	Serbia
Azerbaijan	Kosovo	Tajikistan
Belarus	Kyrgyz Republic	Turkey
Bosnia and Herzegovina	Macedonia, FYR	Turkmenistan
Bulgaria	Moldova	Ukraine
Georgia	Montenegro	Uzbekistan
Latin America and the Caribbean		
Argentina	Ecuador	Nicaragua
Belize	El Salvador	Panama
Bolivia	Grenada	Paraguay
Brazil	Guatemala	Peru
Colombia	Guyana	St Lucia
Costa Rica	Haiti	St Vincent and the Grenadines
Cuba	Honduras	Suriname
Dominica	Jamaica	Venezuela, RB
Dominican Republic	Mexico	
Middle East and North Africa		
Algeria	Jordan	Tunisia
Djibouti	Lebanon	West Bank and Gaza
Egypt, Arab Rep.	Libya	Yemen, Rep.
Iran, Islamic Rep.	Morocco	
Iraq	Syrian Arab Republic	

Table 17.4 continued

South Asia		
Afghanistan	India	Pakistan
Bangladesh	Maldives	Sri Lanka
Bhutan	Nepal	
Sub-Saharan Africa		
Angola	Gambia, The	Rwanda
Benin	Ghana	São Tomé and Principe
Botswana	Guinea	Senegal
Burkina Faso	Guinea-Bissau	Seychelles
Burundi	Kenya	Sierra Leone
Cameroon	Lesotho	Somalia
Cape Verde	Liberia	South Africa
Central African Republic	Madagascar	South Sudan
Chad	Malawi	Sudan
Comoros	Mali	Swaziland
Congo, Dem. Rep.	Mauritania	Tanzania
Congo, Rep	Mauritius	Togo
Côte d'Ivoire	Mozambique	Uganda
Eritrea	Namibia	Zambia
Ethiopia	Niger	Zimbabwe
Gabon	Nigeria	

Source: World Bank (2014) http://data.worldbank.org/about/country-classifications/country-and-lending-groups

Table 17.5 Emerging economies – income classification by Gross National Income (GNI) per capita

Low-income economies ($1,035 or less)		
Afghanistan	Gambia, The	Myanmar
Bangladesh	Guinea	Nepal
Benin	Guinea-Bissau	Niger
Burkina Faso	Haiti	Rwanda
Burundi	Kenya	Sierra Leone
Cambodia	Korea, Dem Rep.	Somalia
Central African Republic	Kyrgyz Republic	South Sudan
Chad	Liberia	Tajikistan
Comoros	Madagascar	Tanzania
Congo, Dem. Rep	Malawi	Togo
Eritrea	Mali	Uganda
Ethiopia	Mozambique	Zimbabwe
Lower-middle-income economies ($1,036 to $4,085)		
Armenia	India	Samoa
Bhutan	Kiribati	São Tomé and Principe
Bolivia	Kosovo	Senegal

Table 17.5 continued

Cameroon	Lao PDR	Solomon Islands
Cape Verde	Lesotho	Sri Lanka
Congo, Rep.	Mauritania	Sudan
Côte d'Ivoire	Micronesia, Fed. Sts	Swaziland
Djibouti	Moldova	Syrian Arab Republic
Egypt, Arab Rep.	Mongolia	Timor-Leste
El Salvador	Morocco	Ukraine
Georgia	Nicaragua	Uzbekistan
Ghana	Nigeria	Vanuatu
Guatemala	Pakistan	Vietnam
Guyana	Papua New Guinea	West Bank and Gaza
Honduras	Paraguay	Yemen, Rep.
Indonesia	Philippines	Zambia

Upper-middle-income economies ($4,086 to $12,615)

Angola	Fiji	Palau
Albania	Gabon	Panama
Algeria	Grenada	Peru
American Samoa	Hungary	Romania
Argentina	Iran, Islamic Rep.	Serbia
Azerbaijan	Iraq	Seychelles
Belarus	Jamaica	South Africa
Belize	Jordan	St Lucia
Bosnia and Herzegovina	Kazakhstan	St Vincent and the Grenadines
Botswana	Lebanon	Suriname
Brazil	Libya	Thailand
Bulgaria	Macedonia, FYR	Tonga
China	Malaysia	Tunisia
Colombia	Maldives	Turkey
Costa Rica	Marshall Islands	Turkmenistan
Cuba	Mauritius	Tuvalu
Dominica	Mexico	Venezuela, RB
Dominican Republic	Montenegro	
Ecuador	Namibia	

High-income economies ($12,616 or more)

Andorra	French Polynesia	Norway
Antigua and Barbuda	Germany	Oman
Aruba	Greece	Poland
Australia	Greenland	Portugal
Austria	Guam	Puerto Rico
Bahamas, The	Hong Kong SAR, China	Qatar
Bahrain	Iceland	Russian Federation
Barbados	Ireland	San Marino

Table 17.5 continued

Belgium	Isle of Man	Saudi Arabia
Bermuda	Israel	Singapore
Brunei Darussalam	Italy	Sint Maarten
Canada	Japan	Slovak Republic
Cayman Islands	Korea, Rep.	Slovenia
Channel Islands	Kuwait	Spain
Chile	Latvia	St Kitts and Nevis
Croatia	Liechtenstein	St Martin
Curaçao	Lithuania	Sweden
Cyprus	Luxembourg	Switzerland
Czech Republic	Macao SAR, China	Trinidad and Tobago
Denmark	Malta	Turks and Caicos Islands
Estonia	Monaco	United Arab Emirates
Equatorial Guinea	Netherlands	United Kingdom
Faeroe Islands	New Caledonia	United States
Finland	New Zealand	Uruguay
France	Northern Mariana Islands	Virgin Islands (US)

Source: World Bank (2014) **http://data.worldbank.org/about/country-classifications/country-and-lending-groups**

economies between 1995 and 2004, with the East Asian and Pacific region (including China) growing the fastest, followed by South Asia, Sub-Saharan Africa and the Middle East and North Africa. The fastest growing country from the advanced economies was the US. Since 2004 pretty much the same trend has continued, with the two main Asian regions posting even faster economic growth over the period 2005 to 2014.

Growth in Latin America and the Caribbean and Europe and Central Asia (including mainly transition economies) also improved their economic performance over this period. In contrast, the advanced economies were hit by the financial crises that fed through into negative growth in 2009, resulting in the US, the euro area and the UK barely posting single-digit growth. For instance, countries in the euro area grew by only an average annual rate of 0.8 per cent from 2005 to 2014, while the US fared better with 1.3 per cent growth. Clearly the banking collapse had a negative economic impact that was mainly felt by advanced economies – it was their banking systems that collapsed – however, the substantial bailout costs and subsequent economic downturn in 2009 and 2010 in many developed economies fed through into weaker growth elsewhere.

Growth prospects for the global economy made by the IMF (2013d) and reported in Table 17.6 illustrate these trends and highlight that emerging markets are expected to grow (in many cases) slightly less up to 2018 compared with their performance over the previous decade. Only advanced economies are expected to substantially increase their growth prospects, and that is because they are reversing weak macroeconomic performance since the mid-2000s. The fastest growing economies in 2013 according to *The Economist* were Mongolia (18.1 per cent), Macau (13.5 per cent), Libya (12.2 per cent), China (8.6 per cent) and Bhutan (8.5 per cent).[3]

---

[3] **www.economist.com/theworldin/2013**

Table 17.6 Real GDP growth (%) – emerging economies

	1995–2004	2005–2014	2018 forecast
East Asia and Pacific	7.1	8.5	7.7
China	9.2	10.1	8.5
Indonesia	2.9	6	6.5
Malaysia	5.2	4.8	5.2
Mongolia	4.5	9.6	8.9
Vietnam	7.3	6.5	5.5
Europe and Central Asia	3.5	4.3	4.3
Bulgaria	1.6	2.7	3.5
Romania	2.5	2.4	3.5
Turkey	4.2	4.3	4.5
Latin America and the Caribbean	2.6	4	3.9
Argentina	1.1	6	3
Brazil	2.5	3.7	4.2
Peru	3.5	6.9	6
Middle East and North Africa	4.5	4.6	4.6
Algeria	4.1	3	3.9
Egypt	4.8	4.5	6.5
Iran	4.9	2.9	2.4
Iraq	4.2	7	8.3
South Asia			
India	6.1	7.5	7
Pakistan	4.2	3.1	3
Sub-Saharan Africa	4.5	5.5	5.5
Equatorial Guinea	39.3	4.1	–7.1
Ghana	4.7	7.4	5.7
Nigeria	6.5	6.8	6.7
South Africa	3.1	3.4	3.1
Advanced economies	2.8	1.4	2.5
US	3.3	1.3	2.9
Japan	1.1	0.7	1.1
Euro area	2.2	0.8	1.6
Germany	0.9	1	1.2
UK	3.3	0.7	1.5

Source: Constructed from data available in IMF (2013d).

Figure 17.3 illustrates the stronger economic performance of emerging markets compared with advanced economies in recent years. One can see the fast growing markets of China, India and Indonesia and also observe how growth in the early 2000s was higher than post banking crises. In contrast, GDP growth rarely exceeds 5 per cent per annum in the developed world and the troubled economies of Spain, Italy, Portugal and Greece following the euro sovereign crises experienced negative growth over 2010–2012. Given these forecasts,

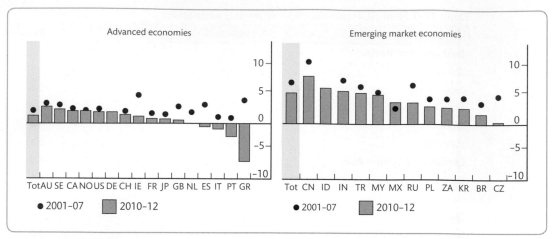

Figure 17.3 Economic growth in advanced and emerging economies

Notes: [1] Average annual real GDP growth, regional totals are weighted averages based on 2005 GDP and PPP exchange rates.
AU = Australia; BR = Brazil; CA = Canada; CH = Switzerland; CN = China; CZ = Czech Republic; DE = Germany;ES = Spain;
FR = France; GB = Great Britain; GR = Greece; ID = Indonesia; IE = Ireland; IN = India;IT = Italy; JP = Japan; KR = Korea;
MX = Mexico; MY = Malaysia; NL = Netherlands; NO = Norway;PL = Poland; PT = Portugal; RU = Russia; SE = Sweden;
TR = Turkey; US = United States; ZA = South Africa.

Source: Bank for International Settlements (2013a) Graph III.1

it is hardly surprising that many banks as well as other businesses are strategically targeting emerging markets for expansion.

17.5   Structural features and trends

This section gives an overview of recent trends that have contributed to shape the current structure of banking systems in emerging markets. First we examine some general trends as well as regulatory developments. We then look at the impact these forces of change have had on the structure and performance of selected banking systems.

The banking systems in emerging countries are heterogeneous, in terms of number and size of institutions, ownership structure, profitability and competitiveness, use of IT and other structural features. In most countries, a few large commercial banks have the majority of the market share and co-exist with a large number of small private (family-owned) banks as well as various savings and co-operative banks. Foreign ownership in the banking sector of emerging markets has increased substantially over the last decade and various banking systems – particularly those in central and Eastern Europe – are dominated by foreign banks.

Another interesting feature is the widespread role of the state in government finance – the majority of the Chinese banking system, for instance, is under direct state control. Of course, since 2008 many advanced economies have seen the role of the state in the banking sector increase, as governments had to rescue banks during the crisis: by the start of 2014 around 45 per cent of the UK retail market was under state ownership. Some of these characteristics are illustrated in the snapshots of Asian and transition banking systems shown in Tables 17.7 and 17.8. Table 17.7 shows that Asian banking markets are relatively larger, in terms of bank

Table 17.7 Banking in Asia

COUNTRY	Bank assets to GDP (%) 2007	Bank assets to GDP (%) 2013	Private credit to GDP (%) 2007	Private credit to GDP (%) 2013	Overhead cost to assets (%) 2007	Overhead cost to assets (%) 2013	Net interest margins to assets (%) 2007	Net interest margins to assets (%) 2013	Branches (per 100,000 people) 2007	Branches (per 100,000 people) 2013	ATMs (per 100,000 people) 2007	ATMs (per 100,000 people) 2013	ATMs (per 1,000 square km) 2007	ATMs (per 1,000 square km) 2013
China	109.5	131.57	99.7	121.49	1.5	1.24	3.7	2.86	n.a.	7.8	n.a.	46.94	n.a.	9.32
Indonesia	31.5	29.96	22.7	25.37	3.8	3.40	6.5	6.35	5.9	10.4	11.3	42.40	10.4	39.79
Korea, Rep.	99.5	98.43	93.1	98.43	1.2	1.2	1.9	2.6	18.4	18.3	235.4	290.03	967.1	1265.79
Malaysia	102.9	120.15	97.0	106.40	1.4	2.8	3.2	4.7	10.7	11.3	39.4	55.50	22.2	36.23
Philippines	35.0	44.9	22.4	29.8	3.6	2.8	4.2	3.7	7.7	8.63	12.7	22.95	24.0	48.73
Thailand	100.9	114.4	89.6	101.9	2.4	1.8	3.6	2.8	9.6	12.16	46.9	104.32	48.7	111.19
Bangladesh	51.8	62.5	34.6	44.6	3.4	2.4	2.5	4.3	7.0	8.19	0.5	6.33	3.7	52.22
India	57.7	65.2	41.1	47.2	2.1	1.7	3.1	3.1	9.0	12.16	3.4	13.27	9.1	38.96
Pakistan	38.8	34.1	27.2	18.1	2.5	2.9	5.1	5.7	7.9	9.33	2.7	6.49	3.6	9.90
REGION	**2007**	**2013**	**2007**	**2013**	**2007**	**2013**	**2007**	**2013**	**2007**	**2009**	**2007**	**2009**	**2007**	**2009**
East Asia Pacific	79.9	42.5	70.7	32.3	2.3	3.7	3.8	4.6	10.5	10.9	69.1	80.5	214.5	239.2
South Asia	49.4	40.5	34.3	34.7	2.7	7.1	3.6	6.1	8.0	8.0	8.4	2.2	3.5	5.5
Eastern Europe & Central Asia	51.8	48.3	41.7	42.1	4.9	3.7	3.9	4.3	25.6	26.9	42.3	55.1	33.1	39
Latin America	42.2	38.8	21.7	31.6	4.5	4.2	5.6	5.7	21.1	22.3	50.7	55.6	10.5	11.8
Middle East & North Africa	58.6	44.1	38.6	36.2	1.7	2.7	2.9	3.6	7.3	9.8	7.8	10.5	3.4	4.7
Sub-Saharan Africa	47.6	34.8	39.1	27.8	4.6	5.1	5.3	5.9	4.9	6.7	13.3	23.7	4.8	9.6

Source: Country Level and Region Level Data on Bank Assets to GDP; Private Credit to GDP are from the World Bank- Financial Development and Structure dataset (updated November 2013); Country Level Data on Branches and ATMs are from the Financial Access Survey Database (IMF, 2013); Region Level Data on Branches and ATMs are from Klapper, L, Martinez-Peria, M.S and Zia, B. (2014) Banking in Developing Nations of Asia: Changes in Ownership Structure and Lending Over the Financial Crisis, Chapter 38 in the Oxford Handbook of Banking, 2nd Edition edited by AN Berger, P . Molyneux and JOS Wilson, Oxford, OUP. Table 1.

Table 17.8 Banking in transition economies

	Number of banks (foreign owned)	Asset share of foreign banks (%)	Domestic credit to GDP ratio (%)	Net interest margin (%)	Non-performing loans (% of total)	EBRD Bank Transition Index
			Post-crisis – 2010			
CEE						
Czech Rep.	37(15)	84.8	75.3	2.68	2.8	4
Hungary	38 (23)	81.3	66.5	3.82	6.7	3.7
Poland	67 (57)	72.3	55.2	3.18	8	3.7
Slovakia	26 (13)	91.6	51.1	2.77	5.2	3.7
SEE						
Bulgaria	30 (22)	84	75.3	3.59	6.7	3.7
Croatia	32 (15)	91	69.6	2.95	7.8	4
Romania	31 (25)	84.3	40.7	4.35	8.5	3.3
Serbia	33 (–)	72.5	45	4.54	16.9	3
Slovenia	25 (11)	29.5	92.7	2.36	6	3.3
FSU						
Estonia	17(14)	98.3	98.8	3.21	5.3	4
Latvia	27 (18)	69.3	103.3	1.57	16.4	3.7
Lithuania	17 (5)	91.5	69.8	1.44	20.8	3.7
Russia	1058 (108)	18.3	44.4	5.08	9.7	2.7
Ukraine	182 (51)	50.8	73.3	4.66	47.9	3

Notes: Data are from country tables in EBRD 'Transition report', various issues, and the EBRD online 'Structural and institutional change' indicators. Some additional data for various years from the World Bank online database. EBRD Index takes values between 1.0 and 4.0+. In case of a missing number in 2010, we use the value from the previous available year. CEE – Central and Eastern Europe; SEE – South-eastern Europe; FSU – Former Soviet Union; – indicates data not available.

Source: Adapted from Bonin *et al.* (2014) Table 2.

assets to GDP, on average, compared with their counterparts in Eastern Europe and Latin America. Branch and ATM coverage is also higher than in other emerging systems, but still low compared with advanced economies.

Table 17.8 provides information on transition economy banking systems and highlights the dominant role played by foreign banks in these systems – apart from in Slovenia (29 per cent foreign bank market share) and Russia (18 per cent share). The characteristics of banking systems vary from country to country and it is impractical to discuss each system individually. It is important, however, in this varied environment, to analyse the main forces of change affecting the structure and efficiency features of banking systems.

17.5.1 Deregulation and financial liberalisation

Banking in emerging markets was traditionally characterised by high levels of government control, with restrictions on borrowing and lending rates and on domestic and foreign entry. In some countries the levels of restriction on financial activities and government intervention in financial markets were so strong (for example, during the Soviet era in the former USSR) that they could be better described as **financial repression**. The main way governments were pursuing financial repression was to maintain the monopoly of the financial sector by state banks, restricting entry of both banks and non-deposit-taking financial institutions and by strictly controlling new financial instruments that could compete with bank deposits. Financial repression could vary from mild to severe and included:

- control over interest rates;
- controls over lending;
- directed lending (loans made at subsidised 'uneconomic' rates to specific politically preferred sectors);
- high reserve requirements;
- restrictions on entry of new banks and other financial intermediaries;
- restrictions on entry of foreign financial intermediaries;
- nationalisation of financial institutions.

Traditionally, there was little incentive to alter these protective banking environments and foster competition. During the 1990s, however, a combination of changes in the global financial markets, macroeconomic pressures resulting from various banking crises and fast technological developments forced governments to deregulate the industry at the domestic level and to open up to foreign competition. These forces continued at a pace until the late 2000s, when the deregulation trend was reversed as a consequence of the global financial crisis.

Although emerging banking systems were least impacted by the crisis, the realisation that many banks had been taking on excessive risks in a light-touch regulatory environment caused both domestic and international bank regulators to reassess the situation. For example, new capital and liquidity rules were put in place under the Basel III regulations, requiring banks to hold more capital and reduce risky assets (see Chapter 7 for details). This regulatory activity (in addition to weak economic growth) is particularly hindering banking sector growth in advanced economies, but it is also having an influence on the emerging world. The growth prospects for many emerging economies have been sluggish; in addition, as regulators are generally becoming more cautious, foreign bank expansion has slowed down. Despite this, at the time of writing (2014), the prospects for banking sector growth, and the opportunities afforded to financial sector investors, remain substantially stronger in emerging markets (particularly in Asia) compared with in the advanced world.

In the liberalisation period preceding the global financial crisis, structural changes occurred in the banking industries of many countries. The main changes at the domestic level, in most emerging banking markets, have been the removal of ceilings on deposit rates and the removal of the prohibition of interest payments on current accounts. These changes were significant because they implied that banks could no longer rely on sources of cheap funding and this put pressure on their profits, thus encouraging them to reorganise their activities and become more market-oriented.

The opening up of banking markets in emerging economies has led to a growing presence of foreign banks (as well as non-bank financial firms) in search of profit opportunities. As a result, most banking markets in emerging countries now depend on foreign institutions to provide capital, technology and managerial expertise. These issues will be discussed in Section 17.5.4.

Deregulation and **financial liberalisation** have long been considered positive forces, as they are supposed to increase banking sector efficiency by imposing competition and removing regulations that distort economic activity. The perceived benefits of deregulation include:

- expansion of financial markets;
- increased competition;
- more choice and cheaper financial products;
- increased innovation as a result of technology developments;
- enhanced consumer welfare;
- fostering of economic growth.

However, beyond the positive aspects, there is now widespread recognition that if deregulation goes too far, it can trigger instability and lead to crisis. On a positive note, financial deregulation has certainly made it easier for intermediaries to cross industry and national boundaries. It has also fostered technological progress, which in turn has reduced costs while stimulating innovation. For example, the computer and telecommunications revolution rendered geographic branching restrictions obsolete. Financial innovation includes the development of new financial instruments, which are now extensively used by emerging countries' banks. Owing to technological advances, emerging economies' banking markets are in a position to 'skip a stage of financial development', rapidly moving from a rather rudimentary system to a fairly advanced one. For example, the rapid development of ATMs, debit and credit cards, telephone and internet banking has pushed developing economies from cash-based transactions to electronic-based transactions, skipping the 'cheques stage'. A good illustration is given in Box 17.1, which shows

BOX 17.1 CHINA BANKING WAR HEATS UP WITH LAUNCH OF ONLINE INVESTMENT APP

The fight for deposits in the Chinese banking system, already at its fiercest in years, has intensified in the past week with the launch of an online investment fund tied to the most popular messaging app.

The fund, which is open to users of WeChat, Tencent's messaging app, is the latest entrant in China's booming market for online investment products that got started half a year ago. For Chinese banks, which have long faced little competition, the Internet funds are eating into their customer base and pressuring them to offer higher deposit rates.

Within two days of its official launch on January 22, Tencent said that its Licaitong fund had attracted more than Rmb1bn ($165mn) of inflows. It has not published any statistics since but the

Shanghai Securities News, an official financial newspaper, estimated that Licaitong has topped Rmb10bn.

It is the most formidable challenge yet to the online investment fund launched in June by ecommerce group Alibaba which has grown to become China's biggest money market fund. As of mid-January, Alibaba said its Yu'E Bao fund had attracted 49m investors and more than Rmb250bn in cash. Although officially classified as money market funds, the Alibaba and Tencent products are increasingly being used by Chinese savers as an alternative to bank accounts.

While banks offer demand deposit rates of 0.35 per cent – a level that is capped by the central bank – Alibaba and Tencent have been offering rates in excess of 6 per cent. At 7.5 per cent, Tencent's

Box 17.1 China banking war heats up with launch of online investment app (*continued*)

rates are about 1 percentage point higher than Alibaba's. That appears to be damping deposit growth at Chinese banks. Bank deposits rose by Rmb9tn in the first half of 2013 but then climbed just Rmb3tn in the second half of the year, after the online investment products began luring cash away. The total invested in the online funds is still less than 1 per cent of the overall amount deposited in Chinese banks, so the short-term impact on banks is expected to be limited.

"But they will soon become a too-big-to-ignore part of the economy," said Victor Wang, an analyst at Credit Suisse. "They are eating banks' desserts today. If the banks don't react, they will take banks' meals tomorrow."

Banks are beginning to fight back against the online funds. The five biggest banks have raised one-year deposit rates to the maximum allowable level – 3.3 per cent, 10 per cent above benchmark rates – but that still leaves them at nearly half the rates offered by the Alibaba and Tencent funds. "It's out of control," an unnamed executive at a

top bank told *Caixin*, a leading financial magazine. The Alibaba and Tencent funds are able to achieve higher returns by directing their customers' cash into the hands of money market funds, which invest in the interbank market and higher-yielding bonds. Alibaba's fund is managed by Tianhong Asset Management, while four companies, including China Asset Management, look after the Tencent fund. Both the Alibaba and Tencent funds have attracted large numbers of new customers in the run-up to the lunar new year, which begins on Friday.

Tencent this week debuted a money-giving function on its WeChat app, playing on the tradition of giving friends and family red envelopes of cash for the new year. This feature has proved popular, allowing it to introduce millions more people to its online payment system and investment fund. Alibaba's Yu'E Bao investment fund attracted 4m new users over the past seven days and daily cash inflows of Rmb10bn, well above its normal average. "Many people were depositing their annual bonuses," said Alibaba.

Source: Rabinovitch , S. (2014) *Financial Times*, 30 January.

the 'war' for deposits between Chinese banks and various money market funds, attempting to attract customers by offering much higher rates and facilitating transactions by using state-of-the-art mobile phone apps.

Emerging markets see the new delivery channels as an important part of the development of their retail and commercial banking activities, both because of the growing availability of IT and telecommunication technologies and the relatively lower cost of delivery compared with bank branches. One particular source of concern in emerging economies related to technological improvements is the so-called **digital divide** in the access to banking services. There is a fear that better-educated and wealthier customers will be able to obtain competitive banking services through the internet whereas the quality of services provided to poorer customers will deteriorate as bank branches are closed, particularly in rural areas. For a detailed discussion on these issues see the work done at the World Bank on constructing the 'The Global Financial Inclusion (Global Findex) Database' and discussed by Demirgüç-Kunt and Klapper (2012).

17.5.2 Role of the state

In the 1980s and early 1990s, in most emerging economies, state-owned banks accounted for the majority of banking sector assets. The banking industry, together with utilities, telecommunications, railways and airlines, was considered too important for the national economy to be left in private hands. Nearly two decades later, governments' share in the banking system has witnessed a substantial reduction. More recently, although state ownership is less prevalent in advanced economies, the fall in the role of the state is noticeable, as shown in Figures 17.4 and 17.5.

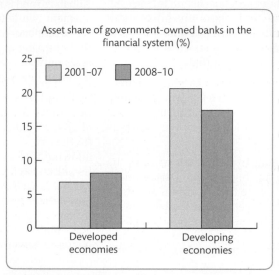

Figure 17.4 Trends in government ownership of banks

Source: World Bank (2013).

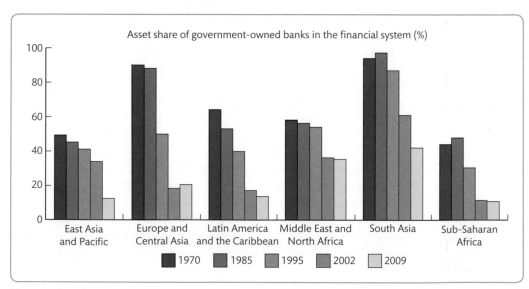

Figure 17.5 Government ownership across developing regions, 1970–2009

Source: World Bank (2013).

In many countries, the decline in state banking is generally attributed to poor performance as a consequence of undue political influence, weak management and the expectation that they would lend (irrespective of cost) to underperforming, state-owned enterprises. This led to a number of bankruptcies of state-owned banks in the banking crises of the 1980s and 1990s and to vulnerable and weak banking sectors. As a response, the governments of many emerging economies introduced reforms that led, among other things, to the gradual privatisation of banking sectors. This helped to restore stability, particularly in Latin America and Central Europe.

Each emerging economy had its own motives for undertaking a process of privatisation of state-owned banks; however, the aims of such programmes were to encourage competition and enhance efficiency of the sector.

Latin American countries launched bank privatisation programmes at different stages during the 1990s; these programmes were part of larger, long-term public sector reforms, with the aim of restructuring public finances, cutting borrowing requirements and deepening the role of the stock markets. The emerging Asian economies, meanwhile, were facing the challenge of returning to private ownership the banks that were nationalised during the 1997–1998 crisis. By the early to mid-2000s, policy makers had become sceptical about the merits of state-owned banking in emerging markets, especially due to their general poor performance and regular bailouts. Also, financial sectors with a strong state ownership presence were typically associated with underdeveloped and inefficient systems. In addition, a large state presence was linked with 'politically motivated' lending, lower banking sector outreach, wider intermediation spreads and slower economic growth.[4] Nevertheless, state banking can have some merits:

● Lending by state-owned banks is less pro-cyclical than lending by private banks.

● State-owned banks may be willing to serve customers in remote areas that private banks do not serve.

● Some countries, such as Thailand, Brazil and Argentina, have used state-owned banks to channel lending to farmers and small and medium-sized enterprises outside the largest cities.

● Lack of basic market and legal infrastructure may be so severe that state-owned banks are the only viable alternative.

Policy makers in most emerging economies seem to consider state ownership of banks as a second-best solution, in 'normal' times at least – during a crisis they may well have to nationalise banks to save them – and are increasingly subjecting the public banking sector to market discipline, treating them in a similar manner to private banks in terms of supervision and other factors. See Box 17.2 for a detailed discussion of the pros and cons of state ownership in banking.

Although the merits of private sector banks may outweigh those for state ownership, it remains the case that in some countries the role of government in the banking system predominates. For example, state banking still accounts for more than 50 per cent of banking sector assets in Algeria, China, Egypt and India. In other countries such as Argentina, Brazil, Indonesia, South Korea, Poland, Russia and Turkey, government-owned banks have a market share between 20 per cent and 50 per cent. The regions of the world with the highest level of banking sector state ownership include Southern Asia and the Middle East and North African regions – see Figure 17.5.

---

[4] See The World Bank (2013) Chapter 4 on direct state interventions for a detailed discussion on the pros and cons of state banking.

BOX 17.2 TWO VIEWS ON THE ROLE OF STATE BANKS

In a recent debate published in the World Bank's 'All About Finance' blog, two academics expressed contrasting views about the role of state-owned banks in promoting financial stability and access.

Franklin Allen, Nippon Life Professor of Finance and Economics, Wharton School, University of Pennsylvania, argues that, despite being outperformed by their private counterparts in terms of long-term resource allocation, 'public banks may enjoy an advantage over private banks in times of crisis and, hence, their merits need to be reassessed.' He goes on to say that 'the real advantage would come when there is a crisis. Rather than having central banks intervene in commercial credit markets, where they have little expertise, the state-owned commercial bank can temporarily expand its role both in terms of assets and loans. This should considerably improve the functioning of the economy and overcome credit crunch problems.

'The financial system can be safeguarded during times of crisis through a mixed system with mostly private banks but one or two are state-owned commercial banks. They would compete with private banks in normal times to ensure a competitive cost structure and prevent corruption, and they would provide useful information to regulators by signalling excess risk-taking or exercise of monopoly power by private banks. However, their real advantage would become evident during a financial crisis. State-owned commercial banks would be a safe haven for retail and interbank deposits, act as a fire break in the process of contagion, and provide loans to businesses – particularly small and medium size enterprises – through the crisis. They could expand and take up the slack in the banking business left by private banks. Listing such banks will ensure full information on them is available and their stock prices will indicate how well they are performing.

'Public banks can play another important role in increasing access to financial services. If the government wishes it to pursue this agenda then it may be helpful to subsidize this kind of activity. In many European countries in the nineteenth and twentieth centuries, the post office provided access to savings accounts and other kinds of financial services that many customers would not otherwise have had. A good example of a public bank that plays these roles is Chile's Banco del Estado, which is entirely owned by the Chilean Government. It is the country's third largest lender and operates in all major segments of the banking market. The fact that it has to compete with private banks ensures it is well run. Banco del Estado also has a long history of promoting access in all parts of the country and to all people. Many other countries might benefit from this type of bank.'

In contrast, Charles Calomiris, Henry Kaufman Professor of Financial Institutions at Columbia University, argues that academic work 'indicates powerfully the negative effects of state-controlled banks on the banking systems of the countries in which they operate and that the winding down of state-controlled banks was rightly celebrated in many countries in the 1990s as creating new potential for economic growth and political reform.'

He goes on to say that there are three main reasons that explain the dismal performance of state-controlled banks. 'First, government officials do not face incentives that are conducive to operating well-functioning banks. They are typically not incentivised to maximise economic effectiveness and they tend not to be trained in credit analysis as well as private bankers. They face incentives that reward politically rather than economically motivated allocations of credit. Second, the politically motivated allocation of funds to crony capitalists has adverse consequences for the political and social system of a region or country. State-controlled banks are a breeding ground for corruption of elected and appointed government officials, the financial regulatory authorities, and the courts. Not only do they stunt the growth of the economy, they also weaken the core political and bureaucratic institutions on which democracy and adherence to the rule of law depend. Third, state-controlled banks are "loss-making machines." Because they are not geared toward profitability or the aggressive enforcement of loan repayment, but rather toward rewarding political cronies with funding, the losses of state-controlled banks pose a major fiscal cost for governments. Those fiscal costs crowd out desirable government initiatives, and given the large size of the losses, can be a threat to the solvency of government and a source of inflationary deficit financing.

'The crisis has only reconfirmed the extreme damage that politically motivated lending can inflict. The quasi-state-controlled US entities Fannie Mae and

BOX 17.2 Two views on the role of state banks (*continued*)

Freddie Mac accounted for more than half of the funding of subprime and Alt-A mortgages leading up to the crisis. There is evidence that political motivations drove the intentional risk taking and deterioration of underwriting standards at those institutions after 2003 – a crucial ingredient in the subprime boom of 2004–2007. Government quotas dramatically increased the funding that Fannie and Freddie had to supply to low-income and underserved borrowers, but the supply of creditworthy low-income and underserved borrowers was limited. Inevitably, lending standards were relaxed. The US experience is not unique. Political motivations drove Spanish Cajas to support a real-estate boom that ended in a massive bust. In Germany, state-controlled banks also made horrible investment decisions, thus reflecting incompetence more than corruption or political motives for channelling funds. Looking back historically, it is clear that state-controlled lending has been a major contributor to unwise and politically motivated risk taking that has ended badly over and over again.

'The huge crisis-related losses of equity capital in the banking system and the subsequent stepping up of regulatory oversight over banks have resulted in a short-term contraction in the supply of credit. This credit crunch magnified the decline of GDP during the recession, and slowed the pace of the recovery. In such an environment, it may seem appealing to pass a law creating a state-owned bank with the goal of re-starting the rapid flow of loanable funds. But such an initiative would be short-sighted. Rather than promoting sustainable growth, it would slow growth over the medium or long run, as funds would be channelled to low-productivity users. A move to support state-controlled banks would also raise systemic risk (as Fannie and Freddie, and the Spanish Cajas clearly show), promote corruption of government officials and institutions, and lead to fiscal losses that could threaten the solvency of government and lead to high inflation.'

Source: The World Bank (2013); 'All about finance' (blog), World Bank.

17.5.3 Mergers and acquisitions

Market-driven consolidation in the form witnessed both in Europe and the United States during the 1990s came later to emerging economies. Before the general liberalisation trend, most banking sector mergers resulted from government efforts to restructure inefficient banking systems (as in many Latin American countries) or from intervention following banking crises (as in East Asian countries). However, following the deregulation and privatisation processes, competition has increased in a number of markets and the M&A trend is becoming more market driven. Cross-border activity is a major feature of M&A in emerging markets since foreign ownership is usually established through the purchase of existing enterprises rather than 'greenfield investment' (new companies).

Consolidation in the financial sector tends to follow broad trends, most noticeably, it tends to be higher when stock markets and bank valuations are high or when banking systems have collapsed and need restructuring via forced consolidation. Total value of global bank M&As peaked in 2008 and 2009 as a result of the global financial crisis, and has fallen back substantially since then. The prospects for increased consolidation in emerging markets emulate expected economic growth prospects:

● Asian economies are likely to see the largest amount and growth in bank M&As up to 2020. Most of this is expected to be domestic deals. There will be continued inter-regional deals with banks from Japan, South Korea, Singapore, Malaysia and also Australia looking to build a broad-based commercial banking presence in the region. Other global banks are more likely to look at developing specialist investment banking, asset management and private banking acquisitions. It has been noted that regulators are increasingly putting limits on foreign acquisition, to constrain domestic purchases, and also Basel III asks for more capital on minority stakes, therefore this may inhibit foreign expansion to some extent. It is important also to note that big banks from the region, especially Chinese banks, are following their large corporate customers around the world and have both made acquisitions and set up greenfield (new) sites:

- Latin America remains the second most attractive market for bank M&As, with most activity taking places in the biggest banking system – Brazil. In addition, some large Latin American banks are following trade flows and making acquisitions in major trading partner countries. Foreign activity in Brazil typically focuses on specialist areas such as private banking, prime brokerage and asset management. However, there has been some consolidation by medium-sized Brazilian banks since 2009. It is interesting to note that Chinese and other Asian banks have entered Brazil but not via M&As and mainly through the set-up of greenfield operations. Elsewhere, the prospects for consolidation are more limited, although some argue there is still potential for more domestic consolidation in Mexico and other Latin American countries such as Colombia and Uruguay.

- Africa presents major M&A opportunities, although many markets remain highly concentrated. The two countries that have experienced most activity are Nigeria (which had a government-forced consolidation aimed at cleaning up the system) and South Africa, with more market-based deals. Other countries such as Kenya offer potential, but political and other risks remain high in many African markets and this tends to deter foreign acquirers.

- Russia and Central Europe experienced some M&A activity. Russia, with around 1,000 banks, offers big opportunities for restructuring, particularly between small and medium-sized institutions. Sberbank, one of Russia's biggest banks, has made acquisitions in the region and also in Turkey. The large number of banks in Poland offers consolidation prospects in the future.

- The prosperity in Gulf countries and elsewhere in the Middle East means that banks from the energy-rich countries are looking to expand into other markets, the recent activity of the Qatari banks being most noticeable in this respect – see Box 17.3.

BOX 17.3 SCOPE FOR CONSOLIDATION IN OVERCROWDED GULF BANKING MARKETS

Only a few years ago Middle Eastern banks were receiving billions of dollars of support from their home governments to fend off the global financial crisis. Now, free from the bad debts that built up at that time, they are striking out with acquisitions across the region and challenging global banks to capture a share of trade between emerging markets.

Mergers and acquisitions have picked up in the past year, as banks such as Qatar National Bank have refashioned themselves as regional champions through deals involving regional operations of European lenders recovering from the crisis. Overcrowded banking sectors in the United Arab Emirates and Bahrain have also started to consolidate.

International banks, many of which are still reviewing which businesses are producing the highest return on capital, are unlikely to invest more in the region, says Redmond Ramsdale, regional director of financial institutions at Fitch Ratings in Dubai. In the meantime, Middle Eastern lenders are likely to be "opportunistic" in their approach to acquisitions. "As Europe recovers from the crisis we may see a stronger interest back in the Middle East," he says. "But this will be medium to longer term."

UAE and Qatari banks received a windfall of deposits during the Arab Spring, becoming flush with capital as expatriates from Syria, Egypt and

BOX 17.3 Scope for consolidation in overcrowded Gulf banking markets (*continued*)

other restive Middle Eastern countries relocated and sought a safe harbour for their savings.

Supported by the development plans of the oil-rich governments of the region, tier one capital ratios of the Gulf's banks are among the highest in the world. Government backing puts the credit ratings of some Gulf banks, such as National Bank of Abu Dhabi, Qatar National Bank and National Bank of Kuwait, on equal pegging with the strongest of international firms. Many banks are redeploying that capital overseas in trade financing or expanding retail lending at home.

Qatar National Bank used its financial strength to embark on a string of acquisitions across north Africa and the Levant which saw it leapfrog ahead of all other Gulf lenders in terms of total assets during 2012.

Few others, however, are using their excess capital to buy weaker rivals – even though transactions have been pushed by governments, either to create national champions in good times or rescue failing lenders in bad. Nevertheless, many markets are ripe for consolidation. With 51 banks in total, the UAE is viewed as one of the most promising markets for mergers and acquisitions. "There's definitely scope for consolidation in the Emirates," says Claudio Scardovi, a managing director at consultancy AlixPartners.

Some Chinese lenders seeking to boost their regional presence may also take an interest in the Emirates, he adds. Lenders including ICBC have grown rapidly since entering the UAE in 2008, catering to an underserved population of Chinese expatriates. Numbers of financial firms are slowly shrinking. This year, First Gulf Bank, controlled by members of the Abu Dhabi royal family, purchased the card payment company Dubai First for $163m, taking control of the firm from Dubai Group, the stricken investment vehicle owned by the emirate's ruler. Soon after, Barclays said it would put its UAE retail banking business up for sale, including its profitable credit card franchise. But not, crucially, its branch licences. These are tightly controlled by the Emirates' central bank and few international lenders have been permitted new storefronts.

Acquisitions seem to provide an exception to the rule, such as HSBC's purchase of Lloyds TSB Middle East last year, through which the bank gained a single branch. Other markets are also starting to consolidate.

Bahrain, the former banking centre of the region, has struggled to recover from the political unrest of 2011, and smaller lenders are consolidating in greater numbers with the encouragement of the kingdom's government. A merger of Elaf Bank, Capivest and Capital Management House completed a rare three-way combination in January. This month, Al Salam Bank agreed to a share-swap merger with BMI Bank, while Khaleeji Commercial Bank began due diligence on a tie-up with Bank Al Khair. Other banks believe that under-banked markets in north Africa and the Levant make more sense as potential entry points than the thinly populated Gulf states.

Emirates NBD and Qatar National Bank expanded into Egypt last year through purchases of franchises from withdrawing French lenders, such as BNP Paribas and Société Générale. But new frontiers in banking are captivating financial groups. "There's a story within the region of new trade and investment corridors," especially between the Middle East and Africa, says one executive at a western financial group, who asked not to be identified. "We're also seeing Iraq as a hugely important new topic of interest."

Iraq, in spite of a spate of recent bombings and other violence, is undergoing something of a gold rush among international financial groups as oil production recovers. Standard Chartered has sought to enter Iraq with three branch launches planned within the next year. And Citibank and JPMorgan are seeking entry points to capitalise upon the rebound in oil production and trade. Gulf lenders are also seeking to make an impact in Iraq. Abu Dhabi Islamic Bank and Qatar National Bank both invested heavily in their Iraqi operations last year. But the market has proven a tough nut to crack for HSBC, which is currently disposing of a majority stake in Dar Es Salaam Investment Bank after a strategic review.

Consolidation has been a feature of both advanced and emerging economies and this trend ultimately feeds through into greater industry concentration, with the usual concerns about big banks and too-big-to-fail safety-net subsidies. However, big banks are often needed to meet the scale of activities demanded by large corporations. As industry in the emerging world expands, so will the banks and other financial firms – it is an inevitable feature of the market process.

17.5.4 Foreign banks

Over the last 20 years foreign banks have become increasingly important in many banking systems and most noticeably in emerging markets. The desire of banks to move to other markets is influenced by factors that are wide and varied. Some of the main reasons put forward for foreign bank entry in emerging (and other) markets have been discussed in Chapter 4.

Claessens and van Horen (2012) present an account of global foreign bank activity examining the features of 5,324 banks operating in 137 countries over the period 1995–2009. Figure 17.6 highlights the extent of foreign bank activity globally and Table 17.9 shows that all regions have witnessed an increase in foreign bank presence since 1995, with Central and Eastern Europe and Sub-Saharan Africa having the highest proportion of foreign bank operators. Foreign banks are generally believed to contribute to greater efficiency and resilience of the financial sector, both because foreign presence implies greater borrowing in local currency (thereby minimising currency mismatches) and because foreign banks can help emerging economies recapitalise their banking systems. Foreign banks may also help enhance financial stability by enabling greater lending diversification and by improving risk management practices. Despite the fact that the benefits

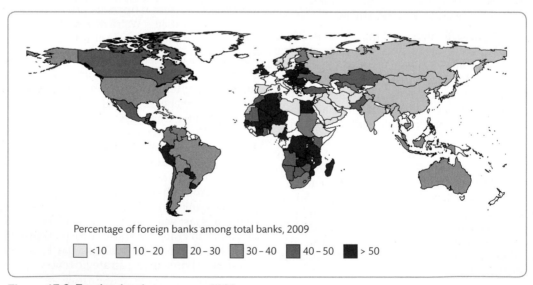

Percentage of foreign banks among total banks, 2009

☐ <10   ☐ 10 – 20   ☐ 20 – 30   ☐ 30 – 40   ☐ 40 – 50   ■ > 50

Figure 17.6 Foreign bank presence, 2009

Source: Claessens and van Horen (2014b).

Table 17.9 Number of banks by host country, aggregates by income level and regions

	1995		2000		2005		2009	
	Number	Share	Number	Share	Number	Share	Number	Share
All countries								
Domestic	3,192	0.80	3,064	0.74	2,861	0.71	2,617	0.66
Foreign	788	0.20	1,069	0.26	1,165	0.29	1,330	0.34
Total	3,980	1	4,133	1	4,026	1	3,947	1
Income groups OECD								
Domestic	1,067	0.82	1,092	0.80	1,102	0.78	1,068	0.76
Foreign	238	0.18	280	0.20	311	0.22	329	0.24
Total	1,305	1	1,372	1	1,413	1	1,397	1
Other high income								
Domestic	79	0.66	74	0.66	63	0.60	62	0.60
Foreign	40	0.34	38	0.34	42	0.40	41	0.40
Total	119	1	112	1	105	1	103	1
Emerging markets								
Domestic	1,484	0.82	1,313	0.74	1,159	0.70	1,011	0.64
Foreign	328	0.18	473	0.26	486	0.30	572	0.36
Total	1,812	1	1,786	1	1,645	1	1,583	1
Developing countries								
Domestic	562	0.76	585	0.68	537	0.62	476	0.55
Foreign	182	0.24	278	0.32	326	0.38	388	0.45
Total	744	1	863	1	863	1	864	1
Region								
Domestic	261	0.82	277	0.81	296	0.81	290	0.76
Foreign	56	0.18	64	0.19	68	0.19	93	0.24
Total	317	1	341	1	364	1	383	1
Eastern Europe and Central Asia								
Domestic	673	0.85	610	0.72	510	0.62	418	0.53
Foreign	115	0.15	235	0.28	310	0.38	374	0.47
Total	788	1	845	1	820	1	792	1
Latin America and Caribbean								
Domestic	604	0.75	485	0.66	400	0.65	369	0.61
Foreign	197	0.25	254	0.34	215	0.35	233	0.39
Total	801	1	739	1	615	1	602	1
Middle East and North Africa								
Domestic	147	0.82	135	0.77	120	0.72	103	0.64
Foreign	32	0.18	40	0.23	46	0.28	57	0.36
Total	179	1	175	1	166	1	160	1
South Asia								
Domestic	134	0.93	144	0.91	149	0.91	141	0.87
Foreign	10	0.07	15	0.09	15	0.09	22	0.13
Total	144	1	159	1	164	1	163	1

Table 17.9 continued

	1995		2000		2005		2009	
	Number	Share	Number	Share	Number	Share	Number	Share
Sub-Saharan Africa								
Domestic	227	0.69	247	0.63	221	0.58	166	0.48
Foreign	100	0.31	143	0.37	158	0.42	181	0.52
Total	327	1	390	1	379	1	347	1

Source: Claessens and van Horen (2014a) p. 302.

that foreign banks can offer to emerging economies are now more widely accepted, a number of concerns remain:

- A large foreign banking presence can reduce the information available to host country supervisors.
- A large foreign banking presence can expose a country to shocks due purely to external events affecting the parent bank.
- Foreign banks 'cherry pick' the best firms, leaving the domestic banking sector with a weakened lending portfolio.
- Foreign banks concentrate on large and more profitable firms, leaving small and medium-sized enterprises for domestic banks.

Overall, however, the significant empirical literature that focuses on foreign bank behaviour (and summarised in Claessens and van Horen, 2012) concludes that increased foreign presence has a positive impact on economic development, apart from in the poorest countries – and this may be because the scale of foreign bank activity in the poorest countries is not too large.

17.5.5 Foreign ownership and regulatory reform

Probably the single most important driving force behind the increase in foreign activity and foreign ownership in emerging banking markets is regulatory reform. During the 1990s and early 2000s many countries engaged in liberalisation programmes aimed at encouraging foreign bank entry. Sometimes this deregulation was due to reform after crises as well as general moves to open up economies to wider access in terms of capital flows and foreign direct investment. Regulatory reforms were designed to strengthen competition, and expansion of trade liberalisation gave additional impetus for structural reforms. Some of the early policy initiatives were designed to achieve a more open capital account and transparent FDI policies and this also facilitated greater foreign bank entry.

A noticeable example of how trade liberalisation can have a substantial impact on an economy is the case of China, and the impact of its joining the World Trade Organization (WTO) in December 2001. Membership of the WTO involves a major commitment to facilitate freer trade in capital, goods and services through the reduction of trade and entry barriers. Under the WTO, China had to make an array of commitments to open its domestic markets to foreign competition – although even by 2014 foreign banks were not permitted to hold a stake of more than 20 per cent in any one bank, and therefore foreigners still cannot have majority control. Table 17.10 illustrates similar limits and other nuances linked to bank entry in Asia.

Table 17.10 Foreign ownership limits in South East Asian banking

Forms	Indonesia	Malaysia	Philippines	Thailand	Vietnam
Acquisition of shares	Since 1992 limited to 49% (51% for ASEAN banks), and increased to 99% in 1999 (for joint venture, since 1989 limited to 85%, increased to 99% in 1999)	Since 1989 limited to 30%, increased to 49% in 2007 (increased to 100% from 49% for Islamic banks)	Since 1994, limited to 60%, increased to 100% in 2000, for new entry on a seven-year-window basis	Prior to 1997, limited to 25%, since 1997 increased to 100%, and has to be reduced to 49% after 10 years	Since 1993, limited to 10%, increased to 30% in 2004 (20% capped on a single strategic investor) (for joint venture, limited to 49%)
Wholly-owned subsidiary	No	No	Yes	Yes	Yes (in 2007)
Full-service branch	Yes	No	Yes	Yes	Yes (in 2007)
Domestic branching for branches and subsidiaries	Up to 10 cities prior to 1999, since 1999 fully open	n.a.	Fully open since 1994	One for branch and four for subsidiaries after the implementation of the Financial Sector Master Plan in 2004	Implicitly restricted for foreign bank branches

Source: Molyneux *et al.* (2014) Table 2.

17.6 Conclusion

After two decades of liberalisation and reform, the banking systems of emerging economies remained fragmented in terms of size, ownership structure, competitive conditions and profitability. Despite these varied characteristics, most countries continued to engage in deregulation and financial liberalisation, in the adoption of new information and telecommunication technologies, as well as extensive privatisation programmes. This has resulted in profound structural changes, ranging from a decrease in the number of banks, an increased presence of foreign financial institutions and a general decline in the role of the state.

Since the global financial crisis of 2007–2009 the trend towards liberalisation and deregulation has reversed, with greater pressures on banks to boost their capital and liquidity and reduce their higher-risk activities. Policy makers in both advanced and emerging markets are more concerned about maintaining safe banking systems than liberalising them further. It is difficult to foresee how long this more cautious banking environment will persist. In some countries a slowdown in the domestic economy is also exacerbating financial sector development. Nevertheless, the economies of seven emerging markets (Brazil, China, India, Indonesia, Mexico, Russia and Turkey) are widely expected to be bigger than the seven largest advanced economies (G7 – Canada, France, Germany, Great Britain, Italy, Japan and US) by 2050 – so the prospects for banking and financial firms in the former remain significant.

Key terms

Bank-based financial systems	Digital divide	Financial liberalisation	Market-based finan-cial systems
Developing countries	Emerging markets	Financial repression	Transition economies
	Financial deepening		

Key reading

Beck, T. (2012) 'The role of finance in economic development – benefits, risks, and politics', in Müller, D. (ed.), *Oxford Handbook of Capitalism*, Oxford: Oxford University Press.

Čihák, M., Demirgüç-Kunt, A., Feyen, E. and Levine, R. (2012) 'Benchmarking financial systems around the world', World Bank Policy Research Working Paper 6175, August, Figure 6, Washington, DC: World Bank.

Claessens, S. and van Horen, N. (2014) 'Foreign banks: Trends and impact', *Journal of Money, Credit and Banking*, Vol. 46, No. 1, pp. 295–326.

Demirgüç-Kunt, A. and Klapper, L. (2012) 'Measuring financial inclusion, The Global Findex Database', World Bank Policy Research Working Paper 6025, April, Washington, DC, World Bank.

Demirgüç-Kunt, A. and Klapper, L. (2013) 'Measuring financial inclusion: Explaining variation in use of financial services across and within countries', *Brookings Papers on Economic Activity*, Spring, 279–394.

The World Bank (2013) *World Development Report, Rethinking the Role of the State in Finance*, Washington, DC: International Bank for Reconstruction and Development/The World Bank.

REVISION QUESTIONS AND PROBLEMS

17.1 How does financial sector development aid economic growth and why is the impact larger in less developed countries?

17.2 Outline the main structural features of emerging banking systems. In general, how do they differ from their advanced economy counterparts?

17.3 Why is the link between finance and growth non-linear? Outline the five main reasons that explain this non-linearity.

17.4 Why does state ownership of banks tend to be associated with a poorly developed financial sector?

17.5 In what circumstances is state ownership preferable to private bank ownership?

17.6 How do foreign banks impact the performance of financial systems? Explain why their influence is found to be greater in emerging markets compared with advanced economies.

17.7 What are the main concerns raised by the role of foreign banks as well as the consolidation process in emerging markets?

17.8 Explain how technology can rapidly impact the behaviour of banks and their customers. In your answer specifically refer to recent mobile phone app development in China.

PART 5

Advanced topics in banking

Banks and markets

18.1   Introduction

Banks are inextricably linked to markets. They obtain their funding not only from traditional retail and corporate deposits but also from other banks via the interbank market. Banks also manage their short-term funding requirements by accessing money markets (which include not only interbank business but also the issue of short-term securities, such as commercial paper). Traditionally, banks have also been major operators in trading (buying and selling) short-term money market instruments, including Treasury bills, trade bills and other short-term instruments such as repurchase agreements (repos). All this activity is undertaken so that banks can manage their predictable (and unpredictable) liquidity positions. In addition, banks have been the mainstay of the foreign exchange market.[1]

Over the last decade or so banks' involvement in markets increased dramatically, partially as a reflection of the trend towards universal banking and also because technological

---

[1] The foreign exchange market (commonly known as forex) is a network of individual investors, businesses, investment management firms, hedge funds, brokers, banks, central banks and governments to buy and sell the currencies of different countries to finance international trade, invest or do business abroad, or speculate on currency price changes. The forex market is considered to be the largest financial market in the world. As of 2013, average daily turnover in global foreign exchange markets was estimated at $5.3 trillion, up from $4.0 trillion in 2010. The growth in global FX market activity between 2010 and 2013 outpaced the 19 per cent rise from 2007 to 2010 reported in the prior survey, but falls short of the record 72 per cent increase (at current exchange rates) between 2004 and 2007 (BIS, 2013d).

advances have made it easier to price and trade an increasingly broader array of complex financial products. Banks have experienced an increasing dependence on financial markets not only as a funding source but also for risk management (hedging) purposes and for undertaking various transactions for their clients. What has emerged is a complex web of interdependence between banks and markets. The past decade has also witnessed the rapid development of a distinct form of financial intermediation: **shadow banking**. In general terms, shadow banking refers to all activities related to credit intermediation, liquidity and maturity transformation that take place outside the regulated banking system.

The aim of this chapter is to outline the key linkages between banks and markets with a particular focus on the recent rise and fall of **securitisation**. Section 18.2 examines the bank intermediation process and compares this to market transactions, highlighting the role of informational asymmetries. It also briefly discusses a new form of financial intermediation, between banks and markets, the shadow banking system. Section 18.3 looks at the evolution of securitisation activity, focusing on the key role played by the US government-sponsored enterprises (GSEs) in promoting the development of a mortgage-backed securities market. We then move on to explain the main processes involved in issuing MBS (and other asset-backed securities). Section 18.4 introduces the modern securitisation process while Section 18.5 discusses the second wave of securitisation with the emergence of collateralised debt obligations (CDOs) and asset-backed commercial paper (ABCP), highlighting how banks were involved in this activity and how it led to big losses. Section 18.6 examines the role of credit-rating agencies and monoline insurers in the securitisation process, and in Section 18.7 we note the broad impact of bank securitisation activity and highlight how such activity will be placed under greater regulatory scrutiny in the future. Finally, in Section 18.8 we discuss the future for the securitisation market, and we outline the proposed financial reforms that aim to restrict bank market activity. Section 18.9 is the conclusion.

18.2 Bank intermediation, markets and information

The main function of banks is to undertake financial intermediation whereby they take low-risk, small and highly liquid deposits and transform these into larger, longer-maturity and riskier loans. Transforming deposits into loans has been the traditional role of commercial banks for centuries (see also Chapter 1). The theory of financial intermediation has emphasised the special role played by banks in screening and monitoring borrowers in the lending process (see Section 1.4.3). For instance, banks have to ensure that they do not lend to bad borrowers (those that will default) and as such they invest substantial resources into systems and procedures (such as credit evaluation of customers, credit scoring and so on) in order to minimise the likelihood of lending to bad customers. More formally, screening is said to reduce adverse selection problems in the loan granting process. The argument goes that borrowers that want to borrow large sums (even at high interest rates) are the most risky and therefore should be screened out as they are the most likely to default. Once bad borrowers have been screened out, then the bank can make loans. However, borrowers' behaviour may change; once granted loans they may then have an incentive not to repay (for instance, if their economic circumstances change) – this is known as moral hazard. As such, banks have to monitor borrowers over the life of the loan so as to minimise the likelihood of moral hazard problems in the lending process. Successful screening reduces adverse selection problems, whereas appropriate monitoring reduces moral hazard.

Put together, screening and monitoring help banks reduce information asymmetries as it provides them with unique (proprietary) information about potential and actual borrowers. Banks are generally regarded as better than markets in reducing information problems as they can get closer to their borrowers over time and adjust their lending (and other) behaviour accordingly. In contrast, market-based financing (bonds and other debt financing) is mostly based on analysts' assessment around a specific point in time. For example, once bonds are issued their terms cannot be renegotiated and information is in the public domain. Market-based financing (and investment banking for that matter) has typically been viewed as transaction-based whereas commercial banking focuses more on relationships (see Section 1.4.3.4 on transaction and relationship banking).

Much of the discussion above focuses on asymmetric information issues between banks and borrowers. In general, where information asymmetries between borrowers and financers are large, then traditional bank intermediation is likely to be more important. When such asymmetries are less important, then market-based financing (based on hard information) will be greater. Some have argued that bank financing is important for small firms whereas as firms become larger they become better suited to market finance. This could be because banks undertake a certification role by signalling a successful medium- to long-term lending relationship. This successful relationship in turn suggests there are minimal adverse selection and moral hazard issues associated with the borrowing firm, therefore making it an appropriate candidate for capital market finance. In other words, bank lending certifies that particular firms have the appropriate information features to be able to tap the financial markets for funding.

Traditionally, banks have been seen to be in competition with the capital market. This spawned a debate as to whether economies that had large banking sectors relative to the size of the economy (so-called *bank-based systems*) resulted in better macroeconomic performance compared with *market-based systems* (those where stock market capitalisation to economy size is relatively large) (see also Section 17.2).

In a bank-based system, banks are the most important source of external financing for firms, although at various extents. Bank–client relationships are close and the universal banking model is widespread. Informational barriers are more significant, as incumbent banks have informational advantages over new entrants. In a market-based system, meanwhile, capital markets usually are the main source of firm financing. Bank–client relationships are typically at arm's length and thus have less contractual flexibility than relationship-based finance.

The US and the UK are viewed as traditional market-based systems whereas Japan and Germany (and most of continental Europe and emerging economies in general) are viewed as bank-based systems. In recent years, the demarcation lines of this common classification of financial systems have become increasingly blurred and it is now normally accepted that bank intermediation and capital market funding activities are complementary. The general consensus that has emerged out of the bank-based versus market-based debate is that it does not really matter whether an economy is bank- or market-based for economic performance – what is most important is that the economy has well-developed banking and financial systems overall. This view has pretty much informed IMF policy actions aimed at promoting financial sector development globally.

18.2.1 The shadow banking system

In addition to the traditional distinction between bank and capital market activities, the growth of shadow banking has strengthened the inter-linkages between banks and markets. Despite a growing interest among both academics and policy makers, there is no comprehensive definition of what constitutes shadow banking.[2] The Financial Stability Board (2011c) defines shadow banking as credit intermediation involving entities and activities outside the regular banking system.[3] Pozsar *et al.* (2010) define shadow banks as financial intermediaries that conduct maturity, credit and liquidity transformation without explicit access to central bank liquidity or public sector credit guarantees. These include finance companies, asset-backed commercial paper conduits, structured investment vehicles (SIVs), credit hedge funds, money market mutual funds, securities lenders, limited-purpose finance companies (LPFCs), and the GSEs. According to the relevant literature, the main components of the shadow banking system (in the US and in the eurozone) include (i) securitisation activities; (ii) collateral intermediation; (iii) money market funds; (iv) the repo market; and (v) hedge funds. In its broader definition, shadow banking also includes investment banks and mortgage brokers.

While measures of shadow banking differ considerably, in the US the system is large and comparable in size to the traditional banking system. In the euro area, the shadow banking system is smaller, representing less than half of the total assets of the banking sector, with some relevant differences among countries (Bakk-Simon *et al.*, 2012). Globally, shadow banking activities were estimated at around $65 trillion in 2011 (up from $26 trillion in 2002), which represents, on average, 25 per cent of the world financial assets and 111 per cent of the world aggregate GDP (Claessens *et al.*, 2012).

Probably the main recent development that reflects the complementarities between bank lending and capital market activities is the increasing importance of securitisation. The evolution and features of the securitisation phenomenon are discussed in Section 18.3 and following. Below we briefly review the other components of shadow banking.

Collateral intermediation

A key function of shadow banking is supporting collateral-based operations within the financial system. This involves the intensive re-use of collateral (which can involve assets of different quality, from investment-grade AAA-rated bonds and Treasury bills to speculative-grade bonds or equities) so that it supports as large as possible a volume of financial transactions (this is also known as *re-hypothecation*, that is the right to re-use the assets received as collateral for other purposes). Collateral intermediation is carried out by a small number of 'dealer banks', most of them classified as systemically important financial institutions (SIFIs) by the Financial Stability Board. The key players in this type of activity are Goldman Sachs, Morgan Stanley, JPMorgan, Bank of America-Merrill Lynch and Citibank in the United States; and Barclays, BNP Paribas, Crédit Suisse, Deutsche Bank, HSBC, Royal Bank of Scotland, Société Générale and UBS in Europe. Outside the US and Europe, only Nomura is active in this market.[4]

---

[2] For a taxonomy of shadow banking see Pozsar *et al.* (2010).

[3] A definition of shadow banking is not straightforward. For a review of the current academic and regulatory attempts to define shadow banking see, among others, Claessens *et al.* (2012), Bakk-Simon *et al.* (2012).

[4] For more detail on collateral intermediation, see Singh and Aitken (2010) and Claessens *et al.* (2012).

Money market funds (MMFs)

Money market funds (MMFs) developed as an alternative to bank deposits and to circumvent regulatory caps on bank interest rates in the United States. MMFs invest in short-term debt, through purchases of certificates of deposits (CDs) and commercial paper (CP) and through repo transactions. Outside the United States, MMFs are less relevant; in the euro area MMFs' balance sheets represent only 4 per cent of the balance sheets of monetary financial institutions (MFIs), although there are substantial country differences (for example, according to ECB statistics, MMFs represent 27 per cent of the total balance sheet of Luxembourg's MFIs and 24 per cent of Ireland's).[5]

The repo market

The repo market is another key component of the shadow banking system, particularly in the United States.[6] According to estimates, the repo market amounted to $12 trillion in early 2010. While there are no official data on the overall size of the repo market in the euro area, market information placed the total value of outstanding repos in the EU at €6.2 trillion at the end of 2011 (Bakk-Simon *et al.*, 2012; ICMA, 2012).

Hedge funds

Hedge funds are also key players in financial markets, although whether they are part of the shadow banking system is debatable.[7] However, hedge funds were part of the complex network of financial intermediaries that was instrumental in the growth of shadow banking, either through their involvement in securitisation activities or in the repo market (Financial Services Authority, 2012).

18.3   The development of the securitisation market[8]

The origins of the **securitisation** business can be traced to the failure of the US Savings and Loans institutions in the mid-1980s. Traditionally, the S&Ls' main business was to collect retail deposits and use these to finance long-term residential mortgages. In the mid-1980s the S&L sector faced collapse because market interest rates increased and therefore the S&Ls had to pay higher deposit rates to maintain funding. However (because of various restrictions), they could not adjust rates on mortgages to cover the increased cost of funding. As such, S&Ls moved into higher-risk commercial property lending to try to generate higher returns: this resulted in substantial losses. Recall that during the 1980s, the US had restrictions on interstate banking so many S&Ls had very concentrated lending portfolios,

---

[5] http://sdw.ecb.europa.eu/

[6] Repos (repurchase agreements) involve an agreement between a cash borrower and a cash lender on the temporary sale of assets for a specified period of time and a certain amount of cash, with interest (repo rate) paid over the duration of the cash holding by the cash borrower (repo seller) to the cash lender (repo buyer).

[7] A hedge fund is an investment fund open to a limited number of wealthy investors and (because of its focus on wealthy/professional investors) is permitted to undertake a wider range of investment and trading activities than other investment funds. There are many different types of hedge funds pursuing a range of activities: in macro funds, for instance, investment and trading strategies are based on movements in macroeconomic indicators such as interest rates, exchange rates and so on.

[8] Baily *et al.* (2008) provide an excellent insight into the evolution of the securitisation business. This section draws information from their work.

which focused on particular geographical areas. This lending concentration resulted in high default rates. The crisis situation faced by the S&L sector led the US authorities to set up the **Resolution Trust Corporation**, an entity that took assets off the S&Ls' books and then sold them on to investors and other banks. This process was not costless – US taxpayers faced losses of around $150 billion – although it did manage to avoid a system-wide collapse.

The process outlined above was the first major securitisation. The process was viewed as a solution to the problem faced by the S&L sector as it freed mortgage lenders from liquidity constraints imposed by their balance sheets. Through the securitisation process, banks no longer had to rely on deposits to make loans; they could make loans and then sell them on to investors in the form of securities to finance the lending activity.

These two different approaches to funding credit have been referred to as the:

- **originate-to-hold model** – where lenders find borrowers, originate loans and then hold these on the balance sheet until maturity (the traditional approach); and

- **originate-to-distribute model** – where lenders find borrowers, originate loans but then sell the loans (re-packaged as securities) on to investors (the securitisation approach).

Prior to securitisation, banks could make only a limited number of loans based on the size of their balance sheets. The new form of financing, however, allowed lenders to sell off their loans to other banks or investors, and the funds raised could be used to increase lending (see Section 18.4.1 for a detailed discussion of the securitisation process).

A major push to the US securitisation trend was led by the development of **mortgage-backed securities (MBS)** promoted by the **government-sponsored enterprises (GSEs)**, notably **Fannie Mae (Federal National Mortgage Association – FNMA)** and **Freddie Mac (Federal Home Loan Mortgage Corporation – FHLMC)**. The GSEs had been established some years earlier to promote home ownership in the US.[9] Mortgages that fit certain rules (known as *conforming mortgages*) could be sold to Fannie Mae and Freddie Mac (see Box 15.1 for US mortgage basics). The GSEs then packaged a geographically dispersed mortgage loan portfolio and sold MBS in financial markets.

Over the 1990s and early to mid-2000s, the securitisation activities of the GSEs were very profitable and their business boomed. The GSEs were key participants in the mortgage market, accounting for much of the expansion of prime mortgage lending in the early 2000s. They also bought sub-prime (higher-risk) loans and expanded that portfolio after 2003.[10] With the rise in sub-prime mortgage defaults (culminating in the credit crunch of August 2007), their portfolios suffered major write-downs, pushing them into losses – Fannie and Freddie had nearly $15 billion of write-downs at the end of 2007 according to their regulator (**Office of Federal Housing Enterprise Oversight, OFHEO**). However, despite these problems, by the end of 2007 they remained by far the largest buyers of mortgages originated, and some 75 per cent of new mortgages written in the fourth quarter of 2007 were placed with Fannie Mae and Freddie Mac. Growing concerns about the value of the

---

[9] The GSEs were established by Congress to direct funds to specific sectors in the economy. Those most involved in mortgage finance include Freddie Mac (established in 1970), Fannie Mae (established in 1938) and the Government National Mortgage Association (Ginnie Mae) (established in 1968). In September 2008 Fannie Mae and Freddie Mac had to be rescued by the US government.

[10] This was in part because Congress encouraged (some critics say pushed) them to provide more loans to low-income borrowers in order to justify the capital advantage they had because of the implicit federal guarantee.

massive portfolio of MBS held by the main GSEs (estimated at $5 trillion) led to a collapse of their share prices in July 2008, and the Federal authorities had to step in and bail them out in September 2008, as explained in Box 18.1. Figure 18.1 illustrates how the US mortgage market works.

It is important to note that while the above discussion has focused on the GSEs, other financial institutions also issued MBS. As the GSEs' original remit was to promote home

BOX 18.1 A HISTORY OF FREDDIE MAC AND FANNIE MAE

1938: Fannie Mae is created during the Great Depression as a government agency to ensure supply of mortgage funds. The aim is to boost banks' capacity to offer home loans by buying up existing loans in exchange for cash.

1968: Fannie Mae is re-chartered by Congress as a shareholder-owned company, funded solely with private capital.

1970: Freddie Mac is created to provide competition in the secondary mortgage market and end Fannie Mae's monopoly.

1971: Freddie Mac introduces the first mortgage-related security.

2003: US policy interest rates hit a low of 1 per cent, further stoking the booming US housing market.

2004: Following an accounting scandal, Fannie and Freddie's regulator, OFHEO, requires the companies to raise their level of core capital 30 per cent above previous levels, in effect capping their ability to purchase mortgages.

2006: A steep rise in the rate of sub-prime mortgage defaults and foreclosures leads a number of sub-prime mortgage lenders to fail. The failure of these companies causes prices in the MBS market to slip.

August 2007: Rising defaults on sub-prime mortgages trigger a global credit crunch.

March 2008: OFHEO gives both companies permission to add as much as $200bn financing into the mortgage markets by reducing their capital requirements.

April 2008: OFHEO report reveals that Fannie and Freddie accounted for 75 per cent of new mortgages at the end of 2007 as other sources of financing pull back on lending.

July 2008: Shares in Freddie Mac and Fannie Mae plummet amid speculation that a bailout of the government sponsored mortgage financiers may be required, and that such a bailout would leave little if any value for current shareholders. Frantic trading . . . in New York drags shares in both companies down to their lowest levels since 1991.

September 2008: The US government seizes control of the troubled mortgage groups in what could become the world's biggest financial bail-out. The government's move, its most dramatic since the start of the credit crisis, is aimed at ensuring the two groups' woes do not cripple the country's housing market or worsen to the point that they fail and send shockwaves through global markets.

 Source: Financial Times (2008) 15 July, 8 September.

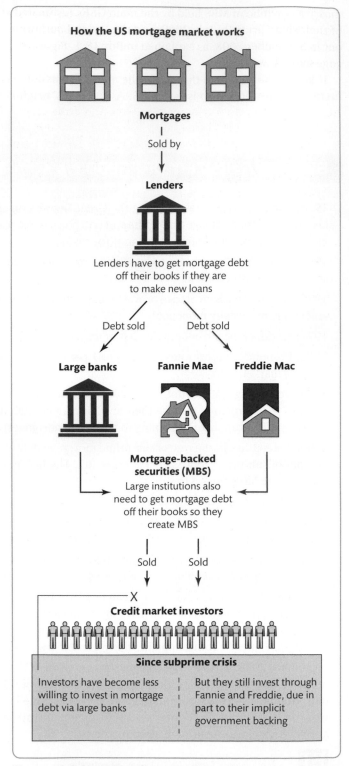

Figure 18.1 How the US mortgage market works

Source: A history of Freddie Mac and Fannie Mae, FT.com, 08/09/08.

ownership to US citizens, they dealt only with mortgages up to a certain size and those that had moderate credit risk features. As such, other institutions were involved in securitising larger 'jumbo' mortgages or those in the higher-risk sub-prime market (see Box 15.1 for definitions).

The growth in the US sub-prime mortgage business (and related securitisations) deserves special mention as this has been attributed as a major culprit of the 2008 financial crisis. Sub-prime mortgage originations grew rapidly from around $200 billion in mid-2003 to more than $500 billion by mid-2004, peaking at around $600 billion in 2005–2006 when they accounted for about 20 per cent of all new US residential mortgages. The attraction of sub-prime mortgages was that they offered higher interest rates than prime (or conforming) mortgages – typically 2 per cent more than fixed-rate prime mortgage lending. In a low interest rate environment this became attractive to banks.

Figure 18.2 illustrates the increasing importance of securitisation, particularly in the sub-prime and Alt-A mortgage market, in the run-up to the 2007 financial crisis. By 2006, around 81 per cent of sub-prime mortgages had been securitised. The tremendous growth in securitisation activity from the early 2000s onwards meant that by 2006 it was driven mostly by non-prime mortgage loans and when sub-prime mortgage borrowers began to default, the securitisation business of such loans collapsed and fuelled the credit crisis. Section 18.4 outlines the securitisation process and shows how particular MBS and ABS structures were created, while Section 18.5 explains the features of CDOs and other instruments.

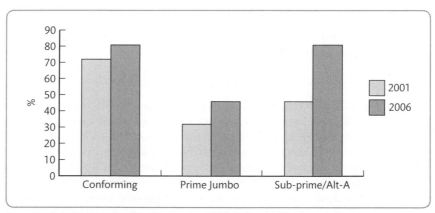

Figure 18.2 Securitisation rates by type of mortgage, 2001 and 2006

Note: Conforming mortgages are those that conform to GSE guidelines and this means that they can be originated and sold to Freddie Mac, Fannie Mae etc. (Loans that do not meet guidelines are known as non-conforming loans.) A jumbo mortgage is a mortgage with a loan amount above the industry-standard definition of conventional conforming loan limits (typically around $420,000 in 2006, and $417,000 in 2011). An Alt-A mortgage is a type of US mortgage that is viewed as riskier than prime mortgages but less risky than sub-prime.

Source: Baily *et al.* (2008) Figure 5.

18.4   Modern securitisation process

Securitisation began in the US in the 1970s with structured financing of mortgage loans by a government-sponsored agency, the Government National Mortgage Association (Ginnie Mae). However, the growth of the securitisation markets started in the mid-1990s: the US market increased from $2.9 trillion in 1996 to $11.6 trillion outstanding at year-end 2007, while the EU market reached $1.97 trillion at year-end 2007 from $7.9 billion in 1996.[11]

After the extended period of growth, global securitisation markets collapsed during the financial crisis of 2008–2009, when securitisation was considered one of the primary causes of the credit market turmoil. Since then, following the generalised loss of investor confidence, most of the new issues have been retained by banks and used as collateral in government refinancing operations. However, despite the weaknesses in the securitisation process revealed by the crisis, policy makers as well as market practitioners acknowledge the potential of securitisation in credit risk transfer and diversification and attempt to revive securitisation by increasing transparency in the market and introducing changes to the securitisation model in terms of simplicity and standardisation (ECB, 2008b).

Traditional securitisation can be defined as the pooling of risky assets and their subsequent sale to a **special-purpose vehicle (SPV)**, which then issues securities. These securities are usually fixed-income instruments, where the principal and interest depend on the cash flow produced by the pool of underlying assets.

According to the Association for Financial Markets in Europe (2014), the process of securitisation is defined as:

> . . . the pooling together of cash-generating assets, such as mortgages, auto loans or SME loans, created by banks and initially funded on their balance sheets, and funding these assets instead by issuing bonds in the capital markets. These bonds are bought by a range of investors - typically banks treasury departments, insurance companies and a range of investment funds. The investors receive regular payments reflecting the interest and principal payments made by the underlying borrowers.

The AFME also clarifies the types of assets that can be securitised:

> The financial assets that support payments on ABS include residential and commercial mortgage loans, as well as a wide variety of non-mortgage assets such as trade receivables, credit card balances, consumer loans, lease receivables, automobile loans, and other consumer and business receivables. Although these asset types are used in some of the more prevalent forms of ABS, the basic concept of securitisation may be applied to virtually any asset that has a reasonably ascertainable value, or that generates a reasonably predictable future stream of revenue. As a result, securitisation has been extended to a diverse array of less well known assets, such as insurance receivables, obligations of shippers to railways, commercial bank loans, health care receivables, obligations of purchasers to natural gas producers, and future rights to entertainment royalty payments, among many others. It is a process by which assets are pooled together and sold as securities.

ABS (asset-backed securities) and MBS (mortgage-backed securities) are the 'original' fixed-income securities resulting from the securitisation of the underlying pool of assets. In Europe and the US the largest components are the RMBS (residential mortgage-backed securities). These are considered traditional 'granular' instruments (i.e. ABS pools have been formed by a large number of small-sized, relatively homogenous consumer-related assets).

---

[11] Securities Industry and Financial Markets Association (SIFMA), **www.sifma.org**.

18.4.1 Creation of an ABS security: participants and functions

Figure 18.3 shows the process of creation of an ABS; securitisation removes financial assets (for example, a pool of mortgage loans) from the balance sheet of the bank. The assets that underlie securitisation transactions are first created when an 'originator', say a bank, makes a loan to a borrower, the 'obligor'. Typically, once the financial asset is created and funded, the bank continues to service the loan, which is the provision of a collection and management function in connection with that loan. As argued by Heffernan (2005), the bank could issue a bond with a bundle of pooled assets acting as collateral, but the credit rating of the bank would be assigned to the new security, the proceeds of the bond would be subject to reserve requirements and the assets included in the computation of the bank's capital ratio. The bank can circumvent these constraints with the process of securitisation.

As illustrated in Figure 18.3, the main participants in a securitisation issue are the following:

- **originator:** the institution (bank) seeking to securitise its assets;
- **sponsor:** the institution that initiates the securitisation process; sometimes the same as the originator, sometimes an agent earning a fee;

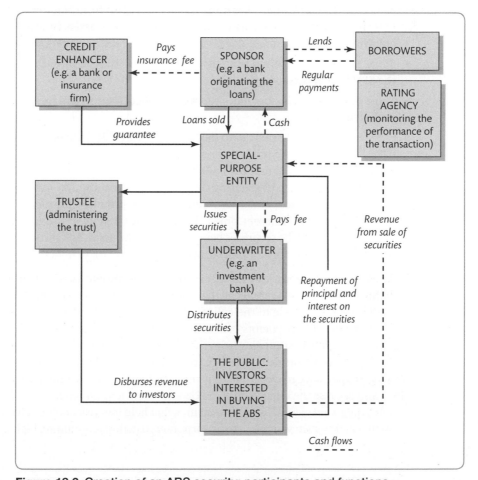

Figure 18.3 Creation of an ABS security: participants and functions

- **special-purpose vehicle:** entity created with the sole purpose of the transaction. The SPV acquires the assets and issues its securities to investors; it is also called 'securitised product issuer';
- **trustee:** impartial third party that monitors the whole deal;
- **custodian:** a party that holds the assets on behalf of the purchaser of the securitised products;
- **servicer:** a party that collects the cash flow on assets and distributes it to either SPV or custodian;
- **underwriter:** an investment bank that markets, distributes and sells the securitised products issued by the SPV.

The following highlights the main stages of the process illustrated in Figure 18.3:[12]

- Stage 1 – the originator makes the mortgage (or other types of) loans.
- Stage 2 – the SPV buys the mortgages (or other loans) from the originator in what is known as a 'true sale'. (Note that many large banks created their own SPVs for this purpose.) The true sale aims to guarantee the separation or 'remoteness' of the cash flows from the underlying assets (mortgages or other loans that have been acquired) from the solvency of the originator. More simply, if the bank that made the loans becomes insolvent then the SPV remains (in theory) legally separate and the loans that have been purchased are protected. The SPV usually has no other function apart from holding the purchased underlying assets and issuing securities backed by the pool of assets (mortgages or other loans) being held. This structure reduces the likelihood of the SPV being placed into bankruptcy.
- Stage 3 – the cash received from investors who buy the (credit-rated) securities issued by the SPV is then passed back to the originator via the SPV.
- Stage 4 – the SPV also appoints a servicer to collect interest and principal payments on the underlying loans.
- Stage 5 – two other key parties to the transaction are the credit enhancer (or swap counterparty) (normally any interest rate risk or currency risk associated with the pool of underlying assets is hedged (or reduced) using a variety of swap transactions) and the trustee, who performs the function of ensuring that money is transferred from the servicer to the SPV and that investors are paid in accordance with the promised priority (investors in the ABS or MBS are paid at different times, different rates and in accordance with varying rules depending on how the securities being backed by the assets are 'sliced and diced' – different tranches of assets back different securities, from low risk to high risk, as explained below.

As Figure 18.3 shows, this all seems rather complicated (and it can be), but one must remember that a critical feature is that if the originator (the bank making the loans) goes bust, there is no recourse to the collateral (the underlying assets) held by the SPV and the servicer ensures that payments on the underlying assets continue to be made and investors that have bought the securities from the SPV still receive interest and principal payments. So (in theory) investors do not have to worry about the risks the bank is taking in its lending activity, all they have to worry about is the credit quality of the underlying assets held in the SPV – and because the regulators in the US and elsewhere classified such SPVs as 'bankruptcy remote', they were viewed as legal structures that held low-risk pools of diversified mortgages (or loans) and as such were seen to be corporate structures containing high-quality collateral.

---

[12] A good exposition of the securitisation process can be found in Marques-Ibanez and Scheicher (2010) and in Casu and Sarkisyan (2014).

Another important feature (see Stage 3 above) is that most securities issued by SPVs were rated by **credit-rating agencies** – Standard & Poor's, Moody's and Fitch. Credit-rating agencies evaluate the credit risk of financial instruments issued by companies (as well as governments and other public bodies). The higher the credit (default) risk associated with a security, the lower the rating and more investors will demand to hold such instruments. (Recall that Standard & Poor's credit-rating scale rates the lowest risk and therefore highest-quality investments as AAA. The credit rating ranges from the aforementioned excellent rating down to poor as such: AAA, AA, A, BBB, BB, B, CCC, CC, C, D. Anything lower than a BBB rating is regarded as high-risk, referred to as speculative grade or a junk bond – see Chapter 4, Table 4.3.)

To assure investors that the ABS or MBS are of a high quality, the SPVs require the credit-rating agencies to rate these securities to reflect the credit risks of the pools of assets backing these securities. While the credit quality of individual loans in the underlying pool of assets may be low, the credit quality (and therefore the credit rating) of the overall portfolio held in the SPV can be increased by pooling the portfolio of risky assets so as to gain various diversification benefits. In addition, the risks of the portfolio could further be improved by various **credit enhancement** techniques, such as third-party guarantees (insurance cover to protect the value of assets), **over-collateralisation** (holding a larger pool of assets than securities issued) and by something known as **excess spread** (originators, namely banks, inject cash into the SPV that will bear certain early losses). All the aforementioned practices, getting the ABS or MBS rated and the various credit-enhancement techniques, were put in place to increase the attractiveness of the securities issued to investors.

There are several methods of credit enhancement and it is not uncommon to see more than one type in a single structured finance transaction. The most common forms are subordination, over-collateralisation and excess spread.

Subordination

Subordination is the process of prioritising the order in which mortgage loan losses are allocated to the various layers of bonds so that the lower-rated junior bonds serve as credit support for the higher-rated senior bonds (i.e. tranching). More specifically, all principal losses on the underlying mortgages go to the most junior bonds first, resulting in a write-down of their principal balance. Similarly, any interest shortfalls will affect the most junior bonds first (see Section 18.4.2 for more details).

BOX 18.2 WHAT IS CREDIT ENHANCEMENT?

Credit enhancement (or credit support) is a risk-reduction technique that provides protection, in the form of financial support, to cover losses under stressed scenarios. Think of credit enhancement as a kind of financial cushion that allows securities backed by a pool of collateral (such as mortgages or credit card receivables) to absorb losses from defaults on the underlying loans.

Thus, it is not the case that through securitisation, poor credit assets somehow 'transform' into solid investments; instead, credit enhancement helps to offset potential losses. Credit enhancement is used in project financings, public–private partnership transactions and structured finance to help mitigate risk for the investors, and has been an accepted practice in bond financing for more than two decades.

Over-collateralisation

Under the over-collateralisation method, the face value of the underlying loan pool is larger than the par value of the issued bonds. So even if some of the payments from the underlying loans are late or default, the transaction may still pay principal and interest on the bonds. For example, if a particular collateral pool's expected performance indicates that the pool would need 40 per cent credit enhancement to support an 'AAA' rating, that rating could not be obtained unless the transaction had 40 per cent more collateral above and beyond the par value of the securities issued.

Excess spread

Excess spread is the additional revenue generated by the difference between the interest rate on the underlying collateral (such as a mortgage interest rate) and the coupon payable on the securities. For example, borrowers whose mortgages are in a given collateral pool may be paying 7 per cent interest, while the coupon of the mortgage-backed security may be 4 per cent. The transaction can then use the excess spread to absorb collateral losses or build over-collateralisation to its target level.

Whatever method a transaction uses, credit enhancement allows for more resources or financial backing for a security than would be available from the underlying assets alone. That way, if the pool ends up experiencing losses, the credit enhancement supporting the bonds should still provide enough buffer to allow for payment to the bonds. Because it provides a kind of safety net, credit enhancement increases the likelihood that bonds with a higher payment priority (senior bonds) will receive their full repayment of principal and timely interest.

18.4.2 Tranching

Another important feature relates to the **tranching** of the liabilities of the SPV so that different types of securities with varying risk and maturity features can be offered to meet varying investor demands. Tranching (from the French for slice) means issuing securities of different risk, duration and other characteristics. In its simplest form, securities issued by the SPV can be broken down into three main 'tranches' and these have different risk–return features: the *senior tranche* (least risky with the highest credit ratings, typically AAA and AA), the *mezzanine tranche* (which are rated, usually BBB and below) and the unrated *equity tranche*. The latter is the most risky tranche of the securitisation deal and is commonly retained by the originating bank on its balance sheet.

In practice, the number of tranches is much higher than three and the senior tranche can be broken into further sub-tranches, which often have the same credit rating but different maturity dates. All tranches are backed by the same pool of risky assets, but if some of the underlying assets default, there is a 'waterfall' of payments such that the equity tranche is the first to suffer losses, followed by the mezzanine tranche and lastly the senior tranche.

In parallel, all payouts coming from the pool first go to the holders of the senior notes, then the mezzanine tranche, and only then would any residual payouts be transferred to equity holders. At least in theory, tranching enables an SPV to split the credit risk and place it with parties that are willing or best able to absorb it.

Example:

An SPV sells four tranches of credit-linked notes with a 'waterfall' structure whereby:

- tranche A absorbs the first 25 per cent of losses on the portfolio;
- tranche B absorbs the next 25 per cent of losses;

- tranche C the next 25 per cent;
- tranche D the final 25 per cent.

Tranches B, C and D are sold to outside investors while tranche A is bought by the bank itself. See Figure 18.4 for an example of this tranching process associated with an SPV asset pool.

Because of the high-risk nature of the equity tranche, traditionally the originators (banks) would hold part of this on their balance sheets to enhance the credit risk of the underlying pool of assets. Holding the equity tranche should also maintain the incentive for originators to continue to monitor the credit quality of the borrowers. However, in the years prior to the 2007–2009 financial crisis, the equity tranche securities were increasingly sold on to speculative investors such as hedge funds. As such, originators (banks) had less incentive to monitor the credit quality of borrowers after the loans had been made because all the risks had been passed on to investors (via the SPV) in the form of securitised assets (MBS and ABS).

Tranching has some advantages and some disadvantages.

Advantages:

- It allows the creation of one or more classes of securities whose rating is higher than the average rating of the underlying collateral asset. This is achieved through the use of credit enhancements, most of which typically come from the originating banks and can be provided in various forms from standby letters of credit to the purchasing of the most junior securities issued by the SPV.

- The equity/first-loss tranche absorbs initial losses, followed by the mezzanine tranches. Thus, the most senior claims are expected to be insulated – except in particularly adverse circumstances – from default risk of the underlying asset.

- Tranching allows investors to further diversify their portfolio.

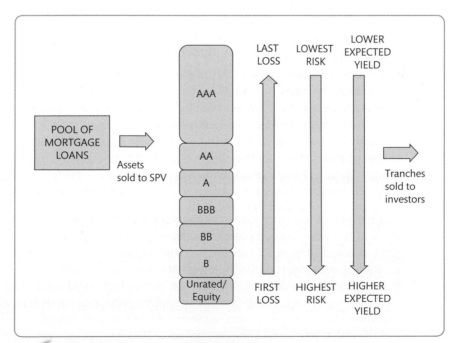

Figure 18.4 Capital structure and prioritisation

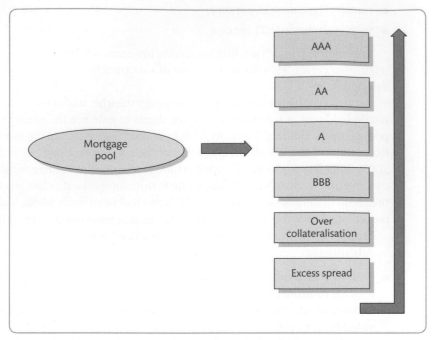

Figure 18.5 Example of tranching and credit enhancement

Disadvantages:

- It adds complexity to deals.
- With increased complexity, less sophisticated investors have a harder time understanding the products offered and therefore are less able to make informed investment decisions.
- Modelling the performance of tranched transactions based on historical performance may have led to the over-rating (by ratings agencies) and underestimation of risks (by end investors) of asset-backed securities. These factors came to light in the sub-prime mortgage crisis.

In the example in Figure 18.5, if there are losses on the pool, those losses would first be allocated to the excess spread. If the losses were greater than the available excess spread, they would be allocated to over-collateralisation. If the losses were greater than both credit enhancements, they would be allocated to the most junior tranche first.

18.5 The 'new wave' of securitisation

The creation of securities known as **collateralised debt obligations (CDOs)** formed a new wave in the securitisation process. In the years preceding the 2007–2009 financial crisis, the tendency had been a departure from the traditional granular securitisation towards the creation of instruments backed by fewer but larger and more heterogeneous assets. The assets backing the new securities, the CDOs, can include high-yield bonds, tranches of other ABS transactions, leveraged loans and often combine securitisation techniques with innovation in credit risk management, such as the use of credit default swaps.

CDO issuers purchased different tranches of MBS and pooled them together with other ABS (backed by car loans, student loans, credit card payments and other assets). They were tranched in a similar fashion as noted above: 'senior' CDOs were backed by highly rated MBS and other ABS, while 'mezzanine' tranches pooled together a higher proportion of junior tranches.

In contrast to an MBS, where the underlying pool of assets was actual mortgages, in the case of CDOs the assets were the securities that received mortgage payments. CDOs, therefore, can be viewed as re-securitised securities. CDOs issued before the financial turmoil frequently were themselves backed by structured securities. This resulted in so-called 'two-layer' or 'double leveraged' securitisations in which structured products were used to fund other structured products. These products are extremely difficult to value in normal times, let alone in periods of turmoil.

Once the ABS and MBS were pooled, these then could be tranched and CDO securities could be issued via SPVs with varying risk–return and maturity profiles. CDOs have been constructed with a variety of assets and have earned different titles, including:[13]

- corporate bonds – collateralised bond obligations (CBOs)
- corporate/leveraged loans – collateralised loan obligations (CLOs)
- BBB ABS – mezzanine CDOs
- tranches of other CDOs – CDO squared (CDO^2).

Again, credit rating agencies were actively engaged in rating the tranches of CDOs and similar securities, and issuers used credit-enhancement techniques to lower the credit risk associated with the various tranches to make them more attractive to investors. The size of US CDO issuance amounted to $300 billion in 2006 and 2007.[14] During 2007, many high-grade CDOs suffered losses, reflecting the mirage associated with the high credit rating of these instruments.

18.5.1 Asset-backed commercial paper

Another important securitised product is **asset-backed commercial paper (ABCP)**. ABCP is (to a certain extent) similar to traditional ABS as it uses a variety of ABS funded by the issue of commercial paper. Marques-Ibanez and Scheicher (2010) note that typically an ABCP uses short-term debt (with maturities starting from one day to several months) to finance a pool of credit assets such as trade receivables, corporate loans, mortgage loans, CDO tranches, or other credit assets obtained from the market, including US sub-prime mortgages.

The underlying assets have relatively long maturities compared with the funding liabilities and as such ABCP structures have large maturity mismatches (or less formally, specific types of SPVs set up by banks, known as **structured investment vehicles (SIVs)**, issue short-term asset-backed commercial paper to finance the assets in the pool and must continue to roll over the issues).

These SPVs that purchase medium- to long-term assets, which they finance by issuing short-term ABCP, are also known as *conduits*. A conduit is an SPV set up by a sponsoring financial institution whose sole purpose is to purchase and hold financial assets from a variety of asset sellers. The conduit finances the assets by selling ABCP to outside investors. The outside investors are primarily money market funds and other 'safe asset' investors. Typically, the originator will provide liquidity support (enhancement and other guarantees) to allay investors' fears about the liquidity mismatch. Many banks (particularly in the US) used this type of structure to hold large pools of medium-term loans in SPV financed by the issue of short-term paper. They could raise short-term finance at attractive terms to hold higher-yielding assets

---

[13] See Marques-Ibanez and Scheicher (2010).
[14] www.sifma.org

in their SPVs that were not subject to onerous capital requirements (which would have been the case if they had been held on-balance sheet).

With the onset of the sub-prime crisis in 2007, liquidity in the ABCP market collapsed, forcing banks to honour the liquidity guarantees that they had made to their SPVs, with many banks having to take these back on to their balance sheets (bearing massive losses as a consequence). Given that the size of the ABCP market was estimated at $1.4 trillion in 2007, the collapse of this activity had serious implications for bank performance. Between July and December 2007, the ABCP market experienced the equivalent of a bank run, when the ABCP outstanding dropped from $1.3 trillion to $833 billion, as documented by Acharya *et al.* (2013) and Covitz *et al.* (2013).

18.6   Types of securitisation

Market professionals agree that securitisation is a structured product, but agreement usually ends there. There are two main different types:

- true sale securitisation;
- synthetic securitisation.

18.6.1   True sale securitisation

In true sale securitisation transactions the originator repackages a pool of assets into tradable securities, which are backed by the assets themselves, and sells it to investors. This is a genuine sale with title passing to the issuer SPV.

The separation of the SPV from the originator also means the third-party investors have no recourse to the originator if the SPV is unable to meet its liabilities to them, aside from any separate security or credit enhancement arrangements included in the securitisation. The true sale process helps to guarantee the separation of the expected cash flows from the underlying assets from the solvency of the originator.

In these cases, the SPV does not have any other function apart from issuing the securities and owning the underlying assets. If the originator goes bankrupt, there is no recourse to the collateral held by the SPV and the servicer ensures that payments on the collateral continue to be made and investors still receive their interest and principal. The credit quality of the securities issued by the SPV is thus delinked from the solvency of the originator, e.g. the bank.

18.6.2   Synthetic securitisation

Synthetic securitisations are issued by banks in order to manage their regulatory capital. In this case the originators do not need funding, their goal is to transfer the credit risk of their portfolio. Synthetic securitisations combine securitisation arrangements with credit derivatives (credit default swaps). In these transactions, the portfolio of assets is not sold to the SPV; instead the originator enters into a **credit default swap (CDS)** or similar arrangement with the SPV (see also Section 18.7).

In synthetic securitisations, the transactions are highly flexible in terms of the asset mix and risk–return characteristics, enabling investors to choose 'tailor-made' tranches to suit their needs. The underlying assets remain on the balance sheet of the originator or arranger, while the SPV holds a pool of CDS that references the assets.

In a synthetic securitisation, the CDS generates a premium payment from the originator or arranger to the SPV. In the event that any of the underlying assets default, the SPV would be responsible for any losses. On the liability side, the SPV still issues fixed-income securities to investors.

18.7 Securitisation, credit-rating agencies and monoline insurers

Banks' increasing involvement in markets via the securitisation process could not have taken place without the role of two important players – credit-rating agencies and **monoline insurers** (that is, entities that provide CDS for specific types of assets).[15]

The credit-rating agencies (CRA) were instrumental in boosting the attractiveness of many securitised assets by assigning ratings to the different tranches of securities issued via SPVs (or SIVs). However, the lack of transparency of various securitised assets – particularly CDOs and ABCP – meant that investors became reliant on the ratings as a guide of the risk–return features of these asset-backed securities. The main agencies – Moody's, Fitch and Standard & Poor's – used complex models to assess the probability of default of the securitised assets and also advised issuers on how to structure the securitised assets (CDOs and the like) so as to minimise funding costs. Put simply, unlike in the corporate bond and other debt markets (syndicated lending), where issues are passively rated, the agencies actively engaged in advising on the creation of increasingly complex structures from which they earned substantial consulting fees. Issuers could shop around to get more attractive ratings. All this resulted in a boom in profits for the credit-rating firms – Moody's profits increased threefold between 2002 and 2006 to $750 million – mainly as a result of fees from advising on securitisation structures.

Since the onset of the 2008 crisis, rating agencies have been accused of being too lenient in rating various tranches in securitisation transactions (particularly the senior tranches). In addition (and as inferred above), various commentators have made allegations about major conflicts of interest arising from the fact that advising and rating securitised assets became a major source of rating agency income and this may have corrupted their incentives for accurately rating the issuers involved in such structures.

As discussed earlier, many of the securitisation structures benefited from credit-enhancement techniques that reduced the perceived risks of the underlying assets backing the ABS, MBS and/or CDO issues. One of the main providers of such enhancement are the so-called monoline insurance companies, major operators being MBIA and Ambac. These had emerged in the US in the 1970s as offering insurance to back municipal bonds. The insurance companies had very strong balance sheets and sold default insurance to issuers of municipal bonds – the municipalities purchased this insurance to obtain higher credit ratings (typically AAA) on the bonds they were issuing and were therefore managing to borrow at lower cost. The monoline insurers earned fees for their services.

Over time, the monoline insurers expanded their activities into the securitisation of MBS and then other ABS and CDOs. At the start of 2008 Bloomberg estimated that seven (AAA-rated) monoline insurance companies insured $100 billion in CDOs linked to sub-prime MBS.

---

[15] Monoline insurance is an insurance company that provides guarantees to issuers, often in the form of credit wraps or credit default swaps, to enhance the credit of the issuer. These insurance companies first began providing wraps for municipal bond issues, then specialised in providing credit enhancement for other types of bonds, such as mortgage-backed securities and collateralised debt obligations.

BOX 18.3 CDS: MODERN-DAY WEAPONS OF MASS DESTRUCTION

As the invasion of Iraq was planned, Warren Buffett pointed to real weapons of mass destruction: derivatives. Reporting earlier this year, the US Financial Crisis Inquiry Commission concluded that over-the-counter derivatives had contributed significantly to the 2007–09 crisis.

Credit default swaps (CDS) came in for particular criticism, for their roles in risky mortgage securitisation and in (toxic) synthetic collateralised debt obligations, and for being central in the $180bn bail-out of AIG (see Box 18.4).

CDS resemble insurance. Buyers receive pay-outs from sellers on a credit event of a particular entity, and in return pay premiums to sellers. CDS are useful for hedging insurable interests. Unlike insurance, however, buyers do not have to have an interest in the entity, and such "naked" CDS have become an efficient way of shorting sovereign bonds.

Ignored by regulators, CDS contracts soared, with gross notional values of CDS positions rising from $1,000bn in 2001 to $62,000bn in 2007. Since then "compression", that is the elimination of redundant positions, has reduced gross values to $26,000bn in 2010, but CDS activity has continued to grow. There is little information about the buyers and sellers of CDS – an information gap the G-20 nations want to close.

Last year academics and commentators pointed to speculators using CDS to attack European sovereign bonds (e.g. "Time to outlaw naked credit default swaps", Wolfgang Munchau, FT, February 28, 2010). An EU Commission task force was set up to investigate, and its released but unpublished report sought to play down the issue.

The task force concluded changes in spreads of CDS and bond markets were mainly contemporaneous, and were equally likely to lead or lag; that there was no evidence of mispricing in sovereign bond or CDS markets; and that there was no conclusive evidence that developments in the CDS market cause higher funding costs for member states.

Unsurprisingly, the task force judged that "in the light of the evidence of the functioning of CDS markets and challenges to implementing a ban (e.g. definition of insurable interest), it may not seem entirely appropriate to consider a ban as a permanent rule". Instead, the still draft EU directive on short selling and CDS calls for transparency and temporary bans in emergency situations.

But were the Commission's findings way off the mark? In a paper* published in July, Giovanni Calice of Southampton University, Jing Chen of Swansea University, and Julian Williams of Aberdeen University came to different conclusions. They investigated potential spillover effects between credit and liquidity spreads in the eurozone sovereign bond market and the sovereign CDS market in the 2010 European sovereign debt crisis.

They found that, prior to the crisis, spreads of bond yields determined CDS spreads, but during the crisis CDS spreads led bond yields. For Ireland, Greece, Portugal and Spain, the transmission effect from the CDS market to bond spreads was large and significant. The authors also found "explosive trends" emanating from the CDS market that, without official intervention, would have resulted in complete market failure for the sovereign debt instruments for several European countries.

Another study** published this year from Joshua Aizenman and Michael Hutchison of the University of California, and Yothin Jinjarak of the University of London, also presented a different picture. Here the authors investigated whether high sovereign debt default risks of financially distressed eurozone countries could be explained by "fiscal space" (government debt/tax ratios) and other economic fundamentals.

They developed a model of pricing sovereign risk, using CDS spreads, for over 50 countries before and after the crisis, related to fiscal space and other factors. They then calculated how actual CDS spreads compared with spreads predicted by the model.

*Liquidity spillovers in sovereign bond and CDS markets. This paper was published as: Calice, G., Chen, J. and Williams, J. (2013) 'Liquidity spillovers in sovereign bond and CDS markets: An analysis of the Eurozone sovereign debt crisis', *Journal of Economic Behavior & Organization*, 85, 122–143.

**What is the risk of European sovereign debt default? Fiscal space, CDS spreads and market mispricing of risk. This paper was published as: Aizenman, J., Hutchison, M. and Jinjarak, Y. (2013) 'What is the risk of European sovereign debt default? Fiscal space, CDS spreads and market pricing of risk', *Journal of International Money and Finance*, 34. 37–59.

BOX 18.3 CDS: modern-day weapons of mass destruction (*continued*)

They showed that the fiscal space of Greece, Ireland, Italy, Portugal and Spain in 2010 was high compared with other countries, so predicted CDS spreads were also higher. But actual CDS spreads were even higher than those predicted, by ratios ranging from Ireland 1.3, Italy 1.4, Spain 1.9, Portugal 2.8 and Greece 3.3. The authors concluded that "the extraordinarily high CDS spreads in [the peripheral economies] in 2010 may be attributed to excessive pessimism and an overreaction to the fiscal deterioration" (though theoretically it might instead reflect future fundamentals).

These two studies suggest that CDS aggravate the eurozone debt crisis. Buyer pressure on CDS spreads can have explosive effects necessitating intervention – bail-outs, support from the new European Financial Stability Facility (EFSF), or purchases of sovereign bonds by the ECB (or soon the EFSF). Moreover, such buyer pressure on CDS appears excessive in relation to the economic fundamentals.

The cost of bail-outs or other support triggered by CDS attacks may largely fall on German shoulders. Last month the German Finance Ministry indicated it would be seeking a Europe-wide ban on naked short-selling of stocks, sovereign bonds and CDS to counter "destructive speculation". Zapping naked CDS may cost much less than bail-outs.

Monoline insurers can provide credit enhancements via two main channels: traditional credit insurance and through the use of CDS. A CDS is similar to credit insurance, but there are major regulatory differences between the two. A CDS transaction (like credit insurance) involves a 'protection buyer' (for example, a CDO bond issuer trying to raise ratings and reduce default risk) and a 'protection seller,' a counterparty who receives a fixed income stream in return for assuming the default risk. CDS, however, are not overseen by any regulatory authority and as such there is no guarantee that in the case of default the seller will have sufficient funds to make full payment.

In general, the purchase of credit protection (via either insurance or CDS) reduces the credit risk of mortgage-backed securities, allowing them to obtain AAA ratings for their bonds. In addition, the credit insurance was provided at relatively low expense because it was believed that the risks were low. All went well until various asset-backed securities went bust following the start of the sub-prime crisis. When, for instance, a CDO issued by the Swiss bank Credit Suisse defaulted during 2006, virtually all its $341 million was wiped out. However, Credit Suisse had bought credit insurance protection from MBIA for its senior tranches (but not mezzanine). While the mezzanine bondholders lost everything, most AAA holders were reimbursed as MBIA had to pay $177 million to cover the losses.

During 2007 the monoline industry made massive losses in the light of the collapse of the sub-prime market and securitised issue business in general. The two top firms posted combined losses of around $4.5 billion and their own AAA ratings were removed. (Ambac's ratings were reduced to speculative grade by Standard & Poor's in July 2009, to CC from triple BBB, after it warned that it would report a $2.4 billion loss.)

As well as monoline insurers, hedge funds and other major insurance companies were very active in the credit protection business. The best example is probably AIG (the second largest general insurance firm in the US in 2008), which reports that it sold a staggering $446 billion in credit insurance (mainly in the form of CDS). See Box 18.4 for details of the AIG involvement in CDS. By the end of 2008, losses on the CDS book amounted to $30 billion and prompted a rescue by the federal authorities in September 2008.

BOX 18.4 AIG SAGA SHOWS DANGERS OF CREDIT DEFAULT SWAPS

In retrospect, a glance at AIG's second quarter 2008 financial statement makes for an interesting read. Buried in that report is a cautionary tale showing just how dangerous credit derivatives can be when combined with insufficient risk management and regulatory oversight – or both sides of these transactions. Unfortunately, few people read the report when it would have been relevant.

The report fully discloses the $446bn in credit insurance AIG sold. The swaps were written out of AIG Financial Products, a non-bank hidden at the heart of the insurance giant. But because AIG wasn't regulated as a bank, it wasn't saddled with any requirements to hold capital against these massive potential liabilities.

A large part of those credit default swaps, about $307bn worth, was bought by European banks in endearingly named "regulatory capital forbearance" trades. By buying such insurance, these banks didn't have to hold capital against their long-term holdings of securities. Another large chunk went to Wall Street firms to hedge their holdings of complicated securities backed by subprime mortgages.

By the end of the year, just this part of this massive book of credit default swaps would cause almost $30bn in losses and trigger what is likely to prove one of the most costly bail-outs ever. Meanwhile, the $307bn "forbearance" book produced a mere $156m in revenue for the first half of last year. These exposures probably represent one of the most skewed risk–reward equations of all time.

AIG did such a booming business selling credit protection because it offered to post generous collateral if the value of the insured securities dropped or if its own credit rating fell. (Other providers, such as the monoline insurers, balked at such terms.) That collateral was meant to give AIG's clients assurance that they were safely hedged. In fact, that sense of safety was always an illusion. Clients hadn't reduced their risk; they had increased it.

That's because the hedges depended on the health of a single institution, AIG, that could never fully compensate counterparties for a big drop in the value of these securities. It might offer to post collateral but, if the market plunged, would AIG even be there to post collateral?

"Derivatives were meant to disperse risk," says Dino Kos, a former Fed official who is now at research boutique Portales Partners. "But at AIG, derivatives were used to concentrate risk."

As the value of the securities insured by AIG plunged, AIG faced a bottomless pit of plunging values and collateral calls that was draining the firm of its cash. By the time AIG was downgraded in mid-September and the Fed had to step in, AIG needed to post $32bn in collateral in the following 15 days – on top of $20bn it had already posted just over the summer. In other words, by demanding the ability to protect themselves through collateral calls and the right to terminate transactions, these counterparties unwittingly triggered AIG's near-death experience.

As the market continued to plunge, AIG and the Fed approached 20 counterparties with an offer to buy these CDOs at a price determined by an independent valuer and then cancel the credit protection on these CDOs. Because these counterparties ultimately received 100 cents on the dollar, the process was reasonably harmonious. That meant both sides were able to avoid another pitfall of the credit default swap market, valuation disputes.

As of year-end, Maiden Lane, a vehicle established by the Fed and AIG, bought about $62bn in face value of these CDOs for nearly $30bn while AIG terminated the credit default swaps, spending $32.5bn recognising $21bn in losses in the process. (In bailing out AIG, the Fed was also handing out tens of billions of dollars more to Wall Street.)

Many players in the financial market stay away from credit derivatives because of the issues the AIG saga raises, including pricing uncertainties, valuation disputes and counterparty risk. "People took risk, which the market never fully reflected in prices, and then looked the other way," says Mark Mckissick, with Denver Investment Advisors. "The whole CDS market was part of the bubble."

18.8   The future of securitisation

The growth in securitisation activity has clearly increased the linkages between banks and markets. From a positive perspective the securitisation trend offers the potential for banks to manage their balance sheets more effectively and to move risks to those most willing to bear it. This can result in a more efficient use of capital resources and a better allocation of risks in the system overall. It also enables banks and other financial intermediaries to generate extra revenue and therefore helps boost financial performance.

While securitisation, well managed and appropriately overseen, can offer such benefits, we know since the advent of the sub-prime crisis that there is a serious negative downside to such activity. Unbridled securitisation activity, misaligned pricing and the emergence of increasingly complex innovations made the market increasingly non-transparent. Risks were not priced appropriately, banks' incentives to screen and monitor borrowers' creditworthiness evaporated, and a spiral of securitisation continued unabated based on the view that property prices would continue to climb.

Since the collapse of the sub-prime lending market from 2007 onwards, the securitisation business has collapsed and banks that were heavily engaged in this activity (both issuing and investing in CDOs and other ABS on their own account) have suffered major losses. As a result, the primary issuance of complex products has almost disappeared and there has been a return to simplicity or 'back to basic' in terms of the characteristics of the securitisation products, which is expected to continue (Casu and Sarkisyan, 2014). Figure 18.6 illustrates the US asset-backed securities issuance (in million $) between 1985 (Q1) and 2012 (Q4) while Figure 18.7 illustrates the global CDO issuance (in million $) between 2000 (Q1) and 2011 (Q4) (in billion $). In the US, total new issuance in 2011 amounted to $124 billion,

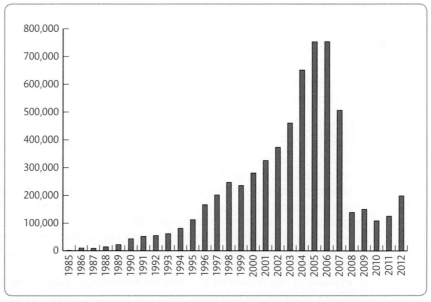

Figure 18.6 US asset-backed securities issuance ($mil), 1985–2012

Source: Data available from Securities Industry and Financial Markets Association (**www.sifma.org**).

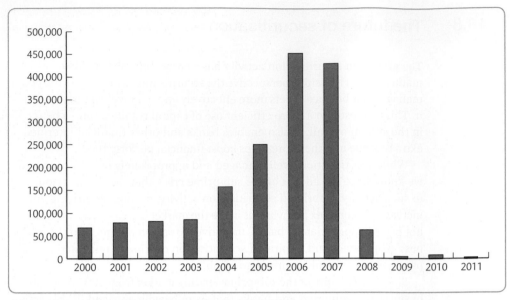

Figure 18.7 Global CDO issuance ($mil), 2000–2011

Source: Data available from Securities Industry and Financial Markets Association (**www.sifma.org**).

down from the 2006 peak of $753 billion. In Europe, total new issuance in 2011 amounted to €207 billion, down from a peak of more than €700 billion in 2008. Residential mortgage-backed securities accounted for 60 per cent of issuance. Within Europe, the largest issuing jurisdictions are the UK and the Netherlands (each accounting for 28 per cent of issuance by value), Spain (accounting for 17 per cent) and Italy (accounting for 14 per cent). Outside the US and the EU there is little current securitisation activity (IOSCO, 2012).

The large losses faced by banks involved in securitisation activity have been a key feature of the global financial sector collapse. Subsequently, US, European and international regulators announced plans to limit securitisation activity. For instance, in 2009, as part of the US government's set of regulatory reforms proposed for the financial system overall, Timothy Geithner, the Treasury Secretary, while outlining a broad array of reforms proposed by the Obama government, noted the following in a written testimony before the House Financial Services Committee:

> In the years preceding the crisis, mortgages and other loans were aggregated with similar loans and sold in tranches to a large and diverse pool of new investors with different risk profiles. Securitisation, by breaking down the traditional relationship between borrowers and lenders, created various conflicts of interest that market discipline failed to correct.
>
> Loan originators failed to require sufficient documentation of income and ability to pay. Securitizers failed to set high standards for the loans they were willing to buy, encouraging underwriting standards to sag. Investors were overly reliant on credit rating agencies, whose procedures proved no match for the complexity of the instruments they were rating. In each case, lack of transparency prevented market participants from understanding the full nature of the risks they were taking.
>
> In response, the President's plan requires securitisation sponsors to retain five percent of the credit risk of securitized exposures; it requires transparency of loan level data and standardization of data formats to better enable investor due diligence and market discipline; and, with respect to credit rating agencies, it ends the practice of allowing them to provide consulting

services to the same companies they rate, requires these agencies to differentiate between structure and other products, and requires disclosure of any 'ratings shopping' by issuers.

Treasury Secretary, Timothy F. Geithner's written testimony
before the House Financial Services Committee, 23 July 2009.

The American Securitisation Forum (ASF) notes that proposed regulations and legislation and related uncertainty as the principal obstacles to the securitisation market's recovery, followed by investors' retreat from the market, accounting charges and public perception. On a more positive note, results of a poll carried out by the ASF asking when mortgage and consumer asset securitisation markets will reach a new equilibrium, indicates hopes of recovery.

Despite the problems with securitisation that became apparent during the 2007–2009 financial crisis (including an over-reliance on ratings, lack of due diligence by investors and inadequate pricing of risk), regulators and policy makers agree that securitisation is also a valuable funding technique and an efficient means of diversifying risk. At the time of writing (2014), work is still in progress to review current national and international initiatives regarding the regulation of securitisation, including measures aimed at enhancing the transparency and standardisation of securitisation products (see proposals by the Financial Stability Board (2012c) and by the International Organization of Securities Commissions (2012)).

As highlighted by IOSCO (2012), securitisation markets have the potential to support economic recovery and there is evidence that investors' appetite is returning. Securitisation is still seen as a viable alternative source of funding for the banking sector at a time when it needs funding diversification. As a consequence, a well-functioning securitisation market would, in turn, support recovery in the real economy. However, there is also concern among issuers that securitisation continues to be stigmatised by sub-prime crisis events. To overcome these problems, regulators are focusing on the following areas:

- risk retention;
- disclosure;
- securitisation processes;
- credit-rating agencies issues.

Risk retention or **'skin in the game'** requirements have been a key focus of regulatory responses since the financial crisis (see Sarkisyan and Casu, 2013). These requirements are intended to avoid misaligned incentives that may be embedded in the 'originate to distribute' model of some securitisation products. This resulted in the introduction of 'risk retention rules' that require banks to maintain an interest in their own securitisations, based on the assumption that retaining 'skin in the game' induces banks to improve screening and monitoring of borrowers. Examples of the proposed rules requiring securitisers to retain a portion of the credit risk in the assets that they securitise include Article 122a of the Capital Requirements Directive (CRD II) in the EU and Section 941 of the 2010 Dodd–Frank Act in the US.

In terms of improved disclosure, in 2010 IOSCO released 'Disclosure principles for public offerings and listings', and it is now developing principles for ongoing disclosure for public offerings and listings of ABS (IOSCO, 2010). Industry initiatives are also focused on improving disclosure through standardisation of documentation and greater transparency of granular data.

In terms of improving securitisation processes, development is sought with particular reference to underwriting and origination practices (such as procedures for accurate assessment of borrowers' capacity to repay), the selection of assets for the pool and investor due diligence. For example, the Financial Stability Board has developed an international principles-based framework for sound underwriting practices of residential mortgages (see FSB 2011c, 2012c).

Finally, discussion is still ongoing on the role of credit-rating agencies. One of the issues discussed relates to the fact that CRA receive a significant amount of information regarding the issuance compared with what is available to either investors or regulators. Current proposals are attempting to assess whether there may be scope for investors and regulators to be given equal access to the information provided to CRAs at the time of the offering and on an ongoing basis thereafter.

18.9 Conclusion

This chapter provides an insight into the involvement of banks in market activities. This involvement can reduce risks (for example, using markets to hedge and manage credit risk more effectively) or it can increase risk (via increased proprietary trading, offering liquidity guarantees for securitised securities, CDS positions, etc.). Nowadays the consensus is that the increasing integration of banks and markets has led to too much risk and regulations need to be put in place to limit such risks occurring again. However, the sluggish economic recovery has started to cast doubts over the extent of regulatory reform. Banks will need to hold more capital and liquidity to back securitisation and other market activity (see Chapter 7 on the introduction of Basel III). Financial innovation will come under greater regulatory scrutiny and will need to be much more transparent. Other participants involved in markets activity closely linked to banks – such as hedge funds, private equity firms, credit-rating agencies and monoline insurers – will also be subject to tougher regulatory oversight.

Key terms

Asset-backed commercial paper (ABCP)	Fannie Mae (Federal National Mortgage Association – FNMA)	Money market funds (MMF)	Over-collateralisation
Asset-backed securities (ABS)	Freddie Mac (Federal Home Loan Mortgage Corporation – FHLMC)	Monoline insurer	Resolution Trust Corporation
Collateralised debt obligation (CDO)	Government-sponsored enterprises (GSEs)	Mortgage-backed securities (MBS)	Risk retention
Credit default swaps (CDS)		Office of Federal Housing Enterprise Oversight (OFHEO)	Securitisation
Credit enhancements		Originate-to-distribute model	Shadow banking
Credit-rating agency		Originate-to-hold model	Skin in the game
Excess spread			Special-purpose vehicle (SPV)
			Structured investment vehicle (SIV)
			Tranching

Key reading

Acharya, V.V., Schnabel, P. and Suarez, G. (2013) 'Securitization without risk transfer,' *Journal of Financial Economics*, 107(3), 515–536.

Bailey, M., Elmendorf, D. and Litan, R. (2008) *The Great Credit Squeeze: How it happened, how to prevent another*, Washington, DC: Brookings Institution.

Bakk-Simon, K., Borgioli, S., Girón, C., Hempell, H., Maddaloni, A., Recine, F. and Rosati, S. (2012) '*Shadow banking in the euro area: An overview,*' ECB Occasional Paper Series, No. 133, April.

Boot, A.W.A and Thakor, A. (2014) 'The accelerating integration of banks and markets and its implications for regulation,' in Berger, A.N., Molyneux, P. and Wilson, J.O.S. (eds), *Oxford Handbook of Banking*, Oxford: Oxford University Press, Chapter 3.

Casu, B. and Sarkisyan, A. (2014) 'Securitization,' in Berger, A.N., Molyneux, P. and Wilson, J.O.S. (eds), *The Oxford Handbook of Banking*, 2nd Edition, Oxford: Oxford University Press, Chapter 15.

Claessens, S., Pozsar, Z., Ratnovski, L. and Singh, M. (2012) '*Shadow banking: Economics and policy*', IMF Staff Discussion Note, 4 December.

Marques-Ibanez, D. and Scheicher, M. (2010) 'Securitisation, instruments and implications,' in Berger, A.N., Molyneux, P. and Wilson, J.O.S. (eds), *Oxford Handbook of Banking*, Oxford: Oxford University Press, Chapter 24.

Sarkisyan, A. and Casu, B. (2013) '*Retained interests in securitisations and implications for bank solvency*', ECB Working Paper Series, No. 1538/April.

REVISION QUESTIONS AND PROBLEMS

18.1 Outline the main differences between bank intermediation and market transactions.

18.2 Explain how relationship lending reduces information asymmetries for banks. Consider whether market transactions can reduce such asymmetries.

18.3 Briefly define shadow banking and the main players in the shadow banking system. Discuss the main drivers for the growth of shadow banking.

18.4 Outline how government-sponsored enterprises (GSEs) were instrumental in creating mortgage-backed securities market in the US.

18.5 Explain the main processes involved in any type of securitisation, whether it be an ABS, MBS or CDOs.

18.6 Discuss the main reasons why banks became so heavily involved in securitisation activity. Highlight the advantages and disadvantages associated with the securitisation phenomenon.

18.7 In the light of the 2007 sub-prime crisis, explain why the credit risks associated with securitisation issues were mispriced.

18.8 Explain the role of credit rating agencies and monoline insurance companies in securitisation activity.

18.9 Discuss the future of securitisation in light of the regulatory proposals aimed at improving processes, transparency and disclosure.

18.10 What is the aim of the implementation of risk retention rules in the context of securitisation?

Chapter 19

Mergers and acquisitions

Learning objectives

- To define bank mergers and distinguish between different types of M&As
- To understand the main trends in bank M&As
- To understand the impact of consolidation on bank performance
- To understand the main drivers of M&As
- To understand the impact of mergers on bank customers (both retail and business)
- To examine whether large bank mergers are motivated by opportunities to exploit implicit too-big-to-fail guarantees

19.1 Introduction

Over the last 20 years one of the major features impacting on global financial systems has been the mergers and acquisitions trend.[1] This has primarily been a consequence of deregulation and innovation (technological and financial). Deregulation has allowed banks to enter new geographical markets and product areas. Technological advances have revolutionised the way banks process transactions (back-office processing), deliver their services to customers (via branches, by phone or on the internet) and make payments.

Financial innovation, characterised by the widespread use of new financial engineering and risk management tools, coupled with the significant involvement of financial institutions in new and broader derivatives and other markets (asset-backed securities, credit default swaps and so on), has been another factor changing the financial landscape.

---

[1] Mergers and acquisitions are usually talked about interchangeably but there is a difference. A merger is usually between firms of roughly equal size and often post merger the name will change to emphasise certain equality. For instance, when Chase Manhattan merged with JPMorgan in the US in 2000, the new name became JPMorgan Chase. In the case of acquisitions, this is usually when a firm is bought out by a larger company and its operations are subsumed under the acquirer's name/brand. For instance, in 2008 Wells Fargo acquired the failing Wachovia. The corporate name Wells Fargo was retained unchanged.

These forces have been very relevant in promoting a wave of merger activity and this trend has been well documented in the consolidation literature.[2] While there is general agreement on the broad forces that have encouraged growth in M&A activity in the banking sector, there remains a lack of consensus as to whether banks in general benefit from M&A activity in terms of improved performance and enhanced shareholder value. In addition, there is a varying picture on other dimensions of the consolidation process such as the impact of M&As on risk, access to finance, the features of acquisition targets and so on.

The aim of this chapter is to provide some useful definitions and a classification of the different types of bank mergers as well as a summary of the main reasons as to why banks merge. In Section 19.2 we define the different types of mergers activities; in Section 19.3 we outline recent M&A trends. In Section 19.4 we discuss the influence of M&A on bank performance. Given that there is a rather mixed picture as to whether bank consolidation boosts performance, this has encouraged researchers to look at alternative reasons as to why banks engage in mergers – so called managerial motives. Section 19.5 therefore focuses on the (non-value-creating) managerial motives for M&As. Section 19.6 outlines the impact of mergers on bank customers. Section 19.7 examines features of product and geographical diversification M&A strategies. Section 19.8 outlines whether the consolidation process has affected systemic risk and also whether large bank mergers are motivated by opportunities to exploit government safety-net subsidies (implicit too-big-to-fail guarantees). Section 19.9 is the conclusion.

19.2   Mergers and acquisitions: definitions and types

Mergers and acquisitions refer to the combining of two or more entities into one new entity. They are often explained by the equation that one plus one equals more than two, because a common motive is to increase the value of the new entity. Although the terms 'mergers' and 'acquisitions' are sometimes used interchangeably to refer to the combination of two (or more) separate enterprises, they have slightly different connotations:

● A merger is when two, usually similarly sized, banks (or any other firms) agree to go forward as a new single entity rather than remain separately owned and operated. Such operation implies the combination of all the assets and liabilities of the two banks.[3]

● An acquisition or takeover is when a bank (the acquirer or bidder) takes over another one (the target or acquired bank) by purchasing its common stock or assets and clearly becoming the new owner.[4]

It is also common to distinguish between horizontal, vertical and conglomerate mergers:

● A horizontal bank merger refers to the merger or the acquisition of a banking firm that operates in the same market and thus produces competitive financial services. A horizontal merger may pose concerns if it creates excessive market power and thus can be blocked

---

[2] See Berger *et al.* (1999), Group of Ten (2001) and DeYoung *et al.* (2009).

[3] In this chapter we refer to 'banks' rather than 'firms' in general, although most definitions are not specific to banks.

[4] Occasionally an individual or group of (usually institutional) investors takes over a firm by means of leveraged buyouts (LBOs). The buyout is *leveraged* because typically a significant amount of LBO financing is borrowed. The acquisition is called an MBO (management buyout) if the group is led by the company's management. For more details see Brealey *et al.* (2012) or Berk and DeMarzo (2011).

by antitrust authorities. Horizontal mergers have been commonplace in the commercial banking industry over the last two decades or so. They are sometimes referred to as horizontal integration and they are fundamentally different from vertical mergers.

- A vertical merger refers to a concentration between firms that have different roles in the same industry. It can take two forms, forward integration and backward integration, depending on whether the firm acquires a distributor or a supplier. Banks typically have higher vertical integration than other firms. Naturally, 'vertical disintegration' runs in the opposite direction, i.e. it occurs when a firm finds it strategically valuable to 'outsource' (purchase from outside vendors) rather than producing certain services in-house. In other words, banks, like any other firms, can decide to sell (divest) businesses. A common type of divesture is the spin-off, i.e. when a bank sells a business or division to a separate independent firm, created through the sale or distribution of new shares. The process of 'deconstruction' of banking services from the originate-to-hold to the originate-to-distribute model (see Chapter 18) can be considered as an example of vertical disintegration.

- A conglomerate merger is one that takes place between companies in unrelated lines of business and does not result in vertical integration. While US antitrust law is not concerned about conglomerate mergers (as they are considered at the worst neutral to competition), EU competition law clearly distinguishes between three types of conglomerate mergers: (a) product-line extension, (b) geographical and (c) pure conglomerate merger.[5]

  - (a) A product line extension occurs when a firm adds a new product to its existing ones by merging with another firm, as in the case of bancassurance.
  - (b) Market extensions take place when the institutions involved in the merger are in the same product market but operate in different geographical markets.
  - (c) Finally, a pure conglomerate merger occurs in all other cases, i.e. there is no functional connection between the merging institutions.

  Box 19.1 describes the emergence of financial conglomerates.

BOX 19.1 THE EMERGENCE OF FINANCIAL CONGLOMERATES

Consolidation in the global banking industry has resulted in the emergence of financial conglomerates that conduct an extensive range of businesses with a group structure. In the European Union, **financial conglomeration** was encouraged by the Second Banking Directive (1989), which enabled banks to operate as universal banks offering the full range of financial services, including commercial banking, investment banking, insurance and other services. In the United States, the passing of the Gramm–Leach–Bliley Act of 1999 enabled banks to establish financial holding companies that can now engage in a full range of financial services (as did the 'Big-bang' reforms in Japan).

Financial conglomerates are defined as a group of enterprises, formed by different types of financial institutions, operating in different sectors of the financial industry. Group organisational structure is believed to bring about, on the one hand, the possibility of exploiting greater cost economies and, on the other hand, the capacity of the group to isolate risk from its different activities. On the revenue side, the ability of financial conglomerates to distribute a full range of banking, securities and insurance services may increase their earning potential and lead to a more stable profit stream. Customers may value a bundled supply of financial services more than separate offers for reasons of transactions and information

➡

---

[5] Kaczorowska (2013) *European Union Law,* Taylor & Francis.

Box 19.1 The emergence of financial conglomerates (*continued*)

costs. Nevertheless, it is argued that such structures may have drawbacks, such as conflicts of interest and concentration of power (Casu and Girardone, 2004). The process of conglomeration in financial services is mainly bank-driven, as banks have been actively expanding into other areas, in particular asset management.

Similar to, but different from, conglomeration is the establishment of jointly owned enterprises offering specialised financial services. In some European countries, for example, savings banks and co-operative banks have set up such jointly owned enterprises that provide asset management, stockbroking and settlement activities as well as insurance, all of which are sold to or distributed by the member institutions of the sector. An example would be the jointly owned investment management firm of the savings bank sector in a country. In economic terms, such jointly owned enterprises provide equal opportunities of marketing and servicing as financial conglomerates. The development of such enterprises as well as co-operation agreements is common in countries such as Austria and Germany.

The trend towards conglomeration can be considered part of a larger trend towards disintermediation and globalisation of financial markets, fostered by financial liberalisation, domestic financial development and new technological possibilities. However, there were several Europe-specific factors that provided a further boost to the growth of financial conglomerates to foster intra-European integration (Allen *et al.*, 2011). Indeed, EU banking and insurance markets are dominated by large pan-European groups. A typical EU financial conglomerate has more than 400 licences in several jurisdictions and several sectors: banking, life and/or non-life insurance, asset management.

Globally systemically important financial institutions (G-SIFIs)

The consolidation trend has resulted in a small number of SIFIs, most of them with a large share of cross-border activity. To address the shortcomings revealed by the crisis, the G20 heads of state committed to enhancing regulation and supervision in a globally consistent way (Basel Committee on Banking Supervision, 2011c). In 2011, the Financial Stability Board released a list of 29 systemically important banks, which are now known as G-SIFIs or G-SIBs (globally systemically important banks).

The list – which is to be updated every year – indicates the G-SIBs and shows their allocation to buckets, corresponding to their required level of additional loss absorbency. G-SIFIs are required to meet higher supervisory expectations for risk management functions, data aggregation capabilities, risk governance and internal controls. These requirements will be phased in starting from January 2016, with full implementation by January 2019 (Financial Stability Board, 2013b).

The regulation of financial conglomerates

The issues relating to the regulation of large, complex groups combining several banking and insurance licences were recognised in the early 1990s. Following recommendations by the Joint Forum, the G10 body of supervisors, the European Union adopted the Financial Conglomerates Directive in 2002. Since 2002, markets have further developed in a direction where the distinction between banking business and insurance business is not always easily discernible and where the largest groups are active in many countries. The 2007–2009 financial crisis highlighted the difficulties in the regulation of large financial conglomerates and the weaknesses of the existing legislative framework, therefore making a revision of the regulatory framework a priority.

In November 2011, the European Council adopted a directive amending the Financial Conglomerates Directive in order to close loopholes and ensure appropriate supplementary supervision of financial entities in a financial conglomerate. The new directive also adapts the supervision of financial conglomerates to the EU's new supervisory structure.

Mergers and/or acquisitions imply a change in management and this is one of the main reasons why they occur. Agency costs, inadequate management and loose monitoring may result in the failure of the bank's internal controls and sub-optimal firm value. In such situations, the *market for corporate control* provides an external governance mechanism and a source of discipline for the managers of publicly held banks. As Henry Manne (1965, p. 113) put it straightforwardly: 'The lower the stock price, relative to what it could be with more efficient management, the more attractive the takeover becomes to those who believe that they can manage the company more efficiently. And the potential return from the successful takeover and revitalization of a poorly run company can be enormous.' Indeed, it is not uncommon nowadays for poorly managed banks to become targets of unfriendly and unsolicited takeovers (so-called *hostile* takeovers).

In the next section we follow the report by the Group of Ten (2001) and provide a systematic list of the main motives, at least in theory, behind consolidation in financial services. Any merger or acquisition should be treated as an investment, therefore the banking firm should be evaluated. This is usually done by calculating the present discounted value of expected future profits. A distinction can thus be made between value-maximising motives and non-value-maximising motives.

19.2.1 Why do banks merge?

Mergers can affect the value of the banking firm by either reducing expected costs or increasing expected revenues. Table 19.1 reports some of the most common motives for M&As in financial services.

Table 19.1 Motives for bank M&As

Value-maximising motives		Non-value-maximising motives
Reduction in costs	**Increase in revenues**	

• Economies of scale and scope	• Increased size allowing firms to better serve large customers	• Management motives:
		  - pursuing personal goals;
		  - own job security;
		  - defensive acquisitions;
		  - increase size to imitate peer firms, etc.

• Replacement of inefficient managers with more efficient managers or management techniques	• Increased product diversification allowing firms to offer customers 'one-stop shopping' for a variety of products	
• Reduction of risk due to geographic or product diversification	• Increased product or geographic diversification expanding the pool of potential customers	
• Reduction of tax obligations	• Increased size or market share making it easier to attract customers (visibility or reputation effects)	• Government motives: - minimisation of social costs associated with bank failure;
• Allowing a firm to become large enough to gain access to capital markets or to receive a credit rating	• Increased monopoly power allowing firms to raise prices	- crisis resolution - willingness to create global national champions;
• Providing a way for financial firms to enter new geographical or product markets at a lower cost than that associated with the *de novo* entry	• Increased size allowing firms to increase the riskiness of their portfolio	- deregulation, etc.

Source: Adapted from Group of Ten (2001).

19.3   Recent trends in bank M&As

Banking sector consolidation was a major recent trend in the US and Europe in the run-up to the 2007–2009 financial crisis, as illustrated in Figure 19.1. One can see that the volume of bank M&A activity increased rapidly from the mid-1990s, peaking in 1998 in the US and a year later in Europe. This trend coincided with the internet boom that fuelled global stock markets over the same period. Bank shares also increased over the period and the increased valuations of banks made it easier for them to finance their acquisitions – at the start of the 1990s the bulk of deals were financed by cash purchases but by the end of the 1990s most acquisitions were financed by banks offering shares to purchase other banks. (Generally, cash purchases are thought to be a better indicator of a good deal compared with share issue financed deals.)

The downturn in markets reversed the late 1990s' consolidation trend, although this seemed to pick up thereafter. Table 19.2 notes some major US bank deals that have taken place since 2000 – note that the last four (JPMorgan Chase/Bear Stearns, Bank of America/Merrill Lynch, JPMorgan Chase/Washington Mutual, Wells Fargo/Wachovia) were all a consequence of the financial crisis. While a number of banks ran large losses and others failed, some banks benefited. For example, Figure 19.2 illustrates how JPMorgan Chase took advantage of the opportunities that arose during the financial crisis in terms of M&A activities.

Many commentators believed that banking systems that suffered most from the crisis (particularly the UK and the US) would eventually experience a major consolidation wave – just to clean up their financial systems – although this has not happened on a major scale, as illustrated in Figure 19.3. On the contrary, there is some evidence that large banks that made major losses during the 2007–2009 financial crisis have had to sell chunks of their international operations in order to boost their capital – from 2009 onwards the overseas expansion of the top US and UK banks (at least) stalled.

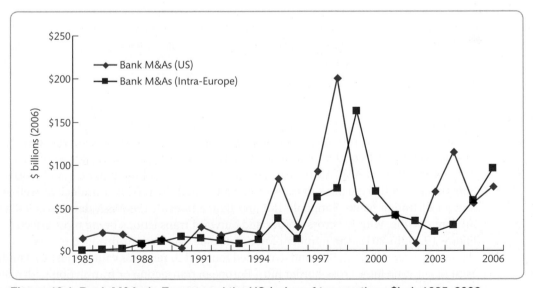

Figure 19.1 Bank M&As in Europe and the US (value of transactions $bn), 1985–2006

Source: DeYoung *et al.* (2009) Figure 1.

Table 19.2 Major US bank M&As since 2000

Year of deal	Acquirer bank	Acquired bank	Name of merged bank	Value of deal ($bn)
2000	Chase Manhattan Corporation	JPMorgan & Co. Inc.	JPMorgan Chase & Co.	33
	Washington Mutual	Bank United Corp.	Washington Mutual	1.5
2004	Bank of America Corp.	FleetBoston Financial Corp.	Bank of America Corp.	42.7
	Regions Financial Corporation	Union Planters Corporation	Regions Financial Corporation	5.9
	SunTrust	National Commerce Financial	SunTrust	7.0
	Wachovia	SouthTrust	Wachovia	14.3
2005	Capital One Financial Corporation	Hibernia National Bank	Capital One Financial Corporation	4.9
	Bank of America	MBNA Corporation	Bank of America Card Services	35
2006	Wachovia	Westcorp Inc.	Wachovia	3.9
2007	Citizens Banking Corporation	Republic Bancorp	Citizens Republic Bancorp	1.0
	Bank of America	LaSalle Bank	Bank of America	21.1
	Banco Bilbao Vizcaya Argentaria USA	Compass Bancshares	BBVA Compass	9.8
	State Street Corporation	Investors Financial Services Corporation	State Street Corporation	4.2
	Bank of New York	Mellon Financial Corporation	Bank of New York Mellon	18.3
	Wachovia	World Savings Bank	Wachovia	25
2008	TD Bank Financial Group	Commerce Bancorp	TD Bank	8.5
	JPMorgan Chase	Bear Stearns	JPMorgan Chase	1.1
	Bank of America	Merrill Lynch	Bank of America	50
	JPMorgan Chase	Washington Mutual	JPMorgan Chase	1.9
	Wells Fargo	Wachovia	Wells Fargo	15.1
2011	Capital One	ING Direct USA	Capital One	9.0
2012	M&T Bank Corporation	Hudson City Bancorp, Inc.	M&T Bank Corporation	3.8
2012	FirstMerit Bank	Citizens Republic Bancorp	FirstMerit Bank	0.91
2013	PacWest Bancorp	CapitalSource Inc.	PacWest Bancorp	2.4

Source: Various editions of the *Financial Times*, *Federal Reserve Bulletin* and SNL Financial.

In Europe, the overall volume of privately driven M&A deals (especially their segment) declined significantly post crisis. The number of bank M&As in 2008 was at the lowest point in a decade. In terms of the total value of transactions, and leaving aside the special effect of the acquisition of ABN AMRO by the consortium of Royal Bank of Scotland, Fortis and Santander in 2008 (the peak in transaction values in 2007 reflects this deal, as well as the merger of Italian banks Sanpaolo IMI and Banca Intesa), the M&A data revealed a significant decline, with EU cross-border and outward transactions being most affected (see Figure 19.4). In 2012, the number of non-domestic transactions dropped to less than half the number recorded in 2008 and decreased fourfold in terms of value to just €10 million. Significantly, no large cross-border intra-European transaction or transaction with a buyer from another EU country took place in 2012 and 2013 (European Central Bank, 2013). In addition to the decline in cross-border M&As, the trend towards divesting non-core activities

JP Morgan Chase
Share price ($)

Then and now

	Q4 2007	Q2 2010
Market value	**$146.9bn**	**$145.0bn**
Total assets	**$1,562bn**	**$2,014bn**
Tier one capital ratio	**8.4%**	**12.1%**
Branches	**3,100**	**5,159**
Employees	**180,667**	**232,939**

Dec 20 2007 Bear Stearns reports third-quarter loss of $859m on hedge fund losses. Shares slide on worries over the bank's liquidity

Mar 16 08 JPMorgan Chase buys stricken Bear Stearns for $2 a share, later raised to $10 a share, after receiving encouragement from the US government

Sep 25 08 JPMorgan acquires banking operations of Washington Mutual for $1.9bn in another government-brokered transaction

May 27 09 Warns on credit card losses related to Washington Mutual

Sept 29 09 Announces shake-up of JPMorgan's top management. Out goes Bill Winters, co-head of investment banking, and in comes Jes Staley, a veteran banker

Nov 19 09 Unveils £1bn deal to buy Cazenove, the UK broker

Feb 15 10 Buys units of RBS Sempra Commodities – a joint venture between RBS, the rescued UK bank, and US utility

group Sempra Energy – for $1.7bn to challenge other banks in raw materials trading

May 12 10 Agrees to give $4bn to Washington Mutual to resolve a dispute that arose after JPMorgan bought the bank

Jun 20 10 Enters talks to buy Gávea Investimentos, a large Brazilian hedge fund and private equity group, in spite of US legislation designed to limit the involvement of commercial banks in such activities

Figure 19.2 JPMorgan's US acquisitions

Source: JPMorgan's US acquisitions pack punch, *Financial Times*, 21/09/10 (Francesco Guerrera).
© The Financial Times Limited. All Rights Reserved.

has been compounded by troubles in the euro area, as several large EU banks have been facing renewed problems (see Box 19.2).

The European Commission (2011) identifies factors that contributed to the contraction in EU banks' M&A activities – on one hand, the re-assessment of risk that was increasingly carried out on a country-specific basis and led to distortions in the money and wholesale markets; on the other hand, the role of governments in the reorganisation of the banking sector, that post crisis largely replaced private M&A activity and resulted in a high level of public ownership.

Table 19.3 summarises the total number of deals (whole company and minority deals – both **domestic** and **cross-border mergers**) of European banks between 2007 and 2013.

EU banks' M&A activity picked up in 2009, particularly with domestic deals. The values of the deals remained modest, however, indicating a clear tendency towards smaller deals. Larger deals in 2009 and early 2010 included the acquisitions of Dresdner Bank by Commerzbank and HBOS by Lloyds TSB as domestic deals, but also the acquisition of Fortis by BNP Paribas,

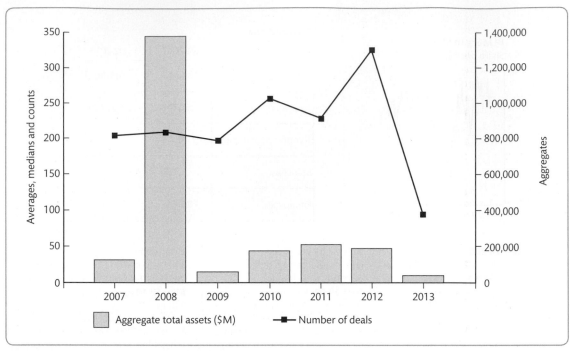

Figure 19.3 Bank M&As in the US, 2007–2013

Note: announcement date (January 2007 to June 2013).

Source: SNL Financial.

BOX 19.2 SANTANDER IN TALKS TO SELL STAKE IN ASSET ARM

Banco Santander is in exclusive talks to sell a stake in its asset management arm to a private equity duo in a move to raise capital and expand the unit. Spain's largest lender by assets is in advanced negotiations with US private equity groups Warburg Pincus and General Atlantic over the sale of a sizeable stake in the business, two people close to the situation said. Both private equity firms have a history of helping their portfolio companies' growth by combining them with additional investments.

The discussion comes as large banks around the world have either sold their asset management units or are merging them with their private banking operations in efforts to increase scale and improve returns. Santander has tried several times to sell the unit, which had €161bn in assets under management at the end of March 2013 across Europe, the UK and Latin America. But analysts said the bank and potential purchasers have previously been unable to agree on a price, in part because almost a third of assets under management are in Santander's economically troubled home market.

The unit was also tarnished a few years ago when its Geneva-based hedge fund investment arm, called Optimal, became embroiled in the Bernard Madoff Ponzi scheme scandal. Santander offered compensation to clients who had invested €2.3bn in Madoff-linked funds through Optimal.

In recent years, asset managers have on average sold for more than 1 per cent of assets under management, according to an analysis by Capital IQ and PwC. If that continues to hold true, that ratio would suggest a price tag of at least €1.6bn for the whole unit.

The asset management business is part of the bank's division headed by Javier Marín, the 46-year-old executive last week named as Santander's chief executive. He replaced Alfredo Sáenz, who retired after being dogged by a criminal conviction that could have seen him banned from banking.

Box 19.2 Santander in talks to sell stake in asset arm (*continued*)

The sale would be the latest in a series of potential capital-raising divestments being considered by Santander, including a partial spin-off of its Mexican subsidiary, and a likely listing of its US auto finance division. The group sold a $1bn stake two years ago in the same US auto finance business to a private equity consortium that included Warburg Pincus.

Mr Sáenz last month confirmed that Santander was in talks to sell the asset management arm, without giving further details. Santander and Warburg Pincus declined to comment, while General Atlantic could not be reached.

 Source: Santander in talks to sell stake in asset arm, *Financial Times*, 05/05/13 (Daniel Schäfer and Miles Johnson).

of Mellon United National Bank by Banco Sabadell, and of UK banks Bradford & Bingley and Abbey by Santander as examples of outward deals. Most of these deals were accelerated or induced by the financial crisis (European Central Bank, 2010c). However, large deals have since dried up as EU banks were badly hit by the sovereign debt crisis from late 2010 onwards and M&A activity plummeted again (see also Chapter 14 on the crises in European banking). The announced merger of the two largest Greek banks, National Bank of Greece and Eurobank, was suspended in the spring of 2013, following pressure from international lenders who feared that the merger could concentrate risk by creating a giant lender with assets of close to 100 per cent of the Greek national output. There are, however, some parts of the financial sector that are benefiting from the troubles that affect large banks (see Box 19.3).

In Asia, the market is more active than in Europe as M&As are seen as a key strategic tool for financial institutions, both domestically and cross-border. The PwC (2011) survey of

Table 19.3 European bank M&As, 2007–2013

Country/area	Total		Domestic		Cross-border	
	No. of deals	Deal value (€mil)	No. of deals	Deal value (€mil)	No. of deals	Deal value (€mil)
Eastern Europe	825	64	549	9.5	276	54.5
France and Benelux	96	1025.2	32	676.0	64	349.2
Central Europe	119	439.4	63	300.0	56	139.4
Nordic countries	77	423	55	37.0	22	386
Southern Europe	222	415.3	127	64.5	95	350.8
UK and Ireland	77	1298.6	30	310.1	47	988.5
Total	1416	3665.5	856	1397.1	560	2268.4

Notes: Domestic M&A when both bidder and target are from the same country. Cross-border M&A when the bidder or the target are from different countries.

Eastern Europe (Bosnia & Herzegovina; Bulgaria; Croatia; Czech Republic; Estonia; Hungary; Latvia; Lithuania; Macedonia; Moldova; Poland; Romania; Russia; Serbia; Slovakia; Slovenia; Turkey; Ukraine); France and Benelux (Belgium; France; Luxembourg; Monaco; Netherlands); Central Europe (Austria; Germany; Liechtenstein; Switzerland); Nordic Countries (Denmark; Faroe Islands; Finland; Greenland; Norway; Sweden); Southern Europe (Cyprus; Greece; Italy; Malta; Portugal; Spain).

Source: SNL Financial and authors' estimations.

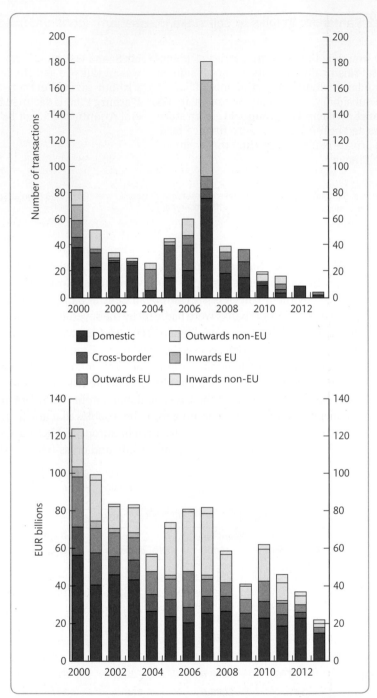

Figure 19.4 EU bank M&As: number and value of transactions, 2000–2012

Source: European Central Bank (2013) Charts 7 and 8.

BOX 19.3 CONSOLIDATION: FRAGMENTED BUSINESS OFFERS HUGE POTENTIAL FOR MERGERS

A recent flurry of deals has spurred hopes that the private banking sector is on the verge of a renewed consolidation wave. In Europe, Credit Suisse this year pounced on Morgan Stanley's regional business. In a deal worth an estimated $150m, it bought the US bank's European and Middle Eastern wealth management operations, with $13bn in assets under management, and doubled the size of its UK business in the process. Also in the UK, asset manager Schroders bought Cazenove Capital in a £424m all-cash deal that marked the biggest take-over in its history. In so doing it has absorbed a venerable City of London institution.

While Morgan Stanley has taken leave of its undersized European unit in its home market it is in the process of buying control of Smith Barney, the US retail brokerage, from Citigroup. It plans to take over the remaining 35 per cent of the business by the end of the year. It follows another US bank, Bank of America Merrill Lynch, last year selling its international wealth management unit to Swiss private bank Julius Baer.

While there are many reasons for these deals, they have a common thread: banks around the world are seeking to strengthen their core businesses while disposing of non-core or undersized units. Universal banks seek to bolster steady-income businesses as they reduce their dependency on volatile trading revenues that are facing stiffer regulatory capital requirements. Large banks have singled out wealth management as a revenue-generating area. They are lured by its high returns and its steady client asset growth rate as the world's private financial wealth, valued in 2011 at $122.8tn by the Boston Consulting Group, is expected to expand further. At the same time, smaller banks struggle to cope with regulation that is pushing up compliance and information technology costs.

A senior financial institution's advisory banker says: "You will see more spin-offs from larger banks and smaller banks merging because of increasing costs for regulatory and IT investments. You can't be a small Ma-and-Pa bank to finance that. You need a certain scale."

One example of such regulation is in the UK, where rules in the Retail Distribution Review ban financial advisers from accepting commissions from product providers. These rules, which came into force in January, are prompting a flurry of deals as hundreds of small independent financial advisers merge or sell out. In theory, there is enormous potential for mergers and acquisitions in a highly fragmented sector. Its top 20 participants worldwide only hold about 50 per cent of assets under management and no single bank has more than a tenth of the market.

The crackdown on tax avoidance could trigger an additional round of mergers, particularly between small Swiss banks struggling to find a business model in the changing regulatory environment. "We believe increased regulation, tax treaties and limitations on the offshore banking model would lead to further pressure on especially the smaller private banks," Kian Abouhossein, analyst at JPMorgan, said in a note to clients. "Private banks, which lack scale or resources to expand in onshore locations, would continue to struggle in the new regulatory environment in our view. As a result we believe the trend of consolidation in the wealth management industry is likely to continue, with some business models becoming unprofitable," the note adds.

While many small institutions are likely to be absorbed into larger entities over the course of the next few years, the world's biggest banks are more likely to be sellers of smaller units rather than looking to embark on large-scale takeovers or mergers. This is because regulators are wary of game-changing mergers and takeovers because of the continuing and fervent debate about banks that are too big to fail and worries about the stability of the financial system.

Shareholders are unlikely to be benevolent towards dilutive and costly transactions that distract banks from their supposed task of handing back money to investors after years of hoarding cash to comply with tighter capital rules. Morgan Stanley's move to take over Smith Barney is a rare exception as the investment bank is diversifying while concentrating most of its wealth management efforts on its vast US home market.

At the same time, there are a number of new entities emerging and entering private banking through acquisitions, namely sovereign wealth

Box 19.3 Consolidation: fragmented business offers huge potential for mergers (*continued*)

and pension funds. One prime example is Aabar Investments, the Abu Dhabi-based investment company, which bought AIG Private Bank from its parent company American International Group a few years ago for SFr307m. Another is the deal by Qatar's al-Thani royal family, through their Precision Capital investment group, to buy the majority of bailed-out Franco-Belgian Dexia's private banking arm for €730m. Bankers say wealth management is appealing to these long-term investors as it is a low-risk, high-return business that depends on decades-long relationships. There will, therefore, be more deals in the pipeline. What looks like a trickle, however, is unlikely to become a torrent in the immediate future.

Source: Consolidation: Fragmented business offers huge potential for mergers, *Financial Times*, 07/05/13 (Daniel Schäfer).

375 senior executives in financial services across 13 Asian regions suggests that Asian financial services are expected to expand rapidly in the medium and long term. The growth in financial services demand is driven by increasingly wealthy, educated and financially sophisticated middle-class customers, sustained economic growth and competitive pressures. In terms of the most attractive M&A markets in Asia, China, Singapore and Hong Kong are the big winners, as shown in Figure 19.5.

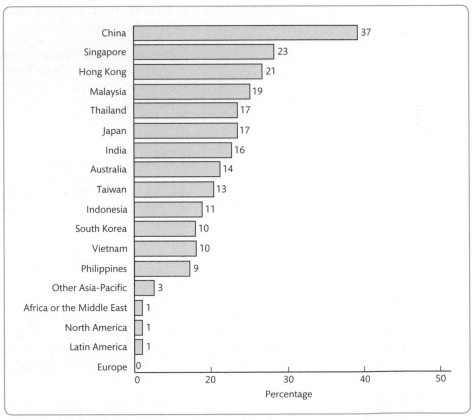

Figure 19.5 Most attractive areas for geographic expansion via M&A

Source: PwC (2011) Figure 13, p. 26.

According to the PwC (2011) survey, the wholesale banking and wealth management sectors are most likely to strategically follow their corporate customers abroad, through cross-border M&As. The other sub-sectors of financial services that are most likely to engage in M&As to enter new markets are investment management and private banking.

19.4 M&A and bank performance

A major motivation for bank M&As is the desire to boost performance (increased profits and higher market valuation via share price increases). Senior executives engaged in M&A activities have to convince the bank owners (shareholders) that the deal will boost performance, either by increasing revenues or by reducing costs. It is unlikely that shareholders will sanction a deal if they believe the acquisition or merger will reduce performance. As such, CEOs make a big deal about the performance-enhancing features of any acquisitions they aim to put in place. Performance gains from mergers emanate from either efficiency improvements or ways in which revenues can increase – namely via market power. The latter relates to bigger banks being able to set prices above competitive levels due to market dominance in particular areas.

A large array of literature has sought to investigate these relationships directly or indirectly. Direct tests seek to establish whether there are cost and/or profit improvements post merger. Studies use either accounting ratios or more sophisticated efficiency estimates to compare pre- and post-merger performance. The consensus view from studies that (mainly) examined bank M&As during the 1980s up to the mid-1990s was that cost and profit improvements resulting from bank mergers tended to be elusive (Berger et al., 1999; Group of Ten, 2001), although since then (particularly for European bank M&As) there appears to have been stronger evidence of performance improvements (DeYoung et al., 2009). Another major part of the literature uses the 'event-study' methodology to gauge market reactions to M&A announcements. The event-study approach aims to evaluate shareholder reactions to merger announcements. The combined effects of the abnormal returns (see Box 19.4) to bidders and targets around the announcement date reflect value creation or destruction for shareholders. This approach is regarded as an indirect measure of the impact of M&As because even if positive abnormal returns are generated (e.g. combined share prices of the acquirer and acquired banks are higher on the M&A announcement date than predicted by the model), it is not clear whether the positive shareholder reaction is due to perceived improvements in performance resulting from greater market power (higher prices) or improved efficiency. The view that emerged from the event studies that examined bank M&As in the 1980s and during the 1990s was that while target shareholders tended to earn strong positive abnormal returns, bidder stockholders earned marginally negative returns – the combined effects being insignificant.

Up until the early 2000s, the general consensus was that there was no strong evidence that bank M&As were performance enhancing and this view directed researchers' attentions to other motives to explain the consolidation phenomena – including objectives geared to maximising CEO remuneration, choosing a 'quiet life' and maximising asset size – as alternative explanations for M&A activity (explained in more detail in Section 19.5).

However, a survey of more than 150 bank M&A studies conducted since 2000 tends to yield a different picture to that outlined above. In general, the more recent literature provides support to the view that North American bank mergers are (or can be) efficiency improving,

BOX 19.4 HOW TO PERFORM AN EVENT STUDY

Event study analysis is a valuable tool in empirical finance. It attempts to measure the impact of merger (or earning) announcements on the value of the firm under the assumption that markets are efficient. A key stage in this analysis is to measure abnormal returns for the acquiring and target banks. This is done by using the difference between the actual bank's stock price and that predicted by a model that extrapolates previous share prices and attempts to indicate what the bank's share price would have been in the absence of the event (the 'normal' return).

The most popular model for normal returns is the 'market model' of the form:

$$R_{it} = \alpha_i + \beta_{im}R_{mt} + \epsilon_{it} \tag{19.1}$$

where R_{it} and R_{mt} are the return on stock i at time t and the return on a country's bank sector index m at time t, respectively. α_i and β_{im} are coefficients to be estimated using regression analysis and are obtained using returns over a period of time *prior to* the event (e.g. a year), while ϵ_{it} is the error term. The abnormal returns (*AR*) can then be calculated as the difference between the actual return and the expected normal return using the following formula:

$$AR_{it} = R_{it} - (\alpha_i + \beta_{im}R_{mt}) \tag{19.2}$$

To make inference about the merger announcement event, abnormal returns should be aggregated into cumulative abnormal returns (CAR) over an arbitrary (and short) time interval (the event 'window') of *j* days (usually three days before and after the event). CAR can be defined as the sum of the abnormal returns in the chosen interval as follows:

$$CAR_{it} = \sum AR_{it} \tag{19.3}$$

T-test statistics will then be used to test, for both the bidder and the target, the null hypothesis of an expected *AR* = 0, i.e. that the event has no impact on the mean (or the variance) of the returns.

although the event-study literature (as before) presents a mixed picture. However, there is incontrovertible evidence that European bank deals have resulted in widespread efficiency gains and value enhancement for shareholders (DeYoung *et al.*, 2009).

One point that should be emphasised is that most academic studies rely on a relatively large sample of bank M&As to investigate whether they boost performance (either profits or stock/share prices) on average. The finding that bank M&As in the US may not boost shareholder returns is just indicating that (on average across all the deals studied) owners may lose out. There will, of course, be deals that boost shareholders' returns. Therefore one has to be careful in discussing the impact of M&As – overall they may not be performance improving, but there may be certain deals that are. As such, the expected performance impact of an individual bank M&A needs to be considered on a case-by-case basis.

As we noted above, there is evidence that (on average) European bank mergers have been good for bank investors, although there are some deals that have clearly been problematic. Box 19.5 highlights how M&As can be value destroying and very risky – and notes the case of the 2007 ABN AMRO deal. In this case a group of banks comprising the Royal Bank of Scotland, Fortis and Santander acquired the Dutch bank. All banks have run into trouble since then and RBS and Fortis had to be bailed out.

BOX 19.5 A WINNER'S CURSE THAT HAUNTS THE BANKING BEHEMOTHS

As governments across the world roll out their plans to re-regulate the financial system, one aspect of the financial debacle receives far too little attention. This is the speed with which great institutions of national importance can be destroyed by ill-judged takeovers.

The phrase *'winner's curse'* barely does justice to the plight of Bank of America after its takeover of Merrill Lynch. So, too, with RBS's acquisition of ABN AMRO; and even more so with Lloyds TSB, where the disastrous purchase of HBOS came after years of prudent behaviour and pedestrian performance.

This is not, of course, a phenomenon that occurs exclusively in the financial world, although the systemic consequences there are often worse because banks are highly leveraged. In the previous cycle, two great pillars of the British industrial establishment, Marconi and Imperial Chemical Industries, reduced themselves to shadows of their former selves with injudicious, badly financed takeovers. At much the same time in the dotcom bubble, Time Warner saw multi-billion value destruction as a consequence of the merger with AOL.

A recurring feature of such disasters is that they are often associated with an overly dominant chief executive. Because of the age-old problem of information asymmetry, it is always difficult for non-executive directors to check and balance a determined CEO. When the CEO is in charge of a complex international financial institution, it is even harder, especially where he has stocked the board with people who lack experience in high finance and cannot understand the financial plumbing.

If it is difficult for non-executives, it is even more so for shareholders who are at one remove from the board. Keith Skeoch of Standard Life, who chairs the UK's Institutional Shareholders Committee, says the shareholder agenda needs to be robust on these issues. Yet it is a measure of how difficult it is for shareholders to restrain a dominant CEO that at RBS most institutions voted in favour of the ABN AMRO deal in spite of the fact that the banking crisis provided an excuse to retreat or renegotiate. In the case of Marconi,

the institutions notoriously egged on the management in carrying out the risky North American cash acquisitions that wrecked the company.

Did banks' risk committees highlight the dangers of rushed acquisitions and inadequate due diligence? Not all banks had risk committees. And one of the problems of these bodies is that they tend to be dominated by accountants who produce splendid matrices of all manner of risks, neatly categorised into hierarchies and pigeonholes.

The danger here is that common sense discussion of the obvious can give way to detailed technical discussion that is remote from the real threats. How many bank risk or audit committees asked simple questions on what had happened to leverage and whether the marked increase in leverage over the past decade posed a serious threat? Another simple, obvious question relates to banks' capacity for collective memory loss. In cycle after cycle, real estate has provided an easy but lethal opportunity for banks to expand loan books. For all the complexity of the current crisis, it remains substantially rooted in real estate. And while the issues to do with toxic paper continue to fester, we are now reaching the point where bad debts in conventional residential and commercial property are exacerbating an already dangerous situation.

What needs to be done to prevent mergers and acquisitions wreaking further damage? First, we need to recognise that it is a very peculiar feature of the so-called Anglo-American model of capitalism that it puts so much resource into an activity that countless academic studies have shown to be generally value destroying for the acquiring shareholders. The evidence seems to suggest that the net effect of mergers and acquisitions is wealth distribution from buyer to seller rather than the efficient capital allocation that its proponents claim. Yet as Lord Myners, City minister, points out, the thrust of the UK Takeover Code is overwhelmingly directed at protecting shareholders in the target company, not those in the acquirer.

In banking, the economic costs of M&A can be even greater because, as currently, it can increase

Box 19.5 A winner's curse that haunts the banking behemoths (*continued*)

concentration and produce banks that are too big to fail or, as in the combined Travelers-Citicorp, too big to be managed effectively. Part of the solution lies in robust competition policy. Yet non-executive directors and institutional shareholders also need to raise their game. A key to doing that is to recognise M&A for what it is: a very high-risk business activity. That is not to say that good takeovers are a chimera. Sir Fred Goodwin did, after all, do a fine job with the acquisition of Nat-West. But that led to hubris, which takes us back to where we started.

19.5 Managerial motives for M&As

The previous section illustrates that – at least from 2000 onwards – there is stronger evidence (particularly in the case of European deals) that M&A activity tends, on average, to increase performance and **shareholder value**. The fact that many earlier merger studies found little evidence of performance improvements encouraged researchers to investigate alternative explanations for the consolidation phenomenon, with particular attention paid to **managerial motives**. Here the argument goes that managers engage in M&As in order to maximise their own utility at the expense of shareholders. Managers' utility may relate to growth if their pay and other benefits are linked to firm size. Similarly, managers' utility may also be related to size if they wish for a **quiet life**.[6] Larger firms may be able to exert greater market power and insulate themselves from various competitive pressures, allowing them to choose a *quiet life*. Another managerial explanation as to why mergers may destroy value is Roll's **hubris hypothesis**, which argues that over-confident managers systematically overestimate the benefits of an acquisition and this therefore results in them over-bidding (paying too much) for targets, leading to value destruction/no performance improvements (Roll, 1986).

Managerial motives for M&As have been investigated in US banking and there does seem to be some evidence that CEO compensation increases with changes in asset size. There is also evidence that CEOs tend to engage in merger programmes more frequently when they can expect to have large compensation increases from acquisitions. Outside the US, the literature on managerial motives for bank mergers is scant, possibly because of the overriding recent evidence that bank mergers are performance enhancing.

---

[6]The quiet life hypothesis was first proposed by John R. Hicks (1935), who noted that the best of all monopoly profits is the quiet life. The quiet life hypothesis posits that banks (firms) with greater market power are less efficient as they are more risk averse than firms in competitive markets. The literature puts forward several reasons to explain managers' choice of a quiet life: (i) if firms can charge prices in excess of competitive levels, managers do not have incentives to minimise costs, thus enjoying a 'quiet life'; (ii) market power may allow managers to pursue objectives other than profit maximisation; (iii) in a non-competitive environment, managers can devote resources to obtaining and maintaining market power, which raises cost and reduces efficiency; (iv) market power allows inefficient behaviour to persist (Berger and Hannan, 1998).

19.6 The impact of M&As on bank customers

A substantial literature investigates the impact of consolidation on bank customers. The early survey literature typically finds that US bank consolidation in the 1980s resulted in lower deposit rates and higher loan rates in more concentrated markets. Studies that focus on the 1990s tend to indicate a weaker relationship between local market concentration and deposit rates. These studies also find evidence that large banks allocate a smaller proportion of their assets to small business loans compared with small banks, and this effect becomes more pronounced for merging banks. These adverse effects on credit availability, however, appeared to be counteracted by the increased credit supply to firms by small incumbent banks. Overall, the early literature suggests that the impact of bank mergers on both the price and availability of banking services is relatively modest.

More recent US studies focus on the effect of bank consolidation on small businesses, with reference to the availability and price of bank services post merger. This stream of research has been influenced not only by the desire to examine possible anti-competitive pricing effects resulting from bank mergers but also by the recent interest in relationship lending and the role of soft (qualitative) and hard (quantitative) information processing in banks' credit decisions. There is some evidence that bank mergers tend to increase rates on unsecured personal loans charged by all banks in the markets in which the merger takes place (although the opposite effect has been observed for interest rates charged on automobile loans). One study examines the specific case of the merger between two US banks (Fleet and BankBoston) and finds that post merger, higher spreads are charged for medium-sized mid-market borrowers (although spreads for small-sized mid-market borrowers remain unchanged) (Calomiris and Pornrojnangkool, 2005). While consolidation is found to have led to lower credit availability for small borrowers, there is also evidence that large banks' decreased lending has been compensated by increased credit from other incumbent (small) banks as well as increased entry of newly chartered (licensed) banks. One interesting (some may say unconventional) study finds that bank mergers in the US relate to higher loan (as well as crime) rates (Garmaise and Moskowitz, 2006).

Mergers can enable banks to acquire proprietary information both to soften lending competition and to increase market share. It has been suggested that as competition increases, the cost of acquiring information about borrowers falls and this can lead to lower loan rates but also inefficient lending decisions. These findings appear to be partially supported by work on Japanese bank consolidation that finds that big bank mergers increase banks' ability to acquire soft information about their corporate borrowers (Ogura and Uchida, 2014).

Evidence on the impact of consolidation on small business lending in Europe (albeit limited) also appears to present rather mixed findings (Montoriol-Garriga, 2008). Various studies on Italian banking have found that interest rates on loans fall when banks with small shares of local banking markets merge, although in the case of large bank deals the results are reversed. Italian bank mergers have also been found to have a substantial adverse effect on credit availability that lasts at least three years after the merger (Bonaccorsi di Patti and Gobbi, 2007). Other work looking at German banking has found that the consolidation trend had no impact on small firm credit availability (Schmieder *et al.*, 2010).

19.7 M&As and bank diversification

An important feature of the consolidation trend in the financial sector has been the strategic focus on both **geographical** and **product diversification**. In the US, the Gramm–Leach–Bliley Act 1999 (also known as the Financial Services Modernization Act) effectively repealed the Glass-Steagall Act of 1933 and granted broad-based securities and insurance powers to commercial banks. Similarly, Japan's 'Big Bang' reforms (also completed in 1999) removed the separation of commercial and investment banking. The 1992 EU Single Market Programme also legislated for a universal banking system. By 2000, therefore, all major financial systems had removed the main product barriers in the financial services sector (although some restrictions remain and vary relating to financial firms' involvement with the non-financial sector – otherwise known as 'commerce').

Product deregulation followed the earlier removal of national bank branching restrictions in various countries. The Riegle-Neal Interstate Banking and Branching Efficiency Act 1994 repealed the McFadden Act of 1927 that inhibited nationwide branching in the US, and similar restrictions were removed in both Italy and Spain in 1992.[7] Deregulation allowed banks the freedom to expand nationally, internationally and across product lines. These changes led to a substantial literature that has sought to identify the impact of these various diversification features.

Diversification (whether geographical or product) was supposed to lead to reductions in risk, although these positive benefits could be offset by shifts to higher-risk portfolios (income streams) and/or greater operational risks. While conventional wisdom in banking argues that diversification tends to reduce bank risk and improve performance, the 2007–2009 financial crisis suggests that aggressive diversification strategies may have resulted in increased risk taking and poor performance (see Box 19.6). Existing studies on the effects of bank diversification have not yet come to a consensus.

One approach to investigating the possible impact of diversification is to study the accounting or stock return features of hypothetical bank-non-bank mergers. The studies that use this approach (mainly investigating the US market) tend to find evidence of risk diversification benefits, particularly in the case of hypothetical bank and life insurance company deals. A recent study by Goetz (2012) investigates how a bank's diversification affects not only its own risk-taking behaviour but also the risk-taking behaviour of competitors, who have not diversified. The author concludes that a bank's risk taking is lower when competitors also have a more diversified business model.

Another strand of the diversification literature uses stock-return event-type studies (see Box 19.4) and these typically reveal mixed findings. Some studies focus on US bank bidder returns and find that significantly higher returns accrue for geographical and product-focused deals. This means that M&As between banks that have a similar business mix, strategies and are based in the same markets tend to do better than diversification-based deals. A number of cross-country European bank merger studies have also found that focused mergers do better

---

[7] One of the main motivations of the Riegle-Neal Act of 1994 was to allow banks to diversify geographic risk. This branching deregulation resulted in the highest-ever five-year run of bank mergers in US history in terms of both the number and the value of the banks acquired.

BOX 19.6 BANK DIVERSIFICATION

With the benefit of hindsight, a big banking riddle looks closer to being solved. For years banks insisted on becoming larger and more diversified, stretching their tentacles right around the globe. Yet finance theory, not to mention plenty of proof on the ground, concluded that universal banking could not, and should not, work. Now that banks are in shrinkage mode again, with the likes of Citigroup literally tearing itself in two, does this spell victory for the latter camp?

Both sides, it seems, were right, but not for the reasons they supposed. Sure, the case against global banks is pretty solid. Executives would bash heads together and boast about cross-selling but in reality there were few synergies across products and borders. And, in theory at least, shareholders should not pay a dime for diversification: they can achieve it far more efficiently

within their own portfolios by owning, for example, a UK retail bank here and a fast-growing Asian lender over there. (See Figure 19.6.)

But global banking shares almost doubled in value over the decade to the end of 2007. Of course, a number of factors such as rampant economic growth and bubbles in many asset classes helped financial companies make a stack of money. But so did leverage. Bernstein, for example, estimates that from 2000 to 2008 the correlation between gross leverage and return on equity for Goldman Sachs was 88 per cent (excluding outlier quarters).

As carry traders appreciate, leverage requires a stable funding platform. A wide geographic spread, therefore, may not have yielded universal banks synergy benefits, but thousands of diversified business streams lowered the volatility of profits. That is handy when gearing up tangible

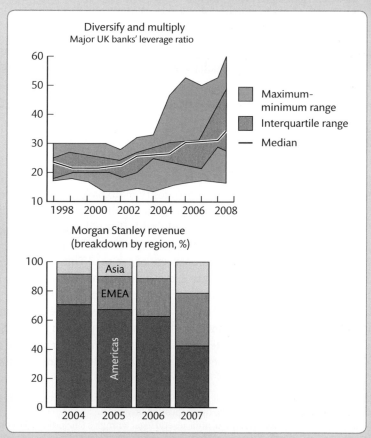

Figure 19.6 Banks diversify and multiply, 1998–2008

Source: Bank of England; Bloomberg.

Box 19.6 Bank diversification (*continued*)

equity by more than 30 times. The trouble was, however, that the combination of lower volatility and benign markets resulted in banks thinking they had a low cost of equity. Thus bigger risks were taken until even the most geographically diversified banks became exposed. Now that excessive leverage is history, so perhaps is the case for universal banking.

 Source: Lex column: Bank diversification, *Financial Times*, 19/02/09.

than diversifying deals in terms of returns to stockholders, although there is evidence that diversifying deals do well – so evidence for Europe is rather mixed.

The recent literature on cross-border mergers involving US and European banks tends to find evidence of no cost efficiency improvements, although there is some evidence of profit efficiency or accounting returns improvements. Other studies that examine diversification focus on a wide range of issues, including:[8]

- potential conflicts of interest associated with commercial bank/investment bank mergers;
- whether banks with securities arms lend more or less to small firms;
- how liquidity shocks and other effects can limit diversification;
- evidence of substantial **conglomerate discounts** (investors value diversified firms less than focused companies, as such conglomerate or diversified firms are not valued as highly as focused firms);
- whether the benefits from diversification are generally offset by fee-income volatility.

In the light of the 2007–2009 financial crisis and the barrage of bailouts and other support provided for 'diversified banks', various legislative moves have sought to restrict bank diversification activity. The most prominent are provisions laid out in the US Dodd–Frank Wall Street Reform and Consumer Protection Act of July 2010, which seeks (among other things) to end 'too big to fail'. The Act clearly states that 'taxpayers will not be on the hook' and the FDIC is prohibited from losing money on systemically important financial intermediaries. In addition, the Volcker rule prohibits banks with federally guaranteed deposits from proprietary trading (i.e. trading using their own capital) and limits investments in hedge funds/ private equity fund sponsorship to 3 per cent of capital.[9] This clearly seeks to limit bank trading activity as well as involvement in hedge fund/private equity areas – although there is no strong evidence that any of this activity led to major bank collapses.

In the UK, an Independent Banking Commission was asked to consider reforms to the banking sector to promote financial stability and competition. On 12 September 2011, the Commission released its Final Report, which sets out views on possible reforms, stating that retail banking is to be ring-fenced from wholesale and investment banking (see Chapter 13

---

[8] See Stiroh (2014) for a review of the diversification literature.

[9] The Volcker Rule was finally adopted, after several legal wrangles (including a lawsuit by community banks), in December 2013, nearly three years after Dodd–Frank was signed into law and two years after the first draft of the rule was put out by the bank regulators (the final version of the Volcker Rule can be found at **www. sec.gov/rules/final/2013/bhca-1.pdf**).

for regulatory changes in UK banking).[10] Also, risk management should become a self-contained, less complex business for retail banking, but remain complex for wholesale/investment banking. Again this inhibits diversified banks' ability to operate in wholesale/investment banking areas.

The common aim of all these proposals for regulatory reforms is to foster financial stability and to ensure that banks are both resilient and resolvable in case of problems. In addition, they aim to limit the implicit guarantees to their respective banking sectors. The predominant view at the time of writing (2014) – particularly in policy circles – is that the higher complexity and excessive agency problems associated with large and complex financial institutions outweigh the benefits of diversification. However, there is also merit to diversification and both sides of the diversification debate are grounded on solid theoretical arguments (see Box 19.6). There is, to date, little empirical evidence that large and diversified financial institutions have fared worse (or indeed that they have cost the taxpayers more money) than smaller institutions with a narrower range of assets and activities. While some activities might be increasing banks' overall risk profile, others are not and may offer financial institutions the opportunity to re-balance their risk exposure and to diversify their revenue streams.

19.7.1 The impact of consolidation on bank entry and other effects

Merger activity can have a significant influence on not only the participants but also other banks and potential entrants to the market. The US literature suggests that mergers encourage new bank charters (licences) and that even the presence of a large bank stimulates new entry into rural banking markets. New entry via merger has also been found to increase the cost efficiency (but not the profit efficiency) of incumbent banks. It has been found (in Italy) that competition in local markets increases the likelihood of M&As (as do higher loans-to-deposits ratios).

Deregulation's positive influence on merger activity is also found. In the US, the deregulation process has been found to increase bid premiums for target banks – as banks are allowed to enter new markets, this pushes up the price of new targets. However, it should be remembered that even though banking systems have been deregulating, the regulatory approval process can act as a constraint on bank merger activity.

19.8 The exploitation of safety-net subsidies and systemic risk

Even prior to 2007, the increased size of banking firms had raised concerns about the risk implications and the repercussions for systemic stability. As banks become larger, irrespective of the performance implications, they may have opportunities to exploit **safety-net subsidies** if they are viewed as 'too big to fail' (TBTF) or 'too big to discipline adequately' (TBTDA). While it is generally recognised that TBTF subsidies are difficult to evaluate, evidence prior to the financial crisis from the US suggested that these were likely to be substantial. Since

---

[10] Independent Commission on Banking (2011) Final Report, September. **http://bankingcommission.independent.gov.uk**

late 2007, the number of bank bailouts (including Citigroup in the US, RBS and Lloyds in the UK, Fortis and Dexia in the Benelux countries, Depfa in Germany, and the main banks in Ireland, Iceland, Spain and Greece) provided further evidence of possible TBTF subsidies. Now we know that some banks are TBTF and the consolidation trend helped feed the system, creating banks that had implicit safety-net subsidies.

Earlier studies on the subject of bank size and safety net subsidies pointed in this direction. One early study suggested that because the top ten largest US banks paid less for funds than smaller banks and operated with lower capitalisation rates, this indicated advantages of TBTF implicit guarantees (Shull and Hanweck, 2001). After the US authorities named 11 US banks as TBTF in 1984, this increased the ratings on new bond issues of these banks relative to other (unnamed) banks.

A literature has emerged focusing on the **merger premium** paid for mega-banks as an indicator of the safety-net subsidy – the argument being that higher premiums will be paid for banks that have implicit bailout guarantees. There is some evidence that significant premiums are paid in mega-conglomerate (more than $100 billion) deals and also large premiums have been paid for targets that have critical size. Overall, even prior to 2007, there were growing concerns about TBTF subsidies resulting from the consolidation process (in the US at least). Now we know that TBTF is a reality that has led many commentators to question the efficacy of bank size and consider the break-up of mega-sized institutions, as illustrated in Box 19.7.

BOX 19.7 OUT TO BREAK THE BANKS

US regulators and lawmakers fear large institutions are still too big to fail. The 2010 overhaul of financial regulation known as the Dodd–Frank Act was supposed to have dealt with the problem. A financial group's failure has been made less likely by limiting risky trading and requiring more loss-absorbent equity capital. Failures have been made easier to handle by allowing the government to wipe out shareholders and forcibly convert debt to equity. International efforts to come up with a global plan to deal with large bank failures are well under way. Higher international capital requirements in a deal known as Basel III are being phased in for banks around the world. But there is a new-found zeal among members of Congress from both parties and from some senior regulators to go further. They want to eradicate the possibility of new bailouts or disastrous collapses and to end the phenomenon of too big to fail.

Barney Frank, the former Democratic congressman who co-authored Dodd–Frank, says the renewed debate is unnecessary. "There is a strange view that if a large institution fails, even though the law doesn't allow for bailouts, there will be overwhelming public pressure to keep them alive," he says. "The notion that there will be an overwhelming demand to keep these firms alive – I just don't know what planet these people have been living on." But Mr Frank has left the stage, along with Sheila Bair, the chairman of the Federal Deposit Insurance Corporation, and Tim Geithner, Treasury secretary. As architects of the post-crisis response, all were invested in the idea that too big to fail had been dealt with. Their departure gives proponents of going further a greater chance of success.

Last week Mr Brown and Mr Vitter, two US Senators, unveiled their latest draft legislation on the topic, which would sharply increase the capital requirements on the largest banks with assets of more than $500bn, forcing them to hold 15 per cent equity against their assets.

Analysts at Goldman Sachs calculate the increased capital is worth about $1.2tn, which would equate to the largest banks forgoing dividends and share buybacks for up to 15 years.

Box 19.7 Out to break the banks (*continued*)

If shareholders accepted that, they would also have to accept a permanently lower return on equity. Many in the industry believe the economics would not work: the biggest banks might have to break up to escape the tougher regime. Mr Vitter and Mr Brown could live with that – and believe others can, too. "If we took that vote today, we'd get upwards of 40 senators," Mr Brown says, adding that he is working with 10 Republican senators to drum up additional support. A majority of the Senate is within reach, he says, though industry lobbyists dispute that count.

What appeals to the members of Congress who might eventually back such legislation is the wave of enthusiasm across the country, particularly in rural districts served by small community banks struggling to compete with their biggest rivals. Camden Fine, who heads Independent Community Bankers of America, the association for the country's 7,000 small banks, says he will expend "every ounce of influence we have in this town" to get legislation passed. There have been several catalysts for action, including JPMorgan's $6bn trading losses last year, which led many to question whether any large institution was truly safe if one of the world's best-managed banks could inflict such damage on itself.

Unlikely cheerleaders for breaking up the banks have emerged, including Sandy Weill and John Reed, who in the 1990s assembled Citigroup, the archetypal financial supermarket. Both have disowned the model, with Mr Weill calling for splits that would leave banks in businesses that are "not going to risk the taxpayer dollars, that [are] not too big to fail".

But the moment that crystallised the sentiment was the admission by the country's top legal official that some banks were "too big to jail". Eric Holder, the US attorney-general, has come under stinging criticism for not prosecuting banks or top bank executives in the wake of the financial crisis.

Asked at a March 2013 hearing whether some banks had escaped prosecution because of their size, Mr Holder surprised the room by conceding the point. "I am concerned that the size of some of these institutions becomes so large that it does become difficult for us to prosecute them when we are hit with indications that if you do prosecute, if you do bring a criminal charge, it will have a negative impact on the national economy, perhaps even the world economy," he said. Mr Holder's statements are considered to be the most explicit admission of concern by a senior Obama administration official regarding the risks posed by big financial groups. "That's what you'd expect to hear from some little tin-horn republic, where certain families that have done wrong escape prosecutions because of their connections," says Mr Fine. "You don't expect to hear something like that in the US."

The more profound unfairness, critics say, is that the biggest banks can borrow more cheaply, feeding a vicious cycle of ever-greater dominance. "I can't find anybody who argues that Dodd–Frank solves too big to fail, other than the big banks who would have to adjust [to a new regime]," says Richard Fisher, president of the Federal Reserve Bank of Dallas. The concern is that banks such as JPMorgan enjoy implicit government guarantees: creditors believe that, as with Bank of New England in 1991 and Citigroup in 2008, the government will find a way to rescue them rather than take the risk that the new tools created by Dodd–Frank could fail, leading to credit freezes and a breakdown in payment networks.

For years this held true. In the past three years credit rating agencies have started to downgrade banks on the assumption that the possibility of a bailout is lower and the funding differential has narrowed. Some analyses find it has disappeared. But even respected figures in the middle, such as Ben Bernanke, chairman of the US Federal Reserve, say it is still apparent.

"Clearly there are grounds for continuing concerns about subsidies associated with too big to fail," says Larry Summers, the former Treasury secretary and economics adviser to President Barack Obama and now a professor at Harvard University. "The steps contained in Dodd–Frank are clearly constructive. But I think we have a long way to go with respect to issues associated

Box 19.7 Out to break the banks (*continued*)

with international resolution, with respect to assuring sufficient capital levels, and with respect to appropriate risk systems. Market evidence does provide some grounds for concern about too-big-to-fail subsidies."

The renewed debate over the size and power of the big banks has alarmed Wall Street lobbyists, who are spending heavily to fight back. "It is of the highest risk and concern," says one top industry lobbyist. Groups are spending millions of dollars to combat the perception that they are protected by the government. The Clearing House, Financial Services Forum and Financial Services Roundtable, three of the biggest trade associations, are all engaged. While both sides have been fighting over the facts, there is also much faith-based rhetoric. "The too-big-to-fail issue has become theological," says Paul Saltzman, head of the Clearing House, which represents the biggest banks. "That is my biggest worry – a debate where facts don't matter. In order to conclusively prove your point, we have to have a crisis, a large bank has to fail and the shareholders, creditors and culpable management need to suffer the consequences without any taxpayer-funded support. No one wants that counterfactual event to occur."

The concern for the banks is that opponents on this issue are not just Democrats such as Mr Summers but also Republicans, including Kevin Warsh, a former Fed governor. Mr Warsh argues that by trying to force the banks into safer activities and branding them systemically important, the problem is getting worse. "If the government chooses select firms to be public utilities atop the business of banking, it is very difficult for the other 7,000 banking institutions to lend and compete," he says. "That is an obstacle to economic growth."

Banks might favour less regulation but they would not favour Mr Warsh's alternative: far more capital and simple leverage ratios that do not allow banks to put less capital against safer assets. Another concern is that the actors are not just former officials or lawmakers but active regulators who have power to force changes. Among

them is Tom Hoenig, vice-chairman of the FDIC, who has also called for significantly higher and simpler capital requirements on large banks. What is new, and what is most worrying for the banks, is that the most powerful regulators at the Fed show little desire to quell the calls from their more feisty colleagues.

Fed officials are considering higher capital requirements, according to people familiar with the discussion, which they could impose without any input from Congress. The FDIC is also considering using its new powers under Dodd–Frank to force divestitures if banks deliver "living wills", designed to show how they could be liquidated, that are deemed inadequate. "The living wills are the thin end of the wedge," says a banker who fears they might be the start of regulators demanding more sweeping changes. In Europe, politicians such as Angela Merkel, the German chancellor, and Michel Barnier, the European commissioner in charge of financial services, warn against going too far, too fast on reform, afraid that the economic recovery will be derailed.

Perhaps, ultimately, Republican leaders in the House of Representatives, Mr Obama or Mr Bernanke will step in and block attempts to hobble the biggest banks, fearing wider repercussions. Members of Congress might be swayed by the grassroots lobbying of small bankers in their districts. But they also like the donations of the biggest groups and are susceptible to the argument that breaking up banks such as JPMorgan would push their business to foreign groups, such as Deutsche Bank or Barclays, that can offer a full suite of products. "I think it's dangerous," says Bill Demchak, chief executive of PNC Financial Services, a bank that, with $300bn in assets, is not large enough to qualify for most of the proposed curbs. "As a selfish competitor does it help us if the bigger banks get hurt more than we do? Yes. But I think it harms our economy."

For now the upper hand is with the reformers. It might be that they have too much momentum to fail.

Box 19.7 Out to break the banks (*continued*)

Three ways to tame Wall Street

Cap size	More capital	Shed risky business
The US already prevents banks from making acquisitions if they possess more than 10 per cent of the nation's deposits. This is true of JPMorgan Chase, Bank of America and Wells Fargo. Proposals to impose further caps on assets or liabilities are, therefore, not without some chance of success. Regulators are focusing more on providing incentives to get smaller, with higher capital requirements for larger institutions. Opponents say that the issue is not really too-big-to-fail but too-interconnected-to-fail and that chopping up Bank of America, with its $2.2 trillion of assets, into five separate companies, does not make the system safer.	With more loss-absorbent equity, banks become less likely to fail and the pressure to deal with failure decreases. The question is how far to go. The Basel III rules agreed internationally already force much more capital into the system. Sceptics argue it is still too little and the system of risk weights is too complicated. Even relatively moderate Fed officials believe that leverage limits, the blunter measure of bank indebtedness, should be lowered. Congressional proposals would go further, with draconian capital levels likely to encourage large banks to break up. Some further tightening of the capital rules has good chances.	Every large institution now needs to submit 'living wills' to regulators to describe how they could be liquidated in the event of a crisis. If regulators find the plans implausible, they can force banks to divest risky operations. Some within the FDIC are keen to start using their new powers, arguing that some banks appear too complex to be dismantled quickly and safely. JPMorgan or Citigroup are unlikely to be told to sell their investment banks tomorrow, but some forced reorganisation, ring-fencing or divestitures are quite likely.

Source: Adapted from Out to break the banks, *Financial Times*, 30/04/2013 (Shahien Nasiripour and Tom Braithwaite). © The Financial Times Limited. All Rights Reserved. Pearson Education is responsible for providing this adaptation of the original article..

Closely related to the arguments linking consolidation to safety-net subsidies are those that consider systemic risk – an area of major concern currently in global banking systems. Some have found that correlations of big-bank stock returns have increased, suggestive of potentially greater systemic risk (e.g. bank share prices move increasingly in the same direction at the same time). Trends in international consolidation (as well as conglomeration) are also likely to increase risks for large complex financial firms. It has been shown that financial sector consolidation can influence liquidity in money markets and the influence depends on divisional capital allocations post merger.

19.9 Conclusion

This chapter provides an insight into recent M&A trends in banking and also examines the impact of the consolidation process on bank performance. We show that the consolidation trend grew in both the US and Europe in the mid-1990s, peaking at the end of the decade, then falling back as a result of the burst of the IT bubble. M&A activity then picked up from the early 2000s, with European deal activity lagging that of the US by around a year or so.

In examining the impact of M&As on bank performance we show that the evidence from the 1990s was pretty mixed (from both stock return event studies and/or cost and profit ratio studies), although in the 2000s there is strong evidence that European M&A activity has been performance enhancing – and evidence on recent US deals remains mixed. We also discuss managerial motives associated with the consolidation process. There is some evidence that small business borrowers may lose out post merger, finding it more difficult to borrow or obtaining credit at higher interest rates. Retail customers may also end up earning less on their deposits and paying more on loans. The deregulation trend has enabled banks to engage in universal activities, spawning a wave of consolidation between banks and non-bank financial firms (including insurance companies, securities firms and so on). Also banks have expanded cross-border to enhance their international activities.

Overall, there is mixed evidence as to whether such diversification is performance enhancing. From the US the consensus appears to be that diversification benefits may accrue if non-traditional income reaches around 25–30 per cent of total income but thereafter any benefits are dissipated by the increased volatility of non-interest income (especially if the bank is engaged in securities activity). Conglomerate discounts appear to be common in universal banking.

Finally, we examine whether large bank mergers are motivated by opportunities to exploit implicit too-big-to-fail guarantees. Evidence prior to mid-2007 pointed in this direction – we now know that this is the case and regulators and politicians are actively discussing restricting mega-bank activity, as reflected in US legislation and proposals in the UK to limit commercial bank securities activity.

Key terms

Conglomerate discounts	Financial conglomeration	Managerial motives	Quiet life
Cross-border mergers	Geographical diversification	Merger premium	Safety-net subsidies
Domestic mergers	Hubris hypothesis	Product diversification	Shareholder value

Key reading

Buch, C. and DeLong, G. (2014) 'Banking globalization: International consolidation and mergers in banking', in Berger, A.N., Molyneux, P. and Wilson, J.O.S. (eds), *Oxford Handbook of Banking*, 2nd Edition, Oxford: Oxford University Press, Chapter 31.

DeYoung, R., Evanoff, D.D. and Molyneux, P. (2009) 'Mergers and acquisitions of financial institutions: A review of the post-2000 literature', *Journal of Financial Services Research*, December.

Garmaise, M.J. and Moskowitz, T.J. (2006) 'Bank mergers and crime: The real and social effects of credit market competition', *Journal of Finance*, 61, 495–538.

Group of Ten (2001) 'Report on consolidation in the financial sector', Bank for International Settlements, Basel: BIS, **www.bis.org/publ/gten05.pdf**

Roll, R. (1986) 'The hubris hypothesis of corporate takeovers', *Journal of Business*, 59, 197–216.

Stiroh, K. (2014) 'Diversification in banking', in Berger, A.N., Molyneux, P. and Wilson, J.O.S (eds), *Oxford Handbook of Banking*, 2nd Edition, Oxford University Press, Chapter 9.

REVISION QUESTIONS AND PROBLEMS

19.1 Outline the main trends in banking sector consolidation since the mid-1990s. What have been the main effects of the consolidation trend?

19.2 Outline the key motives for bank mergers. In your answer discuss whether managerial motives are important.

19.3 Explain the quiet life hypothesis and Roll's (1986) hubris hypothesis.

19.4 Compare the impact of domestic bank deals with cross-border deals. Of these two types of consolidation, which are more likely to be performance enhancing?

19.5 Discuss the impact of mergers on bank customers. Do small businesses lose out as a consequence of the merger trend?

19.6 Examine the influence of product and geographical diversification deals and discuss how such deals may impact on bank performance.

19.7 How are mergers affecting new entry in banking markets?

19.8 In the light of the ongoing turmoil in financial markets, examine whether large bank mergers are motivated by exploiting safety-net subsidies (implicit too-big-to-fail guarantees).

Chapter 20

Bank competition and financial stability

Learning objectives

- To appreciate how to measure the competitive features of banking systems using structural indicators, including concentration ratios and the Herfindahl index

- To understand non-structural indicators of banking sector competition, including the Panzar–Rosse statistic, the Lerner index, the Boone indicator and the persistence of profits (POP) indicator

- To understand accounting and market-based measures of bank risk

- To understand the link between competition and bank risk

- To understand the empirical evidence on the relationship between competition and risk in banking markets

20.1   Introduction

Competition is generally considered an essential force in the economy as it should encourage firms to be more efficient in the way they produce outputs and consequently promote a better allocation of resources. In the banking industry, higher efficiency should entail lower costs, which should then be passed on to bank customers in the form of lower charges, higher deposit rates and reduced lending costs. In addition, competition should have a positive impact on the economy, influencing a broad array of factors that can (i) improve access to finance; (ii) increase competitiveness in other sectors of the economy; (iii) foster innovation and improve the quality of products and services offered; (iv) promote economic growth; (v) widen consumer choice.

However, the issue of the perceived benefits derived from increased competition has always been controversial in banking, as these perceived benefits have to be weighed against the risks of potential instability. As a consequence, the banking industry historically has been heavily regulated. Furthermore, the existence of frictions in banking markets (for example, entry barriers and asymmetric information) causes the welfare theorems associated with perfect competition not to be directly applicable and allow room for the exercise of market power (Vives, 2001). Nevertheless, a healthy degree of rivalry is considered necessary for the dynamic efficiency of an industry and this principle is at the basis of the trend towards fostering greater competition in banking markets all over the world.

The presence of a possible trade-off between competition and stability has always played an important role at the policy level and gained even more prominence in light of events culminating in the global financial crisis of 2007–2009. Questions remain as to whether a certain degree of market power would be beneficial in banking markets to provide incentives for banks to undertake less risky strategies. In this context, the evaluation of competitive conditions and market power becomes increasingly important for policy makers and regulators. Competition authorities often rely on the validity of the structure-conduct-performance (SCP) paradigm and proxy competition with measures of market concentration, such as the n-firms concentration ratio (CR-n) or the Herfindahl–Hirschman index (HHI). Yet recent academic studies have shown concentration to be a poor proxy for competition.

In this chapter, we review the different methods proposed in the academic literature to assess the competitive conditions of banking markets. The research on bank competition has evolved mainly in two directions: the structural and the non-structural approaches. Traditional industrial organisation theory focuses on the SCP paradigm. Market structure is reflected in concentration ratios for the largest firms and the Herfindahl–Hirschman index. This literature is essentially based on the assumption that concentration weakens competition by fostering collusive behaviour among firms. In Section 20.2 we provide an overview of the **structure-conduct-performance (SCP) paradigm**, which uses measures of industry structure and links these to measures of bank performance. The non-structural approaches posit that factors other than market structure and concentration may affect competitive behaviour, such as entry/exit barriers and the general contestability of the market. In Section 20.3 we briefly discuss some of the non-structural indicators of competition, including the Panzar–Rosse H-statistic, the Lerner index, the Boone indicator and the persistence of profits measures. In Section 20.4 we present a comparative analysis of the different measures of competition to establish whether they yield consistent results. In Section 20.5 we outline the link between competition and risk in banking and we introduce different indicators of bank risk, including accounting indicators and market-based measures of risk. We then explore the link in Section 20.6 between competition and risk in banking systems and bring in the debate between the competition-fragility view, which posits that competition induces increased risk taking and therefore is detrimental for stability, and the competition-stability view, which argues the opposite, that is that competition promotes financial stability. We review the results of selected academic studies and attempt to shed some light on this controversial issue. Section 20.7 concludes.

20.2   Structure-conduct-performance (SCP)

The existence of a link between market structure and efficiency was first proposed by Hicks (1935) and the **quiet life hypothesis**. Hicks (1935) argued that monopoly power allows managers a *quiet life* free from competition and therefore increased concentration should bring about a decrease in efficiency. Leibenstein (1966) argued that inefficiencies are reduced by increased competition as managers respond to the challenge.

The analysis of the link between profitability and market structure has a long tradition; however, economists have proposed different interpretations of the results. The alternative theories can be summarised as follows:

1 Market power theories, which include the traditional SCP paradigm and the relative market power (RMP) hypothesis.

2 Efficiency theories, which include the efficient structure hypothesis (x-efficiency (ESX) and scale efficiency (ESS)).

These are reviewed below.

20.2.1 The traditional SCP view

Traditional industrial organisation theory suggests that increased industry concentration lowers the cost of collusion, thus resulting in anti-competitive behaviour and excess profits. The SCP paradigm seeks to explain aspects of the conduct and performance of firms in terms of the structural characteristics of the industries or markets in which they operate. The *structure* (the S in SCP) refers to the structure of the market and includes the number of firms and their absolute and relative sizes, the level of concentration, the extent of product differentiation and the nature of entry conditions.

According to this approach, market structure is expected to influence the way in which firms behave, namely their *conduct* (the C in SCP). The conduct of firms relates to factors such as their pricing behaviour (whether they fix prices through collusion and other forms of strategic behaviour; how they behave in terms of product differentiation, advertising, entry and exit strategies). Conduct, dictated or influenced by structure, in turn determines *performance* (the P in SCP). Firm performance can be measured by a variety of indicators, including profitability, growth, market share, technological progress and efficiency. The most common measures of performance in banking focus either on profitability (return on assets or return on equity) or on prices (loan rates, deposit rates). The traditional SCP is essentially a theory of collusion, its main insight being that the smaller the number of firms in an industry (the more concentrated the industry), the easier it is for firms to collude. Equally, large banks could exploit their market power by setting prices at uncompetitive levels (RMP hypothesis). Shepherd (1982, 1986) argues that differences in performance can be explained by superior efficiency and/or by the influence of factors related to market power. Under this hypothesis, individual market share is the proxy variable for assessing market power.

The theory of the firm literature tells us that the most competitive market outcome is perfect competition where price equals marginal cost. The further price is from marginal cost, the greater the firm's market power and overall profitability. Features of the SCP relationship are illustrated in Figure 20.1.

Early empirical work based on the SCP paradigm focused on the relationship between concentration and performance, measured by profitability. A positive link between concentration and profit was interpreted as evidence that firms act collusively in order to achieve high profits or that dominant firms abuse their market position by acting in an uncompetitive manner to the detriment of consumers. The early empirical work applying the SCP dates back to the seminar work by Bain (1951). A review of the earlier literature is provided by Gilbert (1984); this literature highlights a positive relationship between industry concentration and profits, thus confirming the SCP paradigm.

Figure 20.1 The structure-conduct-performance (SCP) paradigm

20.2.2 The efficient structure hypothesis

Proponents of the SCP paradigm tend to view markets as imperfect in terms of their competitive structure and therefore advocate some form of regulation in order to prevent the abuse of market power. The Chicago School, however, argued that government interference tends to lead to less competition rather than more. A positive link between concentration and profits does not necessarily imply collusive behaviour on the part of firms; it may simply reflect the fact that the larger firms tend to operate more efficiently and therefore make higher profits. This view, which has become known as the **efficient structure hypothesis** (Demsetz, 1973) posits a reverse causality between competition and efficiency: more efficient firms have lower costs, which in turn lead to higher profits. More efficient firms tend to attain large market shares, and consequently the industry becomes concentrated. If all firms operated at similar levels of efficiency, concentration and average profitability would remain low. Because, by definition, concentrated industries contain firms with high market shares, the average level of profit also tends to be higher. However, this correlation between profit and concentration is the result of the underlying relationship between efficiency and profitability. This suggests that regulation or intervention aimed at limiting industry concentration is not an appropriate policy prescription, since it penalises the largest and most efficient firms.

An alternative interpretation of the efficient structure hypothesis suggests firms might have equally good management and technology, but some firms produce at a more efficient scale and therefore have lower unit costs and higher profits. Again, such firms have large market share, which may result in high levels of concentration (this is the *scale efficiency* hypothesis). More concentrated banking sectors will tend to have higher profitability, on average, because large banks are more efficient than their smaller counterparts.

The existence of competing interpretations of the concentration–profitability relationship has produced a vast body of research, which seeks to resolve the issue using empirical criteria. The first application of the efficiency hypothesis to banking is the study of Smirlock (1985). Berger (1995), however, was the first to explicitly test the **efficiency hypothesis** by including specific measures of bank efficiency in his model estimations (previous studies had simply used market share variables to infer efficient behaviour).

20.2.3 Testing the SCP paradigm

To evaluate the SCP paradigm, the first step relates to the measurement of the industry structure. Researchers tend to rely on alternative measures of industry structure characterised by the size distribution of firms. No doubt the choice is strongly influenced by the relative ease with which firm size can be observed – the size of a bank can easily be obtained from a balance sheet (total assets or total deposits). While measures of bank size might be easy to obtain, more complex is the definition of the market in which firms are operating. Traditionally, banking studies consider the national banking market: here the market is defined by the size of total banking sector assets or deposits in a country. This is relatively simple to calculate but a rather crude measure, as it provides only one concentration indicator for the banking system under study. In reality, we know that banks engage in a variety of business areas – consumer loans, mortgages, credit cards, lending to small firms and so on. However, it is difficult to obtain market share information for banks in many of these specific areas and even if this could be obtained, it would be even more difficult to identify the profitability of these specific market segments over time. That is why most studies resort to national market structure indicators and broad bank performance indicators to undertake SCP analysis.

The simplest and most widely used indicator of market structure is the n-firm **concentration ratio** (CR$_n$), which measures the market share of the top n firms in the industry:

$$CR_n = \sum_{i=1}^{n} S_i \qquad (20.1)$$

where S_i = market share of the ith firm, when firms are ranked in descending order of market share.

To put less formally, the 3-firm concentration ratio (CR-3) measures the sum of market shares of the largest three firms; the CR-5 is the market share of the biggest five firms; the CR-10 is the combined market share of the top ten firms, and so on. The n-firm concentration ratio (CR-n) has the advantage of being easily measurable; one needs to know only the total size of the industry and the individual sizes of the top n firms. By focusing only on the share of the top n firms, however, it takes no account of the size distribution of the remaining firms and therefore could lead to biased comparisons. One banking system might look highly concentrated if one considered, say, the CR-3, but it might look less concentrated than a country that had a higher CR-10, as shown in Table 20.1. Here we can see that CR-3 for Country A equals 50 per cent compared with 40 per cent for Country B, thus suggesting the

Table 20.1 Bank size and concentration

Top ten banks ranked from 1st to 10th	COUNTRY A assets market share (%)	COUNTRY B assets market share (%)
1st	20	15
2nd	20	15
3rd	10	10
	CR-3 = 50%	CR-3 = 40%
4th	5	15
5th	5	10
6th	5	10
7th	5	10
8th	5	5
9th	5	5
10th	5	2
	CR-10 = 85%	CR-10 = 97%

former is more concentrated than the latter. However, if we choose the CR-10 to compare market structures, we find that Country A has a CR-10 of 85 per cent but Country B has a higher CR-10 at 97 per cent – suggesting that the latter is less competitive than the former. This indicates that the choice of the number of the largest firms used to calculate the CR-n ratio can lead to inconsistent comparisons of industry market structure.

To deal with this limitation of concentration ratios, one can choose the more data-intensive **Herfindahl-Hirschman index** (HHI) – often just referred to as the Herfindahl index – which (in theory at least) uses information on all firms in the industry.[1] It is defined as the sum of the squares of the market shares of all firms:

$$HHI = \sum_{i=1}^{N} S_i^2 \tag{20.2}$$

where S_i is market share of firm i as before and N is the total number of firms in the industry. In the calculation of HHI, the larger firms receive a weighting heavier than their smaller counterparts, reflecting their relative importance. For example, in an industry with one firm with 100 per cent market share the HHI equals $100 \times 100 = 10,000$. Where there are two firms, both with 50 per cent market shares, the HHI is $(50 \times 50) + (50 \times 50) = (2,500) + (2,500) = 5,000$. If there are five firms with 50 per cent, 20 per cent, 10 per cent, 10 per cent and 10 per cent market shares then the HHI $= 2,500 + 400 + 100 + 100 + 100 = 3,200$. The less concentrated the market, the smaller the HHI. In theory, to calculate the HHI index accurately researchers are supposed to have information on every single firm (or bank) in the industry. While central banks and other regulators have this information, it is often difficult for researchers to obtain information on all banks. It is therefore common to use large samples of banks provided from databases such as SNL Financial, BankScope or Thompson One Banker.

Table 14.13 in Chapter 14, for example, illustrates the HHI and CR-5 assets measures for EU banking systems between 2008 and 2012. The top five banks account for 90.6 per cent of banking assets in Estonia, making it the most concentrated banking system, followed by Lithuania (84.7 per cent), the Netherlands (83.6 per cent) and Finland (80.9 per cent). Germany has the lowest level of concentration with a CR-5 of 33.5 per cent. However, if we use the preferred indicator – the Herfindahl index – one can see that Finland is ranked as most concentrated (with an HHI index of 3,700) followed by Estonia (2,613) and the Netherlands (2,061).

Figure 20.2 illustrates the HHI for equity derivatives contracts – forwards and swaps and options. One can see that in the early 2000s the forwards and swaps business to non-bank clients was heavily concentrated, although this has fallen since, with HHIs of around 1,000.

High levels of industry concentration raise authorities' concerns. Competition authorities (also known as *antitrust* authorities) tend to investigate high concentration levels to ensure that an acceptable level of competition is taking place (see also Box 20.1). However, as we have already noted, just because an industry is concentrated does not necessarily mean that firms are behaving in a monopoly manner – there can be intense competition between the top firms.

Bank conduct is difficult to observe. Tests of the SCP relationship typically aim to relate market structure to performance from which firm conduct is inferred. Once the measure of market structure is chosen, the next step is to choose a bank performance indicator. Usually profits measures such as ROE or ROA are chosen. However, if a specific sector is being analysed, it may be possible to obtain product prices such as the interest rates charged in

---

[1] Hirschman (1945); Herfindahl (1950).

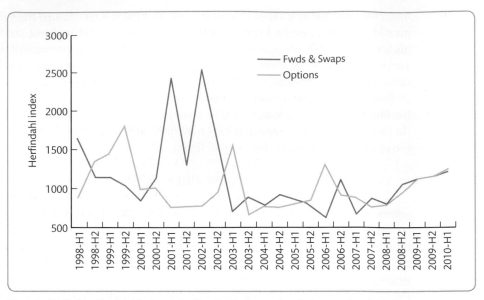

Figure 20.2 Herfindahl index: equity derivatives, bank to non-bank

Source: OECD (2011) Figure 2.11, p. 46.

different markets. Unfortunately, it is often difficult to obtain product prices in different banking markets so researchers stick to bank profitability as the main performance indicator. Most of the empirical banking literature uses simple ordinary least squares (OLS) to estimate the following type of regression:[2]

$$P_{ij} = a + a_1 CONC_j + a_2 MS_{ij} + a_3 \sum BS_{ij} + a_4 \sum MKT_j + u_{ij} \qquad (20.3)$$

where P_{ij} is the profit measure, often the return on equity of bank i in market j; $CONC_j$ is a measure of market structure (HHI or CR-n-firm ratio) in market j; MS_{ij} is a measure of the market share of firm i in market j; BS_{ij} is a vector of bank-specific variables known to have an impact on bank performance for bank i in market j; MKT_j is a vector of market-specific variables that can influence bank performance in market j; and u_{ij} is the error term.

Recall that the model seeks to explain variation in bank performance with a range of bank-specific and market- (or country-) specific variables. The finding of a positive and statistically significant coefficient on $CONC_j$ (a_1) confirms the positive link between profits and concentration, confirming evidence of the traditional SCP paradigm. However, the findings of a positive relationship between concentration and profitability cannot be interpreted unambiguously as the result of collusion and the exercise of monopoly power. If the coefficient of the $CONC_j$ variable loses its explanatory power (a_1 equals to zero or negative) when the variable MS_{ij} is considered (a_2 is positive and significant), this can be read as evidence that bank performance is positively related to firm size and not market concentration, therefore providing support for the efficiency hypothesis, which argues that more concentrated banking sectors containing a high proportion of large banks will tend to have higher profitability on average, because large banks are more efficient than their smaller counterparts operating in more competitive sectors.

---

[2] For more details on the measurement of competition in banking, see Liu *et al.* (2013).

Berger and Hannan (1998) suggest an alternative interpretation of the SCP relationship: they argue that if banks exploit market power, prices should be higher in concentrated sectors than in competitive ones, as banks are able to exercise market power and pay lower rates of interest to depositors (RMP hypothesis). Berger (1995) proposed to test the efficiency hypothesis by extending the traditional SCP equation (equation 20.3) to include specific measures of bank efficiency as follows:[3]

$$P_{ij} = a + a_1 CONC_j + a_2 MS_{ij} + a_3 ESX_{ij} + a_4 ESS_{ij} + a_5 \sum BS_{ij} + a_4 \sum MKT_j + u_{ij} \quad (20.4)$$

where P_{ij} is the profit measure, often the return on equity of bank i in market j; $CONC_j$ is a measure of market structure (HHI or CR-n-firm ratio) in market j; MS_{ij} is a measure of the market share of firm i in market j; ESX_{ij} is a bank-specific x-efficiency measure; ESS_{ij} is a bank-specific scale economies measure; BS_{ij} is a vector of bank-specific variables; MKT_j is a vector of market-specific variables; and u_{ij} is the error term.

The results are interpreted by looking at the sign and significance of the coefficients (a_1 to a_4). In Berger (1995), the MS_{ij} and ESX_{ij} variables are found to be statistically significant in explaining US bank performance, both having a positive effect on profitability. Berger interprets these results as providing evidence that larger banks can do better because they have relative market power, brought about partly through product differentiation. More efficient banks (irrespective of size) earn higher profits because they have superior management and technology. Market concentration and economies of scale are found to be unimportant in influencing bank performance. In interpreting these results, however, Berger sounds a note of caution by pointing to the weak explanatory power of his models.

While there have been other studies that examine SCP and efficiency hypotheses in different countries and regions of the world, the approach broadly taken has pretty much been in line with the methodology suggested by Berger (1995). As in the earlier SCP literature, concentration indicators are still used as the main **structural indicators**. Furthermore, empirical research based on the SCP paradigm often finds the anticipated direction between structure, conduct and performance, although such relationships are usually weak in terms of their statistical significance. To reiterate, an overriding finding from this literature is that market structure does not appear to matter much in explaining bank performance and as such questions whether concentration indicators really can be interpreted as indicators of competitive behaviour.

BOX 20.1 COMPETITION IN UK BANKING

UK regulators are not too happy with competition in the UK banking sector. In 2000, the report on 'Competition in UK banking' (also known as the Cruickshank Report) highlighted a number of concerns about the lack of effective competition. In particular, the Cruickshank report found that:

- the market was highly concentrated, especially for SME banking;

- there was a lack of information provided to personal customers and SMEs, and customers perceived significant barriers to switching current accounts; and

- the banks were effectively in control of the money transmission service, resulting in barriers to entry, poor service levels, high charges and a lack of innovation.

---

[3] There is a large and well-established literature on the measurement of efficiency frontiers, which can be divided into two main streams: parametric techniques, such as stochastic frontier analysis (SFA), and non-parametric techniques, such as data envelopment analysis (DEA). A review of the early literature is provided by Berger and Humphrey (1997), while more recent literature is reviewed by Hughes and Mester (2014).

BOX 20.1 Competition in UK banking (*continued*)

Since then, a number of regulatory interventions have sought to address the problems. Several investigations were carried out, focusing on particular aspects of banking, including personal current accounts, SME banking and cash ISAs. The European Commission also conducted a sector inquiry into retail banking in 2007.

Nonetheless, more than a decade after the report, there has been only limited progress. In addition, the global financial crisis of 2007–2009 has contributed to a worsening of the situation, with concentration increasing in most banking markets. Specifically, as highlighted by the Independent Banking Commission (IBC), most banking markets experienced little change between 2000 and 2007 and saw a marked increase in concentration from 2008 onwards (see Figure 20.3). For example, the total market share of main Personal Current Account of the four largest

banks – Barclays, HSBC, Lloyds Banking Group and Royal Bank of Scotland – fell from 74% in 2000 to 64% in 2008, but increased to 77% in 2010 as a result of the Lloyds/HBOS merger (IBC, 2011).

More recently though, some new competitors have entered the UK retail banking market, for example the establishment of new banks Metro Bank and Virgin Money through the acquisition of Northern Rock. And the Lloyds Banking Group divestments are intended to create an effective 'challenger' bank. The Office of Fair Trading (2012) believes that these changes are a potential turning point for the sector. Coupled with a new regulatory approach by the Financial Conduct Authority, state aid divestments and new entry should help make the market more dynamic and drive strong customer-focused competition.

Sources: Independent Banking Commission (2011); Office of Fair Trading (2012).

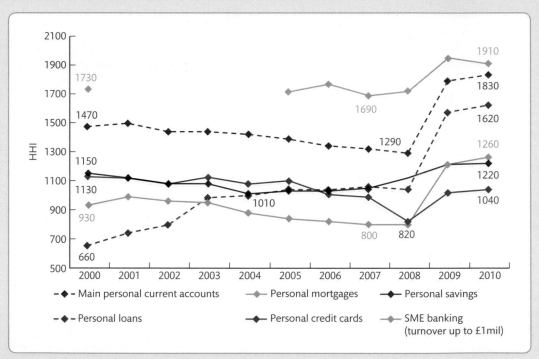

Figure 20.3 Concentration levels in UK retail banking (measured by HHI)

Source: Independent Commission on Banking (2011) p. 167.

20.3 Non-structural measures of banking sector competition

Limitations in the SCP approach have led to the development of the so-called **non-structural indicators**, which have their roots in the **New Empirical Industrial Organization (NEIO)**. The NEIO approaches are based on the direct observation of conduct. More specifically, NEIO studies attempt to evaluate how firms set their prices and quantities. The most widely used non-structural indicators of competition in the banking literature are the Panzar–Rosse H-statistic, the Lerner index and more recently the Boone indicator. Another strand of literature examines the dynamics of banking business using POP indicators of competition.

20.3.1 Panzar–Rosse H-statistic

Rosse and Panzar (1977) and Panzar and Rosse (1987) developed models of oligopolistic, competitive and monopolistically competitive markets and derived a test statistic to distinguish among them. This test has become known as the **Panzar–Rosse statistic** (also known as the **H-statistic** and the *revenue test*). This test is based on the empirical observation of the impact on firm-level revenues of variations in the prices of the factors of production. Built into the test is an explicit assumption of profit-maximising behaviour on the part of the firms. The intuition is straightforward in the cases of perfect competition and monopoly.

Let's consider the impact of a simultaneous equiproportionate increase in all of the firm's factor-input prices (cost of production). This implies an equiproportionate increase in the total cost of producing any given level of output, and an upward shift in the positions of the LRAC (long-run average cost) and the LRMC (long-run marginal cost) functions.

If the market is operating under perfect competition, when a firm's cost of production increases, the market price must increase in exactly the same proportion, so that each firm continues to earn only a normal profit in the long run. The increase in market price will cause a reduction in the level of demand, which in turn will require a decrease in the quantity of output. The required adjustment in the total quantity of output is achieved by a reduction in the number of firms. However, for those firms that survive, total revenue increases in the same proportion as total cost and in the same proportion as the original increase in factor prices. Therefore, in perfect competition, total revenue changes by the same amount as changes in input costs.

Let's now observe firms' behaviour under monopoly conditions (assuming horizontal LRAC and LRMC functions). In this case, to maximise profits, the monopolist must adjust price and output (recall that for profit maximisation, marginal revenue equals marginal cost). As a consequence, an increase in costs (factor prices) causes a decline in the monopolist's total revenue. Therefore, in monopoly, the sum of the elasticities of revenue with respect to each factor price is negative.

The empirical observation of the behaviour of firms in response to a change in input prices is at the base of the Panzar–Rosse test. More specifically, it measures the impact on the firm revenues of changes in costs. The H-statistic is calculated from a reduced form revenue equation and measures the sum of elasticities of total revenue of the firm with respect to the firm's input prices, which can be written as follows:

$$H = \sum_{k=1}^{m} \frac{\partial R_i^*}{\partial w_{ki}} \frac{w_{ki}}{R_i^*}$$

(20.5)

where R_i is the revenues of bank i (* indicates equilibrium values); w_i is a vector of m factor input prices of bank i. Market power is measured by the extent to which a change in factor input prices ∂w_{ki} is reflected in the equilibrium revenues ∂R_i^* earned by bank i. More specifically, H is equal to zero or negative when the competitive structure is a monopoly or a perfectly colluding oligopoly. When H is equal to 1, it indicates perfect competition and $0 < H < 1$ indicates monopolistic competition. Table 20.2 summarises these effects and provides a guide to the interpretation of the H-statistic. Although this was not specified by Panzar and Rosse (1987), it can be shown that under stronger assumptions (in particular a constant price elasticity of demand across bank-size markets and countries), it is also possible to interpret the H-statistic 'continuously' in particular between 0 and 1, in the sense that higher values of H indicate stronger competition than lower values.

The Panzar–Rosse approach has found widespread application in the banking literature due to its modest data requirements, single-equation linear estimation and robustness to market definition. In applying the H-statistic to the banking sector, a methodological choice needs to be made on how to define a bank's production process. The approach to input/output definition traditionally follows the intermediation approach, which was originally developed by Sealey and Lindley (1977) and posits that loans and securities are outputs, whereas deposits, labour and capital are inputs to the production process of banks. Specifically, the input variables commonly used in this type of studies are the average cost of labour, deposits and capital. The Panzar–Rosse revenue test is usually implemented through estimation of the following regression, using bank-level data:

$$ln\,(Revenue_{i,t}) = \alpha + \sum\nolimits_{j=1}^{J}\beta_i w_{j,i,t} + \Theta'X_{i,t} + \eta_{i,t} \tag{20.6}$$

where $Revenue_{i,t}$ is the total revenue of bank i in year t; $w_{j,i,t}$ is the price of factor input j for bank i in market j; $X_{i,t}$ is a vector of exogenous control variables; and $\eta_{i,t} =$ is random disturbance term.

The Panzar–Rosse H-statistic is then defined as:

$$H = \sum\nolimits_{j=1}^{J}\beta_j \tag{20.7}$$

where $j = 1, \ldots J$, and J is the number of inputs included in the calculations.

The dependent variable is defined as the natural logarithm of total revenue (or total revenue over total assets). The decision to consider the total revenue, rather than only the interest part, is to account for the fact that non-interest income has increased dramatically in recent

Table 20.2 H-statistics: interpretation

H-statistics	Competitive environment
$H \leq 0$	Monopoly or collusive oligopoly. In this case, an increase in costs causes output to fall and price to increase. As firms are profit-maximising, they must be operating on the price-elastic portion of their demand function. As a consequence, total revenue will fall.
$H = 1$	Perfect competition. In this case, an increase in costs causes some firms to exit the market. Price will increase and the revenue of the survivor firms will increase at the same rate as the increase in costs.
$0 < H < 1$	Monopolistic competition. In this case, an increase in costs causes revenues to increase at a rate slower than the rate of increase in costs.

years, as has the share of non-interest income from fee-based products and off-balance-sheet activities to total revenue. As discussed above, following the intermediation approach, it is commonly assumed that there are three inputs to the bank production process: deposits, labour and capital. Given these three inputs, the factor input prices are generally defined as follows: 1) the average cost of deposits is defined as interest expenses/total deposits and money market funding; 2) the average cost of labour is calculated as personnel costs/total assets; 3) the average cost of capital is proxied by other non-interest expenses/total assets. The control variables in equation (20.6) can include a number of bank-specific factors, that are relevant to the modern banking business. These are additional explanatory variables which reflect differences in costs, size, risk, structure and product mix and which should, theoretically, stem from the cost and revenue functions underlying the Panzar–Rosse H-statistic. These are generally balance sheet ratios that reflect banks' behaviour and risk profile, and usually include equity to total assets ratio, net loans to total assets ratio, a diversification measure (for example, the proportion of non-interest income among total operating income) and a full set of individual-year dummy variables. The literature also suggests controlling for bank size (the logarithm of total bank assets) since larger banks tend to earn more revenue, *ceteris paribus*, in ways unrelated to variations in input prices. Recall that the two extreme cases of monopoly and perfect competition are identified by $H < 0$ and $H = 1$ respectively.

An important feature of the H-statistic is that the tests must be undertaken on observations that are in long-run equilibrium. In particular, as stated by Molyneux *et al.* (1994) p. 449: 'The empirical test for equilibrium is suggested by the fact that competitive capital markets will equalise risk-adjusted rates of return across banks such that, in equilibrium, rates of return should not be correlated statistically with input prices.' The equilibrium test can be performed by recalculating the Panzar–Rosse H-statistics, replacing the dependent variable in equation (20.6) with the natural log of return on assets (which is equal to net income over total assets). The findings will be interpreted as follows: $H < 0$ would indicate disequilibrium and $H = 0$ would indicate equilibrium. If the market is in equilibrium, then the Panzar–Rosse H- statistic can be meaningfully interpreted.

A study by Sun (2011) investigates the degree of bank competition in the euro area, the US and the UK before and after the introduction of the euro and attempts to assess the impact of the recent financial crisis on bank competition. The results suggest that the level of bank competition converged across euro area countries in the wake of the introduction of the euro; however, the 2007–2009 financial crisis seems to have led to a fall in competition in several countries. The main results of this study (summarised in Table 20.3) seem to indicate a decline in competition since the introduction of the single currency. Indeed, the finding that larger and more financially integrated countries exhibit less competitive behaviour is in line with recent studies (Bikker *et al.*, 2012).

20.3.2 Conjectural variations approach

In the extreme cases of perfect competition and monopoly, firms are assumed to take no notice of other firms' price and output decisions. In the case of monopoly, the monopolist does not consider its rivals (or believes he has no rivals). In the case of perfect competition, each firm is too small to influence market prices. In many markets though, including banking markets, there are a number of firms that have influence over market prices and output quantities and, as such, influence the behaviour of competitors. In this case, each firm will try to anticipate its competitors' reactions to its changes in terms of prices and quantities. What

Table 20.3 Panzar–Rosse H-statistic

	Before EMU	After EMU	Δ pre and post EMU	After crisis	Δ pre and post crisis
Austria	0.583***	0.604***	0.0209	0.707***	0.107
Finland	0.797***	0.550***	−0.247**	0.647***	0.0964
France	0.638***	0.584***	−0.0544	0.625***	0.0414
Germany	0.432***	0.449***	0.0171	0.364***	−0.0849***
Greece	0.816***	0.518***	−0.298***	0.385***	−0.133
Ireland	1.020***	0.754***	−0.266	0.589***	−0.165
Italy	0.878***	0.588***	−0.290***	0.496***	−0.0917***
Netherlands	0.896***	0.407***	0.488***	0.611***	0.204***
Portugal	0.705***	0.679***	−0.0254	0.849***	0.170
Spain	0.704***	0.795***	0.0908**	0.505***	−0.290***
Euro-area	0.699***	0.518***	0.182***	0.444***	−0.0737***
UK	0.506***	0.647***	0.141***	0.618***	−0.0289
US	0.309***	0.425***	0.116***	0.270***	−0.155***

Note: The table displays the estimated average H-statistics of reduced-form bank revenue equations estimated using pooled OLS over the period 1995–2009. The pre-EMU period is 1995–2000; the post-EMU period is 2001–2009. The post-financial crisis period is 2008–2009. All variables in the estimations are annual data from Bankscope.

*p < 0.05;

**p < 0.01;

***p < 0.001

Source: Adapted from Sun (2011) p. 20.

each firm believe its competitors' response to its own actions will be is known as *conjectural variation*.

Models based on the idea that a bank/firm takes into account the reaction of competitors when setting price and output quantities are known as the *conjectural variations (CV) approach*. These models, based on oligopoly theory, were introduced by Iwata (1974), Bresnahan (1982) and Lau (1982).

The conjectural variations approach is built around the principle that profit-maximising firms in short-run equilibrium will choose prices or quantities where marginal costs equal marginal revenues. In contrast to the Panzar–Rosse H-statistic (discussed in Section 20.3.1), the conjectural variation method estimates a structural equation that includes both supply and demand.

More specifically, the CV approach is based on a demand specification, a cost specification and a specification of the interdependence of market participants (the degree of collusion). The degree of competition in the market is evaluated on the basis of the estimated interdependence of market participants. The CV model assumes that firms produce homogenous products and face exogenous market prices; if the price charged by a firm is greater than its marginal cost, the CV model assumes that there is a certain degree of market power (defined as deviation of a firm's pricing to the marginal cost, λ). The parameter λ can therefore be interpreted as a measure of competitiveness. Empirically, the relationship can be written as:

$$P(Q, Y; \alpha) + \lambda QP'(Q, Y, \alpha) = C'(Q, Z; \beta) \tag{20.8}$$

Table 20.4 Interpretation of the CV parameter (λ)

Market structure	Conduct	CV parameter
Perfect collusion (cartel)	A firm expects full retaliation from the competitors. An increase of one unit of output by firm i will lead to an increase in the market output by X/xi units.	$\lambda = \sum_{j \neq i}^{n} x_j/x_i$
Cournot–Nash equilibrium	Firms do not expect any response from the competitors. An increase of one unit of output by firm i will lead to an increase of the market output by X/xi units.	$\lambda = 0$
Perfect competition	An increase in output by one firm has no impact on the market price and quantity.	$\lambda = -1$

where P is the market equilibrium price; $P(Q, Y; \alpha)$ is the market inverse demand function; Q is the market output; and $C'(Q, Z; \beta)$ is the marginal cost. α and β are vectors of exogenous variables that shift the demand and cost functions respectively. In this context, λ is the conjectural elasticity of the industry output to a variation of bank i output, that is it is a measure of the perceived response of the industry to a change in quantity by firm i. The greater the value of λ, the more the firm's pricing deviates from competitive pricing, and therefore the lower the level of competitiveness in the market. The empirical estimation of λ therefore provides a test of firms' competitive behaviour as it can be interpreted, as illustrated in Table 20.4.

Equation (20.8) can be rearranged as:

$$\lambda = \eta(P)\left[\frac{P - MC}{P}\right] \tag{20.9}$$

where $\eta(P)$ is the price elasticity of demand and $[\frac{P-MC}{P}]$ is the well-known **Lerner index** (Lerner, 1934), a conventional measure of market power, calculated as a firm's mark-up over its price (see Section 20.3.3).

The CV method has been widely applied in banking studies, from the early work of Spiller and Favaro (1984), Shaffer (1993), Shaffer and DiSalvo (1994), Berg and Kim (1998) to more recent studies by Bikker and Haaf (2002), Uchida and Tsutsui (2005), Delis *et al.* (2008) and Coccorese (2005, 2009).

20.3.3 Lerner index

The Lerner index of monopoly power (Lerner, 1934) is an indicator of the degree of market power and it is a well-established measure of competition in the banking literature. It represents the extent to which market power allows firms to fix a price above marginal cost (MC). It is based on the assumption that in perfect competition, price equals marginal cost and therefore a measure of the degree to which price exceeds marginal cost provides a useful indicator or measure of market power (this is based on neoclassical theory).

Accordingly, the Lerner index is estimated as follows:

$$L = \frac{P - MC}{P} \tag{20.10}$$

Table 20.5 Lerner index – banks in Asia Pacific (average figures, 2003–2010)

Country	Number of banks*	CR-3**	Lerner index
Australia	48	0.6827	0.2954
China	35	0.5191	0.4343
Hong Kong	32	0.7064	0.4268
India	226	0.3409	0.3093
Indonesia	134	0.4562	0.2653
Japan	597	0.4089	0.3091
Korea	31	0.5057	0.3486
Malaysia	24	0.4563	0.4315
Pakistan	98	0.4376	0.2671
Philippines	78	0.5088	0.3175
Singapore	16	0.9156	0.4889
Sri Lanka	55	0.6165	0.2669
Taiwan	62	0.2719	0.2753
Thailand	64	0.4550	0.3622

Notes: *Number of banks used in the empirical analysis to derive marginal cost measures for calculation of the Lerner; ** CR-3 = 3-bank assets concentration ratio.

Source: Fu *et al*. (2014).

The Lerner index ranges between a minimum value of zero and a maximum value of one. In perfect competition, $P = MC$ so $L = 0$. In monopoly $P > MC$ and if $MC > 0, 0 < L < 1$.

As the Lerner index provides a measure of a firm's market power based on the relationship between its price and marginal cost, the first step is to estimate the marginal cost. There are two ways to estimate marginal cost. The first is simple – using average (variable) costs, defined as the total (variable) costs divided by total assets (or total income). This method has the advantage of being straightforward but not very accurate. The second approach is more complex as it requires the estimation of a cost function. This is usually a translog cost function with a single output (total assets) and three input prices (deposits, labour and physical capital).[4] Table 20.5 illustrates estimates of the Lerner index for banks in the Asia Pacific region indicating that Taiwan has the most competitive banking system with a Lerner index of 0.2719. In contrast, Singaporean banks appear the least competitive (Lerner index of 0.4889).

20.3.4 Boone indicator

An alternative measure of competition, based on the *efficiency hypothesis* (see Section 20.2.2), is the one proposed by Boone (2008), which has become known as the **Boone indicator** and relies on relative profit differences (RPD). This indicator is based on the assumption that competition enhances performance, as efficient banks (i.e. those with lower marginal costs) increase their market share and profits. This effect will be greater, the stronger the competition. As an industry becomes more competitive, given a certain level of efficiency of

---

[4] For more detail, see Liu *et al*. (2013).

each individual bank, the profits of the more efficient banks increase relative to those of less efficient bank counterparts.

The Boone indicator can be estimated from the following simple equation:

$$ln\,(MS)_{i,j} = \alpha + \beta \ln MC_{i,j} \tag{20.11}$$

where $MS_{i,j}$ is the market share of bank i in market j; $MC_{i,j}$ is marginal cost of bank i in market j; and β is the Boone indicator of market power. In this context, the market can be defined in terms of products, for example the loans market, the deposits market, etc.

Recall that the more efficient a firm (or bank), that is the lower its marginal cost, the greater its market share should be, all other things being equal. And the greater the market share, the greater the profits, ceteris paribus. Hence, the estimated β should be negative. As competition intensifies, the slope of the regression should become steeper since inefficient banks are punished more harshly by fiercer competition.

Similarly to the estimation of the Lerner index, the estimation of the Boone indicators requires the computation of the marginal cost, which can be approximated by the ratio of average variable costs to total income (or total assets) or, in a more sophisticated way, it can be derived by the estimation of a translog cost function.

Applications of the Boone indicator to the analysis of competition in banking include van Leuvensteijn *et al.* (2011) and Shaeck and Cihák (2014). The method has a number of appealing properties, including the possibility of evaluating competition in different products/markets. The Boone indicator has a strong theoretical foundation. In addition, the Boone indicator does not impose restrictive assumptions, unlike the Panzar–Rosse H-statistics, which requires the market to be in long-run equilibrium. Finally, it has the same data requirements as the Lerner index. The approach has also attracted some criticism, for example the assumption that because of efficiency improvements, banks increase market share without decreasing prices, that is without passing at least partially the efficiency gains on to consumers. Schiersch and Schmidt-Ehmcke (2010) argue that the empirical application of the Boone indicator is not as robust as its theoretical properties as it doesn't take into account firm size. They argue that the empirical relationship between a firm's efficiency and its profitability does not behave as designed in Boone's theoretical framework, where the most efficient firm is always, by design, also the biggest.

20.3.5 Persistence of profits (POP)

The **persistence of profits (POP)** hypothesis was developed by Mueller (1977, 1986) and focuses on the dynamics of profitability, accounting for the possibility that markets are not in equilibrium when observed. More specifically, the POP hypothesis posits that if entry and exit are sufficiently free to eliminate any abnormal profit, then all firms' profit rates will tend to converge rapidly towards the same long-run average value. The alternative is that some incumbent firm has the capability to prevent imitation, or delay or block entry (inhibiting competition). In this case, abnormal profit tends to persist from year to year, and differences in firm-level long-run average profit rates may be sustained indefinitely. The extent to which firm- or industry-level profits converge to long-run values reflects the degree of competition in the market. The slower the speed of adjustment, the stronger the persistence of profits, the lower the competition.

Empirically, the POP literature focuses on the 'standardised profit rate', which is defined as the difference between the firm's actual profit rate and the average industry profit rate in a given year. As explained by Lipczynski *et al.* (2013), persistence of profitability can be estimated using a first-order autoregressive AR (1) model:

$$\pi_{i,t} = \alpha_i + \lambda_i \pi_{i,t-1} + u_{i,t} \tag{20.12}$$

where $\pi_{i,t}$ is the profit of bank i at time t (for example, the return on assets); and $\pi_{i,t-1}$ is the profit of bank i at time t–1. λ_i represents the strength of profit persistence and can be read as follows: if $\lambda_i = 0$, there is no association between $\pi_{i,t}$ and $\pi_{i,t-1}$. This is the case of perfect competition. If $0 < \lambda_i < 1$, there is a positive association between $\pi_{i,t}$ and $\pi_{i,t-1}$, or evidence of persistence of profit (in the short run).[5]

While there is extensive empirical evidence of the POP hypothesis in various industries, there is only a handful of studies in banking. This is possibly due to the fact that it is relatively difficult to build long time series using banking data. Some of the early work using this approach was undertaken by Berger *et al.* (2000) and Goddard *et al.* (2004). Overall, this literature finds evidence of profit persistence, driven by bank-specific and country-specific characteristics. A recent study by Goddard *et al.* (2011) examines the intensity of competition in 65 national banking industries and reports that the persistence of profit is weaker (i.e. competition is stronger) for banks in developing countries than for those in developed countries. The authors also note that persistence is stronger when entry barriers are high and competition is low.

20.4 Comparing competition measures – are they consistent?

We have introduced a number of competition measures, which are commonly used by academics and regulators alike to estimate the competitive conditions in banking markets. Table 20.6 compares these competition measures for EU banking markets over the period 2000–2009. Looking at the 3-firm concentration ratio (CR-3), Belgium's banking industry shows the highest concentration, with the market share of three largest banks summing up to 85 per cent of the assets of the whole banking system. In contrast, Luxembourg has the lowest level of concentration, with a CR-3 of 0.26 (the market share of the three largest banks represents only 26 per cent of the market's total assets). The HHI shows a different competition pattern to the CR-3 concentration ratio. Looking at the HHI (which includes the market share of all banks in the market) Austria's appears to be the most concentrated banking market. Liu *et al.* (2013) estimate the Panzar–Rosse H-statistic using both the total interest income and the total income as revenue measure. These are the H-stat (II) and H-stat (TI) columns in Table 20.6.

These measures show broadly consistent results (indeed, the correlation coefficient between them is 96 per cent, as reported in Table 20.7). Looking at both H-stat (II) and H-stat (TI), the results suggest that banks in Denmark, France and Luxembourg operate under monopoly conditions, while banks in other countries generate revenue under monopolistic competition.

---

[5] The industrial organisation literature distinguishes between *short-run persistence* (which refers to the degree of correlation between consecutive values of π for the same firm) and *long-run persistence* (which refers to the degree of variation in the long-run average standardised profit rates between firms). A detailed analysis of these concepts is outside the remit of this textbook and we refer the reader to an industrial organisation textbook (Lipczynski *et al.*, 2013).

Table 20.6 Competition measures for selected EU countries (average values, 2000–2009)

Country	No. of bank obs.	CR-3	HHI	H-stat (II)	H-stat (TI)	Lerner	Boone	POP
Austria	1529	0.66	4595	0.58	0.50	9.17	−0.87	0.38
Belgium	352	0.85	2851	0.52	0.56	20.21	−0.89	0.54
Germany	11227	0.69	1067	0.39	0.37	7.30	−0.78	0.34
Denmark	606	0.78	3000	−0.24	−0.13	15.14	−0.39	0.30
Spain	643	0.76	1024	0.02	0.10	25.81	−0.80	0.65
France	1652	0.56	710	−0.46	−0.15	22.71	−0.95	0.46
UK	682	0.57	2251	−0.06	0.01	23.98	0.02	0.53
Italy	2702	0.49	592	0.55	0.49	10.92	−0.15	−0.03
Luxembourg	583	0.26	739	−0.47	−0.03	32.98	−0.22	0.52
Mean	2220	0.62	1870	0.09	0.19	18.69	−0.56	0.41

Note: CR-3 is 3-bank assets concentration ratio; HHI is the Herfindahl–Hirschman index (calculated using asset market shares); H-stat (II) is the H-statistic (using interest income as the dependent variable); H-stat (TI) is the H-statistic (using total income as the dependent variable); Lerner is the Lerner index; Boone is the Boone indicator; POP is the short-run profit persistence parameter λ (ROA as the profit ratio). The measures are calculated using the raw data format from Bankscope over the period from 2000 to 2009, except the CR-3 ratio, which is collected from the World Bank Financial Development and Structure Database (updated at 2010).

Source: Adapted from Liu *et al.* (2013).

To answer the question as to whether the different competition measures are consistent, Liu *et al.* (2013) present a correlation matrix. From Table 20.7, we can see that the Lerner index is significantly correlated with measures of competition derived using the Panzar–Rosse H-statistic (particularly when using interest income as revenue measure) and short-run profit persistence parameter (POP). Competition measures derived from the estimation of the Boone indicator, meanwhile, do not show any significant correlation with other competition

Table 20.7 Correlation matrix for the competition measures

	CR-3	HHI	H-stat (II)	H-stat (TI)	Lerner	Boone	POP
CR-3	1.00						
HHI	0.48	1.00					
H-stat (II)	0.42	0.38	1.00				
H-stat (TI)	0.28	0.30	0.96*	1.00			
Lerner	−0.41	−0.36	−0.715*	−0.59	1.00		
Boone	−0.55	−0.20	−0.21	−0.25	0.23	1.00	
POP	0.17	0.09	−0.40	−0.34	0.67*	−0.32	1.00

Note: CR-3 is 3-bank assets concentration ratio; HHI is the Herfindahl–Hirschman index (calculated using asset market shares); H-stat (II) is the H-statistic (using interest income as the dependent variable); H-stat (TI) is the H-statistic (using total income as the dependent variable); Lerner is the Lerner index; Boone is the Boone indicator; POP is the short-run profit persistence parameter λ (ROA as the profit ratio).

*$p < 0.05$;

**$p < 0.01$;

***$p < 0.001$

Source: Adapted from Liu *et al.* (2013).

measures and seem to contradict the findings of both the Lerner index and the H-statistic. The profit persistence indicator shows significant correlation with the Lerner index but not the other competition measures.

To summarise, from the results presented by Liu *et al.* (2013) it is possible to find consistent evaluation of competitive conditions from the estimation of H-statistic, Lerner index and (to a certain extent) profit persistence. Given their popularity in empirical banking research, this result is reassuring. Structural measures of competition (the CR-n ratio and the HHI) are not good proxies of competition. As for the Boone indicator, although theoretically appealing and relatively easy to compute, doubts remain concerning its effective empirical application.

20.5 Competition and risk in banking

So far we have outlined the different approaches to measuring competition in banking. However, whether competition is a force for good in banking has always been controversial, as the potential benefits deriving from increased competition have to be weighed against the risks of potential instability. The traditional view is that competition would lead to excessive bank risk taking and could therefore result in a higher likelihood of individual bank failure. Bank failures can be costly, can lead to contagion as well as systemic failure (see Chapter 8). As a consequence, the banking industry historically has been heavily regulated. This traditional view is known as the **competition-fragility view** and is sometimes referred to as the **charter value** view of banking according to which banks under greater (actual and potential) competitive pressure choose more excessive risk, thus increasing fragility.

More recently the competition-fragility view has been challenged by various commentators who argue that competition can have a stabilising influence on a banking system. One argument is that as loan interest rates are lower in a competitive system this means that fewer borrowers are likely to default and as such great competition can aid stability. Various theoretical studies point to evidence of this **competition-stability view** that has also been confirmed in a number of empirical studies. Some even find evidence of a U-shaped relationship where competition first reduces stability and then after a certain point aids stability.

In the aftermath of the 2007–2009 financial crisis, supporters of the competition-fragility view point to the house price bubble that led up to the banking crisis – particularly in the US, the UK and Ireland. They argue that banks were competing so aggressively in the lending market (particularly in the market for residential mortgages) that they neglected to accurately estimate the true risk of borrowers. They use the property price bubble as a clear indication that competition in banking leads to increased risk taking, with the now well-known adverse consequences. Another issue brought to the fore by the 2007–2009 financial crisis is that large banks are often deemed to be too big, too interconnected or too complex to fail. In these cases large banks may obtain implicit (or explicit) subsidies via government safety nets (see also Chapter 19). This may increase moral hazard and encourage large banks to take on excessive risks.

Before we can discuss the relationship between competition and risk (and ultimately between competition and financial stability), we need to outline the risk indicators. These are reviewed in Sections 20.5.1 to 20.5.2.

20.5.1 Accounting-based measures of bank risk

The empirical banking literature proposed a number of different measures of risk, ranging from **accounting-based measures** to more complex market-based measures. The simplest are accounting ratios derived from bank accounting information. Two commonly used indicators are the loan-loss provision and loan-loss reserves ratios as higher levels of reserves or provisions can indicate greater banking risk. The ratio of loan-loss reserves to gross loans and the ratio of loan-loss provisions to average gross loans are considered indicators of credit risk. However, these indicators only partly reflect the quality of the loan portfolio, since variation in provisioning across banks may reflect different internal policies regarding problem loan classification, reserve requirements and write-off policies. As such, researchers have sought to use a broader indicator of bank risk, namely, insolvency risk as measured using the **Z-score** indicator. The Z-score has become a popular measure of bank risk and has been widely used in the banking literature (Laeven and Levine, 2009; Čihák *et al.*, 2012b; Lepetit and Strobel, 2013).

20.5.1.1 Z-scores

The Z-score measures the distance from insolvency for a given bank combining bank profitability, capitalisation and volatility of returns. The Z-score is defined as:

$$Z = \frac{\overline{ROA} + \overline{EA}}{\sigma_{ROA}} \tag{20.13}$$

where $\overline{ROA}$ is the average return on assets, $\overline{EA}$ is the average equity capital ratio and σ_{ROA} is the standard deviation of return on assets.

In other words, the Z-score is an indicator of a bank's probability of insolvency as it estimates the number of standard deviations that the bank's profits have to fall below its expected value before its equity becomes negative. The value of the Z-score depends positively on the bank's profitability and capital ratio and negatively on the variability of the bank's profits. A higher Z-score indicates that a bank is more stable, or the less likely it is that the bank will become bankrupt. In other words, a higher Z-score value indicates lower risk.

As with all accounting measures, a limitation associated with using the Z-scores relates to the fact that they are static and backward-looking measures at a point in time. In addition, even if they accurately reflect portfolio quality and risk, managers are likely to have some timing discretion over these measures, and there is evidence that such discretion is exercised in a manner that minimises regulatory costs.

20.5.2 Market-based risk measure

To overcome the well-known shortcoming of accounting measures of risk, researchers have sought to use **market-based measures of bank risk**. These include the volatility of stock prices, Moody's KMV expected default frequency (EDF) and the five-year cumulative probability of default (PD) indicators. Both EDF and PD refer to the probability of default within the short and medium terms (one and five years, respectively) and can therefore be considered representative of all banking risks. In addition, both variables are free from managerial discretion and are usually estimated through an economic cycle (PD estimates are long-run probabilities of default which take into consideration upturns and downturns in the economy).

20.5.2.1   The distance to default model

In order to estimate the insolvency risk of listed banks, it is possible to adapt Black and Scholes' (1973) and Merton's (1974) distance to default (DD) model.

In general terms, the DD model considers equity as a call option on the assets of a firm, with a strike price equal to the face value of the liabilities at time T when the liabilities mature. At time T, if the value of the firm's assets is greater than the face value of its liabilities, then equity holders will exercise their option and pay off the debt holders. If the value of the assets is not enough to fully repay the firm's debts, then the call option loses its value and equity holders will let it expire. In this case, the firm files for bankruptcy and the model assumes that ownership is transferred to the debt holders at no cost, although the payoff for equity holders is zero. In the DD model, the probability of bankruptcy can be estimated as follows:

$$P = N\left(-\frac{ln\left(\frac{V_A}{D}\right) + \left(u - \delta - \left(\frac{\sigma^2 A}{2}\right)\right)T}{\sigma_A \sqrt{T}}\right) \tag{20.14}$$

where P is the probability of bankruptcy; N() is the cumulative normal density function; V_A is the value of assets; D is the face value of debts proxied by total liabilities; u is the expected return; δ is the dividend rate estimated as total dividends over total liabilities + market value of equity; σ_A is the standard deviation of assets (asset volatility); T is the time to expiration (taken to be one year).

In empirical applications of the DD model, V_A and σ_A are non-observable and therefore are commonly proxied following the model outlined by Bharath and Shumway (2008) to estimate the probability of bankruptcy. It is important to note that the market-based measures can be derived only for publicly quoted banks, that is those banks that have equity, bonds, credit default swaps or other publicly traded instruments.

20.6   Bank competition and stability

The impact of bank competition on financial stability remains a highly controversial issue, which is the subject of both academic and policy debates. As clearly illustrated by a recent OECD report:

> Studies exploring the complex interactions between competition and stability in retail and commercial banking come to the ambiguous conclusion that competition can be both good and bad for stability. Policy measures that strike an acceptable balance remain elusive.
>
> OECD (2011)

Theoretical models of the relationship between increased competition and stability reach opposing results, often because of the different assumptions underlying models of bank behaviour. Yet empirical studies may yield different results due to the different measures of competition and risk discussed above.

Table 20.8 summarises some selected studies presenting evidence in favour of and against increased competition in banking.

Table 20.8 Empirical evidence of the competition-stability relationship

Competition-fragility view			Competition-stability view		
Authors	Key variables	Key results	Authors	Key variables	Key results
Rhoades and Rutz (1982)	Competition: CR-3 (deposit) ratio Risk: volatility of ROA; equity/assets; total loans/total assets; net loan losses/total loans	Greater market power, less risk	Jayaratne and Strahan (1998)	Competition: deregulation Risk: NPLs; net loan charge-offs; loan-loss provisions	Deregulation decreases credit risk
Keeley (1990)	Market power: Tobin's q (market to book value of assets) Risk: market value of the banks' capital-to-assets; interest rates on large CDs	Competition encourages risk taking	De Nicolo (2000); De Nicolo *et al.* (2004)	Market power: bank size (total assets) Risk: Z-score	Greater bank size is associated with greater risk and lower charter values
Dick (2006)	Competition: proxied by deregulation Risk: charged-off losses/total loans; loan-loss provisions/total loans	Competition increases credit risk	Boyd and De Nicolo (2005)	Competition: concentration (HHI) Risk: Z-score	Higher concentration leads to higher probability of default Greater bank size is associated with greater risk
Berger *et al.* (2009)	Competition: Lerner index Risk: NPLs/total loans; Z-score; equity/total assets	Banks with greater market power have less risk	Yeyati and Micco (2007)	Competition: H-statistic Risk: Z-score	Competition leads to less risk
Beck *et al.* (2013)	Competition: Lerner index Risk: Z-score	Positive relationship between market power and stability	Uhde and Heimeshoff (2009)	Competition: concentration (HHI) Risk: Z-score	Concentration leads to higher risk

Evidence on the competition-fragility view

Rhoades and Rutz (1982) offer one of the first empirical studies on the relationship between competition and risk in US banking over 1969–1978. They employ the CR-3 deposit concentration ratio as a proxy for (the lack of) bank competition and four alternative risk indicators including the volatility of ROA, equity to assets ratio, total loans to total assets and net loan losses to total loans. The authors provide evidence that Hick's 'quiet life' hypothesis (see Section 20.4) holds and banks with greater market power tend to be less risk-inclined than those operating in competitive markets.

In another study on US banks, Keeley (1990) investigates the relationship between market power, measured as the market to book value of assets ratio (i.e. the Tobin's q) and risk. This latter is measured as the market value of the banks' capital-to-asset and interest rates on large CDs. In line with Rhoades and Rutz (1982), the author provides evidence that bank competition encourages risk taking as institutions with lower market-to-book assets (with less market power) were more likely to take on greater risks.

In a study on the effects of branching deregulation, Dick (2006) contends that banks are more likely to take on more risk when barriers across states are lower and geographic diversification increases. The author employs the ratio of charged-off losses to total loans and loan-loss provisions to total loans as proxies for risk. Evidence indicates that branch deregulation led to greater loan losses, thereby suggesting that competition increases credit risk.

Berger *et al.* (2009) use the Lerner index to measure competition for a sample of more than 8,000 banks across 23 developed nations over 1999–2005. The main findings support the traditional competition-fragility view that banks with greater market power also have less overall risk exposure.

Evidence on the competition-stability view

A number of studies have produced results opposite to those reviewed above, namely that competition appears to be associated with a lower probability of bank failure. For example, in a study on US banks over the period 1975–1992, Jayaratne and Strahan (1998) conclude that deregulation of branching restrictions significantly decreased credit risk (expressed as non-performing loans, net loan charge-offs and loan-loss provisions). A possible explanation for these results is that greater competition encouraged bank managers to carry out better screening and monitoring activities, leading to better credit quality overall.

De Nicolo (2000) and De Nicolo *et al.* (2004) investigated the relationship between bank size, charter value and the Z-score (see Section 20.5.1) as proxy for insolvency risk. The study reveals that greater bank asset size is associated with greater risk and lower charter values. The (debatable) assumption that bigger banks have more market power leads the authors to conclude that competitive banks are less risky.

The empirical analysis carried out by Boyd *et al.* (2006) shows that in US banking, concentration in either deposits or loans markets (measured by the Herfindahl index) leads to higher probabilities of default (as measured by the Z-score). The authors also find that bank size is negatively related to the Z-score, indicating that larger banks face greater risks.

Yeyati and Micco (2007) provide evidence on the relationship between competition and risk for a sample of commercial banks operating in eight Latin American countries over 1993–2002. The authors use the Panzar–Rosse H-statistic (see Section 20.3.1) as a proxy for competition and, as most studies reviewed in this section, the Z-score as a measure for bank risk. One of the key results of the study is that overall competition appears to lead to less risky activities.

Given the conflicting results, the relationship between competition and financial stability is difficult to interpret. It depends on the chosen proxies for competition and risk. It depends on the banking markets analysed (deposit market, loan market, etc.). In addition, it seems to be linked to different types of banks and banking structures.[6] Beck *et al.* (2013) present a comprehensive analysis of attempts to reconcile the different strands of the literature. In addition, the authors explore cross-country heterogeneity in the competition-stability relationship in banking. They find, on average, a positive relationship between market power (measured by the Lerner index) and stability (measured by the Z-score), although there is large cross-country variation in this relationship.

---

[6] A more in-depth discussion of these themes is presented in Casu *et al.* (2012).

20.7 Conclusion

In this chapter we outline the link between banking sector competition and risk. We start by outlining the variety of ways one can measure banking sector competition, highlighting the structure-conduct performance (SCP) paradigm and the use of structural indicators such as concentration ratios and the Herfindahl index. We then go on to explain newer measures of banking sector competition – the so-called non-structural indicators – which include the Panzar–Rosse H-statistic, the Lerner index, the Boone indicator and persistence of profits (POP) measures. We illustrate that these may not always be consistent indicators of banking system competition. Following on from this we describe different ways of measuring bank risk, namely accounting and market-based measures. The main accounting measures include simple ratios such as loan-loss reserves and loan-loss provisions measures of bank credit risk, as well as the bank insolvency risk indicator known as the Z-score. Market-based indicators (other than stock return volatility) can be complicated, and here we briefly outline a distance-to-default bankruptcy prediction indicator of bank risk. Finally, we outline the empirical evidence covering the competition-stability and competition-fragility views.

Overall there is no consensus as to the relationship between competition and risk in banking, as highlighted in the evidence provided in the theoretical and empirical banking literature. A reason for this may be the fact that empirical studies often use different competition measures and risk indicators, as well as varying bank samples and methodologies, to investigate such relationships. So policy makers need to be cautious in implementing policies designed to boost competition unless they are certain such reform does not lead to excessive risk taking. Since the major bank bailouts resulting from the banking sector crash in 2008–2009, various commentators have started to investigate whether government support has resulted in adverse competitive effects. Some argue that banks that were heavily supported by the state have had an unfair competitive advantage over those not supported. Evidence is emerging that such government support had pro-competition effects, although this work remains in its infancy.

Key terms

Accounting-based measures of bank risk	Concentration ratio	Market-based measures of bank risk	Persistence of profits (POP)
Boone indicator	Efficiency hypothesis	New Empirical Industrial Organization (NEIO)	Quiet life hypothesis
Charter value	Efficient structure hypothesis	Non-structural indicators	Structural indicators
Competition-fragility view	Herfindahl–Hirschman index	Panzar–Rosse statistic	Structure-conduct-performance (SCP) paradigm
Competition-stability view	H-statistic		Z-score
	Lerner index		

Key reading

Beck, T., Coyle, D., Dewatripont, M., Freixas, X. and Seabright, P. (2010) *Bailing Out the Banks: Reconciling stability and competition. An analysis of state-supported schemes for financial institutions*, London: CEPR. Available at: **http://dev3.cepr.org/pubs/other/Bailing_out_the_banks.pdf**

Beck, T., De Jonghe, O. and Schepens, G. (2013) 'Bank competition and stability: Cross-country heterogeneity', *Journal of Financial Intermediation*, 22(2), 218–244.

Casu, B., Girardone, C. and Molyneux, P. (2012) 'Is there a conflict between competition and financial stability?' in Barth, J.R., Lin, C. and Wihlborg, C. (eds), *Research Handbook for Banking and Governance*, Cheltenham: Edward Elgar Publishing.

Goddard, J., Molyneux, P., Liu, H. and Wilson, J.O.S. (2011) 'The persistence of bank profit', *Journal of Banking and Finance*, 35, 2881–2890.

Liu, H., Molyneux, P. and Wilson, J.O.S (2013) 'Competition in banking: measurement and interpretation', in Bell, A.R., Brooks, C. and Prokopczuk, M. (eds), *Handbook of Research Methods and Applications in Empirical Finance*, Cheltenham: Edward Elgar.

OECD (2011) *Bank Competition and Financial Stability*, Paris: OECD, Available at: **www.oecd.org/finance/financial-markets/48501035.pdf**

REVISION QUESTIONS AND PROBLEMS

20.1 Outline the main structural measures of competition in banking. What are the main limitations of these measures?

20.2 What does the Herfindahl index tell us about industry concentration?

20.3 What are the main non-structural indicators of competition?

20.4 Explain the main features of the Lerner index and discuss whether it yields similar findings on competition to other non-structural measures.

20.5 What are the main limitations of non-structural competition indicators?

20.6 How do we measure banking system risk?

20.7 Why is the Z-score a preferred accounting measure of bank risk?

20.8 Discuss the two opposing theoretical views, the competition-stability view and the competition-fragility view. Why does the empirical literature provide conflicting results?

20.9 How can more competition lead to greater banking system stability?

20.10 Do state bailouts of major banks distort the competitive environment in banking systems?

Appendix A1

Interest rates, bonds and yields

A1.1   Nominal and real interest rates

Interest rates play a crucial role within the financial system. For example, they influence financial flows within the economy, the distribution of wealth, capital investment and the profitability of financial institutions. It is important to appreciate that an interest rate is a *price*, and that the price relates to *present* claims on resources relative to *future* claims on resources. An interest rate is therefore the price that a borrower pays in order to be able to consume resources now rather than at some point in the future. Correspondingly, it is the price that a lender receives to forego current consumption.

It is common to distinguish between nominal and real interest rates. A *nominal* interest rate is what is normally observed and quoted and represents the actual money paid by the borrower to the lender, expressed as a percentage of the sum borrowed over a stated period of time. The *real* rate of interest is the return if there is no risk and inflation is zero. In most discussions comparing real and nominal interest rates the emphasis is on short-term interest rates and so the focus is on:

$$i = r + P^e \qquad\qquad (A1.1)$$

where
i = nominal rate of interest;

r = real short-term rate of interest;

P^e = a premium based on price expectations (inflation premium).

A1.2   Concept of present value

As we will discuss later on in this appendix, a precise measure of interest rate is yield to maturity. This can be measured on debt market instruments, such as loans and bonds, and requires knowledge of the concept of present value. The present value (PV) of a loan or bond is equal to the current value (i.e. the value today) of a future payment. For instance, to calculate the present value of a one-year £1,000 loan (this is the face value, or FV, of the loan) if the interest rate (r) is 10 per cent we will use the following formula:[1]

$$PV = \frac{FV}{(1 + r)^t}$$ (A1.2)

PV = ?   FV = £1,000

| |
t = today   t = 1 year

$$PV = \frac{FV}{(1 + r)^t} = \frac{£1,000}{(1 + 0.10)^1} = £909$$

This means that given the current interest rate of 10 per cent, today the £1,000 loan is worth £909. To calculate the PV of a two-year loan at the same interest rate:

PV = ?   FV = £1,000

t = today   t = 1 year   t = 2 years

$$PV = \frac{£1,000}{(1 + 0.10)^2} = £826$$

A1.3 Bonds and bond pricing

The concept of PV is often used to calculate the current value of bonds and bond pricing. Bonds are instruments in which the issuer of a bond (the debtor) promises to repay the lender (the investor) the amount borrowed at some pre-determined date in the future in addition to some periodic interest payments before the due date. Because the interest payments paid by the issuer of a bond are fixed, bonds are referred to as *fixed-income securities*. Bonds can be issued by governments and private companies and they pay a periodic cash flow (coupon) at set periods (once every 12 months or every 6 months). At maturity the issuer pays the bondholder the bond's face (or 'par') value. A *zero coupon* bond (also called a discount bond) is a bond paying no coupons that sells at a discount and provides only a payment of par value at maturity.

The present value of the coupon payments will be equal to:

$$PV = \sum_{t=1}^{T} \frac{C}{(1 + r)^t}$$ (A1.3)

$$= \frac{C}{(1 + r)^1} + \frac{C}{(1 + r)^2} + \frac{C}{(1 + r)^3} + \ldots + \frac{C}{(1 + r)^T}$$

Consider a three-year 15 per cent coupon bond. If the bond's face value is £100 and the current interest rate is 10 per cent, the present value will be equal to $\frac{£15}{(1 + 0.10)^1}$ in year 1, $\frac{£15}{(1 + 0.10)^2}$ in year 2 and $\frac{£15}{(1 + 0.10)^3}$ in year 3.

---

[1] Note that this formula can also be written as: PV = FV $(1 + r)^{-1}$.

$$PV = ? \qquad C = £15 \qquad C = £15 \qquad C = £15$$
$$t = \text{today} \qquad t = 1 \qquad t = 2 \qquad t = 3$$

Therefore the PV of the bond coupon payment streams will be equal to the sum of the progression: $13.63 + 12.39 + 11.27 = £37.29$. However, with bonds instruments at maturity the issuer pays the bondholder the bond's face (or 'par') value, which is usually £100 in the UK and $1,000 in the US, so that:

$$FV = £100$$
$$PV = ? \qquad C = £15 \qquad C = £15 \qquad C = £15$$
$$t = \text{today} \qquad t = 1 \qquad t = 2 \qquad t = T = 3$$

It follows that the price of the three-year bond (PB) will be equal to the PV of the coupons plus the PV of the bond's FV:

$$P_B = \sum_{t=1}^{T} \frac{C_t}{(1 + r)^t} + \frac{FV}{(1 + r)^T} \qquad\qquad (A1.4)$$

$$P_B = \frac{£15}{(1 + 0.10)^1} + \frac{£15}{(1 + 0.10)^2} + \frac{£15}{(1 + 0.10)^3} + \frac{£100}{(1 + 0.10)^3}$$

$$P_B = 37.29 + 75.13 = £112.42$$

A1.4 Bonds and yields

For an investor buying a bond, the market price (P) of the bond might be different from the bond's initial face or par value. He will therefore use the bond price (PB), maturity date (t) and coupon payments (C) to infer the return offered by the bond over the investment period. The actual rate of return for holding a bond depends on the price paid for the bond (P), the coupons received relative to the price paid and changes in the price of the bond. We can define the bond's yield to maturity (YTM) as the interest (or more precisely 'discount') rate that makes the present value of a bond's payments equal to its price. The YTM is often viewed as a measure of the average rate of return that will be earned by the investor during the entire time span of the bond.

In the financial press (see Table A1.1), another measure of yield is quoted. This is the current yield, which is equal to the coupon/price of the bond (C/PB). However, the YTM is the most appropriate measure of rate of return, since it includes all aspects of the bond investment, and this can be calculated using a standard discounted cash flow approach as is used to estimate net present values.

To sum up, there are three main elements that determine the annual rate of return an investor is getting on a bond investment:

- **coupon rate:** annual payout as a percentage of the bond's face value;
- **current yield:** annual payout as a percentage of the current market price;
- **yield to maturity:** composite rate of return off *all* payouts, coupon and capital gain (or loss). The capital gain or loss is the difference between face value and the price actually paid for the bond.

Example: yield to maturity of a four-year gilt

Consider the following example of a UK gilt bond selling for £99.15, with a coupon rate of 4 per cent. The bond matures in four years and the par value is £100.

	Coupon	Maturity date	Current price/yield	Price/yield change
4-year	4.000	03/07/2009	99.15/4.02	−0.095/0.028

The yield to maturity is calculated as follows: the coupon payment is £4 (4 per cent of £100), substituting values into the equation A1.3 gives us:

$$£4(1 + r)^{-1} + £4(1 + r)^{-2} + £4(1 + r)^{-3} + £4(1 + r)^{-4} + £100(1 + r)^{-4} = £99.15$$

Yield to maturity (r) = 4.24 per cent.

Note that the YTM can be relatively complicated to calculate manually and it is easier to use web-based bond-yield calculators such as those found at: www.investinginbonds.com.

One important point to note is that yield to maturity (4.24 per cent) is greater than the current yield (4.02 per cent), which in turn is greater than the coupon rate (4 per cent). (Current yield is £4/£99.15 = 4.03 per cent.)

This will always be the case for a bond selling 'at a discount'. In fact, you will always have this:

Bond selling at	Satisfies this condition
Discount	Coupon rate < Current yield < Yield to maturity
Premium	Coupon rate > Current yield > Yield to maturity
Par value	Coupon rate = Current yield = Yield to maturity

A1.5 Yield to maturity – price, maturity, coupon level and frequency of payment and tax

Calculation of the yield to maturity of a bond can obviously change depending on the current price, maturity, coupon rate, frequency of interest payments and tax (on the income from the coupon and possible capital gain if sold before maturity).

Below are some examples:

1. Price

Take the example of the four-year UK gilt shown above and let us assume that the bond is selling for 50 pence more at £99.65, it still has a coupon rate of 4 per cent, matures in four years and the par value is £100. The yield to maturity is calculated as follows:

$$4(1 + r)^{-1} + 4(1 + r)^{-2} + 4(1 + r)^{-3} + 4(1 + r)^{-4} + 100(1 + r)^{-4} = £99.65$$

Yield to maturity (r) = 4.10 per cent (if the current price were 80 pence more at £99.85 the yield to maturity would be 4.04 per cent).

All other things being equal, the yield to maturity declines as the market price approaches par value. In other words, bond prices and yields move in opposite directions.

$$P_B \uparrow \quad \Rightarrow \quad YTM \downarrow$$

2. Maturity

In the same example, assume that maturity is now ten years. That is, the bond is selling for £99.15 and has a coupon rate of 4 per cent, it matures in ten years and the par value is £100. The yield to maturity is calculated as follows:

$$£4(1 + r)^{-1} + £4(1 + r)^{-2} + £4(1 + r)^{-3} + £4(1 + r)^{-4} + £4(1 + r)^{-5}$$

$$+ £4(1 + r)^{-6} + £4(1 + r)^{-7} + £4(1 + r)^{-8} + £4(1 + r)^{-9} + £4(1 + r)^{-10}$$

$$+ £100(1 + r)^{-10} = £99.15$$

Yield to maturity (r) now becomes = 4.11 per cent (if maturity was 20 years this would fall to 4.06 per cent).

All other things being equal, the yield to maturity declines as maturity increases.

$$M \uparrow \quad \Rightarrow \quad YTM \downarrow$$

3. Coupon

Take the same example and now assume that the coupon is set at 5 per cent. That is, the bond is selling for £99.15 and has a coupon rate of 5 per cent, it matures in four years and the par value is £100. The yield to maturity is calculated as follows:

$$5(1 + r)^{-1} + 5(1 + r)^{-2} + 5(1 + r)^{-3} + 5(1 + r)^{-4} + 100(1 + r)^{-4} = 99.15$$

Yield to maturity (r) = 5.24 per cent.

All other things being equal, the higher the coupon, the higher the yield to maturity.

$$C \uparrow \quad \Rightarrow \quad YTM \downarrow$$

Finally, there are two other factors that may influence the YTM. One is the frequency of coupon payments and the other is taxes.

4. The frequency of coupon payments

This can influence the yield to maturity because if coupon payments are made semi-annually then the yield to maturity is calculated by halving the coupon payment and taking account of cash flow over eight six-monthly periods as follows:

$$2(1 + r)^{-1} + 2(1 + r)^{-2} + 2(1 + r)^{-3} + 2(1 + r)^{-4} + 2(1 + r)^{-5} + 2$$

$$(1 + r)^{-6} + 2(1 + r)^{-7} + 2(1 + r)^{-8} + 100(1 + r)^{-8} = 99.15$$

Yield to maturity (r) = 2.62 per cent.

All other things being equal, the greater the frequency in coupon payments, the lower the yield to maturity.

5.   Taxes

Finally, taxes can have a substantial impact on YTM. In the examples above we have assumed no taxes, but of course income from coupons is typically taxable (income tax) as capital gains on sale of the bond may be. Taxes can obviously reduce the size of the net coupon or potential capital gains on the bond if sold before maturity, so one should be aware of potential tax implications when carrying out such calculations.

A1.6   The financial press

Bond prices change daily like shares prices. If you want to keep track of your bond investments, the financial press reports the previous day's closing prices by types of bonds, as illustrated in Table A1.1 which is extracted from the *Financial Times*.

Table A1.1 shows that bond issues are listed in increasing order of residual maturity: shorts, 5–10 years, 10–15 years and more than 15 years. The table also reports *undated* (with no fixed maturity date) and *index-linked* gilts (inflation-linked bonds).[1]

- The title of each bond includes the type of stock, the coupon rate and redemption date (e.g. Treasury, 5 per cent 2014).
- The first column of figures shows the current price in £s (Price £).
- The second column of figures shows the variation on the previous day's price (Day's chng).
- The third column of figures shows the variation on the previous week's price (W'ks chng).
- The fourth column of figures shows the interest or current yield (Int yield).
- The fifth column of figures shows the redemption yield (Red yield).
- Columns 6–9 refer to the redemption yield and show the variation in price on the previous day, week, month and year, respectively.
- The next two columns show the highest and lowest price in the previous 52 weeks (High and Low).
- The last three columns show the nominal total amount in issue (Amnt £m), the last ex-dividend date (Last xd date) and the dates when interest is due (Interest due).

The redemption yield takes into account the capital loss or gain standing on the bond. For instance, take a Treasury bond with 2 per cent coupon and maturity 2016 currently trading at £102.50. Since on redemption you will get back only £100 and there are two years until redemption, that is an average loss of £1.25 every year for every £100 of bonds you own.

Table A1.2 shows a selection of UK government bonds with maturities ranging from 2 years to 30 years with various coupons. The data also reveal that the yield on these gilt-edged securities often varies quite markedly. It is this *spread of yields* paid on the same type of assets (in this case gilt-edged securities) with different terms to maturity that theories of the *term structure of interest rates* seek to explain.

---

[1] For more information and data about the gilt market see also the UK Debt Management Office website: **www.dmo.gov.uk/index.aspx?page=About/About_Gilts**

Table A1.1 Reading the *Financial Times*: UK government bonds

UK GILTS - cash market

www.ft.com/gilts

Mar 18	Price £	Day's chng	W'ks chng	Int yield	Red yield	Red yield Day's chng	W'ks chng	Mth's chng	Year chng	52 Week High	Low	Amnt £m	Last xd date	Interest due
Shorts (Lives up to Five Years)														
Tr 5pc '14	102.17	-0.01	-0.07	4.89	0.35	-0.01	+0.02	+0.01	+0.20	107.15	102.14	40,579	26/02	7 Mar/Sep
Tr 2.75pc '15	101.98	-0.01	-0.05	2.70	0.40	+0.00	+0.01	-0.02	+0.20	104.75	101.95	28,813	13/01	22 Jan/Jul
Tr 4.75pc '15	106.24	-0.02	-0.09	4.47	0.48	+0.01	0.00	-0.01	+0.27	111.26	106.20	37,879	26/02	7 Mar/Sep
Tr 8pc '15	112.95	-0.02	-0.14	7.08	0.43	·	-0.01	-0.02	+0.25	121.28	112.86	10,357	27/11	7 Jun/Dec
Tr 2pc '16	102.50	-0.01	-0.08	1.95	0.64	+0.00	-0.01	+0.01	+0.32	104.92	102.35	32,037	13/01	22 Jan/Jul
Tr 4pc '16	107.81	-0.02	-0.12	3.71	0.80	+0.00	-0.01	+0.02	+0.42	112.66	107.71	34,648	26/02	7 Mar/Sep
Tr 1pc '17	99.16	-0.02	-0.04	1.01	1.25	+0.01	-0.04	-0.04	+0.55	101.91	97.95	23,019	26/02	7 Mar/Sep
Tr 1.75pc '17	102.12	-0.02	-0.07	1.71	0.99	+0.01	-0.03	-0.01	+0.48	105.11	101.45	31,269	13/01	22 Jan/Jul
Tr 8.75pc '17	125.39	-0.04	-0.15	6.98	1.19	+0.01	-0.04	-0.05	+0.58	135.92	125.12	10,879	16/02	25 Feb/Aug
Tr 5pc '18	113.88	-0.03	-0.08	4.39	1.39	+0.01	-0.05	-0.06	+0.62	121.22	113.20	34,398	26/02	7 Mar/Sep
Tr 4.5pc '19	113.13	-0.03	-0.04	3.98	1.73	+0.01	-0.06	-0.08	+0.71	121.28	111.68	35,485	26/02	7 Mar/Sep
Five to Ten Years														
Tr 3.75pc '19	109.71	-0.02	·	3.42	1.87	+0.00	-0.07	-0.08	+0.73	117.57	107.91	28,057	26/02	7 Mar/Sep
Tr 3.75pc '20	109.89	-0.01	-0.01	3.41	2.11	+0.00	-0.07	-0.08	+0.71	118.39	107.76	23,997	26/02	7 Mar/Sep
Tr 4.75pc '20	115.49	·	-0.01	4.11	1.99	0.00	-0.07	-0.08	+0.72	124.76	113.71	32,517	26/02	7 Mar/Sep
Tr 3.75pc '21	109.86	·	+0.03	3.41	2.31	·	-0.09	-0.08	+0.67	118.86	107.30	27,709	26/02	7 Mar/Sep
Tr 8pc '21	138.32	-0.02	-0.02	5.78	2.23	+0.00	-0.09	-0.09	+0.71	152.25	136.23	23,499	27/11	7 Jun/Dec
Tr 1.75pc '22	94.04	·	+0.07	1.86	2.54	+0.00	-0.09	-0.07	+0.65	101.21	90.96	28,360	26/02	7 Mar/Sep
Tr 4pc '22	111.65	·	+0.03	3.58	2.39	·	-0.09	-0.07	+0.65	121.12	108.93	37,045	26/02	7 Mar/Sep
Ten to Fifteen Years														
Tr 5pc '25	120.84	·	+0.18	4.14	2.78	·	-0.11	-0.06	+0.60	133.14	116.51	32,992	26/02	7 Mar/Sep
Tr 4.25pc '27	113.74	+0.02	+0.25	3.74	3.02	0.00	-0.11	-0.08	+0.49	125.44	108.85	29,279	27/11	7 Jun/Dec
Tr 6pc '28	134.93	+0.02	+0.28	4.45	3.04	0.00	-0.11	-0.08	+0.50	149.79	129.51	18,575	27/11	7 Jun/Dec
Over Fifteen Years														
Tr 4.75pc '30	120.31	+0.14	+0.52	3.95	3.18	-0.01	-0.10	-0.09	+0.43	133.06	115.50	28,716	27/11	7 Jun/Dec
Tr 4.25pc '32	113.82	+0.14	+0.51	3.74	3.24	-0.01	-0.10	-0.09	+0.39	125.81	109.05	34,598	27/11	7 Jun/Dec
Tr 4.5pc '34	117.61	+0.15	+0.55	3.83	3.31	-0.01	-0.10	-0.09	+0.33	129.79	112.57	25,501	26/02	7 Mar/Sep
Tr 4.25pc '36	113.96	+0.18	+0.55	3.74	3.35	-0.01	-0.09	-0.09	+0.29	125.51	108.92	25,952	26/02	7 Mar/Sep
Tr 4.75pc '38	123.19	+0.21	+0.63	3.86	3.36	-0.01	-0.08	-0.09	+0.23	135.38	117.68	24,601	27/11	7 Jun/Dec
Tr 4.25pc '39	114.61	+0.19	+0.59	3.71	3.39	-0.01	-0.08	-0.09	+0.20	125.59	109.28	19,280	26/02	7 Mar/Sep
Tr 4.5pc '42	120.02	+0.20	+0.64	3.76	3.40	-0.01	-0.08	-0.09	+0.16	131.41	114.24	26,001	27/11	7 Jun/Dec
Tr 3.25pc '44	96.34	+0.20	+0.58	3.38	3.45	-0.01	-0.08	-0.09	+0.12	104.97	90.69	23,778	13/01	22 Jan/Jul
Tr 4.25pc '46	116.42	+0.24	+0.69	3.66	3.41	-0.01	-0.08	-0.09	+0.09	126.88	109.84	20,873	27/11	7 Jun/Dec
Tr 4.25pc '49	117.57	+0.25	+0.71	3.62	3.40	-0.01	-0.08	-0.09	+0.05	127.61	110.52	19,301	27/11	7 Jun/Dec
Tr 3.75pc '52	107.14	+0.24	+0.66	3.51	3.41	-0.01	-0.07	-0.09	+0.03	116.26	100.30	19,761	13/01	22 Jan/Jul
Tr 4.25pc '55	119.45	+0.26	+0.73	3.57	3.38	-0.01	-0.07	-0.09	+0.02	129.57	111.43	23,416	27/11	7 Jun/Dec
Tr 4pc '60	114.65	+0.27	+0.74	3.50	3.37	-0.01	-0.07	-0.09	+0.02	124.65	106.48	18,764	13/01	22 Jan/Jul
Undated														
Cons 4pc ······ ⊕	97.79	·	+0.68	4.10	4.09‡	-0.01	-0.07	-0.09	+0.02	102.15	90.45	257	22/01	1 Feb/Aug
War Ln 3.5pc ······	83.97	·	+0.52	4.18	4.17‡	-0.01	-0.07	-0.07	+0.15	91.27	77.76	1,938	20/11	1 Jun/Dec
Cn 3.5 pc '61 Aft ······ ⊕	81.81	·	+0.49	·	4.28‡	-0.01	-0.07	-0.07	+0.15	90.64	77.71	17	22/09	1 Apr/Oct
Tr 3pc '66 Aft ······ ⊕	68.68	·	+0.41	4.38	4.37‡	-0.01	-0.07	-0.07	+0.15	76.16	64.91	40	25/09	5 Apr/Oct
Cons 2.5pc ······ ⊕	58.85	·	+0.36	4.26	4.25‡	-0.01	-0.07	-0.07	+0.15	65.43	55.54	177	25/12	5 Ja/Ap/Jul/Oc
Tr 2.5pc ······ ⊕	59.98	·	+0.37	4.18	4.17‡	-0.01	-0.07	-0.07	+0.15	67.81	56.64	287	22/09	1 Apr/Oct
Index-linked				(1)	(2)									
2.5pc '16 ······ (81.6)	338.64	+0.08	+0.14	-2.51	-2.08	-0.01	-0.11	-0.13	+0.77	354.21	337.20	7,899	15/01	26 Jan/Jul
1.25pc '17† (193.725)	110.78	+0.06	+0.14	-1.58	-1.58	-0.02	-0.13	-0.15	+0.89	119.42	109.59	11,846	13/11	22 May/Nov
2.5pc '20 ······ (83.0)	364.72	+0.33	+0.71	-1.11	-0.94	-0.02	-0.12	-0.17	+0.97	393.73	357.72	6,579	07/10	16 Apr/Oct
1.875pc '22† (205.65806)	121.31	+0.14	+0.36	-0.52	-0.52	-0.01	-0.13	-0.15	+0.86	136.90	118.43	15,743	13/11	22 May/Nov
0.125pc '24	104.04	+0.16	+0.49	-0.27	-0.27	-0.02	-0.14	-0.16	+0.77	116.66	100.08	8,688	11/09	22 Mar/Sep
2.5pc '24 ······ (97.7)	330.47	+0.45	+1.33	-0.43	-0.32	-0.01	-0.13	-0.16	+0.75	364.74	319.33	6,821	08/01	17 Jan/Jul
1.25pc '27† (194.06667)	119.22	+0.22	+0.64	-0.14	-0.14	-0.01	-0.11	-0.15	+0.53	135.08	115.11	14,170	13/11	22 May/Nov
0.125pc '29	102.51	+0.30	+0.79	-0.04	-0.04	-0.02	-0.11	-0.15	+0.45	115.32	98.14	14,229	11/09	22 Mar/Sep
4.125pc '30 ······ (135.1)	313.12	+0.81	+2.15	-0.19	-0.12	-0.02	-0.10	-0.16	+0.47	347.63	302.44	4,841	13/01	22 Jan/Jul
1.25pc '32† (217.13226)	124.73	+0.43	+1.10	-0.07	-0.07	-0.02	-0.10	-0.15	+0.31	141.11	119.51	12,760	13/11	22 May/Nov
0.75pc '34 ······ (235.20)	115.55	+0.45	+1.15	-0.03	-0.03	-0.02	-0.10	-0.15	+0.24	129.44	109.97	12,458	11/09	22 Mar/Sep
2pc '35 ······ (173.6)	205.10	+0.47	+1.95	-0.12	-0.06	-0.02	-0.09	-0.14	+0.24	224.90	194.33	9,084	15/01	26 Jan/Jul
1.125pc '37† (202.24286)	127.77	+0.54	+1.35	-0.04	-0.04	-0.02	-0.08	-0.13	+0.13	143.19	121.33	12,132	13/11	22 May/Nov
0.625pc '40† (216.52258)	116.94	+0.54	+1.34	-0.02	-0.02	-0.02	-0.08	-0.13	+0.06	130.39	109.89	11,438	11/09	22 Mar/Sep
0.75pc '47† (207.76667)	127.04	+0.72	+1.78	-0.05	-0.05	-0.02	-0.07	-0.13	-0.04	141.59	117.56	11,687	13/11	22 May/Nov
0.5pc '50† (213.40000)	119.71	+0.73	+1.78	-0.04	-0.04	-0.02	-0.07	-0.12	-0.06	133.71	110.25	11,351	11/09	22 Mar/Sep
0.25pc '52	110.75	+0.74	+1.80	-0.03	-0.03	-0.02	-0.07	-0.12	-0.08	124.13	101.04	9,002	11/09	22 Mar/Sep
1.25pc '55† (192.20000)	155.48	+0.97	+2.41	-0.06	-0.06	-0.02	-0.07	-0.12	-0.07	174.95	143.00	10,169	13/11	22 May/Nov
0.375pc '62	121.41	+0.92	+2.33	-0.06	-0.06	-0.02	-0.07	-0.11	-0.06	139.35	109.00	12,480	11/09	22 Mar/Sep

Table A1.2 UK benchmark government bond yields – 13 May 2014

Maturity	Yield	Today's change	1 week ago	1 month ago
1 month	0.30%	0	0.32%	0.32%
3 month	0.38%	0	0.37%	0.38%
6 month	0.42%	0	0.41%	0.40%
1 year	0.41%	−0.03	0.44%	0.41%
2 year	0.77%	−0.03	0.76%	0.62%
3 year	1.18%	−0.01	1.15%	1.00%
4 year	1.75%	−0.03	1.73%	1.56%
5 year	2.02%	−0.03	2.00%	1.83%
7 year	2.38%	−0.02	2.32%	2.23%
8 year	2.46%	−0.01	2.39%	2.31%
9 year	2.60%	−0.01	2.53%	2.47%
10 year	2.72%	−0.01	2.66%	2.62%
15 year	3.21%	−0.01	3.17%	3.14%
20 year	3.34%	−0.01	3.30%	3.27%
30 year	3.46%	>−0.01	3.44%	3.42%

Source: Financial Times, 13/05/14. © The Financial Times Limited. All Rights Reserved.

A1.7 The term structure of interest rates

The 'term structure' of interest rates refers to the relationship between the term to maturity of a bond and its yield to maturity. Economists and investors believe that the shape of the yield curve reflects the market's future expectation for interest rates and the conditions for monetary policy.

The term structure of interest rates may be defined as the spread of yields generated by the same type of assets with different terms to maturity. The concept of the term structure of interest rates is of relevance only in the case of those assets that have a fixed term to maturity and pay a fixed interest at specified points in time (bonds and other types of financial instruments, such as sterling certificates of deposit).

The term structure of interest rates on a particular type of asset may be represented diagrammatically in a yield curve. The yield in this context is the yield to maturity. As noted above, this yield includes not only the interest income from the asset but also any anticipated capital gain (due to the current price being less than the maturity value) or capital loss (due to the current price being greater than the maturity value).

Typically, the yield curve is drawn for similar-risk securities that have different maturity dates, as shown in Figure A1.1, and demonstrates that long-term bonds (30 years) give higher yields than short-term ones (5 years in the example). This can be considered a 'normal' market's expectations of future interest rates because typically longer-term instruments carry more uncertainty than shorter-term ones and thus should offer higher yields. However, if expectations on the economy are different from normal the yield curve can take different shapes (the two extremes being a flat yield curve, where short- and long-term securities offer the same yield, and inverted, in which short-term securities offer yields higher than the long-term ones).

The yield curve is usually calculated on a daily basis so we can draw a different yield curve for every day. All the major central banks/monetary authorities report yield curve data for

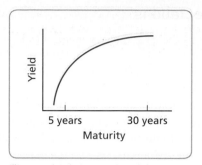

Figure A1.1 Normal yield curve

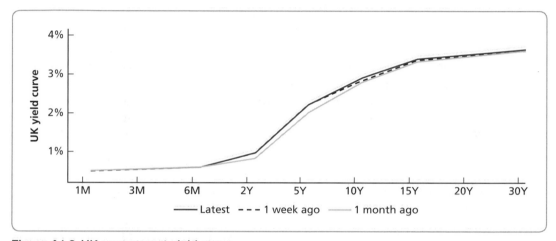

Figure A1.2 UK government yield curve

Source: Financial Times 13/05/14. © The Financial Times Limited. All Rights Reserved.

various instruments. Using the data points in Table A1.2, Figure A1.2 illustrates the shape of the UK government yield curve on 13 May 2014.

A1.8 Theories on the shape of the yield curve

A number of theories have been put forward to explain the various shapes of the yield curve, which may be observed in practice. None of the established theories is wholly satisfactory, and many economists believe that the assumptions required by the theories undermine their practical value. Nevertheless, it is worthwhile summarising the key features of these theories as a basis for more advanced study of yield curves (not covered in this book).

Two main theories seek to explain the shapes of yield curves. These are:

- **expectations theory**, which is subdivided into:
  - pure expectations;
  - liquidity-biased expectations;
  - preferred habitat-biased expectations;
- **market segmentation theory**, which disallows large-scale arbitrage between the various segments of the market.

A1.8.1 Pure expectations

The basis of this theory is that the shape of yield curves is determined by market expectations of future short-term interest rates. If lenders and borrowers expect short-term interest rates to rise, then lenders would wish to invest at the short end of the market, profiting when bond prices had fallen by enjoying higher yields. This would push up short-term bond prices (force down the yield curve for short-maturity bonds). Borrowers would, of course, want to borrow for much longer periods, forcing up the yield for long-maturity bonds. These actions would tilt the curve in an anti-clockwise direction, making it steeper (rising from left to right). However, the theory fails to consider the risks involved, as nobody knows future bond prices (price risk) or future rates of interest (reinvestment risk).

A1.8.2 Liquidity

This theory assumes that the risk associated with investment in bonds increases with their term to maturity. It is argued that this increasing risk will lead investors to require a progressively larger liquidity premium for investing in bonds with a progressively longer maturity. Investors require a premium for bonds not being liquid, e.g. buying long-dated bonds, and this urge to be compensated for holding illiquid assets may be more important than the expectations, which may result in a downward-sloping curve. This premium has an upward bias on the curve. This theory fits closely with the intuitive explanation for the shape of yield curves as discussed above.

A1.8.3 Preferred habitat

This theory argues that investors prefer to match their assets with known liabilities and borrowers will seek to raise funds for a time period that matches their needs. Also, investment institutions may try to match the maturity of their assets and liabilities.

In order to be encouraged to shift out of their preferred habitats, lenders and borrowers will require a premium on the yield to cover the risk that they feel they are being asked to accept. The premium will vary according to the extent that the investor or borrower has to shift from their preferred habitat. Therefore, as there is no reason to believe that the premium will rise uniformly with maturity, the theory is able to explain any shape of yield curve.

A1.8.4 Market segmentation

A lay person might describe this theory as 'a highly structured and inflexible version of the preferred habitat theory'. It assumes that neither investors nor borrowers are able or willing to move along the yield curve to take advantage of arbitrage opportunities.

The reason for this highly inflexible segmentation of the market might be because regulators and/or the investing institutions' own rules require them to keep certain strict percentages of their assets in each of the market's maturity sectors.

Under this theory, the yield curve is constructed from the yield curves of the various segments of the fixed-interest securities market. Some economists regard this theory as unsustainable because it presupposes that there is absolute risk aversion, whereas evidence shows that investors are willing to take risks and arbitrage along the yield curve.

Appendix A2

Introduction to portfolio theory

A2.1   Return, risk and the concept of diversification

The return and risk characteristics associated with different types of securities vary tremendously. For example, the return on a UK Treasury bond is near certain (risk-free). By contrast, the return to be achieved on ordinary equity shares in an average company is far from certain (it carries a positive level of risk). Portfolio theory aims to show that by holding a diversified array of securities, the risk of making a loss on the investment can be reduced. Let's first see how to calculate risk and return.

In order to measure the past performance of a security or a portfolio of securities it is necessary to calculate the actual return on the security or the portfolio taking into account:

● any change in the capital value of the security or portfolio during the relevant time period;

● the dividend or interest payments received on the security or portfolio during the relevant time period.

The single period return may be calculated using the following formula:

$$R_1 = (P_1 - P_0 + D_1)/P_0 \qquad \text{(A2.1)}$$

where:

R_1 = the return obtained by holding the security (portfolio) for the whole of period 1;

P_0 = the market price of the security (portfolio) at the start of period 1;

P_1 = the market price of the security (portfolio) at the end of period 1;

D_1 = the dividend or interest income received on the security (portfolio) during period 1.

Often you will be interested in calculating the multiple period returns. One way to calculate them is by using arithmetic or geometric averages over the period.

The usual way to measure the risk associated with investment in a security is via calculation of the *probable variability of future returns*. In other words, risk may be measured in terms of the variance (or standard deviation) of the expected returns.

Typically, the higher the risk, the higher the variance:

$$\text{Risk}\uparrow \rightarrow \quad \sigma^2\uparrow$$

The variance is the volatility or dispersion of returns. It tells us about the potential for deviation of the returns from its expected value. Look at the example in Table A2.1.

Table A2.1 Case 1: overall expected return on a security

Outcome	Expected return %	Probability of expected return occurring	Expected return weighted by probability %
A	50	0.1	5
B	30	0.2	6
C	10	0.4	4
D	−10	0.2	−2
E	−30	0.1	−3
Total		1.0	10

In Case 1, it is assumed that there are five possible outcomes, A to E. The probability of each outcome occurring is specified on the basis of past experience. For example, there is a 0.1 (i.e. 10 per cent) probability that outcome A will occur. This outcome involves the occurrence of a 50 per cent expected return on the security. If outcomes A to E cover all possible outcomes, then the combined probability must sum to 1.0 (i.e. 100 per cent).

To calculate the overall expected return on the security, the expected return for each possible outcome is multiplied by the probability of that outcome occurring (to give the fourth column in Table A2.1) and the weighted expected returns are summed. Therefore, it may be observed that while the security has possible expected returns ranging from 50 per cent to −30 per cent, the overall expected return is 10 per cent.

More formally, we can express the expected return from a security as:

$$(E)R = p_1R_1 + p_2R_2 + p_3R_3 + \ldots\ldots\ldots + p_nR_n \tag{A2.2}$$

where:

$(E)R$ = expected return

R_i = return in outcome i;

p_i = probability of occurrence of the return R_i;

n = number of outcomes.

Note that in practice future returns and their probabilities are not usually known, so historical average returns from past data relating to the performance of the investment are used as indicators of future returns.

To calculate the variance of the expected return on the security:

- Square the difference between the expected return for outcome A and the overall expected return and multiply the result by the probability that outcome A will occur.
- Repeat this step for each possible outcome.
- Sum the results generated for all possible outcomes.

Thus, for Case 1:

$$\text{Variance} = 0.1(0.5 - 0.1)^2 + 0.2(0.3 - 0.1)^2 + 0.4(0.1 - 0.1)^2$$
$$+0.2(-0.1 - 0.1)^2 + 0.1(-0.3 - 0.1)^2$$

$$= 0.016 + 0.008 + 0 + 0.008 + 0.016 = 0.048$$

The standard deviation is simply the square root of the variance. For Case 1:

$$\text{Standard deviation} = \sqrt{0.048} = 0.2191$$

As a general rule, if an investor wishes to achieve a higher-than-average expected return, they should take on a higher-than-average level of risk.

$$\textbf{Return} \uparrow \quad \rightarrow \quad \textbf{Risk} \uparrow$$

Diversification, that is adding more securities into an existing portfolio, can reduce risk exposure (i.e. the portfolio volatility).

$$\textbf{Diversification} \uparrow \quad \rightarrow \quad \textbf{Risk} \downarrow$$

For a portfolio composed of n securities, the expected return will be equal to the weighted average of the expected returns on the component securities:

$$(E)R_p = w_1(E)R_1 + w_2(E)R_2 + w_3(E)R_3 + \ldots\ldots + w_n(E)R_n \qquad \text{(A2.3)}$$

where:

$(E)R_p$ = weighted average of the expected return of the individual stocks composing the portfolio, where weights are the portfolio weights;

w_n = portfolio weight of stock n, where $n = 1, 2 \ldots n$.

Example

Assume we have a portfolio comprising two equities: the UK supermarket Tesco (trading at 286.25p on 9 April 2014) and Barclays (trading at 238.95 on the same day). Also assume that 70 per cent of the portfolio comprises Barclays shares and 30 per cent Tesco shares. The expected return of Barclays is 20 per cent and for Tesco shares is 4 per cent. The expected return for the portfolio is: $(0.7 \times 0.2) + (0.3 \times 0.04) = 0.14 + 0.012 = 15.2\%$.

While investors cannot escape from the inherent return–risk trade-off, they may nevertheless construct their portfolios in a manner that aims to minimise the risk assumed at any given desired rate of return. *Modern portfolio theory* seeks to explain this behaviour. The theory derives from the seminal work of Markowitz undertaken in the 1950s.

A2.2 Modern portfolio theory

The central principle of modern portfolio theory is that it is possible to construct a portfolio of securities that has a return that is less risky than the return on any individual security contained therein. In order to do this it is necessary that the returns on the individual component securities should not be perfectly correlated. If the performance of securities is affected in an identical way by a particular event, then it is not possible to reduce the risk of being adversely affected by the event simply by holding a portfolio of those securities. The relative variability of returns on two securities is known as their covariance.

The correlation coefficient (ρ) measures the degree to which two variables are linearly related. If there is a perfect linear relationship with positive slope between the two variables, we have a correlation coefficient of 1; if there is a perfect linear relationship with negative slope between the two variables, we have a correlation coefficient of -1; a correlation coefficient of 0 means that there is no linear relationship between the variables. The correlation coefficient (ρ) comprises two elements:

- covariance (the extent to which values move together);
- standard deviations (how tightly values are clustered around the mean in a set of data).

In this context, the correlation coefficient is simply the covariance between the stocks divided by their respective standard deviations. In the case of two stocks, 1 and 2, the correlation coefficient will be calculated as follows:

$$\rho_{1,2} = \frac{\text{Cov}_{1,2}}{\sigma_1 \sigma_2} \qquad \text{(A2.4)}$$

where $\text{Cov}_{1,2}$ is the covariance between the two stocks and is a measure of the extent to which the two assets covary.

To get the correlation, the covariance is divided by the standard deviation to provide a standardised measure between the movements of two different values. (Note that the correlation coefficient falls between -1 (perfect negative) and $+1$ (perfect positive), while zero correlation means that the returns on the two assets are unrelated to each other.)

Hence the variance of the portfolio return σ_p^2, will be equal to the sum of the contributions of the component security variances plus a term that involves the correlation coefficient between the returns of the component securities; or, in symbols:

$$\sigma_p^2 = (W_1\sigma_1)^2 + (W_2\sigma_2)^2 + 2(W_1\sigma_1)(W_2\sigma_2)\rho_{1,2} \qquad \text{(A2.5)}$$

Given this information let us run through the example relating to a portfolio consisting of Tesco and Barclays shares from above. Assume the past standard deviations of Tesco shares were 40 per cent and for Barclays shares 60 per cent. Assume the two stocks are positively correlated – they move in the same direction – but are not perfectly correlated. Assume they are correlated 0.75 ($\rho 1,2 = 0.75$). Recall also that 70 per cent of the portfolio is held in Barclays shares and the remainder in Tesco stock.

The variance of the portfolio is therefore:

$$[(0.7)^2 \times (0.6)^2] + [(0.3)^2 \times (0.4)^2] + 2(0.7 \times 0.3 \times 0.6 \times 0.4 \times 0.75) =$$

$$[0.49 \times 0.36] + [0.09 \times 0.16] + 2(0.0378) =$$

$$0.1764 + 0.0144 + 0.0756 = 0.2664 = 26.64\%$$

So the variance of the portfolio is 26.64 per cent and the standard deviation is:

$$\sqrt{0.2664} = 0.051614 = 5.1614\%$$

Note that the variance of the portfolio return is lower than that of any individual asset, which shows that by constructing a portfolio one is able to diversify risk. Diversification increases the less correlated the stocks are in the portfolio – when stocks in the portfolio are perfectly correlated then there are no diversification benefits.

$$\text{Correlation} \downarrow \ \rightarrow \quad \text{Diversification} \uparrow \quad \rightarrow \quad \text{Risk} \downarrow$$

It must be emphasised that 20 or more different securities is normally thought of as being the minimum number of securities required to achieve significant risk reduction by diversification. Moreover, in order to significantly reduce risk, securities should emanate from different business sectors and ideally from different countries (i.e. international diversification).

A2.3   Efficient (mean–standard deviation) frontier

This section briefly introduces the features of the efficient frontier that can be used to demonstrate the optimal holdings of risky assets for a risk-averse investor. It is otherwise known as the mean–standard deviation frontier as it plots the mean expected return against the standard deviation of a risky asset (the risky asset is constructed by using weights of the two assets in the combined portfolio). Each point on the efficient frontier in Figure A2.1 therefore represents a risky asset.

As the portfolio weights for the two assets range from zero to one, the portfolio goes from one that only combines Security 1 to a portfolio combining only Security 2. As the weights change then the new portfolios plot a curve that includes both Securities 1 and 2. This can be seen in Figure A2.2.

The efficient frontier shows the expected return and risk that could be achieved by constructing different portfolios of the two risky assets. Investors can use this to consider trade-offs between returns (mean returns) and risk (standard deviations) when they choose portfolio weights for their investments. It is important to note that this exposition assumes that investors are not allowed to short-sell (the selling of a security that the seller does not own).

In order to identify the optimal portfolio we have to take into account the risk–return preferences of an investor – this is shown in Figure A2.2 where the investor chooses a portfolio with a 50–50 mix of both Securities 1 and 2. The area inside the frontier is known as a 'feasible region' and this represents feasible but inefficient portfolios as expected return is not maximised for a given risk or standard deviation.

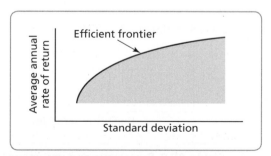

Figure A2.1 Efficient (mean–standard deviation) frontier

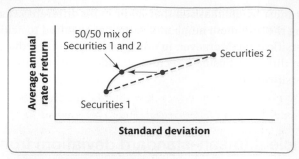

Figure A2.2 Efficient frontier: two risky assets (Securities 1 and 2)

A2.4　Components of risk

The risk associated with the return on a security may be divided into two components:

● Market or systematic risk is the risk related to the macroeconomic factors or market index. Systematic risk is non-diversifiable.

● Unsystematic risk is the firm-specific risk, not related to the macroeconomic environment. Unsystematic risk is diversifiable.

Securities have different proportions of systematic and unsystematic risk. Diversification can reduce firm-specific risk to low levels; however, it cannot eliminate the common sources of risk that affect all firms, as shown in Figure A2.3.

The extent to which the return on an individual equity share moves with the general trend of the average return on the market (i.e. its systematic risk component) is measured by its

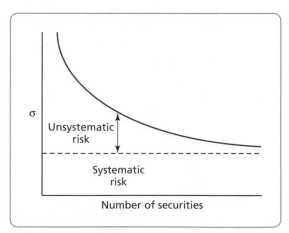

Figure A2.3 Systematic and unsystematic risk: effects of diversification

beta value (β). In particular, β measures the sensitivity of a security's returns to the systematic or market factor and is calculated as follows:

$$\beta_i = \frac{Cov(r_j,r_M)}{\sigma^2 M} \tag{A2.6}$$

where $Cov(r_j,r_M)$ is the covariance with the market divided by the variance of the market.

Some shares (and portfolios) tend to respond strongly to general movements in the market. The returns on other shares (and portfolios) tend to move less markedly and may be relatively stable in the face of major market movements.

The beta value for a company's shares is derived from the capital asset pricing model (CAPM), which is simply the reduction of modern portfolio theory into a single-factor model – with that single factor being called beta (β). Instead of a matrix of covariances between all securities in the market, as shown above, there is only one covariance coefficient: β, the covariance between a security and the market.

The CAPM states that the security's risk premium is proportional to both the beta and the risk premium of the market portfolio. An equity share's β is obtained from an equation that explains the expected return (or required return) from a stock that is calculated as follows:

$$E(r_i) = r_f + \beta_i[E(r_M) - r_f] \tag{A2.7}$$

where:

$E(r_i)$ is the expected return on asset i;

β_i is the beta of asset i;

$E(r_M)$ is the expected market rate of return;

r_f is the risk-free rate of interest.

From the expected return equation shown above, the expected return of a stock, $E(r_i)$, is determined by the risk-free rate (generally given by the rate on the safest investment – usually a government bond such as a UK gilt or US Treasury) plus the β of the security, multiplied by the market risk premium. This is the expected return in excess of that on risk-free securities and thus is calculated as the difference between the expected return on the market portfolio, $E(r_M)$ and the risk-free rate (r_f).

The primary determinant of the expected rate of return is the security's β. The risk-free rate and market risk premium, of course, would be the same for all securities.

If a security cannot match the required rate of return for a certain level of risk, it is considered a poor investment according to CAPM. If a security exceeds the required rate of return, it is considered a good investment according to CAPM.[1]

---

[1] William Sharpe published the capital asset pricing model in 1964 (Sharpe, 1964); for this work he shared the 1990 Nobel Prize in Economics with Harry Markowitz and Merton Miller. Parallel work was also performed by Treynor (1964) and Lintner (1965). For his work on CAPM, Sharpe extended Harry Markowitz's (1952) portfolio theory to introduce the notions of systematic and specific risk.

The interpretation of beta values is straightforward. Quite simply, a market index (such as the FTSE 100) is given a beta value of 1. If an individual equity share has a beta value greater than 1, then the return on this share is prone to fluctuate more than the average return on the market index. For example, if the average return on the market index falls by 10 per cent, the return on the share may fall by 15 per cent – this would mean that the share had a beta value of 1.5. In contrast, if an equity share had a beta value of less than 1, then the return on this share is more stable than the average return on the market. For example, a beta value of 0.3 would imply that a 10 per cent fall in the average return on the market index would be matched by a 3 per cent fall in the return on the share.

A2.5   Security market line

The security market line is a graphical representation of the expected return–beta relationship of the CAPM. Its slope is the risk premium of the market portfolio.

Table A2.2 shows the linear relationship between expected return and beta.

Using the information in Table A2.2, the security market line is shown in Figure A2.4 where beta is on the horizontal axis and expected return on the vertical axis. It can be seen that expected return on an asset with β of zero is 0.03 (or 3 per cent) and for a beta of 1 it is 11 per cent.

The security line is simply a straight line starting from the risk-free point passing through the market portfolio (where $\beta = 1$). Whenever the CAPM holds, all securities must lie on the security market line in market equilibrium. This is because any investor can always obtain the market risk premium $\beta_i (E(r_M) - r_f)$ by holding a combination of the market portfolio and the risk-free rate.

The beta of a portfolio (β_p) is simply the weighted sum of the individual assets in the portfolio (β_i), where weights are the portfolio weights (w_i) so:

$$\beta_p = \sum W_i \beta_i \tag{A2.8}$$

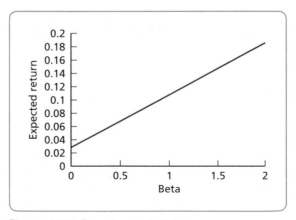

Figure A2.4 Security market line

Table A2.2 Expected return and beta

Risk-free rate (r_f)	Beta (β_i)	Market premium $E(r_i)$ minus (r_f)	Expected return $E(r_M)$
0.03	2	0.08	0.19
0.03	1.5	0.08	0.15
0.03	1	0.08	0.11
0.03	0.5	0.08	0.07
0.03	0	0.08	0.03

A2.6 Portfolio expected returns and the capital asset pricing model

It is argued that rational risk-averse investors will:

- require additional expected returns to compensate for taking on additional risk;
- construct a diversified portfolio of securities.

Therefore, the return that investors require, and the return that the market is willing to pay, will be determined by that component of risk that cannot be eliminated by diversification, i.e. by systematic risk, which cannot be avoided. In other words, the CAPM suggests that:

- the return required on any given security (or portfolio of securities) will depend upon its beta value;
- the total risk associated with the return on any security is irrelevant to the determination of the required return, i.e. because it is relatively easy to eliminate unsystematic risk, investors will not receive any premium for that risk.

The operation of efficient markets in securities should ensure that diversified portfolios containing securities with the same average beta value should attract the same return, irrespective of the total risk associated with the individual securities. If this was not the case then investors holding diversified portfolios would seek to purchase the securities attracting the higher returns (presumably those with greater associated unsystematic risk) and sell securities earning the lower returns. This action would push up the price of the riskier securities and push down the price of the less risky securities. This adjustment would continue until the returns from securities with the same beta values were equalised.

A2.7 Arbitrage pricing theory: a note

An alternative view on stock pricing to CAPM is known as the arbitrage pricing theory (APT). This theory posits that the expected return of a financial asset can be modelled as a linear function of a variety of macroeconomic factors, where sensitivity to changes in each factor is represented by a factor-specific beta. The model-derived rate of return will then be used to price the asset correctly – the asset price should equal the expected end-of-period price discounted at the rate implied by the model. If the price diverges, arbitrage should bring it back into line. Unlike CAPM, which specifies returns as a linear function of only systematic risk, APT may specify returns as a linear function of more than a single factor.

The attraction of APT is that unlike in CAPM one does not have to identify and measure the appropriate market portfolio. However, its main drawback is that it does not specify the underlying macroeconomic factors that are to be used in estimating expected returns (although factors such as growth in real GDP, interest spreads and default probabilities are often used). CAPM, of course, assumes all these macroeconomic factors are taken into account by the market portfolio.

Glossary

Abenomics Refers to the aggressive reforms carried out by Japanese Prime Minister Shinzo Abe since 2012 in an attempt to pull Japan out of recession and deflation and restore growth.

Accounting-based measures of bank risk Indicators of bank risk drawn from the bank balance sheet and profit and loss accounts. These include, for example, loan loss provisions and the Z-score.

Acquis communautaire A French term meaning 'the European Union as it is'; in other words, the rights and obligations that member states of the EU share. The 'acquis' includes all the EU's treaties and laws, declarations and resolutions, international agreements on EU affairs and the judgments given by the Court of Justice. It also includes action that EU governments take together in the area of 'justice and home affairs' and on the Common Foreign and Security Policy.

Adverse selection Refers to a market process in which bad results occur due to asymmetric information between buyers and sellers: the 'bad' products or customers are more likely to be selected.

Agency Within an international parent bank, agencies are offices similar to branches, but with less operative tasks.

Agency capture Refers to the situation where a regulatory process can be captured by producers (banks and other financial institutions) and used in their own interest and advantage rather than in the interest of consumers.

Agency costs These are the costs that principals (typically the owners) have to incur in order to ensure that their agents (the managers) make financial decisions consistent with their best interests.

Alt-A mortgage In the US, a type of mortgage that is less risky than a sub-prime but riskier than an A (i.e. prime) mortgage; 'Alt' is short for *alternative*.

Arbitrage The simultaneous buying and selling of a commodity, or a security, in different markets to take advantage of price differentials.

Arranger In syndicated lending arrangers serve the role of raising finance for an issuer in need of capital. The term is also used in the context of the securitisation process where the arranger bank is an investment bank that acts as the underwriter representing the issuer (the SPV or trust).

Asset-backed commercial paper (ABCP) Short-term borrowing with fixed maturity (less than 270 days) collateralised by a pool of financial assets (e.g. car loans, trade receivables, leases).

Asset-backed securities Securities backed by real or financial assets (e.g. mortgage-backed securities/bonds). Asset-backed securities are otherwise known as collateralised securities.

Asset-based finance A specialised method for providing capital and loans that are secured by machinery, inventory, equipment and/or real estate.

Asset Guarantee Program (AGP) Refers to the US exceptional government support of institutions whose collapse in 2009 would have caused serious consequences to the financial markets and the real economy. It included supporting the value of specific assets held by banks that met certain criteria (namely Citibank and Bank of America) by accepting to absorb a portion of losses on those assets.

Asset–liability management The management of a business in a way that co-ordinates decisions on both sides of the balance sheet. Also known as balance sheet management.

Asset management This can either refer to the managing of an institution's asset side of the balance sheet (e.g. altering the mix of assets to increase returns or minimise risk) or to the function of managing assets on behalf of a customer (asset management *services*).

Asset Protection Scheme (APS) A scheme launched in 2009 by the UK Treasury to protect over £280 billion of Royal Bank of Scotland's financial assets against losses.

Asset transformation The ability of financial intermediaries to transform large denomination assets into smaller units.

Assets What a firm or a person owns or is owed, such as money, securities, equipment and buildings. Assets are listed on a company's balance sheet.

Association for Payment Clearing Services (APACS) APACS was set up in 1985 as a UK-based non-statutory association of institutions delivering payment services to end customers. APACS provides the forum for institutions to discuss non-competitive issues relating to the payments industry.

Automated clearing house (ACH) An ACH transaction is an electronic method of transferring funds for the clearing and settling of payments among financial institutions. Such electronic transactions are substitutes for cheques.

Automated teller machines (ATMs) An unmanned terminal usually operated through the use of a magnetically coded card, which can dispense cash, take instructions on transfer, provide balances, etc.

Back testing In value-at-risk models, back testing is used as an ex-post comparison of the risk measure generated by the model against actual daily changes in portfolio value.

BACS systems (formerly Bankers Automated Clearing Services) A UK system for sending money electronically between banks. It allows automated settlement of accounts between customers, processing direct debits and direct credits, for example.

Bad loans Generally, loans that currently have not been repaid in part or in full (including those in arrears) and thus they are not currently accruing interest or on which interest is not being paid.

Balance of payments A financial statement prepared for a country which summarises the flow of goods, services and funds between the residents of that country and the residents of the rest of the world during a certain period of time.

Balance sheet A financial statement that reports a company's assets, liabilities and net worth at a point in time.

Bancassurance A French term coined to denote the combination of banking and insurance business within the same organisation. It relates to the distribution of insurance products through a bank's distribution channels.

Bank for International Settlements (BIS) An international bank set up in Basel (Switzerland) in 1930 that fosters international monetary and financial co-operation and serves as a bank for central banks. It is the world's oldest international financial organisation.

Bank holding companies (BHCs) In the US a company (so-called top holder) in control of one or more banks. A BHC could also own another bank holding company, which in turn owns or controls a bank. In Europe BHCs are usually referred to as banking/financial conglomerates or groups.

Bank of England Act 1998 A major piece of UK legislation that gave the Monetary Policy Committee sole responsibility for setting interest rates to meet the government's inflation target. The Act also provided for the transfer of responsibility to supervise deposit-taking institutions from the Bank to the Financial Services Authority.

Bank performance Refers to how well a bank is doing. Two commonly used bank performance measures are return-on-assets (ROA) and return-on-equity (ROE).

Bank Recovery and Resolution Directive (BRRD) EU Directive adopted on 15 April 2014 that sets common rules for all 28 member states in relation to when and how authorities will intervene to support troubled banks. The BRRD will be implemented in the eurozone countries through the Single Resolution Mechanism and will likely come into force on 1 January 2015.

Bank restructuring Usually this term refers to the change in structural features of banking markets (e.g. number of institutions operating in the market) through mergers and acquisitions. It can also refer to corporate changes internal to a bank organisation.

Bank runs Refers to the situation where a large proportion of depositors withdraw their savings because they fear that the bank is unsound and about to fail. See also **Banking crisis**.

Bank-based financial systems A type of financial structure where banks play a key role in mobilising savings, identifying viable investments, monitoring the decision of corporate managers and supplying risk management services. Germany and Japan are examples of bank-based systems. The alternative is the **market-based financial system**.

Banker's acceptance A short-term credit investment created by a non-financial firm and guaranteed by a bank. A bank's customer orders his/her bank to pay a sum of money at a future date, typically within six months. When the bank endorses the order for payment as 'accepted', it assumes responsibility for ultimate payment to the holder of the acceptance. At this point, the acceptance may be traded in secondary markets much like any other claim on the bank.

Banking Act (2009) UK legislation aimed at strengthening the resilience of the financial sector and maintaining public confidence by providing tools to the supervisory authorities for dealing with banks and building societies experiencing serious financial distress. The Act created the Special Resolution Regime (SRR) and gave the Bank of England statutory responsibility for systemically important inter-bank payment systems.

Banking and business banking codes Voluntary codes which set standards of good banking practice for banks and building societies to follow when they are dealing with personal or business customers (used in the UK).

Banking book In the context of commercial bank activities, it refers to the bank's core business such as deposits, cash, loans, fixed assets and other illiquid assets.

Banking crisis The situation when individuals and companies lose confidence in the banking system. For example, this may be the result of an actual (or expectations of a potential) run on the banking system. Any event, or series of events, that leads to concerns about the solvency of the banking system can be considered a banking crisis.

Banking Union Refers to the creation of a single centralised mechanism for the supervision and restructuring of banks. In June 2012 the EU leaders committed to creating a banking union for the eurozone members.

Best efforts syndication An arrangement whereby the underwriter in a syndicated contract agrees to do its best to sell the issue to the public at the agreed price but does not guarantee selling the entire issue.

'Big Bang' The name given to 27 October 1986, when the London Stock Exchange (LSE)'s new regulations took effect, allowing banks to own stock broking and jobbing firms and the automated price quotation system was introduced. The new rules allowed banks to undertake a broader range of securities business and resulted in many UK merchant (investment) banks being acquired by foreign institutions.

Bill and Cheque Clearing Systems (BCCS) In Japan, a system that clears bills and cheques which are exchanged between financial institutions located within the same geographical area.

Bill of Exchange A means of payment used in domestic (rarely) and international banking. Defined by the UK Bills of Exchange Act of 1882 as 'An unconditional order in writing, addressed by one person to another, signed by the person giving it, requiring the person to whom it is addressed to pay, on demand or at a fixed or determinable future time, a sum certain in money to, or to the order of, a specified person, or to bearer.'

Bitcoin Digital money and first decentralised P2P (peer-to-peer) payment network that is not controlled by a central authority or bank. It was created in 2009 by the pseudonymous person or group of people Satoshi Nakamoto.

Board of Governors The governing body of the Federal Reserve System, which is responsible for US monetary policy.

BOJ-NET (Bank of Japan Financial Network System) Funds Transfer System In Japan, it is the central bank's funds transfer system and is used to settle interbank obligations including net obligations of participants in the private sector clearing systems.

Bond A document issued by a government or company borrowing money from the public, stating the existence of a debt and the amount owing to the holder of the document (the bondholder). Bondholders use the document to obtain repayment of the loan. Bonds are usually long-term (greater than five-year maturity) and pay fixed rates of interest.

Boone indicator A measure of competition based on the idea that competition enhances the performance of efficient banks which is reflected in higher profits or increased market shares. It is calculated as the elasticity of profits to marginal costs. The more negative the Boone indicator is, the higher the level of competition in the loan market.

Branch A branch office is a key part of the distribution channel and acts as a legal and functional part of the bank, offering a full range of services.

Bridge bank In case of one or more failed institutions in a system, a bridge bank is a temporary financial institution that is established to receive and manage the good assets of the one or more failed institutions.

Broker An intermediary between market makers and investors. Brokers buy and sell securities on behalf of customers and do not take a position in securities.

Building society Mutually owned UK financial institution which issues shares (i.e. accepts deposits) and lends to borrowers mainly for home mortgages.

Call risk The risk that arises when a borrower or bondholder may redeem the security prior to maturity.

CAMELS A rating system used by regulatory and supervisory authorities to evaluate the safety and soundness of financial institutions. The acronym CAMELS refers to the six components of a bank's financial condition that are assessed: Capital adequacy, Asset quality, Management, Earnings, Liquidity and Sensitivity to market risk. Ratings are assigned for each component in addition to the overall rating of a bank's financial condition. The ratings are assigned on a scale from 1 to 5. Banks with ratings of 1 or 2 are considered to present few, if any, supervisory concerns, while banks with ratings of 3, 4, or 5 present moderate to extreme degrees of supervisory concern.

Capital In a balance sheet, capital is the difference between assets and liabilities. Also known as net worth or equity capital, it represents the ownership interest in a business.

Capital adequacy Refers to the level of capital a bank should hold in relation to the regulatory minimum standards, established under the Basel Accord. The amount of capital a bank holds relates to the riskiness of its business activity (both on-balance sheet and off-balance sheet). The more risky a bank's assets (on-balance sheet) and its other activities not recorded as assets (off-balance sheet business including guarantees, commitments, securities underwriting and so on) the more capital it needs to hold.

Capital management Refers to the capital adequacy management techniques used to ensure that the bank keeps an adequate level of capital to comply with regulations.

Capital markets Markets where capital funds (debt and equity) are issued and traded. This includes private placement sources of debt and equity as well as organised markets and exchanges.

Capital risk The decrease in the market value of assets relative to the market value of liabilities. In the case of a bank it refers to the risk associated with losses that have to be borne by its capital reserves. In extreme cases a bank may not have enough capital to cover all its losses and this is when the bank becomes insolvent/bankrupt. Note that capital risk is also used as a general term that refers to losses incurred by an investor where he or she may lose all or part of the principal invested.

Caps A type of option that gives the holder a right to purchase a forward rate agreement 'with hindsight'. For example, an interest rate cap may be bought in order to get protection that the interest rate will not move upwards beyond the level specified by the cap contract.

Cash management and transaction services Offered by large wholesale and/or international banks, cash management and transaction services can include, for instance, electronic funds transfers, cheque deposit services and electronic sending of letters of credit.

Central and Eastern European Countries (CEECs) Acronym used to indicate Central and Eastern European Countries, namely the Czech Republic, Hungary, Poland, Slovakia and Slovenia.

Central bank independence This refers to the level of independence that the central bank of a country has from the government (and political interference).

Certificate of Deposit (CD) A negotiable certificate issued by a bank as evidence of an interest-bearing wholesale time deposit.

Charter value Is the present value of the future profits that a solvent bank would be expected to get from a new business in protected markets. Also known as 'franchise value', it is an intangible asset that includes various factors such as its reputation, customer relationships, scale economies, market structure in the area and so on.

Check 21 In the United States, this term is used to refer to the Check Clearing for the 21st Century Act that became effective on 28 October 2004. The legislation gives banks greater flexibility in converting paper cheques into electronic form to speed up retail payments.

Cheque (UK) or Check (US) A form of payment used in place of cash and payable on demand that instructs a bank to pay the specified sum to the party named on the cheque from funds held on a deposit account.

CHIPS In the United States, the acronym used to indicate the Clearing House Interbank Payments System. It refers to the main bank-owned payments system for clearing large-value, mainly international, payments.

City banks The largest banks in the Japanese banking system that account for over 50 per cent of total banking sector assets.

Clearing Refers to the system whereby payments are settled among banks (or other financial intermediaries) and funds transferred from the account of one institution to the other. In the markets, clearing refers to the process of transferring the ownership of securities (and always involves a clearing house).

Clearing House Automated Payments System (CHAPS) A computerised system that provides a same day guaranteed sterling electronic credit transfer service within the United Kingdom.

Club deal Refers to a loan syndicated by a small number of participating banks, which are not entitled to transfer their portion of the loan to a third party.

Collars Hybrid derivative products, being part forward contract and part option. A collar (as its name suggests) puts an upper and lower bound on price movements.

Collateral An asset that secures repayment on a loan. The main form of collateral is real estate.

Collateralised debt obligations (CDOs) A type of structured asset-backed security. They allow banks to gather together cash-flow generating assets, such as loans, mortgages and bonds, into a special purpose vehicle. Investors will buy tranches in the CDOs that carry different levels of risk and return.

Collateralised loan obligations (CLOs) A type of CDO used by banks to securitise their loan portfolios.

Colonial banks A term used to describe 'British overseas banks' or 'Anglo-foreign banks'. Colonial banks were institutions set up by the British in their colonies and typically only provided services outside the United Kingdom. Note that the term can also be used more generally to describe banks that operate in the colonies of any country.

Commercial bank An institution that undertakes traditional banking activities: deposit-taking, lending and payments services.

Commercial credit Loans and other forms of credit extended to financial and non-financial companies.

Commercial letter of credit (L/C) A document issued by a bank stating its commitment to pay someone a stated amount of money on behalf of a buyer so long as the seller meets very specific terms and conditions.

Commercial paper A short-term unsecured instrument that promises to repay a fixed amount representing the cost of borrowed funds (such as LIBOR) plus interest, on a certain future date at a specific time. Usually issued by companies with a high credit standing. It may be a purely financial instrument or be based on an underlying commercial transaction.

Commitment A legal promise undertaken by a bank to lend to a customer.

Competition Commission Established by the Competition Act 1998, the Competition Commission is an independent body responsible for investigating mergers, markets and conditions and regulation of major UK industries.

Competition policy Government regulations and actions designed to promote competition and restrict monopoly practices by preventing individual firms from having excessive market power.

Competition-fragility view The traditional view that although competition in banking erodes market power, it also lowers profits and results in reduced franchise value that fosters bank risk-taking. It is the alternative to the **competition-stability view**.

Competition-stability view The view that bank risks are greater if there is more market power in the loan markets because loan rates will be higher and customers will find it more difficult to repay their debts. It is the alternative to the **competition-fragility view**.

Competitive pressures Refers to increased rivalry between institutions for customers.

Competitive risk The risk that arises as a consequence of changes in the competitive environment.

Compliance costs The incremental costs associated with complying with regulations.

Concentration ratio Measure used to identify the proportion of total market controlled by the largest firms. In the case of banks, for example, a three-firm concentration ratio measures the proportion of total assets (or total deposits) of the banking sector held by the three largest firms.

Conglomerate discounts Refer to fact that investors tend to value conglomerate or diversified firms less (at a discount) than focused companies.

Consumer credit Loans and other forms of credit extended to the household sector. Otherwise known as retail credit.

Consumer Financial Protection Bureau US agency responsible for consumers' protection in the financial sector.

Contagion The tendency of a financial/banking crisis to spread or spill over from one market to another.

Contractual savings institutions Term used to refer to insurance companies and pension funds whose main funding comes from long-term regular payments (savings) made by individuals/companies. The liabilities of these firms are the long-term future benefits to be paid to policy holders and fund holders.

Convergence This term is widely used to refer to a number of features of the financial system or economy overall. It can relate to: financial regulations across countries becoming more similar as a result of the harmonisation of international regulatory standards, macroeconomic variables such as interest rates, GDP and so on across countries moving to the same level, business practices of banks becoming more similar and so on.

'Convoy system' Term used in Japan to indicate the situation where the Ministry of Finance encouraged healthy banks to acquire those in trouble.

Co-operative banks Traditionally banks that are characterised by mutual ownership; today many co-operative banks have converted into listed institutions.

Corporate banking Corporate banking relates to banking services provided to companies although typically the term refers to services provided to relatively large firms.

Corporate governance Relates to the way outside investors and other stakeholders, such as employees and government, exercise control over senior management and other corporate insiders in order to protect their interests. In banking the situation of governance is complicated because banks are highly leveraged, have opaque business models and they benefit from government safety nets.

Correspondent banking In international banking, banks use correspondent banks to do business in markets where they have no physical presence.

Cost–income ratio A quick test of bank efficiency that can be calculated by dividing non-interest expenses by total income.

Cost of capital Relates to the costs of financing, namely, the expense of raising equity and debt. High-performing banks can raise funds by issuing shares or bonds more cheaply than poor-performing banks. Cost of capital arguments have been used in international banking theory to explain the rationale for overseas expansion.

Costs Derived from the liabilities side of the balance sheet, costs relate to payments that the bank has to undertake including payment of interest on deposits, staff and other operating costs.

Counterparty risk The risk that a party in a financial transaction will default. Counterparty risk is often used to indicate the credit risk on off-balance sheet products.

Countertrade Refers to a variety of commercial mechanisms for reciprocal trade, e.g. barter, switch trading, etc.

Country risk It is the risk that economic, social and political conditions and events in a foreign country will adversely affect a firm's commercial/financial interests.

Covered bonds Debt securities backed by assets such as mortgage loans. Covered bonds are backed by pools of mortgages that remain on the issuer's balance sheet, as opposed to mortgage-backed securities such as collateralised mortgage obligations (CMOs), where the assets are taken off the balance sheet.

Credit checking The process of evaluating an applicant's loan request in order to determine the likelihood that the borrower will repay.

Credit co-operative banks See Co-operative banks.

Credit culture Refers to the fundamental principles that drive lending activity and how management analyses risk. It is generally used in relation to an individual bank's lending and risk management procedures. For example, one may hear a banker say Citibank has a different credit culture to Barclays, implying their loan granting procedures and risk assessments are different in some way. The term can also be used to describe the attitude to borrowing by households, for example, 'US households have a different credit culture to the Japanese', meaning that the former love to borrow whereas the latter do not.

Credit default swaps (CDS) Derivatives that a bank or investor buys to insure a credit risk. If an issuer defaults on a bond or loan, the credit purchaser is compensated at par by the seller of the swap.

Credit easing An unconventional policy tool that implies a central bank's purchase of private sector assets to increase liquidity in the system, make credit more available and ultimately stimulate the economy.

Credit enhancements Protections to cover potential losses via financial support on securitised assets in case of adverse conditions. These risk-reduction techniques enable bankers to convert pools of poorly rated loans or mortgages into highly rated securities. They act as a financial cushion and help improve the credit rating of the structured products or transactions.

Credit facilities Facilities available to individuals and companies such as loans, overdrafts and lines of credit.

Credit guarantee scheme (CGS) One of the measures taken by the UK government in 2008 to help restore the stability of the financial system, protect customers and to boost investors' confidence particularly in the wholesale market. Under this scheme banks could obtain credit guarantees effectively backed by the government in return for a fee.

Credit multiplier A model that illustrates how banks create money determined by the ratio of change in deposits to the change in level of reserves.

Credit philosophy A bank's management's preference for more or less conservative loan granting practices.

Credit-rating agencies Private agencies, such as Standard & Poor's, Moody's and Fitch IBCA, that assess and rate the risk and quality of debt securities, companies, organisations and countries.

Credit rationing A technique used by banks to limit the amount of credit available to a specific segment of customers.

Credit reference agencies Banks use credit reference agencies such as Experian and Equifax in the credit-scoring process to check individuals' identity and credit history when they apply for a loan.

Credit risk The risk that a counterparty defaults on some or all of its contractual obligations. Credit risk in lending operations is the likelihood that a borrower will not be able to repay the principal or pay the interest.

Credit scoring A qualitative evaluation system employed by banks to assess the creditworthiness of an individual or firm that applies for a loan.

Credit transfers Also known as Bank Giro Credits, credit transfers are payments where the customer instructs their bank to transfer funds directly to the beneficiary's bank account.

Credit unions Non-profit financial institutions owned and operated entirely by their members. They provide financial services for their members, including savings and lending. Common in the United States, Ireland and (to a lesser extent) the United Kingdom.

Cross-border mergers Merger operations between institutions headquartered in different countries.

Cruickshank Report A report carried out by the UK government in 2000 looking into the issue of competition in UK banking and headed by Sir Donald Cruickshank.

Currency crisis Typically involves a speculative attack on the currency resulting in a devaluation or sharp depreciation. Authorities will be forced to defend the currency by selling foreign exchange reserves, raising domestic interest rates or imposing capital controls.

Currency forward A derivative contract that allows both the buyer and the seller to hedge against the risk of future fluctuations in currencies.

Currency swaps A transaction in which two counterparties exchange specific amounts of two different currencies at the outset and repay over time according to a predetermined rule which reflects interest payments and possibly amortisation of principal. The payment flows in currency swaps (in which payments are based on fixed interest rates in each currency) are generally like those of spot and forward currency transactions.

de Larosière Report A report published in 2009 by a high-level group on financial supervision chaired by Jacques de Larosière, outlining the proposals for reform of the EU regulatory framework. It contains 31 recommendations on regulation and supervision of EU financial markets and proposes a two-level approach to reforming the EU financial architecture.

Debentures Unsecured obligations of an issuing firm, which are claims only on the general assets of the company.

Debt Management Office (DMO) In the UK it is the Executive Agency of Her Majesty's Treasury. Its key duties include debt and cash management for the UK government, lending to local authorities and managing certain public sector funds.

Default The inability to ultimately fulfil a contractual obligation when it falls due.

Deficit unit Term used to denote the ultimate borrower in a financial transaction.

Deflation A general decrease in price levels that implies an inflation rate below 0 per cent that is caused by a collapse in aggregate demand.

Delegated monitoring One of the theories put forward as an explanation for the existence of banking. It relates to the role of banks as 'monitors' of borrowers.

Demand deposit Current account funds that can be withdrawn at any time without notice. They can be either interest or non-interest bearing. Sometimes known as chequing (checking) accounts.

Demutualisation The process of changing from a mutual company owned by its members (e.g. in the United Kingdom the traditional building societies) to a company owned by shareholders. When the building societies demutualised, their shares became listed on the stock exchange and they converted to banks.

Deposit and lending services Personal banking services that include, for instance, current and savings accounts and consumers' loans and mortgages.

Deposit insurance Where bank deposits of retail customers are insured against loss in the event of bank failure. Deposit insurance schemes can be privately funded (by the banks) or by the government.

Deposit Insurance Corporation An organisation that insures retail customers' deposits. For example, Japan's Deposit Insurance Corporation is a semi-governmental organisation that was established in 1971 with the purpose of operating the country's deposit insurance system, in line with the Deposit Insurance Law.

Deposit-taking institutions/Depository institutions Financial institutions that obtain their funds mainly from accepting savings and/or demand deposits from the general public and provide regular banking services such as chequing and savings accounts.

Deregulation The process of removing or reducing the rules and regulations on an industry with the objective of improving economic efficiency, competition and innovation in the market.

Derivatives Contracts involving rights or obligations relating to purchases or sales of underlying real or financial assets (e.g. gold and shares respectively), or relating to payments to be made in respect of movements in indices (e.g. the London FTSE 100). These rights and obligations are related to – or derived from – the underlying transactions, so they have been given the general name of *derivatives*.

Developing countries Those with a Gross National Income (GNI) per capita of $12,615 or less. The World Bank (2014) classifies economies as low-income (GNI $1,035 or less), lower middle-income (GNI $1,036–$4,085), upper middle-income (GNI $4,086-$12,615) and high-income (GNI $12,616 or more). Low-income and middle-income economies are sometimes referred to as developing countries.

Development banks Multilateral institutions that provide financial support and professional advice for economic and social development activities in developing countries, such as the World Bank. In Japan, a standard type of public financial institution such as, for example, Development Bank of Japan.

Digital divide Gap between those people and communities who have access to information technology (e.g. computers) and those who do not.

Direct debit Regular electronic debiting of funds from an individual's bank account to pay utility bills (electricity, gas, water bills), mortgages, etc.

Direct finance The situation where borrowers obtain funds directly from lenders in financial markets.

Discount A sum of money allowed for immediate payment of a sum due at a later date. If the sum is secured by a bill of exchange, the holder who buys the bill and receives the discount is said to discount the bill.

Discount window Monetary policy tool of central banks that allows eligible banking institutions to borrow money from the central bank, usually to meet short-term liquidity needs.

Disintermediation The process whereby borrowers and investors bypass banks and transact business directly.

Dodd-Frank (Wall Street Reform and Consumer Protection) Act The most comprehensive Wall Street reform in history. It is aimed at avoiding excessive risk taking and at building a safer and more stable financial sector in the US. It became US law in 2010 and was named after Senator Christopher J. Dodd and US Representative Barney Frank, who were the sponsors of the legislation.

Dollarisation When a non-US country either adopts US dollars as a local currency or uses them in parallel to the domestic currency.

Domestic mergers Mergers and/or acquisition operations where both bidder and target are from the same domestic country.

Duration analysis Used extensively as a risk management technique, it is a measure of the average life of an asset's (or liability's) cash flow.

Early warning systems (EWS) Models designed to draw regulators' attention to certain key variables associated with past crisis. These variables can reflect the risk of a single financial institution (micro-prudential approach) or the risk of the financial system as a whole (macro-prudential approach).

E-banking The remote delivery of banking products and services through electronic channels.

E-money E-money includes reloadable electronic money instruments in the form of stored value cards and electronic tokens stored in computer memory.

ECOFIN Council The Economic and Financial Affairs Council is, together with the Agriculture Council and the General Affairs Council, one of the oldest configurations of the Council of the European Union. It is commonly known as the ECOFIN Council or simply 'ECOFIN' and is composed of the economics and finance ministers of the member states, as well as budget ministers when budgetary issues are discussed. It meets once a month.

Economic and Monetary Union (EMU) The name given to the process of harmonising the economic and monetary policies of the member states of the European Union with a view to the introduction of a single currency, the euro.

Economies of scale Cost savings arising from decreasing unit cost of production as output increases.

Economies of scope Cost savings arising from joint production. For example, the costs of a financial institution offering banking and insurance products jointly are lower than the costs of separate firms providing only banking and insurance services.

Efficiency Hypothesis An industrial organisation theory that argues that more concentrated banking sectors containing a high proportion of large banks will tend to have higher profitability on average, because large banks are more efficient than their smaller counterparts operating in more competitive sectors.

Efficient Structure Hypothesis The view that larger firms tend to operate more efficiently, attain large market shares and therefore make higher profits. In empirical tests market share is treated as a proxy for relative efficiency of the firm.

Electronic funds transfer at point of sale (EFTPOS) A system which allows funds to be transferred automatically as goods are bought in a store.

Electronic funds transfer system (EFTS) A system which transfers funds by means of electronic communication rather than paper.

Emerging markets The term 'emerging market' was originally coined to describe a fairly narrow list of middle-to-higher income economies among the developing countries, with stock markets in which foreigners could buy securities. The term's meaning has since been expanded to include more or less all developing countries.

Equator Principles Set out in 2003 and reviewed in 2006, they are a voluntary set of rules in relation to banks' project financing and aimed at the development of socially responsible projects that reflect sound environmental management practices.

Equity In the context of capital markets, equity refers to an ordinary share. In accounting and legal terms, it refers to the financial interests in a firm's assets after prior claims have been made.

Ethical banking A broad term that relates to the principles and policies embraced by a banking firm in relation to the environmental and social impact of its investments and loans (see also **Sustainable banking**).

Euro The euro is the single currency for 18 EU countries.

Euro area/Eurozone/Euroland Expressions used interchangeably to refer to the EU countries that have adopted the euro.

Eurobank Banks and other financial intermediaries that bid for wholesale time deposits and make wholesale loans in a currency or currencies other than that of the country in which they are based.

Eurobond An international bond that may be issued in any currency, other than that of the issuer's home country, and subsequently traded in international markets.

Eurocommercial paper Note sold in London for same-day settlement in US dollars in New York. The maturities are more tailored to the needs of issuers and investors rather than the standard euronote terms of one, three and six months.

Eurocurrency A currency that is held in the form of time deposits in financial institutions outside the home country of the currency, e.g. yen time deposits held in London banks.

Eurocurrency banking This involves banks undertaking wholesale (large-scale) foreign exchange transactions (loans and deposits) with both residents and non-residents.

Euroequities Equities underwritten and distributed to investors outside the country of origin of the issuer.

Euroisation Euroisation occurs when residents of a country extensively use the euro alongside or instead of the domestic currency. For example, this is a process that is common in Central and Eastern Europe.

Euromarkets General term that refers to all the markets in which financial instruments denominated in Eurocurrencies are traded, e.g. Eurobonds, Euroequities, etc.

Euronote A short-term note (usually one, three and six months) issued under a note issuance facility (NIF) or Eurocommercial paper facility.

European Banking Authority (EBA) An independent EU agency established in January 2011 as part of the European System of Financial Supervision (ESFS). It aims to ensure effective and consistent bank prudential regulation and supervision across Europe. Among its main objectives are: to maintain stability in the EU and to safeguard the integrity, efficiency and orderly functioning of the banking sector.

European Central Bank (ECB) The ECB is the central bank for Europe's single currency, the euro.

European Community (EC) Former European Community that was superseded in 1993 by the European Union (EU).

European Currency Unit (ECU) European Currency Unit is a composite currency made up of currencies of the members of the former European Community (EC).

European Financial Stability Facility (EFSF) A temporary rescue facility created by euro countries in 2010 and superseded in 2012 by the European Stability Mechanism (ESM) as a permanent mechanism. It provides financial assistance by issuing bonds or other securities and lending the proceeds to countries under a programme; and, as at 2014, is still operating in parallel with the ESM with the ongoing programme for Greece, Portugal and Ireland.

European Insurance and Occupational Pensions Authority (EIOPA) An independent advisory body based in Frankfurt that is part of the ESFS. Its main responsibilities are to support the stability of the financial system, transparency of markets and financial products and protection of insurance customers and pension scheme members.

European Monetary System (EMS) An exchange rate regime established in 1979 whose main objective was to create closer monetary policy co-operation between Community countries, leading to a zone of monetary stability in Europe. The main components of the EMS were the ECU, the exchange rate and intervention mechanism (ERM) and various credit mechanisms. It ceased to exist in 1999 at the start of Stage Three of Economic and Monetary Union (EMU), when ERM II (Exchange Rate Mechanism II) was established.

European Securities and Markets Authority (ESMA) An independent EU authority created on 1 January 2011 and located in Paris. Its mission is to enhance the protection of investors and ensure stability, integrity, transparency, efficiency and orderly functioning of securities markets in the European Union. Works closely with EBA and EIOPA.

European Stability Mechanism (ESM) The permanent crisis resolution facility for euro area member states established in October 2012. It issues debt instruments in order to finance loans and other forms of financial assistance to euro area countries.

European Supervisory Authorities (ESAs) Refers to three new agencies that since January 2011 oversee the regulation of financial services across Europe, namely: the European Securities and Markets Agency (ESMA); the European Banking Agency (EBA); and the European Insurance and Occupational Pensions Authority (EIOPA).

European System of Central Banks (ESCB) The European System of Central Banks includes the ECB and the National Central Banks (NCBs) of all EU member states (including those that have not yet joined the EMU).

European System of Financial Supervisors (ESFS) Refers to the EU supervisory architecture, and its main purpose is to ensure supervision of the Union's financial system. It consists of the three ESAs; the European Systemic Risk Board (ESRB); the Joint Committee of the ESAs; the competent or supervisory authorities in the member states as specified in the legislation establishing the three ESAs.

European Systemic Risk Board (ESRB) An EU-level body established in 2010 responsible for the macro-prudential oversight of the Union by monitoring the entire financial sector. It is based in Frankfurt and is part of the ESFS. It works in close co-operation with the three ESAs.

European Union (EU) Currently an international organisation of 28 European member states established by the Treaty on European Union (i.e. Maastricht Treaty).

Eurosystem The Eurosystem comprises the ECB and the NCBs of those countries that have adopted the euro. The Eurosystem and the ESCB will co-exist as long as there are EU member states outside the Euro area.

Eurozone crisis The sovereign debt crisis that has been affecting eurozone countries since late 2009. It started after disclosure of underreporting of Greek budget deficits and then quickly spread to other EU countries, including Ireland and Portugal.

Excess managerial capacity Too many managers. Often referred to in the context of bank reorganisations after a merger. For example, when banks merge, the new organisation has two senior management teams, headquarters and a duplication of other managerial functions. A main focus of cost savings post merger is to get rid of this excess managerial capacity by removing duplication of managerial positions. It is also the view that overseas expansion may be driven by the willingness of the bank to extend its scale of operations to achieve a certain size that allows the existing managerial resources to be used more efficiently.

Excess spread In the context of asset securitisation it is the additional revenue generated by the difference between the coupon on the underlying collateral and the coupon payable on securities. It is used as credit enhancer to absorb possible collateral losses.

Exchange controls These are restrictions placed on the movements of funds in a particular currency (or limitations to the convertibility of a currency) by central banking authorities.

Exchange Rate Mechanism (ERM and ERM II) Introduced in March 1979 by the European Community as part of the EMS, the ERM was designed to reduce exchange rate variability and achieve monetary stability in Europe. In May 1999, at the start of Stage Three of the EMU, ERM II replaced the original ERM. Under ERM II, a central rate against the euro is defined for the currency of each member state not participating in the Euro area but participating in the ERM. The mechanism allows one standard fluctuation band of 15 per cent on either side of the central rate. Initially, Denmark and Greece joined ERM II. Since Greece adopted the euro in January 2001, Denmark was the only participant until June 2004, when Estonia, Lithuania and Slovenia joined. In May 2005 Cyprus, Latvia and Malta also joined ERM II.

Exchange rate policy Relates to the control and management of a country's levels of exchange rate for its currency. Governments influence the exchange rate by using the gold and foreign currency reserves held by their central banks to buy and sell domestic currency.

Factoring The purchase by the factor and sale by the company of its book debts on a continuing basis, usually for immediate cash. The factor then manages the sales ledger and the collection of accounts under terms agreed by the seller.

Fair value An accounting term that refers to the best possible estimate of the market prices of certain assets and liabilities using current information about future cash flows and current risk-adjusted discount rates. The alternative is historical cost accounting.

Fannie Mae (Federal National Mortgage Association – FNMA) A US government-sponsored entity and one of America's largest mortgage company providers. It was created in 1938 and became a for-profit, shareholder-owned company in 1968. The large exposures in high-risk mortgages before the housing market crash of 2007 resulted in federal bailout.

Faster Payments Service (FPS) UK new payments service for more than 20 years. Introduced in 2008, it allows internet, phone and standing order payments to be processed almost instantly.

Federal Deposit Insurance Corporation (FDIC) In the US, the FDIC is an independent agency of the federal government that preserves and promotes public confidence by insuring deposits in banks and thrifts for up to $250,000 (see also **Deposit Insurance Corporation**).

Federal Open Market Committee (FOMC) It is the monetary policy making body of the US Federal Reserve System. It is responsible for open market operations and is composed of the seven members of the Board of Governors and five Reserve Bank presidents.

Federal Reserve System (Federal Reserve or Fed) Established in 1913, it is the central bank of the United States. It comprises the Federal Reserve Board, the twelve Federal Reserve Banks, and the national and state member banks. Its primary purpose is to regulate the flow of money and credit in the country.

Fedwire A real-time gross settlement system (RTGS) that links Federal Reserve Banks to other banks and depository institutions. It is an important participant in providing interbank payment services as well as safekeeping and transfer services for US government and agency securities, and mortgage-backed securities.

Finance houses Financial institutions that accept deposits and finance leasing and hire purchase agreements.

Financial asset Term used to refer to claims held by the lender of funds against the borrower in the form of money, bank deposit accounts, bonds, shares, loans etc.

Financial claim A claim to the payment of a future sum of money and/or a periodic payment of money. It carries an obligation on the issuer to pay interest periodically or to redeem the claim at a stated value.

Financial Conduct Authority (FCA) One of the two new regulatory institutions for the UK financial services sector (the other is the Prudential Regulatory Authority), replacing the Financial Services Authority. The FCA was created by the Financial Services Act 2012 and is a separate body from the Bank of England. It is responsible for promoting effective competition, ensuring that relevant markets function well, and for the conduct regulation of all financial services firms.

Financial conglomerates This term defines a group of enterprises, formed by different types of financial institutions, operating in different sectors of the financial industry.

Financial conglomeration The process relating to the creation of groups of financial institutions operating in different sectors (banking, insurance, securities and so on) of the financial industry. A financial institution that undertakes a wide range of different financial activities is known as a financial conglomerate.

Financial deepening Refers to the size of the financial sector relative to an economy. It is typically proxied by domestic private credit by banks over GDP.

Financial deregulation See Deregulation.

Financial derivatives See Derivatives.

Financial futures Futures contracts in an interest rate, stock index, currency or interest-bearing security.

Financial guarantees See Guarantees.

Financial innovation Financial innovation can be defined as the act of creating and then popularising new financial instruments as well as new financial technologies, institutions and markets. It includes institutional, product and process innovation. Institutional innovations relate to the creation of new types of financial firms (such as specialist credit card firms like MBNA, discount broking firms such as Charles Schwab, internet banks and so on). Product innovation relates to new products such as derivatives, securitised assets, foreign currency mortgages and so on. Process innovations relate to new ways of doing banking/financial business, including online banking, phone banking, new ways of implementing information technology and so on.

Financial liability The issuer of a financial claim (borrower) is said to have a financial liability.

Financial liberalisation Generally refers to the process of opening up a market and the relaxation of restrictive practices. Deregulation is required for financial liberalisation to take place.

Financial Policy Committee (FPC) An independent committee at the Bank of England created in 2013 and charged with a primary objective of identifying, monitoring and taking action to remove or reduce systemic risks with a view to protecting and enhancing the resilience of the UK financial system. The FPC has a secondary objective to support the economic policy of the government.

Financial ratio analysis Refers to the use of key ratios to both measure and analyse the performance of a firm. In banking the typical performance ratios are: ROA, ROE, C/I and NIM.

Financial repression A situation where restrictions on financial activities exist and government intervention in financial markets is severe. A financially repressed system is likely to be characterised by a lack of competition in banking and financial markets, and interest rates and other financial market prices do not reflect the underlying economic fundamentals.

Financial Services Act 1986 The Financial Services Act 1986 established the regulatory framework for investor protection in the United Kingdom.

Financial Services Act 2012 The piece of UK legislation that replaced the FSA with the PRA and an FCA. In addition, an expert macro-prudential authority was created within the Bank: the FPC.

Financial Services (Banking Reform) Act (2013) A UK banking bill that received royal assent in December 2013 and that introduced far-reaching reforms to make banks more resilient to shocks, easier to fix when in trouble and to reduce the severity of future crises. Among the key provisions are the introduction of an electrified ring-fence between retail and investment banks and criminal penalties for senior bankers who behave irresponsibly. The Bill also introduced preference for deposits protected under the Financial Services Compensation Scheme if a bank enters insolvency.

Financial Services Action Plan (FSAP) Initiated in 1999 and to last for six years, the FSAP can be considered the European Commission response towards improving the single market in financial services in the EU.

Financial Services Agency In Japan, the governmental agency established in 1998 responsible for supervision and inspection functions of the private sector financial institutions.

Financial Services and Markets Act (2000) (Regulated Activities) Order 2001 The UK legislation that created the Financial Services Authority.

Financial Services Authority (FSA) The Financial Services Authority was established by the Labour government in 1997 as the regulatory body for the whole UK financial services industry. A number of separate regulatory bodies were brought together in the FSA, which also took over the responsibilities that the Bank of England had for supervising banks and other financial institutions. In April 2013 the FSA was replaced by the twin peaks of the FCA and PRA.

Financial Stability Oversight Council (FSOC) Created under the 2010 Dodd-Frank Act, the Council provides comprehensive monitoring of the stability of the US financial system.

Firm-specific advantages One of the theories on the rationale for international banking. For example, firms have financial, economic, business and other advantages specific to their own operations that enable them to undertake international activities.

Fiscal policy One of the five major forms of economic policy conducted by governments, fiscal policy relates to changes in the level and structure of government spending and taxation designed to influence the economy.

Fixed-rate assets and liabilities Fixed-rate assets and liabilities carry rates that are constant throughout a certain time period (e.g. one year) and their cash flows do not change unless there is a default, early withdrawal or an unanticipated prepayment.

Floating-rate debt Debt instruments that pay a variable (as opposed to fixed) rate of interest.

Floating-rate note A medium-term security which carries a floating rate of interest which is reset at regular intervals, usually quarterly or half-yearly, in relation to some pre-determined reference rate, typically LIBOR.

Floors A type of option. An interest rate floor is similar to a cap except that it protects an investor or depositor against a floating rate of interest falling below a specified lower or floor level.

Foreign debt crisis Situation of financial turmoil that occurs when a country is unable to service its foreign debt, such as in the case of a sovereign debt crisis or private debt crisis (or both). See, for example, Europe's debt crisis started in 2010.

Foreign direct investment (FDI) The movement of capital across national frontiers in a way that grants the investor control over the acquired asset. Thus it is distinct from portfolio investment which may be cross-border, but does not offer such control. Firms which undertake FDI are known as multinational enterprises.

Foreign exchange risk The risk that exchange rate fluctuations affect the value of a bank's assets, liabilities and off-balance sheet activities denominated in foreign currency.

Foreign Exchange Yen Clearing System (FXYCS) In Japan, the FXYCS was established in 1980 to facilitate clearing of yen payments for cross-border financial transactions.

Forfaiting In international banking, the situation where the exporter agrees to surrender the rights to claim for payment of goods or services delivered to an importer under a contract of sale, in return for a cash payment from a forfaiting bank. The forfaiting bank takes over the exporter's debt and assumes the full risk of payment by the importer. The exporter is thereby freed from any financial risk in the transaction and is liable only for the quality and reliability of the goods and services provided.

Forward rate agreement (FRA) A common type of forward contracts that gives the agents involved the opportunity to hedge against interest rate risk thereby 'locking in' the future price of the assets.

Forwards In a forward contract, two parties agree to exchange over-the-counter (OTC) a real or financial asset on a prearranged date in the future for a specified price.

Freddie Mac (Federal Home Loan Mortgage Corporation – FHLMC) A US government-sponsored enterprise created in 1970 and one of America's largest mortgage company providers. The large exposures in high-risk mortgages before the housing market crash of 2007 resulted in federal bailout.

Free banking A school of thought that maintains that the financial sector would work better without regulation, supervision and central banking.

Funds transfer pricing (FTP) A process used to determine the relative performance of different business units within a bank that considers assets and liabilities simultaneously. It can significantly contribute to optimise a bank's risk/return profiles and is carried out via the treasury division.

Futures contracts An exchange traded contract generally calling for the delivery of a specified amount of a particular commodity, or financial instrument, at a fixed date in the future.

Gap analysis Gap analysis is possibly the best-known interest rate risk management technique. The 'gap' refers to the difference between interest rate sensitive assets and interest rate sensitive liabilities over a specific time horizon.

Geographical diversification Refers to the expansion of the supply of a bank's financial products and services into different geographic locations or markets.

Gilt-edged securities UK government bonds.

Global onshore private banking business The business of offering banking and investment services to wealthy (high net worth) individuals in their own country (onshore). Wealthy individuals that have their personal finances managed outside their home country (e.g. UK billionaires who place their funds in Swiss banks) are said to be undertaking offshore private banking activity. The word 'global' comes from the fact that there are a number of firms that offer such services in many countries, such as Citigroup Private Bank and UBS. Note also that many banks use the term 'global' to signify that their services are available to an international clientele as well as to indicate that they have substantial international operations.

G-SIBs Global Systemically Important Banks. See SIFIs and G-SIFIs.

G-SIFIs Global Systemically Important Financial Institutions. These can be banks, insurance companies or other financial institution. See SIFIs and G-SIBs.

Globalisation General term used to describe the world-wide integration of both capital and money markets.

Governing Council The main decision-making power of the ECB.

Government bonds Bonds issued on behalf of (or backed up by) the government.

Government safety net Public policy regulation designed to minimise the risk of bank runs, it includes deposit insurance and the lender-of-last-resort function.

Government-sponsored enterprises (GSEs) Enterprises created by the US Congress to perform a key role in the country's housing finance system, namely to provide liquidity, stability and affordability to the mortgage markets. Examples are Fannie Mae and Freddie Mac.

Gramm-Leach-Bliley Act Legislation passed in 1999 whereby US banks can establish financial holding companies and engage in the full range of financial services areas, such as securities underwriting, insurance sales and underwriting and investment banking business.

Guarantees These are traditional off-balance sheet exposures, where a bank has underwritten the obligations of a third party and currently stands behind the risk, for example standby letters of credit and acceptances.

Hard information Refers to verifiable data that as a result of technological process can be summarised into numerical scores, and it can be stored and transmitted electronically. For example, in bank lending, the credit scoring data.

Hedge fund A private investment fund that trades and invests in various assets such as securities, commodities, currency and derivatives on behalf of its clients.

Hedging Reducing risk by taking a position that offsets existing or expected exposures. Hedging is the avoidance of risk by arranging a contract at specified prices which will yield a known return.

Herfindahl-Hirschman index (HHI) Often just referred to as the Herfindahl index, it is a measure of market concentration calculated as the sum of the squares of the market shares of all firms operating in the market.

High net worth individuals (HNWIs) Wealthy personal (retail) customers. Definitions vary but typically refer to individuals with more than US$1 million or more in investable assets (the limit is usually US$30 million for *ultra* HNWIs.

Hire services (hire purchase) A transaction in which customers pay for the cost of the asset, together with the financing charges, over the hire period and take legal title on the equipment at the time of final payment (or there may be a nominal purchase option fee at the end of the payment period).

Home and office banking systems (HOBS) Banking facilities provided in the home or office through the means of a TV screen, personal computer or telephone.

Horizontal FDI A theory in international banking that associates the existence of multinationals in a country to trade barriers that make exporting costly.

H-statistic A non-structural measure of market competition based on the empirical observation of the impact on firm-level revenues of variations in the prices of the factors of production. Built into the test is an explicit assumption of profit-maximising behaviour on the part of the firms. When $H = 1$, it indicates perfect competition; $0 < H < 1$ monopolistic competition; and $H \leq 0$ monopoly or collusive oligopoly.

Household information files (HIFs) Information databases containing financial files and other characteristics of households. Data are usually used for marketing purposes.

Hubris hypothesis A managerial explanation as to why mergers may destroy value according to which over-confident managers systematically overestimate the advantages of an acquisition and therefore pay too much for targets, leading to value destruction/no performance improvements.

Impaired loan Situation that occurs when it is likely that all amounts due on a loan will not be collected.

Income statement See Profit and loss account.

Independent Commission on Banking An independent body set up in 2010 with the task of investigating possible reforms for promoting financial stability and competition in the UK banking markets and to make recommendations to the government.

Indirect finance The situation where borrowers obtain funds indirectly from lenders through financial intermediaries.

Inflation risk The probability that an increase in the price level for goods and services will unexpectedly erode the purchasing power of a bank's earnings and returns to shareholders.

Information asymmetries The imperfect distribution of information among parties to a contract. They can create situations of adverse selection and moral hazard.

Information memo In the syndicated lending process, the memo prepared by the arranger specifying the terms of the transaction. Also known as bank-book.

Innovative (or new product) stage When a good or service is produced to meet a new consumer demand or when a new technology enables the creation of innovative goods.

Inspection Term relating to when bank regulators demand to inspect the books (financial accounts) and managerial practices of a bank. Inspection is often undertaken on the bank's own premises.

Instruments of portfolio constraint Instruments that may be imposed by the authorities for the aims of monetary policy that constrain the portfolio structure of financial institutions, with the purpose of influencing credit creation and, possibly, the type of lending taking place.

Insurance services Insurance products protect policyholders from various adverse events. Policyholders pay regular premiums and the insurer promises compensation if the specific insured event occurs. There are two main types of insurance – life insurance and general (or property and casualty) insurance.

Interbank Usually refers to short-term wholesale loans traded between banks.

Interest rate risk Defined as the risk arising from the mismatching of the maturity and the volume of banks' assets and liabilities as part of their asset transformation function.

Interest rate swaps A transaction in which two counterparties exchange interest payment streams of differing character based on an underlying notional principal amount. The three main types are coupon swaps (fixed rate to floating rate in the same currency), basis swaps (one floating rate index to another floating rate index in the same currency), and cross-currency interest rate swaps (fixed rate in one currency to floating rate in another).

Interest spreads Difference between interest paid and interest owned, e.g. if interest paid on deposits averages 4 per cent and interest earned on assets equals 10 per cent then the interest spread is 6 per cent.

Intermediary An intermediary links borrowers and lenders either by acting as an agent or by bringing together potential traders, or by acting in place of a market.

Internationalisation General term used to describe the substantial increase in the presence of banks and other financial institutions doing business outside their domestic markets.

Intervened bank In bank resolution terminology, an intervened bank refers to an insolvent or non-viable institution whose control is in the hands of the authorities.

Investment banking Financial business that involves dealing mainly with corporate customers and specialises in securities markets activities including underwriting, trading, asset management and corporate restructuring (e.g. mergers and acquisitions) advisory activities.

Investment intermediaries In the United States, a term to designate mutual funds, investment banks, securities firms and finance houses whose liabilities are usually short-term money market or capital market securities.

Investment products Generally speaking these are services and products offered to retail customers that include for example mutual funds (known as unit trusts in the UK), investment in company stocks and various other securities related products (such as savings bonds).

Invoice discounting services Similar to factoring, invoice discounting services involve a narrower service where the discounting company collects sales receipts but the firm still manages its ledger.

Islamic banking A type of banking particularly common in South and South-East Asia, the Gulf Co-operation Council Countries and other countries, that offers products and services that do not charge or pay interest.

Japan Post Bank A Japanese bank which was formerly part of the Post Office Savings Bank and was privatised in 2007. It is now part of the Japan Post Holdings postal and financial services group.

Jobber A firm, or individual, in the stock exchange responsible for quoting prices to and trading securities via brokers.

Key performance indicators (KPIs) Financial (e.g. asset quality) and non-financial (e.g. customer satisfaction) factors that management monitors and reviews against the company's strategic objectives.

Lamfalussy process A procedure established in February 2001 by a Committee of Wise Men chaired by Alexander Lamfalussy, for improving the effectiveness of the EU's securities market regulatory process.

Large and complex banking groups (LCBGs) Financial institutions with such a large asset size and business complexity that their failure would most probably result in contagion as it would affect other institutions and harm the stability of the financial markets.

Leasing A financial technique for obtaining the use of an asset by contracting a series of payments over a specific period. The grantor of the lease (the lessor) remains the owner of the leased property throughout the term of the lease and receives payments from the lessee.

Least-cost resolution In the context of bank restructuring, the generally accepted principle that the bank resolution should be carried out in a manner that minimises the cost for the resolution authority, deposit insurer or the government.

Legal risk The risk that contracts that are not legally enforceable or documented correctly could disrupt or negatively affect the operations, profitability or solvency of the bank.

Lender of last resort (LOLR) The understanding that the central bank will always stand ready to lend money to a bank or number of banks experiencing a crisis if they cannot obtain finance from market sources.

Lerner index of monopoly power A non-structural indicator of the degree of market power that represents the extent to which market power allows firms to fix a price above marginal cost. It is based on the assumption that in perfect competition, price equals marginal cost and therefore a measure of the degree to which price exceeds marginal cost. It ranges between 0 (P = MC in perfect competition) and 1 (P > MC in monopoly), and $0 < L < 1$ if MC > 0.

Letter of credit A document issued by a bank stating its commitment to pay someone a stated amount of money on behalf of a buyer so long as the seller meets very specific terms and conditions.

Leverage Usually refers to the debt to equity ratio; the higher the proportion of debt over equity the greater the leverage (or gearing). The leverage ratio for banks refers to the Tier 1 capital to assets ratio that regulators expect to range between a minimum of 3 to 4 per cent depending on a specific bank's characteristics.

Liabilities The debts and other financial obligations of a firm or an individual.

Liability management The process whereby banks manage liabilities and buy in (i.e. borrow) funds when needed from the markets for interbank deposits, large-sized time deposits and certificates of deposit.

Liikanen Report A set of proposals published in October 2012 on reforming the banking sector in Europe prepared by a group chaired by Mr Erkki Liikanen, Governor of the Bank of Finland. The central recommendation is to legally separate (ring-fence) risky activities from core banking activities.

LIBID (London Interbank Bid Rate) The rate at which a bank is willing to buy funds in the international interbank markets.

LIBOR (London Interbank Offered Rate) The rate at which a bank is willing to lend funds (wholesale money) in the international interbank markets.

LIMEAN The mean of LIBID and LIBOR.

Liquid asset An asset that can easily be turned into cash at short notice.

Liquidity The ability of an institution to pay its obligations when they fall due.

Liquidity crisis A situation where depositors demand larger withdrawals than normal and banks are forced to borrow funds at an elevated interest rate. A liquidity crisis is usually unpredictable and can be due to either a lack of confidence in the specific bank, or some unexpected need for cash. Liquidity crises can ultimately result in 'a run' and even the insolvency of the bank.

Liquidity management Those activities a bank should carry out to ensure that holdings of liquid assets are sufficient to meet its obligations as they fall due, including unexpected transactions.

Liquidity risk The risk that a solvent institution is temporarily unable to meet its short-term monetary obligations.

Loan commitments Promises to lend up to a pre-specified amount to a pre-specified customer at pre-specified terms.

Loan policy A fundamental part of the credit process whereby the lending guidelines that bank employees follow to conduct lending business are formalised.

Loan rate Term used in the process of loan pricing to indicate the price of the loan.

Loan sales A loan sale occurs when a bank originates a loan and then decides to sell it to another legal entity, usually a financial intermediary. Where the bank is selling only part of the loan then the operation is called loan participation or loan syndication.

Location advantages One of the theories on the rationale for international banking.

Longer-term refinancing operations A process by which the ECB provides financing to banks in the euro area. In the wake of the crisis the ECB has provided liquidity to banks using LTROs with maturities of up to 36 months.

Long-term credit banks A private credit institution that provides long- and medium-term finance to the corporate sector.

Macro-hedging When a bank uses futures (or other derivatives) to hedge the entire balance sheet (the aggregate portfolio interest rate risk).

Major British banking groups (MBBGs) According to the British Bankers Association, MBBGs currently include: Santander UK Group; Barclays Group; HBOS Banking Group; Lloyds Banking Group; The Royal Bank of Scotland Group.

Management risk The risk that management lacks the ability to make commercially profitable and other decisions consistently. It can also include the risk of dishonesty by employees and the risk that the bank will not have an effective organisation.

Managerial motives Alternative explanations to performance and efficiency motives for bank consolidation phenomenon based on the idea that managers engage in M&A operations in order to maximise their own utility at the expense of shareholders (see also **Quiet life** and **Hubris hypothesis**).

Market capitalisation Market value of a company's outstanding equity.

Market flex language In a syndicated loan contract it is the right given to underwriters/arrangers to change the structure and conditions of the borrowing (e.g. changes in interest rates and covenants) in order to attract enough commitment from participants in financing the loan.

Market maker An institution that quotes bid and offer prices for a security and is ready to buy and sell at such prices.

Market maker of last resort (MMOLR) The evolution of the lender of last resort from the traditional idea of a provision that should apply only to solvent but illiquid banks, to one that has to meet the liquidity needs of dysfunctional financial markets.

Market-based financial systems A type of financial structure where well-functioning markets will reduce inherent inefficiencies associated with banks and play a key role in promoting economic growth. The US and UK are examples of market-based systems. The alternative is the **bank-based financial system.**

Market-based measures of bank risk Measures of bank risk that are not accounting-based such as: the volatility of stock prices; Moody's KMV Expected Default Frequency (EDF); and the five-year cumulative probability of default (PD) indicators.

Market risk The risk of losses in on- and off-balance sheet positions arising from movements in market prices. This type of risk pertains in particular to short-term trading in assets, liabilities and derivative products, and relates to changes in interest rates, exchange rates and other asset prices.

Market segmentation A systematic process whereby different types of groups are identified (segmented) for target marketing purposes.

Mature product stage A stage in the product life cycle when growth has started to slow and defending market share becomes the chief concern. Additionally, more competitors have stepped forward to challenge the product at this stage, some of whom may offer a higher-quality version of the product at lower price. Customers are more aware of the product's features and also are likely to become more price-sensitive (demand for the product in the home market becomes more elastic). At this stage, the producer is likely to benefit from scale economies so production costs fall. When a product or service reaches maturity, foreign expansion becomes likely.

Maturity The length of time elapsing before a debt is to be redeemed by the issuer.

Medium-term notes (MTNs) Medium-term debt securities that pay floating rates of interest.

Merchant bank A British term to indicate an investment bank, that is a financial institution that specialises in securities markets activities such as underwriting and trading and advising on such issues as mergers and acquisitions. Merchant banking is also a term used in the United States to refer to investment banks that acquire equity stakes in companies either for strategic or temporary investment purposes.

Merger premium In a merger operation, the premium that an acquiring bank is willing to pay for the target bank over and above the market value of the target bank's stock. Merger premiums are typically proportional to the potential gains from the merger operations; in banking they may also be higher for banks that have implicit bailout guarantees.

Mergers and acquisitions (M&As) The combination of two (or more) institutions through partnering or purchase.

Micro-hedging When a bank hedges a transaction associated with an individual asset, liability or commitment.

Modern banking As opposed to traditional banking, modern banking refers to the new ways of doing banking business as a result of the forces of change. Generally used to emphasise the fact that banks have become full-service financial firms operating in many different sectors of the financial industry (banking, insurance, pensions, investments and so on) in both their home and international markets.

Modern international banking Refers to the process of expansion of banks overseas in recent years.

Monetary aggregates A series of measures for the money supply, including narrow and broad measures. Usually termed as M1, M2, M3 and M4.

Monetary policy Relates to the actions taken by central banks to influence the availability and cost of money and credit by controlling some measure (or measures) of the money supply and/or the level and structure of interest rates.

Monetary Policy Committee (MPC) An independent nine-member panel that is responsible for setting the short-term base interest rate and more generally for the UK monetary policy decisions.

Monetary transmission mechanism Describes the process through which monetary policy decisions affect the real economy and inflation level.

Money Money is represented by the coins and notes which we use in our daily lives; it is the commodity readily acceptable by all people wishing to undertake transactions. It is also a means of expressing a value for any kind of product or service. This, of course, is the most common and narrowest definition of money. For monetary policy purposes broader definitions of money can include coins and notes plus bank deposits and other items.

Money market Short-term financial market usually involving large-value (wholesale) assets with less than one year to maturity.

Money market funds (MMFs) Type of mutual funds that invest in highly liquid and low-risk securities such as government securities and certificates of deposits.

Money transmission services The activity of financial intermediation exercised, for instance, by the means of: the collection and transfer of funds (e.g. credit transfers); the transmission and execution of payment orders (e.g. cheque payments and other payments media); and the offsetting of debits and credits.

Monitoring Checking on borrowers' behaviour and ability to repay their loans through the life of the loan.

Monoline insurer Bond insurer that provides guarantees to issuers, often in the form of credit wraps or credit default swaps, to enhance the credit of the issuer. These insurance companies first began providing wraps for municipal bond issues, then specialised in providing credit enhancement for other types of bonds, such as mortgage-backed securities.

Moral hazard It is a situation that arises when a contract or financial arrangement creates incentives for the parties involved to behave against the interest of others.

Mortgage-backed bonds Bonds traded mainly in the United States which pay interest on a semi-annual basis and repay principal either periodically or at maturity, and where the underlying collateral is a pool of mortgages.

Mortgage-backed securities (MBS) These are securities backed by a collection of mortgages.

Mortgage equity withdrawal Relates to home owners borrowing against the increased value of their property (capital gains), by taking out additional housing equity loans.

Multinational banking Refers to banks having some element of ownership and control of banking operations outside their home market.

Mutual funds An institution that manages collectively funds obtained from different investors. In the United States they are referred to as mutual funds; in the United Kingdom, unit trusts.

National central banks (NCBs) Within the Eurosystem, the central banks of the 18 European Union member states whose common currency is the euro.

National Competent Authorities (NCAs) Authorities responsible for conducting the banking supervision in the euro area.

National consolidation The reduction in the number of banks in a system generally due to mergers and/or acquisitions between domestic institutions.

National debt management policy One form of economic policy conducted by governments that is concerned with the manipulation of the outstanding stock of government debt instruments held by the domestic private sector with the objective of influencing the level and structure of interest rates and/or the availability of reserve assets to the banking system.

Negative equity The situation where the market value of a property is less than the outstanding mortgage loan.

Net interest margin (NIM) A common measure of bank performance that is equal to gross interest income minus gross interest expense.

New Empirical Industrial Organization (NEIO) Describes techniques for the estimation of competition in an industry. It refers to development of the so-called 'non-structural approaches' that are based on the direct observation of firms' conduct and on the evaluation of how firms set their prices and quantities.

New member states (NMSs) Refers to the ten countries that joined the EU on 1 May 2004, namely Cyprus, the Czech Republic, Estonia, Hungary, Latvia, Lithuania, Malta, Poland, Slovenia and the Slovak Republic.

NIM-8 (countries) Refers to the former transition countries. This includes the Central and Eastern European countries (CEECs) (Czech Republic, Hungary, Poland, Slovenia and the Slovak Republic) and the three Baltic States (Estonia, Latvia and Lithuania).

Non-deposit-taking institution (NDTI) A general term used to refer to financial institutions whose main activity is not to take deposits, such as insurance companies, pension funds, investment companies, finance houses and so on.

Non-performing loans (NPLs) Non-performing loans are loans on which debtors have failed to make contractual payments for a predetermined time.

Non-structural indicators This refers to the empirical competition literature in banking that moves away from the assumption that concentration and competition are inversely related and argues that competition should be measured ignoring market concentration. Non-structural indicators of competition include the Panzar–Rosse H-statistic, the Lerner index, the Boone indicator and the persistence of profitability (POP) measures.

Note A certificate of indebtedness like a bond, but used most frequently for short-term issues.

Note issuance facility (NIF) A medium-term arrangement enabling borrowers to issue short-term paper, typically of three or six months' maturity, in their own names. Usually a group of underwriting banks guarantees the availability of funds to the borrower by purchasing any unsold notes at each rollover date or by providing a standby credit. Facilities produced by competing banks are called, variously, revolving underwriting facilities (RUFs), note purchase facilities and Euronote facilities.

Off-balance-sheet (OBS) activities Banks' business, often fee-based, that does not generally involve booking assets and taking deposits. Examples are swaps, options, foreign exchange futures, standby commitments and letters of credit.

Off-balance sheet (OBS) management This refers to those activities banks should carry out to control and limit their exposure derived from off-balance sheet transactions.

Off-balance-sheet (OBS) risk This relates to the risks incurred by a bank in dealing with contingent, non-traditional banking activities such as guarantees and letters of credit.

Office of Federal Housing Enterprise Oversight (OFHEO) In the US was an independent body responsible for ensuring the stability, liquidity and affordability of the US mortgage market and for overseeing two GSEs: Fannie Mae and Freddie Mac. In 2008, it was incorporated into the newly created Federal Housing Finance Agency.

Office of the Comptroller of the Currency (OCC) The OCC is an independent bureau of the US Department of the Treasury, set up in 1863 to regulate all banks chartered by the Federal Reserve.

Official bank rate (also referred to as 'policy rate' or 'base rate') In the UK, the Bank Rate is the overnight interest rate at which the Bank of England lends to financial institutions. In setting this key rate the Bank considers the amount at which banks borrow from each other overnight.

Offshore banking Banking activity undertaken by institutions that are located outside the country of residence of the customer, typically in a low-tax jurisdiction (e.g. Bahamas and Bermuda) and that provide financial and legal advantages.

Open market operations (OMOs) These operations are the most important tools by which central banks can influence interest rates and therefore the amount of money in the economy. The principle is that the central bank will influence the level of liquidity and the level and structure of interest rates within the financial system by purchasing or selling government debt to the non-bank private sector.

Operating risk This relates to the possibility that operating expenses might vary significantly from what is expected, producing a decrease in income and a bank's value.

Operational risk The risk associated with the possible failure of a bank's systems, controls or other management failure (including human error).

Option The contractual right, but not the obligation, to buy or sell a specific amount of a given financial instrument at a previously fixed price or a price fixed at a designated future date. A traded option refers to a specific option traded on official markets. A call option confers on the holder the right to buy the financial instrument. A put option involves the right to sell.

Ordinary shares Security representing the claim to the residual ownership of a company. Known as common stock in the US. (See **Equity**.)

Originate-to-distribute model When banks distribute (i.e. 'sell') the loans they originate to investors rather than hold them until maturity. (See **Originate-to-hold model**.)

Originate-to-hold model When banks use deposits to fund loans with the intention to keep them on their balance sheets until maturity as opposed of selling them to investors (See **Originate-to-distribute model**.)

Over-collateralisation In the context of asset securitisation it is the holding of a larger pool of assets than securities issued. It is used as credit enhancer to absorb possible collateral losses.

Over-the-counter (OTC) An informal dealer-based market.

Own Funds Directive EC directive adopted by the Council of Ministers in April 1989. The aim was to harmonise the definition of capital for all EU credit institutions in line with the 1988 Basel I recommendations.

Ownership advantage In international banking, one of the theories for explaining overseas expansion is based on the idea that banks expand overseas to enjoy direct benefits derived from their technological expertise, marketing know-how, production efficiency, managerial expertise, innovative product capability and so on.

Panzar–Rosse statistic See H-statistic.

Payment system Any organised arrangement for transferring value between its participants.

Peer group A set of individual banks that are grouped following analytical criteria such as size, business mix, ownership, etc.

Peer group analysis Used by banks to compare the financial performance against other similar-sized banks with similar characteristics and business mix (i.e. a peer group). In the context of EWS, for example, the aim of peer group analysis is to identify a possible area of underperformance and other differences that could imply supervisory concern.

Pension services Pension services offered via banks are known as private pensions. These are distinguished from public pensions that are offered by the state. Contributions paid into the pension fund are invested in long-term investments with the individual making contributions receiving a pension on retirement (a retirement income is generated by the purchase of annuities).

Persistence of profits (POP) This argues that if in a market entry and exit are sufficiently free to eliminate any abnormal profit, then all firms' profit rates will tend to converge rapidly towards the same long-run average value. The extent to which firm- or industry-level profits converge to long-run values reflects the degree of competition in the market. The slower the speed of adjustment, the stronger the POP, the lower the competition.

Plastic cards These include credit cards, debit cards, cheque guarantee cards, store cards, travel and entertainment cards and 'smart' or 'chip' cards.

Portfolio risk The risk that a particular combination of projects, assets, units or else in the portfolio will fail to meet the overall objectives of the portfolio due to a poor balance of risks. In the case of a bank loan portfolio, for example, it is the risk that the initial choice of lending opportunities will prove to be poor, in that some of the alternative opportunities that were rejected will turn out to yield higher returns than those selected.

Preference shares Shares which pay a fixed dividend and rank ahead of ordinary shares in liquidation. Known as preferred stock in the US. (See **Equity**.)

Price elasticity of demand A measure of the degree of responsiveness of demand to a given change in price.

Price stability A situation of stability in the level of prices of goods and services that protects the purchasing power of money.

Prices and incomes policy One type of economic policy of a government intended to influence the inflation rate by means of either statutory or voluntary restrictions upon increases in wages, dividends and/or prices. Widely used in the United Kingdom during the 1960s.

Primary market Market in which securities are traded between issuers and investors, thereby raising additional funds for the issuing firm.

Prime rate One of several base interest rates used as an index to price commercial loans.

Principal–agent problems An economic theory concerning the relationship between a principal (for example, a shareholder) and an agent of the principal (for example, a company manager). It involves the costs of resolving conflicts of interest between the principals and agents (agency costs).

Private banking Specialist banking, investment, estate planning and tax services provided to wealthy (high net worth) personal customers.

Private deposit-taking financial institutions Privately owned financial intermediaries funded mainly by deposits from the public. The distinction between private and public deposit-making institutions is usually made when one describes a banking system that has both private and government-owned banks, such as in Japan.

Private equity finance A type of service offered to firms that need to raise finance and that can be distinguished according to two main types: formal and informal. Formal equity finance is available from various sources including banks, special investment schemes, and private equity and venture capital firms. The informal market refers to private financing by so-called business angels – wealthy individuals that invest in small unquoted companies. Private equity finance can refer to both large and small equity stakes.

Private non-deposit-taking financial institutions Privately owned financial intermediaries that do not take deposits, including a wide variety of securities, insurance and other firms.

Private sector purchaser A UK bank resolution procedure whereby all or part of a failing bank's business (its shares or property, i.e. assets and liabilities) are transferred to a commercial purchaser.

Privatisation process The process of conversion from a government-controlled company to a public limited company often through a sale or flotation on the stock market.

Process of deconstruction The process of deconstruction generally refers to the separation of banks' lending function into different component parts (i.e. origination, funding, servicing and monitoring) that can be provided by different financial institutions.

Product diversification This refers to a bank's diversification into more than one product market.

Product (production) diffusion This relates to the pattern of customer or firm adoption of a new product, service or production process. For example, if a new mortgage product is offered by a bank and then all other banks start offering a similar product in a short period of time then this product can be said to have fast diffusion among banks. Diffusion simply refers to the rate of take-up by potential users of the new product, process or service.

Product life cycle The stages of development that new products go through from introduction to decline.

Profit and loss account (income statement) A document that reports data on costs and revenues and measures bank performance for a given financial year.

Profit margin A common measure of profitability that is equal to earnings before income taxes to total operating income and takes into account both interest and non-interest income.

Profits Revenues minus costs.

Proprietary trading The practice of a bank making investments with its own money (thus bearing the risk of trading losses) rather than on behalf of a customer, so as to make a profit for itself. See also **Volcker Rule** for the proposed prohibition of speculative proprietary trading.

Prudential regulation Regulations governing the supervision of the banking system, e.g. licensing criteria, capital adequacy requirements, etc.

Prudential Regulation Authority (PRA) One of the two new regulatory institutions for the UK financial services sector (the other is the Financial Conduct Authority), replacing the Financial Services Authority. The PRA was created by the Financial Services Act 2012 and is part of the Bank of England. It is responsible for the prudential regulation and supervision of banks, building societies, credit unions, insurers and major investment firms.

Public financial institutions Government institutions like public development banks that deal with the provision of public credit (e.g. lending, public securitisation, public portfolio investments, etc.). They are common in both developing and developed countries (e.g. Japan, Canada).

Public-Private Investment Program (PPIP) Created in 2009 in the US in the context of TARP to help restart the markets for legacy mortgage-backed securities (i.e. originally issued prior to 2009).

Quantitative easing An unconventional monetary stimulus designed to inject money directly into the economy when official interest rates are close to zero. The central bank purchases assets (government bonds, equities, houses, corporate bonds or other assets from banks) from private business using new money created electronically.

Quiet life In the industrial economics literature this hypothesis argues that monopoly power allows managers to benefit from a 'quiet life', free from competitive pressures, and therefore increased concentration should bring about a decrease in efficiency.

Rate-sensitive assets and liabilities Assets and liabilities that can be re-priced within a certain time period (e.g. 90 days); therefore the cash flows associated with rate-sensitive contracts vary with changes in interest rates.

Recapitalisation Term used to refer to a change in the way a firm is financed resulting from an injection of capital.

Refinancing risk The risk that the cost of rolling over or re-borrowing funds will rise above the returns being earned on asset investments.

Regional banks In Japan, banks with a regional focus specialised on retail and SMEs (small and medium-sized enterprises).

Regulation The setting of specific rules of behaviour that firms have to abide by – these may be set through legislation (laws) or be stipulated by the relevant regulatory agency (for instance, the Financial Conduct Authority and Prudential Regulation Authority in the United Kingdom). See also re-regulation.

Regulatory forbearance The possibility given by the regulatory authorities to insolvent banks of staying in operation for the sake of avoiding systemic risk.

Regulatory risk The risk associated with a change in regulatory policy. For example, banks may be subject to certain new risks if deregulation takes place and barriers to lending or to the entry of new firms are lifted.

Reinvestment risk The risk that the returns on funds to be reinvested will fall below the cost of funds.

Relationship banking When there is a close and long-term relationship between the banks and the firms they lend to. Among the key benefits are lower monitoring costs for the banks, the continuous role of the banks in serving firms' financial needs (e.g. in response to new investment opportunities), mutual confidence and loyalty.

Remote payments These are payment instruments that allow remote access to a customer's account.

Repos (repurchase agreements) Securities that can be sold for a finite period, but with a commitment to repurchase usually at an agreed price and at a stated time.

Representative office Representative offices can be set up by banks in risky markets abroad as the cost of running such small offices is negligible, and they can easily be closed if commercial prospects are not good.

Reputation risk The risk that strategic management's mistakes may have consequences for the reputation of a bank. It is also the risk that negative publicity, either true or untrue, adversely affects a bank's customer base or brings forth costly litigation thereby affecting profitability.

Re-regulation This term describes the process of implementing new rules, restrictions and controls in response to market participants' efforts to circumvent existing regulations.

Reserve requirement The proportion of a commercial bank's total assets which it keeps in the form of liquid assets so as to comply with regulatory reserve requirements.

Resolution Trust Corporation A temporary US government agency, the first of its kind, created in 1989 and charged with the task of taking assets off the Savings & Loans (S&Ls) books and then selling them on to investors and other banks.

Resolved bank A bank that, as a result of a crisis, has been acquired by the authorities ('intervened') and eventually is either liquidated, taken over, recapitalised or other.

Retail or personal banking Banking services provided to the household (consumer) sector.

Return on assets (ROA) A common measure of bank profitability that is equal to net income/ total assets.

Return on equity (ROE) A common measure of bank profitability that is equal to net income/ total equity.

Revenues The revenues, generated by the assets of a bank, include: interest earned on loans and investments; fees and commissions (interest and non-interest revenue); and other revenues (e.g. from the sale of businesses).

Revolving lines of credit A commitment by a bank to lend to a customer under pre-defined terms. The commitments generally contain covenants allowing the bank to refuse to lend if there has been a material adverse change in the borrower's financial condition.

Revolving underwriting facilities (RUFs) Similar to a NIF but differs from it because issuers are guaranteed the funds by an underwriting group which buys the notes at a minimum price.

Ring-fencing The key recommendation of the Vickers and Liikanen reports that implies that banks should separate their retail and SME deposit-taking business from investment and wholesale business.

Risk-adjusted return on capital (RAROC) A risk-adjusted profitability measurement and management framework for measuring risk-adjusted financial performance and for providing a consistent view of profitability across businesses.

Risk–asset ratio A ratio that sets out to appraise a bank's capital adequacy on the basis of a bank's relative riskiness.

Risk culture This refers to corporate values and people's behaviour within an organisation that affect risk propensity and risk management decisions.

Risk management Risk management is a complex and comprehensive process, which includes creating an appropriate environment, maintaining an efficient risk measurement structure, monitoring and mitigating risk-taking activities and establishing an adequate framework of internal controls.

Risk measurement The process of quantification of risk exposure.

Risk retention This refers to regulation that requires banks to retain a portion of the credit risk in the assets that they securitise. This is based on the assumption that by retaining 'skin in the game' (i.e. an interest in their own securitisations) banks should have a greater incentive to improve the screening and monitoring of their borrowers.

Rogue trader A trader who recklessly makes speculative deals without authorisation with the intention of deriving higher monetary benefits for themselves.

Rogue trader risk The risk that rogue traders within the organisation create huge losses by trading in high-risk investment.

Safety-net subsidies Safety nets that confer both benefits (arising from their presence) and subsidies. These latter by definition are transfers of resources across groups; they occur when, for example, the government provides safety net-related financial services below their fair price (i.e. there is a misallocation of resources because if, for example, deposit insurance is fairly priced, there are no subsidies).

Savings and Loans Association (S&Ls) The most important type of savings institutions in the United States; also known as thrifts.

Savings bank A financial institution whose primary function is to offer savings facilities to retail customers. Traditionally savings banks were mutual institutions (like building societies in the United Kingdom and thrifts in the United States), i.e. they were established and controlled by groups of people for their own benefit. Today savings banks' business has become more diversified and many have become listed.

Screening The action undertaken by the less-informed party to determine the information possessed by the informed party. For example, the action taken by a bank before giving a loan to gather information about the creditworthiness of a potential borrower.

Second Banking Co-ordination Directive (2BCD) A milestone in the harmonisation of EU banking laws, the 1989 Second Banking Co-ordination Directive established EU-wide recognition of single banking 'passports' issued in any member state as well as the principle of home-country supervision with minimum standards (including capital) at the EU level. In addition, the directive allowed banks to operate as universal banks.

Secondary market A market in which previously issued securities are traded.

Securities house A non-bank organisation that specialises in brokerage and dealing activities in securities.

Securities Markets Programme Started in May 2010 to address tensions in certain market segments that hampered the monetary policy transmission mechanism in the eurozone. Under the SMP, the ECB could intervene by buying from banks on the secondary market the securities that it normally accepts as collateral. The programme was terminated in September 2012.

Securities underwriting The procedure under which investment banks provide a guarantee to a company that an issue of shares (or other capital market instruments) will raise a specific amount of cash. Investment banks will agree to subscribe to any of the issue not taken up.

Securitisation The term is most often used narrowly to mean the process by which traditional bank assets, mainly loans or mortgages, are converted into negotiable securities which may be purchased either by depository institutions or by non-bank investors. More broadly, the term refers to the development of markets for a variety of new negotiable instruments, such as FRNs in the international markets and commercial paper in the United States, which replace bank loans as a means of borrowing. Used in the latter sense, the term often suggests disintermediation of the banking system, as investors and borrowers bypass banks and transact business directly.

Settlement An important element in the processing of large-value funds transfers, settlement is the transfer of funds from the payer's financial institution to the payee's financial institution with respect to the payment order.

Settlement or payment risk A risk typical of the interbank market; it refers to the situation where one party to a contract fails to pay money or deliver assets to another party at the time of settlement.

Shadow banking All activities related to credit intermediation, liquidity and maturity transformation that take place outside the regulated banking system.

Shareholder value This refers both to the value of the firm to shareholders and to the management principle of maximising the worth of a corporation to shareholders. A bank can create shareholder value by pursuing a strategy that maximises the return on capital invested relative to the (opportunity) cost of capital (the cost of keeping equity shareholders and bondholders happy).

Shinkin banks Co-operative not-for-profit financial institutions operating in Japan. Their membership is composed of local residents and small and medium-sized enterprises.

Systemically important financial institutions (SIFIs) These are large, complex and interconnected financial firms – almost exclusively banks – whose distress or failure would cause considerable damage to the world financial system (see also G-SIFIs, G-SIBs).

Signalling In an adverse selection problem, the term refers to actions of the 'informed party' and can imply, for instance, the offer of a warranty or guarantee.

Single Bank Resolution Fund (SBRF) Set up under the control of the Single Resolution Board, the fund should provide medium-term funding support while the bank is restructured. It should be funded by contributions of the banking sector.

Single EU passport Also known as the 'Single European Banking Licence', it ensures that EU-incorporated banks which are authorised within their own country's regulations (e.g. UK banks authorised by the FSA) are automatically recognised as banks in any part of the European Union by virtue of their home country recognition.

Single Euro Payments Area European Union project that aims to create an integrated market for all electronic euro payments within Europe.

Single market A single market represents the creation of one area with common policies and regulations in which there is free movement of goods, persons, services and capital.

Single Resolution Board (SRB) A committee consisting of representatives of the ECB, the EC and the relevant national authorities with broad powers for the resolution of troubled banks.

Single Resolution Mechanism (SRM) A single system in the eurozone for the timely and effective resolution of troubled banks.

Single Rulebook A single set of harmonised prudential rules for financial institutions across the EU provided by the EBA.

Single Supervisory Handbook A set of guidelines to be compiled by the EBA to promote a level playing field for the supervision of the 28 European Union countries and avoid fragmentation within the Single Market.

Single Supervisory Mechanism (SSM) It is a component of the Banking Union through which the ECB will be responsible for specific supervisory tasks related to the financial stability of all euro area banks as well as banks in other (non-euro area) member states voluntarily joining the SSM. The main aims of the SSM will be to ensure the safety and soundness of the European banking system and to increase financial integration and stability in Europe.

Skin in the game See **Risk retention**.

Small and medium-sized enterprises (SMEs) In the EU SMEs are defined as companies with less than 250 employees and either an annual turnover not exceeding €50 million or a total balance sheet not exceeding €43 million. The term is also widely used to refer to small businesses in general.

Soft information Data that cannot be reduced to numbers and can be based on opinions, rumours, long-term relationships with customers, etc. A typical example in banking is relationship lending.

Solvency The ability of an institution to repay obligations ultimately.

Solvency Ratio Directive EC directive agreed in July 1989. The aim was to harmonise the solvency ratios (capital adequacy ratios) for credit institutions (in line with Basel I 1988 proposals).

Sovereign risk Relates to the risk associated with a government default on bond or loan repayments.

Special Liquidity Scheme (SLS) A scheme introduced by the Bank of England in April 2008 (and closed in January 2012) to improve the liquidity position of the banking system by allowing banks and building societies to swap their high-quality mortgage-backed and other securities for UK Treasury Bills for up to three years.

Special-purpose vehicle (SPV) An entity created solely for a specific, limited and temporary purpose or activity. It can be created through a variety of entities, such as trusts, corporations, limited partnerships and limited liability companies, and used in structured finance transactions such as securitisations to isolate certain company assets or operations.

Special Resolution Regime (SRR) Introduced by the Banking Act 2009, the SRR may be adopted by supervisory authorities in the case of UK banks or building societies experiencing financial difficulties. This special resolution regime offers three options: stabilisation, bank insolvency and bank administration.

Specialist banking Banks specialised in the supply of specific products and services as opposed to universal banking.

Standardised products The final stage of the product life cycle where the product is uniform and undifferentiated and competition between producers is based solely on price.

Standby letter of credit Similar to the commercial L/C. The standby L/C is issued by the importer's bank and obligates that bank to compensate the exporter in the event of a performance failure. The importer will pay a fee for this service and will be liable to its bank for any payments made by the bank under the standby L/C.

Standing facilities Central bank facilities available to counterparties on their own initiative. For example, the Eurosystem offers two overnight standing facilities: the marginal lending facility and the deposit facility.

Standing orders These are instructions from the customer (account holder) to the bank to pay a fixed amount at regular intervals into the account of another individual or company.

Sterling commercial paper A collective name for sterling-denominated short-term unsecured notes issued by corporate borrowers. The majority are issued at maturities of between 15 and 45 days.

Stockbrokers See **Broker**.

Stress testing Simulation techniques used to try to gauge the ability of a financial institution to deal with extreme scenarios such as a crisis and establish whether the institution is at risk of failure.

Structural deregulation This refers to the opening up, or liberalisation, of financial markets to allow institutions to compete more freely. Specifically, this process encompasses structure and conduct rules deregulation (such as the removal of branch restrictions and credit ceilings, respectively) and not prudential rules.

Structural indicators In the context of competition literature, typical structural indicators are the Herfindahl-Hirschman index and the concentration ratios.

Structure-conduct-performance (SCP) paradigm A traditional industrial organisation theory that hypothesises that market concentration weakens competition by fostering collusive behaviour among a handful of firms thus resulting in abnormal profits.

Structured investment vehicle (SIV) A type of structured SPV used in the short-term asset-backed commercial paper (ABCP) market. They are also known as *conduits*.

Sub-prime mortgage lending Residential mortgages issued to individuals who are at high risk of default because of their poor credit histories (e.g. late payments or bankruptcy). Interest rates are typically higher on sub-prime compared to *prime* (conventional) mortgages in order for the credit firms to compensate themselves for carrying a higher than average credit risk.

Subsidiary In international banking a subsidiary is a separate legal entity from the parent bank that has its own capital and is organised and regulated according to the laws of the host country.

Sudden stop This refers to a sudden and typically large reduction in international capital inflows or a sharp reversal in aggregate capital flows to a country, likely taking place in conjunction with a sharp rise in its credit spreads.

Supervision A term used to refer to the general oversight of the behaviour of financial firms.

Supervisory re-regulation Defined as the process of implementing new rules, restrictions and controls in response to market participants' efforts to circumvent existing regulations (e.g. bank capital adequacy rules).

Surplus unit Term used to denote the ultimate lender in a financial transaction.

Sustainable banking This generally refers to the situation where banks' business decisions to lend or invest take into account environmental and social implications in addition to financial and economic performance.

Swap A financial transaction in which two bodies agree to exchange streams of payment over time according to a predetermined rule. A swap is normally used to transform interest rate or foreign exchange cash flows from one form into another. Fixed interest cash flows may be swapped for variable cash flows, or/and different currencies can be swapped. (See **Currency swaps** and **Interest rate swaps**).

Syndicated loans Syndicated loans are a special category of loans in which an arranger bank, or group of arrangers, forms a group of creditors on the basis of a mandate to finance the company (or government) borrower.

Systematic credit risk The risk associated with the possibility that default of all firms may increase over a given time period because of economic changes or other events that impact large sections of the economy.

Systemic risk The risk faced by a financial system, resulting from a systemic crisis where the failure of one institution has repercussions on others, thereby threatening the stability of financial markets.

Tail risk A higher than expected risk of an investment moving more than three standard deviations away from the mean.

Technology Term used to indicate the use of modern machines and systems, e.g. computers, internet, electronics, circuits and so on.

Technology risk This occurs when technological investments do not produce the anticipated cost savings in the form of either economies of scale or scope; it also refers to the risk of current systems becoming inefficient because of the development of new systems.

Temporary public ownership (TPO) In the UK, it involves a short-term situation where the government acquires all the shares of a failing bank.

Term Asset-Backed Securities Loan Facility A funding facility created in 2009 by the US Fed to help market participants meet the credit needs of households and small businesses by supporting the issuance of asset-backed securities collateralised by loans of various types to consumers and businesses of all sizes.

Thrifts See **Savings and Loans Associations**.

Too big to fail (TBTF) The cases of TBTF, as well as 'too important to fail', are examples of moral hazard caused by the government safety net. Because the failure of a large (or strategically important) bank poses significant risks to other financial institutions and to the financial system as a whole, policymakers may respond by protecting bank creditors from all or some of the losses they otherwise would face.

Trade-off between safety and returns to shareholders This is the trade-off between total capital and ROE.

Trading book Bank activities classified for regulatory purposes that are market-related such as derivatives and bonds. These are activities that are not traditional (e.g. loans) and are also characterised by high liquidity and ease to trade.

Traditional banking As opposed to modern banking, traditional banking refers to mainstream deposit and lending activity.

Traditional foreign banking In international banking, this involves transactions with non-residents in domestic currency that facilitate trade finance and other international transactions.

Tranching In the securitisation process, it refers to the issuing of securities carrying different levels of risk, duration and other characteristics. Typically three main types of tranches can be identified: senior (AAA rating), mezzanine (BBB and below) and equity tranche (unrated).

Transactional banking Financial services or products provided by the bank to a firm in exchange of a fee that does not imply any form of relationship or future business. Transactional banking involves 'arm's length' transactions rather than relationships.

Transaction costs The costs associated with the buying and selling of a financial instrument (e.g. cost of searching, cost of writing contracts, etc.).

Transition economies A term used to describe former communist countries that have been transforming their planned economies to market economies.

Treasury A division within banks that acts as a 'bank's bank' and is responsible for the management of liquidity, and capital and balance sheet requirements.

Treasury bill (or T-bill) A financial security issued through the discount market by the government as a means of borrowing money for short periods of time (usually three months).

Troubled Assets Relief Program (TARP) A plan authorised by the US Congress in October 2008 through which the US government acquired assets and equity from financial institutions. Its main aims were to strengthen banks' financial positions – by indirectly improving their capital strength – to provide greater confidence in the system and to restart economic growth.

Trust banks In Japan, banks that perform commercial banking activity, but whose main function is asset management for retail and other customers.

Turner Review A 2009 report published in the UK by Lord Turner on how to respond to the global banking crisis. It covers the need for: banks to be better capitalised; credit agencies to be more closely supervised; and excessive pay scales of bankers to be reduced. It also highlights the need to reform the supervisory framework both in the UK and at a pan-European level.

Twin crises These are crises episodes that occur simultaneously such as a currency crisis and a banking crisis (e.g. Asian crisis) or banking crises followed by sovereign debt crises (e.g. eurozone crises).

UK Financial Investments Ltd (UKFI) Created in November 2008 as part of the UK's response to the financial crisis. It is responsible for managing the government's shareholdings in the Royal Bank of Scotland Group and Lloyds Banking Group.

Underwriting See **Securities underwriting**.

Underwritten deal A type of syndication where arrangers guarantee the entire commitment, and then syndicate the loan to other banks and institutional investors. If they cannot fully subscribe the loan, they absorb the difference and may later try again to sell to investors.

Unit trust A UK institution that manages collectively funds obtained from different investors (see **Mutual funds**).

Universal bank An institution which combines its strictly commercial activities with operations in market segments traditionally covered by investment banks, securities houses and insurance firms, and this includes such business as portfolio management, brokerage of securities, underwriting, mergers and acquisitions. A universal bank undertakes the whole range of banking activities.

Universal banking Under the universal banking model, banking business is broadly defined to include all aspects of financial service activity – including securities operations, insurance, pensions, leasing and so on.

Unlisted securities market Market for dealing in company stocks and shares that have not obtained a full stock exchange quotation.

Unsystematic credit risk Also known as firm-specific credit risk, this is derived from 'micro' factors and thus is the credit risk specific to the holding of loans or bonds of a particular firm.

VaR (value at risk) VaR is a technique that uses statistical analysis of historical market trends and volatilities to estimate the likely or expected maximum loss on a bank's portfolio or line of business over a set time period, with a given probability. The aim is to get one figure that summarises the maximum loss faced by the bank within a statistical confidence interval.

Venture capital Share capital or loans subscribed to a firm by financial specialists when these companies are considered to be high risk and would not normally attract conventional finance.

Vertical FDI A type of FDI that describes overseas investment as a consequence of differences in international factor prices (e.g. wages, raw materials).

Vickers Report The most far-reaching reform of British banking in modern history. It was issued in September 2011 by the Independent Commission on Banking chaired by Sir John Vickers. Its main recommendations relate to ring-fencing retail banking from investment/wholesale banking, boosting capital resources and various measures aimed at increasing competition in UK banking.

Visegrad countries These are the following four Central European states: Czech Republic, Hungary, Poland and Slovakia.

Volcker Rule Part of the 2010 Dodd-Frank Act that aims to constrain risk taking at banks by introducing a ban from trading on a proprietary basis (subject to certain exceptions) and by restricting investment in hedge funds and private equity by commercial banks. Paul Volcker is an American economist who was chairman of the Fed from 1979 to 1987.

Wholesale banking The borrowing and lending of large amounts of money usually between banks or other financial organisations, through the interbank market.

Zengin Data Telecommunication System (Zengin System) The main retail payments system in Japan that clears retail credit transfers.

Z-score A bank-specific indicator of distance from insolvency that combines bank profitability, capitalisation and the standard deviation (volatility) of profits. The Z-score depends positively on bank profits and capital ratio and negatively on profits variability; so a higher (lower) Z-score indicates that a bank is more (less) stable, or the less (more) likely it is that the bank will fail.

References and further reading

Accenture (2013) 'Regulatory implications of rogue trading', **www.accenture.com/us-en/blogs/regulatory_insights_blog/archive/2013/03/22/rogue-trading.aspx**

Account Market **www.oft.gov.uk/shared_oft/reports/financial_products/OFT1005rev**

Acharya, V.V. (2010) 'Failures of the Dodd Frank Act', *Financial Times*, 15 July.

Acharya, V.V., Schnabl, P. and Suarez, G. (2013) 'Securitization without risk transfer', *Journal of Financial Economics*, 107(3), 515–536.

Adrian, T., Ashcraft, A.B. and Cetorelli, N. (2013) 'Shadow bank monitoring', New York Fed Staff Report 638.

Aghion, P., Angeletos, G.M., Banerjee, A. and Manova, K. (2010) 'Volatility and growth: Credit constraints and the composition of growth', *Journal of Monetary Economics*, 57(3), 246–265.

Aghion, P., Bacchetta, P., Rancière, R. and Rogoff, K. (2009) 'Exchange rate volatility and productivity growth: The role of financial development', *Journal of Monetary Economics*, 56(4), 494–513.

Aghion, P., Fally, T. and Scarpetta, S. (2007) 'Credit constraints as a barrier to the entry and post-entry growth of firms', *Economic Policy*, 22(52), 731–779.

Aghion, P., Howitt, P. and Mayer-Foulkes, D. (2005) 'The effect of financial development on convergence: Theory and evidence', *Quarterly Journal of Economics*, 120(1), 173–222.

Aizenman, J., Hutchison, M. and Jinjarak, Y. (2013) 'What is the risk of European sovereign debt defaults? Fiscal space, CDs spreads and market pricing of risk', *Journal of International Money and Finance*, 34, 37–59.

Akerlof, G.A. (1970) 'The market for "lemons": Quality uncertainty and the market mechanism', *The Quarterly Journal of Economics*, 84(3), 488–500.

Alfon, I. and Andrews, P. (1999) 'Cost–benefit analysis in financial regulation: How to do it and how it adds value', *Journal of Financial Regulation and Compliance*, 7(4), 339–352.

Allen, F., Beck, T., Carletti, E., Lane, P., Schoenmaker, D. and Wagner, W. (2011) *Cross-border Banking in Europe: Implications for financial stability and macroeconomic policies*, London: Centre for Economic Policy Research (CEPR).

Altunbas, Y., Kara, A. and Marques-Ibanez, D. (2010) 'Large debt financing: Syndicated loans versus corporate bonds', *The European Journal of Finance*, 15(5), 437–458.

Anonymous (2012a) 'Mexican banks: From tequila crisis to sunrise', *The Economist*, 22 September.

Anonymous (2012b) 'Press 1 for modernity', *The Economist*, 28 April.

Anonymous (2013a) 'Leaving the Old Lady', *The Economist*, 15 June.

Anonymous (2013b) 'What caused China's cash crunch?', *The Economist*, 4 July.

Arcand, J.L., Berkes, E. and Panizza, U. (2012) 'Too much finance?', IMF Working Paper, WP/12/161.

Association for Financial Markets in Europe (2014) 'Europe: The market at Crossroads', **http://www.afme.eu/WorkArea/DownloadAsset.aspx?id=10823**

Athey, S., Atkenson, A. and Kehoe, P.J. (2005) 'The optimal degree of discretion in monetary policy', *Econometrica*, 73(5), 1431–1475.

References and further reading

Augar, P. (2014) 'Reckless: The rise and fall of the City', *Financial Times*, 16 January.

Ayadi, R., Llewellyn, D.T., Schmidt, R.H., Arbak, E. and De Groen, W.P. (2010) *Investigating Diversity in the Banking Sector in Europe. Key developments, performance and role of co-operative banks*, Brussels: Centre for European Policy Studies.

Ayadi, R., Schmidt, R.H. and Carbo Valverde, S. (2009) *Investigating Diversity in the Banking Sector in Europe: The performance and role of saving banks*, Brussels: Centre for European Policy Studies.

Ayyagari, M., Demirguc-Kunt, A. and Maksimovic, V. (2011) 'Small vs. young firms across the world: Contribution to employment, job creation, and growth', The World Bank Policy Research Working Paper Series, 5631, April.

Baily, M.N., Elmendorf, D.W. and Litan, R.E. (2008) 'The great credit squeeze: How it happened, how to prevent another', Brookings Institution, May.

Bain, J.S. (1951) 'Relation of profit rate to industry concentration: American manufacturing, 1936–1940', *Quarterly Journal of Economics*, 65(3), 293–324

Bakk-Simon, K., Borgioli, S., Giron, C., Hempell, H., Maddaloni, A., Recine, F. and Rosati, S. (2012) 'Shadow banking in the euro area: An overview', ECB Working Paper Series, No. 133, April, **www.ecb.europa.eu/pub/pdf/scpops/ecbocp133.pdf**

Bank for International Settlements (2009a) *79th BIS Annual Report 2008/09*, June, **www.bis .org/publ/arpdf/ar2009e.pdf**

Bank for International Settlements (2009b) 'Issues in the governance of central banks', A Report from the Central Bank Governance Group, May, **www.bis.org/publ/othp04.pdf**

Bank for International Settlements (2012) 'Innovations in retail payments', May, **www.bis.org/ cpmi/publ/d102.pdf**

Bank for International Settlements (2013a) *83rd Annual Report*, June, **www.bis.org/publ/ arpdf/ar2013e.pdf**

Bank for International Settlements (2013b) 'Foreign exchange turnover in April 2013: Preliminary global results triennial central bank survey', September, **www.bis.org/publ/rpfx13fx.pdf**

Bank for International Settlements (2013c) 'Statistics on payment, clearing and settlement systems in the CPSS countries, figures for 2012', December, **www.bis.org/cpmi/publ/d116.pdf**

Bank for International Settlements (2013d) 'Triennial central bank survey of foreign exchange and derivatives market activity', December, **www.bis.org/publ/rpfx13.htm**

Bank for International Settlements (2013e) 'Triennial central bank survey of foreign exchange and derivatives market activity', September, **www.bis.org/publ/rpfx13ir.pdf**

Bank for International Settlements (2014) 'Highlights of the BIS international statistics', *BIS Quarterly Review*, March.

Bank of England (2007a) Financial Stability Report, Issue No. 22, October, **www.bankofeng- land.co.uk/publications/Documents/fsr/2007/fsrfull0710.pdf**

Bank of England (2007b) 'Proposals to modify the measurement of broad money in the United Kingdom: A user consultation', Quarterly Bulletin, Q3, **www.bankofengland.co.uk/ publications/Documents/quarterlybulletin/qb070304.pdf**

Bank of England (2008) 'Financial stability and depositor protection: Special resolution regime', Cm7459, July, **www.bankofengland.co.uk/publications/Documents/other/ financialstability/financialstabilitydepositorprotection080722.pdf**

Bank of England (2012a) *Annual Report*, June, **www.bankofengland.co.uk/publications/Pages/annualreport/default.aspx**

Bank of England (2012b) 'The framework for the Bank of England's operations in the sterling money markets', June, **www.bankofengland.co.uk/markets/sterlingoperations/redbook.htm**

Bank of England (2013a) 'Asset purchase facility', Quarterly Report, Q1, **www.bankofengland.co.uk/publications/Documents/other/markets/apf/apfquarterlyreport1304.pdf**

Bank of England (2013b) Quarterly Bulletin, Volume 53, No. 1, Q1.

Bank of Japan (2012) 'Payment, clearing and settlement systems in Japan, CPSS – Red Book – 2012', **www.boj.or.jp/en/paym/outline/pay_boj/pss1212a.pdf**

Bank of Japan (2013) 'Financial system report', October, **www.boj.or.jp/en/research/brp/fsr/index.htm/**

Barclays PLC (2008) *Annual Report*, February, **www.barclays.com/content/dam/barclayspublic/docs/InvestorRelations/AnnualReports/AR2008/2008-barclays-bank-plc-annual-report.pdf**

Barker, A. (2013) 'EU agrees deposit guarantee scheme deal', *Financial Times*, 18 December.

Barker, A. (2014) 'EU reaches deal on final piece of banking union', *Financial Times*, 20 March.

Barker, D. and Holdsworth, D. (1993) 'The causes of bank failures in the 1990s', Federal Reserve Bank of New York Research Paper, 9325.

Barth, J.R., Caprio, G. and Levine, R.E. (2013) 'Measure it, improve it. Bank regulation and supervision in 180 countries 1999–2011', Milken Institute, April.

Basel Committee on Banking Supervision (1988) 'International convergence of capital measurement and capital standards', Bank for International Settlements, July, **www.bis.org/publ/bcbs04a.pdf**

Basel Committee on Banking Supervision (1993) 'The supervisory treatment of market risks', Bank for International Settlements, April, **www.bis.org/publ/bcbs11a.pdf**

Basel Committee on Banking Supervision (1996) 'Amendment to the Capital Accord to incorporate market risks', Bank for International Settlements, January, **www.bis.org/publ/bcbs24.pdf**

Basel Committee on Banking Supervision (1997a) 'Core principles for effective banking supervision', Bank for International Settlements, September, **www.bis.org/publ/bcbs30a.pdf**

Basel Committee on Banking Supervision (1997b) 'Principles for the management of interest rate risk', Bank for International Settlements, September, **www.bis.org/publ/bcbs29a.pdf**

Basel Committee on Banking Supervision (2000) 'Principles for the management of credit risk', Bank for International Settlements, September, **www.bis.org/publ/bcbs75.pdf**

Basel Committee on Banking Supervision (2001a) 'Consultative document. Operational risk, supporting document to the New Basle Capital Accord', Bank for International Settlements, January, **www.bis.org/publ/bcbsca07.pdf**

Basel Committee on Banking Supervision (2001b) 'Overview on the New Basel Capital Accord. Consultative document', Bank for International Settlements, January, **www.bis.org/publ/bcbsca02.pdf**

Basel Committee on Banking Supervision (2004) 'International convergence of capital measurement and capital standards. A revised framework', Bank for International Settlements, June, **www.bis.org/publ/bcbs107.pdf**

References and further reading

Basel Committee on Banking Supervision (2006) 'International convergence of capital measurement and capital standards. A revised framework. Comprehensive version', Bank for International Settlements, June, **www.bis.org/publ/bcbs128.pdf**

Basel Committee on Banking Supervision (2010a) 'Principles for enhancing corporate governance', Bank for International Settlements, October, **www.bis.org/publ/bcbs176.htm**

Basel Committee on Banking Supervision (2010b) 'Report and recommendations of the Cross-Border Bank Resolution Group', Bank for International Settlements, March, **www.bis.org/publ/bcbs169.pdf**

Basel Committee on Banking Supervision (2010c) 'Revisions to the Basel II Market Risk Framework', Bank for International Settlements, December, **www.bis.org/publ/bcbs193.pdf**

Basel Committee on Banking Supervision (2011a) 'Basel III: A global regulatory framework for more resilient banks and banking systems', Bank for International Settlements, June, **www.bis.org/publ/bcbs189.pdf**

Basel Committee on Banking Supervision (2011b) 'Basel III: A global regulatory framework for more resilient banks and banking systems', Bank for International Settlements, December, **www.bis.org/publ/bcbs189.pdf**

Basel Committee on Banking Supervision (2011c) 'Global systemically important banks: Assessment methodology and the additional loss absorbency requirement', Bank for International Settlements, November, **www.bis.org/publ/bcbs207.pdf**

Basel Committee on Banking Supervision (2011d) 'Global systemically important banks: Assessment methodology and the additional loss absorbency requirement', Bank for International Settlements, July, **www.bis.org/publ/bcbs201.pdf**

Basel Committee on Banking Supervision (2011e) 'Operational risk – supervisory guidelines for the advanced measurement approaches', Bank for International Settlements, June, **www.bis.org/publ/bcbs196.htm**

Basel Committee on Banking Supervision (2011f) 'Principles for the sound management of operational risk', Bank for International Settlements, June, **www.bis.org/publ/bcbs195.htm**

Basel Committee on Banking Supervision (2011g) 'Range of methodologies for risk and performance alignment of remuneration', Bank for International Settlements, May, **www.bis.org/publ/bcbs194.pdf**

Basel Committee on Banking Supervision (2013a) 'Basel III: The liquidity coverage ratio and liquidity risk monitoring tools', Bank for International Settlements, January, **www.bis.org/publ/bcbs238.pdf**

Basel Committee on Banking Supervision (2013b) 'Consultative document. Revised Basel III leverage ratio framework and disclosure requirements', Bank for International Settlements, June, **www.bis.org/publ/bcbs251.pdf**

Basel Committee on Banking Supervision (2013c) 'Fundamental review of the trading book: A revised market risk framework', Consultative Document, Bank for International Settlements, October, **www.bis.org/publ/bcbs265.pdf**

Basel Committee on Banking Supervision (2013d) 'Report to G20 leaders on monitoring implementation of Basel III regulatory reforms', Bank for International Settlements, August, **www.bis.org/publ/bcbs260.pdf**

Basel Committee on Banking Supervision (2014) 'Consultative document. Basel III: The net stable funding ratio', Bank for International Settlements, January, **www.bis.org/publ/bcbs271.pdf**

Basel Committee on Banking Supervision and International Association of Deposit Insurers (2010) 'Core principles for effective deposit insurance systems', Bank for International Settlements, December, **www.bis.org/publ/bcbs192.pdf**

Bassett, W.F., Lee, S.J. and Spiller, T.W. (2012) 'Estimating changes in supervisory standards and their economic effects', Finance and Economics Discussion Series, Divisions of Research & Statistics and Monetary Affairs, Federal Reserve Board, 2012–2055.

Beck, T. (2012a) *Banking Union for Europe Risks and Challenges*, London: Centre for Economic Policy Research (CEPR), **www.voxeu.org/sites/default/files/file/cross-border_banking.pdf**

Beck, T. (2012b) *The Role of Finance in Economic Development – Benefits, Risks, and Politics*, in Müller, D. (ed.), *Oxford Handbook of Capitalism*, Oxford: Oxford University Press.

Beck, T., Büyükkarabacak, B., Rioja, F. and Valev, N.T. (2012) 'Who gets the credit? And does it matter? Household vs. firm lending across countries', *The B.E. Journal of Macroeconomics*, 12(1), 1935–1690.

Beck, T., Coyle, D., Dewatripont, M., Freixas, X. and Seabright, P. (2010) *Bailing out the Banks: Reconciling stability and competition, an analysis of state-supported schemes for financial institutions*, London: Centre for Economic Policy Research (CEPR).

Beck, T., De Jonghe, O. and Schepens, G. (2013) 'Bank competition and stability: Cross-country heterogeneity', *Journal of Financial Intermediation*, 22(2), 218–244.

Beck, T., Demirgüç-Kunt, A. and Maksimovic, V. (2006) 'The influence of financial and legal institutions on firm size', *Journal of Banking and Finance*, 30(11), 2995–3015.

Beck, T., Demirgüç-Kunt, A., Laeven, L. and Levine, R. (2008) 'Finance, firm size, and growth', *Journal of Money, Credit and Banking*, 40(7), 1379–1405.

Beck, T., Levine, R. and Loayza, N. (2000) 'Finance and the sources of growth', *Journal of Financial Economics*, 58(1–2), 261–300.

Beltratti, A. and Stulz, R.M. (2012) 'The credit crisis around the globe: Why did some banks perform better during the credit crisis?', *Journal of Financial Economics*, 105(1), 1–17.

Benston, G.J., Eisenbeis, R.A., Horvitz, P.M., Kane, E.J. and Kaufman, G.G. (1996) *Perspectives on Safe and Sound Banking: Past, present, and future*, Cambridge, MA: The MIT Press.

Berg, S.A. and Kim, M. (1998) 'Banks as multioutput oligopolies: An empirical evaluation of the retail and corporate banking markets', *Journal of Money, Credit and Banking*, 30(2), 135–153.

Berger, A.N. (1995) 'The profit–structure relationship in banking: Tests of market power and efficient structure hypotheses', *Journal of Money, Credit and Banking*, 27(2), 404–431.

Berger, A.N. and Hannan, T.H. (1998) 'The efficiency cost of market power in the banking industry: A test of the "quiet life" and related hypotheses', *The Review of Economics and Statistics*, 80(3), 454–465.

Berger, A.N. and Humphrey, D.B. (1997) 'Efficiency of financial institutions: International survey and directions for future research', *European Journal of Operational Research*, 98(2), 175–212.

Berger, A.N., Bonime, S.D., Covitz, D.M. and Hancock, D. (2000) 'Why are bank profits so persistent? The roles of product market competition, information opacity and regional macroeconomic shocks', *Journal of Banking & Finance*, 24(7), 1203–1235.

Berger, A.N., Demsetz, R.S. and Strahan, P.E. (1999) 'The consolidation of the financial services industry: Causes, consequences, and implications for the future', *Journal of Banking & Finance*, 23, 135–194.

References and further reading

Berger, A.N., Kick, T., and Shaek, K. (2014) 'Executive board compensation and bank risk taking', *Journal of Corporate Finance*, in press.

Berger, A.N., Klapper, L.F. and Turk-Ariss, R. (2009) 'Bank competition and financial stability', *Journal of Financial Services Research*, 35(2), 99–118.

Berk, J.B. and DeMarzo, P.M. (2011) *Corporate Finance*, 2nd Edition, Boston, MA: Prentice Hall.

Bernanke, B.S. (2003) 'Constrained discretion and monetary policy', Speech before the money marketeers of New York University, New York, 3 February, **www.federalreserve.gov/ BOARDDOCS/Speeches/2003/20030203/default.htm**

Bernanke, B.S. and Reinhart, V.R. (2004) 'Conducting monetary policy at very low short-term interest rates', *The American Economic Review*, 94(2), 85–90.

Bernet, B. and Walter, S. (2009) *Design, Structure and Implementation of a Modern Deposit Insurance Scheme*, Vienna: SUERF Studies. **http://www.suerf.org/download/studies/ study20095.pdf**

Bertay, A.C., Demirgüç-Kunt, A. and Huizinga, H. (2013) 'Do we need big banks? Evidence on performance, strategy and market discipline', *Journal of Financial Intermediation*, 22(4), 532–558.

Bessis, J. (2009) *Risk Management in Banking*, 3rd Edition, London: John Wiley & Sons.

Bharath, T.S. and Shumway, T. (2008) 'Forecasting default with the Merton Distance to Default Model', *Review of Financial Studies,* 21(3), 1339–1369.

Bikker, J.A. and Haaf, K. (2002) 'Competition, concentration and their relationship: An empirical analysis of the banking industry', *Journal of Banking & Finance*, 26(11), 2191–2214.

Bikker, J.A., Shaffer, S. and Spierdijk, L. (2012). 'Assessing competition with the Panzar–Rosse Model: the role of scale, costs, and equilibrium', *Review of Economics and Statistics*, 94(4), 1025–1044.

Black, F. and Scholes, M. (1973) 'The pricing of options and corporate liabilities', *The Journal of Political Economy*, 81(3), 637–654.

Blinder, A.S. and Zandi, M. (2010) 'How the Great Recession was brought to an end', Princeton University, **www.economy.com/mark-zandi/documents/End-of-Great-Recession.pdf**

Blundell-Wignall, A., Wehinger, G. and Slovik, P. (2009) 'The elephant in the room: The need to deal with what banks do', *Financial Market Trends*, 2, 1–26.

Board of Governors of the Federal Reserve System (2012) *99th Annual Report*, **www.federal-reserve.gov/publications/annual-report/files/2012-annual-report.pdf**

Board of Governors of the Federal Reserve System (2013) 'The Federal Reserve system: Purposes and functions', **www.federalreserve.gov/pf/pdf/pf_complete.pdf**

Boissay, F., Collard, F. and Smets, F. (2013) 'Booms and systemic banking crises', ECB Working Papers Series, No. 1514, February.

Bonaccorsi di Patti, E. and Gobbi, G. (2007) 'Winners or losers? The effects of banking consolidation on corporate borrowers', *Journal of Finance*, 62, 669–695.

Bonin, J., Hasan, I. and Wachtel, P. (2014) 'Banking in transition countries', in Berger, A.N., Molyneux, P. and Wilson, J.O.S. (eds), *The Oxford Handbook of Banking*, 2nd Edition, Oxford: Oxford University Press, Chapter 39.

Boone, J. (2008) 'A new way to measure competition', *The Economic Journal*, 118(531), 1245–1261.

Boot, A.W.A. (2000) 'Relationship banking: What do we know?', *Journal of Financial Intermediation*, 9(1), 7–25.

Boot, A.W.A. and Thakor, A. (2014) 'Commercial banking and shadow banking: The accelerating integration of banks and markets and its implications for regulation', in Berger, A.N., Molyneux, P. and Wilson, J.O.S. (eds), *The Oxford Handbook of Banking*, 2nd Edition, Oxford: Oxford University Press, Chapter 3.

Bouma, J.J., Klinkers, L. and Jeucken, M. (2001) *Sustainable Banking: The greening of finance*, Sheffield: Greenleaf Publishing.

Bowman, D., Cai, F., Davies, S. and Kamin, S. (2011) 'Quantitative easing and bank lending: Evidence from Japan', Board of Governors of the Federal Reserve System, International Finance Discussion Papers, **www.federalreserve.gov/PubS/ifdp/2011/1018/ifdp1018.pdf**

Boyd, J.H. and De Nicolo, G. (2005) 'Bank risk-taking and competition revisited', *The Journal of Finance*, 60(3), 1329–1343.

Boyd, J.H., De Nicolo, G. and Jalal, A.M. (2006) 'Bank risk-taking and competition revisited: New theory and new evidence', IMF Working Paper, WP/06/297.

Braithwaite, T. (2012) 'Banks confront a post-crisis world of tougher regulations and lower profits', *Financial Times*, 30 September.

Braithwaite, T. and Chon, G. (2013) 'Volcker Rule comes of age in spite of protests', *Financial Times*, 10 December.

Brammertz, W., Akkizidis, I., Breymann, W., Entin, R. and Rustmann, M. (2011) *Unified Financial Analysis: The missing links of finance*, Chichester: Wiley.

Brealey, R.A., Myers, S.C. and Marcus, A.J. (2012) *Fundamentals of Corporate Finance*, 7th Edition, New York: McGraw-Hill/Irwin.

Bresnahan, T.F. (1982) 'The oligopoly solution concept is identified', *Economics Letters*, 10(1–2), 87–92.

Brierley, P. (2009) 'The UK Special Resolution regime for failing banks in an international context', Bank of England Financial Stability Paper, No. 5, **www.bankofengland.co.uk/research/Documents/fspapers/fs_paper05.pdf**

British Bankers' Association (1996) *Banking Business. An Abstract of Banking Statistics*, Volume 13.

British Bankers' Association (1999) *Banking Business. An Abstract of Banking Statistics*, Volume 16.

British Bankers' Association (2004) *Banking Business. An Abstract of Banking Statistics*, Volume 21.

British Bankers' Association (2005) *Banking Business. An Abstract of Banking Statistics*, Volume 22.

British Bankers' Association (2008) *Banking Business. An Abstract of Banking Statistics*, Volume 25.

British Bankers' Association (2011) *Banking Business. An Abstract of Banking Statistics*, Volume 28.

British Bankers' Association (2012) *Banking Business. An Abstract of Banking Statistics*, Volume 29.

British Bankers' Association (2013) *Banking Business. An Abstract of Banking Statistics*, Volume 30.

British Private Equity & Venture Capital Association (2010) 'A guide to private equity', **www.bvca.co.uk/Portals/0/library/Files/Website%20files/2012_0001_guide_to_private_equity.pdf**

Brunnermeier, M.K., Crocket, A., Goodhart, C., Persaud, A. and Shin, H. (2009) 'The fundamental principles of financial regulation', Geneva Reports on the World Economy, London: Centre for Economic Policy Research (CEPR).

Buch, C. and DeLong, G. (2014) 'Banking globalization: international consolidation and mergers in banking', in Berger, A.N., Molyneux, P. and Wilson, J.O.S. (eds), *The Oxford Handbook of Banking*, 2nd Edition, Oxford: Oxford University Press, Chapter 31.

Bullard, J. (2013) 'The global battle over central bank independence', Central Banker, Federal Reserve Bank of St. Louis, Spring, **www.stlouisfed.org/publications/cb/articles/?id=2344**

Burrows, O., Learmonth, D. and McKeown, J. (2012) 'RAMSI: A top-down stress-testing model', Bank of England Financial Stability Paper, 17, **www.bankofengland.co.uk/research/ Documents/fspapers/fs_paper17.pdf**

Calice, G., Chen, J. and Williams, J. (2013) 'Liquidity spillovers in sovereign bond and Cds markets: An analysis of the Eurozone sovereign debt crisis', *Journal of Economic Behavior & Organization*, 85, 122–143.

Calomiris, C.W. and Pornrojnangkool, T. (2005) 'Monopoly-creating bank consolidation? The merger of Fleet and Bankboston', NBER Working Paper, No. 11351.

Capgemini (2012) 'World payments report', **www.uk.capgemini.com**

Capgemini and Efma (2011) 'World retail banking report', **www.uk.capgemini.com**

Capgemini and Efma (2012) 'World retail banking report', **www.uk.capgemini.com**

Capgemini and RBC Wealth Management (2012) 'World wealth report', **www.capgemini.com**

Carbó-Valverde, S., Kane, E.J. and Rodriguez-Fernandez, F. (2013) 'Safety-net benefits conferred on difficult-to-fail-and-unwind banks in the US and EU before and during the Great Recession', *Journal of Banking & Finance*, 37(6), 1845–1859.

Casu, B. and Girardone, C. (2004) 'Financial conglomeration: Efficiency, productivity and strategic drive', *Applied Financial Economics*, 14(10), 687–696.

Casu, B. and Sarkisyan, A. (2014) 'Securitization', in Berger, A.N., Molyneux, P. and Wilson, J.O.S. (eds), *The Oxford Handbook of Banking*, 2nd Edition, Oxford: Oxford University Press, Chapter 15.

Casu, B., Girardone, C. and Molyneux, P. (2012) 'Is there a conflict between competition and financial stability?' in Barth, J.R., Lin, C. and Wihlborg, C. (eds), *Research Handbook on Banking and Governance*, Cheltenham: Edward Elgar Publishing.

CEA (2010) 'Insurance Distribution Channels in Europe', 39, **www.insuranceeurope.eu/ uploads/Modules/Publications/cea-statistics-nr-39–distribution.pdf**

Chapman, J. (2011) 'CDs: Modern day weapons of mass destruction', *Financial Times*, 11 September.

Chui, M., Domanski, D., Kugler, P. and Shek, J. (2010) 'The collapse of international bank finance during the crisis: Evidence from syndicated loan markets', *BIS Quarterly Review*, September, 39–49.

Čihák, M., Demirgüç-Kunt, A., Feyen, E. and Levine, R. (2012a) 'Benchmarking financial systems around the world', The World Bank Policy Research, Working Paper No. 6175, August.

Čihák, M., Maechler, A., Schaeck, K. and Stolz, S. (2012b) 'Who disciplines bank managers?', *Review of Finance*, 16, 197–243.

CIMA (2004) 'Maximising shareholder value: Achieving clarity in decision making', Technical Report, **www.valuebasedmanagement.net/articles_cima_maximizing_shareholder_ value.pdf**

Claessens, S. and Kose, M.A. (2013) 'Financial crises: Explanations, types, and implications', International Monetary Fund Working Paper, 13/28.

Claessens, S. and Laeven, L. (2003) 'Financial development, property rights, and growth', *Journal of Finance*, 58(6), 2401–2436.

Claessens, S. and van Horen, N. (2012) 'Foreign banks: Trends, impact and financial stability', IMF Working Paper, WP/12/10.

Claessens, S. and van Horen, N. (2014a) 'Foreign banks: Trends and impact', *Journal of Money, Credit and Banking*, 46(1), 295–326.

Claessens, S. and van Horen, N. (2014b) 'Location decisions of foreign banks and competitor remoteness', *Journal of Money Credit and Banking*, 46(1), 145–170.

Claessens, S., Ratnovski, L. and Singh, M.M. (2012) 'Shadow banking: Economics and policy', IMF Staff Discussion Note, **www.imf.org/external/pubs/ft/sdn/2012/sdn1212.pdf**

Clews, R., Salmon, C. and Weeken, O. (2010) 'The Bank's Money Market Framework', *Quarterly Bulletin*, Bank of England, Q4, **www.bankofengland.co.uk/publications/Documents/quarterlybulletin/qb100404.pdf**

Coase, R.H. (1937) 'The nature of the firm', *Economica*, 4(16), 386–405.

Cocco, J.F. (2013) 'Evidence on the benefits of alternative mortgage products', *Journal of Finance*, 68(4), 1663–1690.

Coccorese, P. (2005) 'Competition in markets with dominant firms: A note on the evidence from the Italian banking industry', *Journal of Banking & Finance*, 29(5), 1083–1093.

Coccorese, P. (2009) 'Market power in local banking monopolies', *Journal of Banking & Finance*, 33(7), 1196–1210.

Competition Commission (2002) 'The supply of banking services by clearing banks to small and medium-sized enterprises: A report on the supply of banking services by clearing banks to small and medium-sized enterprises within the UK', March. **webarchive.nationalarchives.gov.uk/+/www.competition-commission.org.uk/rep_pub/reports/2002/462banks.htm#full**

Competition Commission (2006) 'Store cards market investigation', March. **www.competition-commission.org.uk/assets/competitioncommission/docs/pdf/non-inquiry/rep_pub/reports/2006/fulltext/final_report.pdf**

Corporation of London (2002) 'Financing the future. The London Principles', **www.cityoflondon.gov.uk/services/environment-and-planning/sustainability/Documents/pdfs/SUS_financingfuture.pdf**

Court des Comptes (2013) 'Dexia: A high cost with persistent Risk', Thematic Public Report, July.

Cour-Thimann, P. and Winkler, B. (2013) 'The ECB's non-standard monetary policy measures. The role of institutional factors and financial structure', ECB Working Papers Series, No. 1528, April.

Covitz, D., Liang, N. and Suarez, G.A. (2013) 'The evolution of a financial crisis: Collapse of the asset-backed commercial paper market', *The Journal of Finance*, 68(3), 815–848.

Credit Suisse First Boston (1997) 'Credit Risk+ a credit management framework', ©1997, Credit Suisse First Boston International, **www.csfb.com/institutional/research/assets/creditrisk.pdf**

Cruickshank, D. (2000) 'Competition in UK banking', A Report to the Chancellor of the Exchequer, The United Kingdom for the Stationery Office, 21.

Cumming, C. and Hirtle, B. (2001) 'The challenges of risk management in diversified financial companies', *Economic Policy Review*, 7(1).

Damodaran, A. (2013) 'Equity risk premiums (ERP): Determinants, estimation and implications', available on SSRN at **http://dx.doi.org/10.2139/ssrn.2238064**.

Danielsson, J. (2000) 'VaR: A castle built on sand', *The Financial Regulator*, 5, 46–50.

Danielsson, J. (2002) 'The emperor has no clothes: Limits to risk modelling', *Journal of Banking & Finance*, 26(7), 1273–1296.

Davies, M. (2010) 'What's it like running a bank? Good, bad or ugly?', Guest Opening Speech, Wolpertinger Conference, Bangor Business School, September (Unpublished).

De Nicolo, G. (2000) 'Size, charter value and risk in banking: An international perspective', Board of Governors of the Federal Reserve System, International Finance Discussion Paper No. 689.

De Nicolo, G., Bartholomew, P., Zaman, J. and Zephirin, M. (2004) 'Bank consolidation, internationalization and conglomeration: Trends and implications for financial risk', *Financial Markets, Institutions and Instruments*, 13(4), 173–217.

Delis, M.D., Varlagas, P.T. and Staikouras, K.C. (2008) 'On the measurement of market power in the banking industry', *Journal of Business Finance and Accounting*, 35(7–8), 1023–1047.

Dell'Ariccia, G., Igan, D. and Laeven, L. (2012) 'Credit booms and lending standards: Evidence from the subprime mortgage market', *Journal of Money, Credit and Banking*, 44, 367–384.

Deloitte (2013) 'Future of bank treasury management. A profession in focus', March, **www .deloitte.com/assets/Dcom-UnitedKingdom/Local%20Assets/Documents/Industries/ Financial%20Services/uk-fs-future-bank-treasury-management.pdf**

Demirgüç-Kunt, A. and Klapper, L. (2012) 'Measuring financial inclusion. The Global Findex Database', The World Bank Policy Research, Working Paper 6025, **http://elibrary.worldbank .org/doi/pdf/10.1596/1813–9450–6025**

Demirgüç-Kunt, A. and Klapper, L. (2013) 'Measuring financial inclusion: Explaining variation in use of financial services across and within countries', Brookings Papers on Economic Activity, Spring, 279–394.

Demirgüç-Kunt, A., Love, I. and Maksimovic, V. (2006) 'Business environment and the incorporation decision', *Journal of Banking & Finance*, 30(11), 2967–2993.

Demsetz, H. (1973) 'Industry structure, market rivalry and public policy', *Journal of Law and Economics*, 16(1), 1–9.

DeYoung, R. (2014) 'Banking in the United States', in Berger, A.N., Molyneux, P. and Wilson, J.O.S. (eds), *The Oxford Handbook of Banking*, 2nd Edition, Oxford: Oxford University Press, Chapter 34.

DeYoung, R., Evanoff, D.D. and Molyneux, P. (2009) 'Mergers and acquisitions of financial institutions: A review of the post-2000 literature', *Journal of Financial Services Research*, 36, 87–110.

DeYoung, R., Peng, E. and Yan, M. (2013) 'Executive compensation and business policy choices at US commercial banks', *Journal of Financial and Quantitative Analysis*, 48(01), 165–196.

Diamond, D.W. (1984) 'Financial intermediation and delegated monitoring', *The Review of Economic Studies*, 51(3), 393–414.

Diamond, D.W. and Dybvig, P.H. (1983) 'Bank runs, deposit insurance, and liquidity', *The Journal of Political Economy*, 91(3), 401–419.

Dick, A.A. (2006) 'Nationwide branching and its impact on market structure, quality and bank performance', *Journal of Business*, 79(2), 567–592.

Dowd, K. (1996) *Competition and Finance: A new interpretation of financial and monetary economics*, London: Macmillan.

Ernst and Young (2013) 'World Islamic Banking Competitiveness Report 2013–14. The Transition Begins', **http://emergingmarkets.ey.com/wp-content/uploads/downloads/2013/12/ World-Islamic-Banking-Competitiveness-Report-2013–14.pdf**

European Banking Authority (2013) 'Warning to consumers on virtual currencies', EBA/ WRG/2013/01, **www.eba.europa.eu/documents/10180/598344/EBA+Warning+on+ Virtual+Currencies.pdf**

European Central Bank (2006) 'Financial stability review', December, **www.ecb.europa.eu/pub/ pdf/other/financialstabilityreview200612en.pdf??a26f4bc9093173998888fa2693f6ccc6**

European Central Bank (2008a) 'Covered bonds in the EU financial system', December, **www .ecb.europa.eu/pub/pdf/other/coverbondsintheeufinancialsystem200812en_en.pdf**

European Central Bank (2008b) 'Securitisation in the Euro Area', *ECB Monthly Bulletin*, February. **www.ecb.europa.eu/pub/pdf/mobu/mb200802en.pdf**

European Central Bank (2008c) 'Ten years of the Stability and Growth Pact', *Monthly Bulletin*, October, **www.ecb.europa.eu/pub/pdf/mobu/mb200810en.pdf**

European Central Bank (2009a) 'Credit default swaps and counterparty risk', August, **www.ecb .europa.eu/pub/pdf/other/creditdefaultswapsandcounterpartyrisk2009en.pdf**

European Central Bank (2009b) 'Financial stability review', December, **www.ecb.europa.eu/pub/ pdf/other/financialstabilityreview200912en.pdf??7e1073aa7dd961b1248c19c2fecbf696**

European Central Bank (2010a) 'Beyond ROE: How to measure bank performance', Appendix to the Report on EU banking structures, September, **www.ecb.europa.eu/pub/pdf/other/ beyondroehowtomeasurebankperformance201009en.pdf**

European Central Bank (2010b) 'The ECB's monetary policy stance during the financial crisis', *Monthly Bulletin*, January, **www.ecb.europa.eu/pub/pdf/other/art1_mb201001en_pp63–71en.pdf**

European Central Bank (2010c) 'EU banking structures', September, **www.ecb.europa.eu/pub/ pdf/other/eubankingstructures201009en.pdf**

European Central Bank (2011a) 'The monetary policy of the ECB', **www.ecb.europa.eu/pub/ pdf/other/monetarypolicy2011en.pdf?536dd5e934d206858a2d6d1b5e52d4d3**

European Central Bank (2011b) *Monthly Bulletin*, July, **www.ecb.europa.eu/pub/pdf/mobu/ mb201107en.pdf**

European Central Bank (2012a) 'A fiscal compact for a stronger economic and monetary union', *Monthly Bulletin*, May, **www.ecb.int/pub/pdf/other/art1_mb201205en_pp79–94en.pdf**

European Central Bank (2012b) 'Monetary and fiscal interactions in Europe', *Monthly Bulletin*, July, **www.ecb.int/pub/pdf/other/art1_mb201207en_pp51–64en.pdf?fbc950d904a5d4 d27be6cf98c733a294**

European Central Bank (2013) 'Banking structure report', November, **www.ecb.europa.eu/ pub/pdf/other/bankingstructuresreport201311en.pdf**

European Commission (2007a) 'Report on the Retail Banking Sector Inquiry', Commission Staff Working Document, January, **http://ec.europa.eu/competition/sectors/financial_ser- vices/inquiries/sec_2007_106.pdf**

European Commission (2007b) 'Review of the Lamfalussy Process. Strengthening supervisory convergence', Communication from the Commission to the European Parliament and the Council, COM (2007) 727.

European Commission (2009) 'Five years of an enlarged EU. Economic achievements and challenges', DG Economic and Financial Affairs, **http://ec.europa.eu/economy_finance/ publications/publication14078_en.pdf**

European Commission (2011) 'European Financial Stability and Integration Report', Commission Staff Working Paper.

European Commission (2012) 'A roadmap towards a Banking Union', Communication from the Commission to the European Parliament and the Council, COM/2012/0510.

European Commission (2013a) 'Europe 2020 in a nutshell. Taking stock of the Europe 2020 strategy for smart, sustainable and inclusive growth', Communication from the Commission to the European Parliament, the Council, the European Economic and Social Committee and the Committee of the Regions, COM(2014) 130.

European Commission (2013b) 'A Single Market for growth and jobs: An analysis of progress made and remaining obstacles in the member states', Report from the Commission to the European Parliament, the Council, the European Central Bank, the European Economic and Social Committee, the Committee of Regions and the European Investment Bank, COM(2013) 785 final.

European Commission, Joint Research Centre (2009) 'Possible models for risk-based contributions to EU deposit guarantee schemes', June, **http://ec.europa.eu/internal_market/bank/docs/guarantee/2009_06_risk-based-report_en.pdf**

European Economic and Social Committee (2012) 'Obstacles to the European Single Market', Findings of the Single Market Observatory (SMO) Status, July.

European Parliament (2014) 'Review of the new European System of Financial Supervision (ESFS), Part 1: The work of the European supervisory authorities (EBA, EIOPA and ESMA)', **www.europarl.europa.eu/RegData/etudes/etudes/join/2013/507446/IPOL-ECON_ET(2013)507446_EN.pdf**

European Systemic Risk Board (2011) *Annual Report*, **www.esrb.europa.eu/pub/pdf/ar/2011/esrbar2011en.pdf?7fe54d5c524714d16500e1806638e7ac**

Federal Reserve Board (2005) 'Monetary policy and the economy', Chapter 2 in *The Federal Reserve System: Purposes and Functions*, pp.15–25, 9th Edition Board of Governors of the Federal Reserve System, Washington DC **www.federalreserve.gov/pf/pdf/pf_2.pdf**

Federal Reserve Board (2010) 'Advisory on interest rate risk management', **www.federalreserve.gov/newsevents/press/bcreg/bcreg20100107.pdf**

Federal Reserve Board (2014) 'Consumers and mobile financial services 2014', Board of Governors of the Federal Reserve System, March, **www.federalreserve.gov/econresdata/consumers-and-mobile-financial-services-report-201403.pdf**

Federal Reserve System (2005) 'Purpose and functions', Board of Governors of the Federal Reserve System, **www.federalreserve.gov/pf/pf.htm**

Federal Reserve System (2011) 'The 2010 Federal Reserve Payments Study: Noncash payment trends in the United States: 2006–2009', April, **www.frbservices.org/files/communications/pdf/press/2010_payments_study.pdf**

Federal Reserve System (2013) 'The 2013 Federal Reserve Payments Study: Recent and long-term payment trends in the United States: 200–2012. Summary Report', December, **http://fedpaymentsimprovement.org/wp-content/uploads/2013_payments_study_summary.pdf**

Fiechter, J., Ötker-Robe, I., Lyina, A., Hsu, M., Santos, A. and Surti, J. (2011) 'Subsidiaries or branches: Does one size fit all?', IMF Staff Discussion Note, March (SDN/11/04).

Filardo, A. and Yetman, J. (2011) 'Key facts on central bank balance sheets in Asia and the Pacific', Bank for International Settlements, 6 December.

Financial Services Authority (2009) 'The Turner Review. A regulatory response to the global banking crisis', March, **www.fsa.gov.uk/pubs/other/turner_review.pdf**

Financial Services Authority (2010) 'Revising the Remuneration Code', Consultation Paper, 10/19, **www.fsa.gov.uk/pubs/cp/cp10_19.pdf**

Financial Services Authority (2011a) 'The failure of the Royal Bank of Scotland', Financial Services Authority Board Report, December, **www.fsa.gov.uk/pubs/other/rbs.pdf**

Financial Services Authority (2011b) 'Revising the Remuneration Code – feedback on Cp10/19 and final rules', Policy Statement, PS10/20, **www.fsa.gov.uk/pubs/policy/ps10_20.pdf**

Financial Services Authority (2012) 'Assessing the possible sources of systemic risk from hedge funds, A report on the findings of the FSA's Hedge Fund Survey and Hedge Fund as Counterparty Survey', **www.fsa.gov.uk/static/pubs/other/hedge-fund-report-aug2012.pdf**

Financial Stability Board (2011a) 'Key attributes of effective resolution regimes for financial institutions', October, **www.financialstabilityboard.org/publications/r_111104cc.pdf**

Financial Stability Board (2011b) 'Policy measures to address systemically important financial institutions', November, **www.financialstabilityboard.org/publications/r_111104bb.pdf**

Financial Stability Board (2011c) 'Shadow banking: Scoping the issues', April, **www.financialstabilityboard.org/publications/r_110412a.pdf**

Financial Stability Board (2011d) 'Thematic review on mortgage underwriting and origination practices', March, **www.financialstabilityboard.org/publications/r_110318a.pdf**

Financial Stability Board (2012a) 'Global shadow banking monitoring report 2012', November, **www.financialstabilityboard.org/publications/r_121118c.pdf**

Financial Stability Board (2012b) 'Principles for sound residential mortgage underwriting practices', April, **www.financialstabilityboard.org/publications/r_120418.pdf**

Financial Stability Board (2012c) 'Strengthening oversight and regulation of shadow banking. An integrated overview of policy recommendations', Consultative Document, November, **www.financialstabilityboard.org/publications/r_121118.pdf**

Financial Stability Board (2012d) 'Thematic review on deposit insurance systems, peer review report', February, **www.financialstabilityboard.org/publications/r_120208.pdf**

Financial Stability Board (2013a) 'Thematic review on resolution regimes, peer review report', April, **www.financialstabilityboard.org/publications/r_130411a.pdf**

Financial Stability Board (2013b) 'Update of group of global systemically important banks (G-SIBs)', November, **www.financialstabilityboard.org/publications/r_131111.pdf**

Financial Stability Forum (2008) 'Report of the Financial Stability Forum on enhancing market and institutional resilience', April, **www.financialstabilityboard.org/publications/r_0804.pdf**

Fiordelisi, F. (2007) 'Shareholder value efficiency in European banking', *Journal of Banking & Finance*, 31(7), 2151–2171.

Friedman, M. (1969) *The Optimum Quantity of Money*, London: Macmillan.

Friedman, M. (1968) 'The role of monetary policy', *The American Economic Review*, 58(1), 1–17.

Fu, X., Lin, Y. and Molyneux, P. (2014) 'Bank competition and financial stability in Asia Pacific', *Journal of Banking & Finance*, 38, 64–77.

Gapper, J. (2008) 'After 73 years: The last gasp of the broker-dealer', *Financial Times*, 15 September.

Garmaise, M.J. and Moskowitz, T.J. (2006) 'Bank mergers and crime: The real and social effects of credit market competition', *Journal of Finance*, 61, 495–538.

Genetay, N. and Molyneux, P. (1998) *Bancassurance*, London: Palgrave Macmillan.

Gilbert, R.A. (1984) 'Bank market structure and competition – a survey', *Journal of Money, Credit and Banking*, 16(4), 332–354.

Girardone, C. and Snaith, S. (2011) 'Project finance loan spreads and disaggregated political risk', *Applied Financial Economics*, 21(23), 1725–1734.

Goddard, J., Molyneux, P. and Wilson, J.O.S. (2004) 'Dynamics of growth and profitability in banking', *Journal of Money, Credit and Banking*, 36(6), 1069–1090.

Goddard, J., Molyneux, P. and Wilson, J.O.S. (2009a) 'Crisis in UK banking: Lessons for public policy', *Public Money and Management*, 29, 276–284.

Goddard, J., Molyneux, P. and Wilson, J.O.S. (2009b) 'The financial crisis in Europe: Evolution, policy responses and lessons for the future', *Journal of Financial Regulation and Compliance*, 17, 362–380.

Goddard, J., Molyneux, P. and Wilson, J.O.S. (2014) 'Banking in the European Union: Deregulation, crisis and renewal', in Berger, A.N., Molyneux, P. and Wilson, J.O.S. (eds) *The Oxford Handbook of Banking*, 2nd Edition, Oxford: Oxford University Press, Chapter 35.

Goddard, J., Molyneux, P., Liu, H. and Wilson, J.O.S. (2011) 'The persistence of bank profit', *Journal of Banking & Finance*, 35, 2881–2890.

Goetz, M. (2012) 'Bank diversification, market structure and bank risk taking: Theory and evidence from U.S. commercial banks', **www.bostonfed.org/bankinfo/qau/wp/2012/qau1202.pdf**

Goff, S. (2011) 'Just the facts: The Vickers Report', *Financial Times*, 12 September.

Goff, S. (2013) 'Born from the Reverend Henry Duncan, a brief history of TSB', *Financial Times*, 6 September.

González-Páramo, J.M. (2010) 'The challenges of credit risk management: Lessons learned from the crisis', Speech given at the Bank of International Settlements by the Member of the Executive Board of the European Central Bank, 26 May, **www.bis.org/review/r100528d.pdf**

Goodhart, C.A.E. (1987) 'Why do banks need a central bank?', *Oxford Economic Papers*, 39(1), 75–89.

Goodhart, C.A.E., Hartmann, P., Llewellyn, D., Rojas-Suarez, L. and Weisbrod, S. (1998) *Financial Regulation: Why, how and where now?* London: Routledge.

Gray, S. and Talbot, N. (2006) 'Monetary operations', in Hammond, G. and Blake, A. (eds) *Handbooks in Central Banking*, London: Centre for Central Banking Studies, Bank of England.

Greenbaum, S.I. and Thakor, A.V. (2007) *Contemporary Financial Intermediation*, 2nd Edition, Amsterdam, Boston, MA: Elsevier Academic Press.

Gros, D., Alcidi, C. and Giovanni, A. (2012) 'Central banks in times of crisis: The Fed vs. the ECB', CEPS Policy Briefs, No. 276, July, pp. 3–5.

Group of Ten (2001) 'Report on consolidation in the financial sector', Bank for International Settlements, **www.bis.org/publ/gten05.pdf**

Guerrera, F. (2010) 'JPMorgan's US acquisitions pack punch', *Financial Times*, 21 September.

Hagendorff, J. (2014) 'Corporate governance in banking', in Berger, A.N., Molyneux, P. and Wilson, J.O.S. (eds), *The Oxford Handbook of Banking*, 2nd Edition, Oxford: Oxford University Press, Chapter 4.

Hagendorff, J. and Keasey, K. (2012) 'The value of board diversity in banking: evidence from the market for corporate control', *The European Journal of Finance*, 18, 41–58.

Hagendorff, J., Keasey, K. and Vallascas, F. (2013) Size, Risk and Governance in European Banking. Oxford: Oxford University Press.

Hammond, G. (2012) 'State of the art inflation targeting', Bank of England, CCBS Handbook, No. 29, February.

Heffernan, S. (2005) *Modern Banking*, Chichester: John Wiley & Sons.

Heinemann, F. and Jopp, M. (2002) 'The benefits of a working European retail market for financial services', Report to the European Financial Services Round Table, Institut für Europäische Politik, Berlin, **http://ftp.zew.de/pub/zew-docs/div/erffinal.pdf**

Hempel, G.H. and Simonson, D.G. (2008) *Bank Management*, 5th Edition, New York: John Wiley & Sons.

Herfindahl, O.C. (1950) *Concentration in the US Steel Industry*, New York: Columbia University.

Hicks, J. (1935) 'Annual survey of economic theory: The theory of monopoly', *Econometrica*, 3(1), 1–20.

High-Level Expert Group on Financial Supervision in the EU (2009) 'Report (de Larosière Report)', February, **http://ec.europa.eu/internal_market/finances/docs/de_larosiere_report_en.pdf**

High-Level Expert Group on Reforming the Structure of the EU Banking Sector (2012) Final Report (Liikanen Report), October, **http://ec.europa.eu/internal_market/bank/docs/high-level_expert_group/report_en.pdf**

Hirschman, A.O. (1945) *National Power and the Structure of Foreign Trade*, Berkeley, CA: University of California Press.

HM Treasury (2012) 'Banking reform: Delivering stability and supporting a sustainable economy', June, **www.gov.uk/government/uploads/system/uploads/attachment_data/file/32556/whitepaper_banking_reform_140512.pdf**

Hoelscher, D.S. and Quintyn, M. (2003) 'Managing systemic banking crises', IMF Occasional Paper, No. 224, August.

Hughes, J. and Mester, L. (2014) 'Measuring the performance of banks: Theory, practice, evidence, and some policy implications', in Berger, A.N., Molyneux, P. and Wilson, J.O.S. (eds), *The Oxford Handbook of Banking*, 2nd Edition, Oxford: Oxford University Press, Chapter 10.

Hunter, G. S. (2013) 'Scope for consolidation in overcrowded Gulf banking markets', *Financial Times*, 9 October.

ICMA (2012) 'Shadow banking and repo', ICMA European Repo Council, **www.icmagroup.org/assets/documents/Maket-Practice/Regulatory-Policy/Repo-Markets/Shadow%20banking%20and%20repo%2020%20March%202012.pdf**

Independent Commission on Banking (2011) *Final Report*, September, **http://bankingcommission.independent.gov.uk/**

Institute of International Finance (2009) 'Risk Culture, reform in the financial services industry: Strengthening practices for a more stable system', The Report of the IIF Steering Committee on Implementation (SCI), Institute of International Finance, Washington DC, December, **www.iif.com/download.php?id=rvQQAgKiCMM**

Institute of Risk Management (2012) 'Risk culture: Guidance from the Institute of Risk Management', London: Institute of Risk Management, **www.theirm.org/media/885907/Risk_Culture_A5_WEB15_Oct_2012.pdf**

International Finance Corporation (2007) 'Banking on sustainability, financing environmental and social opportunities in emerging markets', **www.ifc.org/wps/wcm/connect/1bba68804886595eb902fb6a6515bb18/FINAL_IFC_BankingOnSustainability_web.pdf?MOD=AJPERES&CACHEID=1bba68804886595eb902fb6a6515bb18**

International Monetary Fund (2004) 'The Treatment of nonperforming loans in macroeconomic statistics', An Issue Paper Prepared for the December 2004 Meeting of the Advisory Expert Group on National Accounts.

International Monetary Fund (2007) 'Compilation guide on financial soundness indicators: Experience with the co-ordinated compilation exercise and next steps', Statistics Department, October, **www.imf.org/external/np/pp/2007/eng/101807a.pdf**

International Monetary Fund (2012a) 'Japan: Financial sector stability assessment update', IMF Country Report, No. 12/210, **www.imf.org/external/pubs/ft/scr/2012/cr12210.pdf**

International Monetary Fund (2012b) 'The quest for lasting stability', Global Financial Stability Report, April, **www.imf.org/external/pubs/ft/gfsr/2012/01/pdf/text.pdf**

International Monetary Fund (2012c) 'Restoring confidence and progressing on reforms', Global Financial Stability Report, October, **www.imf.org/external/pubs/ft/gfsr/2012/02/pdf/text.pdf**

International Monetary Fund (2012d) 'Enhancing Financial sector surveillance in low-income countries – financial deepening and macro-stability', IMF Board Paper, April, **www.imf.org/external/np/pp/eng/2012/041612.pdf**

International Monetary Fund (2013a) 'European Union: Publication of financial sector assessment programme documentation – technical note on deposit insurance', IMF Country Report, March, **www.imf.org/external/pubs/ft/scr/2013/cr1366.pdf**

International Monetary Fund (2013b) 'Transition challenges to stability', Global Financial Stability Report, October, **www.imf.org/external/pubs/ft/gfsr/2013/02/pdf/text.pdf**

International Monetary Fund (2013c) 'Unconventional monetary policies. Recent experience and prospects', April, **www.imf.org/external/np/pp/eng/2013/041813a.pdf**

International Monetary Fund (2013d) 'World economic outlook', April, **www.imf.org/external/pubs/ft/weo/2013/01/pdf/text.pdf**

Investment Management Association (2011) Ethical Investing in Funds, **www.investmentfunds.org.uk**

IOSCO (2010) 'Disclosure principles for public offerings and listings of asset backed securities', Final Report, April, **www.iosco.org/library/pubdocs/pdf/ioscopd318.pdf**

IOSCO (2012) 'Global Developments in securitisation regulation', International Organization of Securities Commissions, CR09/12, June, **www.iosco.org/library/pubdocs/pdf/IOSCOPD382.pdf**

Ito, T. and Mishkin, F.S. (2004) 'Two decades of Japanese monetary policy and the deflation problem', NBER Working Paper, No. 10878, November, **www.nber.org/papers/w10878**

Iwata, G. (1974) 'Measurement of conjectural variations in oligopoly', *Econometrica*, 42(5), 947–966.

Jahan S. (2012) 'Inflation targeting: Holding the line', International Monetary Fund, **www.imf.org/external/pubs/ft/fandd/basics/target.htm**

Japan Post Bank (2012) *Annual Report*, **http://www.jp-bank.japanpost.jp/en/aboutus/pdf/en2012_all.pdf**

Jayaratne, J. and Strahan, P.E. (1998) 'Entry restrictions, industry evolution, and dynamic efficiency: Evidence from commercial banking', *Journal of Law and Economics*, 41, 239–273.

Jensen, M.C. and Meckling, W.H. (1976) 'Theory of the firm: Managerial behavior, agency costs and ownership structure', *Journal of Financial Economics*, 3(4), 305–360.

Jorion, P. (2007) *Value at Risk: The new benchmark for controlling market risk*, 3rd Edition, New York: McGraw-Hill.

Joyce, M., Tong, M. and Woods, R. (2011) 'The United Kingdom's quantitative easing policy: Design, operation and impact', *Quarterly Bulletin*, Bank of England, Q3, **www.bankofengland. co.uk/publications/Documents/quarterlybulletin/qb110301.pdf**

Kaczorowska, A. (2013) *European Union Law*, 3rd Edition, London: Routledge, Taylor & Francis Group.

Kanaya, A. and Woo, D. (2000) 'The Japanese banking crises of the 1990s: Sources and lessons', IMF Working Paper, WP/00/7 **www.imf.org/external/pubs/ft/wp/2000/wp0007.pdf**

Keeley, M.C. (1990) 'Deposit insurance, risk and market power in banking', *The American Economic Review*, 80(5), 1183–1200.

Kiff, J. and Morrow, R. (2000) 'Credit derivatives', *Bank of Canada Review*, Autumn, 3–11.

King, M. (2012) 'Twenty years of inflation targeting', Speech given at the Stamp Memorial Lecture, London School of Economics, **www.bankofengland.co.uk/publications/Documents/ speeches/2012/speech606.pdf**

King, R.G. and Levine, R. (1993) 'Finance and growth: Schumpeter might be right', *Quarterly Journal of Economics*, 108(3), 717–737.

Klapper, L., Laeven, L. and Rajan, R.G. (2006) 'Entry regulation as a barrier to entrepreneurship', *Journal of Financial Economics*, 82(3), 591–629.

Klapper, L., Martinez-Peria, M.S. and Zia, B. (2014) 'Banking in the developing nations of Asia: An overview of recent changes in ownership structure', in Berger, A.N., Molyneux, P. and Wilson, J.O.S. (eds), *The Oxford Handbook of Banking*, 2nd Edition, Oxford: Oxford University Press, Chapter 38.

Kneer, C. (2013) 'The absorption of talent into finance: Evidence from U.S. banking deregulation', De Nederlandsche Bank.

Koch, T.W. and MacDonald, S.S. (2009) *Bank Management*, 7th Edition, Mason, OH: South-Western, Cengage Learning.

Koopman, G.-J. (2011) 'Stability and competition in EU banking during the financial crisis: The role of state aid control', *Competition Policy International*, 7, 8–21.

KPMG (2010) 'Risk management – a driver of enterprise value in the emerging environment', **www.kpmg.com/IN/en/IssuesAndInsights/ThoughtLeadership/KPMG_Risk_ Management_Survey_2011_1.pdf**

KPMG (2013) 'Major Australian banks: Full year results 2012', Financial Institutions Performance Survey, **www.kpmg.com/AU/en/IssuesAndInsights/ArticlesPublications/Financial-Institutions-Peformance-Survey/Major-Banks/Documents/major-australian-banks-year-end-2012v2.pdf**

Kydland, F. and Prescott, E. (1977) 'Rules rather than discretion: The inconsistency of optimal plans', *Journal of Political Economy*, 85, 473–490.

Laeven, L. and Levine, R. (2009) 'Bank governance, regulation and risk taking', *Journal of Financial Economics*, 93(2), 259–275.

Laeven, L. and Valencia, F. (2008) 'Systemic banking crises: A new database', IMF Working Paper, WP/08/224, **www.imf.org/external/pubs/ft/wp/2008/wp08224.pdf**

Laeven, L. and Valencia, F. (2012) 'Systemic banking crises database: An update', International Monetary Fund Working Paper, WP/12/163.

Laeven, L. and Valencia, F. (2014) 'Resolution of banking crises: The good, the bad, and the ugly', in Claessens, S., Kose, M.A., Laeven, L. and Valencia, F.(eds), *Financial Crises: Causes, consequences and policy responses*, Washington, DC: International Monetary Fund.

References and further reading

Landier, A. and Ueda, K. (2009) 'The economics of bank restructuring: Understanding the options', IMF Staff Position Note, SPN/09/12, June.

Lau, L.J. (1982) 'On Identifying the degree of competitiveness from industry price and output data', *Economics Letters*, 10(1–2), 93–99.

Leibenstein, H. (1966) 'Allocative Efficiency vs."X-Efficiency"', *The American Economic Review*, 56(3), 392–415.

Lepetit, L. and Strobel, F. (2013) 'Bank Insolvency risk and time-varying Z-score measures', *Journal of International Financial Markets, Institutions and Money*, 25, 73–87.

Lerner, A.P. (1934) 'The concept of monopoly and the measurement of monopoly power', *Review of Economic Studies*, 1(3), 157–175.

Lewis, M.K. and Davis, K. (1987) *Domestic and International Banking*, Cambridge, MA: The MIT Press.

Lintner, J. (1965) 'The valuation of risk assets and the selection of risky investments in stock portfolios and capital budgets', *The Review of Economics and Statistics*, 47(1), 13–37.

Lipczynski, J., Wilson, J.O.S. and Goddard, J. (2013) *Industrial Organization: Competition, Strategy and Policy*, Harlow: Pearson.

Liu, H., Molyneux, P. and Wilson, J.O.S. (2013) 'Competition in banking: Measurement and interpretation, in Bell, A.R., Brooks, C. and Prokopczuk, M. (eds), *Handbook of Research Methods and Applications in Empirical Finance*, Cheltenham: Edward Elgar.

Llewellyn, D.T. (1999) 'The economic rationale for financial regulation', FSA Occasional Papers Series, No. 1, **www.fsa.gov.uk/pubs/occpapers/op01.pdf**

Loan Market Association Syndicated Loan – Glossary, **www.lma.eu.com/uploads/files/ Syndicated_Loan_glossary[1].pdf**

Manne, H.G. (1965) 'Mergers and the market for corporate control', *The Journal of Political Economy*, 73(2), 110–120.

Markowitz, H. (1952) 'Portfolio selection', *The Journal of Finance*, 7(1), 77–91.

Marques-Ibanez, D. and Scheicher, M. (2010) 'Securitisation, instruments and implications', in Berger, A.N., Molyneux, P. and Wilson, J.O.S. (eds), *The Oxford Handbook of Banking*, Oxford: Oxford University Press, Chapter 24.

Masters, B. (2013) 'Gargantuan task of Libor probes becomes clearer', *Financial Times*, 1 November.

Masters, B. (2013) 'Risk management progress has been small, says banking study', *Financial Times*, 28 July.

McCauley, R., McGuire, P. and von Peter, G. (2010) 'The architecture of global banking: From international to multinational?' *BIS Quarterly Review*, March, 25–37.

McGuire, C.L. (2012) 'Simple tools to assist in the resolution of troubled banks', Other Operational Studies, World Bank, No. 12342, **http://siteresources.worldbank.org/EXTFINANCIALSECTOR/ Resources/Bank_Resolution_Toolkit.pdf**

McKinsey (2011) 'Day of reckoning? New regulation and its impact on capital-markets businesses', **www.mckinsey.com/App_Media/Reports/Financial_Services/McKRegulation_capital_ markets.pdf**

McKinsey (2012) 'Value creation in European banking', **www.mckinsey.com/**

Merton, R.C. (1974) 'On the pricing of corporate debt: The risk structure of interest rates', *The Journal of Finance*, 29(2), 449–470.

Mishkin, F.S. (2011) 'Monetary policy strategy: Lessons from the crisis', NBER Working Paper No. 16755, **www.nber.org/papers/w16755.pdf**

Mishkin, F.S. (2000) 'What should central banks do?', *Federal Reserve Bank of St Louis Review*, November–December.

Moe, T.G. (2012) 'Shadow banking and the limits of central bank liquidity support: How to achieve a better balance between global and official liquidity', Levy Institute of Bard College, Working Paper, No. 712.

Molyneux, P., Lloyd-Williams, D.M. and Thornton, J. (1994) 'Competitive conditions in European banking', *Journal of Banking & Finance*, 18(3), 445–459.

Molyneux, P., Nguyen, L.H. and Xie, R. (2014) 'Foreign bank entry in South East Asia', *International Review of Financial Analysis*, 30, 26–35.

Montoriol-Garriga, J. (2008) 'Bank mergers and lending relationships', ECB Working Papers, September, **www.ecb.europa.eu/pub/pdf/scpwps/ecbwp934.pdf**

Moody's Analytics (2011a) 'Banking industry survey on stress testing', **www.moodysanalytics. com/Microsites/Global-Marketing/2011/Stress-Testing-Survey**

Moody's Analytics (2011b) 'Implementing High value funds transfer pricing systems', **www .moodysanalytics.com/~/media/Insight/Quantitative-Research/Enterprise-Risk-Modeling/2011/2011–01–09-Implementing-High-Value-Fund-Transfer-Pricing-Systems. ashx**

Moore, E. (2011a) 'Decision to abolish cheques reversed', *Financial Times*, 12 July.

Moore, E. (2011b) 'PPI misselling – "nothing was separated and explained"', *Financial Times*, 13 May.

Mueller, D.C. (1977) 'The persistence of profits above the norm', *Economica*, 44(176), 369–380.

Mueller, D.C. (1986) *Profits in the Long Run*, Cambridge: Cambridge University Press.

Mueller, H. (1994) 'Credit policy: The anchor of the credit culture', *Journal of Commercial Lending*, 76(11), 29–36.

Murphy, E. (2013) 'Who regulates whom and how? An overview of US financial regulatory policy', Congressional Research Service, **www.fas.org/sgp/crs/misc/R43087.pdf**

Nakamoto, S. (2009) 'Bitcoin: A peer-to peer electronic cash system', **https://bitcoin.org/ bitcoin.pdf**

Nasiripour, S. and Braithwaite, T. (2013) 'Out to break the banks', *Financial Times*.

National Audit Office (2012) 'The creation and sale of Northern Rock Plc', Report by the Comptroller and Auditor General, 17 May, **www.nao.org.uk/wp-content/ uploads/2012/05/121320.pdf**

National Audit Office (2013) 'The Comptroller and Auditor General's Report to the House of Commons', HM Treasury Resource Accounts 2012–13, **www.nao.org.uk/wp-content/ uploads/2013/07/HMT-Accounts-2012–13.pdf**

OECD (2011) 'Bank competition and financial stability', **www.oecd.org/finance/financial-markets/48501035.pdf**

Office of Fair Trading (2004) 'Store cards', March, **www.oft.gov.uk/shared_oft/reports/ financial_products/oft706.pdf**

Office of Fair Trading (2007) 'SME banking', OFT937, August, **http://webarchive.nationalarchives .gov.uk/20140402142426/http://www.oft.gov.uk/shared_oft/reports/financial_products/ oft937.pdf.**

Office of Fair Trading (2008) 'Personal current accounts in the UK', July, **www.oft.gov.uk/shared_oft/reports/financial_products/OFT1005.pdf**

Office of Fair Trading (2010a) 'OFT's response to the consumer focus super-complaint', June, **www.oft.gov.uk/shared_oft/super-complaints/OFT1246.pdf**

Office of Fair Trading (2010b) 'Review of barriers to entry, expansion and exit in retail banking', November, **www.oft.gov.uk/shared_oft/personal-current-accounts/oft1282**

Office of Fair Trading (2012) 'Competition in UK banking', Speech at the seminar on 'A competitive banking sector: Challenges in a post-crisis environment', organised by MLex in association with Lloyds Banking Group, **www.oft.gov.uk/shared_oft/speeches/2012/speech0212.pdf**

Office of Fair Trading (2013) 'Review of the personal current account market', OFT1005rev, January, **www.oft.gov.uk/shared_oft/reports/financial_products/OFT1005rev**

Ogura, Y. and Uchida, H. (2014) 'Bank consolidation and soft information acquisition in small business lending', *Journal of Financial Services Research*, 45, 173–200.

Oliver Wyman (2011) *The Future of Banking in Emerging Markets*, London: Oliver Wyman.

Panzar, J.C. and Rosse, J.N. (1987) 'Testing for monopoly equilibrium', *Journal of Industrial Economics*, 35(4), 443–456.

Parks, T. (2005) *Medici Money: Banking, metaphysics, and art in fifteenth-century Florence*, New York: WW Norton & Company.

Payments Council (2013) 'Quarterly statistical report', **www.paymentscouncil.org.uk/**

Perignon, C. and Smith, D.R. (2010) 'The level and quality of value-at-risk disclosure by commercial banks', *Journal of Banking and Finance*, 34, 362–377.

Philippon, T. (2010) 'Financiers vs. engineers: Should the financial sector be taxed or subsidized?', *American Economic Journal: Macroeconomics*, 2(3), 158–182.

Plender, J. (2009) 'A winner's curse that haunts the banking behemoths', *Financial Times*, 12 July.

Plenderleith, I. (2012) 'Review of the Bank of England's provision of emergency liquidity assistance in 2008–09', Report presented to the Court of the Bank of England, **www.bankofengland.co.uk/publications/Documents/news/2012/cr1plenderleith.pdf**

Power, M., Ashby, S. and Palermo, T. (2013) 'Risk culture in financial organisations, a research report', **www.lse.ac.uk/researchAndExpertise/units/CARR/pdf/Final-Risk-Culture-Report.pdf**

Pozsar, Z., Adrian, T., Ashcraft, A. and Boesky, H. (2010) 'Shadow banking', Staff Report, Federal Reserve Bank of New York, 458, **www.newyorkfed.org/research/staff_reports/sr458.html**

PwC (2007) 'Guide to key performance indicators: Communicating the measures that matter', **www.pwc.com/gx/en/corporate-reporting/assets/pdfs/uk_kpi_guide.pdf**

PwC (2009a) 'Balance sheet management benchmark survey', December, **www.pwc.com/en_GX/gx/banking-capital-markets/assets/balance-sheet-management-benchmark-survey.pdf**

PwC (2009b) 'Financial instruments under IFRS. A guide through the maze', **www.pwc.com/gx/en/ifrs-reporting/Financial_instruments_Guide_maze.jhtml**

PwC (2011) 'Emerging opportunities, financial services M&As in Asia', **www.pwc.tw/en_TW/tw/publications/events-and-trends/assets/e253.pdf**

PwC (2012) 'The risk culture survey', **www.pwc.com/en_US/us/insurance/publications/assets/pwc-erm-survey-report.pdf**

PwC (2013) 'Brave new world: New frontiers in bank M&As', **www.pwc.lu/en/corporate-finance/docs/pwc-journal-banking-manda.pdf**

Rabinovitch, S. (2014) 'China Banking war heats up with launch of online investment app', *Financial Times*, 30 January.

Rajan, R.G. and Zingales, L. (1998) 'Financial dependence and growth', *American Economic Review*, 88(3), 559–586.

Reinhart, C.M. and Rogoff, K.S. (2009) *This Time is Different: Eight centuries of financial folly*, Princeton, NJ: Princeton University Press.

Reinhart, C.M. and Rogoff, K.S. (2011) 'From financial crash to debt crisis', *American Economic Review*, 101(5), 1676–1706.

Resti, A. and Sironi, A. (2010) *Risk Management and Shareholders' Value in Banking*, Chichester: John Wiley & Sons.

Rhoades, S.A. and Rutz, R.D. (1982) 'Market power and firm risk: A test of the 'quiet life' hypothesis', *Journal of Monetary Economics*, 9(1), 73–85.

Rioja, F. and Valev, N.T. (2004a) 'Does one size fit all?: A reexamination of the finance and growth relationship', *Journal of Development Economics*, 74(2), 429–447.

Rioja, F. and Valev, N.T. (2004b) 'Finance and the sources of growth at various stages of economic development', *Economic Inquiry*, 42(1), 127–140.

Roll, R. (1986) 'The hubris hypothesis of corporate takeovers', *Journal of Business and Economic Statistics*, 59, 197–216.

Rose, P.S. and Hudgins, S.C. (2010) *Bank Management & Financial Services*, 8th Edition, Singapore: McGraw-Hill/Irwin.

Rosse, J.N. and Panzar, J.C. (1977) 'Chamberlin vs. Robinson: An empirical study for monopoly rents', Studies in Industry Economics, Research Paper No. 77, Stanford University, California.

Rybczynski, T. (1983) 'The industrial finance systems: Europe, U.S. and Japan', Research Institute of Industrial Economics, Working Paper 113, **www.ifn.se/eng/publications**

Saigol, L. (2013) 'RBS apologises for Cyber Monday technology breakdown', *Financial Times*, 3 December.

Sano, H. and Hirata, N. (2010) 'Japan scales back Japan Post privatisation', Reuters, 24 March.

Sarkisyan, A. and Casu, B. (2013) 'Retained interests in securitisations and implications for bank solvency', ECB Working Paper Series, 1538 (April), **http://www.ecb.europa.eu/pub/pdf/scpwps/ecbwp1538.pdf**

Saunders, A. and Cornett, M.M. (2012) *Financial Markets and Institutions*, New York: McGraw-Hill/Irwin.

Sawada, M. (2013) 'Measuring the effect of postal saving privatization on the Japanese banking industry: Evidence from the 2005 general election', *Pacific-Basin Finance Journal*, 21(1), 967–983.

Schaeck, K. and Čihák, M. (2014) 'Competition, efficiency, and stability in banking', *Financial Management*, 43(1), 215–241.

Schäfer, D. (2013) 'Consolidation: Fragmented business offers huge potential for mergers', *Financial Times*, 13 May.

Schäfer, D. and Johnson, M. (2013) 'Santander in talks to sell stake in asset arm', *Financial Times*, 5 May.

Schiersch, A. and Schmidt-Ehmcke, J. (2010) 'Empiricism meets theory: Is the Boone-Indicator applicable?' Discussion Papers of DIW Berlin 1030.

Schmieder, C., Marsch, K. and Forster-van Aerssen, K. (2010) 'Does banking consolidation worsen firms' access to credit? Evidence from the German economy', *Small Business Economics*, 35(4), 449–465.

Scorpio (2012) 'Scorpio Partnership Private Banking Benchmark 2012', **www.scorpiopartnership .com**

Sealey, G.W. and Lindley, J.T. (1977) 'Inputs, outputs and a theory of production and cost at depository financial institutions', *Journal of Finance*, 32(4), 1251–1266.

Select Committee on the European Union (2003) 'Towards a Single Market for finance: The Financial Services Action Plan', House of Lords, 45th Report, **www.publications.parliament. uk/pa/ld200203/ldselect/ldeucom/192/192.pdf**

Sender, H. (2009) 'AIG saga shows dangers of credit default swaps', *Financial Times*, 6 March.

Schaeck, K. and Cihák, M. (2014) 'Competition, efficiency, and stability in banking', *Financial Management*, 43(1), 215–241.

Shaffer, S. (1993) 'A test of competition in Canadian banking', *Journal of Money, Credit and Banking*, 25(1), 46–61.

Shaffer, S. and DiSalvo, J. (1994) 'Conduct in a banking duopoly', *Journal of Banking & Finance*, 18(6), 1063–1082.

Shambaugh, J.C. (2012) 'The euro's three crises', Brookings Papers on Economic Activity, 12 March, **www.brookings.edu/~/media/Projects/BPEA/Spring%202012/2012a_Shambaugh.pdf**

Sharpe, W.F. (1964) 'Capital asset prices: A theory of market equilibrium under conditions of risk', *The Journal of Finance*, 19 (3), 425–442.

Shepherd, W.G. (1982) 'Economies of scale and monopoly profits', in Craven, J.V. (ed.), *Industrial Organization, Antitrust, and Public Policy*, Boston, MA: Kluwer Nijhoff.

Shepherd, W.G. (1986) 'Tobin's Q and the structure performance relationship: Reply', *American Economic Review*, 76, 1205–1210.

Shinkin Central Bank (2012) *Annual Report*, **www.shinkin-central-bank.jp/e/financial/pdf/ all_2012.pdf**

Shiratsuka, S. (2010) 'Size and composition of the central bank balance sheet: Revisiting Japan's experience of the quantitative easing policy', Globalization and Monetary Policy Institute, Federal Reserve Bank of Dallas, WP N. 42.

Shotter, J., Jenkins, P. and Massoudi, A. (2012) 'UBS updates Facebook status', *Financial Times*, 31 July.

Shull, B. and Hanweck, G. (2001) *Bank Mergers in a Deregulated Environment: Promise and peril*, Westport, CT: Quorum Books.

Singh, M.M. and Aitken, J. (2010) 'The (sizable) role of rehypothecation in the shadow banking system', IMF Working Paper, 10/172, **www.imf.org/external/pubs/ft/wp/2010/wp10172.pdf**

Sinkey, J.F. (2002) *Commercial Bank Financial Management*, 6th Edition, New York: Macmillan.

Smirlock, M. (1985) 'Evidence of the (non) relationship between concentration and profitability in banking', *Journal of Money, Credit and Banking*, 17(1), 69–83.

Soble, J. (2013) 'Japan's biggest banks profit under Abenomics', *Financial Times*, 31 July.

Spiller, P.T. and Favaro, E. (1984) 'The effects of entry regulation on oligopolistic interaction: The Uruguayan banking sector', *RAND Journal of Economics*, 15(2), 244–254.

Standard & Poor's (2010) *A Guide to the European Loan Market* (January). **www.lcdcomps .com/d/pdf/European_Loan_Primer.pdf**

Standard & Poor's (2011) *A Guide to the Loan Market,* September, **www.lcdcomps.com/d/pdf/ LoanMarketguide.pdf**

Standard & Poor's (2012) 'Sovereign ratings and country T&C assessment histories', **www .standardandpoors.com/spf/upload/Ratings_US/TC_Assessment_Histories_1_4_13.pdf**

Statistics Bureau (2013) 'Statistical handbook of Japan, Ministry of Internal Affairs and Communications of Japan', **www.stat.go.jp/english/data/handbook/index.htm**

Stiroh, K. (2014) 'Diversification in banking', in Berger, A.N., Molyneux, P. and Wilson, J.O.S. (eds), *The Oxford Handbook of Banking*, 2nd Edition, Oxford: Oxford University Press, Chapter 9.

Stolz, S.M. and Wedow, M. (2010) 'Extraordinary measures in extraordinary times. Public measures in support of the financial sector in the EU and the United States', ECB Occasional Paper Series, 117, July, **www.ecb.europa.eu/pub/pdf/scpops/ecbocp117.pdf**

Sun, Y. (2011) Recent Developments in European Bank Competition, IMF Working Papers, WP/11/146. **www.imf.org/external/pubs/ft/wp/2011/wp11146.pdf**

Taleb, N. (1997) 'The world according to Nassim Taleb', *Derivatives Strategy*, 2(1), 37–40.

Teitelbaum, H. (2013) 'NSFR implementation uncertain after Basel III compromise on LCR phase-in', *Financial Times*, 22 January.

Tett, G. (2013) 'Watch out for the rate hike hit to banks', *Financial Times*, 13 June.

The Banker Database, **www.thebankerdatabase.com**

The Governing Council of the European Central Bank (2011) 'Guideline of the European Central Bank on monetary policy instruments and procedures in the Eurosystem', Official Journal of the European Union, **www.ecb.int/ecb/legal/pdf/02011o0014–20130103-en.pdf**

The Norinchukin Bank (2012) *Annual Report*, **www.nochubank.or.jp/en/ir/annual_report/ pdf/ar_2012_.pdf**

Toyoda, M. (2013) 'Reconsidering central bank independence: The changing roles and functions of central banking', Harvard Law School, **www.law.harvard.edu/programs/about/pifs/ education/llm/2012–2013/masahiro-toyoda-if-seminar-paper-spring-2013.pdf**

Treasury Committee (2011) 'Competition and choice in retail banking', 9th Report of Session 2010–11, House of Commons, **www.publications.parliament.uk/pa/cm201011/cmselect/ cmtreasy/612/612i.pdf**

Treynor, J.L. (1964) 'How to rate management of investment funds', *Harvard Business Review*, 43, 63–75.

UBS (2012) *Annual Report*, **www.ubs.com/global/en/about_ubs/investor_relations/ annualreporting/2012.html**

UBS (2014) 'Bitcoins and banks. Problematic currency, interesting payment system', UBS Global Research, **www.ubs.com/investmentresearch**

Uchida, H. and Tsutsui, Y. (2005) 'Has competition in the Japanese banking sector improved?' *Journal of Banking & Finance*, 29(2), 419–439.

Uchida, H. and Udell, G. (2014) 'Banking in Japan', in Berger, A.N., Molyneux, P. and Wilson, J.O.S. (eds), *The Oxford Handbook of Banking*, 2nd Edition, Oxford: Oxford University Press, Chapter 36.

Uhde, A. and Heimeshoff, U. (2009) 'Consolidation in banking and financial stability in Europe: Empirical evidence', *Journal of Banking & Finance*, 33, 1922–1311.

US Department of the Treasury (2013) 'The financial crisis five years later. Response, reform and progress', September, **www.treasury.gov/connect/blog/Documents/FinancialCrisis5Yr_vFINAL.pdf**

Valdez, S. and Molyneux, P. (2013) *An Introduction to Global Financial Markets*, 7th Edition, London: Palgrave Macmillan.

van Leuvensteijn, M., Kok Sorensen, C., Bikker, J.A. and van Rixtel, A.A.R.J.M. (2011) 'Impact of bank competition on the interest rate pass-through in the euro area', *Applied Economics*, 45(11), 1359–1380.

Van Rompuy, H. (2012) 'Towards a genuine economic and monetary union', Report by President of the European Council Herman Van Rompuy, June and December, **www.consilium.europa.eu/uedocs/cms_Data/docs/pressdata/en/ec/134069.pdf**

Vives, X. (2001) 'Competition in the changing world of banking', *Oxford Review of Economic Policy*, 17(4), 437–479.

Walker, D. (2009) 'A review of corporate governance in UK banks and other financial industry entities', Final Recommendations, November, **webarchive.nationalarchives.gov.uk/+/http://www.hm-treasury.gov.uk/d/walker_review_261109.pdf**

Wilson, J. (2012) 'Germany's small banks fight to keep privileges', *Financial Times*, 2 December.

World Bank (2013) 'Rethinking the role of the state in finance', Global Financial Development Report, **http://econ.worldbank.org/**

World Council of Credit Unions Statistical Report, **www.woccu.org/publications/statreport**

Yeyati, E.L. and Micco, A. (2007) 'Concentration and foreign penetration in Latin American banking sectors: Impact on competition and risk', *Journal of Banking & Finance*, 31, 1633–1647.

Index

Note: page numbers in **bold** denote glossary references.